FOUNDATIONS OF ACCOUNTING

Edited by
RICHARD P. BRIEF
New York University

A GARLAND SERIES

Proceedings of the Seventh International Congress of Accountants 1957

GARLAND PUBLISHING, INC.

NEW YORK & LONDON 1988

For a list of Garland's publications in accounting, see the final pages of this volume.

Reproduced from a copy in the American Institute of Certified Public Accountants

Library of Congress Cataloging in Publication Data

International Congress of Accountants (7th : 1957 : Amsterdam, Netherlands)
Proceedings of the Seventh Inmternational Congress of Accountants, 1957.
p. cm. — (Foundations of accounting)
Held 9th-13th September, Amsterdam. Reprint.
ISBN 0-8240-6142-X (alk. paper)
1. Accounting—Congresses. 2. Comparative accounting—Congresses.
3. Budget in business—Congresses. I. Title. II. Series.
HF5603.I62 1957
657—dc 19 88-18048

Design by Renata Gomes

The volumes in this series are printed on acid-free, 250-year-life paper.

Printed in the United States of America

PROCEEDINGS

OF THE SEVENTH INTERNATIONAL CONGRESS

OF ACCOUNTANTS 1957

The English translations of the texts and addresses supplied in other languages have been provided by the authors and speakers on their responsibility

The ideas expressed in the papers represent the personal views of the authors

proceedings

OF THE SEVENTH INTERNATIONAL CONGRESS

OF ACCOUNTANTS 1957

9th–13th September, Concertgebouw Amsterdam

Printed by Meijer Wormerveer

CONTENTS

PART ONE

GENERAL

PART TWO

BUSINESS SESSIONS

PART THREE

APPENDICES

PART ONE (GENERAL)

SPONSORING BODIES

NEDERLANDS INSTITUUT VAN ACCOUNTANTS
(NETHERLANDS INSTITUTE OF ACCOUNTANTS)

491, Herengracht, Amsterdam

VERENIGING VAN ACADEMISCH GEVORMDE ACCOUNTANTS
(ASSOCIATION OF UNIVERSITY TRAINED ACCOUNTANTS)

38, Ten Hovestraat, The Hague

CONGRESS COMMITTEE

J. KRAAYENHOF, PRESIDENT
PROF. A. M. VAN RIETSCHOTEN, VICE-PRESIDENT
R. BESANÇON, EC.DRS.
PROF. A. GOUDEKET
MR. B. MORET, EC.DRS.
H. C. TREFFERS
J. VOGEL, EC. DRS.

Secretariat

A. L. DE BRUYNE, SECRETARY
MR. C. BOERTIEN, ADJUNCT SECRETARY

Ladies Committee

MRS. A. M. VAN RIETSCHOTEN, PRESIDENT
MRS. H. L. VAN DEN BOSCH
MRS. A. L. DE BRUYNE
MRS. A. L. DEMENINT
MRS. A. GOUDEKET
MISS W. INGENHOES
MRS. A. C. J. DE JONG
MRS. J. DE JONG
MRS. A. TH. E. KASTEIN
MRS. J. KRAAYENHOF
MRS. J. LOS
MRS. W. H. MERCKEL
MRS. J. G. DE WEGER

BUSINESS SESSIONS COMMITTEE

PROF. A. GOUDEKET, Chairman
PROF. A. M. VAN RIETSCHOTEN

Sub-Committees for:

Principles for the Accountant's Profession

L. VAN ESSEN LZN., *Chairman*
C. BAKKER, EC. DRS.
DR. A. TH. DE LANGE
H. DE LEEDE
A. STRAATEMEIER

Budgeting and the Corresponding Modernization of Accounting

PROF. DR. A. MEY, *Chairman*
J. J. N. VAN HOUT
J. P. SLOT, EC. DRS.
P. J. VAN SLOTEN, EC. DRS.
A. F. TEMPELAAR

The Verification of the Existence of Assets

A. C. J. JONKERS, EC. DRS., *Chairman*
R. BURGERT, EC. DRS.
W. J. VAN DUIN
PROF. A. A. DE JONG
H. F. DE WIJS

Business Organization and the Public Accountant

H. REINOUD, *Chairman*
S. C. BAKKENIST, EC. DRS.
C. H. A. J. JANSSENS
J. A. M. F. LINDNER, EC. DRS.
R. W. STARREVELD

The Internal Auditor

J. DE JONG, EC. DRS., *Chairman*
A. C. J. DE JONG
J. KEUZENKAMP, EC. DRS.
P. C. LOUWERS
W. N. A. F. H. STOKVIS

Ascertainment of Profit in Business

G. L. GROENEVELD, EC. DRS., *Chairman*
PROF. J. BRANDS
J. H. C. LAMAN, EC. DRS.
L. J. M. ROOZEN, EC. DRS.
J. A. RIJPKEMA

OTHER COMMITTEES

Social Events Committee

H. C. TREFFERS, *Chairman*
H. P. DE BOER
H. L. VAN DEN BOSCH
J. INGWERSEN
MR. A. TH. E. KASTEIN
J. LOS, EC. DRS.

Reception and Registration Committee

J. VOGEL, EC. DRS., *Chairman*
A. L. DEMENINT, EC. DRS.
W. C. KOPPENBERG
D. KUIJPER CZN.
G. PAAR
J. SPOORMAKER, EC. DRS.

Publicity Committee

R. BESANÇON, EC. DRS., Chairman
P. H. BOSCHMA

Finance Committee

MR. B. MORET, EC. DRS., Chairman
J. C. BECK

CHAIRMEN OF THE BUSINESS SESSIONS

TUESDAY MORNING

Principles for the Accountant's Profession

ARTHUR B. FOYE, C.P.A., United States of America

TUESDAY AFTERNOON

Budgeting and the Corresponding Modernization of Accounting

H. HJERNØ JEPPESEN, DENMARK

The Verification of the Existence of Assets

G. F. KLINGNER, F.C.A., IRELAND

WEDNESDAY AFTERNOON

Business Organization and the Public Accountant

PROF. B. J. S. WIMBLE, C.A. (S.A.), F.S.A.A., SOUTH AFRICA

The Internal Auditor

WP F. C. J. BUSCH, GERMANY

FRIDAY MORNING

Ascertainment of Profit in Business

A. VEYRENC, FRANCE

PROGRAMME OF THE CONGRESS

MONDAY, 9TH SEPTEMBER

10.30 hrs	Divine Service in the Westerkerk conducted by the Rev. J. H. Sillevis Smitt, President of the Netherlands Bible Society and Chief of the Protestant Chaplains of the Royal Netherlands Navy
10.30 hrs	High Mass, celebrated in the St. Nicolaaskerk
14.15 hrs	Opening Session 1. Address by Sir Harold G. Howitt, G.B.E., D.S.O., M.C., D.C.L., F.C.A., President of the Sixth International Congress on Accounting, London 1952 2. Address by His Royal Highness, the Prince of the Netherlands 3. Address by His Excellency Dr. G. M. J. Veldkamp, State Secretary of Economic Affairs 4. Opening Address by Mr. J. Kraayenhof, President of the Congress
16.30 hrs	Cocktail Party at Krasnapolsky Hotel for Delegates and their Ladies presented by the Sponsoring Bodies
20.15 hrs	Reception by the President and the Vice-President of the Congress and Mrs. Kraayenhof and Mrs. Van Rietschoten

TUESDAY, 10TH SEPTEMBER

10.00 hrs	Business Session *Principles for the Accountant's Profession*
14.30 hrs	Business Session *Budgeting and the Corresponding Modernization of Accounting*
14.30 hrs	Business Session *The Verification of the Existence of Assets*
10.00 hrs	Visit by the ladies to the Rijksmuseum (also 14.30 and 15.30 hrs)
14.30 hrs	Visit by the ladies to Asscher's Diamant Maatschappij (Asscher's Diamond Company), Amsterdam
14.30 hrs	Visit by the ladies to Amstel Brouwerij (Amstel Brewery), Amsterdam
18.30 hrs	Delegates' Dinner at Carlton Hotel
20.30 hrs	Round Trip through the canals, presented by the Municipal Council of Amsterdam

PROGRAMME OF THE CONGRESS

WEDNESDAY, 11TH SEPTEMBER

11.00 hrs	Meeting of the Leaders of the Delegations at Amstel Hotel
14.30 hrs	Business Session *Business Organization and the Public Accountant*
14.30 hrs	Business Session *The Internal Auditor*
14.00 hrs	Visit by the ladies to the Fashion Parade at Hotel Bouwes, Zandvoort, organized by Maison Vogelzang
14.45 hrs	Visit by the ladies to the Fashion Parade at Victoria Hotel, Amsterdam, organized by Offerman Couture
20.30 hrs	Concert by the Concertgebouw-Orchestra conducted by Dr. Eduard van Beinum – Soloist: Hans Henkemans, piano – Presented by the Municipal Council of Amsterdam The programme comprised the following works: 6th Symphony, Franz Schubert – Piano Concerto K.V. 453, Wolfgang Amadeus Mozart – 3rd Symphony, Willem Pijper – L'oiseau de Feu, Igor Strawinsky

THURSDAY, 12TH SEPTEMBER

8.30 hrs	Excursions: The Enclosing Dyke – De Hooge Veluwe – Netherlands Open Air Museum in Arnhem – Royal Trade Fair in Utrecht – The Hague – Gouda/Het Westland – Bird Park in Alphen aan den Rijn – Rotterdam – Amsterdam
21.00 hrs	Visit to the Rijksmuseum in Amsterdam on the invitation of the Government The Minister of Economic Affairs and the State Secretary of Economic Affairs received a limited number of delegates

FRIDAY, 13TH SEPTEMBER

8.30 hrs	Visit by the ladies to Flower Auctions at Aalsmeer
10.00 hrs	Business Session *Ascertainment of Profit in Business*
14.30 hrs	Closing Session – Addresses by: Mr. J. Kraayenhof, President of the Congress Prof. A. Goudeket, Chairman of the Business Sessions Committee Mr. R. Besançon, ec. drs., Chairman of the Publicity Committee Mr. H. C. Treffers, Chairman of the Social Events Committee Mr. S. Prakash Chopra, B.A., B. Com., A.C.A., F.C.A. (India), President of the Institute of Chartered Accountants of India Mr. J. A. De Lalanne, C.B.E., M.C., B.A., C.A. (Canada) on behalf of the English-speaking guests Dr. Jakob Viel (Switzerland) on behalf of the German-speaking guests Prof. Avv. Rag. Giovanni Sensini (Italy) on behalf of the French-speaking guests
21.00 hrs	Ball

MONDAY, 9TH SEPTEMBER

DIVINE SERVICE, WESTERKERK

Minister: The Reverend J. H. Sillevis Smitt, President of the Netherlands Bible Society and Chief of the Protestant Chaplains of the Royal Netherlands Navy.
Organist: Simon C. Jansen, Precentor-organist of the Westerkerk.
Vocalist: Aafje Heynis, Contralto.

1. INTROITUS

2. PSALM, *sung by the congregation*

1 All people that on earth do dwell,
Sing to the Lord with cheerful voice;
Him serve with mirth, His praise forth tell;
Come ye before Him and rejoice.

2 The Lord ye know is God indeed;
Without our aid He did us make;
We are His folk, He doth us feed,
And for His sheep He doth us take.

3 O enter then His gates with praise;
Approach with joy His courts unto;
Praise, laud, and bless His name always,
For it is seemly so to do.

4 For why, the Lord our God is good;
His mercy is for ever sure;
His truth at all times firmly stood,
And shall from age to age endure.

3. PRAYER

Our Father, which art in heaven
Hallowed be thy name
Thy kingdom come
Thy will be done in earth
As it is in heaven
Give us this day our daily bread
And forgive us our trespasses

As we forgive them that trespass against us
And lead us not into temptation
But deliver us from evil
For thine is the kingdom
The power and the glory
For ever and ever. Amen.

4. THE LESSON FROM THE OLD TESTAMENT. *Daniel 6. 1–10.*

1 It pleased Darius to set over the kingdom an hundred and twenty
princes, which should be over the whole kingdom;
2 And over these three presidents; of whom Daniel was first; that the
princes might give accounts unto them, and the king should have no
damage.
3 Then this Daniel was preferred above the presidents and princes, be-
cause an excellent spirit was in him; and the king thought to set him
over the whole realm.
4 Then the presidents and princes sought to find occasion against Daniel
concerning the kingdom; but they could find none occasion nor fault; for
as much as he was faithful, neither was there any error or fault found in him.
5 Then said these men, We shall not find any occasion against this Daniel,
except we find it against him concerning the law of his God.
6 Then these presidents and princes assembled together to the king, and
said thus unto him, King Darius, live for ever.
7 All the presidents of the kingdom, the governors, and the princes, the
counsellers, and the captains, have consulted together to establish a
royal statute, and to make a firm decree, that whosoever shall ask a
petition of any God or man for thirty days, save of thee, O king, he shall
be cast into the den of lions.
8 Now, O king, establish the decree, and sign the writing, that it be not
changed, according to the law of the Medes and Persians, which alter-
eth not.
9 Wherefore king Darius signed the writing and the decree.
10 Now when Daniel knew that the writing was signed, he went into his
house; and his windows being open in his chamber toward Jerusalem,
he kneeled upon his knees three times a day, and prayed, and gave
thanks before his God, as he did aforetime.

5. CHORAL-PRELUDE, played by the organist
Ich ruf zu dir, Herr Jesu Christ – J. S. Bach (1685–1750)

6. THE LESSON FROM THE NEW TESTAMENT. *St. Luke 10. 38–42.*

38 Now it came to pass, as they went, that he entered into a certain village:
and a certain woman named Martha received him into her house.
39 And she had a sister called Mary, which also sat at Jesus' feet, and
heard his word.
40 But Martha was cumbered about much serving, and came to him, and
said, Lord, dost thou not care that my sister hath left me to serve alone?
bid her therefore that she help me.

41 And Jesus answered and said unto her, Martha, Martha, thou art careful
and troubled about many things:
42 But one thing is needful: and Mary hath chosen that good part, which
shall not be taken away from her.

7. ARIOSO, *sung by the contralto*

Dank sei Dir, Herr.
Du hast Dein Volk mit Dir geführt,
Israël hindurch das Meer.
Wie eine Herde zog es hindurch.
Herr, Deine Hand schützte es;
In Deiner Güte gabst Du Ihm Heil.

G. F. Händel (1685–1759)

8. HYMN, *sung by the congregation*

1 Praise to the Lord! the Almighty, the King of creation!
O my soul, praise Him, for He is thy health and salvation!
All ye who hear – Now to His temple draw near,
Serve Him in glad adoration!

2 Praise to the Lord! Who o'er all things so wondrously reigneth,
Shielding thee gently from harm and from fainting sustaineth;
Hast thou not seen – How thy desires have been
Granted in what He ordaineth?

3 Praise to the Lord! Who doth prosper thy work and defend thee,
Surely His goodness and mercy here daily attend thee;
Ponder anew – What the Almighty can do,
If with His love He befriend thee!

4 Praise to the Lord! Oh let all that is in me adore Him!
All that hath life and breath come now with praises before Him!
Let the Amen – Sound from His people again,
Gladly for aye we adore Him.

9. THE ADDRESS, by the Reverend J. H. Sillevis Smitt:

The text of my sermon can be found in Daniel Chapter VI, verse 10:

'Now when Daniel knew that the writing was signed, he went into his house; and his windows being open in his chamber toward Jerusalem, he kneeled upon his knees three times a day and prayed and gave thanks before his God, as he did aforetime'.

My dear friends—this Daniel was an exceptional man. If we read through our Bible we shall find that the Bible describes all the human weaknesses of the great men of faith:—

Noah—drunkedness, Jacob—craftiness
Abraham—fear and cowardness
David—lust, fear and even murder,

all except for *one* man; he is portrayed without that stress of weakness; in Daniel there was no weakness and man could find no guilt in him.

Daniel was extremely busy, cares and problems piled on his desk; just like an accountant. But what else can be expected of a man who was prime minister of a World Empire. He was, without exception, as busy as the modern man of to-day. Let us look at the modern man as we know him, is he not burdened above his strength, more pushed than pushing, more driven than driving, he is in fact more slave than the youngest bell-boy, but yet this Daniel possessed an inner rest—of which we are lacking—so rich that he was a prophet and seer.

Daniel can also be classed as an extremely capable man, but this is the least of his qualities. Cleverness is a gift and not a virtue. If this congress is lacking anything—may God make it a true and great success—it is certainly not lacking in brains. If ever there was an outstanding unique collection of brains it was the League of Nations and yet it became a failure. No my friends, there was never a shortage of brains in the World but let us take a good look as to how the situation is nowadays.

When failures arise in the world of to-day, we are inclined to blame the inefficiency of the acting bodies, but have failures anything to do with our brains? I am convinced that the cause of all failures is not here in our heads but here in our hearts. We are not lacking brains, we are lacking character.

This man was incorruptible, maybe this is the reason why the King decided to put him in charge of the whole realm as a sort of super controller, super administrator and accountant with the special commission to look after the vast and detailed business with honesty and efficiency.

Deeply, basically honest he had apparently no price; no one could buy him or his favours. Just fancy the temptation Daniel was exposed to—temptation of money and temptation of power—surely these are the two most corrupting temptations that exist on this earth. But nowhere in the Bible can one read that Daniel yielded to power but it can be found that he preferred to kneel and pray to his God three times a day. The love of money which we all know as the root of all evil did not once grip his temptation.

I started my sermon by telling you that Daniel was an exceptional man and once more I wish to stress this point. The same was said of Daniel as was said of our Lord. His enemies looked for a weak spot in his armour —they convicted him of sin—they looked for a leakage but they could find nothing. They sought with the fingers of the searchlight of their jealousy and hate but their results were always negative. With us it is exactly the opposite, the only ones who do not see our faults are ourselves. But for all this fault-finding and mockery he did not shrink from his responsibility. He was courageous and a man without fear. He had no fear for *man* and that is saying something! Kings and enemies could not scare him. He had no fear to live and certainly no fear to die. Nothing could stop him from doing what he thought to be his duty. This man was true to his job; he was true to his King, his conviction, his job and himself. He preferred to die sticking to his standards than live by the grace of betrayal of his standards. He started as a youth on the road of true conviction, believing and giving his faith to his God and we find him in his good old age still on that same road of true conviction; just the same man, quiet, brilliant, fearless, steadfast and everyone's servant but let it not be forgotten he was nobody's slave, except God's.

What was the secret to this man's greatness and strength? What was the key to his wisdom and courage, of his moral strength and invincibility? What hidden secret could be found behind a man so unconquerable—giving thanks to God and yet knowing he was hunted down to death by his enemies.

The secret my friends lies in one's house, in your house and mine. What sort of house do you live in? How many rooms can be found in your home? Maybe you have a sitting room, a lounge, pantry, study, bedroom, bathroom and even an attic or cellar. But still I feel we have missed one out. If Jesus should say to you, and he does, go you into your closet, would you, could you do it? Have you a closet?

The waiting room and consulting room of psychiatrists are crowded because the closets are empty. We are harassed, driven beyond endurance. We become neurotic and seem to fall to pieces, are in full conflict with ourselves, our wives and fellow-people. Do we ever stop to ask ourselves as to why we become in such a state of affairs, surely if we should ask ourselves this question the answer would be the open window to Jerusalem; the secret to Daniel's strength and greatness. His open window and regular contact with his God was the first rule in his life. His work occupied his whole day, but still he found time to give thanks to his God three times a day. So burdened as he was he could be found in his closet. Threatened as he was by his enemies still he was present in his closet, on the *budget* of his life God was not the closing but the first entry.

Before the opening of this Congress I would like to ask you one question, have you your daily meeting with God? Have you amongst all the rooms in your home that one little room—the closet? You cannot do without it—meeting God—being with Jesus Christ everyday, there is your rest, that inner relaxation we need so badly; in company with the Lord, men can see things in their right proportion, there and then anger comes to rest, one finds correction of thought, plans, intentions, you acquire a clear vision of the difference between right and wrong, the unburdening of cares, the help, comfort and strength which you cannot do without. The inner restoration and forgiveness is found for faults and sins. Guidance is waiting for you. You are recharged with confidence, strength and courage; temptation is conquered, fear is overcome, there is wisdom, rest, quietness and sympathy. Let me give you an illustration of this:–

During the war I was stationed in Milford Haven, and it was part of my job to visit our mine sweepers, at that time fishing trawlers converted into useful warships. It was mid-winter and very early in the morning I found myself on board the mine sweeper that I intended to sail with. The skipper welcomed me on board and immediately asked me if I would like a cup of coffee. You can of course imagine my reaction to such a question and down we went into his cabin. It was extremely cosy, the stove was burning and I was given a steaming hot cup of coffee. All of a sudden I saw to my surprise a plant on the table, it was a beauty, so fresh and green and in perfect condition. I inquired as to how such a plant, which after all needs fresh air and light, could exist in such an atmosphere, in such a cabin with artificial light and no sun. The skipper immediately demonstrated; he opened the hatch of his cabin, in flowed the daylight and he said 'Here is the secret; everyday for one hour the hatch remains open, the light and fresh air flows in and there you see the result'.

Light and strength are two things we need so much, especially light in the dark and gloomy world of to-day. I read in an American book the story of a truck going over the river to a suburb factory. The truck was loaded with drums and on arriving was unloaded and the drums were brought downstairs to the cellar. The lids were removed from the drums and the contents revealed—a dark colourless lifeless paint.

A man enters with a small tube in his hand; an uncanny mysterious light is shining out of the tube. He moves the tube over all the drums and the lids are put back in their place. A miracle has happened: the paint has become light-giving. We can see our clocks and watches in the dark. Under Jesus' hand we become light-giving. Thus the contact with Jesus changes us from children of darkness into children of light.

My third illustration is that of *power*. My hobby is stone collecting, I love to saw, grind and polish. If you use a thin metal disc to saw with and nothing happens the disc is the loser, but if you put some diamond dust on the rim it makes all the difference; the saw is kept going at a high speed and the hardest stone can be sliced. The disc is more than a conqueror. Are you a conqueror? We should be conquerors! In our temptation our hardship and devastating duties let our life be embedded everyday by the spirit of Jesus Christ. A voice sounds from far away over all the participants of this congress. It is a voice of wisdom and love, a voice of one who knows what is in man and what he needs, and it says:

'enter into thy closet; my father which seeth in secret shall reward thee openly. But seek ye first the Kingdom of God and his righteousness and all these things shall be asked unto you'.

Amen.

10. VOCAL-SOLO, *by the contralto*

a God is my shepherd,
I want for nothing
My rest is in the pleasant meadows,
He leadeth me where quiet waters flow!
My fainting soul doth He restore,
and guideth me in the ways of peace,
to glorify His name.
And though in death's dark valley my steps must wander,
my spirit shall not fear,
for Thou art by me still;
Thy rod and staff are with me,
and they shall comfort me.

A. Dvořak (1841–1904)

b I will sing new songs of gladness,
I will sing Jehovah's praises
upon a tenstringed psaltery.
Ev'ry day will I extol Thee,
and will bless Thy holy name.
Great is God and great His mercy;
who shall tell of all His greatness?
who shall His power declare?
My song shall be of praise and honour,
and of Thy glorious acts,
Thy works are wonderful,
past our knowing.
Yea, men shall tell of Thy great kindness,
and of Thy wond'rous might,
and my voice shall proclaim aloud Thy glory.

A. Dvořak (1841–1904)

II. PRAYERS

Almighty God, from whom all thoughts of truth
and peace proceed
Kindle we pray thee
in the hearts of all men the true love of peace
and guide with thy pure
and peaceable wisdom
those who are entrusted with the government
of the nations of the earth
that in tranquillity thy Kingdom
may go forward
till the earth be filled with the knowledge
of thy love
through Jesus Christ our Lord. Amen.

O Lord, we beseech thee mercifully
To receive the prayers of thy people
Which call upon thee
And grant that they may both perceive
And know what things they ought to do
And also may have grace and power
Faithfully to fulfil the same
Through Jesus Christ our Lord. Amen.

Oh God of truth and light
Bless we pray thee with the enlightening and guidance
Of thy Spirit
All who participate in the great
Undertaking of this congress

So that all their endeavours in words and deeds
May lead to the glory of thy name
And serve the benefit of the people they
Represent and all mankind in general
Through Jesus Christ our Lord. Amen.

Almighty God, who has given us grace at this time
With one accord to make
Our common supplications unto thee
And dost promise that when two or three
Are gathered together in thy name
Thou wilt grant their requests
Fulfil now, O Lord
The desires and petitions of thy servants
As may be most expedient for them
Granting us in this world knowledge of thy
truth and in the world to come life everlasting. Amen.

Teach us, our God and King
In all things thee to see
And what we do in anything
To do it as for thee. Amen.

12. HYMN, *sung by the congregation*

1 O God, our help in ages past,
Our hope for years to come,
Our shelter from the stormy blast,
And our eternal home.

2 Under the shadow of Thy throne
Thy saints have dwelt secure;
Sufficient is Thine arm alone,
And our defence is sure.

3 Before the hills in order stood,
Or earth received her frame,
From everlasting Thou art God,
To endless years the same.

4 A thousand ages in Thy sight
Are like an evening gone,
Short as the watch that ends the night
Before the rising sun.

5 Time, like an ever rolling stream,
Bears all its sons away;
They fly forgotten, as a dream
Dies at the opening day.

6 O God, our help in ages past,
Our hope for years to come,
Be Thou our guard while troubles last,
And our eternal home.

13. THE BLESSING

6 The grace of our Lord Jesus Christ
And the love of God
And the communion of the Holy Ghost
Be with you all

Amen.

MONDAY, 9TH SEPTEMBER

HIGH MASS, ST. NICOLAASKERK

The High Mass was celebrated by the Rev. J. Aarts, assisted by the Rev. Dr. P. Dreesen, S. J. and the Rev. W. Switzar.

VENI CREATOR

Veni Creator Spiritus,
Mentes tuorum visita,
Imple superna gratia
Quae tu creasti pectora.

Qui diceris Paraclitus,
Altissimi donum Dei,
Fons vivus, ignis, caritas,
et spiritalis unctio.

Tu septiformis munere,
Digitus paternae dexterae,
Tu rite promissum Patris
Sermone ditans guttura.

Accende lumen sensibus:
Infunde amorem cordibus:
Infirma nostri corporis
Virtute firmans perpeti.

Hostem repellas longius,
Pacemque dones protinus:
Ductore sic te praevio
Vitemus omni noxium.

Per te sciamus da Patrem,
Noscamus atque filium,
Teque utriusque Spiritum
Credamus omni tempore.

Deo Patri sit gloria,
Et Filio, qui a mortuis
Surrexit, ac Paraclito,
In saeculorum saecula. Amen.

V. Emitte Spiritum tuum et creabuntur.
R. Et renovabis faciem terrae.

OREMUS

Deus, qui corda fidelium sancti Spiritus illustratione docuisti, da nobis in eodem Spiritu recta sapere et de ejus semper consolatione gaudere. Per Christum Dominum nostrum. Amen.

THE ADDRESS, by the Reverend Dr. P. Dreesen, S. J.:

MEINE LIEBEN BRÜDER UND SCHWESTERN IN CHRISTO,

Sie wollen mir gestatten einige Worte an Sie, meine verehrten Teilnehmer am siebten internationalen Kongreß zu richten.

Es war eine sehr gute Initiative, diesen Kongreß für die katholischen Teilnehmer mit einer Heiligen Messe zu eröffnen.

Ihr Kongreß wird ohne Zweifel vor allem einen Austausch von Gedanken und Anregungen auf dem Gebiete Ihrer Wissenschaft bezwecken. Dennoch liegt bei einem Kongreß der Schwerpunkt nicht ausschließlich in der rein wissenschaftlichen Ebene. Ist es nicht vielmehr so, daß das Wertvolle zu einem erheblichen Teil auch liegt in dem Kontakt, der zwischen Vertretern verschiedener Länder und Nationen hergestellt wird? Durch diese Begegnungen entsteht eine Einheit, eine Verbrüderung, wenn ich es so sagen darf, aus der Wertschätzung und Respekt für die andern erblüht etwas, das für die Erhaltung unserer Welt wirksamer ist als welche Abrüstungskonferenz es auch immer sein dürfte.

Nun, wo ist ein stärkeres Band der Einheit untereinander zu finden, als in Christo, der das Fundament und der Grund echter gegenseitiger Anerkennung und Liebe zwischen Menschen ist.

Deshalb können Sie – wie mir scheint – diesen Kongreß nicht sinnvoller eröffnen, als gerade durch die gemeinsame Feier des Kreuzopfers und durch die gemeinsame Teilnahme am Leibe Christi.

Deshalb wollen wir auch diese Heilige Messe für Ihre persönlichen Anliegen und für das Gelingen Ihres Kongresses Gott darbringen.

Möge unter Gottes Segen Ihr Aufenthalt in den Niederlanden sich fruchtbar und bereichernd auswirken.

MY DEAR BRETHREN IN JESUS CHRIST,

For many of you this is not the first time you have come to this country; and most of you, I suppose, have already read about Holland. So you will have noticed that Holland, and more especially this town of Amsterdam, have always been places for international contacts to take place. Formerly it was commerce, which brought nations together here, now it is the International Court of Justice, the Palace of Peace and the numerous congresses.

Now the aim of a congress is a double one: the exchange of scientific results and human ideas on the one hand, and the opportunity for personal interviews with members of foreign nations on the other. From either point of view you are in a most favourable atmosphere in our country.

But the foundation of the unity of all people, and its most radical cause, is our unity in our Lord Jesus Christ. That is why I think the organising committee has done very well indeed in assembling you here, before the congress starts.

Here, in this church dedicated to Saint Nicolas, Amsterdam's patron Saint, we are to unite around the altar; together we are to celebrate Holy Mass, in order to implore God's blessing on this congress, its work and its members. For where could we better be united in Christ than around his own Sacrifice of the Cross?
I sincerely hope and pray that in these days God will abundantly pour down his blessing upon you; also that your stay here will be a time in which contacts and friendships will grow among you based on God's presence in every single man. An ever increasing appreciation and understanding may arise among members of all nationalities, all of them children of one and the same Father in Heaven.
If our meeting will help to achieve this, you will at the end rightly look back upon a good congress.

CHÈRS FRÈRES,

Si je m'adresse en dernier lieu à vous, les participants de langue française, qui êtes venus à ce septième congrès international, c'est pour la seule raison que j'ai suivi l'ordre alphabétique des trois langues utilisées au congrès.
Vous aussi, vous avez accepté l'invitation des organisateurs à commencer ce congrès par une messe solennelle, parce que vous êtes convaincus que l'on ne trouve nulle part une unité plus solide entre les hommes que dans le Christ Notre Seigneur. N'est-il pas vrai que l'estime profonde des hommes entre eux ne se fonde solidement que sur la présence de Dieu dans l'homme, présence qui nous demande, selon le précepte du Christ, à aimer les autres comme nous-mêmes.
Et c'est précisément cette estime mutuelle, née de la rencontre personnelle, qui est, avec l'échange des données scientifiques, l'aspect le plus important d'un congrès international.
Maintenant que le progrès de la technique a créé la possibilité illimitée de s'entretuer, nous avons plus que jamais besoin de compréhension mutuelle, de respect et d'amour pour sauver la paix du monde, voire l'humanité elle-même.
Vraiment, il n'est pas de meilleure façon de commencer ce congrès sinon par la célébration du sacrifice de la messe. Cette messe sera offerte à Dieu à votre intention, d'abord pour que ce congrès réussisse et pour implorer la bénédiction divine sur vous-mêmes et sur tous ceux qui vous sont chers.
J'espère qu'à travers de tout ce que ce congrès vous apportera, vous réussirez à trouver Dieu dans les autres participants.
Alors vous retournerez dans votre pays, l'esprit enrichi, le cœur plein de joie et d'une charité plus vivante.
C'est ce que je vous souhaite de tout cœur.

MONDAY, 9TH SEPTEMBER

OPENING SESSION

MR. J. KRAAYENHOF, PRESIDENT OF THE CONGRESS, IN THE CHAIR

The President was introduced by Sir Harold G. Howitt, G.B.E., D.S.O., M.C., D.C.L., F.C.A., President of the Sixth International Congress on Accounting, London, 1952.

SIR HAROLD G. HOWITT:

I have been invited formally to introduce the President of this Seventh International Congress of Accountants in that I was President of the Sixth International Congress in London in 1952. If, in this sense, I am being privileged to carry the torch, I can but wish I was still competent to bear it into this hall in true Olympic style.

The high standard of the accounting profession in Holland is well-known throughout the world and this is confirmed by the fact that in the comparatively short history of these congresses this is the second which has been held in your country, the other one having been in 1926. I feel sure that this Congress will be as happy and as useful as was the previous one.

I have looked at the record of the proceedings of the 1926 Congress and it is clear how carefully the subjects for discussion were then chosen to cover the current problems. The same care has obviously been taken in selecting subjects for the present Congress. They include not only subjects related to our profession as such and the ever-widening scope of our responsibilities, but also problems arising from the urge of the modern age in which we live including the impact of inflation on accountancy records.

In 1926 also great care was taken for the entertainment and the social needs of your visitors. We have a saying in my country that 'All work and no play makes Jack a dull boy'. This is certainly true of accountants, and of ladies also, and we look forward with great enthusiasm to enjoying the traditional hospitality of your country so clearly in evidence in the programme that is before us.

It would be an impertinence for me to say any more at this stage; it is now my pleasure to vacate the Chair and to ask Mr. Kraayenhof to take over as President of the Congress. I wish you, Sir, all success and happiness in your task. *(applause)*

THE PRESIDENT:

Thank you, Sir Harold, for your kind co-operation in getting the presidency of this congress started and for your friendly words. I feel that the best thing I can do is to try and follow in your steps, with a view to attaining that the pleasant remembrances of international congresses, brought back home by so many of us in 1952 from London, may be continued through the present Congress.

Your Royal Highness, Your Excellency, Ladies and Gentlemen, Undoubtedly, I am acting as the spokesman of all the participants of this Congress when in the first place I welcome His Royal Highness, the Prince of the Netherlands, and express our sincere thanks for his willingness to attend this opening session and to address the Congress.

Your Royal Highness may be assured that we deem this to be a great favour and a new proof of your highly appreciated interest in the important events in our country, especially when such events are taking place on an international basis.

I am very pleased indeed to inform our guests from abroad at this moment that Her Majesty the Queen has expressed the desire to meet a deputation of the delegates on Thursday afternoon at the Royal Palace in Soestdijk.

You will appreciate, of course, that only a small number of delegates can be chosen to join; they will receive the invitation in due course.

I also particularly welcome His Excellency Dr. Veldkamp, State Secretary of Economic Affairs, whose duties include matters relating to our profession. The Minister of Economic Affairs is, much to our regret, unable to attend.

I am glad to inform you that Dr. Veldkamp has agreed to say a word of welcome to the Congress on behalf of the Netherlands Government.

Furthermore, I welcome the Governor of the Queen for the Province of North Holland, Dr. Prinsen, the Deputy-Burgomaster of Amsterdam, our host-city, Dr. De Roos and our other special guests.

Before I invite His Royal Highness to open the Congress, I feel I should say a few words about the use of the English language in this session by Dutch speakers. As this Congress takes place in the Netherlands, the Dutch language naturally is among the official languages of the meeting. But as we have realized that the greater part of our visitors might not have succeeded in learning Dutch before their arrival here, we have decided for simplicity to use, in this session as well as at the closing of the Congress, the language which is spoken, or at least understood, by the great majority of the visitors, that is the English language, with an interpretation in French and in German. I, in advance, apologize for the mistakes that you will undoubtedly hear, but in this point—of course—I am speaking only for myself.

In the business sessions each of the four languages may be used by the speakers, as the number of hear-phones fully covers the needs at these sessions, assuming that the Dutch colleagues can follow the discussions in the other languages without a receiver.

I may now call upon His Royal Highness, the Prince of the Netherlands.

HIS ROYAL HIGHNESS, THE PRINCE OF THE NETHERLANDS:

In my life I have had and have many different functions to perform, but I want to tell you that I consider it a real privilege to be invited to open this Seventh International Congress of Accountants. It gives me particular pleasure to see that from professional circles all over the globe so many have responded to the invitation to meet here and exchange views, even though that meant travelling long distances to reach this capital of the Netherlands.

As you gather here for what I am sure will prove to be an important and valuable conference, you must certainly remember with appreciation how, after the last war, the professional organisations of the United Kingdom and Ireland in 1952 resumed in London the series of international gatherings in which you periodically take stock of your position and problems. And we in Holland, on our part, recall that in 1926, after the first world-war, the Netherlands Institute of Accountants had a similar privilege and pleasure of contributing to the resumption of international contact here in Amsterdam.

The real significance of professional congresses like yours is, I feel primarily to be seen in the usefulness of open-minded discussion of the many problems which must face you, for surely the accountants won't be the world's only example of a body of hard-working responsible men and women without worries, problems or difficulties.

However, a not less interesting, and perhaps even more far-reaching, objective can be attained by assemblies like this. It is unfortunately a fact that many and serious conflicts and disputes in the world arise from insufficient knowledge of, and lack of appreciation and respect for, the opinions of other people.

Even in these days we are all liable to adapt ourselves to a considerable extent to the ideas and habits of our national, professional and social surroundings, and very often only too readily use our own outlook on life as the criterion with which to judge or measure the views and behaviour of other people. But international congresses, which provide opportunities for a down-to-earth discussion of professional problems as well as real personal contact between representatives of many nations, can do much towards promoting a better mutual understanding. And this, in its turn, goes a long way towards respect for and appreciation of opinions and a way of life differing from our own.

You may perhaps think that a specialised congress of this kind may be able to make only a small contribution in this direction, but I know from my own experience of international gatherings, that you can even surprise yourselves by the measure of goodwill that you can produce. That is why I wish to congratulate you on coming here in such great numbers and, if I may use the phrase, in such great variety too.

Now, a well-prepared discussion of professional problems in an international gathering is undoubtedly of great importance to the advancement of every profession and of the work done in many fields of business and government service. It seems to me, however, that there is a particular reason why everything I have said applies especially to the profession of which so many distinguished members are together in this hall this afternoon.

I feel sure, that as accountants not one of you will contradict me when I say that important decisions are very often based, wholly or partly, on the opinions expressed by accountants, either in their capacity of auditors or in that of advisers. Those decisions are mostly related to economic and financial matters which, as we all know, dominate for a large part the relations between individuals and between the numerous smaller and larger communities of modern society.

It is for this reason that it is surely not an overstatement to say that accountants, in promoting fairness and honesty in all kinds of financial statements and presentations, make a valuable contribution to the founding of human relations on principles of truth and justice.

A profession which in this way can do much for that improvement of human relations, which we so sorely need, must obviously itself give an example of international co-operation in the study of professional problems and of international understanding. That is the particular reason why I mentioned that —in my opinion— your profession is definitely on the right course with the organisation of regular international congresses on such a world-wide scale.

Accountancy today may be regarded as a science as well as a profession. As with almost every other sphere of human activity, it becomes more complicated and more exacting every year. Gone forever are the days of which the American philosopher Thoreau wrote: 'Instead of a million, count half a dozen, and keep your accounts on your thumb-nail'.

Of course, the world's back-room boys, those incredible inventors and scientists, are trying to help you with their clever mechanical brains and fantastic mathematical robots; but it may well be that even these aids to calculations are in many ways adding to, rather than substracting from, your problems, if only because the very principles on which you work must always have a human element and must always manifest human characteristics.

It is only natural that this modern world, by its magnificent achievements in the technical field, displays a special interest in the material aspects of all walks of life. It is to be feared, however, that the importance of material prosperity sometimes takes too large a place in the thoughts and activities of man.

A profession like yours, which in particular occupies itself with economic and financial matters and is surrounded as it were by an atmosphere saturated with materialism, is peculiarly susceptible to this danger. I see, however, that you do not need a warning against this as you have decided to start your proceedings with a discussion on the principles of your profession, a topic which is in itself of a spiritual rather than of a material character.

For an outsider —and I most certainly, despite my varied activities, cannot claim sufficient knowledge of your noble profession— it is interesting to see how and on what grounds your profession performs its principal function. In his certificate the accountant expresses his professional opinion as the result of his examination and audit. And this certificate is accepted throughout the free countries of the world as the hall-mark of reliability of financial statements. Surely only in a society where the individual has freedom of thought and freedom of speech can such an instrument be successfully applied as a confidence-inspiring factor in economic and financial matters.

That is to say, a high degree of appreciation by society for the judgment of the individual members of your profession is a prerequisite for the performance of your profession's function.

It seems to me that you will only be able to reach this goal if you succeed in feeling yourselves members of a fraternity which is based on mutual understanding and appreciation, which would promote and strengthen feelings of friendship and goodwill.

There are already many signs of a widespread desire in the world in general

J. Kraayenhof, President of the Congress

Professor
A. M. van Rietschoten
President of the Netherlands
Institute of Accountants
and Vice-President of the
Congress Committee

J. G. de Weger, ec. drs.
President of the
Association of University
Trained Accountants

to achieve a greater measure of world brotherhood, which in its turn would considerably contribute to a lasting world peace. But as such a brotherhood must be based on those sentiments of understanding and goodwill of which I have just spoken, it is clear that intellectual professions such as yours must do their best to achieve this goal.

I now leave you to your discussions in the hope —even with the conviction— that this international gathering will be one more valuable contribution to the great work and aim of your profession. *(applause)*

THE PRESIDENT:

The enthusiastic reception you have given to the inspiring address of our royal guest is a clear manifestation of the strong desire for international understanding and co-operation which lives in the hearts of all of us. May this be a token of this week's proceedings and of the many personal contacts they will bring to us. Your Royal Highness, we are very grateful to you for your remarks, so full of significance and challenge.

In the name of the Congress I thank you most heartily. I may now call upon His Excellency Dr. Veldkamp.

HIS EXCELLENCY DR. G.M. J. VELDKAMP, STATE SECRETARY OF ECONOMIC AFFAIRS:

I feel it to be a privilege and a pleasure to bid you a hearty welcome, on behalf of the Government, to this Seventh International Congress of Accountants. In particular I welcome the many hundreds of foreign participants who have come to this country from every part of the world to attend this interesting congress. It is a reason for particular gratification that for the second time in the history of international accountants' congresses a Dutch invitation has been accepted by the competent organizations in so many countries. I think I may interpret this as an international acknowledgement of the high standards which have long characterized the Dutch accountant's profession, as organized in the sponsoring bodies.

Another cause of satisfaction is that this international congress is to be held in the Netherlands, a country which has always been internationally minded and has ever set the greatest store by good external relations. For centuries past, foreign trade, as a result of this country's geographical position, has held a prominent place among the activities of its population. To maintain and increase the prosperity of this small, densely populated country with but scant natural resources an intensive economic intercourse with other countries will always be indispensable.

It is partly on this consideration that the Netherlands has ever been an ardent advocate of international economic co-operation and played a leading part in the international consultations on this subject, frequently taking the initiative to start or activate such consultations. This holds true of the co-operation among European countries in the various ways in which it has found expression, as well as of world-wide co-operation as embodied, for example, in the General Agreement on Tariffs and Trade.

In this connection, however, I am also thinking of the economic collaboration between the Netherlands, Belgium and Luxembourg, the most advanced and concrete instance of economic partnership between a number of countries in these post-war years. In my opinion the Benelux countries have thereby proved to the world that by voluntary co-operation between free and independent nations, sustained by mutual confidence and understanding, results can be obtained which redound to the benefit of all partners. If, Mr. President, these principles also inform your Congress, we need not, I am sure, doubt the success of this international gathering of so many eminent experts.

I have wished, Ladies and Gentlemen, to devote a few words to the age-old international orientation of this country and its people so that the many participants from abroad may feel at home here and this congress may apply itself with the greater assiduity to the problems it has set itself to solve.

That the problems with which modern accountancy has to deal direct and indirect are manifold these days, need hardly be stressed before this expert company.

To promote and guarantee truthfulness in financial accounting by government departments as well as business undertakings is among the high duties of the accountant, on whom the most exacting demands are made by the constantly shifting influences to which our social life is exposed. And it seems warranted to make particular mention here of the practical significance of the profession with regard to the collection of direct taxes, which in modern national communities has become an indispensable but very complicated business.

Besides this task, Mr. President, of ensuring truthfulness in financial accounts, to which I have just referred, a matter which I deem of surely no less social importance is the contribution the accountant makes to the efficient functioning of public services and commercial undertakings. This holds especially true of our time, now that the tempestuous pace at which technology advances, providing new ways of creating material wealth, confronts us with ever new problems brought on by their practical application.

Although man's ingenuity and his never flagging energy will go on creating novel and unthought-of ways of production, he will still have to face a shortage of physical means. For this reason an efficient use of available resources will continue to claim our closest attention. I need not explain before this learned company that also in this field much is expected of the expert knowledge and devotedness of your profession now and in the future. You are among those who should be able to give directions for achieving the highest possible degree of efficiency in man's work.

The strong development of accountancy all over the world affords a clear proof of the still rising demand for the highly qualified services the accountant can offer. This rising demand shows itself also in the Netherlands, in business as well as in official circles.

The task with which the present-day accountant is faced is a multifarious one. A periodical reflection on this task, for which these international congresses offer an opportunity, may well, I think, have a highly stimulating effect on the development of accountancy and thus — in view of the important place the accountant holds in our society — on the evolution of our social life.

The fact that so many leading men of the accountancy profession have come to Holland from all over the world to attend this congress prompts me to express a desire and a hope that your talks may be fruitful and that the personal acquaintanceships to be established here may confirm and enhance your mutual esteem. *(applause)*

THE PRESIDENT:

His Excellency, Dr. Veldkamp, has given us a warm welcome in the name of the Netherlands Government, with a special address to the many hundreds of visitors from abroad, and including a special reference to the growing importance of the accountant's profession, both nationally and internationally.
Your Excellency, we have greatly appreciated your attendance at this opening session and your speech. And I take this opportunity of gratefully acknowledging your kind invitation, on behalf of the Government, to all visitors of the Congress to a special visit to the Rijksmuseum on Thursday evening, followed by a reception for the leaders of the delegations and their ladies.
This brings me to the social events in our programme presented to us by the Municipal Authorities. First there is the performance on Wednesday evening by the Concertgebouw Orchestra, conducted by Dr. Eduard van Beinum. Without boasting, it may be said that this Orchestra, as well as its conductor, has a world fame.
Secondly, there is on Tuesday evening the round trip through the canals and the harbour of Amsterdam, the most attractive and typical way of getting acquainted with our beautiful city, nearly 700 years old.
Mr. Burgomaster, will you please accept our warmest thanks for these tokens of the well-known hospitality of the capital of the Netherlands?
Before proceeding to my opening presidential remarks, it seems proper to introduce to you the other persons sitting with me at this table. I ask each to rise after I have called his name, and you might applaud them together when they all stand.
First, the vice-president of the Congress, Professor Van Rietschoten, who also officiates as the president of the Netherlands Institute of Accountants;
then Dr. De Lange, vice-president of that Institute;
Mr. De Weger, the president of the Association of University Trained Accountants, the second of the two sponsoring bodies of this Congress;
the members of the Congress Committee, Mr. Besançon, Professor Goudeket, Mr. Moret, Mr. Treffers and Mr. Vogel,
and its secretary, Mr. De Bruyne,
all of whom have shared with the vice-president and myself the burden of the preparatory work —and the headaches— involved in organizing this Congress;
and last but not least, the six chairmen of the business sessions
Mr. Busch of Western Germany,
Mr. Foye of United States of America,
Mr. Hjernø Jeppesen of Denmark,
Mr. Klingner of Ireland,
Mr. Veyrenc of France
and Professor Wimble of South Africa. *(applause)*
The registrations for this Congress, I am glad to inform you, have by far

surpassed the estimates we had originally made. There are 104 accountancy bodies represented, from 40 different countries. Our office has issued 2850 admission cards, of which 1650 are for visitors from abroad, including 750 ladies, and 1200 are for members of the two sponsoring bodies, including 500 ladies.

As these numbers permit only a very brief introduction to each other, may I ask all delegates, visitors and their ladies from abroad to rise together, to enable the members of the sponsoring bodies and their ladies to welcome them. *(applause)*

For the rest, I would refer to the list of visitors which is included among your papers to find the names of all those whom you want to meet. You will notice from that list that we enjoy a great number of visitors, who distinguish themselves in the profession and that we have both veterans and younger people.

Much to our regret you will not find the name of Mr. George O. May of United States of America, the last available visitor to the Congress in St. Louis (U.S.A.) in 1904, which has been listed as the first international congress in our field.

Mr. May, well-known to many of you, is still a fighter for truth in economics and accounting, as appears anew from his recent articles in professional periodicals. We invited him to this Congress as our guest of honour, and it was with great sorrow that we learned he could not arrange to come. I may take it for granted that it meets with your approval to send him a cable with greetings from this gathering. *(applause)*

It took 22 years before, in 1926, the next, that is the second international Congress was held, the congress we are still proud to have received in this country. A glance at the list of the visitors to that congress and to the one of the present Congress, more than 30 years later, will show you that we have some old-timers among us. We may take it for granted that they enjoyed their stay in Amsterdam in 1926, for —to our great pleasure— they have come again.

We deeply regret that we have lost through death the very able and enthusiastic president of the 1926 Congress, Mr. E. van Dien, as well as some of his close co-operators.

On the other hand, I am happy to state that quite a number of Dutch colleagues who were responsible for the set up in 1926 are still alive, and that many of them are present this afternoon. It will give them great satisfaction that the then younger generation has the privilege of organizing another international congress in the Netherlands.

It is only natural that the Congress Committee of to-day cherishes the hope to equal our 1926 record. But an old Dutch saying gives the cautious warning not to praise the day before the night.

In two respects it will not be easy to match our previous record. The first of these is the problem of accommodating so many guests. In 1926 we had 200 members and ladies from other countries; this time there are, as I have mentioned, 1650.

Serious arrears in the building of new hotels have resulted from the second world-war and from the scarcity of labour and materials in the succeeding years. The Congress Committee has, however, succeeded in providing accommodation for everyone, but should there be serious shortcomings in this respect, please do not hesitate to call upon the secretariat. We certainly wish to make your stay in Amsterdam as comfortable as possible.

The second reason why it will be difficult to outdo the 1926 congress is of a more national character; that congress proved to have been of great significance for the development of the principles of accountancy in our own country. For a long period, indeed, some of the papers delivered there exercised a stimulating influence on our basic professional philosophy.

This recognition was not the least of the motives that encouraged the sponsoring bodies to extend at the meeting in 1952 their invitation for this seventh congress: it was hoped and expected that the profession in the Netherlands would benefit anew by a world-wide exchange of opinions on certain important problems and by personal contacts with the men behind such opinions.

I have indicated that a certain amount of courage was needed to extend an invitation for a congress like this. At this moment, feeling that the sponsoring bodies must render an account of their accomplishments, I recognize that courage alone would not have secured any good result, had we not also encountered such heart-warming willingness to co-operate and assist, both from abroad and in our own country.

In the first place, there was the invaluable and indispensable help from the secretariat of the last congress, Mr. MacIver and his staff. The Congress Committee wishes to express its best thanks for this ever-ready support and experienced advice. We, in our turn, will try our best to give similar assistance to the sponsoring bodies of the next congress.

But we also found full preparedness in many countries to deliver papers on the chosen subjects; many dozens of colleagues from all parts of the world have undertaken to serve as leaders or members of the discussion-panels, whilst others are taking the responsibility, as chairmen and vice-chairmen, for the proceedings in the business sessions. This co-operation has made it possible to realize our strong wish to internationalize to the greatest possible extent the fulfilling of the functions of this Congress.

It is obvious that, apart from this, we had to call upon a large number of members of the two sponsoring bodies to make the machinery of the organization running.

To all these willing helpers, we are most grateful.

Before dealing with the business aspects of this Congress, I think I should now say a few words about some of the social events, apart from those offered by authorities which I have already mentioned.

There is, in the first place, the dinner to-morrow evening, at which we hope to meet all the special delegates. We greatly regret that lack of accommodation makes it impossible for us to invite their ladies as well, but I am sure that friends will take care of these 'one-evening-grass-widows', maybe by taking them out on the boat-trip through the canals!

Then there is the special ladies programme, which I very much hope will be enjoyed by all of them.

I presume that in making their choice there must have been influence from the men's side, as some hundreds registered for a visit to some industry or other. I hope the husbands will forgive our taking many of the ladies to a diamond establishment and another group to a brewery!

On Thursday there are the excursions for all of the visitors. We appreciate it highly that hundreds and hundreds (I guess about 1600) have registered for a trip through the country or for museum-going. I hope you will like the beauty of the Dutch countryside, with its wide landscape, its attractive scenery, its picturesque mills and its lakes and rivers, and that you will enjoy some paintings and architecture of old as well as modern schools.

As for the forecast of the weather on the day of our excursions, much to my regret I am not in a position to take any responsibility or to give any assurance. Among the Facts about Holland in the preliminary issue of the Congress News you will find comforting information about our climate; evil tongues claim, however, that this country has no climate but that it is favoured by different weather conditions. So let us hope for the best!

I would now submit to you what we have arranged as far as the business sessions are concerned. As for the selection of the subjects to be discussed at this Congress, we asked for the opinion of the participating bodies on a list of 13 subjects of which our sub-committees had made a synopsis. It is not my intention to sum up all the reasons why the six subjects on the programme have been chosen, but I should like to say a few words about each of them.

In the last decades private enterprises have succeeded in spreading their interests to an increasing extent beyond the borders of their own country. As a corollary, the trade in securities has more and more assumed an international character.

Consequently the growth of our profession, which was first developed on a more national scale, is now confronted with problems which compel us to compare internationally the differences in the performance of our function. This is one of the main reasons why the subject 'Principles for the Accountant's Profession' has been chosen for the first plenary session of this Congress.

Ever since private commercial enterprise has played a vital role in production, the profit obtained has been the determining factor for its functioning. Therefore the reporting about the financial results of the enterprise is one of the main objects on which the expert opinion of an auditor is required. Thus it is our professional duty to reflect upon the meaning of profit and upon the means of ascertaining the profit. This reflection is the more necessary since capital investments have become of increasing importance for the running of an enterprise, which involves that long-term developments effect the organization of the business. Amongst these developments changes in value, either through the market or through the currency, have a strong bearing on the business' policy. Consequently it is thought that the problem of 'The Ascertainment of Profit in Business' should be dealt with in the other plenary session.

In performing their auditing function, accountants act on the one hand on behalf of third parties interested in the accounts rendered by the management of its stewardship, and on the other hand they act on behalf of the management itself. Their functioning on behalf of parties other than the management has greatly influenced the concept of the auditor's responsibility for a fair presentation of the company's assets and liabilities in the balance sheet. The evolution of this

concept induces a renewed exchange of views and a further investigation of the principles determining the auditor's responsibility. Therefore the subject of one of the business sessions is: 'The Verification of the Existence of Assets'.
The requirements which have to be met by an efficient management control have led to a development of systems which are collectively called 'budget control'. The application of a system of budget control presents many problems, including those in the field of administrative organization. For this reason, 'Budgeting and the Corresponding Modernization of Accounting' has been chosen as a subject for discussion.
The growing importance of control on behalf of management has still other implications. At first the auditor generally functioned as an independent accounting expert, that is, as a public accountant. As business increased in size and complexity, another branch of the profession came into being. Within the enterprises, and exclusively on behalf of the management, another function was to be fulfilled, namely, that of the internal auditor. Regarding the present day views on this youngest branch of the profession, a great divergency exists as to the functional position of the internal auditor and the scope of his duties. At the session on Wednesday afternoon colleagues of different nationalities will exchange ideas on this topical subject:' The Internal Auditor'.
Both his audit and his advisory functions confront the auditor with problems in the field of business organization. During the past decade various trends have developed within the profession. These developments have led to the setting apart of one of the sessions for the subject: 'Business Organization and the Public Accountant'. It is felt that in future this subject will ask for more attention on the part of the practitioners of our profession.
We greatly appreciate that all colleagues who took part in the written preparation of the exchange of views have done so with expert skill and knowledge; and we are especially indebted to them in that, by keeping close to the time schedule, they enabled us to send out the 31 printed papers on the six subjects concerned to congress members as early as May of this year, thus making it possible for their valuable contents to be studied in time.
I must at this stage say a special word on the translation work that had to be done on the papers, as it was decided to furnish an English translation of all the French, German and Dutch papers, English being —and I can say this without fear of discriminating against any other language— the leading language in our profession.
I doubt whether any of you have ever had to make, or check, a translation of papers like these into or from your own language. Well, I can tell you, from my own experience, that it is the most frightful work that can be imposed upon you. All those who have assisted in doing this disagreeable but responsible job have therefore earned appreciative applause from all of us. *(applause)*
I hope that the solution we were able to find to the difficult problem of the use of different languages will prove to be satisfactory, and I apologize in advance for the inconvenience that undoubtedly remains in this respect for those of our visitors whose language could not be added to the list.
As for the discussions in the business sessions, I know that the members of the panels have done, and are doing, important preparatory work to improve the

debates at the sessions. We are very grateful for their activity and feel sure it will greatly improve the results of the business section of the Congress.

This seems the appropriate moment to deal with what we may expect to be the 'results of the business part'. In this connection we have to bear in mind the following facts. Our profession is still a very young one. Its most essential function is the satisfaction of the need for an independent opinion on financial statements, a need that has only assumed great and world wide importance during recent decades. An international exchange of opinions has hardly started as yet, and is by no means organized systematically. Besides this, in various countries the national development of the profession shows a strong subservience to local circumstances and/or statutory regulations.

Consequently, in a meeting of representatives of so many different countries, and of such a large variety of bodies, any resolution could only be of a very general nature. Moreover, it is my firm belief that the profession cannot be built up on such resolutions and that they would endanger rather than promote further development. Therefore, and in line with the objectives of former congresses, the Congress Committee does not intend to put forward any resolution or recommendation on the problems dealt with.

The main objectives were and are:

firstly, to reach a better understanding of the various views on the subjects under discussion; that is, to learn from one another the points on which we agree, as well as on the how and why with respect to the points on which we differ; and secondly, to stimulate the study of the theory and techniques of the profession throughout the world.

I now come to the end of my address.

In our preparatory work we have tried to avoid all foreseeable risks which might endanger the success of this Congress. However, in the year behind us we have been confronted with one overwhelming danger that had not been calculated by any of us, namely, the threat of a new war. This risk has demonstrated itself in a severe way; it is not even a full year ago that we, in Europe, felt very close to war. By Heaven's grace the immediate threat seems to have been averted; so we have been able to come together to hold our Congress. I sincerely hope that we will all be happy and gay together, although we are well aware of the fact that the dark shadow on the world has not yet disappeared.

At the opening of the 1952 Congress in London the president, Sir Harold Howitt, described the world situation at that moment in the following words: 'It is sad to reflect that, although the tragedies of two world wars are within the memories of most of us, we do not even yet seem to have learned our lesson'.

In re-reading this, and having to recognize that since 1952 only little progress has been achieved, I could not help recollecting how more than 300 years ago a still-quoted Dutch poet, named Camphuysen, expressed himself thus: (freely translated by me)

Oh, were all people sane and wise,
and striving to do well,
the earth would be a paradise!
Now often she's a hell.

Both reflections unmistakably point to the individuals as bearers of the ultimate responsibility for the welfare of the world, and not to nations or groups of nations, neither to political parties nor labour unions nor to any association of employers or scientists. It is each of us, individually who, by his personal attitude towards his fellow-men, exercises a good or a bad influence on the final outcome.

As accountants we are members of a calling which has a strong personal character; in doing our job we are individually responsible. Our profession has retained, and must retain, this characteristic even where in public practice extensive duties have asked for large partnerships of accountants.

In the papers for to-morrow morning's business session it anew has been put before us that truth and fairness are guiding principles for the profession; and it is for each of us individually to live up to these principles.

In this way everyone, according to his abilities and his place, will contribute to peace and justice in the world, as His Royal Highness has pointed out to us in such a convincing way. Seen in this light, there is more idealism to guide us in our profession than is generally assumed by outsiders and than is accepted by even some of ourselves.

With this stimulating aspect in mind, I am glad to declare the proceedings of the Seventh International Congress of Accountants started. *(applause)*

SOCIAL EVENTS

MONDAY, 9TH SEPTEMBER

Cocktail Party at Krasnapolsky Hotel

After the opening session, the Councils of the two sponsoring bodies, The Netherlands Institute of Accountants and The Association of University Trained Accountants, gave a cocktail party at Krasnapolsky Hotel.

Here the Vice-President of the Netherlands Institute of Accountants and the President of the Association of University Trained Accountants, Dr. A. Th. de Lange and Mr. J. G. de Weger, ec. drs., with Mrs. De Lange and Mrs. De Weger, welcomed a great number of delegates of the foreign organizations and many Dutch congress officials.

This well-attended party that lasted till half past six, afforded an excellent opportunity for a first encounter with new friends and also in many cases of meeting old friends again.

Reception in the Concertgebouw

The President of the Congress, Mr. J. Kraayenhof and the Vice-President, Professor A. M. van Rietschoten, with Mrs. Kraayenhof and Mrs. Van Rietschoten welcomed the visitors from abroad and many members of the Dutch sponsoring bodies and their ladies in the grand hall of the Concertgebouw. This hall, in which the opening session had been held in the afternoon, had a festive aspect, being decorated with flowers and lighted effectively. In the small hall films about Holland were shown; several lobbies had been fitted up as bars, the Dutch Inn and the Congress Bar especially proved highly popular. More than 2000 guests were present in the Concertgebouw on this evening.

TUESDAY, 10TH SEPTEMBER

Visit by the Ladies to the Rijksmuseum

The Ladies Committee had organized a visit to the Rijksmuseum for this day. The interest shown in an inspection of the art treasures in this museum was such that three groups had to be formed, meeting at 10.00, 14.30 and 15.30 hours respectively.

The 'Nightwatch' by Rembrandt, his 'Masters of the Cloth Guild' and many other famous paintings attracted a great deal of attention.

Visit by the Ladies to Industrial Places

For the afternoon two visits to Amsterdam industries had been organized. The visit to Asscher's Diamond Company lasted about an hour and was followed up by a tea-party offered in the restaurant of the rowing and sailing club 'De Hoop' on the river Amstel. The visit to the Amstel Brewery could not cover the whole plant, as rebuilding work had rendered part of the brewery inaccessible. This was made good by an enlightening motion picture and some interesting demonstrations.

Delegates' Dinner at Carlton Hotel

After the apéritif, held from 18.30–19.30 hours, Mr. Kraayenhof opened the dinner which was given at Carlton Hotel. Guests of honour were H. R. H. the Prince of the Netherlands; His Excellency the State Secretary of Economic Affairs, Dr. G. M. J. Veldkamp; the Governor of the Queen for the Province of North Holland, Dr. M. J. Prinsen; and the Deputy-Burgomaster of Amsterdam, Dr. A. de Roos.

To all official delegates of the bodies invited an invitation had been sent to attend this dinner and most of them had accepted the invitation. Unfortunately, the available room in the Carlton Restaurant did not make it possible to invite the delegates' ladies as well.

Besides the guests of honour and the delegates from abroad, a number of special guests were at the table. The annexes include a list of the names of all of the guests and the menu and list of toasts.

The following addresses were given:

THE PRESIDENT:

Your Royal Highness, Your Excellency, Ladies and Gentlemen, It is my great honour and pleasure to welcome you to this dinner, which I sincerely hope will be a festival occasion for all of us; a festivity, because we are together as friends from 40 different countries in all parts of the world.

To-night we shall refrain from any discussion on what possibly divides us on professional topics; rather we shall enjoy what unites us, namely the desire to co-operate in every possible way, to achieve greater mutual appreciation and a readiness to support each other, whenever necessary.

It is in this connection that I feel the strong desire to say a special word of welcome to His Royal Highness, the Prince of the Netherlands. On many occasions Your Royal Highness has been a most eminent ambassador of goodwill for the Netherlands in visiting a large number of countries near and far. On the occasion of this Congress, you are performing this function in an excellent way in your own country; firstly, by attending our opening session, where you were kind enough to give us such a stimulating address; and again to-day, as we foregather in this limited group of official delegates, by favouring us with your distinguished presence. I am convinced that all delegates to this Congress will return home with the strong feeling that both Her Majesty the Queen and Your Royal Highness are in high sympathy with the important events in the life and strivings within their nation; and that they give an uplifting example in respect of goodwill to all mankind. May we, therefore, offer our respectful tribute to You, as well as our deepest gratitude.

I very much regret to have to inform you having received a message from His Excellency the Minister of Economic Affairs, Professor Zijlstra, that duties of office prevent him from attending this dinner, as he originally planned. Then, too, I am happy to welcome once more in our midst His Excellency the State Secretary of Economic Affairs, Dr. Veldkamp; the Governor of the Queen

for the Province of North Holland, Dr. Prinsen; the Deputy-Burgomaster of Amsterdam, Dr. de Roos, and our other special guests. From these special guests I may mention by name Dr. W. F. Schokking, because he will be speaking to you at this dinner. Mr. Schokking has been in the Cabinet as Minister of Defence and is now a member of the „Raad van State", the highest advisory body to the Crown.
We are very grateful that they have all accepted our invitation.
For the sponsoring bodies it is a great event, indeed, to be the hosts of nearly 300 special delegates from so many countries, representing more than 100 accountancy bodies. Having you all together is a delightful thing, but it confronts us anew with the language problem. In the story of the Tower of Babel, the Bible teaches us that if everyone was left to speak his own language, there would be chaos. And what is worse, our tower would never be finished! To avoid this disagreeable situation we had to decide on one language to be mainly used at this dinner and, out of respect to the majority of our guests, we have chosen English. But as, much to our regret, no interpretation into other languages is practicable at this dinner, we decided to have the toast to the guests from abroad proposed in French and in German as well and to ask for the response in either of the three languages.
I sincerely hope that you will all engage in lively conversation with your neighbours, irrespective of possible language difficulties. In that way, I am sure, we shall enjoy a pleasant and not too formal gathering, which will be completely in accord with the desire expressed to me by our distinguished guests and undoubtedly with your own wishes as well.
You will now allow me to say a few explanatory words in French and in German as to the use of the English language.

Maintenant je voudrais m'adresser un moment à mes amis qui parlent la langue française. Pour les Associations organisatrices de ce congrès, c'est un grand événement d'être les hôtes d'environ 300 délégués spéciaux représentant plus de 100 organisations professionnelles. Nous sommes très heureux d'être réunis ensemble, mais la diversité des langues nous a causé des problèmes. En ce rapport, je me permets de vous rappeler l'histoire de la Tour de Babel, dans laquelle la Bible nous enseigne que, si tout le monde ne parlait que sa propre langue, le Chaos en résulterait et, ce qui est pire, la construction de la tour ne serait jamais finie!
Afin d'éviter cette situation désagréable, nous étions obligés de nous décider à nous servir principalement d'une seule langue à ce dîner, et dû au respect envers la majorité de nos hôtes, nous avons choisi l'anglais. Cependant, comme à ce dîner on ne peut pas, à notre grand regret, pratiquer d'interprétation en d'autres langues, nous nous sommes décidés à prononcer trois toasts à nos invités de l'étranger: en anglais, en français et en allemand.
J'espère vivement que vous vous engagerez à une conversation vivante avec vos convives, nonobstant les difficultés éventuelles de la langue. De cette façon, je suis sûr que cette réunion ne sera pas trop formelle et que vous vous réjouirez réellement, ce qui sera en harmonie parfaite avec le désir exprimé par nos hôtes distingués, de même que —sans doute—avec le vôtre.

Ich möchte jetzt auch ein direktes Wort an die deutsch sprechenden Gäste richten und zwar bezüglich des Problems der Sprachenschwierigkeiten bei einer so sprachegefärbten Gesellschaft. Hoffentlich haben Sie schon alles verstanden von dem was ich auf englisch oder auf französisch gesagt habe. Ein Festdiner, wie wir dies heute Abend miteinander haben, kann Ansprachen wohl noch vertragen, Uebersetzungen sicherlich nicht. Ich habe mich daher veranlaßt gesehen, mich selbst der englischen Sprache, die Sprache die die Mehrheit unserer Gäste versteht, zu bedienen und die Redner zu bitten, dasselbe zu tun. Es wird aber eine wichtige Ausnahme gemacht werden, und zwar für die an die ausländischen Gäste zu richtende Ansprache. Diese wird von drei verschiedenen holländischen Herren auf englisch, französisch, bezw. deutsch gehalten, und auch in diesen drei Sprachen aus den Kreisen der Gäste beantwortet werden. *(applause)*

THE PRESIDENT then proposed the toast to Her Majesty the Queen.

Thereupon HIS ROYAL HIGHNESS, THE PRINCE OF THE NETHERLANDS proposed the toast to the Heads of States of all Nationalities present at the dinner.

THE PRESIDENT:

Now a toast will be proposed to the guests from abroad, but I will first tell you something about it, because otherwise things might go otherwise than we have intended. There will be only one toast to the guests from abroad, that is not in order to save a drink, it is only to save time. The toast will be introduced by three speeches.

Mr. Van Rietschoten will be the first and he will speak in English. Mr. Besançon will be the second and he will speak in French and Mr. de Weger will be the third and he will speak in the German language.

Mr. Van Rietschoten is the President of the Netherlands Institute of Accountants and is also officiating, as you saw yesterday evening and also yesterday afternoon, as Vice-President of the Congress; Mr. Besançon is a member of the Congress Committee and Mr. De Weger is President of the Association of University Trained Accountants.

Now after these three gentlemen have spoken to you, I will propose the toast to the guests from abroad; so if you think they deserve it, you might applaud after they have spoken, but they will not lift their glass.

We could, of course, not make the same restriction as to the gentlemen who will be kind enough to respond to this toast. So Mr. Marquis Eaton, who will be speaking on behalf of the English speaking guests, after his speech, may lift his glass in response to the speech of Prof. Van Rietschoten. After their speeches Mr. Veyrenc and Dr. Bredt can do the same in response to the speeches in French and in German. So then you can perhaps lift your glasses three times. May I now call upon Prof. Van Rietschoten.

PROF. A. M. VAN RIETSCHOTEN, President of the Netherlands Institute of Accountants and Vice-President of the Congress, speaking to the guests from abroad in the English language:

Your Royal Highness, Your Excellency, Mr. President, Ladies and Gentlemen, It is a privilege and a pleasure to me to welcome our guests from abroad in the mother language of our profession, the English language. I think that all of you will agree with me that the professional bodies represented at this congress play a prominent part in the development of our profession and members take their duties towards them very seriously. To many a delegate his professional association counts among his most exacting employers.

As a group the accountancy bodies throughout the world look to me like a large family whose members are scattered all over the world. It being impossible to meet frequently, it has proved feasible to bring about the reunion of the family every five years, except when there happens to be a war on. But that means that it is quite an event to have the whole family together. In part because we wanted to show our professional friends from abroad the resurrection of this country after the war the Dutch bodies in 1952 invited you to come and hold your next meeting in Amsterdam. The editor of the English journal 'The Accountant' in a recent article referred to this city as the Venice of the North, because of her many canals. He may not have realized that Amsterdam resembles Venice in yet another respect. The Venetians of the Middle Ages were the traders and freight carriers of the world and the Netherlands' people, especially the merchants of Amsterdam, have taken over this function after the sea-routes to the Far East and to America had been discovered. From the 16th century onwards our prosperity has for a good part been based on our trade on the East. After the second world-war, however, circumstances have changed fundamentally. The trade with the East is to a great extent lost to us and we have fallen back on our own resources.

The density of population in this country is about three times that of the most populous state in the United States of America. While in the State of New York live about 300 people per square mile, we have more than 900. To a country with small natural resources such a change in circumstances constitutes a challenge. With Toynbee, many consider the answer a community gives to a challenge to make history. We only have our personal abilities to help us to make the most of our new situation. We like to think that with foreign aid so graciously extended to us, we have not been entirely unsuccessful. That is one of the reasons why we feel somewhat proud to be your hosts for these few days. We sincerely hope that you will enjoy your stay with us and that you will be able to get some impression of the situation we live in. Many of you have had to travel great distances to reach this country. We are most grateful to you for having taken all this trouble and we thank you most heartily. We feel greatly stimulated by your presence, and if it so happens that the proceedings of this Congress benefit our profession, this will be due to you, our guests from abroad. *(applause)*

MR. R. BESANÇON, member of the Congress Committee, speaking to the guests from abroad in the French language:

Altesse Royale, Monsieur le Secrétaire d'Etat, Monsieur le Président, Mesdames, Messieurs,

En préparant cette allocution en langue française dont vous, M. le Président, m'avez fait l'honneur de me charger, il m'est passé par l'esprit un mot récent d'une fillette française. S'étonnant, peut-être pour la première fois de sa vie, de la complexité du monde au delà des frontières de son propre pays, elle demanda à sa mère 'Est-ce que les autres pays ont aussi une histoire de France?' Voilà une question bien plus intéressante que la réponse, du reste inconnue, parce qu'elle exprime avec une simplicité touchante le point de départ, bien des fois, de réflections et de délibérations sur des questions et des problèmes internationaux.

Admettons, M. le Président, qu'en nous occupant de la situation professionnelle dans un autre pays, il nous arrive parfois de demander aussi: 'Est-ce qu'ils ont comme nous un Ordre d'Experts Comptables, un Institute of Chartered Accountants ou un Nederlands Instituut van Accountants?'

Ainsi, pour comprendre la position professionnelle ailleurs, et peut-être aussi pour en juger, nous partons inconsciemment de la situation dans notre propre pays, c'est à dire nous estimons les autres à notre mesure, et il va sans dire qu'une telle méthode n'aboutit à aucun résultat.

Pour comprendre et apprécier, tant dans la vie personnelle que dans la vie professionnelle, les conceptions, les idées, les façons de faire, toutes différentes des nôtres, il nous faut tout d'abord nous débarrasser des erreurs d'un égocentrisme individuel ou national, et nous placer, libres d'esprit, sans préjugés quelconques, en face des problèmes résultant de la diversité frappante qui existe encore dans tout les domaines de notre belle profession.

M. le Président, l'inspiration pour cette thèse m'a été donnée par nos invités étrangers de ce soir et par le chaleureux acceuil que notre invitation à ce congrès a reçu de la part des autres membres des associations professionnelles dont ils sont les représentants. Le fait que plus de 1600 collègues étrangers avec les dames assistent au congrès nous a vraiment réjoui de grand cœur. Avouons humblement, qu'en même temps, nos pauvres cœurs ont été saisis par la lourde responsabilité d'organiser un congrès digne d'une assistance tellement nombreuse et compétente.

La visite de tant de centaines d'éminents confrères est pour nous une preuve incontestable que le désir de ranimer le contact international dans un esprit confraternel, amical et sans préjugés, est partout vivant.

Cela nous a donné l'élan et la force de surmonter les difficultés toujours inhérentes à l'organisation d'un tel événement.

C'est pour cette raison, M. le Président, que nous voulons remercier de tout cœur les délégués d'être venus (et bien souvent de très loin) et d'avoir accepté notre invitation d'être présent ce soir. Et nous les prions de bien vouloir exprimer aux associations qu'ils représentent notre profonde reconnaissance pour l'appui inestimable que nous avons reçu, et des associations elles-mêmes et de tant de leurs members. *(applause)*

MR. J. G. DE WEGER, EC. DRS., President of the Association of University Trained Accountants, speaking to the guests from abroad in the German language:

Königliche Hoheit, Exzellenz, Herr Präsident, Meine Damen und Herren!

Es ist mir eine besondere Ehre bei dieser feierlichen Gelegenheit einige Worte – in deutscher Sprache – an Sie richten zu dürfen. Daß die Teilnehmer an diesem Kongreß, darunter recht viele deutschsprechende, in so großer Zahl und mit den besten Gefühlen internationaler Verbundenheit aus aller Welt nach Amsterdam gekommen sind, ist für uns in Holland sehr erfreulich. Diese große Teilnahme war für uns eine extra Anregung alles daranzusetzen den glatten und möglichst befriedigenden Verlauf des Kongresses sicherzustellen. Schon im voraus möchte ich denjenigen, die auf diesem Kongreß einen aktiven Beitrag zur Weiterentwicklung unseres Berufes liefern wollen, von Herzen danken. Wir sind ihnen deswegen sehr verbunden.

Während Ihres kurzen Aufenthaltes in unsrer Hauptstadt werden Ihnen bereits die kleinen Schilder aufgefallen sein, welche die in vielen Sprachen verständliche Bezeichnung 'Het Atoom' tragen. Diese Schilder zeigen den Weg zur Ausstellung, die von seiner Königlichen Hoheit im Vorwort zum Ausstellungskatalog als die erste internationale Ausstellung, welche die Benutzung der Kernenergie zu friedlichen Zwecken zum Gegenstand hat, gekennzeichnet wurde. Bei dem Besuch dieser Ausstellung empfinden wir Gefühle des Staunens und der Freude über die Möglichkeiten die uns der Gebrauch dieser fast unvorstellbaren Kraft- und Wärmequellen in Aussicht stellen. Gerade diese ungeheuren Möglichkeiten sollen den Inhabern und Geschäftsführern aller in Betracht kommenden Unternehmungen von ihrer großen Verantwortlichkeit hinsichtlich der Benutzung dieser Energie durchdringen.

Es wurde im Kreis unserer deutschsprechenden Kollegen schon eher gesagt: wir leben dem Atomzeitalter entgegen. Dies bedingt Anpassung. Technisch gilt es nicht nur die Bändigung und Steuerung der Atomprozesse, sondern auch die fortschreitende Automatisierung und die Errungenschaften auf dem Gebiet der Elektronics. Soziologisch betrifft es die Anpassung an neue Arbeitsspannen, an andere Arbeitsorte und -methoden. In moralischer Hinsicht schließlich besteht diese Anpassung zumal in der Beherrschung dieser Elementargewalt, die der Schöpfer uns freigibt, in dem Fernhalten der Vernichtungen und in der Förderung des positiven Gebrauchs zum eigenen Nutzen des Unternehmens, zum Nutzen des Landes und Volkes, ja – und der Schritt ist kleiner als je – zum Nutzen der Menschheit.

Der Wirtschaftsprüfer hilft den Unternehmern, die bewußt und mit voller Energie ihre Mitarbeit zum neuen Zeitalter geben, nachdem sie in den eben vergangenen Jahren viele Folgen des Krieges überwunden haben. Ihre Tatkraft möge nur dem Guten dienen, auch wenn ihnen unvermutete Möglichkeiten geboten werden sollten. Ich glaube, daß man nicht schwarzseherisch zu sein braucht, vielmehr mit Vertrauen der Zukunft entgegensehen kann.

Die Aufgabe des Wirtschaftsprüfers ist von der des Unternehmers verschieden. Ersterer prüft und berät, ist jedoch nicht dazu berufen selbst die Zügel zu führen. Kann aber sein Einfluß zum Guten nicht sehr groß sein? Besteht für den Wirtschaftsprüfer, der an der Wiege vieler Entwicklungen stehen darf, nicht ganz besonders die Möglichkeit dem Frieden und dem Wohlstand zu dienen? Kann und soll er darum auch nicht im wohlverstandenen Interesse des Unternehmens..... und in dem der Menschheit solche Gelegenheiten benutzen und damit helfen einer etwaigen negativen Wirkung Einhalt zu tun, andererseits aber die positive Wirkung bestens zu fördern?

Die Feststellung, daß wir dem Atomzeitalter entgegenleben, soll unser Tun

unbedingt mit bestimmen und uns auch auf diesem Kongreß nicht unberührt lassen. Bei der Behandlung der Fachprobleme soll die zu erwartende große Umwälzung und die dadurch bedingte Anpassung im Hintergrund unsres Denkens stehen. Es mögen daneben die Stunden der Erholung, die wir hier zusammen erleben, ein gutes Zeichen sein für eine glückliche Zukunft, die wir unsrer Nachkommenschaft so sehr wünschen.
Wenn wir gleich den Toast auf unsere geehrten Gäste ausbringen, so bitte ich Sie dabei auch speziell an das Wohl und Glück derjenigen zu denken, die nach uns kommen, unserer Kinder und Kindeskinder. *(applause)*

HIS ROYAL HIGHNESS, THE PRINCE OF THE NETHERLANDS at this point interrupted and addressed some words in Spanish to the Spanish-speaking guests.

THE PRESIDENT then proposed the toast to the guests from abroad.

MR. MARQUIS G. EATON, President of the American Institute of Certified Public Accountants, responding to the toast for the English-speaking guests:

Your Royal Highness, Excellency, Mr. President, Ladies and Gentlemen,
The several meetings of the Congress have until now been serious occasions, as was entirely proper.
I hope, then, that you will forgive me if I find something amusing in my present situation.
It occurs to me that it is somewhat more humorous than appropriate that a man from Texas should undertake now to respond on behalf of the so-called English-speaking guests.
In Texas and in England, to mention only two of the great English-speaking countries, we use many of the same words but we pronounce them all differently, and in most cases we use them with different meanings.
In Texas and in England we speak the same language only in the loosest sense of the word.
I was reminded of this again the other day when in Northern England Mrs. Eaton and I stopped at a roadside hotel for lunch. When we entered the place, I found an individual who at high noon was dressed exactly as I am now. Some previous experience with English custom told me that this signified that he was some sort of functionary of the establishment.
When I asked him whether we might be served with lunch his reply was 'Straight away'.
In Texas we would use the word 'straight', as in the shortest distance between two points; and the word 'away' meaning 'not here'. In Texas usage, however, the man's reply seemed to have little relevance to my problem.
But, from some brief contact with English, as it is spoken in England, I felt that I had a choice of two possible meanings: Either the man intended to say that we could be served at once, or he meant to tell me that if I would move directly forward in the way I was facing I would find the dining room.
As I say, in Texas and in England, we speak the same language only at scattered points.
And as to our cousins in Scotland, we only pray to the same God.
But to return to my duty. I will make a run at it —which translated into English I think means I will give it a go.

It is a pleasant thing indeed when a guest can feel an unreserved sense of gratitude to his host. The arrangements for this meeting, the skill and energy which have gone into its planning, bespeak a generous and friendly nation. Those of us from the English-speaking countries who have come to sit down in friendship with our professional colleagues feel warmed and richly rewarded. But as I speak of the gratitude of the English-speaking guests toward our host accountants, I should like in a personal way, and as an American, to acknowledge also the gratitude my country has felt toward The Netherlands through all the several hundred years of the history of the New World.

Most of us who came from the United States to this meeting in Amsterdam took ship at Nieuw Amsterdam, which has lately come to be called New York. We recall that from 1607 you gave hospitality near Leyden to a band of Puritans, 35 of whom in 1620 joined a group to sail for America on a small vessel called the Mayflower.

They landed at Plymouth, on our Cape Cod, and are known by us with affection and respect as the Founding Pilgrim Fathers.

We remember also that in 1792 your country, always a passionate partisan of freedom, made the first friendly gesture toward an infant republic calling itself the United States of America. On April 19 of that year the States-General of The Netherlands recognized the United States, and on October 8 concluded with our ambassador John Adams a treaty of friendship and commerce. In that same year John Adams bought a mansion in The Hague which thus became the first legation building to be owned abroad by our new nation.

Shortly thereafter the Amsterdam banking house of Van Staphorst Brothers made a loan of $ 2,000,000 to the Congress of the United States. The house in which this took place may still be found at Number 280 Singel in this city. Other Dutch banking houses followed with loans of 30,000,000 guilders, equivalent to $ 300,000,000 to-day. Under the circumstances of the times these loans must be regarded as having been advanced at heavy risk. They constituted The Netherlands Marshall Plan for America.

These were no small gestures, coming as they did from a great commercial and maritime power.

Entirely aside from my own country's obligation to our host, all of the accountants represented here are indebted to The Netherlands for holding in 1926 the 2nd International Congress of Accountants, which was in fact the first of the current modern series.

When, in these troubled times, we accountants from the various countries of the world meet together, we are conscious of the stresses that would tear apart the friendships which sovereign nations should, on moral grounds and in their own self-interest, hold for each other.

One of the day-by-day and never-ending difficulties arises from differences in the languages we speak. What a great nuisance it is that we should speak in so many tongues, and be forced to communicate our most intricate thoughts by means of translation, which is slow and costly and must often be inexact. What a great boon to mankind it would be if we all could form our thoughts, and communicate them, in one great universal language. It is difficult to believe that many of our present strains could survive such an event.

In the meanwhile the greatest single bulwark against tensions between nations is friendly international trade and investment. The more one nation trades with another, the more each elevates its conditions through the use of the other's goods of commerce, the stronger are forged the links of mutual advantage—links which themselves are not the weakest of the materials of friendship. I need not dilate on the connection between our science of accounting, and international trade and investment. We have all found in the history of commerce and industry, and in the history of accounting, the evidence that they have developed and expanded hand in hand—that without any question whatever they are mutually dependent. We have seen how, until accounting began to take on the principles of its present form, commerce was limited to small concerns, and to restricted geographical areas, in which firsthand knowledge could serve as substitute for accounts.

Fortunately, and as I believe inevitably, the development of accounting has until now followed much the same course in all of the industrial and trading countries. It has become the single language in which business results, and business status, are expressed throughout the world. To that important extent we accountants have in our custody, for administration to the greatest good of all mankind, a significant part of the universal language we all desire.

I do not believe that I overdramatize my point when I say that these conditions present us with responsibility, and opportunity, of first magnitude in affairs. We will discharge that responsibility to the extent that we guide the future course of accounting to adopt the best practices, in whatever country these may originate, and shape it so that we achieve the greatest practical uniformity in accounting principle, in standards of financial reporting and disclosure, in the concept of independence of the auditor, and in the many other things which, taken together, make up present-day accounting and the profession of accountancy. It will never be said of the accountants of the world that they failed to bring to full usefulness in the affairs of mankind the part of the universal language which was within their keeping.

In closing, I express this wish for our profession of accountancy: May she continue forever to be distinguished for her vital role in building toward a better world social order. *(applause)*

MR. A. VEYRENC, President of the Conseil Supérieur of the Ordre National des Experts Comptables et des Comptables Agréés, responding to the toast for the French-speaking guests:

Altesse Royale, Monsieur le Secrétaire d'Etat, Monsieur le Président, Mesdames, Messieurs, Au nom de mes collègues français, j'ai d'abord le devoir de prier votre Altesse Royale d'agréer l'expression de notre profonde déférence et de notre respectueuse sympathie. En rappelant en quelle haute estime le peuple de France tient votre Altesse, laissez-moi vous dire combien la délégation française a été touchée de vous voir présider la séance inaugurale du Congrès.

Je veux maintenant remercier de tout cœur notre collègue hollandais—Monsieur René Besançon – des souhaits de bienvenue qu'il vient de nous adresser avec tant de gentillesse et auxquels nous avons été particulièrement sensibles.

Ils confirment l'ambiance confraternelle qui préside aux travaux du VIIe Congrès International d'Experts Comptables.

Mes collègues français et moi-même ne pouvons que nous féliciter de ce que les Pays-Bas, renommés de longue date pour la cordialité de leur acceuil, aient été désignés pour organiser ce Congrès.

Il nous est très agréable de nous trouver dans votre belle cité d'Amsterdam, joyau de la Hollande, qui jouit d'une réputation si hautement justifiée aussi bien pour ses beautés naturelles que par la place importante qu'elle occupe dans le domaine international des affaires, le rôle de premier plan qui est le sien, non seulement comme capitale des Pays-Bas, mais encore comme centre commercial et bancaire débordant largement les frontières de votre beau pays.

Les français n'ont pas oublié non plus que, il y a trois siècles, leur illustre compatriote Descartes trouva, sur la terre hospitalière de Hollande, la sereine quiétude qui lui permit d'élaborer les plus célèbres de ses œuvres.

Sans entrer dans le détail des questions techniques soumises à l'étude du Congrès, je voudrais seulement rappeler que la comptabilité se présente partout comme un instrument nécessaire et efficace de la productivité dans les entreprises. Il est donc d'un grand intérêt que soient confrontées, dans des assises internationales comme celle-ci, les opinions de professionnels qualifiés de toutes nations afin de pouvoir dégager de leurs échanges de vue et de leurs communs efforts, toutes conclusions susceptibles d'orienter l'exercice de la profession vers les techniques modernes les plus aptes à favoriser la gestion des entreprises et accroître leur efficience.

Sur le plan humain, l'intérêt de ces congrès n'apparaît pas moindre. De telles manifestations ne peuvent que contribuer à intensifier nos relations culturelles, à resserrer nos liens réciproques de confiance et de bonne confraternité. Ces contacts et ces travaux poursuivis en commun nous font mieux connaître les uns les autres et substituent à certains préjugés qui peuvent peut-être exister, un climat international de mutuelle compréhension et d'estime réciproque. Ils constituent un moyen de rapprochement qui, tout en favorisant les progrès techniques, développe en même temps un esprit de solidarité entre nations également éprises de liberté et d'esprit pacifique.

En vous félicitant du grand succès du septième Congrès International d' Experts Comptables, qu'il soit permis aux members de la délégation française d'exprimer à tous leurs collègues hollandais leurs sentiments de confraternelle sympathie et de cordiale gratitude.

Ils prient très respectueusement votre Altesse Royale d'agréer, pour la nation néerlandaise, leurs vœux ardents de Paix et de Prospérité, et de bien vouloir présenter à sa Majesté la Reine leurs hommages les plus déférents. *(applause)*

DR. ING. OTTO BREDT, President of the Institut der Wirtschaftsprüfer, Germany, responding to the toast for the German-speaking guests:

Königliche Hoheit, Exzellenz, Herr Präsident, meine Damen und Herren, liebe niederländische Kollegen!

Im Auftrage der Delegationen der deutschsprachigen Länder habe ich die Ehre und die ganz besondere Freude, Ihnen für diese wunderbaren Tage in Amsterdam und für die Ansprache, die Sie an uns gerichtet haben, unseren herzlichsten Dank auszusprechen. Als wir vor 5 Jahren mit freudigem Danke Ihrer Einladung zustimmten, den nächsten internationalen Accountants-Kongreß hier in Amsterdam zu veranstalten, waren wir uns von vornherein darüber klar, daß dieser Kongreß, genau so wie der sechste in London, ein voller Erfolg werden würde. Zwei Dinge waren es, die uns in dieser Ansicht bestärkten: Die alte, traditionelle und schon sprichwörtlich gewordene Gastfreundschaft der Niederlande und die in der ganzen Welt bekannte Meisterschaft unserer niederländischen Kollegen in der Organisation und in fachlicher Beziehung. Seit dem Londoner Kongreß sind 5 Jahre ins Land gegangen. In diesen 5 Jahren sind wir Ihnen immer näher gekommen, wir haben Sie immer näher kennengelernt und, ich darf es offen bekennen, immer mehr schätzen gelernt, so daß wir heute in unseren Herzen Ihre Freunde geworden sind. Wir haben mit Ihnen vor 2 Jahren in Scheveningen Ihr 65-jähriges Jubiläum miterleben dürfen. Sie haben uns dort gezeigt, wie man die Realität des Alltags im Kampf um das Brot, das tägliche Brot, in meisterhafter Weise harmonisieren kann mit den Idealen, die Sie in Ihrem Innern tragen. Doch damit nicht genug. Sie haben uns auch gezeigt, wie man den Ernst des Alltags mit dem Frohsinn der Freizeit verbinden kann zu dem, was Sie Ihr Leben hier in den Niederlanden nennen. Dafür danken wir Ihnen ganz besonders.

Es liegt ein tiefer Sinn in diesen internationalen Veranstaltungen. Nicht etwa nur der, daß die Kollegen aus aller Welt hier zusammenkommen, um ihre praktischen Fragen, ihre Erfahrungen und Gedanken auszutauschen. Noch weit mehr erscheint uns der Sinn darin zu liegen, daß wir hier auf diesem Boden persönliche Beziehungen anknüpfen können, Beziehungen von Mensch zu Mensch und damit auch von Volk zu Volk. Und nun, meine lieben Kollegen aus aller Welt, werden Sie mit mir wissen, warum dieser Siebente Internationale Accountants-Kongreß hier in Amsterdam veranstaltet wurde, ich möchte sogar sagen, veranstaltet werden mußte: weil hier in den Niederlanden uns vorgelebt wird, wie man internationale, wie man nationale, wie man menschliche Beziehungen gestalten soll. Lassen Sie uns damit diesen Siebenten Internationalen Kongreß zu einem weiteren Baustein auf dem Weg in die Zukunft werden lassen. Lassen Sie uns aber nie vergessen, daß mit dem Ernst der fachlichen Arbeit der Frohsinn und die Freude der geselligen Veranstaltung verbunden werden, damit wir das Leben zu dem machen, was des Lebens wert ist und was es menschenwürdig macht. Gestatten Sie mir, daß ich das, was ich Ihnen am heutigen Abend sagen möchte, in diesem Sinne in einem Reim ausklingen lasse:

Habt Freude in Herzen, auch wenn's weh manchmal tut
Mit Lachen und Scherzen geht's noch einmal so gut.

Und nun gestatten Sie mir, als letztem der ausländischen Redner, daß ich Sie alle, meine lieben Kollegen aus aller Welt, auffordere, das Glas zu erheben und auf unsere niederländischen Gastgeber zu trinken. *(applause)*

DR. W. F. SCHOKKING, proposing the toast to the accountancy profession:

Your Royal Highness, Your Excellency, Mr. President, Ladies and Gentlemen, I feel impressed by the degree of perfection in the organization of this Congress. This afternoon when at home, I received a letter from your secretariat, telling me that I should deliver my speech to-night at 10.16. My first reaction was:

do I indeed need a warning to stay sober until that time? Judging from the good time we had, I dare say this warning was not quite superfluous. But nevertheless I hope you will be content with my present state of mind.

May I be serious now?

I look upon it as a great honour that your President, Mr. Kraayenhof, asked me some time ago to deliver a short address to this honourable company to-night.

Generally speaking, Mr. Kraayenhof is not the man dependent on the help of others. However, he knew of my great interest in your profession and its great importance for the structure of our modern society, and therefore I dared not disappoint him. Maybe you, too, know his kind way of asking you to help him.

It is on record how your profession started; how it developed and has reached this summit in a period of less than a century.

In our present day your profession has become an indispensable element in governmental affairs and in business.

Professionally your garments are not the hood and gown. You do not wear wigs. Your modest, yet most efficient, mighty and spectacular tool is your fountain-pen. I must confess, too, it is a very special one, as it needs no refilling; its flow is continuous and never runs out.

Being away from your countries—and as far as your Dutch colleagues present here are concerned, away from their offices—you will hardly realize what the temporary blocking up of this flow may mean to your clients or employers now that the nib has come to rest for a short period.

I wonder whether your clients or employers enjoy a happy breathing space. No cross-examination on accounts, on sheets of balance etc., etc.

Now that you are away, I wonder on the other hand, in how far a kind of feeling of unrest and feeling of unsettlement is developing since your clients and employers are foregoing the benefit of your wise auditing. I am told that they are relying to such an extent on your most valuable advice, that they will only find their bearings the moment you have come back to their rescue.

It is not your clients and employers only, it is the whole governmental and business-sphere in the world, which cannot do without your wisdom and helpful assistance.

If sheer modesty should forbid you to believe me, I want to prove the truth of what I have said by telling you a story. I should like to add: this is not the same as telling you stories!

Two students went abroad for a holiday. At a certain moment they found they had no money left. Both of them wired their daddies: 'Nearly broke Stop What must we do?'

One father wired: 'Do not worry; wait some more days; I shall have more bank-notes printed at short notice'.

This gentleman was most fervently in favour of the theory that inflation is the most workable solution for financial difficulties. Moreover one of his basic ideals was to have one's debts paid by others in future.

The father of the second cabled: 'Return to-day'.

The latter was: an accountant.

May I wind up with the following?

Your scientific training as accountants is a guarantee that economic and financial problems can be reduced to their real proportions.

According to my conviction, your scientific training implies mastering the know-how of getting rid of so-called important items, mastering the art of clarifying the facts and data. Your education implies that an authoritative advice should be based on character and qualification.

Last not least, the power and capacity to convey this well-founded advice to the client or employer in question.

As I understood from the address at the opening session, in the international field much more is required on all hands in your profession than was the case in the past.

Since the second world-war there is a steady increase in the rate in which the evolution proceeds. I feel privileged that to all appearances you are not only living up to expectations but are taking the lead and going ahead unswervingly.

I do not mean to say that the responsibility of your clients, whether ministers or government-officials or directors of companies are concerned, has been taken over or should be. Not by any means!

Your profession, however, has brought about a work of art. It has created a 'responsibility of your own'. A creation because it is something new, which was not there before.

And now I want to raise my glass in honour of your profession, most valuable and indispensable in our modern world. *(applause)*

MR. J. F. DOWLING, President of the Institute of Chartered Accountants of Scotland, responding to the toast to the accountancy profession:

Your Royal Highness, Your Excellency, Mr. President, Mr. Schokking, Ladies and Gentlemen, As you Mr. President have indicated, the honour of replying to the toast which Mr. Schokking has proposed in such encouraging terms has fallen to me, because I am privileged to be President for this year of the oldest existing Accountancy Body in the world, The Institute of Chartered Accountants of Scotland. I speak of the age of my own Institute with due humility in the presence of our Italian colleagues, because while the Scottish Institute was founded no longer ago than 1854 the first Association of Accountants of which there is any record, the Collegio de Raxionati was founded in Venice as early as 1581. The vicissitudes of history are, however, such that my Institute has the longest continuous existence of the Accountancy Bodies of the present day. In this city I would like to acknowledge the special debt which the profession in Scotland owes to the Netherlands. I refer to the fact that George Watson, the first Scots accountant to set up in public practice, learned his bookkeeping here in the Netherlands. In Edinburgh you may still see accountbooks in his writing which open with the words: 'Laus deo ady primo July 1674 in Rotterdam'. We have been reminded this evening that our profession is a relatively young one and in that connection I would like to tell you a story which has as its basis the game of golf. That game is, we are told, one which was invented in the Netherlands, but in Scotland we too play golf. Some years ago we had in Scotland a visit from an Indian Prince who made his way to St. Andrews. And there he was fascinated to see this game being played. He gave instructions that full details were to be obtained and ordered the officials in his own country immediately to prepare for his playing on his return. That was done and the day came when the Prince had to play his first game. There he stood with a lovely new bag of clubs and a nice white ball on the tee. His attention was directed to the green some 350 yards away in which a flag moved gently on the breeze. With beginner's luck his first shot was a beauty—right down in the middle. When he was handed another club, he again did supremely well, and the ball finished about a yard from the hole. He asked for further instructions, and was handed a putter. He was told to put the ball not in the hole but 2 inches to the left. He did this exactly as directed. He then asked for additional instruction. He was told at that point to remove his turban from his head, throw it on the ground, stand on it in anger and shout 'Confound it, I've missed it'.

Mr. President, I don't see we miss anything if we admit we are a young profession and have much to learn. I think we can take encouragement from the progress we have made but at the same time we should ask ourselves the question whether there is a reasonable hope and expectation that our progress will continue, and that the influence which the accountant exerts, will expand further in the years ahead, to the greater benefit of the industrial and commercial life of the world. I suggest the answer to that question should be an emphatic 'yes'. I take that view because we can show not only that we are alert to the scope and need for further progress, but also that we are active in its pursuit. Not the least of the evidence to that effect is the holding of this great Congress where accountants of many nations meet together. Here developments which are taking place are reviewed and their merits are discussed. New ideas are brought forward and debated, and I am sure we shall not be sluggish in our acceptance of the good in them. I am confident, Mr. President, that our approach to these matters improves considerably on that of the University student of whose work his tutor said: 'Mr. Smith's work contains much that is good and much that is new, but that which is good is not new and that which is new is not good'.

It has been suggested that where there is one accountant he will produce an acceptable set of figures, but that where there are two or more accountants they will produce an argument. That is probably an overstatement. But it is true to say that there are accounting questions on which there are differences of opinion amongst accountants. I do not think that this is to be regretted; on the contrary it is from the resulting discussion and debate that the correct answer often emerges. This is neither the time nor the place to discuss the differences.

Instead I prefer to turn to some matters of fundamental importance to the responsible exercise of our profession on which I suggest we are all in agreement. The first of these is that the accountant must always bring to the performance of his functions, integrity and independence. The second is that the accountant should always be prepared to exercise his personal judgment. I am sure there is general agreement that the accountant must be ready to answer the call to do so and be equipped to merit the privilege, and accept the responsibility, of expressing a carefully considered and soundly based personal opinion.

And the third point relates to standards of professional conduct. It would not, I think, be disputed that—to put it at its lowest—qualified accountants throughout the world observe standards of professional conduct at least as high as those of any other profession. I have mentioned very briefly three matters which I think are to be regarded as of primary concern to us and I venture to suggest that we are in agreement on them. If I am right in that view, it seems to me that we have in them factors which operate to bind accountants together, irrespective of the part of the world in which they practise their profession and in spite of natural differences of opinion on other questions.

Mr. President, Sir, one of our difficulties is that accounting terminology does not yet have universally accepted meaning. But that will, I hope, be achieved some day. The confusion which can sometimes arise from the use of words which can have different meanings is illustrated by the story of the man who wished to construct his family tree. To that end he worked hand in hand with an expert and he was horrified to find in the course of his enquiries that one of his ancestors had committed a murder and had died an untimely death on the electric chair. The expert assured him there was no cause for alarm—that particular ancestor would be described in the family tree as one who had occupied the Chair of applied electricity in a well-known public institution, and had died in harness.

Mr. President, in these days when many countries, including my own, depend for their very existence on international trade, members of the accountancy profession cannot afford to be parochially minded.

A Congress, such as this, attended by accountants from all over the world is a good prophylactic against parochialism. I feel certain we can learn much from each other and thus add to the store of knowledge on which we can draw when we are called upon to discharge that duty which I hope will always lie in the path of the qualified accountant, and which none should wish to shirk—the giving of that invaluable service to the communities of the world which consists in the expression of impartial and informed opinion on accounting and allied questions based on a critical analysis, by a trained and independent mind, of all the relevant facts and circumstances.

On behalf of my profession, I thank you, Mr. Schokking, for the way in which you have proposed this toast and you, Ladies and Gentlemen, for the manner—the perhaps not surprisingly warm manner—in which you received it. *(applause)*

MR. W. H. LAWSON, President of the Institute of Chartered Accountants in England and Wales, proposing the toast to the Congress Committee:

Your Royal Highness, Your Excellency, Ladies and Gentlemen,

I am sure that you would all like to drink just one more toast, a toast to the Congress Committee. They are, of course, the representatives of our hosts to-night, The Netherlands Institute of Accountants and The Association of University Trained Accountants. Our hosts are giving us the most wonderful evening, and I'm sure this evening will remain in our memories as one of the most happy occasions of this whole congress. Now this is not the time to propose a vote of thanks to the Congress Committee, we were told yesterday that in Holland we must not praise the day before the night. Nevertheless, I hope I

may be allowed to say on behalf of all the guest bodies that we do feel that the congress has started magnificently and we are seeing the result of this tremendous work which has been put into its organization by the committee, and its President, Mr. Kraayenhof, and if I may add, with an extremely able secretariat, led by Mr. De Bruyne and Mr. Boertien.
We realize that the success of this congress is not due only to organization, and we appreciate enormously the wonderful friendliness and kindliness of our hosts. In these days it is not always that 40 countries agree about anything, but I'm quite sure that we all agree to-night in thanking from our hearts our hosts and the Congress Committee for all they're doing for us. Your Royal Highness, Your Excellency, Ladies and Gentlemen, I ask you to rise and drink to the Congress Committee. *(applause)*

THE PRESIDENT:

I may make a few remarks, more or less in a professional way, in which of course I will try to avoid any point on which we might be divided. I would have to confess to you, that it would not be a fair statement, if I would say that I did not know that Mr. Lawson would ask to speak to propose the toast to the Congress Committee, but I can assure you that I did not know that what he was going to say would be an overstatement! But now he has done so, I can only accept his nice and kind words on behalf of the Congress Committee and of the sponsoring bodies of whom many members shared the work with us, and to say to you all that we thank you very much for coming; beaucoup de remerciements que vous êtes venus; tausend Dank daß Sie gekommen sind! *(applause)*

The dinner ended at 11.30 p.m.

Round Trip by boat

In the evening the other participants in the Congress and the ladies made a round trip by boat through the partly illuminated canals and harbours of Amsterdam. This trip was tendered by the Municipal Council of Amsterdam. About 1500 visitors took part in the trip. The fleet consisted of 20 of the well-known Amsterdam sightseeing boats.

WEDNESDAY, 11TH SEPTEMBER

Meeting of Leaders of Delegations, Amstel Hotel

At 11 hours a meeting of the leaders of delegations took place at Amstel Hotel. This meeting was followed by a lunch in the same hotel, offered by the President of the Congress to the attendants of the meeting and their ladies.

Visit by the Ladies to Fashion Parades

The Ladies Committee had organized two fashion parades viz. one at Victoria Hotel in Amsterdam and another at Hotel Bouwes in Zandvoort. The show at Victoria Hotel was presented by Offerman Couture and that at Hotel Bouwes by Maison Vogelzang. Both shows attracted lively interest.

Concert

Even though Muse did not stand at the cradle of the accountancy profession, its growth has never been affected. Muse did attend the Congress, however. The Large Hall of the Concertgebouw had accommodated the plenary session of the Congress during the daytime, but in the evening of 11th September it was claimed by Muse. On the rostrum from which the members of the panel had held their discussions in the afternoon, the Concertgebouw Orchestra took their traditional places that evening to give a gala concert offered by the Municipal Council of Amsterdam.

The orchestra has such an international fame that it is superfluous to expatiate on it. Without national chauvinism it may be stated that, first for many years under the conduct of Willem Mengelberg and thereafter under its present conductor Eduard van Beinum, the Concertgebouw Orchestra ranks as one of the leading orchestras in the world.

As was to be expected at such a gala evening for an international gathering, a varied programme had been composed. It comprised works from various periods of music literature, works of different character, which enabled the orchestra to show its special qualities in respect of musical interpretation, expression and virtuosity both as ensemble and in the separate groups of instruments.

The concert opened with the 6th symphony by Schubert, composed in the years 1817–18; it was followed by Mozart's piano concerto in G-major (KV 453), with the soloist Hans Henkemans, who is reputed to be one of the best interpreters of Mozart's oeuvre. Besides as a pianist Henkemans has also a reputation as a composer; he is a prominent Dutch contemporary composer.

After the interval the programme was devoted to works of modern composers: Igor Strawinsky, whose 75th anniversary is being celebrated this year, and Willem Pijper, one of the most outstanding figures among the Dutch composers, who died in 1947. Maybe the greater part of the audience will have heard Pijper's Third Symphony, which is considered to be his best and most characteristic work, this evening for the first time, unless known to them from recordings.

In addition to explanatory notes to the other works played, the programme gave a short analysis of this latter symphony written by Hans Henkemans, who was one of Pijper's pupils.

The evening was concluded by work from the Russo-French maestro Strawinsky. In the suite from his well-known ballet 'The Firebird' Eduard van Beinum got an opportunity to make the orchestra display all its colourful beauty, a worthy conclusion of an artistic manifestation of the Congress.

During the interval the Deputy-Burgomaster of Amsterdam, Dr. A. de Roos and Mrs. De Roos, welcomed a number of special delegates.

THURSDAY, 12TH SEPTEMBER

Excursions

No business sessions were held on this day. The Congress Committee had enabled the visitors from abroad to select a trip out of a programme of nine. About

1450 guests had registered for these excursions and they were joined by about 200 Dutch participants.
The trip to the Enclosing Dyke and the excursion to The Hague were very popular and were joined by 385 and 360 guests respectively.
The other excursions went to:
The National Park 'De Hooge Veluwe', combined with a visit to the Kröller-Müller Museum,
Arnhem and the Netherlands Open Air Museum there,
Utrecht, where, on the invitation of the Board of the Royal Dutch Trade Fair, the autumn fair was visited,
Gouda, combined with a visit to a flower auction in Aalsmeer, and a trip through Het Westland, centre of vegetable- and fruit-growing,
Alphen aan den Rijn, where the bird park 'Avifauna' was visited. During this excursion a call was also made at Amsterdam's airport 'Schiphol',
Rotterdam, in which town a bus trip and a tour by boat were made to give impressions of the reconstruction work and to see the harbours.
The excursions were in general made by coach, though some were made by boat. Departure was between half past eight and half past nine in the morning. In the course of the afternoon everybody returned to Amsterdam.

Reception by H. M. the Queen at the Royal Palace, Soestdijk

In the afternoon of this day a number of delegates, together with the members of the Congress Committee, paid their respects to Her Majesty The Queen at the Royal Palace in Soestdijk, Queen Juliana having graciously provided an opportunity for this visit.
A short excursion to the 'Atom' Exhibition had been arranged for these delegates and their ladies in the morning.

Visit to the Rijksmuseum and Government Reception

Their Excellencies, the Minister of Economic Affairs and the State Secretary of Economic Affairs, had invited a number of delegates to a reception in the festively-decorated Restaurant of the Rijksmuseum; in consequence of the limited accommodation the number of persons invited had to be restricted.
Their Excellencies had also invited all participants in the Congress and their ladies to visit the Rijksmuseum and the special exhibition of French Decorative art 'From Gothic to Empire'. Many availed themselves of this opportunity.

FRIDAY, 13TH SEPTEMBER

Visit by the Ladies to Flower Auctions, Aalsmeer

More than 800 ladies had registered for participation in a visit on Friday morning to one of the two flower auctions in Aalsmeer.
Two groups departed for this trip to Aalsmeer. After having visited this Dutch flower-centre the ladies had coffee on their way back to Amsterdam, which was reached before lunchtime.

Ball

After the closing session on Friday afternoon the Concertgebouw was again the meeting place for about 2000 Congressionists and their ladies, this time for a pleasant and sociable farewell party.

The flower-decorations in the grand hall gave this building a new and gay look. Dance music was provided by two orchestras. In the small hall an entertaining cabaret programme was staged. All lobbies and bars were in use this evening. The Concertgebouw was crowded but not beyond capacity.

The cold buffet, served most attractively by the Carlton Hotel in the circular hall, was highly appreciated by the visitors.

FRIDAY, 13TH SEPTEMBER

CLOSING SESSION

MR. J. KRAAYENHOF, PRESIDENT OF THE CONGRESS, IN THE CHAIR

THE PRESIDENT:

Ladies and Gentlemen, my dear friends!

It is not possible to describe the feelings of gratitude in the hearts of the councils and members of the sponsoring bodies for what this week has been and has produced.

In 1952 we asked for the responsibility for the organization of this Congress, and you were good enough to give us your confidence.

But as regards the spirit in which these Congress days would be lived through, the responsibility was, we realized, solely a matter for the participants in the Congress.

And I do not exaggerate when I say that the outcome of this week has by far surpassed what we had dared to hope for.

The members of the Congress Committee and I were fully aware of certain weak spots in what could be arranged for you. But, from the very beginning we have found a friendly willingness to accept things as they presented themselves. Personal kindness and co-operation have been the leading principles of the Congress family during the whole week.

The repeated interest shown in our Congress by our Royal Family has undoubtedly been a heartwarming experience for all of us. The profession has been greatly honoured by H. M. the Queen as well as by H. R. H., the Prince of the Netherlands.

The same applies to the Netherlands Government and the Burgomaster and Aldermen of the City of Amsterdam. It surely has been made clear that it was not only we who wanted to show you that we were glad you had come, but that the same sentiments were also felt by our country as a whole and by the City of Amsterdam, in particular.

When I arrived at the Congress building last Monday, I received a most agreeable surprise, when I saw all the national colours fluttering in the wind around this building. Perhaps you had the same feelings as I had. But I feel you should know that it was not the Congress Committee which put up these flags: it was done by order of the City authorities!

But having expressed our gratitude for the assistance of those not belonging to our Congress community, I would now express my heartiest thanks for, and highest appreciation of, the work of our Congress-Secretariat. Mr. De Bruyne as

Secretary, Mr. Boertien as Assistant Secretary and Miss De Muynck and the staff of the office she was leading have done a wonderful job. Mr. De Bruyne and Mr. Boertien have directed the extensive preparatory work with indefatigable devotion to the cause of the Congress and with unconquerable optimism. May I ask them all to rise: I think they earn the warm applause of us all. *(applause)*
I will now tell you a little story which crossed my mind this week when one of my Dutch friends, referring to my somewhat lyrical words about the Netherlands at the opening session, asked me, whether my presentation had been fair, since I had not mentioned that in some parts our country is indeed a 'frog-land'. Dismal critics even say that instead of 'in some parts' one should say 'in some respects', but I do hope that none of you will go home with that feeling.
Reflecting upon the incessant energy displayed by Mr. De Bruyne and his staff, who were often nearly driven desperate, this expression 'frog-land' reminded me of a story which, I feel, I must now tell you.
A little frog was happily jumping along in the meadow. It was getting dark, so it did not notice a bucket, filled with milk, that had been left behind by mistake. Our poor frog jumped into the bucket and then soon discovered that he could not manage to jump out again. He scrambled faster and faster on all fours, spurred on by the energy of despair. After some time, however, he had to contemplate the probability that he would never succeed in getting out. Then, at daybreak, when, over-fatigued, he was near to giving up its seemingly useless efforts, all of a sudden our brave little frog felt a support under his small hind legs: his energetic and relentless tramping had produced a good knob of butter!

Now I would mention the Vice-President and the other members of the Congress Committee, some of whom will say a few words to you on what has happened under their special responsibility. Our Committee work started as early as 1953, since when we have been labouring together as good friends to achieve the best result. I wish now to thank them most heartily for this fine experience of good co-operation.
Then I would like to thank all of the other co-operators. Most of them are represented on the platform: the sponsoring bodies; the co-presidencies and the discussion panels for the business sessions; the sub-committees for the subjects; the sub-committees for the organizational work, the social events, the finance and the press, including the colleagues from abroad, who have assisted us so wonderfully in preparing the daily editions of the Congress News.
An important, and sometimes spectacular, part in this week's proceedings has been played by this Concert Hall and the other rooms in the building. As Amsterdam still has a shortage of halls for congresses of this size, we had no other choice than this attractive, but old-fashioned building. For the fact that, notwithstanding this, it has been possible to organize the functions of this Congress in such a satisfactory way, we are indebted to a high degree to the manager of this building, Mr. A. Verbruggen. And to-night, at the closing ball, I have every reason to believe that you will see a further example of what imagination and good co-operation can achieve. Mr. Verbruggen, may I ask you to come to the platform to enable us to show our appreciation of your part in the success of this Congress. *(applause)*

I now call upon Professor Goudeket, who, as a member of the Congress Committee, has led the work for the business sessions.

PROF. A. GOUDEKET:

At the request of our President, I want to tell you a little about that part of our Congress which was assigned to me, as a member of the Congress Committee. At first I thought this might be rather difficult in view of the fact that I do not feel too dissatisfied about the result of the work, but, fortunately, as soon as I started ordering my thoughts the task became easier, owing to the circumstance that I did not do the work alone but was strongly supported by Prof. Van Rietschoten.

Moreover, Prof. Van Rietschoten and I did not do so very much. We started by requesting the assistance of as many sub-committees as there were subjects to be tackled. And it was our colleagues forming these committees who did the job on our behalf. If we can be satisfied, it seems that we owe the result in the first place to their achievement. Yet when the result is further analyzed, the conclusion is that this would be too much honour even for what our friends in the sub-committees have done.

For, in the first instance, they in their turn invited their colleagues in foreign countries and in Holland to do the actual work, such as writing a paper, being the rapporteur or acting as discussion leader, as a panel member, chairman or vice-chairman. And when I recollect what was required of them in respect of the contents of the papers, the summaries and the preparation of the discussions, I feel that we must direct our thanks almost exclusively to the teams you have seen on the platform during the various sessions.

In our desire to have everything done as thoroughly as possible we even tried now and then to influence the opinion of a panel member. At this moment we feel happy that we did not succeed in doing so. To our sincere thanks I should like to add our apologies for what we made them suffer, as well as our appreciation of the sporting way in which they took it and for the friendly way in which they finally did what they considered to be best. Concluding as far as the session teams are concerned, I should like to say that we Netherlanders are deeply grateful for this fine co-operation with our friends all over the world.

As I look around, I see some of these gentlemen sitting in the hall with rather proud faces. I am sorry for them, because after further study of the problem I have come to the conclusion that they will have to share with others the honour I originally felt inclined to give to them. An element of paramount importance has led to the fact that we can feel rather satisfied; that element is the audience, that is the visitors of the sessions themselves.

To you, indeed, we really owe this result. The good mind you brought along created a stimulating atmosphere during our congress, particularly in the business sessions, which were of such a high level that everything was not best or better but good. If a panel member was speaking rather lengthy, we watched you show your patience; if someone did not speak loud enough, you accepted it. Generally speaking, the translation system was very satisfactory and the interpreters are entitled to our sincere thanks. If now and then, however, it was

MEMBERS OF THE CONGRESS COMMITTEE

R. Besançon, ec. drs.

Professor A. Goudeket

Mr. B. Moret, ec. drs.

H. C. Treffers

J. Vogel, ec. drs.

SECRETARIAT

A. L. de Bruyne
Secretary

Mr. C. Boertien
Adjunct Secretary

H.M. The Queen received over sixty delegates at the Royal Palace, Soestdijk

When the photograph was taken not all of them had reached the terrace.

not 100%, you did not blame anyone, and if a headphone refused to function, you changed it, if there were any sets left!

We who prepared and those who produced the sessions could not have wished for a kinder audience. We are all most thankful to you; it is nice indeed to work under such circumstances. Just as it is in business life, I have first dealt with the human side. But in conclusion I should like to spend a short time on the material things. The proof of the pudding is in the eating: I think we may be satisfied about the choice of the subjects that were eventually selected with your preliminary advice.

It is true that the panel system was not perfect; but it will always remain difficult to prepare a discussion with members who come from all over the world. It will be worthwhile to give this method our positive consideration for future congresses, and if we all make up our minds to work it as good as possible, I am sure we shall succeed. Further points for future consideration are: should there be simultaneous sessions and what should be the number of subjects? The translation system naturally gives certain inconveniences during the discussions, but we are all willing to accept these, recognizing the great benefit of the system for those friends who do not know the different languages.

This is the moment to mention the kind co-operation of Mr. Wilfrido Castillo Miranda from Mexico, who for the sake of our Spanish-speaking friends has willingly translated into Spanish the papers on five of the subjects. Unfortunately, these translations could not be multiplied before the sessions were held, but we will see to it that they are circularized as soon as possible.

One thing is very important for a successful discussion, namely, that those who discuss do not fully agree. That element of the preparation was the easiest one: we agreed completely in not agreeing fully on the details. That is good, because back of all the disagreement is the absolute desire of all colleagues in all countries to perform their professional duties on the highest possible level. This being a fact, the permanent friendly and collegial contact will gradually lead to a complete agreement on the basic elements of the professional performance.

Mr. President, I hope I have complied with your requirements. Please allow me to end with an auditor's certificate:

I am of the opinion that this Congress has given a fair view of the actual situation in the professional world about the subjects we dealt with, and of the profit resulting from a closer and still more friendly co-operation on professional matters between accountants all over the world. *(applause)*

THE PRESIDENT:

And now I ask Mr. Treffers, the member of the Congress Committee especially concerned with the social events and the accommodation, to give a short review of his activities.

MR. H. C. TREFFERS:

When our President asked me yesterday to make a short report in this closing session on the social events, I felt myself in a rather difficult position.

Firstly, this is the only thing I have had to do without the support of the colleagues of my sub-committee whose names are mentioned on page five of our programme.

Secondly, I do not know whether you, Gentlemen, have ever succeeded in getting a good idea of a nice dress on the basis of a description given by your lady. Yet I am being asked to make an unqualified report on the fashion shows.

Finally, I feel as if I am giving a professional opinion before the balance-sheet has been prepared, because I am doing this before we see the results of a very essential event, namely, to-night's ball.

On the other hand, Mr. President, I have accepted your request with great pleasure since it gives me the opportunity of thanking our guests not only because so many of them have accepted our invitation for the various events and for their fine co-operation but also for the way they have kept to our time schedule.

I will now give a short account of the various events. First, I must tell you that even those of us who were literally in the picture received a new surprise as to what flowers can do, and I think this is the right moment to thank Mr. Noyons and our florist, the firm of Frankenhuysen-Corona, for the manner in which they succeeded in transforming this hall for our Monday evening's reception.

And speaking about this event, I do hope that it gave our guests the opportunity of getting acquainted with one another..... and with the rather complicated location of the various rooms in this Congress building.

As to the boat trip on Tuesday night, we gathered the impression that it was enjoyed by many of you. And as I had to answer some inquiries about this subject,..... it was not my committee which had stopped the rain before you embarked.

As to the dinner party on that same night, the Congress Committee has asked me to tell you how much we enjoyed the excellent speeches made by our guests. We regret that one of them could only be delivered some 20 minutes after it was scheduled.

Coming now to the concert presented to us by the Municipality of Amsterdam, I hope you will agree with me when I say that we are most grateful for the very fine performance the Concertgebouw Orchestra, its conductor Dr. Eduard van Beinum and the soloist Mr. Hans Henkemans have offered us.

Regarding the excursions, I must first confess that we had arranged to have the normal Dutch weather on that day in order to give you a good impression of our country under normal weather conditions. But I hope you will understand that it was not according to our plans that many of you had to wait a long time in the cold wind before some of the coaches arrived. For this I am indeed very sorry, although I trust you nevertheless got a favourable impression of some of the typical parts of this country.

As for to-night's ball, I can only say: just come and see for yourself. Of course, I hope that you will have a very enjoyable night.

I think this session gives especially us gentlemen the best opportunity to thank most cordially the members of the Ladies Committee for the very charming and efficient way in which they succeeded in entertaining our ladies when we were at the business sessions or occupied with other professional duties such as a dinner party.

Coming to a conclusion in this matter of the social events, I must tell you that I learned from the sixth Congress in London that in addition to the business sessions the social events are a most important contribution to the success of international congresses, because one of the best ways in which so many people from different countries all over the world can come to a mutual understanding is to meet one another and to speak with one another in circumstances under which all guests are having a good time. If we have succeeded a little in achieving this, the Congress Committee will feel really satisfied.

(applause)

THE PRESIDENT:

I myself now wish to say a few words about the meeting of the leaders of the delegations of all the accountancy bodies represented at this Congress. On Wednesday morning we had—as I see it—a very constructive talk, mainly with regard to the future: when and where the next congress, the 8th of the series, will be held. There seems to be full agreement that it will be 1962. As for the place, five invitations were presented in a very charming and convincing way, by representatives of India, of the State of Maryland in the United States of America, of the American Institute of Certified Public Accountants, of Italy and of Australia. At the end of the discussions thereon, the delegate of Italy was kind enough to withdraw his invitation in favour of that of the American Institute, having regard to the fact that the latter would happily coincide with the Institute's 75-year jubilee. Regarding the invitation of India I was asked to call upon Mr. Chopra in this session, which I now gladly do.

MR. S. PRAKASH CHOPRA, President of the Institute of Chartered Accountants of India:

Mr. President, I am grateful to you for this opportunity.

Ladies and Gentlemen, I am taking this opportunity of making an announcement which, I have no doubt, will be very much liked by all of you here. Before I do that, however, I must confess—having come here—I cannot resist the temptation of saying how happy my colleagues from India and I have been during our stay here; the conduct of the deliberations has been done in a most able manner and we are full of admiration for the President and all his colleagues in Holland. This has been my first visit to Holland and I assure you, and I am sure my colleagues join with me in this, that we could not have had a happier time. Now to come to the announcement: this is with regard to the invitation that we gave, a cordial invitation to the Congress Committee, a request that the next Congress might be held in India. This letter was sent by me to your President on my arrival or soon after my arrival in Amsterdam. This was also a follow up on an invitation that we had given after the last International Accountancy Congress. At the time of the meeting of the leaders of delegations, however, I learned that a similar invitation had been received from the American Institute of Certified Public Accountants and it also appeared that in 1962 they will be having their 75th anniversary—I hope I am correct. In view of this and in view of the feelings of a large number of us that we should give an opportunity to the American Institute to have their celebration in the same year and the same place as when and where they are going to have the 8th International Accountants Congress, I announce that I would like to retire, if I may use a clumsy phrase, in favour of the invitation by the American Institute of Certified Public Accountants. Mr. President and Ladies and Gentlemen, this is not to say that we withdraw our invitation. We give you an open invitation. As and when you find it convenient, we shall be only too happy to receive you all in our country and I hope we shall do justice to an invitation to persons that come from countries who are in a position to give such tremendous hospitality. And so far as our profession is concerned I do not think it is all that young. The Institute to which I belong is very young, that is, it was founded in 1949, but that was a finale to a profession that had gone on for a large number of years. We shall look forward to meeting all of you in our country some time or other and I shall certainly look forward to visiting America, if I can, or at least some of my colleagues will visit America at the next International Congress. Once again, Sir, thank you very much for this opportunity and all that you have done for us here. Thank you. *(applause)*

THE PRESIDENT:

After this most graceful withdrawal of India, three invitations remain. As agreed upon in our meeting the Councils of all Bodies will be consulted and taking into account their information, the decision will be taken as soon as possible. The Secretariat of this Congress will function on all matters that may come up, until the ultimate decision has been reached.
I now call upon Mr. Besançon, who as a member of the Congress Committee had the responsibility for the publicity and the press. The 'Congress News' was produced under his personal direction.

MR. R. BESANÇON:

Mr. President, Ladies and Gentlemen,
You, Mr. President, have asked me to report about the publicity part of our work. Well, there is a certain type of man which we do not particularly like, i.e. the would-be accountant. Yet I am afraid I have to confess that my co-member, who has shared all my troubles, and I have acted this week as would-be publishers and on top of that even as would-be editors.
We were very lucky that we had the invaluable help of an expert, Mr. Spaan, who literally worked the whole week day and night, to keep things journalistically as straight as possible. We are very much indebted to him and I want to thank him most heartily for everything he did. We have tried very hard to learn from him. However, a week is but a short time and, speaking for myself, I still feel quite unprepared to go in for an examination on even the most basic principles of what I, with due respect, may call the publicity-science.
Mr. President, if you want me to give some impressions of my amateurish editorship, I surely must mention the most pleasing fact that as an editor one is fully entitled to ask other people to do the actual work. In our case we asked for the collaboration of nine colleagues to write the reports on the business sessions in English, French and German. Their collaboration was given with a heart-warming enthusiasm.

Within the limited scope of these articles, naturally, a full account of the discussions was impossible and was not intended either. In my opinion the reports gave a lively impression of the debate and I want to express here our most heartfelt thanks to these nine colleagues

Mr. H. Paul Cemach	M. J. Lievens
Mr. N. T. Summerscale	Herr W. Grah
Mr. P. C. Louwers	Herr Dr. W. Ostrowski
M. M. K. F. Dehoux	Herr K. Warth
M. J. Goubaux	

who gave up a large part of their 'Congress-time' to this important task.
But Mr. President, I discovered still another feature of the editors' work which, however, seemed to me to be definitely unpleasant.
As editors we had to use our pencil mostly for what I perhaps might describe as mutilating the bodies of magnificent speeches. It certainly is a purely negative, and therefore a disagreeable, task to cross out and to cut away.
When doing this distressing work, we felt an increasing need to apologize to the authors, who had all succeeded so well in the composition of their speeches. They can rest assured that the ill-treatment of their 'brain children' was as painful to us, as it undoubtedly must have been to them.
Mr. President, as there will certainly come another opportunity to thank the many members of the sponsoring bodies who have helped us most generously in many ways, I will not venture to do so here. In conclusion, I would now summarize the final impression of our work in these words:
We had the experience of a heart-warming and enthusiastic co-operation given by many for one single purpose. *(applause)*

THE PRESIDENT:

May I now make a few personal remarks.
I have explicitly avoided referring to any wish to promote international uniformity in any field of our professional work. That is why I stressed at the opening of the Congress that no resolutions or recommendations would be aimed at; thus keeping in line with former congresses, a line which will, I think, have to be followed by future congresses.
In my personal opinion, however, this does not mean that no beginning of an attempt should be contemplated to come to some sort of unification, to begin with in such countries in which at least a comparable level of accountancy has been reached. In learning from each other at international congresses and by means of studying each other's publications, in course of time there should be a more precise exchange of opinion on some points between such countries, possibly leading to conclusions which could influence the standards and proceedings. I have particularly in mind the field on which we are the sole experts, that is, on the auditing of financial statements. The divergencies on auditing standards in the various countries are still significant and I must acknowledge that I have no good arguments when I am asked to explain them.
It is more in this field than in that of accounting principles that the full responsibility lies, as I feel it, on our shoulders.

The second subject I would bring to your attention is that of education for the profession.

Naturally, it is generally recognized that education for our profession is absolutely essential for its future. I will refrain from giving any views on problems arising from education under current circumstances, but I think I might mention some of the reasons why the international exchange of views in regard to this subject would seem to be valuable.

There are several ways, as far as education goes, of becoming a good accountant; and I would not at this moment in any respect suggest preference for a one track educational system. But different systems of education should have many aspects in common.

This realization gives rise to other questions.

Should education for the profession only include preparation for the general professional knowledge required for qualification or should there be alternative schedules for specialization in different fields? Or again, to what extent should practical training form a part of the preparation for qualification?

The spectacular developments in the fields of physics and chemistry appeal to-day to the attention and the imagination of young people everywhere. And for those with an above-average intelligence this often decides their choice of a career.

How, therefore, should education for our profession be made inviting and attractive enough for a large number of gifted young people?

Some co-ordination of educational schemes seems to me essential for proper international understanding and co-operation in the wide field of our profession. Without wishing to prejudice either the Congress Committee or the Councils of the sponsoring bodies in any of these fields, I venture to recommend further consideration of these subjects.

Before ending my address I should mention to you the receipt of many cables of good wishes for our Congress. I cannot read them all to you, but I may make an exception for the one received from Mr. George O. May, in answer to our cable on behalf of the opening session: 'Warm thanks for kind message; regret absence; wish you all a successful meeting'.

Furthermore, I feel I should mention, with great appreciation, the receipt this morning of this week's issue of the English journal, 'The Accountant', already containing a full report on our opening session.

I am now going to call upon some of the delegates who will be so kind as to say a few parting words.

Mr. De Lalanne of Canada, speaking for the English-speaking guests.

MR. JAMES A. DE LALANNE:

Mr. President, may I be permitted to say a few words before we adjourn.

Ladies and Gentlemen,

I have been asked by our colleagues to attempt to express our feelings at this time as we are about to return to our homes—some far—some near—after this very pleasant visit to Amsterdam.

As President of the Canadian Institute, I am very happy and proud to be entrusted with this task as Canada and Holland have had most friendly associations and many mutual interests in all walks of life for a very long time. In the Province of Quebec—where I live—we have a bi-lingual situation and where it happens that we are using our two legal languages—French and English—and there is occasion to move a vote of thanks—it is considered good taste to express our appreciation in the native tongue of the guest speaker. Unfortunately, Mr. President, my inability to speak the language of our host Institutes precludes my following our recognized practice and I offer my sincere apologies.

I am sure that you realize that what I shall be able to say in the short time available will be only a slight indication of our thoughts at this time.

Words cannot adequately express our feelings, but I assure you that each and every one of us will carry away happy memories of the many new contacts we have made and in particular your kindly reception and the hospitality we have enjoyed during the past five days—all too short for us—but—no doubt—long and arduous ones for you.

First, may I acknowledge the honour conferred on the leaders of the various delegations and others when they were received so graciously—yesterday afternoon—by Her Majesty the Queen.

It was a particularly pleasant occasion for my fellow Canadian and myself since Her Majesty—as Crown Princess—resided for several years in Canada and one of Her lovely Princesses was born in our country.

Secondly—It was very gratifying to us all to note the high esteem in which your Institutes—and our profession as a whole—are held in this country—as evidenced by the gracious presence of His Royal Highness, The Prince of the Netherlands and members of the Government, at our opening session and at that delightful dinner on Tuesday evening.

Much has already been said by others in praise of the astounding energy and skill with which the Congress Committee and its supporting secretariat have planned and organized this gathering and I shall not attempt to go over the ground again.

The despatch, tact and courteous manner in which negotiations and correspondence—in a score of languages—were conducted with the 140 member organizations in 40 widely separated countries and with all those participating in the technical sessions has been little short of amazing.

One example of this was the very polite manner in which your secretary inquired as to whether any typographical error may have occurred or whether there was some other dire reason that the President of the Canadian Institute was listed as a mere Chartered Accountant (C.A.) whereas most of the other members of our party carried the higher rank of Fellow (F.C.A.).

My answer is—of course—that the Quebec Provincial Institute by which I am licensed has no authority in its charter to grant fellowships. I hope that is the reply given by our secretary but I would not dare to ask what confidential explanation may have passed between our Secretary and yours, Mr. President.

I mention the foregoing only as an illustration of the meticulous and methodical manner in which the records were audited in accordance with good accounting practice and procedure and to exemplify the care taken to ensure perfection in the highest degree feasible in the circumstances.

The physical arrangements for our accommodation and our various needs and for the technical sessions must have produced innumerable complications—all of which have been dealt with in your very efficient manner.
And when we speak of that magnificent concert and the other extra-mural activities I think I might best describe our feelings by repeating the words used by the President of the American Institute that 'you have again proved by your hospitality that you are a very friendly and most generous nation'.
I am sure that our ladies would wish me to express their sincere appreciation for the most interesting programme provided for them and for the many courtesies extended by the President and members of the Ladies Committee.
And so, with that preamble and on behalf of all the visitors and members of their families it is my honour and privilege to convey to you, Mr. President—to you Mr. Vice-President and to all members of the sponsoring bodies—our heartiest congratulations with sincere appreciation of the magnificent contribution which you have added to the advancement of our profession throughout the world by your able and conscientious promotion and conduct of this Seventh International Congress of Accountants 1957—and our many thanks for the innumerable courtesies extended to us—all of which cannot help but engender even better understanding and co-operation between the nations represented at this gathering.
Met de beste wensen tot wij elkaar weer ontmoeten. *(applause)*

THE PRESIDENT:

For all of the guests from abroad: Mr. De Lalanne's last words were Dutch! I now will call upon Prof. Sensini of Italy, who will address you in French. After his address, Dr. Viel of Switzerland, will follow in German.
As far as my expectations go, a part of our English-speaking guests might not be able to understand these gentlemen by lack of interpretation in this session into English. For this I apologize, but I may take it that they will graciously accept to be shut out for a moment, recognizing their obvious advantage in this respect during the whole week. They may take it that friendly words only will be said, so they might join in the applause if they wish to do so. Prof. Sensini speaking for the French-speaking guests:

PROF. AVV. RAG. GIOVANNI SENSINI:

Monsieur le Président, mes chèrs Confrères et cher Monsieur De Lalanne!
Au sujet du remarquable travail de notre Comité, permettez-moi d'en faire un petit bilan: en effet, nous sommes des Experts Comptables, donc quelquefois, même nos travaux exigent un bilan! Dans notre cas on peut nous envier; il présente uniquement des 'actifs'.
En première ligne, voilà, la splendide impression, l'inoubliable souvenir d'Amsterdam, cette capitale magnifique! La beauté de cette ville en effet, reste intacte, même quand il pleût, et son sourire est chaleureux même quand il fait froid; donc elle est une merveilleuse et délicieuse ville et par conséquent le chef-d'œuvre de notre Congrès.
Nous avons écouté des exposés techniques très remarquables, dont les extraits occuperont une place d'honneur dans nos bureaux. Je suis sûr que très souvent

nous serons obligés, et avec plaisir, de consulter les savantes dissertations de nos éminents collègues.
Pour conclure, il faut mettre à l'actif de notre bilan, l'agréable occasion de se rencontrer et de faire de nouvelles connaissances, en renforçant les relations anciennes et amicales.
J'espère qu'on se rencontrera bien souvent et que nous aurons la fortune de pouvoir nous serrer la main à l'occasion de nombreux congrès à l'avenir.
Et voilà le magnifique bilan de ce Congrès 1957!
C'est encore un plaisir particulier de savoir que le prochain aura lieu dans cinq ans aux Etats Unis, à l'occasion du jubilé de l'Association de nos Collègues d'outre-mer.
C'est l'unique raison pour laquelle je n'ai pas insisté à proposer l'Italie. Quand même, j'espère que mon pays aura l'honneur d'être désigné pour le Congrès suivant.
Enfin, permettez-moi, Mon Président, Monsieur le Vice-Président et Messieurs les Membres du Comité, de vous exprimer ma parfaite reconnaissance. Je vous prie de ne pas considérer mes simples mots comme des expressions conventionnelles. Non! J'aimerais que vous puissiez comprendre mes sentiments au fond de mon cœur, que, hélas, avec mon pauvre français, je ne suis pas capable d'exprimer. Je crois fermement parler aussi au nom de mes collègues, qui avec moi – et non sans émotion! – vous disent:
Au revoir en 1962! Auf Wiedersehen in fünf Jahren! Let us hope to see you again in 1962! *(applause)*

THE PRESIDENT:

I now call upon Dr. Viel, speaking for the German-speaking guests.

DR. JAKOB VIEL:

Herr Vorsitzender! Meine Damen und Herren!
Es ist eine besondere Liebenswürdigkeit der Kongreßleitung, daß sie den Vertreter der kleinen Schweiz aufgerufen hat, an der heutigen Schlußsitzung im Namen der deutschsprechenden Kongreßteilnehmer das Wort zu ergreifen. Vielleicht tat sie das auch, weil – wie Sie alle wissen – ein silbernes Band die Schweiz mit Holland verbindet: der Vater Rhein. Bei uns ein unbändiger Junge, der in mutwilligen Sprüngen von Fels zu Fels hinunterspringt, hat er im Verlaufe seiner langen Reise, bevor er sich ins Meer der Unendlichkeit ergießt, Muße genug, sich darauf zu besinnen, wie man sich unter gesitteten Menschen zu benehmen hat und welche Manieren die Holländer bei seinem Eintritt in ihr Land von ihm erwarten. So paßt er sich der Umgebung an und anerbietet sich auch Träger eines regen gegenseitigen Güterverkehrs und damit auch Mittler einer engen Verbundenheit unserer beiden Völker zu sein.
Und nun, meine Damen und Herren, gestatten Sie mir noch ein kurzes Wort des Dankes an die Kongreßleitung.
Wir Buchsachverständige sind gewohnt, Bilanzen zu ziehen, und so werden wir es auch über den Amsterdamer Kongreß tun. Da steht auf der Aktivseite zunächst der Posten angenehmster Erinnerung an eine schöne, malerische Stadt mit liebenswürdigen Menschen, an den unvergeßlichen Besuch im Schloß

Soestdijk und an das wunderbare Symphoniekonzert im Concertgebouw. Als Aktivum vermerken wir uns weiter das Erlebnis eines gewaltigen Potentials an Fachwissen und Erfahrungen, das sich hier manifestierte und auf dessen Grundlage sich ein befruchtender kollegialer Gedankenaustausch entfaltete. Und schließlich sind als dritter Aktivposten zu nennen die menschlichen Beziehungen, die wir unter Kollegen neu anknüpfen oder, wo sie bereits bestanden haben, vertiefen durften. Auf der Passivseite – um der Vollständigkeit halber auch diese zu erwähnen – mag vielleicht bei diesem und jenem Kongreßteilnehmer der Posten einer gewissen körperlichen Ermüdung ob der Fülle des uns während einer ganzen Woche Gebotenen stehen. Er wird sich aber bald in das Eigenkapital persönlichen Gewinnes aus der Veranstaltung verwandeln. So haben wir also allen Grund, der Kongreßleitung unseren herzlichen und aufrichtigen Dank auszusprechen. Wir waren die Nutznießer einer tadellosen Organisation, eines vorbildlich vorbereiteten Kongresses und werden unseren Kollegen zu Hause mit Begeisterung davon berichten.
Nochmals innigen Dank, Herr Kraayenhof, an Sie und an alle Ihre tüchtigen Mitarbeiter. *(applause)*

THE PRESIDENT:

I thank you for the applause given to each of the three gentlemen who all expressed themselves in such kind terms.
As for the friendly words spoken to me personally and to my co-members of the Congress Committee, I may say the following.
When Sir Harold Howitt, who – in parenthesis – very much to his and our regret had to go back to London on urgent duties on Wednesday morning already, introduced me to you as your president, he wished me, on my thorny path, both happiness and success.
As for the happiness: from the very beginning you have given it unconditionally to me and my countrymen. This accounts for half, or perhaps even more, of the success which, according to the many kind assurances which were given to me, so abundantly fell to us. The other part of the success we owe to all those who have co-operated in such a fine way in the tremendous preparatory work and during the congress-days.
Now, except for to-night's ball, we have reached the moment of parting. I wish you all a safe return to your homes and hope that we part with such remembrances that we all can join in the wish: 'Au revoir' at a future Congress! And herewith I declare that the proceedings of this Congress have come to an end. *(applause)*

PART TWO

BUSINESS SESSIONS

PRINCIPLES FOR THE ACCOUNTANT'S PROFESSION

Morning session: Tuesday, 10th September 1957

Chairman:	ARTHUR B. FOYE, C.P.A., United States of America
Vice-chairmen:	DR. ERNST ALLET, Austria[1] ASBJØRN GLOMSTEIN, Norway[2] N.R. MODY, B. Com., F.C.A., India
Panel members:	
Discussion leader:	L. VAN ESSEN LZN. *Nederlands Instituut van Accountants*
Rapporteur and author of a paper:	SIR THOMAS B. ROBSON, M.B.E., M.A., F.C.A. *Institute of Chartered Accountants in England and Wales*
Authors of papers:	CARMAN G. BLOUGH, M.A., LL.D., C.P.A. *American Institute of Certified Public Accountants*
	ÖIAR I. CASSEL, Civ. Ekonom. *Föreningen Auktoriserade Revisorer, Sweden*
	DR. A. TH. DE LANGE *Nederlands Instituut van Accountants*
	WP. DR. HEINRICH WOLLERT *Institut der Wirtschaftsprüfer in Deutschland e.V.*
Other members of the panel:	PAUL BUSUTTIL, F.M.I.A. *Malta Institute of Accountants*
	W. LESLIE MCDONALD, F.C.A. (Canada) *Canadian Institute of Chartered Accountants*
	U. SHEIN *Burma Accountancy Board*

[1] The deputy of Prof. Dr. L. L. Illetschko
[2] Mr. Glomstein was not able to attend this meeting.

PAPER

by

SIR THOMAS B. ROBSON, M.B.E., M.A., F.C.A.

The Institute of Chartered Accountants in England and Wales

I. Introduction

The activities of the accountant's profession are world wide. The principles which should govern its actions are universal. Truth and fairness should be the outstanding characteristics of our profession everywhere. The greater the impact of accounting thought in one country upon the thought of accountants in another the closer shall we come to universal understanding and application of fundamental accounting principles. That is one of the reasons why we of the profession in the United Kingdom are delighted to take part in this congress and why we believe that, if the highest interests of the profession as a whole are to be assured, properly qualified accountants of one country should be able, under their own professional designations, to work in other countries in friendly co-operation with the skilled accountants of those countries.

Whatever may be his nationality or place of residence, every accountant needs integrity, independence of mind, perception and impartial judgment as well as technical ability and knowledge. He needs the ability to set out clearly and concisely the conclusions at which he arrives and the facts on which they are based. These qualities are fundamental and this paper assumes their presence in those who have to decide how best in particular situations to apply the principles to which the paper refers.

While my remarks are devoted primarily to the principles which are relevant to those who are engaged as public accountants or as their employees, I do not overlook the importance of the other branch of our profession comprising accountants engaged as employees in industrial and commercial concerns or elsewhere. The latter are a substantial proportion of accountants—nearly one third of the members of my own Institute are so engaged—and I hope that they will feel that much of what I have to say about the principles applicable to public accountants is also relevant for those not in public practice.

II. Functions of the Public Accountant

The main function of the public accountant is to audit accounts as an independent examiner who is not employed in the organisation whose accounts he examines. In the United Kingdom the development of this function has received its main impetus from the early appreciation by shareholders in companies of the need for an independent expert to examine on their behalf the accounts presented to them by directors and to report whether those accounts present a true picture of the position and results of the company: in other countries it has developed out of a desire by managements themselves to demonstrate to their shareholders that the accounts presented to them have this characteristic.

British company law requires that the annual accounts of every company shall be audited. The law also provides that (except in a special class of companies of the family type) the auditors shall be either members of certain recognised British accountancy bodies or persons having similar qualifications obtained abroad. Annual audits are also required by the regulations of many organisations which are not subject to company law.

The public accountant has also other duties besides auditing.He prepares accounts for businesses needing them and advises the proprietors on the implications of the facts which the accounts shew. He prepares computations of clients' profits for taxation purposes, submits these on their behalf to the authorities and negotiates agreement of the tax liabilities which arise. In addition he makes investigations and reports on the financial position and past profits of businesses for prospectus and other purposes and his advice is sought either in an independent capacity or on behalf of one of the parties in the formulation of schemes of amalgamation and the valuation of businesses. He provides secretarial or share registration services for companies, gives advice on cost accounting, budgetary control and management accounting and the financial and accounting organisation of businesses, assists in the administration of deceased estates, acts as trustee in bankruptcies or as liquidator in the winding up of companies or as receiver or trustee on behalf of debenture holders. He also acts from time to time as an arbitrator in disputes on financial matters and, subject to what I say about directorships under the heading of 'Independence', he may act as a director of companies.

The public accountant's field of activity in the United Kingdom is, therefore, too extensive for detailed consideration in this paper. The comments which follow will, therefore, be confined to the principal functions mentioned and to matters related thereto.

III. Independence of the Auditor

It is essential that the auditor should be independent of those who are responsible for the accounts which he audits. This is recognised by British company law which prescribes that no director or other officer or servant of a company shall be eligible for appointment as its auditor; nor may the auditor be a partner or employee of an officer or servant of the company unless it is one of the family type of companies to which I referred above.

Many public accountants who act as directors of companies of which they are not auditors do not regard such directorships as impairing their independence in their work as auditors of other companies. Some accountants, however, make a practice of not accepting directorships of any company lest knowledge acquired by them as auditors of one company might influence, or be suspected of influencing, their judgment in their capacity as directors of another company.

There is no rule of law in Britain to the effect that the ownership of a financial interest in a company by its auditor, or the existence of a family relationship between him and any of its officers, necessarily implies a lack of independence. If, however, a financial interest or a family relationship were such that a person could not easily act objectively and with complete independence in the capacity of auditor, then he would be expected to refrain from accepting or continuing in that appointment. Such a position might arise if the accountant were to have a financial interest which is material in relation to the capital of the company or to his personal resources.

The fact that a public accountant who is auditor of a company gives advice to its management is not regarded as implying a lack of independence on his part, but an extension of such services beyond advice, to the point where the accountant participates in management and shares in executive decisions would usually impair his independence and, therefore, his suitability for appointment as auditor. On matters short of this point it is obviously in the interests of all concerned that the best available advice shall be obtained by a company on taxation problems, finance, accounting systems and organisation and other matters with which its auditor is well qualified to deal by reason of his professional skill and knowledge of the company's affairs without in any way departing from his position of independence. Practical experience in the United Kingdom and elsewhere, over a long period of years, does not provide evidence that the widespread practice of rendering valuable advice in this way impairs in the slightest degree the independence of the public accountant in making his report as auditor.

IV. Auditor's Reports and Responsibility

The report in which the auditor states his conclusions upon the work which he has done is of paramount importance both to himself and to his clients. In this paper there is little space for comment on reports other than those on the annual accounts of companies; and even on those the comments must be brief.

In some countries the auditor of a company signifies his approval of its annual accounts by the mere addition of his signature to them; in others, including the United Kingdom and most of the other English speaking countries, he does so by presenting a formal signed record of his opinion of the accounts submitted to him. My preference is to follow the latter course as this procedure serves to emphasise that the accounts are the responsibility of the directors, not of the independent auditor who reports upon them, and, moreover, it enables the auditor to state clearly his opinion with any reservations he wishes to make.

Under United Kingdom law the auditor of a company is appointed by, and addresses his report to, the shareholders. Neither he nor the shareholders can limit his responsibility for his report and for the performance of the work which he has to do in order to be able to present it. If he is negligent and the company suffers as a result he may be sued by the company for damages; if his negligence is of such a nature or magnitude as to involve him in penalties under the criminal law he must be prepared to meet the consequences. In his capacity as auditor he has, however, no responsibility under civil law to third parties such as bankers and others with whom he is not in contractual relationships.

As regards the form and contents of his report, my view is that the simpler and more forthright the expression of the auditor's opinion on the annual accounts of a company, the greater its utility to the shareholders. In my opinion the report should be divested of all unnecessary verbiage and its terms should be reduced to saying whether in the opinion of the auditor, subject to any reservations stated in the report, the accounts shew a true and fair view of the state of the company's affairs as at the date of the balance sheet and of the profit or loss for the year, or other financial period, ended on that date. We have not quite reached this position in Great Britain but shall be very close to it if Parliament adopts recommendations made by my Institute for the elimination of certain matters now required by company law to be mentioned in the auditor's report; for example, he is at present required in all cases to say whether proper books have been kept and whether he has obtained all the information he has required whereas these are matters which in our view need be referred to only where the auditor is not satisfied.

I do not think there is any need for the report to define the scope of the auditor's examination of a company's accounts unless this is necessary for a proper appreciation by the shareholders of the opinion stated in his report. If the auditor has done with satisfactory results all the work which was necessary to enable him to express a clear opinion, then in my view he does not help the shareholder by either a long or short description of the technical processes which he has followed.

In the United Kingdom it is no part of the auditor's duty to include in his report recommendations on policy or criticisms on policy grounds of the actions of the management. I believe that in some countries the auditor is expected not only to report his view of the validity of the accounts but also to make a recommendation to the shareholders as to whether they should accept the report of the directors. The auditor in my country has no duty of this kind, his responsibilities in the work laid upon him are heavy enough and I, for one, am glad that the additional burden is not laid upon him.

The foregoing is concerned with the auditor's report on the annual accounts of a company. It does not deal specifically with reports on the auditing or preparation of annual accounts of sole traders and partnerships, though the same broad principles apply to them, with the distinction that the scope of an examination of the accounts of a private trader or firm and of the accountant's responsibility for that examination depends upon the arrangements made between the accountant and his client and upon the extent to which the client is aware of any limitations on the scope of the work done. Reports on such accounts should be so drawn that the client and any other person reading them are made aware of the responsibility which the accountant has undertaken and should contain all the reservations necessary, whether as regards limitations imposed by the client on the scope of the work or as to the validity of the accounts or otherwise. The terms of the report should be such that a reasonably informed reader would not be led to infer that the association of the accountant's name with the accounts implies that they are more reliable than is warranted by the circumstances.

This does not imply any duty on the accountant to state in his report that the profits shewn in the accounts of his client are not the same as those which are assessable to taxation. Taxable profits in the United Kingdom are computed in accordance with the taxation laws which differ in important respects from the generally accepted accounting principles by which the profits shewn in accounts are determined. This fact is well understood by the taxation authorities and any comment on the matter in the accountant's report would, therefore, be regarded as redundant. Indeed, one of the important tasks of the public accountant is to negotiate with the Inland Revenue authorities the adjustments required in order to compute the taxable profits from the figures in the accounts. The authorities rightly expect the accountant to be honest and frank in his dealings with them on behalf of his client but they are well aware that his report to his client is relevant only to the fairness of the accounts as such.

The foregoing slight sketch of some of the requirements with which the public accountant's report should comply would be incomplete without emphasis on the need for maintenance of standards such that reliance can be placed upon accountants' reports wherever they may be studied. Only if this need continues to be fully met can our profession continue to enjoy the international status to which it has attained through years of endeavour and achievement.

V. Auditor's Duty

The duty of an auditor of a company, as that duty is seen in the United Kingdom, is to make an examination of such a nature and extent as to enable him properly to give a report of the kind already described. The requirements of such an examination were stated in the English courts some sixty years ago in words which still apply. The judge said:

> 'It is the duty of an auditor to bring to bear on the work he has to perform that skill, care and caution which a reasonably competent, careful and cautious auditor would use. What is reasonable skill, care and caution must depend on the particular circumstances of each case.' (Kingston Cotton Mill case, 1896)

Accountants in my country regard it as fundamental that the auditor should use his own judgment, experience and discretion in deciding the extent and nature of his work in particular matters and we would consider inappropriate any attempt to prescribe detailed rules for his compliance. It is for the auditor to justify his decision if he is later charged with having failed in his duty.

British practice recognises that in all but small or exceptional cases, the auditor who will eventually have to sign a report stating whether the accounts submitted to him shew a true and fair view cannot be expected to make a complete and detailed check of all transactions; indeed that such a check would be neither necessary nor practicable. The auditor examines and takes into account the nature and efficiency of the system of internal control, including the extent and nature of any internal audit, and decides in the light of his judgment and experience the tests which are necessary to enable him to form and express a responsible opinion on the accounts. The extent to which his tests need go into detail, in order that he may be satisfied as to the nature and efficacy of the systems in use and form his opinion on the accounts themselves, differs according to the results of his tests and the circumstances which he meets. In large well organised businesses the proportion of the transactions which need detailed examination is much smaller than in businesses where the system of internal control is defective.

How far the existence of an internal audit will enable the independent auditor to reduce his own work is a matter for him alone to decide, bearing in mind his responsibility to form an independent opinion on the accounts. Consultation with internal auditors as to the nature and scope of their work and access to their reports on the work done by them are relevant matters for consideration by the independent auditor in deciding the scope of his own examination, but he alone must make the decision bearing in mind his responsibility and that the extent of his examination must be reasonable in the circumstances. His opinion of the efficiency of the internal audit will be material to his decision.

British practice also recognises that a great deal of the work undertaken by auditors can properly be delegated by them to members of their own staffs provided that proper control is exercised by the principals. Methods of control and supervision vary, but it is usually regarded as essential to an audit and all similar types of work that the auditor's staff should be required to prepare proper working papers for review by supervisory members of the staff and ultimately by the principals. Such working papers contain two types of information, firstly the composition of the various items in the accounts and secondly a record of the work carried out, including the enquiries made and information received. Arrangements are sometimes made with the officers and staff of companies whereby they prepare certain schedules for the auditor or make available copies of schedules prepared for their own purposes. Provided that such schedules are checked as necessary before being incorporated in the working papers, accountants do not regard this practice as offending against the general principle that the work of the audit should be done by the auditor or by staff employed by him.

VI. Education and Training

The methods of training students to become public accountants differ greatly as between countries and as between accountancy bodies and in dealing with training I have space only for remarks on the methods of qualification followed by The Institute of Chartered Accountants in England and Wales.

The qualities needed in a chartered accountant (in addition to those of character and those which come from technical knowledge and experience) have been summarised as follows in the booklet of general information which my Institute issues to persons who contemplate training for membership:

'Unless a candidate has reasoning power, an aptitude for figures and a sound knowledge of elementary mathematics he is not likely to succeed in the examinations, although an extensive knowledge of mathematics is not necessary. The ability to be concise and lucid, both orally and in writing, is important and a thorough knowledge of the English language is therefore essential.

Patience and concentration are necessary in dealing with both routine work and involved financial transactions. Powers of observation and deduction, as well as quickness in grasping facts, are particularly valuable in carrying out financial investigations of various kinds and in detecting fraud. Readiness and ability to accept responsibility and to act on his own initiative are as vital to an accountant as they are to members of the other great professions, such as medicine and the law. Tact, the power to inspire confidence and the ability to supervise and plan the work of others, are qualities which are essential if the accountant is to achieve success after qualification.'

My Institute considers that a candidate who has the foregoing qualities and has attained a good standard of general education, proved by his having passed an appropriate examination, has a reasonable prospect of being able to be trained to become a chartered accountant.

The process of training involves a period (normally five years) of practical training as an apprentice in the office of a member of the Institute practising in England or Wales and the passing of the Institute's professional examinations. There are two of these. The first, taken about half way through the period of apprenticeship, is in accounting, auditing, taxation, costing, general commercial knowledge and elementary law. The second taken at the end of the period, is in advanced accounting, auditing, taxation, general financial knowledge, cost and management accounting, and the law relating to companies, liquidations, receiverships, contracts, bankruptcy, trusts and other kindred matters.

The Institute attaches the utmost importance to thorough practical training in public accountancy obtained in the course of working as an apprentice in a member's office. It is the combination of this practical training as an apprentice with the attainment of theoretical standards indicated by the results of the examinations and the right kind of personal character which we regard as qualifying a student to be admitted as a chartered accountant. We do not regard experience or training obtained in any other way as being an acceptable substitute. Some countries and other accounting bodies may have different views, and be willing to accept training in a university or in the office of a government department or an industrial concern, but we are not prepared to do so.

VII. Rules of Professional Conduct

Unlike some other countries, the profession in the United Kingdom has no formal written code of ethics.

We regard it as essential that a public accountant shall be honest with himself and with others, a man of integrity, character and common sense, that he shall do unto others as he would that they should do to him and that he shall do all he can to maintain the esteem in which his profession is held by the public; but we do not have a detailed code of conduct telling him how to regulate his actions to attain these desirable ends. Much is left to the conscience and sense of responsibility of the individual accountant. If he fails to live up to the standards expected of him the disciplinary machinery of the accountancy body of which he is a member comes into operation. In serious cases the penalty may be exclusion from membership, involving loss of the right to describe himself by the professional designation to which membership of the accountancy body has hitherto entitled him. This disciplinary machinery is operated by the accountancy body itself and there is no appeal from its decision.

My own Institute's charter states that one of its objects is the enforcement of strict rules of conduct as a condition of membership; but its written rules are few in number. Convictions for offences against the law of the land, legal or financial incapacity arising from lunacy or bankruptcy and the like, wilful breach of the Institute's bye-laws and failure to pay its dues are mentioned in the regulations as matters providing grounds for disciplinary action against a member, as are also such matters as connivance in the improper use of a member's name in professional work which he does not control and the improper acceptance or giving of commissions or sharing of profits of or with others without the client's consent. Perhaps, however, the most important of the written rules is one which provides that conduct discreditable to a member is a ground for disciplinary action but does not specify the conduct which is discreditable.

Advertising, improper solicitation and circularisation for public accountancy work are not specifically prohibited in the written rules but have always been treated by the Institute as being discreditable acts. The determination of whether a particular act constitutes advertising is a matter for consideration on the facts, but a strict view is taken and even the use of heavy type for insertion of names in directories and the insertion of announcements in the general newspapers of changes in the addresses of offices and in the constitution of firms are viewed as reprehensible. The insertion in the newspapers in the United Kingdom of what are known in some countries as professional cards would not be tolerated, nor would approaches to non-clients with requests for professional work.

It is an unwritten but well understood rule that the affairs of clients must be treated as matters which are strictly confidential. A breach of this confidence would be a discreditable act unless it occurred in circumstances in which the accountant was legally obliged to break the recognised rule. Such a legal obligation exists only in exceptional circumstances.

Being in a position of trust, a public accountant must be scrupulous in matters where his personal interests may be involved and unless he obtains the consent of his clients he should refrain from using for his own benefit confidential information obtained in the course of his duties. He must not act for clients on opposite sides in a transaction without the consent of both; he must not purport to be independent if he is not so in fact. He must not accept nomination as auditor of a company without first ascertaining from the auditor whom it is proposed to displace whether there is any professional reason why the nomination should be declined.

There are no references in the Institute's regulations to the basis on which fees should be charged and there are no official scales, but the council of the Institute has stated that fees should normally be calculated according to the type of work done, the grade of person engaged on it and the time occupied. The council deprecates the charging of fees computed solely by reference to results, particularly where the remuneration is for services rendered in taxation recovery claims.

There is not the slightest objection to a public accountant co-operating with members of other professions in order to secure the best possible advice for his client on matters where the facts make joint advice desirable, but the sharing of profits on such work with persons other than public accountants is prohibited in my Institute unless the client concerned gives his consent.

The public accountant is personally responsible for his actions and those of his employees. This does not prevent him from joining in partnership with other public accountants and practising with them under a firm name; a very large proportion of the public accountants in the United Kingdom are practising in partnerships in this way. Many of these partnerships have been in existence for a century or longer and some of the firm names do not now represent the names of any of the present partners. In view of the importance attached to the personal qualities and responsibility of public accountants they do not form themselves into corporate bodies as is done in some other European countries; and indeed the British company law recognises the personal nature of the profession by prohibiting a corporate body from being appointed auditor of a company.

VIII. Professional Standards

As has been indicated, there is no prescription in detail of the nature and extent of the work which an auditor of a company is expected to do in the United Kingdom. These are matters for his own judgment and this fact emphasises the importance of high qualification and sound training.

The Companies Act, 1948 does not standardise the form in which accounts of companies have to be submitted but prescribes the minimum of information which they must shew. My Institute, which would regard standardisation of the form of accounts as undesirable and restrictive of progress, issues authoritative recommendations to its members on important matters of accounting principles in company accounting and these have been found most useful to members of the profession and business men generally, but the Institute does not issue recommendations on auditing procedure. There are, therefore, no detailed directives on the form of accounts or on auditing practice; the public accountant makes his own decisions in the light of his experience and the circumstances of the company concerned and determines his procedures in particular cases accordingly. We believe that this freedom for the individual to use his initiative, without the encroachment on his independence which official directives would involve, is not only precious to those who believe in liberty but is best calculated to make for sound development of technique and for the independence of mind which is an essential characteristic of the public accountant.

IX. Conclusion

I commenced this paper by emphasising the international nature of the accountancy profession. I would like to end with the same thought. The whole aim of the profession is to provide skilled services for the assistance and protection of business activities wherever they are carried on. The overriding principle which governs our profession is that the individual accountant should be properly qualified by suitable training, experience and examination and by his inherent honesty and independence of mind to carry out the important duties which rest upon him. It is these qualities and not his race, nationality or place of residence which determine his suitability for his task. In the opinion of the council of my Institute, an opinion with which I profoundly agree, any step which disregards these qualities and imposes tests based on other factors is detrimental to the development of our profession and to the country taking the step; the holding of this congress and its six predecessors give ample support for this opinion.

I realise that the space allotted to me for this paper has enabled me to touch only briefly upon some of the more important aspects of my task and, moreover, has compelled me to confine my remarks almost exclusively to an exposition of the United Kingdom point of view and to the position of my own Institute in particular. On a number of the matters there is much more to be said both from the United Kingdom standpoint and from the standpoint of the profession in other countries and in the latter respect I am relying upon the contributors of other papers to fill some of the gaps which I have left. It is my sincere hope that the limitations of my own paper will induce others to raise in the discussion points which need to be brought into prominence in order that the subject of principles for the profession may be dealt with worthily by the congress.

PAPER

by

CARMAN G. BLOUGH, M.A., LL.D., C.P.A.

American Institute of Certified Public Accountants

I. FUNCTION

The practices of most of those who held themselves out as public accountants in the United States prior to 1900 sprung from the needs of management for expert help in setting up bookkeeping systems, in keeping the accounts, and in preparing statements from them. Even today, most of the work of many of the public accountants who serve small businesses is limited to this type of service and to assisting clients in the settling of problems growing out of the income tax laws.

However, certified public accountants in the United States have gained their position of high regard mainly because they have met the needs of present and prospective investors and credit grantors for an independent report which can be relied upon as assurance that the representations of the management of an enterprise, as set forth in the financial statements, are dependable. It is basic to our concept of the public accountant's primary function that he is reporting upon management's representations, and that he has important responsibilities to outside third parties who may rely upon his report.

This function of the professional certified public accountant (CPA) can become significant only when a substantial number of enterprises have been organized with capital obtained from outside the management. The first businesses of this kind to be developed in the United States to any significant degree were our railroads and other early public utilities. Since much of the capital for these enterprises came from Great Britain, it was only natural that the first professional accountants to perform this type of independent audit function in the United States were those who were sent over from England and Scotland; naturally the British investors would have more confidence in their reports.

By the end of the first quarter of this century, a large number of corporations, financed by persons or financial institutions having no connection with the management, had taken their place in the American industrial picture. During the last 30 years, corporations of this kind have multiplied and grown both in size and in number, until today they do a tremendous proportion of the business done in our country. With this development, it was inevitable that the need would increase for the services of the public accounting profession in reporting to public investors and to outside credit granting agencies on the financial representations of management. Also, we have recently been seeing a trend towards reliance by governmental regulatory agencies upon the reports of professional CPAs.

II. Independence

Since it is the auditing of accounts (we customarily refer to it as the examination of financial statements) and the expression of an opinion with respect to the fairness of the financial statements presented by management that really marks our profession, independence ranks high among our auditing standards. Preparation of tax returns, representation of clients before the Treasury Department, the installation of bookkeeping and accounting systems, the development and analysis of financial information for management purposes, the preparation of budgets, and all of the other functions commonly performed by professional public accountants could be performed just as effectively if the accountants were not independent of the management. However, without independence of his client, the auditor is not in a position to review the decisions of its management in the objective manner that is so essential to the performance of his obligations to those outsiders who rely upon his opinion.

Because the public must rely upon the representation of the professional accountant and because the maintenance of high standards of work in that capacity is necessary, each state, territory, and possession of our country recognizes a public interest in this area sufficient to justify the regulation of the practice of accountancy and restricts the use of the designation 'Certified Public Accountant' or 'CPA'. We also have, in the Codes of Ethics of our American Institute of Certified Public Accountants and the various state societies of CPAs, in the rules and regulations of some of the state boards of accountancy, and in the regulations of our United States Securities and Exchange Commission, criteria for determining when an auditor is not to be considered independent. Basically, they recognize that no matter how independent an auditor actually is, and knows himself to be, he should do everything possible to avoid even the slightest appearance of lack of independence. Unless the public has confidence in his independence, the usefulness of his auditing services is very materially diminished.

III. Certificate Responsibility

No matter how effectively the auditor may perform his work of examining the financial statements of a client, the action which finally makes it useful, either to the management or to the public to which the financial statements may be presented, is his report on the results of his work. Unless he states clearly the nature of the work he has performed and the responsibility he takes for the fairness of the financial statements with which he permits his name to be associated, what he did in the course of his examination may become relatively useless.

It seems clear that, under our concepts of the auditor's functions, he has a material responsibility to the public when he issues an opinion. Aside from legal obligations, our American Institute of Certified Public Accountants has taken the position that the auditor, in his report, shall state whether the financial statements are presented in accordance with generally accepted principles of accounting, and whether such principles have been consistently observed in the current period in relation to the preceding period. It has also taken the position that informative disclosure in the financial statements is to be regarded as reasonably adequate unless otherwise stated in the report. With respect to the opinion, a member of the Institute is also charged with seeing that the report either contains an expression of opinion regarding the financial statements taken as a whole or an assertion to the effect that an opinion cannot be expressed. When an over-all opinion cannot be expressed, he is required to state the reasons therefore. In all cases where the auditor's name is associated with financial statements, the report should contain a clear-cut indication of the character of the auditor's examination and the degree of responsibility he is taking. He must, of course, have a sound basis for any opinion expressed.

The extent of the auditor's legal liability is very difficult to outline and certainly one who is not a lawyer should not undertake to do so. However, in view of the fact that these are the considered requirements placed on its members by such a responsible professional body as the Institute, it may be presumed that the courts would take judicial notice of such rules in the case of any litigation in which they were pertinent.

On the other hand, the auditor is not a guarantor and should not be held liable for errors in judgment if he had reasonable grounds on which to base a judgment. It should also be realized that, under present day thinking in our country, the ordinary examination incident to the issuance of an opinion respecting financial statements is not designed and cannot be relied upon to disclose defalcations and similar irregularities, although their discovery frequently results. If a CPA were to attempt to discover defalcations and similar irregularities, he would have to extend his work to a point where its cost would be prohibitive. It is generally recognized that good internal control and surety bonds provide effective measures of protection from such frauds.

Under the terms of our auditing standards, it is not only permissible, but the auditor has an obligation to limit his responsibility for financial statements if the scope of his examination has been restricted so that he has not been able to satisfy himself with respect to material items, or if the circumstances of the examination were such as to make it impossible for him to satisfy himself with respect to something material. In his engagement of the auditor, the client sometimes limits the extent of the examination. This definitely has an influence on the accountant's responsibility, since he has no right to do what his client has forbidden him to do. On the other hand, the client cannot place limitations on the scope of the examination and also insist that the auditor take the usual responsibility for the statements.

In any situation in which the client is required to obtain an unqualified expression of opinion from the auditor, he must permit the auditor to take whatever steps he considers necessary to professionally satisfy himself with respect to the statements. Since underwriters, bankers, substantial investors, and governmental authorities regulating the issuance of securities often insist on having a reputable auditor's opinion on which they can rely, it seems obvious that in financing, whether international or domestic, the auditor must have the right to extend the scope of his audit to whatever degree he considers necessary if he is to be in a position to issue a report that is acceptable.

It must be recognized that there may be situations in which the auditor will be unable to satisfy himself even though the client has in no way restricted the scope of his examination. This is often true where the facts of the situation are such that the auditor is simply not able, and no auditor with complete freedom would be able, to satisfy himself with respect to the fairness of the representations. In such cases, the auditor has an obligation to make his position clear by stating the limitations on his examination and by qualifying his opinion or disclaiming an opinion.

In any assignment in which the auditor's name is to be associated with financial statements, it must be remembered that, after he has submitted his report, he has no further control over it. Since this is so, it is difficult to determine to what extent others may ultimately rely on the fact that he has prepared a report. Accordingly, it seems to me, he should always word his report in such a way that anyone relying upon it will not be misled as to what the auditor thinks about the financial statements.

If the statements are prepared from books without audit, that fact should be clearly disclosed and the auditor should make it clear that he is not in a position to take any responsibility for the fairness of the statements. If he has a significant qualification with respect to the accounting principles that have been followed in the preparation of the statements, he should make that clear and indicate the nature of the difference. If he has made an audit, but the audit is inadequate to reach a conclusion, he should make that clear and disclaim an opinion on the statements as a whole.

On the other hand, if his work has been sufficient to give him a sound professional basis for expressing an opinion and he has an unqualified opinion that the statements are a fair presentation, he should say so. The client who engaged him is entitled to the benefit that can flow from his professional approval of the statements, and the user of them who attaches significance to the auditor's name should have the benefit of knowing that he considers the information to be fairly presented.

Where statements are to be filed with a governmental agency which requires special forms of presentation or that specific procedures be followed in the preparation of the statements, the auditor should be advised as to their intended use, and should satisfy himself that the governmental regulations have been observed, before releasing the statements for that special purpose. On the other hand, the regulatory or other governmental authority has a responsibility for satisfying itself that the accountant knew that the statements were to be filed. Where government regulations merely require that statements be in accordance with generally accepted accounting principles, of course no special form or other consideration need be given as long as the auditor does express the opinion that the statements are prepared in conformity with generally accepted accounting principles.

Auditing standards, and particularly the differences in them from one country to another, are, of course, quite important in cases in which international financing is involved. The investors in any nation in which securities of companies located in other countries are being sold, need assurance that the auditors who report on the financial statements have standards comparable to those of the accountants who report on the financial statements that they are accustomed to seeing in their own countries.

In this connection, the existence of authoritative groups to define and promote the application of auditing standards and accounting principles, the influence of the government in regulating or directing accounting practices, the extent to which accounting procedures are flexible enough to meet special problems and may be experimented with, the practices as to types of disclosure, the independence of the auditor from the client, the extent of ethical standards and methods of enforcing them, the differences in the auditing procedures, the extent of government regulation as to audit programs, the existence of standard forms of reporting promulgated by the government or other authoritative bodies, and differences between basic underlying audit philosophies, may all be important in determining the extent to which the users of financial statements in one country are likely to have confidence in the reports of auditors from other countries.

IV. Task

In the task of auditing the accounts of a company, the procedures to be followed in any given situation must be determined in the light of the circumstances. Certain auditing procedures are always considered essential whenever the items to which they relate are material. For example, confirmation of bank balances by direct communication with the banks is considered essential in practically all cases. Confirmation of the balances of accounts receivable by direct communication with the debtor is considered essential in all cases in which it is practicable and reasonable if the amounts are significant. Observation of the inventory taking, usually accompanied by test countings, is considered essential in all cases where practicable and reasonable and the amounts of inventory on hand are material. Securities are inspected and counted. These are only examples of commonly recognized auditing procedures.

However, even with respect to these procedures, the extent to which accounts receivable may be confirmed or the extent of the physical test counts of the inventories, for example, will depend upon the nature and effectiveness of the internal controls and the type of records that are kept in the individual case. As a matter of fact, there is practically no phase of the audit which is not dependent, insofar as the detail to which it is carried is concerned, upon the effectiveness of the system of internal control that is found to be present after careful study.

Except in small businesses where there is little or no internal control, we do very little detailed checking. Our audits consist of sampling and testing to the extent which seems appropriate in the light of the reliance which the auditor feels can be placed upon the integrity of the records as a result of what he learns about the internal checks and controls that have been established and the way in which he finds they have been carried out. It follows that one of the first and most important steps in any examination is to determine the nature of the internal controls that have been set up and then to determine whether the controls are in fact functioning.

Most of the work in an audit is carried on by the auditor or his immediate employees. It is not uncommon to have employees of the client do the clerical work in preparing schedules and exhibits of various kinds, but before the auditor has any right to rely upon them, he must check them sufficiently to assure himself that they have been accurately prepared. There are situations in which the auditor may, for one reason or another, rely for part of the work upon another accountant. For example, the auditor whose client's main office is in one part of the country may retain another independent certified public accountant to do the necessary audit work at a distant branch. Frequently, a United States auditor will engage an auditor in another country to make the audit of a foreign branch or subsidiary. In such cases it is usual for the principal auditor to lay out the program of work which is to be followed by the other accountant and the nature of the working papers. In these situations, the second accountant, in effect, acts as the agent of the first.

Sometimes a client will hire another accountant to audit a branch or a subsidiary. In such situations the principal accountant may state that his opinion is expressed in reliance upon the other auditor's report with respect to a certain portion of the financial statements. This is in itself a qualification of his own opinion. In situations in which the auditor states that he is relying upon another auditor's statement, if a filing with our Securities and Exchange Commission is involved, the certificate of the other auditor must also be filed.

V. Ability

When an independent certified public accountant undertakes to perform an examination leading to an auditor's opinion, he holds himself out as one who is proficient in accounting practice and auditing procedure. To obtain that proficiency as a professional man, he must receive the kind of training that is adequate to fit him for being a professional man. This means that he must not only have a thorough technical training in accounting and auditing principles and procedures, he must acquire the ability and habit of considering dispassionately and independently whatever facts are disclosed by his examination. These qualities can be acquired only through a combination of training and experience.

In the United States, the regulation of the professional practice of accounting rests in the hands of the individual states, possessions and territories, and the District of Columbia. All of these 53 governmental divisions have passed some form of legislation relating to the practice of public accounting within their jurisdictions. All of them include a substantial examination among the requirements. It is a matter of satisfaction within the accounting profession in our country that all of the states, possessions and territories, and the District of Columbia now use the same CPA examination, prepared by the American Institute of Certified Public Accountants.

The American Institute is the only national organization of certified public accountants in the United States. In addition, the CPAs in each state or other certifying governmental unit have an organization of their own. The Institute has no authority over these state societies, but actually exercises a great deal of influence over them toward the development of uniform policies due to the fact that the members of the various state societies who are active as officers and committee members are almost always members of the American Institute as well. The pronouncements of the Institute are recognized as high authority by the state groups, and also by governmental agencies, financial institutions, and others interested in accounting matters.

During the early part of the century, most of the accountants in the United States acquired their training and skills in accounting and auditing almost entirely from experience as employees working under others. In recent years, however, most of the young men who have entered the profession have also acquired substantial educational background. The trend of thinking for the future seems to be definitely in the direction of requiring more extensive training in colleges and universities, and less experience, before admitting persons to the practice of public accountancy.

In the summer of 1956, an independent commission of leading CPAs and educators, after four years of study, issued a statement of recommendations entitled 'Standards of Education and Experience for Certified Public Accountants'. The commission's recommendations were long-run in their nature and anticipated that ultimately professional programs on a post-graduate basis would be developed as a means of training college graduates specifically for careers as CPAs in public accountancy. They contemplated that limited internship programs would be developed as part of each professional curriculum.

The Institute is studying these recommendations but has neither adopted nor rejected them. However, since the various governmental divisions operate separately of each other in developing legislation of this kind, and since there are many CPAs in our country who believe that a certain amount of actual experience in the practice of public accounting is necessary before one is qualified to make an independent examination, it must be anticipated that it will be years before there is uniformity, if that ever becomes the case.

In the auditing field it seems to me that experience is more important in relation to education than it is in many other areas of a CPA's practice, such as taxation and some of the fields of 'management services' discussed later in this paper. Accordingly, it may be presumed that the extent to which education supersedes experience in the requirements for the CPA certificate will depend, in part at least, upon the extent to which these other professional activities of the CPA expand in relation to auditing.

Regardless of the progress that may be made toward higher educational requirements before a person may become a CPA, it seems obvious that much more must be done in the way of organized direction of advanced adult education for accountants after they are in the profession. They must keep abreast of developments not only in business but, more important, in the standards and procedures of auditing and in the evolution and application of principles of accounting. The American Institute is encouraging the development of advanced training courses for practitioners and members of their staffs and, along with others, has prepared course material on some subjects. However, much more must be done in this whole field.

VI. Rules of Professional Conduct and their Supervision

We have long passed the point where anyone seriously argues that the individual accountant should set his own standards of professional conduct. It is generally agreed that he should be governed by rules or regulations of professional organizations or of governmental boards. Left only to his own judgment, the conclusions of even the best intentioned may be distorted by his own experiences and relationships.

Most of the rules of professional conduct are fairly broad and leave varying degrees of flexibility within which individual judgments must be made. There are many situations which are not covered specifically by the codes and the individual must use his own judgment as to what is the professionally ethical thing for him to do. Self discipline is an essential professional characteristic and it should take him far beyond the literal obligations required by law or by the professional societies. However, the criteria by which the well-intentioned individual may judge his own standards are much more likely to be sound and lead to proper conclusions if they have been established by the combined efforts of many members of the profession and are based upon long experience.

No one set of rules of professional conduct governs the public accountants in the United States. The American Institute has established rules which are binding on its own members. Practically all of the state societies and other such groups have their own rules of professional conduct which are binding on their members. In addition, state agencies for the regulation of public accounting, usually known as state boards of accountancy, are sometimes authorized by law to establish rules which are binding on every person who has received his certificate as a Certified Public Accountant in their jurisdictions. Thus, a member of the American Institute might be subject to three different sets of rules. Fortunately, however, the different sets of rules are not dissimilar.

One universally recognized rule of professional conduct is that the confidential relationship of the accountant with his client must not be violated. Without the consent of his client, he is obliged to keep all information concerning the client's business to himself unless he is required by an order of a court of proper jurisdiction to reveal it. Even then, the statutes of some of our states have granted privileged communication to the accountant so that in those states he may not be required to disclose the client's secrets even in a court proceeding.

The Institute's rules of professional conduct also, in substance, forbid the accountant to express an opinion on the statements of a company if he has a substantial financial interest in it where it is financed by public distribution of securities. However, where the statements are to be used as a basis of credit, without there being public distribution of securities, a substantial financial interest in the client does not preclude his expressing an opinion, provided his report discloses such interest.

It should be noted that, while the Institute's rules limit the auditor in expressing an opinion if he has a financial interest in the enterprise which is substantial, the rules of our Securities and Exchange Commission state that he shall not be considered independent if he has *any* financial interest, direct or indirect. It should be noted, too, that the SEC retains the right to examine any relationship that may exist between an accountant and his client to determine whether an accountant is in fact independent in a particular situation. The Commission has on more than one occasion found that numerous relationships between an accountant and his client, no one of which in itself would have been sufficient to find him lacking in independence, were in the aggregate so significant as to lead the Commission to a ruling that the relationship of the auditor with his client was not conducive to an independent decision on his part. An accountant will not be considered independent by the SEC with respect to any enterprise with which he is, or was during the period of the report, connected as a promoter, underwriter, voting trustee, director, officer or employee.

Professional services for a fee contingent upon the findings or results of the services are also generally forbidden by the Institute's rules of conduct. However, this rule does not apply to cases involving taxes where the findings are those of the tax authorities or to fees fixed by courts or other public authorities which are therefore of an indeterminate amount at the time when the engagement is undertaken.

The practice of the profession of accountancy as a corporation is forbidden by the preponderant majority of the codes of professional conduct, including the Institute's, though there are still quite a few states in which it is permitted. However, the practice of accountancy under a corporate form is quite uncommon today, even by those who are not subject to any prohibitions.

Occupations incompatible with public accounting are generally prohibited, although no specific occupations are named in the codes as being incompatible with that of the practice of a certified public accountant. Presumably any occupation which casts doubt on the independence of the CPA as an auditor, or which might serve as a 'feeder' to his practice, would be held to be incompatible.

Cooperation with other certified public accountants who are also members of the American Institute of Certified Public Accountants is not only considered proper under the Institute's rules of professional conduct, it is strongly advocated by the leaders of our profession. Such cooperation is also extended to independent accountants who are members of an association similar to the American Institute in foreign countries. Thus the use of correspondent firms in carrying out parts of an examination where a branch or a subsidiary is located in a different city or country is quite common. Also, the cooperation of two accounting firms in handling an assignment which is too big for either of them alone is considered appropriate. On the other hand, there is a definite prohibition against the certified public accountant's splitting fees with the laity. He is also forbidden to accept fees or commissions from vendors of goods or services, the purchase of which the accountant has recommended. It is considered inappropriate for accountants and non-accountants to form a partnership for the practice of public accounting.

VII. Consultative Capacity

The growth of activities in the field of 'management services' is one of the significant recent developments in our profession. The opportunities for increasing service to the client and of obtaining additional and profitable engagements are great. There are, however, many problems of professional conduct, specialized personnel, relations with other professional groups, and the like, which have not been completely solved. By the term 'management services', I refer to those services to business management which a CPA or a firm of CPAs may be qualified to perform in addition to the conventional and traditional services rendered by the public accountant. By 'traditional services', I have primarily in mind auditing, tax service, preparation of financial statements of various types, and consultation and advice on matters of accounting principles or procedures, which have always been considered an important part of the services of a CPA.

The question has often been raised as to whether the accountant can engage in 'management services' for his client and still maintain the degree of independence which is considered essential in an audit engagement. Ordinarily, this should present no serious difficulty, since a 'management service' is given in the form of a study, a survey, or as advice, and no managerial decisions are made and put into effect by the accountant. Nevertheless, it must be recognized that there may be situations in which the accountant is asked to take responsibility for the conduct of some phase of business management for a time or accepts responsibility for management action to such an extent that he would not be able to view the financial representations with sufficient objectivity to be considered independent. It seems to me that the propriety of any such relationship would have to be a matter of judgment in the individual situation and that, whenever a service to management is of such a nature that it might have a coloration of lack of independence, the accountant should choose between acting in such a consultative capacity and acting as the company's independent auditor, since he could not rightly do both.

Regardless of how much we expand into the 'management service' area we must not lose sight of the fact that our prestige is based upon our accomplishments as auditors. Our ability to continue to fill the needs of those outside of the management of a business, who rely on financial statements for assurance that the representations of management are fair and reasonable, is the heart of our claim to professional recognition. It is only in that function that we can claim abilities that cannot be found in others. It has seemed clear to me, therefore, that when we talk about 'Principles for the Accountant's Profession', we must place primary importance upon those principles which govern our activities as independent auditors.

PAPER

by

ÖIAR I. CASSEL, M. ECON.

Föreningen Auktoriserade Revisorer, Sweden

The accountant's profession has not developed along the same lines in all countries. Today, however, we demand of a practising accountant that he shall be a person on whose impartial judgement we can rely. His work must be of a high standard. Leading institutions therefore arrange training and examinations and confer professional titles in some form. In many countries they also issue rules for professional conduct.

This paper aims to show how we in Sweden look upon the main principles of the accountant's profession, and it will deal particularly with questions on which the Swedish conception seems to differ from that of other countries.

1. *The Origin of the Accountant's Function in Sweden*

As early as in the seventeenth century the Swedish iron and timber works had on their staffs 'assistants' who examined the accounts and made out a report to the proprietor. These 'assistants' saw to it that the accounts were kept correctly, and that the business of the enterprise as a whole was administered with care and in accordance with instructions. This was in other words an early form of internal auditing.

Gradually it became more usual for the ownership of the business enterprises to be divided up on several hands. One might say that not until the arrival of the limited liability companies did the auditor's function acquire its present form. The auditor nowadays has to watch over the interests not merely of a particular person but of a multitude of shareholders. Creditors also very often pay regard to the fact that their debtors' accounts have been audited by an expert.

The Companies Act, 1944, lays down rules for rendering of accounts, thereby protecting the interests of shareholders and creditors. The Act also requires a limited liability company to insert in their published annual report statements regarding annual turnover, assessed and insured values of plant, as well as remunerations and salaries paid to the members of the Board and different categories of employees, all of which is intended as information to Commerce and Industry in general. In examining the annual accounts the auditor has to pay a certain regard also to these general interests.

2. *The Accountant's Function according to Swedish Law*

The Companies Act, 1944 agrees as regards auditing in all essentials with the Acts relating to financial associations, banks and insurance companies and requires a limited liability company to have one or more auditors. When the share capital issued or the registered maximum capital exceeds five hundred thousand Kronor there must be at least two auditors, and when it exceeds two million Kronor, at least one of them must be an authorized public accountant. With regard to the auditor's qualifications, the Act lays down that he shall be of age, a Swedish citizen domiciled within the country, and that he shall possess such knowledge of financial conditions as the company's activities may call for.

Auditors are usually elected by the shareholders for the period up to the next annual Shareholders' Meeting. A Shareholders' Meeting may at any time relieve the auditor of his appointment. At the request of a qualified minority at a Shareholders' Meeting, a special auditor may be appointed by the County Council besides the one elected by the Meeting.

3. *The Auditor's Report—his Responsibility*

The auditor's report is the document which presents to owners, creditors, and others interested, the form, scope and result of his work. Swedish practising accountants usually draw up their reports in fairly literal accordance with the rules laid down in the Companies Act.

The Act mentions firstly a statement on the result of the auditor's examination. In order to comply with this rule it is customary for the auditor to enumerate in his report most of the duties of an auditor, that are specified in the Act, and state that he has examined the company's books, other records, and annual accounts, made or checked up an inventory, and carried out such other examination as has been deemed necessary. The same paragraph of the Act provides that the auditor shall ascertain whether the organisation and control of the company's financial administration is satisfactory, but this is generally not included in the auditor's report.

The Act further stipulates that the auditor's report shall contain a statement as to whether there is cause for remarks in regard to the annual account, the bookkeeping, the inventory, or the administration of the company's affairs in other respects. We find here the unique regulation, which is peculiar to Sweden and Finland, that the auditor shall examine, and issue a statement of opinion on the administration of the company's affairs. The purpose of this is presumably that the auditor shall bring to the knowledge of the shareholders any administrative measures that are of such nature and scope that they might conceivably influence the shareholders' opinion in the matter of granting the Board discharge from responsibility.

The report shall include any remarks caused by the auditor's examination, and shall also contain statements of opinion regarding the approval of the balance sheet, the discharge from responsibility of the Board and the Managing Director, and the proposed disposition of the profits. Certain special statements are required in the case of a parent company, when the assets have been written up, or when the company has a pension fund.

The auditor's report is filed with the authorities as an official document together with the company's annual accounts. The latter shall be provided with the auditor's endorsement on the balance sheet and the profit and loss account that these agree with the company's books.

As the auditor's reports of the larger companies often receive a wide publicity, the accountant, in order to avoid damaging the reputation of his client, must consider carefully whether any matter of a serious nature which he may have observed really calls for a remark on his part. It is therefore comparatively rare to find a remark in a published auditor's report. Before including a remark in his report the auditor will usually confer with the Managing Director or the Board. Thus a remark in the auditor's report may be avoided in those cases where it is possible for the company to bring about a correction before the annual accounts are made up.

An auditor can be ordered to pay compensation for damage suffered by the company if he or his assistant wilfully, or by omissions in carrying out his commission, has caused the damage. He may also be made liable for losses sustained by shareholders, creditors, or other third party if he causes such losses wilfully or by failure to comply with the provisions of the Companies Act and the Articles of Association. If the company has several auditors, they will be jointly liable for the damages. A penalty may also be inflicted upon the auditor if he deliberately, or through gross carelessness, gives incorrect or misleading information regarding the company's affairs, or neglects to pass criticism on the administration when called for, or if he improperly discloses any matter that has come to his knowledge during the audit, and he was aware, or should have been aware that it might cause damage. A penalty for unauthorized disclosure of information can also be imposed on the auditor's assistants. Further, an auditor who fails to comply with the rules in respect of the contents of an auditor's report also becomes liable to a penalty.

Unless the accountant has been asked to make up, or assist in making up his client's returns for income tax assessment, he is in Sweden not held responsible for whether the enterprise has complied with the statutory taxation regulations. Should he find, however, that his client runs a risk of being assessed for a considerably higher amount than that set aside for income tax as shown in the balance sheet, it is the auditor's duty—unless he can get the balance sheet amended to call attention to the matter in his report. He does not do this in the interests of the Treasury; in this case it is the interests of the shareholders and creditors he is thinking of. Should it be a company's policy wrongfully to evade taxation, this cannot be regarded as compatible with good administration, and the auditor should endeavour to obtain correction by applying to the Manager or the Board of Directors. What has now been said has regard also to other financial legislation.

In many countries practising accountants work on principles so similar in character that one might say that the significance of a clean auditor's report is that nothing has been left out of the annual accounts that might affect the position of the enterprise or the result of its activities, or is of such importance that it should be brought to the notice of the shareholders or creditors. Even non-professionals should consequently be able to rely on a report of this kind issued by an accountant in a foreign country. For this reason it is very important that an accountant should not be able to evade responsibility by simply leaving out some sentence which is normally included in all auditor's reports, since the significance of this omission might not easily be apprehended by a foreigner. If a foreign auditor's report contains a criticism which is perhaps worded in vague terms, a non-professional reader should consult an accountant in his own country. Should this accountant fail to understand the significance of the criticism, he should be able, through his own professional association, to apply to the association of the country in question and receive from them an interpretation of what, in principle, the wording of the report implies.

What has been said above applies to reports of auditors commissioned by a Meeting of Shareholders to audit the company's accounts and administration.

It is of course hardly necessary nor possible to achieve uniformity as regards the wording of reports rendered by practising accountants in respect of all other kinds of commission. In these cases the accountant should state in his report the name of his client, and possibly also the object of the commission, in order to indicate clearly to whose interests he has paid special regard. He should also state the nature and scope of the work, and should then underline any restrictions which the client may have imposed and which he would not have observed if he had been permitted to draw up the programme for his work himself. Provided the auditor's report is sufficiently informative, he should not be liable for damages which arise by his omission to carry out some examination which might have been expected of him, or by his carrying out the examination in a way which differs from the methods commonly used by accountants.

4. *Working Methods*

The Swedish Companies Act lays down no rules for the detail work of an audit. All that an auditor has to go by is the general conception among practising accountants of what an examination of accounts should comprise, and how it should be carried out. No standards have been published in Sweden. A certain guidance may, however, be obtained from the commentary to the Companies Act, which is presumably intended to be an account of the methods practised in the early 1940's.

The commentary mentions that the detailed examination of vouchers, postings and footings of accounts is often entrusted to a person who is either employed by the enterprise, or has been appointed by the accountant and the management of the enterprise jointly. Some of the large business enterprises have arranged for internal audit on modern lines. The examiner, or the audit department, submits a report to the appointed auditor, who in his report generally mentions the detailed audit undertaken by the examiner or the audit department, as the case may be.

In cases where the auditor does not carry out the detailed audit himself or assisted by his own staff, he will as a rule give or approve instructions for this work, and then satisfy himself by test checks that it is being carried out correctly. In many cases the auditor, or his staff, will anyhow perform some detail checking in order to get more direct contact with the detailed accounts, while at other times he may only carry out such test checks that are called for by his examination of the balance sheet and the profit and loss account.

In cases where the auditor has been asked to carry out the detailed audit, the scope of his work will depend upon the degree of internal control exercised within the business enterprise. If the latter's organisation is of a high standard in this respect, it is considered that much of the auditing could be done by random tests, e.g. the checking of cash receipts, sales and purchases. Cash disbursements, however, are still very often subjected to a full examination, probably due to the fact that auditor and client may find it difficult to agree upon the extent of internal check necessary.

The common usage among Swedish professional accountants as regards the detailed auditing of accounts is held in respect by clients and others interested. It covers most of the problems in the field of detail examination. There is, however, still some considerable doubt regarding the extent to which random sampling instead of full examinations can be permitted, and the methods to be applied in these examinations. It must, however, be a matter of great importance that a common usage be established in regard to effective random sampling.

The Companies Act does not mention any division of work in those cases, where several auditors have been appointed. However when a professional accountant carries out an audit with a non-professional, it frequently happens that it is the former who devotes most time to the examination of the accounts, while the non-professional auditor, who often possesses a special experience of the client's field of activity, may be able to make useful observations during his examination of the administration, and thus complements the professional auditor's more general experience.

5. *Leading Institutions*

Although the Companies Act permits an audit to be carried out exclusively by non-professionals—except in the case of the large companies—we have in Sweden institutions which are responsible for maintaining a body of professional accountants of a high standard. The Companies Act mentions authorised public accountants and approved examiners of accounts.

Under their regulations established by the King in Council, the Chambers of Commerce, of which there are 12, have the right to authorise accountants for practising the profession of a public accountant and to approve examiners of accounts. The authorized public accountants shall, with certain exceptions, devote their activities exclusively to auditing, whereas the approved examiners may have another profession and occupy themselves with auditing as a side line. As this paper is to deal exclusively with professional accounting, the approved examiners have merely been mentioned in passing.

Out of the 310 authorised public accountants, about 210 are members of the Authorised Public Accountants' Association (Föreningen Auktoriserade Revisorer).

While the Companies Act makes certain minimum provisions regarding the competence of an auditor and the carrying out of an audit, which, although exacting, still leaves it open to non-professionals to carry out an audit, the Chambers of Commerce have placed very high demands on the qualifications of an authorised public accountant. For the members of the Authorised Public Accountants' Association—hereinafter called the Association—these demands have been made even more stringent in respect of professional conduct. The different demands placed on an authorized public accountant by the Companies Act, the Chambers of Commerce, and the Association, will be discussed under separate headings.

6. *Independence*

In order that the auditor's opinions shall always bear the stamp of impartiality, it is essential that his position should be independent.

The Companies Act prescribes in this respect that an auditor shall be of age, that he shall not hold an office in the company or in other way occupy a position subordinate to or dependent on a member of the Board, managing director or other officer in the company who handles the accounting, financial administration, or has the control thereof, or to any such person's spouse or close relation (parents, children, brothers, sisters, or brothers-in-law).

The statutes of the Chambers of Commerce require that an authorised public accountant shall not be under any restriction as to his person or property, and shall have a reputation for honesty, uprightness and good conduct. There are also further regulations—applicable to all audit commissions—which correspond to those of the Companies Act in respect of independence of position, but which also prescribe that an authorised public accountant may not undertake an audit if otherwise there are special circumstances which are likely to shake confidence in his impartiality in the performance of his duties. An authorised public accountant may not carry on or be an active partner in a business enterprise of any kind whatsoever, nor may he hold a salaried public or private office, other than employment with an authorised public accountant. Exemptions may be granted after investigation of each special case.

The Association's statutes, which in this respect are much the same as those of the Chambers of Commerce, lay down that a member may not undertake other than organisational commissions if he is in a position of dependence on any person who holds a high office in the client's business. The same rule applies where a member has a direct or indirect interest in a business enterprise if the commission results in his issuing a report that may become accessible to a third party. Such interest is for instance the holding of one or more shares or participating rights in the business and, although not specially stated in the Association's statutes probably also the granting of loans to an enterprise or security given for the fulfillment of an enterprise's obligations. As position of dependence should probably also be regarded cases in which an accountant receives besides the audit fee a privilege in the form of a loan, security or otherwise, which might conceivably influence his impartiality in the performance of his commission. The customary staff rebates, that the accountant may be allowed on purchases of the client's goods, can, however, be regarded as permissible.

The Association's statutes prohibit a member from carrying on in addition to his accounting work any activity of such a nature or scope that it may adversely affect his position as an authorised public accountant.

7. *Ability*

To be admitted by a Chamber of Commerce as an authorised public accountant the applicant must have taken an Economics Degree at a Swedish College of

Economics in the subjects of business administration, law, and economics, and have been awarded at least the grade 'cum laude approbatur' in the two first-mentioned subjects. He must also have proved by work in practice—e.g. duly certified service with an authorised public accountant—his aptitude for the profession of accountancy and such employment must as a rule have been held for at least 5 years.

To be admitted to membership of the Association an applicant must be an authorised public accountant, and for at least one year prior to his application he shall have carried on in a satisfactory manner, and be still carrying on his professional activities.

An authorised public accountant must thus have a university degree of a qualifying class. The time taken to complete the studies at the College of Economics is usually 3½ years. The subject of business administration includes a short course in auditing, which can be completed in one term along with the other studies.

The actual training for accountancy does not begin until the student enters the employment of an authorised public accountant as an assistant at the age of about 25. This is an ordinary salaried appointment, without, as a rule, any contractual undertakings on either side. The training in the accountant's office consists solely of practical work. Theoretical instruction for assistants has been arranged by the Association at intervals of a few years in the form of short courses. There is no form of accountancy examination. After five years of practical work, the assistant applies to a Chamber of Commerce to be admitted as an authorised public accountant. He has then to submit a testimonial given by his employer, stating in detail the work having been undertaken by the assistant and his aptitude for the profession.

Swedish literature on the subject of auditing is, unfortunately, not very frequent. There is no special journal devoted wholly to the problems of auditing, and the articles on auditing which appear in the rest of the special press are few and far between.

In connection with its annual meetings the Association generally arranges lectures and discussions on one or more questions of topical interest. The Association also arranges informal meetings, when the members can air their differences of opinion on special problems.

By his university training and his practical experience in an accountant's office, the authorised public accountant has had opportunity to acquire a good general knowledge. The curriculum of the Colleges of Economics, however, also includes a compulsory special course in accounting organisation, bookkeeping technique and administration. The instruction given is of a very high class, and enables the students to acquire a sound knowledge of the developments in these fields.

8. *Professional Conduct*

It is not enough that the individual accountant himself must be possessed of independent judgement and of competence, there must also be respect for the whole profession. Every accountant must be sure that if in a certain situation he acts in accordance with the rules laid down for professional conduct, he can count on the support of the whole profession and of his individual colleagues, and on receiving understanding from his client and others concerned with his commission.

The Companies Act mentions a penalty for an auditor who without special reason discloses any matter that may have come to his knowledge during the audit. Further regulations regarding an authorised public accountant's conduct in relation to his clients are to be found in the statutes of the Chambers of Commerce, which, besides the obligation to observe secrecy, also lay down that the accountant shall carry out the audits entrusted to him with honesty, zeal and care, conscientiously and to the best of his ability. The statutes also provide that in the case of a dispute regarding the fee, the matter shall be submitted to the Accountant's Board for arbitration.

The Association's regulations regarding a member's professional conduct in carrying out his commissions are essentially the same as those of the Chambers of Commerce. The statutes of the Association further prescribe that a member shall also in other respects observe the professional ethics of public accounting. This brief regulation is, however, of a far-reaching nature, and affects the member's relations with his clients and colleagues, with the whole profession, and with commerce and industry in general. It is an outward expression of the fact that certain ethical rules exist in the form of a usage generally accepted among the members of the Association.

The question of the fee plays an important role in the relations between the accountant and his client. There is no generally accepted system for the calculation of the fees, in any case not in the form of an approximate scale of charges. A member may probably not, however, calculate his fee according to what the client may be able to achieve as a result of the accountant's work, nor may he accept a commission or other considerable remuneration as a result of dealings between the client and a third party. It should be mentioned here that under the provisions of the Companies Act, the audit fee shall be fixed by the Shareholders' Meeting. The auditor will, however, sometimes charge an additional fee for detailed audit and consultations.

The client must be able to rely on the protection afforded by the rule of secrecy. This does not mean, however, that the accountant is prohibited from consulting his colleagues in his own firm or elsewhere on important matters of principle concerning a certain client. This is often necessary in order that the accountant shall be able to feel sufficiently certain of the standpoint he intends to take. The client's name should not be mentioned in these discussions, nor should any circumstances be mentioned in such a way that they might disclose the identity of the enterprise.

There is in the relations between members of the Association particularly one unwritten law which seems to be generally applied, namely, the rule that if a member is offered a new commission, before accepting it he must find out whether the audit has previously been carried out by a colleague, and if such proves to be the case, he should confer with the latter as to his reason for relinquishing the commission. The purpose of this is to afford the new auditor an opportunity to judge whether he shall accept the appointment, and if he does so, to derive benefit from the other's experiences. Ordinary courtesy also demands that if a member is asked to carry out an audit or other commission in co-operation with a colleague, who may have previously carried out the commission alone or with a non-professional auditor, he shall inform his colleague before accepting the commission. The latter then will have the opportunity to resign his appointment if he finds it compatible with his client's and his own interests to do so.

A direct approach to a potential client with offers of unreasonably low fees or better service than offered by other colleagues, constitutes a breach of the rule regarding professional ethics in relation to the profession in general.

Professional conduct in the relations between colleagues is affected to some extent by the forms in which the accounting activity is carried on. Nowadays it would seem to be less usual for an authorised public accountant to carry on his practice singly, with possibly a few assistants. In some cases co-operation between accountant colleagues takes the form of sharing an office and certain members of the staff. The trend of developments, however, appears to be increasingly towards audit offices in the form in which they occur in the Anglo-Saxon countries, among others. This, however, applies only to the external form, since according to Swedish law a firm of auditors may not be appointed to audit a limited liability company. For this purpose a physical person has to be appointed. Other types of audits, too, are mostly in the nature of a personal relationship between the client and the accountant, even though in carrying out the audit the latter may be assisted by one or more assistants. The Companies Act stresses this personal relationship by pointing out that when appointing an auditor, the Meeting of Shareholders may stipulate that the auditor shall not employ any assistants in carrying out the audit—a stipulation which would seem to be rather unreasonable, at any rate when it is a question of large audits.

In the case where an internal audit department of a high standard is responsible for the detailed audit of current business transactions, it would seem suitable that the appointed auditor should not spend his time on detail work but should concentrate instead on studying the whole. It is quite understandable that under those circumstances the client might prefer to deal with certain specific persons as auditor and deputy auditor instead of entrusting himself to a firm of auditors.

A member of the Association may not offer employment to any person in the employ of a colleague without first having conferred with the latter. To express criticism of a colleague's opinion without first having heard his side of the matter is of course not acceptable.

Correct professional conduct towards the profession in general demands that the restrictive rules regarding advertising, contained in the statutes of the Association, shall be observed. Apart from the short particulars in a telephone book or directory, a member may not insert more than twelve short advertisements during a year. Advertising is, in fact, quite unusual with Swedish professional accountants.

The authorised public accountant has undoubtedly a duty towards Commerce and Industry in general to co-operate actively with his clients in keeping the standard of accounting on such a high level that it will gain general credence with the public.

9. *Consultative capacity*

The special examinations and investigations regarding the position, results and administration of enterprises, or units within an enterprise, which an accountant may be commissioned to undertake, either as an appointed auditor or in no connection with an audit, are carried out on the same principles as an ordinary audit. As mentioned, however, the report is drawn up in a different way, it is not published, and it does not carry the same far-reaching responsibility.

An authorised public accountant is often engaged as a permanent or temporary consultant in matters relating particularly to accounting and other administrative questions, and may often give informal recommendations based on his examinations and studies. The duty of an accountant to carry out his work conscientiously and to the best of his ability would mean in this connection that the accountant may not pretend to be able to give advise in matters with which he is not sufficiently acquainted, and that he must in such cases refer his client to an expert. This also applies to consultation on financial and taxation matters. Any responsibility which an accountant incurs by negligence in advisory matters is probably of a purely moral nature.

10. *Combination of Auditing and Consultative Capacities*

The impropriety of approving or suggesting measures which one later on has to examine critically, is often given as a reason why the accountant should abstain from any consultation which has a direct connection with the audited enterprise's administration or accounting. For an auditor to attend the Board Meetings is regarded by many as being directly incompatible with professional ethics. On the other hand it is possible that the auditor may be asked quite informally to give his opinion prior to a matter being dealt with by the Board, and he will then do so by mentioning several different ways of solving the problem, or by giving different reasons why he considers one way to be more practicable than another. It is quite usual for the management to discuss with the auditor the setting up of the annual accounts before they are made out in their final form.

It must be deemed to be quite justifiable, and many times even suitable, for the auditor to give an opinion on organisational matters in respect of, for instance, the tasks of the accounting personnel or book-keeping matters in general. It should also be possible for the accountant to give advice in other matters concerning administration and taxation without this preventing him from auditing the enterprise's accounts and administration.

INLEIDING

van

DR. A. TH. DE LANGE

Nederlands Instituut van Accountants

I. FUNCTIE

Bij de beoordeling van de functie, de taak, de verklaring en de verantwoordelijkheid van de accountant in Nederland dient wel te worden bedacht, dat in dat land de positie van de accountant geheel is bepaald geworden door het vrije spel der krachten, voortkomende uit de behoeften van het verkeer en de ontwikkelingsdrang van de beoefenaren van het beroep. Een wettelijke regeling van het accountantsberoep is ondanks uitgeoefende aandrang en ondernomen pogingen nog niet tot stand gekomen. Er bestaat geen wettelijk verplichte controle op de jaarrekeningen van naamloze vennootschappen. Voorschriften met een wetgevend karakter omtrent door de accountant te verrichten werkzaamheden en door hem in acht te nemen regelen ontbreken nagenoeg geheel; zij hebben althans geen wezenlijke invloed op de beroepsvervulling uitgeoefend. Rechterlijke uitspraken, welke de accountant een grondslag voor zijn beroepsuitoefening zouden kunnen bieden, worden evenmin aangetroffen.

Wel hebben de grondslagen voor het accountantsberoep een codificatie gevonden in de statuten en reglementen van het Nederlands Instituut van Accountants, met name in het Reglement van Arbeid en de Ereregelen, welke laatste reglementen sedert korte tijd gelijkluidend zijn aan de Voorschriften inzake de beroepsuitoefening van de Vereniging van Academisch Gevormde Accountants. Deze codificatie is bij het Instituut reeds vrij spoedig na zijn oprichting tot stand gekomen en daarna enkele malen uitgebreid en aangepast aan de ontwikkeling van het beroep. De reglementsbepalingen zijn te beschouwen als de resultaten van de gedachtenwisseling van de beroepsbeoefenaren omtrent hetgeen als fundamenteel voor de beroepsuitoefening moet worden aangemerkt. De ware inhoud van de reglementen kan dan ook alleen worden begrepen na kennisneming van de uitgebreide literatuur, welke zich in de loop der jaren heeft gevormd in de vorm van boekwerken, tijdschriftartikelen, verslagen van studievergaderingen, rapporten van studiecommissies, e.d. Slechts met behulp daarvan kan men zich een beeld van de stand van het beroep in Nederland vormen.

In de formulering van de grondslagen voor het accountantsberoep heeft vooral prof. dr Th. Limperg Jr een belangrijk aandeel geleverd. Op basis van zijn leer van het gewekte vertrouwen hebben de opvattingen omtrent de functie, de taak en de verantwoordelijkheid van de accountant, alsmede omtrent de draagwijdte van zijn verklaring zich nader ontwikkeld. Zo wordt thans algemeen in Nederland de functie van de accountant gezien als het voldoen aan de behoefte aan het oordeel van de onafhankelijke deskundige op het gebied van de controle, de administratieve organisatie en de bedrijfseconomie. Deze behoefte kan ontstaan zowel in het maatschappelijk verkeer als bij de topleiding van een bedrijf. In het eerste geval komt zij voort uit de wens van aandeelhouders, schuldeisers en andere belanghebbenden bij de financiële positie en uitkomsten van het bedrijf, of van enig onderdeel daarvan, zich te laten voorlichten omtrent de juistheid van overgelegde cijfers en de interpretatie daarvan voor bepaalde doeleinden. Vervult de accountant zijn functie ten behoeve van de bedrijfsleiding, dan heeft zij ten doel de directie te informeren omtrent de wijze, waarop de aan haar ondergeschikte leiders hun bevoegdheden hebben gebruikt en omtrent de resultaten van het beleid van hogere en lagere leiders. In beide gevallen is de functie van de accountant gebaseerd op het onafhankelijk oordeel van de deskundige op de hiervoren aangeduide gebieden. Uit deze omschrijving volgt reeds, dat het van de accountant verlangde oordeel meer omvat dan de boekhoudkundige juistheid van cijferopstellingen; het strekt zich tevens uit tot het beeld, dat de cijfers bij de lezer oproepen.

De vraag, waarvoor de accountant zich bij de vervulling van zijn functie steeds ziet gesteld, is, of de verslaglegging tezamen met de inhoud van de verklaring (het rapport van de accountant), de lezer een getrouw en volledig beeld geven van alle factoren, welke voor zijn oordeelsvorming van betekenis zijn. Daarbij gaat het niet zozeer om de formele juistheid van de cijfers, maar vooral om de bedrijfseconomische inhoud daarvan. Zo gaat het niet alleen om de grootte van het totale resultaat der onderneming, maar ook om de analyse daarvan naar de oorzaken, indien en voorzoverre deze analyse noodzakelijk is om zich omtrent de werkelijke winstgevendheid van het bedrijf een oordeel te vormen; aldus worden de incidentele winsten of verliezen gescheiden van de normale winstbronnen.

Het is begrijpelijk, dat de hiervoren omschreven controlerende functie van de accountant verbonden is geworden met een adviserende functie, welke met name ten opzichte van de bedrijfsleiding wordt vervuld. Waar de administratie een zo bij uitstek belangrijk waarnemingsinstrument voor het bedrijfsgebeuren is en de accountant door de controle van deze administratie dit bedrijfsgebeuren zo intens, nauwkeurig en kritisch waarneemt, ligt het voor de hand, dat de directie van het bedrijf behoefte heeft haar gedachten omtrent het gevoerde en te voeren beleid te toetsen aan die van de accountant, daarbij profiterende van diens bedrijfseconomische kennis. Daarnaast heeft zich in de loop der jaren met de toeneming van de deskundigheid van de accountant op dit terrein een zelfstandige adviserende functie ontwikkeld, los staande van de vervulling van de controlerende functie.

II. Onafhankelijkheid

De behoefte aan een onafhankelijk oordeel schept de noodzaak te bezien onder welke omstandigheden de onafhankelijkheid van de accountant gewaarborgd is. Deze onafhankelijkheid heeft een juridisch en een economisch aspect, maar is daarnevens een kwestie van karakter, van begrip voor de aard van de functie. De accountant moet zich bewust zijn van het belang van zijn verklaringen en van de beslissingen, welke daarop worden gebaseerd. Dit geldt voor alle accountants, ongeacht de juridische vormgeving van hun werkzaamheden voor het maatschappelijk verkeer, voor de bedrijfsleiding of voor de overheid.

Het begrip van de accountant voor de aard van zijn functie is mede daarom van belang, omdat de economische onafhankelijkheid naar haar aard gemakkelijk kan worden aangetast. Bij de formulering van zijn oordeel zal de accountant in dienstbetrekking zowel als de openbare accountant zich moeten hoeden voor overwegingen, gericht op het behoud van de dienstbetrekking of van de relatie, welke de onafhankelijkheid verloren doen gaan.

Het juridische aspect van de onafhankelijkheid van de accountant heeft betrekking op de gezagsverhouding, op de vraag, of de accountant een ondergeschikte dan wel een nevengeschikte functie vervult. Op dit punt lopen de posities van de openbare accountants en van de functionarissen in dienstbetrekking uiteen. De laatstbedoelden, waartoe behoren de interne accountants van de bedrijven en de overheidsaccountants, zijn ondergeschikt aan hun werkgevers. Uit dien hoofde zullen zij tegenover derden geen verklaringen kunnen afgeven, welke betrekking hebben op verantwoordingen van hun werkgevers, ook al kunnen zij tegenover hun superieuren van een onafhankelijk oordeel doen blijken. Zij missen in het maatschappelijk verkeer de autoriteit van een onafhankelijke functionaris. Dit brengt mede, dat alleen de openbare accountants verklaringen, bestemd voor het maatschappelijk verkeer, kunnen afgeven, terwijl de accountantsverklaringen, welke de bedrijfsleiding en de overheid als zodanig behoeven, zowel door openbare accountants als door accountants in dienstbetrekking kunnen worden verstrekt.

III. Verklaring en verantwoordelijkheid

Degenen, te wier behoeve de accountantswerkzaamheden worden verricht, nemen kennis van de uitkomsten van deze werkzaamheden in de door de accountant als sluitstuk van zijn arbeid afgelegde verklaring. Onder een verklaring wordt verstaan elke mededeling, hetzij schriftelijk of mondeling gedaan, hetzij in de vorm van een korte formule of van een meer of minder uitgebreid rapport, waarin een oordeel wordt kenbaar gemaakt. Het uitspreken van een oordeel, het afgeven van een verklaring doet de verantwoordelijkheid voor de juistheid van de verklaring ontstaan. In Nederland spreekt men van de verantwoordelijkheid van de accountant, indien gedacht wordt aan de vaktechnische verplichtingen, welke op de accountant met betrekking tot de vervulling van zijn functie rusten. Deze vaktechnische verplichtingen rusten op de accountant, onverschillig of ook een financiële sanctie op de niet-nakoming van de verplichtingen bestaat. Zou deze sanctie bestaan, dan spreekt men van de aansprakelijkheid voor de juistheid van de verklaring. Uit een beroepsoogpunt is de verantwoordelijkheid uiteraard veel belangrijker dan de aansprakelijkheid; de financiële gevolgen van het niet-nakomen van de vaktechnische verplichtingen zijn van minder gewicht voor de accountant dan het hem opzeggen van het vertrouwen voor de toekomst.

De inhoud van de verklaring moet gedekt zijn door een deskundig onderzoek, dat die inhoud rechtvaardigt. Dit betekent, dat de verrichte werkzaamheden de verklaring moeten kunnen dragen. Van meer belang is evenwel, dat de verklaring alleen dan geen groter vertrouwen opwekt dan gerechtvaardigd is, indien het onderzoek gericht is geweest op een rationele doelstelling. De verantwoordelijkheid voor de juistheid van de verklaring reikt dan ook verder dan de inhoud van de verklaring; zij strekt zich uit tot het doel van het onderzoek. Door het aanbrengen van ondoelmatige beperkingen in de doelstelling ontneemt de accountant aan de verklaring haar betekenis en wekt hij bij de ondeskundige lezer een groter vertrouwen dan op grond van de verrichte werkzaamheden gerechtvaardigd is.

Vermeden dient te worden een opsomming van de verrichte werkzaamheden te geven; voor de niet-deskundige lezer en zelfs veelal voor de deskundige lezer is het niet mogelijk te beoordelen, of de opsomming een beperking van de betekenis van de uitkomst van het onderzoek inhoudt. Daarom wordt erop aangedrongen de conclusie van de verrichte arbeid zo eenvoudig mogelijk te formuleren; bij de controle van de jaarstukken zal men kunnen volstaan met de enkele akkoordverklaring of handtekening.

Hiermede zijn wij gekomen aan de omvang van de verantwoordelijkheid van de accountant voor zijn verklaring. Met name doet dit vraagstuk zich voor bij de goedkeurende verklaring van de jaarstukken van de onderneming, maar het vraagt evengoed een beantwoording, in geval de verklaring voortvloeit uit bijzondere onderzoekingen op het gebied der controle of van bedrijfseconomische aard. Kort geformuleerd: hoever reikt de betekenis van het oordeel van de accountant, welk vertrouwen mag de lezer in de verklaring stellen. Zoals in de aanvang van dit referaat reeds is opgemerkt, vindt de Nederlandse accountant bij de beantwoording van deze vraag geen steun in wetgevende bepalingen en rechterlijke uitspraken. Hij zal de vraag, of de verrichte werkzaamheden de afgifte van een verklaring rechtvaardigen, moeten beantwoorden aan de hand van de normen, welke in het maatschappelijk verkeer zijn gegroeid met betrekking tot de omvang van het vertrouwen, dat de lezer in een bepaalde verklaring kan stellen. De maatschappelijke norm is de toetssteen voor de omvang van de verantwoordelijkheid, welke de accountant door de afgifte van de verklaring aanvaardt. Deze norm is uiteraard niet altijd even hoog geweest; met de ontwikkeling van het beroep heeft zij een bepaald niveau bereikt, een niveau dat enerzijds aan de behoefte aan zekerheid voor de lezer voldoet, anderzijds niet hoger is gesteld dan de vaktechniek toelaat.

De inhoud van deze norm is aan de accountants en aan hen, die krachtens hun belang van accountantsverklaringen kennis nemen, bekend, ten dele op grond van jarenlange ervaring, ten dele op grond van de omschrijvingen, welke men daaromtrent in de vakliteratuur, en voor een deel ook in de reglementen, kan aantreffen. Uiteraard zal bij de vervulling van nieuwe functies door de accountants de juiste norm aanvankelijk niet of onvoldoende bekend zijn; zo kan men stellen, dat, terwijl de normen van vertrouwen voor de verschillende controlerende functies van de accountant thans gevestigd zijn, de normen in de adviserende functies nog geenszins vaststaan en daaromtrent meningsverschillen kunnen worden waargenomen. Onder deze laatste omstandigheden is het noodzakelijk, dat de accountant de draagwijdte van de verklaring nader aangeeft, opdat bij de lezer daarover geen misverstand ontstaat. Met de voortgaande ontwikkeling van bepaalde functies zal blijken, in hoeverre het verkeer het aanleggen van andere normen verkiest en in hoeverre door de accountant daaraan kan worden voldaan. Met name in dergelijke ontwikkelingsperioden doet de accountant verstandig te zorgen, dat geen overdreven betekenis aan zijn verklaring kan worden gehecht.

Ook naar de groepen van belanghebbenden, tot wie de accountantsverklaring is gericht of voor wie zij is bestemd, heeft de norm van vertrouwen een verschillende inhoud. Men kent de publieke verklaringen voor aandeelhouders en schuldeisers en de niet-publieke verklaringen voor commissarissen en directie. Voor de publieke accountantsverklaring zal de eis ten aanzien van de verificatie van de details minder ver gaan dan voor de niet-publieke verklaringen voor de functionarissen van het bedrijf. De gepubliceerde jaarstukken geven een globaal beeld van de uitkomsten en van de financiële toestand van het bedrijf; dat beeld behoeft de werkelijkheid niet meer nauwkeurig aan te geven dan nodig is om een indruk van die werkelijkheid te krijgen en om een verkeerde indruk te voorkomen. Het accountantscertificaat bij deze jaarstukken heeft slechts betrekking op dit globale beeld. De cijferopstellingen, welke aan de commissarissen worden verstrekt, zijn aanzienlijk meer gedetailleerd; de gegevens, welke de directie hanteert, zijn uiteraard het meest volledig. Zowel commissarissen als directie hebben deze gegevens nodig voor de richtige vervulling van hun functie, zodat zij zeker willen zijn van de juistheid van de overgelegde specificaties. Onder deze omstandigheden strekt de goedkeurende verklaring van de accountant zich uit tot de jaarstukken en alle daarop betrekking hebbende specificaties en toelichtingen. Een en ander betekent, dat door de afgifte van een publieke verklaring de accountant een minder ver gaande verantwoordelijkheid voor de juistheid van de gepubliceerde cijfers aanvaardt dan door het uitbrengen van een rapport aan commissarissen; dit rapport schept op zijn beurt een minder omvangrijke verantwoordelijkheid dan het rapport aan de directie.

Bij het verlenen van bijstand in belastingzaken aanvaardt de accountant tegenover de fiscus de verantwoordelijkheid voor de juistheid van alle in besprekingen en rechtsgedingen met de fiscus overgelegde cijfers en van alle daarop schriftelijk of mondeling verstrekte toelichtingen, tenzij door hem het tegendeel uitdrukkelijk is gesteld. Op basis van de door de accountant gegarandeerde juistheid van de feitelijke gegevens kan deze de belangen van zijn cliënt behartigen door de verdediging van een voor de belastingplichtige zo gunstig mogelijke wetsinterpretatie.

Ongeacht evenwel of de accountant de onderneming bijstaat in de verzorging van de belastingzaken, hij zal zich moeten overtuigen, dat de door de onderneming verschuldigde belastingen in de balans zijn verwerkt. De ontwikkeling van de Nederlandse fiscale wetgeving in de na-oorlogse jaren heeft aanleiding gegeven tot een nadere bezinning op de belastingverplichtingen van de onderneming. Meermalen wordt de accountant voor de situatie gesteld, dat de toepassing van de belastingvoorschriften medebrengt de fiscale aanvaarding van lasten, welke in de jaarstukken van de onderneming eerst in een later jaar als zodanig tot uitdrukking komen; met name is dit het geval, indien de fiscus de berekening van afschrijvingen op duurzame activa toestaat, welke door de onderneming eerst in latere jaren wordt toegepast. Onder deze omstandigheden heeft de onderneming niet alleen een verplichting uit hoofde van de belastbare winst, maar tevens een latente belastingverplichting uit hoofde van in de toekomst nog te dragen lasten. De accountant zal de goedkeurende verklaring slechts kunnen afgeven, indien in de balans met deze latente belastingverplichtingen rekening is gehouden.

De financiële positie en uitkomsten van het bedrijf worden niet alleen beheerst door fiscale, maar ook door economische voorschriften van de overheid. De laatstbedoelde voorschriften kunnen betrekking hebben op prijs- en produktieregelingen en op de declaratie of afdracht van gelden aan daartoe ingestelde fondsen van publiekrechtelijke aard. De vraag, in hoeverre de goedkeurende accountantsverklaring bij de jaarrekening mede omvat de waarborg voor een richtige naleving van deze voorschriften, heeft aanleiding gegeven tot de instelling van een studiecommissie vanwege het Nederlands Instituut van Accountants; het door deze commissie uitgebrachte rapport is evenwel nog niet gepubliceerd.

Uit de voorgaande beschouwingen volgt, dat de accountant met zijn verklaringen geen onbeperkte verantwoordelijkheid aanvaardt. De beperkingen van deze verantwoordelijkheid zijn evenwel begrepen in de norm van vertrouwen, welke in het verkeer is ontstaan. Daarom is het in het algemeen onnodig de grenzen van de verantwoordelijkheid in de verklaring op te nemen. Er kunnen evenwel omstandigheden optreden, waardoor de accountant genoodzaakt is zijn verantwoordelijkheid ten opzichte van de gestelde norm te beperken. Het ligt in de rede, dat de formulering van de nauwer getrokken grenzen der verantwoordelijkheid geschiedt door het aangeven van de beperkingen ten opzichte van de norm.

IV. Taak

In de voorafgaande beschouwingen is gebleken, dat de verantwoordelijkheid voor de deugdelijkheid van de verklaring door de accountant slechts kan worden aanvaard, indien de daartoe te verrichten arbeid is uitgevoerd. Welke arbeid zal moeten worden verricht in elk voorkomend geval en welke vaktechniek moet worden toegepast, wordt onderzocht in de leer der accountantscontrole. Het zou ons te ver voeren de vaktechniek hier nader uiteen te zetten. Wij zullen ons beperken tot enkele facetten van het vraagstuk.

In Nederland wordt de accountantspraktijk algemeen uitgeoefend met behulp van medewerkers en assistenten; de medewerkers onderscheiden zich van de assistenten door het bezit van een accountantsdiploma. Dit betekent, dat slechts een deel van de uit te voeren werkzaamheden door de accountant, die de verklaring ondertekent, zelf wordt verricht, en dat de verklaring voor een goed deel is gebaseerd op de mededelingen van de ondergeschikten omtrent het resultaat van hun werkzaamheden. Deze omstandigheid brengt evenwel geen beperking van de verantwoordelijkheid van de accountant mede. Hij heeft zorg te dragen voor een zodanige regeling der werkzaamheden, dat daardoor geen onvolkomenheden in de controle ontstaan. De accountant zal zich moeten overtuigen zowel van een goede organisatie als van een goede uitvoering van de controle.

De organisatie van het bedrijf is van grote betekenis voor de aard en de omvang van de te verrichten taak. De functieverdeling kan in het te controleren bedrijf zodanig geregeld zijn, dat zelfs van een mogelijkheid van controle geen sprake kan zijn. Dit kan ook het geval zijn, indien de administratie onvoldoende is ontwikkeld. Onder dergelijke omstandigheden zal de accountant zijn controlewerkzaamheden eerst kunnen aanvangen, nadat de gebleken bezwaren zijn opgeheven. De ervaring leert, dat het op peil brengen van de organisatie en van de administratieve inrichting in belangrijke mate aan de accountant wordt opgedragen. Hij heeft dan de gelegenheid de bestuurlijke en administratieve organisatie aan te passen aan de behoeften van de controle-techniek en te bevorderen, dat de controle zo eenvoudig mogelijk kan worden gehouden.

V. Vakbekwaamheid

De deskundigheid, waarover de accountant moet beschikken, strekt zich uit over de gebieden van de controle, de administratieve organisatie en de bedrijfseconomie. De vereiste deskundigheid wordt uiteraard in hoge mate bepaald door de vraagstukken, waarvoor de accountant zich in zijn beroepsuitoefening ziet gesteld. De snelle maatschappelijke ontwikkeling heeft deze vraagstukken voortdurend van karakter doen veranderen, waardoor de praktiserende accountant genoodzaakt is zijn deskundigheid steeds aan de gewijzigde behoefte aan te passen. Dit betekent, dat de vakbekwaamheid van de accountant geenszins uitsluitend afhankelijk is van de genoten opleiding, maar tevens van zijn bereidheid de vaktechnische ontwikkelingen te volgen. Deze ontwikkelingen mogen op het terrein der controle reeds van belang zijn, op de gebieden van de administratieve organisatie en van de bedrijfseconomie, met name van de interne organisatie van het bedrijf, zijn de ontwikkelingen van zodanige omvang, dat men zich met recht kan afvragen, of het mogelijk geacht moet worden dat de praktiserende accountant deze kan volgen. Voor bepaalde onderdelen van de administratieve organisatie (het gebruik van elektronische apparatuur en automatisering) en van de bedrijfseconomie (marktonderzoek en fabrieksorganisatie) zal dit bepaald niet mogelijk zijn. Daaruit is de opkomst van andere deskundigen mede te verklaren, maar tevens richt deze ontwikkeling de aandacht op de noodzaak en de mogelijkheden van specialisatie binnen het accountantskantoor. Hoewel men in Nederland een open oog heeft voor deze beroepsvraagstukken, kan men niet zeggen, dat de bestudering daarvan de te volgen weg reeds duidelijk heeft leren kennen, zodat te dezer plaatse niet verder op dit onderwerp kan worden ingegaan.

Het is duidelijk, dat de dynamiek van het accountantsberoep haar stempel op de opleiding dient te drukken. Het onderwijs mag het aanleren van parate feitenkennis en bepaalde vakgrepen weliswaar niet verwaarlozen, het zal zich moeten richten op het bijbrengen van begrip voor de aard van de vraagstukken, van het vermogen de problemen te onderkennen en van de methoden, volgens welke deze tot oplossing kunnen worden gebracht.

In Nederland kan men het accountantsdiploma verwerven door het afleggen, hetzij van het accountantsexamen aan een instelling van Hoger Onderwijs, hetzij van de examens van het Nederlands Instituut van Accountants. In het eerste geval wordt het onderricht gegeven aan een Universiteit, waaraan een Faculteit der Economische Wetenschappen is verbonden of aan een Economische Hogeschool. Aan een instelling van Hoger Onderwijs is de accountantsopleiding georganiseerd als een voortgezette studie na het doctoraalexamen in de economische wetenschappen, welk laatste examen een volledige economische opleiding afsluit. Het Nederlands Instituut van Accountants organiseert voor hen, die na de middelbare school geen hoger onderwijs genieten, een reeks van examens, waaronder examens in de economische vakken, de administratieve organisatie en de controleleer; tevens draagt het Instituut zorg voor de cursussen, welke voor de onderscheidene examens opleiden.

Het onderscheiden karakter der beide opleidingen brengt mede, dat de universitaire opleiding als een dagstudie is opgezet, terwijl het onderwijs van het Nederlands Instituut van Accountants in de avonduren wordt gegeven. In laatstbedoeld geval is het voor de studerenden mogelijk zich overdag in de praktijk te bekwamen. Dit neemt niet weg, dat ook bij de academische studenten in de accountancy de gewoonte bestaat in de jaren na het doctoraalexamen in de economische wetenschappen een functie bij een accountantskantoor of in het bedrijfsleven te aanvaarden. Op deze wijze hebben beide groepen van studerenden de gelegenheid naast de theoretische vorming de nodige praktische ervaring op te doen.

VI. Gedragsregels

In het kader van dit referaat is het niet mogelijk de gedragsregels, welke bij de beroepsuitoefening in Nederland in acht plegen te worden genomen, volledig te behandelen. De op dit punt geldende regels kunnen slechts in grove lijnen worden aangegeven.

Met betrekking tot de vormen van beroepsuitoefening kan worden opgemerkt, dat volgens de reglementen van het Instituut de openbare accountant zijn beroep alleen mag uitoefenen voor eigen rekening als zelfstandig gevestigd accountant, dan wel voor gemene rekening, in maatschap met een of meer leden van het Instituut of van een daarmede gelijkgestelde vereniging. In deze bepaling komt het persoonlijke karakter van de beroepsuitoefening naar voren; zij heeft in het bijzonder de beroepsuitoefening door of in dienst van naamloze vennootschappen onmogelijk gemaakt. Het bedoelde voorschrift zou echter tevens verhinderen, dat de openbare accountant zich associeert met een niet-accountant ter verkrijging van een samenwerking op een ander gebied, bijvoorbeeld op dat der administratieve organisatie. Daarom is het aan de leden in het vrije beroep toegestaan een maatschap met niet-leden van het Instituut aan te gaan, mits geen verklaringen in de zin van certificaten omtrent juistheid worden afgegeven, noch daartoe leidende opdrachten worden aanvaard.

De samenwerking met collega's in maatschapsverband werpt het interessante vraagstuk van de verantwoordelijkheid van elk der maatschapsleden voor de verklaringen, afgegeven door de maatschap dan wel een harer leden, op. Te dezer plaatse moet worden volstaan met de mededeling, dat de reglementen van N.I.v.A. en V.A.G.A. voorschrijven, dat een openbare accountant, die zijn praktijk uitoefent in maatschapsverband, verplicht is zodanige voorzieningen te treffen, dat hij zich in redelijkheid overtuigd kan houden, dat de arbeid van de medevennoot en diens verklaringen aan de reglementen voldoen. Deze verplichting reikt evenwel niet verder dan de algemene grondslagen van de onderzoekingen, waaronder worden verstaan zowel de in de reglementen vastgelegde algemene beginselen van beroepsuitoefening als de beginselen, volgens welke de werkprogramma's worden opgesteld.

Omtrent de hoogte van de tarieven, welke de accountants ter honorering der opdrachten in rekening mogen brengen, bestaan in het vrije beroep geen voorschriften, afspraken of algemeen aanvaarde gewoonten. De gebruikelijke wijze van berekening van het honorarium komt tot uitdrukking in de reglementsbepaling, dat de accountant in het vrije beroep geen andere vergoedingen mag aanvaarden, dan waarop hij uit hoofde van de omvang, de aard en de betekenis van de opdracht aanspraak heeft en dat hij geen vergoedingen mag bedingen, welke afhankelijk zijn van de uitkomst van de arbeid.

Tenslotte zij vermeld, dat het de leden in de vrije beroepsuitoefening is verboden reclame te maken of vergoedingen te geven voor het hun bezorgen van opdrachten.

VII. Reglementering en toezicht

De vraag kan gesteld worden, of de gedragsregels dienen te worden omschreven in reglementen van beroepsorganisaties, dan wel of het aanbeveling verdient de reglementering achterwege te laten en de werkzaamheden en normen uitsluitend te doen bepalen door de accountant zelf op grond van zijn door opleiding en ervaring verworven kennis. In Nederland is deze vraag reeds vele jaren geleden beantwoord ten gunste van de reglementering door de beroepsorganisatie, hoewel de beroepsvoorschriften van de Vereniging van Academisch Gevormde Accountants eerst na de tweede wereldoorlog tot stand gekomen zijn. Men heeft echter zorgvuldig vermeden de reglementering tot een handleiding bij de beroepsuitoefening te maken. Slechts algemene beginselen zijn in de voorschriften vastgelegd; de accountant zelf blijft voor de beslissing staan, hoe in elk bijzonder geval te handelen. De reglementen voor de beroepsuitoefening bevatten dan ook slechts een relatief gering aantal bepalingen. Dit biedt het voordeel van de mogelijkheid van een verdere ontwikkeling van de beroepsopvattingen binnen het kader der bestaande reglementering. In deze ontwikkeling heeft de door het Instituut ingestelde Commissie van Advies inzake Beroepsaangelegenheden een belangrijk aandeel. Deze Commissie houdt zich niet alleen bezig met het verstrekken van door leden van het Instituut gevraagde adviezen; door kennis te nemen van de publieke verklaringen van de accountants heeft zij gelegenheid ook op eigen initiatief adviezen te verstrekken. Daarnaast onderzoekt zij op verzoek van het Bestuur van het Instituut bepaalde beroepsvraagstukken en brengt zij daarover rapporten uit, welke als regel ter algemene kennis van de leden worden gebracht. Hoewel de inhoud van deze rapporten in geen enkel opzicht bindend voor de leden is, oefent de zienswijze van de Commissie niettemin een belangrijke invloed op de ontwikkeling van de beroepsopvattingen uit, mede door de discussies, welke naar aanleiding van de rapporten plegen te worden gevoerd.

VIII. Adviezen

De adviserende functie heeft betrekking op de problemen van administratieve organisatie en bedrijfseconomie. Vooral de behandeling van bedrijfseconomische vraagstukken is in de laatste decennia op de voorgrond gekomen, met name wat betreft de vragen van financiering, kostprijsberekening en winstbepaling. In verband hiermede rijst de interessante vraag van de aard van de verantwoordelijkheid voor de juistheid van de gedane mededelingen in de adviserende functie. Uiteraard kunnen hier slechts enkele punten worden aangestipt.

Vooropgesteld dient te worden, dat onder de geschetste omstandigheden de accountant geraadpleegd wordt om zijn deskundigheid. Dit betekent, dat de accountant alleen dan verantwoordelijkheid voor zijn adviezen kan dragen, als hij de vereiste deskundigheid waarlijk bezit. In de voorgaande beschouwingen is reeds tot uitdrukking gekomen, dat de bedrijfseconomische vraagstukken door de maatschappelijke en algemeen economische ontwikkelingen een zeer breed terrein bestrijken en dat een volledige deskundigheid van de accountant op al deze terreinen niet meer mag worden verwacht. Met name op de terreinen van verkooppolitiek (marktorganisatie, prijspolitiek) en van interne organisatie (rationele arbeidsmethoden, loonstelsels) kunnen slechts specialisten de nodige deskundigheid opbrengen. Dit betekent, dat de accountant, wil hij de volle verantwoordelijkheid voor de door hem verstrekte adviezen kunnen aanvaarden, zich beperkingen ten aanzien van de onderwerpen van zijn activiteit zal moeten opleggen, tenzij hij in de organisatie van zijn kantoor de nodige specialisten weet op te nemen. Uiteraard rijzen dan vraagstukken met betrekking tot de verdeling van de verantwoordelijkheid voor de uitgebrachte adviezen, waarop in het kader van dit referaat niet kan worden ingegaan en waaromtrent in Nederland nog geen gevestigde opvattingen bestaan.

Voorts dient de vraag te worden gesteld, of, gegeven de deskundigheid van de accountant voor het uitbrengen van het advies, aan het advies van de accountant dezelfde betekenis moet worden gehecht als aan dat van een andere deskundige. In dit verband kan worden opgemerkt, dat in vele gevallen de controlerende accountant en niet een andere deskundige zal worden aangezocht te adviseren wegens zijn bekendheid met de bijzondere omstandigheden in het bedrijf, waarop het advies betrekking zal hebben. Met name zal dit het geval zijn bij die vraagstukken, waarin de cijfermatige gegevens en de organisatorische en persoonlijke verhoudingen in het bedrijf, ook buiten het concrete deelprobleem, waarom het gaat, een belangrijke rol spelen. In deze gevallen zal immers de waarde van het advies in hoge mate afhankelijk zijn van de nauwkeurige kennis van deze gegevens en verhoudingen en van de wetenschap, welke betekenis aan de gehanteerde gegevens en aan de verhoudingen moet worden toegekend en of zij als betrouwbaar kunnen worden aangemerkt. Het is duidelijk, dat in dergelijke gevallen de deskundige, niet-accountant, in de beoordeling en de beantwoording van het vraagstuk bij de accountant van het bedrijf ten achter staat. Maar tevens staat vast, dat de accountant bij het uitbrengen van zijn advies zich bewust moet zijn van zijn verantwoordelijkheid voor de betrouwbaarheid en de wijze van interpretatie der gehanteerde gegevens.

Het voldoen aan deze verwachtingen door de controlerende accountant moge in den regel niet veel bezwaren ontmoeten, moeilijker wordt het vraagstuk indien het advies van een accountant wordt gevraagd in een bedrijf, waarin hij geen controlerende functie vervult. Dan staat hij in beginsel gelijk met elke andere deskundige. Toch mag niet worden voorbij gezien, dat het verstrekken van de opdracht aan de accountant veelal gebaseerd zal zijn op het algemeen vertrouwen in het oordeel van de accountant over vraagstukken, waarin de waarneming van het bedrijfsgebeuren door middel van de administratie een belangrijke rol speelt. Dit zal de accountant noodzaken zich omtrent de reële inhoud der gehanteerde gegevens een oordeel te vormen en hun juistheid vast te stellen. Dit betekent, dat ook zonder een controle-opdracht aan de accountant deze de overgelegde gegevens niet zonder meer zal kunnen aanvaarden. Hoewel de vertrouwensnormen in de adviserende functies nog niet zo scherp vaststaan als in de controlerende functies, mag toch veilig worden gesteld, dat bij de opdrachtgever ten aanzien van de accountant verwachtingen bestaan, die uiteraard niet mogen worden beschaamd. Het afzien van de beoordeling van de bruikbaarheid der cijfers zal in sommige gevallen tot de onaanvaardbaarheid van de opdracht, in andere gevallen tot een voorbehoud in het advies moeten leiden.

IX. Combinatie controlerende en adviserende functie

Velen zijn van mening, dat in de combinatie van de controlerende en adviserende functie van de accountant het gevaar kan zijn gelegen, dat de accountant door zijn adviezen zijn objectiviteit bij de uitoefening van zijn controlerende functie verliest. Het wil mij voorkomen, dat, wanneer het advies op de juiste wijze wordt gegeven, d.w.z. wanneer het op de juiste gegevens en deskundigheid is gebaseerd en waarlijk het karakter van een advies draagt, dit gevaar niet behoeft te bestaan. Daartoe dient het karakter van het advies nader te worden bezien.

Het vraagstuk van de collisie van de adviserende met de controlerende functie is met name van belang in de gevallen, waarin het gevraagde advies betrekking heeft op het door de bedrijfsleiding te voeren beleid. Van een beleidsvraagstuk kan worden gesproken, indien de te nemen beslissing afhankelijk is van het oordeel omtrent de te verwachten ontwikkelingen van voor de beslissing bepalende factoren. Zou het vraagstuk elk beleidselement missen, zouden m.a.w. de voor de handelwijze bepalende factoren vaststaande grootheden zijn, welke naar hun aard geen toekomstige ontwikkelingen kennen, dan zou de opstelling van het advies alleen deskundigheid op het betreffende gebied van kennis vereisen en zou een onbevredigend advies slechts kunnen worden geweten aan onvoldoende deskundigheid. Zodra evenwel beleidselementen het gedrag van de bedrijfsleiding bepalen, wordt het persoonlijke inzicht in bepaalde toekomstige ontwikkelingen van doorslaggevend belang. Hoewel het begrijpelijk is, dat menige bedrijfsleider het oordeel van een ander over deze ontwikkelingen wil vernemen, wil het mij voorkomen, dat de accountant met het oplossen van beleidsvraagstukken op de verkeerde weg zou zijn. Hij zou daarmede trouwens een der meest essentiële elementen van de bestuursfunctie overnemen, in stede van zich te bepalen tot de adviserende en de controlerende functie. De adviserende taak houdt onder deze omstandigheden in ervoor te zorgen, dat de bedrijfsleiding, alvorens haar beleidsbeslissing te nemen, volledig op de hoogte wordt gesteld van alle voor de besluitvorming belangrijke factoren en dat geen daarvoor van belang zijnde overweging door onvoldoend inzicht in de aard van het vraagstuk buiten beschouwing wordt gelaten. Hierbij kan de accountant richting geven aan zijn advies door bepaalde mogelijke ontwikkelingen te veronderstellen en onder deze veronderstellingen de gevolgen voor het beleid aan te geven. Op grond van een aldus geformuleerd advies zal de bedrijfsleiding echter zelf haar besluit moeten nemen, haar beleid moeten bepalen. De accountant zal zich, zowel in zijn controlerende als in zijn adviserende functie, ervoor moeten hoeden in het beleid van de bedrijfsleiding te treden. Zo goed als hij in de controlerende functie niet het beleid zelf, maar de verslaglegging daarvan zal moeten beoordelen, zal hij in de adviserende functie niet omtrent het beleid zelf moeten adviseren, maar moeten zorgdragen, dat alle voor dat beleid bepalende factoren in hun juiste betekenis ter kennis van de beleidsman komen. Onder deze omstandigheden zal bij een vakbekwame uitoefening van de adviserende functie geen collisie met de controlerende functie behoeven te worden gevreesd.

Translation

PAPER

by

DR. A. TH. DE LANGE

Nederlands Instituut van Accountants

I. Function

When appraising the function, the duties, the certificate and the responsibility of the public accountant in the Netherlands it should be borne in mind that the position of the accountant in that country has evolved entirely out of the free play of forces arising from the needs of business intercourse and the desire for development of those practising the profession. Notwithstanding repeated representations and endeavours, there has as yet been no statutory regulation of the accountancy profession. The law does not require that the annual accounts of public companies be audited. Legislative directives concerning the duties to be performed by the accountant are almost completely lacking; those that do exist have at least had no essential influence on the practice of the profession. Judicial rulings on which the accountant might base the exercise of his profession are just as little in evidence.

True, the principles of the profession of accountancy in the Netherlands have been codified in the statutes and regulations of the Netherlands Institute of Accountants, particularly in the rules regarding professional duties and in those on professional conduct. Recently a similar wording was given to the regulations of both the Netherlands Institute of Accountants and the Association of University Trained Accountants. This codification was established fairly soon after the foundation of the Institute and has been amplified from time to time and adapted to the development of the profession. The rules and regulations are to be regarded as the results of the exchange of views among practising accountants upon matters which they have considered fundamental to the exercise of their profession. Their true content can therefore only be understood by studying the extensive literature that has been built up in the course of the years in the form of books, articles, reports of professional meetings and research committees, etc. Only with the aid of these publications it is possible to form a clear picture of the state of the accountant's profession in the Netherlands.

In the formulation of the principles on which the auditing function of the accountancy profession is based a particularly important contribution was made by Professor Th. Limperg Jr. His theory regarding the creation of confidence served as the basis for the closer development of the conceptions concerning the function, the duties and the responsibility of the auditor, as well as of the full bearing of his certificate. Thus, the function of the auditor is now generally regarded in the Netherlands as the fulfilment of the need for judgment by an independent expert in the field of auditing, accounting organization and business economy. This need may arise both in the business relationships within society and in the top management of an enterprise. In the first case it stems from the wish of shareholders, creditors and other parties interested in the financial position and results of a business undertaking, or of a part thereof, to be advised as to the correctness of figures provided and as to their interpretation for certain purposes. If the auditor fulfils his function on behalf of the business management, his aim is to inform the management of the manner in which the departmental heads of the firm have used the powers conferred upon them and of the results shown by the policy of higher and lower members of the managerial staff. In both cases the auditor's function is based upon his independent judgment as an expert in the fields mentioned. From this description it follows that the judgment required from the auditor comprises more than the verification of sets of figures from a book-keeping point of view; it also extends to the state of affairs which the figures conjure up to the reader. The question always facing the accountant in the fulfilment of his function as an auditor is whether the accounts together with the contents of the auditor's certificate (the report of the auditor) give the reader a fair and complete picture of all factors which are necessary to help him form his judgment. In this respect it is not so much a matter of the formal correctness of the figures as of their significance from the aspect of business economy. Thus it is not only a question of the amount of the total profit shown by an undertaking but also of the analysis of the results in order to determine the sources of profit, if and in so far as such an analysis is necessary in order to form a judgment of the real profit-earning capacity of the undertaking. Thus, the incidental profits or losses should be separated from the normal sources of profit.

It is understandable that the auditing function of the accountant has come to be associated with an advisory function, which is more especially fulfilled on behalf of the management. Whereas the accounting administration is such a pre-eminently efficient instrument for recording the course of affairs in a business, and whereas the professional accountant, when auditing the accounting records, is observing the course of affairs so intensely, accurately and critically, it is natural that the management of the business feels the need to test its own ideas concerning past and future policy against the ideas of the accountant, thereby profiting by his expert knowledge. With the growing skill of the professional accountant in the domain of management and business economics, an independent advisory function has developed over the course of the years, distinct from the auditing function.

II. Independence

The need for an independent judgment makes it necessary to consider in what circumstances the independence of the accountant can be assured. Independence has not only a juridical as well as an economic aspect, but it is also a question of character, a question of the accountant's understanding of the nature of his auditing function. The auditor must be aware of the importance of his certificates, and of the decisions based on them. This applies to all auditors, irrespective of the juridical constitution of their activities in business intercourse, for company managements or for government departments.

The auditor's understanding of the nature of his function is also of importance since his economic independence may easily be affected. When expressing his opinion, the auditor, either in the employment of others or as a public accountant, must beware of considerations aimed at retaining his employment or business relationship, which would nullify the independence.

The juridical aspect of the auditor's independence is related to the question of authority, that is to say whether the auditor occupies a subordinate or an independent position. In this respect the position of public auditors differs from that of auditors in whole-time employment. The latter, including internal auditors and auditors in government service, are subordinate to their employers. For this reason they cannot issue to third parties any certificates relating to accounts rendered by their employers, even though in their relations with their employers they show an independent judgment. In business intercourse they have not the authority attributed to an independent auditor. This means that certificates intended for public use can be given only by public auditors, while certificates required by a company management or a government department can be provided either by auditors in their employ or by public accountants.

III. Certificates and Responsibility

Those for whom the professional accountant performs his duties as an auditor are notified of the results of his work by means of the certificate which he issues at the conclusion of his examination. By a certificate in this sense is meant any communication, whether in the form of a short statement or of a more or less comprehensive report, in which a judgment is expressed; such a judgment may even be expressed in a verbal report. When expressing a judgment or issuing a certificate, the auditor is responsible for the correctness of his certificate. In the Netherlands the auditor's responsibility is spoken of in relation to the obligations resting on the professional accountant in the performance of his duties. The auditor has these professional obligations irrespective of whether he is subject to a financial sanction if he fails to comply with them. If there is such a sanction the auditor is said to be liable for the correctness of his certificate. From a professional point of view the auditor's responsibility is naturally much more important than his liability; the financial consequences of a failure to comply with professional obligations are less damaging to an auditor than the withholding of confidence in him in the future.

The contents of the certificate must be backed by a skilled examination which justifies those contents; in other words, the work performed must be such as to support the certificate. What is more important, however, is that it is only when the investigation has been planned and carried out with a rational object in view that the certificate arouses no greater confidence than is justified. The auditor's responsibility for the correctness of his certificate therefore extends beyond the formal contents of the report to include the object of the audit. By introducing irrelevant restrictions in the object in view the auditor deprives his certificate of its significance and awakens in the inexpert reader a greater confidence than is justified by the work performed.

It should be avoided to give a summary of the work performed; the layman and sometimes even the expert will be unable to judge whether the summary is intended to limit the significance of the outcome of the examination. For this reason auditors are urged to formulate the conclusions they arrive at in the simplest possible terms; after auditing the annual accounts of an undertaking it should be sufficient for the auditor to state simply that he has found them correct or merely to apply his signature.

This brings me to the problem of the extent of the auditor's responsibility for his certificate. This problem arises in particular with regard to the unqualified certificate attached to a company's annual accounts, but it is equally deserving of an answer if the certificate relates to a special investigation or to an examination for management purposes. In short, how far does the significance of the auditor's judgment extend and what confidence may the reader place in the auditor's certificate? As stated at the outset, in answering this question the Netherlands auditor receives no support from statutory provisions or judicial rulings. He must answer the question as to whether the work he has performed justifies the issue of a certificate taking into account the standards that have come to be accepted in business intercourse regarding the confidence an interested reader may place in a certificate. The standard accepted in the business world is the touchstone for the extent of the responsibility which the auditor accepts in issuing his certificate. Naturally, this standard has not always been as high as it is now; with the development of the profession it reached a certain level, a level which on the one hand satisfies the reader's need for reliability, and on the other hand is no higher than the professional technique permits.

The implications of this accepted standard are familiar to the auditors, and to those who concern themselves with auditor's certificates as interested parties, partly as a result of years of experience and partly by virtue of the definitions to be found in the professional literature and to some extent in the rules and regulations of the professional bodies. Naturally, when the professional accountants undertake new duties the applicable standard will at first be unknown or only very vaguely known; thus it may be said that whereas the standards of confidence in the various auditing functions of the accountant are now established, the standards as regards his advisory functions are as yet by no means established and are subject to some differences of opinion. In these latter circumstances it is necessary for the professional accountant to specify carefully what his certificate is intended to cover in order that no misunderstandings shall be created amongst those who read it. With the continued development of certain functions it will appear to what extent other standards are preferred by the parties concerned and in how far the accountant will be able to meet these standards. During such periods of evolution the accountant will be wise to take especial care that no exaggerated significance can be attached to his certificate.

The standard of confidence also has different connotations to the interested parties to whom the auditor's certificate is directed or to whom it is given.

There are public certificates for shareholders and creditors and private certificates for directors and managements. The demands as regards the verification of details will be less exacting for an auditor's public certificate than for his private certificate prepared for the purposes of the company's officials. The published annual accounts give a global picture of the results and of the financial position of the undertaking; that picture need not show the reality any more accurately than is necessary to give a general impression of the reality and to avoid a mistaken impression. The auditor's certificate on these annual accounts is concerned only with that global picture. The sets of figures presented to the directors are considerably more detailed, and the data in the management's hands are naturally the most complete. The directors as well as the management need such detailed statements in order to be able to fulfil their duties properly, and they wish to be assured of the correctness of the returns put before them. In these circumstances the auditor's certificate includes the annual accounts with all the schedules and explanations pertaining to them. The foregoing implies, that in issuing a public certificate the auditor accepts a less comprehensive responsibility for the correctness of the published figures than when he issues a certificate to the directors of an undertaking; this certificate in its turn creates a less comprehensive responsibility than a certificate to the management.

When rendering assistance in fiscal matters the auditor accepts responsibility towards the tax authorities for the correctness of all figures presented in discussions with them or in law suits and for all written or verbal explanations to those figures, unless he explicitly states the contrary.

On the basis of his guarantee of the correctness of the factual data, the auditor can safeguard the interests of his client by defending the interpretation of the law most favourable to the tax-payer.

Irrespective, however, of whether the auditor assists the undertaking in fiscal matters, he will have to satisfy himself that the taxes owed by the enterprise are included in the balance sheet. The development of fiscal legislation in the Netherlands in the postwar years has given cause for a closer consideration of an undertaking's tax-obligations. The auditor is often faced with a situation in which the application of the fiscal regulations entails the acceptance of charges which will not appear as such in the company's accounts until a later year. This is especially the case when the tax authorities permit depreciation allowances on fixed assets that will not be taken up by the company until some years later. In such circumstances the company is not only liable to taxation on its taxable profit for the year, it also has a latent liability to taxation by reason of the charges to be borne in the future. The auditor can approve the accounts only if this latent liability to taxation has been provided for in the balance sheet.

The financial position and results of an undertaking are controlled not only by the fiscal but also by the economic regulations of the government. The economic regulations may relate to prices, to production and to the declaration or the remittance of money to certain public funds. The question in how far the certificate of the auditor on the annual accounts constitutes an assurance that these regulations have been properly observed has led to the appointment of an investigatory committee on behalf of the Netherlands Institute of Accountants;

the report made by this committee has, however, not yet been published.

From the foregoing considerations it follows that the auditor in issuing his certificate does not accept an unlimited responsibility. The limitations of his responsibility, however, are comprised in the standard of confidence prevailing in business intercourse. For this reason it is, generally, unnecessary for the auditor to specify the limits of his responsibility in his certificate. Circumstances may arise, however, which oblige the auditor to limit his responsibility in relation to the existing standard. It stands to reason that restrictions of the responsibility are formulated by indicating them in comparison to the standard.

IV. Duties

It has been explained that the auditor can only accept responsibility for the validity of his certificate provided that the work to justify the certificate has been carried out. The work to be performed in each given case and the professional techniques to be applied are dealt with in the theory of auditing. It would exceed the scope of this paper to enter into a discussion of professional techniques. It will be sufficient for our purposes to touch upon a few aspects only.

In the Netherlands an auditor generally practises with a staff of qualified accountants and with assistants, the latter having no accountant's diploma. This means that only a part of the work undertaken is actually performed by the principal himself who must sign the certificate, and that therefore the certificate is based largely upon the communications of subordinates on the results of their work. This does not, however, limit the auditor's responsibility. It is up to the auditor to apportion the duties in such a way that no deficiencies arise in the auditing work: he must ensure that the audits are as well organized as they are properly carried out.

The organization of the undertaking whose accounts are to be audited has a very important bearing on the nature and volume of the work performed by the auditors. The division of responsibilities in the undertaking in question may be such that no audit can possibly be carried out. This may be the case when the accounting organization is underdeveloped. In such circumstances the auditor will not be able to start an audit until his comments have been taken care of. Experience shows that the professional accountant is entrusted in large measure with the duty of bringing the organization and the accounting system of a firm up to standard. He is thereby in a position to adapt the managerial and accounting organization to the requirements of the auditing technique and to ensure that the audit can be carried out as efficiently as possible.

V. Professional Skill

The professional skill which the accountant is required to possess extends over the fields of auditing, accounting organization and business management. The skill demanded is naturally determined to a high degree by the problems facing the accountant in the fulfilment of his professional duties. The rapid development of society continuously changes the character of these problems, and the accountant has accordingly been obliged to match his skill to the modifications

CHAIRMEN OF THE BUSINESS SESSIONS

WP. F. C. J. Busch,
Germany

Arthur B. Foye, C.P.A.,
United States of America

H. Hjernø Jeppesen,
Denmark

G. F. Klingner, F.C.A.
Ireland

A. Veyrenc, France

Professor B. J. S. Wimble,
South Africa

Registration

in the requirements. This means that the accountant's skill is by no means exclusively dependent upon the training he has received; it also depends upon his readiness to follow developments affecting his profession. While these developments may have an important bearing on auditing technique, in the fields of accounting organization and business management, particularly as regards the internal organization of business undertaking, the developments have been such that it may well be asked whether the practising accountant can possibly be expected to follow them. It will decidedly not be possible for him to follow the development in certain branches of accounting organization (for instance the application of electronic equipment and automation) and of business management (market research and factory organization). This explains the emergence of other experts, although these developments also call attention to the necessity and the possibilities of specialisation within the professional accountant's office. While accountants are alert to these professional questions in the Netherlands, it cannot be said that the study so far undertaken has shown clearly the course to be followed, so that at present no more can be said about this subject.

It is evident that the dynamic nature of the accountancy profession should set its seal upon the methods of professional training. The educational system may certainly not neglect the teaching of a ready knowledge of facts and technical procedures, but it should also particularly be directed to give students an understanding of the nature of the subjects, and teach them the ability to recognize the problems and the methods of solving them.

In the Netherlands an accountant's diploma can be obtained either by passing the accountancy examinations at an institution for higher education or by passing the examinations of the Netherlands Institute of Accountants. In the first case the student receives his instruction at a University to which a faculty of economic sciences is attached, or at a College of Economics. In such an institution for higher education the training in accountancy is as a post–graduate study following the doctoral examination in the economic sciences, the latter examination concluding a complete education in economics. The Netherlands Institute of Accountants organizes a series of examinations for students who have had no higher education after leaving secondary school; the subjects in which they must satisfy the examiners include branches of economics, accounting organization and auditing. The Institute is also responsible for the courses preparatory to the various examinations.

By virtue of the different character of the two systems of education, the university course is organized as a day-time study, whereas the Netherlands Institute of Accountants gives its instruction in evening classes. In the latter case the students have the opportunity to acquire practical proficiency during the day. The academic students for their part usually take up a post in an accountant's office or in industry in the years after graduation in the economic sciences. In this way both classes of students have the opportunity to acquire practical experience in addition to their training in theory.

VI. Rules of Conduct

Within the scope of this paper it is impossible to deal fully with the rules of conduct observed by practising accountants in the Netherlands. A rough outline of the applicable rules is all that can be given here.

With regard to the forms in which the profession of accountancy is practised it may be remarked that, according to the Institute's regulations, the public accountant may only practise his profession for his own account as an independently established member of the profession, or in partnership with one or more members of the Institute or of an equivalent association. This provision emphasises the personal character of the accountancy profession; in particular it has made it impossible for the profession to be practised by, or in the service of, limited companies. The said provision would also, however, prevent public accountants from entering into association with someone who is not an accountant, with the object of working together in another field, for example that of accounting organization. Therefore, members in practice are permitted to form a partnership with non-members of the Institute, provided no auditors' certificates are issued or assignments accepted which would lead to the issue of such certificates.

Co-operation with fellow accountants in a partnership gives rise to the interesting question as to what extent the individual partners are responsible for the certificates issued by the firm or by one of its members. It will suffice here to say that under the regulations of the Netherlands Institute of Accountants and the Association of University Trained Accountants a public accountant practising in partnership with others is in duty bound tc take such steps as to ensure that he may be reasonably convinced that his partner's work and certificates satisfy the regulations. This obligation, however, does not go beyond the general principles of the examinations, by which are understood the general principles governing professional practice, as laid down in the regulations, and the principles according to which the audit programmes are drawn up.

As regards the fees which professional accountants may charge in payment for their services there exist no directives, agreements or generally accepted customs. The usual method of fixing fees finds expression in the professional rule that an accountant in practice may accept no other remuneration than that to which he is entitled by virtue of the extent, nature and significance of his assignment, and that he may claim no remuneration that depends upon the outcome of his work.

Finally, it should be mentioned that professional accountants in practice are not allowed to advertise, or to offer payment in return for the procurement of work.

VII. Regulations and Supervision

The question may be asked whether the rules of conduct to be observed should be defined in the regulations of professional bodies, or whether such regulations were better dispensed with and the standards left entirely to be determined by the auditors themselves by virtue of their training and experience. In the

Netherlands this question was answered many years ago in favour of the regulations made by professional bodies, although the regulations of the Association of University Trained Accountants were not laid down until after the Second World War. Nevertheless, the professional bodies have carefully avoided making their rules and regulations into a manual of auditing procedure. What they lay down are just the principles of professional practice; the auditor himself is left to decide how he must act in individual cases. This has the advantage of allowing the continued development of professional points of view within the framework of the existing regulations. The Advisory Committee on Professional Matters appointed by the Council of the Institute plays an important part in this development. Apart from giving advice requested by members of the Institute, this Committee also proffers advice on its own initiative based on its study of the public certificates issued by practising accountants. In addition it inquires into certain professional matters at the request of the Council of the Institute and brings out reports on them, which are as a rule brought to the general notice of the members. Although the contents of these reports are in no respect binding upon the members, the views of the Committee nevertheless exercise a profound influence on the development of professional ideas, partly as a result of the discussions which usually follow the report.

VIII. Advice

The advisory function of professional accountants is concerned with problems of accounting organization and business management. In recent decades the handling of matters of business economy has received a marked impetus, particularly in connection with questions of financing, costing and profit analysis. Here, too, the interesting question arises as to the nature of the accountant's responsibility for the correctness of the information he provides in his advisory function. Naturally only a few points can be touched upon here.

In the first place it is important to note that the accountant is consulted because he is an expert in the field of business economics in its widest sense. This implies that he can only accept responsibility for his advice if he really has the expert knowledge required. As has already been pointed out, owing to the developments in business society and in general economics, the field of business management is now very wide and the accountant can no longer be expected to have a detailed knowledge of all its many aspects. Particularly in matters of sales policy (market organization, price policy) and of internal organization (rational working methods, wage systems) the requisite skill is possessed by specialists only. Consequently, if the accountant wishes to accept full responsibility for the advice he gives he must restrict the subjects on which he is willing to be consulted, unless he has the necessary specialists in his office to deal with the subjects concerned. Naturally, problems then arise with regard to the division of responsibility for the advice given; this matter, about which established views do not yet exist in the Netherlands, cannot be dealt with here.

Another question that should be asked is whether, supposing the accountant has the skill needed to give the advice, the same significance can be attached to his advice as to that of another expert. In this connection it may be remarked that in many cases the auditor and not an other expert will be asked for advice, because of his familiarity with the special circumstances prevailing in the enterprise which asks for his advice. This is especially evident in matters in which statistical data and the organizational and personal relationships within the business, also outside the concrete facts of the problem, play an important part. In such cases the value of the advice will of course largely depend upon the exact knowledge of these data and relationships, and upon the knowledge what significance may be attached to them and whether they may be regarded as reliable. Obviously, the company's auditor is better able to give the right judgment and answer in these circumstances than the expert who is not a professional accountant. It must be recognized, however, that when giving his advice the accountant must be aware of his responsibility as regards the reliability and the interpretation of the data.

Although the auditor will generally be able to satisfy these expectations without much difficulty, a complication arises when he is consulted for advice by an enterprise, which is not being audited by him. In principle he is then in the same position as any other expert. It should not be overlooked, however, that the professional accountant is frequently entrusted with such work because of the general confidence placed in his judgment on matters in which the observation of a firm's operations by means of the accounting organization plays an important part. This will oblige him to inquire into the real content of the data provided and to ascertain their correctness. This means, even when he is not called upon to audit the data, that it is not permissable for the professional accountant to accept them at their face value. Although the standard of confidence in the advisory function of an accountant is not so sharply defined as it is in his auditing functions, it is nevertheless safe to assert that the client has expectations that must naturally not be disappointed. Where the professional accountant is not able to check the usefulness of the figures he will in some cases have to refuse the assignment; in others he will give his advice with reservations.

IX. Combination of Auditing and Advisory Functions

Many are of opinion that where the public accountant acts in an auditing as well as in an advisory capacity, there may be a danger that he will lose his objectivity as an auditor because of the advice he has given. It seems to me that if the advice is rendered in the right way, that is to say if it is based on the proper information and skill and truly has the character of advice, then this danger no longer exists. This calls for a closer examination of the character of the advice.

The problem of a conflict between the advisory and the auditing function is especially of importance in those instances in which the advice requested has a bearing upon the policy to be conducted by management. One may speak of a policy problem when the decision to be taken depends upon judgment concerning the expected developments of the factors determining the decision. If the problem should lack any policy element, in other words if the factors determining the line of conduct were fixed quantities, which according to their nature are not subject to future developments, then the formulating of the advice would only require expert knowledge in the particular field and an unsatisfactory advice could only be attributed to insufficient expert knowledge. However, as soon as policy elements determine the management's line of conduct, personal insight into future developments becomes of conclusive importance. Although it is understandable that many managers like to have the opinion of someone else on these future developments, it appears to me that the auditor would be on the wrong track if he claimed to solve policy problems. In doing so he would indeed be taking over one of the most essential elements of the management function, instead of restricting himself to the advisory and to the auditing function. Consistently with this, the accountant in exercising his advisory function would take care that the management, before taking a decision, is fully informed of all factors which are of importance in taking a decision and that no consideration which may be of importance is left out of account, due to insufficient insight into the nature of the problem. At the same time the accountant can give some guidance in his advice by assuming certain possible developments and by indicating the consequences of management action under these assumptions. On the basis of an advice rendered in such a form the management will itself, however, have to take the decision and determine its policy.

In the exercise of both his auditing and his advisory functions the public accountant must beware of intervening in the management of a business. Just as in his capacity as an auditor he will have to judge the accounts kept by the undertaking and not the managerial policy, so in his capacity as an adviser it will be his duty not to advise on the managerial policy but to ensure that all the factors affecting that policy are brought, with their proper significance, to the knowledge of the management. In these circumstances there need be no fear that the properly exercised advisory function of the public accountant will clash with his function as an auditor.

REFERAT

von

WIRTSCHAFTSPRÜFER DR HEINRICH WOLLERT

Institut der Wirtschaftsprüfer in Deutschland e.V.

I. Die Errichtung des Berufes im Jahre 1931

Der Wirtschaftsprüferberuf in Deutschland ist unter der Schockwirkung der Wirtschaftskrise der Jahre 1930/31, insbesondere unter dem Eindruck einiger großer Skandale, wie des Zusammenbruchs der 'Nordwolle' und des 'Fawag'-Konzerns, ins Leben gerufen worden. Bis dahin fehlte eine solche Einrichtung im deutschen Wirtschaftsleben völlig. Und doch haben die Spuren dessen, was bis dahin an ähnlichen Einrichtungen in Deutschland vorher vorhanden war, auch auf den Wirtschaftsprüferberuf abgefärbt.

Vorhanden waren bis zu diesem Zeitpunkt vereidigte Bücherrevisoren, Treuhand- und Revisionsgesellschaften, die in der Hauptsache von Banken gegründet waren und in ihrem Interesse sowie unter ihrer Kontrolle wirkten, und endlich Prüfungsverbände für Genossenschaften.

Trotz aller dieser Einrichtungen kam es jedoch bis zum Jahre 1931 in Deutschland nicht zu einer einheitlichen Ausgestaltung des Prüfungswesens.

Die als Folge der Wirtschaftskrise eingeführte Neuerung bestand darin, daß durch eine Notverordnung vom 19.9.1931 die Prüfung der Jahresabschlüsse der Aktiengesellschaften und der Kommanditgesellschaften auf Aktien durch 'sachverständige Prüfer' (Bilanzprüfer) angeordnet wurde. Nur wenig später wurde diese Pflichtprüfung auch auf die Wirtschaftsbetriebe der öffentlichen Hand ausgedehnt.

In beiden Fällen wurde die Prüfung durch besondere Verordnungen den 'öffentlich bestellten Wirtschaftsprüfern', und zwar neben Einzelpersonen auch Wirtschaftsprüfungsgesellschaften übertragen. Die besondere – ja geradezu kuriose – Eigentümlichkeit der damaligen Situation kennzeichnet sich dadurch, daß ein Berufsstand, der 'öffentlich bestellten Wirtschaftsprüfer' überhaupt noch nicht existierte.

Aus diesem Grunde schloß das damalige Deutsche Reich mit den ihm zugehörigen Ländern einen Vertrag, die sogenannte 'Ländervereinbarung', in dem die Grundsätze vereinbart wurden, nach denen in den einzelnen Ländern Wirtschaftsprüfer öffentlich bestellt und vereidigt werden sollten.

Diese Ländervereinbarung kann man die 'Magna Charta' unseres Berufsstandes nennen, denn sie bildete die im wesentlichen einheitliche Grundlage für die Errichtung und Entwicklung des Berufsstandes bis zum Ende des Krieges im Jahre 1945; auf ihr beruht das Berufsrecht der Wirtschaftsprüfer, das unserem Beruf das ihm eigentümliche Gepräge eines freien Berufes mit öffentlich-rechtlicher Verantwortung gegeben hat.

Die nach 1945 in den einzelnen neu errichteten Ländern Deutschlands erlassenen Berufsordnungen stellen sich, ebenso wie die zur Zeit den zuständigen Gesetzgebungsorganen des Bundes vorliegende bundeseinheitliche Neuregelung des Berufsrechts, im wesentlichen nur als Modifikationen des auf der Grundlage der Länderverordnung beruhenden Berufsrechts dar.

Bevor ich jedoch auf das Berufsrecht unseres Standes eingehe, ist es erforderlich, dass ich mich zunächst den dem Berufsstand vom Gesetzgeber übertragenen und von der Wirtschaft freiwillig zugewiesenen Aufgaben zuwende, da nur von hier aus unser Berufsrecht verständlich wird.

II. Die Aufgaben des Wirtschaftsprüfers

1. *Die aktienrechtliche Pflichtprüfung*

Erste und zunächst einzige Aufgabe, die ausschließlich dem neuen Berufsstand der Wirtschaftsprüfer im Jahre 1931 vom Staat übertragen wurde, war die bereits erwähnte Pflichtprüfung der Jahresabschlüsse der Aktiengesellschaften und Kommanditgesellschaften auf Aktien durch einen Wirtschaftsprüfer, der jährlich von der Hauptversammlung zu wählen ist.

Die fundamentale Bedeutung dieser Aufgabe läßt sich daran erkennen, daß ein nicht geprüfter Jahresabschluß nichtig ist, mit der Folge, daß sämtliche auf ihm beruhenden Beschlüsse ebenfalls nichtig sind.

Die sich aus der gesetzlichen Abschlußprüfung ergebende Aufgabe gliedert sich in

a. Prüfung
b. Schriftliche Berichterstattung
c. Erteilung, Einschränkung oder Verweigerung des Bestätigungsvermerks.

Die Prüfung hat sich nach § 135 AktG unter Einbeziehung der Buchführung und des Geschäftsberichts auf den Jahresabschluß zu erstrecken, wobei nicht nur die formelle Übereinstimmung mit den Bucheintragungen festzustellen, sondern auch materiell zu prüfen ist, ob insbesondere

a. die einzelnen Abschlußpositionen ordnungsmäßig (Inventur) nachgewiesen (§ 129 AktG in Verbindung mit § 39 HGB),

b. unter Beachtung der gesetzlichen Vorschriften angemessen bewertet (§ 133 AktG),

sowie

c. klar und übersichtlich entsprechend den Gliederungsvorschriften (§§ 131, 132 AktG)

ausgewiesen worden sind, und die dem Abschluß zu Grunde liegende Buchführung sowie die sonstigen Unterlagen ordnungsmäßig und beweiskräftig sind.

Die Prüfung, ob andere gesetzliche Bestimmungen, wie z.B. des Steuer-, Preis- und Devisenrechts beachtet worden sind, fällt nur soweit unter die Aufgaben des Abschlußprüfers, als hiervon die einzelnen Posten des Jahresabschlusses berührt werden.

Die Prüfung von Unterschlagungen gehört weder nach dem Gesetz noch nach Auffassung des Berufes zu den Aufgaben des Abschlußprüfers; es bedarf hierzu eines besonderen Auftrages.

Richtschnur für die Abschlußprüfer sind neben den allgemeingültigen Grundsätzen ordnungsmäßiger Prüfung im wesentlichen die gesetzlichen Vorschriften.

Das Charakteristikum der gesetzlichen Abschlussprüfung als Ordnungs- und Gesetzmäßigkeitsprüfung kommt auch in der Pflichtprüfung des Geschäftsberichts des Vorstandes zum Ausdruck.

Die Pflicht zur Erstattung eines Prüfungsberichts folgt aus § 139 AktG, wonach dem Vorstand und dem Aufsichtsrat, letzterem als Vertreter der Aktionäre der geprüften Gesellschaft, also den beiden Organen, die für die Feststellung des Abschlusses in der Regel gesetzlich zuständig sind, schriftlich zu berichten ist, ob nach dem Ergebnis der Prüfung die für die Aufstellung des Jahresabschlusses erlassenen gesetzlichen Vorschriften eingehalten sind.

Im Gegensatz zu einer Entscheidung des Bundesgerichtshofes vom 15.12.1954 (BGHZ 16/17), nach der entsprechend den gesetzlichen Vorschriften die wirtschaftlichen Verhältnisse der Gesellschaft im Prüfungsbericht nicht zu erörtern seien, ist es jedoch von jeher berufsüblich gewesen, im Prüfungsbericht – meist in einem besonderen Teil – auch zur wirtschaftlichen Lage, insbesondere zur Vermögenslage, dem Finanzaufbau, der Liquidität und Rentabilität des Unternehmens, und zwar im Vergleich zu den Ergebnissen des Vorjahres, zusammenfassend Stellung zu nehmen.

Ausser dem nach § 139 AktG vorzulegenden Prüfungsbericht hat der Abschlußprüfer schließlich nach § 140 AktG den sogenannten 'Bestätigungsvermerk' zu erteilen, einzuschränken oder zu verweigern. Sofern die gesetzlichen Voraussetzungen für die Erteilung des uneingeschränkten Bestätigungsvermerks erfüllt sind, lautet dieser wie folgt:

'Nach dem abschließenden Ergebnis meiner (unserer) pflichtmäßigen Prüfung auf Grund der Bücher und der Schriften der Gesellschaft sowie der vom Vorstand erteilten Aufklärungen und Nachweise entsprechen die Buchführung, der Jahresabschluß und der Geschäftsbericht, soweit er den Jahresabschluß erläutert, den gesetzlichen Vorschriften'

Der Abschluß ist mit dem vom Abschlußprüfer erteilten Bestätigungsvermerk zu veröffentlichen. Er unterrichtet damit die Öffentlichkeit über das Ergebnis der Abschlußprüfung und begründet dadurch deren Vertrauen in die Ordnungs- und Gesetzmäßigkeit des Abschlusses.

In der Erteilung des Bestätigungsvermerks findet demnach die öffentlichrechtliche Funktion des Abschlußprüfers ihren sinnfälligen Ausdruck.

Der Abschlußprüfer muß den Bestätigungsvermerk versagen oder einschränken, wenn er bei seiner Prüfung Mängel feststellt, die die Erteilung des Bestätigungsvermerks entweder überhaupt nicht, oder nur in einschränkender Form rechtfertigen. Die Gründe für eine Versagung oder Einschränkung des Bestätigungsvermerks sind im wesentlichen im Gesetz selbst nicht festgelegt. Die Entscheidung hierüber ist vielmehr grundsätzlich in das pflichtmäßige Ermessen des Abschlußprüfers gestellt, für dessen Entscheidung aber die gesetzlichen Vorschriften und die vom Berufsstand entwickelten Grundsätze ordnungsmäßiger Abschlußprüfung als Richtschnur dienen müssen.

Die vorstehend dargelegten Grundsätze für die Prüfung, Berichterstattung und Erteilung des Bestätigungsvermerks sind – mit geringfügigen Modifikationen – auch für die Durchführung der übrigen, auf gesetzlicher Grundlage beruhenden, Prüfungsaufgaben maßgebend. Darüber hinaus sind diese Prinzipien der Ordnungs- und Gesetzmäßigkeit leitende Richtschnur für die gesamte Berufstätigkeit der Wirtschaftsprüfer geworden.

Aus den vorstehenden Ausführungen könnte der Schluß gezogen werden, daß der Ermessensspielraum des Wirtschaftsprüfers bei gesetzlichen Abschlußprüfungen weitgehend durch die zwingenden gesetzlichen Bestimmungen eingeengt sei.

Diese Schlußfolgerung wäre jedoch nicht gerechtfertigt. Denn innerhalb der gesetzlichen Rahmenvorschriften hat der Abschlußprüfer fundamentale Entscheidungen hinsichtlich des Umfanges und der Methode der Prüfung, der Anlage und Ausgestaltung des Prüfungsberichtes und schließlich der Beurteilung des Prüfungsergebnisses nach eigenem pflichtmäßigen Ermessen zu treffen. Die Bedeutung dieser Entscheidungen ergibt sich daraus, daß von der Erteilung des Bestätigungsvermerks Gedeih und Verderb des Unternehmens selbst sowie Dritter, und schließlich auch Ruf und Existenz des Wirtschaftsprüfers abhängen können.

2. *Die weiteren auf gesetzlicher Grundlage beruhenden Aufgaben*

Die Fülle dieser weiteren gesetzlichen Pflichtprüfungen läßt sich im wesentlichen in zwei große Kategorien, nämlich

a. die der wiederkehrenden Gesamtprüfungen und

b. die der begrenzten Sonderprüfungen

einteilen.

Zu den wichtigsten wiederkehrenden Gesamtprüfungen, die, wie die aktienrechtliche Pflichtprüfung, fast ausschließlich im jährlichen Turnus, und zwar sowohl für die Unternehmen privater Rechtsform, als auch für den Bereich der öffentlichen Wirtschaft vorgeschrieben sind, gehören die der Rechnungsabschlüsse der privaten Versicherungsunternehmen und Bausparkassen, sämtlicher privater Kreditinstitute und der Wirtschaftsbetriebe der öffentlichen Hand.

Die Kategorie der Sonderprüfungen hat vor allem durch die Währungsumstellung im Jahre 1948 eine erhebliche Ausweitung und eminente Bedeutung erfahren. Hierzu gehört insbesondere die Prüfung der DM-Eröffnungsbilanzen und der Vorschläge für die Neufestsetzung der Kapitalverhältnisse der Aktiengesellschaften und Gesellschaften mit beschränkter Haftung sowie der Umstellungsrechnungen sämtlicher Geldinstitute, Versicherungsunternehmen und Bausparkassen.

Auf die Fülle der Gesetze und Verordnungen, die Inhalt und Umfang dieser Pflichtprüfungen im einzelnen regeln, kann hier nicht näher eingegangen werden.

3. *Der sonstige Tätigkeitsbereich*

Von den wichtigsten Funktionen, die der Berufsstand neben seiner Eigenschaft als gesetzlicher Prüfer ausübt, seien hier nur genannt:

a. die Prüfung von Jahresabschlüssen derjenigen Unternehmungen, die einer

Pflichtprüfung nicht unterliegen, die Erstattung von Gutachten aller Art für Privatunternehmungen, die öffentliche Hand und die Gerichte,

b. wirtschaftliche und steuerliche Beratung,

c. die Tätigkeit als Schiedsrichter, insbesondere bei Auseinandersetzungen zwischen Gesellschaftern, als Liquidator, Konkurs- und Vergleichsverwalter sowie als Testamentsvollstrecker und Treuhänder.

Zusammenfassend darf gesagt werden:

In den 25 Jahren seit Errichtung des Berufes sind Berufsstand und Aufgaben organisch zusammen gewachsen. Der Berufsstand nimmt heute innerhalb der sonstigen wirtschaftsberatenden und prüfenden Berufe, wie z.B. der vereidigten Buchprüfer, der Steuerberater und Helfer in Steuersachen, eine anerkannte Spitzenstellung ein und ist in seiner Bedeutung für die deutsche Wirtschaft nicht mehr wegzudenken.

III. Das Berufsrecht

1. *Die Notwendigkeit eines Berufsrechts*

Angesichts der Bedeutung und des Umfanges der soeben erwähnten Aufgaben ist es verständlich, daß der Staat – wie auch bezüglich anderer freier Berufe mit besonderer Verantwortung gegenüber der Allgemeinheit oder öffentlich-rechtlichen Funktionen – schon bei der Errichtung des Berufes im Jahre 1931 in der bereits genannten 'Ländervereinbarung' auf die Gestaltung und Entwicklung des Berufsrechts der Wirtschaftsprüfer einen maßgebenden Einfluß genommen hat.

Die nachfolgende kurze Darstellung der wichtigsten Grundsätze unseres Berufsrechts beruht auf der Berufsordnung für die Angehörigen des wirtschaftlichen Prüfungs- und Treuhandwesens vom 20.12.1946, die sich regional auf den Bereich der Länder der ehemaligen britischen Besatzungszone (Nordrhein-Westfalen, Schleswig-Holstein, Niedersachsen und Hamburg) erstreckt, und die die größte Ähnlichkeit mit der ehemaligen Ländervereinbarung aufweist.

2. *Die wesentlichsten Elemente des Berufsrechts*

Der Auslese nur geeigneter (physischer) Personen für den Beruf des Wirtschaftsprüfers dienen die Bestimmungen über:

a. das Zulassungs- oder Vorprüfungsverfahren,

b. das Prüfungsverfahren,

c. das Bestellungsverfahren

sowie für Wirtschaftsprüfungsgesellschaften das Anerkennungsverfahren.

Im *Zulassungs- oder Vorprüfungsverfahren* für natürliche Personen muß der Bewerber nachweisen, daß er seiner Persönlichkeit nach für den verantwortungsvollen Beruf eines Wirtschaftsprüfers geeignet ist, in geordneten wirtschaftlichen Verhältnissen lebt und mindestens 30 Jahre alt ist, sowie, daß er eine praktische Tätigkeit von insgesamt 6 Jahren (davon 4 Jahre im Prüfungswesen) ausgeübt und ein abgeschlossenes wirtschaftswissenschaftliches, juristisches oder technisches Studium absolviert hat.

Von letzterem Erfordernis kann nur in Sonderfällen abgesehen werden.

Gegen die Ablehnung des Antrags auf Zulassung ist die Beschwerde an die

Hauptstelle für das wirtschaftliche Prüfungs- und Treuhandwesen gegeben, die endgültig entscheidet.

Im *Prüfungsverfahren* muß der Kandidat seine fachliche Qualifikation durch

a. die Anfertigung einer wissenschaftlichen Hausarbeit,

b. zwei schriftliche Klausuren

und die Ablegung einer mündlichen Prüfung unter Beweis stellen.

Die Prüfung erstreckt sich im wesentlichen auf folgende Gebiete:

a. Buchhaltung und Jahresabschluß sowie die Betriebswirtschaft in allen ihren Spezialzweigen,

b. das Bürgerliche- und Handelsrecht unter besonderer Berücksichtigung des Wirtschaftsrechts,

c. das Steuerrecht,

d. das Berufsrecht.

Nach Ablegung der Prüfung wird der Kandidat im *Bestellungsverfahren* auf seinen Antrag hin von der jeweils zuständigen staatlichen Behörde (für Nordrhein-Westfalen der Bundesminister für Wirtschaft) zum öffentlichen Wirtschaftsprüfer bestellt und anschließend vereidigt.

Der Eid des Wirtschaftsprüfers lautet:

'Ich schwöre, daß ich die Aufgaben und Pflichten eines öffentlich bestellten Wirtschaftsprüfers gewissenshaft und unparteiisch erfüllen, Verschwiegenheit bewahren und die von mir verlangten Gutachten gewissenhaft und unparteiisch erstatten werde'.

Nach der Vereidigung erhält der Wirtschaftsprüfer eine Bestellungsurkunde und wird in die Liste der öffentlich bestellten Wirtschaftsprüfer eingetragen.

Eine Eigentümlichkeit des deutschen Berufsrechts, die nur aus der historischen Entwicklung verstanden werden kann, besteht darin, daß neben Einzelprüfern auch Gesellschaften in der Rechtsform von Kapital- und Handelsgesellschaften mit denselben Rechten und Pflichten wie Einzelpersonen als Wirtschaftsprüfungsgesellschaften anerkannt werden können.

Die Anerkennung von Kapital- und Handelsgesellschaften als Wirtschaftsprüfungsgesellschaften ist im wesentlichen davon abhängig, daß die Vertretung der Gesellschaft nach außen nur durch Personen mit der Qualifikation eines Wirtschaftsprüfers ausgeübt werden darf.

Darüber hinaus soll auch im Prinzip durch besondere Bestimmungen über die Kapitalbeteiligung an den Wirtschaftsprüfungsgesellschaften ein Abhängigkeitsverhältnis gegenüber Dritten, nicht dem Berufsstand angehörigen natürlichen und juristischen Personen vermieden, und dadurch irgendeine Einflußnahme auf die für die Tätigkeit der Gesellschaft verantwortlichen Personen ausgeschlossen werden. Ohne hier auf die hinsichtlich der Wirtschaftsprüfungsgesellschaften bestehenden Kontroversen eingehen zu wollen, läßt sich sagen, daß die Wirtschaftsprüfungsgesellschaften eine für die Berufsausübung unerläßliche Assoziationsform, vergleichbar den partnership des anglo-amerikanischen Rechtskreises, darstellen.

Als die wichtigsten Prinzipien, die vornehmlich das für die Ausübung des Berufes unerläßliche, insbesondere auch moralische, Fundament legen und garantieren sollen, sind hier zu nennen:

a. die Grundsätze über die Berufsausübung,

b. die Bestimmungen über die Sicherung dieser Berufsgrundsätze.

Sie stellen das eigentliche Standesrecht des Berufes dar, das nur zum Teil kodifiziert ist, zum nicht unwesentlichen Teil dagegen als ungeschriebenes Gewohnheitsrecht Geltung gewonnen hat.

Als wesentlichste Berufsgrundsätze sind hier zu nennen:

a. die Hauptberuflichkeit,
b. die Eigenverantwortlichkeit,
c. die Unabhängigkeit,
d. die Verschwiegenheit,
e. die Unparteilichkeit,
f. das Verbot der Werbung und die Bestimmungen über den Mandatsschutz.

Das Postulat der *Hauptberuflichkeit* läßt sich dahin kennzeichnen, daß die spezifischen Prüfungs- und Beratungsaufgaben die Arbeitskraft des WP ganz oder überwiegend in Anspruch nehmen müssen, und der Wirtschaftsprüfer weiterhin in seiner Eigenschaft als gesetzlicher Abschlußprüfer keinerlei hiermit nicht vereinbare Nebentätigkeiten, insbesondere kaufmännischer oder gewerblicher Art, als Angestellter – sofern er nicht im Dienste einer Wirtschaftsprüfungsgesellschaft steht – oder als Beamter ausüben darf.

Das Wesen der *Eigenverantwortlichkeit* besteht darin, daß der WP in seiner Berufsausübung keinerlei Weisungen von dritter Seite unterliegen darf.

Im Angestelltenverhältnis darf ein WP entweder nur als zeichnungsberechtigter Vertreter eines Einzelwirtschaftsprüfers oder einer Wirtschaftsprüfungsgesellschaft, im letzteren Falle regelmäßig in der Stellung eines Prokuristen, tätig sein.

Dabei darf jedoch auf die Entscheidungsfreiheit eines angestellten WP keinerlei Einfluß von Seiten seines Dienstherrn ausgeübt werden.

Das Postulat der Eigenverantwortlichkeit verlangt ferner, daß der WP auch *tatsächlich* in der Lage sein muß, die sich aus seiner Tätigkeit ergebende Verantwortlichkeit zu tragen. Er darf sich daher zur Erfüllung seiner Aufgaben nicht einer unbegrenzten Anzahl von Gehilfen bedienen. In der Regel dürfen daher einem WP nur 5 Assistenten zur Seite stehen.

Der Berufsgrundsatz der *Unabhängigkeit* ist Gegenstand ganz besonders eingehender, überwiegend auf gesetzlicher Grundlage beruhender, Regelung gewesen.

Ohne auf diese höchst komplizierten Bestimmungen hier eingehen zu können, läßt sich die Quintessenz dieses Berufsgrundsatzes dahin zusammenfassen, daß ein Wirtschaftsprüfer oder eine Wirtschaftsprüfungsgesellschaft zum gesetzlichen Abschlußprüfer dann nicht gewählt werden darf, wenn aus verwandtschaftlichen Beziehungen oder auf Grund wirtschaftlicher Abhängigkeit eine Einflußnahme möglich sein könnte, ohne dass *tatsächlich* irgendein Einfluß ausgeübt zu werden brauchte.

Von besonderer Bedeutung gerade für Wirtschaftsprüfungsgesellschaften, ist die Vorschrift des § 137 II AktG, nach der schon eine unmittelbare oder mittelbare Kapitalabhängigkeit der Prüfungsgesellschaft von dem zu prüfenden Unternehmen oder umgekehrt, die Tauglichkeit dieser Wirtschaftsprüfungsgesellschaft als gesetzlicher Abschlußprüfer ausschließt, und die Nichtigkeit der Prüfung zur Folge hat.

Man darf sagen, dass auf normativem Wege das Postulat der Unabhängigkeit hinreichend scharf bestimmt ist.

Eine ganz andere, sich einer gesetzlichen Regelung entziehende Frage ist die der *tatsächlichen* Unabhängigkeit, die insbesondere in der Form der Mandatsabhängigkeit dann gefährdet sein kann, wenn ein Wirtschaftsprüfer einem machtvollen Großunternehmen gegenübersteht, und dieses Mandat für seine Existenzgrundlage von entscheidender Bedeutung ist. Zweifellos sind hier die von mehreren Wirtschaftsprüfern gebildeten Arbeitsgemeinschaften, ebenso wie Wirtschaftsprüfungsgesellschaften, vor einer solchen Abhängigkeit besser geschützt, da sie in der Regel über eine bessere Streuung ihrer Mandate verfügen.

Letzten Endes läßt sich aber das Postulat der Unabhängigkeit nur durch charakterliche Eigenschaften der Person, nicht aber durch Normen verwirklichen.

Das Prinzip der *Verschwiegenheit* ergibt sich schon aus den allgemeinen Berufsgrundsätzen. Darüber hinaus ist der Wirtschaftsprüfer durch seinen Berufseid ausdrücklich zur Verschwiegenheit verpflichtet. Außerdem ist durch die Vorschrift des § 300 des Deutschen Strafgesetzbuches eine Verletzung dieser Verschwiegenheitspflicht unter Strafe gestellt.

Als Korrelat dieser Verschwiegenheitspflicht steht dem Wirtschaftsprüfer ein Zeugnisverweigerungsrecht über berufliche Angelegenheiten gegenüber den Gerichten zu, gleichwie dem Anwalt und dem Arzt.

Als wesentliches Element der Berufsgrundsätze ist schließlich die ebenfalls im Berufseid gelobte *Unparteilichkeit* des Wirtschaftsprüfers zu nennen, die zusammen mit der Unbefangenheit letzten Endes nur durch eigene, sorgfältige Gewissensprüfung gewährleistet werden kann. Sie kennzeichnet sich im Prinzip darin, daß der Wirtschaftsprüfer bei allen seinen Aufgaben und Urteilen sich so verhalten muß, daß sein Verhalten der Kritik eines unparteiischen Dritten in jeder Richtung standhalten kann. Interessenkonflikte können bei Zusammentreffen von Beratungsaufgaben mit Prüferfunktionen auftreten. Hier sollte die Beratung niemals bis zur verantwortlichen Durchführung dessen gehen, was später der Prüfung und Begutachtung unterliegt. Eines der beiden Mandate müßte dann niedergelegt werden. Dasselbe gilt dort, wo der Wirtschaftsprüfer nach genauer Gewissensprüfung nicht in der Lage ist, seine persönlichen Interessen eindeutig hinter die des Mandanten zu setzen. Alle diese Erwägungen reichen bereits weit in den ethischen, daher einwandfrei nicht kodifizierbaren Bereich der Grundsätze herein, die Ruf und Wert der Persönlichkeit ausmachen.

Das *Verbot der Werbung* beruht auf der Erwägung, dass eine Werbung mit den grundlegenden Prinzipien eines freien Berufes mit öffentlich-rechtlicher Verantwortung unvereinbar ist.

Nach dem Berufsgrundsatz des *Mandatsschutzes* ist jede Gebührenunterbietung als unstandesgemäß verboten. Die Mindestgebühren für die Durchführung der aktienrechtlichen Pflichtprüfung sind in einer amtlichen Gebührenordnung festgesetzt. Bei Übernahme eines Mandates besteht die Übung, den bisher tätigen Wirtschaftsprüfer hierüber zu informieren und ihn ggfs. über die Gründe seines Ausscheidens zu befragen.

3. *Die Sicherung der Berufsgrundsätze*

a. Es liegt auf der Hand, daß die besten Rechtsnormen und Grundsätze in Anbetracht der Unzulänglichkeit der menschlichen Natur oft nur Theorie blieben, wenn nicht Vorsorge getroffen wäre, daß ihre Einhaltung von einer übergeordneten Instanz überwacht und ihre Verletzung geahndet würde.

Entsprechend alter Tradition freier Berufe mit öffentlich-rechtlichen Funktionen werden die Aufgaben der Überwachung der Berufstätigkeit der Wirtschaftsprüfer und Wirtschaftsprüfungsgesellschaften und der Ahndung von Verstößen gegen die Berufsgrundsätze oder das Standesrecht von den Berufsangehörigen selbst – in Form der Selbstverwaltung – wahrgenommen.

Zu diesem Zweck sind sämtliche Wirtschaftsprüfer und Wirtschaftsprüfungsgesellschaften obligatorisch in den Landeskammern für das wirtschaftliche Prüfungs- und Treuhandwesen – Körperschaften des öffentlichen Rechts mit dem Recht der Selbstverwaltung unter staatlicher Aufsicht – und diese wiederum in einer Hauptkammer zusammengeschlossen.

Die wirksamste Gewähr für die Einhaltung und Fortbildung der Berufsgrundsätze bietet die Institution der Ehrengerichtsbarkeit, die durch Ehrengerichte bei den Landeskammern und durch den Ehrengerichtshof bei der Hauptkammer, als letzter Berufungsinstanz, ausgeübt wird.

Die Ehrengerichte können auf folgende gesetzlich bestimmte Strafen bei Verletzung des Standesrechts erkennen:

a. Verwarnung,

b. Verweis,

c. Geldstrafe bis DM 5.000,–.

d. die Feststellung, daß der angeklagte Wirtschaftsprüfer oder die Wirtschaftsprüfungsgesellschaft unwürdig ist, weiterhin den Beruf eines Wirtschaftsprüfers bzw. einer Wirtschaftsprüfungsgesellschaft auszuüben.

Diese letzte schwerste Strafe hat die Zurücknahme der Bestellung des öffentlich bestellten Wirtschaftsprüfers bzw. der Anerkennung als Wirtschaftsprüfungsgesellschaft durch die staatlichen Behörden zur Folge.

Die Entscheidung der Ehrengerichte und des Ehrengerichtshofes werden laufend in einer amtlichen, von der Hauptkammer für das wirtschaftliche Prüfungs- und Treuhandwesen herausgegebenen Sammlung veröffentlicht.

Schließlich ist in diesem Zusammenhang noch zu erwähnen, daß die Berufsbezeichnungen 'Wirtschaftsprüfer' und 'Wirtschaftsprüfungsgesellschaft' besonderen strafrechtlichen Schutz genießen.

Während die Landeskammern und die Hauptkammer öffentlich-rechtliche Funktionen ausüben, gehören die Berufsangehörigen dem Institut der Wirtschaftsprüfer e.V. in Deutschland – einem rechtsfähigen Verein des Privatrechts – auf rein freiwilliger Grundlage als Mitglieder an.

Die verschiedenen Aufgaben des Instituts lassen sich zusammenfassend dahin kennzeichnen:

a. Vertretung der beruflichen Interessen des gesamten Berufsstandes gegenüber Dritten, insbesondere den staatlichen Behörden und Institutionen gegenüber,

b. fachliche Förderung der Berufsangehörigen und des Berufsnachwuchses.

In einem Hauptfachausschuß und verschiedenen Fachausschüssen, die sich aus Berufsangehörigen zusammensetzen, wird die 'Meinung des Berufes' gebildet, in Fachgutachten niedergelegt, und werden diese laufend veröffentlicht. Die Fachgutachten sind zwar nicht gesetzliche Normen, stellen jedoch die autoritative Auffassung des gesamten Berufsstandes dar.

Schließlich gibt das Institut die anerkannte Fachzeitschrift des Berufsstandes 'Die Wirtschaftsprüfung' heraus und pflegt die Beziehungen zu den ausländischen Berufskollegen.

IV. Die Haftung des Wirtschaftsprüfers bzw. der Wirtschaftsprüfungsgesellschaft

Ein auf die Einhaltung der Berufsgrundsätze mindestens von außen her wirkendes Mittel ist die Verantwortlichkeit der Berufsangehörigen in Verbindung mit der daraus folgenden vermögensmäßigen und strafrechtlichen Haftung.

Verletzt der Wirtschaftsprüfer (Wirtschaftsprüfungsgesellschaft) seine vertraglichen Pflichten, so haftet er, ggfs. auch für seine Gehilfen, dem Auftraggeber – grundsätzlich jedoch nicht Dritten gegenüber – auf Ersatz des durch seine Pflichtverletzung entstandenen Schadens.

Der Wirtschaftsprüfer (Wirtschaftsprüfungsgesellschaft) kann durch Vertrag seine Haftung der Höhe nach beschränken, jedoch nicht ausschließen.

Hinsichtlich seiner wichtigsten Aufgabe, nämlich der gesetzlichen Abschlußprüfung, ist die Haftung bei fahrlässiger Pflichtverletzung auf DM 100.000,– kraft Gesetzes beschränkt.

Zur Deckung von Schadenersatzansprüchen sind die Wirtschaftsprüfer und Wirtschaftprüfungsgesellschaften gesetzlich verpflichtet, eine Berufshaftpflichtversicherung mit einer Mindestversicherungssumme von DM 100.000,– für den einzelnen Schadensfall abzuschließen. Die Höhe der hierfür zu zahlende Prämie richtet sich naturgemäß nach dem personellen Umfang des Büros.

Die Wirtschaftsprüfer und ihre Gehilfen unterstehen grundsätzlich in derselben Weise wie alle anderen Personen im Staatsgebiet der Bundesrepublik Deutschland den allgemeinen strafrechtlichen Normen.

Daneben gelten für die Durchführung der gesetzlichen Abschlußprüfungen noch besondere strafrechtliche Vorschriften (vgl. § 302 AktG; § 150 GenG; § 137 VAG), nach denen u.a. falsche Berichterstattung und Verletzung der Verschwiegenheitspflicht mit Gefängnis oder Geldstrafe zu ahnden sind.

V. Der Bestätigungsvermerk in internationaler Beurteilung

Mit Vorstehendem habe ich versucht, die Grundlagen und Grundsätze unseres Berufes in Deutschland nach wesentlichen Gesichtspunkten darzulegen und sie damit dem internationalen Urteil der auf diesem Kongress zusammengekommenen Berufskollegen unterstellt. Ich möchte mein Referat nicht abschließen, ohne Möglichkeiten zur Erörterung zu stellen, nach denen dem Bestätigungsvermerk, der bedeutungsvollsten Ausdrucksform unserer beruflichen Betätigung über den klar abgrenzbaren nationalen Bereich hinaus, internationale Bedeutung beigelegt werden könnte.

Hierbei möchte ich von folgenden Erwägungen ausgehen:

1. Nach allgemeiner, international anerkannter Überzeugung ist der Jahresabschluß nach den Grundsätzen eines ordentlichen Kaufmanns aufzustellen, mögen diese auf allgemeiner Übung oder auf Gesetzesvorschriften beruhen.

Die wichtigsten dieser Grundsätze sind die der Klarheit und der Wahrheit, der Ordnung und der Vorsicht.

2. Nach allgemeiner Gepflogenheit hat sich die Prüfung auf die Einhaltung dieser Prinzipien zu erstrecken, wobei der Umfang der einzelnen Prüfungshandlungen, bestimmt durch die Umstände, in das sachverständige und pflichtmäßige Ermessen des Prüfers gestellt ist.

3. Ist nach diesen Grundsätzen bilanziert und geprüft worden, so kann ein diese Tatsachen bestätigender Vermerk erteilt werden.

Ob im Einzelfall die vorstehend genannten Prinzipien für die Erteilung des Bestätigungsvermerks tatsächlich maßgebend gewesen sind, hängt von der persönlichen und fachlichen Qualifikation des Prüfers ab.

Entsprechen diese den allgemeinen und international anerkannten Berufsgrundsätzen, so begründet der Bestätigungsvermerk allgemeines Vertrauen in die Ordnungsmäßigkeit des Abschlusses. Insoweit kann demnach auch von einer internationalen Bedeutung gesprochen werden.

Je einheitlicher und eindeutiger nach Form und Inhalt seine Fassung ist, umso verkehrssicherer und verkehrsfähiger ist der Bestätigungsvermerk auch im internationalen Bereich.

Mir scheint demnach eine entscheidende Aufgabe internationaler Zusammenkünfte wie dieses Kongresses darin zu liegen, die Grundsätze der Berufsauffassung und Berufsausübung als die entscheidenden Grundlagen unseres Berufes in den verschiedenen Ländern zu erkennen, gegebenenfalls anzugleichen und damit ihnen und ihren Ergebnissen internationale, d.h. schließlich auch völkerverbindende Geltung zu verschaffen. Ich bin überzeugt, daß auch dieser Kongress uns auf diesem Weg ein beachtliches Stück weiterbringen wird.

Translation

PAPER

by

WIRTSCHAFTSPRÜFER DR HEINRICH WOLLERT

Institut der Wirtschaftsprüfer in Deutschland e.V.

I. The Establishment of the Profession in 1931

Accountancy as a professional institution was established in Germany as a result of the shock of the financial crisis of the years 1931 and 1932, and particularly as a result of several big scandals, such as the collapse of the firm 'Nordwolle' and that of the 'Fawag' concern. Up to that time such an institution was absent from German business life. And yet what did exist prior to that time in similar institutions in Germany left its marks on the accountant's profession.

Up to that time there existed sworn auditors, trust-and audit companies, the latter were mainly set up by banks and worked on their behalf as well as under their control, and finally there were audit institutions for co-operatives.

In spite of all these institutions, there was no uniformity in accountancy in Germany prior to 1931.

The innovation introduced as a result of the financial crisis consisted in the promulgation of an emergency decree on 19th September 1931, making compulsory the audit of annual financial statements of Stock Companies (Aktiengesellschaften) and of Limited Partnership Companies (Kommanditgesellschaften auf Aktien) by 'professional auditors' (balance sheet auditors). Shortly afterwards, this compulsory audit was extended to public enterprises.

In both instances, the audit was entrusted to the authorized public accountants, both to individuals and to audit companies. The peculiarity of the situation of those years is characterized by the fact that there was no profession of 'authorized public accountants' (öffentlich bestellte Wirtschaftsprüfer) in existence as yet.

For this reason the then German State concluded an agreement with its federated Länder, the so-called 'Länder-Agreement' in which the principles were agreed according to which accountants were to be publicly invested and sworn in the individual Länder.

This Länder-Agreement may be called the Magna Charta of our profession, for in essence it provided the uniform basis for the establishment and development of the profession until the end of the last war in 1945; in this Agreement, the legality of the accountant's profession has been anchored that gives our profession its typical character of a free profession with responsibility to the public.

The new professional regulations in the different newly formed Länder of the German Federal Republic proclaimed after 1945, represent only minor modifications of the professional code laid down in the Länder ordinance, just as the re-arrangement of the professional code on a federal basis which is at present being considered by the competent federal legal authorities.

However, prior to discussing the professional code, it is imperative that I first refer to the tasks which have officially been conferred upon the profession and which have been referred to us voluntarily by the business world, since only a comprehension of these will render understandable our professional code.

II. The Duties of the Wirtschaftsprüfer

1. *Compulsory Audit under Company Law*

As already mentioned, the first and initially only task which was exclusively conferred upon the new authorized public accountants by the State in 1931, was the compulsory audit of the annual financial statements of Stock Companies and Limited Partnership Companies, by a public accountant annually elected at the stockholders' meeting.

The fundamental significance of this task can be recognized from the fact that an annual balance sheet which has not been audited is considered void and as a consequence, all resolutions based upon it are equally void.

The duties relating to the legal audit of the financial statements are subdivided as follows:

a. Audit

b. Written Report

c. Issue of either a clean or a qualified certificate, or refusal to issue a certificate.

In accordance with article 135 of the Company Law, the audit must cover the annual financial statements by taking into consideration the accounting records and the annual report, whereby not only the formal agreement with the books has to be checked but it must be materially examined, in particular whether:

a. The individual items of the financial statements have been properly shown in accordance with good accounting principles (inventory) (article 129 of the Company Law) and in conjunction with article 39 of the Commercial Code.

b. Whether they have been properly valued, taking into consideration the legal provisions (article 133 of the Company Law), as well as

c. Whether they have been shown clearly, in conformity with legal balance sheet requirements (articles 131 and 132 of the Company Law), and whether the books upon which the closing balance sheet is based as well as all other relevant documents are in good order and can be considered conclusive evidence.

The verification concerning observance of other legal regulations such as concerning taxation, price and currency regulations has bearing upon the duty of the auditor only when individual items of the closing balance sheet are affected by them.

The verification of whether embezzlements have taken place is not the task of the auditor either; according to both the law and the professional standards in such cases, a special mandate must be given.

Next to the generally accepted principles of a regular audit, the auditor uses the legal provisions as a yardstick.

One of the characteristics of the legal audit as one of correctness and legality is the compulsory audit of the financial report of the Management.

The compulsory rendering of an audit report derives from article 139 of the Company Law according to which a written report must be submitted to the Management and the Board of Directors, to the latter in its capacity of representative of the shareholders of the company whose accounts are audited, that is to say to the two bodies which are as a rule legally competent to establish the annual balance sheet; this report must state whether the legal regulations for the establishing of the closing balance sheet have been observed as proved by the results of the audit.

Contrary to a decision by the Federal Supreme Court of 15th December 1954 (BGHZ 16/17) upholding the legal regulations that the financial circumstances of the company must not be disclosed in the audit report, it has been a custom in professional circles to summarize and discuss the financial position of the business, particularly as far as the capital, the liquidity and earning capacity are concerned, as compared with the previous year. This part of the report is usually contained in a separate chapter.

Apart from the audit report in accordance with article 139 of the Company Law, the accountant is held, according to article 140 of the Company Law to either issue a clean or a qualified certificate or to refuse the certificate. If the legal conditions for the issuance of an unqualified certification have been met, the latter is worded as follows:

> Subsequent to the conclusive results of my (our) legal audit of the books and documents of the company and of the information and evidence submitted by management, the books, the closing balance sheet and the annual report, as far as the latter elaborates upon the financial statements, all correspond to the legal regulations'.

The closing balance sheet must be published with the certification issued by the auditor. Thus the public is informed of the results of the audit and its faith in the legality and correctness of the closing balance sheet is justified.

The issuance of the certification is therefore the logical expression of the official function of the auditor.

The auditor must refuse or limit the certification if he discovers some flaws during the audit which either do not justify the issuing of the certification at all or do so in a qualified form only. The reasons for refusing or qualifying a certification are not laid down by law as such. The decision is rather left to the auditor's judgment in conscientiously carrying out his duty as a matter of principle: His decision must, however, be guided by the legal regulations and the principles developed by the profession which bear upon correct auditing.

The above mentioned principles of auditing, reporting and issuing of the certification are also valid—with minor modifications—for the carrying out of other audit tasks which are based upon legal regulations. Moreover, these principles of correctness and legality have become the guiding principles for the entirety of the professional activities in accountancy.

From the above one might be inclined to draw the conclusion that the margin of judgment available to the accountant in legally compulsory audits is greatly narrowed down owing to the compulsion exercised by the law.

Such a conclusion however would be unjustified. For within the framework of the legal regulations, the auditor must take his own fundamental decisions regarding scope and method of audit, the structure and shape of the audit report and finally the evaluation of the results of the audit according to his own judgment and conception of duty. The significance of such decisions is proved by the fact that the welfare of the business itself and that of others as well as the reputation of the auditor may depend on the issuance of the certification.

2. *Further Duties based upon Legal Provisions*

The multitude of these additional legally compulsory audits can be subdivided into two large categories, namely:

a. Recurring general audits
b. Limited special audits.

Among the most important recurrent general audits recurring annually, which like the audit under Company Law are compulsory for private as well as for state owned enterprises, there are: Yearly closing balance sheets of private insurance companies, building societies, all private credit banks and public utility companies.

The category of special audits was considerably extended and gained great significance particularly as a result of the currency reform of 1948. This includes particularly the audit of DM-Opening Balance Sheets and the proposals for the establishment of the capital position in private and public Limited Liability Companies as well as the conversion into D. Marks of the accounts of all financial institutes, insurance companies and building societies.

The multitude of laws and ordinances which regulate the contents and extent of these compulsory audits cannot be discussed in detail here.

3. *Other Duties*

Among the most important functions carried out by the members of the profession, apart from their function as authorized auditors, the following are mentioned:

a. Audit of financial statements of enterprises which are not subject to compulsory audit, the rendering of expert opinions of all types for private businesses, for public enterprises and the courts.

b. Advisory activity in the fields of industry and taxation.

c. Activity as arbitrator, particularly in disagreements between partners, as liquidator, as administrator in cases of bankruptcy or composition settlements, and as executors of wills and as trustees.

In conclusion, I should like to say the following:

In the 25 years since its inception, the profession and its duties have grown organically. The profession nowadays occupies a leading position among the other advisory services in business, such as sworn accountants, tax experts, tax advisers, and has become a permanent feature of the German economy.

III. The Professional Code

1. *The Necessity of a Professional Code*

Considering both significance and extent of the duties mentioned above, it is understandable that the State has taken a decisive influence upon the formation and development of the professional code of the accountants already at the time when the profession was officially instated by virtue of the Länder-Agreement of 1931; this development is identical to that of the other professions which have either special public responsibilities or official functions.

The following short outline of the most important principles of our professional code is based upon the professional regulations for members of the Auditor's and Trusteeship Organisations of 20th December, 1946 which covered the area of the Länder of the former British Zone of Occupation (North-Rhine Westphalia, Schleswig Holstein, Lower Saxony, and Hamburg); these regulations have a great similarity to the former Länder-Agreement.

2. *The Most Important Elements of the Professional Code*

The selection of only suitable (physical) persons for the profession of accountant is governed by regulations regarding:

a. The procedure of admission, or pre-examination
b. The examination procedure
c. The investment procedure

Additionally, for audit companies there is
The procedure of recognition.

The *procedure of admission or pre-examination* for physical persons imposes the condition upon the candidate of proving that as an individual he is suitable for the responsible position of accountant, that he is living in settled financial circumstances and that he is at least 30 years of age; furthermore, that he has completed a 6 years' stage of practical work (four of which in the profession).

Furthermore, he must have taken his university degree in economic science, law or engineering.

This last requirement may be dropped in special cases only.

There is a possibility of appealing against the rejection of an application for admission with the Central Office of Auditors' and Trusteeship Organisations. Its decision is final.

The *examination procedure* requires the candidate to prove his professional competence by:

a. The writing of a scientifical paper at home
b. Two written papers in the presence of examiners, and the taking of an oral examination.

The examination covers mainly the following branches:

a. Book-keeping and preparation of annual balance sheets as well as Business Economics in all its specialized branches
b. Civil and Commercial Law with particular regard to Economic Law
c. Taxation Law
d. The Professional Code.

After having passed the examination, the candidate is invested in the profession upon his request by the competent governmental authority (in North-Rhine Westphalia this is the Federal Minister of Economics) in an *investment procedure* and is subsequently sworn in.

The accountant's oath is as follows:

'I swear that I shall fulfil the tasks and duties of an authorized public accountant conscientiously and impartially, that I shall keep the professional secret and that I shall render the expert opinions required of me conscientiously and impartially.'

After having taken the oath, the accountant receives an investment charter and is entered into the register of authorized public accountants.

One special feature of the German professional code which can only be understood in the light of the historical development consists in the fact that apart from individual accountants, companies in the form of joint-stock companies may be recognized as audit companies vested with the same rights and duties as the individual accountants.

The recognition of joint-stock companies as audit companies is mainly dependent on the condition that the representatives of the company who deal with third parties must be qualified accountants.

Beyond that and as a matter of principle there exist special regulations governing the participation in the capital of such audit companies in order to avoid any dependence on others, i.e. physical or juridical persons that do not belong to the profession, and to exclude any influence from being exerted upon the persons responsible for the company's business. Without wishing to enter into the pros and cons of audit companies in Germany, I should like to say that the audit companies represent a form of association which is indispensable to the execution of the profession and which can be best compared to the Anglo-American partnerships.

Among the most important principles which are to lay the indispensable foundation and in particular the moral foundation for the professional practice, I should like to mention the following:

a. The principles governing the professional practice
b. The regulations concerning the safeguarding of these professional principles.

These represent the actual professional code of the accountants, a code which has only partly been codified but whose remaining, rather significant part has acquired validity as an unwritten rule of custom.

The most important professional principles are as follows:

a. Accountancy practice as a main occupation
b. The accountant's personal responsibility

c. Independence
d. Keeping the Professional Secret
e. Impartiality
f. Prohibition of advertising and of competition among accountants.

The requirement that the *accountant must practise his profession as a main occupation* is characterized by the fact that the specific tasks of audit and advice must wholly or mainly occupy the energy of the accountant and moreover, the accountant in his capacity of legal auditor of financial statements must refrain from any other additional activities which are not in harmony with his main occupation, such as commercial or trade activities or occupation as an employee—unless he is employed by an audit company—or as an official.

The essence of having to *act on his own responsibility* is that the accountant must not be exposed to any pressure in the form of orders from outside when carrying out his professional duties.

If an accountant is employed, he may only be active as the deputy of an accountant entitled to sign on behalf of the firm, or as the representative of an audit company; in the latter case he must always be invested with power of attorney.

In such instances, however, the employer must in no way impair the freedom of decision of an accountant in his employment.

The condition of an accountant assuming responsibility on his own account requires the accountant *actually* to be able to shoulder the responsibility arising out of his duties. In performing his task he must not therefore use an unlimited number of assistants. As a rule, not more than five persons may assist the accountant.

The professional principle of *independence* has been the subject of particularly detailed regulations which to a great extent are based on legal provisions.

Without going into the details of these highly complicated provisions here, the essence of this professional principle can be summarized as follows: An auditor (or an audit company) must not be appointed legal auditor if there is a possibility of undue influence being exerted upon him (it) as a result of relationship or economic dependence without any such influence *necessarily* being exerted.

Particularly in the case of audit companies, article 137 II of the Company Law is of special significance; according to this article, any direct or indirect dependence of the audit company as regards invested capital by the business whose accounts have to be audited or vice versa excludes the acceptability of such an audit company as legal auditor, and its audit would be void.

One might say that the condition of independence has been adequately regulated.

An entirely different question which does not fall within the law is that of the economic independence which might be endangered particularly in the case of dependence on the mandate where the accountant is faced with a powerful large enterprise, which engagement might be of decisive significance as a basis of his existence. No doubt the partnerships formed by a number of accountants as well as audit companies are better protected from such dependence since as a rule they have at their disposal a better distribution of their mandates.

In the last resort, the condition of independence can only be fulfilled by the personal qualities of the individual rather than by regulations.

The principle of keeping the *professional secrecy* derives already from the general professional principles. Beyond that, the accountant is expressly obliged by his oath to observe the rules of professional secrecy. Moreover, any infringement of this obligation to observe the rules of professional secrecy is punishable in accordance with article 300 of the German Criminal Code.

Correlated to the duty to observe the professional secret is the accountants' right of refusing to give testimony before the courts much in the same way as doctors and lawyers have.

Another essential element of the professional principles is the accountant's *impartiality*, a requirement which is also contained in the professional oath; this impartiality, together with his unbiased attitude can in the last resort only be guaranteed by the accountant's own careful scrutiny of his conscience. It is in principle characterized by the fact that the accountant in performing all his duties and giving all his judgments must behave in such a manner that it can withstand in every respect any criticism that might be forthcoming from an impartial outsider. There might be conflicting interests arising out of a coincidence of advisory tasks with the functions of auditor. In such instances, the advisory activity should never go so far as to be responsible for the carrying out of anything that would be subjected to audit and certification later on. In that case, one of the two mandates would have to be dropped. The same is valid in cases where the accountant, after scrupulous examination of his conscience finds that he is not in a position to put his personal interests unequivocally behind those of his client. All these considerations touch closely upon the ethical sphere of those principles which go to make the reputation and the value of the personality and can therefore not strictly be embodied in any code.

The *prohibition of advertising* is based upon the consideration that publicity is incompatible with the basic principles of a liberal profession with responsibilities to the public.

According to the professional principle of *non-competition among accountants*, any undercutting of fees is prohibited as unprofessional. The minimum fees for the carrying out of a compulsory audit under Company Law have been laid down in an official table of fees. When an accountant is appointed legal auditor of a company for the first time, it is customary to inform the former auditor of this appointment and, if deemed necessary, to ask him why his engagement has not been renewed.

3. *Safeguarding the Professional Principles*

It is obvious that the best legal standards and principles would often remain just theory unless care was taken by a superior body to supervise adherence thereto and to prosecute any violation thereof.

In accordance with an old tradition of the liberal professions that exercise public functions the tasks of supervising the professional activities of the auditors and audit companies as well as the tasks of prosecuting any violation of the professional principles or of the professional code have been taken over by members of the profession themselves—in the form of self-administration.

For this purpose, all auditors and audit companies are joined compulsorily in the Länder Chambers of Auditors' and Trusteeship Organisations which are corporations under public law with the right of selfadministration under government control; these Länder Chambers are in turn united in a Central Chamber.

The most efficient guarantee for the observation and development of the professional principles is the institution of the professional Council jurisdiction which is practised by the professional Councils of the Länder Chambers and that of the Supreme Professional Council, as the highest authority of appeal of the Central Chamber.

The professional Councils are empowered to pronounce sentences laid down by law in cases of violation of the professional code as follows:

a. Caution
b. Reprimand
c. Fine up to DM 5,000
d. Finding that the accused auditor or audit company has been found unworthy of continuing to practise public accounting.

This latter heaviest punishment is followed by a withdrawal of the investment of the officially appointed auditor or of the recognition of the company as an audit company by the competent authorities.

The decisions of the professional councils are currently published in an official publication issued by the Central Chamber of Auditors' and Trusteeship Organisations.

It should further be mentioned that the professional nomenclature of 'auditor' and 'audit company' ('Wirtschaftsprüfer' and 'Wirtschaftsprüfungsgesellschaft') is legally protected.

While the Länder Chambers and the Central Chambers are exercising functions under public law, the members of the profession belong to the 'Institut der Wirtschaftsprüfer', Registered Society of Germany,—an association possessing legal personality under private law—on a purely voluntary basis.

The different duties of the Institute may be summarized as follows:

a. Representation of the professional interests of the entire profession before third parties, particularly before the authorities and official institutions

b. Promoting the professional interests of the members as well as of the new generation of accountants.

In a Central Professional Committee and several Professional Sub-Committees composed of members of the profession, the 'professional opinion' is being formed and laid down in expert bulletins which are currently published. The expert opinions do not represent legal regulations; however they do represent the authoritative opinion of the entire professional group.

Finally, the Institute issues the wellknown journal of the profession 'Accountancy' ('Die Wirtschaftsprüfung') and entertains relations with foreign confrères.

IV. Liability of the Auditor or Audit Company

One of the means of guaranteeing the upholding of the professional principles is the reponsibility of the members of the profession coupled with the resulting liability; this latter relates to property as well as to penal law.

If the auditor (the audit company or their assistants) violate their contractual duties, such auditor or audit company are liable to the client—as a matter of principle not to third parties—for restitution of any loss incurred as a consequence of his dereliction of duty.

The auditor (audit company) can limit the amount of his (its) liability by contract but cannot exclude it.

As far as the accountant's most important task, namely the legal audit of the annual financial statements is concerned, his liability is limited to DM 100,000 by law in cases of negligent dereliction of duty.

In order to cover any claims of restitution, the auditor and audit companies are legally bound to conclude a professional indemnity insurance for a minimum amount of DM 100,000 per individual instance of possible loss. The amount of the premium due for this insurance varies according to the number of personnel of the accountants' office.

The accountants and their assistants fall as a matter of principle under the general penal legislation in the same way as all other persons do who are within the boundaries of the German Federal Republic.

In addition, there are special penal regulations governing the execution of legal audits of annual financial statements (vide articles 302 of the Company Law; 150 GenG; 137 VAG), according to which i.a. false reporting and violation of the professional secrecy are punishable by imprisonment or a fine.

V. The Certification Judged in the Light of International Relations

With the above I have endeavoured to explain the bases and principles of our profession in Germany according to their essential characteristics and have thus submitted them to the international judgment of our confrères who have forgathered at this Congress. I should not like to close my paper prior to having submitted for discussion some possibilities according to which form of expression of our professional activities could be given international significance beyond the clearly defined national sphere.

In doing so, I am moved by the following considerations:

1. According to internationally recognized principles, the financial statements have to be established in conformity with sound business whether these principles be based upon custom or upon legal provisions.

The most important of these principles are those of clarity and truth, of correctness and care.

2. According to general practice, the audit has to cover the observance of these principles whereby the scope of the audit, determined by circumstances, is left to the expert and conscientious discretion of the auditor.

3. If the statements have been prepared and the audit carried out according to these principles, a certification can be issued which will confirm these facts.

Whether the principles quoted above have actually determined the issuance of the certification in any individual case depends on the personal and professional qualifications of the auditor.

If these latter correspond to the general internationally recognized professional principles, the certification justifies general confidence in the correctness of the financial statements. In this respect one may therefore also speak of an international significance.

The more uniform and unequivocal the certification will be drawn up as regards its form and contents, the more reliable and capable it will be for being used in international business transactions.

It seems therefore to me that it is one of the decisive tasks of international meetings like this Congress to recognize the principles of professional conceptions and professional practices as the decisive bases of our profession in the different countries and if need be to adapt them to one another and thus to attach international validity to these principles and the conclusions arrived at: That is to say, a validity which will be yet another means of bringing the nations more closely together. I am convinced that this Congress too will carry us considerably further along this road.

DISCUSSION

CHAIRMAN: MR. ARTHUR B. FOYE, C.P.A. (U.S.A.)

CHAIRMAN:

It is a very great pleasure to be here this morning, both for you and for me, at this session. The Seventh International Congress opened yesterday, as I think most of you were here, with a fine meeting, a fine opening session under the very strong leadership of Mr. Kraayenhof and with an inspiring keynote address by His Royal Highness the Prince of the Netherlands. And then last night we were made personally welcome, in this very room, by a reception and were greeted by Mr. and Mrs. Kraayenhof and by Prof. and Mrs. Van Rietschoten. And so we have opened the congress and we have been made welcome. To-day we are opening the business sessions of this Congress. Of course during this week we shall discuss many subjects of great interest to accountants and naturally we want to start with fundamentals. So this morning the session is to be devoted to the subject of the Principles for the Accountant's Profession. In each of the countries that are represented here, these principles have evolved under the intelligent leadership of the accountants in those countries, and we are fortunate to have the essence of those principles distilled for us by a panel and in the papers that some of the panel members have written. Yesterday Prince Bernhard said, very truly, that the subject we are to discuss this morning was one that has a large spiritual element as well as a material element; for the principles are founded on things partly of the spirit and partly material. And it is a good thing for us to be reminded of that, because in our profession we do not live for bread alone. We live, not only for the service we render clients, but for the service we render to the business public and to the public at large. It is in those responsibilities and with the cognizance of them that we are this morning going to deal with this subject of the Principles. The panel that you have before you is made up of a discussion leader, of a group of people who wrote papers and then some other members of the panel. The discussion leader is Mr. Van Essen of the Netherlands. My special colleagues sitting at the elevated table are the two Vice-Chairmen of this meeting who support me, Mr. Mody and Dr. Allet. Mr. Mody of India, Dr. Allet of Austria. Mr. Van Essen occupies the centre place on the platform and will be the discussion leader. Five of the panel members prepared papers. Those papers were distributed to the delegates and I was going to say I was sure—I better say that I hope—that all of you read them. However, the papers are in your hands, you will find them exceedingly interesting.

Those who prepared the papers are: Sir Thomas Robson of England, who is also the Rapporteur of this meeting, Mr. Carman Blough of the United States; Mr. Cassel of Sweden; Dr. De Lange of the Netherlands and Dr. Wollert of Germany.

Then there are three other panel members for the purpose of discussion of the papers: Mr. Busuttil of Malta, Mr. McDonald of Canada; and Mr. U. Shein of Burma.

The plan of the meeting is that Mr. Van Essen will guide and lead the discussion. The essence of the papers will be presented to you by Sir Thomas Robson. The panel will discuss these papers. We asked the delegates, in correspondence, to submit questions on the papers. Four of the delegates were good enough to send in comments and questions. We appreciate their doing it and they will be recognized. The time will not permit the full discussion of the comments and all of the questions, but Mr. Van Essen will select certain of the questions for discussion by the panel. Because of the size of the gathering it is not possible to permit discussion from the floor and as you have all had the opportunity to submit questions, questions from the floor will probably not be entertained again because of lack of time. I think we are dealing with one of the most important subjects that accountants should deal with in this matter of the principles that guide our profession. And it is a pleasure to turn this meeting over to our discussion leader Mr. Van Essen.

MR. L. VAN ESSEN LZN. (Netherlands)

Ladies and Gentlemen, As the President, Mr. Foye, has already pointed out, a summary has been prepared by Sir Thomas Robson of the different papers and I now want to call upon Sir Thomas to read this summary.

SIR THOMAS B. ROBSON (United Kingdom)

INTRODUCTION

Our participation here shews the world wide nature of our profession, and our belief that the principles which should govern it are universal. Accountants need the basic qualities of character and competence, but they need also the benefits which come from contacts with other accountants, from the impact of mind on mind and the discussion of common problems.

The profession itself in every country needs a like impact; it can obtain this by participation in congresses such as this, by the despatch of its members to work in other countries and by the contact which it maintains with accountants from abroad who work within its own country.

FUNCTIONS

The principal function of public accountants is to audit the annual accounts of companies for the benefit of shareholders.

In some countries the law neither requires audits nor prescribes the qualifications of auditors. In some countries every company must have an audit, whilst in others it is required only for companies in which the investing public have interests. In some countries only persons with specified qualifications may act as auditors of companies, whilst in others qualifications are required only in companies in which the public are interested.

In most countries accountants also perform other functions. They advise on accounting and system matters, and investigate the accounts of businesses whose owners desire to dispose of them or to obtain additional capital. In some but not all countries they act as directors of companies other than those which they audit, as receivers or trustees in bankrupt and other estates, as liquidators of companies, as expert witnesses in the courts, as arbitrators in disputes on financial matters, and as advisers on taxation.

Other accountants perform functions as whole-time financial directors and controllers, chief accountants or internal auditors of particular companies. These may not have the same independence as accountants in public practice, but they regard themselves as bound none the less to comply with the principles of the profession.

INDEPENDENCE OF AUDITORS

Independence is a fundamental requirement for an auditor. Unless he is independent of those whose accounts he examines, there can be no assurance that he will be objective and impartial in his reports.

Most advanced countries have regulations designed to secure that only the truly independent person shall be an auditor. They, therefore, treat as ineligible those who are directors, officers and employees of the company audited; some of them also exclude persons having a financial interest in the company. In some countries the degree of independence required for the auditors of public companies is greater than for privately owned family concerns.

The fact that an accountant gives advice to a company is not in general (though not everywhere) regarded as impairing his independence as its auditor as long as he does not participate in executive decisions.

REPORTS AND RESPONSIBILITY

Some countries have specific regulations as to the contents of an auditor's report; others leave this matter to his discretion. The form and contents of the reports, therefore, differ greatly. In one country a simple signature by the auditor on the accounts may imply his approval. In another a signed opinion stating that the accounts shew a true and fair view is considered necessary, or such an opinion together with an indication of the scope and nature of the work done in the audit. In some countries the opinion has to be accompanied by a statement that the accounts comply with the regulations of the country where they are issued or are based on the consistent application of accepted accounting principles. In others the auditor's report has also to include a recommendation that the shareholders should approve the accounts and the proposals of the management.

Whatever form a report may have, it should be clear, concise and forthright, and should indicate unmistakably the opinion which the auditor has formed and the reservations to which it is subject; if he cannot form an opinion he should say so. The work which precedes the report should be carefully planned and skilfully and accurately performed; the report itself should not imply that it deserves a greater measure of reliance than the work done justifies.

In some countries the auditor's legal responsibility for defects in his work (apart from criminal acts) and in that of his staff is to the company alone, but in others it extends to third parties who suffer by his negligence. Whilst the auditor of a private client's accounts may accept his client's instructions limiting the scope of his audit, the auditor of a company may not in general accept such limitations.

In most countries the personal financial liability of the auditor for failure in his duty is unlimited, though in some it is restricted by law to a specified maximum on each audit. The auditor of a company is not a guarantor and he should not normally be held responsible for defalcations which the management has failed to detect.

AUDITOR'S DUTY

His duty is to ascertain and report whether the accounts presented to him shew a fair view of the state of affairs and profits. His work for this purpose differs according to the circumstances, the importance of particular items in relation to the fairness of the accounts as a whole, the size of the company, the system of internal control and its effectiveness, the scope and efficiency of any internal audit. He has to evaluate these and decide for himself the form and extent of his examination.

Reliance on tests and samples as opposed to detailed and complete checks is well recognised as a practical necessity. Any other course would be wholly impracticable in large organisations; it would make the cost of the audit prohibitive and would not make it more effective for its primary purpose.

The auditor must use skill and care and exercise character and intelligence. He must see that his own staff follow his example, for in all but the smallest audits he needs to delegate important duties to them. Delegation of those duties to employees of the company whose accounts are under audit is not appropriate.

EDUCATION AND TRAINING

Recruits for the profession need to be persons of character, intelligence and ability, with an aptitude for figures, power of clear, concise and grammatical self-expression and a sound general education. Their training differs widely between countries and between professional bodies.

In some countries long practical training in the office of a public accountant, accompanied by study of professional subjects and the passing of examinations of high standards, is regarded as essential. In others the attainment of a university degree in economics or a similar subject is required; in some of these this has to be followed by practical experience over a series of years and the passing of professional examinations, whilst in others it is possible to pass the examinations and acquire a diploma without practical experience.

In some countries the qualification consists of admission to membership conferred by the professional institutes themselves; in others it is a diploma conferred by a public authority or a university.

RULES OF PROFESSIONAL CONDUCT

In most countries where there is a highly developed accountancy profession its ethical standards are similar to those of the older professions such as medicine and law.

In some countries endeavours have been made to formulate codes of ethics containing rules of conduct, whilst in others those concerned prefer to state broad principles of conduct without detailed formal written regulations. Failure to live up to the standards expected involves the responsible person in penalties for his fault.

In general, a member of the profession is required to be a man of conscience and integrity, honest with others and with himself, one who does unto others as he would wish to be done to him, one who seeks always to keep the profession high in public esteem. Advertising and improper solicitation of business, undercutting of fees and approaches to the clients of other accountants are improper. The sharing of fees with non-accountants without the client's consent and the determination of fees as a percentage of the benefit of the accountant's work to the client are disapproved. The maintenance of professional secrecy about a client's business is essential.

PROFESSIONAL STANDARDS

The profession in every country has much to learn from the experience of others. International congresses and conferences confined to one nation or institute are of the greatest benefit not only to those who attend but also to those who afterwards hear about them. The availability of accountancy literature and of a forum for discussion of opinions and ideas is also very important.

Some institutes issue their own recommendations on principles and procedures; others confine their activities to the examination of candidates for qualification and the exercise of discipline over their members. In some countries attempts have been made to standardise the form of accounts, in some a large measure of freedom is left as to the form but the extent of the disclosure to be made in the accounts is prescribed, whilst in others these matters are left for determination by the individual company and its auditors. It is not, therefore, possible to say that there is any detailed international standard in these matters, except that accounts in every country should have the qualities of truth and fairness and be the result of the consistent application of recognised principles.

CONCLUSION

The need for these essential qualities emphasises the international character of our profession and of the principles which should guide it. Wherever we work our aim should be to serve our clients with the highest possible skill and to provide all the protection in our power for their businesses wherever they may be located or conducted.

Race, nationality and place of residence are not the factors which determine the suitability of the accountant for his task; any failure to recognise this will hurt both the profession as a whole and the country where the failure occurs. The real determinant of the success or otherwise of the profession in any country is whether its members have the right character and ideals, the requisite training, ability and experience, a firm grasp of accounting principles, a sincere desire to serve their clients and the honesty and independence of mind without which the highest service to their clients cannot be given.

Opening Session

Monday night's Reception

DISCUSSION

MR. L. VAN ESSEN LZN. (Netherlands)

I thank you, Sir Thomas, for this very useful summary. And now, Ladies and Gentlemen, to start our discussion, I should like to call on Mr. McDonald to put the first question.

MR. W. LESLIE MCDONALD (Canada)

Dr. De Lange in his paper dealing with the principles of the profession in the Netherlands indicates that in issuing a public certificate the auditor accepts a less comprehensive responsibility for the correctness of the published figures than when he issues a certificate to the directors of an undertaking. In turn, he indicates that there is even a greater responsibility in a certificate to management. In Canada the auditor is appointed by the shareholders, to report to the shareholders on the financial statements presented by the directors at the annual meeting. It, therefore, seems strange to a Canadian that the auditor should have any greater responsibility than he assumes when reporting to shareholders, and I wonder if Dr. De Lange would care to give us some further explanation about this.

MR. L. VAN ESSEN LZN. (Netherlands)

Now I call on Mr. De Lange to give the first reply, but as Mr. De Lange is going to speak in Dutch, it will be necessary for our panel members to have a receiver. Everything arranged now? Then I call on Dr. De Lange.

DR. A. TH. DE LANGE (Netherlands)

Mijnheer de voorzitter, dames en heren, De vraag welke Mr. McDonald heeft gesteld vereist in de eerste plaats een bezinning op de doelstellingen van de contrôle. Het is duidelijk, dat Mr. McDonald, afgaande op de omstandigheden in de Engels sprekende landen, zijn aandacht in de eerste plaats richt op de verklaring van de accountant voor hetgeen wij in Nederland plegen te noemen het 'maatschappelijk verkeer', dat zijn al diegenen, die belang hebben bij de uitkomsten van de controle, die belang hebben bij de verklaring van de accountant. In Nederland in ieder geval wordt, naast deze ongetwijfeld zeer belangrijke, zo niet belangrijkste, functie van de accountant, vervuld de functie ten behoeve van de bedrijfsleiding, ten behoeve van de dagelijkse leiding zowel als ten behoeve van de toezicht houdende functionarissen, in het bijzonder de Raad van Commissarissen. Het is in Nederland dan ook zo, dat de beide doeleinden van de uitvoering van de opdracht in het oog worden gehouden en dat in de verslaglegging daarvan blijkt, een verslaglegging die zich dan daarin uit, dat naast de meer of minder korte verklaring ten behoeve van het maatschappelijk verkeer een rapport wordt uitgebracht aan de Raad van Commissarissen en/of de Directie. En nu gaat de opmerking van Mr. McDonald in het bijzonder over dit onderscheid in de functie van accountant, in de doelstelling van het onderzoek, omdat naar gelang de doelstelling de verslaglegging verschillend zal zijn en daarmede de verantwoordelijkheid. Het gaat dus niet om een verschil in verantwoordelijkheid in die zin, dat men voor de ene verklaring een andere verantwoordelijkheid zou hebben dan voor de andere, dat het akkoord bij de ene verklaring iets anders zou betekenen dan bij de andere verklaring; akkoord is uitcraard akkoord. Maar waar het om gaat is, dat men zich akkoord verklaart met een omvang van gegevens, die bij de verklaring zijn gevoegd en die dus inhoud geven aan de verslaglegging, waarop de verklaring betrekking heeft. In Nederland onderscheidt men een verschil in verantwoordelijkheid bij de verklaring tegenover, zeg nu maar eenvoudigweg, aandeelhouders en de verklaring tegenover de commissarissen, omdat de verklaring tegenover aandeelhouders betrekking heeft op het globale beeld van de vermogenspositie en de resultaten, zoals die blijken uit de jaarstukken van de onderneming, terwijl het rapport aan de Raad van Commissarissen of aan de Directie meerdere gegevens ter nadere specificatie bevat en de verklaring dus mede deze nadere specificaties omvat.

De accountant is dan ook niet verantwoord alleen deze specificaties op te nemen ter vergroting, als het ware, van het rapport, zonder dat hij de juistheid daarvan heeft nagegaan. Hij zal zich van de juistheid van de gedetailleerde gegevens moeten overtuigen en voor de juistheid dus verantwoordelijk zijn.

Dit in de eerste plaats ten aanzien van de opmerking van Mr. McDonald, wat betreft de situatie, waarin de accountant zich bevindt. Maar als men zich afvraagt, hoe het vraagstuk van de verantwoordelijkheid voor het rapport aan directie en commissarissen ligt, dan valt nog een ander punt in het oog, dat is de vraag welke verantwoordelijkheid heeft de accountant voor hetgeen niet in het rapport is opgenomen; dat is het vraagstuk, dat in het bijzonder onze aandacht verdient te hebben. De accountant mag immers niet de kans lopen te worden aangesproken door de Raad van Commissarissen met de vraag: waarom hebt gij ons dat niet medegedeeld? Juist het achterwege laten van de informatie, welke voor de uitoefening van de functie door de Raad van Commissarissen en de Directie noodzakelijk is, schept de verantwoordelijkheid voor de accountant, de verantwoordelijkheid voor het niet hebben gerapporteerd van datgene, dat voor de betrokkenen belangrijk is. Men ziet hier duidelijk naar voren komen het verschil in verantwoordelijkheid ten opzichte van aandeelhouders en van bedrijfsleiding. Tegenover aandeelhouders behoeft men niet zo uitgebreid in de verslaglegging te zijn als tegenover de bedrijfsleiding, omdat de aandeelhouders geen belang hebben bij een zo gespecificeerde verslaglegging als voor de Raad van Commissarissen en de Directie noodzakelijk is.

Mijnheer de voorzitter, ik wil het hier voorlopig bij laten.

Mr. Chairman, Ladies and Gentlemen, The question raised by Mr. McDonald requires that we should firstly consider the actual object of the audit. Mr. McDonald, basing his thoughts on conditions pertaining to English speaking countries, has, naturally, thought firstly about the report or certificate of the auditor for public use, for, what we call, business intercourse, embracing all those, who are interested in the results of the audit, in the public statement of the auditor. In the Netherlands, in addition to this public function which is extremely important and may even be the most important of the auditor, the auditor also has another function—as regards the daily management of the enterprise and also with regard to the various supervisory officials and the board of directors. Consequently, in the Netherlands, these two functions have to be taken into account. In the way of reporting by the Dutch auditor, this is also clearly apparent.

In addition to what has briefly to be stated to shareholders there is a more detailed report, interesting management and the board of directors.

Mr. McDonald, in his question, did in particular raise the problem of the significance of these different functions and the two forms of reporting. The resulting difference in responsibility is not actually a difference in the nature of responsibility, the difference is not, that for one of the reports the responsibility is different than that for the other report. Obviously the significance of one of the responsibilities cannot be different from that of the other, but the fact is that in reporting to the board of directors one does declare one's approval with a number of data which supplement the 'annual' account of the management. Consequently in the Netherlands we can distinguish a difference in the responsibility involved in the certificate to shareholders and that involved in a report submitted to the board of directors. The report submitted to shareholders only deals with the total picture, with the position as far as assets and liabilities are concerned and with the results as shown by the various accounting documents of the undertaking, whereas the report submitted to the board of directors examines a number of data in greater detail, and these data, in that particular case, then also become the responsibility of the auditor, which is not the case with a report submitted to the shareholders only. The auditor cannot in his report submitted to the board of directors simply accept the specifications, which are handed to him by the employees of the business, he must also examine the correctness of the records, and consequently accept full responsibility.

This, I believe, replies to Mr. McDonald concerning the position of the auditor. But when we go a little further into the examination of the reports by a Dutch auditor to the board of directors, we must take into account another consideration which is: what is the responsibility of the auditor as regards what is not stated in the report? That is a question which, in my opinion, deserves to be examined, because the accountant should not run the danger of having the board of directors asking—'why did you not inform us about this?' It is precisely in this matter of the omission of information, essential for the board of directors and the management, that the responsibility of the auditor lies: the responsibility for having failed to report on something that is of importance to those concerned. And here we see clearly the real difference between responsibility to the shareholders and responsibility to the management. In the report submitted to shareholders it is not necessary to be as detailed as in the case of a report submitted to the management or to the board of directors, because only the latter are interested in a detailed report of this kind. Mr. Chairman, that is all I wish to say at the moment.

MR. L. VAN ESSEN LZN. (Netherlands)

Thank you, Mr. De Lange. Are you satisfied Mr. McDonald?

MR. W. LESLIE MCDONALD (Canada)

I think it may largely be a matter of semantics. Perhaps I have a somewhat different understanding of the precise meaning of the word responsibility than Dr. De Lange. It seems to me that, of course, audit engagements vary in difficulty and in the amount of work that has to be done, but once an accountant has accepted instructions and decided what he should do and has indicated what he is prepared to give his opinion on, I think he is responsible and just as responsible in one form of report as he is in another form of report. I rather think, as I say, it may be semantics, and it may be that Dr. De Lange is only indicating that a report to the directors is a more difficult assignment and involves more work.

MR. L. VAN ESSEN LZN. (Netherlands)

Thank you. Is there someone wanting to make an additional remark on this subject?

MR. CARMAN G. BLOUGH (U.S.A.)

I would like to comment on that very briefly. In the United States it is not customary to submit long reports to management for the very large companies. That information customarily comes from the internal staff. But there are a great many cases among smaller companies where the public accountant is asked to submit a long form report for the use of management. However, it is quite customary also in our country for bankers to request the opportunity to see these long form reports, as a result of which the auditor must recognize that whenever he is submitting a long form report it is likely to find itself in the hands of creditors. Accordingly, it is quite important that he should recognize that there should be no discrepancy between the two and that the short form report should contain all the significant information that is essential to a fair reflection of the condition of the business and the results of its operations. A great deal of the other information which goes into the long form report cannot be audited in detail. However, the auditor has a responsibility for satisfying himself that in so far as it is material in relation to the statements as a whole, not just with respect to the individual schedule but in relation to the statements as a whole, it is not materially misleading, and he is also obliged to indicate to what extent he has, through audit procedures, satisfied himself with respect to the other information.

MR. L. VAN ESSEN LZN. (Netherlands)

Thank you, Mr. Blough. Any other additional remark?

DR. A. TH. DE LANGE (Netherlands)

Mijnheer de voorzitter, dames en heren, Inderdaad gaat het vraagstuk niet om een verschil in aard van de verantwoordelijkheid, zoals ik ook in mijn eerste opmerkingen al heb uiteengezet, maar om hetgeen noodzakelijk medegedeeld moet worden aan de bedrijfsleiding. Dit vraagstuk doet zich voor, als de informatie, welke de bedrijfsleiding van haar eigen organen ontvangt, naar het oordeel van de accountant onvoldoende, onvolledig dus, of onjuist is.

De accountant heeft zorg te dragen – en dat is zijn verantwoordelijkheid – dat al diegenen die kennis nemen, in welke functie dan ook, van de mededelingen van de accountant de juiste indruk van de werkelijkheid krijgen. Voorzover dus de verslaglegging daarin te kort schiet zal het noodzakelijk zijn, dat de accountant aanvullende mededelingen doet. En het is begrijpelijk dat die aanvullende mededelingen ten opzichte van aandeelhouders veel beperkter kunnen zijn dan ten opzichte van de Raad van Commissarissen of de Directie of welk ander orgaan dan ook.

Mr. Chairman, Ladies and Gentlemen, It is not a question here of a difference in the nature of the responsibility, but of a difference between what you have to report to the shareholders and what to the board of directors and the management. This problem arises, when the information which the management or board obtains from its own accounting department is incomplete or even incorrect in the opinion of the accountant. It is the auditor's task—and herein lies his responsibility—to ensure that all those, whatever their function, who see the information he supplies, shall obtain a true picture of the situation. If the report presented by the management should give an insufficiently clear picture, it is necessary for the auditor to give additional information, and it is comprehensible that such additional information can be much briefer for shareholders, than if it is called for by the management or the board of directors or any other body.

MR. L. VAN ESSEN LZN. (Netherlands)

Thank you, Mr. De Lange. And now I should like to pass over to another question and to call on Mr. U. Shein to put this question.

DISCUSSION

MR. U. SHEIN (Burma)

Ladies and Gentlemen, I wish to put the following question: Is the auditor responsible, in principle, for detecting irregularities committed?

This question is one that always has been raised both in professional and other circles and it is in my opinion one of material interest to all engaged in the accountant's profession. The main point which springs to my mind with regard to irregularities is, does it mean fraud or the faults in the staff employed by a concern or does it refer to the trading irregularities?

Then to the second point. I would very much doubt whether any accountant acting as an auditor would be in the position to be categorical as to whether trading irregularities due to the management's fault have in fact taken place, as he cannot be expected to know the day-to-day trends in the business of each and every one of his clients. He can be expected, of course, to point out to his clients any breaches of the laws of the country in which the operations are carried out. For instance, if it is due to the fact that the client may not have been aware of some point of company or other law which an auditor, through his wider experience, is cognizant of. Here, in my opinion, the auditor clearly has a duty to point out the law to his clients.

Coming to misappropriation and fraud by the employees, the problem here is, to my way of thinking, far more difficult. Undoubtedly, a large majority of frauds detected during the course of the audit could be detected by the management, if their own internal organization were better. It would appear, therefore, to me, that one of the essentials in preventing irregularities is to see that the client runs an efficient, up-to-date system of internal check, where such checking is done by other than those directly responsible for the original entries. This whole question seems to me to be one of great interest.

MR. L. VAN ESSEN LZN. (Netherlands)

Thank you, Mr. Shein. I now call upon Dr. Wollert to give the answer.

DR. HEINRICH WOLLERT (Germany)

Meine Damen und Herren, Ich möchte diese Frage mit einem klaren Nein beantworten. Ich halte den Abschlußprüfer nicht für verantwortlich, auch Unterschlagungen und ähnliche kriminelle Akte festzustellen. Um diese, meiner Meinung nach klare Antwort etwas näher zu begründen, scheint es mir wichtig zu sein, auf die Aufgabe des Abschlußprüfers mit einigen Worten einzugehen. Die wirtschaftliche Abschlußprüfung des Wirtschaftsprüfers hat sich darauf zu erstrecken, daß der Abschluß nach den Grundsätzen der Wahrheit, der Klarheit, der Vorsicht sowie nach den hierfür bestehenden gesetzlichen Vorschriften aufgestellt und die dem Abschluß zugrunde liegenden Bücher und Nachweise nach dem Prinzip der Ordnung und der kaufmännischen Sorgfalt geführt sind. Hiervon hat sich der Prüfer mit seiner Fachkunde, der beruflichen Sorgfalt und der durch die Umstände gebotenen Vorsicht, ich möchte sagen, mit einem gewissen beruflichen Störungsgefühl, zu überzeugen. (Um den Übersetzern die Übersetzung des Ausdrucks 'Störungsgefühl' zu erleichtern schlage ich vor: professional sensibility for detecting irregularities). Die Beurteilung der Geschäftsführung auf die Zweckmäßigkeit ihrer Maßnahmen hin gehört im Regelfall nicht zu den Aufgaben des Abschlußprüfers. Wichtig ist, daß das Unternehmen nach einem System arbeitet, durch das die Verbuchung sämtlicher Geschäftsvorfälle gewährleistet und mindestens in sich wechselseitig kontrolliert wird. Für diese Schutzmaßnahmen ist die Leitung des Unternehmens verantwortlich. Diese Schutzmaßnahmen verstehen wir unter dem Sammelbegriff 'interne Kontrolle'. Ich bin der Meinung, daß der Prüfer nur insoweit verpflichtet ist, daß er sich von dem Vorhandensein und der Wirksamkeit dieser internen Kontrolle laufend überzeugt. Hierdurch trägt der Prüfer prävenirend dazu bei, die Möglichkeiten von Unregelmäßigkeiten und Unterschlagungen einzuschränken. Ich bin der Meinung, daß weder Auftraggeber noch die Öffentlichkeit mehr von dem Prüfer erwarten könne, als die Erfüllung dieser Funktion. Es sei denn, daß der Prüfer einen speziellen Auftrag erhalten hat, Unterschlagungen und Irregularitäten zu entdecken. Aber auch in diesem Falle wird der Prüfer klug genug sein, nur einen solchen Auftrag entgegenzunehmen, der in sich so abgegrenzt ist, daß er nicht in das Unwegsame hinein gerät. Ebensowenig, wie das Vorhandensein der Feuerwehr den Ausbruch von Feuer verhindert, oder die Existenz der Polizei in jedem Falle in der Lage ist, jeden Diebstahl zu entdecken, ebensowenig bin ich der Meinung, daß der Prüfer im Rahmen seiner Abschlußprüfung verpflichtet wäre, Unterschlagungen aufzudecken. Wenn er nicht verpflichtet ist, kann er auch nicht dafür verantwortlich gemacht werden. Diesen Tatbestand und diese Lage hat auch das deutsche Institut der Wirtschaftsprüfer in einem Fachgutachten aus dem Jahre 1937 festgestellt.

Die Einstellung des Berufs zu diesem Punkt kommt auch dadurch zum Ausdruck, daß die allgemeinen Geschäftsbedingungen, die wir im allgemeinen in Deutschland zur Grundlage der vertraglichen Beziehungen zwischen unseren Mandanten und uns machen, ausschließen, daß der Prüfer für die Aufdeckung von Unterschlagungen im Rahmen einer normalen Abschlußprüfung verantwortlich ist.

Ladies and Gentlemen, I would like to answer this question with a very definite No. I am of the opinion that the auditor who has to examine the final accounts is not responsible for detecting irregularities and similar criminal offences. In order to explain this definite answer in a little more detail, it seems to me to be important to describe the function of the auditor in a few words. It is the auditor's duty to see that the final balance sheet has been drawn up in accordance with the principles of truth, clarity, care and according to the applicable legal rules and regulations. He must ascertain that all the books and documents relative to the audit have been kept in an orderly manner and in accordance with commercial principles. The auditor has to convince himself of this with his expert knowledge, his professional thoroughness, and the caution which may be indicated by the circumstances, I might even say, with a sort of professional sensibility for detecting irregularities. As a rule, the auditor has not to express an opinion on the competency and soundness of the decisions of the management. It is important that the business should work to a system which guarantees that everything is recorded and that as much as possible is counter checked. It is the management which is responsible for the measures covered by the term 'Internal Control'. In my opinion the auditor is responsible only to the extent that he must convince himself of the existence and efficiency of this 'Internal Control'. The auditor plays a preventive part here, in reducing the possibility of irregularities etc. I am of the opinion that neither the management nor the public can expect more of the auditor than the fulfilment of this function, unless the auditor has received a special engagement to look for irregularities. But in this case too, the auditor will be intelligent enough to accept such an engagement only when it is limited in such a way that he doesn't get led too far afield. I don't think that the existence of a fire service prevents fires from breaking out, nor does the police, in every case, prevent or even discover every theft, and no more, in my opinion, can the auditor in his examination of the balance sheet be put under any obligation to discover irregularities. If he has no such obligation, he cannot be held responsible for it. This position has been recognized by our German Institute in an expert opinion dating back to 1937. The attitude of the profession is also expressed by the fact that the general terms which we in Germany usually conclude as a basis for the contractual relationship between our clients and ourselves, excludes the possibility of the auditor being held responsible for the detection of irregularities in the normal annual audit.

MR. L. VAN ESSEN LZN. (Netherlands)

Thank you, Mr. Wollert. Are you satisfied, Mr. Shein?

MR. U. SHEIN (Burma): Yes.

MR. L. VAN ESSEN LZN. (Netherlands)

Is there someone who wants to make an additional remark about this question? Sir Thomas Robson?

SIR THOMAS B. ROBSON (United Kingdom)

In the U.K. no specific duty is laid upon an auditor of a company to detect irregularities. His duty under our company law is to report to the shareholders by whom, or under authority from whom, he is appointed, whether the balance sheet shows a true and fair view of the state of affairs as at the balance sheet date and the profit and loss account shows a true and fair view of the profit for the year. It follows, however, from this duty that before the auditor can express such an opinion he must do his best to ensure that there have been no irregularities, the effect of which would be so material as to prevent the accounts from showing a true and fair view. For example, a failure to make adequate investigation regarding some of the assets appearing in the balance sheet, might well result in the auditor being held liable for negligence in a court of law if the result of his failure were that the balance sheet showed assets which the company did not possess on the balance sheet date because they had been misappropriated. On the other hand irregularities by subordinate employees, though occasioning loss to the company, may not prevent the account from showing a true and fair view. For example: if cash has been stolen during the financial year the theft will have reduced the company's profit, but the reduced profit shown in the account will still be a true and fair view of the profit for a year.

The detection and prevention of irregularities by subordinate employees, without the knowledge of the directors, are in my opinion primarily matters for the directors. It is for them to see that their accounting system and internal control arrangements are such as to safeguard the company's assets. A U.K. auditor would pay special attention to the systems in operation and would consider possible loopholes for irregularities. He would examine carefully any weakness and investigate thoroughly any circumstances which arouse his suspicion. But his enquiries in this connection are primarily to see if the accounts submitted to him can be relied upon. He cannot pretend to assume the director's responsibility for the proper conduct of the company's affairs and he does not pretend, nor does his report imply, that there are no irregularities which his audit has not brought to light.

As a general statement of the U.K. point of view, both in law and from the professional standpoint, I do not think I can improve upon the word used by one of our judges in our Court of Appeal as long ago as the year in which I myself was born, when he said: 'It is the duty of an auditor to bring to bear on the work he has to perform, that skill, care and caution which a reasonably competent, careful and cautious auditor would use. What is reasonable skill, care and caution must depend on the particular circumstances of each case.'

MR. L. VAN ESSEN LZN. (Netherlands)

Thank you, Sir Thomas. Now Mr. De Lange says he has a few brief comments.

DR. A. TH. DE LANGE (Netherlands)

Mijnheer de voorzitter, dames en heren, Ik zou graag naar aanleiding van de opmerkingen van Dr. Wollert twee korte opmerkingen willen maken, die mij van principiële betekenis lijken. In de eerste plaats heeft Dr. Wollert gewezen op het bestaan van een contractuele verhouding tot de opdrachtgever. Ik zou daar slechts deze opmerking over willen maken, dat naar Nederlandse opvattingen de contractuele verhouding en dus de beperking in de contrôle, die bij die verhouding tot stand is gebracht, geen betekenis kan hebben tegenover derden, die van de contractuele beperkingen niet op de hoogte zijn, daargelaten nog, of de beperking als zodanig doelmatig is. In de tweede plaats heeft Dr. Wollert gewezen op de noodzakelijkheid van een zeker beroepsgevoel om fraude, onregelmatigheden, te ontdekken. Ik geloof, dat wij kunnen stellen: niet elke fraude zal door de accountant worden ontdekt. Men zou verkeerd doen de indruk te wekken, dat de accountantscontrôle het ontdekken van onregelmatigheden garandeert. Noodzakelijk is echter, dat de contrôlewerkzaamheden van de accountant op dit ontdekken gericht moeten zijn. Het gaat dus niet om de vraag of de ene accountant een beter gevoel heeft voor het ontdekken dan de ander, maar of zij beiden de bekwaamheid hebben voor het nemen van die contrôlemaatregelen, die het ontdekken zo goed mogelijk verzekeren.

Mr. Chairman, Ladies and Gentlemen, Pursuing the remarks made by Dr. Wollert, may I add two small comments, which seem to me to concern questions of principle. First of all, Dr. Wollert, in his statement, drew our attention to the existence of a contractual relationship between the auditor and his client. There I would comment that according to Netherlands practice, the contractual relationship and the limitation which is introduced by the contract itself, as to the purpose of the audit, can have no relevance as far as third parties are concerned, who have not been informed of these limitations, ignoring the question whether such limitations are appropriate or not. In the second place, Mr. Wollert also drew our attention to the need for a certain professional feeling for detecting fraud and irregularities. I believe we can say that the auditor will not discover every fraud. I think we should do wrong to create the impression that the accountant's audit guarantees that all irregularities will be found. Nevertheless the accountant's activities should aim at detecting irregularities. It is not therefore a question of whether or not one accountant has more intuition than another in detecting fraud, but of whether both have sufficient skill to apply audit procedures which provide the best possible guarantee of fraud etc., being detected.

MR. L. VAN ESSEN LZN. (Netherlands)

Is there anyone who wants to make remarks? Wollen Sie noch das Wort ergreifen, Dr. Wollert?

DISCUSSION

DR. HEINRICH WOLLERT (Germany)

Ich habe nicht festgestellt, daß noch neue Fragen aufgetaucht sind. Soweit ich Sie verstanden habe, haben Sie im wesentlichen nur das kommentiert, was ich gesagt habe.

I don't think that any new questions have been raised. I think, in the main, you have only commented on what I said.

MR. L. VAN ESSEN LZN. (Netherlands)

Thank you, gentlemen. Then I should like to pass over now to another problem and I call on Mr. Cassel to put the question.

MR. ÖIAR I. CASSEL (Sweden)

Mr. Chairman, Ladies and Gentlemen, In Sweden partnerships are not legally allowed as auditors of limited liability companies. Instead the auditors are appointed individually. I should like to know now what is the auditor's professional responsibility, if he works in partnership with other professional auditors. Would this be a question of individual or of joint responsibility? If joint liability would be the case, how far does this responsibility extend and what measures should be taken by the partnership to enable this responsibility to be borne?

MR. L. VAN ESSEN LZN. (Netherlands)

Thank you, Mr. Cassel. May I call on Mr. Blough to give a reply?

MR. CARMAN G. BLOUGH (U.S.A.)

In the United States it is customary for accountants to form partnerships for the professional practice of accounting. As a matter of fact probably most of the auditing in the U.S. is done by partnerships. Mr. Cassel has asked about the professional responsibility of the individual partners and the selection of partners and their obligations.

I might say first that a professional partnership legally is in the same position as any business partnership. In other words, every partner is unlimitedly liable for any partnership action which is taken by another partner. But apparently it is not the legal obligation Mr. Cassel is interested in as much as the professional obligation. It seems to me that any accountant who enters into partnership with another accountant has a professional obligation or responsibility for determining that that other accountant is competent and qualified in every way to be his partner in the professional practice of accounting. He must satisfy himself that his partners are professionally qualified, that they have integrity, that they have independence, and that he can place complete reliance upon what they do and take full responsibility for their work. The obligation of a partnership in the professional practice of accounting in the U.S. is one of joint and several responsibility. Every partner must stand behind the work that is done by his partners and, therefore, he must satisfy himself that his partners are the kind of men who can do the work that he would like to stand behind. We have a number of partnerships in the U.S. that have more than 100 partners. That necessitates such a thorough organization of procedures and practices, and methods of testing the work of the various offices and of the various partners, that each partner can be completely satisfied that all of his partners are maintaining the professional standards and have the qualities that they should have for him to continue with them in the joint practice of accounting.

It means that they must be fully satisfied that a man has these qualities before he is taken into the partnership, and if they discover that by chance one has been received into the partnership who is not so qualified, they must take steps to see that he is removed from the partnership.

Now we have another kind of partnership project that occurs occasionally, which is in the nature of a joint undertaking by two or more firms. Sometimes an undertaking is so large that one firm—not one of the larger firms, but one of the smaller firms or say an individual practitioner—cannot handle the engagement with his own organization. He may then call in some other accountants or partnership of accountants to work with him jointly. Under these circumstances he has the same responsibility, in my opinion, for satisfying himself as to the work which is done by those with whom he associates himself in that way that he would have if he entered into a complete partnership. Usually under these circumstances one of the firms will take the responsibility and will use the other as an assistant. But if they sign separately, in other words, if they act jointly and each of the accountants or each of the firms signs the report, each is responsible fully for the work of the other and therefore each has a responsibility to satisfy himself or itself, if it is a partnership, that the other party or parties to the project are qualified, that they are independent, that they have integrity and that they have done a professional job on that particular engagement.

MR. L. VAN ESSEN LZN. (Netherlands)

Thank you, Mr. Blough. And in addition to this question there is another question and I now call upon Mr. Paul Busuttil to put this question.

MR. PAUL BUSUTTIL (Malta)

My question is in connection with the responsibility of the auditor when certifying the annual account of holding companies. This type of enterprise is becoming increasingly popular. We in Malta are as yet not familiar with holding companies. What we know of the ramifications of holding companies is from accountancy text books, generally U.K. text books. Owing to modern warfare we in Malta are now unable to rely for our living on the strategic value of our island country so at the moment our Government has embarked on a programme to change the economic structure of the Island from strategic to industrial. It would, therefore, be interesting to know for us accountants what is the statutory position of the auditor as regards his responsibility, when during his audit he has to rely on the annual accounts of one or more subsidiaries whose accounts have been audited abroad. May I put the question in a skeleton form. What responsibility has the auditor who certifies the financial statements of a parent company for the correctness of particulars included in such statements relating to a subsidiary company whose annual accounts have been certified by an auditor whose practice is established abroad?

MR. L. VAN ESSEN LZN. (Netherlands)

Thank you, Mr. Busuttil. I think it would be best to call again on Mr. Blough to answer this question too.

MR. CARMAN G. BLOUGH (U.S.A.)

Did I understand you to say the statutory obligation or did you mean the professional obligations? I hesitate to answer from the standpoint of a statutory obligation because there is no statutory obligation so far the practice in the U.S. is concerned. The only place where the law comes into the matter there is in connection with the filing of statements with our Securities and Exchange Commission, where companies are seeking to sell their securities in Interstate commerce or through the mail or where they have their securities listed on one of our national securities exchanges. Any such company has to file statements with the Securities and Exchange Commission.

In those circumstances, the commission has laid down some rules with respect to the obligations of the certifying accountant which are as close to the statutory as I could place it in our country. Those rules in general provide for the inclusion or the exclusion of subsidiaries in consolidation in such a way as to most fairly present the results of the enterprise and its condition as a whole, and where subsidiaries are not included in consolidation, if they are material, their statements must be submitted separately. Now, if the statements are submitted separately, then the auditor's certificate, covering those statements, is required to be filed regardless of whether it is that of a foreign accountant or of a U.S. accountant. However, in most instances, and we have a great number of these holding companies in our country, practically all of the subsidiaries, a great many of them at least, are included in consolidation. There are some rules which specify that certain types of companies, in certain countries where exchange restriction etc. exist, should not be included in consolidation. But getting down to the basic question, the responsibility of the auditor, when he does include in his consolidation the statements of subsidiaries that have been certified to by other accountants, legally as far as this rule of the S.E.C. is concerned, either he must take full responsibility for the statements, or if he relies and states that he does rely on the statements of other accountants, then the certificate of those other accountants must be filed. So much for the statutory phase of it. I'd like to deal a little bit with the professional aspects of it as I see them. It seems to me that any accountant who includes in a consolidation, to which he certifies, the statements of subsidiaries that are certified to by other accountants, has a professional responsibility to satisfy himself that that work was done in a qualified manner, and that the information contained in those statements was audited in such a manner that he himself can take the responsibility for it. That involves not necessarily any supervision over the audit but it certainly involves consultation with respect to the way in which the audit of the subsidiary is to be carried out and a review and analysis of the statements with the representatives of the subsidiary's auditors, or whatever else is necessary to satisfy himself that those statements are of such a nature that they meet the standards which he himself or which his firm would be willing to take responsibility for.

Very often relationships are established between accountants in the U.S. and accountants in other countries, sometimes accountants in the U.S. do not even audit all the subsidiaries in the U.S. Other accountants in the U.S. may audit a subsidiary or some subsidiaries which are included in the consolidation. Regardless of whether it is a foreign accountant or a U.S. accountant, the auditor who is submitting the report on the consolidation, in my opinion, has a professional obligation to satisfy himself that the audit was carried out on a professional basis equivalent to what he himself considers appropriate. A good many of the firms in the U.S. have relationships with firms of auditors both in the U.S. and in other nations throughout the world, where their past experiences are such that, through exchanges of ideas, through reviews of procedures, through possibly the exchange of personnel from time to time, there is built up a full understanding between the two auditors or auditing firms as to what is expected on the part of one by the other.

In those circumstances, long experience may be such that the certifying auditor can accept the other auditor's report on a subsidiary without any further consideration, knowing from past experience and past relationships that the job has been done in such a way as to meet his standards. On the other hand, if it is a new connection or if it is one in which he is not so sure, then he has an obligation, through reviewing procedures, reviewing the papers, possibly even specifying in advance the procedures which he wishes to have carried out, to satisfy himself that that information is such that he can take the responsibility for it, when he includes it in the consolidation and signs the certificate covering the consolidation.

MR. L. VAN ESSEN LZN. (Netherlands)

Thank you, Mr. Blough. Now, owing to the time I should like to pass over to another question and I should like to ask Mr. McDonald to put this question.

MR. W. LESLIE MCDONALD (Canada)

Mr. Cassel indicates in the paper he has prepared that in Sweden where the issued or registered capital exceeds a certain amount, the Law requires that there be at least 2 auditors. The question which I have been asked to put along these lines is: is the appointment, by enterprises above a certain size, of more than one auditor desirable? If there are no objections to this, what is the position as regards the professional responsibility of each auditor appointed? Is each entirely responsible for the whole or each for a part of the whole? In the latter case, how is the responsibility of each to be determinated? Also, may the auditors to be appointed be partners in the same firm?

MR. L. VAN ESSEN LZN. (Netherlands)

Thank you, Mr. McDonald. And now I call upon Mr. Cassel to give us the answer.

MR. ÖIAR I. CASSEL (Sweden)

Mr. Chairman, Ladies and Gentlemen, I may say that in some cases it may be desirable to have more than one auditor. For instance, if the majority of shares in a limited liability company are held by two or three groups of shareholders. In such cases we very often have two or more professional auditors appointed. In other cases it may be desirable to have, beside the professional auditor, also a layman who is well acquainted with the company's line of business.

The reason for this Swedish point of view seems to be the legal requirement in Sweden that the auditors have to consider and comment upon the management's administration of the company's affairs in general. Now, if there is more than one auditor, with us each is considered entirely responsible for the whole, both legally and professionally. I may say, however, that part of the detail work of the audit, of course, may be divided between the auditors, but still each auditor is at least legally responsible for the whole. In Sweden there is no rule against two auditors in the same company being partners of the same audit firm, but I may say that it is not usual. I think it may be an open question whether this form of arrangement serves a useful purpose or not.

MR. L. VAN ESSEN LZN. (Netherlands)

Thank you, Mr. Cassel. Are there any comments? No?

Ladies and Gentlemen, as I said already, time is going on and I must devote some minutes to the discussion out of the audience. As Mr. Foye already said in his opening speech, there are some gentlemen in this audience who have been so kind as to send in very interesting questions concerning the subjects we are discussing this morning. We are very thankful for receiving these comments and these questions. The gentlemen I have in mind are:

Mr. J. S. Seidman of New York, Monsieur Charles Corbin, Alger, Mr. W. L. Barrows of Birmingham, Monsieur Robert Coste, Clermont-Ferrand and Mr. C. Bakker of Amsterdam. May I ask these gentlemen to stand for a moment.

Thank you gentlemen. Owing to lack of time, it will be totally impossible to handle the comments in question in full. But some of them I should like to put. I do not intend, also owing to this lack of time, to ask these gentlemen to come to the platform, but I will read the questions in a somewhat abbreviated form.

The first question I should like to read is the following:

In the paper by Mr. Wollert it is set forth that in Germany there are minimum fees for carrying out compulsory audits under German Company Law. I wonder on what factors the fee schedule is based. How does it allow for variations to take into consideration size, nature of business, condition of records, availability of underlying vouchers, special transactions and all of the other things that defy uniformity of fee. I also wonder whether in actual practice the minimum fees prescribed tend to become the maximum fees. I call on Dr. Wollert to give the answer.

DR. HEINRICH WOLLERT (Germany)

Ladies and Gentlemen, I would like to answer this question in English. I hope you will understand me well.

Our fee system is a minimum fee system and consists, in general, of two parts. One part is the per diem rate, and the other part is a flat rate fee, depending on the balance sheet sum, of which it is a proportion. So the more time you need for your work the more you have to charge according to per diem rate; the bigger the balance sheet sum, the higher the flat rate, although, this flat rate is degressive. That means a small balance sheet sum gives you the chance to charge a relatively higher flat rate than does a big balance sheet sum. I mentioned that the fee system is a minimum fee and you were asking me whether there is any danger of the minimum fee becoming a maximum fee. The reason why we have these minimum fees in Germany is to avoid competition by money, by fees, by some other—I may not say colleagues.

Also the State and the Court both of which are very keen on paying only small fees, have learned that quality costs more, so, the better the quality, the higher the fee; with this I would not like to say that a high fee is the best proof of quality. So, on the average, there is no danger of the minimum fee being used also as a maximum fee.

We usually charged higher than the minimum fee, because we believe we do the best work; for this we need more money and more fees.

MR. L. VAN ESSEN LZN. (Netherlands)

Thank you, Dr. Wollert.

Ladies and Gentlemen, Another question is this one: In countries where the profession is regulated by law, is it the custom in most of them for the right to practise to depend on the extent of the professional experience which the individual has obtained, or on the examinations which the individual has passed, not necessarily after obtaining experience in practice. I might call on Sir Thomas to answer this question.

SIR THOMAS B. ROBSON (United Kingdom)

Mr. Chairman, I think that question has really been answered in the papers which are summarized in my Rapporteur's Summary. The question is not capable of a simple answer which covers the whole of the different conditions in the countries here represented, for the conditions in these countries and the measures of training differ very greatly from one country to another. Some countries and some professional bodies in other countries insist on both practical training and experience in addition to the passing of examinations. Others recognize university examinations without previous experience. Others again permit or propose to permit recognition of such examinations after they have been followed by practical experience for a period of years. Some require the practical experience to be in work for a public accountant; others recognize practical experience gained in industry or in Government service. All one can say, I think, is this: that in every progressive body the methods of training and qualification are under constant review. But the number of countries and institutions represented in this congress and the great variety of their circumstances indicate how wide are the possibilities of differences in point of view. These differences are found in practice in very considerable degree. I do not think myself that the question could be answered in a way which would have any hope of finding general acceptance in the Congress.

MR. L. VAN ESSEN LZN. (Netherlands)

Thank you, Sir Thomas. Now another question which is put before me is this one:

Dr. Wollert says in his paper that as a rule the number of assistants in Germany is limited to 5 assistants to one accountant. Is this practical? There can be engagements that need more than 5 assistants to one accountant and is it not necessary that the number of assistants per accountant differs with the nature of the audit? In some cases 5 can be even too many.

I call on Mr. Wollert to answer this.

DR. HEINRICH WOLLERT (Germany)

First, it would seem that a misunderstanding has arisen out of my paper. It is not the case that we have the rule of one Wirtschaftsprüfer and five assistants on each job. To clarify, I wish to say that the word 'assistants' does not mean youngsters, they may be much older than the qualified man. This ratio of 1 : 5 is to be applied to the staff of the accounting firm as a whole. The reason is to be seen in the endeavour of our profession to avoid the unethical multiplication of the work of a qualified man through the use of a multitude of unqualified persons. You may ask me why exactly 1 : 5? Well, I must say that we have had this ratio in our professional law for the past 25 years; it has been arrived at through experience, and I must say it has worked well. We have the feeling that the proportion 1 : 5 is just big enough to have some help and just small enough to enable us to supervise the work of the assistants, supervised by a qualified person, by the Wirtschaftsprüfer.

MR. L. VAN ESSEN LZN. (Netherlands)

Thank you, Mr. Wollert.

Ladies and Gentlemen, I am now going to try to summarize this morning's discussions.

For your guidance: I am going to speak in Dutch.

Dames en Heren, Nu wij dan gekomen zijn aan het slot van de discussies van deze ochtend, wil ik proberen in het kort het besprokene samen te vatten. En als ik dit dan tracht te overzien, dan kom ik tot deze slotsom, dat onze besprekingen voornamelijk betrekking hebben gehad op de verantwoordelijkheid van de accountant; daarop heeft zich ons debat voor het grootste gedeelte geconcentreerd. Hoe komt dat? Is dat bij andere beroepen ook zo, dat men steeds spreekt over zijn verantwoordelijkheid? Ik doe een greep. Een bus-chauffeur – wat is zijn taak? Hij moet in ontvangst nemen de vervoerprijs, hij moet erop letten, dat er geen passagiers in de bus zitten die niet hebben betaald, hij moet voorzichtig zijn bij het sluiten en openen van de deuren, anders veroorzaakt hij ongelukken. Heeft die man verantwoordelijkheid? Natuurlijk, vanzelfsprekend. En daarom spreekt hij daar niet over. Een ander beroep – een bakker – wat doet die? Een bakker koopt meel en andere ingrediënten, hij bakt daarvan brood. Maar als dat brood niet voldoet aan de kwaliteitseisen, als dat brood te weinig vaste stof bevat of te licht van gewicht is, dan wordt hij op z'n vingers getikt door de keuringsdienst voor waren. Draagt die bakker verantwoordelijkheid? Natuurlijk, vanzelfsprekend, en daarom spreekt hij daar niet over. Als ik een ander beroep noem – het beroep van de arts. Het beroep van de arts eist een grondiger opleiding dan dat van de bus-chauffeur en dan dat van de bakker. Draagt de dokter verantwoordelijkheid? Natuurlijk, een zware verantwoordelijkheid, want van zijn adviezen, van zijn voorschriften kan afhangen het leven van zijn patiënt. De dokter moet er dus voor zorgen, dat die adviezen, dat de voorschriften die hij geeft worden gegeven met de grootst mogelijke zorgvuldigheid en nauwgezetheid, met inachtneming van alle omstandigheden, die op dat advies, op dat voorschrift van invloed kunnen zijn en gebaseerd op een grondige kennis van ziekteverschijnselen en van geneesmiddelen. Die dokter draagt dus verantwoordelijkheid en toch, over de verantwoordelijkheid van de arts wordt, voor zover mij bekend, niet zo vaak meer gedebatteerd. Maar als hij nalatig is of blijk geeft van grove onkunde, dan wordt hij bestraft.

Hoe komt het nu, dat onder de accountants zo vaak gesproken wordt over hun verantwoordelijkheid? Ik geloof dat ik daarvoor verschillende oorzaken kan aanwijzen; ik zal niet volledig kunnen zijn, maar enkele wil ik er toch noemen.

De eerste dan: de eerste oorzaak van dat voortdurend spreken over verantwoordelijkheid zie ik in de jeugd van het beroep. Het accountantsberoep is jong, jonger dan de meeste beroepen waarvoor een opleiding nodig is zoals die van de accountants. U weet het, de Engelse accountants kregen een Royal Charter in 1880. Het accountantsberoep heeft zich in de V.S., naar wij hebben kunnen lezen in de inleiding van Mr. Blough, eerst ontwikkeld in de laatste 30 jaren tot op de hoogte waarop het nu staat. In Duitsland heeft de grote opbloei van het Wirtschaftsprüfer-Beruf eerst plaatsgevonden – Dr. Wollert heeft het gezegd in zijn inleiding – na de tweede wereldoorlog. En in Nederland? Het Nederlands Instituut van Accountants is opgericht in 1895, maar de grote opbloei van het beroep is ook pas vele jaren later gekomen. En dus is het begrijpelijk, dat de beoefenaars van een zo jong beroep als het accountantsberoep is nog steeds bezig zijn om de omvang, om de grenzen van hun verantwoordelijkheid af te tasten.

Vervolgens zou ik willen noemen: de accountant is in zijn functie van controleur geroepen om zijn deskundig, zijn onafhankelijk oordeel te geven over de verantwoording die anderen afleggen van hun bestuur. Hij verklaart door zijn handtekening of door zijn korte of lange verklaring, of die verantwoording al dan niet geeft een betrouwbaar beeld, een juist beeld van de resultaten van het bestuur. En mede op grond van dat onafhankelijke, van dat deskundige oordeel krijgen de bestuurders décharge. Ook daarom is het wel duidelijk, dat de vraag, hoe ver de accountantsverantwoordelijkheid reikt, een belangrijke vraag is.

En dan ten slotte: behalve de opdrachtgever nemen ook anderen kennis van het oordeel dat de accountant geeft over de al of niet juistheid van een verantwoording. Verzekerden, crediteuren e.d. en die crediteuren en die verzekerden hebben met die accountant geen ander contact, dan dat zij kennis nemen van zijn oordeel, neergelegd in zijn handtekening, in zijn verklaring. En ook tegenover hen draagt de accountant verantwoordelijkheid en het is van belang vast te stellen, hoe ver die verantwoordelijkheid reikt.

En dus – wij hebben vanmorgen voornamelijk gesproken over de verantwoordelijkheid, zóveel dat bij iemand de vraag zou kunnen opkomen: is de titel waaronder onze besprekingen van vanmorgen zijn gehouden, wel juist? Had die titel niet beter kunnen luiden: de verantwoordelijkheid van de accountant, in plaats van – zoals nu – grondslagen voor het accountantsberoep? En ik meen toch die vraag ontkennend te moeten beantwoorden, want naar mijn mening vormt het besef van onze verantwoordelijkheid, het gevoel voor onze verantwoordelijkheid, de grondslag voor onze beroepsuitoefening.

Er is over die verantwoordelijkheid, over de verschillende aspecten van die verantwoordelijkheid, vanmorgen gesproken. Er zijn vragen aan de orde geweest, die betrekking hebben op de verhouding tussen de verklaring die de accountant geeft bij de jaarrekening en het uitvoerige rapport dat hij uitbrengt aan de directie en commissarissen. Er is gesproken over de vraag, of de accountant verantwoordelijkheid draagt en hoever die verantwoordelijkheid strekt voor het ontdekken van onregelmatigheden. Er is gesproken over de verantwoordelijkheid van de accountants die samenwerken in maatschapsverband, over de verantwoordelijkheid die de accountant van een moedermaatschappij heeft voor de jaarstukken van de dochtermaatschappij, die door een andere accountant, meestal in het buitenland, zijn geverifieerd. Alles, vragen met betrekking tot de verantwoordelijkheid.

En als ik mij nu afvraag, of uit die botsing van meningen de waarheid naar voren is gekomen, de waarheid in dien zin, dat zij zou inhouden een communis opinio, een gemeenschappelijke mening die wij allen delen, dan zeg ik 'neen', daarvoor liggen de meningen in sommige opzichten nog te ver uit elkaar. Maar het is uitermate belangrijk, en daarvoor hebben wij vanmorgen de gelegenheid gehad, dat wij althans hebben kunnen kennis nemen van elkaars meningen. Het kennen van elkaars meningen is het eerst nodige ten einde te komen tot een eenparigheid van mening. En dus is naar mijn mening deze ochtend van groot nut geweest.

En nu ben ik dan, dames en heren, gekomen tot het eind van mijn samenvatting die, met het oog op de tijd, kort heeft moeten zijn, en ik zou willen eindigen met een enkele zin uit het prae-advies van Sir Thomas Robson waar hij zegt in zijn conclusie:

> 'The whole aim of the profession is to provide skilled services for the assistance and protection of business activities wherever they are carried on. The overriding principle which governs our profession is that the individual accountant should be properly qualified by suitable training, experience and examination and by his inherent honesty and independence of mind to carry out the important duties which rest upon him. It is these qualities and not his race, nationality or place of residence which determine his suitability for his task'.

Ik meen, dat deze woorden ons allen uit het hart gegrepen zijn. Hiermee wil ik dan mijn korte samenvatting besluiten.

And now I want to call upon Mr. Foye to resume the presidency of this meeting.

Ladies and Gentlemen, We have now come to the end of this morning's discussion and I will attempt to summarize briefly what has been said. Trying to survey what was discussed here this morning, I have come to the conclusion that our discussion has dealt mainly with the problem of the accountant's responsibility. The greater part of our debate has, indeed, concentrated on that particular point. Why? Is that also the case with other professions? Is the question constantly: the responsibility of the member of the profession? Let us take a bus-driver. What is his task? He must take the fares, he must see that there are no passengers within his bus that haven't paid fares, he must see that there are no accidents when passengers board the bus or leave the bus. Does this man have responsibility? Of course he has, that speaks for itself. And therefore: he does not speak about it. Let us take another job—a baker. A baker buys flour and he bakes bread, but when that bread does not meet the legal requirements of quality, if the loaf has not got the required weight, he will, undoubtedly, be punished by the food inspection. He is responsible for the quality and the weight of the loaf he produces. That goes without saying. And therefore: his responsibility is not discussed. May I now take another profession—a doctor. A medical doctor must have a better background and training than the bus-conductor or the baker. Does the doctor have responsibility? Of course he has, a very heavy responsibility, because it is on his prescription, on his advice that the life of the patient may depend. Consequently, the doctor must see that his prescription and advice is given with the greatest possible competence and care. He must take into account all the circumstances bearing upon this advice or prescription, and he must base himself on a fundamental and detailed knowledge of any symptoms of illnesses and of any possibilities of cure. As far as I know, however, the responsibility of the doctor is not a question that is very frequently discussed nowadays. Though he may indeed be punishable, if he acts with negligence.

Why then, if that is the general situation, is there so much discussion about the responsibility of the accountant? I believe I may be able to put forward here some of the reasons; I could not hope to be complete, but some of the reasons I will mention. Firstly, the reason why we constantly speak about our responsibility lies, I believe, in the very youth of our profession. We are not a very old profession. As you know the English accountants received their Royal Charter in 1880. The profession of accountants in the U.S., as we read in Mr. Blough's report, has only developed to its present standards during the last 30 years. In Germany the development of public accountancy as a profession does, in fact, date from after the Second World-War. In the Netherlands the Institute was founded in 1895, but the great development of our profession didn't come until many years later. And it is consequently quite comprehensible that those who practise such a young profession as the public accountant's, must still constantly be concerned with defining their responsibilities.

As another cause I might state the following. In his function as an auditor, the accountant is called upon to give his expert and independent opinion on the management, as exercised by others. He certifies whether the statements give a fair and correct view of the Company's affairs and results. And it is partly on the basis of this independent and expert judgement, that the management is discharged. That is why the question of the accountant's responsibility is of tremendous importance.

Finally, one other reason: it is not only the clients, but others, too, who acquaint themselves with the auditor's report, creditors and others, and they have no other contact with the auditor except through his report, except through his certificate. And the accountant therefore also has a responsibility to third persons, and it is, of course, important to define the extent of that responsibility.

And consequently this morning we have spoken mainly about responsibility. To such an extent that one might wonder whether the title of this morning's meeting had been well chosen. Should we not have entitled our meeting this morning, 'The Accountant's Responsibility' rather than 'Principles for the Accountant's Profession'. I do not believe that that is the case. I would reply in the negative. For in my opinion, the conception of our responsibility and our feeling of responsibility are, in fact, the basic principles for our profession.

We have gone into some detail about the various aspects of this responsibility this morning, questions have been raised dealing with the relationship between the published certificate and the more detailed report which the auditor submits to the board of directors and the management. The question has also been asked, as to what extent the auditor can be held responsible for discovering irregularities. The question has been raised concerning the responsibilities of accountants working in partnership; concerning the responsibility of an accountant working for a parent company, also for reports submitted by affiliated companies, audited abroad. All these questions are of considerable importance for us.

And when I consider these matters and try to see whether the truth, in the sense of a common opinion, has indeed evolved from the divergent opinions and discussions during this meeting, I would say No, because there has been too great a difference of opinion on certain points. We could not arrive at absolute truth. But what is of considerable importance is that we have been able to become acquainted here, this morning, with each other's opinions, and that is essential in order to arrive in future at a common opinion—and that, indeed, is the great usefulness of our discussion this morning.

I have to come to a conclusion, Ladies and Gentlemen. I've had to be very brief in this summary, in view of the short time at our disposal, but I would like to end up by quoting a few words of Sir Thomas Robson's, who says:

'The whole aim of the profession is to provide skilled services for the assistance and protection of business activities wherever they are carried on. The overriding principle which governs our profession is that the individual accountant should be properly qualified by suitable training, experience and examination and by his inherent honesty and independence of mind to carry out the important duties which rest upon him. It is these qualities and not his race, nationality or place of residence which determine his suitability for his task'. And I believe that we all heartily agree with these words. This concludes my short summary, and I will now call upon Mr. Foye to resume the presidency of this meeting.

CHAIRMAN:

The papers and the discussions have emphasized the international character of our profession; they have emphasized the common basis of integrity and independence, and I think the similarities of the principles, even though there are variations in their application, and in this give and take of the discussion I think we have all been informed and stimulated to the extent, I hope, that you will either read or reread the papers in the light of the discussion. I believe that we have this morning made a significant contribution to a broader and deeper understanding of the principles of accounting on which our profession is based. I shall ask vice-chairman Mody to come to the rostrum and to express the appreciation not only of ourselves but of the audience to the panel for their service.

Vice-chairman, MR. N. R. MODY (India)

Mr. Chairman, Ladies and Gentlemen, It is with great pleasure that I rise to thank the rapporteur and the panel for their work this morning. At an international congress of this description, the purpose of the panel is to bring out the salient points in the papers and stimulate interest in the subject. I have no doubt you will agree with me that this morning's panel has succeeded in performing both these functions. But for their work, the excellent material contained in the papers would not have been emphasized for our benefit. Indeed, Sir Thomas has himself pointed out, rather modestly I should say, in his brilliant and thought-provoking paper, that 'it is my sincere hope that the limitations of my own paper will induce others to raise in the discussion points which need to be brought into prominence in order that the subject of principles for the profession may be dealt with worthily by the congress'.

The panel has certainly succeeded in doing this and its leader, Mr. Van Essen has very efficiently guided the panel debate into its proper perspective. Therefore, Ladies and Gentlemen, I extend the grateful thanks of this house to the rapporteur and the members of the panel for the able manner in which they have done full justice to the task allotted to them by the Congress Committee.

CHAIRMAN:

Now I shall ask our other vice-chairman, Dr. Allet, to close the session.
Dr. Allet will speak in German.

Vice–chairman, DR. ERNST ALLET (Austria)

Verehrte Damen und Herren, sehr geehrter Herr Präsident! Durch die fortschreitende Industrialisierung einerseits und die dadurch bedingte Zusammenballung von Fremdkapital andererseits hat der Wirtschaftprüferberuf in den letzten Jahrzehnten einen eminenten Aufschwung empfangen, wie kaum ein anderer Beruf. Die Entwicklung der berufsständischen Grundlagen war daher auch in dieser Zeit sehr bewegt, ganz besonders auch in Österreich, in Deutschland und im übrigen Europa. In den einen Ländern stärker, in den anderen Ländern wieder etwas schwächer.

Jedenfalls ist diese Entwicklung aber noch nicht als abgeschlossen zu betrachten. Es war daher heute für alle anwesenden Damen und Herren sehr interessant, eine international vergleichende Betrachtung zu hören und Anregungen zu erhalten. Ich darf jetzt ganz besonders dem Herrn Präsidenten dieser Arbeitssitzung, Mr. Foye, für seine ausgezeichnete Leitung der Sitzung und Vorbereitung der Sitzung und für seine Mühewaltung danken und schließe hiermit diese Arbeitssitzung.

Ladies and Gentlemen, Mr. Chairman, As a result of progressive industrialization on the one hand, and the concentration of foreign capital on the other, the profession of auditor has undergone a development in recent decades the like of which scarcely any other profession has seen. There have accordingly been lively developments too as regards the principles of the profession, particularly in Austria, Germany and other European countries, more marked in some than in others. This trend cannot be considered as having come to an end as yet, and therefore it was very interesting for the ladies and gentlemen present to be able to listen to-day to an international comparative study of the question and to receive suggestions. Now I must thank the chairman of this business session, Mr. Foye, for his excellent management and preparation of the session and for all the efforts he has made. And herewith I declare this session closed.

BUDGETING AND THE CORRESPONDING MODERNIZATION OF ACCOUNTING

Afternoon session: Tuesday, 10th September 1957

Papers by: Page

Chairman:	H. Hjernø Jeppesen, Denmark
Vice-Chairmen:	P. J. Tinoco, Venezuela Dr. Jakob Viel, Switzerland Prof. K. Kurosawa, Japan
Panel members:	
Discussion leader:	Prof. Dr. Abram Mey* Nederlands Instituut van Accountants
Rapporteur and author of a paper:	WP Herbert Rätsch *Institut der Wirtschaftsprüfer in Deutschland e.V.*
Authors of papers:	S. Prakash Chopra, B.A., B. Com., A.C.A., F.C.A. (India) *The Institute of Chartered Accountants of India*
	Joseph Pelej, C.P.A. *American Institute of Certified Public Accountants*
	A. F. Tempelaar *Nederlands Instituut van Accountants*
	J. P. Wilson, F.C.W.A., A.C.I.S. *Institute of Cost and Works Accountants, U.K.*
Other members of the panel:	R. van Iper *Nationaal College der Accountants van België*
	J. R. Leitch, C.A. Institute of Chartered Accountants of Scotland
	Paul Loeb* La Société des Experts-Comptables Français
	Carl Henrik Witt *Föreningen Auktoriserade Revisorer, Sweden*

* Prof. Mey acted as Mr. Loeb's substitute in view of the latter's indisposition

REFERAT

von

WIRTSCHAFTSPRÜFER HERBERT RÄTSCH

Institut der Wirtschaftsprüfer in Deutschland e.V.

I. Bessere Betriebsführung durch Planung und Kontrolle

Analog zur internationalen Entwicklung gewinnen neuerdings auch in Deutschland die Methoden der Planung und Kontrolle zunehmend an Bedeutung. Die Gründe hierfür sind mannigfach: hohe Besteuerung; angespannte Lage des Kapitalmarktes; scharfe binnen- und außenwirtschaftliche Konkurrenz; Verkürzung der Arbeitszeit; steigende Arbeits- und Stoffkosten; zunehmende Sättigung der Märkte und damit verbundene hohe Elastizität der Nachfrage; neue technische Entwicklungen, durch die die Produktionsverfahren revolutioniert werden und die eine rasche Anpassung und erhebliche Investitionen verlangen. Alle diese Einflüsse zwingen die Betriebe, ihre Leistung in einem Ausmaß zu steigern, wie es mit unsystematischen, punktuell ansetzenden Maßnahmen nicht erreicht werden kann. Es hat sich vielmehr weitgehend die Einsicht durchgesetzt, daß ein systematisches geistiges Durchdringen aller Betriebsfunktionen und ihres organischen Zusammenhanges unerläßlich ist, wenn man den Betrieb sicher steuern will.

Hierzu gehört zunächst eine ständige Kontrolle der erzielten Leistung; darüber hinaus müssen die Grundsätze der Geschäftspolitik ständig unter zukunftsbezogenem Aspekt neu durchdacht werden, weil man sich nicht darauf verlassen kann, daß die in der Vergangenheit bewährten Methoden auch in Zukunft zum Ziel führen werden. Nur dieses Wechselspiel von *Kontrolle* der vollbrachten Leistung und *Planung* der zukünftigen Leistungsziele ermöglicht eine den Betriebs- und Marktbedingungen organisch angepaßte Geschäftsführung und eine nachhaltige Steigerung der Ertragskraft des Betriebes.

Die Durchführung von Kontrolle und Planung ist Aufgabe des Rechnungswesens, das sich dabei zwar in weitem Umfang der Hilfe der Einkaufs-, Produktions- und Verkaufsabteilungen bedient, das aber allein verantwortlich ist für die systematische Durchführung der Planungs- und Kontrollarbeit und für die sinnvolle Aufbereitung des zusammengetragenen Zahlenmaterials. In seiner traditionellen Form ist das Rechnungswesen jedoch nicht geeignet, diese neuen

Aufgaben zu bewältigen. Bilanzen und Gewinn- und Verlustrechnungen liegen in der Regel erst vor, wenn Fehler nicht mehr reparabel und vorhandene Chancen verpaßt sind; außerdem kann das traditionelle Rechnungswesen keine Auskunft über die Höhe des erzielten Leistungsgrades geben, weil ihm der Maßstab fehlt, mit dem Kosten und Leistungen beurteilt und die Ursachen von Erfolgsveränderungen exakt berechnet werden können. Organisation und Arbeitsweise des Rechnungswesens müssen daher den neuen betriebspolitischen Zielsetzungen angepaßt werden. Dies bedeutet dreierlei:

1. Die Abrechnungsunterlagen müssen *analytisch* bearbeitet werden. Dabei kommt es darauf an, Maßstäbe für Kosten und Leistungen zu entwickeln und zu zeigen, wie sich Kosten und Leistungen bei Veränderungen der Betriebs- und Marktbedingungen verhalten.
2. Die Zahlen der Vergangenheit müssen *kurzfristig* bereitgestellt werden, um noch rechtzeitig bei Fehlentwicklungen eingreifen zu können.
3. Es müssen *Planungen* für die zukünftigen Geschäftsperioden angestellt werden, um Chancen und Risiken richtig beurteilen und behandeln zu können.

II. Die Praxis der Planung und Kontrolle in Deutschland

1. *Die Bildung von Standards*

Beginn und Voraussetzung jeder Kontroll- und Planungsarbeit ist die Entwicklung von Standards. Als Standard bezeichnen wir jede einen betrieblichen Tatbestand kennzeichnende Zahl mit Maßstabcharakter. Es gibt Mengen-, Zeit-, Leistungs-, Kosten-, Erlös- und Gewinnstandards. Die Standards werden entsprechend dem Entwicklungsstand des Rechnungswesens im jeweiligen Betrieb nach mehr oder weniger verfeinerten Methoden gebildet. Grundsätzlich kann man drei Verfahren unterscheiden:

a. Die Standards werden als *Durchschnittswerte* aus den Abrechnungsunterlagen der Vergangenheit entwickelt. Derartige Erfahrungswerte eignen sich vor allem für Kostenvorausschätzungen, da die Wahrscheinlichkeit groß ist, daß der Durchschnitt der Vergangenheit auch in Zukunft realisiert werden kann. Für Zwecke der Leistungsmessung sind solche Standards aber unbrauchbar, weil in den Durchschnittswerten der Vergangenheit auch alle Unwirtschaftlichkeiten enthalten sind.

b. In Konzernunternehmen werden zuweilen *Betriebsvergleichswerte* der Standardisierung zugrunde gelegt, indem man die Betriebsergebnisse eines *guten* Konzernbetriebes zum Standard erklärt. Ein solcher Standard ist zwar auch nur ein Erfahrungswert; er hat aber im Vergleich zum Durchschnittsstandard nach Methode *a.* den Vorteil, dass er eine bestimmte Leistungshöhe repräsentiert.

c. Das beste und bei uns heute allgemein angestrebte Verfahren besteht darin, die Standards mit wissenschaftlichen Methoden *analytisch* zu ermitteln. Da analytisch ermittelte Standards einen vollkommenen Leistungsmaßstab darstellen, nennt man sie auch *Richt-* bzw. *Planwerte* (z.B. Plankosten). Die wichtigste Methodik für die Bildung von Richtwerten ist das *Experiment.* Experimentell ermittelt werden z.B. alle Zeitstandards (Arbeitsstudie), die Standards für produktionsbedingte Materialverluste (z.B. Späne, Einspannenden, Abbrand usw.), aber auch kompliziertere Standards wie etwa Richtwerte für den Umsatz je Verkäufer oder den Umsatz für jede DM Werbeaufwand.

Lange Zeit hindurch war umstritten, ob die Standards auf der Basis optimaler, normaler oder tatsächlicher Betriebsbedingungen ermittelt werden sollen. Optimale Standards kennzeichnen eine Bestleistung, normale Standards die bei normalen Bedingungen erzielbare Leistung, erreichbare Standards hingegen die bei den tatsächlichen Voraussetzungen mögliche Leistung.

Im allgemeinen hat man sich bei uns dafür entschieden, gleichzeitig mit normalen und erreichbaren Standards zu arbeiten. Der optimale Standard wird grundsätzlich nicht mehr angewendet, weil wir unsere Kontroll- und Planungsarbeiten von Illusionen frei halten wollen.

Das Arbeiten mit einem doppelten Standard ist wohl insbesondere zur richtigen Erfassung und Zurechnung der Verantwortung bei Mehr- oder Minderleistungen erforderlich. Da der Beschäftigungsgrad, das Produktionsverfahren und die Auftragszusammensetzung ganz überwiegend außerhalb der Einflußsphäre der technischen Abteilungsleiter liegen, gibt man diesen *erreichbare* Standards vor, weil nur der erreichbare Standard den jeweiligen Betriebsbedingungen angepaßt ist und wegen seiner Situationsgerechtigkeit einen echten Leistungsanreiz bildet. Die Unwirtschaftlichkeiten, die durch Abweichen vom normalen Beschäftigungsgrad, von der normalen Auftragszusammensetzung und von dem normalen Produktionsverfahren verursacht werden, dürfen aber nicht einfach außer Acht gelassen werden. Für diese Abweichungen sind die Geschäftsleitung, der Vertrieb und der Einkauf verantwortlich, die ihre Dispositionen daher am normalen Standard ausrichten müssen. Durch Messung des Unterschiedes zwischen normalem und erreichbarem Standard gewinnt man einen Maßstab für die Beurteilung der einkaufs-, vertriebs- und allgemeingeschäftspolitischen Maßnahmen.

Das Arbeiten mit erreichbaren Standards bedeutet natürlich, daß man auf die – arbeitstechnisch mancherlei Vorteile bietende – *starre* Standardisierung verzichten und zur *flexiblen* Budgetierung übergehen muss. Standards werden also nicht nur für normale Betriebsbedingungen, sondern für alle praktisch möglichen Betriebsbedingungen festgesetzt.

Soweit die Standards Wertstandards sind, werden sie auf Tageswertbasis gebildet. Dies ist eine selbstverständliche Konsequenz aus der Tatsache, daß bei uns die Kosten- und Leistungsrechnung grundsätzlich zum Tageswert durchgeführt wird. Weichen die Tageswerte von den Anschaffungswerten ab, dann werden die vorhandenen Bestände in der Regel sofort auf den Tageswert umgewertet. Liegt der Tageswert unter dem Anschaffungswert, dann wird die Differenz direkt über Gewinn- und Verlustkonto ausgebucht. Ist der Tageswert jedoch höher als der Anschaffungswert, dann ist zur Einhaltung des Niederstwertprinzips die Einschaltung eines Bestandsgegenkontos erforderlich, das bilanziell als Wertberichtigungskonto aufzufassen ist und entsprechend dem Verbrauch der aufgewerteten Bestände über Gewinn- und Verlustkonto aufgelöst wird.

Standards wurden zunächst nur für einzelne, besonders wichtige Erfolgskomponenten gebildet, z.B. Verbrauchsmengen wichtiger Materialien, Ausschußquoten, Umsatzleistungen je Kopf im Handel usw. Dabei blieb es jedoch nicht. Eine große Zahl deutscher Betriebe ist heute dabei, *alle Betriebsvorgänge systematisch* zu standardisieren, d.h. neben der Istrechnung eine komplette Standard- bzw. Planwertrechnung aufzubauen. Besonders weit sind diese Bemühungen im Bereich der Kostenrechnung fortgeschritten, wo neben der Istkostenrechnung die sogenannte Standard- oder Plankostenrechnung vielfach praktiziert wird.

Während die Problematik der Standardisierung der Fertigungsabteilungen weitgehend gelöst ist, bestehen nach wie vor gewisse Schwierigkeiten bei der Standardisierung der Verwaltungsdienststellen. Es ist bisher nur in wenigen Fällen gelungen (z.B. in Schreibzimmern), exakte Leistungsmaßstäbe für Büroarbeiten zu finden. Dies ist in erster Linie darauf zurückzuführen, daß die Verwaltungsarbeit in Deutschland nicht sehr stark spezialisiert ist, so daß sich das Leistungsbild eines Verwaltungsangestellten aus sehr viel verschiedenen Komponenten zusammensetzt, die nicht ohne weiteres auf einen Nenner gebracht werden können. Als Ausweg verbleibt für den Verwaltungssektor die Methode, auf Grund von Erfahrungswerten durchschnittliche Verbrauchssätze zu errechnen, die den Verwaltungskostenstellen in Form von Limitbudgets vorgegeben werden.

2. *Die Verwendung von Standards für die Betriebskontrolle*

Das Prinzip der ausgebauten Planwertrechnung besteht darin, den monatlichen Istkosten und -erlösen sowohl normale als auch erreichbare Standardkosten und Standarderlöse gegenüberzustellen. Um einen vollen Wirkungsgrad der Rechnung zu erzielen, werden die Standardkosten und -erlöse für jede Kostenstelle und jeden Kostenträger im Detail ermittelt. Aus den Abweichungen, die sich zwischen Standardwerten und Istwerten ergeben, kann mit großer Sicherheit berechnet werden, durch welche Faktoren der Gewinn des jeweiligen Monats beeinflußt worden ist. Abnorme Entwicklungen werden kenntlich gemacht und die Geschäftsleitung hat dann die Möglichkeit, hieran ihre weiteren Maßnahmen zu orientieren, indem sie den Einfluß der positiven Faktoren fördert und den der negativen Faktoren zurückdrängt.

Im Rahmen der Planwertrechnung werden im allgemeinen folgende Abweichungen ausgewiesen:

a. Preisabweichung: Die Preisabweichung ergibt sich nach der Formel 'Tagesfestwert × Istverbrauch minus Tagesistwert × Istverbrauch'. Die Preisabweichung wird nur ermittelt, wenn der Betrieb mit Festwerten rechnet, nicht dagegen bei der Verwendung von beweglichen Tageswerten.

b. Beschäftigungsabweichung = Standardkosten der Istbeschäftigung minus Standardkosten der normalen Beschäftigung. Grundsätzlich muß die Beschäftigungsabweichung von der Geschäftsleitung (falsche Investitionspolitik), vom Verkauf (zu geringer Absatz trotz vorhandener Absatzmöglichkeiten) oder vom Einkauf (ungenügende Rohstoff- und Energiebeschaffung) verantwortet werden. Verschlechtert sich jedoch die Beschäftigung infolge von technischen Störungen, die durch Unachtsamkeiten bei der Fertigung auftreten, so muß der entstehende Verlust auch dem Fertigungsbereich zugerechnet werden.

Die Beschäftigungsabweichung wird nach herrschender Auffassung nicht den

Produkten zugerechnet, sondern über Gewinn- und Verlustkonto ausgebucht. Die Kostenträger sind daher stets nur mit normalen fixen Kosten belastet, um ihr Erfolgsbild nicht ungerechtfertigt zu verschlechtern.

Neuerdings wird auch die Frage lebhaft diskutiert, ob man den Produkten überhaupt fixe Kosten belasten soll. Das Verfahren, die fixen Kosten unter Umgehung der Kostenträgerkonten direkt auf Gewinn- und Verlustkonto zu buchen, nennt man bei uns Grenzplankostenrechnung, womit angedeutet werden soll, daß die Kostenträger nur mit proportionalen Kosten = Grenzkosten belastet werden. Diese Methode entspricht dem amerikanischen direct costing. Ebenso wie in Amerika ist auch bei uns eine erhebliche Skepsis gegenüber der Grenzplankostenrechnung zu beobachten. Die Vertreter der Grenzplankostenrechnung begründen ihr Verfahren damit, dass die fixen Kosten der Betriebsbereitschaft nicht durch die monatliche Produktion verursacht würden und es daher nicht möglich ist, diese Kosten den Kostenträgern nach dem Verursachungsprinzip zuzurechnen; vielmehr komme es in der Kostenrechnung allein darauf an, die Fixkostentragfähigkeit der einzelnen Produkte exakt zu berechnen, die sich aus der Differenz zwischen Erlös und proportionalen Kosten ergibt. Je höher diese Differenz ist, umso förderungswürdiger sei ein Produkt und umgekehrt. Dem wird nun von den Vertretern der Vollkostenrechnung mit viel Berechtigung entgegengehalten, dass verschiedene Produkte sehr unterschiedliche maschinelle und personelle Produktionsgrundlagen benötigen und dass diese Unterschiede von der Kostenrechnung nicht einfach ignoriert werden dürfen. So können einzelne Artikel nur auf Hochleistungsdrehbänken hergestellt werden, während für andere Produkte normale Drehbänke vollkommen genügen. In solchen Fällen binden die einzelnen Produkte unterschiedliche Kapitalbeträge, was auch in einer unterschiedlichen Belastung durch Kapitalkosten zum Ausdruck kommen muß.

Die Grenzplankostenrechnung hat sich daher bisher noch nicht in stärkerem Umfang durchsetzen können. Wo sie jedoch praktiziert wird, entfällt der Ausweis einer Beschäftigungsabweichung im Rahmen der Plankostenrechnung vollkommen. Statt dessen wird imRahmen der Ergebnisrechnung die Deckung der fixen Betriebsbereitschaftskosten durch den Bruttogewinn nachgewiesen.

c. Verfahrensabweichung: Standardkosten des Standardverfahrens minus Standardkosten des Istverfahrens.

d. Abweichung wegen veränderter Auftragszusammensetzung: Standardkosten der normalen Auftragszusammensetzung minus Standardkosten der tatsächlichen Auftragszusammensetzung.

e. Verbrauchsabweichung: Tageswert × erreichbarer Standardverbrauch minus Tageswert × Istverbrauch. Unter erreichbarem Standardverbrauch versteht man den Verbrauch, der sich nach Abzug eines evtl. Mehrverbrauches durch zu geringen Beschäftigungsgrad, abweichendes Produktionsverfahren oder abweichende Auftragszusammensetzung ergibt. Die Verbrauchsabweichung ist also die Abweichung, die von den einzelnen Kostenstellen selbst verursacht wird und daher auch von diesen verantwortet werden muß. Im einzelnen umfaßt die Verbrauchsabweichung folgende Verbrauchsdifferenzen: Standardmaterialverbrauch minus Istmaterialverbrauch (hinsichtlich Materialmengen und Materialarten); Standardzeitverbrauch minus Istzeitverbrauch; Standardstundenleistung minus Iststundenleistung; Standardkosten der Arbeits- bzw. Maschinenstunde minus Istkosten der Arbeits- bzw. Maschinenstunde.

f. Absatzabweichung: Standardumsatz minus Istumsatz. In dieser Abweichung kommen folgende Einflüße zum Ausdruck: geringere Verkaufsmengen, schlechtere Verkaufspreise, höhere Preisnachlässe, schlechtere Artikel- und Sortenzusammensetzung des Umsatzes, höhere Retouren.

Die Masse der deutschen Betriebe ist nach wie vor zentral organisiert. Daher werden im allgemeinen die im Rahmen der Planwertrechnung erarbeiteten, auch die *Einzelheiten* der Wirtschaftlichkeitsentwicklung in den verschiedenen Abteilungen und Unterabteilungen berücksichtigenden Erkenntnisse lediglich den *oberen* Betriebsinstanzen mitgeteilt. Diese beschließen dann ihrerseits die notwendigen Maßnahmen und erteilen den nachgeordneten Dienststellen entsprechende Anweisungen.

In den fortschrittlichen Betrieben setzt sich aber immer stärker die Erkenntnis durch, daß es nicht ausreichend ist, nur die oberen Instanzen über die Kostenentwicklung zu orientieren, da gerade die unteren und mittleren Management-Stufen einen gerade zu entscheidenden Einfluß auf die Kostengestaltung haben und die Wirtschaftlichkeit des Betriebes daher weitgehend von der Mitarbeit der Meister und Abteilungsleiter abhängt. Soweit man in diesen Betrieben dazu übergegangen ist, das Rechnungswesen stärker in den Betrieb hineinzutragen, verfolgt man zunächst nur die Absicht, die Kostenstellenleiter kostenbewußter zu machen, indem man ihnen an Hand der Abrechnungsbögen und insbesondere der Abweichungen zwischen Ist- und Plankosten zeigt, welche Möglichkeiten sich für Kosteneinsparungen und Leistungssteigerungen bieten.

Voller Erfolg kann diesen Bemühungen aber nur beschieden sein, wenn bestimmte Voraussetzungen erfüllt werden. Zunächst müssen die für die Kostenstellenleiter bestimmten Berichte so gestaltet werden, daß sie dem Denken des Betriebsmannes entsprechen. Darum werden zweckmäßigerweise nicht allein Kosten*werte* berichtet, sondern zu jedem Wert möglichst auch die entsprechenden *Mengen* angegeben, weil erfahrungsgemäss die Menge für den Techniker aussagefähiger ist als der Wert. Außerdem ist es zweckmäßig, die Kosten besonders herauszustellen, die von den Kostenstellenleitern tatsächlich *beeinflußt* werden können.

Wenn die Übermittlung der Kostenunterlagen an die Kostenstellenleiter in den deutschen Betrieben nur relativ langsam voranschreitet, so liegt das nicht daran, daß man die Zweckmäßigkeit eines solchen Vorgehens leugnet, sondern hat seinen Grund in personellen Schwierigkeiten des Rechnungswesens. Es ist ja nicht damit getan, daß die Plankosten und Abweichungen den Abteilungsleitern mitgeteilt werden. Der Wert der Plankostenrechnung wird vielmehr erst dann voll ausgeschöpft, wenn das Rechnungswesen dafür sorgt, dass die Abteilungsleiter aus dem übersandten Zahlenmaterial auch Schlußfolgerungen ziehen. Dieses, von den Amerikanern treffend 'follow through' genannte Schlußglied der Plankostenrechnung erfordert engsten Kontakt zu den betreffenden Betriebsstellen, der sich nur herstellen lässt, wenn die Leute des Rechnungswesens einen nicht unerheblichen Teil Dienstzeit im Betrieb verbringen. Dieser Zeitaufwand ist umso größer, je weiter und je ungeschulter der Kreis der in die Plankostenauswertung einbezogenen Dienststellenleiter ist, und übersteigt heute in der Regel bei weitem das Ausmaß, das unsere Rechnungswesenabteilungen personell zu leisten imstande sind. Erst wenn dieser Engpass überwunden ist, können auf diesem Sektor weitere Erfolge erwartet werden.

3. *Rentabilitäts- und Finanzplanung*

Die Betriebe, in denen eine Kontrollrechnung auf Standardbasis bereits eingeführt ist, wollen auf dieses Instrument nicht mehr verzichten. Sie haben jedoch feststellen müssen, dass die Anforderungen, die von der Betriebspolitik an das Rechnungswesen gestellt werden, allein mit einer solchen Nachrechnung nicht erfüllt werden können. Die Geschäftsleitung braucht vielmehr darüber hinaus *kurzfristige* und wenn möglich *vorausschauende* Informationen. An diesem Punkt hat die weitere Entwicklung der Standardrechnung in Deutschland eingesetzt.

Eine Verbesserung erzielt man bereits dadurch, dass man über einzelne besonders wichtige Tatbestände wöchentlich oder sogar täglich berichtet. Daraus ergibt sich die Möglichkeit, bei Fehlentwicklungen sofort einzugreifen. Die tägliche Berichterstattung ist heute weitgehend üblich geworden auf dem Finanzsektor in Form des ausgebauten Geldstandberichtes und im technischen Bereich, der die wichtigsten Verbrauchs- und Leistungswerte ebenfalls in Tagesberichten verfolgt.

Diese Berichterstattung von Einzelzahlen vermittelt aber keinen Überblick über die Entwicklung des Gesamtbetriebes und den jeweiligen Stand der für die Geschäftsleitung vor allem wichtigen Größe, nämlich des Gewinnes. Zudem ist sie keine auf die Zukunft ausgerichtete Vorschaurechnung. Die letzte Stufe eines ausgebauten Systems des betriebspolitischen Rechnungswesens ist daher erst dann erreicht, wenn der Monatsgewinn entweder im voraus geschätzt (Prognoserechnung) oder geplant wird (Gewinnplanung auf der Grundlage des Kosten- und Erlösplanes). Der Unterschied zwischen Prognosegewinn und Plangewinn besteht darin, dass der Prognosegewinn eine möglichst genaue Vorschätzung des tatsächlichen Gewinnes des kommenden Monats darstellt, während der Plangewinn ein bestimmtes Leistungsziel für den kommenden Monat setzen soll.

Auch derartige Planungen werden heute bei einer Reihe von deutschen Unternehmungen bereits in der Praxis durchgeführt, wobei man den Gewinn am Monatsbeginn an Hand der Verkaufs- und Produktionsplanung und der vorhandenen Standards plant und laufend über die während des Monats eintretenden Veränderungen und Abweichungen berichtet.

Die Tatsache, dass die Verkaufs- und Produktionsplanung bei uns recht flexibel gehandhabt wird, so daß im Laufe des Monats noch viel geändert werden kann, bringt Vor- und Nachteile mit sich. Der Vorteil liegt darin, dass sich die Betriebe eine hohe Elastizität bewahrt haben, die es ihnen ermöglicht sich schnell an neue Bedingungen anzupassen. Diese Elastizität ist ein wichtiges betriebspolitisches Aktivum. Die Kosten-, Erlös- und Gewinnplanung wird jedoch durch häufige Planänderungen erheblich erschwert. Insbesondere ist es unmöglich, die Pläne als unbedingt zu erreichende Leistungsziele aufzufassen. Sie haben vielmehr ganz eindeutig den Charakter einer Prognoserechnung, die zeigt, welche Kosten, Erlöse und Gewinne bei Einhaltung der Planung entstehen werden. Dies bedeutet aber bereits eine große Hilfe für die Geschäftsleitung, weil ohne Schwierigkeiten ersehen werden kann, was man durch Planänderungen verliert und gewinnt.

Parallel zur Gewinnplanung wird die Finanzplanung durchgeführt. Sie beruht grundsätzlich auf dem gleichen Ausgangsmaterial: dem Absatz- und Produktionsplan, dem daraus entwickelten Einkaufsplan und den Kosten- und Erlösplänen. Dabei wird nach den international bekannten Grundsätzen für die laufende Finanzplanung vorgegangen. Interessant ist in diesem Zusammenhang aber die Tatsache, daß neuerdings dem Problem der Abschreibung im Rahmen der Finanzplanung ganz besondere Aufmerksamkeit geschenkt wird. Im *laufenden* Finanzplan erscheinen die Abschreibungen zwar nicht, weil dieser nur die Kosten berücksichtigt, die auch zu Ausgaben führen, was hinsichtlich der Abschreibungen nicht gilt. Wohl aber hat die Abschreibung eine ganz große Bedeutung für die *Investitionsplanung.*

Wir können Investitionen aus drei Quellen finanzieren:

1. aus am Markt aufgenommenem Eigen- und Fremdkapital;
2. aus Gewinnen, wozu auch überhöht angesetzte Risikoposten in der Bilanz gehören;
3. aus Abschreibungen.

Solange der Kapitalmarkt beengt ist und die Gewinne stark besteuert werden, sind die Abschreibungen eine vergleichsweise sehr ergiebige Finanzierungsquelle. Voraussetzung ist allerdings, dass sie auch tatsächlich in Höhe des Ansatzes in der Kostenrechnung verdient, daß sie steuerlich in voller Höhe anerkannt und daß sie außerdem nicht zur Ersatzbeschaffung benötigt werden. Hieraus ist ohne weiteres ersichtlich, daß zwischen Kosten- und Investitionsplanung ein sehr enger Zusammenhang besteht, da der geplante Abschreibungsbetrag einen wesentlichen Teil des in der folgenden Periode verfügbaren Investitionsspielraumes darstellt. Von den für die Neu-investitionsfähigkeit der Abschreibungen maßgebenden Faktoren ist derjenige am wichtigsten, ob die Abschreibung für Ersatzbeschaffungen benötigt wird. In gewisser Vereinfachung kann hierzu gesagt werden, dass die Notwendigkeit der Ersatzinvestition umso geringer ist, je geringer das Alter des Anlagenbestandes ist. Da unsere nach dem Krieg wieder aufgebauten Betriebe im allgemeinen mit einem sehr modernen Anlagenpark arbeiten, kommt der Frage der Abschreibung sowohl in der Gewinn- als auch in der Investitionsplanung erhebliche Bedeutung zu.

III. Die Bedeutung der modernen Methoden des Rechnungswesens für das Wirtschaftsprüfungswesen

Die modernen Methoden des Rechnungswesens werden vom deutschen Wirtschaftsprüfungswesen stark beachtet. Sowohl im Rahmen der Prüfungs- als auch in der Beratungspraxis sind die Wirtschaftsprüfer bemüht, sich die bei der Weiterentwicklung des Rechnungswesens ergebenden Möglichkeiten zunutze zu machen.

1. *Bedeutung im Rahmen der Prüfungspraxis*

a. Verbesserte Organisation des Rechnungswesens als Folge der Planung

Es ist eine bekannte Tatsache, dass die Betriebe bei der Einführung der Planung zunächst bemüht sein müssen, hierfür die notwendigen organisatorischen Grundlagen zu schaffen. In der Regel zeigt sich schon bei den vorbereitenden Arbeiten, daß die dem Rechnungswesen zugrundeliegenden *Uraufschreibungen* ungenügend und unzuverlässig sind und dass die *Schlüssel*, mit denen die Kosten zugerechnet werden, nicht die wünschenswerte Exaktheit besitzen. Für die Planung müssen alle unzulässig vereinfachenden Abrechnungsmethoden aufgegeben und durch exakte Lösungen ersetzt werden. Die Kostenstellenrechnung wird verfeinert und im Endergebnis zeigen sich häufig nicht unerhebliche Änderungen im Selbstkostenwert der Kostenträger.

Diese intensive Organisationstätigkeit, die der Einführung der Planung vorausgeht, ist für den Wirtschaftsprüfer von unschätzbarem Wert, da sie in jedem Falle die Zuverlässigkeit des Rechnungswesens erhöht. Vor allem erleichtert sich dadurch die Inventur der Material- und Fabrikatebestände und die Prüfung des Wertansatzes der Halb- und Fertigfabrikate.

b. Beurteilung der Richtigkeit des ausgewiesenen Gewinnes

Der Bestätigungsvermerk des Wirtschaftsprüfers beinhaltet nicht nur die Versicherung, dass die Buchführung, der Jahresabschluß und der Geschäftsbericht, soweit er den Jahresabschluß erläutert, den gesetzlichen Vorschriften entsprechen, sondern soll auch gewährleisten, daß der Jahresabschluß die wirtschaftliche Lage des Unternehmens zutreffend zum Ausdruck bringt. Die Überzeugung, daß dies der Fall ist, kann der Prüfer – abgesehen von der Durchsicht der Bücher – nur dadurch gewinnen, daß er

a. bestimmte Standardvorstellungen von den typischen Markt-, Konkurrenz- und Produktionsbedingungen der betreffenden Branche besitzt, und
b. die zukünftigen Risiken des Geschäfts in Rechnung stellt.

Das deutsche Prüfungswesen arbeitet sehr weitgehend mit Standards, die meist auf Erfahrungen aus dem Zeit- und Betriebsvergleich beruhen, wobei dem Wirtschaftsprüfer seine intime Kenntnis verschiedener Betriebe derselben Branche sehr nützlich ist. Da auch die steuerliche Betriebsprüfung mit sehr genauen und weitreichenden Standards arbeitet, muß der das Unternehmen finanziell und steuerlich beratende Wirtschaftsprüfer mit mindestens gleichwertigen Standardunterlagen an seine Arbeit gehen.

Das Arbeiten mit Standards ermöglicht es dem Prüfer zu beurteilen, ob die von der Gesellschaft vorgelegten Unterlagen im Rahmen des Normalen und damit Wahrscheinlichen liegen. Ergeben sich Abweichungen zwischen Standards und Istwerten, dann können auf diese Weise Fehler im Rechnungswesen bzw. Verlustquellen im Betrieb nachgewiesen werden.

Besitzt der zu prüfende Betrieb eigene Standards, dann erleichtert sich für den Prüfer die Arbeit erheblich. Er braucht seine eigenen Standards nur noch mit denen des zu prüfenden Betriebes zu vergleichen, um sicher zu gehen, dass die vom Betrieb genannten Ursachen für die negative oder positive Entwicklung des Geschäftsganges zutreffen. Dabei muß der Wirtschaftsprüfer Wert darauf legen, mit möglichst globalen, die großen Zusammenhänge kennzeichnenden Standards auszukommen. Es kann nicht seine Aufgabe sein, seine eigenen Standardvorstellungen soweit auszubauen, daß sie auch die Arbeitsergebnisse einzelner Kostenstellen einbeziehen. Dies würde die Prüfung zu umfangreich gestalten und außerdem eine so genaue Kenntnis der Besonderheiten des jeweiligen Betriebes voraussetzen, wie sie nur bei einem langjährigen Beratungsverhältnis entstehen und verlangt werden kann.

Keine Bilanzierung kann als zutreffend bezeichnet werden, wenn sie nicht die zukünftigen Geschäftsrisiken berücksichtigt. Gerade die Prüfung der Posten mit erhöhtem Risiko gehört zu den wichtigsten Pflichten des Wirtschaftsprüfers. Diese Aufgabe wird erheblich erleichtert, wenn das zu prüfende Unternehmen über eine gute Kosten-, Erlös-, Gewinn- und Finanzplanung verfügt. Wenn sich der Prüfer davon überzeugen kann, daß die Planungen der Gesellschaft in der Vergangenheit zuverlässig waren, wird er sich bei der Prüfung des Jahresabschlusses auch die Planungen für das kommende Geschäftsjahr ohne größere Einschränkungen zunutze machen können. Hier wird also ein sehr enger Zusammenhang zwischen Wirtschaftsprüfung und Unternehmensplanung erkennbar.

2. *Bedeutung im Rahmen der Beratungspraxis*

Es ist eine Besonderheit des deutschen Wirtschaftsprüfungswesens, daß die eigentliche Prüfungspraxis stark im Vordergrund steht, während die Beratungspraxis weniger stark ausgebildet ist. Soweit die Beratungspraxis einen nennenswerten Umfang hat, befaßt sie sich fast ausschließlich mit finanzwirtschaftlichen und steuerlichen Fragen. Die produktions- und absatzwirtschaftliche Problematik wird dabei nur am Rande berührt. Gerade in der produktions- und absatzwirtschaftlichen Sphäre liegt aber das eigentliche Anwendungsgebiet der verfeinerten Standard- und Planungsrechnung.

Die Einrichtung und Überprüfung von betrieblichen Standard- und Planungsrechnungen sowie die Hilfeleistung bei der Analyse von Abweichungsrechnungen liegt daher nicht im engeren Arbeitsbereich des deutschen Wirtschaftsprüfers, sondern wird in der Regel von besonderen Betriebsberatungsinstituten vorgenommen oder von den Betrieben in eigener Regie durchgeführt. Dies kann sich jedoch sehr rasch ändern, wenn z.B. bei einer Veränderung der Konjunkturlage die Verlustquellenforschung und -beseitigung alle anderen Probleme an Bedeutung übertreffen sollte. Aus diesem Grunde muß sich das deutsche Wirtschaftsprüfungswesen zumindest personell in die Lage versetzen, den Unternehmen auch bei der Lösung dieser Probleme beratend zur Seite stehen zu können.

Translation

PAPER

by

WIRTSCHAFTSPRÜFER HERBERT RÄTSCH

Institut der Wirtschaftsprüfer in Deutschland e.V.

I. Improved Management Techniques Resulting from Budgeting and Control

The world over more and more attention is being paid to the problems of budgeting and control; of late increasing importance has been attached in Germany to the study of methods of budgeting and control. There are many reasons why this should be so, chief among them are perhaps high taxation, the difficulty of borrowing money on satisfactory terms, the severity of competition both in domestic and foreign trade, the shorter hours now worked, rising costs of labor and materials, the fact that markets are becoming more and more saturated with goods and are consequently developing into buyers' markets, new technical discoveries which have revolutionized methods of production and forced businesses to throw over long-established practices and policies at a moment's notice and to embark on large programs of capital expenditure. Such considerations are now forcing businesses to increase their efficiency to an extent that would be out of the question if they continued to rely only on self-operating controls unrelated to other factors. In Germany it is now the generally accepted view that unless real hard thought is given to all aspects of an undertaking's activities, to the relation of these aspects one with another and with all other related factors, it is quite impossible to secure the efficient management of a business.

To achieve this aim the prime requisite is clearly that the management should have continuous control over what happens in the business, and the complementary requisite is a management always ready and willing to reconsider even the fundamentals of existing policies in the light of future potentialities; no management should ever rely on the assumption that methods which have succeeded and justified their adoption in the past will necessarily be attended with success in the future. The secret of conducting a business so as to make the maximum use of its productive capabilities and of its selling opportunities, and to secure that the profit-earning capacity of the business consistently rises, lies in sensing the correlation between *control* of performances and *budgeting* for the future production program.

It is the task of the accounting department to institute systems of control and budgeting. It will, of course, have to call on the buying, production and selling departments for assistance in carrying out its task; but it must bear the sole responsibility for the smooth running of the systems introduced, and for the workmanlike assembling of the statistical data produced. Accounting procedures, however, at least in their traditional forms, cannot cope with these new demands. Balance sheets and profit and loss accounts invariably see the light of day at a date when any chance of retrieving errors which have been made or of undoing any harm already done are past. Traditional accounting procedures, again, can supply no information as to the efficiency of the business; they cannot produce data which make it possible to compare cost with performance or to trace in detail variations in earning power to their source. Reorganisation of the accounting department, therefore, is necessary, and its methods of operating must be altered, in order to enable it to measure up to the novel demands that the new aims make on it. This involves three matters:

1. Accounting records must be treated *analytically*. The essence of the problem is to set up standards by which cost and performance can be measured and to be able to show how cost and performance vary in relation to each other when production conditions and selling conditions change.

2. All records of what has happened must be summarised at *short intervals*, so that, if mistakes have been made, it is still possible to take corrective action.

3. Forward-looking *budgets* must be constructed to enable the management to gain a balanced view of the opportunities available and of the risks involved, and to decide on action accordingly.

II. Budgeting and Control as practised in Germany

1. *The Construction of Standards*

The construction of standards is the basis on which all budgeting and control must rest. By a 'standard' we mean every figure which characterises, by the method of measuring it, something that exists as a business fact. There are thus standards of quantity, of time, of performance, of cost, of revenue, and of profit. Some businesses employ elaborate standards; others are content with rather more primitive ones. It will depend in each case on the degree of efficiency possessed by the accounting department of the business in question. There may be said to be, basically, three different procedures:

a. The 'standard' may be an *average figure* computed from accounting records reflecting the transactions which have taken place. Figures of this kind, resting on what is known to have happened, are well suited for use in making estimates of future costs. There is a very considerable probability that the average of the past can be repeated in the future. But such standards must not be used for the purpose of measuring performance, because average figures compiled from what has happened inevitably also contain some components which reflect the less satisfactory aspects of the activities of the business.

b. In large concerns the standard may be based on the comparable figures of other factories; for instance, the figures of a *known first-class factory* of the group may serve as the standard. Essentially a standard of this kind is also based on what is known to have happened, but it has the advantage, as compared with the average standard described in *a.*, that it does reflect a known level of performance.

c. The best procedure, and the one to which we universally incline to-day, is to arrive at standards *analytically*, making use of scientific methods for this purpose. As analytically ascertained standards constitute a perfect measurement of performance they are often called '*marker-bases*' or '*budget bases*' (for instance, budget costs). The most important guide in constructing marker-bases is *practical experiment.* All time-standards are arrived at empirically (by means of work-study), and empirical methods are also employed to arrive at standards of spoilage resulting from productive processes (for example, swarf, scrap, ashes etc.) and even to arrive at more complicated standards, such as, for instance, the marker-bases for turnover per salesman or for the relationship between turnover and the money spent on advertising.

For a long time it was an unsettled question whether standards should be based on ideal, on normal or on actually expected operational conditions. By ideal standards we mean those based on reaching the highest imaginable level; normal standards represent what can be achieved under normal conditions, attainable standards, on the other hand, represent the level reachable in existing circumstances.

In Germany the tendency is now to use the normal and the attainable standards together at the same time. We have decided that hopes that bear no relation to reality are not a sound basis for budgeting computations and control planning; consequently ideal standards have gone completely out of use.

We have found it necessary to use dual standards in order to ensure that the responsibility for over-par or under-par performance is laid at the door of the proper persons and that it is correctly assessed. Obviously the intensity of employment, the processes in use and the type of order are very largely outside the sphere of influence of the individual managers of the production departments and it is therefore the proper course to set standards which are *attainable* by them in the conditions under which they have to work and which offer them a real incentive to attain these standards. But equally obviously deviations from the standards relating to intensity of employment, to processes in use or to the type of order, brought about by the fact that the undertaking is a thoroughly inefficiently run business, cannot be simply ignored. For such deviations the management, the buying department or the selling department, are responsible, and it is their task to harmonise their practices with the normal standards. Measuring the difference between the normal standard and the attainable standard makes it possible to set up a yard-stick by which to assess the success of the measures decided on by the buying or selling departments and generally of the 'top-level' policy of the business. The use of attainable standards naturally involves giving up any attempt at *rigid* standardisation (however much such methods commend themselves to the accounting department) and adopting the practice of *flexible* budgeting. Standards may be constructed not only for normal manufacturing processes, but for pretty well all the operations of a business.

If the standards are money standards they should be based on current prices ruling. This is the logical consequence of the practice, followed generally in Germany, of evaluating costs and operations on the basis of the current prices ruling. If such prices vary from the costs of acquisition, it is usual, at any rate, to reassess the stocks on hand at once, to accord with price changes. If the ruling price is less than the cost of acquisition, the difference will be charged direct to the profit and loss account. If the ruling price is higher than the cost of acquisition, any departure from the principle of the lower of cost of market is considered improper; a suspense account is therefore set up to carry the necessary adjustment, until such time as it, or a part of it corresponding to the materials consumed, can be passed to profit and loss account.

As a start standards were constructed only for the special constituents of profit-earning capacity which are of particular importance, for instance, for the quantities of important raw materials consumed, for ratios of spoilage and, in trading concerns, for the turnover per person concerned. But that was not the end of it. Many German undertakings are now going over to constructing standards systematically for the whole of the transactions their business engages in, that is to say, side by side with the actual accounting record to build up a complete range of standard or predetermined costs. This tendency has, of course, been most marked in undertakings which have already made it a practice to maintain standard cost accounts (or predetermined cost accounts) alongside their normal accounts. While the whole range of problems connected with standardising the work of the manufacturing departments has been largely solved, the standardising of the work of the administrative units still constitutes a source of difficulty. Only in a few cases, one of which is typing pools, has it been possible to arrive at any exact measurement of the amount of work performed by persons who do office work. This is due in Germany to the fact that we do not seek to 'specialise' office work to any great degree. The output of an office worker is thus the total of many various tasks which cannot all be reduced to one denomination. The only way of overcoming the difficulty in regard to office work seems to be to compute average allowances for expenses based on known previous expenditure and to allocate them to the various office units in the form of limit-budgets.

2. *The Use of Standards for Controlling Operations*

The object of a developed system of recording predetermined costs is to enable a comparison to be made monthly between the actual figures for costs and revenues and the normal as well as the attainable standard costs and standard revenues. To make the figures as fully informative as possible standard costs and standard revenues are computed in detail for every cost center and for every cost unit. From the resultant variances between the standard figures and the actual figures it is possible to ascertain in terms of figures with a high degree of accuracy the factors which have influenced the profits for the month in question. The calculations will disclose any abnormal features and enable the management to adopt appropriate measures so that it can give full rein to positive factors or draw a tight rein on negative factors.

The main types of variances thrown up by predetermined costs are the following:

a. Price variances: The formula for these is: Fixed current price multiplied by actual consumption less actual current price multiplied by actual consumption. Price variances can be ascertained only when the business uses fixed prices, not when it uses variable current prices.

b. Activity variances, that is to say: Standard costs of the actual employment less standard costs of normal employment. The general rule is that the responsibility for an employment variance lies either with the management (unsuitable machinery purchased), with the selling department (sales too small despite existing opportunities) or with the buying department (unsatisfactory purchases of materials or fuel and power). But it can be caused by technical faults which can be laid at the door of a production unit, in which case it must find expression in the figures pertaining to production. It is generally thought that the employment variance should not be transferred to the cost of the articles produced, but should be written off to the profit and loss account. Cost units should always bear only the normal fixed expense, otherwise the results they show are unfairly biassed to their disadvantage.

Recently there has been much discussion over the question whether fixed expense should be charged to the cost of the articles produced at all. The method of charging fixed expense directly to the profit and loss account and not via the accounts of the cost units is called in Germany Grenzplankostenrechnung (marginal standard costing). The intention implicit in the choice of this title is to bring out that the essence of the theory is that cost units should only be charged with variable expense (that is to say, with marginal costs). In America the corresponding method is called 'marginal costing'. The theory of marginal standard costing is viewed in both Germany and America with not a little scepticism. The advocates of marginal standard costing make a strong point of the fact that fixed expense, due to the fact that the factory is ready and in a condition to operate at all, is not caused by the production which goes on month by month. In fact, they maintain, a causal relationship cannot be called in aid to justify charging fixed expense to the cost units; they go further, taking the line that the sole purpose of costing is to compute as near as possible a figure for each individual article produced representing its capacity to carry the load of fixed expense, which must be, of course, the difference between the amount the article sells for and the total variable costs. The larger this difference is, the more advantageous it is to sell the article; and the converse applies correspondingly. The point is made by the upholders of 'full' costs, and their point has very considerable substance, that the articles produced differ from each other in requiring the use of very different quantities of mechanical power and of labor to produce them; and that these differing requirements cannot be simply overlooked in the costings. A good example is the comparison of articles produced with the aid of a high capacity lathe and other articles produced on a standard lathe. In such cases the different articles produced are directly derived from very different capital outlays, and this fact must be reflected in the varying charge for the expense of 'capital'.

The propagation of the theory of marginal standard costs has consequently not been attended by a large measure of success. Where it is used, the predetermined costs will show no employment variance whatever. On the other hand the amount which can be said to be due to the fact that the factory is ready and in a condition to operate at all will appear as a counter-item to gross profit in the profit and loss account.

c. Process variances: Standard costs of the standard process less standard costs of the actual process.

d. Variances caused by variation in the type of order: Standard costs of the normal type of order less standard costs of the actual type of order.

e. Consumption variances: Current prices multiplied by attainable standard consumption less current prices multiplied by actual consumption. The expression 'attainable standard consumption' means the net consumption after deducting from it any possible excess consumption arising from the fact that the intensity of employment is under-par or that there are process variances or type of order variances. The consumption variance is thus a variance which is brought about by conditions in the cost centers themselves and is therefore their responsibility. The following are sub-categories of consumption variance: Standard materials consumption less actual materials consumption (in regard to both the quantities and the qualities of materials consumed), standard time taken less actual time taken, standard output per hour less actual output per hour, standard cost per labor-hour and per machine-hour less actual cost per labor-hour and per machine-hour.

f. Sales variances: Standard turnover of goods less actual turnover of goods. The following can in various ways influence this variance: that the quantities sold are too small, that selling prices are too low, that allowances on sales have been granted too liberally, that goods have been pressed on unsuitable customers, that returns are too high.

A high degree of centralization continues to be the most marked organisational characteristic of the bulk of German enterprises. In consequence, the knowledge obtained from the use of predetermined costs of *the details* of the extent to which departments and sub-departments are operating profitably or otherwise remains locked up in the archives of the *top-level managers*, who decide on the action that seems necessary to them and issue corresponding instructions to the departmental managers subordinate to them.

In progressive undertakings it is becoming more and more the accepted view that it is wrong to allow information as to the results shown by costing to remain the private secret of the top-level management; but that, on the contrary, it is the lower and middle grades of managers who have an absolutely decisive influence on how costs work out; and that whether the undertaking is operating profitably or not so operating can depend very largely on the extent to which the cooperation of foremen and under-managers is enlisted. Where such enterprises have taken the decision that factory officials shall be cognizant of the accounting aspect of all that goes on in the factory the first step has been to make the managers of cost centers more conscious of the costs of the unit under their managership. The usual way of doing this has been to supply them with the standard cost sheets, and to make particularly clear to them the variances between predetermined costs and actual costs; from these figures they can judge what are the possibilities of saving expenses and of increasing output. But full success can only be expected from these measures provided certain definite requirements are not ignored. In the first place, the statements which the managers of the cost centers are required to digest must be in a form that makes an appeal to their understanding and habits of mind. It is therefore generally better not to confine the contents of the reports to statements of costs expressed *in terms of money* but, as far as possible, to add information as to the corresponding *quantities* involved. It is a well-known fact that technicians appreciate statements depicting quantity movements far more readily than those which merely portray money movements. Secondly, one of the essential features of the statements should be the clear prominence which is given to that expense which the cost center manager can actually influence.

Actually the practice of putting all the data regarding costs at the disposal of cost center managers is spreading comparatively slowly in Germany. This is due to the fact that on the accounting side men with the ability to implement the scheme are extremely rare and hard to find, and not to any theoretical objections to the object of the scheme. The task is by no means fully completed when the statements of predetermined costs and the relative variances are put in the hands of the cost center managers. Full value can only be extracted from statements of predetermined costs when the accounting department is in a position to ensure that the cost center managers draw the requisite conclusions from the figures supplied to them. This is the final link in the chain, and is aptly described by the American expression 'the follow through'. Its essential feature is the building up of very close contact with the responsible officials in the factory. But that is only possible if the officials in the accounting department spend quite a large proportion of their time in the factory; and the time that will have to be spent in the factory will be all the greater when the number of officials who must be drawn into the scheme to make full use of the predetermined costings is large. Equally the fact that they are totally unversed in such matters will make greater demands on the time of members of the accounting department. It will be found in general, that the time needed to carry out this scheme efficiently far exceeds the time that members of the accounting department of German undertakings can possibly devote to it. Victory on this front of the battlefield can only be looked for when means have been found to circumvent this obstacle.

3. *Budgeting for Profit Margins and Financial Budgeting*

Undertakings which use standard costs as their costing system never show a desire to abandon them. In the past they will have discovered for themselves that costings in the form of 'historical' costs simply cannot cope with the demands that the technique of management in all its phases makes on the accounting department. They will also have discovered that the management must have information *at short intervals* and, if possible, information which is *forward-looking*. This is the stage that many German undertakings have reached and the stage from which the further development of standard costing is setting out.

The first and most obvious improvement is to institute a system of reporting on individual, but specially important, subjects weekly, if not daily. This makes it possible to take corrective action immediately, if things are going wrong. To-day daily reports are the normal thing, as a general rule, in financial matters, in the form of the expanded statement of cash resources, and in matters concerned with production, in the form of day-to-day reporting on movements of important raw materials and on output achieved.

But this method of reporting on special fields affords the management no conspectus of how the business as a whole is progressing, and no clue as to what is happening to that most important of all factors, the profit. Moreover, it offers no revelation of what may be expected in the future. The last stage of a fully developed system of accounting for productive processes is therefore only reached when monthly profits are either estimated in advance (forecasting) or are predetermined (predetermination of profits on the basis of budgeted costs and revenues). The difference between profit forecasting and predetermination of profits is that the former reflects an estimate, made as accurately as possible, of the actual profit for the coming month, and the latter sets a definite target for the coming month.

Predetermined costings of this kind are to-day an established institution in a number of German enterprises. The profit is predetermined at the beginning of the month by reference to selling budgets, production budgets and other existing standards. Currently during the month changes which take place and variances which are thrown up are made the subject of reports.

The fact that in Germany very flexible methods are adopted in regard to selling budgets and production budgets, with the consequence that it is possible to make many alterations in the course of a month, has advantages and disadvantages. It is an advantage that undertakings have maintained a high degree of elasticity, which enables them to adapt themselves to new conditions very quickly. This elasticity is an important business asset. But the budgeting for expense, revenue and profit is considerably hampered if the budgets are frequently changed. One major disadvantage is that it becomes impossible to look on the budgets as targets which must be hit. They tend to acquire the nature of forecasts, merely prognosticating what expense, revenue and profits will arise if the budget is adhered to. But it should not be overlooked that even this provides considerable assistance to the management as it enables them to see without difficulty what is gained and what is lost by altering their budgets.

Financial budgeting may be undertaken on parallel lines with profits budgeting. The underlying data are the same for both, for the selling and production budgets, as for the buying, expense and revenue budgets which derive from the first two budgets. The principles which can be regarded as governing the methods of short-term financial budgeting are in fact accepted by all countries. In this connection it is of interest that very great attention has recently been paid to the problem of the extent to which depreciation may be said to fall within the province of financial budgeting. In a *short-term* financial budget the provision for depreciation obviously has no place because it only has regard to expense which will lead to cash disbursements and that is not so in the case of depreciation. On the other hand it is of very great importance in connection with budgeting for capital outlays.

Capital outlays can be financed from three sources:

1. share capital and loan capital subscribed by money market interests,
2. profits, and for this purpose excessive provisions for eventualities count as profits,
3. depreciation provisions.

While the present restrictions on the money market last and while profits are heavily taxed, provisions for depreciation constitute, in comparison with the other two possibilities, an abundant source of capital. It is, of course, essential that the amount of the provision for depreciation has actually been earned, that all of it is recognised by the tax authorities as an allowable deduction and that the money is not required to pay for replacements. Enough has been said to indicate that there is a very close connection between expense budgeting and capital outlay budgeting, as the amount that is budgeted for depreciation determines largely the limits within which capital outlays will be feasible in the following financial period. The most important point in connection with the general problem of paying for capital outlays out of depreciation provisions is whether money is required for replacements. It is perhaps not simplifying the situation too much to lay down as a general proposition that the less the age of the fixed assets generally, the less will correspondingly be the necessity for replacements. Such German factories as have had to be rebuilt since the war generally have very modern equipment. Consequently the question of depreciation plays a very large part in profit budgeting as well as in capital outlay budgeting.

III. Modern Methods of Accounting and the Accountancy Profession

German accountancy circles have watched the development of modern accounting methods very closely, intent to discover what possibilities it holds for them, not only as auditors but also as consultants on matters within their professional cognizance.

1. *Effects on Audit Work*

a. Better organisation of accounts after introduction of budgeting

It needs scarcely be pointed out that businesses which decide to institute budgetary methods must first of all set up a properly organised basis on which the new methods can function. Usually the preparatory investigations of the position make it quite clear that the *original records* of transactions, on which the whole subsequent accounting inevitably rests, are not informative enough and that they can be very unreliable; furthermore, that the *ratios* used for allocating expense and other matters to costs are all other than accurate. It is of the essence of sound budgeting that all short-cut methods which sacrifice accuracy to simplicity, must be discarded and replaced by methods which ensure accurate computations. The costing of cost centers will be elaborated, and not unusually it turns out that the cost basis of the cost units, as used hitherto, is nowhere near correct.

The preliminary work that must be done to reorganise the system from top to bottom, before the introduction of budgetary planning can be even thought of, must result in the whole accounting system of the business being made much more dependable. This is, of course, of very great value to the auditor, chiefly, perhaps, because it eases his tasks of checking the inventories of materials and manufactured products and of forming an opinion as to the accuracy of the pricing of goods in process and of finished goods.

b. Assessing the correctness of profits shown

The certificate of a German auditor (Wirtschaftsprüfer) embodies not only the assurance that 'the books of account, the annual accounts and that part of the manager's report which comments on the annual accounts have been prepared in the manner required by law', but it ought also to constitute an assurance that the annual accounts, as presented, properly and fairly disclose the financial and economic position of the business. Apart, of course, from his inspection of the books of the business, the auditor can rely on only two other aids to support his conviction that he was justified in signing the certificate to the accounts, namely:

a. any knowledge he possesses, derived from his experience of the 'standard' conditions as regards selling opportunities, competition and manufacturing techniques of the type of business he is dealing with,

b. his assessment of the future dangers inherent in carrying on that type of business.

German auditors are accustomed to make considerable use of standards, which mostly owe their origin to the experience of generations of accountants, and obviously if the auditor has an inside knowledge of the affairs of comparable enterprises in the same line of business it will be of great value to him. Officials of the Revenue who investigate the affairs of taxpayers have behind them a fund of accurate and comprehensive standards; it behoves the practising accountant who is called upon to advise his client as to financial and fiscal problems to have at his disposal a fund of standards possessing at least equal efficacy.

The auditor who makes use of standards in his work is in a position to judge whether the figures submitted by his client are within the range of the normal and consequently of the probable, or not. If, moreover, the figures submitted as the 'actual' figures diverge from what he knows should be the standard, he may very well be able to put his finger on some erroneous accounting procedure or perhaps on where the business is losing money.

If the business that he is auditing has its own standards, the auditor's task is made materially lighter. He needs then only compare his own standards with those of the business he is auditing, and he will be able to determine with confidence whether the reasons given by the management of the business for the success or failure of its affairs are the true ones. The auditor should take care, in his use of standards, to confine himself as far as possible to really comprehensive standards and standards which delineate only major trends. It should not be his function to acquire such detailed knowledge of the affairs of his client that he is in a position to discuss standards relating to the production of individual cost centers. In the first place he could only acquire such knowledge if he carried his audit much further than practitioners consider necessary, and even then it would have meant that he had spent time on acquiring detailed knowledge of the special points affecting that business of a kind that an auditor only acquires who has acted as consultant to the business for many, many years. That is not what is normally expected of him.

Accounts which do not take into consideration the future dangers that the business may have to face can never be described as true and correct. One of the most onerous duties that an auditor has to undertake is to form a balanced view of the correctness of the provision for risks where the danger is not insubstantial. It eases the auditor's burden very much if the business he is auditing can show that it has a good system of budgeting for expense, revenue, profits and financial matters. If the auditor can satisfy himself that the budgets of the undertaking have been reliable in the past, he would normally be justified in his audit of the annual accounts of an undertaking, in according substantial credence to the budgets for the forthcoming financial year. At this point the very close connection between auditing and budgeting becomes apparent.

2. *Effect on Consultative Work*

It is a peculiarity of the accountancy profession in Germany that it is the exception rather than the rule for German practitioners to devote any substantial amount of time to consultative work. Auditing is certainly the major function of most practitioners. Where practitioners engage in consultative work to any extent, their sphere is practically always financing or taxation problems. They have scarcely ever even ventured across the border of the territory constituted by the whole range of problems associated with production and selling techniques. Yet that territory is the home of the production and selling problems which await treatment at the hands of a specialist qualified in the finer points of standard costing and predetermined costing.

The construction of systems of standard costing and of budgeting (and their subsequent examination in the course of an audit) and assistance in the breaking down of variance statements is not, as has been seen, considered to fall within the scope of the normal professional functions of a German practitioner. Usually it is done by special companies or firms which make a business of selling advice, or it is carried out by the staff of the undertaking concerned. This situation might change very suddenly if, for instance, boom conditions were to cease, and the paramount questions which every business was asking became 'What is the source of our losses' and 'How are we to stop them'. This is the reason why German professional accountants must take care that every one of them has qualified himself so that he may be in a position to offer advice to his client on the solution of such problems.

PAPER

by

S. PRAKASH CHOPRA, B.A., B. COM., A.C.A., F.C.A. (INDIA)

The Institute of Chartered Accountants of India

In India we are still in the process of evolution. We are just getting to grips with the economic problems facing us. In this International Congress it is my intention only to highlight some of the outstanding problems that face the Accountants in India and to bring out such special features as are arising or are likely to arise consequent upon the adoption of the modern concept of measurement or control by under-developed countries anxious to catch up with the economic progress in advanced countries in their efforts to secure a decent standard of living for their nationals in a democratic and peaceful manner.

Modern Accounting is no longer a record of book-keeping entries, reflecting merely the state of affairs of a business house. Over the years it has developed into an instrument of control and a tool for management. Accountancy has not only to keep pace with the advance in technical and scientific knowledge in all spheres more particularly its commercialisation but has also to be in a position to give answers with the requisite speed.

One of the special features of the modern business and industry is the size which tends to grow bigger and bigger. Generally management is for the most part, in the hands of persons who have virtually no personal financial stake therein. This becomes much more so in cases in which the industry or trade is in the hands of the State. In economically under-developed countries or in countries attempting a socialistic pattern of society, the tendency is increasingly towards running industries under State control or ownership, and that poses a problem of its own. In India, for instance, a line of demarcation has lately been laid down in respect of the spheres of industrial activity, that is to say, as between what are popularly known as the Public (or State) Sector and the Private Sector respectively. Under the declared industrial policy of the State, the key or basic industries are generally the concern of the State though in some cases there may be mixed economies i.e. the Public and the Private Sectors working jointly; while the consumer goods industries, small scale industries and industries not falling within the Public Sector have been left over to the Private Sector. In course of time there is every likelihood of an increasing shift in favour of State owned industry possibly because of the necessity *a.* to step up production at the required pace, *b.* to expand employment opportunities, and *c.* to reduce inequalities in income and wealth to achieve more even distribution of the economic power.

Increased overall productivity aimed at achieving a substantial increase in national income presupposes greater efficiency and more intensive utilisation of the available resources with complete elimination of all avoidable waste. So that we have to think and think intensively, in the words and spirit of the popular saying 'Think before leap', and pool all experience and knowledge, our own as well as of others including the 'Know How' – to produce a complete and fool-proof plan or scheme of working. Detailed calculations of the expected performances prepared by financial, commercial and technical experts have to be used as the base and an estimate of the probable happenings called the 'Budget', produced.

Such a plan to be of practical utility, is expressed in terms measurable and comparable, involving as it does, an element of convertibility or production which is the sum total of the final product after the conversion of raw materials and effort. 'Units' are employed as the measure or yard-stick. The 'Units' may be in terms of quantities of raw materials, man-hours, machine-hours, horse-power, units of products, or money values. They can be expressed in quantititative terms prevalent in relation to particular commodities or industries and/or can also be expressed in specialised terms or in terms of money value. In the latter case, allowance is made for the rise or fall in general prices.

The best expressed Budget (or the Master Budget) is in the form which is adopted for the presentation of the final results, e.g. the Balance Sheet or Statement of Assets and Liabilities, Income & Expenditure Account, etc. The Master Budget is further broken down into sections, e.g. sales and/or sales cost budget, and so on. These different budgets are further sub-divided till you reach the most elementary production points. All this is in effect an analysis and further analysis of figures representing real goods.

There was a time when it was almost the fashion to treat the budget, the financial accounts and the cost accounts as separate water-tight compartments and hence separate functions. Now in any good accounting system they form part of the integral whole, and the budget framed by careful forecasting forms the basis of the 'Standards' set for costing. By investigations into quality control, job evaluation, time and motion study, plant lay out, lay out for production and the like, the budgets or standards are under constant review and an attempt towards progressive improvement is made. While the main budget is, as a rule, for the year, it is split up into periods of time over the year and is subject to revision from time to time according to plan – which is known as the flexible budget method.

After its final adoption by the management, the Plan or budget is launched in the form of commencement of production or business, as the case may be, and the results of the actual happenings are recorded in the appropriate accounts. By comparing the actuals from time to time during the course of working with the budgeted figures it is possible to study causes of the variances and to remove inefficiencies. As a matter of fact the budget is the friend of the management at all levels. The performer, that is, the human performer, knows in advance what is expected. The people above him know what to expect of him and he knows what to expect of the people below. Delegation of responsibility without any expensive team of supervisors thus becomes possible. In fact, worked in a proper spirit, the performer becomes his own boss.

To make things easier the use of ultra technical terms in such schemes has to be avoided and they have to be worded in simple language. Any new scheme involving radical changes should be introduced by stages and in a manner likely to bring home its utility and efficiency to the performers. Further it would be found that the human nature reacts more sympathetically and readily if it is made to appear that the new method is an attempt to supplement and not to supplant.

In India the extent to which modern methods of accounting are used, varies from industry to industry and from unit to unit. This is due in part to the present stage of economic development and in part to the dearth of qualified personnel. Only after the independence of the country have any serious and sustained efforts emerged for real progress. The Institute of Chartered Accountants of India was established in 1949. The First Five Year Plan ended 1955–56 brought about some improvement in industrial production. The Second Five Year Plan which is considered ambitious by some and not going far enough by others, lays particular emphasis on the need for the training of technical and managerial personnel. It may be mentioned, however, that during the past few years attempts have been made for the introduction of uniform costing in industries e.g. jute. And the introduction of improved accounting methods has also been attempted in some, e.g. oil and petroleum companies, steel mills, textile mills. Following recent nationalisation, the Insurance Corporation may be one of the largest single units, perhaps the largest, with decentralised accounting and central overall control. Other large scale industries, such as coal, both in the Private and the Public Sectors, heavy chemicals, electric supply undertakings, cement, paper and manganese are stated to be in the process of introducing the latest methods.

In India the State Departments are also now thinking along these lines. The Government of India have set up a special Department to study and further such working so far as it might be practicable. The Planning Commission, India, has set up a wing to carry on research and investigations in this behalf. All these attempts are yet in their infancy, and the results of their researches and experiments are awaited with interest. The main trend of their approach concerns the method and manner of job evaluation and productive estimation. One feature peculiar to the scheme of management accounting in a State Department or enterprise is that the civil servant or other employee working therein is generally a permanent servant and his services are not easily terminable. The impersonality of approach is greater here than in any enterprise under private control. Parliamentary control at times tends to produce a certain element of nervousness or lack of confidence in the minds of the civil servant for which reason he is disinclined to take risks. It appears that the budgetary standards control method should prove particularly useful and place the civil servant employee or the Minister in Charge in a stronger position to answer critics.

Turning next to some of the other typical problems arising in economically under-developed countries working to a plan and/or attempting a welfare State with an eye on social justice:

a. Return on Capital. What should be deemed to be Capital employed? And what should be the basis of 'Return'? The Tariff Commission in India has been allowing a return on Block at original cost plus a smaller return on circulating capital employed when determining the cost of production for purposes of deciding whether an industry is entitled to, or is justified in claiming, protective Tariffs. On the other hand, in some 'cost plus' contracts, return on capital is given in the form of profit on turnover. There are also businessmen who would like a 'risk rate of return' on the total value of assets of the industry. It is argued that the Equity Shareholders carry the risk in respect of all liabilities and hence should be entitled to the difference between the interest or return payable on all other finance and the risk rate of Return on total Capital employed. For example, if Debenture Loans were raised at 5 % and the normal dividend expectation of an Equity Shareholder was 10 %, then for purposes of cost of production calculation the interest on the Debenture Loan finance employed should be taken at 10 %. Similarly in the case of sundry credits or deposits, the interest calculation should be done the same way. My view is that such an approach may lead to absurd results: it does not seem equitable and would tend to increase the cost of production to an abnormally high figure. The correct approach would appear to me to be that the actual interest on all finance other than Equity Capital should be calculated and Equity Capital given a risk rate of return which should take into account the risk taken in regard to other liabilities. Another interesting point that arises here is about the return on General Reserves which are the property of Equity Shareholders. Should they be taken as part of Equity Capital or as a separate item? It is opined by some that they should be treated as part of Equity Capital. In this connection it is submitted that this may not be in accordance with facts or law. In most countries, there is restriction in regard to repayment of capital but not to the same extent in regard to distribution of reserves in the form of dividends. The reserves are, therefore, like call deposits by shareholders except that they cannot be called back by the shareholders but can be distributed amongst the shareholders by the Directors. In these circumstances what suggests itself is that the return on Reserves may be taken at a rate lower than the rate of return on Equity Capital but higher than loan capital.

b. Depreciation Funds. The role of depreciation funds in financing as well as the mode and extent of charging depreciation as an expense also need consideration. It has been argued that depreciation should be calculated on the replacement or current value of the assets. The main argument in favour of this contention is that by means of depreciation charges a business house is supposed to accumulate funds required for replacement of assets and an attempt is made to keep the real capital intact. This school of thought approaches the problem from the point of view of investors particularly Equity Shareholders. According to them the fact that depreciation is primarily an apportionment of the cost of the assets over different periods of time during their life is of secondary importance. And yet it is felt that the adoption of the replacement value or current value theory in regard to depreciation would lead to inflationary tendencies already existing and would also lead to social injustice. At any rate there would appear to be an invidious distinction between a bank depositor and an investor in Equity Capital when he is given the proposed favoured treatment.

In matters like these, there can be three possible approaches: there is the seller or the manufacturer's point of view, the consumer's point of view, and the State's point of view representing the society as a whole. While the seller would like to earn profits and be also in a position to retain his real capital intact, the buyer would like to buy as cheaply as possible in order to keep down his cost of living or the cost of further manufacture. The State, on the other hand, would like a balance between the two, with an eye to equitable distribution of wealth or power. During a period of rising prices, if the replacement or current value theory is adopted, the cost of sales would obviously be higher. The additional cost would have to be paid by the buyer. Even assuming that this additional cost is justified with a view to ensuring future production, it is for consideration whether this additional amount should be left with the seller or should be shared amongst the different factors of production including wage earners, and the State in the form of taxation. In connection with any suggestion to step up depreciation charges we have to bear in mind that the consumer is already paying a higher amount for the maintenance of the old machinery at the prevailing market prices and is being deprived of the use of new machinery which even though more expensive is likely ultimately to be more economical. It may sometimes be found that if the original cost of machinery were taken at the replacement value and depreciation were calculated at appropriate rates over the spent up life, the resultant written down value would not materially differ from the book value. This is perhaps due to the fact that the machinery is generally either fairly old or has been purchased in the recent past at almost the current prices. On this point I would say that, even though the depreciation charges need not be stepped up, it might still be necessary to create a reserve out of the profits for the eventuality of replacement. A proper balance between savings and consumption has to be maintained. Savings, however, should not be confused with legitimate costs.

c. Source of profits. The matter of determination of the source of profit poses an interesting problem. A country or a society may either sell its goods in a raw material form or convert them into finished goods for sale. When the sale is in converted form, it would be appropriate to separate the profit on the sale of raw material from that on conversion. Take, for instance, jute: at any particular moment of time the cost of the raw material and the cost of conversion can be calculated separately. The difference in the price of the finished product, and the price of the raw material consumed therein can be compared with the cost of conversion to find the profit or loss on conversion. There are cases, however, in which such analysis and comparison on an international basis may not always be possible, e.g. coarse or short staple Indian cotton which cannot be exported and can only be converted into cloth within the country. Such analysis will prove useful in fixing the location of an industry and to the management in determining future policy.

d. Aids. This is one of our peculiar problems, that is to say—How to treat the value of 'aid' in accounts? Such 'aid' may take the form of supply of plant and machinery free or at a concessional price and/or value of trained personnel placed at our disposal. Accounting for the former is comparatively simple. Depreciation can be calculated on the market price of the Plant & Machinery, although nothing or a part only of the price may have been paid. Suitable credit can be given to an appropriate account or to the party which may be a State Department. The value of the skilled labour so made available is, however, a little more difficult to determine. Should that be taken as expenditure incurred by the party giving the aid or should it be on the basis of costs that would have been incurred, had such skilled labour not been made available? Should we consider this aid to be in the nature of experimental expenses or what? As against this there is the question what the consumer can bear.

e. Of late the element of uncertainty in forecasting has become more complex, for the bank rates in certain European countries have been rising unexpectedly. It almost looks as if the Bank rate is losing its sanctity. A large number of contracts were based on the prevailing English bank rate but as the result of the sudden rise in the bank rate the cost of supply from Britain and some other countries went up unexpectedly. Devaluation followed by the raising of the bank rate appears to have shaken faith in Sterling which had past traditions to its credit.

The popular belief that a rise in bank rate is deflationary does not appear to me to be really true. The obvious result of a rise in the bank rate is an increase in interest charges payable to the bank and over the time to other depositors and investors. The cost of production goes up with the consequential increase in price resulting in a demand for a wage rise. Such increase in bank rate has also the effect of making it more difficult for economically under-developed countries e.g. India, to borrow from producing countries particularly when interest rates in the former countries are lower than in European countries.

Further in Planned Economy, it becomes essential sometimes for the State to have some knowledge of or supervision over the affairs of the trade and industry in private hands. With the introduction of the budgetary standard control methods this should become easier.

In India amongst other things an attempt is being made towards some sort of standardisation in the form of presentation of accounts. A start has been made under the Indian Companies Act whereunder a form for the Balance Sheet and a Schedule for the Profit & Loss Account has been prescribed. There may even be a good case for having separate forms of account for different industries to suit their individual requirements or for purposes of collecting statistics subsequently to act as an aid for determining overall policies.

In respect of some of the problems raised above I have attempted to give some answers. Yet I am sure the learned and experienced members of the Conference will be able to throw much valuable light thereon, as the same or similar problems may have arisen elsewhere and may have been solved or may be under active and serious consideration.

PAPER

by

JOSEPH PELEJ, C.P.A.

American Institute of Certified Public Accountants

The last two decades of our century have witnessed revolutionary changes in management philosophy and management techniques. While in the earlier stages of our industrial development management was primarily concerned with production, marketing and other operating matters, our social, scientific and technological advances have created new demands and have affected so materially the size and complexity of our business and industrial enterprises that the administrative function has become one of management's principal concerns. In organizations of any size, 'management' is no longer the responsibility of the few. Authority has been delegated and managerial responsibility has been established at various levels. This has led to demands for improved methods of planning, controlling and coordinating the activities of the enterprise. In developing these improved methods, the concepts of the accounting function have undergone significant changes.

Historical Accounting

The old and narrow concept, which is still quite prevalent, regards accounting as being essentially historical in character, chiefly concerned with the recording of past transactions in conventional accounts, the paying of bills, calculation of taxes and the preparation, periodically, of financial statements designed principally to give an account, in conventional financial terms, of management's stewardship. Internally, historical accounting may provide a basis for the formulation of general financial policies. Aside, however, from furnishing management with historical financial data for comparison with like data for prior periods, historical accounting makes relatively little contribution to operational planning and control.

Management Accounting

Today, we hear a great deal about 'management accounting' by which we refer to that phase of the accounting function which is directly concerned with aiding management's planning and administrative tasks and which, in essence, is a change in perspective from the contemplation of historical results to the more fruitful planning of future operations and evaluation of the results against predetermined plans. It has to do with methods to enable management to plan and coordinate operations for future periods and to determine (1) the extent to which established plans and objectives are being met, (2) the efficiency of performance and (3) responsibility for performance in relation to established goals. It also serves to indicate to management the course of action that might be taken to effect cost reductions and to improve operating results. Thus, 'management accounting' covers a much broader field than is usually associated with the historical concept of accounting. It is concerned with the planning function through budgeting, the control function through the use of standards and other measurements of performance and with adequate methods and procedures to provide a basis for effective reporting to management by areas of responsibility.

Elements of Budgeting

Budgeting has come to be recognized as one of the most effective aids to management, particularly when it is conceived not only as serving the planning function but also as a basis for effective control over all phases of the operations of the business as well as a guide to future action. The design and operation of the budget requires the adoption of sound principles of (1) organization and utilization of personnel, (2) operational controls and (3) management reporting, to integrate and coordinate the efforts of practically every section of the business towards the attainment of over-all management objectives. Today's concept of management embraces every level and area of authority in the company responsible for carrying out some part of the company's program. This includes not only the top executive group, but the successive levels of authority in sales, production, general administration and, in fact, any area of company operation where effective planning and control are required. A soundly conceived plan of budgetary control provides greater opportunities for the extension of the usefulness of the accounting function to all these levels.

It also becomes apparent that a successful budget system must be based on a sound plan of organization in which each department and administrative group must understand the objectives of its particular activity and its relationship to the objectives of the company as a whole. Departmental relationships, lines of responsibility, and spheres of authority must be clearly defined and logically assigned. Fixing responsibility of specific individuals for efficient performance in accordance with the established plans is a fundamental concept of budgetary control. However, if specific individuals are to be held responsible for performance, they must know precisely what they are responsible for, and to whom. They must be vested with necessary authority, and clear-cut policies and procedures must be established to enable those accountable for performance to function properly. Failure to do this will cause departmental activities to get out of focus with over-all company objectives and result in duplication or waste of effort.

Coordinated effort of all departments of the business is essential to the successful operation of the budget. It follows that department heads and supervisors should take an active part not only in the preparation of the budget but also in making its operation effective. In fact, this collective effort is important in establishing acceptance on the part of managers and department heads of their responsibility to perform in accordance with established plans. The accountant's function is principally that of consulting with department heads in the course of preparing the budget, supplying them with essential data, coordinating departmental plans, integrating them with company-wide objectives and presenting the complete budget to top management for approval.

Sales Forecasts

Proper planning is at the base of most successful business operations. It may be informal, intuitive or subconscious, or it may assume the proportions of a highly organized and scientific forecasting operation. While a small business can, as a rule, be successfully run without formalized plans (yet seldom without any planning), the need for organized forecasting becomes greater in larger business organizations. Sales forecasts are most important parts of the budget structure since they directly influence the production, expense and other budgets which are geared to the requirements estimated on basis of the sales forecast. The point to which this function needs to be expanded and the degree of accuracy with which sales forecasts can be made depend upon a variety of factors, such as the competitive situation, the company's position in the market, the nature and variety of its products, its position in the industry, its distribution methods, the effect upon its own operations of business trends in other industries and of general business conditions and many others. So essential is this function that an ever-increasing number of the larger organizations have established marketing research divisions whose staff of trained analysts and statisticians makes extensive studies of the various economic and other factors affecting the company's business with a view to assisting sales management in arriving at the sales potential for a given budget period as well as on a long-term basis. By virtue of its studies of the markets, the research staff is also in a position to offer suggestions for improvements in marketing methods.

Inventory Budgets

When the sales budget has been established, steps can be taken to ascertain whether or not the estimated sales volume will yield a satisfactory profit in terms of return on the capital invested. This involves careful consideration of the pricing and marketing policies and costs with regard to each product and preparation of a sound inventory budget. Maintaining inventories at the most economical levels and stabilization of inventories at these levels are important objectives of modern budgeting and accounting methods.

In dealing with the inventory problem, accountants have resorted to varying techniques, most of which fall into the 'sound business judgment' category. However, in recent years the scientific approach of operations research has provided accountants with powerful tools for the selection, evaluation and correlation of the factors involved in the problem in such a way as to produce vastly improved solutions which could not be obtained by the conventional methods.

Budget Standards

When the sales and inventory budgets have been agreed upon, budgets can be prepared of the cost of production and distribution of the anticipated sales volume and of the expenses involved in the administrative services. These budgets are designed for the purposes of cost control. Effective control involves comparison of actual with anticipated performance with a view to ascertaining the reasons for the variances between them so that appropriate action may promptly be taken where the need for corrective measures is indicated. This concept of control differs materially from the old methods of comparing actual results for corresponding periods. It presupposes the establishment of standards and aims at fixing responsibility for performance.

The task of setting standards, particularly for factory expenses, calls for maximum cooperation and active participation of the operating personnel and department heads at all levels of managerial or supervisory responsibility as well as of the laboratory and other technicians and methods analysts. The historical approach to the setting of standards has many serious disadvantages, the most important of which, perhaps, is that standards based on past experience are influenced by the inefficiencies of the past and their use may, therefore, easily lead to serious inequities through penalizing the efficient operator and permitting the inefficient one to perpetuate his inefficiencies. The best standards are those which are based upon engineering analyses and measurements with a view to ascertaining best performance under a given set of circumstances. These so-called engineered standards are developed through time and motion studies, job analyses, work load studies, calculations of manpower requirements, etc. The important thing, however, is to make certain that everyone concerned understands how the standards were produced and that they are regarded as fair and equitable by those whose performance they are intended to measure. The first objective is to gain organization-wide acceptance of the philosophy of control through the use of standards and to educate the organization in the utilization of the information which the system produces.

Flexible Budget

Certain elements of manufacturing expenses vary with the levels of production, such as indirect materials, or they may remain fixed regardless of the production level, such as depreciation, taxes, and insurance or they may be semi-variable in character such as foremen's wages which will vary with the number of shifts worked and not directly with production volume. This difference in the behavior of expenses in relation to production is taken into account in what is known as the flexible budget in which the various elements of departmental expense are computed in relation to varying production capacity. The flexible budget provides management with more effective means for the evaluation of actual performance because the goals and standards can be set to correspond to the same levels to which the actual performance data relate.

Evaluating Performance

An essential element of the system of budgetary control is the manner in which performance is evaluated against the established yardsticks and the methods followed in explaining and presenting the variances. This evaluation must be made from realistic viewpoints which take proper cognizance of the plans established for the unit whose performance is being evaluated and the nature and extent of its operations, the objective being to segregate the total variance for the unit as between those components which can be traced to inefficiency or deviations from established plans caused by decisions of its own supervision and those which have been caused by outside influences or inefficiencies of other units of the company or by decisions of top management. This form of analysis calls for the exercise of a large degree of objectivity, an understanding of the operations in many departments and proper coordination of the results.

The question therefore arises as to who should assume the responsibility for the evaluation of performance and the analysis of variances. From the standpoint of good control, this operation should not be the sole responsibility of personnel in the department whose performance is being evaluated. Where it is, the explanations frequently take the form of excuses and there is, moreover, the danger of providing opportunities for the concealment of serious irregularities. The prevalent practise therefore is to delegate this task to the accountant who is thus placed in a position of making an important contribution to management in its quest for ways of improving the operations. However, he cannot discharge this function successfully if he should also be charged with or assume the responsibility for taking action or for effecting the desired improvements. His is the task of disclosing, reporting and making his facilities available to further such corrective steps as management may decide to take. The evaluation and analysis process holds the promise of greatest success where it is a joint effort of the accountant with personnel in the departments being evaluated and it is the wise accountant indeed who emphasizes the cooperative rather than the critical nature of his participation in this most important task. The effectiveness of a system of standards and budgets depends to a great extent upon the approach to the establishment of the yardsticks, organization of the evaluation of performance against them and the quality of the reporting of the results of such evaluation to all levels of management.

Reporting on Performance

The budget will not in itself accomplish the desired results. Its effective use requires complete management support and the development of a reporting system which clearly fixes responsibility for performance, which promotes action and which ensures that the information to promote it reaches those who have the knowledge, the authority and the will to take whatever measures are needed to be taken. Generally speaking, the required action may be of the type intended to correct deficiencies in performance as indicated by unfavorable variances of actual results from standard. Or it may be of the long-range type intented to improve the standard of performance in the future through modification of objectives and policies, more efficient facilities, methods and personnel.

The system of reporting should meet the requirements of all levels of supervision and provide for the integration of reports at the lower levels into reports for top management control. There is no uniform pattern, but in the design of the reports the two principles of 'responsibility accounting' and 'management by exception' should be observed. At the lower levels of supervision, this means that the reports should be restricted to information relating to those phases of the operations over which the individual to whom the report is issued has control. The data contained in these reports should be of immediate interest to the recipients and the reports should be timed with due regard to the interval required to take corrective action before it may be too late.

Particularly at the lower levels of responsibility, the inclusion in reports of figures, which the recipients cannot recognize as relating to their own responsibility and to the operations over which they have control, leads to distrust of the reports and eventual deterioration of the system. This is not to say that in order, for example, to reflect in the report the total cost of a department or other unit of responsibility it may not be desirable or necessary to include data beyond those reflecting the direct responsibility of the department or unit. In most cases, it is advisable to distinguish between controllable and non-controllable expenses and to segregate the two groups clearly in the reports.

The man best fitted to correct inefficiencies and reduce costs is the man closest to the operations. Thus, the foreman, concerned as he is with the day-to-day operations, might be furnished with simple reports on a daily basis whereas the plant superintendent might make better use of information furnished him on a weekly basis. The top production official, being more concerned with trends and performance over the longer term might best be served with reports on a monthly basis. Most important of all, every effort should be made to ensure that the significance of the data in the reports is fully understood by the recipients. For this purpose, the analysts should take the keenest interest in the operations, frequently visit the operational centers, familiarize themselves with the jargon of the workers and with plant terminology with a view to being able to interpret the figures simply and intelligently and in language (oral or graphic) which the operating men can readily understand. An educational program for supervisors and others participating in compiling and administering the budget may be found extremely helpful. Such a program provides for instruction meetings in which discussions are held on such points as definition and purpose of the budget, definition and methods of determination of cost elements, classification of manufacturing overhead expenses, explanation of forms to be used in preparing the budget, description and explanation of reports to be provided and how they can be used to control costs.

Obviously, as operations expand and the area over which control must be exercised increases, it becomes more and more difficult, in fact, impossible for executives to oversee, check and follow up every detail of the operations under their charge. Even if it were possible for them to do this, they would be deprived of the time and energy for purposeful, creative thinking. Reporting by exception has therefore become an accepted device to conserve executive time and improve the usefulness of reports as promoters of action. In reporting on performance in a well-planned operation, only the more important deviations from the established plans as shown by a comparison of actual performance with predetermined standards should require the attention of top management.

Modernizing the Accounting System

In order to produce the data required to attain the budget objectives, far-reaching revisions in the accounting system are frequently necessary. The accounting records must reflect costs and expenses by areas of responsibility as laid down in the plan of organization. Within each area, appropriate account classifications must be provided to permit ready comparisons of the figures representing actual against predetermined performance. This involves a careful re-examination of the chart of accounts to ensure that the transactions are recorded in such a manner as to preclude intermingling in one account of figures pertaining to different responsibilities or the recording in the same account of several types of expenses. Once the usefulness of the system has been recognized by management, the demands on the accountant for more detailed and current information increase rapidly. These demands make it necessary for the accountant to introduce improved methods and procedures to produce the required data quickly and efficiently. To ensure timeliness of the reports, the work of periodically closing the accounts must in many cases be speeded up through more extensive use of labor-saving devices and other techniques. The tremendous technological advances in office equipment design in recent years, including electronic data processing equipment, are of great assistance to the accountant not only in keeping clerical costs within economical limits but in more promptly meeting the demands for information vital to management in making more informed decisions.

Long-range Planning

This paper has briefly dealt principally with some of the more important aspects of short-term budgeting and with certain features considered essential to making the system effective. Attention should, however, be directed to the importance of long-range planning. Long-range plans should include the development of a sales program with due regard to extension of markets, modification of product lines, improvements in methods of distribution as well as a program for the improvement of production through better use or expansion of production facilities, improved inventory management and improvements in methods to reduce the costs of operations. Personnel development and training programs are an essential part of such long-range plans. They should of course also include a sound plan of financing to meet the costs of expansion and other costs connected with the execution of the long-term plans. Integration of the period budget with long-term plans is essential so that decisions can be made with due regard to the future growth and development of the company.

Audit Implications

A few words should be said about the effect of budgets upon the function of the auditor. Proceeding on the premise that in formulating the audit program, both as to nature and extent, the auditor relies heavily upon the condition of the system of internal accounting control, we are led to the conclusion that the system of budgetary control, when effectively administered, should improve the effectiveness of the auditor's work since it strengthens the system of internal accounting control. Refinements in the chart of accounts resulting from the introduction of a system of budgetary control enable the auditor to make a better analysis of the operations. If the analyses of and reporting on the variances have been properly organized, a review of these analyses and reports might furnish the auditor with significant clues to more effective distribution of audit emphasis and effort. Because of the critical review of variances and the action which they invite, there is usually much greater care exercised under a budget system in the coding and subsequent processing and recording of revenues and expenditures. This results in greater reliability of the figures recorded in the accounts. For the same reasons, errors and irregularities are more likely to be detected. It is well known that, frequently, gross errors or fraud are disclosed not through audit procedures but through persistent investigation of questions first raised by personnel in operating departments concerning figures which are out of line with the operators' intimate knowledge of the operations.

The challenge to the accountant to aid management in planning, controlling and improving complex operations is today greater than ever before. In trying to meet this challenge, the forward-looking accountant has excellent opportunities for the exercise of his best technical skills, for creative and imaginative thinking and for gaining acceptance of his function as a real tool of modern management.

INLEIDING

van

A. F. TEMPELAAR

Nederlands Instituut van Accountants

I. Inleiding

Ten tijde van het in 1926 in Nederland gehouden Internationale Accountantscongres was het onderwerp 'budgettering in de onderneming' vrijwel onbekend. De referaten 'Standard costs as a basis of management and industrial control'[1] zou men als voorstudies van budgettering kunnen beschouwen.

In de dertig jaren tussen 1926 en heden zijn in een zeer omvangrijke literatuur vele facetten van de budgettering beschreven. Niettemin is het onderwerp nog steeds actueel. In dit referaat beperk ik mij tot enkele belangrijke aspecten en tot de praktische toepassing door middengrote en kleinere ondernemingen in ons land.

De steeds groter wordende risico's voortvloeiende uit de anticipatie op toekomstige omstandigheden en de groter wordende behoefte aan delegatie van functies hebben in de onderneming hun invloed doen gelden op de aard en de omvang van de administratie. Er is behoefte ontstaan aan een administratie, welke de leiding – op de verschillende niveaus van autoriteit – inzicht verschaft in de te verwachten consequenties van de voorgenomen anticipatie en in de werkelijke ontwikkeling in vergelijking tot de gestelde verwachtingen, zowel wat de onderneming in haar geheel als wat de activiteiten van elk der organen afzonderlijk betreft.

De traditionele boekhouding kan aan deze behoefte niet voldoen. Zij is uitsluitend historie-beschrijving van financiële data en geeft de leiding geen andere informatie dan de jaarlijkse, in comptabele volgorde opgestelde, balans en resultatenrekening. Zij moet daarom worden gemoderniseerd en omgevormd tot een apparaat voor progressieve oriëntatie.

Naast de historie wordt ook de verwachting een element van administratie. Vergelijking tussen verwachting en uitvoering worden van betekenis, o.a. voor correctief toezicht van de leiding en voor heroriëntatie t.a.v. de uitgestippelde gedragslijn.

Het moderne administratieve systeem vereist als verantwoordelijke leider een

[1] Inleidingen op dit congres door C. Hewetson Nelson, Prof. J. Anton de Haas, Prof. J. G. Ch. Volmer en William Kemp.

dynamisch georiënteerde persoon met kritische aanleg en onderlegd in bedrijfs-economische problemen. De statische boekhoudersfiguur, wiens denken en handelen alleen op comptabele vraagstukken gericht waren, is als chef niet meer op zijn plaats.

II. Budgettering en budgettaire controle als middel van informatie voor de bedrijfsleiding

Op het C.I.O.S.-congres 1951 te Brussel werd budgettering als volgt omschreven[1]:

1. An instrument for orientation in the field of activity and for building up a policy.

2. An instrument of guidance, planning and control of organisation, private as well as public ones (a.o. a means to the delegation of authority and to the coordination of activities; a control of efficiency).

Budgettering is een *middel*. Budgettering is geen toverformule, welke een gebrek aan bekwaamheid in de leiding kan compenseren. Het kan de leiding niet vervangen; integendeel, *alleen onder voorwaarde van een bekwame directie kan budgettering doeltreffend zijn.*

De grondslagen voor het budgetteren zijn voor elke onderneming gelijk, doch de praktische uitwerking moet zijn aangepast aan de aard en de organisatie van elk individueel bedrijf.

Budgettering is alleen dan van nut voor de leiding, wanneer het systeem als volgt wordt toegepast:

1. De budgettering als gecoördineerd systeem van plannen ten behoeve van de leiding[2].

2. De budgettering als middel voor de functionele taakverdeling en de budgettaire controle als instrument voor de controle op de uitvoering.

3. De budgettaire controle ten dienste van het continueel volgen en het analyseren van bedrijfsresultaten.

Indien niet op deze wijze toegepast, degradeert het totale systeem tot een variant van het boekhouden en zal het niet leiden tot de gewenste modernisering van de administratie.

1. *De budgettering als gecoördineerd systeem van plannen ten behoeve van de leiding*

De steeds verdergaande industrialisatie en mechanisatie vergen van de ondernemingen steeds belangrijker wordende investeringen in materiële en in mentale waarden, waarbij moet worden geanticipeerd op toekomstige omstandigheden. Dit dwingt de leiding van een onderneming zo systematisch mogelijk vooruit te zien[3]. De leiding moet plannen opstellen, waarin de door haar uitgestippelde gedragslijn t.a.v. het bestuur van de onderneming tot uitdrukking

[1] Zie het samenvattend rapport 'The flexible and variable budget' van Prof. Dr. A. Mey en E. Beekman.

[2] Men kan 'de leiding' onderscheiden naar het niveau van autoriteit, met in de top van de autoriteits-pyramide de top-leiding. In het kader van het in dit referaat aan de orde gestelde vraagstuk van de budgettering heeft dit onderscheid m.i. geen principiële betekenis, zodat ik het in deze inleiding niet toepas.

[3] 'Gouverner c'est prévoir' (Fayol).

wordt gebracht en waarin de vermoedelijke gevolgen van dit bestuur op de rentabiliteit en de vermogenspositie zijn berekend.

De plannen moeten op reële aanwijzingen (marktanalyse, statistische informatie e.d.) en niet alleen op intuïtie berusten. Men mag niet het risico lopen door 'fata morgana's' misleid te zijn.

Van dominerend belang zijn de activiteitsbegrotingen op lange termijn, bijv. van 3 tot 5 jaren. Hieruit vloeien enerzijds voort de kapitaalsbegrotingen, eveneens op lange termijn en anderzijds de exploitatiebegrotingen op korte termijn. Alleen op langere termijn geprojecteerd kan de leiding nagaan of haar doelstellingen kunnen worden verwezenlijkt en zo ja, onder welke voorwaarden[1]. Zij is hierdoor tevens in staat bij afwijkende omstandigheden zich snel te heroriënteren en dienovereenkomstig de gepaste maatregelen te nemen. De kapitaalsbegrotingen, welke op deze activiteits-plannen zijn gebaseerd, geven inzicht in de behoeften aan nieuwe investeringen en in de volgorde in urgentie.

Voor elke belangrijke investering zal tevens een afzonderlijke begroting moeten worden opgesteld van de behoefte aan middelen (incl. eventuele additionele investeringen in voorraden en vorderingen!) en van de met deze investering te bereiken resultaten. De verwachtingen van de commerciële en van de technische man moeten op deze wijze kritisch worden beoordeeld, zo nodig gecoördineerd en worden aangevuld met calculaties van de administratieve man. Alleen op deze wijze toegelicht kan de leiding beslissen en de verantwoordelijkheid voor haar besluit dragen.

Elk jaar resp. elk seizoen wordt de begroting voor de komende 3 of 5 jaren opgesteld. De begroting voor het eerste jaar is de exploitaite-begroting, welke gedetailleerd is. De begrotingen voor de volgende jaren zijn alleen in grote lijnen[2].

De verwachtingen van verkoop in het komende jaar en de produktiecapaciteit zijn het uitgangspunt van alle overige budgetten op korte termijn (inkoop, produktie, de hiermede samenhangende exploitatiekosten enz.). Deze budgetten moeten worden gecoördineerd en zullen aldus leiden tot de begrote, functioneel gedetailleerde resultatenrekening en de begrote balans.

Het deelnemen aan het tot stand komen van de budgetten (stimuleren en coördineren) vormt een belangrijke activiteit van de moderne administratieve leiding. Zij vertegenwoordigt tevens het bedrijfseconomisch element in de budgettering.

2. *De budgettering als middel voor de functionele taakverdeling en de budgettaire controle als instrument voor de controle op de uitvoering*

Als plan ten behoeve van de leiding heeft het budget weinig invloed op de

[1] Het opstellen van deze plannen zal eenvoudiger zijn voor bedrijven, die de toekomstige markt beter kunnen peilen dan voor die bedrijven, waar deze prognose minder 'reëel' kan zijn. Niettemin moeten ook de laatste trachten hun plannen op te stellen. Men wordt hierdoor *gedwongen* zich voortdurend op de toekomstige ontwikkeling van de onderneming te bezinnen.

[2] In de literatuur wordt veel meer aandacht geschonken aan de jaarbegrotingen dan aan de plannen op lange termijn, ofschoon de laatstgenoemde voor het inzicht van de leiding in de toekomstige ontwikkeling van meer belang zijn.

inrichting van de administratie. In feite is het budget niet meer dan een administratieve uitwerking van het plan.

De budgettering grijpt meer in de administratie in, wanneer zij wordt gehanteerd als middel voor de functionele taakverdeling.

De delegatie van functies is een van de essenties van de moderne bedrijfsvoering. De directeur, die alles zelf wil doen of in elk detail gekend wenst te worden, mislukt als leider. De leiding moet de vereiste delegatie toepassen teneinde 'to have time to think'. Voorwaarde is uiteraard, dat er bekwame medewerkers zijn, waaraan kan worden gedelegeerd.

De gedelegeerde functies dienen nauwkeurig omschreven en begrensd te zijn. Steeds dient op elk niveau van autoriteit de mogelijkheid van controle op de uitvoering te bestaan. De administratie kan in deze voor de leiding een onmisbare steun zijn, door zowel de *opdracht* als de resultaten van de *uitvoering* weer te geven en deze onderling te vergelijken. De toepassing van standaardkosten[1], budgetten en budgettaire controle is op dit vergelijken (van *opdracht* en *uitvoering*, van *toegestane* en *werkelijke kosten*) toegespitst.

Zij stelt de leiding in staat de uitvoering effectief te controleren en hierdoor meer te delegeren. Zonder deze middelen is het niet meer mogelijk een grote of middengrote onderneming doeltreffend te leiden.

In het kader van dit referaat beperk ik mij t.a.v. de budgettering als opdracht en de budgettaire controle tot de volgende opmerkingen.

a. De budgetten zijn kwantitatieve plannen, door middel van prijzen tot waarden herleid. Bij het bepalen van de offers, welke mogen worden gebracht, wordt uitgegaan van normatief gestelde verhoudingen[2] (o.a. op basis van standaardreceptuur, tijdstudies en andere statistische analyses). Ook de prijzen voor de waardering der hoeveelheden dienen als norm bedoeld te zijn (te bereiken verkoopprijs, te betalen inkoopprijs).

b. De budgetten worden per verantwoordelijke functionaris (zowel van de hoofdafdelingen als van de hulpafdelingen van de onderneming) opgesteld. Hierbij pleegt de leiding met haar medewerker(s) overleg, doch behoudt zich zo nodig de eindbeslissing voor, teneinde de door haar uitgestippelde beleidslijn te kunnen realiseren. De verantwoordelijke functionarissen (chefs) dienen deze budgetten als opdracht te beschouwen.

c. Bij belangrijke wijzigingen in de te verwachten omstandigheden dienen de budgetten gewijzigd te worden ('flexible budgeting'). Ingeval de werkelijke hoeveelheid prestatie-eenheden afwijkt van de begrote dient het desbetreffende budget van toegestane offers overeenkomstig te worden herleid (variabele budgettering). In verband hiermede worden de offers per afdeling onderscheiden naar de graad van afhankelijkheid van het volume prestaties[3].

d. De registratie van de uitvoering dient met dezelfde rubriceringen en onder dezelfde benamingen te geschieden als in de budgetten is toegepast.

[1] 'I believe I am justified in saying that no succesful budgetary control can be exercised without the use of standard costs, but that in turn no system of standard costs can effectively operate without a budgetary plan'. (Prof. J. Anton de Haas; Referaat Internationaal Accountantscongres 1926).

[2] De exactheid, waarmede deze normen worden bepaald, is afhankelijk van de aard van het bedrijfsproces en van de bedrijfsgrootte.

[3] De indeling 'variabel' en 'constant' is in het algemeen te grof.

e. De afwijkingen tussen 'opdracht' en 'uitvoering' worden geanalyseerd en gerubriceerd naar soort. De belangrijkste onderscheidingen zijn: hoeveelheidsafwijkingen in verkoop c.q. in productie; afwijkingen van de gestelde normen, zowel wat hoeveelheden[1] als wat waarden c.q. prijzen betreft; afwijkingen tengevolge van onjuiste begroting; incidentele verschillen.

De invloed van wijzigingen in de vervangingswaarde van belangrijke grond- en hulpstoffen op het resultaat der onderneming dient afzonderlijk tot uitdrukking te worden gebracht.

f. Van de aldus geanalyseerde verschillen ontvangt de leiding periodiek een overzicht. De betrokken functionarissen ontvangen een gedetailleerde opgave betreffende hun afdeling. De periodiciteit dezer overzichten varieert per onderneming. Zij moet zodanig zijn, dat de gegevens – gezien hun relatieve belang – actueel blijven en correctief ingrijpen door de leiding tijdig mogelijk is. Voorkomen is beter dan genezen. Het is daarom noodzakelijk, dat reeds bij het nemen van een besluit tot het doen van uitgaven, dus bij 'het bestellen', de consequenties ervan t.o.v. de opdracht worden nagegaan.

g. Zowel in de budgetten als in de registratie van de werkelijke mutaties dienen alle op de afdeling betrekking hebbende exploitatiekosten te zijn opgenomen. Ingeval de geplande hoeveelheid prestaties geringer is dan op grond van de beschikbare capaciteit mogelijk is, zal een evenredig deel van de vaste lasten voor deze capaciteit als verlies buiten de afdelingsoverzichten blijven en rechtstreeks op de algemene resultatenrekening verantwoord worden[2]. De afschrijvingen op gebouwen, machines e.d. moeten zijn gebaseerd op de vervangingswaarde dezer activa. Een zelfde beginsel geldt voor het gebruik van materialen en producten[2].

h. Budgettaire controle is ook noodzakelijk t.a.v. de investeringsbedragen in geval van nieuwe investeringen. Verschillen betreffen hier voornamelijk prijsverschillen en afwijkingen van het plan. Het accent van de controle ligt voor deze uitgaven bij 'het bestellen'.

Het behoeft geen nader betoog dat het gehele systeem van 'budgetair management' alleen dan goed kan functioneren, wanneer de administratie op de in de sub a t/m h gestelde voorwaarden is ingesteld.

3. *Budgettaire controle ten dienste van het continueel volgen en het analyseren van bedrijfsresultaten*

Met behulp van voorgecalculeerde, functioneel gedetailleerde kostprijzen wordt van de geleverde prestaties het resultaat bepaald. Dit resultaat zou zijn behaald, indien zich geen afwijkingen zouden hebben voorgedaan van de in de calculaties en de budgetten vóóronderstelde bedrijfsomstandigheden. De sub 2 besproken analyse van de verschillen geeft een inzicht in de gevolgen van de afwijking van de werkelijke bedrijfsomstandigheden tot de vooronderstelde. Het op basis van de voorgecalculeerde kostprijzen berekende resultaat wordt met deze verschillen gecorrigeerd.

[1] Dit geldt ook voor het beheer van voorraden of vorderingen, hetgeen door middel van gecalculeerde en begrote rente-bedragen tot uitdrukking wordt gebracht.

[2] De belangstellende lezer zij o.a. verwezen naar 'The flexible and variable budget'; referaat van Prof. Dr. A. Mey en E. Beekman op C.I.O.S.-congres 1951.

CLOSE-UPS OF THE BUSINESS SESSIONS

Tuesday afternoon in the Grand Hall

Tuesday afternoon in the Grand Hall

Tuesday morning in the Grand Hall

Tuesday afternoon in the Small Hall

De budgettaire controle is op deze wijze niet alleen het middel om doeltreffend toezicht te houden op de activiteiten van het personeel aan wie gedelegeerd is, doch staat tevens ten dienste van het continueel volgen van de bedrijfsresultaten en het analyseren ervan.

Uit het voorgaande blijkt, dat in de administratie alle bedrijfshandelingen worden getoetst aan ter beschikking staande begrotingen en normen. Van de administrateur, die de verschillen moet analyseren en interpreteren, wordt naast deskundigheid objectiviteit en tact geëist. Hij moet een goed contact hebben met chefs en eventueel lagere niveaus van autoriteit, waarin hij alleen dan zal slagen, wanneer hij zal trachten hun taal te verstaan en te spreken. Hij mag niet verlangen, dat men zijn – voor velen vaak moeilijk begrijpelijke – administratieve taal verstaat.

III. Mogelijkheden van toepassing bij middengrote en kleinere ondernemingen

Hetgeen in dit hoofdstuk wordt opgemerkt betreffende de ervaringen met het budgetteren in Nederland, heeft geenszins de pretentie van volledigheid. In de eerste plaats kan alleen de persoonlijke ervaring worden weergegeven. Bovendien zou het onmogelijk zijn in het korte bestek van dit prae-advies een volledige weergave van alle toepassingen in ons land te geven.

De eigen ervaring en contacten met anderen leren, dat de toepassing van budgettering en budgetcontrole voor middengrote en kleinere bedrijven veel beperkter is dan voor de grote ondernemingen. De techniek van de vergelijking van uitkomsten met normen is in de fabricatorische uitvoering meer ontwikkeld dan in andere sectoren van het ondernemingsbeheer. Gestimuleerd door het streven naar verbetering van de productiviteit wordt de administratie thans meer ingeschakeld voor het beheersen van de rendementen en de kosten. De gewoonte neemt toe de afdelingsrendementen betreffende het gebruik van materialen, van arbeids- en van machinetijd in periodieke overzichten aan de bazen en chefs voor te leggen en met hen te bespreken. Op deze wijze worden bazen en chefs mede betrokken in het zoeken naar de oorzaken van verspilling.

Er is een streven merkbaar ook die afdelingskosten, waarop de chef invloed kan uitoefenen, te begroten en de afwijkingen tussen begroting en werkelijkheid met hem te bespreken. Een werkelijk normatief stellen dezer kosten komt echter nog weinig voor. Meestal worden de bedragen van het recente verleden als basis gekozen. Het systeem blijft hierdoor een – verbeterde – historische kostenvergelijking.

Als alles omvattend huishoudplan wordt het stelsel van budgetten bij de middengrote en kleinere bedrijven vrijwel nergens toegepast. Begrotingen van jaaromzetten komen wel voor, doch zijn veelal zeer grof en meer als extrapolatie van het verleden dan als ware opdrachten te beschouwen. Een op schrift gesteld plan voor meer jaren ontbreekt bij de meeste ondernemingen. De afzonderlijke begroting voor nieuwe investeringen komt bij sommige bedrijven wel voor.

De administraties stellen voorcalculatorische kostenverdeelstaten op, met het doel de afdelingstarieven te calculeren. Reële afdelingsbudgetten met opdrachten aan afdelingschefs zijn deze opstellingen echter niet. Met behulp van deze afdelingstarieven wordt periodiek een overzicht van resultaten samengesteld, waarbij deze zijn geanalyseerd naar de sub 2 genoemde soorten afwijkingen. Zij verschaffen de directie inzicht in de ontwikkeling van het resultaat ten opzichte van vorige perioden. De publicatie komt echter veelal te laat – minimaal 3 à 4 weken na afsluiting van de periode[1] – om nog voldoende actueel te zijn voor het nemen van correctieve maatregelen. Sommige bedrijven hebben deze leemte ondervangen door tussentijdse statistische informaties.

Het beginsel van de vervangingswaarde wordt voor het bepalen van de verkoopprijs veelal wel toegepast. De invloed van een zich wijzigend prijspeil van grondstoffen e.d. op de resultaten van de onderneming wordt door sommige bedrijven bepaald. Men maakt hierbij gebruik van extra-comptabele positieoverzichten van voorraden.

De publicaties betreffende de toepassing van budgettering door grote bedrijven zijn in ons land als studiemateriaal van groot nut geweest. Niettemin moet het als een leemte worden beschouwd, dat voor de kleinere eenheden nog weinig is geschreven. Hetgeen bij de enkele grote ondernemingen mogelijk is, kan nl. niet zonder meer bij de vele kleinere bedrijven worden toegepast. De organisatorische omstandigheden zijn geheel anders. Het klimaat is vaak minder gunstig voor toepassing van budgettering. Ik noem bijv. de volgende omstandigheden:

a. De organisatorische afstand tussen leiding en uitvoering is veel geringer, waardoor de delegatie van functies minder is afgerond. De controle op de uitvoering geschiedt meer door directe waarneming, waardoor de behoefte aan een budget (als middel voor de functionele taakverdeling) veel minder door de directie wordt gevoeld[2].

b. De kleinere onderneming kan de markt minder goed overzien dan het grote bedrijf. Het maken van plannen houdt dus meer onzekerheden in. Berekeningen worden hierdoor minder aantrekkelijk. Intuïtie staat meer op de voorgrond, mede door het persoonlijk element, dat de directie aan de organisatie geeft.

c. Het bepalen van normen is vaak minder goed mogelijk, enerzijds omdat het apparaat voor het vaststellen dezer verhoudingen veelal ontbreekt en anderzijds, omdat vaak vele varianten voorkomen met beperkte toepassing per variant[3].

d. In de directies van de middengrote en kleinere bedrijven is er naast de commerciële en de technische directeur veelal geen bedrijfseconomisch geschoolde leider. Het belang van de administratie wordt dan alleen op lager niveau vertegenwoordigd. Het introduceren van een moderne administratie kan in dit geval minder eenvoudig worden, vooral wanneer de directie a priori afkerig is van de administratieve medewerking, welke de moderne administratie ook van haar en haar medewerkers vraagt. Hierbij komt, dat niet iedere administrateur een goede verkoper van zijn ideeën is, dan wel zelf niet begrijpt, wat voor de onderneming wel en wat *niet* toepasselijk is. Zonder daadwerkelijke steun van de directie kunnen de niet-administratief georiënteerde lagere organen

[1] Het samenstellen van deze overzichten is een relatief zware belasting voor de administratie.

[2] Het nut van het delegeren wordt niet door iedere directie begrepen. Men is geneigd (te) veel zelf te doen, tot schade van de onderneming.

[3] Typebeperking wordt wel meer dan voorheen, doch nog altijd te weinig toegepast.

slechts langzaam van het nut ener moderne administratie worden overtuigd.

Het zijn o.m. deze omstandigheden, welke de toepassing van het budgetsysteem in middengrote en kleinere ondernemingen vertragen en soms slechts ten dele mogelijk maken. Men zal er daarom voor moeten waken de 'theorie', welke men aan de hand van de voorbeelden van de grote bedrijven heeft geleerd, zonder meer op de kleinere eenheden toe te passen.

De minder gunstige omstandigheden voor budgetteren zijn voor de desbetreffende bedrijven geen reden niet naar het praktisch mogelijke te streven. In dit verband doe ik de volgende aanbevelingen:

a. Een betrouwbare kostprijsberekening. Bij het calculeren van zoveel mogelijk normatieve verhoudingen uitgaan; invloeden van vermijdbare onderbezetting moeten worden geëlimineerd.

b. Een begroting van de opbrengsten en offers in het komende jaar (of seizoen), zo nodig op basis van critisch geëxtrapoleerde gegevens van het recente verleden. De begroting moet afdelingsgewijze worden opgesteld, waarbij onderscheid moet worden gemaakt in offers, waarop de afdelingschef invloed kan uitoefenen en offers, waarop dit niet of praktisch niet mogelijk is. Voor het variabel houden van de begroting zullen de offers voorts worden onderscheiden in direct variabel, vertraagd variabel en constant.

c. Periodieke statistische overzichten van de belangrijkste bedrijfsgegevens per afdeling, waarbij de werkelijkheid wordt vergeleken met de begroting resp. met voorgecalculeerde verhoudingen. De gegevens betreffen de prestaties van verkoop en van productie, het verbruik van materialen, arbeids- en machinetijd (efficiëntierendementen en bezettingsgegevens), de door chefs te beïnvloeden afdelingskosten, kwaliteitssortering van producten e.d. Met behulp van prijzen en kostprijscalculaties kan de voorgecalculeerde winst op verkopen worden bepaald en kunnen de hoeveelheidsverschillen (efficiëntie en bezetting) worden gewaardeerd. De directie ontvangt op deze wijze op zeer korte termijn gegevens, welke een beeld geven van de richting, waarin de belangrijkste delen van het bedrijfsresultaat zich ontwikkelen. De meeste gegevens zullen op veel korter termijn dan per maand of periode van 4 of 5 weken kunnen worden gepubliceerd. Het voordeel van de snelle informatie prevaleert boven het nadeel, dat deze informatie omtrent het resultaat niet in een administratief sluitend verband ligt.

d. Vergelijking van de overige exploitatiekosten. Van de uitgaven, welke niet door de afdelingschef beïnvloed kunnen worden, wordt eveneens een vergelijking tussen begroting en werkelijkheid gemaakt. Het is niet noodzakelijk, dat dit per afdeling geschiedt. Het oordeel over de toelaatbaarheid van de vertraagde aanpassing van de kosten aan een gewijzigde bedrijfsbezetting[1] zal aan de administrateur moeten worden overgelaten[2].

e. Volledig geanalyseerde tussentijdse resultatenrekening. Teneinde de eenheid van

[1] Wanneer men vooraf reeds in afzonderlijke begrotingen voor afwijkende bezettingsgraden de aanpassing bepaald heeft, kent men wel de mate van de aanpassing der offers, doch nog niet het tempo.

[2] In middengrote en kleinere ondernemingen kunnen vele kosten zich slechts in vertraagd tempo en vaak dan nog onvoldoende aan een zich wijzigende bezetting aanpassen. De grove indeling in variabele en constante kosten leidt in geval van de automatische aanpassing van de begroting volgens het systeem van de variabele budgettering tot een onjuist inzicht in de gevolgen van de gewijzigde bezetting.

conceptie te bewaren en de onderlinge aansluiting der verstrekte overzichten vast te stellen dient enkele malen per jaar, n.m.m. drie à vier malen, een volledige resultatenrekening te worden samengesteld, waarbij de resultaten per afdeling zijn geanalyseerd en gegroepeerd naar de op blz. 224 sub e genoemde soorten afwijkingen. De uitkomsten van deze resultatenrekeningen moeten een bevestiging geven van hetgeen tussentijds met behulp van de statistische informaties reeds als ontwikkeling van het resultaat is aangegeven.

f. Bezinning op de toekomst. Het blijft onder alle omstandigheden noodzakelijk, dat men zich door middel van het opstellen van plannen, hoe globaal ook, steeds weer bezint op de toekomstige ontwikkeling van de onderneming. Voorts zal van iedere belangrijke investering een begroting van de totale behoefte aan middelen en van de te bereiken rentabiliteit moeten zijn gemaakt vóór de directie een beslissing neemt.

IV. Betekenis van de budgettering voor de accountantscontrole

Door de budgettaire controle worden de afwijkingen t.o.v. de verwachtingen resp. de normen afzonderlijk en naar de gedelegeerde verantwoordelijkheden tot uitdrukking gebracht en tevens de oorzaken blootgelegd. (Onderscheid der verliezen naar plaats resp. naar kostensoort; afwijkingen in efficiëntie, resp. in bedrijfsbezetting; gevolgen van foutieve projectie enz.). De kosten worden aldus beter meetbaar, terwijl tevens de verantwoordelijkheden voor de afwijkingen scherp gesteld worden. 'Onverklaarbare' verschillen zullen spoedig blijken[1], hetgeen preventief werkt voor onregelmatigheden.

Een dergelijke analytische administratie verscherpt de interne controle veel en is daarom ook voor de controlerende accountant een belangrijke steun. Zij geeft hem de mogelijkheid de kosten in relatie te brengen tot de geleverde prestaties en 'ontoelaatbare' verschillen (evt. fraude) in de uitgaven te constateren. Zonder de meetbaarheid van kosten en de interne analyse zou hem dit veel minder gelukken.

De accountant kan zich bovendien – ook tussentijds – een beter oordeel vormen omtrent de ontwikkeling in de onderneming. Dit is van belang voor zijn beschouwingen in het accountantsrapport en voor zijn periodiek gesprek met de directie, dat n.m.m. behalve op belangrijke controle-opmerkingen ook op de ontwikkelingen in de onderneming (organisatie, resultaat en vermogenspositie) betrekking moet hebben.

De vraag op welke onderdelen de accountant zijn controle-plan moet wijzigen i.v.m. het budgetsysteem moge ik onbesproken laten.

[1] Dit geldt te meer omdat de totale bedragen over vele afdelingen verdeeld zijn, meer dan in de traditionele boekhouding voorkomt.

Translation

PAPER

by

A. F. TEMPELAAR

Nederlands Instituut van Accountants

I. Preface

When the International Congress of Accountants was for the first time held in Amsterdam in 1926 budgeting in business was hardly known. The reports on 'Standard costs as a basis of management and industrial control'[1] may be considered as preparatory studies on budgeting and budgetary control.

Since then a comprehensive literature has been published, discussing many aspects of budgeting. Nevertheless the subject has not lost its interest and current importance.

In this paper I confine myself to some important aspects of budgeting and to its practical application by medium-sized and smaller companies in our country.

The increasing risks involved in the anticipation of future business circumstances and the growing necessity of delegating authority and initiative have had their influence on the character and scope of accounting. It has been felt necessary to create a system of accounting, which could furnish the management—on each level of authority—with information on the expected consequences of the planned forecast and on the actual performance in comparison with the forecast. This information covers the activities of the enterprise as a whole as well as of the parts of the organisation.

The conventional double-entry system of former days could not render these services. That system is merely historical recording of financial facts and gives the management only information about the Balance Sheet and the Profit and Loss Account once a year. That system should be modernized and transformed into an instrument for the information of progressive management. In addition to history forecasts should also become an element of accounting. The comparison between expectation and performance, between the planned and the actual results with a break-down of the divergencies according to their origin, is of great significance for the corrective supervision of management and for the changing—when necessary—of future plans.

This modern form of accounting requires of the chief accountant that he should have dynamic and critical faculties and be skilled in the solution of

[1] Reports for the 1926 Congress, written by C. Hewetson Nelson, Prof. J. Anton de Haas, Prof. J. G. Ch. Volmer and William S. Kemp.

business problems: a person who is interested and experienced only in bookkeeping procedures is not capable of being placed in charge.

II. Budgeting and Budgetary Control as a Tool of Management

At the C.I.O.S.-Congress in 1951 at Brussels the following definition of budgeting was given[1]:

1. An instrument for giving direction to activity and for policy making.
2. An instrument of guidance, planning and control of organisation (private as well as public) as a means to the delegation of authority and to the coordination of activities; and as a control of efficiency.

Budgeting is an *instrument*. It is not a magic formula that will compensate for a serious lack of ability on the part of the management. It cannot be a substitute for management. On the contrary budgeting can only give good results when applied by a competent management.

The principles of a system of budgeting are the same for every company, but its practical application should differ with the nature and the internal organisation of each company.

A system of budgeting can but serve as an instrument of management if it is applied:

1. As a coordinated set of plans for management[2].
2. As a means of delegation of authority and initiatives and as an instrument for control of performance.
3. As a means of control applied to continuously scrutinize the company's results. If not applied in this way, budgeting will only be a variety of a normal system of bookkeeping and therefore will not result in a modernization of the accounting-system.

1. *Budgeting as a coordinated set of plans for management*

Ever growing industrialisation and the application of mechanisation demand increasing investment in tangible assets and in mental ability. Management must anticipate future circumstances and conditions and plan systematically[3], there must be plans in which the policy of management is expressed and calculations are made of the expected consequences of this policy on the profitability and the financial position of the company.

These plans should not only be based on intuition, but should be supported by reasonable deductions based on market-research, statistics etc. The 'expedition' must not set its course on a mirage.

General long term activity programming—i.c. for 3 to 5 years—is of the utmost significance. From these plans can be derived long term capital budgets and operational budgets for shorter periods.

Only with these long term programs will it be possible for management to consider whether the goals set can be achieved and if so under what conditions[4].

[1] 'The flexible and variable budget', report of Prof. Dr. A. Mey and E. Beekman.

[2] In this paper I shall not make a distinction between the management of the several levels of authority.

[3] Gouverner c'est prévoir (Fayol).

[4] If it is not possible to make a reliable forecast of future market conditions, the making of such plans will not be simple. Nevertheless management must try, as by doing so everybody is forced to study changes in business conditions continually.

This also enables management to adjust its plans to the change of conditions and to take the necessary steps in time.

Capital-budgets based on such activity plans picture the future needs and the scope of new investments and show them in the sequence of their urgency.

For each important capital investment a special budget must be made, giving the capital requirements (including additional investment in inventories etc.) and the results to be achieved. The expectations of the sales manager and the technical engineer should be tested and completed by calculations of the cost accountant. Only when supplied with this information can management take well-founded decisions.

Every year the activity plans for the next three or five years must be planned. The plan for the first year is an operating budget, which goes into details. The plans for the following years give only broad outlines[1].

The sales forecast for the coming year together with the figures about production capacity are the base for all other short term budgets (purchases, production, costs etc.). These budgets must be coordinated and be combined in a master budget and a forecast of the Profit and Loss Account.

Assisting in the compilation of the budgets (i.e. stimulating and coordinating) and seeing to it that they are based on the principles of management economics is part of the important activities of modern accounting.

2. *Budgeting as a means of delegation of authority and initiative and as an instrument of control of performance.*

Budgeting as a plan for management has in itself little or no influence on accounting procedures: in reality the budget is no more than working out the plan in an accounting form.

Its influence on accounting is much greater when budgeting is used to delegate authority and initiative and to control actual performance.

Delegation is one of the essentials of modern business building. The manager who likes to do everything himself or to be consulted in every detail, will fail. The management must delegate in order 'to have time to think'. This presupposes of course that there are capable subordinates, to whom functions can be delegated.

These functions should be precisely defined and outlined. On every level of authority there must be the means of controlling the execution of the instructions. Here the accounting system can render indispensable services to management by recording in figures both the *instructions* as well as the results of *execution*. By comparing the corresponding figures management is able to supervise the activities of those to whom functions have been delegated.

The application of standard costs[2], budgets and budgetary control is based on this comparison of *instruction* and *execution*, of *estimated* and *actual costs*. This system enables management to exercise an effective control and therefore to delegate as

[1] In literature more attention is paid to the operating budgets than to long term plans, though these plans give better information about future developments.

[2] 'I believe I am justified in saying that no successful budgetary control can be exercised without the use of standard costs, but that in turn no system of standard costs can effectively operate without a budgetary plan' (Prof. J. Anton de Haas; Report International Congress of Accountants 1926).

much as possible. Without these tools it is no longer possible to manage effectively a large or medium-sized company.

Concerning budgeting (as a set of instructions) and budgetary control I restrict myself to making the following remarks.

a. Budgets are quantitative plans, expressed in monetary terms. The costs, that will be incurred, are based on standards[1] (standard formulae, job analyses and time studies and other statistical analyses). The prices used for expressing the quantities in monetary terms must be seen as a directive to be achieved (selling price to be attained; purchase price to be paid).

b. A budget is made for every responsible departmental manager (of the manufacturing departments, and of the auxiliary service departments, such as boilerhouse, maintenance etc.). In making these budgets management should consult the executives, but must retain the right of making final decisions in order to be able to determine the alternate policy.

These budgets are to be considered as instructions for the responsible departmental managers.

c. On the occurrence of material changes in forecasted business conditions budgets have to be adapted ('flexible budgeting'). Whenever the actual volume of output diverges from the forecast the cost allowances of the departments in question should be adapted accordingly ('variable budgeting'). The various costs of each department should consequently be distinguished according to their dependence on the volume of output[2].

d. When recording performance actual figures should be classified under the same heads as those used in the budgets.

e. Variances (between *instruction* and *performance*) should be analysed and classified. The most significant classifications are: variance in volume (of sales or output); deviations from standards in both quantities[3] and prices; variances on account of 'errors in budgeting' and miscellaneous differences. When changes occur in the replacement value of stocks of raw materials, finished goods etc. the influence of these changes on the company's profits should be separately brought out.

f. Management should periodically receive reports concerning these differences between the results and the budget. The responsible departmental managers should receive detailed information concerning their departments. The frequency of these reports may vary from company to company. However, the figures must by all means be sufficiently timely to enable management to exert its corrective influence. Prevention is, of course, better than cure. It is therefore necessary to realize the consequences of all expense as and when a decision is taken to purchase.

g. Both in budgets and in records of actual figures *all* items of a department's cost of operation should be included. In case the planned volume of output is

[1] The accuracy of these standards depends on the nature of the processes and on the size of the company.

[2] The distinction between 'variable' and 'fixed' costs is generally speaking too broad.

[3] This applies also to the control of the volume of inventories (stocks) and receivables by means of comparing the cost of the actual investment to that foreseen in the budget. This cost can be measured by means of a standard rate of interest, whether to be paid or not.

smaller than the available capacity allows for, a proportionate part of the fixed cost-burden of the capacity will have to be considered as a loss to be charged directly to the Profit and Loss Account and should not be considered part and parcel of the department's result[1]. Depreciation on buildings, plant, equipment etc. ought to be based on the replacement value of these assets. The same principle of valuation holds good for raw materials etc. consumed in production and for the cost of goods sold[1].

h. Budgetary control should also be applied to the amounts to be invested in fixed assets. In this matter divergencies will mostly concern changes in prices and deviations from the plan. As in the case of operational costs (see *f*) the crux of controlling this expenditure lies in prevention, i.e. in putting the purchase order to the test of the budget.

It needs no further elaboration to illustrate that the ability of the accounting department to handle the data of the budget as well as those of actual performance is essential to meet the requirements of budgetary management given in the points *a* to *h* inclusive above.

3. *Budgetary control as a means of control applied to continuously scrutinize the company's results.*

By means of the pre-calculated cost prices determined for each department the financial result of the sales or the output is ascertained. This result would have been achieved if there were no deviations from the circumstances and conditions which were assumed when making the budgets.

The analyses of the variances discussed above under 2 supplies information as to the reasons for differences between the actual circumstances and the circumstances assumed when making the budgets. The result ascertained by means of the pre-calculated cost prices is adjusted according to these variances.

Applied in this way the system of budgetary control is not only a means of supervisory control of management, but it also renders service when reviewing the company's results.

When accounting is done in the way described above all activities are measured by and analysed on the basis of the available budgets and standards. The accountant (or the controller) who must analyze and interpret the variances, must not only be an expert in his field but must also possess objectivity and tact.

He must have good relations with the executives and other responsible employees. He will only succeed when he tries to understand and to speak their 'language' as his accounting language is often difficult to understand for non-experts.

III. Possibilities for Practical Application in Medium-Sized and Smaller Companies

What is said in this chapter about the practical application of budgeting and budgetary control in the Netherlands does not pretend to be complete. In the first place only personal experience can be reported. Moreover it would be

[1] cf. 'The flexible and variable budget', report of Prof. Dr A. Mey and E. Beekman at the C.I.O.S.-Congress 1951.

impossible to give a complete picture of all applications in our country. Based on my experience and on viewpoints of colleagues I am of opinion that the practical application of budgeting and budgetary control in medium-sized and smaller companies is much more restricted than in the larger units. The procedure of comparing results or output with standards is more developed in factory production than in other spheres of business management. Stimulated by efforts to improve productivity, accounting procedure is nowadays more and more used as a means for controlling efficiency of production and expenses. It is becoming still more common practice to produce periodical statements of efficiency achieved in every department as regards consumption of materials, direct labour time and machine time. These statements are issued to the responsible supervisors and to foremen and thoroughly discussed with them. In this way these employees are obliged to think out for themselves the causes of waste and to take steps to eliminate these causes in future.

There is a tendency to budget the departmental costs that are controllable by departmental managers and to discuss with them the differences between actual and estimated costs. Only occasionally, however, these costs are measured against a standard. In most cases the figures of the previous year are taken as a basis for estimating such costs. The system applied in this way is, therefore, just a—possibly improved—historical comparison of expenses.

The budget system as a completely comprehensive plan of operations for a certain period is practically nowhere applied in medium-sized and smaller companies. Estimates of annual turnover are sometimes available. They are mostly very rough, and only based on the figures of the past. Therefore they cannot be considered as a real plan for action.

A plan of activity for several years ahead is only seldom available. A special budget for new investment is drawn up in more instances.

In order to determine cost rates for each department, the accounting department makes up pre-calculated cost allocation sheets, but these are not real budgets with instructions to the departmental managers. The cost rates for each department are used to calculate the cost price of the products. They can also be applied for preparing periodical statements of results, which are analyzed and classified in the same way as mentioned above. They supply management with information as regards the trend of the results compared with former periods (*but not compared with goals to be achieved*). The figures produced in this way are often too late—they are available at best 3 to 4 weeks after the end of the period[1]—and are therefore too old to be of use for taking corrective steps for the immediate future. Some companies have dealt with this difficulty by preparing interim statistical information.

When ascertaining cost or fixing selling prices the consumption of raw materials and the depreciation on fixed assets are frequently valued on the basis of replacement values. Only some companies determine separately the influence which changing price levels of raw materials etc. have had on the results of the company. For this purpose use is made of supplementary statements specifying the quantities of raw materials etc. in regard to which there is a risk of changing prices.

[1] Compiling these statements is a rather heavy burden on the accounting departement.

Much knowledge has been published in our country by means of handbooks or periodicals about the application of budgeting and budgetary control in *large* companies. Little has been published about the application in smaller units, which certainly is a pity because the conditions for applying the system in smaller companies are different from those in large ones. The organisation is quite different. The 'climate' is often less favourable for budgeting. As examples I mention the following conditions:

a. The functional distance between management and actual performance is much shorter, which means that the delegation of functions is less complete. The delegated functions are less clearly defined.

The supervision of performance is more effected by visual and other direct observations. Therefore the need of a budget (as a means for the delegation of authority and initiative) is much less felt by the management[1].

b. The smaller company is in a lesser position to get an overall picture of the market than the larger unit. Plans are much more uncertain as regards their possible realisation, so that calculations are less dependable. Intuition comes more into its own, partly because of the personal touch which the management gives to the organisation.

c. The determination of standards is often rather difficult, even not possible at all, as the organisational set-up for fixing standards is mostly not available. Moreover there are often many varieties in production which only have a restricted application per variation[2].

d. In the top-management of medium-sized and smaller companies consisting probably of sales—and technical—directors there is often no chief accountant skilled in management accountancy. Then the accounting function is represented at a lower level of ability and authority. The introduction of a modern accounting system may then be less easy, especially if management dislikes a priori the idea of observing accounting instructions and requirements.

The introduction of a modern accounting system is also hampered if the accountant cannot 'sell' his ideas or does not understand himself which accounting procedures are applicable and which are not applicable in the company. Without the active cooperation and help of top-management it certainly takes time to convince the managers and executives of the usefulness of a modern accounting system.

In my opinion these conditions are the reasons, why the application of budgeting and budgetary control in medium-sized and smaller companies is often delayed or not in existence. In many of these companies an application of budget procedures similar to those, which are used by larger enterprises will not give the expected results, and thus lead to disappointments. We must be well aware of this.

However, such less favourable conditions are not an argument for aban-

[1] In spite of the less favourable conditions for delegating the management of medium-sized and smaller companies must try to delegate as much as possible. Not every manager is convinced of the necessity to delegate. He is inclined to do too much himself, which is not good for the company.

[2] Standardisation is applied more than in the past though still insufficiently. Limitation of the range of products and standardisation must be emphasized.

doning the aim of modernising the accounting-system to the extent practicable. To obtain this I would put forward the following recommendations:

a. Reliable cost-calculations. These should be based on standards as much as possible. The allocation per unit of fixed overheads should be based on the potential output of the production departments under normal conditions and not on actual output.

b. An estimate of the total sales and costs for the next year (or season). In case there are no precise plans estimates must be based on the figures of previous years. The estimates must be made for every important department of the company (see page 232 under *b*.) The costs of each department should be distinguished as between controllable and non-controllable costs. (Controllable from the viewpoint of the departmental manager.) In order to make the estimates 'variable', the costs must also be distinguished between variable, semi-variable and fixed costs.

c. Periodical statistical information about the significant activities of the important departments of the company. In these statements actual figures are compared with estimates (and with pre-calculated ratios) for the volume of sales and output, consumption of raw materials (value as well as efficiency), direct labour and direct machine time (efficiency of production and volume variances), the controllable costs of the department, the ratio concerning assortment of production as regards quality. The profits from sales or services rendered can be calculated from the pre-calculated cost prices. On the basis of the same prices and rates the important volume variances can be expressed in money. Although the costing system may not be complete, the management can be informed in this way about the trends of the significant aspects of the business results at the earliest moment. Most of these figures can be produced at much shorter intervals than a month or a 4- or 5-weekly period. The advantage of this quick information is greater than the disadvantage that the figures are not derived from a balanced set of double entry books.

d. Control of the 'non-controllable' costs. A comparison between the estimated and actual figures should also be made for this expenditure. It is not necessary to make this comparison for every department separately. The accountant (or the controller) has to adjust the estimated amounts in case of a change in volume of production[1]. In my opinion only this officer can determine to what extent the total amount of an expense may be influenced by the actual change in volume[2].

e. Interim Profit and Loss Account with full analysis of the results. In order to maintain uniformity in the conception of the interim statistical statements of the results and to prove that such information is sufficiently in accordance with the results shown by the books, 3 to 4 times a year a complete Profit and Loss Account has to be drawn up. The results of the latter statement must be analyzed and classified in the manner explained on page 232 under number *e*.

[1] In medium-sized and smaller companies many costs adjust themselves only slowly and insufficiently to movements in the level of activity. When applying variable budgeting the rough distinction between 'variable' and 'fixed' costs results in a misleading picture of the real variance in volume.

[2] When separate budgets are drawn up in advance to suit various assumed levels of activity, the *amount* of adjustment of the costs is known, but not the *time* in which the adjustment must take place. This must be judged by the accountant.

f. Reflection on the future. The management must always consider the future development of the company, if possible by making plans or otherwise by making rough estimates. Before deciding upon an investment the total need of capital and the profitability of this investment must be calculated.

IV. The Significance of Budgeting for the Auditor

By budgetary control attention is focussed on deviations from forecasts and from standards. These variances are analyzed departmentally according to the delegated responsibility and are classified, so that information can be given about their causes (identifying losses to the cost centre or to the type of cost; distinguishing between losses due to variances in efficiency and in volume of output, due to uneconomical investments etc.). This results in a better judgment of the expenses and in a proper determination of the responsibility for the variances. Unjustifiable expenses will soon come to light[1], which may act as a preventive against irregularity and fraud.

Such an analytical accounting-system strengthens the internal control and is, therefore, of very great significance for the auditor. It enables him to measure the costs against the performances and to detect 'inadmissable' divergencies (e.g. fraud). Without the help of such a systematic internal scrutiny it would be a much more difficult problem for him to make his audit effective.

The modern accounting-system enables the auditor to get a clear picture of the situation of the company at short intervals, this providing him with the data to be commented upon on his long-form audit report and for his periodical discussion with management. When meeting management he should not only deal with questions and comments resulting from his audit, but also discuss the development in the condition of the company, and the various aspects of general management such as the organisation, the results and the financial position.

I feel that I should not discuss the problem as to how the audit programs can be modified when budgeting and budgetary control are applied.

[1] Also because the amounts are broken down to many departments, to a greater extent than is afforded by the conventional accounting system.

PAPER

by

J. P. WILSON, F. C. W. A., A.C.I.S.

The Institute of Cost and Works Accountants, U.K.

1. Introduction

The purpose of this paper is to consider the effects which the introduction of Budgeting has had upon the principles and practice of accounting. It is possible that some of these effects were not specifically intended when Budgeting was introduced, but have been a natural yet unforeseen outcome of Budgeting. In this paper an attempt is made to analyse these effects and to set them out in a rational order.

2. Definition

For the purpose of this paper the term Budgeting is assumed to include the full operation of Budgeting, which is frequently described as Budgetary Control, and in addition Standard Costing which can be considered as detailed Budgeting, particularly in its application to the costs of products.

3. The Effect upon the Principles of Accounting

The general effect of the introduction of Budgeting upon the principles of Accounting has been to promote the use of an Accounting System to provide more and better information. In other words an Accounting System is now required to do more work than it has ever done before, and if this is to be accomplished successfully and without undue clerical effort, the accounting practices must be carefully designed. Particular instances of improved information are as follows:

31. *Management Accounting*

The introduction of Budgeting has greatly extended the use which is made of accounting information as the basis for action by the Management of a business. A distinction might be drawn between this use of accounting information, which can be described as Management Accounting, and the use of accounting information as a means of safeguarding the assets of a business, which might be termed

Ownership Accounting. The Annual Profit and Loss Account and Balance Sheet, while to some extent used for Management Accounting purpose, have primarily been a report to the owners upon the progress of their business and the value of their property. The use of accounting for ownership purposes has a direct value. It is essential, for example, to keep accounts of the transactions with each customer in order to render statements promptly and correctly and to obtain payment of monies due. Management Accounting has an indirect value. It provides information which has a value only in so far as it is used by the Management of a business as the basis for its decisions or for its control of the business in conformity with the decisions taken. For this purpose accounting information must be made available quickly at frequent intervals. For example, Ownership Accounting may require the presentation of a Profit and Loss Account and Balance Sheet once a year, although in this connection the practice is growing for companies to present their shareholders with financial results every six months or even every quarter; but Management Accounting requires the presentation of a Profit and Loss Account and Balance Sheet every month. In addition the content of these financial statements must be more informative if they are to be used as the basis for management action, and this has largely been made possible by the incorporation of budget figures.

32. *Explanation of Financial Results*

Prior to the introduction of Budgeting a Profit and Loss Account prepared on conventional accounting lines would show the profit or loss that had been made in the period, but would not readily show the explanation of this profit or loss. It would usually have been possible to ascertain from such a Profit and Loss Account for a period of six months or more the major long term factors contributing to the result achieved, but this form of statement would not have been sufficiently sensitive to show the reasons for the results of a period as short as one month. By the introduction of Budgeting it has been possible to revise the form of short period Profit and Loss Accounts so that not only is shewn the result achieved, but this result is measured against the standard result planned and attention drawn to divergences from plan. It is a further advantage that the preparation of financial results by a system which provides for the explanation of these results is a check upon the accuracy of the results. Where the accounting system is such that explanation of the results cannot be readily obtained, an inaccurate result may be unwittingly accepted.

33. *Improvement in the Value of Information Provided*

An important effect of the introduction of Budgeting upon Accounting has been to show that in the past accounts have been designed in many cases to give information under certain headings which is of little or no value, and not to give other information which is really valuable. For example, many accounting systems have been designed to analyse actual expenditure to specific orders or products. By this means the excess costs being incurred have been buried from sight by being split over a large number of so-called actual cost accounts. Upon the introduction of Budgeting, procedures of Accounting have been redesigned to show instead the more valuable information concerning the excess costs—the amounts, the departments in which they arise and their causes.

34. *Accounting Control of Performance*

The introduction of Budgeting has given rise to the use of the accounting system to provide information for the control of performance. This information which can be provided as a matter of routine at frequent intervals, and with a much greater degree of accuracy owing to the integration of such statistics within the Accounting System, is far more effective for the control of performance than statistics prepared in isolation from the Accounting System, or impressions gained from spasmodic inspections. For example, statistics of sales performance in respect of volume, selling prices and pattern of sales, and of production performance in respect of output and efficiency, can be incorporated within the accounts. The accounting control of cost performance can also be effected on the following lines.

341. The use of Budgeting and Standard Costs enables costs to be controlled by their measurement against the standards embodied in the Budgets and Standard Costs. The significant statistics are the variances between standard cost and actual cost and by the employment of the appropriate accounting techniques these variances can be analysed to such causes as:

Material Prices
Material Usages Efficiency
Labour Wage Rates
Labour Efficiency
Over- or Under-Spending
Capacity Employed
Revision of Budgets due to External Causes.

The careful analysis of variance to causes enables a better control of performance to be maintained, because the effects on cost of external events such as a National Wages Award, or a fall in market demand leading to unused manufacturing capacity, can be segregated from the effects on cost due to the performance of the Management.

In the presentation of information for the control of performance it is essential that the information should be provided under the headings of the individuals responsible for the performance. For example, sales statistics might be presented in respect of each Sales Area in order to control the performance of the Area Sales Manager; or production and cost statistics might be prepared in respect of each production department in order to control the performance of the Departmental Manager.

35. *Decentralised Cost and Performance Control*

The use of Budgeting to provide information for the control of performance by laying emphasis upon the results achieved by the individuals controlling departments of the business has had the effect of devolving performance and cost control upon departmental managers and in some cases to the supervisors of sections of a department. This development has necessitated a change in the accounting system to give an analysis of costs to departments in place of an analysis to jobs carried out. It is the departmental manager's responsibility to control the cost of the jobs on which he is engaged in order to produce the most favourable variance possible. By this means the departmental manager is stimulated to keep closely informed about the work passing through his department, so that an analysis of actual costs to jobs is in general unnecessary.

36. *Stock Valuation*

Where the principles of Budgetary Control have been adopted to the extent of using standard prices for the valuation of materials, the accounting is not only simplified but clearer information is presented to Management. The use of standard prices for materials enables detailed stores accounts in quantity and value to be eliminated, and requires a stores control account only to be maintained in value. Clearer information is available to Management because movements of prices are segregated in a purchase price variance account and the stock account then reflects movements in the volume and mix of the materials held. It does not necessarily follow that the valuation of stock at standard material prices involves the acceptance of this valuation for the Annual Accounts to be presented to the owners of the business, as the valuation at standard material prices can be adjusted for this purpose.

4. The Effect upon the Techniques of Accounting

The effect of the introduction of Budgetary Control upon the techniques of Accounting will also largely depend upon the degree to which Budgetary Control has been adopted. In certain cases its use might be limited to the measurement of figures, obtained by normal accounting processes, in which case the effect upon the technique of accounting would be very small. The effect is much greater when Budgetary Control has been extended to include Standard Costing integrated within the accounting system. In these circumstances features of the effect upon accounting are as follows:

41. *Frequency and Speed of Presentation of Financial Results*

The introduction of Budgetary Control by making accounts an instrument of control has necessitated the preparation at frequent intervals, usually of one month, of a Profit and Loss Account and Balance Sheet. It has also necessitated presentation as soon as possible after the end of the period under review. The improvement in the speed of presentation is mainly a matter of conscious effort on the part of the Accounting Department, but the following techniques have been found of value for this purpose:

411. The adoption of a full method of Standard Costing whereby the value of Stock and Work in Progress is ascertained automatically from the accounts without the necessity for any physical stock-taking or detailed valuation of stock.

412. The adoption of 13 four weekly accounting periods or 12 periods of 4 or 5 weeks in each year.

413. The use of valued Goods Received Notes to avoid any delay due to late receipt of suppliers' invoices.

42. *The Use of Stock Control Accounts*

421. Prior to the introduction of Budgetary Control the accounting technique widely used for ascertaining the consumption of materials was by the formula

Value of Opening Stock
add
Purchases
substract
Value of Closing Stock.

The disadvantages of this method are:

4211. There is no accounting control over stocks.

4212. It is necessary to list all stocks, either from quantity stock records or by physical stock-taking, at the end of each period.

4213. The pattern of usage of the material is not revealed, such as the value of raw material used in each department or the cost value of despatches of finished goods to each class of customer.

422. With the introduction of budgetary control and standard costing the possibility of using stock control accounts has been increased by the following advantages:

4221. The use of standard prices for materials simplifies stores accounting, and renders unnecessary stores accounts carrying prices or values and the calculations to ascertain the appropriate price for each issue.

4222. The use of standard cost accounting techniques, whereby cost variances are eliminated at the purchase analysis stage or as they arise in the departmental operating accounts, enables work in progress and stocks of finished goods to be valued in the accounts at known standard costs. Despatches of finished goods to customers by extension at the appropriate product standard costs can therefore be credited to the work in progress account or finished stock account at the same value at which they were previously debited.

423. The major effects of the use of stock control accounts under the foregoing conditions have been:

4231. An accounting control of stocks at very little cost.

4232. The elimination of period-end stock-takings and valuations.

4233. The positive valuation of the usage of material by the valuation of issues, giving an analysis of usage to the various departments for comparison with standard usage and establishing departmental material usage efficiencies.

4234. The positive ascertainment of the cost of goods sold by the valuation of actual despatches at the appropriate product standard cost. This positive method can be applied in two forms:

42341. The goods despatched as recorded on each invoice can be extended at standard cost, so arriving at a standard cost of sales for each despatch. This method is sometimes known as the Double Pricing Method, as the invoices are priced with the sales value and the cost of sales value.

42342. The sales invoices for a period are summarised to show the total quantity of each product sold and these totals extended by the appropriate standard costs of the products to give a total cost of sales.

The advantage of a positive ascertainment of cost of sales is that an analysis of this cost can be prepared parallel to an analysis of sales, and therefore dependent upon the detail in which these analyses are prepared, the resultant standard profit can be analysed to products, markets, areas or even customers. This information is of considerable value for the explanation of the financial results of each period (See Section 32).

43. *The Interpolation of Assessments into Accounts*

The introduction of Budgetary Control, especially as extended to Standard Costing, has resulted in the accounts of a business carrying a much larger proportion of figures which are not facts so much as assessments. It is possible that under normal accounting systems prior to the introduction of Budgetary Control the only assessments were the value of stock and the depreciation written off fixed assets. Under an accounting system incorporating standard costs it must be recognized that the following figures entering into the accounts are examples of assessments rather than of facts:

Depreciation
Standard cost of production
The transfer of charges from the Administrative and Service Departments to the departments served
The value of stocks when carried at standard prices.

Further examples of assessments are the various valuation of departmental production used in order to analyse the total departmental variance, the following example being taken from the Oil Refining Industry:

Standard Cost of Actual Yield	
	Yield Efficiency Variance
Standard Cost of Throughput at Standard Rate of Operation	
	Rate of Throughput Variance
Standard Cost of Throughput at Actual Rate of Operation	
	Capacity Employed Variance
Allowed Cost of Throughput at Actual Rate of Operation	
	Spending Variance
Actual Departmental Cost	

While a modern accounting system commences with the hard facts of the money paid out for plant, supplies, wages and expenses and ends with the hard fact of money received from customers for the sale of its products, there is between these hard facts the interpolation of assessments, such as these shown above, which are the means of providing the Management with valuable information for control purposes. By their nature these figures cannot be completely substantiated but nevertheless they serve to present a picture, in which detail may not be necessary and from which lessons can be drawn.

44. *The Segregation of Policy or Abnormal Items*

Regard for the distinction between Ownership Accounting and Management Accounting affects the accounting treatment of provisions which as a matter of financial prudence may be made in the annual accounts as presented to the owners of the business. If these provisions, as for the heavy writing down of stock values or abnormal depreciation, are not to distort the accounts as presented for management purposes, it is necessary to segregate such items. (See line 28 of Appendix A.) The acceptance of this practice is all the more necessary in view of the increasing tendency to integrate cost accounts within the general accounting system.

45. *The Classification of Revenue Expenditure*

Prior to the introduction of Budgetary Control the customary analysis of revenue expenditure was by the nature of the expense such as Materials, Wages, Salaries, Electricity, etc. With the introduction of budgetary control it has become necessary to analyse expenses to the departments by which the expense is incurred. For general accounting purposes it is still necessary to obtain an analysis of expenditure by the nature of the expense. To meet both of these requirements the following arrangements can be made:

451. The adoption of a two-part code for the classification of revenue expenditure, the first part indicating the department incurring the charge and the second part the nature of the expense.

452. A first analysis of revenue expenditure to the accounts covering the nature of the expenditure. Subsequently by means of a credit in a special Transfer Account the same expenditure can be debited in the accounts for the departments of the business.

453. Definition in the departmental budgets of the classifications of expense controllable by, and therefore chargeable to, each department.

454. The establishment of the principle that in the primary analysis of expense all expenditure should be charged to the departments responsible, and no charge should be made to any departments on an arbitrary percentage basis.

455. The inclusion of notional departments, such as General Works—Administration and Personnel, for those expenses which are controllable by the Works Management and not by departments as commonly understood.

46. *Collaboration between the Accountant and other Functions of the Business*

The developments in accounting consequent upon the introduction of budgetary control have reduced the self-sufficiency of the accountant. The accounting system by taking into its purview a much greater range of the operations of the business, as distinct from being confined to those transactions involving the passing of money, has become more dependent upon the recording procedures throughout the business for the provision of its basic data. It is therefore essential that in laying down any recording procedures within a business the requirements for accounting purposes should be considered. The accounting system is also required to incorporate budgeted figures in the production of which the accountant may take only a part. For example, the budgeted figures of Sales may be very largely the work of a market analyst in the Sales Department; the budgeted cost of the material content of a product may be largely the work of a chemist; and the budgeted conversion cost of a product may be largely the work of a time study engineer. The tendency would appear to be for the other departments of the business to provide the physical standard whether of sales, material used or time taken on different processes, and for the accountant to convert this data into terms of money.

47. *Modern Form of Monthly Profit and Loss Account*

An example of one of the many possible forms of Monthly Profit and Loss Account used primarily for management purposes is set out in Appendix A. This form has been simplified, as for example by the exclusion of year-to-date figures, so that the principles can be clearly shown. The main feature of such a form of Profit and Loss Account is the explanation of the final result for the period by the comparison of actual with budgeted performances. The following are more detailed comments with reference to the lines of the form:

1. In this statement the intention is to show separately the results of Manufacturing and Trading. The Manufacturing Account would be amplified as necessary by supporting schedules giving further detail.

7. The Departmental Cost Savings or Excesses would be analysed on supporting schedules showing the performance of individual departments.

13. Budgeted Sales are shown as a measure of the actual sales achieved and the resulting difference analysed to gain or loss of sales value in respect of volume or selling prices. This is an example of the interpolation of an assessment into the accounts.

13–19. Using a positive method of ascertaining cost of sales by the evaluation of despatches, it is possible for the results shown on lines 13–19 of this statement to be analysed on supplementary schedules to product groups, markets, sales areas etc.

20–22. Selling and Distribution Expenses could also be analysed on supplementary schedules to the departments, and therefore the individuals, responsible for the expenditure.

24. The Profit and Loss Account on this statement is designed to bring together the results of the different activities of the business.

27. The profit for management purposes shown on this line is intended to be the net financial result achieved by the Management during the period, as explained by the foregoing figures on the statement. It should be a real measure of the Management's success or failure, undistorted by any provisions made for Ownership Accounting purposes.

28–29. While it is vitally necessary to show the profit for management purposes as on line 27, the Management of a business will normally require to know the profit for each period, and particularly for the year to date, in terms of the annual profit. For this reason line 28 shows the adjustment to be made to the profit for management purposes to arrive at a profit on the annual accounts basis. In this particular example it has been assumed that it is the practice for annual accounts purposes to write down finished stocks to a figure substantially lower than the standard production cost: as in this period finished stocks have been reduced the effect of the adjustment is to increase the profit calculated on the annual accounts basis. A member of the Management who is interested in the annual profit as reported to the owners of the business would therefore direct his attention to the final line of the statement.

APPENDIX A

Form of Monthly Profit and Loss Account

		£	£	£
1. MANUFACTURING ACCOUNT				
2. Actual Cost of Production				110,000
3. Adjust for Cost Savings (+) or Excess (—)				
4. General:	Material Prices	— 9000		
5.	Capacity Employed.	— 4000		
6.	Budget Revisions	— 5000	— 18,000	
7. Departmental:	Material Usage Efficiency	+ 2000		
8.	Labour: Wage Rates	— 1000		
9.	Labour: Efficiency	+ 5000		
10.	Spending	+ 2000	+ 8,000	— 10,000
11 Standard Cost of Production				100,000
12. TRADING ACCOUNT				
13. Budgeted Sales				160,000
14. Adjust for Gain (+) or Loss (—)				
15.	Volume		— 6,000	
16.	Selling Prices		— 4,000	— 10,000
17. Actual Sales.				150,000
18. Less Standard Production Cost of Goods Sold				120,000
19.				30,000
20. Less Selling and Distribution Expenses: Budgeted			10,000	
21.	Adjust for Cost Saving (+) or Excess (—)		— 2,000	
22.	Actual Selling Expenses			12,000
23. Profit on Trading				18,000
24. PROFIT AND LOSS ACCOUNT				
25. Profit on Trading	(line 23)			18,000
26. Net Excess Cost of Production	(line 10)			— 10,000
27. Total Profit for Management Purposes				8,000
28. Adjustment to Annual Accounts Basis				+ 3,000
29. Net Profit before Taxation on Annual Accounts Basis				£ 11,000

DISCUSSION

CHAIRMAN: MR. H. HJERNØ JEPPESEN, Denmark

CHAIRMAN:

Ladies and Gentlemen, It is my great privilege to welcome you all to this session. Before I deliver a few opening remarks I should like to introduce to you your colleagues on the platform. They being the vice-chairmen, the discussion leader, the rapporteur, the authors of papers and three other members of the panel. I should like to present to you the vice-chairmen, first Dr. Jakob Viel from Switzerland, Mr. Pedro Tinoco from Venezuela and Prof. Dr. Kurosawa from Japan who has come the long way over the North Pole to attend this meeting. The vice-chairmen will be so kind as to assist me in the presidency of this meeting. In the programme you will see Mr. Paul Loeb from France mentioned as the discussion leader. But owing to his health, he has requested that his task be taken over by Prof. Dr. Mey from Holland. Prof. Mey is so kind as to replace Mr. Loeb in that function. The rapporteur who is also author of a paper, is Mr. Herbert Rätsch from Germany and the other authors are Mr. Prakash Chopra from India, Mr. Joseph Pelej from the United States of America, Mr. Tempelaar from Holland and Mr. Wilson from the United Kingdom.

The other members of the panel are Mr. René van Iper from Belgium, Mr. Leitch from the United Kingdom and Mr. Witt from Sweden.

I consider it a good decision of the Congress Committee to make Budgeting and the Corresponding Modernization of Accounting one of the subjects of our Congress. Technical development and discoveries in that field have forced the businesses to introduce large programmes of capital expenditure.

In analogy with that development the tools of management have developed as well. Budgeting is one of these tools par excellence. We in our profession know that management cannot perform its task without having a well-functioning budget system at its disposal. The accountants render their services not only as auditors, but also as advisers and consultants. You are in possession of the published papers which are the basis for the discussions to-day. We know that many colleagues have prepared their questions and remarks carefully for the benefit of all others, and I now open this session and ask the discussion leader Prof. Mey to take over.

PROF. DR. ABRAM MEY (Netherlands)

I thank you, Mr. Chairman, for introducing me as the discussion leader and I regret very much that it is necessary for me to replace my colleague Loeb on his personal request, as a consequence of his not being too well disposed to-day. I now give the floor to Mr. Rätsch of Germany, as the rapporteur, who will introduce the problem.

MR. H. RÄTSCH (Germany)

VORLIEGENDE STELLUNGNAHMEN

Erfreulicherweise haben die über das Thema 'Planung' referierenden Kollegen ihre Beiträge inhaltlich sehr verschieden gestaltet und darüber hinaus eine Anzahl wichtiger Fragen unterschiedlich beantwortet.

Die fünf vorliegenden Referate bieten daher trotz ihrer Kürze eine umfassende und lückenlose Darstellung des gegenwärtigen Wissens über Methoden und Probleme der Planung. Andererseits wird aber auch erkennbar, daß sich die Praxis der Planung noch im Entwicklungsstadium befindet; einheitliche, international anerkannte Lösungen sind daher nicht für alle Fragen gefunden worden.

Analysiert man die einzelnen Referate daraufhin, welche besonderen Erkenntnisse sie im Rahmen der gesamten Vortragsreihe beisteuern, dann ergibt sich folgendes Bild:

Der niederländische Beitrag von Herrn A. F. Tempelaar setzt sich besonders intensiv mit der Problematik der Planung in Klein- und Mittelbetrieben auseinander. Der indische Beitrag von Mr. S. Prakash Chopra beleuchtet die Fragen der Planung unter dem Aspekt einer staatlich gelenkten Volkswirtschaft. Im britischen Referat von Mr. J. P. Wilson dominiert die Fragestellung, welche Einflüsse die Planung auf das gesamte Rechnungswesen ausübt und welche Konsequenzen sich daraus für den Accountant ergeben, während die Ausführungen unseres amerikanischen Kollegen Mr. J. Pelej in erster Linie auf die Bedeutung der Planung für die Unternehmensführung Bezug nehmen. Mein eigener Beitrag zielt im wesentlichen darauf ab, eine elastische Planungspraxis zu empfehlen, wie es in einer vielseitig strukturierten Volkswirtschaft mit hohem Exportanteil und starken Expansionstendenzen unumgänglich erscheint.

VORAUSSETZUNGEN FÜR DIE EINFÜHRUNG EINER UMFASSENDEN BETRIEBSPLANUNG UND DER BUDGETÄREN KONTROLLE

Faßt man die Ergebnisse der fünf vorliegenden Referate zusammen, so können folgende drei Voraussetzungen für die Einführung einer Betriebsplanung genannt werden:

1. Die Bereitschaft der Unternehmensführung (des "management") und der Beschäftigten zur Planung und Kontrolle, denn ohne das Vorhandensein einer grundsätzlichen Bereitschaft und eines guten Betriebsklimas werden die Erfolge moderner Verfahren des Rechnungswesens gefährdet.
2. Klare Zielsetzungen des "management" über den Umfang der Planungen und der budgetären Kontrollen und Einbeziehung auch der unteren Instanzen in die Planungs- und Kontrollarbeiten zur Ermittlung zuverlässiger Planwerte und zur Erreichung einer verantwortungsbewußten Mitarbeit aller Beteiligten.
3. Das Vorhandensein einer funktionsfähigen Betriebsorganisation und eines reibungslos arbeitenden Rechnungswesens, denn ohne eine ausreichende

Organisation und ohne ein ausreichendes Rechnungswesen ist eine wirksame Planung in Frage gestellt und der übrigen betrieblichen Daten gegeben. Nur ein voll funktionsfähiges Rechnungswesen kann als 'tool of management' dienen.

DIE BEDEUTUNG DER BETRIEBLICHEN PLANUNG UND DER PLANUNGSKONTROLLE

Alle Referenten sind sich darüber einig, daß die Planung eine eminente betriebswirtschaftliche Bedeutung besitzt. Interessant sind jedoch die unterschiedlichen Begründungen dieser Stellungnahme. Während der indische Kollege in der Planung eine Voraussetzung für die Produktionssteigerung in einer sich entwickelnden Volkswirtschaft sieht, betonen die Vertreter der liberal organisierten Volkswirtschaften Amerikas, Englands, Hollands und Deutschlands den unternehmerischen Aspekt.

Für die private Unternehmung ist die Planung eine Notwendigkeit:

1. weil eine kapitalintensive Produktion bei schnellem Wechsel der Marktbedingungen ein erhebliches Risiko beinhaltet, und
2. weil die wachsenden Betriebsgrößen eine Delegation der Leitungsfunktion und damit zusammenhängend eine intensivierte Kontrolle erforderlich machen.

Ausgehend von dieser durch einen hohen Stand der wirtschaftlichen Entwicklung bestimmten Notwendigkeit der Modernisierung des Rechnungswesens lassen sich die Aufgaben der betrieblichen Planung als Instrument der Unternehmensführung wie folgt zusammenfassen.

Die betriebliche Planung und die Planungskontrolle dienen:

1. der laufenden Beobachtung der Marktverhältnisse;
2. der Orientierung der Geschäftspolitik;
3. der laufenden Beobachtung der Kosten und Leistungen;
4. der Steigerung der Wirtschaftlichkeit;
5. der Förderung einer verantwortungsbewußten Mitarbeit aller im Unternehmen Beschäftigten.

DIE TECHNIK DER PLANUNGSVERFAHREN UND DER BUDGETÄREN KONTROLLE

Alle fünf Referenten stimmen darin überein, daß das "Budgeting" für den Betrieb eine dreifache Aufgabenstellung beinhaltet:

die Planung als solche;
die Kontrolle;
die Koordinierung.

Allerdings ist die Planung lediglich ein Instrument der Unternehmensführung; sie kann das "management" nicht ersetzen. Ihre Funktion wird am besten erfüllt, wenn man in einem geschlossenen System budgetiert. Alle Bereiche und Ebenen des Unternehmens müssen erfaßt werden. Ausgehend von der Absatz-, Produktions-, Einkaufs-, Finanz- und Ergebnisplanung der Gesamtunternehmung verzweigt sich die Planung pyramidenförmig bis zu den letzten Kostenstellen.

Die Technik der Planung bedient sich hierbei zunächst der Ermittlung maßstabgerechter Standards, die z.B. Mengen-, Zeit-, Leistungs-, Kosten-, Erlös- oder Gewinnstandards sein können, und die entweder auf Grund eingehender analytischer Arbeiten oder in Anlehnung an Durchschnitts- oder Vergleichswerte festgelegt werden. Soweit die Standards Wertstandards sind, werden sie auf Tageswertbasis gebildet, weil die Kosten- und Leistungsrechnung grundsätzlich nur dann aussagefähig ist, wenn sie mit Tageswerten rechnet.

Längere Zeit hindurch war umstritten, ob die Standards auf der Basis optimaler, normaler oder tatsächlicher Betriebsbedingungen ermittelt werden sollten, und man hat sich heute mehr für die normalen und praktisch erreichbaren Standards entschieden, weil die Planungs- und Kontrollarbeiten frei von Illusionen gehalten werden sollen.

Das Arbeiten mit praktisch erreichbaren Standards bedeutet allerdings, daß man auf die arbeitstechnisch einfachere starre Planung verzichten und zur flexiblen Planung übergehen muß, d.h. Standards werden nicht nur für konstante, sondern auch für alle praktisch möglichen Betriebsbedingungen und Kapazitätsstufen festgesetzt.

Die Erkenntnisse aus der Planung und der Planungskontrolle schließlich werden für die Unternehmensführung durch die Berichterstattung erschlossen. Diese muß vor allem schnell erfolgen, um Mängel möglichst umgehend abzustellen und Chancen rechtzeitig wahrnehmen zu können.

Je nach der Managementsebene, für die ein Bericht gedacht ist, ändert sich die Technik der Berichterstattung. Für Berichte an das Top-Management gilt die Regel des 'management by exception', da die oberen Stellen nicht mit umfangreichem Berichtsmaterial überlastet werden sollen. Unteren Managementstufen ist demgegenüber nach dem Prinzip des 'responsibility accounting' zu berichten. Diese Stellen sollen alle Einzelheiten, die zur Steuerung ihres Bereiches erforderlich sind, erhalten; dabei kommt es darauf an, die von den unteren Instanzen zu verantwortenden Kostenelemente getrennt von den nicht zu verantwortenden Kostenelementen auszuweisen.

DIE EINFLÜSSE VON BETRIEBSTYP UND BETRIEBSGRÖSZE AUF DIE BETRIEBLICHE PLANUNG

Von ganz wesentlicher Bedeutung für die betriebliche Planung sind schließlich
der Betriebstyp und
die Betriebsgröße,
die beide sowohl für die Anwendbarkeit einer Planung überhaupt als auch für den Umfang der Planung bestimmend sind.

Ganz allgemein läßt sich hierzu sagen, daß die Brauchbarkeit moderner Planungs- und Kontrollverfahren zunächst von der Branchenzugehörigkeit des Unternehmens abhängt. Produktionsbetriebe sind im allgemeinen einer Planung leichter zugänglich als Handelsbetriebe, und je höher der Anteil der Massenfertigung an der Gesamtproduktion ist, desto erfolgreicher kann die betriebliche Planung als Instrument der Unternehmensführung zur Anwendung gelangen.

Betrachtet man diese Schlußfolgerung unter dem Gesichtspunkt der Betriebsgröße, so ergibt sich daraus zwangsläufig, daß auch der auf Massenfertigung ausgerichtete Großbetrieb Vorteile in der Anwendung und Auswertung der Planung vor dem Mittel- und Kleinbetrieb besitzt, und zwar einmal auf

Grund der breiteren Anwendungsmöglichkeiten und der breiteren Basis des Rechnungswesens und zum anderen auf Grund der im Großbetrieb meistens besser zu lösenden Fragen der personellen Besetzung.

Unter den hier vorliegenden Referaten hat sich gerade Herr Tempelaar mit diesem Fragenkomplex auseinandergesetzt und dargelegt, daß die Klein- und Mittelbetriebe auf dem Gebiet der betrieblichen Planung hinter den Großbetrieben zurückgeblieben sind, obwohl auch im Klein- und Mittelbetrieb durchaus Anwendungsmöglichkeiten für das "Budgeting", so z.B. für eine Planung und Kontrolle der Kosten und der Finanzverhältnisse, bestehen.

DIE BEDEUTUNG DER BETRIEBLICHEN PLANUNG UND DER PLANUNGSKONTROLLEN FÜR DAS WIRTSCHAFTSPRÜFUNGSWESEN

Faßt man die uns hier vorliegenden Referate zusammen, so ergibt sich das eindeutige Bild, daß in der betrieblichen Planung und in der Planungskontrolle große Möglichkeiten für bessere, schnellere und zuverlässigere betriebliche Entscheidungen und für eine Steigerung der Wirtschaftlichkeit beschlossen liegen.

Die Planung und die Planungskontrolle führen zu einer ständigen Überwachung des Betriebsgeschehens bei gleichzeitiger Analyse der Abweichungen von den gesetzten Standards, und es ist selbstverständlich, daß die Ergebnisse dieser ständigen Kontrolle nicht nur für den Betrieb, sondern auch für den Accountant ein wichtiges Hilfsmittel zur Beurteilung der Betriebssituation in der Unternehmensentwicklung darstellen.

Die Planungswerte und die Auswertungsergebnisse werden somit als Bestandteile des betrieblichen Rechnungswesens zu wesentlichen Ausgangswerten, sowohl für die Durchführung der reinen Prüfungsarbeiten als auch für die Ausführung der dem Accountant übertragenen Beratungsaufgaben, und es wird daher mit eine wichtige Aufgabe der Accountants sein, in der Praxis die betriebliche Planung und die Planungskontrolle zu fördern. Damit dienen wir einerseits der Unternehmensführung der von uns betreuten Unternehmen und verbessern andererseits die Ergebnisse unserer eigenen Berufsarbeit.

MATTERS DISCUSSED

The fact that the papers on budgeting contributed by my colleagues differ widely from each other in content and, moreover, advance quite dissimilar solutions of a number of major problems, makes my task more than usually rewarding.

Though short, the five papers submitted set out the present state of our knowledge of the methods and problems of budgeting comprehensively and exhaustively. But they show clearly that the practice of budgeting is still in its infancy; and they remind us that there are still questions, to which no answers, generally accepted internationally, exist.

If one were to ask oneself in what way the various papers submitted contributed to the general aims of our Congress, I think that the answer would be on the following lines:

The Dutch paper by Mr. A. F. Tempelaar stresses the difficulties in the practice of budgeting that small and medium-sized businesses experience. The Indian paper by Mr. S. Prakash Chopra views problems of budgeting as one aspect of the greater problem of how a government can effectively steer the whole economy of its country. Mr. J. P. Wilson's British paper is very largely concerned with the influence of budgeting on accounting procedures generally and on the tasks devolving on an accountant; while our American colleague, Mr. J. Pelej, emphasizes the importance of budgeting from the point of view of management. I have in my own contribution put forward a strong plea for elasticity in the practice of budgeting, an obvious requirement in a many-sided economy, largely dependent on its export trade and subject to strong expansive pressures.

WHAT IS INVOLVED IN THE INTRODUCTION OF COMPREHENSIVE SYSTEMS BOTH OF BUDGETING FOR PRODUCTION AND OF BUDGETARY CONTROL

If one analyses carefully the points made in the five papers, there emerge three considerations which seem to be essential to the introduction of a system of budgeting for production:

1. The readiness of the management and of the workers to accept budgeting and the necessary budgetary controls, since, if this readiness is lacking and if relations in the business are unhappy, all the fruits of employing a progressive system of accounting may be lost.

2. Definite ideas on the part of the management regarding the scale on which the schemes of budgeting and the budgetary controls are to operate; co-operation with the lower ranges of the management in working out the schemes of budgeting and of the budgetary controls, not only with a view to making the predetermined costs reliable, but also with the object of giving all concerned the feeling that they are actively participating in working out the schemes.

3. The existence of a sound set-up from the managerial point of view and of an accounting system that functions smoothly. Without adequate organisation and without an adequate system of accounting efficient budgeting and the information it ought to produce cannot be guaranteed. Unless the system of accounting is operating smoothly, it cannot be the 'tool of management'.

VALUE OF MANAGEMENT BUDGETING AND OF BUDGETARY CONTROLS

All contributors agree that management budgeting is a matter of prime importance to a business. But it is interesting to note the differing reasons given for this view. My Indian colleague looks on budgeting as the pre-requisite for boosting output in an expanding economy, while the representatives of the free-market economic systems of America, Great-Britain, the Netherlands and Germany put the profit-earning aspect first.

Budgeting is essential to any undertaking run on business lines, because

1. the heavy capital investment in plant and the fickleness of markets mean that it is never free from risks, and

2. the incessant expansion of undertakings necessitates the delegation of managerial functions and, in consequence, tighter methods of control.

We thus start from the need to modernise the theory and practice of accounting, to compel it to reach the high level of efficiency attained by industry at the present time. Then we can proceed to describe the tasks of management budgeting as the tool of management as embracing: Management budgeting and budgetary control for the purpose of

1. maintaining a continuous watch on market developments,
2. giving guidance in connection with the general policies of the business,
3. maintaining a continuous watch over costs and output,
4. increasing profit-earning capacity,
5. strengthening the sense of solidarity among all members of the staff.

METHODS OF DRAWING UP SCHEMES FOR BUDGETING AND BUDGETARY CONTROL

All five papers are unanimous in attributing three functions to management budgeting

planning, (budgeting in the strict sense)
controlling,
co-ordinating.

Planning (or budgeting) is clearly a contrivance that the management must operate, and not a substitute for management itself. It will work most successfully if it is set up as a self-contained system. All departments and all levels of the undertaking must be included. The starting point must be the planning of sales, of output, of purchases, of financial resources and of results, which should embrace the whole undertaking; the planning must be extended until it has penetrated every cost centre.

Budgeting in practice concerns itself in the first place with setting up standards, based on the accurate measurement of some object—quantity, time, output, costs, revenues or profits standards are possible kinds of standard — and determined after careful analysis of the facts or by reference to average or comparable bases. If money standards are employed, they will be based on current prices ruling, on the ground that no computations of costs and output have any real meaning unless based on current prices.

For a long time it was an unsettled question whether standards should be based on ideal, or on normal, or on actually expected conditions. The balance of professional opinion to-day favours the employment of normal and actually attainable standards, because budgetary calculations and the relative budgetary controls must have a solid foundation of real fact.

The employment of actually attainable standards means that one cannot operate on a system of rigid budgeting, which is much easier to work from the accounting point of view, but must operate on a flexible budgeting system, that is to say, standards must be set up not only for normal manufacturing processes, but for pretty well all the operations of a business, and they must cover every stage of production.

The key that unlocks the knowledge acquired by budgeting and budgetary controls and makes it available to the top-level management is the system of reporting. The essential thing about reporting is that the information is made available quickly, so that weaknesses may be dealt with promptly and opportunities grasped before they have passed.

The type of report prepared must be adapted to the requirements of the particular level of management for which it is intended. If the report is to go to the top-level management, it must conform to the 'management by exception' rule, as persons working at that level must not be burdened with a mass of detail. Below that level the 'responsibility accounting' rule applies. Lower levels should be in possession of all the information requisite to enable them to control operations in the field allotted to them. This also means that those elements of costs for which those levels of management can be held responsible must be distinguished from those elements for which they carry no responsibility.

TYPE OF BUSINESS AND SIZE OF BUSINESS IN RELATION TO MANAGEMENT BUDGETING

Finally,

the type of business, and

the size of the business

have a considerable effect on management budgeting, since both are factors in determining whether a budget can be made at all, and, if so, in what detail it can be made.

One can say generally that the usefulness of modern systems of budgeting and budgetary controls to an undertaking depends on the kind of business it is engaged in. It is generally easier to apply budgetary methods to a manufacturing business than to a purely merchanting business; and the probability that success will attend the employment of management budgeting as the tool of management is greater where the proportion of the total output consisting of serially manufactured goods is high.

Applying this line of reasoning to the size of the undertaking, it needs no proof that the undertaking which produces serially manufactured goods on a really large scale will have advantages over the medium-sized or small undertaking in the matter of getting the most out of budgeting, for two reasons, first of all, the accounting system, being much more developed, will offer greater scope for elaboration of budgeting methods, and secondly, the larger undertaking can usually afford more highly qualified staff.

Mr. Tempelaar in his paper devoted considerable space to this question, and showed that medium-sized and small undertakings have not gone so far in introducing management budgeting as larger undertakings have done, although there are fields open to medium-sized and small undertakings where they could effectively make use of budgeting methods, such as budgeting for, and budgetary controls on, costs and financial resources.

VALUE OF MANAGEMENT BUDGETING AND BUDGETARY CONTROLS TO THE AUDITOR

It is the unanimous conclusion of all the papers submitted that management budgeting and budgetary controls make it possible for managements to arrive at decisions based on a sounder view of facts and fortified by more detailed knowledge; they will also be able to do it more quickly. These are factors which enhance the profit-earning capacity of the business.

Budgeting and budgetary control result in everything that goes on in a business being permanently under observation and disclose at the same time the extent of variances from any standard which has been fixed. Clearly the fact that all happenings are permanently subject to control cannot fail to be a valuable aid not only to the management but also to the accountant, in assessing the situation of the undertaking.

The data used for budgeting and the deductions drawn from evaluating such data are thus assimilated to the factory accounting system and provide the ground work not only for audits in the strict sense, but also for the investigation of any problems on which the accountant may be asked to advise. The accountant has in consequence, a strong interest in seeing that everything is done to encourage budgeting and budgetary control. And, in fact, in doing so, we are not only helping the managements of undertakings to which we owe duties, but also we are improving the quality of our own professional work.

PROF. DR. ABRAM MEY (Netherlands)

I think, Colleagues, that we must be very thankful to our colleague Rätsch for his excellent 'resumé' of the various papers. I imagine we may take up five important points for our further discussions.

First of all, the conditions which the accountant should take into consideration when introducing budgetary control; second, the importance of the system of budgetary control; third, the technique of budgetary control; fourth, the influence of the size of the business and, last but not least, the importance of budgetary control for the auditor's work.

I think that we may discuss first which are these general conditions. This is a basic problem. We heard Mr. Rätsch speaking about a 'mental climate' and a delegation of authority in his introduction. I think Mr. Pelej that you will have something to say about the conditions mentioned as well as about that mental climate.

MR. JOSEPH PELEJ (United States of America)

Ladies and Gentlemen, As you all no doubt know, books have been written in answer to that question. I shall try in two or three minutes to indicate some of the more important matters which in my opinion the accountant should take into consideration before—and during—the introduction of the system of budgetary control.

First is the establishment of an effective plan of organization in which authorities and responsibilities are clearly defined. This is of the utmost importance since fixing responsibility for performance is one of the principal objectives of the system.

Secondly, I think that a thorough review of existing practices and procedures should be made to correct, insofar as practicable, the more obvious defects in the existing system, procedures and practices. This should be done before the system is installed because, if improvements can be made before the installation, the budget will be more workable and practicable. It seems to make little sense to set budget figures for inefficient or unnecessary operations. Among other things consideration should be given to the mechanization of certain procedures heretofore carried out by hand, the rearrangement of the departmental functions and responsibilities, etc.

Thirdly, I consider the appointment of a budget-director, that is a person responsible for the introduction and co-ordination of the budget and the follow-up and subsequent reporting on its operations, of utmost importance. This is frequently one of the most important functions of the accountant.

And fourthly, the system of accounts and management reporting should be reorganized so as to ensure that management is being furnished with essential information for important management-decisions promptly and in the simplest possible terms.

As to the 'mental attitude', I may point to the following:

1. Every effort should be made to obtain a thorough understanding of the philosophy of budgetary control by management and to procure management's fullest support. This often necessitates important changes in the viewpoint of management as regards the delegation of authorities and

responsibilities and a recognition on the part of management of the accountant's function as advisor and interpreter rather than a recorder of figures relating to passed transactions.

2. I believe it is important to make certain that the objectives of the system are clearly understood by supervisory personnel which is to be held responsible for performance. And this I think should include personnel at the lowest possible supervisory level. It is the man closest to the operations that can do the most good in improving them.
3. I should make sure that the supervisor whose performance is to be measured understands the manner in which the measurements, yardsticks or standards have been arrived at for these standards. And I should make very sure that these persons are in agreement with the basis and consider them fair and equitable.
4. Insofar as possible, incentives should be provided for personnel not only to meet the budgetary standards but to improve them. I should also like to point out the need to make every effort to meet the views of those who are expected to meet the budgetary goals.

My general reasons for emphasizing these factors—and there are many others—are:

1. Co-operation at all levels of management is essential. It is axiomatic that people will not co-operate with what they do not understand. This is particularly true as far as practical operating men are concerned who for the most part are technicians with little or no training in accounting and control procedures associated with the accounting function.
2. Unless properly introduced, personnel expected to meet the budgetary standards will become confused and suspicious and will block all future attempts to make the system work.
3. Unless properly introduced, management itself will lose confidence and withdraw its support.

PROF. DR. ABRAM MEY (Netherlands)

I thank you, Mr. Pelej. Ladies and Gentlemen, We have observed that Mr. Pelej is a real expert in this field. Only there is one thing more. Just before he came here, he attended a conference in London about 'operational research' and other things of that kind, so that he really has the very latest information about everything that has to do with budgeting and budgetary control, even with the help of mathematics. It may be reserved for the later discussion.

There was something in what he said that makes me ask our rapporteur what his opinion is about the possibility of introducing budgetary control in the case of a firm which still has the traditional accounting system, and on the other hand, what are the demands to which the chief-accountant in the firm in question must answer in order to meet the requirements of budgeting.

MR. H. RÄTSCH (Germany)

Die ausgebaute Planrechnung besteht ja darin, daß man den Istkosten und Erlösen sowohl die normalen als auch die erreichbaren Standardkosten und Erlöse gegenüberstellt. Die Untersuchung der Abweichungen, die sich dann ergeben, ist m.E. mit eine der haupsächlichsten Aufgaben des Accountants. Denn diese Abweichungen zeigen ja, welche Faktoren den Gewinn beeinflussen. Diese Untersuchungen, die der Accountant vorzunehmen hat, sind ungewöhnlich wichtig, denn anomale Entwicklungen werden dadurch kenntlich gemacht, und die Geschäftsleitung hat dann auf Veranlassung des Accountants die Möglichkeit, den Einfluß positiver Faktoren zu fördern und den Einfluß negativer Faktoren zurückzudrängen. Wir kennen da z.B. Preisabweichungen, Beschäftigungsabweichungen, Abweichungen wegen eines veränderten Auftragsbestandes, Verbrauchsabweichungen, Absatzabweichungen. Ich möchte sagen, daß in den fortschrittlichen Betrieben sich immer mehr die Erkenntnis durchsetzt, daß es nicht ausreichend ist, wenn nur die höchsten Instanzen, d.h. Vorstandsmitglieder und Geschäftsführer eines Unternehmens über diese Abweichungen orientiert werden, und daß nur sie von einer bestimmten Kostenentwicklung Kenntnis erhalten. Gerade die mittleren und unteren Instanzen haben oft einen entscheidenden Einfluß auf die Kostengestaltung und die Wirtschaftlichkeit des Betriebes oder einzelner Betriebsteile hängt also von der Mitarbeit dieser Abteilungsleiter, Meister oder wie man sie nennen will, entscheidend ab.

Standard costing in its developed form involves, as we all know, comparing actual costs and revenues with normal and with attainable costs and revenues. The investigation of the variances which such a comparison throws up, is in my view one of the most important tasks of the accountant, since the variances obviously disclose what factors are influencing profits. These investigations which the accountant must carry out, are extremely important, since any developments out of the normal are definitely made clear by such investigations, and the management, thanks to the activities of the accountant, is then in a position to stimulate positive factors and to repress negative factors. In this connection we have price variances, employment variances, variances caused by variation in the type of order, consumption variances, sales variances. It is certainly my view that in progressive undertakings it is becoming more and more generally recognised that it is not sufficient that merely the top-level management, that is to say, executive or managing directors and their deputies, should be in possession of information regarding variances and should have access to knowledge of the direction in which they are pointing. But it is just the lower and middle grades of managers who have often a decisive influence on how costs work out; and whether the whole undertaking or particular departments of it are operating profitably can thus depend on the extent to which the co-operation of these under-managers and foremen, or whatever they are called, is enlisted.

PROF. DR. ABRAM MEY (Netherlands)

I thank you, Mr. Rätsch. So I suppose it would not do to introduce budgetary control without the conditions mentioned being fulfilled.

Mr. Wilson, I think you can give me, in a few words, your answer about it. Please make it short.

MR. J. P. WILSON (United Kingdom)

Mr. Chairman, I would not disagree with anything that Mr. Pelej has said but he gave a counsel of perfection and we have to operate budgetary control or attempt to operate it (I hope we do operate it) in an imperfect world. I would say that if the introduction of budgetary control had always to wait upon the establishment of a rational organization and all the other prerequisites that Mr. Pelej has laid down, then in many cases budgetary control would never be introduced at all. Between what we can do and what we would like to do is the danger that we do nothing at all. I would say that the intro-

CONCERT-GEBOUW

H.R.H. The Prince of the Netherlands at the Delegates' Dinner
To the left of H.R.H.:
the President of the Congress, Mr. J. Kraayenhof;
the Governor of the Queen for the Province of North Holland, Dr. M. J. Prinsen;
Mr. Marquis G. Eaton, U.S.A.; Dr. W. F. Schokking; Mr. W. H. Lawson, U.K.
and Professor A. Goudeket
To the right of H.R.H.:
the State Secretary of Economic Affairs, Dr. G. M. J. Veldkamp;
the Vice-President of the Congress, Professor A. M. van Rietschoten
and Mr. J. T. Dowling, U.K.

duction of budgetary control can be introduced based upon an assumed rational organization, that it might very well be effective and in fact might even point the way to the establishment of rational organization. After all there is not one system of budgetary control. You take the circumstances of the business and you apply to that business the system of budgetary control, standard-costing, the accounting system which is suitable; in other words a system which really must be tailor-made for that particular business. It may be that in certain cases you have to start off with a provisional system. You have to accept some crude standards perhaps, but they may be very good for their purpose. So, they might do the job and do it very well. Therefore I say, don't let us wait until the last button is sewn on the last tunic of the last soldier before we invade. After all a budgetary control system can be like a flower, a plant, it can grow. It can start from fairly small beginnings, it can be rough, but it can achieve something really effective, probably fairly soon, and perhaps it can become really polished after a number of years.

PROF. DR. ABRAM MEY (Netherlands)
Thank you, Mr. Wilson. I think that Mr. Pelej will agree that we do not have to wait for the last soldier and the last button on his tunic. But may I go on, please. That is something for private discussion between you two. May I ask Mr. Leitch to tell us something about his opinion, because Mr. Leitch warns us to be careful of some dangers. Mr. Leitch the floor is yours.

MR. J. R. LEITCH (United Kingdom)
Mr. Chairman, Ladies and Gentlemen, I feel that to-day there may be a tendency to overburden management with too much accounting information and statistical analyses to the extent that business acumen is overcast by masses of figures. The danger is that too much emphasis is inclined to be placed on figures which consequently become the master and not the servant of those who are using them. Management cannot avoid responsibility for decisions—and I would like to emphasise this point—by attempting to base them too closely on figures supplied by the accountant; management must still use business acumen and commonsense. There must be many factories, particularly of the small or medium size, where the accountant and his staff work very hard to produce under whatever system you like—budgetary control, or otherwise—operating statements promptly, when the state of affairs disclosed thereby would have been obvious to a casual observer walking round the factory, or, even to the canteen manageress.

PROF. DR. ABRAM MEY (Netherlands)
I thank you, Mr. Leitch. I think Mr. Tempelaar will be so kind as to answer Mr. Leitch's remarks and ease his mind with regard to that overburdening of management by our information statements.

MR. A. F. TEMPELAAR (Netherlands)
Mijnheer de voorzitter, Ik zal de eerste zijn om te bevestigen, dat overdrijving in informatie terzake van details vermeden moet worden, maar wil toch het

risico, waarop door de heer Leitch wordt gewezen, niet zonder meer uit de weg gaan. De heer Leitch heeft gelijk voor al die gevallen waarin het systeem, waarover wij hier discussiëren inclusief de gehele informatie van statistieken en cijferopstellingen, zou ontaarden in een automatische demonstratie. Iets, wat we in de praktijk inderdaad wel tegenkomen: 'hier hebt u de cijfers, er zijn nog meer cijfers beschikbaar, zoekt u zelf maar uit wat u wilt'. Dit heeft als gevolg, dat de leiding bedolven ligt onder een hoop gegevens, waarmede ze niet werken kan. Zelf kan zij niet uitzoeken wat wel en niet belangrijk is. Daartoe ontbreekt haar de tijd en de lust.

Wij moeten dus de waarschuwing van de heer Leitch wat dit betreft volkomen onderschrijven. Anderzijds zou ik toch ook naar voren willen brengen, dat ik een groter gevaar zie, wanneer men de leiding te weinig gegevens geeft om – reëel goed geïnformeerd – te kunnen beslissen. Hoe en wat wij moeten doen, hebt u in de referaten kunnen vinden. Ik geloof, dat ik het in verband met de tijd hierbij kan laten, mijnheer de voorzitter. We aanvaarden wel de waarschuwing, maar aan de andere kant laten we niet te bang zijn om reorganisaties, als in de referaten bedoeld, door te voeren.

Mr. Chairman, I would be the first to confirm that we have to avoid exaggerations in giving management informative data, but on the other hand I would like to say a word about Mr. Leitch's point. He is right as far as the system we are now discussing and all the statistical information and figures might degenerate into an automatic proof. We come across this in practice: 'Here are the figures; there are more too; you must look yourself to see if you can find what you want'. The result is that the management becomes buried under a mass of useless data. To that extent we must agree entirely with Mr. Leitch. But I must also say that I feel there is greater danger in giving the management too little information to allow it to come to realistic, well-informed decisions. It cannot sort out what is important and what is not, having neither the time nor the inclination to do this. That is all I need say, I think, Mr. Chairman. We accept the warning, but, on the other hand, we must not be afraid to introduce the reorganizations referred to in the papers.

PROF. DR. ABRAM MEY (Netherlands)

Thank you, Mr. Tempelaar. I think you can compare the conduct of an organizing expert, who overburdens management with informative data, with the Dutch saying that the housewife must not give her husband more to eat than he can consume. The same holds good for the relation between the accountant and everyone in his client's business who is in a responsible position. But there is another problem, there is another danger. We have seen everything from above so far, but you can see it from the point of view of the executive personalities with lower functions. I remember, Mr. Pelej, you pointed in your paper to some danger on the lower executive level. May I ask you to explain that danger?

MR. JOSEPH PELEJ (United States of America)

Well, the point that I tried to make in my paper was that a budget is not something that top-management should put in its drawer and forget about. A budget is a means to an end and not an end in itself.

PROF. DR. ABRAM MEY (Netherlands)

Yes, but may I interrupt you? It is especially about the danger at the lower levels that I wanted your remarks.

MR. JOSEPH PELEJ (United States of America)
I am coming to that.

PROF. DR. ABRAM MEY (Netherlands)
Will you make it short?

MR. JOSEPH PELEJ (United States of America):
A budget is a co-operative effort, in its planning as well as in its execution. As many supervisory employees as possible should be brought into the scheme, because only then will a budget accomplish its purposes.

PROF. DR. ABRAM MEY (Netherlands)
Yes, I think that this is the thing I needed. The lower executives are, as Mr. Pelej says in his paper, inclined (sometimes at least) to see these budgeted amounts as grants for expenditure, is it not so, Mr. Pelej? And especially with regard to authorisation budgets in governmental services that danger is present. Is that not the problem?

MR. JOSEPH PELEJ (United States of America)
Well, that is where the accountant's function comes in. In the preparation of the budgets the accountant should act as co-ordinator and it is up to him, in collaboration with the departmental supervisors and departmental employees, to decide whether the amounts to be budgeted meet the general business objectives, and appear reasonable and necessary. Also, once the budget is established, it does not mean that no revisions will be made while it is in operation. The budgetary amounts should be reviewed in the light of changing conditions continually. They have to be diminished if there is a possibility of accomplishing the objectives at less than the budgeted costs.

PROF. DR. ABRAM MEY (Netherlands)
Thank you. I may now turn to another subject. Mr. Chopra, will you make a short remark about your idea that this introduction on budgetary control is seen by all those writing papers too much from the side of the Western capitalist countries? But, please, we are short of time. May I ask you to pose the problem as briefly as possible?

MR. S. PRAKASH CHOPRA (India)
Mr. Chairman, Ladies and Gentlemen, I promise I will be short. I noticed that in the rapporteur's summary he has, and up to a point rightly, drawn a distinction between the paper that I have written and the papers that have been written by the others. I noticed also that he mentioned that possibly that is due to a difference between a liberal economy and maybe what I would call a planned economy and others that are called competitive economies. I have found, when I have been going round the different countries, that, in effect there is very little difference in regard to the approach on the subject. Unfortunately, however, there is more emphasis—at least to my way of looking at it—on either competition or in regard to seeking new markets or, for that matter,

on high rates of taxes. I see no reason why we should say that management-accounting is primarily necessary in the case of a competitive economy. It is just as necessary for a planned economy as it is for a competitive economy. One of the main reasons why this is so, is as follows: in a planned economy, when you have a very large number of persons who are not businessmen, but civil servants, and who have to follow a plan and who have no personal stakes in it, they need a certain amount of guidance. A management accounting system will give guidance to people who are implementing a plan and would also act as a check in regard to the work that they are performing. Well, I do not think I will dilate on that very much, because there will be others who would like to say something about it.

PROF. DR. ABRAM MEY (Netherlands)

I thank you, Mr. Chopra and I am glad to hear that—according to your opinion—in Government business and in Government-guided business, budgetary control is just as much required as in competitive industries. I fully agree.

But now I should like to turn to the chapter on the technique of budgeting and there is first the problem of quantitative factors in the establishment of standards and I think that Mr. Rätsch, as the rapporteur, will put some questions about this and bring some problems forward, especially with regard to the normal, optimal and actual conditions in establishing standards.

MR. H. RÄTSCH (Germany)

Ich glaube, daß man bei der Festlegung von Standards weitgehend analytisch vorgehen muß, d.h. also, daß man an dem 'Experiment', um Standards festzustellen, nicht vorbei kommt. Nun gibt es natürlich eine Anzahl von Standardbegriffen, z.B. optimale Standards, normale Standards und, wie wir sie nennen, erreichbare Standards; diese sind mit 'attainable standards' übersetzt worden und daraus hat sich eine gewisse Debatte ergeben. Ich möchte sagen, optimale, also ideale Standards, sind Bestleistungen, die kaum jemals erzielt werden und in denen manchmal etwas Illusion steckt. Wir sollen uns ja aber gerade im Rechnungswesen und bei der Budgetierung von Illusionen freihalten.

Normale Standards sind diejenigen Standards, die man bei normalen Betriebsbedingungen erreichen kann und erreichbare Standards sind, wenn ich das so sagen darf, Standards, die bei tatsächlichen Voraussetzungen eine mögliche Leistung bewirken.

Wir arbeiten aus den Gründen, die ich eben anführte, nicht mit optimalen Standards, sondern wir arbeiten mit normalen und erreichbaren Standards. Das Arbeiten mit einem doppelten Standard bringt natürlich etwas mehr Arbeit mit sich, als wenn man nur mit einem einzelnen Standard rechnet, doch glaube ich, daß das Arbeiten mit doppelten Standards bei richtiger Erfassung und richtiger Zurechnung der Verantwortung bei Mehr- oder Minderleistungen das Entscheidende und Erforderliche ist. Faktoren, wie die Beschäftigungsgrade, das Produktionsverfahren, die Auftragszusammensetzung, liegen ja alle außerhalb der Einflußsphäre der technischen Abteilungsleiter und daher gibt man diesen Abteilungsleitern, damit sie Freude an ihrer Arbeit haben, erreichbare Standards vor, weil nur der erreichbare Standard wegen seiner, ich möchte sagen Situationsgerechtigkeit, einen echten Leistungsanreiz bildet.

Herr Professor Mey, ich weiß nicht, sollen wir jetzt auch schon über Bewertungsfragen sprechen? Sonst wäre das alles, was ich zu sagen hätte.

I think that one must employ analytical methods for the most part in order to establish standards, that is to say, that in arriving at standards one must substantially base oneself on empirical methods. Of course there are a number of theories as to what is a standard; standards are most commonly divided into three types: ideal standards, normal standards, and standards based on what is in practice reachable which we call (and have translated as) 'attainable' standards. On this point there has been some discussion. I define ideal standards as those based on reaching the highest imaginable level; such a level is in practice scarcely ever reached and the standards are really of a somewhat illusory nature. Of all people, accountants should shun wishful thinking, and in no field so definitely as in budgetary control.

Normal standards represent what can be achieved under normal conditions, while attainable standards represent the level reachable in existing circumstances, if I may so put it.

For the reasons I have just given we make no use of ideal standards, but we do employ normal and attainable standards. Making use of double standards inevitably causes somewhat more work as compared with the use of single standards. But I believe that the employment of double standards, if they are soundly planned and if they ensure that results above par or below par will be laid at the door of the right person, can be made to work very satisfactorily. The essential thing is that departmental managers are offered a real incentive to attain a standard. Factors such as the intensity of employment, the process used and the type of order are outside the sphere of influence of the departmental manager. We therefore offer him, in order to give him as much encouragement as possible, attainable standards, because the attainable standard is the only standard which can offer him genuine encouragement, being, if I may say so, the only standard 'tailored' to fit the actual conditions. Professor Mey, I don't know if you want me to go on with questions of valuation. I have said all I have to say on the topic under discussion.

PROF. DR. ABRAM MEY (Netherlands)

Not at the moment, Herr Rätsch. We shall be dealing with that in a moment. Mr. Wilson, I think you can give your opinion about these different standards. We thank Mr. Rätsch for his explanation of the problem of the quantitative measurement of performances.

MR. J. P. WILSON (United Kingdom)

Mr. Chairman, On this particular point I do think that there are different standards, but if I may come back to a point which I hoped to have made earlier, and that was that you must have your system suited to the particular circumstances of the business, I think that in many cases it might be highly desirable to keep on record your attainable standards and at the same time to use a standard which is adapted to the conditions as you actually find them.

Now, the difference between those two standards will, of course, come up in the form of a variance of imperfect conditions and that can be a very useful figure. But, if that figure is going to come up time after time, month after month, until you get used to it, and if management cannot do anything about those imperfect conditions, well then it may be just as well to discontinue the use of your ideal standard and to lose sight of your imperfect condition variance. That would lead us then to what I think my colleague Mr. Rätsch calls his 'attainable standard'. And on this point of attainable standard I would make this plea. Do have these standards so that they are attainable. Do not set your standard so high that the executives and departmental managers that have to work to these standards, just cannot make them, get discouraged and therefore lose faith in the system and by so doing bring about a distinct psychological disadvantage. My advice on this particular problem would be: set your standard within reach, let your departmental managers and your foremen taste blood, let them have some credit variances. I think that is an important psychological point.

PROF. DR. ABRAM MEY (Netherlands)

Thank you, Mr. Wilson. And Mr. Pelej, as America is the Fatherland of standards, I would ask you if it is possible for you to tell us, briefly, what your opinion is about what Mr. Rätsch and Mr. Wilson said regarding standards.

MR. JOSEPH PELEJ (United States of America)

I have very little to add as far as the basis for their determination is concerned, but I would like to point out that I would use attainable standards in dealing with supervisory personnel at the lower levels. I would not introduce the so-called ideal standards into statements for their information, because the ideal standard is something that supervision at the lower levels can do absolutely nothing about. It is a question for top-management to deal with that.

PROF. DR. ABRAM MEY (Netherlands)

Thank you, Mr. Pelej. Now I think, Ladies and Gentlemen, that we must go on and attack the next problem which follows that of the quantities. It is the problem of the values in cost-calculation. The notion *replacement value* has been mentioned several times in the papers. And now there is Mr. Prakash Chopra from India who has some rather critical remarks to make about the opinions of most of us.

So I would ask you, Mr. Chopra, to be so kind as to make your remarks about the use of replacement value, but do not go too far into the dangerous monetary problem, nor enter the field of politics or other ones, which will lead us off the path.

MR. S. PRAKASH CHOPRA (India)

I notice that I have again been reminded to keep away from politics and economics. I thought that so far as we accountants are concerned we have to take into account economics all the time, when we are dealing with facts and figures which really determine costs of different types. Coming to my subject, on this question of replacement cost: as we all know there is a fair amount of literature on the subject and there is no point in my repeating what has often been said. But in view of there being a difference of opinion amongst ourselves on the panel, perhaps I might mention that I do differ with the concept that as far as possible depreciation should be charged on the basis of replacement value of assets.

In fact this is partly connected with another point that I mentioned in my paper, that is, regarding the return on equity-capital. This whole problem really lends itself to three possible approaches: (I) when you look at it from the point of view of the manufacturer with greater emphasis on the equity-holders in a company, and (II) when you look at it from the point of view of the consumers and (III) when you look at it from the point of view of the State, which has to maintain the balance between the consumer and the manufacturer. In fact you might mention a third party, which is often there and which exists as much in one type of economy as another; that is, labour. We often talk about an increase in labour wages resulting in inflation in one way or the other. If we start approaching the manufacturer's profits in the same way and from the same angle, we might get extraordinary results. Perhaps we would find that the suggestion I have attempted to make in my paper would find favour with a lot of us and that is this: that while we certainly make a provision for the rising cost of assets that have to be replaced, it does not mean that the additional amount so required should be charged to the profit and loss account in such a manner that the whole of it is charged to cost of production, without drawing upon the profit margin, resulting in unnecessarily higher prices. Perhaps the additional cost could be divided between the consumer, the manufacturer and the State by means of taxes. Whatever be the approach, this is where economics come in. I have the feeling that the practice of charging depreciation on replacement costs causes inflation. When there is inflation, there is a further attempt to chase it. It is like chasing your bets. You find that it is not always a particularly happy approach. You do not achieve satisfactory results.

PROF. DR. ABRAM MEY (Netherlands)

I thank you, Sir. Only many of us will not agree with you, because to state that costs have risen will not consequently cause higher selling-prices. May I now ask Mr. Loeb to say something about replacement value, because in France, as you know, there has been a great need to look into the problems of inflation and the devaluation of money.

MR. PAUL LOEB (France)

Je crois que l'emploi de la valeur de remplacement dans les budgets se justifie pour autant que le budget est une construction pour l'avenir et non pour le passé. Par conséquent il faut se rapprocher le plus possible de valeurs futures, mais il ne faut pas négliger l'aspect de contrôle qui fait comparer des valeurs actuelles avec des valeurs antérieurement prévues. La comptabilité budgétaire permet de séparer l'influence de variations de valeurs dues à des événements extérieurs à l'entreprise, de respecter la règle du contrôle qui impose les mêmes conditions pour les faits prévus et pour les faits réels.

Well, I think that the use of the replacement value in the budget is justified insofar as this budget itself is meant for the future and not for the past. Consequently one has to get as close as possible to future values, but one should not, of course, ignore the control aspect which compares present values with values forecast earlier on. Budget accounting enables you to isolate the influence of variations in values which result from external events and at the same time to abide by the auditing rules which require that the same conditions be applied to forcasts of facts and to actual facts.

PROF. DR. ABRAM MEY (Netherlands)

I thank you, Mr. Loeb. I should like to ask Mr. Wilson to give his opinion about the point of using replacement value in accounting.

MR. J. P. WILSON (United Kingdom)

Mr. Chairman, My immediate point about the use of replacement value is this, that cost accounts are intended to convey to management information about their business, what is going on. Well now, there is no one who can say to-day that inflation is not going on and that money is not losing its value. Therefore, just on those general grounds I give my opinion that replacement values, the use of replacement values, should be reflected in your accounts somewhere. In other words, that the accounts should tell the management of the business how it is being affected by changes in money values.

Now, my colleague Mr. Chopra has made the point that he thinks that the use of replacement values might be inflationary. I would think it was the reverse, that the non-use of replacement values tends to inflate profits, to make profits seem to be greater than they really are and by so doing makes management more prepared to accept price increases, such as wage increases, in other directions.

PROF. DR. ABRAM MEY (Netherlands)

I thank you, Mr. Wilson. May I conclude from what you said that it is your opinion that the whole accounting system has to be kept in replacement values during the year, or in what way do you see the solution of this problem, because this is a very important question.

MR. J. P. WILSON (United Kingdom)

Mr. Chairman, Exactly how it is done is too big a question to discuss here.

PROF. DR. ABRAM MEY (Netherlands)

Yes, but in principle?

MR. J. P. WILSON (United Kingdom)

In principle, yes, I say that we must take replacement-values into accounts fully.

PROF. DR. ABRAM MEY (Netherlands)

Thank you. May I ask Mr. van Iper—what way is followed in your country? In Belgium do you use replacement value or do you use historical values, in other words: traditional methods?

MR. RENÉ VAN IPER (Belgium)

En Belgique, Monsieur le Président, il est d'usage de faire intervenir dans la mesure du possible le prix de remplacement, quand nous établissons le budget.

La Belgique, les dernières années, n'a heureusement plus connu de fortes dépréciations de sa monnaie.

Il est donc assez facile pour nous de tenir compte pour nos standards de prix de remplacement, leur différence d'une année à l'autre ayant pu être de 2, 3 voire même 5%.

In Belgium, Mr. Chairman, we always try to use the replacement value as far as possible, when we prepare our budget. Belgium, fortunately, has not experienced any marked decrease in money values for a while now. It is therefore a fairly easy matter for us to employ the replacement value as the standard, since the differences are merely of the order of 2, 3, or, perhaps, 5 per cent from one year to another.

PROF. DR. ABRAM MEY (Netherlands)

Thank you, so much. I will ask Mr. Tempelaar to speak. He has something to tell us regarding his opinion on the application of the replacement value.

MR. A. F. TEMPELAAR (Netherlands)

Voorzitter, Mag ik mij beperken tot een opmerking, die de heer Loeb maakte, want wanneer wij over de vervangingswaarde gaan uitweiden, komen wij in twee internationale congressen nog niet klaar. De heer Loeb heeft in zijn antwoord gezegd, dat hij voor de vergelijking, dus voor de budgetaire contrôle, de historische waarde wil aanhouden. Ik zou hier het volgende amendement op willen geven. Wanneer het gaat om vergelijking in kwantiteiten, dus wanneer men verschillen in hoeveelheden moet waarderen, zou ik beslist niet op historische waarde waarderen, want die verliezen zijn heden gemaakt.

May I merely mention Mr. Loeb's comment, for if we go into all the details of the replacement value, we shall not say all there is to say in two international congresses. Mr. Loeb said in his reply that for the purpose of comparison, i.e. for budget control, he wants to keep to the historical value. Here I would like to suggest an amendment to this and to say that if we are making a comparison of quantities, in other words if we have to value quantitative differences itself, I would certainly not do it on the basis of historical value, because the differences (losses) occur in the present.

PROF. DR. ABRAM MEY (Netherlands)

I thank you, Mr. Tempelaar. I think we have to say that your first indication was right. We can't go on to discuss everything about replacement value, because it is too big a problem. There is another question connected with it, and that is the problem of so-called 'fixed cost' and the 'allocation of fixed cost', or 'particularisation of fixed cost', which is also the problem of so-called 'uncontrollable cost'. Mr. Witt, this is something that is your hobby, I suppose?

MR. CARL HENRIK WITT (Sweden)

Yes, I like the subject. When dealing with the question of the distribution of fixed cost and cost of auxiliary departments I would like you to bear in mind that most of the budgets are made out on the basis of an assumed activity of a certain sale's or production department. Based on this assumption the various costs of the department are calculated, looking back historically or trying empirically to arrive at the correct figures. These expected costs are then related to the assumed activity resulting, for instance, in an estimated percentage of cost. If this percentage of costs is applied to the actual activity of the department, it is reasonable to expect that the budget-figure would be a fairly correct measurement of such costs as, for instance, wages, materials in production, etc.

Whereas on the other hand with fixed costs, such as depreciation, the contrary might be the case, when the activity differs. I expect that the general answer would be that the function of the budget is also that of task-setting, and that in the event of the activity falling below what is planned, the decreasing budget-cover of the fixed cost will influence the department heads to find ways of cutting down such cost. If, on the other hand, the activity is higher than expected, it is believed that it will not be possible to make use of such extra budget-cover as will be incurred in fixed cost. According to my opinion those fixed costs are generally very hard to change in such a way that any marked effect can be traced in the short time budget. There may, however, be a risk that the department head in the event of excess-cover of fixed costs, will have a tendency to look upon the budgetary result as a whole and consider everything well and good, although he has exceeded the cover of other kinds of cost. If on the other hand there is a loss in the department caused by lack of cover re-fixed cost, he may easily start to distrust budgeting and show a lack of enthusiasm. No items should, according to my opinion, be entered into a budget, unless the person responsible has a possibility of influencing them inside the budget period.

PROF. DR. ABRAM MEY (Netherlands)

I thank you, Mr. Witt. And now I would ask Mr. Loeb to speak. He wished to say something about the problem of the flexible and the variable budget in the same context as the problem of the fixed costs and the particularisation of the fixed costs.

MR. PAUL LOEB (France)

Je crois qu'on pourrait prendre comme définition de flexible-variable la définition suivante, qui répond à l'organisation du coût des produits. J'appellerais budget flexible, le budget qui s'étend sur une période, dans laquelle les frais fixes ne sont pas changés, c.à.d. pour de faibles variations, pour de faibles variations de capacité, de production ou même de valeur les frais fixes ne changent pas, il n'y a que les frais variables qui changent, n'est-ce pas; c'est le budget flexible. Au contraire j'appelle budget variable le budget dans lequel les frais variables ont changé naturellement, mais en plus les frais fixes également ont changé plus ou moins, pas tous, dans la même proportion, parce que les frais fixes sont plus ou moins fixes. Rien n'est proportionnel, rien n'est fixe, mais les frais fixes varient tout de même quand la structure de l'affaire varie ou quand il se produit des variations importantes dans le degré de l'activité. Dans ces conditions on refait un nouveau budget, qu'on peut appeler budget variable et qui est caractérisé par le fait que les frais fixes ont changé. L'ensemble des frais fixes a changé; certains sont restés peut-être fixes, mais certains autres ont varié.

I think that we can take as definitions of 'flexible' and 'variable' budgets the following definitions which are in accordance with the structure of the costs of products. I would refer to the flexible budget as being the budget which covers a period during which fixed costs have not changed, that is, in other words, with very small variations.

Small variations in capacity, production or even in value, will not cause the fixed costs to change, only variable costs will change. That is the flexible budget. I would say that the variable budget on the other hand is a budget in which variable costs have changed, of course, but in which fixed costs have also changed more or less, not all necessarily in the same proportion, because fixed costs are more or less fixed. Nothing is proportional, nothing is fixed, but fixed costs do, nevertheless, vary with changes in the structure of the concern, or when there are considerable variations in the amount of business. Under such conditions you prepare a new budget, which you may call a variable budget, which is characterized by the fact that the fixed costs have changed. In fact it is the totality of fixed costs which has changed, but some of these costs may remain unchanged and others will have changed.

PROF. DR. ABRAM MEY (Netherlands)

Merci, M. Loeb. And now I would call on Mr. Tempelaar and ask him if it is possible for him to give in one or one and a half minutes the Dutch opinion on this problem. Mr. Tempelaar?

MR. A. F. TEMPELAAR (Netherlands)

It has taken the experts 20 years.

PROF. DR. ABRAM MEY (Netherlands)

Therefore you can do it now in a minute and a half.

MR. A. F. TEMPELAAR (Netherlands)

I hope so. Ik geloof, dat er ten aanzien van hetgeen de heer Witt naar voren heeft gebracht, een zeker misverstand moet bestaan. Wanneer de heer Witt zegt, dat we uitsluitend met de 'controllable cost' te doen hebben in bedrijfsoverzichten, heeft hij duidelijk het oog op de kostensoorten, die door de betrokken afdelingschef kunnen worden beheerst. Dit heb ik in mijn referaat eveneens opgemerkt. Van betekenis is echter tevens, dat hier weer die hoeveelheidskwestie een rol speelt. Wanneer het gaat om hetgeen 'controllable' is, dan moet men niet alleen naar kosten – kostensoorten – kijken, doch ook de hoeveelheden in aanmerking nemen. Denkt u bijv. maar eens aan de mogelijkheid, die elke afdelingsleider heeft om de tijd te vermorsen. Deze vermorsing – of neemt u desnoods maar stilstand door andere oorzaken – moet gewaardeerd worden. Hier komen we eigenlijk op een punt, waarvan ik zoëven zei, dat de geleerden er twintig jaar over gedaan hebben en het er nog niet allemaal over eens zijn. Het Nederlandse standpunt meen ik in het algemeen wel zo te mogen stellen: er is een causaal verband tussen de hoeveelheid prestaties, welke men op grond van de projectie aantrekt (door het investeren in gebouwen, machines e.d.) en de kosten, welke deze aanschaffingen met zich mede brengen. Dit causale verband is ontstaan op het moment van de aanschaffing. Men kan dus als het ware (en ik doe het nu maar heel kort, mijnheer de voorzitter) zeggen dat er kosten zijn, welke per *eenheid beschikbare prestatie of capaciteit*, kunnen worden uitgedrukt. Wanneer zo'n eenheid prestatie om een of andere reden verloren gaat, is het noodzakelijk dit verlies tot uitdrukking te brengen. Dit verlies betreft dan o.m. de kosten – op basis van vervangingswaarde – welke aan de desbetreffende eenheid op grond van eerder genoemd causaal verband moeten worden toegekend. Het is dus naar onze mening absoluut noodzakelijk de vaste kosten, die in het algemeen ontstaan doordat men met 'durable means of production' te doen heeft, in het budget van de afdeling op te nemen en aldus het verlies aan hoeveelheden – bijv. ingeval van 'idle capacity' – te waarderen, of eventueel een winst bij extra gebruik van capaciteit uit te drukken.

Voorzitter, het vraagstuk van de calculatie van vaste kosten in de kostprijs ten behoeve van de aanbiedingsprijs en de hiermede verband houdende 'marginal costing' wilde ik thans onbesproken laten.

I hope so. On the question raised by Mr. Witt there seems to be some misunderstanding. When he says that we are only concerned with the 'controllable cost', he refers doubtlessly to costs over which the department manager concerned can exercise influence. I mentioned this myself in my paper. But one should not forget that quantity also plays a role here. When it is a matter of what is 'controllable', we should take into account not only costs and types of cost but also quantities. Think, for instance, of the opportunity every departmental manager has to waste time. And this waste of time, or 'standing idle' due to other causes, must be evaluated and taken into account. Here we have actually come upon a point which, as I remarked a moment ago, has occupied the experts' attention for twenty years, and on which they are still not in agreement. But I think I may say that in general the view we take in Holland is that there is a causal relation between the quantity of output resulting from projects planned (by investment in buildings, machinery, etc.) and the costs these involve.

This causal relation comes into existence at the time the machinery etc. is purchased. One can say, as it were, (and I am putting it very concisely here, Mr. Chairman) that there are costs which can be expressed *per unit of available output or capacity*. When such a unit is lost for some reason or other, the loss should be recorded. This loss refers, among other things, to the costs—on the replacement value basis—which must be allocated to the unit concerned on the grounds of the causal relation mentioned. It is, therefore, absolutely essential, in our opinion, to include the fixed costs which, in general, arise because one is concerned here with durable means of production, in the department's budget in order to value the loss in quantity, due, for example, to idle capacity—or to record any profit arising from extra capacity.

I cannot enter here into the question of the calculation of fixed costs into the cost-price to arrive at the price at which the goods are finally offered and the associated matter of marginal costing.

PROF. DR. ABRAM MEY (Netherlands)

I thank you, Mr. Tempelaar. I am glad that you did not enter into the field of marginal costing, but I am glad too that in your opinion it is very clear that idle capacity, not required for production, cannot be considered as a cost-factor. I suppose now, Gentlemen, that there is another chapter to discuss, viz. that about the relation of budgetary control and the size of the business. I will leave it for what it is for the moment, and ask my panel to jump straightaway into the problem of its importance for the auditor's verification and for the auditor's work. What is the importance to it of budgetary control? Mr. Leitch, I think that you have a definite opinion about that. Will you be so kind?

MR. J. R. LEITCH (United Kingdom)

Mr. Chairman, Ladies and Gentlemen, I hold the opinion that it is open to question whether a good system of budgetary control and standard costing necessarily eases the burden of the auditor. I should have thought that the auditor would have been much more concerned about the general internal audit carried on by his client's staff, and whether there was a system of budgetary control and standard costing, or not, was not necessarily a matter which concerned him.

PROF. DR. ABRAM MEY (Netherlands)

Thank you, Mr. Leitch. I am glad to say that I believe our colleague Rätsch is of quite a different opinion; so I might ask Mr. Rätsch for his views on the matter.

MR. H. RÄTSCH (Germany)

Ich habe durchaus Verständnis für die Auffassung von Mr. Leitch, nur glaube ich, daß wir gleich noch folgendes sagen können. Wir Wirtschaftsprüfer selbst arbeiten ja mit Standards und das Arbeiten mit externen Standards erleichtert unsere Prüfung. Wir haben Betriebsvergleiche usw. mehr. Auch die Steuerbehörde ist ja in großem Umfang in der Lage Betriebsvergleiche anzustellen; sie hat das Material zur Verfügung. Standards, bzw. die von der Gesellschaft zu treffenden Untersuchungen der Abweichungen der Istzahlen von den Standards, und das ist doch wohl wichtig, können meines Erachtens bei unseren Prüfungshandlungen nicht ganz außer acht gelassen werden. Wir haben durch die Kontrolle dieser Abweichungen, durch ihre Untersuchung, eine Möglichkeit festzustellen, wie das innerbetriebliche Kontrollgefüge des Unternehmens arbeitet. Und den Umfang unserer Prüfungsarbeiten stellen wir ja wohl weitgehend darauf ab, ob dieses innerbetriebliche Kontrollgefüge funktionniert oder ob es nicht funktionniert, und da haben wir an Hand der Abweichungen doch ein wirklich gutes Material. Ich möchte daher sagen, daß die Standards uns einen Gradmesser geben für die Intensität unserer eigenen Tätigkeit; insoweit ist meines Erachtens also unsere Arbeit unmittelbar durch die von der Gesellschaft vorbereiteten Planungsunterlagen berührt.

While I fully appreciate Mr. Leitch's point of view, I think that the following should not be lost sight of. We auditors definitely do make use of standards; and the employment of external standards certainly eases our task. We all have our own comparative data acquired from the audits we do. Our taxation officials are, of course, in a position to build up comparative data on a far more elaborate scale; they have access to the necessary information. In my view it would be quite wrong, when undertaking the audit of a company, completely to ignore standards or any explanations put forward by the company to explain why actual figures deviated from a standard; and I think that this is a matter of major importance. Checking up on these variances, really going into them, makes it possible for the auditor to discover how the company's system of internal check is working. We would all admit that the extent of the audit we decide to make depends largely on whether the system of internal check is functioning properly or not. It is the variances which provide us with reliable material on which to base our judgement. I think, therefore, that I can definitely say that standards provide us with a means of establishing the intensity of the work we feel necessary to devote to the audit, and to that extent, I feel, our work is directly effected by the data used by the company to compile its standard costs.

PROF. DR. ABRAM MEY (Netherlands)

I thank you, Mr. Rätsch. I should like to ask my colleagues Mr. Pelej and Mr. Wilson if it is possible for them in the two minutes we still have to state their opinions. Mr. Pelej for one minute and Mr. Wilson for one minute, please.

MR. JOSEPH PELEJ (United States of America)

Mr. Chairman, I want to say that I concur with everything that Mr. Rätsch has said. As auditor, I would feel much more comfortable about my work, if the company had a system of budgetary control, if for no other reason than that it would give me an opportunity to learn more about the operations which the figures reflect.

PROF. DR. ABRAM MEY (Netherlands)
Mr. Wilson?

MR. J. P. WILSON (United Kingdom)
Mr. Chairman, I too am quite sure that the auditor does a better audit-job if he has behind him the information that is conveyed by a system of budgetary control and standard costs. As an industrial accountant having to cope with auditors I would probably say that perhaps I do not like that quite as much; and that is probably what my colleague Mr. Leitch is thinking, that the auditors might be a little more difficult with him, because they have the weapons in their hands to be difficult. But let me say that when I put on my shareholder's hat, I am very glad that auditors are increasingly having the benefit of budgetary control and standard-cost-systems to help them to do a good audit.

PROF. DR. ABRAM MEY (Netherlands)
So, Mr. Wilson, you are glad, too. Just a minute ago I said I am glad, Mr. Leitch, that Mr. Rätsch is of a different opinion. It was not, Mr. Leitch, because I knew before that the match would be one to three, but for another reason. Suppose we agreed about everything here in the discussion, Ladies and Gentlemen, there would be no reason to go on holding congresses like this and that would be a very great pity for all of us. Now we have to switch over to the free discussion, and there are some Gentlemen who have asked to say a few words in that free discussion. The first is Mr. Lawrence Robson of the United Kingdom, then Mr. Van Sloten, then Mr. Wayne Keller, Mr. Van Hout and Prof. Anthony. Oh, and Mr. Diephuis. Sorry, Mr. Diephuis, that I forgot your name. May I ask these gentlemen to come to the platform and take their seats here, in order that we do not lose any time by coming up and down from the platform one by one.

Gentlemen, we have twenty minutes time, so I may ask these Gentlemen to make it short. Mr. Robson, may I ask you first to put your question to the panel?

MR. LAWRENCE ROBSON (United Kingdom)
Mr. Chairman, Ladies and Gentlemen, I must pay tribute to the panel for the excellent way they have handled this subject this afternoon, and in doing so I am sure I am speaking for all the delegates. I wish to make two points. Firstly, during the past twenty years we have witnessed considerable changes in accountancy techniques. Both in industry and in the professions the accountant is now expected to think in terms of financial planning involving budgetary control and standard costs, as opposed to the production of historical accounting information confirming what has happened after the event. The accountant of to-day is expected to exercise day-to-day financial control of an undertaking in relation to agreed attainable budgets of performance. The profession is indebted to our American colleagues who in the last twenty or thirty years have produced a great deal of literature in regard to these techniques, which are now having

the attention of the profession in most countries represented at this Conference.

One of the major problems posed by the papers this afternoon constitutes a challenge to the profession to study ways and means of improving the training and education of the accountant in order to enable him to grapple with the highly specialised problems with which he must deal if either in industry or in the profession he is to undertake the responsibilities of providing management with day-to-day financial control in relation to carefully developed budgets of all operating costs both functionally and by product. In view of the ever widening fields of responsibility within commerce and industry in which the accountant has to play his part, the whole problem of training the accountants of the future might well be a suitable subject for the next International Conference.

I don't think there is any easy answer to the problem; during a recent visit to the United States I talked to American friends in the profession and learned that some firms recruit young men from the university with engineering degrees and train them in the techniques of budgetary control and standard costs. They claim that they find men with this combined training well able to undertake important installation work for clients in the field of management accounting. It is my own view that accountants trained in professional offices, while becoming expert in audit and taxation work, and acquiring the ability to undertake the legal responsibilities of accountants in the field of trusteeships, receiverships and liquidations, are not thereby fully equipped to deal with installation work in the sphere of management accounting, which has become a highly specialised field of accountancy endeavour calling for considerable experience in industry and in the techniques of installing schemes of financial control based on budgetary control and standard costing.

I recall my own days as an articled clerk when I had my first view of modern factory organisation. For many years a large-scale factory appeared to me to be an impenetrable forest of machinery. The accountant in industry to-day, if he is to help management compile budgeted expenditure and the appropriate standards of performance in both time and money for highly specialised industrial processes, must familiarise himself with those processes and the equipment used, otherwise he is unable to discuss these problems with the technicians whose responsibility it is to operate such processes at reasonable standards of efficiency. It is imperative therefore that the accountant of to-day should have a thorough understanding of the whole structure of industrial management. The professional accountant is being increasingly called upon to advise upon and even install modern management accountancy techniques, and my second point therefore is that some training within industry is essential in order to enable him to carry out this work satisfactorily. This means taking a much longer view of the training of the professional accountant, which appears to indicate the necessity for creating opportunities for specialised training after the general accountancy qualification has been obtained.

PROF. DR. ABRAM MEY (Netherlands)

Thank you very much, Mr. Robson. These were important points you were referring to. May I ask Mr. Wilson as a fellow-countryman of Mr. Robson's for an answer? I think this gentleman will agree very quickly.

MR. J. P. WILSON (United Kingdom)

On this point of the supply of trained accountants, I think that I am very much in agreement with what Mr. Robson has said. If I could point out what I would consider to be the principal things to be required of men that were coming to do this work, this skilled work, I would say that the first thing that they should possess is character and the second quality is that of a trained mind. Personally I don't think it matters which way a man has come up, whether he started off as an engineering apprentice, as an articled clerk to an accountant or whether he started in the wages office of an industrial concern—or even whether he was a University man that read for the Bar. I don't think the initial training matters. I think the important points are the qualities of the man himself. And then I think—if only we can convey these new ideas and they are fairly new—well not new but only now being widely accepted, if we can convey and teach the new ideas of what the accountant can do in this sphere and the tremendous value of it, well then I think that the problem will sort itself out.

PROF. DR. ABRAM MEY (Netherlands)

I thank you for your opinion—but you bring us back to the starting point of the mental conditions for introducing budgetary control. Now I may call upon Mr. Diephuis who is in a position to ask us something about psychological facts and what they have to do with mental conditions. Mr. Diephuis, please be so kind.

MR. G. DIEPHUIS (Netherlands)

Mijnheer de voorzitter, Ik heb ten aanzien van de budgettering vele goede dingen en een enkel minder goed ding gelezen in de referaten en in deze discussie gehoord. Toch is het mij misschien vergund, nu ook ten aanzien van al die goede dingen van het 'principle of exception' gebruik te maken, door u te wijzen op een gevaar van psychologische aard bij het toepassen van het systeem. Ik wil dit nog naar voren brengen en daaromtrent aan het panel nog gaarne een vraag stellen. In het systeem worden bij de toepassing ervan de afwijkingen in het schijnwerperlicht van de leidinggevende organen geplaatst. Daardoor kunnen deze afwijkingen gemakkelijk een indruk wekken, die groter is dan de werkelijke betekenis ervan. Dit gevaar bestaat vooral, wanneer het 'principle of exception' wordt toegepast, waarbij namelijk de afwijking buiten het integrale beeld van de uitvoering wordt geplaatst. Hierdoor kan zij niet in haar juiste proporties worden beoordeeld, en zal alleen maar op de afwijking als zodanig kunnen worden gelet. Naar mijn mening worden daardoor de resultaten dan niet in het juiste licht geïnterpreteerd, waardoor de behandeling van de afwijking niet juist kan geschieden. Dit veroorzaakt gemakkelijk psychologische spanningen, waardoor de goede verstandhouding en de noodzakelijke samenwerking tussen leider en sub-leider resp. uitvoerder in gevaar komen. Mijn vraag is nu, of het panel met mij van mening is, dat hier een werkelijk gevaar voor de werking van het systeem bestaat resp. dreigt en zo ja, of het dan misschien de middelen kan aangeven om dit gevaar zoveel mogelijk uit te bannen respectievelijk te bezweren.

Mr. Chairman, concerning budgeting I have heard and read in the reports a number of arguments in favour and also several arguments not in favour. Regarding these points I should like to avail myself of the 'principle of exception' and draw your attention to a danger of a psychological nature in the application of this system. In stating this point I would like at the same time to put a question to the panel.

Where this system is applied, the management directs its spotlight mainly on deviations. These deviations may consequently easily seem greater than they actually are. This danger exists especially when the 'principle of exception' is applied by which deviations are shown apart from the complete picture of executive management. Consequently they cannot be judged in their real proportions, and attention will be focussed on the deviations as such. Because of this the results will not, in my opinion, be correctly interpreted so that the deviations cannot be dealt with properly. This tends to cause a psychological tension which is detrimental to a good understanding between the top and lower levels of management. My question to the panel would be: Do you agree that a real danger to the functioning of the budgeting system lies herein, and if so, could you suggest some means of reducing or eliminating this danger?

PROF. DR. ABRAM MEY (Netherlands)

I must ask Mr. Rätsch to answer Mr. Diephuis on that problem of these psychological conditions.

MR. H. RÄTSCH (Germany)

Ich glaube, daß es natürlich außerordentlich wichtig ist, daß man in einem guten Betriebsklima, das nun einmal da sein muß, auch die Frage der nicht so großen Wichtigkeit dieser Abweichungen sehen muß. Natürlich, wenn Abweichungen da sind, dann entsteht sofort einmal die Schuldfrage, und es will sich selbstverständlich niemand schuldig fühlen. Andererseits kann man, wenn etwas erreichbar ist, dieses Erreichbare auch tatsächlich den Leuten mitteilen, denn das Erreichbare sollte ihr Ziel sein und ohne eine Zielsetzung – auch in den einzelnen Betriebsabteilungen – glaube ich, kommt man nicht weiter. Ich glaube also, daß das psychologische Moment auf diesem Gebiet nicht überschätzt werden sollte.

I believe that it is, of course, extremely important that in the good atmosphere which you must after all have in a business, one should also study the question of the not so great importance of these variances. Naturally, if there are variances, the question of who is responsible for them at once arises, and no one particularly wants to take the responsibility. But on the other hand, if something can be attained, then the attainable aim should be made known to the workers, for that should be their target, and without that target—even in the separate departments of a business—you would not get very far. I am therefore of the opinion that the psychological factor in this field should not be overestimated.

PROF. DR. ABRAM MEY (Netherlands)

Danke Ihnen. I am afraid—with regard to Mr. Rätsch's answer— of coming into conflict now with my friend, Mr. Leitch, again; but we cannot prolong that discussion. So I call now on Mr. Van Sloten. I give you the floor, Mr. Van Sloten, to state your problem.

MR. P. J. VAN SLOTEN (Netherlands)

Mijnheer de voorzitter, Ik zou graag even willen aanknopen bij uw mededeling in het begin van de zitting, dat mr. Pelej zo juist een conferentie in Londen heeft bijgewoond, waar de betekenis van 'operational research' voor het bedrijfsleven aan de orde is geweest. Het geeft mij eigenlijk aanleiding tot een tweetal vragen: ik zou in de eerste plaats graag willen weten of we de 'operational research' zelfs in die zin een betekenis kunnen toekennen, dat het beschikken over de resultaten daarvan op de duur als een belangrijke voorwaarde voor een doelmatige budgettering en een goede budget-administratie gezien zal moeten worden. In de tweede plaats zou ik willen vragen of het panel van mening is, dat de mathematisch-statistische methoden van de "operational research" ook een principiële wijziging zullen brengen in de wijze van het bepalen van het bedrijfsbeleid, zodat wij op de duur zelfs de mogelijkheid onder ogen zouden moeten zien dat er geen plaats meer zou overblijven voor vrije, soms min of meer intuïtieve beslissingen van de ondernemers. Of is het panel van mening, dat de genoemde methoden van 'operational research' toch niet meer zijn dan een technisch hulpmiddel, dat bij het bepalen van slechts enkele onderdelen van het bedrijfsbeleid goede diensten kan bewijzen.

Mr. Chairman, I would like to refer back to your statement that Mr. Pelej quite recently attended a conference in London where the techniques of operational research were being discussed. And this leads me to put two questions. Firstly, I would like to know whether such importance can be ascribed to operational research that having its results at one's disposal is a pre-requisite for good budgeting and good accounting.

Secondly, I would like to ask whether the panel is of the opinion that the mathematical and statistical methods of operational research will bring about fundamental modifications in the manner in which management takes decisions, so that possibly in future there may be no more room for free decisions made by management, which are sometimes taken more or less intuitively. Or is the panel of the opinion that the methods of operational research are no more than a technical expedient, which can render good service only as regards a limited number of the decisions of management?

PROF. DR. ABRAM MEY (Netherlands)

I thank you, Mr. Van Sloten. Ladies and Gentlemen, I am inclined to observe that Mr. Van Sloten seems to be anxious that the top-manager will be replaced by a kind of 'automatic pilot', but I will ask Mr. Pelej to answer about that, because he is particularly up to date on operational research.

MR. JOSEPH PELEJ (United States of America)

As far as I can make out, Mr. Chairman, and Ladies and Gentlemen, operational research is no more going to replace management than accounting will. Operational research is another managerial aid. It is a scientific approach to business problems which most of us know has been developed during the war and is now being applied to business transactions. As far as budgeting is concerned, I believe that operational research can make very important contributions in producing optimum solutions to questions of sales forecasting, preparation of production-schedules, production-controls, optimum inventory levels and so on. As Sir Charles Goodeve put it, 'Experience is getting used to the problem, but research is trying to find a good solution to it'.

PROF. DR. ABRAM MEY (Netherlands)

Thank you, Sir. Mr. Wilson, please.

MR. J. P. WILSON (United Kingdom)

The point that I want to make I can make quite briefly, and that is this, if you consider the use that is made of the information provided by the accountant, it is really used for two things—as the basis for management taking decisions, and secondly as the basis for management exercising control, to see that those decisions are carried out. Now as I see it, the cost information which is supplied to Management for making decisions will be part only of the raw material of the people engaged on operational research. But on the other hand I can quite see that operational research will work in the reverse direction and will provide better information on which to base budgets and all other plans.

PROF. DR. ABRAM MEY (Netherlands)

I thank you, Mr. Wilson. Ladies and Gentlemen, is it not curious that we —accountants—have been discussing the whole afternoon about budgeting and other kinds of things and no one has yet said a word about the standardization of office work, because all of us have to do with office work in practice. May I call upon Mr. Van Hout to put his question about standardization in regard to office work.

MR. J. J. N. VAN HOUT (Netherlands)

Mijnheer de voorzitter, Als ik naar aanleiding van wat u daar zegt dus ook een enkele vraag zou willen stellen, dan betreft dit inderdaad de wijze, waarop voor bepaalde kostengroepen of kostensoorten standaarden of normen kunnen worden vastgesteld. Zowel de heer Rätsch als de heer Pelej zijn bij hun inleidingen vrij uitvoerig stil blijven staan bij de betekenis van de standaarden en van de noodzaak van vergelijking van de uitkomsten van de werkelijkheid met de gestelde standaarden. Ook is daarbij gewezen op de onderscheiding, die moet worden gemaakt tussen empirisch vastgestelde standaarden en analytisch vastgestelde standaarden, terwijl de heer Rätsch ook nog spreekt over standaarden ontleend aan andere bedrijven.

Beiden drukken zich in hun inleidingen zeer positief en met klem van argumenten uit voor de analytisch vastgestelde standaard. Het is mij duidelijk, dat op verschillende terreinen de analytische standaard inderdaad de voorkeur verdient, om niet te zeggen de enig juiste is, terwijl de vaststelling daarvan niet op te grote bezwaren hoeft te stuiten. Op andere terreinen, en ik denk daarbij in het bijzonder dus aan de kantoor- en administratieve werkzaamheden, ook aan diverse soorten van indirecte arbeid, lijkt het mij veel moeilijker om langs analytische weg tot vaststelling van standaarden te komen. Ik zou het zeer op prijs stellen, indien uw panel ook nog iets zou willen zeggen over dit probleem, m.a.w.: zijn de geachte inleiders van mening, dat ook voor kantoorwerkzaamheden en indirecte arbeid analytische standaarden kunnen worden vastgesteld, en zo ja, is het mogelijk om dit in het kort aan te geven? Dank u.

Mr. Chairman, If I may put one question with regard to what you just said, it is one concerning the possibility of establishing standards or norms for certain costs or groups of costs.

Mr. Rätsch and Mr. Pelej in their papers went at some length into the importance of standards, and into the need for comparing the actual results with the standards set. Mention was also made of the distinction that must be made between standards arrived at empirically and those arrived at by analysis, and Mr. Rätsch also mentioned standards derived from other industrial undertakings. In their papers both were strongly in favour of standards determined by analysis, supporting this with many arguments. It is clear to me that in many fields the analytical standard must be preferred, if not the only proper method, while it should not be too difficult to determine. But in certain other fields, and here I am thinking in particular about office and bookkeeping work and various types of indirect labour, it appears to me to be far more difficult to establish standards by means of an analytical procedure. I would be very grateful if the panel would say something about this problem. In other words, are the panel members of the opinion that for office workers and for other indirect labour it is possible to establish analytical standards, and if so, could they give some details?

PROF. DR. ABRAM MEY (Netherlands)

I think, Mr. Pelej, that you pointed in your paper to the problem which Mr. Van Hout has brought forward, so may I ask you for your answer?

MR. JOSEPH PELEJ (United States of America)

The establishment of standards for office workers in the U.S. is receiving considerable attention. The setting of standards of this type of work is facilitated in the larger organizations where office work can be divided into specific highly routinized tasks. The difficulty increases when the same workers perform many different jobs, although some office tasks can be relatively easily measured and expressed in terms of units such as postings to accounts, handling of identical pieces of paper, such as invoices and so on.

PROF. DR. ABRAM MEY (Netherlands)

Thank you, Mr. Pelej.

Now I would call upon Mr. Wayne Keller, and I will ask you to make your comments very short, because we are coming to the end of the session. I think Mr. Keller has two features to mention about the possibilities and practices he is used to in America, which are very important.

MR. I. WAYNE KELLER (United States of America)

Mr. Chairman, Ladies and Gentlemen, The very excellent papers prepared for this session have emphasized the contribution which effective budgeting makes to the management of a business. However, for the most part they have seemed to deal with the comparisons of actual results with standard and budgeted allowances which are made at the close of each month. In the United States many companies have found that by the time these analyses become available production conditions have changed and the reports have lost some of their value for cost control purposes. They are records of the extent to which operations were controlled in relation to the budget, but they are not control tools of maximum effectiveness.

Comparisons of actual costs with standards and budgets are needed by factory managers during a month if they are to achieve maximum effectiveness in controlling the costs for which they are responsible. This is accomplished by making daily comparisons of actual amounts with standard allowances for significant items of cost such as raw materials, labour and supplies. Allowances expressed in units of material and hours of labour per unit of production are given to production clerks in the factory.

These clerks summarize the actual costs in units, not in monetary values, apply the unit allowances to the actual units of production and determine the deviations from the budgeted allowances. These comparisons are made for each working shift, normally three shifts in each day, and for each day. This provides an immediate measurement in terms of units rather than in monetary values which can be used to initiate corrective action while production is in progress. Production foremen have found such comparisons to be of great assistance in aiding them to meet their budgeted costs.

Some companies have gone further and apply the unit allowances by detailed cost items to the quantity of production scheduled. When these production schedules and the related unit allowances for each class of labour, and each kind of material are given to the foreman, he can plan his work to better advantage. The daily variance reports, expressed in units, then tell him if he achieved his plans for that day. He does not have to wait for the monthly variance reports showing monetary values to take corrective control action.

PROF. DR. ABRAM MEY (Netherlands)

Thank you, Mr. Keller. And I may inform you and the audience that it has been a custom in Holland for some time to use a technical quantitative daily control of efficiency in the way you tell us is your daily practice in your company. But that daily quantitative control is also taken up in the records in a comparison of required costs and actual costs. So what we get is a mutual check on the daily technical control and the control by the records, so that we can really bring technical-internal-check and administrative-internal-check into harmony with each other. It is very important and very stimulating for us to hear that in America the same practices are applied too. I now call upon Mr. Anthony.

PROF. R. N. ANTHONY (United States of America)

Mr. Chairman, At the conclusion of this interesting and stimulating discussion of where we are now in the field of management accounting, I hope that one or two panel members might be willing to comment on where we are likely to go in the near future; that is, what are likely to be the most significant developments in the field of accounting, say before the time of our next meeting?

PROF. DR. ABRAM MEY (Netherlands)

Thank you, Prof. Anthony, for that question: what will be the future. Well, the future is our next congress, I suppose. But, Mr. Tempelaar, you can say a few words about the panel's opinion with regard to Mr. Anthony's question.

MR. A. F. TEMPELAAR (Netherlands)

Mijnheer de voorzitter, Ik zal proberen de sluier van de toekomst iets op te lichten.

Wat is de toekomstige ontwikkeling? Mijn persoonlijke visie is dat de administratie steeds meer het middel zal worden voor de ondersteuning van de leiding. Dit beginsel, dat de laatste dertig jaar het streven is geweest, zal verder worden voortgezet en zal natuurlijk met de ontwikkeling van de techniek verder worden geperfectioneerd. Ik verwacht niet, dat er plotseling iets heel nieuws uit de lucht zal vallen, doch meen, dat alles wat er in de toekomst wat betreft de administratieve ontwikkeling zal komen, een verbetering zal zijn van hetgeen we nu al regelmatig nastreven. Ik wil hierbij het accent in het bijzonder leggen op de ondersteuning van de functies van management door de administratieve organen. In dit verband wil ik vooral de nadruk leggen op die ondernemingen, welke niet van zo grote omvang zijn. De tijd voor de discussie heeft ons helaas geen gelegenheid gegeven om ook deze ondernemingen aan een beschouwing te onderwerpen (afgezien dan van wat daarover in de referaten is geschreven). Gaarne maak ik thans toch even van de gelegenheid gebruik om op te merken dat, als wij de ontwikkeling van de administratie eens op een kortere termijn dan misschien door prof. Anthony is bedoeld, willen zien, de taak van de accountant in de eerste plaats is ernaar te streven, dat de administratie steeds meer de leiding ondersteunt, o.a. door haar steeds meer op rationele wijze van gegevens te voorzien. Er ligt voor ons een grote taak om dit in het bijzonder te doen voor de kleinere bedrijven; ik bedoel daarmede niet de ambachtsplaatsen, maar de middengrote en kleinere bedrijven, zoals er talloze in ons land, maar ook in Amerika zijn. Voor deze kleinere eenheden is voor ons als accountants de taak weggelegd, om de administratie te ontwikkelen, opdat ook daar de leiding de juiste gegevens verkrijgt.

De techniek zal wel verder gaan met toepassingen van de elektronika, maar ik ga hierop wegens onvoldoende kennis hieromtrent niet verder in.

Mr. Chairman, I will try to throw some light on the future. How will things develop in the future? I think that the accounting department will tend increasingly to become a means of support to management. This principle, which has been the goal in the last thirty years, will continue and be further perfected as new techniques develop. I do not anticipate that anything completely new will suddenly drop from the sky, but I feel that all future developments—as far as the bookkeeping and accounting are concerned—will be an improvement of what we are already regularly attempting to do. But I want to lay the emphasis on the support of the functions of management by the accounting department, and especially in the not so large firm.

We have not really had time in our discussion to refer to medium-sized and smaller businesses, except for what has been said in the papers. I should like to take this opportunity to say that if we desire to see the accounting develop rather more rapidly than envisaged by Professor Anthony, the accountant's task is in the first place to attempt to see that the accounting department is a constant support to the management, among other things, by supplying figures on an ever more rational basis. A great task lies for us in doing this particularly for the smaller firms. I do not mean one-man businesses, but the medium-sized and smaller undertakings such as exist in considerable numbers in our country and even in America. It is our job as accountants to develop the accounting procedure in the smaller firms in such a manner that there, too, the management obtains the proper information. Technique will go ahead, with the application of electronics, but I know insufficient about this to go into the matter further.

PROF. DR. ABRAM MEY (Netherlands)

Dames en Heren, Ik moet mij nu – naar de algemene gedragsregel – omstellen op mijn moedertaal om de samenvatting te geven. Eigenlijk is het niet nodig om nog een samenvatting te geven, want we hebben alles, ook de toekomst al besproken. Maar toch, wat hebben we gezien vanmiddag? Wij hebben gezien, dat door de budgettaire contrôle het administratie-apparaat, dat in zijn wezen retrospectief georiënteerd is, door de besproken verandering, zijnde de invoering van de budgettaire contrôle, is geworden een prospectief instrument voor het bedrijfsbestuur. Niet alleen voor het bestuur van een industrieel bedrijf. Hetzelfde kan ook gezegd worden voor de openbare bestuurslichamen; maar daar wil ik hier niet op ingaan, want dat valt iets buiten het onderwerp, hoewel het toch genoemd is. Wij hebben een behandeling gekregen van de systematische verwerking van de verwachting. Men kan een bedrijf niet besturen zonder verwachting, maar men kan ook geen verwachting hebben zonder dat men die verwachting vastlegt, opdat men de gronden van zijn verwachting ook weer kan contrôleren en kan nagaan. Wij krijgen dus eigenlijk een tweeling-instrument: budgettering en administratie, zodat dus mogelijk wordt om op zeer korte termijn – dagelijks hebben wij gehoord, maandelijks hebben we gehoord, wekelijks ligt ertussenin – te vergelijken verwachting, normstelling met werkelijkheid; na te gaan, wat zijn de verschillen en wat veroorzaakt de verschillen; liggen hier beleidsfouten, liggen hier fouten in de uitvoering, zijn de gedelegeerde initiatieven wel uitgevoerd zoals het verwacht werd, zoals het behoorde? En kunnen wij hier dan niet meteen invoeren, dat wat men tegenwoordig bedrijfssignalering noemt, maar wat toch eigenlijk niets anders is dan de individualisering van de budget-contrôle op de lagere niveaux van de stratificatie van de leiding; invoeren dat elke persoon aan wie een zekere taak is toegewezen een gegeven krijgt omtrent de uitvoering van zijn taak. Aldus is hij betrokken bij de vaststelling van de taak en het bepalen van het betrekkelijke normatieve gegeven, zodat deze persoon dus in staat is om zelf na te gaan, wat zijn de afwijkingen uit derzelver oorzaken. Hij kan zich zelf realiseren welke fouten er zijn gemaakt en dus bij zijn chefs, voordat de opmerking komt 'wat is er gebeurd' reeds komen met de zelf ontdekte fouten en met de voorstellen om die fouten te herstellen en voortaan te verhinderen. Aldus wordt alles wat we tot dusverre gedaan hebben en weer als nieuwe gedachten voor de bedrijfssignalering naar voren zien gebracht ingevoegd in dat tweeling-systeem van budgettering en administratie, waarvan de delen elkaar voortdurend contrôleren en die mogelijk maken wat Limperg indertijd introduceerde in zijn organisatiedictaat als 'het correctieve bewindvoeren'. Correctief bewindvoeren is een noodzakelijkheid omdat de mens nu eenmaal fouten maakt, omdat er een onmogelijkheid is om nauwkeurig vooruitzichten te bepalen. Men kan wel vooruitzichten bepalen, men kan rekenen en men kan daarbij methoden toepassen van 'operational research', men kan allerlei analyses maken, men kan verwachtingen hebben, maar het is altijd nodig om deze te verifiëren en na te gaan en te zien waar eventuele fouten liggen. Er zijn nl. ook beleidsfouten en misschien zijn de fouten van de bewindvoering die gecorrigeerd moeten worden veel belangrijker dan de fouten van de efficiency in de uitvoering in de fabriek. Maar willen we dat, dan moeten wij ook een systeem van budgettering invoeren, dat voldoet aan de technieken die hier vandaag besproken zijn.

Dan moeten we marktanalyse gebruiken, dan moeten we standaarden maken voor de uitvoering, dan moeten we in huidige waarde en niet in historische uitgaven calculeren, dan moeten we niet spreken van niet-contrôleerbare kosten, maar we moeten ons realiseren dat alle kosten contrôleerbaar zijn. Dit zijn ook de kosten van het gebruik der duurzame produktiemiddelen, omdat het aantal werkuren dat de machine gedraaid heeft meetbaar en dus contrôleerbaar is en de kosten van één werkeenheid (bijv. één werkuur) altijd in het tarief berekenbaar zijn. Eigenlijk wisten we dat allang, maar we hebben het niet van den beginne af in het systeem der kostprijsberekening opgenomen. En dan komt natuurlijk de vraag: is dat alles slechts bestemd voor de grote onderneming? Wij hebben dat punt in onze discussie vanmiddag moeten overslaan. Nee, dames en heren, het is volgens het oordeel van het panel, waar we mee samengewerkt hebben, niet alleen voor de grote onderneming, het is ook voor de middelmatige onderneming, het is ook voor de kleine onderneming. Maar ieder die dit toepast moet dit natuurlijk toepassen als een verstandig en goed accountant – andere zijn er hopelijk niet – en moet natuurlijk de dingen naar de juiste verhouding bepalen en naar de juiste maat toepassen. Ten slotte, er is een groot belang dat we met de bestudering van deze vraagstukken voortgaan.

De discussie van vanmiddag heeft uitgewezen, dat we er nog lang niet zijn. Maar een voortschrijden in deze richting is er sedert het accountantscongres van 1926 dan toch wel duidelijk merkbaar geweest. Ik dank u.

Ladies and Gentlemen, I must follow the prescribed procedure and revert to my mother tongue to make the summary. Actually it is not necessary to give such a resumption, because all the subjects desired have been discussed in a rather concentrated way; even our expectation, with regard to the future development of the use of this instrument.

We have, nevertheless, seen this afternoon that by the introduction of budgeting and budgetary control the accounting procedures, which were originally of a retrospective character, have been basically modified. By the introduction of corresponding budgeting, accounting is no more an instrument of registration only. It is at the same time a prospective instrument for management, and not only for business and industrial administration. The same principles of managerial budgeting and accounting can be applied to public administration. But I will not enlarge upon this subject, though it has been mentioned in the discussion, because it does not belong to the subjects as prescribed for our inquiry into this problem.

Budgeting implies a systematic elaboration of managerial expectations. Business cannot be managed without anticipations, but one cannot work with them efficiently without their elaborate classification and systematization. During the execution of plans one must necessarily keep in mind the bases of one's expectations, in order to check them with the actual development and to change the measures taken, when circumstances change. In this way we get a 'twin-set' instrument for management: budgeting and accounting.

It now becomes possible to compare—daily, weekly, monthly, as we have heard—the expectations with reality, normative data with figures recording performances. Moreover, it becomes possible to analyse what the causes are of the differences found. These causes may be managerial misapprehensions, misconstructions or mistaken anticipations. On the other hand they may be mistakes in the execution by some of the co-operators; are the delegated initiatives executed as they ought to be? All this concerns the flexibility of the budget.

We introduce—and did already introduce in our practice in this field—what is nowadays called administrative signalling. This is nothing else than the individualisation of budgetary control of all centres of responsibility; the higher ones as well as those on the lower levels of authority in the stratification of managerial functions. Every person who has responsibility for task-execution will have—apart from his instruction—a qualitative measure—a quantification of his task. In that way he becomes related to the fixation of his task in relation to management as a whole. He himself is connected with the fixation of normative data for the execution of his task. And as a consequence he is enabled to control all work executed under his competence. He himself can state the causes of the mistakes made under his responsibility and possibly the imperfection of his orders. He realizes what has taken place. He has the possibility to report to his superiors about what has happened, before they call him to account for it. When reporting his own mistakes he has an opportunity of presenting to his chiefs a proposal as to how to prevent them in future.

In the way of this method, which we have already applied for years, the idea of signalling expresses the necessity of delegation of responsibility just one step further. It may be called a new thought, when considered from its own point of view. All in all, it is an indispensable element in our 'twin-set' system of budgeting and accounting, of which the parts continually verify each other. In this way the system is the instrumentation of that kind of administration which Limperg introduced under the name of 'corrective management'. Such management

—the adjusting element of it—is required, because people do make mistakes in their activities and because perfect foresight does not exist. One can, and even must, foresee, calculate, apply the best, the most scientific method in doing so. Thus one can approach the most perfect methods of estimating. But it will always remain a working-hypothesis, which has to be compared with the actual facts, which requires the breaking down of differences and analysis of their causes in order to adjust the measures taken on the hypothetical basis. Let us be aware that there is the possibility of managerial mistakes. They need adjustment even more than the mistakes caused by neglect (of attention) and other elements of inefficiency in the execution in the factory.

Only if we want to reach that goal, must we introduce budgetary systems as we discussed this afternoon. Then we have to use market-analysis, we have to establish standards for the execution of the work, we have to calculate in actual—up to date—value and not in figures of expenses in the past. Then we have to control cost and we have to avoid the idea of costs which are uncontrollable. The cost of durable means of production are controllable, but we have to apply the right method. The number of working-hours a machine is in action is measurable as well as the number of hours the machine has to work for a product. The notion 'working-unit' is connected with capacity and with the 'lifetime' of machines and buildings. I refer here to my presentation of the respective part of Limperg's theory at the C.I.O.S. Congress at Brussels in 1951.

The cost of a working-unit can be calculated and in the tariff it can be expressed per hour or per performance. Such tariffs were known, but mostly we did not apply them in the right way in cost accounting, before the idea that the machine is a stock of working-units was introtroduced.

Finally there is the problem: is all this not only applicable to big enterprises? We had to omit it in our discussion, because of lack of time.

No, definitely no, ladies and gentlemen, the opinion of the international panel, which co-operated in the preparation of this discussion, is that the system has to be applied in all kinds of management, in huge, medium and small enterprises—as a matter of course. But it has to be applied by intelligent accountants—there are no others I hope—and it is obvious that they will regulate all the measures in the required proportions. If that is done, good results can be obtained.

Nevertheless, these problems must undoubtedly be studied further, our discussions of this afternoon have shown that this subject is far from being exhausted, though considerable progress has been made since 1926, when accountants met for the first time in an international gathering with representatives from all over the world.

CHAIRMAN:

Ladies and Gentlemen, You have now heard the discussions and Prof. Mey's summary of the essential points of the debate. I have no doubt that some here to-day do not agree with some of the opinions here mentioned. Different people have different views as to what is the best way, but I express the hope that the discussions have given you some new ideas and a stimulus for your work in the future. One of the objectives of a congress is to stimulate research to develop even higher standards of technique in the accountant's work. Progress there must be in the help given to management and I hope we have succeeded in making our tools a little better.

Mr. Jacob Viel will now come to the microphone.

Vice-chairman, DR. JAKOB VIEL (Switzerland)

Meine Damen und Herren, Ich darf wohl im Namen von Ihnen allen sprechen, wenn ich dem Herrn Vorsitzenden, dem Herrn Diskussionsleiter und allen Mitgliedern des Panels, speziell den Herren Referenten, herzlich danke für die kompetente Art und Weise, wie sie die Verhandlungen geführt und das Problem der Budgetierung behandelt haben.

Die Herren Referenten haben uns einen guten Überblick gegeben über den Stand der Budgetierung in ihren Ländern und auch über ihre persönlichen

Auffassungen. Es ist ja interessant festzustellen, wie sich, angebahnt durch die ursprünglichen Zeitstudien für Elementarfunktionen, ausgelöst durch Taylor, über die Standardkostenrechnung schließlich das umfassende Budget, das Betriebsbudget entwickelt hat. Wenn auch die Entwicklung in den einzelnen Ländern unterschiedlich gewesen sein mag, so werden doch die zunehmende Kostenintensität, der verschärfte Konkurrenzkampf und die wachsenden Betriebsgrößen überall die Erkenntnis darüber gefördert haben, was man mit dem Betrieb an unerbittlichen Konsequenzen auf sich genommen und wie man sich zu verhalten hat.

Der moderne Unternehmer muß vor allen Dingen Planer sein, eingedenk des Ausspruchs von Robert Bridges: 'die Weisheit liegt in der meisterhaften Bewältigung des Unvorhergesehenen'. Wir Wirtschaftsprüfer haben in der Planung immer noch Pionierarbeit zu leisten und ich bin überzeugt, meine Damen und Herren, daß unser Amsterdamer Kongreß uns erneut bewußt werden ließ, wie bedeutsam die Aufgabe ist, die wir im Dienste der Wirtschaft zu erfüllen haben.

Ladies and Gentlemen, I think I may speak for all of you when I warmly thank the Chairman, the discussion leader and all the members of the panel and especially the authors of the papers, for the competent way in which they have led the debate and treated the problem of budgeting. The authors have given us a good survey of the state of budgeting in their respective countries and also of their personal views.

It is interesting to see how, starting from the original time studies for elementary functions, prepared by Taylor, via the standard cost accounting, we finally get to the comprehensive budget, the business budget. Although the course of development in the various countries may have been different, the progressing intensity of cost, heightened competition and the growing size of businesses have nevertheless increased knowledge everywhere, of the inexorable consequences one has taken upon oneself with a business, and how one has to behave.

The modern business man must above all things be a planner, remembering Robert Bridges' saying: 'Wisdom lies in mastering the unforeseen'. We auditors still have to do pioneer work in planning, and I am convinced, Ladies and Gentlemen, that our Amsterdam Congress has shown us once again how important the function is that we fulfil in the service of economics.

CHAIRMAN:

Prof. Kurosawa from Japan will now close the session.

Vice-chairman, PROF. K. KUROSAWA (Japan)

Mr. Chairman, Ladies and Gentlemen, I want to address a few words of thanks to the Chairman for his excellent performance. He has led this session on 'Budgeting and the Corresponding Modernization of Accounting' most successfully. It is a topic which has become the most important problem in professional as well as in managing circles, in modern business enterprises throughout the world. Allow me to say a word in the Japanese language to express my feelings: 'Domo Arigato!' which means: Thank you very much.

THE VERIFICATION OF THE EXISTENCE OF ASSETS

Afternoon session: Tuesday, 10th September 1957

Papers by page

Chairman:	G. F. Klingner, F.C.A., Ireland
Vice-chairmen:	Dr. A. R. Rojansky, C.P.A., F.A.C.C.A., Israel Prof. Avv. Rag. Giovanni Sensini, Italy
Panel members:	
Discussion leader:	WP Prof. Dr. Ernst Knorr *Institut der Wirtschaftsprüfer in Deutschland e.V.*
Rapporteur and author of a paper:	J. A. de Lalanne, C.B.E., M.C., B.A., C.A. (Canada) *Canadian Institute of Chartered Accountants*
Authors of papers:	Donald J. Bevis, C.P.A. *American Institute of Certified Public Accountants*
	R. Burgert, Ec. Drs. *Vereniging van Academisch Gevormde Accountants* *The Netherlands*
	Claude Paquet, HEC. *Chambre Nationale des Experts-Comptables* *Diplômés par l'Etat, France*
	Sir Richard Yeabsley, C.B.E., F.C.A., F.S.A.A. *The Society of Incorporated Accountants, U.K.*
Other members: of the panel:	M. Hussain Chaudhury *Pakistan Council of Accountancy*
	G. D. Stewart, F.I.A.N.Z., F.P.A.N.Z. *Incorporated Institute of Accountants of New Zealand*
	Prof. B. J. S. Wimble, C.A. (S.A.), F.S.A.A. *Transvaal Society of Accountants*

PAPER

by

J. A. DE LALANNE, C.B.E., M.C., B.A., C.A. (CANADA)

Canadian Institute of Chartered Accountants

I. Introduction

The terms of reference for this assignment stipulate that 'the valuation of assets is considered a separate subject' and that it is not to be discussed in this paper.

What is asked for is an outline of the author's views as to 'the procedures which should be carried out by the auditor to satisfy himself as to whether the physical volume or quantity of assets is correctly stated in the client's accounts and of any variations in procedure as regards:

a. audit of annual accounts;

b. investigations.'

I shall presume that verification of the existence of assets must be considered in two parts; firstly, that the particular asset, whatever type it may be, is either physically in existence or that the right to it does exist, and secondly, that the physical asset or the right belongs, in fact, to the individual or company whose accounts are under audit.

The first audit usually calls for certain procedures and verifications which need not be repeated to the same extent in subsequent examinations; also, the same tests need not all be repeated every year, but over a cycle of years all phases of the client's operations should be covered in reasonable detail, having regard to the client's own system of internal control and the extent and effectiveness of any independent internal audit.

Before discussing the methods and procedures which I suggest should be adopted by the auditor to satisfy himself of the existence of various types of assets, and to avoid repetition throughout these comments, I express the general view that personal observation or inspection by the auditor, where feasible, should be the starting point for all verification.

I realize that for many types of assets this is only a partial verification and does not necessarily prove ownership. On the other hand, in addition to other merits, it has the advantage of giving the auditor a first-hand knowledge of the assets and the nature of the undertaking with which he is dealing, the size of the client's operations and a general knowledge of the procedures and of the division of duties as between the responsible employees.

While it is sometimes essential that a physical inspection be made of certain types of assets at or near the date of the fiscal year end, with control being maintained as circumstances dictate or permit, I feel very strongly that such a verification should be supplemented by other 'surprise' counts or confirmations, especially for those assets which fall within the current or liquid class.

Without such additional safeguards and the knowledge by employees (even officers of the company) that no further inspection is likely to be made until the next year end or periodical fixed audit, there is much more opportunity for substitution and/or misappropriation of funds, securities or inventories and for systematic defalcation in customers' balances, even before the auditor has completed his current task. The frequency of such surprise tests will be dependent on many factors—and to be most effective, should be varied from time to time both as to date and procedure.

Now a few comments on the various types of assets.

Fixed assets with little or no turnover, which cannot normally be substituted (e.g. land and buildings).

The extent of the investigation to be made in connection with these assets will depend on the nature of the business, the number of properties, their size, and their location, but it is most important that, if practicable, the auditor should from time to time visit all properties, view any additions or demolitions, note the type of structure and become familiar with the uses to which they are put. This not only satisfies the auditor that the properties actually exist but it gives him information which is of assistance, for instance, in interpreting the particulars contained in the relative deeds or supporting documents and in forming an opinion as to the adequacy of accumulated depreciation and of depreciation rates in use. In most instances the time of the visit or the frequency is not a very serious matter so long as the records indicate that the properties are in reasonably full operation.

The second step is a thorough examination of the deeds and such registrations as may be required by the governing political authority. Where the properties are numerous and it is not feasible for the auditor to examine in detail all the supporting deeds and documents, he should ensure that his client maintains a proper record of all properties with particulars of all acquisitions, disposals and abandonments. Where such record exists, a comprehensive test is usually sufficient.

As part of his programme, the auditor should, of course, scrutinize all minutes, agreements and contracts, examine the relative tax bills and insurance policies and adopt such other practices as might seem appropriate to ensure that there are no prior liens on any of the assets.

Fixed assets (with a lower turnover) which are difficult to substitute (e.g. machinery and equipment, furniture and fittings, vehicles, etc.).

Periodical scrutiny of machinery and equipment and a careful check of all additions, replacements and disposals would normally suffice for fixed machines and equipment. For movable equipment such as office machines and vehicles, a physical inspection and comparison of serial numbers is the most effective verification.

In large undertakings, it is normally not practicable for the auditor to make frequent detailed verifications of the existence of all the assets falling within this class and therefore more reliance must be placed on the client's own records.

In industries such as transportation, trucking and construction where the owners generally adopt a numbering system of their own for rolling stock and other pieces of equipment, the auditor is more likely to be able to make appropriate test checks and establish controls to assist him in determining that the relative assets are satisfactorily accounted for.

Current assets (with a higher turnover) which can more easily be substituted (e.g. stocks of raw materials, work in process and finished goods).

In the matter of inventories, the situation is more complex and personal inspection by the auditor from time to time is most desirable. Three important factors are:

The physical existence of the product.
The quality or grade of the merchandise in question—and its condition.
The ownership.

Confirmation of existence and of quantities should not normally be too difficult in the case of *raw materials* and *finished goods*, where a physical inspection can be carried out and when suitable and adequate records are maintained for receiving and shipping and of movement within the plant.

It is difficult to separate a study as between 'physical existence' and 'valuation' as the auditor will no doubt wish to compare the quantities and qualities with invoices for recent deliveries to the plant and to ensure that the styles and qualities listed for the stock on hand are in agreement with the relative particulars recorded by the supplier in his invoices. Special care should be taken to ensure that the materials or supplies are actually owned by the company and taken into its accounts and that they have not been received on consignment.

As regards *finished goods* procedure is somewhat the reverse of that for raw materials in that studies should be made of production and of quantities represented in sales, with appropriate inquiry as to whether packaged goods still remain in the ownership of the client or may have been packed and invoiced prior to the inventory date but held for later shipment.

Work in process is usually one of the most difficult for an auditor to verify and in this connection he must, to a great extent, rely on the accuracy of the client's cost or working records—supplemented by such personal observation as may be practicable.

I appreciate that there are many types of business where it is virtually impossible for the auditor to carry out, either himself or through his associates, anything more than a cursory inspection of stocks. In these instances, it is necessary for him to pay much more attention to the company's records of purchases, production and sales, the rates of wastage learned through experience, possibility of theft and pilfering, obsolescence, and all the other factors which go to reduce quantity and quality.

He must also satisfy himself:

Of the sufficiency and accuracy of the client's records and his method of stocktaking.

Of the practices adopted in establishing quantities and grades of merchandise and in determining slow-moving and/or obsolete stocks.

That there was a simultaneous closing (so-called cut off) of receiving, production and shipping records co-incident with the commencement of the actual count.

That there was adequate control of the movement of stocks within the plant during the period of stocktaking in instances where production and shipping must, of necessity, continue uninterrupted.

Claims or rights incorporated in documents, which can be easily substituted (e.g. securities, bills receivable, warehouse certificates and cash).

While in many types of business it is desirable and necessary to make actual physical counts of cash, securities and bills receivable at the fiscal year end, I suggest that physical counts with an element of surprise are the most effective, especially as regards the discovery of substitution or other types of defalcation.

Maintenance of control during any physical inspection of assets of this type is extremely important with special cognizance being taken of 'due dates' and 'endorsements'—where applicable.

Where it is necessary to prove existence and/or title by means of written confirmation, the form of the request or of the confirmation to be returned should be carefully designed so as to include all relevant facts, and disclosure of any accounts which might be temporarily dormant.

Where more than one party has an interest or responsibility in any transaction, confirmation should be obtained from each—e.g., bills receivable under discount.

Certain organizations such as stock exchanges stipulate that the independent auditor reconcile and confirm bank balances both as of the audit date and as of a date subsequent thereto.

This practice has considerable merit in the case of other types of assets included in the group under discussion.

Long-term loans or receivables

These are normally covered by some type of document such as a notarial deed or formal contract. The auditor should ascertain whether all legal requirements of these documents have been met by the borrower and appropriate steps should be taken to ensure the existence of any security which may have been pledged against the respective asset. For example, in the case of negotiable securities, confirmation or inspection should be made. Where the security is in the nature of a fixed asset, other documents as well as tax bills and insurance policies should always be inspected, confirmed and, where observation by the auditor is not feasible, other inquiries made as to the existence of the security and that there are no prior liens or rights against the security pledged.

Short-term receivables

The nature and size of the business and other relevant factors will usually dictate the procedure to be followed in verifying receivables, e.g., the extent of the coverage, the frequency of inspection and of direct communication with debtors, either in positive or negative form of confirmation.

In addition, extensive tests should be made of the source of the charges, the terms of credit, experience of collection, the method by which the debtor pays, whether for the exact charges or by lump sum payments, and whether any items appear to be in dispute.

Credit notes issued subsequent to closing date should also be scrutinized to ascertain whether any applied to the period under audit and the reasons for and effect of the issue of same.

This is another instance where it is difficult to separate verification of 'existence' and of 'valuation'.

Investigations

In the case of investigations where the auditor is in a less favourable position to form an opinion on the adequacy of the system of internal control and where time dictates a more restricted examination of the accounts than in the case of a general audit, the auditor must consider the nature of the business concerned, the volume of its operations, the comparison of both its balance sheets and operating accounts over a period of years with a thorough inquiry into any assets or liabilities, income or expenditures which would appear out of line in the final period as compared with the experience in prior years.

Where feasible, observation of the physical stock on hand is most important and in many instances the engagement of independent specialists may be desirable except in cases where, for instance, the purchaser of a business can send in his own experts to appraise the quality and quantity and value of stock. In the case of an appraisal for purchase or sale of a business, for example, the auditor is seldom capable of expressing an opinion on the realizable value of properties such as land, buildings and machinery, and it may not be practicable for him to make a physical inspection of all properties. The report of any recognized independent appraisers specially engaged for the purpose or who may have carried out a recent inspection of the properties would be most helpful in such a case.

One of the problems which often confronts the auditor in the case of an investigation is the secrecy which must be maintained, sometimes coupled with urgency. This occurs in various ways and for many reasons but limits considerably the extent to which the auditor may have access to certain of the basic records and often precludes his discussing underlying principles with the persons who actually must carry them into effect. Consequently, investigations impose on the auditor greater need for sound judgement, tact and capacity to work under pressure and he must give due consideration to trends in the particular business and in the industry in so far as statistics may be available, bearing in mind the dangers of placing too much reliance on comparisons even of companies in the same type of business.

II. General

As regards certain of the points specifically referred to in the 'terms of reference', my views are as follows:

The auditor is justified in examining certain assets less frequently than once a year, e.g. distant properties where it can be seen that buildings and equipment and other facilities are being used to reasonable capacity for the company's operations and where he has no reason to believe that they have been sold, destroyed or abandoned.

In determining the frequency of stocktaking and the examination of assets and in fixing the time and scope of such inspection, consideration should be given to the possibility of substitution and the frequency of movement.

Stocktaking at the close of the fiscal year does prove the existence of the particular materials or other assets as at that date and, if a complete coverage can be made simultaneously, minimizes the possibility of substitution or transfer between departments or warehouses. This method is necessary and desirable for many industries and particularly where it is impractical to maintain perpetual inventory records, or where a gross profit method of computation is not feasible.

On the other hand, the speed with which an overall count must be made for some types of operation sometimes offsets the advantages which accrue and more satisfactory results are obtainable through periodical checks of stocks throughout the year, and a normal experience determined as regards wastage, shrinkage, pilferage and the like. Surprise test counts at times other than the closing date are normally found most advantageous in detecting frauds, thefts and other forms of misappropriation. I do not suggest, however, that this should eliminate entirely physical checks of stocks at the year end.

Where practical limitations reduce the opportunity for the auditor to make personal inspections, he will be more dependent on perpetual or other inventory records maintained by the client and must pay particular attention to the client's method of control, internal checks or audits carried out by his own staff or by independent persons, and must apply such other yardsticks as may be available to him in determining quantities and qualities.

I consider that attendance at physical stocktaking and the inspection of cash and securities are most important in verifying the accuracy of balance sheet items. As regards cash and securities, the auditor will normally assume full responsibility for a personal or independent verification. Unless he is so required by his terms of engagement, he should not assume the responsibility for the actual stocktaking of merchandise but should co-operate and assist in such stocktaking to whatever extent he feels desirable or as requested and should observe the methods and procedures to satisfy himself that quantities are being properly recorded and that the descriptions of the various types of goods are such that will permit the client's staff to place proper valuations on the inventories.

Wherever possible, a study should be made of the accounts for the period subsequent to the date of the balance sheet with particular reference to cash received, deposited, collection of accounts receivable, discounts allowed and sales of merchandise in relation to the inventories listed as on hand at the year end. For example, an abnormal falling off in sales following the close of the year might indicate insufficient stock on hand to make the required deliveries and suggest further tests.

The obtaining of written confirmation directly from depositories such as bankers, consignees and warehousing companies and from third parties in the case of advances, loans and receivables is, in my opinion, a key part of every audit or investigation. The frequency and manner in which these may be requested is a matter for each individual assignment but should not preclude occasional inspection by the auditor.

Where assets are held in custody for others, verification should be carried out in a similar manner.

In regard to the extent that an auditor requires expert knowledge as to the nature of the assets of the company, this is certainly always an advantage, and in some instances may be essential, possibly more often for valuation rather than for verification of existence. However, in both instances the usual general rules would apply and if the auditor has made a comprehensive study of the client's products, method of operation and control of stocks, he should normally not need specific technical knowledge for adequate stocktaking.

In assignments where the auditor does not have sufficient technical knowledge to carry out an adequate stocktaking by himself, he would be well advised to engage independent experts to assist him if his terms of engagement or the local law under which he practises requires him to personally make a physical count—independent of the client's staff.

If, on the other hand, the responsibility for compiling the inventory rests with the client, the auditor would not normally engage independent experts, unless he had reason to believe that styles and/or quantities were not being correctly stated or in cases where sufficient data were not available to him to form an opinion as to the thoroughness of the procedures adopted by the client.

As to the question of technical suitability, I would not think that the auditor could be expected to pass on the suitability of each and every item appearing in the inventory. He would, of course, take the precaution to inquire as to orders in hand and the client's ability to fill such orders, to ascertain that the stocks are not excessive in relation to current sales—or shipments—and in comparison with inventories required in the past and that there have not been an unduly large number of returns by customers.

Provided quantities and qualities were correctly stated, the question of possible obsolescence due to pending inventions or a tapering off in demand due to general business conditions would be a matter of concern for those placing the appropriate value on the stocks in question.

The auditor's responsibility is governed either by the statute under which he practises, or by his terms of reference.

Except for such matters as may be specifically excluded in the terms of engagement, the client may reasonably expect that the auditor has satisfied himself on all material facts not subject to a qualification in his report. I would not consider, however, that the auditor's responsibility would in any way be reduced by his lack of technical knowledge, in so far as third parties are concerned, even if he has been relieved by the client of certain responsibilities.

III. Conclusion

In the foregoing, I have restricted my comments to the classification of assets and types of business which are most common and have not attempted to discuss other types which appear less frequently in financial accounts.

However, in all instances, existence, ownership or title can best be proven by the application of the same general principles—which may be summed up as follows:

Actual count or personal observation.

Written confirmation or other documentary evidence where physical inspection is not feasible or appropriate.

Comprehensive examination of the client's records.

Intelligent study of the client's practices and procedures.

Exercise of sound judgement and meticulous care on the part of the auditor in the planning of this programme, having in mind the importance of variation in coverage, methods and timing.

PAPER

by

DONALD J. BEVIS, C.P.A.

American Institute of Certified Public Accountants

I. Introduction

The ultimate objective of the auditor in the ordinary examination of the annual accounts of an enterprise or in an investigation of special matters is the expression of an informed opinion or conclusion on the financial statements of the enterprise or on the matters under investigation.

This paper deals with the problems or questions that are encountered in that phase of the examination or investigation relating to the verification of the existence of assets. The word 'verification' is used hereafter not in the sense of 'proving something to be *true*' or of 'establishing the *truth* of something', but in the auditor's accepted sense of establishing or proving the *general fairness* of the matter under investigation by relying upon a system of carefully devised testing.

For the purpose of this discussion it is presumed that the auditor is a professional man and conducts himself in accordance with the ethics and standards of his profession. The generally accepted auditing standards (as distinguished from auditing procedures) of independent certified public accountants in the United States require that the examination or investigation be performed by a person having adequate technical training and proficiency as an auditor, that in so far as the assignment is concerned he maintain an independence in mental attitude, and that he exercise due professional care in the performance of his work. In performing the examination it is essential that the work be adequately planned and supervised; that there be a proper study and evaluation of the existing internal control for the purpose of determining the extent of the audit tests to be performed; and that sufficient competent evidential matter be obtained through inspection, observation, inquiries, and confirmations to afford a reasonable basis for an opinion.

II. Audit of Annual Accounts

The principle has been established that the financial statements upon which the auditor is reporting are the representations of management. Management has the direct responsibility for the maintenance of an adequate and effective system of accounts and for safeguarding the assets. The auditor's representations are expressed in his report or opinion, which reflects his personal judgment as to the general credibility and fairness of the statements. His examination is not designed and cannot be relied upon to detect defalcations and other similar irregularities, particularly those that involve collusion.

It is important to recognize at this point that the auditor, in connection with his examination of the annual accounts, usually is asked to give his opinion on the income statement, as well as the balance sheet. Therefore, in determining the procedures to be followed in the verification of the existence of assets, appropriate consideration must be given to all aspects of the examination, and not to the balance sheet alone, and to the fact that some audit procedures are designed to test the validity of figures in both statements.

The auditor in rendering the usual opinion on the financial statements does not state that he has made an exact and complete verification of the figures on the statements. The objectives of an audit do not require such an extensive scrutiny. Furthermore, it cannot be presumed that the figures should be exact figures. Accounting values of most items in financial statements cannot be determined exactly. They are subject to many variable factors, including accounting conventions, industry practices, and judgments of individuals. The determination of those values also is often complicated by the inability to measure exactly the physical volume or quantity of the assets.

The auditor's opinion is the opinion of an expert in accounting and auditing, based upon an adequate examination for the purposes required of the underlying data. The scope of his examination takes into consideration, and its extent will vary in accordance with, the materiality of the separate items in, or affecting, the financial statements and the relative degree of risk of occurrence of material inaccuracies. Since the fairness of the financial statements will be more seriously affected by a misstatement of a material item, a relatively greater amount of evidential matter must be examined or tested in support of a material item than would be necessary in support of an immaterial item. Greater attention must also be given to those items or spheres of activity in which material error or fraud could be expected to exist, in contrast with those items which are least susceptible to error or fraud.

The auditor need not, except in the most unusual case, make a detailed audit of all transactions. The nature of the audit procedures employed and the extent of the tests of the records and selected transactions are a matter of judgment and will depend to a large degree upon his appraisal of the adequacy of the system of internal control. One of the principal purposes of internal control is to minimize the possibility of error or irregularity. The more adequate and effective the system, the less extensive the amount of testing that is required. Where internal control is limited or restricted, a more comprehensive audit and a greater amount of testing will be required. Ordinarily, the small concern will have a weak system of internal control, the medium sized concern will have an adequate system, and the large concern will have an extensive system. The system of internal control of the large organization is usually typified by the existence of some degree of internal audit.

In summary, therefore, it can be stated that the nature and extent of the specific audit procedures to be employed in the verification of the existence of assets depend upon: (1) the materiality of the item to be audited, (2) the probability of finding material inaccuracies, and (3) the evaluation of the system of internal control, including the methods followed by the enterprise in physically controlling and accounting for the assets.

III. Investigations

In a special investigation the audit procedures to be employed will depend upon the character and purpose of the examination and the type of report desired from the auditor. The nature and extent of these procedures may vary for several reasons from what would be required in the examination of the annual accounts. In the first place, the purpose of the examination may dictate that different procedures be employed. Secondly, a greater or lesser degree of assurance on the part of the auditor may be required, with a consequent expansion or reduction in the audit procedures employed and the extent of their application, depending again upon the purpose of the examination and the expected results. Further, in a special investigation the auditor usually is restricted to a specific item or one phase of the operation of an enterprise. Because of this limitation and the resultant inability to obtain reasonable knowledge of the whole, he is in a less favorable position to form an opinion on the adequacy of the system of internal control, and he is not in a position to benefit from the knowledge he obtains from other audit procedures and tests that would be performed in the examination of the annual accounts. Hence, the audit procedures employed may have to be more comprehensive, and the extent of his tests of the item or phase of the operations may have to be greater than might otherwise be necessary in order to give him the assurance he requires to render the expected opinion.

In any event, if the investigation involves the issuance of a report by the auditor, the substance of the generally accepted auditing standards mentioned previously in this paper still applies.

IV. Types of Assets

Irregularities due to fraud or dishonesty are more apt to occur when the asset is readily accessible and mobile, has a relatively high value, and is easily negotiable or convertible into funds. Assets that have these characteristics include the following:

1. Cash—which ordinarily can be used by the abstracter without major difficulty of conversion,
2. Marketable securities and other negotiable instruments—which are readily negotiable without endorsement into cash or its equivalent,
3. Stocks of raw materials, work in process, and finished products—the use of which by fraudulent conversion depends upon their ready marketability or use by the possessor,
4. Certain types of machinery and equipment, furniture and fixtures, etc.—which have the same characteristics as the inventory items mentioned above, and
5. Bank account balances, receivables, and certain securities—the improper use of which requires only fraudulent endorsement or forgery.

It is to these types of assets that greater auditing attention and more extensive tests need be applied in order to assure the auditor that, as of the date of the annual accounts or investigation, there is a reasonable presumption of the existence of these assets. It will be observed that the greater risk generally lies in items that are classified as current assets, as distinguished from fixed assets. It is also to be noted that the greater risk lies in items that have a higher turnover and can more easily be substituted. There usually is little exposure in fixed assets with little or no turnover, and which normally cannot be substituted, such as land and buildings or intangibles.

The probability of bookkeeping errors also has some relationship, if it does not vary directly, with the rate of turnover. The larger the number of bookkeeping entries required, the greater the statistical chance for error. Bookkeeping and accounting errors also may arise out of incompetence, inattention, or improper supervision. The auditing procedures employed should take these factors into consideration.

V. Audit Techniques

The techniques that the auditor follows in the verification of the existence of assets, in the examination of the annual accounts or in a special investigation, can be summarized as follows:

1. Analysis and review of data in the company's files and records and data obtained by the auditor in the course of his examination,
2. Observation of accounting and internal control procedures,
3. Inspection of physical assets, documents, and other supporting evidence,
4. Confirmation of items shown on the records by direct communication with an authoritative person in a position to verify the items,
5. Inquiry of officers and employees, legal counsel, etc. and
6. Computation of figures in the records or books of account.

In the majority of cases each of these techniques must be applied before the auditor can obtain satisfaction as to the general fairness of any item under investigation. For example, with respect to stocks of raw materials, work in process, and finished products, the auditor will have to analyze and review data pertaining to the purchasing, receiving, and accounts payable departments to satisfy himself that the company has title to the inventory. He will have to observe the procedures followed in taking physical inventories and inspect selected items. Often he may have to obtain confirmation as to inventory belonging to outsiders or out on consignment, and he will make inquiry of officers and employees as to obsolete and excess inventory items. Tests will have to be made of the arithmetical accuracy of the inventory prices, extensions, and tabulations.

It is the composite knowledge that the auditor obtains from all required procedures and tests that enables him to express an opinion on the matters under investigation. He does not rely completely upon any single procedure, such as physical stocktaking.

DONALD J. BEVIS

VI. Physical Stocktaking

The presence of the auditor during the time of physical stocktaking usually provides the best independent means of verifying the accuracy of balance sheet items. Without having the knowledge that comes from direct contact with physical stocktaking, the auditor is not in a position to appraise whether the procedures are good and should result in a reasonable determination of the inventory for accounting purposes. He must rely, otherwise, on representations of management of the company and the people directly responsible for taking the inventory. His observation of the procedures followed and inspection of selected items give him some direct assurance as to the bona fides of the inventory.

Physical stocktaking provides a check on the reliability of the accounting procedures and costing techniques through a comparison, with all of its ramifications, of priced physical inventories or physical quantities with the inventory amounts shown by the accounting records. The correctness of interim financial statements of an enterprise (or the year-end statements if physical inventories are taken in advance of the end of the year) depends to a major extent upon the accounting and cost procedures employed to produce them.

Physical stocktaking, by developing and pointing out differences, is thereby a means of checking and proving the adequacy of internal organization and other phases of internal control. For example, are the established procedures for the control of receiving and shipping of materials functioning properly? Have reasonable safeguards been provided to prevent theft of valuable merchandise? The best way of satisfactorily answering these questions is to be able to demonstrate that opening inventories, plus purchases and production, equal sales, plus closing inventories. There are few cases, however, where it is necessary or worthwhile for the auditor to spend the time required to ascertain that quantitative relationship if it has not been established by the company. There are other tests that can be performed in a lesser amount of time that not only will give him reasonable answers to this question, but also will answer many other questions as to the adequacy of other related and unrelated accounting and internal control procedures. Internal control, once instituted, cannot be presumed to be continuous in all aspects; it frequently breaks down through discontinuance of checks and of operations believed to be in effect by management, but which are no longer carried out.

The foregoing discussion of physical stocktaking has been directed primarily to stocks of raw materials, work in process, and finished products. The observations or conclusions are, however, applicable to other types of assets that are subject to physical control procedures. For example, the verification of the existence of cash on hand, securities and other negotiable instruments, and items of machinery and equipment can be accomplished by a physical inventory. The results of the physical inventory also can give some assurance as to the adequacy of the internal control procedures.

Certain characteristics of physical stocktaking are also present in the examination of receivables and other assets. Trial balances or detailed listings of these assets are an essential part of the examination process, although in the case of receivables they cannot be conclusive as to their bona fides. Direct confirmation from the debtor is the best means of proving the existence and authenticity of receivables.

VII. Date of Physical Examination of Assets

If the major purpose of the verification of the existence of assets is to establish their general fairness as of the date of the audit, obviously the ideal would be to have a complete and simultaneous inventory and check of all items on that date. This would eliminate the possibility of substitution to cover up shortages, and the additional auditing procedures and tests required in the reconcilements of inventories of assets at one date to the amounts shown in the accounts at another date. On the other hand, a practice of taking all inventories on the audit date eliminates any benefits that can come from surprise examinations, and normally only discloses conditions existing at one time and not during the year. When inventories are taken during the year or at odd times, the element of surprise sometimes can be injected. By having more frequent contact, the possibility of unobserved breakdowns in control procedures is considerably lessened. More frequent contact also should give the auditor greater assurance as to the fairness of the income account.

The observance of a practice of complete and simultaneous inventory is of greater importance in special investigations. In such cases, because of the restricted nature of the examinations, the auditor usually does not have the same degree of familiarity with the system of internal control as he does in the audit of the annual accounts. Therefore, he cannot place as much reliance on the internal accounting and, from the standpoint of his reporting responsibilities, he normally is not concerned with it.

For various reasons the ideal seldom can be attained, particularly in the examination of the annual accounts. Many companies take their physical inventories of raw materials, work in process, and finished stock at a time when the inventories are lowest, or when production demands are the least, or when there is the greatest availability of man power. These dates will not necessarily coincide with the end of the fiscal year. Perpetual inventory controls and records are an essential part of the operations of other companies. The reliability of these controls and records is checked throughout the year by comparison with physical inventories; no complete annual inventory is taken. As a part of his examination, the auditor makes tests of these physical inventories.

Also many companies, because of the limitations of time on their employees, prepare detailed listings and analyses of their receivables one or two months in advance of the end of the fiscal period. These listings must be used by the auditor. There can be no objection to this practice if there is reasonable internal control. Furthermore, since a very large number of companies close their accounts on a calendar-year basis, auditors, because of practical limitations on their own time and personnel, have encouraged their clients to take their inventories at other dates. This has also had a salutary effect on the client; his audit has not been subjected to extreme pressures of time and urgency, with the attendant chances for error and neglect.

In brief, the further the practices of the company and the auditor depart from the ideal, the tighter and more effective the system of internal control, and the more extensive the audit procedures and tests must be. In this connection, however, it should be noted that the degree of adequacy of internal control is not always uniform between assets or phases of the operation of a company. This can result in relatively more or less extensive audit tests in some areas than in others.

It is not practicable to set forth a precise rule as to the date of physical examinations of assets, or the intervals between such examinations, by the auditor. These determinations must be based upon the accounting and control procedures followed, the rate of turnover of the assets, their convertibility or negotiability, and the probability of occurrence of material inaccuracies in the accounts since the previous inventory. All of these factors are interrelated and the timing, or frequency, of the physical examinations will have a direct relationship with the seriousness of the findings.

If the accounting and control procedures are relatively poor, there exists the possibility of shortages and material inaccuracies in the accounts. Obviously in such cases there cannot be much authority attached to tests performed by the auditor far in advance, or for a period far in advance, of the date of the annual accounts or investigation. Unless he repeats these tests at or near the audit date, he cannot obtain reasonable satisfaction with the accounts at that time. The converse of this proposition is also true—the more reliable the accounting and control procedures, the less extensive the audit tests and the further the time of the physical examination can be separated from the audit date.

Likewise, it is generally true that, where turnover is slow, the frequency of the audit tests can be reduced. Where turnover is higher, the chance of bookkeeping errors is greater; accordingly, less reliance can be placed on tests performed in the past and more reliance must be placed on current control procedures and audit tests.

The element of surprise can be important in the application of auditing tests, in that there is a better chance of disclosing shortages or irregularities if the person being audited does not have advance information. However, with the increase in the size of business and the number of transactions, and the consequent improvement in internal controls, the detection of fraud and embezzlement is no longer considered by the user of audits to be of major importance; and, accordingly, the usual examination is not designed for that purpose, although the discovery of irregularities frequently results.

On the basis of the propositions developed in this paper and under the assumption of adequate internal control, it would appear that the auditor is justified in examining certain assets less frequently than once a year. These would include fixed assets, such as land, buildings, machinery and equipment, and assets that have been held in bond or to which access has been restricted. Further, it would appear that physical inventories of raw materials, work in process, and finished products (or at least a substantial portion thereof) should be taken at least once during a year; and the auditor should be present during the period of inventory taking to observe the procedures followed and make tests of the quantities. Physical examinations of material amounts of cash and securities and other negotiable instruments should be made as of the audit date, or reasonably close thereto. In all cases there is the presumption that the auditor will make some review of the intervening transactions between the time of the physical examination and the date of the audit.

VIII. Other Procedures

Since 1939 the auditor in the United States has been required to observe inventories and confirm receivables where either of these assets represents a significant proportion of the current assets or of the total assets of a concern. There has been no substantive change in these mandatory procedures since that time. Failure to apply these procedures, where they are practicable and reasonable, in general precludes expression of an opinion on the fairness of the financial statements taken as a whole. Many people felt when these procedures (particularly the requirement for observation and attendance at inventory taking) were adopted that they took the auditor out of his proper sphere and placed upon him responsibilities for which he was not equipped, either by training or in personnel, to assume. Subsequent experiences have demonstrated, however, that the auditor was capable of meeting his new responsibilities. The new procedures required the auditor to be familiar with the company's inventory plans and organization and to be present during the period of inventory taking to satisfy himself that a reasonable inventory was being taken. The new procedures did not take away from the company its responsibility for taking the inventory and the determination of quantity, quality, and condition of the inventory items.

There are no acceptable alternative procedures to these required procedures, using 'alternative' in the sense of equal value, effectiveness, or rank. Any other procedures employed in lieu of the mandatory procedures can only be considered to be substitute or other procedures, but not alternative procedures.

It is difficult in a paper of this length to give adequate consideration to these 'other' procedures. They will vary with differences in practices between companies and with the nature of the items under investigation. Two examples, however, can be cited. In the case of the verification of receivables, investigations of subsequent collections and adjustments have been made in lieu of confirmation with the debtors. Verification of the existence of merchandise being held by depositories or on consignment with outsiders has been made by direct communication with the holder or consignee, instead of by physical inspection. The use of these other procedures can give the auditor some satisfaction, but certainly not the assurance he obtains from following the procedures of direct confirmation of receivables and observation or inspection of the physical inventories.

In some areas of the audit process where physical determinations are an important factor, physical evidence is not always the best evidence. For example, in the case of a cash count the bona fides of coin and currency can usually be established by inspection. However, better proof of the authenticity of a check included in that count can be obtained by confirmation, rather than by inspection.

IX. Ownership of Assets

During the course of an examination it is frequently found that the company has in its possession assets belonging to other parties. In the verification of the physical existence of these assets the same audit procedures should be followed as in the case of assets owned by the company. The principal auditing problem in such situations arises in establishing the accountability of the company to the third party.

X. Use of Independent Experts

Ordinarily, in his verification of the existence of assets for the purpose of expressing an opinion on the annual accounts, the auditor does not need specific technical knowledge of the products or manufacturing processes to satisfy himself as to their existence, quantity, quality, and condition. It is the company's responsibility to organize and take the inventory; it is the auditor's responsibility only to satisfy himself as to the general fairness of the inventory. In making his examination, in addition to observing the physical stocktaking procedures, he performs certain other audit tests, which in the aggregate give him the information he needs to express an opinion. If internal control is reasonably adequate, the auditor can ordinarily obtain independent corroboration and technical assistance from the company's own experts. This fact, together with the knowledge that comes from his other auditing procedures, normally would eliminate any necessity to get outside technical assistance.

A detailed discussion of these other procedures is outside the scope of this paper; but a listing of a few of the more important procedures and policies of the company, of which the auditor would have knowledge through his tests, and which would aid him in reaching an opinion, would include:

1. Purchasing policies,
2. Receiving and shipping controls,
3. Material handling procedures,
4. Use of formulas, bills of material, parts lists, etc.,
5. Policies with respect to scrap and obsolescence, and
6. Quality control and inspection.

There are, however, some situations where the auditor might desire outside technical assistance. In the case of special investigations, for example, of a processor of drugs and chemicals or a jewelry firm, the auditor could find the advice of independent experts to be necessary before he could form an intelligent opinion on the inventory, because of his limited knowledge of the internal control and accounting procedures and his lack of technical knowledge of the business.

XI. Conclusion

The foregoing discussion of the problems or questions that are encountered by the auditor in the verification of the existence of assets has not at all exhausted the subject. There are many fields that require further exploration and investigation. There are other areas where there are still differences of opinion between equally competent professional auditors. It is to be hoped that this Seventh International Congress of Accountants through the interchange of ideas among people of good will will aid in the further development of a relatively new, but most needed profession.

INLEIDING

van

R. BURGERT, EC. DRS.

Vereniging van Academisch Gevormde Accountants

I. Begrip Inventarisatie

Bij inventariseren gaan de gedachten onwillekeurig uit naar het inventariseren van goederenvoorraden; wij geven er echter de voorkeur aan het begrip inventarisatie in ruimer verband te bezien en het vraagstuk te behandelen met betrekking tot alle activa in de onderneming. Wij willen nl. onder inventariseren verstaan het kwantitatief waarnemen van de activa der onderneming ter toetsing van de juistheid van de voorstelling in de administratie van de hoeveelheid van deze activa. Wij beperken ons daarbij tot het hoeveelheidsgezichtspunt en laten het waarderingsprobleem buiten beschouwing.

II. De plaats van inventarisatie in het controleplan bij de controle ter certificering van de jaarrekening

A. Algemeen

Bij de controle van de jaarrekening wordt aan de inventarisatie veelal een belangrijke rol toegedacht bij de controle van de balans. Wij moeten echter bedenken, dat de accountantsverklaring niet alleen betrekking heeft op de balans, maar tevens op de daarbij behorende resultatenrekening. Dit heeft tot gevolg, dat de accountantscontrole meer omvat dan een zelfstandige controle der individuele balansposten en dat zij antwoord moet geven op de vraag of de omzettingen in de verschillende vermogensbestanddelen, welke uit de verrichte beheersdaden voortvloeien, in de jaarrekening als geheel gezien, op de juiste wijze zijn weergegeven. Daarbij is de resultatenrekening te beschouwen als een voorstelling van de verrichte beheersdaden, die invloed hebben op de grootte van het vermogen, terwijl de balans te beschouwen is als een specificatie van het eindvermogen, welke, uitgaande van een ook in samenstelling gegeven beginvermogen, op rekenkundig juiste wijze voortvloeit uit de verrichte beheersdaden. De accountantscontrole moet zich dan ook richten op het gehele omzettingsproces geld–goederen–geld. Wij willen, met het doel de functie van de inventarisatie in het geheel van controlemaatregelen duidelijk te maken, het controleplan in een – voorlopig eenvoudig – handelsbedrijf bespreken.

B. Controleplan handelsbedrijf

Aannemende, dat alleen contante zaken worden gedaan, en geen andere vermogensbestanddelen aanwezig zijn dan goederenvoorraad en geld, is de gehele kringloop als volgt voor te stellen:

	begin-balans	*transacties*	*eind-balans*	
goederen-beweging	BV +	QI — QV	= EV	(in hoeveelheden)
		resultatenrekening		
geld-beweging	BS +	VG — IG	= ES	(in geld)

waarin: BV = beginvoorraad (hoeveelheden en waarde)
QI = inkopen in quantiteiten
QV = verkopen in quantiteiten
EV = eindvoorraad (hoeveelheden en waarde)
VG = verkopen in geld
IG = inkopen in geld
BS = beginsaldo
ES = eindsaldo

(De schematisch bedoelde aanduiding der Resultatenrekening is uiteraard alleen juist in het geval van gelijkblijvende voorraad.)

Voor het vervolg wordt aangenomen, dat de posten uit de beginbalans gecontroleerde grootheden zijn, hetgeen bij doorlopende controle ook het geval is.

De accountantscontrole behoort gebaseerd te zijn op een volkomen determinering van beide vergelijkingen, welke determinering verkregen is, wanneer telkens drie van de vier termen gedetermineerd zijn. Het is onverschillig, welke drie termen door de controlewerkzaamheden zullen worden gedetermineerd; doelmatigheidsoverwegingen zullen de keuze der te determineren factoren beheersen. Inkopen en verkopen komen in beide formules voor, daardoor omvat de controle maximaal:

1. inkopen
2. verkopen
3. eindvoorraad goederen
4. eindsaldo geldvoorraad.

a. Controle goederenbeweging

1. *Inkopen*

De juistheid der geboekte inkopen kan gecontroleerd worden aan de hand van externe stukken: de inkoopfacturen. Ten aanzien van de kwantitatieve juistheid der geboekte inkopen vormen de inkoopfacturen een absoluut bewijs, mits voor elke inkoopfactuur de afgescheiden bewaarfunctie heeft verklaard, dat de in de inkoopfactuur vermelde goederen inderdaad zijn ontvangen en mits ook kwaliteitscontrole heeft plaatsgevonden.

Om aansluiting te krijgen bij de controleformule der geldbeweging moet tevens worden gecontroleerd, dat het rekenkundig verband tussen kwantiteit, prijs en geldsom op de inkoopfacturen juist is en dat de inkoopsprijzen aanvaardbaar zijn.

2. *Verkopen*

De controle op de verkopen is moeilijker dan die op de inkopen. Het handelsgebruik brengt mee, dat de verkoper de verkooprekeningen uitstuurt; daardoor kan de controle op de verkopen niet op basis van externe stukken geschieden. Nog belangrijker is, dat het gevaar van onvolledigheid der registratie bij de verkopen groter is dan bij de inkopen. Volledigheid der geregistreerde inkopen voorlopig veronderstellende, is het daarom doelmatig de verkopen uit de formule der goederenbeweging als onbekende te nemen en de formule dus zo te stellen:

$$QV = BV + QI - EV.$$

Inventarisatie van de eindvoorraad, gepaard gaande met detailcontrole op de inkopen stelt ons in staat de verkopen kwantitatief te controleren.

Er dient dan nog verband gelegd te worden met de geldbeweging; daartoe moet QV in de in kwantiteiten luidende formule worden omgerekend in geld, hetgeen beoordeling van de verkoopprijzen noodzakelijk maakt. In zeer eenvoudige gevallen kan de totale geldomzet onmiddellijk worden bepaald door de gevonden verkochte kwantiteit te vermenigvuldigen met de verkoopsprijs. Bij wisselende verkoopsprijzen of bij bepaalde stelstels van kortingen kan echter detailcontrole op de verkoop noodzakelijk zijn. Nadat de identiteit van QI en IG enerzijds en van QV en VG anderzijds in de beide formules van geld- en goederenbeweging is vastgesteld, zijn beide formules volkomen gecontroleerd.

b. Plaats van de inventarisatie in het controleplan

Uit het bovenstaande volgt, dat de inventarisatie niet een op zichzelf staand controlemiddel is, maar een schakel in een sluitend geheel van controlemiddelen. De gehele controlearbeid is gericht op de determinering van – in ons geval voorlopig – twee vergelijkingen; deze determinering is verkregen, indien van n termen er n–1 gedetermineerd zijn. De keuze van de onbekende term is een vraag van doelmatigheid. Daaruit vloeit voort, dat de verkopen in de formule der goederenbeweging, zoals hierboven omschreven, als onbekende wordt genomen. Een tweede doelmatigheidsgrond schuilt in het feit, dat een goedkeurende accountantsverklaring mede dekt de aanwezigheid en het bestaan van de op de balans verschijnende voorraad goederen en geld.

Daarom bevat het controleplan:

1. controle van de inkopen;
2. inventarisatie der voorraden geld en goederen.

Bij de controle van de registratie van het omloopproces komt uiteraard ook de vraag op, of de registratie volledig is. In het kader van het besproken controleplan kan de vraag naar volledigheid alleen betrekking hebben op de inkoop.

Volledigheid der inkopen werd dan ook uitdrukkelijk voor-ondersteld. Onvolledigheid van òf inkopen òf verkopen zou niet onontdekt blijven, slechts compenserende onvolledigheid van inkopen èn verkopen beide zou zich aan het oog van de accountant onttrekken. De accountantscontrole kan nl., mathematisch gesproken, wel concluderen tot volledigheid van de registratie van afhankelijke grootheden, echter niet tot volledigheid van de registratie van onafhankelijke grootheden. Ten aanzien van de laatste steunt zij uiteindelijk op de interne organisatie, terwijl hier ook de algemene regel geldt, dat de accountant niet verantwoordelijk kan zijn voor de juiste en volledige registratie van transacties, die hij niet heeft kunnen kennen.

c. Vorderingen en schulden

Wij veronderstelden contante betaling. Wanneer wij deze veronderstelling laten vallen, moeten we de twee formules als volgt wijzigen:

1. goederenbeweging : $BV + QI - QV = EV$
2. beweging der schulden : $BS + IG - U = ES$
3. beweging der vorderingen : $BS + VG - O = ES$
4. geldbeweging : $BV + O - U = EV$

waarin U = betaling van schulden
O = ontvangst van debiteuren.

De formule der goederenbeweging is onveranderd gebleven, de formules 2, 3 en 4 betekenen slechts verdere detaillering van de formule der geldbeweging. Als nieuwe termen verschijnen U en O, en hier bestaat hetzelfde alternatief als ten aanzien van I en V: op in wezen dezelfde gronden, zal als regel detailcontrole der uitgaven de voorkeur verdienen.

In een het gehele omzettingsproces omvattend controleprogramma behoren dus voor te komen:

a. inventarisatie voorraden;
b. inventarisatie debiteurensaldo;
c. inventarisatie geldmiddelen.

Van inventarisatie der schulden wordt niet gesproken; dit wordt duidelijk, wanneer we de controleformule voor de beweging der schulden nog eens nader bezien:

$$BS + IG - U = ES.$$

IG is te ontlenen aan de formule der goederenbeweging en U aan de formule der geldbeweging. Het eindsaldo is dus volkomen gedetermineerd. Inventarisatie der schulden kan daaraan niets toevoegen; inventarisatie van activa heeft zin, omdat het te kwader trouw onttrekken van activa direct voordeel kan opleveren, hetgeen niet het geval is met het onttrekken van schulden. Detailcontrole der schulden op basis van de verrichte betalingen in de volgende periode vindt plaats als verificatie van de juistheid der individuele crediteuren-rekeningen.

c. Controleplan produktie-onderneming

Wanneer wij onze abstractie verder verminderen en thans overstappen op produktie-ondernemingen, dan ontstaat de noodzaak, de formule voor de goederenbeweging verder te detailleren, zonder dat daarvan enige invloed uitgaat op de formules der beweging van vorderingen en schulden en de geldbeweging. Deze detaillering is als volgt uit te werken:

grondstof: BV + QI — EV = QM.
produktie: BV + QM — EV = V.

waarin QM = materiaalverbruik.

Andere produktiekosten dan materiaalverbruik laten wij in deze inleiding buiten beschouwing. De formule voor de grondstoffen is volkomen identiek met die voor de goederenbeweging der handelsonderneming. Het enige nieuwe gezichtspunt is, dat de omzetting van materiaalverbruik in produkt moet worden gecontroleerd. We kunnen hierop niet uitvoerig ingaan en daarom volstaan we met de opmerking, dat de controle op deze omzetting behoort te berusten op calculatienormen, welke in het onderzoek moeten worden betrokken. Behalve de voorraad grondstoffen moet ook de voorraad eindprodukten geïnventariseerd worden. Het feit echter, dat de produktie tijd kost, doet bovendien voorraden goederen in bewerking ontstaan. Doelmatige organisatie der produktie brengt vaak mee, dat het produktieproces in fasen wordt gesplitst, waarbij elke fase als een op zichzelf staand produktieproces beschouwd wordt. Naast een voorraad gereed produkt ontstaan dan goederen in bewerking en voorraden halffabrikaat, welke echter niet tot principiële veranderingen aanleiding geven.

d. Inventarisatie overige activa

Tot nu toe hadden onze beschouwingen slechts betrekking op de controle van de omloop van het vlottend bedrijfskapitaal. Daarenboven kunnen we nog te maken krijgen met vaste activa en beleggingen. Ook voor deze activa is de inventarisatie geen op zichzelf staand controlemiddel. Het ontstaan in hoeveelheid en soort der hier bedoelde activa blijkt bij de controle der geldbeweging. Inventarisatie van deze activa is naast controlemiddel op het werkelijk bestaan van in de balans vermelde bezittingen tevens een middel tot controle van de volledigheid der geldontvangsten, omdat tegenover het *niet meer* aanwezig zijn van vroeger wel aanwezige activa de ontvangst van een corresponderend bedrag aan geld of andere waarden geconstateerd moet worden.

III. Techniek der inventarisatie in het kader van de controle der jaarrekening

Wij zijn thans gekomen tot een bespreking van de techniek der inventarisatie, waarbij wij zullen trachten antwoord te geven op de vragen *wanneer, hoe vaak* en *hoe* de verschillende vermogensbestanddelen geïnventariseerd moeten worden.

Onze voorgaande beschouwingen houden reeds een antwoord in op de vraag, *wanneer* geïnventariseerd moet worden. Wij spraken nl. steeds van inventarisatie van de *eind*voorraad, van het *eind*saldo. Integrale inventarisatie op de balansdatum vloeit logisch voort uit de controle van het gehele omloopproces. Slechts bij volledige inventarisatie op één moment wordt de zekerheid verkregen, dat tijdelijke substitutie van het ene goed in het andere, met het doel een tekort te bemantelen, niet mogelijk is c.q. niet onontdekt kan blijven. Daar echter ook inventarisatie tijd kost, wordt dit ideaal slechts in uitzonderingsgevallen benaderd. Het principe heeft echter betekenis, omdat het ons leert, dat aan niet volledig simultane inventarisatie risico's verbonden zijn. Deze risico's zijn groter, naarmate de aard van de te inventariseren activa een grotere mogelijkheid van substitutie inhoudt. Naar dit gezichtspunt zou men de posten, welke normaliter op de balans voorkomen, in de volgende groepen kunnen onderscheiden, waarbij echter in het kader van deze inleiding niet naar volledigheid kan worden gestreefd:

1. *Geldmiddelen, de geldvorm naderende vorderingen* (bank/girotegoeden), *waardepapieren aan toonder*

Hier zijn de substitutiemogelijkheden zo groot, dat simultane inventarisatie zo goed mogelijk benaderd moet worden door integrale inventarisatie op de balansdatum. Een gelukkige omstandigheid is, dat inventarisatie dezer activa vrij snel kan verlopen; soms omvat de inventarisatie niet meer dan het kennisnemen van bevestigingen van derden-bewaarders met niet betwijfelbare betrouwbaarheid (banken bijv.). De grote mate van substitueerbaarheid en ten dele de zeer talrijke mutaties brengen voorts mee, dat ter verkrijging van een check op de interne controle inventarisatie meerdere malen per jaar gewenst is met daarop aansluitend detailcontrole in a-chronologische volgorde.

Een aanwijzing voor de aanwezigheid van periodieke opbrengsten gevende waardepapieren wordt reeds verkregen door de regelmatige verantwoording dezer opbrengsten. Toch kan inventarisatie niet gemist worden, gedeeltelijk op grond van mogelijke vervreemding tussen vervaldag en tijdstip van inventarisatie, gedeeltelijk door de mogelijkheid van verpanding zonder dat deze invloed heeft op de verkrijging der periodieke baten.

2. *Tot het vlottend bedrijfskapitaal behorende roerende goederen*

Tot deze groep behoren de goederenvoorraden: grondstoffen, halffabrikaten, gerede produkten, handelsgoederen. Hier is de substitutiemogelijkheid belangrijk kleiner dan bij de eerste groep, de inventarisatie echter veel moeilijker en tijdrovender. Beide omstandigheden leiden er vaak toe, dat de eis van absolute simultaneïteit niet gehandhaafd wordt. Men komt dan tot de volgende mogelijkheden, waarbij aan de interne controle hogere eisen te stellen zijn naarmate men zich verder van volledige, simultane inventarisatie verwijdert.

a. Inventarisatie gedurende een kortere of langere periode rond de balansdatum, met aanvullende controle op de mutaties, welke zich gedurende de inventarisatieperiode voordoen;

b. Permanent partiële inventarisatie. Daarbij wordt meerdere malen per jaar telkens een gedeelte van de voorraden geïnventariseerd, zodanig, dat gedurende het gehele boekjaar alle goederen minstens één keer worden opgenomen. De gedeelten van de voorraad, welke in één keer worden geïnventariseerd, worden gekozen met inachtneming van het gezichtspunt der substitueerbaarheid. Uit deze partiële inventarisatie kan de overtuiging geput worden, dat de voorraadadministratie voortdurend, en dus ook op de balansdatum, de werkelijke voorraad aangeeft.

Onder ideale organisatorische omstandigheden en bij perfecte interne controle is het denkbaar, dat de overtuiging van overeenstemming tussen voorraad en voorraadadministratie aan de interne controle wordt ontleend. Hierbij toetst de accountant de interne controle voortdurend door inventarisatie van daartoe gekozen goederen, gepaard gaande met detailcontrole van mutaties, liggende kort vóór en na het inventarisatietijdstip. Het gedeeltelijk werken in omgekeerde volgorde, nl. uitgaan van de goederen en daarna de registratie in de voorraadadministratie opzoeken, verdient aanbeveling. Bij de keuze der te inventariseren goederen moet er weer rekening mede gehouden worden, dat goederen, welke onderling vrij gemakkelijk substitueerbaar zijn, gezamenlijk worden geïnventariseerd. Het overvalselement is, indien toetsing der interne controle op de voorgrond staat, van groot belang. Dit element ontbreekt volkomen bij inventarisatie op vooraf vaststaande tijdstippen.

In sommige gevallen is het mogelijk en/of gewenst de inventarisatie te vervangen door alternatieve controlemiddelen. Afloopcontrole is doeltreffend, wanneer de voorraad i.v.m. onvermijdelijke seizoensfluctuaties in de aanvoer, produktie of afzet, na de balansdatum tot nul nadert. Ook voor goederen in bewerking komt afloopcontrole in aanmerking en wel sterker, naarmate de aard van het produktieproces meer nadert tot het uiterste geval van langdurige stukproduktie. Identificatie en waardering lopen hierbij ongemerkt in elkaar over. Men kan dan uitgaan van de registratie der kosten per order, welke, na vaststelling van het stadium van voortgang, vergeleken kunnen worden met de voorcalculatie. Advies van technische deskundigen, externe of interne, mits organisatorisch vrijstaande van produktie en registratie, is vaak nodig. Constatering der financiële afwikkeling na de balansdatum is echter meestal doeltreffender.

Tenslotte zijn er goederen, welker identificatie zo moeilijk is, dat bijstand van deskundigen bij de inventarisatie niet gemist kan worden.

3. *Tot de vaste activa behorende roerende goederen*

Tot deze groep rekenen we de roerende goederen, zoals machines, transportmiddelen, meubilair, etc. Deze hebben een lange omlooptijd, relatief weinig mutaties en de substitutiemogelijkheid varieert van vrij groot tot zeer gering. Hier is ook nog te onderscheiden tussen 'directe' produktiemiddelen en meer 'indirecte'. Bij een volledige bezettingsgraad volgt de voortdurende aanwezigheid van de eerste groep via de standaard-calculatie reeds uit de bereikte produktie en in die omstandigheden treedt de inventarisatie als controlemiddel dan ook sterk op de achtergrond. Ontbreken de geschetste voorwaarden, dan vervaagt de grens tussen beide groepen en is inventarisatie niet te vermijden. Voorwaarde daarvoor is administratieve individualisering der verschillende objecten. Het is als beproeving van de interne controle vaak gewenst de inventarisatie voor een deel te verrichten, uitgaande van de administratie en voor een ander deel uitgaande van de objecten zelf om daarna de opneming in de administratie te verifiëren. Wat de frequentie der inventarisatie betreft, lijkt een programma, waarin gedurende een periode, gelijk aan de kortst voorkomende levensduur, alle activa één keer worden opgenomen, bij goede interne organisatie voldoende.

Aanvullende controle wordt verkregen door verband te leggen met de polis van brandverzekering en daarbij behorende taxatierapporten.

4. *Onroerende goederen*

Bij onroerende goederen culmineren de sub 3 genoemde eigenschappen; er komen echter twee nieuwe juridische kenmerken bij. Het eerste is, dat hier bezit niet geldt als volkomen eigendomstitel. De rechtsregels, welke bij de overdracht van onroerend goed in acht genomen moeten worden en de vraag, hoe het eigendomsrecht van onroerend goed bewezen kan worden, zijn niet in alle landen dezelfde. Hierop kunnen wij niet nader ingaan. Voor ons land geldt, dat kennisneming van het eigendomsbewijs, als regel een notariële koopakte, aangevuld moet worden met een recherche naar de inschrijving in de openbare registers. De inventarisatie krijgt daardoor een formeel karakter. Omtrent de gewenste frequentie der 'inventarisatie' is van belang, hoe de bevoegdheid tot vervreemding (en bezwaring, waarover straks) bij de te controleren onderneming is geregeld. Ligt deze in handen van één persoon, dan is jaarlijkse recherche naar de toestand op de balansdatum vereist. Is deze zo geregeld, dat voor vervreemding (en bezwaring) de medewerking nodig is van een toezichthoudend orgaan (als regel de raad van commissarissen), dan geeft kennisneming van de notulen van de vergaderingen dezer organen al een aanknopingspunt. In dat geval is eigendomsonderzoek met grotere intervallen dan een jaar verantwoord te achten.

Het tweede juridische kenmerk is, dat onroerende goederen bezwaard kunnen worden. Controle-technisch kan men bezwaring gelijk stellen met partiële vervreemding. Daarom is onderzoek naar de bezwaardheid, welke eveneens blijkt uit openbare registers, nodig. Omtrent de frequentie gelden dezelfde overwegingen als omtrent de constatering van de eigendom zijn gegeven.

5. *Onlichamelijke zaken*

Wij ontmoeten hier allereerst:

a. handelsvorderingen

Voor de inventarisatie van vorderingen geldt, dat het bestaan der individuele vorderingen kan worden afgeleid uit hun voldoening na de balansdatum (afloopcontrole). Kan de afloop niet binnen een aanvaardbare termijn worden geconstateerd, dan moet men overgaan tot de controle van het ontstaan der vordering, aangevuld met beoordeling van de vraag, of de rechtsverhouding tot de debiteur meebrengt, dat de vordering terecht nog niet is voldaan. Deze werkzaamheden hebben nog als nevenfunctie, dat zij kunnen leiden tot een oordeel over de vraag, of in de loop der controleperiode de boekingen op de individuele debiteurenrekeningen juist zijn geweest.

Naarmate men meer kan rekenen op de medewerking van de overige deelnemers aan het economisch verkeer, komt naast de bovenbeschreven techniek het gebruik van saldobevestigingen in aanmerking. Voor vorderingen, welke resultaat zijn van rekening-courantverhoudingen is dat zelfs noodzakelijk, omdat ten aanzien van deze vorderingen de afloop/ontstaanscontrole niet mogelijk is. Saldobiljetten verdienen de voorkeur in landen, waar betaling met cheques overheerst. Bij overwegend giroverkeer is de afloopcontrole niet minder effectief te achten.

Veelal vormen de handelsdebiteuren een zo omvangrijk complex, dat het doelmatig kan zijn het onderzoek naar het bestaan der geregistreerde individuele vorderingen op de balansdatum te vervangen door een frequente, onregelmatige, partiële toetsing gedurende de controleperiode van de te boek staande vorderingen. Hierbij kan zowel de techniek van de afloop/ontstaanscontrole worden toegepast als die van de saldobevestigingen. Evenals bij de partiële voorraadopname veronderstelt deze werkwijze een sterke interne controle.

b. Overige vorderingen

Ten aanzien van vorderingen, niet voortvloeiende uit de regelmatige stroom van goederen of diensten, is de saldobevestiging het enig mogelijke controlemiddel. Evenals bij effecten geldt, dat de regelmatige verantwoording van periodieke baten bij rentedragende vorderingen de inventarisatie niet overbodig maakt.

c. Vorderingen, belichaamd in een hoogwaardig waardepapier

Wij hebben hier op het oog wissels, accepten, e.d., welke de crediteur bepaalde bewijsrechtelijke voordelen bezorgen en waarbij betaling nooit plaats vindt zonder uitlevering van het waardepapier. Het bestaan der vorderingen wordt door de betreffende waardepapieren volledig bewezen.

d. Vorderingen, belichaamd in gewoon incassopapier

Het incassopapier als intern geproduceerd stuk heeft onvoldoende gezag om het bestaan der vordering te bewijzen. Inventarisatie van dit papier heeft dan ook geen andere betekenis dan van beproeving der interne organisatie.

e. Vorderingen, waarvoor zekerheid gesteld is

Naast de controle op het bestaan dezer vorderingen zelf is, indien zij als zodanig in de balans worden vermeld, controle van het onderpand nodig; deze kan omvatten:

1e. verificatie van inschrijving in openbare registers;
2e. inventarisatie onderpanden;
3e. verificatie garantieverklaringen, borgtochten.

6. *Immateriële waarden*

Het feitelijk bestaan dezer waarden op een bepaald tijdstip is alleen doeltreffend te controleren, wanneer zij betreffen in openbare registers ingeschreven rechten (merkenrecht, octrooirecht). Het verifiëren aan de hand van de verkrijgingscontracten is overigens de enig mogelijke controle, hoewel daardoor vaak geen zekerheid wordt verkregen omtrent de vraag, of sedert de verkrijging geen vervreemding zonder verantwoording van de tegenwaarde heeft plaats gevonden.

7. *Activa, eigendom van derden*

Vaak komt de figuur voor, dat de onderneming houder of bezitter is van activa, die aan derden in eigendom toebehoren, zonder dat dit verband houdt met de essentie der bedrijfsvoering zoals dat bijv. bij een veem het geval is.

Ten aanzien van het inventarisatie-vraagstuk behoort geen onderscheid gemaakt te worden tussen deze activa en die, welke eigendom der onderneming zijn. De hierbedoelde waarden van derden behoren bewaard en geadministreerd te worden op dezelfde wijze als de goederen, welke wel eigendom der onderneming zijn. De rechtsverhouding tot de eigenaar behoort als verplichting te worden geregistreerd, ook al is het niet algemeen gebruikelijk de betreffende waarden, alsmede de corresponderende verplichtingen in de balans tot uitdrukking te brengen. Ze zijn bij de inventarisatie volledig in aanmerking te nemen. Controle-technisch klemt dit te meer, wanneer het gaat om waarden, welke substitueerbaar zijn met soortgelijke of zelfde waarden, welke wel eigendom der onderneming zijn.

IV. Betrekkelijke betekenis van de inventarisatie van goederenvoorraden als controlemiddel en aanvullende controlemiddelen

In de rijk geschakeerde werkelijkheid zijn er vele situaties, waarin de betekenis van controle-arbeid slechts betrekkelijk is. Ondanks dit algemene gezichtspunt, moeten we hier toch nog aandacht schenken aan de betrekkelijke betekenis van de inventarisatie als controlemiddel.

Alleen in eenvoudige gevallen, d.w.z. waar de identificatie geen moeilijkheden biedt, de telling niet veel tijd kost, aanvoer en afvoer tijdelijk geblokkeerd of eenvoudig geregistreerd kunnen worden, kan inventarisatie in de zin van waarnemen en tellen volkomen doeltreffend zijn. Aan deze voorwaarden is heel vaak in meerdere of mindere mate niet voldaan. Het is daarom ook niet mogelijk, dat de accountant een absolute verantwoordelijkheid voor de juistheid der voorraadcijfers kan aanvaarden. Deze verantwoordelijkheid kan niet anders dan relatief zijn, variërende met de aard der goederen, de omvang van de voorraad en de overige omstandigheden. Hoe zwaarder deze factoren aan de mate van zekerheid afdoen, hoe meer de nadruk gelegd moet worden op aanvullende (niet: alternatieve) controlemiddelen. Deze bestaan in hoofdzaak uit een beoordeling van het voorraadcijfer, in zijn geheel, groepsgewijze of zelfs per goederensoort, op aanvaardbaarheid binnen het geheel van de bedrijfsuitoefening. Zonder dit aanvullend onderzoek uitputtend hier te kunnen behandelen, wijzen wij op de volgende mogelijkheden, welke zich t.a.v. de goederenvoorraden voordoen:

1. vergelijking werkelijke voorraad met gebudgetteerde voorraad als resultante van beginvoorraad – inkoopbudget en verkoopbudget;
2. onderzoek van de goederenbeweging in de volgende controleperiode;
3. bepaling van de omzetsnelheid en vergelijking van dit kengetal met ervaringscijfers;
4. idem bruto-winstmarge;
5. onderzoek naar de waarschijnlijkheid van speculatieve voorraden op grond van het prijsverloop.

V. INVENTARISATIE BIJ ONDERZOEKEN MET BIJZONDERE DOELSTELLING

Deze onderzoeken hebben meestal een eenmalig karakter. Daardoor is inventarisatie van alle terzake doende activa op één bepaald tijdstip vaak de enig mogelijke werkwijze. Bovendien vloeit uit het incidentele karakter van het contact met de te controleren onderneming voort, dat de kwaliteit van de interne organisatie en interne controle buiten het gezichtsveld van de accountant komt te liggen; deze omstandigheid brengt ook mede, dat bij investigations de medewerking van deskundigen eerder nodig is dan bij de doorlopende controle van de jaarrekening. Het principe van de simultaneïteit moet daarom als regel ten volle in aanmerking worden genomen.

Het controleplan wordt mede ingesteld op de vraag, bij welke onjuiste voorstelling de gecontroleerde onderneming belang heeft. Bij de controle der jaarrekening langs de lijnen van de gegeven formules is inventarisatie een positief controlemiddel tot vaststelling van een der grootheden uit de kringloopformule. Het belang bij onjuiste voorstelling van de grootte van bepaalde activa kan er bij investigations toe leiden, dat controle van de omvang dezer activa negatief moet geschieden en dan is inventarisatie een ongeschikt controlemiddel. Ter verduidelijking noemen wij als voorbeeld het geval van een onderzoek naar de juistheid van de omzet, waarbij de onderneming belang heeft deze zo hoog mogelijk voor te stellen. Ook in dat geval zou men zich op het eerste gezicht kunnen baseren op controle door middel van de formule $BV + QI - EV = QV$. Het belang van de gecontroleerde onderneming zou er toe kunnen leiden, dat $BV + QI$ zo groot mogelijk, en EV zo klein mogelijk wordt voorgesteld. Het is duidelijk, dat men dan de eindvoorraad niet door inventarisatie kan controleren, omdat het eenvoudig is een stuk van de voorraad aan de waarneming van de accountant te onttrekken. Bij investigations is dan ook de plaats van de inventarisatie in het controleplan niet zonder meer gelijk te stellen aan die bij de controle van de jaarrekening. Het doel van het bijzonder onderzoek is daarvoor beslissend en er is een zo grote veelheid van doelstellingen denkbaar, dat een uitvoerige casuïstiek onvermijdelijk zou zijn. De noodzakelijk beperkte omvang van deze inleiding laat deze behandelingswijze niet toe.

Translation

PAPER

by

R. BURGERT, EC. DRS.

Vereniging van Academisch Gevormde Accountants, Netherlands

I. Conception of Stocktaking

In using the term 'stocktaking' we normally think of the listing of stock in trade but here it is preferred to use 'taking stock' in a broader sense as relating to all the assets of an undertaking. Taking stock in this broader sense is the observation in quantities of the assets in order to verify the accuracy of the figures given by the books. In this way we restrict ourselves to quantities only and leave out any question of valuation.

II. The place of Stocktaking in the Audit Programme for the Annual Accounts

A. General

In the audit of the annual accounts an important place is usually given to stocktaking in so far as the balance sheet is concerned. We have to consider, however, quite rightly, that the auditor's report covers not only the balance sheet but the statement of income as well. Consequently the audit comprises more than checking the individual items of the balance sheet only: it has also to answer the question whether the movements of assets and liabilities during the period under review, are recorded correctly. Moreover, the statement of income has to be considered as presenting the results of transactions which affect the size of the company's net assets or business capital, whereas the balance sheet has to be considered as a specification of the net assets or business capital at the closing date which, proceeding from an initial business capital has emerged with arithmetical correctness from the acts of management. Thus the audit has to direct its attention to the opening position, the whole process of mutation: cash–goods–cash, and the closing position. In order to make clear the place of 'taking stock' of assets in audit procedures, we will discuss first the audit programme for a trading company operating on very simple lines.

B. Audit programme of a trading company

Assuming that both purchases and sales are for cash and that no other assets exist apart from stocks and cash, the whole cycle of operations can be presented as follows:

Balance sheet beginning of year		Transactions of year	Balance sheet end of year	
Stocks:	OS +	GP — GS	= CS	Flow of goods
		Income-statement		
Cash:	OB +	MS — MP	= C B	Flow of money

in which O S = opening stock (quantities and value, the first equation, however, is in principle to be understood as running in quantities only)
GP = goods purchased in quantities
GS = goods sold in quantities
CS = closing stock (same qualification as given for O S)
MS = sales, expressed in money
MP = purchases, expressed in money (cost of goods sold)
OB = opening balance
CB = closing balance

(It should be noticed, that the above scheme of the income-statement is only correct in the case of stocks remaining constant.)

In what follows it is assumed, that the balance sheet at the beginning of the year was subject to audit in the previous year, which is indeed the case with a continuing audit.

The audit should be based on a full solution of both equations; this is obtained, when for each equation three of the four terms have been satisfactorily determined. It is immaterial which three of the four factors will be determined by the audit procedures: it is only a matter of expediency, which of the terms are chosen. Purchases and sales appear in both equations; as a maximum the audit comprises the examination of both quantities and values of purchases, sales, closing stocks and closing cash balance.

a. Auditing the flow of goods

1. *Purchases*

The correctness of the purchase records can be checked by making use of external documents, i.e. the vouchers. As far as the quantities are concerned, the vouchers are satisfactory proof, provided the storekeeper has declared for every invoice that the goods therein mentioned have been received and provided that both quantity and quality have been tested and approved.

In order to tie in with the equation-formula of the flow of money the arithmetical relationship between quantity, price and amount on the purchase vouchers must be checked and the prices examined to ensure that they are acceptable.

2. *Sales*

The audit of the sales is more difficult than that of the purchases. Commercial practice provides that invoices are sent by the seller; as a result the audit of the sales cannot be done on the basis of external documents. More important still, the danger of incompleteness in recording sales is greater than in the case of purchases. Therefore, assuming for the time being, that the purchases have been recorded accurately and completely, it is expedient to treat sales as the unknown factor in the equation of the flow of goods as follows:

$$GS = OS + GP - CS$$

Checking of the closing stock, together with a detailed examination of the purchases enables us to ascertain the quantities sold.

Relationship has still to be established between the flow of goods and the flow of money: to do this GS in the equation-formula of the quantities has to be converted into money (MS); and this makes it necessary to review the selling prices. In the simplest cases the total value of sales can be determined by multiplying the quantities sold by the selling prices. Varying sales prices or certain systems of allowances and discounts will, however, make a more detailed audit of money-sales necessary. When it has been established, that GP and MP on the one hand, and GS and MS on the other are identical in both equations these formulas of the flow of goods and of the flow of money will have been checked effectively.

b. Stocktaking in the audit programme

It follows from the above, that stocktaking is not an isolated audit procedure, but a link in a chain of audit procedures. In the example used the whole audit is aimed at determining the correctness of the two equations: this is obtained, when out of n factors n–1 have been determined. The choice which factor will be taken as unknown is a matter of expediency. For the above-mentioned reason the sales in the equation of the flow of goods, are being taken as the unknown factor. A second reason for choosing the sales as an unknown factor lies in the fact, that the auditor's report covers the verification of the existence of the stocks of goods and the cash balances appearing in the balance sheet.

Therefore the audit programme will include:

1. checking of the purchases,
2. verification of stocks of goods and cash balances.

Obviously, in checking the recording of the flow of goods, the question naturally arises, whether or not the records are complete. In the framework of the audit programme described above, the question of completeness can only refer to the purchases. That is why we deliberately assumed the completeness of the purchases. Incompleteness of either purchases or sales would be detected, only compensating omissions of purchases and sales might escape the auditor's notice. In general a proper audit can only ascertain the completeness of the records of dependent (in a mathematical sense) quantities and values when the completeness of any independent elements can be taken for granted, provided the relation between both is determinable. Assurance of the completeness of the purchases must be derived from an effective system of internal control. It goes without saying that the auditor cannot be held responsible for the correct recording of transactions which cannot possibly come to his attention when performing his audit with professional skill and care.

c. Accounts receivable and accounts payable

So far we have assumed payment in cash for purchases and sales. If we now drop this assumption, we have to extend the formulas as follows:

1. flow of quantity of goods : $OS + PQ - SQ = CS$
2. movements of payables : $OB + MP - O = CB$
3. movements of receivables: $OB + MS - R = CB$
4. flow of cash : $OB + R - O = CB$

in which: O = payments to creditors
R = receipts from debtors

The formula of the flow of goods has remained unchanged, formulas 2, 3 and 4 are only further extensions of the formula of the flow of cash. New factors are O and R, and here the same alternative exists as for P and S: for the same reasons detailed previously, the checking of the payments will be preferable to that of the receipts. In an audit programme which comprises the whole of the flow of goods and money, the following should be included:

a. verification of the existence of the stocks
b. verification of the existence of the accounts receivable
c. verification of the existence of the cash on hand

Nothing is said about taking stock of the accounts payable; this will become clear, when we further review the formula for the movement of the payables:

$$OB + MP - O = CB$$

MP can be derived from the formula of the flow of goods after verification of prices and O from the formula of the flow of cash. The closing balance is therefore completely determined. Nothing can be added thereto by verification of the existence of the payables.

There is sense in stocktaking of assets, because the taking away of assets may give a direct advantage to the person effecting same, which is not the case with payables. A detailed verification of payables by checking the accounts with payments effected in the following period serves to ascertain the correctness of the individual accounts payable only.

C. Audit programme of an industrial enterprise

When we broaden our outlook and turn to manufacturing undertakings, the formula for the flow of goods has to be further broken down:

$$\left.\begin{array}{ll}\text{raw materials:} & OS + GP = M + CS \\ \text{production} & : OS + M = GS + CS\end{array}\right\}\text{Quantities}$$

in which M = quantities used in manufacturing. The formulas for the movements of receivables, payables and the flow of cash are not affected.

Production costs other than usage of raw materials are ignored in this paper. The formula for raw materials is identical with the one for the flow of goods in a trading company. The only new aspect is, that the conversion of raw materials into finished products has to be checked, an aspect which cannot be dealt with in detail; suffice it to mention, that the check on this conversion should be based on costing standards.

Stocktaking not only applies to stocks of raw materials but also to stocks of finished products. However, as production takes time, there will always be work in progress too. Efficient organisation of production often involves the splitting up of the process into stages: and each stage may then be considered as a separate process. Apart from a stock of finished products, there will thus be a stock of work in progress and stocks of partly-manufactured articles. This, however, does not affect the principle involved.

D. Taking stock of other assets

Up till now, reference has only been made to the audit of movements in the current assets. Apart from those, we have to deal with fixed assets and investments too. Taking stock of the latter is, like the stocktaking of current assets, not an isolated audit procedure. The auditor will come across the quantity and the nature of any additions to these assets when auditing the flow of cash. Apart from being a check on the existence of assets shown in the balance sheet, stocktaking of these assets also supports the audit of cash receipts; assets which no longer exist, must have resulted in a corresponding receipt of cash or some other acceptable entry.

III. The Mechanics of Stocktaking in the Framework of the Audit of the Annual Accounts

Now the mechanics of stocktaking will be dealt with by answering the question *when*, *how often* and *how* stocktaking of the different assets should be done.

The previous considerations already included an answer to the question, *when;* all the time we have referred to stocktaking of the *closing* stock or *closing* balance. Stocktaking of all stocks on the date of the balance sheet is the ideal aim in auditing the flow of transactions. Only when all the stocktaking can be done simultaneously, can one be sure that temporary substitution of one asset by another, so as to cover up any shortage, has not taken place. As, however, stocktaking takes time, this goal can only be achieved in exceptional cases. The principle, however, has its merits, because it shows us, that every stocktaking which is not complete and simultaneous involves risks. If the nature of the assets permits easy substitution these risks become larger. From this angle we can broadly group the items, normally appearing in a balance sheet, as follows:

1. *Cash, cheques, bills, bearer securities, etc.*

The possibilities of substitution are here so great that stocktaking should come as near as possible to being simultaneous by carrying out a complete stocktaking on the date of the balance sheet. Fortunately, stocktaking of these assets can be done fairly quickly; in many cases the stocktaking can be reduced to seeing the confirmations of third parties with undoubted reputation (e.g. banks). In those cases where substitution can easily be effected and where there is a rapid conversion of the assets concerned, it is necessary to undertake in addition to the normal year-end checks some interim checks according to circumstances. It is essential that such interim checks should be on a 'surprise' basis, preferably linked with other, more detailed checks.

Income in the form of interest and dividends etc. derived from the various assets provides an additional evidence of their existence, but because of various circumstances which may arise, such as sales of such assets, or their being charged as security for a loan between the due date of the income and the closing accounting date, stocktaking must still take place.

2. *Other current assets*

In this category we reckon stocks of goods such as raw materials, partly finished products, finished products, trading stock etc. The possibility of substitution is appreciably smaller than with the assets dealt with in the previous paragraph. Stocktaking, however, is much more difficult and takes much more time. Consequently the principle of strict simultaneousness will not always be adhered to.

The more the system adopted deviates from the strict simultaneous process the tighter the system of internal control must be. Accordingly the following alternatives can be distinguished:

a. Stocktaking carried out during a longer or shorter period round about the date of the balance sheet, with supporting check on the movements arising during the period concerned.

b. Continuous stocktaking during the year, each time covering only some part of the stock in accordance with a timetable, so that by the year-end all parts of the stock have been covered at least once. The goods to be examined at the same time should be so chosen as to avoid the possibility of substitution.

This partial continuous stocktaking may give us the conviction that the records will show continuously, and consequently also on the date of the balance sheet, the actual stock on hand.

In the case of a well-organized system of internal control, it may be possible to rely on internal control for assurance that the stock-records are in accordance with the actual stocks. In this case the auditor must test the system periodically by stocktaking of selected articles, together with a detailed check of the movements immediately before and after the time of stocktaking. It is preferable to vary the method of approach occasionally by starting from the goods and subsequently looking for the entries in the stockrecords and vice-versa. In selecting the articles to be tested, it should be borne in mind, that articles which can be easily substituted, should be examined simultaneously. The surprise element is very important for testing the system of internal control. This element is non-existent in the case of stocktaking on dates fixed in advance.

In some cases it is possible and/or desirable to replace the stocktaking with alternative audit procedures. A check on ultimate disposition can be very effective particularly in the case when owing to seasonal fluctuations in supply, production or turnover, the stock diminishes to practically nothing after the

BEFORE THE OPENING SESSION

H.R.H. The Prince of the Netherlands greeting
Sir Harold G. Howitt, G.B.E., D.S.O., M.C., D.C.L., F.C.A.,
President of the Sixth Congress in London in 1952

BEFORE THE DELEGATES' DINNER

H.R.H. The Prince of the Netherlands speaking with
Mr. Arthur B. Foye, U.S.A. and with the President, Mr. J. Kraayenhof

date of the balance sheet. A check on the subsequent disposition is also advisable on goods in the course of production and more so when the manufacturing process bears the nature of a prolonged piece-production, such as shipbuilding etc. Identification and valuation merge into each other unnoticed. The starting point may then be the cost records for every order, which after the measure of progress has been ascertained, may be compared with the budget. It is often necessary to obtain advice from external or internal technical experts; the latter should, if possible, be independent both of production and bookkeeping. However, it is usually more effective to establish the financial settlement after the date of the balance sheet.

Finally there are items which are so difficult to identify that help from experts cannot be avoided in carrying out a stocktaking.

3. *Fixed assets transferable by delivery*

Generally the following assets belong to this category: machinery, transport-vehicles, furniture etc. They have a comparatively long life and are rarely convertible into other assets, while the possibility of substitution varies considerably. Distinction should be made between means of production which are more of a direct character and those which are more of an indirect character. When the factory is working at full capacity the quantity of the first category can be established on the basis of the output achieved by using costing standards: in these circumstances stocktaking as an audit procedure is of minor importance. When the conditions described above do not exist, the demarcation line disappears between the two categories and stocktaking cannot be avoided. It is essential for stocktaking that the different objects are clearly identifiable in the records. In order to test the system of internal control it is often desirable to vary the method of approach to the stocktaking, by starting partly from the records and partly from the assets. As far as the frequency of the stocktaking is concerned, it is considered that the period between two successive stocktakings covering all the assets, should be equal to the shortest life, provided the system of internal control is appropriate. Additional check is often obtained by comparison with valuation reports attached to fire insurance policies etc.

4. *Fixed assets transferable by deed*

The items under this category have as a general rule a long life, very few movements and small risk of substitution. However, as distinct from those in the previous paragraph two legal aspects arise. The first is that possession does not necessarily mean ownership. Legal rules, which have to be observed in conveying immovables together with the question of how the ownership of immovables can be proved, are not the same in all countries. We cannot discuss this in more detail. In the Netherlands it is necessary in the case of land and buildings, in addition to the inspection of the title deed (which is generally a deed drawn up by a notary-public), to obtain confirmation from the register of real estate. Stocktaking in this case therefore takes on a more formal character. As regards the frequency of taking stock, consideration should be given to the company's regulations that have been laid down as to the authority to alienate (or mortgage about which more will be stated later). If this authority is in the hands of one person only, confirmation of ownership should be obtained at the date of every balance sheet. If however the regulations are such that alienating (or mortgaging) is only possible through a supervisory body (as a rule the board of directors) then the minutes of the meetings making the decision will evidence a change immediately. In this case verification of ownership at longer intervals than one year may be considered adequate. The second legal aspect is that in the Netherlands immovables may be mortgaged; as far as the mechanics of auditing are concerned a mortgage may be considered as a partial alienation. Therefore verification of the mortgage-position is necessary, and this likewise appears from information obtained from the registrar of real estate. As far as the frequency is concerned, the same principles apply as those relating to ownership.

5. *Accounts receivable*

a. Trade-debts

The method of verification of the existence of these assets consists in checking the payments received subsequent to the date of the balance sheet. When payment has not taken place within a reasonable period, it is necessary to verify the origin of the receivable in question, incorporating a review of any special credit terms allowed to the customer. These procedures serve an additional purpose, in that they assist in forming an opinion as to whether the entries in the sales ledger during the period under review are correct. As an alternative to the procedures described above circularisation may be considered, provided there is co-operation from the other parties concerned. In the case of balances on current accounts circularisation is the only effective method, because in this case verification of origin and subsequent payment is impossible.

Circularisation is preferable in those countries where payments are usually made by cheque. Where payments are usually made by bank transfer (traders-credit) verification of subsequent payment can be considered as an equally effective check. In many cases the accounts receivable are very numerous. Then it may be expedient to substitute for verification on the balance sheet date, a system of frequent tests at irregular intervals during the period under review. Either of the two methods may then be applied. As in the case of continuous stocktaking a good system of internal control is essential.

b. Other accounts receivable

As regards accounts receivable not resulting from the regular flow of goods, circularisation is the only reliable procedure. As in the case of securities, reconciliation with periodical interests received does not imply that stocktaking can be disregarded.

c. Negotiable instruments

Under this heading we would classify bills of exchange, acceptances etc. which give certain legal advantages to the holder and in the case of which payment is never made without the handing over of the relative documents. The existence of these receivables is fully substantiated by the documents.

d. Receivables, incorporated in collection bills

The collection bill, being a document prepared internally, is not sufficient proof of the existence of the receivable: as a result stocktaking of these documents serves no other purpose than that of testing the internal organisation.

e. Accounts receivable, partly or wholly secured

When these receivables are shown as such in the balance sheet both the receivables themselves and the underlying security should be verified. This may involve:

1. verification of entry in any register open to the public
2. stocktaking of the underlying securities
3. verification of guarantees, pledges etc.

6. *Intangibles*

The existence of such assets can only be effectively verified, when they relate to rights entered in registers open to the public (trade marks, patent rights etc.). Otherwise verification by means of the contracts by which the rights have been acquired is the only other possibility. In these cases it is often difficult to be quite sure that no alienation of the asset has taken place.

7. *Assets, owned by third parties*

It often occurs, that the company has in its possession assets, which in fact belong to third parties, this being unconnected with the real character of the business, as is the case e.g. with a bonded warehouse. As regards the problem of stocktaking no distinction should be made between these assets and those belonging to the company. The assets of third parties should be kept and accounted for in the same way as goods which are the property of the company. The legal position vis à vis the owner should be recorded as a liability, although it is no general practice to account for these assets and corresponding liabilities in the official balance sheet. In stocktaking, however, they should be fully taken into account. As far as the mechanics of the audit are concerned this is more important still whether goods which are the property of the company, can be substituted by the goods owned by third parties.

IV. Relative Significance of Stocktaking of Stocks of Goods as an Audit Procedure and Additional Procedures

In practice many situations arise in which audit procedures have only a relative significance. Notwithstanding this general point of view, attention must nevertheless be paid to the relative significance of stocktaking as an audit procedure. Only in simple cases, that is to say where (*a*) identification presents no difficulty, (*b*) counting does not take much time, and (*c*) supply and despatch can be controlled during the period of the examination, can stocktaking in the sense of observation and counting be fully effective. Very often, however, these ideals do not exist all at the same time. Therefore it is frequently not possible for the auditor to take full responsibility for the correctness of stock figures. This responsibility can therefore only be a relative one, varying in respect of the nature of the goods, the size of the stocks and other circumstances.

The more these factors diminish the degree of certainty, the more stress has to be laid on additional (not alternative) audit procedures. These consist mainly of arriving at a well-founded judgement on the stockfigure either in total, per category or even per article. Without discussing these additional procedures in any detail, the following possibilities, which may be helpful, are suggested:

1. Comparison of actual stock with the budgetted stock resulting from the opening stock, the purchase budget, and the sales budget.
2. Review of the flow of goods in the next accounting period.
3. Comparison of the turnover speed with that of previous periods.
4. Comparison of gross profit margin with that of previous periods.
5. Examination of the probability of speculative stocks in consequence of price movements.

V. Stocktaking for Special Investigations

Investigations as a rule are for a specific purpose only; usually there is no repeat and they bring the auditor into contact with the company concerned only once. As a result stocktaking of all relevant assets simultaneously is usually the only possible procedure. Very often there is no ample opportunity to assess the quality of internal organization and control. This also entails the necessity of attracting more readily the assistance of specialists when making an investigation than in the regular audit of the annual accounts. The principle of simultaneousness has to be followed as closely as possible and the programme of work has to be drawn up keeping in mind the possibility of some misrepresentation of the figures in the interests of those whose undertaking is being investigated.

In auditing the annual accounts along the lines previously suggested, 'taking stock' is a reliable procedure to establish whether the presentation in the records of the flow of goods and of money during the year is correct and whether the balances at the year-end do exist. The existence of an interest to give an incorrect picture of the flow of goods and money and of the size of certain assets will, in the case of investigations, lead to a critical examination in order to ascertain whether all the assets have been completely accounted for and in those cases stocktaking is insufficient. To clear this point we give as an example the case of an examination of the correctness of the turnover, the business in question having an interest to state the turnover figure as high as possible. On the face of it, it might appear possible to base the examination on the formula $OS + GP - CS = GS$. The business concerned may like to state $OS + GP$ as high as possible, and CS as small as possible. It is clear that the size of the closing stock cannot be checked by means of a stocktaking, because it is quite easy to keep part of the stock away from the auditor's survey. In investigations therefore it is not always possible to attach to stocktaking the same purport in the audit programme as in the case of an audit of annual accounts. The terms of reference of the investigation are the deciding factors. However, there are so many types of investigation that it will be appreciated that the small scope of this paper cannot possibly deal with all of these problems.

RAPPORT

par

CLAUDE PAQUET, HEC.

Chambre Nationale des Experts Comptables diplômés par l'Etat, France

I. INTRODUCTION

Définition et utilité de l'inventaire

Le premier texte légal faisant mention de l'inventaire est l'ordonnance de Colbert de 1673 dont l'article 8 prescrit:

'Seront aussi tenus tous les marchands de faire dans le même délai de six mois (après la publication de la présente ordonnance) inventaire sous leur seing de tous leurs effets mobiliers et immobiliers et de leurs dettes actives et passives, lequel sera récolé et renouvellé de deux ans en deux ans'.

Lc Code de Commerce de 1807 reprend l'idée dans son article 9:

'Le commerçant est tenu de faire tous les ans, sous seing privé, un inventaire de ses effets mobiliers et immobiliers, et de ses dettes actives et passives, et de le copier, année par année, sur un registre spécial à ce destiné'.

Enfin un décret du 22 Septembre 1953 a modifié ce dernier article en stipulant:

'Elle (toute personne physique ou morale ayant la qualité de commerçant) doit également faire tous les ans un inventaire des éléments actifs et passifs de son entreprise et arrêter tous ses comptes en vue d'établir son bilan et le compte de ses pertes et profits. Le bilan et le compte 'Pertes et Profits' sont copiés sur le livre d'inventaire'.

Depuis 1673 un inventaire doit donc être effectué par les commerçants tous les deux ans, puis tous les ans depuis 1807. Mais aucune définition de l'inventaire n'a été donnée par la loi. En matière civile divers textes citent l'inventaire (mais sans jamais le définir) à propos des dissolutions de communauté, successions...

La définition de l'inventaire a été donnée soit dans des ouvrages de comptabilité, soit au cours de jugements. Je retiendrai celle donnée le 20 septembre 1884 par le Tribunal de Commerce de la Seine:

'L'inventaire est un relevé complet, sans lacunes ni omissions, un dénombrement détaillé, article par article, de tous les éléments, soit d'actif soit de passif; tout doit être appelé, examiné, chiffré'.

Dresser un inventaire consiste donc à établir une liste de *tous* les éléments, positifs (actif) ou négatifs (passif) du patrimoine d'une personne physique ou morale. Cette opération est rendue obligatoire pour les commerçants tant par la loi commerciale ou fiscale que par des considérations économiques afin de pouvoir 'faire le point', tout comme un capitaine de navire le fera chaque jour, et dégager le résultat obtenu entre deux inventaires successifs.

Tout comme le capitaine redressera éventuellement la marche de son navire pour rattraper l'écart constaté entre le but assigné et le point atteint, le commerçant qui se sera fixé un budget constatera un écart entre prévisions et réalisations et rectifiera en conséquence ses méthodes de gestion.

II. Généralités sur le contrôle de l'inventaire

a. But du contrôle

S'il est indispensable de dresser un inventaire, encore faut-il que celui-ci soit exact. Son contrôle s'impose pour être certain de son exactitude, et, partant, de celle des divers postes du bilan. Mais, à mon sens, il ne suffit pas de vérifier cette exactitude. Il faut connaître les raisons *profondes* de la modification, d'un inventaire à l'autre, des divers postes du bilan. Il ne suffit pas comme on le voit, hélas trop souvent, d'affirmer que le poste 'Immobilisations' par exemple, a augmenté parce que l'on a acheté des machines, ou que le poste 'Disponibilités' a diminué parce que l'on a moins d'argent. Ce sont là des vérités premières.

Il faut lier les diverses modifications constatées dans l'inventaire, d'une part entre elles (par exemple les Disponibilités ont diminué dans les mêmes proportions que les Dettes) et d'autre part avec les postes du bilan qui ne font pas l'objet de l'inventaire, tels que les réserves (par exemple les Disponibilités ont diminué parce que les réserves ont été distribuées) ou les Résultats[1] (par exemple les Disponibilités ont diminué par suite de pertes).

En un mot il faut rattacher les modifications des emplois entre elles et avec celles des origines.

On pourra alors se servir de l'inventaire des divers postes du bilan et des comptes d'exploitation et de résultats, pour obtenir une image dynamique de la vie de l'entreprise pendant une période donnée et non plus seulement aboutir à une position statique à un moment donné. C'est toute la différence qui existe entre le cinéma et la photographie.

D'autre part le contrôle de l'inventaire permettra de vérifier l'organisation interne de l'entreprise et les moyens mis en œuvre pour contrôler régulièrement les mouvements des biens à l'intérieur de celle-ci:

une augmentation exagérée de certains postes de l'actif (stocks par exemple) peut provenir d'une mauvaise organisation du service des achats ou l'on passe des commandes sans s'occuper de celles déjà passées par le voisin, ou (s'il s'agit des clients) d'une mauvaise organisation du service de recouvrement des créances. Ces faits doivent, semble-t-il, être signalés par le contrôleur aux ayants-droit de l'entreprise qui lui ont demandé d'en contrôler la gestion.

b. Objet du contrôle

Le plus souvent, lorsque l'on prononce le mot 'inventaire', on pense Valeurs

[1] A propos du poste 'Résultats', il est bien entendu que celui-ci doit être réparti en charges et produits d'exploitation et en pertes et profits hors exploitation.

d'exploitation c'est-à-dire Stocks. Evidemment l'inventaire des stocks est un des problèmes les plus délicats de l'inventaire, mais ce n'est pas le seul; et si l'on admet que l'inventaire de tout l'actif doit être effectué on pense plus rarement à vérifier le passif exigible. Ce point mérite cependant un contrôle sérieux.

Je n'ai pas l'intention de dresser ici la liste des biens et dettes à inventorier. Cela serait non seulement fastidieux, mais aussi inutile, car nous étudierons plus loin la manière de faire l'inventaire des divers chapitres apparaissant au bilan.

c. Epoques du contrôle

Diverses méthodes peuvent être envisagées pour contrôler les existants tant en ce qui concerne l'époque que la fréquence des contrôles. D'aucuns pensent qu'un inventaire annuel suffit, d'autres estiment que les contrôles doivent être plus fréquents, d'autres enfin sont d'avis qu'un inventaire complet n'a besoin d'être effectué qu'à de longs intervalles, supérieurs à la durée de l'exercice.

1. L'inventaire annuel

L'inventaire annuel soulève une controverse entre les tenants de l'inventaire effectué à la date du bilan, et ceux qui préfèrent instaurer un inventaire tournant.

Cette dernière méthode implique qu'un plan de contrôle soit préalablement établi et scrupuleusement observé, plan dans lequel aucune catégorie de valeurs à inventorier ne doit être omise, et qu'une comptabilité en quantités soit tenue pour permettre de suivre les mouvements entre l'inventaire effectué et la fin de l'exercice. Il y aura intérêt à vérifier simultanément plusieurs catégories de valeurs, choisies si possible de façon à pouvoir établir un rapprochement dans les variations constatées d'un inventaire à l'autre dans les quantités de chaque catégorie. Ainsi il serait bon de vérifier simultanément les stocks de produits finis, et les comptes des clients. Mais les recoupements seront difficiles si l'on s'en tient là; aussi préférons-nous l'inventaire de fin d'exercice.

L'inventaire tournant a le gros avantage de permettre de ne vérifier à la fois que certaines des valeurs possédées par l'entreprise et de ne pas obliger à arrêter celle-ci pendant un temps parfois assez long.

Néanmoins un de nos collègues, Monsieur Parenteau, a pensé à effectuer le calcul suivant. Si dans une entreprise les frais fixes représentent 40 % du chiffre d'affaires, et si l'arrêt de l'entreprise dû à un inventaire complet se monte à trois jours de travail, soit 24 heures sur 2.000 dans l'année, cet arrêt ne coûte à l'entreprise que 0,48 % de son chiffre d'affaires. Or comme l'inventaire tournant ne peut s'effectuer que dans le cas où une comptabilité matières est tenue, et que celle-ci coûte certainement plus cher que ½ % du chiffre d'affaires, l'argument en faveur de l'inventaire tournant tombe.

Je ne rejetterai pas pour autant la comptabilité matières, car elle a d'autres avantages que celui de permettre de ne pas effectuer l'inventaire au moment du bilan; elle seule permettra d'effectuer des recoupements entre les entrées et les sorties... de stocks, de créances, ou de dettes et de surveiller ainsi la marche de l'entreprise en cherchant à éliminer le coulage, sans parler des fraudes volontaires effectuées par les dirigeants.

Et pourquoi tiendrait-on la caisse en 'inventaire permanent' si l'on n'en faisait pas autant pour les marchandises qui représentent des capitaux autrement importants?

L'inventaire de fin exercise a le grand avantage d'être effectué à la date à laquelle le bilan sera dressé. Mais son contrôle ne pourra être effectué par l'expert comptable que par la suite; en effet l'immense majorité des entreprises clôture leur exercice comptable le 31 décembre et le contrôleur ne peut les vérifier toutes au même moment.

Ma préférence personnelle irait donc théoriquement au second procédé ci-dessous décrit:

2. Inventaires multiples par exercice

Ces inventaires multiples ont-ils un intérêt pour le contrôle du bilan? Il est indiscutable que cette méthode prend beaucoup de temps et coûte plus cher à l'entreprise que le procédé de l'inventaire unique; elle oblige par ailleurs à tenir l'inventaire permanent. Mais le contrôleur externe pourra alors assister à l'un des inventaires exécutés dans le courant de l'exercice et suivre dans la comptabilité matières les mouvements existant entre cet inventaire et celui effectué en fin d'exercice et qu'il n'aura pu contrôler.

Si un contrôle efficace doit être réalisé je pense donc que là est le meilleur procédé: inventaire en cours d'année effectué sous les yeux du contrôleur externe et comptabilité des quantités mise à sa disposition pour vérifier les mouvements ayant eu lieu entre cet inventaire et la date du bilan, où un second inventaire aura été dressé en dehors de sa présence.

Ce second inventaire, dont les opérations auront été vécues par le contrôleur interne, devra être organisé comme d'ailleurs le premier, de telle manière que son résultat soit exact. J'en reparlerai plus longuement ci-dessous.

3. Inventaires raréfiés (moins d'un par exercice)

Ce procédé, qui implique la tenue d'une comptabilité quantitative peut être, à mon sens, envisagé pour certains actifs qui varient peu. Je pense aux immobilisations. Mais pour la grande majorité des biens de l'entreprise, il me semble que le système est insuffisant et qu'un inventaire doit absolument être effectué au moins une fois dans l'année.

d. Pratique du contrôle

Trois points devront être examinés pour que le contrôle soit correctement effectué:

- Existence matérielle des biens portés à l'inventaire
- Propriété de ces biens
- Valorisation de ces biens.

Je traiterai les deux premiers points, le troisième, fort important, ayant été expressément rejeté de l'objet du présent rapport.

III. Modalités du contrôle de l'inventaire

Le mode de vérification dépendra essentiellement de la nature des biens inventoriés.

a. Les Immobilisations corporelles: elles sont de deux sortes:

1. Les immeubles (terrains et constructions). Il y a lieu pour vérifier leur appartenance à l'entreprise de s'assurer que celle-ci les a acquis et ne les a pas recédés.

Le premier terme de cette proposition n'entraîne qu'une vérification facile sur laquelle il n'y a pas lieu de s'étendre: le contrôleur se fera présenter les actes propriété: statuts pour les apports, actes d'achats ou de succession pour les autres modes d'acquisition. Un cas est plus délicat à résoudre celui des bâtiments construits par l'entreprise. Souvent on pourra se faire présenter des mémoires d'entrepreneurs; parfois l'entreprise ayant construit par ses propres moyens, il faudra s'assurer de l'existence même de la construction. Si le terrain sur lequel le bâtiment est construit n'appartient pas à l'entreprise, le bâtiment lui-même lui serait loué s'il ne lui appartenait pas non plus; il y aura lieu de se faire présenter le bail du terrain qui serait aussi celui du bâtiment s'il y avait location. Si le terrain appartient à l'entreprise, le bâtiment lui appartiendra par accession sauf contrat contraire passé entre les parties, lorsque le constructeur-locataire du terrain résiliera son bail. S'il n'y a pas de locataire dans ce bâtiment il appartiendra au propriétaire du terrain.

Il faut d'autre part s'assurer du fait que les immeubles ayant appartenu à l'entreprise ne sont pas sortis de son patrimoine. Il suffira de se rapporter au registre des transcriptions immobilières tenu par le conservateur des hypothèques.

2. Les Matériels et Mobilier divers: Les biens meubles possédés par l'entreprise sont présumés lui appartenir (Art. 2279 du Code Civil).

On procédera donc à leur comptage et on se fera présenter les factures d'achat. Si certains 'meubles' ont été, soit-disant, fabriqués par l'entreprise il faudra s'assurer que ce ne sont pas des biens loués. On recherchera les sorties de stocks des matières ayant servi à leur fabrication, s'il existe une comptabilité matières. On pourra aussi rechercher dans le poste de frais de loyers et locations qu'il n'y a aucune trace de prise en charge de location de ces 'meubles' à des tiers. Enfin en vérifiant les comptes de mobilier et matériel et les existants, on s'apercevra peut-être que des achats d'immobilisations ont été passés en charges et les immobilisations ainsi immédiatement amorties.

Il est bon d'obtenir de l'entreprise qu'elle tienne une fiche par bien meuble acquis en y indiquant les caractéristiques de l'objet, sa date et son mode d'acquisition, le nom des vendeurs, etc...

A noter que, en France, pour les véhicules automobiles, la propriété sera prouvée par la carte grise.

Pour effectuer l'inventaire des divers matériels, un expert comptable n'est pas toujours compétent et devra souvent se faire assister d'un spécialiste qui peut d'ailleurs, en cas de contrôle annuel (et non dans les investigations spéciales) être un technicien de l'entreprise. Qui, autre qu'un technicien, fera rapidement la différence entre un broyeur Carr et un broyeur Krupp, par exemple?

b. Les Immobilisations en cours

Comme pour les immobilisations corporelles ci-dessus, on vérifiera l'existence matérielle de l'immobilisation, puis on recherchera l'origine: mémoires d'entrepreneurs, ou sorties de magasins de matières et heures de travail affectées à ces productions.

c. Les Immobilisations incorporelles

1. le Fonds de commerce: Il existe évidemment. Mais il peut y en avoir plusieurs correspondant à divers lieux de vente. Le Registre du Commerce donnera à ce sujet toutes indications utiles.

2. Les Brevets – Licences...: Des actes d'acquisition de ces biens pourront être présentés. En France l'Office National de la Propriété Industrielle pourra donner d'utiles précisions sur les brevets déposés et leurs origines (acquisitions, inventions de l'entreprise).

3. Les Dépôts et cautionnements: Il faudra connaître leurs divers dépositaires et les interroger pour s'assurer qu'ils n'ont pas remboursé les sommes à eux déposées.

4. Les Prêts à plus d'un an: Se traiteront comme les dépôts et cautionnements.

5. Les Titres de participation: Ils ne se différencient des titres de placement que par le but de leur acquisition, qui est confirmé par la quantité de titres possédés. Je traiterai cette question avec les titres de placement.

d. Les Valeurs d'exploitation

Ainsi que nous l'avons vu ci-dessus il est bon que l'expert comptable puisse assister à l'inventaire.

Etablir l'inventaire à la date du bilan n'est pas toujours possible; en tout cas le plus souvent le contrôleur ne peut y assister; aussi, je m'excuse de le répéter, vaut-il mieux procéder à un inventaire complet à une période rapprochée de la date fatidique et suivre en comptabilité matières les entrées et sorties entre les dates de l'inventaire et du bilan.

J'omets volontairement de spécifier la manière dont l'inventaire doit être effectué, de nombreux ouvrages ayant traité cette question (classement préparatoire des stocks – arrêt des opérations, répartition du personnel en équipes difficulté de mesurer certains stocks, volumes difficiles à évaluer, etc....).

J'attirerai par contre l'attention sur le fait que le dénombrement ne suffit pas. Encore faut-il dénombrer *tout* ce qui appartient à l'entreprise et *seulement* ce qui lui appartient:

– Il faut être certain que tout a été inventorié, aussi bien les objets qui, géographiquement, sont dans l'entreprise, que ceux qui sont entre les mains de tiers. Seul un examen sérieux de la comptabilité matières peut permettre de se faire une opinion sur ce point. On s'assurera que toute inscription au débit des comptes de stocks (ou de leurs comptes subdivisionnaires, y compris les comptes d'achats) a fait l'objet d'une entrée en comptabilité matières.

– D'autre part on s'assurera que tous les objets entrés en comptabilité matières et inventoriés ont fait l'objet soit d'une acquisition s'il s'agit de marchandises ou matières, soit d'une sortie de stocks de matières s'il s'agit de produits. Dans ce dernier cas on retombe dans le même problème que celui posé par les immobilisations en cours, mais cette question est plus facile à résoudre pour les stocks par le procédé ci-après.

Il semble y avoir intérêt en ce qui concerne les stocks quels qu'ils soient (matières ou produits), à essayer de suivre en comptabilité leur évolution ultérieure, c'est-à-dire rechercher les emplois ou les sorties de stocks soit pour la fabrication, soit pour la vente. Il est évident qu'il faudra alors vérifier que les sorties concernent les stocks inventoriés et non des stocks produits ou achetés depuis. Autrement dit nous retombons dans l'exploitation de la comptabilité matières et son contrôle avec un inventaire ultérieur à celui que l'on vérifie.

Le problème n'est donc que déplacé. Il semble qu'il ne puisse être résolu que par la tenue d'une comptabilité non seulement des stocks appartenant à l'entreprise, situés dans l'entreprise et à l'extérieur, mais aussi de ceux n'appartenant pas à l'entreprise et se trouvant dans son enceinte. Le contrôleur devra s'assurer que les biens entrés en comptabilité matières l'ont été en comptabilité générale; de même pour les sorties.

Remarquons au passage qu'une comptabilité quantité n'est pas toujours facile à tenir. Certains produits augmentent de poids ou de volume (produits hygrométriques, fumiers en comptabilité agricole); d'autres diminuent, soit par évaporation (essence) ou dessication naturelle (savon en paillettes); d'autres enfin se transforment (produits oxydables).

e. Les comptes de Tiers débiteurs

Ici il est impossible de parler de quantités sans avoir recours à l'évaluation monétaire. Je ne passerai sous silence que le problème des provisions pour dépréciation. Il est évident qu'il ne faut pas, pour vérifier ces divers comptes, se contenter de vérifier que les relevés de comptes (balances) concordent avec le compte général, mais s'assurer que les opérations économiques ou juridiques affectant l'entreprise ont toutes été correctement enregistrées en comptabilité et par conséquent que les données de la comptabilité correspondent aux réalités. Le procédé le plus simple est d'interroger les débiteurs pour savoir s'ils sont d'accord sur les chiffres indiqués par l'entreprise créancière. Encore peut-il y avoir discordance entre les deux contractants, des chevauchements d'écriture étant toujours possibles dans le temps. Mais il faut aussi rechercher la cause de ces créances et la rattacher à un autre mouvement de comptes.

La naissance d'une créance a une origine (vente, profit, prêt de capitaux etc....) dont la réalité devra être démontrée (bordereau de livraison, contrat de prêt, intérêts se rapportant au dit contrat...). Il y aura aussi lieu de s'assurer que la créance existe toujours et c'est sur ce seul point qu'une réponse du débiteur pourra avoir quelque valeur s'il indique avoir réglé sa dette par tel ou tel moyen[1].

f. Les valeurs financières

1. Les titres de placement, auxquels je rattache les titres de participation. Ces titres sont ou non, selon leurs espèces, représentés matériellement.

– Les titres ayant donné lieu à représentation matérielle seront présentés au contrôleur, ou à défaut un relevé de dépôt entre les mains d'un tiers en tiendra lieu. Il faudra s'assurer que le tiers est sérieux et que son relevé n'est pas fantaisiste. En général il s'agira d'une banque ou d'un agent de change, en lesquels on peut avoir confiance; parfois d'un créancier gagiste dont on se fera fournir le

[1] NB: Il y a lieu de remarquer qu'un compte en banque est une créance envers un banquier (à moins qu'il ne s'agisse d'une dette) et que sa vérification se rattache à celle des comptes de tiers et ne présente généralement aucune difficulté spéciale.

contrat de prêt et qui n'a aucun intérêt à prétendre détenir plus de titres qu'il n'en a entre les mains.

– Les titres non matériellement représentés: ce sont des parts de Sociétés et les droits des associés résultent uniquement des statuts et des cessions ultérieures. Il faudra donc se faire communiquer leurs statuts par les sociétés en cause et leur demander si l'entreprise contrôlée est toujours associée et combien de parts elle possède.

Le procédé de vérification de l'existence du titre par l'examen des cessions ultérieures est parfois applicable en cette manière.

2. Les effets de commerce: Pour vérifier leur existence on ne peut que rarement se les faire présenter car la vérification est le plus souvent effectuée assez longtemps après l'inventaire et les effets sont alors passées en d'autres mains. On s'assurera alors de leurs négociations, cessions ou règlements ultérieurs par tous moyens (bordereaux d'escompte ou d'encaissement, confirmation de réception par le cessionnaire, etc....) et d'autre part on vérifiera l'origine des effets et leur cause, afin de s'assurer non plus de leur existence mais de la raison d'être des effets pour pouvoir par la suite les valoriser.

3. L'encaisse. Le mieux est de la compter au moment de l'inventaire. A défaut de ce contrôle il y aura lieu de se faire présenter la 'comptabilité matières des espèces' et de pointer les entrées et les sorties effectuées entre le contrôle et l'inventaire, en s'attachant à rechercher les causes des mouvements d'espèces, c'est-à-dire en contrôlant les pièces de caisse. Le contrôle matériel de l'encaisse devra avoir lieu impromptu afin de déjouer les tours pendables d'un caissier ou d'un directeur indélicat. (Se méfier des encaisses trop importantes.)

g. Les Dettes

Ainsi que je l'ai indiqué au début du présent rapport, les dettes doivent aussi être inventoriées et leur inventaire contrôlé. On recherchera l'origine de la dette et on s'assurera de son existence actuelle. On pourra, pour ce faire, interroger les créanciers qui fournissent des relevés, et pointer les paiements ultérieurs, ce qui permettra en outre de vérifier, plus ou moins, que toutes les dettes ont été comptabilisées.

Parfois lorsqu'il s'agit de dettes fiscales ou parafiscales, le calcul de la dette pourra être effectué et l'existence de cette dette prouvée par le simple fait que ce calcul était impossible à la date de l'inventaire (je pense ici à l'impôt sur les bénéfices dont la base ne peut être connu qu'après l'inventaire et dont le taux n'est souvent connu que quelques mois après).

h. Le Compte de Résultats

Il peut paraître curieux de parler du Compte de Résultats à propos de l'inventaire. Je veux seulement signaler que les charges doivent être étudiées afin d'assurer qu'aucun investissement n'y a été porté, qui aurait dû constituer un actif (voir spécialement les comptes: Entretien et réparations, Fournitures faites à l'entreprise, Fournitures de bureau). De même il faudra rechercher si dans les ventes ou plus normalement dans les profits exceptionnels ne se trouvent pas les prix de vente d'immobilisations vendues qui n'auraient pas été retirées de l'actif.

D'autre part on s'efforcera de vérifier que toutes les charges se rapportent aux exercices écoulés (vérification des 'Charges payées d'avance') et que les charges restant dues ont été comptabilisées soit dans les comptes de dettes ci-dessus étudiés, soit au compte de régularisation 'Charges à payer'.

IV. CONCLUSION

La vérification sérieuse de l'inventaire ne peut s'effectuer que par le contrôle des mouvements de valeurs à l'intérieur de l'entreprise. Ces mouvements sont dus à des raisons économiques ou juridiques qu'il s'agit d'analyser. Le contrôle externe de l'inventaire ne peut être effectif que si un contrôle interne et une organisation comptable sérieuse existent comprenant une comptabilité matières et une comptabilité prix de revient.

Nous avons vu que pour chaque poste vérifié, il fallait rechercher l'origine du bien ou de la dette, et bien souvent ce que ce bien ou cette dette est devenu ultérieurement. En effet toute la comptabilité est axée sur la réalité et c'est pourquoi le procédé dit 'à parties doubles' est universellement employé: Tout a une origine – Tout a une destination. Lavoisier disait: 'Rien ne se crée, rien ne se perd, tout se transforme'. Il me paraît évident que ce grand savant a ainsi énoncé non seulement ce qui est devenu un axiome de chimie, mais encore un des grands principes auxquels nous ne saurions trop souvent nous référer dans le domaine de la comptabilité.

Translation

PAPER

by

CLAUDE PAQUET, HEC.

Chambre Nationale des Experts Comptables diplômés par l'Etat, France

I. Introduction

Definition and object of stocktaking

The first French law that mentions stocktaking is the ordinance of Colbert, issued in 1673, in which article 8 rules:

'All merchants must, within the period of 6 months following the publication of this ordinance, take stock of all their movable and immovable assets and all their book debts and liabilities; the list of the inventory must be signed by them and must be re-examined and renewed every two years'.

The Commercial Code of 1807 again expresses the same idea:

'Yearly every merchant must take stock of his movable and immovable assets, and his book debts and liabilities and register them, year after year, in a special register, which has to be signed by him'.

Lastly a decree dated the 22nd of September 1953 modified this last article by stipulating:

'They (meaning every corporation or person carrying on business) must, equably, each year take stock of assets and liabilities of their firm and balance the accounts in order to draw up a balance sheet and profit and loss account. The balance sheet and the profit and loss account are registered in the stocktaking book'.

From the above it appears that since 1673 businessmen have had to take stock every two years and since 1807 they must do it every year. But so far the law has not yet given any definition of stocktaking. In civil matters several texts quote stocktaking (but without defining it) in connection with inheritance, dissolution of partnerships, etc.

The definition of stocktaking has been given either in books on book-keeping or in legal verdicts.

I shall quote the verdict of the Court of Commerce of Seine passed on the 20th of September 1884:

'Stocktaking is a complete statement, without blanks or omissions, a detailed enumeration, item after item, of all the elements, whether they are assets or liabilities; every thing must be named, examined, written in figures'.

Therefore stocktaking consists in establishing a list of all positive or negative elements of the financial status of a person or a corporation. Businessmen are not only forced to take stock by commercial or fiscal law, but also by economic factors, in order to be able to take bearings just as a captain of a ship will do every day, and also in order to ascertain the results obtained between two successive stocktakings.

Just as a captain will, if necessary, rectify the sailing of his ship in order to overtake the difference between the assigned destination and the point which has been reached, a businessman who has fixed his own estimates, will ascertain a difference between expectations and realizations and consequently will rectify his business-policy accordingly.

II. General Remarks on Stocktaking as an Element of Control

a. Purpose of stocktaking-control

If stocktaking is necessary, it will at least have to be correct. From its function as an element of control follows that one has to be sure of its correctness and consequently also of the correctness of the various items of the balance sheet. But, in my opinion, verifying this correctness is not enough. It is necessary to know the reasons for changes in the various items of the balance sheet, from one stocktaking to another. For instance, it is not sufficient to state that the fixed assets have increased because machines have been bought, or that the liquid assets have decreased because there is less money at hand. Unfortunately one can see too often that such superficial explanations are given. It is necessary to seek the relationship between the various changes that have taken place in the items of the inventory (for instance liquid assets have decreased in the same proportion as creditors) and also the relationship with other items of the balance sheet, such as the reserves (for instance liquid assets have decreased because reserves have been distributed) or the relationship with the Profit and Loss Account (for instance liquid assets have decreased owing to a loss).

In short, it is necessary to link the changes in the items with each other and also with their respective causes.

It is clear that one can use the inventory of the different items of the balance sheet and the trading and profit and loss accounts, in order to obtain a dynamical picture of the life of the firm during a given period instead of a static view of its position. It is a similar difference as there is between cinematography and photography.

On the other hand the inventory will give us a check on the internal organization of the firm and all the means put in operation to check regularly the movements of goods inside it: an exaggerated increase of some items of the assets (stocks for instance) can be caused by a faulty organization of the purchase-department where one person may place orders without paying any attention to the orders which have already been placed by someone else; or — (with regard to debtors) — it can be caused by a faulty organization of the financial department. It appears to me that those facts must be pointed out by the auditor to the owners of the firm who asked him to audit its management.

b. Object of stocktaking-control

Usually, when one uses the word 'stocktaking', one thinks of the 'Working-Values', in other words: stocks. It is obvious that taking stock of goods or merchandise is one of the most delicate problems of stocktaking, but it is not the only one; and taking it for granted that the inventory of all the assets should be taken, one rarely thinks of verifying the claimable liabilities. Yet this point deserves a serious examination.

I do not intend to draw up a list now of goods and debts, which should be subject to an inventory. Not only would this be dull, but it would also be useless as we shall study the way of taking the inventory of the various items of the balance sheet in the following pages.

c. Time of Control

Various methods of checking the stock on hand can be considered, as regards the time as well as the frequency of verifications. Some think that a yearly stocktaking is enough, others are of opinion that verification ought to be more frequent, lastly others consider a complete inventory only necessary at long intervals, longer than the financial year.

1. The annual stocktaking

Annual stocktaking raises a discussion between the defenders of a stock taken at the date of the balance sheet, and those who prefer to establish a method of taking the stock in parts, periodically throughout the year.

This last method implies that a plan of checking is previously drawn up and scrupulously fulfilled in the course of a year—a plan in which no category of goods may be left out. Further it implies that the accounts must be kept in quantities in order to be able to follow the changes which have taken place between the date of stocktaking and the end of the financial year. It will be of importance to check simultaneously several groups of items, chosen, if possible, so that a ratio can be established between the changes which have been found in the quantities of each group, from one stocktaking to another. Therefore it would be a good thing to check the stocks of manufactured goods and the customers accounts simultaneously. But cross-checking will be difficult if one does not go further into the matter; therefore we do prefer the inventory taken at the end of the financial year.

Periodical stocktaking in parts throughout the year offers the great advantage of checking only a part of the values owned by the firm at a time and it does not entail that the firm has to be closed for some time.

However, one of our colleagues, Mr. Parenteau, has made the following calculation. If in a firm the fixed costs represent 40 % of the turnover, and if closing the firm owing to a complete stocktaking amounts to three working days, being 24 hours on 2000 hours of the year, closing costs the firm only 0,48 % of its turnover. However, periodical stocktaking (in parts) can only be applied when stock-accounts are kept, and as the cost of keeping these accounts is certainly higher than ½ % of the turnover, the outcome of the calculation will not be in the favour of periodical stocktaking.

But it is not a reason why I shall reject stock-accounts for they offer other advantages than the one of not having to take stock on the date of the balance sheet—only stock-accounts open the possibility of linking the inward and outward flow of goods, debts or claims, and of observing the development of the firm while any weak spots that may entail losses will be eliminated, to say nothing of fraudulent dealings of the management of that firm.

And why are cash-accounts kept on a permanent basis, while the same is not done for the goods which involve much more capital?

Stocktaking at the end of the financial year has the advantage that it is effected on the date of the balance sheet. But the auditor will only check it later on, for the great majority of the firms close their financial year on December 31st and the auditor cannot verify the stocks of all these firms at the same time.

In theory, I think I prefer the second procedure which will be described in the following paragraph.

2. Frequent stocktakings during the financial year

Are these frequent stocktakings important for the audit of the balance sheet? There is no doubt that this method takes much time and costs the firm more money than the method of taking stock once a year; further this method necessitates permanent stock-records.

But it will be possible for the (external) auditor to be present at one of the inventories taken during the financial year and he will be able to follow the changes that have taken place in this inventory till the end of the financial year, when another inventory will have been taken without him being present.

If a real control must be attained I think that is the best method to take an inventory during the financial year, under the supervision of the external auditor, while the stock-records, showing the quantities of the goods, are placed at his disposal in order to verify the movements which have taken place between this inventory and the date of the balance sheet when a second inventory is taken without his presence.

This second inventory, which is effected under the supervision of the internal controller, will have to be organized, like the first one, that is to say in such a way that its results are correct. I shall revert to this subject more extensively below.

3. Occasional stocktakings (less than once a year)

This method, which implies quantitative stock-accounts can, in my opinion, be considered for certain assets which do not fluctuate much. I am thinking of fixed assets. But I am of opinion that it is insufficient for the great majority of firms and that it is necessary to take an inventory at least once a year.

d. Essential points of stocktaking

Three points must be examined in order to carry out the audit properly:
— Physical existence of the stocks shown on the stocktaking list,
— Property of these goods,
— Valuation of these goods.

I shall only discuss the first two points. The third one which deals with a very important subject has on purpose been left out of this report.

III. Methods of Auditing the Inventory

The method of examination will depend chiefly on the nature of the goods of which an inventory has to be taken.

a. Fixed assets

There are two kinds of fixed assets:

1. Real estate (land and buildings)

In order to verify that these assets belong to the firm it is necessary to ascertain that the firm has acquired them in a proper manner and has not withheld them from third parties.

This verification is quite simple and so it is not necessary to dwell further on this subject: the auditor will have the property-certificates shown to him, i.e. the articles of association for the assets brought into the firm at its foundation, the deeds of purchase or the deeds of succession for the assets acquired later. It will be more difficult if the buildings have been built by the firm. Often it will be possible to examine the contractor's bills; if the firm has constructed the buildings by its own means it will be necessary to ascertain the actual existence of the buildings. If the ground on which the buildings have been erected does not belong to the firm, the buildings themselves will be rented if they do not belong to the firm either; therefore it will be necessary to examine the lease of the ground as this lease will also refer to the buildings. If the ground belongs to the firm, then the buildings will also belong to it except in case a contrary clause exists between the two parties, in which event the builder of the premises, who is also the tenant of the land, will revoke the lease. If there is no tenant of the buildings, they will belong to the landowner.

On the other hand it is necessary to ascertain that buildings which belong to the firm, remain part of its possessions. It will be sufficient to refer to the registrar of transfers and mortgages.

2. Equipment and various movable assets

Movable goods which are in the possession of the firm are legally considered to be its property. Therefore, the auditor will proceed to verify their quantity and the purchase invoices will have to be handed to him. If certain movables have been manufactured by the firm it will be necessary to ascertain that they have not been rented from a third party. The raw materials which have been used for their manufacture will have to be traced by the auditor, which will only be possible if there are stock-records of the raw materials. Also a proof could be found in the fact that there is no trace of any charges for hiring those movables from third parties. Finally by verifying the accounts of the equipment and other movable assets with the inventories which are actually present, we could perhaps find out whether any purchases of fixed assets have been charged to the profit and loss account and therefore have been written-off immediately.

It is advisable for the firm to have a card for each item of its movable assets, stating its characteristics, when and how it was acquired, the name of the sellers, etc.

I may observe that in France it is possible to prove the property of motor cars by the 'carte grise'.

An auditor is not always competent to take the inventory of various types of machinery and equipment and often he will have to call in the help of a specialist who may be a technical man of the firm, in the event of annual audits (but not for special investigations). For instance who else but a technical man could quickly see the difference between a mill constructed by 'Carr' and one made by 'Krupp'.

b. Fixed assets under construction

As stated above for the fixed assets, the physical existence of these assets will be checked, then their origin will be traced: contractors' bills, use of raw materials and working hours put into their production.

c. Intangible Assets

1. The business

Obviously it exists. But there may be several branch-offices in different places. The Trades Register will give all the necessary indications on this subject.

2. Patents, licences

The purchase-deeds of these rights could be presented. In France 'L'Office National de la Propriété Industrielle' will give accurate information about the patents which have been taken out and their origin (purchased patents, inventions of the firm).

3. Deposits and caution money

It will be necessary to know the persons or bodies with whom the money has been deposited in order to find out that the sums have not been paid back.

4. Loans granted for a period longer than one year

These will be treated like deposits and caution money.

5. Shares in subsidiary companies

These barely differ from stocks and shares which have been bought for investment purposes and which are verified by the number of the titles owned. I shall discuss these shares together with the stocks and shares.

d. Stocks in trade

As we have seen above, it is advisable that the auditor is present at the stocktaking.

It is not always possible to take the inventory at the date of the balance sheet and usually the auditor cannot be present. Therefore, I apologize for repeating it, it would be better to take a complete inventory at the nearest possible date and to follow the incoming and outgoing flow of goods, between the date of the inventory and the date of the balance sheet.

Intentionally I am not going into details about the way the inventory has to be taken, many books have treated this matter (preliminary classification of the stocks, suspension of business or work, distribution of the staff in gangs, difficulty in measuring certain stocks, difficulty in estimating the volume of certain goods, etc.).

On the other hand I may call your attention to the fact that counting alone is not sufficient. Yet it is necessary to count everything that belongs to the firm and only what belongs to it.

It is necessary to be sure that an inventory of every thing has been taken, the things which are on the premises of the firm as well as those which are in hands of third parties.

Only a serious examination of the stock-records will give sufficient ground to form an opinion on that particular point. One will have to be sure that every entry on the debit-side of the stock-accounts (or of their sub-accounts including the purchase-accounts) corresponds with an entry in the stock-records.

On the other hand it will be necessary to make sure that every entry appearing on the stock-accounts and of which an inventory has been taken, corresponds either with a purchase (if it concerns merchandise or raw materials) or with the consumption of raw materials (if it concerns manufactured goods). In the last case we come across the same problem as the one which arises with regard to fixed assets under construction, but it is easier to solve this problem when it concerns goods, as will appear below.

As regards goods, whatever they are (raw materials or manufactured goods) it seems important to try and follow their way throughout the accounts, that is to say to trace their issue from the stocks to the manufacturing accounts or the sales accounts. It is obvious that subsequently it will be necessary to verify that the issue has come from the stocks of which an inventory has been taken and not from stocks which have been produced or bought since. In other words we revert once again to the stock-records of raw materials and their verification with an inventory which is taken later than the one which is part of a balance sheet which is being audited.

So the problem has only been shifted. It seems that it can only be solved by keeping records not only of stocks which belong to the firm (kept within the firm as well as outside it), but also of stocks which do not belong to it, but are within its walls. The auditor will have to ascertain that the goods which have been entered into the stock-records are also entered into the general accounts; the same applies to the goods which have been issued from the stocks.

By the way, we may point out that it is not always easy to keep stock records which show quantities. Some goods can increase in weight or in volume (goods that absorb moisture, for instance manure), others decrease, either because they evaporate (petrol) or because of natural desiccation (soap in flakes); lastly there are goods that change nature (oxidizable goods).

e. Debtors

In this connection it is impossible to speak of quantities, without taking the monetary value into account. I am going to pass by the problem of making sufficient provision for bad or doubtful debtors.

It is clear that it is not sufficient to verify that the schedule of the balances of the various individual accounts tallies with the debtors' account in the general ledger, but one must ascertain that all the transactions affecting the firm have been registered correctly and consequently that the accounts are in accordance with reality. The simplest method is to send statements of account to the debtors, in order to find out whether they agree with the balances stated. Still there may be a difference between the figures of the two parties as transitory entries may occur.

But it is also necessary to find out the cause of the claim on the debtor and thus to link it up with changes in other accounts. Every claim has an origin (sale, profit, loan) which will help to prove its existence (delivery-note, contract of a loan, interest due on a loan). It is also necessary to find out whether the claim still exists on the date of the balance sheet and in this respect a reply from the debtor can be of some use if he indicates when and how he settled his debt.

f. Assets with a monetary character

1. Bonds and Shares (with which I am connecting shares in subsidiary companies)

These titles are or are not, according to their origin, embodied in securities.

Bonds and Shares which are actually embodied in certificates, will be shown to the auditor; if this is not possible, a statement of deposit in hands of a third party will take their place. Generally it will be a bank or a stock-broker who can be trusted; sometimes it will be a mortgagee whom we shall approach and who has no interest in pretending that he has more securities than he really has in hands.

The titles which are not embodied in certificates are the rights of shareholders in limited companies and the rights of partners which are derived from the articles of association and from any changes that have taken place. Therefore the auditor will have to enquire into the articles of association of the limited companies concerned and it will be necessary to ask them if the firm under audit actually is a partner and how many shares it owns.

Sometimes it is possible to verify the transfer of the shares into the name of the firm, in order to ascertain their actual existence.

2. Bills Receivable

It is seldom, that bills receivable can be shown to the auditor, in order to verify their existence, because in most cases the examination is carried out rather a long time after the date of the balance sheet and the bills have passed into other hands in the meantime. It will be necessary to attain certainty about the endorsements and the ultimate settlement of every bill, by all possible means (payment notes, confirmation of receipt by the drawee, etc.). On the other hand it will be necessary to verify the origin of each bill, and to find out the reason why it was drawn in order to be sure of its material background.

3. Cash in hand

The best thing to do is to count it at the time of the balance sheet. If this check cannot take place, it will be necessary to examine the cash accounts and to seek the connection of the incoming and the outgoing flow of money with the other assets, especially during the period between the last cash-audit and the date of the balance-sheet. The audit of cash at hand will have to take place at unexpected moments in order to take an unreliable cashier or manager by surprise (beware of large sums of cash at hand).

g. Creditors

As I said at the beginning of this report, it will also be necessary to take an inventory of the debts due to creditors and to check this inventory. The origin of the debt and its actual existence will have to be ascertained. In order to do so the creditors who furnish statements could be questioned, and the payments could be checked with their statements. Besides, this examination will bring to light whether all debts have been accounted for on the date of the balance sheet.

Sometimes when fiscal or semi-fiscal debts are concerned, the calculation of the debt can be executed and the existence of this debt can be proved by the mere fact that this calculation was impossible at the time of the balance sheet. (Here I am thinking of the profit tax which can only be calculated after the balance sheet is ready and the rate of which often is only known a few months later.)

h. The Profit and Loss account

It may seem strange to speak of the profit and loss account when we are dealing with the inventory. I only want to point out that the charges have to be studied in order to ascertain that no investment which should have formed an asset has been entered on this account (examine especially the accounts of maintenance and repairs, supplies to the firm, office appliances). It will also be necessary to find out that the sales or the extra-ordinary profits do not comprise the returns of fixed assets which have been sold, but which rightly should not have been withdrawn from the assets.

On the other hand it will be necessary to verify that all the charges refer to the financial year which is being audited and that all the expenses which remained due, have been accounted for either in the debt-accounts or in the transitory account: 'Expenses to be paid'.

IV. Conclusion

It is only possible to verify the inventory seriously if the movements of the values inside the firm are followed. Those movements result from legal or economical causes and have to be analysed. The external audit of the inventory can only be effective if an internal check and a proper system of accounting, including stock-accounts for the goods and raw materials and cost-accounts for the manufactured articles, exist.

We have seen that for every item which has been discussed, it is necessary to look for the origin of the good or of the debt, and that in many cases it is necessary to know what has become of this good or of this debt. Indeed all book-keeping is based on reality and this is the reason why the method of 'double entry book-keeping' is used universally.

Every thing has its origin. Every thing has its destination. Lavoisier said: 'Rien ne se crée, rien ne se perd, tout se transforme'. It seems obvious to me that this great scientist has expressed what has become not only an axiom of chemistry, but also one of the great principles to which we cannot refer often enough in accountancy.

PAPER

by

SIR RICHARD YEABSLEY, C.B.E., F.C.A., F.S.A.A.

The Society of Incorporated Accountants, U. K.

As practising Accountants, we are concerned with this feature in two capacities —as Auditors and as reporting Accountants. In the former our duties are subject to statutory requirements, in the latter by the terms of reference accepted, implied or limited in terms. It may be well to note that while the subject matter is not directly concerned with the valuation of assets, the existence of an asset implies ownership of something of some value. For the purpose of this paper let us assume that existence and ownership is that with which we are at present concerned.

Firstly, let us consider our duties as Auditors and, in particular, under the Companies Acts operative in Great Britain, now codified in the Companies Act 1948. The Ninth Schedule to that Act enumerates the matters to be expressly stated in the Auditor's Report and opens with this significant paragraph:

> 'Whether they have obtained all the information and explanations which to the best of their knowledge and belief were necessary for the purposes of their audit.'

However, no precise direction is given by the Statute as to the steps he should take to enable him to report to the Members without qualification that in his opinion... the Balance Sheet gives a true and fair view of the state of the Company's affairs at the date thereof. Therefore, let us note the judicial pronouncements on the duty of an Auditor that have been made arising from legal proceedings against Auditors:

> 'The duty of an Auditor is to verify the facts which it is proposed to state in the Balance Sheet and to verify them using ordinary and reasonable care and skill.'
>
> Lord Justice Warrington – In re The City Equitable Fire Insurance Co., Ltd. (1924)

> 'Such I take to be the duty of the Auditor; he must be honest – that is, he must not certify what he does not believe to be true, and he must take reasonable care and skill before he believes that what he certifies is true. What is reasonable care in any particular case must depend upon the circumstances of that case.'
>
> Lord Justice Lindley – In re The London & General Bank Ltd. (1895)

> 'It is the duty of an Auditor to bring to bear on the work he has to perform that skill, care and caution which a reasonably competent, careful and cautious Auditor would use.

What is reasonable skill, care and caution must depend on the particular circumstances of each case.'

Lord Justice Lopes – In re The Kingston Cotton Mill Co. Ltd. (1896)

'The Auditor most undoubtedly does undertake very considerable responsibilities, and is liable for the proper discharge of his duties, and if by the neglect of his duties or by want of reasonable care... damage is caused to the company as such he is responsible for that damage... He has got to bring to bear upon those duties reasonable and watchful care... the company look to him to protect their interests... It is quite easy for me to lay down... in general terms what the duty of an Auditor is, it is very much more difficult... to apply that duty to the particular case... It cannot be disputed that when an Auditor returns to the Shareholders an entry of cash in hand he must have taken reasonable steps to ascertain that the cash was in hand... He has the same duty to discharge in regard to the verification of the cash as he has with regard to the verification of the securities...'

The London Oil Storage Co., Ltd. v. Seear Hasluck & Co. (1904)

These cases deal with the subject in general and with certain assets in particular but we should also note the following dealing with particular types of assets:

'It is no part of an Auditor's duty to take stock. No one contends that it is. He must rely on other people for details of the Stock-in-trade in hand.'

Lord Justice Lindley – In re The Kingston Cotton Mill Co., Ltd. (1896)

'An Auditor is not, in my judgment, ever justified in omitting to make personal inspection of securities that are in the custody of a person or company with whom it is not proper that they should be left.'

Chancery Division – In re The City Equitable Fire Insurance Co., Ltd., (1924)

'I think he (the Auditor) must take a certificate from a person who is in the habit of dealing with and holding securities, and who he on reasonable grounds rightly believes to be, in the exercise of the best judgment, a trustworthy person to give such a certificate.'

Court of Appeal. Ibid.

'He (the Auditor) is entitled to see the Company's books and the materials for their books, and also to ask for explanations. But he is not called on to seek for knowledge outside the Company, or to communicate with customers or creditors... There was certainly no duty cast on the Auditor to take stock.'

The Irish Woollen Co., Ltd., v. Tyson and others. (1900)

Concluding a review of the legal position, I again refer to the City Equitable case which may well be regarded as the most important recent case on the subject and quote Lord Justice Sargant, who said, 'In my judgment it would not be right that auditors should deliberately adopt a standard of verification less than the ordinary, below the ordinary standard, because the persons with whom they are dealing are persons of specially high reputation.'

To summarize the legal position in regard to Auditors:

1. They must obtain all the information they consider necessary for their audit, and in this context it is submitted that information includes verification.

2. In the verification of assets stated on the Balance Sheet they must use ordinary and reasonable care and skill.

3. What is reasonable care depends on the circumstances of each case.

4. What is skill in this context has been judged by reference to current practice—as evidenced by the ordinary standards enunciated by expert witnesses from the Accountancy profession as that which a reasonable competent careful Auditor would use.

5. They may rely on the certificates of others to the extent that they judge the others to be trustworthy persons and it would not be reasonable and practicable for them to insist on a personal inspection of items covered by the certificates.

6. They are not bound to *take* stock but are bound to make a reasonable and proper investigation... of the Stock Sheets.

7. They must take reasonable steps to ascertain that an item 'Cash in hand' stated on the Balance Sheet was represented by Cash in hand.

One very important conclusion can be drawn from all this, namely that the Auditor must verify the existence of assets and he is to assess the extent to which this is necessary in the particular case judged by applying ordinary and reasonable care and skill.

Clearly, this judgment will be influenced by (a) the nature of the asset, (b) the extent and efficiency of the system of internal check or audit, (c) degree, i.e. size of the undertaking and the relative importance of the item in question.

a. Nature of the Asset

It would not be appropriate in such a paper to attempt to indicate the steps of verification that might be taken in respect of each type of asset but observations on certain types will serve to indicate the procedures considered appropriate to similar items and cases but what is said in regard thereto must be subject to the later remarks under headings (b) and (c).

Fixed Assets

It is clearly necessary to verify documents of title to such assets as Land, Buildings—whether held on Freehold or Leasehold tenure. Their physical existence should, where practicable, be verified by visual inspection, and the same applies to Plant, Machinery and the like. The Plant Register should be examined and appropriate test checks made with the Plant in position; the use of codings and coding plates affixed to the Plant can assist the Auditor in identifying the items in question. Such inspection may disclose redundant or obsolete plant and raise the question of their valuation. In this connection, the arrangement of the position of Plant & c. should be noted and photographic records may prove of value. The continued use of assets and revenue therefrom after the date of the Balance Sheet is clearly evidence of their existence—e.g. ships. There are many cases where visual inspection may not be practicable—I refer to those which for one reason or another are inaccessible to the Auditor, for example, such assets abroad. Consider underground mines or alluvial mines, rubber and tea plantations, oil wells and the like. Here it is obvious that some indirect form of verification, quite apart from that of legal title is all that can reasonably be expected. Here again, photographic records are of some value but appropriately worded certificates from the local auditors or officials and the Directors should be obtained.

Intangible Assets

These include such items as Goodwill, Trademarks, Patents and the like. Except in the case of Goodwill, their existence depends on the legal ownership thereof which can be verified in appropriate manner. Goodwill is often the name given to the excess of the sum paid for a business or assets associated therewith over the values attributed to the net physical assets acquired. Having been verified on its first appearance in the Balance Sheet, little, if anything, can be done on the audit of subsequent Balance Sheets. The imprecise nature of this asset is recognized by all, both as to what it is intended to cover and the notional nature of the sum attributed to it in the accounts.

Trade Investments and Investments in Subsidiary Companies

Here the Auditor is concerned with the legal ownership of such investments and to some extent to the value thereof. To the extent that they represent shares in companies he will take cognizance of the nature and extent of the Auditors' report on the last accounts available, and in certain cases, of the standing of the Auditor.

To the extent that the investment represents monies advanced or balance due on current account a certificate would be obtained from an appropriate official confirming the amount thereof.

Government Securities and other investments

The Auditor will verify the legal ownership of such investments but the question of their value will be to some extent dependent on the nature of the operations of the company possessing them, for example, Banks, Investment Trusts, Finance Companies and Commercial concerns.

Reference to the nature of the company possessing the type of asset gives one the opportunity of referring in more detail to the extent to which certificates might properly be accepted from persons holding them at the date of the Balance Sheet. As stated earlier herein, the classic legal case in the British Courts on this subject was In re City Equitable Fire Insurance Co., Ltd. (1924). In this case charges were made against the Auditors of the company of negligence in respect of the audit of the accounts of the company for certain years. One of the three charges was their failure to detect and report to the Shareholders the fact that a number of the Company's securities which were in the hands of Ellis & Co. (the Company's Stockbrokers of which the Chairman of the Company, a Mr. Bevan, was senior partner) were being pledged by that firm to its customers.

In the Court of Appeal the Master of the Rolls said he thought that it was going too far to say that under no circumstances can a certificate from a Stockbroker be accepted. In the case of a large institution like the City Equitable Company, with a considerable amount of investments to make and sell, it may well be a convenient method of business to have large blocks of securities in the hands of the Company's brokers. The Auditor must in all cases decide whether the person from whom he takes a certificate is in the habit of dealing with and holding securities, and whether he can reasonably regard him as a trustworthy person to give a certificate. This ruling adds to the Auditor's responsibility as compared with what it would be if it had, for example, been ruled that he can take a banker's certificate but not any other person's. However, it leaves with the Auditor the judgment to make as to what is reasonable in all the circumstances of the particular case and as Lord Justice Sargant said, 'It would not be right that Auditors should deliberately adopt a standard of verification less than the ordinary, below the ordinary standard, because the persons with whom they are dealing are persons of specially high reputation.'

It is submitted that practitioners would all agree that current practice is at least in line with the legal pronouncements.

Current Assets

Under this heading it is proposed to deal with only two main items, namely Stock and Debtors, as the matter of Cash at Bankers and in hand may be regarded as covered in what has already been said.

Stock in Trade

The legal authorities make it clear that it is no part of the Auditor's duty to *take* stock, which must mean the original listing of the quantities of the physical stock, the pricing and valuation thereof; this clearly is the duty of Management and the primary responsibility for the accounts presented to the Shareholders is clearly placed by Section 149 of the Companies Act 1948 upon the Directors.

What should the Auditor do by way of verifying the existence of Stock in Trade? Until recent years it was probably well nigh universal practice in Great Britain to accept the Stock Sheets, suitably endorsed by those responsible for listing, supervision prices and extensions, as evidence of the existence of the Stock. For stocks in bond, certificates were and are accepted while for stocks in warehouses of third parties certificates were and still are accepted in appropriate cases. In certain cases also verification was obtained by reference to subsequent proceeds, e.g. in the case of certain crops & c.

However, it is becoming much less uncommon for an Auditor to make such tests as he is able to do as to the quantities of the larger items included in Stock.

There can be no question of his holding himself out as an expert in such matters; it is obvious that a person with fraudulent motives could mislead and indeed deceive an Auditor, both as to the quantity and quality of certain items. Numerous cases will come to one's mind and it is not proposed to give even any obvious examples. The Auditor should be careful to make it clear to the Management that his visual examination is a cursory one and limited to his inadequate technical knowledge and he does not hold himself out as an expert Stocktaker or Valuer. It is suggested that this is desirable so as to avoid a possible charge by Directors that they were aware that the Auditor made a visual check and relied on it in relief of the duties that otherwise they would have carried out.

However, within the limits mentioned it is submitted that the best practice does require some steps to be taken to verify by visual means the existence of the stocks listed on the Stock Sheets wherever this is possible and practicable without technical knowledge to do so. Such verification will obviously include a test of the larger items, a review of the stocktaking system generally, including a test of quantities with such Financial and Stock Records that exist. It is submitted that the Auditor is at great risk and, indeed, failing in his duty if he does no more than test some prices and extensions and check the additions but otherwise relies on a certificate of the Management and this risk exists even though the item Stock in Trade is stated on the Balance Sheet 'as valued by the Management.'

As to the receipt of certificates as evidence of the existence of stock held by others, much of what is said in regard to certificates of safe keeping of investments applies equally here. Each case must be considered on its merits and while there should be no element of distrust, the Auditor will naturally enquire in certain cases 'Why are the stocks so situated?' 'How often are they inspected?' 'Who covers the fire and burglary risk and on what quantities or values?' 'How often is the stock so held turned over in terms of usage?'

Sundry Debtors or Accounts Receivable

Under previous headings reference has been made to the verification of existence ex post facto and it is thus that the debts due are in the main dealt with. The composition of the debt recorded in the books and its subsequent payment, together with an examination by way of test of the method of invoicing and of the rendering of statements, of tests of the goods outwards records and the like are also part of such verification. Except in the case of loans or cash advances material in amount, it is most unusual for Auditors in Great Britain to require confirmation from debtors of their balances. In this connection the extract given earlier herein from the Irish Woollen Case may be noted, 'He (the auditor) is not called on to seek for knowledge outside the Company, or to communicate with customers or creditors.'

b. Internal Check or Audit

As has already been said, it is primarily the responsibility of the Directors to submit proper accounts to the Shareholders and it is their responsibility also to ensure by appropriate safeguards within the organization that the records of assets and liabilities, of sales and cost thereof are adequate and that the affairs of the Company are dealt with efficiently. They are primarily responsible that there are reasonable safeguards to ensure that the assets of the Company are not depleted by fraudulent conversion and it is with these matters well in mind that appropriate steps should be taken within the organization. These may be by way of supervision of activities, the re-arrangement of duties, systems of authorizations and the like. In some cases there may also be set up a more formal system, or indeed department, devoted to internal audit. Size of the concern and the scope of its operations may well require the latter and with the advent of electronic Accounting this is becoming of increasing importance. Interim work by the Auditor directed, as is the work of the internal audit staff, to the verification of the transactions and to ensuring that the records do disclose factual matter may well be not only desirable but essential. It is in this field of internal audit and interim audits that much can be done to satisfy the Auditor and he will examine with care not only the procedure laid down within the Company but also the extent to which they are, in fact, being applied. The efficacy of the internal check or audit will affect the extent of the Auditor's verification and while he may report to the Directors on weaknesses therein it is his responsibility, once on notice to take appropriate steps to satisfy himself as to the items in the accounts and if he is unable to do so he should report accordingly to the Shareholders.

c. DEGREE

In viewing the extent of verification, it is evident that account must be taken not only of what is said previously but also of the size of the undertaking and the relative importance of the item in question—herein also lies the question of judgment by the Auditor. Observe also the following extract from the judgment of Lindley L. J. in the London & General Bank Case (1895).

> 'What is reasonable care in any particular case must depend on the circumstances of that case. Where there is nothing to excite suspicion, very little enquiry will be reasonable and quite sufficient; and in practice, I believe, business men select a few cases haphazard, see that they are right and assume that others like them are correct also.'

While this indicates that test checks are likely to be regarded as reasonable, clearly the extent thereof must be conditioned by the efficacy of the system of internal check and audit as assessed by the Auditor himself. Should there be obvious loopholes or indeed grounds for suspicion, then he is required to probe as far as it is necessary to satisfy himself as to the items in question and if need be to qualify the terms of his report to the Shareholders.

Before leaving the matter of Auditors appointed under Statutory provisions such as the Companies Acts 1948, it is noted that Auditors appointed under other Statutes may be required to state specifically, as, indeed, they are, for example, in the case of Building Societies and Trustee Savings Banks, certain verifications that they are carried out.

Most of what has been said earlier relates to the position of Auditors appointed under the Companies Act but we, as Accountants, are called upon to report on the accounts of sole traders, partnerships and as investigating accountants for some particular purpose, e.g. in regard to possible purchase of an undertaking.

In such cases, the degree of verification is determined by the terms of appointment and the Accountant, in his report, will state the scope and the limitations of his responsibility.

It is important to note that the use in the report of the term 'audit' without qualification may fairly be taken to imply verification of the results and position disclosed and reliance may be placed upon it. The work of an accountant is of a technical character and if he is employed as an expert he is expected to bring to bear the skill associated therewith. His report should be in precise terms and the work he does should be such as to verify the substantial accuracy of the statements reported upon consistent with limits of the technical ability expected of such a person, the terms of his appointment and the degree of limitation specifically stated in his report to those appointing him.

In connection with Prospectuses, Offers for sale and applications in regard to the granting of quotations and permission to deal, the London Stock Exchange require that there shall be submitted to the Share and Loan Department by the Auditors a letter confirming 'that they have satisfied themselves that Stocks and Work in progress (if any) have been properly taken and valued throughout the period covered by their report.' Clearly, such a letter must be so worded as to indicate the extent to which the Auditors were unable to satisfy themselves in regard thereto.

On the subject of disclaimer of responsibility, it is of interest to note that where the Auditor of a Holding Company is not also the Auditor of each of the companies whose accounts are consolidated, he will qualify his report on the consolidated statement by including such words as, 'including the accounts of certain subsidiaries that are not audited by me'—thus disclaiming direct responsibility for the verification of the assets &c. of those subsidiaries that are included in the consolidated statement.

While reference has been made herein to Case Law and judgments over fifty years old, it is submitted that the principles therein enunciated are as valid today as when they were stated. Great developments have taken place, not only in the growth of Companies and the registration of Companies with Limited Liability under the Companies Acts, but also in the form of accounting. With all this, the experience and qualification of those engaged on Auditing has increased and with it the general standard of auditing has been raised. The law cases indicate that the judges place reliance on the evidence of practitioners on matters of professional practice and the reasonable standard of skill that might be expected in particular circumstances and we do well to ensure that the standard of each of us is not less than is ordinarily acceptable and that the high standard expected of us is maintained.

In conclusion, was not Shakespeare right when he said in 'Othello', 'Be sure of it, give me the ocular proof?'

DISCUSSION

CHAIRMAN: MR. G. F. KLINGNER, F.C.A. (Ireland)

CHAIRMAN:

It is to me a very great pleasure and a very great honour indeed to have been asked to preside at this session to-day. And speaking on behalf of the organization which I represent here, the Institute of Chartered Accountants in Ireland, I wish to convey on behalf of my Institute our gratitude to the Congress for having permitted me to take the chair. The subject this afternoon, as you know, is titled 'The Verification of the Existence of Assets'. Mr. Foye, in introducing the session this morning, referred to the fact that this morning's subject was possibly somewhat more spiritual than material. Well, I think the operation is now reversed. This subject to-day decidedly is practical and very material and is one which we all have to deal with in our everyday practice and I am sure you agree with me that it is a very well chosen subject as a contrast to the subject of this morning. Now I would like first of all to introduce the persons on the platform with me and I would ask each one to stand when I mention their names so that you will be more familiar with them. Firstly I have to tender an apology from Mr. Lopez of Uruguay who was to be one of the Vice-Chairmen, but I received a letter from him last week, at home before I left for Amsterdam, saying that he very much regretted, through illness, that he was not permitted to travel and asking me to extend his sincere apologies for his absence. I propose, when I return home, with your permission to write to Mr. Lopez and say how sorry we were that he is not here, and wish him a speedy recovery.

Now I would like to introduce first the two Vice-Chairmen, to my left Prof. Sensini of Italy, and Dr. Rojansky from Israel. Then we have the Discussion leader: Prof. Dr. E. Knorr of Germany. And we have then the five authors of papers including one who is the rapporteur. The first name is that of the rapporteur Mr. De Lalanne from Canada, then there is Mr. Donald J. Bevis of America, Mr. Burgert of the Netherlands, Mr. Claude Paquet from France and Sir Richard Yeabsley, C.B.E., from England.

Those, Ladies and Gentlemen, are the five authors of the papers and I am sure that you agree that we are very grateful indeed for all the trouble involved in writing the papers. Last of all we have three other members of the panel with us, firstly Mr. M. Hussain Chaudhury from Pakistan, Mr. G. D. Stewart from New Zealand and Prof. B. J. S. Wimble from South Africa.

And, Gentlemen, that composes the team. So there remains for me at this stage to say that the procedure will be rather similar to this morning. I will, in a moment, hand over the proceedings to Prof. Knorr. The rapporteur, Mr. De

Lalanne will give a brief summary of the papers which will take about fifteen minutes, then there will be the discussion by the panel lasting about an hour, after which there will be twenty minutes for free discussion; and with that I now hand over to Dr. Knorr to take charge of this meeting.

PROF. DR. ERNST KNORR (Germany)

Meine sehr verehrten Damen und Herren,

Der Abschnitt der Aussprache unserer heutigen Nachmittagssitzung zu diesem Gegenstande der Inventarisierung soll beginnen mit dem Bericht unseres Herrn Kollegen De Lalanne, der sich in ganz ausgiebiger Weise mit diesem Stoffe befaßt hat. Einen entscheidenden Teil seines Berichtes haben Sie bereits in gedruckter Form vor sich liegen. Herr De Lalanne wird jetzt die Freundlichkeit haben eine Zusammenfassung seiner Gedanken und Ausführungen hier mündlich vorzutragen.

Ladies and Gentlemen, the discussion this afternoon on our subject, The Verification of the Existence of Assets, will start with the report from our colleague Mr. De Lalanne. He has dealt with this material in a very exhaustivemanner, and you already have an important part of his report before you in print. Mr. De Lalanne will now be kind enough to give us a summary of his paper and of his ideas in general. May I now call on Mr. De Lalanne to read his summary.

MR. J. A. DE LALANNE (Canada)

INTRODUCTION

The terms of reference for this discussion specifically exclude the question of valuation. It is virtually impossible to segregate the verification of existence and relative valuation in the case of some assets, but we have done our best to deal in the main with aspects where this conflict is least evident.

The authors are representatives of five different countries, three in Europe and two in North America, and while the basic plans and methods of approach were different in each instance, the conclusions as to our responsibilities and the recommendations as to procedures were very similar.

EXISTENCE AND OWNERSHIP

To begin with, all agreed that the topic presented a twofold inquiry; firstly, the proving on the one hand that the particular asset did actually exist, at the date of the balance sheet, in physical or some other form, and secondly, that the title or right thereto was actually vested in the owner as recorded.

INSPECTION AND OBSERVATION

There seemed to be unanimous conviction that under most circumstances and, wherever feasible, observation, or as one called it, 'ocular proof', is the surest evidence of existence, and that verification of ownership requires varying techniques dependent on the nature of the asset and other relevant factors.

It was recognized too that frequency of inspection by the auditor will vary widely—having regard to—

the size of the organization under audit;

the location of the various plants, warehouses or other places of business;

effectiveness of the internal organization and control;

DURING THE INTERVAL OF THE GALA CONCERT

Dr. A. de Roos, Deputy-Burgomaster of Amsterdam and Mrs. De Roos greeting Dr. Otto Bredt (Germany) and Mrs. Bredt

AT THE GOVERNMENT RECEPTION

Third from left Professor Dr. J. Zijlstra, Minister of Economic Affairs with Dr. G. M. J. Veldkamp, State Secretary of Economic Affairs and Mrs. Veldkamp (first and second from left) receiving Professor Dr. Th. Limperg Jr. and Mrs. Limperg, Netherlands (first and second from right) who were introduced by the President of the Congress

Thursday night at the Rijksmuseum on the invitation of the Government

the opportunity for and possibility of substitution;

the practices adopted by management in determining stocks on hand; and other considerations.

It is suggested that in the case of immovables, for example, at least for distant or out of the way properties, the auditor would be justified in making personal inspections less frequently than once a year if he had other means of satisfying himself that such properties had not been demolished or transformed.

On the other hand, there was fairly general agreement that other types of assets, especially those falling within the current class, should be inspected by the auditor on an average of at least once a year.

Simultaneous inspection by the auditor of all assets of the same type is considered to be the ideal, but it is appreciated that this can seldom be attained and hence the problem is to find the best substitute in each individual case.

It is suggested that cash and marketable securities should normally be inspected, or confirmed, as of—or close to—the date of the balance sheet, and preferably at other times throughout the year when an element of surprise can be injected.

As regards inventories of raw materials, work in process and finished goods, the same general principles apply and the closer the inspection to the closing date, the less possibility there would be of shortages developing, provided the internal control of stocks in the interim was satisfactory and adequate. On the other hand, inspections and counts of stocks under pressure at a year end sometimes lose their effectiveness and might better be replaced by more calm and searching observation of quantities and qualities throughout the year.

For assets such as notes and accounts receivable, I find that there is an increasing tendency towards the detailed audit being carried out prior to the year end, which again affords more opportunity for appropriate analysis and scrutiny of the accounts, the obtaining of written confirmation or reports where deemed desirable and the follow through of subsequent credits before the date when the auditor must append his report to the annual accounts.

OWNERSHIP

On the question of ownership, the practices in the various countries seem quite similar, e.g., inspection and perusal of

Property deeds, registrations, progress estimates and billings of contractors for land and buildings.

Suppliers' invoices and receiving records for other purchases and scrutiny of purchase agreements or contracts where such exist.

Registrations on certificates for marketable securities or endorsements if carried in street names.

Identifying documents and public registrations in the case of patents, copyrights and the like.

Confirmation of title by the auditor is considered of prime importance as is also the maintenance of appropriate record of any goods received on consignment or of assets carried for others where it is the business of the client to deal in assets which are the property of others.

PROCEDURE

Reference was made in some of the papers to statutory requirements and legal decisions in the matter of stocktaking.

In Great Britain, there have been, over the years, many judicial pronouncements which held that—

'It was no part of the auditor's duty to take stock';

and in regard to confirmation—

'I think he (the auditor) must take a certificate from a person who is in the habit of dealing with and holding securities and who he, on reasonable grounds rightly believes to be in the exercise of the best judgment a trustworthy person to give such certificate.'

and in another case—

'In my judgment it would not be right that auditors should deliberately adopt a standard of verification less than ordinary, below the ordinary standard because the persons with whom they are dealing are persons of specially high reputation'.

In the United States—since 1939—the auditor has been required to observe inventories and confirm receivables where either of these represents a significant proportion of the current assets or of the total assets of a concern. At first it was apparently felt that observing of inventories might take the auditor out of his proper sphere and impose upon him responsibilities for which he was not equipped to assume, either by training or personnel. However, as it has developed, the new procedure has not taken away from the company any of its responsibility for taking the inventory but has merely required the auditor to familiarize himself with the client's organization and plan for stocktaking and through personal observation satisfy himself of the adequacy, thoroughness and effectiveness of the method of determining quantities and qualities and the condition of stock and by making such tests by personal inspection and count as he may deem advisable.

While it was not always the case and regardless of present legal requirements, the foregoing practice now appears to be receiving more universal recognition as desirable and often essential procedure if the auditor is to express a constructive opinion on the inventories.

The frequency and extent of the coverage by the auditor by personal inspection will depend to a considerable degree on the completeness of the company's records of purchases, sales, movement within the plant, internal control, perpetual inventory records where such exist, and his method of stocktaking.

RESPONSIBILITIES

It seems to be an established principle in all countries that it is the responsibility of management to maintain an adequate and effective system of accounts, to adopt the appropriate controls for the safeguarding of the properties and other assets and to prepare such financial statements and reports as are required by the owners, and that it is the responsibility of the auditors to report or express an opinion on the correctness or fairness of such representations of management.

It is the general view too that, with the ever-increasing imposition of new taxes and the ramifications of governmental and other controls, the responsibility of the auditor goes far beyond the detecting of shortages, substitution by design or accident, and other forms of defalcation, matters now dealt with to a greater degree by management.

The auditor's basic responsibility in this connection is to carry out such tests as he may deem necessary to satisfy himself that the client's organization is so designed and functions effectively to ensure that any malpractices should come to light before they reach undue proportions. This, of course, does not relieve the auditor of any responsibility in carrying out his own tests and particularly those which might disclose any misrepresentations in the accounts which could arise through collusion between responsible officials.

Recommended practice is to avoid stereotyped forms of audits and to vary the audit programme both as regards content, procedure and time of inspection, bearing in mind that there must always be a certain amount of overlapping so as to maintain an element of doubt as to when any phase of the undertaking may be subject to scrutiny by the auditor.

In some countries such as Canada, the auditors of incorporated companies are appointed by the shareholders and report to such shareholders. The regulating legislation stipulates minimum disclosure and the matters on which the auditors must report but no attempt is made to dictate the procedure he should adopt to enable him to form an opinion.

Some organizations such as governing bodies of stock exchanges go somewhat further and stipulate the minimum inquiry and procedures which must be followed by the auditor. As regards other countries, I understand that in some instances auditors still report to the directors from whom they receive their appointment and not necessarily directly to shareholders.

INVESTIGATIONS

The annual audit normally covers the overall operations of the particular business, while investigations often are restricted to one or more specific items or phases. In these circumstances, the procedure to be followed and the form of report by the auditor will depend on the terms of reference, the nature of the business, the time element and other factors. In most instances, the auditor will not have had the same opportunity of acquainting himself with the internal organization and the effectiveness of any internal control or internal audit and will probably find himself in the position of having to take a more active part in the organizing and planning of any stocktaking, particularly of materials and stock in trade. In such cases, too, he will probably find it necessary to undertake a simultaneous check of the various similar types of assets and to adopt alternative methods of verification which might not normally be adopted as extensively in the case of an annual audit.

In special types of investigation, the auditor is more likely to require outside technical advice to a greater extent than would apply in the case of an annual audit.

CONCLUSION

To sum up, in regard to the major issues listed in the terms of reference, the general consensus seems to be that:

Stocktaking considered in its broad sense is an essential part of any audit.
Personal inspection is generally the surest evidence of existence.
For assets which can more easily be substituted, inspections with an element of surprise will be found most effective.
The time, frequency and coverage of any inspection will depend on the nature and size of the undertaking, the extent and effectiveness of the internal control and other pertinent factors.
Practices and procedures will of necessity differ widely in the case of investigations as compared with annual audits.
The auditor need not ordinarily have expert technical knowledge of all phases of the operation and, provided he uses reasonable care and skill combined with sound judgment, he would be considered competent to carry out an intelligent and adequate verification of the existence of assets.

PROF. DR. ERNST KNORR (Germany)

Meine Damen und Herren, Es ist sicher in Ihrem Sinne, wenn ich Herrn Kollegen De Lalanne für diese so überaus gedrängte und doch übersichtliche Zusammenstellung aller Gesichtspunkte, die unseren Gegenstand betreffen, herzlich danke. Ich denke, wir werden im Laufe des Nachmittags noch mehrmals die Möglichkeit haben Herrn De Lalanne zu Einzelfragen zu hören. Die Mitglieder des Panels und alle an der schriftlichen Vorbereitung dieses Gegenstandes beteiligten Herren haben zum Teil vor dem Kongreß, zum Teil in einer Vorbesprechung gestern, überlegt, wie aus dieser Fülle von Stoff für die verhältnismäßig kurze Zeit das Beste herausgewählt werden kann. Es bliebe einmal die Möglichkeit, eine große Zahl von Einzelfragen kurz zu besprechen, wie aber auch einige wenige, besonders bedeutsame Fragen herauszuschälen, um ihnen mehr Zeit und Aufmerksamkeit zu widmen.

Wir haben uns übereinstimmend für die letztere Lösung entschieden und haben einige wenige Fragen herausgeschält, von denen wir hoffen, daß auch Sie es gutheißen, wenn wir gerade sie herausstellen und eingehender erörtern. Es bleibt uns ja allen deutlich, daß der ganze Bereich in zwei Stunden immer nur einiges bearbeiten lassen kann, während wir im übrigen ja die Zeit, die wir hier zusammen sind, benutzen können um die Fragen, die man nicht in so kurzer Zeit besprechen kann, weiter aufzustellen. Würden Sie mir erlauben, daß ich Ihnen die Fragen, die wir in diesem Kreise Ihnen besonders vortragen wollten, einmal vorlese.

Ist der von Herrn Kollegen Bevis betonte Unterschied zwischen großen, mittelgroßen und kleinen Unternehmungen tatsächlich für unsere Fragengruppe von Bedeutung? Das ist die erste Frage. Die zweite ist beschränkt auf die Güterbewegung. Welche Revisionsarbeiten sind erforderlich zur Feststellung der Richtigkeit der Darstellung in der Buchführung desjenigen was vorhanden sein soll, und zwar wiederum für die große, mittelgroße und kleine Unternehmung? Inwiefern beteiligt sich der Wirtschaftsprüfer an der Feststellung desjenigen was tatsächlich vorhanden ist, ebenfalls für die große, mittelgroße und kleine Unternehmung?

Die dritte Frage: die Simultaninventur wird von allen Referenten als ein vielfach unerreichbares Ideal angesehen. Welche sonstigen Prüfungsmittel aber stehen, besonders im Falle der großen Unternehmung, an Stelle der Simultaninventur zur Verfügung?

Und die vierte Frage: welche Prüfungsmittel, die sich auf die Feststellung des Vorhandenseins gerade von Forderungen beziehen, haben den Vorzug?

Ich brauche Ihnen nicht zu verschweigen, daß wir eine weitere Frage auch als ähnlich bedeutsam herausgestellt haben, aber wir haben uns mit Rücksicht auf die Begrenzung in der Zeit entschließen müssen, von der Erörterung dieser Frage, wenigstens im Augenblick, abzusehen.

Nun, wenn wir in dieser Folge vorgehen, möge Herr Kollege Burgert als Erster zu der ersten Frage, die ich schnell wiederholen darf, Stellung nehmen, das ist die, ob der vom Kollegen Bevis betonte Unterschied zwischen großem, mittelgroßem und kleinem Unternehmen tatsächlich von Bedeutung ist.

Darf ich Herrn Kollegen Burgert bitten.

Ladies and Gentlemen, no doubt you would like me to express your hearty thanks to our colleague De Lalanne for his very concise yet lucid summary of all aspects of our subject. I imagine that in the course of this afternoon we shall have an opportunity to hear Mr. De Lalanne speak on various questions. The members of the panel and all those who helped to prepare this subject in writing, some of them before the congress, some of them at the preliminary meeting yesterday, have in fact discussed how to make the best selection out of the abundance of material, in view of the comparatively short time at our disposal. We can discuss a large number of questions briefly or a few particularly important questions at greater length. We have unanimously decided on the latter course and have selected a few essential questions, hoping that you will agree if we announce them and proceed to discuss them at length. The whole range cannot, of course, be dealt with thoroughly in two hours. We can use the time at our disposal to discuss the matter as best possible in the time available. Now, I should like to read out the questions which we should like to see discussed.

First of all, the question which Mr. Bevis has emphasized—The difference between large, medium size and small concerns—is that of importance to our particular question? The *Second* question is restricted to the movement of goods—What audit procedures are considered necessary to establish the correctness of the presentation in the accounts of the quantities that ought to be present, and again for the large, the medium size and the small concern. And further, to what extent does the auditor participate in establishing what is really present also in large concerns, medium size concerns and small concerns.

Question number *three*—simultaneous stock-taking is described as an unattainable ideal by all authors of papers, or nearly unattainable. What other checks are possible, particularly in the case of the large concern, to replace simultaneous stock-taking?

Question number *four*—what audit procedures purporting to verify the existence of receivables are to be preferred? Of course, there are other questions of similar importance, but as we do not have much time at our disposal we have had to decide, not to embark on a discussion of these, at least not for the time being. Now if we are to adopt this procedure, I must call on Mr. Burgert to speak on the first question, which is whether the distinction which Mr. Bevis has drawn between large, medium size and small concerns is of real importance.

May I ask Mr. Burgert to address the congress?

MR. R. BURGERT (Netherlands)

Inderdaad acht ik deze onderscheiding voor een vruchtbare discussie van betekenis, indien zij niet gemaakt wordt aan de hand van een criterium, zoals bijv. de grootte van de omzet, het aantal arbeiders, maar aan de hand van een criterium ontleend aan de contrôle-techniek.

Het komt mij voor, dat het meest doeltreffende onderscheidingscriterium gevonden kan worden in de kwaliteit van de administratieve organisatie en interne contrôle. Voorts zullen wij ons moeten baseren op slechts één soort opdracht, nl. een opdracht tot het verrichten van werkzaamheden, die gericht zijn op een goedkeurende verklaring bij de jaarrekening voor een open vennootschap.

I certainly do regard this distinction as of value to a fruitful discussion, as long as it is not made on the basis of a criterion such as, for example, the size of the turnover, the number of workers, but on the basis of a criterion derived from the technique of audit. It seems to me that the most effective criterion for making this distinction can be found in the standard of the bookkeeping and accounting organization and of the internal audit. For the rest, we shall have to base our arguments on one type of commission only, namely, a commission to perform those operations which have as their aim the approval of the annual accounts of a public company.

PROF. DR. ERNST KNORR (Germany)

Darf ich die anderen Herren Mitglieder des Panels und Mitarbeiter fragen, ob sie in diesem Augenblick hierzu noch etwas zu sagen wünschen. Wir hatten in der Vorbesprechung ja den Eindruck, daß Herr Kollege Burgert das Wesentliche hierzu sagen würde. Dann darf ich sicher Ihr Einverständnis damit unterstellen, daß wir zu der zweiten Frage übergehen, die nun mehr ins Detail geht. Darf ich sie selbst noch einmal vorlesen, oder – auch hier wollte Herr Kollege Burgert als erster das Wort nehmen – wollen Sie selber dann die Frage noch einmal vorlesen am Beginn Ihrer Ausführung? Sonst kann ich es gerne übernehmen.

May I ask the other members of the panel whether they wish to add anything to this as yet?
During yesterday's meeting we gathered the impression that Mr. Burgert would say the essential. Then I may take it that you agree to our passing on to the second question which goes into greater detail. Now, shall I read the question once again? Or Mr. Burgert might read the second question himself, before his address, as he will again be the first to speak on the subject. Otherwise I can do it.

MR. R. BURGERT (Netherlands)

De tweede vraag luidt dus, beperkt tot de goederenbeweging: Welke contrôlewerkzaamheden worden nodig geacht om de juistheid vast te stellen van de voorstelling in de boekhouding van de hoeveelheden, die aanwezig behoren te zijn resp. voor the small concern, the medium-sized concern en the large concern? Het tweede deel van deze vraag is dan: In hoeverre neemt de accountant deel aan de vaststelling van datgene, wat werkelijk aanwezig is. Ook deze vraag successievelijk te behandelen voor the small concern, the medium-sized concern en the large concern. Bij de beantwoording van deze vraag zal men van mij wellicht de weergave verwachten van algemeen aanvaarde Nederlandse opvattingen. Ik wil daartoe ook een poging doen, maar daarbij moet ik op de voorgrond stellen, dat over de onderhavige materie thans in ons land nog een discussie gaande is. Het contrôle-programma dat ik in mijn inleiding kort geschetst had, geldt, dunkt mij, naar algemene Nederlandse opvattingen voor het small concern. In dat geval omvat de accountantscontrôle dus een volledige contrôle van de goederenkringloop, omvattende een detailcontrôle van de inkoop, gevolgd door zelfstandige vaststelling van de eindvoorraad en ten slotte afleiding uit deze twee grootheden en de bekende beginvoorraad van de omvang der verkoop. Om misverstand te voorkomen wijs ik er nog op, dat het kwantitatieve verband in de goederenbeweging overal daar, waar er een vast verband bestaat tussen hoeveelheid en waarde, of tussen inkoopprijs en verkoopprijs, ook in geldbedragen gelegd kan worden. De voorraadopname is in dit geval, het geval dus van de kleine onderneming, een simultane inventarisatie op de balansdatum. Het lijkt mij nuttig om ons in dit verband ook af te vragen welke betekenis de accountantsverklaring voor deze kleine onderneming heeft. Naar mijn mening houdt de accountantsverklaring in dit geval dan de zekerheid in, dat zowel de gegevens in de resultatenrekening als die in de balans op grond van een volkomen onderzoek juist zijn bevonden. De accountantsverklaring kan echter bij een small concern niet inhouden, dat de registratie ook inderdaad volledig is geweest. In mijn inleiding heb ik reeds vermeld, dat het onderzoek in principe niet kan leiden tot ontdekking van de weglating uit de registratie van elkaar compenserende inkopen en verkopen. Krachtens de gemaakte veronderstelling is bij het small concern de interne contrôle onvoldoende sterk om de volledigheid der registratie te garanderen. Wanneer ik nu vervolgens overga tot de middelgrote onderneming, dan ga ik me waarschijnlijk bewegen op het terrein, waar de meeste Nederlandse accountants het grootste deel van hun werk vinden. Het werkprogramma is voor het medium sized concern wel zo te typeren, dat als uitgangspunt de contrôle op de goederenbeweging op dezelfde wijze geschiedt als bij het small concern, maar bekortingen zijn mogelijk, zodra, uitgaande van één gecontrôleerde onafhankelijk variabele, andere elementen in de resultatenrekening in totaal, door middel van een verbandcontrôle kunnen worden geverifieerd. Ten aanzien van de inventarisatie geldt, dat de interne contrôle als regel voldoende sterk is om de in mijn inleiding besproken permanent partiële inventarisatie in de plaats te stellen van de simultane inventarisatie op de balansdatum, indien aan de laatste moeilijkheden verbonden zijn of indien deze laatste te tijdrovend zou zijn. Bij zeer sterke interne contrôle komen dan zelfs test counts in aanmerking. De mate van zekerheid, welke de accountantsverklaring biedt, berust bij het medium sized concern nog op dezelfde basis als bij het small concern, maar is bovendien belangrijk toegenomen. De interne organisatie en contrôle, door de accountant onderzocht en regelmatig getest, heft in dit geval de bij het small concern bestaande onzekerheid omtrent de volledigheid van de registratie op. De discussie in ons land loopt nu over de vraag, in hoeverre bij de contrôle van de goederenbeweging, bij effectieve interne contrôle, de detailcontrôle op de inkopen verminderd kan worden. Het is mijn mening, die echter niet als algemeen aanvaard kan gelden, dat de detailcontrôle op de inkoop sterk beperkt kan worden, wanneer het gaat om een groot aantal gelijksoortige transacties en wanneer het mogelijk is door contrôle van het prijsverloop in de tijd na te gaan, of het verband tussen geregistreerde ingekochte hoeveelheid en de totale koopsom juist is.

Wanneer ik dan ten slotte de gestelde vraag bezie voor het large concern, dan moet men naar mijn mening stellen, dat het totaal van de contrôle-werkzaamheden, uit te voeren door de interne en externe accountant, gezamenlijk te vergelijken is met dat voor het medium-sized concern. Een verdere uitwerking zal ons brengen tot een bespreking van de verhouding tussen de interne en de externe accountant. Wij zouden dan naar mijn mening ver buiten ons eigenlijke onderwerp komen en daarom ga ik daarop verder niet in.

Wanneer ik ten slotte het hele terrein nog eens overzie, dan zouden wij waarschijnlijk wel kunnen zeggen, dat de contrôletechniek in Nederland is opgebouwd vanuit het small concern en het medium sized concern, terwijl wij uit de inleidingen de indruk krijgen, dat in Engeland en Amerika de opbouw voornamelijk plaats vond vanuit het large concern. Het uiteindelijk verschil is wellicht in twee vragen weer te geven. De eerste vraag: of het vasthouden aan de consequente beoordeling van de goederenkringloop niet noodzakelijk is om tot een effectieve beoordeling te komen van het bedrijfsresultaat en van hetgeen als voorraad op de balans behoort te verschijnen. En dan de vraag, die vooral voor ons Nederlanders geldt: moeten wij in Nederland niet diepgaand de vraag bestuderen, in hoeverre de detailcontrôle, met name op de inkoop, bij perfecte interne contrôle verminderd kan worden.

The second question—limited to the movement of goods—reads then as follows: What audit operations are considered necessary in order to determine the accuracy of the bookkeeping figures regarding the quantity of goods that should be on hand, and this for the small concern, the medium-sized concern and the large concern respectively. The second part of this question then is: how far must the auditor take part in the job of ascertaining what stocks are actually present. This question likewise to be dealt with from the point of view of the small, the medium-sized and the large concern respectively .

You will probably expect me to reflect the opinions generally accepted in the Netherlands in answering this question. I shall make an attempt to do this, but I should point out first of all that deep discussion of the matter in question is at present going on in our country. The audit programme which I had outlined in my introduction applies, it seems to me, as far as the ideas generally accepted in the Netherlands are concerned, to the small concern. In that case, then, the audit covers a complete control on the circulation of goods, comprising a detailed check of the purchases, followed by independent determination of the final stock and finally the derivation, from these two quantities and the known amount of the initial stock, of the size of sales. In order to avoid any misunderstanding, I would point out that quantitative relations in the movement of goods can always be expressed in money terms as well, where there is a fixed relationship between quantity and value, or between the buying and the selling price. The stock check is in this case, viz., the case of the small concern, a simultaneous stock-taking on the day the balance is struck.

It would be useful, I think, if we were also to ask ourselves in this connection what significance the auditor's statement has for this small concern. In my opinion, in this case the auditor's statement contains the assurance that both the particulars in the profit and loss account and in the balance sheet have been found correct after a complete check. The auditor's statement in the case of the small concern cannot, however, imply that the registration, too, has, indeed, been complete. I have already mentioned in my introduction that, in principle, his inquiries cannot lead to the discovery of the omission in the registration of purchases and sales which cancel each other out. By virtue of the supposition made, the internal audit in the case of the small concern is not strong enough to guarantee the completeness of the registration.

If I now pass over to the medium-sized concern, I shall probably be entering the field where most Dutch auditors find the greater part of their work. The programme of work in the case of the medium-sized concern can be characterized by saying that, as the point of departure, the check on the movement of goods takes place in the same way as in the small concern, but short-cuts are possible as soon as, on the basis of one independent variable that has been checked, one can verify the totals of other elements in the profit and loss account by means of linked checks. As regards the check of stocks, the internal audit is usually reliable ehough to substitute the permanent-partial check discussed in my introduction for the simultaneous stock-taking on the day the balance is struck, should the latter check involve difficulties or require too much time. One can even make do with test counts, if the internal audit is very highly developed. The degree of certainty offered by the auditor's statement remains on the same basis as in the case of the small concern, but is, moreover, considerably greater. In this case the uncertainty existing in the case of the small concern regarding the completeness of the registration is removed by the internal organization and the internal audit, investigated and regularly tested by the auditor.

The discussion going on at the moment in our country concerns the question as to how far the detailed check on purchases can be limited in carrying out the audit of the movement of goods, when it is known that the internal audit is effective. It is my opinion—though this must not be taken as the generally accepted opinion—that we can, indeed, limit the detailed check on purchases very considerably when there is a large number of similar transactions and when it is possible, by examining the price trend during the period concerned, to ascertain whether the relation between the quantity registered as having been purchased and the total amount paid is correct.

Considering, finally, the question as it regards the large concern, one must, to my view, say that the whole body of audit operations to be carried out by the internal and the external auditors together is comparable to that for the medium-sized concern. If we take the matter any further than this, we shall find ourselves discussing the relation between the internal and the external auditor. In my opinion this would lead us far away from our proper subject, and consequently I shall not go any further into the matter than this.

Reviewing the whole field once more, to conclude with, we could probably say that in the Netherlands the technique of audit has been built up on the basis of the small and the medium-sized concern, while we gather the impression from the introductions that in England and America this technique has been built up mainly on the basis of the large concern. The ultimate difference may, perhaps, be illustrated by two questions. The first is: whether it is not essential to keep to the consistent appraisal of the circulation of goods in order to arrive at an effective appraisal of the business results and of what ought to appear as the stock on the balance sheet. And the second—which applies to us Dutchmen in particular: must we not devote careful study in the Netherlands to the question as to how far the detailed check, particularly of the purchases, can be limited, when a perfect system of internal audit is in operation.

PROF. DR. ERNST KNORR (Germany)

Darf ich Ihnen, Herr Kollege Burgert, auch für diese Ausführungen danken. Erlauben Sie mir noch eine kurze Nachbemerkung zur Frage eins. Herr Kollege Burgert hat zur Frage Stellung genommen, ob die Größe der geprüften Unternehmung für unseren Fragenbereich von Bedeutung sei. Die Fragestellung heißt aber praktisch ja auch die Bejahung. Darüber hinaus aber haben gerade die letzten Ausführungen des Kollegen Burgert uns ja belegt, wie auch grundsatzverschieden schon die Prüfungsmaßnahmen sein müssen, je nach der Größe des Betriebes um den es sich handelt. Wir brauchen auf die Frage gerade deswegen nicht mehr einzugehen, weil ich glaube, daß darin volle Übereinstimmung besteht.

Nun hatte Herr Kollege Prof. Wimble den Wunsch sich zu dieser Frage zwei weiter zu äussern. Ist es Ihnen recht, daß Sie jetzt das Wort dazu nehmen?

May I thank Mr. Burgert for these remarks?

Now there is one thing I should like to add to what Mr. Burgert has said—as to whether the size of the concern is of importance to us. In his opinion that is so, but Mr. Burgert's final remarks in particular have shown us, that there can even be differences of principle in audit measures dependent upon the size of the business. We must not go any further into this matter, for I think we are all in agreement on this point. Now Prof. Wimble would like to talk on question two. Would you like to speak now, Professor Wimble?

PROF. B. J. S. WIMBLE (South Africa)

Mr. Chairman, I do not think either part of these two questions really can be answered in a cut and dried way. I think that, as so much depends upon the nature of the business in question and the type of goods, it is very difficult to lay down anything that must invariably be done. And I think one point that perhaps hasn't been stressed enough is that, even in the same concern, it is desirable to vary the audit procedure as much as possible from year to year. The checking of the records kept by a business depends, I think, not so much on whether it is a big or medium-sized or small concern, but on whether the system of internal control in the firm in question is satisfactory or not. If it is satisfactory then I think that small test checks, sampling here and there, will be quite adequate. But even if it is a big or medium-sized concern, and the system of control is not adequate, it may be necessary to extend various checks and possibly, in an extreme case, to do a complete check of the quantitative stock records. With regard to the question of the auditor's responsibility for actually ensuring that stocks are on hand, again I don't think any hard and fast rule can be laid down. I would like to know from the representatives of various countries where physical stock-taking does seem to be the general rule, whether it hasn't to be departed from occasionally. It seems to me that there must be cases where it is quite impossible for the auditors to take any responsibility for the stock at all.

The sort of businesses that I have in mind are dealers in precious stones, where the auditors wouldn't be in a position to know whether the stocks were genuine; dealers in chemicals, where it would be very difficult to know the composition of the stocks, and dealers in works of art, where the auditors might not be in a position to know whether the works were genuine or whether they were copies.

PROF. DR. ERNST KNORR (Germany)

Thank you. May I now call on Sir Richard to address the meeting?

SIR RICHARD YEABSLEY (United Kingdom)

The question posed is what are the procedures which are considered necessary to establish the correctness of the presentation in the accounts of the quantities that ought to be present, in the small concern, the medium and the large concern respectively. It then goes on to ask to what extent is the auditor to participate in establishing what is really present. The extent and character of the audit depends largely on the terms of appointment or contract. The extent may be limited if the terms of the contract permit and the limitations are clearly stated, but where, as in the U.K., the scope of the audit required in regard to Limited Companies is set forth in the Statute, there can be no limitation. In such cases the auditor must satisfy himself on the matters he is required to review by the exercise of reasonable care and skill or to make appropriate qualifications in his report in terms on those matters on which he is unable to satisfy himself. In my view, our Statutes do not put an obligation on the auditor to so review the accounts as to ensure they are what they ought to be, if by this is meant a perfect accounting. That surely is the responsibility of management and the auditor is often not qualified nor in a position to say for example, whether unproductive expenditure ought to have been incurred. However, while he may rely on the responsibility of management to exercise an appropriate system of internal check, he must satisfy himself that there is such a system and that it is efficiently operated. To the extent that it is not, he must take such further steps as are necessary to satisfy himself that the financial position and trading results disclosed are fairly stated. Defalcations may be reflected in accounts in two ways. Firstly, the accounts may be correctly stated, but assets belonging to the company wrongly withdrawn during the year and charged directly or indirectly against the results disclosed by the accounts under review. Secondly, the accounts may be wrongly stated, for example the assets overvalued, or non-existent items included therein to offset such assets wrongly withdrawn from the company.

In the first case the accounts are accurate, but not what they ought to be, in the second, they are what they ought to be but they are not accurate.

Having taken reasonable steps to satisfy himself—and what are reasonable steps must depend on the particular circumstances of each case—it is submitted that no claim would effectively lie against the auditor in respect of defalcations covered in the first case. However, the onus of proof by the auditor as to whether reasonable steps were taken in the second case I quoted, where the accounts do not fairly state the true position, is obviously much greater.

In this connection, we in my country recall the words of Lord Justice Lopez in the classic case of the Kingston Cotton Mills, decided over 60 years ago and may I take a short quotation from it: 'Auditors must not be made liable for not tracking out ingenious and carefully laid schemes of fraud when there is nothing to arouse their suspicion and when these frauds are perpetrated by tried servants of the company and are undetected for years by the directors.'

It is submitted that in essence the legal position of the auditor is little or no different in the case of small, medium or large concerns. The techniques he adopts will, however, differ according to the system of internal check employed and the degree of dispersion of duties and it would seem to follow that the larger the concern the more the auditor must be able to rely on the system of internal audit and check and it is for management to ensure that their responsibility is fully discharged. Beyond this I have nothing to add to what I have said in my paper on Stock in Trade in particular.

PROF. DR. ERNST KNORR (Germany)

Thank you, Sir Richard. May I now call on Mr. Bevis.

MR. DONALD J. BEVIS (U.S.A.)

I concur with Prof. Wimble in that a definite and categorical answer cannot be given to either part of this question. In the first place, the required or necessary audit procedure will depend on the nature of the business under examination. Secondly, the audit procedures employed must be developed and programmed, on the basis of the accounting and internal control procedures in effect. Thirdly, the extent of audit testing will vary with the degree of satisfaction that the auditor obtains in the course of his examination. In other words, the auditor must adapt his procedures to what he finds. However, as a general rule, I think it can be stated that a small concern will have a weak system of internal control, the medium size will have an adequate system of internal control, and the large concern will have an effective system of internal control, including some degree of internal audit. That is the subject for tomorrow afternoon's discussion.

There are, however, several statements that can be made in response to these questions. The auditor is presumed to have a reasonable knowledge of the accounting procedures followed and the results they are expected to produce. With respect to quantities that ought to be present, his knowledge would be based upon his review (including such test checks as are deemed to be necessary in his judgment) of those procedures followed by the organization in controlling the movement of goods from purchase or manufacture to ultimate disposition, including the practices followed in the receipt and shipment of inventories and their control in the course of manufacturing or warehousing.

As to the second part of the question, the auditor generally has no responsibility, as such, for establishing what inventories are really present. His responsibility, except in unusual cases, is limited to being in a position to determine whether or not the amounts shown for inventories in the financial statements have been fairly stated. In making this determination the auditor should have knowledge of, and participate in the discussions of, the physical stock-taking procedures proposed to be employed by the client. He should be present during the period of inventory-taking to make such observations and tests of procedures followed and inventory quantities, as he deems appropriate in the circumstances. Finally, he will have to make certain tests of the inventory pricing and the mathematical accuracy of the compilations and computations. If physical stock-taking occurs at a date other than the date of the examination, then obviously he will have to make such tests of the records between these dates as would be appropriate in the circumstances.

Prof. Wimble raised certain questions with regard to the auditor's responsibility and what he can do in those situations where he is not presumed to have a real knowledge of the inventory quantities. I believe that the auditor can obtain some knowledge through continued association with his client. This knowledge comes from the intimate relationship he has with the records and his familiarity with the past history of the organization. Furthermore, in those situations where internal control is obtained through numbers of people involved, it would require extensive collusion, in my opinion, in order to have anything really go wrong with inventories of that character, just because of the nature of the manufacturing process. There are, however, certain situations where it might be advisable to call in experts, but I think these are definitely in the minority and do not occur very often, and again, to lay down categorical rules to be followed in such cases seems to me to be outside of the question at this meeting. I think I should add that it is the composite knowledge that the auditor obtains from all his procedures and tests that he has employed that enables him to express his opinion. He does not rely solely upon his observation of the inventory or any individual part of the examination but he does rely upon what he obtains through the sum total of his review.

PROF. DR. ERNST KNORR (Germany)

May I now ask Mr. De Lalanne to join the discussion?

MR. J. A. DE LALANNE (Canada)

Mr. Chairman, I think we all agree on the general procedures we should follow in the verification of the inventory. The only place where I would find it difficult to apply rules across the board is in the classifying as to small, medium or large companies, because what we might consider in Canada quite a nice large audit would not necessarily be considered more than a very minor assignment in some of the other countries, particularly those we have spoken of. I suggest that one must take into consideration both the size of the company and also all the various internal controls and other factors which have been raised by previous speakers.

I might raise two or three points for consideration that have not been mentioned as yet. One is, that in Canada I do not think that we can say that we are not responsible or that we can be relieved in any way of responsibility for inventory taking or testing by merely adding a notation to the balance sheet —which at one time was the practice—such as 'Inventories as certified by the Management'. The general feeling now in our country is that this is merely a statement without any real significance and if the inventory turned out to be very different from that as shown, the auditor would still be jointly liable with the management to the same extent as would apply if the reference had not been made. Unless we include a qualification in our report we really do not relieve ourselves of our responsibility. There are two points that I would like to raise in addition to that matter. First, the question of mechanical checking or listing of inventories, and especially when they are carried out at year-ends or at any time when there is a deadline for the date of filing a report or submitting of statements. The tendency in our country now is to get away almost entirely from mechanical checking whether it be a matter of inventories or of any other listings, and to take more time to study the basic entries; in the case of stocks, to pay much more attention to quantities and sizes, the saleability, the age, the movement and the amount of stock being carried in relation to foreseeable requirements and the like; also when we are depending on internal auditors, not only to ascertain that the internal auditors have satisfied themselves, but to study meticulously the reports of the internal auditors and the adjustments that they have made and to ensure that the books of accounts have been adjusted appropriately to the figures which the internal auditors have established from their studies.

The other point is that where stocktakings are being observed by auditors and particularly in the larger company, I suggest that planning with the management in advance of the stocktaking is a very important part of the auditor's responsibility and a great aid to him in observing the procedures and in the follow up afterwards which has been described by Mr. Bevis.

Those, I think, are the only points in my memorandum, Mr. Chairman, which have not been covered by other speakers.

PROF. DR. ERNST KNORR (Germany)

Thank you. Would Mr. Burgert like to say something about that?

MR. R. BURGERT (Netherlands)

Naar aanleiding van het door de vorige sprekers naar voren gebrachte zou ik met name nog even stil willen staan bij de vraag, of zij wel evenveel betekenis hechten als wij in Nederland aan de juistheid van de resultatenrekening. Men krijgt zo de indruk, dat in het betoog van de vorige sprekers toch wel de contrôle op de balans in het bijzonder op de voorgrond wordt gesteld.

Ik zou dit wat nader willen illustreren door de twee voorbeelden van Sir Richard Yeabsley nog eens de revue te laten passeren. Sir Richard heeft twee gevolgen onderscheiden, in het eerste is er sprake van een onrechtmatige onttrekking aan het bedrijfsvermogen, welke ten laste van de resultatenrekening is gebracht. Sir Richard vindt, dat de jaarrekening dan is 'accurate, but not what it ought to be'. Ik geloof dat we in dit geval ten aanzien van de resultatenrekening alleen maar van 'accurate' zouden kunnen spreken, wanneer deze onttrekking als 'non-operational loss' tot uitdrukking was gebracht.

In het tweede geval is een onttrekking aan het ondernemingsvermogen aan het oog onttrokken door een te hoge voorstelling van andere activa. Hier noemt Sir Richard de jaarrekening 'not accurate' maar wel 'what it ought to be'. Naar mijn gevoel is het laatste alleen het geval, wanneer de vereiste overboeking in dit geval duidelijk uit de rekening blijkt of in het verslag is toegelicht en niet leidt tot een te hoge voorstelling van het vermogen.

Het spreekt wel van zelf, dat wanneer we deze vraag bezien, we het bekende recept uit de economie moeten toepassen: 'go to the margin and find the truth' en moeten veronderstellen dat het gaat om een onttrekking van zeer wezenlijke grootte. Ik kan dan, geloof ik, ook Sir Richard niet volgen bij zijn onderscheiding van deze twee criteria voor juistheid, namelijk 'accurate' en 'what it ought to be', ik geloof dat er maar één criterium is en dat is, dat de gehele jaarrekening, bestaande uit resultatenrekening én balans een juiste voorstelling moet geven, in de eerste plaats van de grootte en de samenstelling van het vermogen en in de tweede plaats van de wijze, waarop de winst of het verlies is behaald.

Ik meen dan ook, dat in het eerste voorbeeld van Sir Richard in principe naar onze Nederlandse opvattingen, de accountant te kort zal schieten tenzij de boeking als een 'non-operational loss' duidelijk zal blijken.

Ik ben het wel met Sir Richard in algemene zin eens, dat de accountant niet in de eerste plaats gezien moet worden als een ontdekker van fraude. Maar daarbij wil ik toch wel in aanmerking nemen, dat de grenzen tussen onjuiste voorstellingen, in verband met onrechtmatige onttrekkingen aan de ene kant, en die, in verband met onjuiste voorstellingen van wat feitelijk is gebeurd, aan de andere kant, niet scherp te trekken zijn. Feitelijk betekent dit, dat wanneer we niet voortdurend op de eerste, op fraudes dus, bedacht zijn, ook de tweede onjuiste voorstelling gevaar loopt niet ontdekt te worden. Dan immers worden vermogensverminderingen voortgevloeid uit onrechtmatige handelingen en vermogensverminderingen door verliezen uit economische oorzaken dooreengemengd.

In view of what the preceding speakers have said, I should just like to ask whether they attach as much importance as we do in the Netherlands to the accuracy of the profit and loss account. One gathers the impression that in what the preceding speakers have said the main emphasis is laid on the balance sheet.

I should like to illustrate this further by going over the two examples quoted by Sir Richard Yeabsley. Sir Richard distinguished between two results; in the first there is a question of the assets of the company having been wrongly withdrawn and charged against the results. In this case, Sir Richard is of the opinion that the accounts are 'accurate, but not what they ought to be'. I think that in this case, as far as the profit and loss account is concerned, we should only be able to speak of it being 'accurate', if this withdrawal were shown as a 'non-operational loss'. In the second case it is a question of a withdrawal of the company's assets being concealed by putting other assets at too high a figure. In this case Sir Richard says the accounts are 'not accurate' but that they are 'what they ought to be'. I feel that this is only so, if the required transfer is clearly apparent, in this case, from the accounts, or is explained in the report, and does not lead to an overstatement of the assets.

It goes without saying that in considering this question, we have to apply the well-known formula in economics: 'Go to the margin and find the truth' and must suppose that a withdrawal of real size is involved. I don't think I can agree with Sir Richard as regards the distinction he makes between these two criteria of accuracy either, that is to say, between 'accurate' and 'what it ought to be'. I believe there is one criterion only, and that is that the entire accounts, consisting of the profit and loss account *and* the balance sheet, must accurately reflect the situation, in the first place as regards the size and the composition of the assets, and in the second place as regards the way the profit or the loss has been arrived at.

I am accordingly of the opinion that in the first of Sir Richard's examples, in principle, according to our Dutch conception of things, the auditor will not have fulfilled his task properly unless the entry is clearly apparent as a 'non-operational loss'. I am in agreement with Sir Richard in the general sense that the auditor must not be regarded primarily as a detector of fraud. But I would remark that it is not possible to draw a clear line between wrong statements connected with wrongful withdrawals on the one hand and wrong statements of what has actually happened on the other. In practice this means that if we are not continually on the look-out for the first, that is, for fraud, the second type of wrong statement runs the risk of passing undetected. In that case, reductions of the assets resulting from illegal transactions are mixed up with reductions of assets resulting from losses due to economic causes.

PROF. DR. ERNST KNORR (Germany)

Ich danke Ihnen, Herr Kollege Burgert.

Meine Damen und Herren, wenn aus dem kleinen hier versammelten Kreise niemand mehr das Wort nehmen möchte zu dieser Frage, möchte ich auch vorschlagen, daß wir die Diskussion beschließen, ohne daß wir sie als erschöpft ansehen können, damit wir auch noch zu den anderen Fragen kommen, denn bei unserer Zeiteinteilung hatten wir zunächst nicht angenommen, daß wir soviel Zeit zur Besprechung des bisher Besprochenen in Anspruch nehmen würden. Aber ich möchte wohl hoffen, daß Sie mir darin zustimmen, daß wir keine der hier spontan erwachsenen Äußerungen entbehren möchten. Wenn schon in diesem kleinen Kreise sich ergibt, daß auf dem Wege zum gemeinsamen Ziel zu zuverlässigen Vermögens- und Bestandsfeststellungen verschiedene Wege führen, ist es umso eher verständlich, daß bei der großen Zahl von Tausenden Accountants in jedem Lande verschiedene Wege beschritten werden. Ich möchte das nicht einmal bedauern, denn diese Berufsarbeit kann ja unmöglich einheitlich und mechanisch und gleichartig sein, sie muß schon sehr individuell sein, wenn nur das Ziel nicht nur angestrebt, sondern nach weiterer Möglichkeit auch erreicht wird.

Darf ich nun vorschlagen, daß wir dann zur Frage 3 übergehen? Ich darf sie noch einmal in Ihr Gedächtnis zurückrufen, ohne Ihr Erinnerungsvermögen gering anschlagen zu wollen: sie lautet nach der mir vorgelegten Fassung: Simultaninventur wird von allen Referenten als ein vielfach unerreichbares Ideal betrachtet; welche sonstigen Prüfungsmittel stehen besonders im Falle der Großunternehmungen an Stelle der Simultaninventur zur Verfügung?

Zu dieser Frage wollen aus diesem Kreise wieder mehrere Herren das Wort nehmen. Ist es nun recht, wenn Herr Kollege Stewart das Wort zunächst nimmt?

Thank you, Mr. Burgert. Ladies and Gentlemen, if no one else wishes to comment on this matter, I should now like to suggest that we come to the end of this part of our discussion, while admitting that we haven't exhausted the subject. I think that we now ought to go on into the next question, as we had not actually expected to take up as much time as we have done on the first questions. But I hope that I may take it that you agree with me when I say that we would not have liked to do without any of the spontaneous comments that have been made this afternoon; we have heard this afternoon that various methods are adopted for the verification of the existence of assets, and if we found that among such a comparatively small number of accountants, it is obvious that there must be a great difference of opinion among all the many thousands of accountants at work in the various countries. I cannot regret that, for our professional work cannot be uniform and mechanical, but must always be highly individual if we are not only to aim at a goal but to seek further possibilities.

May I now suggest that we go on to question 3. I may remind you how that question reads, although I am sure you all have good memories—but anyway, may I read it to you again—Simultaneous stock-taking is considered as an almost unattainable ideal by nearly all the authors of the papers presented here. What other checks are possible, particularly in the case of the large concern, to replace simultaneous stock-taking? Quite a number of people would like to talk on this point, perhaps Mr. Stewart will make a start.

MR. G. D. STEWART (New Zealand)

The question says that simultaneous stock-taking has been regarded by the members of the panel as a 'mostly unattainable ideal' and it goes on to ask what other checks are possible particularly in the case of large concerns. The questioner says that all authors agree that it is an 'ideal'; my reading of the papers is not that. To me the majority agreed that continuous stock-taking is preferable, particularly in the case of larger companies. It is desirable audit procedure for the auditor to be present at certain times in connection with the stock-taking, to verify the physical existence of the stock. He can verify certain large items; he can review the stock-taking system employed by the company; and he can review the methods employed by the people who are put on to do the job. Stock-taking requires good organization. The auditor who has checked the methods employed in taking the stock is in a better position to be satisfied when he comes to verify the existence of this very important asset.

The main place to go to for verification of work in progress, I consider, would be the costing records; one would have to see that the goods were subsequently sold or transferred to finished stocks and also do a review of outstanding work orders. (Some of these things have been mentioned by other speakers earlier, I am afraid I cannot help a certain amount of repetition.)

Management is responsible for stock-taking. The auditor has to guard against becoming a stock-taker or a valuer. He can form a better opinion of the value and the existence of stock by actual inspection.

Thus I would say that actual attendance is desirable to verify:

1. that stock-taking is properly planned and controlled;
2. that the company's employees are doing the work effectively, and
3. that the stock appears to be correctly recorded as to description and quantity.

The audit development in recent years has been towards the verification of the internal check and test checks of actual transactions. Continuous stock-taking lends itself to this development. The auditor can reduce other detailed checking if he is satisfied that the stock-taking has been done seriously and efficiently. The auditor's certificate must be of greater value if he has been present at or, connected with, some part of the stock-taking. It is much more valuable surely, if he has seen what is happening: the ocular proof which was referred to earlier. It may not be possible to do this every year, in every audit. An auditor could, it is suggested, attend and observe say every three or four years to satisfy himself that the company's methods are efficient and that the work is properly carried out. By doing so I consider that he would be in a stronger position to give his certificate, to say that the value of the assets is a true and fair one. Being present at the continuous stock-takings does pose practical difficulties for the auditor, and I think it would be a useful point for our discussion as to the way in which and the extent to which the auditor should arrange to attend continuous stock-taking so as to satisfy himself in a manner comparable with the manner he adopts at a simultaneous stock-taking. I think, we have to adjust ourselves in our auditing to altered methods and to the altered size of businesses, and it appears to me that we have to adjust ourselves to simultaneous stock-taking, which is really the only logical method for the very large concerns. Thank you.

PROF. DR. ERNST KNORR (Germany)

Thank you, Mr. Stewart.

Ich möchte gern vorschlagen, daß wir dann zur Frage 4 übergehen. Ich darf auch diese Frage noch einmal vorlesen: Welche Prüfungsmittel, die sich auf die Feststellung des Vorhandenseins von Forderungen beziehen, haben den Vorzug? Eine Frage, die ja je nach der Bedeutung, die der Posten 'Forderungen' in der Bilanz hat, ein größeres oder geringeres Gewicht, aber immer ein Gewicht haben wird. Zu dieser Frage, darf ich nun annehmen, wird Herr Kollege Hussain Chaudhury zuerst das Wort nehmen. Bitte sehr.

I would like to suggest that we go on to our fourth question. I will read out this question again too. What audit procedures purporting to verify the existence of receivables are to be preferred? This is a point which varies in importance, according to the size of the items, receivables in question. I think that Mr. Hussain Chaudhury would like to comment on this point first of all.

MR. M. HUSSAIN CHAUDHURY (Pakistan)

The question of verifying the receivables as disclosed by the management in a balance sheet is a matter of vital importance to an auditor and presents him with some complications in selecting the procedure that he should preferably adopt to satisfy himself as to the accuracy and exactness of the figure of receivables. Unlike some other assets, this asset cannot be verified by what has been termed an 'ocular proof', being very much of an abstract nature. This factor warrants special attention and consideration from the auditor in the matter of the adoption of some convincing method to justify the certification of this class of asset. The verification procedures will vary in different cases. The most satisfactory and soundest method, preferable in all cases, is a direct 'confirmation' by the persons and organizations under obligation, secured in a way free from all interference and influence by the management.

Confirmatory letters issued by the organization may be either in a positive or negative form.

Some countries, like America, are said to have already adopted such procedures; but here we are dealing with the question on an international level. In other countries, such a step on the part of the auditor would be construed as lying outside the scope of his duties. Such methods are, however, to be recommended for universal application, since the practice of direct confirmation almost puts the auditor in direct touch with the third parties in the matter of ascertainment of their obligations towards the organization being audited —the most authentic way of satisfaction for the auditor, and for the respective parties too.

Notwithstanding all that has been said in favour of the above method, there are certain drawbacks, as luck will have it. The vital question that confronts the auditor, and rather perturbs him, is the 'silence' of some of the parties to whom such confirmatory letters are addressed. Naturally, there will be some cases in which the auditor will receive neither a confirmation of the amount involved nor any other communication. The problem before him would be whether he should treat such silence as a sign of confirmation of the accuracy of the balance or a denial of it. Silence cannot be treated as a denial, but it would be risky to take it as a confirmation.

The adoption of the negative method would tend to nullify the whole object of verification. Mention may be made here of cases where fictitious debits are created in the name of parties who do not exist. Accordingly, no confirmation will be received. What a fantastic and ridiculous situation would emerge, if the auditor were to take the silence as confirmation in such cases.

The auditor has no authority over third parties; confirmations or denials cannot therefore be secured by force. Thus the auditor has either to satisfy himself by 'other means' or to qualify his report regarding the amount remaining unconfirmed.

The following measures may, however, be adopted by the auditor in order to judge the fairness of the figures, keeping in view the circumstances governing the particular business and the applicability of such methods to the case in question:

1. The auditor should carefully spot the items which may have been outstanding for a long time, probe deeply into each to find out its nature, and carefully observe what efforts have been made to recover the amount, before it is barred by limitation.
2. The auditor should further pick up some material items and examine the position as regards recoveries during the ensuing period. Reasonable recoveries in the subsequent period will go a long way to satisfy the auditor as to the correctness of the figure.

No hard and fast rule can, however, be laid down in the matter of verification of receivables. Much will depend on the circumstances of the case, the extent of internal check applied, the nature of business under audit, the volume of receivables in ratio to other assets, etc. The auditor's discretion and sound judgement play a very important role in devising the most suitable check in any particular case to satisfy himself as to the correctness, fairness or exactness of the figures. Thank you.

PROF. DR. ERNST KNORR (Germany)
Mr. Paquet would you like to follow now?

MR. CLAUDE PAQUET (France)
Vous me permettez d'abord de rappeler l'idée primordiale qui a été développée par tous les rapporteurs et reprise dans l'introduction de cette séance par Monsieur De Lalanne, à savoir que l'inventaire simultané est un idéal le plus souvent irréalisable. En partant de cette constatation il semble que l'on soit obligé pour vérifier l'existence des créances commerciales de procéder successivement à deux contrôles, le premier le contrôle de la naissance de la créance. Toute créance a une origine qu'il faut rechercher, afin de s'assurer de son existence. Cette origine pourrait être un prêt de capitaux, un profit exceptionnel, un produit dû à l'activité normale de l'entreprise, évidemment le plus souvent ce sera une vente. Ainsi faut-il rattacher la naissance de la créance, c.à.d. une augmentation de l'actif, soit à une diminution de ce même actif, soit à une augmentation du passif, ou éventuellement à ces deux mouvements simultanés qui peuvent se produire dans le bilan. Le deuxième contrôle serait la vérification de l'existence actuelle de cette créance. Sachant que la créance existait à un moment donné, il faut encore vérifier qu'elle n'est pas éteinte. On ne pourra le vérifier qu'en demandant au débiteur s'il est d'accord sur la dette qu'il a envers l'entreprise. Et ici nous avons évidemment deux possibilités, le débiteur reconnaît l'existence actuelle de cette dette et il n'y a naturellement pas de problèmes; deuxième possibilité: il n'est pas d'accord, il ne reconnaît pas la dette. Ici il y a encore deux cas. Il peut ne pas reconnaître cette dette, parce qu'il n'est pas d'accord sur l'origine de celle-ci; nous retombons à ce moment dans la première partie du contrôle qu'il faudra pousser plus avant, et qui dans certains cas ne peut d'ailleurs être solutionnée que devant les tribunaux. Ou bien, il n'est pas d'accord, il ne reconnaît pas cette dette, parce qu'il prétend de l'avoir réglée, il faudra rechercher de quelle manière il s'est libéré et contrôler dans la comptabilité de l'entreprise créancière ou soi-disant telle, contrôler l'existence du payement. Dans l'un ou l'autre cas: reconnaissance par le débiteur de sa dette, ou non-reconnaissance de sa dette, il faudra que l'expert se persuade de la réciprocité des deux comptabilités. J'entends par là que l'une des entreprises peut tenir en comptabilité des écritures d'acceptation ou de création d'effets et considérer cette acceptation comme un payement; alors que l'autre ne comptabilise le payement de l'effet, comme si c'était uniquement le règlement de la créance elle-même. Des divergences peuvent donc apparaître entre plusieurs comptabilités. Ces divergences étant de pure forme, de même, si l'entreprise créancière a escompté les effets tirés sur son débiteur, elle peut ne plus avoir tracé dans sa comptabilité de cette créance, qui, cependant, existe effectivement jusqu'au payement de l'effet, son échéance. Et cette non-apparition, si je peux dire, de la créance peut être compensée par une dette éventuelle envers le banquier escompteur, dette qui n'apparaîtra qu'à l'échéance de l'effet, si celui-ci est impayé.

Je me permets maintenant de dire un tout petit mot qui est un tout petit peu en dehors de la question. Je voulais faire remarquer, qu'en Grande-Bretagne ou également aux Etats-Unis ainsi que l'ont fait remarqué à la fois le rapporteur général et dans leurs rapports M. Yeabsley et M. Bevis, l'audit existe depuis de nombreuses années; il est autant permis par la pratique, que par la jurisprudence de poser des normes de vérification. En France aucune méthode officielle n'a été mise au point. Ce que je vous dis à l'instant est une opinion plus ou moins personnelle. Actuellement néanmoins la Chambre Nationale des Experts-Comptables diplômés par l'Etat, qui est l'une des grandes associations françaises d'experts-comptables, a créé enfin en février dernier seulement, une Commission d'Etudes sur la certification des bilans, dont le président est d'ailleurs parmi nous ce soir. Les conclusions de cette commission seront présentées d'ici quelques jours les 21 et 22 septembre à un congrès qui doit avoir lieu à Lille, et sont à peu près les suivantes: tout d'abord la certification des bilans est une mesure d'affinissement des affaires et pour les actionnaires qui auront plus de garantie en ayant un bilan certifié par une personne honorable et d'autre part pour les pouvoirs publics, les administrations, les banques etc. Cette certification aboutirait, je vous rappelle que ce n'est qu'un projet, à un rapport assez étoffé, mais qui resterait confidentiel, et à une lettre de certification, qui, elle serait publique ou à peu près publique, que l'on pourrait donner à toute personne. Les normes et méthodes de certification, de vérification n'ont, par contre, pas été discutées, de façon très nette, et ils restent encore à voir.

On a pensé naturellement aux méthodes anglosaxones, mais également à une autre méthode peut-être un peu plus récente, qui serait le contrôle budgétaire, que l'on pourrait appliquer à beaucoup d'entreprises. De toute façon l'idée pour le moment n'est qu'en l'air, on ne sait pas exactement où l'on va. Je crois qu'il est intéressant cependant de vous tenir au courant de ces projets.

If you will allow me, I should like to recall the basic idea which was developed by all the authors and taken up again in the introduction to this meeting by Mr. De Lalanne. That is to say that simultaneous stocktaking is an ideal which is usually unattainable. If we start from this observation, it seems we are obliged, in order to verify the existence of receivables, to take two successive steps. The first is the check on the origin of the receivable item. Every receivable has some origin, which must be searched for in order to verify its existence. It may be a capital loan, any exceptional profit, the product of the normal activity of the undertaking, while obviously, in most cases, it will be a sale. It is consequently necessary to link the origin of the receivable, that is to say, an increase in the assets, either to a reduction of these same assets, or to an increase in the liabilities or, possibly, to both these simultaneous movements, which can appear on the balance sheet.

The second control would be the verification of the continued existence of this receivable. Knowing that the item existed at a certain moment, we must still verify that it still exists.

This can only be verified by asking the debtor if he agrees that he has this debt to the undertaking. There are two possibilities here; the debtor admits that the debt exists, whereupon there is no further problem, or he doesn't admit the existence of the debt. There are two situations here as well; he cannot admit the claim because he is not in agreement as regards its origin. This brings us back to the first possibility, which has to be investigated further, and in certain cases can be solved only by resort to law. Or, secondly, he does not admit to the debt, because he alleges he has paid it; and we then have to find out the way he paid it. This can be checked from the accounts of the firm in question. In both cases—admission or non-admission of the item by the debtor—the auditor will have to see that the accounts of both firms concerned agree. By this I mean that the one firm may keep in its accounts records of acceptance or bills and consider these as payments, whereas the other party does not bring the payment into account until actually made. Differences can therefore appear between various systems of bookkeeping. If the undertaking which has the claim has discounted the bill issued to his debtor, there may be no trace left in his accounts of this credit claim, which exists nevertheless, until the moment the bill is paid. And this non-appearance of the credit can be compensated by a possible debt to the banker, who has paid the bill. This would appear only when the bill has been paid, if it is paid, of course.

I would now like to add here a very few words, which are a little outside the scope of the question. I would like to say that in Great Britain and the U.S. as was pointed out by the general rapporteur and in the reports of Messrs. Yeabsley and Bevis, audit has existed for quite a number of years and both practice and law permit norms of verification to be laid down. In France no special method has been developed. This, of course, is a personal opinion. As recently, however, as last February, the Chambre Nationale des Experts-Comptables diplômés par l'Etat, which is one of our large organizations of accountants, set up a commission to study the certification of balance sheets; the chairman of that commission is present among us to-day. The findings of this commission will be submitted in a few days time, on 21st and 22nd September, to a congress to be held in Lille; they consist roughly of the following: first, the certification of the balance sheets is a healthy measure both for shareholders who would receive better guarantees by having their balance sheets certified by a qualified person, and secondly for the public authorities, administrations, banks, etc. This certification would lead to a fairly lengthy report which would, however, remain confidential, and a briefer certificate which would be made public, or at least available to any person requesting it. The standards and methods of certification, of verification, have not, however, been fully discussed up to now, and we must see how things develop.

We have, of course, had the British methods in mind, but also a rather more recent method, viz. budgetary control, which could be applied to a great number of undertakings. Up to now the idea is still in the air, we do not know where we are going. I thought it worth while, however, to inform you of these plans.

PROF. DR. ERNST KNORR (Germany)

Merci bien, Monsieur Paquet.

Meine Damen und Herren. Es wollte sich zu diesem Gegenstande auch noch äußern, erneut Herr Kollege De Lalanne und die Herren Kollegen Prof. Wimble und Burgert. Mit Rücksicht darauf aber, daß wir noch einen Beitrag von Herrn Kollegen Densem – Mr. Densem hier? – hören wollten, würde es wohl zu schätzen sein, wenn wir diese Beiträge nun zurückstellten. Ich darf auch an dieser Stelle sicher mit Ihrem Einverständnis feststellen, daß wir in einer so kurzen Arbeitstagung immermehr nur die Fülle der Gesichtspunkte und Probleme sehen, ohne sie auch nur annähernd erschöpfend würdigen zu können. Das wird auch in den Jahren nach diesem Kongreß, in denen wir das alles ja weiterentwickeln wollen, unsere Aufgabe sein. Wenn Sie demnach einverstanden sind, möchte ich jetzt Herrn Densem das Wort zu einem Aussprachebeitrag geben, der in den Abschnitt – wie wir ihn nennen – 'free discussion' hineinfällt.

Thank you, Mr. Paquet.

Ladies and Gentlemen, Mr. De Lalanne would like to speak again on this point, and also Prof. Wimble and Mr. Burgert. But our colleague Mr. Densem wants to take part in the debate. Is Mr. Densem here? I think we had best call on Mr. Densem first, and I think at this stage I may say with your approval that we cannot exhaust all the many aspects of this problem in so short a business session as this. We shall have to do that in the years following this congress, in which we will have to study all these problems further. I may take it that you will agree with me when I now call on Mr. Densem to read his paper. His contribution will come under the heading 'free discussion'.

MR. W. G. DENSEM (United Kingdom)

Mr. Chairman, Ladies and Gentlemen, I really have a question I wish to ask, which has been half answered already. I was very concerned with the insistence which is now put on the attendance by auditors at stock-takings. It is, to my mind, merely part of the general auditing procedures. But, when one reads the literature that is written on this subject, one is left in doubt whether it is always understood that it is merely an auditing procedure. And one wonders whether, in the minds of some accountants and, possibly, in the mind of some clients, there is doubt as to the exact responsibility of the auditor. Mr. De Lalanne has already said that the whole responsibility for taking the inventory rests upon management. I am concerned that we in our profession make certain that our position as auditors is fully understood, and that we are not held to be in any way stock-takers.

PROF. DR. ERNST KNORR (Germany)

Meine Damen und Herren, Darf ich hören ob auch in kleinerem Kreise noch das Wort gewünscht wird? Ich habe den Eindruck, daß Herr Kollege De Lalanne noch mancherlei sagen möchte und sehr zu kurz gekommen ist, ja? Wollen Sie noch einiges sagen? Darf ich Ihnen das Wort noch einmal geben?

Ladies and Gentlemen, may I ask whether anybody else would like to take the floor. I think that Mr. De Lalanne has quite a few comments that he would like to put forward, and he has not been given much time to do so, so far. Would Mr. De Lalanne like to address us again?

MR. J. A. DE LALANNE (Canada)

Mr. Chairman, My comments will be very brief. I would just like to mention that there appears to be a great tendency to lay particular stress on the verifying of accounts receivable which appear in the records, whereas it seems to be that there is also a responsibility on the auditor to ensure to the best of his ability that everything which should be set up in the records is actually recorded. When I stated in the summary that it was not feasible always to separate the verification of existence and valuation, I was particularly referring to accounts receivable. I appreciate that a great many auditors do not place much confidence in direct communication with debtors, for reasons with which I must agree. I realize, too, that normally, if a debtor finds something wrong with a confirmation which has been mailed to him by the client with a request to reply to the auditor, nine times out of ten and probably more often, he will speak to the clerk in the client's office with whom he has been dealing and tell him that there is something wrong with the statement. Of course, that clerk is generally the very person who knows that there was something wrong with it before it was sent out. However, notwithstanding that weakness, I still contend that direct communication with debtors has its advantages and above all creates a very good moral influence on employees.

I consider, too, that in the case of verification of receivables the best time to carry out the detailed check is at the time of the interim audit. And in that connection I might mention that in Montreal, Canada, my home town, our Investment Dealers' Association has just recently changed its regulations to permit the verification of balances during any period not more than 90 days prior to the audit date. That was done mainly because of the speed with which the accounts had to be checked in busy periods, generally calendar year end and hence they could not always be given thorough scrutiny. Another point I would like to make is that in auditing accounts receivable I think there again we should get away from mechanical checking and listing, and that we should do what one of my associates of the United Kingdom always refers to as auditing in depth and that we should pay more attention to the nature and origin of the charge, how it is billed, terms of credit and all the other relative aspects, rather than simply listing down a group of figures, adding them up and finding that they agree with the book totals.

The last point about which I would have spoken, if we had more time, is the different treatment, which, I find, is sometimes given to bills and notes receivable as compared with accounts receivable. It seems to me that in that instance it is all the more desirable that we should have direct communication with the debtors, as well as the normal confirmation by the banker or other person holding the notes, to obtain the debtor's admission as to the existence and due date of the note. Here again I consider that mere verification of the note is not sufficient—it should be traced back and compared with the relative open account in the books, if there is one, to find out just how old such account is and whether in fact it is a good receivable. That is probably a question of valuation, but I suggest it comes into the verification of existence as well. I think that covers the main points of which I would have spoken, had there been more time.

PROF. DR. ERNST KNORR (Germany)

Mr. Burgert also has a few words to say.

MR. R. BURGERT (Netherlands)

Ik zou nog graag iets in het midden willen brengen over de keuze van de contrôlemiddelen gericht op de contrôle van vorderingen, nl. de saldobiljetten en de contrôle door middel van wat de Engels sprekende heren noemen 'subsequent payment'. Ik heb er in mijn inleiding al op gewezen, dat waarschijnlijk de voorkeur in de Angelsaksische landen voor saldo-bevestigingen wel gezocht moet worden in de daar bestaande betalingsgewoonten. In landen echter met een sterk ontwikkeld giroverkeer verdient, wanneer het althans handelsvorderingen zijn die door remises per factuur worden afgewikkeld, de methode van afloopcontrôle, contrôle dus door middel van 'subsequent payment', de voorkeur. Deze contrôle immers levert voor de inmiddels afgewikkelde vorderingen tevens een feilloos oordeel over de volwaardigheid daarvan. Afloopcontrôle is, dunkt mij, alleen mogelijk aan de hand van girostukken, omdat uit deze girostukken altijd duidelijk blijkt, in de eerste plaats door wie de betaling is verricht, en in de tweede plaats wanneer zij is verricht.

I should just like to say a word about the choice of the means of audit aimed at verifying the accounts receivable, namely balance slips and verification by means of what our English friends refer to as 'subsequent payment'. I have already made reference in my introduction to the fact that the reason for the preference shown in the Anglo-Saxon countries for verifications of balances must be sought in the methods adopted in these countries for making payments. In countries where a great deal of payment is done by means of transfer accounts, at least in the case of commercial accounts receivable, which are settled by remittances as per invoice, the 'subsequent payment' method of verification deserves preference. For this type of verification makes it possible to arrive at a definite opinion as to the completeness of the claims, which in the meantime have been settled. Subsequent payment verification is, it seems to me, only possible on the basis of transfer (giro) account slips, since these slips show clearly, firstly, who made the payment and, secondly, when the payment was made.

PROF. DR. ERNST KNORR (Germany)

Möchte nun hier noch jemand das Wort? Ja – Mr. Bailey – aber wir werden es nicht schaffen. Dann möchte ich Ihr Einverständnis damit unterstellen, daß ich noch einiges Zusammenfassendes sage und dann dem Herrn Präsidenten den Schluß der Versammlung überlasse.

Meine Damen und Herren, erlauben Sie mir zunächst noch ein Wort des Dankes an Herrn Kollegen Prof. de Jong, an Herrn Kollegen Jonkers und Herrn Kollegen Van Duin. Diese drei Herren haben auch sehr konzentrierte und auf das Ziel gesteuerte Ausführungen beitragen wollen, aber wir werden mit Rücksicht auf den festgesetzten Zeitplan nicht dazu übergehen können auch diese Ausführungen zu hören. Umsomehr drängt es mich, diesen Herren für ihre fleißige Mitarbeit, die nun hier nicht zu Ihren Ohren kommt, zu danken. Und nun zur Zusammenfassung.

Meine Damen und Herren, bei dieser Fülle von Gesichtspunkten, die zum Teil von mehreren Sprechern von verschiedenen Gesichtswinkeln aus beleuchtet worden sind, ist es schwer noch etwas zu sagen, ohne die Ausführungen der Referente überhaupt zu beeinträchtigen. Ich möchte mich deshalb auf die Unterstreichung einiger weniger Gesichtspunkte beschränken, bei denen überwiegend übereinstimmende Beurteilung in den verschiedenen hier vertretenen Ländern vorliegt, zum Teil aber auch eine verschiedenartige Betrachtung.

Ich glaube, es ist nachdrücklich darauf hingewiesen worden, wie wichtig die Feststellung und Festhaltung der Eigentumsverhältnisse ist. Das geschieht nach meiner Beobachtung länderweise sehr unterschiedlich. Es bedeutet in einer Unternehmung, die intakt ist, natürlich nichts Wesentliches, ob sie nur Besitz oder auch Eigentum in ihrem Aktivvermögen hat; in dem Augenblick aber, in dem die sichere Zahlungslage auch nur in Frage gestellt wird, ist natürlich die Unterscheidung zwischen Besitz und Eigentum deswegen wesentlich, weil – auf längere Zeit – die Unternehmung nur über ihr Eigentum verfügen kann und nicht über den Besitz, der im Eigentum der Lieferer etwa auf Grund des Eigentumsvorbehaltes steht, der im deutschen Rechtskreis eine sehr erhebliche, manchmal recht erschwerende Bedeutung hat.

Die Frage des persönlichen Augenscheins, darin sind wir sicher einig, tritt für den Prüfer mit der Größe der Unternehmung immer mehr zurück. Wer kann in einer großen Unternehmung, selbst wenn er schon im Laufe des Jahres Teilprüfungen vornimmt, sich des persönlichen Augenscheins bedienen, um die Feststellung der Bestände zu treffen? Der Rückgriff auf die inneren Prüforgane, den insbesondere Herr Kollege De Lalanne sehr stark betont hat, hat naturgemäß das Bedenken, daß es sich ja um Funktionäre der Unternehmung, die wir prüfen sollen, handelt. In diesem Zusammenhange ist mir der Hinweis darauf sehr wertvoll erschienen, daß die Prüfer ja doch immer mehr von den Inhabern und nicht von den Geschäftsführern der Organe verpflichtet und auch ihnen verantwortlich sein sollen.

Zur Verantwortung:

Wir sind alle bereit, jede für unseren Beruf mit unseren Berufsmitteln überhaupt vertretbare Verantwortung zu übernehmen. Je mehr Verantwortung wir übernehmen, desto stärker kann ja der Anspruch auf das Vertrauen zu unserem Bestätigungsvermerk sein, und umgekehrt, je mehr Vertrauensanspruch wir für unseren Bestätigungsvermerk erheben, desto mehr müssen wir bereit sein, Verantwortung zu übernehmen. Aber, das ist sicher auch heute deutlich geworden, es gibt Grenzen dort, wo das Physische sich sehr stark einschaltet.

Angeklungen nur ist der Gesichtspunkt der schwebenden Geschäfte, die mir deswegen so wesentlich erscheinen, weil gerade auch im internationalen Verkehr ja schwebende Geschäfte letzthin – die Kupferpreisschwankungen machen das deutlich – ein wesentlich stärkeres Gewicht erlangt haben, als das je vorher der Fall war. Daß eine übersichtliche Rechnungslegung der Unternehmung uns die Feststellung der Bestände wesentlich zu erleichtern vermag, bedarf keiner Betonung, es ist dort, wo der Prüfer mehrere Jahre oder noch längere Zeit hintereinander dieselbe Unternehmung prüft, ja ohne weiteres möglich, solche Schwächen oder gar Mängel, die er in der Übersichtlichkeit eines Rechnungswesens findet, zur Abstellung anzuempfehlen und wohl auch die Abstellung durchzusetzen. Im ganzen glaube ich, wird der heutige Nachmittag die Bestätigung dafür abgegeben haben, daß die Zweifel, die bei der Auswahl gerade dieses Gegenstandes den umsichtigen Vorbereitern des Kongresses doch auch vorgeschwebt haben, nicht begründet sind. Wenn ich darf, möchte ich auch Ihre ungeteilte Aufmerksamkeit bei der heutigen Beratung so werten, daß Ihnen nicht nur der Gegenstand, sondern auch die verschiedenartige Betrachtung und Würdigung durch Vertreter der verschiedenen Länder, verschiedener Sprachen, verschiedener Rechtssysteme, doch wert gewesen ist, in zwei Stunden behandelt zu werden. Ich möchte mich, um Ihre Zeit nicht über Gebühr in Anspruch zu nehmen, auf diese Bemerkungen beschränken, nicht ohne Ihnen für Ihre Aufmerksamkeit, die für uns der Grund der, wie ich glaube sagen zu dürfen, fruchtbaren Besprechung war, herzlich zu danken, besonders aber auch meinen Herren Kollegen aus dem Panel und nicht zuletzt auch den beteiligten Dolmetschern, die dazu beigetragen haben, daß wir uns in einer Sache, in der uns die Sprachen nicht trennen dürfen, auch gut verständigen konnten. Ich danke Ihnen.

I should like to give you a short summary and I shall then ask the Chairman to conclude the meeting.

Ladies and Gentlemen, to begin with I should like to express our thanks to Prof. DeJong, and to our colleagues, Mr. Jonkers and Mr. Van Duin. These three colleagues have done a great deal of hard work on their contribution, but unfortunately we do not have sufficient time to ask them to read them to us. That is an additional reason for me to thank these gentlemen cordially for the work they have done. Now to my summary.

Ladies and Gentlemen. It is difficult to say anything further on this abundance of views which have been expressed—many speakers approaching the subject from different directions—without prejudice to what the main authors have already said. I will, therefore, confine myself to emphasizing a few views on which there is predominantly agreement in the various countries represented here, though there is not agreement in all of them. I think it has been pointed out how important it is to verify the situation as to the assets, and I gather that procedures vary greatly from country to country.

When a firm is doing well, it doesn't really matter greatly whether its assets consist merely of holdings or also of its own property. But when the firm's liquidity is in question, then, of course, the difference between proprietorship and ownership becomes essential because in the long run the firm can only dispose of its property and not of its holdings, which are the property of the supplier on the grounds of the property proviso, which in German Law has very great significance and often involves complications.

Now, as to ocular stock-taking we are surely all agreed that this becomes more and more difficult for the auditor, the larger the concern is.

Which auditor, even if he has carried out partial audits during the year, can apply a personal ocular stock-taking check of all items in a large firm, in order to verify the stocks? Reliance on the internal audit department, which Mr. De Lalanne in particular has strongly emphasized, has naturally the drawback that these are the employees of the firm, whose records we have to audit. In this connection it seems very important to me to bear in mind that the auditors must be under an obligation towards the owners, and not so much to the managers, and must be responsible to these owners too. Now I should like to say something about the problem of responsibility. All of us are prepared to assume the responsibilities proper to our profession. The more responsibility we assume, the more confidence others will have in the certificate we issue. And, vice versa, the more confidence we claim our clients can have in our certificate the readier we must be to assume responsibility. But it has surely become clear to-day that where there is a large physical element, certain limits impose themselves. Now, pending business transactions have only been mentioned in passing. I think these are very essential because—especially in international business—they have recently assumed greater importance than even before—as the fluctuations in the prices of copper have shown. It needs no saying that a good system of accounting in the firm itself can make the task of verifying the existence of assets very much lighter for us. Where an auditor has examined the books of the same firm for several years running, it is easy for him to see to it that certain weaknesses or omissions in the organization of the accounting system are remedied, and usually he succeeds in getting these faults remedied. I think, generally speaking, that this afternoon has shown us that the doubts the cautious organizers of this congress had concerning the choice of the subject for this meeting were ill-founded. I think that I may also take it that the attention that you have shown has proved that not only the subject was of interest to you but also the varying ways in which representatives of various countries and various legal systems have commented on it, and I think you found it worth while to listen to these discussions for two hours this afternoon.

In order not to make too great a demand on your time, I should like to confine myself to these comments, though I should also like to thank you for your attention, for us the justification for what I think I may call our fruitful discussions. I should also like to thank my colleagues on the panel and also the interpreters who have helped us to understand one another on a matter in which difference of language must not be allowed to divide us. I thank you.

CHAIRMAN:

Ladies and Gentlemen. It only remains for me now to bring the session to a close. It would, I think, be quite presumptuous on my part to attempt to make any comment or summary on this very interesting subject which has been discussed this afternoon; that has been so ably done by Prof. Knorr. It does seem to me, however, that, if any justification is required to the holding of congresses of this sort, we had it here this afternoon. I had the honour of having on the platform with me representatives of twelve different countries, we have had the privilege and pleasure of hearing an expression of views from the members of the panel representing nine different countries. It is very interesting to hear all these different views. They do emphasize that this question of the verification of the existence of assets has taken on quite a new emphasis in recent years. It is very different from what it was when I was learning my profession, I know, and the emphasis merely seemed to be slightly different in the view of some of the representatives. But the fact is, there is a problem here, there are new techniques to be learned, and I am quite sure that we all have gained very much from this afternoon's discussion. Before I leave the rostrum I would just like to thank my two vice-chairmen for their co-operation and the members of the panel for theirs. We had a very interesting meeting last evening for two hours, and I can only say that I wish all the meetings I have at home were conducted in such a friendly and charming manner.

I shall now ask the vice-chairman Dr. Rojansky to propose the vote of thanks to the members of the panel.

Vice-chairman, DR. A. R. ROJANSKY (Israel)

Mr. Chairman, Ladies and Gentlemen. It is a privilege to be called upon to express the thanks of the audience to the members of the panel. Our profession is in the course of development, perhaps more than any other profession; and despite that, many basic problems have not only been left unsettled, but they are even undefined, for instance, the jurisdiction of our profession has not yet been decided upon. I just want to draw your attention to the collusion in certain countries between lawyers and accountants. Anyhow, we as auditors have to serve our clients to the best of our ability, we have to be faithful to them, to ourselves and to the profession as a whole. We have to utter our opinion based on our knowledge, and our advice must be based upon our opinion. These two are indivisible. We cannot and should not find ourselves in the position of a lawyer, to remind you of that classic case, when a client came to a lawyer and wanted to hire him and presented to him his case and the lawyer after listening to him and studying the case said to him 'Do you want me to give you my honest opinion?' 'No', said the client, 'I prefer your professional advice'. We as auditors do not accept that, for us our advice is our opinion and our opinion is our advice. And to achieve that goal, we have to study, to analyse and to exchange opinions. We had the privilege this afternoon to make a very important step towards that goal. We had a very distinguished and efficient leader of discussions, we had five authors who have presented excellent addresses and studies and we had other members of the panel who conducted their discussions on a very high level. I think that this has really brought us a step forward and this is the real way we have to proceed in the future too.

I am sure that I shall be expressing the feelings of the audience if I offer to all the members of the panel our sincere thanks for their time and effort which has been so successful and beneficial.

Vice-chairman, PROF. AVV. RAG. GIOVANNI SENSINI (Italy)

Mr. Chairman, Ladies and Gentlemen. It is a pleasure to me to have the honour of thanking the Chairman, Mr. J. F. Klingner, and extending to him the most sincere wishes from the participants for guiding the work of this session.

Mr. Klingner and I have worked under different flags, which, however, by chance have the same colours (Mr. Klingner shows the two flags waving them).

Eire and Italy, even if far removed from each other, have many geographic and economic characteristics in common, and I am therefore doubly pleased to thank him on the meeting's behalf.

I was able to ascertain the care with which he has arranged and directed our work so that it could be accomplished in the most satisfactory way within the given time.

I wish we could meet again and have a Chairman, as kind (in the widest meaning of the word) as Mr. Klingner.

BUSINESS ORGANIZATION AND THE PUBLIC ACCOUNTANT

Afternoon session: Wednesday, 11th September 1957

Papers by: Page

Chairman:	PROF. B. J. S. WIMBLE, C.A. (S.A.), F.S.A.A., South Africa
Vice-Chairmen:	ERIC ORREBY, Sweden B. W. S. O'CONNELL, F.C.A., F.S.A.A., South Rhodesia
Panel Members:	
Discussion leader:	H. REINOUD *Nederlands Instituut van Accountants*
Rapporteur and author of a paper:	F. M. RICHARD *Compagnie Nationale des Experts-Comptables, France*
Authors of papers:	S. C. BAKKENIST, Ec. Drs. *Nederlands Instituut van Accountants*
	J. E. HARRIS, B. Com., F.A.C.C.A. *Association of Certified and Corporate Accountants, U.K.*
	SVANTE KIHLMAN, Ekon. mag. *Föreningen C.G.R., Finland*
	G. L. PHILLIPPE *Controllers Institute of America*
Other members of the panel:	DR. FERNANDO BOTER Y MAURI, *Ilustre Colegio Oficial de Titulares Mercantiles de Barcelona, Spain*
	R. KEITH YORSTON, F.C.A. (Aust.) *The Institute of Chartered Accountants in Australia*
	SHALOM PROSHAN *Association of Certified Public Accountants in Israel*

RAPPORT

de

F. M. RICHARD

Compagnie Nationale des Experts-Comptables, France

I. Historique de la profession d'expert-comptable en France

La profession d'Expert-Comptable fait l'objet en France, d'une réglementation légale (Ordonnance du 19 septembre 1945) qui a, entre autres mérites, celui de préciser le rôle de l'Expert-Comptable dans la vie économique.

En fait, les textes légaux rappellent les missions habituellement confiées à l'Expert-Comptable:

'Est Expert-Comptable, le technicien qui, (en son propre nom et sous sa responsabilité) fait profession habituelle d'organiser, vérifier et redresser les comptabilités et les comptes de toute nature'.

'L'Expert-Comptable peut aussi analyser par les procédés de la technique comptable, la situation et le fonctionnement des entreprises sous leurs divers aspects: économique, juridique et financier'.

Les mots placés entre parenthèses: (en son propre nom et sous sa responsabilité), permettent de distinguer entre l'exercice de la profession à titre libéral comportant l'assujettissement à des règles de conduite professionnelle, d'indépendance, de discipline rigoureuse, d'avec l'exercice salarial de la profession; distinction qui se retrouve dans des professions voisines, par exemple, les licenciés en droit inscrits à un Barreau comme Avocats, ou au contraire les licenciés en droit exerçant la fonction salariée de chef du service juridique ou contentieux dans une entreprise.

II. Les missions de l'expert-comptable et la gestion des entreprises

L'évolution de la structure des entreprises, les profondes modifications dans la désignation des 'hautes directions', leurs groupes de recrutement et la formation des cadres supérieurs,

L'évolution que d'aucuns qualifient de révolution économique, sociale et politique du monde industriel,

La tendance à la concentration industrielle,

Le développement du machinisme, de la technologie, de l'organisation scientifique du travail,

La complexité croissante des entreprises modernes, ont modifié le caractère des missions confiées à l'Expert-Comptable.

Rares sont les taches limitées à la révision des comptes, à l'assistance dans les questions fiscales et juridiques.

A partir du moment ou l'on aborde l'organisation d'une comptabilité ou d'un service administratif lié à la comptabilité, l'interprétation d'un bilan ou d'une situation, l'analyse d'une société, l'Expert-Comptable entre en contact avec toutes les fonctions de l'entreprise qui constituent un ensemble harmonieusement coordonné en vue d'atteindre les objectifs fixés par la direction.

Il est impossible de dissocier les renseignements chiffrés des réalités économiques, techniques et humaines de l'entreprise. Les mesures comptables doivent être un guide, comme les mesures en médecine alertent le médecin mais ne remplacement pas l'examen clinique.

La mise en place et la surveillance d'un système de prix de revient, le contrôle budgétaire, l'analyse des ventes et des coûts de distribution, l'établissement d'un programme financier sont inséparables de l'organisation de la production, des stocks et de la vente, et l'Expert-Comptable se trouve amené à quitter le domaine de la technique comptable pure.

L'efficacité de l'intervention de l'Expert-Comptable l'oblige donc à intervenir dans des domaines qui ne lui auraient pas été ouverts il y a de cela quelque vingt ans.

Il semble que d'ores et déjà l'Expert-Comptable peut accepter des missions de Conseil de Gestion et de Contrôle de Gestion, en vue de l'application aux entreprises des techniques que nous examinerons dans les lignes qui suivent.

III. Les instruments de contrôle de gestion

Il n'est pas inutile de passer en revue les instruments du contrôle de gestion, car leur utilisation montre que le contrôle de gestion est le domaine d'élection des professionnels de la comptabilité.

La comptabilité traditionnelle est l'instrument le mieux conçu pour la gestion; les défauts qu'on lui reproche parfois – tel sa rigueur mathématique – ne sont que l'excès de ses qualités.

Il suffit d'adapter à ces fins la comptabilité financière ainsi que la comptabilité industrielle, appelée dans notre pays: Comptabilité analytique d'exploitation, pour en obtenir les services nécessaires: rapidité, précision limitée aux chiffres significatifs, adjonction aux renseignements monétaires (francs) des données d'exploitation (journées ou heures de travail, unités produites, poids, etc....). Il serait inconcevable qu'au nom d'une prétendue rigidité de système on se privât d'une méthode parvenue à un haut degré de perfectionnement.

Ajoutons qu'en France, l'adoption volontaire par la plupart des entreprises (probablement 90 % dans les grandes entreprises, 60 % dans les moyennes entreprises et 40 % dans les petites entreprises) d'un plan comptable national normalisé dit: 'Plan Comptable 1947' permet d'envisager de fructueuses comparaisons entre firmes de la même profession.

L'utilisation des prix de revient standard ou autres formules de coûts prédéterminés, permet les contrôles souhaitables des coûts de production, de distribution ou administratifs, liés le plus souvent au contrôle budgétaire.

Le contrôle par sections homogènes, assez voisines des centres de coûts, permet d'exercer un contrôle budgétaire aux échelons de base de la hiérarchie et portant sur des unités opérationnelles décentralisées et nombreuses.

Les discussions de doctrine portant sur les méthodes d'imputations de frais; le traitement des écarts dus à l'activité de l'entreprise, de la production ou de la distribution; l'utilisation du direct-costing, ont eu le mérite, sinon d'apporter des solutions définitives, mais au moins de diffuser largement ces techniques et de les faire comprendre de ceux susceptibles de les appliquer dans les cas particuliers ou l'une ou l'autre de ces méthodes est la plus efficace.

Toutes les ressources de la statistique ne semblent pas encore été utilisées pour dégager d'un ensemble de faits comptables, de données statistiques tant internes qu'externes à l'entreprise: les tendances, comportements, mécanismes, relations existant entre les faits observés.

On peut envisager le développement de l'application statistique comme moyen de prévision, d'action et de contrôle, mais aussi comme moyen d'analyser les différentes fonctions de l'entreprise.

La statistique est de plus une des branches de la Recherche Opérationnelle.

IV. Les informations de décision

L'évolution de la comptabilité en tant qu'instrument de gestion, a été influencée dans ses concepts de:

1. Temps,
2. Langage,
3. Buts.

1. Le facteur 'Temps' a entraîné l'abandon de la comptabilité historique, enregistrant le passé ou le présent très récent, pour tendre à enregistrer le présent immédiat, c'est à dire saisir les faits à l'instant même où ils se produisent.

Une image illustrant cette différence de conception est la comparaison du 'livre de bord' et du 'tableau de bord', sur un navire. Il est certes utile de tenir un 'livre de bord' relatant toutes les données d'un voyage, les points successifs, les consommations, les bâtiments rencontrés, etc.... rapport que le commandant du navire présentera à sa compagnie de navigation quand le voyage sera terminé. Mais d'autres préoccupations nécessitent le fonctionnement d'un 'tableau de bord' où s'inscrivent, à l'instant même, les données essentielles de la vie et de la marche du navire: vitesse, pression vapeur, nombre de tours auxquels fonctionnent les machines, sondages, radar, direction, etc....

Dans l'entreprise, le 'livre de bord' – comptes et bilans – répond à des besoins très différents de ceux des informations de chaque jour, heure, opération, produit, etc.... ce sont ces dernières informations que la comptabilité de gestion s'efforce de fournir.

2. Le 'langage monétaire' correspond à l'aspect financier, mais il n'est pas le langage commun de l'entreprise. Une large fraction de l'entreprise agit et pense

dans d'autres unités d'expression; heure, poids, volume, unités produites, etc.... c'est le langage de l'exécutant, et il est évident que toute une partie de la comptabilité informative doit être donnée dans ces unités de mesure.

On peut d'ailleurs prévoir que cette évolution se poursuivra vers l'enregistrement comptable de mesures techniques (températures, pressions, délais, mélanges, etc.).

3. Dans l'optique du comptable financier, l'information est une fin en soi, elle est dite: de 'connaissance' portant sur des faits du passé ou du présent, et l'on peut considérer que sous cet angle, si cette information est exacte, précise et rapide, le comptable a déjà rempli avec succès un rôle important.

Mais le chef d'entreprise et ceux à qui il délègue une partie de ses responsabilités, n'ont pas le temps, ni peut être la tournure d'esprit nécessaire, pour examiner une masse d'informations, en tirer celles utiles, et l'on est arrivé à demander au comptable d'isoler les informations devant déclencher une décision, une action.

Les comptabilités doivent donc sélectionner les 'informations de décision'; à cette seule condition les comptabilités sont dynamiques et motrices.

V. Le rôle de l'expert-comptable: critique, conseil et controleur externe, en matière de gestion

Ces trois rôles de l'Expert-Comptable, représentent non seulement vis à vis de l'entreprise des activités bien différentes, mais reposent sur des principes, des comportements, des limitations qu'il convient d'examiner.

L'observation des faits économiques de l'entreprise, du fonctionnement des diverses divisions, la confirmation ou l'infirmation de ces observations par les renseignements du bilan et des comptes de résultats, peuvent amener l'Expert-Comptable à formuler sur la gestion une appréciation ou des critiques, mais à notre avis, cette opinion ne doit pas dépasser la limite de la compétence personnelle de l'Expert-Comptable. Si l'appréciation tient compte d'avis techniques extérieurs, il convient d'en mentionner la source et l'étendue.

Un rapport sur la gestion devra rappeler les conditions dans lesquelles la mission a été confiée, par qui elle a été demandée et dans quels buts, et être transmis au seul mandant, évitant tout ce qui pourrait avoir un caractère public.

On note donc la différence de conception avec un rapport sur la sincérité et l'exactitude du bilan, et du compte de résultats, que peut remettre un Expert-Comptable, et qui est destiné à de nombreux tiers par rapport à l'entreprise et même au public en général.

Dans son rôle de conseil, l'Expert-Comptable, nanti de la confiance de son client, devra mesurer l'étendue morale de ses responsabilités, d'autant plus grandes que son conseil sera sollicité sur des problèmes généraux de l'entreprise orientation, programmes, politiques, et non seulement sur des questions d'organisation à un niveau opérationnel.

C'est dans le rôle de contrôle que l'Expert-Comptable reprend contact avec son domaine traditionnel puisque, la Fonction Administrative, telle que l'a définie FAYOL est: 'Prévoir, Organiser, Commander, Coordonner, Contrôler'.

Ce contrôle consistera à mettre en place, dans une perspective beaucoup plus large que celle de la comptabilité, un système permettant de mesurer l'activité de l'entreprise, d'en prévoir et d'en contrôler les résultats, et de mettre à la disposition des divers responsables, les informations nécessaires pour que leur action soit mieux coordonnée et plus efficace.

VI. L'ÉVOLUTION DU RÔLE DE L'EXPERT-COMPTABLE DANS SON RÔLE DE CONSEIL ET CONTROLEUR DE GESTION

Comment la mission traditionnelle de vérificateur de comptes, de conseil juridique et fiscal, d'organisateur comptable, évolue-t-elle vers le conseil et le contrôle de gestion?

Les problèmes d'organisation comptable entraînent presque toujours l'étude de structures administratives, non seulement de ce qu'il convient d'appeler 'l'administration' proprement dite, mais aussi l'administration de la production et l'administration de la vente.

Comment peut-on organiser efficacement un service de paye, un contrôle du prix de revient de la main d'œuvre, sans examiner le système de lancement de fabrication, de planning, d'étude des tâches et des postes de travail, etc....

L'établissement d'un plan de trésorerie amène l'Expert-Comptable à s'intéresser au planning d'approvisionnement en fonction des programmes de production.

Le problème de la facturation à la clientèle est lié au processus des commandes, gestion des stocks et des approvisionnements, etc.... Il y a toujours un 'fait comptable' à la fin d'une série d'imprimés.

Tout document comptable est l'aboutissement d'un processus administratif.

Il est donc naturel que l'Expert-Comptable étudie et soit amené à suggérer des réformes concernant l'administration de l'entreprise.

L'Expert-Comptable peut également être saisi des mêmes problèmes lors de l'examen financier de l'entreprise.

La vérification du bilan et des comptes de résultats conduit à leur analyse et à leur interprétation, puis à la recherche des causes qui sont à l'origine des situations – favorables ou non – que ces causes soient techniques ou commerciales.

L'Expert-Comptable, après avoir exposé ses constatations et son opinion – dans la limite de ses compétences – est amené à suggérer des solutions, éventuellement à participer à leur application.

Les fonctions d'une entreprise sont en général tellement diversifiées que l'organisateur-conseil doit lui-même céder la place à un spécialiste de l'industrie ou du commerce considéré.

Dans des industries relativement simples – dans le sens qu'elles ne font pas appel à des techniques hautement scientifiques – par exemple le textile laine et coton, la chaussure, ce sont les ingénieurs spécialisés dans ces domaines qui paraissent les plus aptes à résoudre les problèmes relevant à la fois d'une technique industrielle et de l'organisation.

L'Expert-Comptable semble le mieux susceptible de grouper autour de lui une équipe permanente de semi-spécialistes complétée, lorsque cela est nécessaire, par des spécialistes purs – l'Expert-Comptable réalisant la synthèse des diverses disciplines mises en jeu.

VII. Spécialisation de l'expert-comptable dans le conseil de gestion

Le diplôme français d'Expert-Comptable, considéré comme étant du niveau d'une licence, comporte outre la connaissance approfondie de la technique comptable, une excellente formation juridique, fiscale, mathématique et économique.

La diversité des domaines étudiés confère une forte culture générale en tant que culture technique; l'expérience, l'exercice de la profession libérale peuvent conduire ces 'généralistes' de l'expertise comptable à des spécialisations.

Nombreux, parmi les meilleurs des Experts-Comptables français, se sont ainsi dirigés vers l'expertise judiciaire qui est une conception très particulière du système judiciaire français; d'autres Experts-Comptables font une brillante carrière dans la révision des comptes, l'organisation comptable, la surveillance des comptabilités, etc.

Un petit nombre est spécialisé dans les études de prix de revient, les questions budgétaires, la recherche de la rentabilité et de la productivité des entreprises, la statistique, la comparaison inter-entreprises et inter-professions.

Ce n'est encore qu'exceptionnellement que certains Experts-Comptables acceptent actuellement des missions de Conseil de Gestion, mais un effort de formation est en cours, qui doit permettre de pallier cette absence relative de spécialisation.

Sous l'égide du Commissariat Général à la Productivité qui fonctionne au sein du Ministère des Affaires Economiques, il a été créé en France, avec l'appui des organismes professionnels les plus représentatifs, un organisme de recherche et d'enseignement dénommé:

'Institut de Perfectionnement dans les Méthodes de Contrôle de Gestion'.

Cet institut vise à former aux disciplines de direction générale et de contrôle de gestion des entreprises, les techniciens que leur formation spécialisée d'ingénieur, d'organisateur, de juriste, d'expert-comptable, n'avait pas préparés à la diversité des problèmes soulevés par la conduite et le contrôle d'une affaire.

Partant d'une culture de base acquise dans les Universités ou les Grandes Ecoles, l'Institut dispense aux uns – ingénieurs, organisateurs, juristes – la compréhension des problèmes comptables et financiers; aux autres – experts-comptables, cadres comptables et administratifs – l'initiation aux problèmes de l'organisation industrielle; et à tous, l'utilisation de la comptabilité, de la statistique, des mathématiques, comme instruments de prévision et de contrôle.

De plus, l'Institut est le lieu de rencontre de cadres de direction, de spécialistes de la comptabilité et de professeurs, et permettra par cette confrontation de disciplines et d'expériences de faire progresser les méthodes comptables en les adaptant aux problèmes complexes posés par la gestion des entreprises.

Il faut également signaler la création d'Instituts d'enseignement pour les carrières d'Organisateur Conseil et de Technicien Commercial, et l'adjonction au programme de certaines écoles préparant au diplôme d'Expert-Comptable, de cours spécialisés en Contrôle de Gestion.

Il paraît ainsi souhaitable et possible de donner une orientation nouvelle, à titre de spécialisation, au diplôme d'Expert-Comptable en France.

VIII. Conclusion

Le Conseil et le Contrôle de Gestion – que nos Confrères américains appellent Controllership – est en voie de devenir dans les entreprises, une fonction aussi courante que celle de production, distribution, financement. Cette fonction peut, soit être dévolue à un seul homme de l'entreprise, ou répartie entre plusieurs collaborateurs selon leur compétence, et la structure des affaires.

Il paraît probable, dans un proche avenir, que les Expert-Comptables français, en plus grand nombre, s'orienteront vers le Conseil et le Contrôle de Gestion. A ce titre, l'Expert-Comptable sera consulté pour organiser les services et méthodes de contrôle et en surveiller le bon fonctionnement.

Les grandes entreprises rechercheront la compétence, l'expérience, l'indépendance des Experts-Comptables, soit pour les organisations proprement dites du contrôle, soit pour l'évaluation et l'appréciation de leurs propres services par comparaison avec des applications existantes.

Les entreprises de moyenne importance demanderont à l'expert-comptable la création et la mise en place des dispositifs de prévision, de gestion et de contrôle, l'établissement de diagnostic d'entreprise, etc....

Il n'est pas d'exemple que le besoin ne créé l'organe capable d'y répondre.

Les Experts-Comptables intéressés par cette question, soit se spécialiseront dans le Contrôle de Gestion, soit s'associeront afin de grouper les professionnels capable de répondre aux besoins de l'économie nationale, mais la formation de base sera toujours l'expertise comptable.

Certains membres de ces groupements devront être spécialisés dans:
Prix de Revient, Contrôle Budgétaire,
Statistique, Préparation mathématique des décisions,
Organisation industrielle,
Organisation commerciale,
Organisation financière,
Organisation générale.

Ils feront appel, chaque fois que cela sera nécessaire, à des techniciens, des ingénieurs en particulier, pour étudier les problèmes strictement techniques.

Du point de vue éthique professionnelle, les règles de conduite de la profession libérale d'Expert-Comptable, s'appliquent aux missions acceptées et accomplies dans le domaine du Conseil de Gestion, ceci implique que l'Expert-Comptable n'acceptera de mission que s'il est complètement qualifié, soit personnellement soit en collaboration avec un collègue lui-même qualifié.

Translation

PAPER

by

F. M. RICHARD

Compagnie Nationale des Experts-Comptables, France

I. Historical Notes on the Profession of Public Accountant in France

The profession of public accountant in France is legally organized (Decree of September 19th, 1945), which has, amongst other merits, the one of precising the role of the public accountant in economic life.

As a matter of fact, the legal regulation recalls the missions usually carried on by the public accountant.

> 'Is considered as Public Accountant, the technician who [in his own name and under his responsibility] makes a usual profession of organizing, auditing, correcting accounts and accounting of every nature'.
>
> 'The Public Accountant also analyses, through accounting procedures, the situation and development of business, under their various aspects: economic, legal, and financial'.

The words between brackets: 'in his own name and under his responsibility' stress the difference between the accountant 'in practice' subject to rules of professional conduct, independance and strict discipline—from the profession carried on as a salaried profession—differences also to be found in like professions—for instance a jurist with a degree of Master of Law, can be registered as a Barrister at the Bar or else can be employed as head of the legal department of a company.

II. The Tasks of the Public Accountant and the Management of Enterprises

The evolution of the structure of firms, the deep alterations in the choice of 'top management', in the selection and training of executives,

The evolution, sometimes called revolution, of the industrial world in its economic, social and political aspects,

The tendency to industrial concentration,

The development of machinism and technological progress,
The growing complexity of modern business,
have modified the tasks entrusted to the public accountant.

It is seldom that such tasks are limited to auditing or assisting the client in tax or law problems.

From the moment the accountant is involved in organizing an accounting system or an administrative department linked with the accounting department, or has to interpret a balance sheet, to analyse a corporation, the public accountant is in contact with all the functions of the business which constitute an overall system, harmoniously co-ordinated in order to reach the goals set out by the management.

It is impossible to separate the figures from the economic, technological facts and human realities of the business.

Accounting measures must be a guide—just as in medicine: temperature, blood pressure, etc. call the attention to the doctor,—but there are no substitutes to a clinical examination.

Organizing a cost system, a budgetary control, a sales and distribution costs analysis, a financial plan, cannot be separated from production planning, inventories and sales and therefore the Public Accountant has to leave his realm of pure accounting.

In order to attain an efficient result, the public accountant has to enter into fields in which he would not have ventured some twenty years ago.

It seems that now the public accountant can already accept missions as management consultant and management controller and also to apply techniques which will be reviewed in the following chapters.

III. The Instruments of Management Control

It is interesting to pass under review the instruments of management control, as their utilisation will show that management control is the elective field of accounting practitioners.

Accounting by tradition is the best conceived instrument for management, the defects which are sometimes pointed out against it—such as its mathematical strictness—are but the excess of its virtues.

It is only necessary to adapt in view of the objectives of management, the financial accounting and cost accounting —which bears in France the name of 'exploitation analytical accounting'—in order to obtain the needed services: quickness, precision limited to significant figures, disclosure apart of monetary information (in francs) of production figures (number of work-days or work-hours, units produced, weights, etc.). It would be inconceivable that under the pretext of its rigidity, the accounting system should be discarded when it has attained such a high degree of development.

Let us add that in France, the majority of firms (probably 90 % of big concerns, 60 % of middle size firms, and 40 % of small businesses) have adopted the uniform national accounting plan, named '1947 Uniform accounting plan' which renders possible interesting comparisons between firms in the same trade.

The adoption of standard cost prices or other predetermined costs enables desirable controls of production costs, as well as of distribution or administrative costs, generally linked with budgetary control.

Control by 'homogeneous sections' similar to 'cost centers' renders possible the budgetary control at basic levels of hierarchy dealing with operational units, numerous and decentralized.

Doctrinal discussions on: methods of allocating expenses, the treatment of activity variances—either production or sales variances—, direct costing method, have had the merit, if not to bring final solutions, at least to disseminate these techniques and to teach them to those likely to apply same to the particular cases where one or the other method is best suited.

All the resources of statistics do not seem to have been employed in view of bringing out from a mass of accounting facts, of statistical data whether internal or external to the firm, the trends, mechanisms, relations existing between the facts under survey.

One can foresee the development of statistics as a means of forecasting, of action and control and also as a means of the analysis of the various functions of a business.

Statistics is also one of the branches of operations research.

IV. The Information of Decision

The evolution of accounting as a tool of management has been influenced in its concepts of:

1. Time;
2. Language;
3. Objectives.

1. The 'time' factor has led to abandon historical accounting recording the past or even the recent present, tending to record the immediate present to seize facts at the very moment when they happen.

A picturesque illustration of these two different concepts would be the comparison of a 'log-book' and a 'dash board' on a ship. It is undoubtedly necessary to keep a log-book, recording all the facts and events of a crossing: the successive points, fuel consumptions, other boats met en route..., this report being presented by the captain to the steamship company when the trip is over. But other needs render necessary the functioning of a dash board which shows instantly the essential facts of the life and run of the ship: speed, steam pressure, r.p.m. at which the machines run, radar findings, direction, etc.

In a business the log-book—accounts and balance sheet—answers needs very different from daily information or information by hour, operation, product, etc. such are the information that management accounting endeavours to show.

2. The 'monetary language' conveys the financial aspect, but it is not a common language in business. A large fraction of the business act and think in other units or means of expression: hour, weight, volume, units produced, etc. such is the language of the productive man, of the layman, and therefore it is evident that 'informative' accounting must be kept in these units of measurement.

Very likely this evolution will go as far as accounting recording of technical figures (temperatures, pressures, delays, mixes, etc.).

3. For the financial accountant the information is an end in itself. Financial accounting could be called 'information of knowledge' dealing with facts of past and present—and from this point of view, one must admit that if the information is correct, precise and promptly rendered, the accountant has already successfully filled an important role.

But the manager or the executives to whom he delegates part of his responsibilities have not the time, or perhaps have not the mind to examine a mass of information in order to select the relevant ones and therefore the accountant must choose, isolate the information which should bring forth a decision, an action.

Accounting must therefore make a choice of 'information of decision', this being the necessary condition of a dynamic accounting.

V. The Role of the Public Accountant as Adviser and External Controller of Management

These roles of the public accountant represent, with regards to the client, not only very different activities, but are also based on principles, working attitudes and limitations which should be examined.

The observation of the economic facts of a business, of the functioning of its various divisions, how these observations are confirmed or not, through the information given by the balance sheet and the profit and loss account, may bring the public accountant to formulate criticism or appreciation of management, but in our opinion, this opinion must not go beyond the personal capability of the public accountant. If such an appreciation takes into account other opinions on technical points, due reference should be made to such opinions, mentioning both their scope and sources.

A report on management should recall the conditions under which it was asked to the public accountant, who asked for this report, and to what purposes. It should be communicated only to this person, avoiding all communication of a public nature.

This is apparently a difference of concepts with the usual audit report on the correctness and sincerity of the balance sheet and profit and loss account, which is intended to many people outside the company and even the public at large.

As an adviser, the public accountant, entrusted with the confidence of his client, must measure his moral responsibility the more important when his advice is sought for, on overall problems of the company: politics, programs and not only on the routine organization questions at an operational level.

It is as such that the public accountant re-enters his traditional field, as according to Fayol the administrative function is 'to forecast, to organize, to command, to coordinate, to control'.

This control will consist in the organization, in a much wider perspective than accounting, of a system which will permit to measure the activity of a business, to forecast and control its results and to communicate to all levels of management the necessary information so that their action is well coordinated and efficient.

VI. The Evolution of the Role of the Public Accountant as a Management Consultant and Controller

What has been the evolution of the public accountant, acting up to now, mainly as auditor, adviser on tax and law questions, organizer of accounting systems and procedures, towards the new tasks of management consultant and controller?

Problems of accounting systems and procedures, will almost invariably lead to the study of the administrative structure not only in the sense of 'administration' pure and simple, but administration of production and distribution.

The efficient organization of a payroll department, of a cost and labor control system, leads to the study of the existing methods of production planning and control, of work measurements and job evaluation.

The forecasting of a financial budget must be studied by the accountant in connection with the inventory and purchase program in function of the production planning.

Even the simple problems of billing to customers is linked with incoming orders procedure, inventory control and purchasing. There is always an 'accounting fact' at the end of a series of forms. Every accounting document is the end and result of administrative procedure.

It is therefore evident that the public accountant has to study the administrative procedure of the business and may be brought to advise certain changes.

The public accountant may also be confronted with the same problems when he audits and studies the financial situation of the business.

The audit of a balance sheet and profit and loss account leads to their analysis and interpretation, then to the disclosure of the causes which originated the situation—favorable or unfavorable—technological or commercial causes.

The public accountant after he has disclosed his findings and opinion in the limits of his competence, is brought to suggest solutions and eventually to participate in their application.

The activities of a corporation are generally so diversified that the management consultant himself must bring in a specialist of the industry or trade under consideration.

In industries with relatively simple techniques—in the sense that they do not call for highly scientific technics—for instance, wool and cotton textiles, shoe manufacturing—the engineers specialized in these fields seem best suited to solve problems pertaining both the manufacturing and management of production.

The public accountant himself is probably best suited to gather round him a permanent team of semi-specialists, completed when this is necessary with full specialists; the public accountant realizing the synthesis of the various disciplines engaged.

VII. The Specialization of the Public Accountant as Management Consultant

The French diploma of certified public accountant, considered to be of the level of a 'master' degree, covers, apart from an advanced knowledge of accounting techniques, an extensive training in law, taxes, and to a lesser degree in mathematics and economics.

Such a vast array of fields give a thorough general culture—as a technical culture—but only experience, the practice of the profession as public accountant can lead these 'generalists' of accounting to some specializations.

Many among the ablest French public accountants, have become 'judiciary accountants' which is a very particular concept of the French legal system; other public accountants make a brilliant career as auditors or in organizing accounting systems or in controlling accounts.

A small number have been specialized in cost accounting, budgetary accounting, control of return and productivity in business, statistics, inter-companies or inter-professions comparisons.

It is only exceptional that some public accountants presently accept tasks as management consultants but efforts of training are under way which will palliate this relative lack of specialists.

Under the sponsorship of the General Commissary to Productivity, a section of the Ministry of Economic Affairs, it has been recently created in France, with the support of the most influential professional bodies, a research and educational institute named:

'Institute for the Development in Methods of Controllership'.

The objectives of this institute is to teach the art and techniques of topmanagement and controllership to the specialists: engineers, consultants, jurists, public accountants who, due to their specialized education, are not prepared to meet the very complex problems of management and controllership.

Starting with a solid basic culture dispensed in universities and scientific institutes, this institute for controllership teaches: to the engineer, the jurist, the consultant: the understanding of accounting and financial problems; to the public accountant and the accountant: the notions of industrial organization, and to the two groups: how to use accounting, statistics, mathematics, as tools for budgeting and control.

Moreover this institute will be a meeting point for executives, accountants and professors and will permit through the confrontation of disciplines and experiences, the promotion of management accounting in adapting accountancy to the needs of the complex problems to be solved in modern management.

It should also be reported the creation in France of a school for management consultants and for sales managers, and that some of the existing schools of accountancy, preparing for the certificate of public accountant have added to their tuition an optional course of controllership.

It therefore seems possible and desirable to give a new orientation to the French diploma of public accountant, with a specialization in controllership.

VIII. Conclusion

Management consultancy and controllership tend to become an established function in business, just as usual as production, sales or finance.

This function may be exercised either by one person in the firm or be divided between several executives according to their ability and depending on the structure of the business.

It seems possible in the near future that French public accountants in a greater number will be attracted by controllership. As such, the public accountant will be consulted to organize control departments and their methods and supervise their efficiency.

Large firms will seek the skill, experience and independence of the public accountant to organize their control and budget departments, or to evaluate their existing departments in comparison with others.

Medium size firms will ask from the public accountant, the creation and setting up of: forecasting, planning, budgeting, control, the appraisal of their overall organization.

The public accountant will either specialize in controllership or will enter into partnership with specialized practicians in order to meet the needs of industry, but their basic education will remain public accountancy

Some branches of these partnerships will be, for instance:

Costing and budgetary control,
Statistics, mathematical preparation of decisions,
Industrial organization,
Distribution organization,
Financial organization,
General organization.

Whenever necessary they will ask the advice and co-operation of technicians, engineers, for instance, to investigate the technical problems.

As to ethics, the rules of professionnal conduct of the existing bodies of public accountants will be applicable to the new tasks assigned to and accepted by the public accountants in the field of controllership. It implies therefore that public accountants will accept such missions only if they feel fully qualified, either personally or in co-operation with qualified colleagues.

INLEIDING

van

S. C. BAKKENIST, EC. DRS.

Nederlands Instituut van Accountants

I. DE FUNCTIES VAN DE PUBLIC ACCOUNTANT

Om het verband tussen de public accountant en de organisatie van het bedrijf op te sporen is het m.i. noodzakelijk aan te geven, welke functies in Nederland de public accountant vervult. Ik zoek voor het omschrijven van deze functies aansluiting bij de beschouwingen, die Van Rietschoten heeft gewijd aan de functies van het accountantsberoep[1]). Het wil mij namelijk voorkomen, dat Van Rietschoten een omschrijving van de inhoud van de functies heeft gegeven, die algemeen door de Nederlandse beroepsgenoten wordt aanvaard.

De functie valt in drie delen uiteen:

1. Onafhankelijk controleur van de administratie van een bedrijf, welke controle uitmondt in een zo mogelijk goedkeurende verklaring bij de rekening en verantwoording, welke periodiek, al dan niet publiekelijk, door de leiding aan eigenaars van het in het bedrijf geinvesteerde vermogen moet worden overgelegd.

De kring van belanghebbenden bij deze accountantsverklaring beperkt zich veelal niet tot de eigenaars, respectievelijk aandeelhouders; er is een veel ruimere kring van belanghebbenden. In Nederland vatten wij deze ruime kring van belanghebbenden bij de accountantsverklaring samen in de term 'het maatschappelijk verkeer', en wij spreken in deze functie dan ook van controleur ten behoeve van het maatschappelijk verkeer.

2. Daarnaast, en veelal gelijktijdig met de vervulling van de sub 1. genoemde taak ten behoeve van het maatschappelijk verkeer, treedt de accountant op als *controleur ten behoeve van de bedrijfsleiding.*

Met het groter worden van de bedrijven neemt de afstand tussen directie en uitvoering toe. De administratie gaat een steeds belangrijker plaats innemen als bron, waaruit de topleiding de gegevens put, waarop het bedrijfsbeleid wordt gebouwd en als middel om na te gaan in welke mate de uitvoering overeenkomstig de bedoelingen van de topleiding heeft plaatsgevonden. Maatregelen moeten dus worden getroffen om de juistheid van de administratieve gegevens te verzekeren. De public accountant kan deze taak economisch en doeltreffend combineren met de controle-werkzaamheden, welke hij voor de sub 1. genoemde taak moet vervullen. Vertrouwt de topleiding hem deze taak toe, dan treedt hij op als controleur ten behoeve van de bedrijfsleiding.

3. De kennis en ervaring, die de accountants zich voor en door hun beroepsuitoefening verwerven, maken hen tot een deskundige op het gebied van de bedrijfseconomie, de administratieve organisatie en de controle. Dientengevolge kon de accountant worden tot *bedrijfseconomisch adviseur van de bedrijfsleiding*.

Deze adviseursfunctie zal echter steeds als nevenfunctie bij de controletaak worden uitgeoefend. Zij is een welhaast logisch uitvloeisel van deze controletaak.

II. Controletaak en personele organisatie

Voorwaarde voor een doeltreffende controle is een zodanige functieverdeling tussen de personeelsleden, dat controle van de administratie de accountant in staat stelt tot een onafhankelijk oordeel over de juistheid van de rekening en verantwoording te geraken.

De in Nederland algemeen aanvaarde richtlijn is, dat er een duidelijke scheiding moet zijn tussen de beherende, de bewarende en de registrerende taken in het bedrijf. Alleen dan ontstaat er in het bedrijf interne controle en mag worden verwacht, dat de administratie, welke door de accountant wordt gecontroleerd, en op welke controle hij zijn oordeel over de juistheid van de overgelegde rekening en verantwoording baseert, een betrouwbaar beeld geeft van het bedrijfsgebeuren in de periode, waarop deze betrekking heeft. Het is de plicht van de accountant, dat hij zich bij de aanvang van zijn controle-arbeid een oordeel vormt ten aanzien van de personeelsorganisatie en de ontworpen taakverdeling in het te controleren bedrijf. Komen hierin naar zijn oordeel, gezien vanuit zijn controle-functie, leemten voor, dan ligt het op zijn weg hierop de aandacht van de leiding te vestigen, ten einde te bewerkstelligen, dat hierin de door hem noodzakelijk geoordeelde veranderingen worden aangebracht. Geconstateerd mag worden, dat door het bedrijfsleven keer op keer onbewust tegen genoemde grondregel wordt gezondigd. In vele gevallen blijven dan, na kortere of langere tijd, de gevolgen niet uit. Op deze wijze oefent de accountant dus als uitvloeisel van zijn controle-arbeid een belangrijke invloed op de personele organisatie van het door hem te controleren bedrijf uit.

III. De public accountant en de administratieve organisatie

De public accountant komt, zowel ten behoeve van de controle van de rekening en verantwoording als ten behoeve van de controle voor de bedrijfsleiding, voortdurend in aanraking met de administratie in het bedrijf. In Nederland definieert men de public accountant als een deskundige op administratief en bedrijfseconomisch gebied. Bemoeienis van de accountant met de administratieve organisatie spruit dus én voort uit zijn controle-functie én uit zijn specifieke deskundigheid.

Ik meen, dat de opvatting thans vrij algemeen in Nederland wordt gehuldigd, dat de functie van de administratie is geëvolueerd, van verslaglegging van de plaatsgevonden bedrijfsgebeurtenissen ten behoeve van het afleggen van rekening en verantwoording, – in welke functie de administratie als een last werd gevoeld door de bedrijfsleiding – tot registratie van het bedrijfsgebeuren ten behoeve van het bedrijfsbestuur (tool for management). Met name ten gevolge van het groter worden van de bedrijven, is de behoefte aan instrumenten in handen van de bedrijfsleiding voor het besturen een klemmende eis geworden. Het is gebleken, dat een doeltreffende administratieve organisatie een van de meest waardevolle gereedschappen kan zijn. Hiermede wil echter nog niet gezegd zijn, dat in het merendeel van de Nederlandse bedrijven, waar men deze administratieve organisatie zou mogen verwachten, een 'up to date' organisatie inderdaad reeds wordt aangetroffen. Omdat de accountantscontrole in Nederland niet steunt op een wettelijk voorschrift, bestaat er tussen de bedrijfsleiding en de public accountant veelal een sfeer van vertrouwen, waardoor zijn controletaak zowel de controle van de rekening en verantwoording als de controle ten behoeve van de bedrijfsleiding omvat. Het is met name de laatste taak, die de public accountant ten volle confronteert met de ontwikkeling van de administratieve organisatie, opdat dit onderdeel waarlijk worde tot een instrument ten behoeve van het bedrijfsbestuur.

Hier ligt voor de public accountant een belangrijk werkterrein. De bedrijven hebben dringend behoefte aan deskundige voorlichting. Ten dele moeten zij nog op de hoogte worden gebracht van de ontwikkelingen, die zich op het gebied van de administratieve organisatie bezig zijn te voltrekken. Ten dele moeten zij nog van de waarde van de uitbouw van hun administratieve organisatie in deze richting worden overtuigd. De beschouwingswijze, dat de administratieve organisatie tot een minimum omvang beperkt moet blijven èn uit kostenoverwegingen èn ten einde bureaucratisering van het bedrijf te voorkomen, heeft nog allerminst afgedaan. Daarbij komt, dat de 'produktieve' waarde van de administratie alleen maar tot zijn recht kan komen als de opzet van de administratie door deskundigen geschiedt, die dit werkterrein ter dege beheersen en voorts actieve belangstelling voor het hanteren van het administratieve apparaat bij de bedrijfsleiding weten te wekken. Alleen dan kan de administratieve organisatie een levend onderdeel van de gehele organisatiestructuur worden. Alleen dan wordt de administratie het cement, dat de afdelingen (bouwstenen) tot een hecht geheel samenbindt. Anders is het gevaar groot, dat de administratie als het zand in het raderwerk van de organisatie wordt beschouwd.

Naast de administratie ten behoeve van het periodiek afleggen van rekening en verantwoording (financial accounting), zie ik dus het administratief geheel ten behoeve van het bedrijfsbestuur (management accounting). Tot het laatste gebied reken ik dan de kostprijsadministratie, de bedrijfsbegroting, de variabele budgettering en de resultatenberekening op korte termijn. Voor ieder dezer deelgebieden is het ontwikkelen van normcijfers voor kosten, prestaties en opbrengsten van grote betekenis.

Ten behoeve van het bestuur neemt de bedrijfsbegroting met een taakstellend karakter een centrale plaats in. Bedrijfsbegroting te zamen met normcijfers bieden de mogelijkheid de toelaatbare kosten en de te verwachten prestaties per afdeling te vermelden naast de taken en bevoegdheden, die door de hoogste bedrijfsleiding worden gedelegeerd. Op deze wijze kan de controlerende taak van de public accountant een hecht fundament voor de beoordeling worden gegeven.

Sinds kort dient zich een nieuwe ontwikkeling aan op het terrein van de administratieve organisatie in de persoon van de 'controller'. Ik meen, dat de inhoud van de controllerstaak het best kan worden afgeleid van de omschrijving, die ik in het C.P.A. Handbook aantrof, te weten: 'Planning for profits and providing suitable profit control machinery' [2]). In vele gevallen maakt de controller deel uit van het hoogste bestuurscollege.

Ik acht om twee redenen deze ontwikkeling belangrijk. Ten eerste omdat de hoge plaatsing van de controller in de hiërarchie duidelijk illustreert de grote betekenis, die aan het besturen van de administratieve organisatie wordt toegekend. Ten tweede omdat in de omschrijving van de inhoud van de controllerstaak het vooruitschouwende element, dat in de administratie moet worden gebracht, is neergelegd. Op deze wijze tekenen zich drie stadia in de ontwikkeling van de administratie af:

a. De boekhouding ten behoeve van het periodiek afleggen van rekening en verantwoording. De instelling moet hiertoe in hoofdzaak terugschouwend zijn.

b. De administratie ten behoeve van het besturen van het bedrijf, eigenlijk ten behoeve van de dirigerende leiding, gericht op het heden.

c. De administratie ten behoeve van de controllerstaak, welke inhoudt het voorbereiden van maatregelen ter verzekering, respectievelijk verbetering van de winstgevendheid voor de nabije en verdere toekomst, gericht dus op de toekomst.

Op deze beschouwingen over de controllerstaak wil ik enkele opmerkingen over de taak van de administratie ten behoeve van het voortdurend streven van de bedrijven naar opvoering van de productiviteit, met name de arbeidsproduktiviteit, laten volgen. Een goede administratie stelt kosten en prestaties voortdurend tegenover elkaar en brengt regelmatig de afwijkingen ten opzichte van de gestelde normcijfers onder de aandacht van de verantwoordelijke functionarissen in het bedrijf. Voorts vindt de hoogste bedrijfsleiding in dergelijke overzichten de grondslag voor de beoordeling van de efficiency van de onderscheiden bedrijfsonderdelen. Dit middel, ik zou willen spreken van de indirecte methode, mag zeker niet onvermeld blijven naast de rechtstreekse aanpak van de opvoering van de produktiviteit door organisatie-deskundige en efficiency-ingenieur.

Voorts mag het streven van de bedrijven tussentijdse resultatenoverzichten, bij voorbeeld kwartaaloverzichten, te publiceren en het streven de periode, welke verstrijkt tussen de balansdatum en het moment, waarop de jaarrekening wordt overgelegd, zoveel mogelijk te bekorten, niet onvermeld blijven. Ook deze ontwikkelingen stellen nieuwe eisen aan de administratieve organisatie en maken heroriëntering van de controle-arbeid van de accountant noodzakelijk.

Ten slotte de mechanisatie van de administratie. Naarmate de omvang van het administratieve werk toeneemt èn door de groei van de bedrijfsomvang èn door verruiming van de functionele inhoud van de administratieve taak, neemt de mogelijkheid mechanische hulpmiddelen toe te passen toe. Mechanisatie is behalve uit kostenoverwegingen ook belangrijk uit het oogpunt van versnelling van het tempo, waarin belangrijke overzichten beschikbaar komen. Bemoeienis met de uitbouw en omvorming van de administratieve organisatie verplicht de public accountant tevens tot het op peil houden van zijn deskundigheid op dit gebied. Uiteraard sluit dit de mogelijkheid van het te hulp roepen van externe specialisten op het terrein van de mechanische administratie niet uit. De accountant trede in dergelijke gevallen echter niet terug, omdat het zijn taak blijft aan te geven welke functies de mechanische apparatuur dient te vervullen en welke organisatorische maatregelen moeten worden getroffen om een doeltreffend functioneren in het administratieve geheel te verzekeren.

Ik hoop erin geslaagd te zijn het ruime en fascinerende werkterrein te schetsen, dat de administratieve organisatie de public accountant biedt. Het ligt binnen het bereik van zijn deskundigheid en het hangt ten nauwste met de doeltreffende vervulling van zijn controle-functie samen. Overigens mag uit mijn beschouwingen, ik vermeld dit met name ten behoeve van de buitenlandse beroepsgenoten, niet de conclusie worden getrokken, dat de Nederlandse accountants allen reeds in zo ruime mate bemoeienis met de omvorming van de administratieve organisatie van de Nederlandse bedrijven hebben. Wel meen ik, dat de wenselijkheid van een dergelijke ruime bemoeienis vrij algemeen in Nederlandse vakkringen wordt ingezien. Het N.I.v.A. en de V.A.G.A. bevorderen, dat in de leden- en studievergaderingen regelmatig referaten worden gehouden, welke een stimulans in deze richting uitoefenen.

IV. De deskundigheid van de public accountant en het werkterrein van de organisatie-deskundige

De na-oorlogse ontwikkeling noopt de Nederlandse ondernemers, èn als gevolg van een voortdurend stijgend loon- en prijspeil, èn als gevolg van een algemeen heersende arbeidsschaarste, alles in het werk te stellen om de arbeidsproduktiviteit op te voeren. Ook van overheidswege wordt voor dit streven intensief propaganda gemaakt, omdat alleen langs deze weg het welstandsniveau kan worden verhoogd. Zonder twijfel zijn sinds 1945 aanmerkelijke resultaten bereikt. Het inzicht wint veld, dat de externe organisatie-adviseur hierbij waardevolle diensten kan bewijzen. Zonder aarzeling mag worden vastgesteld, dat er in Nederland in verhouding tot de potentiële behoefte een groot tekort aan bekwame organisatie-deskundigen bestaat. Tot op dit moment bestaat er geen officiele opleiding, noch aan de Nederlandse Universiteiten, noch aan de Hogescholen, voor dit vrije beroep. Degenen, die op dit moment met succes als zodanig in Nederland optreden, zijn allen self-made men. De voorbereidingen van het Nederlands Hoger Onderwijs tot het instellen van een opleiding voor organisatie-deskundigen zijn reeds ver gevorderd. In 1953 heeft een speciaal voor dit doel ingestelde Staatscommissie over deze opleiding rapport uitgebracht[3]). Maar niet alleen bij overheid, bedrijfsleven en hoger onderwijs, ook in accountantskringen staat dit vraagstuk in het middelpunt van de belangstelling[4]).

De accountant heeft als logisch uitvloeisel van zijn controle-functie bemoeienis met administratief-organisatorische vraagstukken. De bedrijfseconomie moet behalve voor de accountant ook voor de opleiding van de organisatie-deskundige een belangrijk leervak zijn. Er is dus een verwantschap wat de theoretische scholing betreft. Het is verklaarbaar, dat in de kring van de Nederlandse accountants reeds geruime tijd de vraag in bespreking is of het niet op de weg van de accountants ligt ook de verbetering van de organisatie van de gecontroleerde bedrijven tot voorwerp van activiteitsontplooiing te maken. Men vraagt zich af of de accountants, indien zij nalaten in deze richting hun werkterrein uit te breiden, niet gevaar lopen te zijner tijd het verwijt te horen, dat zij in gebreke zijn gebleven.

De accountant is verantwoord het werkterrein van de organisatie-deskundige te betreden, wanneer aan twee voorwaarden is voldaan:

1. Hij moet hiertoe de vereiste vakbekwaamheid bezitten.

2. Hij moet hierdoor geen schade toebrengen aan de doeltreffende vervulling van zijn basisfunctie, de controlefunctie[5]).

De gedachtenwisseling over de vakbekwaamheid van de accountant wordt vertroebeld, wanneer men de vraag van de mogelijkheid van vakbekwaamheid zowel voor de controlerende functie als voor de organisatorisch-adviserende functie toespitst op het individu. Het gaat er niet om of een individuele persoon zich zowel de theoretische scholing als praktische ervaring voor beide werkterreinen kan eigen maken. Zowel de accountantsfunctie als de organisatorisch-adviserende functie wordt in de praktijk door organisaties, door kantoren, vervuld. De accountant is geen alleen-werkend deskundige. Hij werkt veelal in maatschapsverband met één of meer collega's samen en deze samenwerking wordt in vakkringen toegejuicht, omdat dit de vakbekwaamheid door uitwisseling van ervaring en periodieke gemeenschappelijke bespreking vergroot. Daarnaast beschikt ieder accountantskantoor over een staf assistenten, waartussen arbeidsverdeling bestaat en die per opdracht onder een gediplomeerd accountant werken. De accountantsfunctie wordt door groepen van in één verband samenwerkende personen vervuld.

Een soortgelijke ontwikkeling valt, wat de arbeid van de organisatie-deskundige betreft, waar te nemen. Ook hier samenwerking van één of meer deskundigen, geassisteerd door een kleine staf organisatie-assistenten. De assistentenstaf voor het organisatiewerk is veelal kleiner en minder gelaagd dan mogelijk is voor het accountantswerk.

De vraag van de deskundigheid moet dus worden geprojecteerd op het accountantskantoor. Kan deze organisatie zich de deskundigheid eigen maken, zowel voor de accountantsfunctie als voor de organisatorisch-adviserende functie? Dit is een vraag van personeelsselectie en personeelskeuze, welke vraag naar mijn mening zonder aarzeling met 'ja' kan worden beantwoord. Het is mogelijk, maar men bedenke dan echter, dat het, behoudens in uitzonderingsgevallen, niet mogelijk is dat van deze formatie personen deel zullen uitmaken, die zich terecht als deskundige op beide werkterreinen mogen aandienen. Dit is een praktische onmogelijkheid, omdat deskundigheid uit drie elementen is opgebouwd:

a. theoretische scholing;

b. practische ervaring;

c. aanleg en karaktereigenschappen.

Ook al is het in uitzonderingsgevallen mogelijk, dat begaafde personen, die gemakkelijk en snel studeren, de examens afleggen die voor beide beroepen aanstonds worden vereist, dan nog zal het onmogelijk blijken de vereiste praktische ervaring, die voor ieder der beroepen jaren vraagt, te verwerven en te onderhouden. Tenslotte meen ik, dat aanleg en karaktereigenschappen voor deze beroepen van wezenlijk verschillende inhoud zijn.

Mijn conclusie is dus, dat het accountantskantoor, dat werkelijk het werkterrein van de organisatie-deskundige gaat betreden, een binnen het kantoor volledige specialisatie van assistenten, medewerker(s) en vennoten zal moeten tot stand brengen. De volgende stap zal dan zijn, dat men binnen het organisatiewerk opnieuw een specialisatie zal moeten bevorderen. Het is namelijk op zich zelf weer zo breed en gevarieerd – de ontwikkeling is nog allerminst tot stilstand gekomen – dat tussen de kantoren, die op dit terrein opereren, reeds een zekere specialisatie zich aftekent, terwijl dit evenzo noodzakelijk is binnen ieder kantoor.

Aan de psychologische kanten van het organisatiewerk, evenals aan bedrijfssociologische aspecten wordt steeds meer betekenis toegekend. Vandaar dat sommigen van oordeel zijn, dat in het team dat aan een organisatie-opdracht werkzaam is ook de psycholoog en socioloog moeten zijn opgenomen. Want steeds meer wint de zienswijze veld, dat het scheppen van een doeltreffende organisatie niet alleen een vraagstuk is van het brengen van technische hulpmiddelen in de juiste verhouding ten opzichte van elkaar, maar vooral in het scheppen van de juiste menselijke verhoudingen (human relations) in het bedrijf. Ten behoeve van het opsporen van de weerstanden, die er in dit opzicht in de bedrijven bestaan, alsmede ten behoeve van de invoeringsfase kan de kennis en ervaring van socioloog en psycholoog waardevol zijn. Want, men kan niets opleggen, men moet overtuigen en overreden. Hiertoe is veel geduld, tact, vasthoudendheid en overredingskracht noodzakelijk. Het vereist een zich volledig inleven in de sfeer van het onderhavige bedrijf; een intensief contact met de betrokken functionarissen. En hier is weer een volledig afwijkende instelling in vergelijking tot de controle-arbeid. De accountant-controleur en zijn assistenten moeten afstand bewaren, mogen niet op al te vriendschappelijke voet met de functionarissen in het te controleren bedrijf staan. De zienswijze wordt zelfs verdedigd, dat het team, dat een bedrijf controleert, slechts enkele jaren achtereen hetzelfde bedrijf mag controleren. Dan moet bewust roulering worden nagestreefd, ook al betekent dit het verloren gaan van detailkennis en ervaring, in de achterliggende jaren door de controle-arbeid opgebouwd.

V. Argumenten pro en contra het betreden van het werkterrein van de organisatie-deskundige

Twee stadia in de bemoeienis van de accountant met de organisatie moeten duidelijk worden onderscheiden:

a. een bemoeienis, die noodzakelijk voortvloeit uit en verbonden is met vervulling van zijn *functie*. Bemoeienis dus met de personele en administratieve organisatie;

b. een bemoeienis, die kan voortvloeien uit zijn *deskundigheid*. In dit geval heb ik het oog op de ruimere bemoeienis met de organisatie als organisatie-deskundige.

In de voorgaande paragraaf meen ik te hebben aangetoond, dat het accountantskantoor in staat is zich de vereiste deskundigheid voor de ruimere bemoeienis met de organisatie te verwerven. De vraag blijft nog te beantwoorden of deze uitbreiding van werkterrein gewenst is. Gewenst vanuit een doeltreffende vervulling van de accountantsfunctie gezien; gewenst vanuit de behoefte van het bedrijfsleven gezien.

Allereerst de argumenten 'pro'. Hiervoor is reeds geconstateerd, dat er een tekort is aan vakbekwame organisatie-adviseurs. Uitbreiding van het aantal, door ontplooiing van activiteit door accountants, kan dus, vanuit het bedrijfsleven gezien, alleen maar worden toegejuicht. Dan is er zelfs nog een bijkomend argument. De accountant heeft reeds contact met een groot aantal bedrijven. Vele bedrijven staan thans nog aarzelend en argwanend tegenover het inschakelen van organisatie-deskundigen, omdat zij maar moeilijk kunnen aanvaarden, dat buitenstaanders in staat zouden zijn belangrijke verbeteringen in de organisatie van het bedrijf tot stand te brengen. Voorts staan de bedrijven steeds aarzelend tegenover het binnenhalen van een buitenstaander in het bedrijf. Hier liggen ongetwijfeld belangrijke psychologische weerstanden, die vrijwel op slag zouden zijn overwonnen, wanneer die buitenstaander de bekende en vertrouwde accountant kan zijn. De man, respectievelijk het kantoor, waarmede reeds vele jaren de meest vertrouwelijke vraagstukken worden besproken.

Voor de kleinere bedrijven en middelgrote bedrijven is het ongetwijfeld voordelig, wanneer zij bij hun eigen accountant steun kunnen vinden, voor het oplossen van organisatorische vraagstukken. Zelfs indien hun accountant zich niet op alle punten met de gespecialiseerde vakman kan meten. Bedacht moet worden, dat de organisatie-vraagstukken met het groter worden van de bedrijven tot ontwikkeling komen en zich zelfs eerst dan voor gedetailleerde analyse lenen.

Het argument dat men vaak in accountantskringen hoort, dat de accountant het bedrijf reeds kent, mag niet onvermeld blijven. De oriënterende bestudering van het bedrijf, steeds de eerste fase van een organisatie-onderzoek, kan hierdoor belangrijk worden bekort. Dit argument verliest overigens aan waarde, wanneer een speciale staf binnen het kantoor voor dit werkterrein is gevormd. Nauw hiermede verbonden is het argument, dat de accountant een blijvend contact met het bedrijf, ten behoeve van zijn controle-arbeid, onderhoudt. Hij kan dus beter dan de buitenstaander-organisatie-deskundige, erop toe zien, dat de gepropageerde maatregelen niet verwateren. Ook dit argument verliest aan kracht naarmate de opvatting algemeen wordt, dat de taak van de organisatie-deskundige niet eindigt met het uitwerken van voorstellen tot verbetering. Juist dan komt de moeilijkste fase, de invoering; het aanbrengen van veranderingen in werkmethode, taakverdeling en organisatie-structuur. Sommigen propageren reeds een permanent contact tussen bedrijf en organisatie-deskundige, ten behoeve van regelmatige bewaking van de organisatie, respectievelijk een periodieke 'check-up'.

Onder de argumenten 'contra' behoort in de eerste plaats de vrees te worden genoemd, die sommigen hebben dat de controlefunctie in gevaar komt, omdat de onbevangenheid van de accountant wordt verminderd[6]). Men denkt dan met name aan de gevallen, dat de door de accountant, en dan als organisatie-deskundige, gepropageerde veranderingen in de organisatie minder succesvol blijken te zijn. De noodzaak kan zich voordoen, dat de accountant aan bedrijfsleiding en/of aandeelhouders hiervan melding moet maken en dan, zo wordt door hen gesteld, ontstaat het gevaar dat de accountant, in de positie gebracht in afkeurende zin te moeten rapporteren over zijn eigen organisatie-arbeid, hiermede de hand zal lichten. Het is moeilijk dit argument op zijn juiste waarde te schatten. Wel is het interessant melding te maken van het feit, dat aan dit aspect ook in hoofdstuk 25 van het C.P.A.-Handbook (U.S.A.) aandacht is geschonken. De conclusie is daar, dat de 'independence' van de accountant niet in gevaar wordt gebracht.

In ieder geval verliest dit argument veel aan betekenis, wanneer de controletaak door de ene afdeling en de organisatorisch-adviserende taak door een andere afdeling wordt verricht.

Tegenover het hiervoor, onder de argumenten 'pro', betoogde, dat het bedrijf er gemakkelijker toekomt de eigen accountant in te schakelen voor organisatie-werk, moet worden gesteld, dat ik bij vele bedrijven heb menen waar te nemen, dat men maar moeilijk kan geloven, dat het accountantskantoor terecht pretendeert op zo'n ruim gebied de vereiste deskundigheid te bezitten. Men aanvaardt gemakkelijker de deskundigheid van specialisten op beperkte gebieden. De verruiming van werkterrein gaat in tegen de normale maatschappelijke ontwikkeling, die de bedrijven op hun eigen werkterrein waarnemen, namelijk beperking van werkterrein ter opvoering van de specifieke deskundigheid op een beperkter gebied. Men wil nog wel aannemen, dat het accountantskantoor deskundig is op het administratief-organisatorisch gebied, omdat accountant en administratie begrippen zijn, die voor de bedrijven bijeen behoren. Wellicht voelen de bedrijven onbewust ook het verschil in karaktereigenschappen, die voor beide functies, accountant en organisatie-deskundige, vereist zijn.

Een ontwikkeling van het accountantskantoor, in die zin, dat naast een afdeling voor de accountantsfunctie een afdeling ontstaat voor de organisatorisch-adviserende functie, zal worden bemoeilijkt door het feit, dat de volwaardige organisatie-deskundige niet behoeft te beschikken over het accountantsdiploma. Maar dan kunnen deze deskundigen nooit tot de top van het kantoor doordringen, dat wil zeggen in de maatschap worden opgenomen, omdat de reglementen van de leidende beroepsorganisaties, het Nederlands Instituut van Accountants (N.I.v.A.) en de Vereniging van Academisch Gevormde Accountants (V.A.G.A.) associatie met niet-leden verbieden. Dit verbod vindt zijn oorzaak in de overweging, dat geen waarborg voor deskundigheid aanwezig is ten aanzien van de leiding van de beroepsarbeid, wanneer één of meer leden van de maatschap ongediplomeerd zijn. Voorts stelt het reglement van arbeid voor de vennoten de gemeenschappelijke verantwoordelijkheid tegenover de beroepsorganisatie voor elkaars arbeid. Hoe verklaarbaar dit voorschrift vanuit accountantsstandpunt gezien ook is, het zal voor de organisatie-deskundige onaanvaardbaar zijn en met name de bekwamen nopen uit de formatie te treden. Dit zal nog meer klemmen, wanneer eenmaal de Universiteiten en Hogescholen ook voor organisatie-deskundige opleiden. Deze personen zullen zich, èn wat theoretische scholing èn wat maatschappelijke standing van hun vrije beroep betreft, de gelijkwaardigen van de accountants achten. Daarom is de kans groot, dat de organisatie-afdeling van het accountantskantoor een overgangsfase zal blijken te zijn gedurende de periode, dat het vrije beroep van organisatie-deskundige nog niet tot volle wasdom is gekomen.

Literatuur-overzicht

1) A. M. van Rietschoten. Enkele beschouwingen over de functies van het accountantsberoep. Rede uitgesproken bij de aanvaarding van het ambt van buitengewoon hoogleraar aan de Universiteit van Amsterdam op 20 november 1950.

2) C.P.A.-Handbook (U.S.A.). Chapter 25.

3) De opleiding van deskundigen op het gebied van leiding en organisatie van bedrijven. Rapport uitgebracht door een hiertoe ingestelde Commissie van Advies op 4 augustus 1953.

4) H. Reinoud. Enkele opmerkingen omtrent de toekomstige ontwikkeling van de organisatie-deskundigheid van de accountant. 14 november 1953. Zie ook het verslag van de discussies in 'De Accountant' van januari en mei 1954.

5) Ook in het Wetsontwerp tot wettelijke regeling van het accountantswezen wordt de controle-functie als de hoofdfunctie van de accountant omschreven.

6) Zie het artikel van Prof. Dr H. J. v. d. Schroeff in het Maandblad voor Accountancy en Bedrijfshuishoudkunde, oktober 1947, getiteld: 'Enige opmerkingen over mogelijkheden en wenselijkheden van een verbijzondering in de uitoefening van het accountantsberoep'.

Translation

PAPER

by

S. C. BAKKENIST, EC. DRS.

Nederlands Instituut van Accountants

I. The Function of the Public Accountant

If we wish to consider the relationship between the public accountant and business organisation, we must first define the functions of the Public Accountant in the Netherlands. I shall base the 'definition' on the views Prof. Van Rietschoten has put forward on the subject, because I feel that he has defined the content of the various functions in a way that is generally accepted by my Dutch colleagues.

The function can be sub-divided under three headings:

1. Independent auditor of an organisation's administration. The audit culminates in the issue of a report on the accounts, whenever possible unqualified, which is submitted — publicly or in private, as the case may be — to the owners of the capital invested in the organisation.

In many cases interest in this report is by no means limited to the owners and shareholders; interest is far more widespread than that. In the Netherlands this wider circle of interested parties is referred to as 'the business community' and we therefore speak of *the auditor performing his task on behalf of the business community.*

2. In addition to the exercise of his controlling task on behalf of the business community, and often simultaneously and interwoven with the task referred to under 1. above, the auditor exercises a *controlling function on behalf of management.*

As the size of business undertakings increases, there comes into being an ever widening gulf between top management and executive direction. The administration becomes of increasing importance as the source which supplies top management with the data on which policy is based, and as a means of ascertaining to what extent planned policies were in fact executed. This makes it necessary to ensure that the information issued by the administration is factually correct. The public accountant can combine the task of providing that assurance with his tasks referred to under 1. above, and this combination is both economical and practical. If management entrusts him with this task, he exercises a controlling function on behalf of management.

3. The knowledge and experience which accountants acquire in the course of

their practice, qualify them as experts in the fields of business economics, administrative organisation, and audit. Consequently, the accountant can become *an adviser to management on business economics.*

This advisory function will, however, always be a task subsidiary to the controlling (audit) task; it can indeed be considered as a logical consequence of the controlling function.

II. The Controlling Function in Relation to Allocation of Duties

It is a condition of effective control that there should be such a distribution of duties amongst the staff (of the organisation) as will enable the accountant, as a result of his audit, to form an independent opinion on the correctness of the accounts.

In the Netherlands the principle is generally accepted that there must be a clear segregation between management duties, duties involving the responsibility for cash, goods, etc., and finally the task of recording. Only in these circumstances can there be effective internal check and only then can it be expected that the administration which is being audited by the accountant, on which audit he bases his judgment as to the correctness of the accounts, does indeed give a reliable picture of what happened in the organisation in the period to which the accounts relate. It is the accountant's duty to form at the beginning of his auditing task a judgment regarding the staff arrangements and the distribution of tasks in the organisation he is auditing. If, in his opinion, and seen from a viewpoint of his auditing function, there are weaknesses, then it is his duty to draw the attention of management to these weaknesses in order to bring about that the changes which he considers necessary are duly made. It should be said here that businesses are again and again unconsciously violating the basic rule mentioned above. In many cases the consequences of doing so show up sooner or later. It is thus that the accountant exercises, as a result of his auditing task, an important influence on the staff arrangements of the organisation he is auditing.

III. The Public Accountant and Administrative Organisation

The public accountant is, as a result of his auditing the accounts and also as a result of his auditing on behalf of management, permanently in touch with the administration of the undertaking. In the Netherlands one defines a public accountant as an expert in administrative matters and questions of business economics. The accountant's concern with the administrative organisation results thus both from his auditing task and from his special expertise.

I think that it is now the general opinion in the Netherlands that there has been an evolution of the function of the administration from reporting past events for the purpose of compiling the annual accounts —in which function management considers the administration to be a burden—to the recording of events on behalf of executive management, i.e. into a tool for management. The increase in the size of business units has brought about an urgent need to supply management with the proper tools. It has been shown that efficient administrative organisation can be one of the most effective tools. That is not to say, however, that the majority of Dutch businesses in which one could expect such an administrative organisation has, in fact, got an up-to-date organisation. The audit of accounts by accountants is not prescribed by law in the Netherlands, and this often brings about an atmosphere of confidence between management and the public accountant which results in his auditing task comprising both the audit proper and the control on behalf of management. It is particularly this latter task which confronts the public accountant with the development of administrative organisation so that he may contribute to its development into a really valuable tool for management.

This is thus an important field of activity for the public accountant. Business urgently needs expert advice. In some cases management still need to be informed of developments which are constantly occurring in the field of administrative organisation. In some cases they still have to be convinced of the value of building up their administrative organisation in that direction. The view is still prevalent that administration must be restricted to a minimum:

a. to keep down costs, and

b. in order to avoid tieing up the business in red tape.

It should also be noted that the 'productive value' of the administration is only realised if the administration is set up by experts who are really at home in this work and who also know how to interest management in making full use of the administrative set-up. Only if this is done can the administration become a living part of the whole organisation structure; only then can the administration be the link which holds together the various departments as cement holds together the individual bricks. In any other circumstances there is a great danger that the administration will be considered as a spanner in the works.

I see thus a two-fold task for the administration:

a. To provide the necessary data for the accounts (financial accounting).

b. Administration for management (management accounting).

Into the latter group I count costing, budgeting, budgetary control, and the calculation of interim results. In each of these fields it is important to set standards for expense, performance and proceeds.

The budget can be seen as a definition of the task of the business and it therefore occupies a prominent place in the control of operations by management. Budget together with standards make it possible to lay down the admissible costs and the expected performance of every department, in addition to laying down the tasks and authority which are being delegated by top management. The auditing duties of the public accountant can thus acquire a sound basis on which to examine the results.

There has recently been a new development in the field of administrative organisation, viz. the appearance of the 'controller'. In my opinion the task of the controller can best be defined by referring to the definition contained in the C.P.A. handbook, viz. 'Planning for profits and providing suitable profit control machinery'. In many cases the controller is a member of top management.

I consider this development important for two reasons. Firstly, because the controller's position on the highest management level clearly illustrates how much importance is attached to the leadership of the administrative organisation, and secondly, because the definition of the controller's task clearly illustrates that it is the administration's task to look to the future. We can thus distinguish three stages in the development of the administration:

a. Book-keeping with the purpose of providing the data for the accounts; the tendency here is to look backward all the time,

b. Administration in order to manage the undertaking, i.e. on behalf of top management and concerned with events just happening,

c. Administration to enable the controller to fulfil his task which includes the taking of steps to ensure, or to improve, the profitability of the immediate and distant future, i.e. forward-looking all the time.

Having considered the controller's task, I would like to follow with some observations on the task of the administration in connection with the continuous endeavours of businesses to increase productivity, and mainly the productivity of labour work. A good administration continuously compares costs and performance and regularly shows up to the responsible managers deviations from set standards. Top management is in a position to base on such reviews their judgement of the efficiency of the various parts of the organisation. This method, which I will call the indirect method, must surely be noted next to that direct approach to the increase of productivity by the organisation expert and the efficiency engineer.

I must not omit to mention the wish of business people to have published interim results, for example, quarterly results, and to shorten as much as possible the period elapsing between the end of the financial year and the presentation of the accounts. These developments also confront the administration with new demands and make it imperative that the accountant should review his audit task.

Finally, the mechanisation of the administration.

The increase of administrative work as a result of the growth of business on the one hand and of the wider interpretation of the functional content of the administrative task on the other hand, increases the possibility of using mechanical aids.

Quite apart from considerations of cost, mechanisation is also important in order to speed up the availability of important data. If the public accountant is to concern himself with building up and reforming the administrative organisation, it becomes imperative for him to be an expert, and to be up-to-date, in this field. Naturally, this does not exclude the possibility of calling in external specialists in mechanised methods of administration. Even in such cases, however, the accountant should not just fade out of the picture, because it remains his task to lay down which functions the machines are to carry out and what steps have to be taken as regards the organisation, in order to ensure an efficient functioning of the administration as a whole.

I hope I have succeeded in sketching the wide and fascinating task which administrative organisation offers to the public accountant, a task which falls within the limits of his expert knowledge and is most closely connected with the efficient exercise of his controlling function. Primarily for the benefit of colleagues from abroad, I would add that it must not be concluded from my remarks that all Dutch accountants are already to a really large extent concerned with the reorganisation of the administration of Dutch undertakings. I do think, however, that the desirability of concerning themselves therewith is generally recognised in Dutch accountancy circles. The Netherlands Institute of Accountants (N.I.v.A.) and the Association of University Trained Accountants (V.A.G.A.) see to it that papers are regularly read to meetings of members and students which stimulate thought in this direction.

IV. The Expert Knowledge of the Public Accountant and the Field for the Specialist in Organisation

The post-war development forces Dutch employers, as a result of a continuing rise of wages and prices, and also as a result of the general scarcity of labour, to try everything possible in order to increase the productivity of work. The Government carries on extensive propaganda to the same effect, realising that this is the only way to raise the standard of living. No doubt substantial results have been achieved since 1945. It is being realised that the external adviser on organisation can make a valuable contribution in this matter. It can be stated without hesitation that, compared with the potential need, there exists in the Netherlands a great shortage of suitable management consultants.

Up to now, there is no official training system in existence for this profession, neither in the Universities nor in higher education. The men who at the moment successfully carry out this work in the Netherlands are all self-made men. Preparations are well advanced for a training system for management consultants. A Royal Commission was specially set up for this purpose and reported in 1953. The subject is the centre of attention, not only for the Government, business, and educational authorities, but also in accountancy circles.

As a logical consequence of his controlling function, the accountant is concerned with questions of administration and organisation. Business economics must be an important subject not only for the accountant but also in the training of management consultants. There is therefore a relationship as far as theoretical education is concerned. It is understandable that Dutch accountants have for some time been discussing whether it would not be up to them to include the improvement of the organisation of those undertakings which they audit amongst their tasks. The question is being asked whether the accountants will not sooner or later be reproached if they fail to extend their activities in this direction.

The accountant is justified to enter the field of advising an organisation if two conditions can be fulfilled:

1. He must have the necessary expert knowledge.
2. He must not, by doing so, detract from the value of his basic function which is that of auditor.

Consideration of the question whether the accountant possesses the necessary expert knowledge is becoming more difficult if one relates the question of possessing the necessary knowledge, both for the controlling and for the advising function, to a particular individual. The point is not whether a particular individual can acquire the necessary theoretical knowledge and practical experience for both fields of activity, because in practice both the function of accountant as also the function of management consultant is being carried out by organisations, i.e. by practices. The accountant is not an expert who works on his own. He usually works in partnership with one or more colleagues and this co-operation is welcomed by the profession because the exchange of experience and mutual discussion are beneficial to all taking part. Furthermore, in every accountant's office there is a staff of clerks who work under the direction of qualified accountants and amongst whom the work is distributed. The accountant's function is therefore carried out by groups of persons working together.

We have seen a similar development in the work of management consultants, i.e. one or more experts working with the assistance of a small staff of clerks. The staff of assistants in consultancy work is usually smaller and less differentiated than is possible in accountancy work.

The question of expertness must therefore be related to the accountancy practice. Can the practice acquire the expert knowledge that is necessary to carry out both accountancy work and consulting work? This is a question of staff selection and choice which I think can, without hesitation, be replied to in the positive. It is possible, but it must be remembered that, apart from exceptional cases, the group will not contain persons who can justifiably claim to be experts in both fields. That is a practical impossibility because there are three elements to be considered:

a. Theoretical training
b. Practical experience
c. Aptitude and character

Even though it is possible in exceptional cases that gifted persons who learn easily and quickly, succeed in passing the examinations which will shortly be demanded for both professions, it will still remain impossible to obtain and keep up-to-date the necessary practical experience, the acquisition of which is a matter of years in each of these professions. It is finally my opinion that the aptitude and character which is required for these professions is materially different. My conclusion is therefore that the accountancy practice which enters upon the field of consulting will have to bring about within the office complete specialisation of partners and staff. The next step will then have to be a further specialisation within the field of consulting because this field is again so wide and varied—the development is by no means concluded—that one begins to see a certain amount of specialisation as between different practices, and this is equally important within every office.

Increasing attention is being paid to the psychological and sociological aspect of consultancy work. That has led many people to conclude that the consultancy team must include psychologists and sociologists. It is being increasingly realised that the creation of an efficient organisation is not just a question of installing suitable technical devices, but primarily the creation of the right human relations within the undertaking. In dealing with the resistance that is being encountered in this connection, and also in connection with the implementation, the knowledge of the sociologist and psychologist can be of great value. It is not a question of giving orders but it is necessary to convince and to persuade. This requires much patience, tact, tenacity and persuasive power. The consultant must absorb the atmosphere of the client's undertaking. He requires intensive contact with the staff. Here again, we have quite a different position compared with audit work. The auditor and his staff must maintain a certain distance and they must not get too friendly with the client's executives. It has even been said that a team which is auditing a client's books should only do so for a number of successive years, and then there must be a change of personnel, even if that entails the loss of certain detailed knowledge and experience that has been acquired during the past years.

V. Arguments for and against entering the Field of Consultancy

We must therefore distinguish two phases of the accountant's concern with the organisation:

a. A concern which necessarily flows from, and which is connected with, the execution of his *function* as an auditor, viz. concern with the staff distribution and administrative organisation.

b. A concern which can result from his being an *expert.* In this connection I am referring to the wider concern with the organisation as a consultant.

In the previous paragraph I have indicated that the accountancy practice is in a position to acquire the necessary expert knowledge for the wider concern with the organisation. That, however, leaves open the question whether this extension of activities is indeed desirable:

a. from a point of view of ensuring the effective persecution of the accountant's basic function, and

b. from the point of view of the needs of the business community.

I will deal first with the arguments in favour. In this connection I have already mentioned that there is a shortage of suitable consultants. An increase in their number as a result of extending the activities of accountants can therefore be welcomed by the business community. There is here an additional argument. The accountant is already in touch with a great number of undertakings. Many firms are at this moment still doubtful and suspicious of the intervention of the consultant because they find it difficult to accept that outsiders should be in a position to bring about important improvements in the organisation of the undertaking. Moreover, there is always a hesitation to call in an outsider. These are no doubt important psychological obstacles which can be cleared out of the way almost instantly if the outsider can be the accountant who is known and trusted; the man or the practice with whom one has been discussing for many years the most confidential questions.

For the smaller and medium sized firm it is no doubt advantageous if they can get from their own accountant the help that is required for the solution of their organisational problems, even if the accountant cannot in all respects compete with the specialist consultant. It must be remembered that questions of organisation are only coming to the foreground as the size of the undertaking increases, and only then do they become suitable for detailed analysis. The argument which is often heard within the profession that the accountant already knows the client must not be forgotten. The preliminary survey of the undertaking which is always the first stage in a consultant's investigation can therefore be reduced in duration. This argument, however, loses part of its force when the practice has a specialized staff for business consultancy. Closely connected herewith is the argument that the accountant remains in perpetual contact with the client in connection with the audit. He is thus in a better position than the outside consultant to see that the recommendations are not watered down. However, this argument also loses force as the view is gaining ground that the consultant's task does not finish with the preparation of recommendations. This is followed by the most difficult phase, the implementation; the changing of working methods, the distribution of tasks, and the building of the organisation structure. From some quarters there is already propaganda for a permanent contact between consultant and client in order to ensure constant supervision of the organisation or a periodical check-up.

Dealing with the arguments against, we must mention in the first place the fear expressed by some people that the audit function is being endangered because the impartiality of the accountant is being reduced. They think particularly of the cases in which the changes in the organisation brought about by the accountant in his function as a business consultant prove to be less successful. Those holding this view say that this can put the accountant in the position where he has to make an adverse report on his own work as a consultant, and the danger is that he will not do so. It is difficult to say what there is in this argument but it is interesting to record the fact that the matter has been considered in Chapter 25 of the C.P.A. handbook. The conclusion there is that the independence of the accountant is not endangered.

In any case, this argument loses importance if the audit is carried out by one department and the consultancy work by another department.

As against the argument which has been mentioned under the arguments in favour, viz. that the client finds it easier to bring in his own accountant for consultancy work, it must be stated that in many undertakings I have felt that one is not prepared to believe that the accountancy profession is rightly claiming to possess the necessary expert knowledge in such a wide field. One finds it easier to accept the expert knowledge of specialists in limited fields. The extension of the field of activities goes against the normal development in the community, which the clients recognise in their own fields of activity, and which is towards greater specialisation in a limited field. One is perhaps prepared to accept that the accountancy practice are experts in the field of administrative organisation because 'accounting' and 'administration' are terms which seem to belong together, but subconsciously clients somehow feel the difference in character which is required for the two functions of accountant and consultant respectively.

Development of the accountancy practice in the direction that next to a department for accountancy work there comes into being a department for consultancy work, is being made more difficult by the fact that a qualified consultant need not have an accountancy qualification. That means, however, that these experts cannot rise to the top level in the accountancy practice, i.e. become partners, because the by-laws of the leading accountancy bodies, the Netherlands Institute of Accountants (N.I.v.A.) and the Association of University Trained Accountants (V.A.G.A.) prohibit partnership with non-members. The reason for this prohibition is the consideration that there is no guarantee of expert direction of the professional work if one or more of the partners is unqualified. Moreover, the rules and regulations of the profession lay down the partners' joint responsibility to the accountancy body for each other's work. However understandable these rules may be when seen from an accountant's point of view, it is a position that will be unacceptable to the consultants, and especially the brilliant ones will decide to sever the connection. This problem will become more urgent when the Universities and higher education have started to turn out consultants. These people will, both as regards theoretical education and status of their profession, feel themselves the equals of the accountants. There is therefore a great chance that the consultancy department of the accountancy practice will turn out to be a temporary phase during the period in which the profession of consultant is not yet fully developed.

PAPER

by

J. E. HARRIS, B. COM., F.A.C.C.A.

Association of Certified and Corporate Accountants, U.K.

I. The Purpose of the Paper

The purpose of this paper is three-fold and its divisions can broadly be enumerated as follows:

1. To examine the extent to which the internal organization of a business affects the certificate given by a public accountant in his capacity as auditor.
2. To study whether a 'business organization' is itself a suitable subject for appraisal,—that is to say, whether the organization, as distinct from the financial transactions and results thereof, can be evaluated or audited so that a certificate as to its efficiency could be given by a public accountant.
3. To discuss—if 'business organization' is found to be a suitable subject for auditing—whether it is practicable and or desirable for a public accountant to extend his customary audit in this respect; and whether such an extension of an audit ought to be made compulsory by law or whether it ought to be treated only as a possible additional service of the public accountant available if requested.

II. Customary Financial Audit

Throughout this paper discussion will be restricted to what are known in the United Kingdom as limited companies since the audit of these companies is obligatory by law. Such audits have been required by law in the United Kingdom only since 1900 and the most recent legislation affecting the law relating to the audit of companies was enacted in 1948. The vast majority of businesses and bodies other than limited companies are not subject to a compulsory audit and therefore have freedom of action in deciding the limit and scope of the duties of their auditors if any; therefore, if this restriction were not placed on the discussion the permutation of possibilities would be such as to necessitate continuous qualifications distracting to the main theme.

To ascertain the extent, if any, to which the internal organization of a business affects the certificate to be given by the auditor, it is obviously necessary to set down and to examine exactly what the auditor is required by law to state in his audit report. The main relevant requirements of the Companies Act 1948 in this connection are as follows:

1. Whether they (the auditors) have obtained all the information and explanations which to the best of their knowledge and belief were necessary for the purposes of their audit.

2. Whether, in their opinion, proper books of account have been kept by the company, so far as appears from their examination of those books, and proper returns adequate for the purposes of their audit have been received from branches not visited by them.

3. (1) Whether the company's balance sheet and profit and loss account dealt with by the report are in agreement with the books of account and returns.

(2) Whether, in their opinion and to the best of their information and according to the explanations given them, the accounts give the information required by the Act in the manner so required and give a true and fair view:

a. in the case of the balance sheet, of the state of the Company's affairs as at the end of its financial year; and

b. in the case of the profit and loss account, of the profit or loss for its financial year.

It is clear, therefore, that there is a minimum amount of information which the auditor must be able to obtain before he can satisfy himself sufficiently about the affairs of the company to enable him to give a full and unqualified audit report. It is also obvious, to generalize, that the efficiency or otherwise of the organization clearly has a bearing on the amount of work which the auditor must perform before he can feel satisfied as to his ability to give his report. To set a limiting case, varying with the size and nature of the business there is plainly a set of conditions which, irrespective of the amount of detail work performed by the auditor, are such that it would be impossible for him to satisfy himself as to the state of the Company's affairs at the end of the financial year or as to what is a fair view of the profit or loss made by the Company during its financial year.

Apart from this it will have been noted that the auditor is required to report upon the adequacy of the books of account. This, of course, constitutes a further minimum requirement which, if not satisfied must lead the auditor to qualify his certificate. Having regard to this, it is certainly within the spirit of his function, although beyond what the letter of the law requires, if the auditor advises at the earliest possible moment as to what he considers to be the least efficient parts of the business organization, and what changes are, in his view, the minimum necessary to enable him to give an unqualified certificate, bearing in mind his statutory duties. The advantages of this course of conduct require no elaboration.

In my opinion, to this extent and this only, it is the function of the auditor as such to give advice. As will be seen later, I am of the opinion that the public accountant can make an increasingly valuable contribution to business organization and thereby more widely benefit the national economy. However, both in practice and theory, I think it vital to maintain as a separate and distinct function the work of the public accountant in his capacity as auditor from work which is either voluntary on his part or requested of him in extension of that necessitated by the audit. My view of the need for maintaining this clear division of duty results from the structure of companies and the reason for and purpose of the appointment of auditors. It has to be recalled that auditors are appointed by the shareholders of a Company to report to them and therefore to confirm the accuracy or otherwise of the financial results of the organization presented by the officers of that organization. It is true of course that in a very large number of small companies the directors and shareholders are the same people. Nevertheless it would be both impractical and, in my view, a retrograde step for the present legal requirements of an audit report to be variable according to the size of the business. Furthermore, in my opinion, the present obligations are the minimum irrespective of the size and nature of the company concerned. If these views are sound, it follows that the shareholders must receive regularly from an unbiased qualified observer his views on the financial results and position of the Company entrusted by them to the directors. Moreover, the increasing size of business organizations is resulting in an ever growing number of cases where the only link with the company of the majority of its directors is in their capacity as directors, so that in effect the Board to which has been entrusted the running of the company in turn passes on that trust in all respects excepts overall policy to the various executives of the company. This, in my view, strengthens the need for an impartial annual review, which is in essence the content of the annual audit by an independent public accountant. To summarize, therefore, the public accountant in his capacity as auditor is called upon to report on what has happened and not to give advice or to say what might have happened if an alternative set of circumstances had been in existence.

III. The Extent to which a Business Organization determines the Course of an Audit

The minimum limit already having been noted in relation to the inefficiency of a business organization, it is apparent that the better and more efficient the organization the greater will be the help it can give to the auditor in his annual review of the financial results. For example, bearing in mind the size and multitude of operations in most businesses, the system and extent of internal check within the organization is of importance to the Public Accountant when assessing the amount of detailed checking which he feels it necessary to perform in the course of the audit. Apart from the needs of the auditor, it is also plainly in the interests of the organization itself, firstly to arrange its affairs so as to reduce the possibility of fraud within the organisation and secondly to show the results of established policies as early and as continuously as possible. To this extent the internal and external audits are often complementary and interdependent in application. Furthermore, the definition of responsibility within the organization, the segregation of duties according to measurement and control, the creation of objective and standard conditions so that variances therefrom can be quickly noted and explained, the planning, routing and scheduling of information are all factors which the public accountant, as the external auditor, would take into account in determining his approach to and the extent of the audit. To put this particular aspect briefly, therefore, for practical reasons the larger the organization the greater is the necessity for the external auditor to rely on sampling rather than exhaustive checks.

To summarize this section, in my view, whilst the structure and efficiency of the organization can materially assist and determine the approach of the public accountant in his capacity as auditor this does not, and should not, take away from him any part of his ultimate responsibilities to the shareholders who have appointed him. Thus the relationship of the auditor to the shareholder is one of kind and not of degree whilst the extent to which a Business Organization determines the course of an audit is one of degree and not of kind.

IV. Business Organization—subject for Evaluation and Audit

Having argued the case that it is not a function of the auditor as such to give advice except within the strict limits discussed, it is now necessary to consider whether the duties of the auditor can and ought to be extended so that his certificate would cover not only the financial results of the organization but the efficiency and structure of that organization. However, before attempting to discuss that question it is first necessary to decide whether methods and organizations of business can be usefully evaluated and whether, therefore, they could reasonably be brought within the scope of an audit.

The study of workshop methods has long been accepted as necessary to achieve efficiency, but the need for examining what may briefly be termed the administrative organization, methods and clerical routine has become widely recognized as a necessity only in relatively recent years. Most public accountants would, however, agree that there is from their own experience considerable evidence of the need for an examination of many of their clients' clerical routines and procedures; inevitably unless an organization is reviewed from time to time, parts of its structure and many of its routines are retained long after the need for them has disappeared or long after the circumstances which brought about their existence have considerably changed. This growing need for a regular or even continuous examination of methods and appraisal of results has given rise to the development of internal auditing as a tool of management control. Formerly the prime purpose of internal audit was the detection and prevention of fraud together with checking the accuracy of numerous accounting entries; these functions are now more usually and more aptly described as internal check. In the largest undertakings the internal audit department is further segregated from the organization and methods section, the latter being concerned primarily with the efficiency of procedures whereas the former concerns itself mainly with the results of those procedures. Thus there has been evolved a method of appraising the results of established policies and of assessing to what extent those policies have been implemented.

However, evaluation and audit are not synonymous; evaluation necessitating an element of opinion to a far greater degree than is consistent with what is normally meant by auditing. In order to evaluate or to appraise, it is first necessary to know exactly what are the required or desired objectives as well as the policy that has been established to achieve them. The objectives may well vary from business to business and it must always be remembered that the origination of policy is the prerogative of management alone. Perhaps it may be agreed that given the desired results and an established policy as basic premises, in theory at least there is possible the most efficient method to achieve those results. If that were the case it would be possible to audit—in the sense of verifying facts—and thus compare what had taken place with what it was assumed ought to have happened. But even if this argument is sound in theory, in my view the complexity as well as the magnitude of operations remove the possibility of objectivity and therefore one of the essential requirements of audit in practice.

Thus, to summarize this section whilst I believe that there is equally a need for maintaining a review of the organization and clerical procedures as there is for the surveillance of workshop and general production methods and procedures, it is nevertheless submitted that their evaluation can never be as objectively audited and reported as can the financial results of an undertaking. In the last analysis the possible results of alternative methods are dependent on subjective and not objective tests.

V. Extension of Compulsory Audit

Having reached the conclusion that a firm's organization and methods together with the results thereof ought to be regularly appraised, it is now necessary to examine whether such an appraisal should be made part of an obligatory audit. My view is that an extension of a statutory audit in this direction would be unsound both in theory and practice. Firstly to generalize, the less objective it is possible to make an evaluation, the more do the conclusions drawn depend on the calibre and training of the person making it. To generalize further the more the conclusions are based on opinion rather than fact the more dangerous is it to require these conclusions to be stated as a matter of law. Secondly it is usually the case that there is more than one solution to or method of dealing with any business problem. Thus, anybody appraising organization and methods can never achieve more than to contrast the results not with alternative facts but with what he imagines would have been the results if different methods had been adopted. There would be, therefore, the possibility, if such an audit were to take place annually or at other regular intervals, of there being continuous doubts as to the efficiency of the directors raised in the minds of shareholders, themselves unable to appreciate the full significance of various factors involved. The directors, on the other hand, would constantly have to defend policies, without for obvious practical reasons, being able to acquaint shareholders with the full details or circumstances which determined the policy. If, alternatively, the report following such an audit were couched in terms so as to avoid any criticism of the methods already adopted the auditor's work may easily degenerate into a time-wasting and meaningless exercise. Thirdly, and in my view of more fundamental importance, is the need to ensure that responsibilities and power do not become divorced. The directors of a company ultimately have to bear the responsibility for the satisfactory running of a business and it is therefore essential that they should have the ultimate power—not only in theory but in practice. In my opinion it would place the directors in an invidious position if they were subject to constant surveillance by statutory auditors who were in a position to state what in their view ought to have been done. The directors can in one sense be regarded as trustees of the shareholders and it is on the basis of factual results and not on possible alternative achievement that they should be judged by those shareholders.

VI. Possible Extension of the Function of the Accounting Profession

I now turn to whether it is useful and/or desirable to utilize the public accountant in reviewing and commenting upon the organization and procedures of a business, not as part of any obligatory audit but as a function suggested either by the public accountant himself or requested by the Company concerned. In my view it is desirable particularly where an internal audit is not already established that such an extension of the public accountant's work should take place. It therefore remains to be discussed whether such work should be performed by a firm of public accountants specializing in this field or whether it ought to be undertaken by what may be described as the 'public accountant general practitioner'. In the latter case this could mean either the Company's auditor for statutory purposes or another public accountant but one not necessarily specialising in this particular work.

Dealing first with the specialist firm, there has been, particularly since the last world war, a considerable development in this field in the United Kingdom though there are now but a handful of large leading firms in this connection. There has been, however, in my country a further development whereby some of the larger firms of public accountants have set up within their organizations departments which specialize in what has become known as Management Consulting. Bearing in mind the increasing breadth of knowledge which is now required of the general practitioner in relation not only to audit but also particularly to taxation, bankruptcy and company law, it is probably too much to expect him also to be a specialist in the fields of management accounting, costing and business methods.

One of the main advantages of employing the specialist Management Consultant introduced by a Company to report on its 'organization and methods' is that a clear division between that of audit for the benefit of shareholders and that where a report is prepared primarily for the assistance of the directors is thereby maintained. On the side of experience, the specialist Management Consultant is normally somebody who has had not only an accounting but also an industrial training and therefore is much more in a position to envisage the detailed implications of a policy which he may suggest, than is the public accountant who has received his training and experience in the field of public accounting.

Moreover, in my view, the study and training required for the purpose of the current professional accountancy examinations are not ordinarily calculated to give the Public Accountant the psychological approach necessary for dealing with the problems of management accounting. Although the outlook and examinations of the Public Accounting bodies may be slowly changing nevertheless the public accountant is necessarily more concerned with results of the past rather than the expectations of the future; an audit necessitates his concerning himself with what has happened rather than what is likely to happen. On the other hand when dealing with the problems of organization, methods and management accounting the results of the past are primarily utilized and considered only as a tool in the hands of management in order that they may better judge what course of action to follow and what results it is hoped will be achieved in the future.

In practice, however, apart from the limited availability of specialist firms, the size and nature of a very large number of businesses is not such as to warrant or make economic the employment of specialists; furthermore, not having been used to this service in the past many managements would not be conscious of its existence or aware of its potential benefit. From a practical viewpoint, therefore, it is clear that the general practitioner has a wide field of action in this particular sphere and, provided a harmonious relationship can be established, there does not appear to be any theoretical objection to such advisory work being undertaken for a Company by a public accountant who is not the auditor of the organization concerned. On the other hand, it would seem that the statutory auditor is, in these circumstances, better qualified for the task as his general background knowledge of the organization and of the personalities within it may to a considerable extent offset his lack of theoretical training in this particular sphere. Furthermore, as previously emphasized, this work must necessarily be kept separate from that in connection with the statutory audit; nevertheless during the audit he is in a position to obtain information and detail which would be of inestimable value to him when advising on the organization. His experience, rather than his training, would enable him to be of considerable help to a client in an advisory capacity and moreover the employment of the one public accountant for the two purposes may well result in economies to the company concerned.

VII. Conclusion and Summary

In conclusion and to summarize, it is my view that the present statutory audit function of the Public Accountant should remain carefully segregated from any other service he may render his clients. Whilst I believe that the organization of a business is a subject for evaluation, nevertheless I do not think that it should be included as part of a statutory audit. Finally although I acknowledge the pre-eminence of skill of the specialist, I believe that the Accounting Profession through the Public Practising Accountant can make an increasingly valuable contribution to the industrial and commercial world. The present generation has seen the start of a development which I hope and believe will continue.

PAPER

by

SVANTE KIHLMAN, EKON. MAG.

KHT Yhdistys – Föreningen CGR, Finland

I. The Importance of Business Organization

One of the most important assumptions in order that a business enterprise should be able to work with success is, that its organization is effective. The greater the business is, the more important it becomes for the enterprise itself to have a well planned organization.

When carrying out an audit the organization influences it to the extent, that with regard to the control point of view, a well planned organization creates greater security as to the correctness of the accounts and the balance sheet, whereas a faulty organization places greater demands upon the accountant, and calls for disproportionately more work from him when he has to convince himself of the reliability of the material.

II. The Audit of Business Organization

Special legal regulations in Finland

According to old custom, which in the year 1895 was incorporated in the law, regarding a share company, which is the most usual form of company, it is the accountant's liability to examine and to present to the Annual General Meeting a report, not only upon the Company's 'räkenskaper' (accounting, record keeping and balance sheet) but also upon the company's 'förvaltning' (management). 'Förvaltningen' is defined by Professor Oskar Sillén, Sweden, as comprising, in translation 'all measures and actions which the management of a business make or ought to make in order to achieve the aims of the enterprise's activity (usually understood:) within the framework of the prevailing law and good business practice'. It is incumbent upon the General Meeting, annually, after having read the accountant's report, to confirm the balance sheet and profit and loss account, and to determine either to release the management from responsibility for the activities up to the end of the year of work, or otherwise to withhold this release from responsibility, with its resultant consequences. Sweden has corresponding legal regulations.

'Förvaltningen' is, as may be understood from the definition, given a very wide conception which embraces the enterprise's activity in its entirety, and business organization, now under discussion, is only a part of this management.

Accountants in Finland, as well as in Sweden, have thus a legal liability to examine, and also to form an opinion of the business organization in its entirety. In this respect there may exist a difference, at least in principle, as compared with other countries. Consequent upon this, the basis for the accountant's attitude in the present questions is different. This is of importance to bear in mind when reading the following statement. It should be specially observed, that, in the question of the accountant's liability of examination, it is not justifiable in Finland to make any difference between that part of the business organization which comprises accountancy, or has direct connections with it and the other part of business organization.

The accountant's competency

On the other hand there is reason to make a certain discrimination between the mentioned parts of business organization, in respect of the accountant's competence to examine them. The liability of examination which is placed upon the accountant in Finland, pre-supposes that he stands on a high level in respect of theoretical knowledge, practical experience and power of judgment. To the greatest possible extent endeavours have been made to achieve this object by prescribing for authorization, final examination at a University of Economics, as an obligatory basis, and in addition, by placing high demands upon experience within business life, as a pre-requisite to be able to apply to participate in the special accountant's examination, which requires yet further studies. It may possibly be asked how the accountant can, in any case, be thought to possess sufficient competence for the judgment of the whole of business organization. To this it can be replied, that from the authorities' and business life's viewpoint it is not expected that the accountant, besides his own special sphere of accounting, should also have, in respect of all other spheres of business organization, a greater, or even an equally extensive knowledge and experience as the enterprise's management he is appointed to supervise. It is not thus expected that he shall be an all round expert with greater qualifications in all spheres than everybody else, neither does one expect that every year he shall examine in detail everything referring to the business organization. But one has knowledge of the accountant's general qualifications, and when he fulfils his task with reasonable conscientiousness and the judgement which is required of an accountant, in order, in a general way, to assess the business organization, one considers oneself justified in setting great store on his opinion.

The judgement of the organization's efficiency and comments thereon

Contrary to previous practice, when the whole audit work was done all at one time after the closing of the books, the audit is now made, as a rule, since the introduction of auditing as a profession, continuously during the year. As a result of this the accountant has sufficient time and possibilities, as far as is necessary, to examine the details of the business organization. Auditing work is of course chiefly directed towards the examination of the accounting material. Therefore the accountant in the first place examines those parts of the business organization which are connected with accounting. And of those parts, internal control in its various forms takes a prominent place, because the extent of the accountant's own examination of the accounting is directly dependent upon the construction of the internal control and its effectivity. Regarding the other parts of the business organization the auditor can form a certain judgement already when checking the accountancy material and thereby facts can come to light which give him reason to make special investigations. For the rest these parts of the organization are examined to the extent motivated by their importance for the enterprise and within the limits of the accountant's competency.

The examination results in an estimation of the organization's effectivity with special regard to obvious faults and short-comings. Such points it is the duty of the accountant to comment upon. It is to the advantage of the enterprise that a necessary amendment is made as soon as possible, and the accountant therefore is right in immediately pointing out to the management that he has found something requiring correction, and not to delay his remarks until later, possibly until the final audit of the year. In other words, the accountant should so direct his work, that the enterprise in good time makes arrangements, so that criticisms at the final audit become superfluous.

When observing possibilities for improvements in the organization, it is natural that the accountant should draw the attention of the management thereto. In particular the enterprise may expect of the accountant that he sees to it that an adequate internal control is brought into existence in order to increase the safety in the custody of the assets and the reliability of figures.

The accountant should take care that his comments and suggestions of possibilities for improvement should not take such a form, that, as a result thereof, he even indirectly attempts to lead the enterprise. If serious weaknesses in the organization which are pointed out, are not corrected by the management, it is, however, justified for the accountant to consider if he can remain as auditor of the enterprise as otherwise his audit report after completed work may be negative, or he perhaps cannot give a report at all. Information hereon to the management of the enterprise very probably leads to a correction, since the management otherwise take upon themselves an increased responsibility for the possible damage resulting to the business from the faulty organization. The accountant should also give attention to the fact that as a result of his examination and criticism the management of the business are not lulled into a false sense of security, that the auditor has taken upon himself the responsibility that the organization is the best possible and is continuously corrected. This in certain cases can happen very easily. But it would mean that the accountant had taken upon himself part of the management's duties and responsibilities, which naturally may not take place, as this would undermine the accountant's independent position in relation to the management.

In examination as to how the organization functions and also when considering alterations, it would be of great help for the accountant to have at his disposal a written plan of the organization, showing the various employees' positions, authority, seniority, chief duties etc. Such a plan would in many cases be of still greater advantage for the enterprise itself. The accountant has therefore every reason to endeavour to exercise influence so that such tables should be compiled to a greater extent than now appears to be the case. Another step forward would be to introduce written working instructions. These, however, should neither be constructed nor applied in such a manner that would lead to too great a rigidity.

Supervision that the organization functions according to instructions from the management

It should be stressed that it is the management's business to see to it that the organization functions in accordance with the directives given by them. The accountant's task is only to control that the management actually fulfils this duty, in regard to which he naturally in the first place should direct his attention to the internal control. That this functions satisfactorily is of special interest to the accountant, also because, as has already been stated, it is a condition that he shall have the possibilities, to a greater extent, to rely upon it in his audit work. Unfortunately, however, it happens that the management make changes in the organization without at all thinking how and in which manner these will influence the pre-arranged internal control system. As a result a gap can appear in the accountant's plan of examination without his knowing anything of it. An accountant should therefore continually keep himself informed regarding all such alterations in the organization and changes of staff in positions which are connected with the internal control.

III. The Accountant and his Advice Concerning the Business Organization in the Enterprise he Audits

Advice—a natural supplement to criticism

It is one thing to draw attention to the fact that something should be altered but another thing, comprising one step further, to give advice as to how the alteration should take place. The conception of audit includes the first task but not the second. However, an auditor is appointed by the owners of a business with a view to his helping them as their trusted representative. And the accountant naturally helps the owners of the business by giving assistance to their enterprise. When one sees the accountant's task against this background, one must consider that he does not fulfil his commission so well as would be possible, if he only limits himself to point out weaknesses, but fails to give advice as to how they should be corrected, despite his having a definite opinion hereon, based on his knowledge and experience. And it is to be supposed that the accountant in most cases has a definite opinion as to how a thing should be altered. Because, if he is capable to judge and criticise a matter which his task pre-supposes, he should also be capable of knowing how it should be arranged. It is thus to be considered correct that the accountant, beside the actual audit work, also to the extent possible, assists the enterprise by giving advice concerning the business organization.

When an accountant puts forward his remarks on some point, it is to be expected that the management of the business, in the first place, turn to him to hear his opinion as to how the detail in question in the organization should be altered, because it is obvious that the accountant, before he brings forward the matter, has basically acquainted himself regarding it. Since the accountant's comments will certainly result in his being asked for advice, it cannot be thought significant that he first should await an enquiry before he gives his advice. It should not therefore be considered of any importance whether it is the enterprise which asks, or the accountant who offers advice. The chief point is that the questions should be handled in the quickest possible manner and the most effective way.

The extent of advice limited by the accountant's competence

A limitation in giving advice concerning the business organization is only effected by the accountant's competency to give it. As previously pointed out, no one expects the accountant to be an expert within all sections of business organisation and the accountant should strictly refrain from giving advice on questions, for the judgement of which he has not the necessary ability. The accountant has thus, from case to case, by exercising the necessary self-criticism, carefully to consider, whether he can actually find himself competent to give advice. It cannot be denied, that such an assessment of his own competence puts great demands upon the accountant's capacity to practice self criticism. It is neither easy nor pleasant to establish one's own limitations and pass them on to others. The accountant's training to give an objective judgement, should, however, create good presumptions for him to come to a correct result. On the other hand self criticism must not be converted to unjustifiable lack of appreciation of his suitability as adviser. An accountant should realize that apart from the fact that he possesses a basic theoretical education, in most cases he has a considerably more extended experience than most other possible advisers. He probably operates in many spheres with which they have no experience, and deals furthermore in his activities with such business enterprises as they never reach. Furthermore the accountant must observe, that through his activity in the enterprise, he has acquired a thorough knowledge of its organization and problems, and that it takes considerable time and expense before anyone else can acquire for himself a corresponding knowledge. Finally an accountant has no reason to withdraw himself just because a question touches upon the sphere of another professional group, but independently of this, he should decide for himself whether or not he has the necessary competence for the problem in question.

An accountant's advice must not be mistaken as an order

It has previously been stated regarding the auditing of the organization, that the accountant's activity should not lead to his taking over the direction of the business organization. In the question of giving advice there is reason to still further stress this point. It should be strongly emphasized, that it is the management of the enterprise which is primarily responsible for the business organization. When an accountant gives advice as to how an alteration should be affected, also when he gives advice unsolicited, it should be clear both for the accountant himself and for the management, that it is only a question of advice, which the management are free either to accept or reject, and that the responsibility for the results of an alteration made according to the advice, or that the advice is not acted upon, exclusively falls on the management of the enterprise. The accountant has the possibility to point out that his advice is only in the nature of a suggestion, by presenting several alternative proposals, and it would appear advisable that he should always, if only the question permits, offer the management the opportunity of considering different solutions. This naturally does not prevent him recommending one of the alternatives. Since otherwise misunderstandings can so easily arise, it is important that the staff also have it clearly understood by themselves, that the opinion expressed by the auditor in discussions regarding alterations, is not to be understood as an order from his side, but that amendments can only be put into practice in the ordinary line of authority from the management.

Apprehension that the accountant's objectivity and integrity shall be risked

Owing to the special legal provisions previously mentioned, in Finland, as well as in Sweden, at least purely in principle, perhaps a more sceptical attitude should be taken than in other countries, to the suitability of an accountant giving advice concerning business organization. One can be apprehensive that an accountant may feel himself bound by the advice he gives, and withhold himself from commenting upon faults in the organization which have arisen by the enterprise following it. First and foremost it can be established that the accountant cannot consider himself bound by, or responsible for, a suggestion, where it is later found out that at the time of giving his advice he had not the knowledge of all the circumstances influencing the matter. Furthermore it may happen that the actual conditions have changed after the advice had been given, so that it appears unsatisfactory under prevailing conditions, although it was good and well motivated when given. For such a fatality the accountant can neither blame himself nor be criticised by others, since one cannot expect greater capacity in him than in others to anticipate the future development. It would be desirable that the accountant should protect himself against later possible forthcoming doubts in these connections, as well as against a misunderstanding of what his advice meant, by giving his advice together with the circumstances in written form, or at least, to make notes for his own guidance. Such a line of action demands, however, considerable extra time and can therefore only come into question in very important cases. In other than the above mentioned respects there is no reasonable cause to suppose that an accountant should judge a matter differently at a later point of time than at an earlier one. The prospects of an accountant being placed in the necessity of criticising the results of his own advice, regarding business organization, appear thus to be small, and apprehension for objectivity, unjustifiable. The accountant therefore has every reason to observe, that from the point of view of the enterprise, if he endeavours to avoid giving advice in questions in which he is competent, he must appear ungracious, and the accusation could be expected, that the accountant purposely wishes to provide himself with the opportunity of making remarks later by standing aside, waiting to see how the matter develops, so that at a suitable moment he can step forward and be wise after the event. It has also been suggested that giving advice might cause doubts as to the accountant's integrity. In this respect it can, however, be argued that it must be considered easier for an accountant to overcome his own purely personal ambitions concerning the results of his advice, than to overcome the temptation to give way to demands from the management's side in matters which have nothing to do with the giving of advice. Such demands could indicate that the accountant should not make comments or not even mention facts which according to good auditing custom should be presented and furthermore be associated with the threat that otherwise he would be dismissed. If he has sufficient moral strength to deal with the latter case, there certainly should be sufficient to deal with the first as well.

Larger organization tasks

Sometimes alterations can be considered which are of such dimensions, that they require considerable work in investigation and planning before a suggestion for re-organization can be submitted for the management's deliberation. Also, even though the initiative to such an alteration emanates from the accountant, it cannot be considered correct that he starts with the work without a special order from the management, as such a larger undertaking can no longer be considered to arise out of the task of auditing. An accountant should remember that he is only an alternative adviser, and should avoid making himself indispensable and thereby obstructing the enterprise's possibilities to utilize other advisers.—Especially for greater re-organization it is natural that the management consider whether they should avail themselves of external experts. By this the accountant can be of service to the enterprise by giving advice as to persons suitable for the work. Since it is the enterprise which should be helped and not the accountant, the enterprise itself should be the employer of the experts and not the accountant. With his detailed knowledge of the business the accountant, however, can be of great help for an external expert by assisting him in his work. A considerable amount of otherwise necessary investigations could thus be eliminated and expenses reduced, and moreover a better result could be achieved. It would appear therefore desirable that the accountant so far as possibilities allow him, should place himself at the disposal of the enterprise in this connection.—However, it is often the case that the management also wish to entrust work of this nature to their auditor. One cannot, however, reckon with the fact that an accountant just at any time, with short notice, can spare sufficient extra time for such laborious special work. The enterprise should therefore be understanding towards the accountant in case he should consider that he cannot see any possibility of assisting.

The accountant's right in respect of organization tasks in an enterprise, to utilize his experience from the organization of other enterprises, has sometimes been doubted. The predominant opinion, even in business life, is, however, that organization and control systems cannot be monopolized or held secret. However, an accountant should, in connection with questions of organization, also carefully observe his duty not to disclose his other clients' business secrets.

IV. Advice to Enterprises which the Accountant does not Audit

The accountant's training and experience lead to the fact that into his sphere of work can be counted the giving of advice concerning business organization also in such enterprises which he himself does not audit. In Finland, however, not a single public accountant has devoted himself to such work as his chief occupation.

On the assumption that the management of a business shall have full freedom to utilize the experts which they consider best in every special case, there should be no objection against an accountant taking it upon himself to give advice to an enterprise which is audited by another public accountant. The reason for calling in another accountant, need not give offence to the ordinary auditor and for example it can be that the other has concentrated upon, or had more experience of, the sphere in question, or also, that one would like to have an opinion from someone who is not influenced by previous impressions of the enterprise. Naturally both parties should show all the consideration which is due to a good colleague. Co-operation, as previously mentioned regarding external experts, has to be established.

V. Conclusion

The above analysis gives expression to the opinion that the public accountant, with his knowledge and his experience, should endeavour to help the enterprise to improve its business organization. But it perhaps should be stressed, that this should not lead to the result that the accountant loses sight of his specific task, —to audit.

The attitude of accountants has also changed in accordance therewith, which factor was given notable expression at the last Northern Countries' Accountants Congress in Helsingfors in 1954, where this fact was witnessed both during discussions, in the speeches and in the press. The business world's attitude is in agreement: it expects that the accountant shall be an adviser to a much larger extent than previously. In particular small enterprises which have not qualified employees, have great need of help and they often choose auditors especially with the thought of having a good adviser in respect of their business organization.

PAPER

by

G. L. PHILLIPPE

Controllers Institute of America

I have been asked to discuss the financial organization associated with the larger industrials in the United States and how the services of the public accountant fit into this picture.

My comments will of necessity be limited to my own experience in business, which has been with General Electric Company. However, I would say that General Electric Company's relationship with its public accountants—and its need for their services—probably are fairly typical of those of other large manufacturers in the United States.

The functions carried out by our accounting organization also are typical of those of other companies. The form may be somewhat different because General Electric Company has probably advanced further than some American corporations in (a) decentralization of the operating responsibilities and (b) definite divorcement of the headquarters staff organization from operating functions.

I. Nature of the Business

It might help to give you a brief summary of General Electric Company's operations:

1. Our annual sales volume for 1956 was about $ 4 billion. This was more than twice the Company's sales seven years before, and we expect the volume to double again within the next eight years.

2. Employment averaged more than 280 000 individuals last year.

3. Ownership of the Company is divided among over 360 000 Share Owners, no one of whom owns as much as 1/10th of 1 % of the outstanding stock.

4. Our products vary, in size, from a turbine-generator selling for several million dollars to a lamp bulb which retails at less than twenty cents; in complexity, from a simple light socket to an electronic computer or a complicated gun fire control for the Armed Services.

5. Our products and services are sold under sales contracts which vary from simple open accounts, installment sales for appliances, and long-term contracts for large apparatus, to involved target incentive pricing on Government con-

tracts for aircraft gas turbines and to contracts for operation of a Government plutonium facility.

6. There are some 159 manufacturing plants in the United States and Canada with sales offices, service shops or wholesale houses in another 350 locations. We also have factories and sales offices in approximately 55 cities in Latin America and other foreign locations.

The domestic and Canadian organizations consist of more than 100 Product Departments with sales volumes ranging from $ 5 million to $ 200 million per annum. Each Department has sole responsibility for a specific line or related lines of products. It has its own General Manager and under him the various functional managers, such as Manager-Engineering, Manager-Manufacturing, and Manager-Finance. The Manager-Finance of a Department is fully the equivalent of the Comptroller or chief financial officer of an outside business of similar size.

Product Departments manufacturing similar or related products are combined into Divisions of five to eight Departments under a Division General Manager. The Divisions are grouped into four broad groups—Apparatus, Consumer Products, Industrial Components and Materials, and Electronic, Atomic and Defense Products, each under an Executive Vice President. Neither the 20 Division General Managers, nor the four Executive Vice Presidents, have any staffs. Their assignments are to advise, counsel and appraise the over-all operations of the Departments and to participate in their forward planning. Responsibility for operation of the business at a profit is placed on the *Department* General Manager.

II. Financial Organization of the Business

How do we tie all this together for accounting purposes.

The Manager-Finance of each Product Department has his own complete set of accounts. He is responsible for the accounting, financial control and reporting of his Department. Another very important part of his work is as financial counsel for the Department General Manager and the other functional managers in the day-to-day operation of the business, the measurement of operating results, budgeting, forecasting and forward planning.

The Manager-Finance of each Department is appointed by and reports to the Department General Manager. His appointment is based, however, on nominations by the Comptroller and the Comptroller may request his removal at any time for lack of technical competence or performance. We have no difficulty in the operation of this functional responsibility of the Manager-Finance to the Comptroller. The need for this special relationship, which exists only in the financial and legal areas, is well recognized by the organization.

As previously stated, each Department has its own accounts which are maintained in accordance with general accounting principles established by the Comptroller. The Department reports its operating results, the condition of its balance sheet accounts and certain supplementary operating statistics monthly to headquarters on the basis of standard definitions and procedures. Other than this standard form of reporting and the maintenance of its balance sheet valuations in accordance with principles established by the Comptroller, the Manager-Finance has complete freedom to establish his own system of reporting and internal control and is encouraged to exercise his ingenuity and initiative in this respect.

At headquarters, the Comptroller's organization includes an Accounting Operations Department which receives the financial data sent in by the Product Departments, consolidates it with the Company's general accounts and issues the consolidated financial statements and reports. I might add that the accounting reports from the Product Departments are transmitted to headquarters by telegraph, received in the form of a punched tape, consolidated and printed on our statement forms by electronic data processing equipment.

The over-all planning, study and research necessary to support this system of accounting is provided by seven staff or Services components comprised of experts in their fields. These Services are:

General Accounting
Tax Accounting
Personnel Accounting
Cost Accounting
Measurements
Office Procedures, and
Financial Personnel Development

They provide the advance study and analysis necessary for development of our financial policies, teach and advise the operating personnel in the interpretation and application of our accounting procedures, and assist the Comptroller in the analysis and presentation of the Company's financial reports to top management, the Share Owners, the Government and the public generally.

In addition, we have a staff of some 110 Traveling Auditors who are responsible to the Comptroller for examination of the accounts of all components of the Company and its subsidiaries. Their audits are made on the same professional standards as those generally followed by independent accountants. In addition, our Traveling Auditors devote special attention to the Departments' adherence to the Company's established Accounting Procedures, to operating efficiencies and economies and to the detection of fraud or misappropriation.

III. Problems Encountered

I do not intend to give you the impression that with this organization we have solved all the problems of accounting for a large manufacturing enterprise. I only *hope* that we have recognized most of them. But perhaps this outline indicates how we are approaching them.

One of the major problems generated by our decentralization program—both for ourselves and for the public accountant—has been the *rapid increase in the number of Managers-Finance who send reports directly to the Comptroller's organization.* Not so many years ago, the Comptroller could reach the entire operating financial organization by talking to some eight or ten Divisional Comptrollers. Now we deal separately with over 120 Managers-Finance.

This matter of numbers was first a problem in connection with *personnel requirements*. Fortunately, the Company had had an organized program for the recruiting and training of college graduates for positions in our accounting organization for over 35 years. In addition to formal classroom training and practical accounting experience in our plants, many of the abler recruits had served on our Traveling Auditors' staff, which we have used as an advanced financial training ground as well as a tool for insuring the integrity of our accounts.

We did not, of course, have as many top grade men as we would have liked —one never does—but thanks to the foresight of my predecessors we had a large enough group of well qualified men to enable us to place a Manager-Finance next door to each Department General Manager, where his analysis and interpretation of the figures and his financial counsel could be most effective.

Our Financial Personnel Development Service continues this program by recruiting over 300 college graduates each year and by providing training courses and adequate on-the-job training for them. This Service also facilitates company-wide promotion opportunities and carries on advanced training for the older men.

Communication is another problem which decentralization has made more difficult—and at the same time—more important. We of course have the usual flood of letters, instructions and manuals—sometimes I think we defeat our own communications by their sheer volume.

My staff and I attempt to maintain more *personal* contacts with our Managers-Finance through regional and national meetings with them, through periodical field visits and meetings on specific subjects. This is an area where we have much to learn.

The mere *mechanics of handling and processing such a large volume of data* is a tremendous problem. As I indicated, we are utilizing the newest and largest electronic equipment available but it is not yet entirely adequate for business' needs. Our Office Procedure Service is constantly studying the problem, promoting maximum utilization of machines, and encouraging the design of electronic data processing equipment specifically for accounting needs. Too many of our present computers seem to have been designed for the engineer's requirements and merely adapted for office use.

IV. Relationship with Public Accountant

If I have been successful so far in creating the impression I was aiming for, you will understand that General Electric Company has a galaxy of top accounting talent, a well developed internal audit program and a staff capable of solving our accounting problems. What use then have we for public accountants? What service can the public accountant perform for us that cannot be performed equally well by our own organization?

The first that the public accountant can and does contribute to General Electric Company is '*independence*'.

The Company's responsibility for the integrity of its financial reporting is to some 360000 Share Owners—considerably more than its 280000 employees.

These Share Owners must rely on these reports for information as to the progress and security of their investment. Many of them have no direct contact with the affairs of the Company. Even the Share Owners who have some contact as employees actually can have little conception of the over-all picture of the Company's business.

The responsibility of a publicly held Company in the United States to the Share Owners is much larger than is indicated by the number of Share Owners because of the investment in our large companies by life insurance companies, savings banks, mutual investment trusts and other organizations which, while they count as only one Share Owner in the records, are investing the savings of thousands of individuals.

Seventeen of the Company's nineteen Directors, whom the Share Owners have elected as their representatives, have no connection with the Company except as Directors. Only two of the Directors are officers of the Company—the President and the Chairman of the Board.

The management of General Electric Company is a 'professional' management in the sense that all of the officers were advanced to their positions because of their abilities. None of them represent large ownership interests in the Company. Most of them are the college recruits of 25 to 35 years ago. They are really *stewards* to whom the Directors have entrusted the operation of the business.

Under these circumstances, it seems desirable—even essential—that the Share Owners of the Company be supplied with evidence that the facts and figures reported to them by the management which runs their business for them have been reviewed and examined by someone who is independent as well as expert on the subject. Such evidence is desirable from the point of view not only of the Share Owners but also of the management which makes the representation.

Apart from an independent report of stewardship to the *owners* of the Company, I would suggest that we as business managers in today's system of free enterprise have a public responsibility. Large corporations today touch the lives of great numbers of peoples. We have a responsibility to deal fairly with our Share Owners in sharing the gains or losses from the business, to pay fair wages, to charge prices which reflect value, to further scientific progress in our field, and to be a good citizen in all matters. It is in our own enlightened self interest to report on how we have discharged these responsibilities. The public accountant's opinion, or stamp of approval, adds to the validity of such reports.

I have been talking about the advantages and benefits of the independent public accountant's opinion from a purely voluntary standpoint, which is the basis on which many of our present large companies commenced their relationships with the public accountants. As a practical matter, for a publicly held corporation, such as General Electric Company, it is no longer purely a matter of choice.

Companies whose securities are registered for sale by the Securities and Exchange Commission are required to include an independent public accountant's certificate in any prospectus offering new securities. The Commission also has established very stringent rules with respect to the independence of a public accountant—for example, no shares of stock in a company being audited may be owned by any member of the independent accounting firm.

The Company's listing contract with the New York Stock Exchange also requires an audit by and certificate from independent public accountants. Most banking and other financial institutions as a matter of good business practice will require a public accountant's certificate before consideration of a request for financing.

The evidence that management's facts and figures are to be relied upon is contained, of course, in the report of the independent public accountant. Let us see just what this report means. If, as is most likely, the auditor gives his opinion without qualification, the report will be brief. It will identify the financial statements covered and state that an examination has been made 'in accordance with generally accepted auditing standards'. It will then state that the statements present fairly the financial position of the company as of a specified date and the results of its operations for the period then ended in conformity with generally accepted accounting principles applied on a basis consistent with the preceding year.

Does this mean that the public accountant is saying that he has checked each and every transaction and is, in effect, insuring that every penny has been properly accounted for? Of course not. The main purpose of an audit is to enable the public accountant to express an opinion on the financial statements as a whole. To do this he examines or tests accounting records of the company and other supporting evidence by methods and to the extent he deems appropriate in the special circumstances for each case. Such a test examination could not be expected to and is not designed to disclose all irregularities, if any exist, although, of course, it is very possible that major irregularities would be uncovered if they had not already come to light in the ordinary course of events as a result of the operation of the system of internal control. Such systems of internal check and control are the subject of continuous review. The public accountant, therefore, studies:

1. The accounting policies and procedures of the company
2. The system of internal check and control
3. The reports of the company's own internal auditors.

He can then determine what tests he will apply, and how and to what extent he will apply them, to satisfy himself that the records of the company present fairly the elements making up its financial statements. Such test examinations will then be the basis for his report.

My remarks, of course, are based largely upon a big operation where the skill and integrity of financial personnel are as high as we can make them; where proper internal check and control exist; and where internal auditing is of a high order. It would appear that the smaller the operation the more difficult it is to obtain the checks and balances necessary for good internal control. It is in this situation that additional skills of the public accountant must be brought into play to determine the method and the extent of tests to be employed.

I have heard the view expressed that having accounts audited is a duplication and a waste of money. We do not subscribe to that view. As a matter of fact, our accounts have been audited since 1897. Let me digress for a moment to refer back to the early annual reports of General Electric. The present Company was incorporated on April 15, 1892, and the first report on this Company covered the period to January 31, 1893. Financial statements were presented but they were not audited. Instead they bore the signature of an officer of the Company below the magical notation E & O E, which, I believe, stands for 'errors and omissions excepted'. It is interesting to observe that this notation continued to be used in the published statements until 1905, after which it was omitted. The first audit report appears in the Sixth Annual Report of the Company and covered the two years ended January 31, 1898, so you can see the present Company had only been in existence for a few years before the value of an independent audit was recognized and, of course, the Company has had an annual audit ever since.

As a sidelight, it is interesting to observe that from 1906 to 1918 our auditors were identified in their reports as 'Chartered Accountants'. This, of course, is the British designation, which indicates how recently the profession of 'Certified Public Accountants' has developed in the United States. In 1900 there were approximately 250 CPA's, by 1920 about 5000, and at the end of 1954 some 50000.

Looking over these annual reports also gives one some idea of the change which has taken place in procedures of public accountants over the years. The Company's first audit report in 1898 described in great detail just what the auditors did, and it obviously involved a tremendous amount of detailed checking. As the Company grew in size and complexity, it became impossible for the auditors to continue this volume of detailed work. By a gradual process the Company's internal control systems and present type of auditor's examination evolved. The auditor's reports grew more brief until we have the present two-paragraph report. Now to return to the point I was attempting to make, it is our view that the duplication of effort as between our own organization and the public accountants is small indeed. We have and we recognize a great responsibility to the 360000 people who own the business. We feel that when we present them with financial statements, which are the reports of our stewardship, these owners are entitled to have the word of an independent expert that the statements show in fact what they purport to show.

I have been discussing the advantages of the public accountant's audit to the large corporation. For the medium sized and smaller concern, the intensive study and review which the public accountant must make of the system of internal check in order to determine the extent to which he can rely upon it in his audit is of very valuable assistance. The public accountant is interested not only in how the system is supposed to function but also in how it does operate. Disclosure of weaknesses are reported to the client with a view to having them corrected. We have found their work in this connection helpful in General Electric despite our larger organization, checks and controls and extensive internal audits.

To the smaller concern, the public accountant is a valued business counselor whose view from the outside and whose wide knowledge of business skills are very helpful.

In the large corporation, we find the public accountant's services most valuable in our unusual transactions and in new developments. They have much more opportunity than the accountant in industry to be conversant with controversial points of accounting principles or techniques. A company may wish to merge with another, or split off a portion of its business, or acquire another company, or make a stock split, or pay a dividend in stock. For example, their judgment and experience were of considerable aid to us in adopting the LIFO basis of inventory valuation. We have been talking to them about how we should recognize the effect of inflation on our plant values and depreciation. On these, on complicated tax questions, on ways to present data in registration statements, their background of experience gives us a valued test of the procedures and recommendations our own staff has developed. Other times we are merely seeking someone who understands our business and background with whom we can talk over our problems. I know that our public accountant's viewpoint and mature judgment has been of great personal benefit and reassurance to me.

DISCUSSION

CHAIRMAN: PROF. B. J. S. WIMBLE, C.A. (S.A.), F.S.A.A., SOUTH AFRICA

CHAIRMAN:

Ladies and Gentlemen, It is a great honour for a small country like South Africa, small in population if not in area, to be asked to nominate a chairman for one of the business sessions of this congress in this beautiful city. I should like to express the sincere thanks of the Joint Council of the Societies of Chartered Accountants in South Africa to the Congress Committee. To-day we are to discuss Business Organization and the Public Accountant. I am sure that you are all anxious to hear what this panel of eminent men think about this topic. It is a topic of great interest to the accountant, whether he is in public practice or whether he is in industry. I shall not, therefore, waste any-more of your time, but it is my pleasant duty to introduce to you those taking part in this afternoon's proceedings.

The Vice-Chairmen of this meeting—I will ask each one to stand up as I call his name—are Mr. Orreby of Sweden and Mr. O'Connell of Southern Rhodesia.

The rapporteur and author of a paper is Mr. Richard of France. The authors of the other papers are Mr. Bakkenist of the Netherlands, Mr. Harris of the United Kingdom, Mr. Kihlman of Finland and Mr. Phillippe of the United States of America. The other members of the panel are Dr. Boter of Spain, Mr. Proshan of Israel and Mr. Yorston of Australia. I will now call upon the discussion leader to take over.

MR. H. REINOUD (Netherlands)

Mr. Chairman, Before I start asking Mr. Richard to read his summary of the papers, I should first like to make a preliminary remark with regard to the translation of the paper of Mr. Bakkenist. Mr. Bakkenist has used in the Dutch language the words 'administratieve organisatie', 'administratie' and 'administratieve gegevens'. These words have been translated in the English version by 'administration', 'administrative organization' and 'administrative data'. This is not quite right. As regards the Dutch word 'administratie', it should be kept in mind that the English word 'administration' and the French word 'administration' have a somewhat different shade of meaning. The English word and also the French word is more related to management, and, for instance, policy formulation. In the Anglo-Saxon countries the words 'administratieve organisatie', are usually translated as: 'organization and methods concerning accounting and record keeping', or abbreviated: 'accounting organization'. And in France it is probably the phrase 'organisation comptable' or 'organisation de la comptabilité' that comes nearest to the Dutch concept of 'administratieve organisatie'. May I now ask Mr. Richard to read to us his summary?

MR. F. M. RICHARD (France)

Afin de traiter tous les aspects de ce vaste sujet, le schéma suivant avait été suggéré aux rapporteurs:

a. L'importance de l'organisation de l'entreprise pour l'expert-comptable agissant en qualité de réviseur des comptes
b. L'organisation de l'entreprise en tant qu'objet de vérification et d'appréciation de la part de l'expert-comptable
c. L'expert-comptable en tant que conseiller en matière d'organisation, en tant que cette fonction découle de ses responsabilités de réviseur des comptes
d. Si l'expert-comptable joue un rôle actif en ce qui concerne l'organisation des services comptables et/ou de l'organisation des autres fonctions de l'entreprise, est-ce que ces fonctions sont susceptibles de nuire à son objectivité en tant que réviseur des comptes dans la même entreprise
e. Le rôle de l'expert-comptable en tant que conseil en organisation
f. L'influence de la dimension de l'entreprise.

On ne peut manquer d'être impressionné par les opinions de plusieurs des rapporteurs sur l'importance croissante de la Comptabilité de Gestion, usant de nouvelles techniques issues de la Comptabilité Financière, mais visant à d'autres buts et répondant à ses propres concepts.

D'une façon presque unanime, les rapporteurs attirent l'attention des praticiens de la comptabilité sur les responsabilités des experts-comptables acceptant des missions d'Organisation, de Conseiller de Gestion, ou de Contrôleur, missions qui ne doivent jamais être confondues avec les responsabilités en tant que réviseur des comptes.

M. Svante Kihlman de Finlande, pense que

L'expert-comptable, grâce à ses connaissances et son expérience, doit s'efforcer d'aider l'entreprise à améliorer son organisation. Mais on doit peut-être insister sur le fait que ceci ne doit pas conduire à perdre de vue sa tâche spécifique: la vérification des comptes.

L'attitude des comptables change donc en fonction de ses nouvelles missions.

Le monde des affaires accepte cette évolution: il espère que le comptable sera un conseiller dans une plus large mesure que précédemment. En particulier les petites entreprises qui n'ont pas les collaborateurs spécialisés ont grand besoin d'une aide, et ils choisissent souvent les experts-comptables, en pensant qu'ils trouveront auprès d'eux de bons conseils en matière d'organisation de leur entreprise.

De l'avis de M. Svante Kihlman, l'étendue des conseils donnés par l'expert-comptable est limitée par sa compétence en tant que réviseur des comptes.

Personne n'attend de l'expert-comptable qu'il soit un expert dans tous les domaines de l'organisation de l'entreprise, et l'expert-comptable doit éviter de donner un avis sur des questions sur lesquelles il n'a pas la qualification nécessaire. L'expert-comptable doit par conséquent, selon les cas d'espèces, et au moyen d'une autocritique, considérer soigneusement s'il s'estime lui-même compétent pour donner un avis.

M. J. E. Harris d'Angleterre, pense que

Le statut actuel de révision des comptes exercée par l'expert-comptable doit rester soigneusement séparé de tout autre mission qu'il peut être appelé à remplir auprès de ses clients. Tout en croyant que l'organisation de l'entreprise est un sujet d'appréciation et d'évaluation, je ne pense néanmoins pas que ce sujet doive rentrer dans la mission statutaire de révision des comptes. Finalement, bien que je reconnaisse la prééminence d'aptitude du spécialiste en organisation, je pense que la profession comptable, au moyen de l'expert-comptable indépendant, peut apporter une contribution importante au monde industriel et commercial. La génération contemporaine a vu le commencement d'une évolution qui, j'espère, et je crois, continuera.

M. J. E. Harris pense que

Il est vital de maintenir séparée et distincte la fonction de l'expert-comptable en tant que réviseur des comptes (Commissaires aux Comptes), de tout autre travail qu'il effectuerait spontanément ou sur demande, en dehors des travaux nécessaires à la révision des comptes.

et que:

On demande à l'expert-comptable, en sa qualité de réviseur des comptes de dire ce qui est arrivé, et non pas de donner un conseil ou de dire ce qui serait arrivé dans d'autres circonstances.

La séparation des fonctions de réviseur des comptes étant clairement définie par rapport à la mission de Conseiller de Gestion, ainsi que la possibilité d'évolution de la fonction comptable, M. J. E. Harris écrit:

Toutefois il y a, dans mon pays, une évolution par laquelle certains parmi les plus grands Cabinets d'experts-comptables ont mis sur pied dans leur organisation des sections, qui se spécialisent dans ce qu'on appelle le Conseil de Gestion.

M. G. L. Phillippe des Etats-Unis, apporte son expérience dans l'une des plus grosses sociétés américaines.

Cette Société a une galaxie de comptables experts de grand talent, un programme de contrôle interne très développé, et un personnel capable de résoudre nos problèmes comptables. Comment pouvons-nous utiliser les experts-comptables? Quels services l'expert-comptable peut-il remplir qui ne pourrait pas aussi bien être rempli par un professionnel de notre propre organisation?

La première contribution que l'expert-comptable peut et doit apporter est 'l'Indépendance'.

M. G. L. Phillippe reconnaît que

Leur expérience nous permet de bénéficier de leur évaluation des procédures et méthodes qui ont été élaborées par notre propre personnel. Dans d'autres cas nous rechercherons seulement quelqu'un capable de comprendre notre entreprise et son environnement et avec qui nous pouvons discuter sur nos problèmes. Je sais que le point de vue de notre expert-comptable et son jugement mûri ont été d'un très grand profit et une garantie en ce qui me concerne.

Le rapport de M. Bakkenist de Hollande, donne une vue complète et détaillée de l'évolution de la fonction d'expert-comptable dans son pays.

Les connaissances et l'expérience que l'expert-comptable acquiert pour l'exercice de sa profession et au moyen de cet exercice, en fait un expert en matière d'économie d'entreprise, d'organisation d'entreprise et de révision des comptes. C'est ce qui a permis à l'expert-comptable de devenir un conseiller de gestion.

Cette fonction de conseil est toutefois exercée en tant que fonction supplémentaire à sa mission de révision des comptes. C'est presque la suite logique de son travail.

La croissance des entreprises a nécessité d'une façon impérative l'élaboration de nouveaux instruments dans les mains de la direction de ces entreprises pour qu'elles puissent remplir leurs fonctions de direction. Il a été prouvé qu'un système comptable efficace est l'un des meilleurs instruments de direction, ceci n'implique néanmoins pas que dans la plupart des entreprises hollandaises où l'on pourrait s'attendre à trouver une organisation comptable moderne, celle-ci existe déjà.

Un bon système comptable compare les coûts et la production et soumet régulièrement les écarts par rapport aux standards, aux personnes hiérarchiquement responsables. De plus la direction générale peut baser son jugement, en ce qui concerne l'efficacité de chacun des services, sur de tels rapports. Cette manière de perfectionner la productivité, que j'aimerais appeler la manière indirecte, doit certainement être retenue en plus de la manière directe qui consiste à faire appel à des Conseils en Organisation.

L'entrée de l'expert-comptable dans le domaine du contrôle de gestion est justifiée s'il remplit deux conditions:

1. Il doit posséder la connaissance suffisante.
2. Ceci ne doit pas porter préjudice à sa fonction de base qui est la révision des comptes.

M. Bakkenist apporte la conclusion de son rapport

En espérant que j'ai réussi à donner une description générale du vaste et fascinant domaine que l'organisation comptable ouvre à l'expert-comptable.

Il y a aux Pays-Bas un manque considérable de Conseillers en matière d'organisation et de problèmes de gestion proportionnellement aux besoins existants. Jusqu'à présent il n'y a pas d'enseignement officiel en vue de cette profession libérale, ni dans les Universités ni dans les Collèges commerciaux. Les Conseils de Gestion qui exercent actuellement se composent d' hommes qui se sont formés eux-mêmes. Un projet est actuellement bien avancé pour la création d'un programme d'enseignement de Contrôle de Gestion dans les Universités hollandaises. En 1953 une Commission Royale désignée spécialement à cet effet, a publié un rapport sur ce programme. Non seulement le Gouvernement, les entreprises et les Universités sont intéressés dans cette question, mais aussi les experts-comptables.

On peut se poser la question: Dans le cas où les experts-comptables n'étendraient pas leur domaine d'action dans cette direction, ne risquent-ils pas qu'on leur reproche plus tard d'avoir échoué à ce sujet?

En France les mêmes problèmes d'évolution des entreprises ont amené les experts-comptables à s'intéresser vivement aux travaux de comptabilité de gestion.

Il paraît probable, dans un proche avenir, que les experts-comptables français, en plus grand nombre, s'orienteront vers le Conseil et le Contrôle de Gestion. A ce titre, l'expert-comptable sera consulté pour organiser les services et méthodes de contrôle et en surveiller le bon fonctionnement.

Les grandes entreprises rechercheront la compétence, l'expérience, l'indépendance des experts-comptables, soit pour les organisations proprement dites du contrôle, soit pour l'évaluation et l'appréciation de leurs propres services par comparaison à des applications existantes.

Les entreprises de moyenne importance demanderont à l'expert-comptable la création et la mise en place des dispositifs de prévision, de gestion et de contrôle, l'établissement de diagnostic d'entreprise, etc.

Il n'est pas d'exemple que le besoin n'a pas créé l'organe capable d'y répondre.

Plusieurs expériences de formation au contrôle de gestion sont en cours et notamment un 'Institut pour le perfectionnement dans les méthodes de Contrôle de Gestion', a été créé.

Soit que les experts-comptables se spécialiseront dans le Contrôle de Gestion, soit qu'ils s'associeront afin de grouper les professionnels capables de répondre aux besoins de l'économie nationale, la formation de base sera toujours l'expertise comptable.

Ils feront appel, chaque fois que cela sera nécessaire, à des techniciens, des ingénieurs en particulier, pour étudier les problèmes strictement techniques.

Du point de vue éthique professionnelle les règles de conduite de la profession libérale d'expert-comptable s'appliquent aux missions acceptées et accomplies dans le domaine du Conseil de Gestion; ceci implique que l'expert-comptable n'acceptera de mission que s'il est complètement qualifié, soit personnellement soit en collaboration avec un collègue lui-même qualifié.

In order to treat this very broad subject under its various aspects, the following canvass was suggested to the authors of papers:

a. The importance of business organization for the accountant in his capacity as an auditor

b. The organization of a business as a subject of evaluation and audit

c. The public accountant as an adviser on the subject of organization in so far as this is part of his regular duties as an auditor ('derived' consulting activities)

d. If the public accountant is concerning himself intensively with the organization of the accounting and record keeping system and/or with the rest of the organization this will endanger his objectiveness in the performance of his auditing function with the same enterprise

e. The public accountant as an independent adviser on organization

f. The influence of the size of the enterprise.

One cannot fail to be impressed by the opinions of several authors on the growing importance of Management Accounting, using new techniques derived from Financial Accounting but aiming at different targets and following its proper standards.

Almost unanimously the authors call the attention of the practitioners on the responsibilities of the public accountants accepting missions of Organization, Consultancy, or Controllership, never to be confused with the responsibilities of the Auditor.

Mr. Svante Kihlman from Finland thinks

The public accountant, with his knowledge and his experience, should endeavour to help the enterprise to improve its business organization. But it perhaps should be stressed, that this should not lead to the result that the accountant loses sight of his specific task, to audit.

The attitude of accountants has also changed in accordance therewith.

The business world's attitude is in agreement: it expects that the accountant shall be an adviser to a much larger extent than previously. In particular small enterprises which have not qualified employees, have great need of help and they often choose auditors especially with the thought of having a good adviser in respect of their business organization.

In Mr. Svante Kihlman's opinion, the extent of advice given by the public accountant is limited by his competence as auditor.

No one expects the accountant to be an expert within all sections of business organization and the accountant should strictly refrain from giving advice on questions, for the judgement of which he has not the necessary ability. The accountant has thus, from case to case, by exercising the necessary self criticism, carefully to consider, whether he can actually find himself competent to give advice.

Mr. J. E. Harris from England thinks

The present statutory audit function of the public accountant should remain carefully segregated from any other service he may render his clients. Whilst I believe that the organization of a business is a subject for evaluation, nevertheless I do not think that it should be included as part of a statutory audit. Finally although I acknowledge the pre-eminence of skill of the specialist, I believe that the accounting profession through the public practising accountant can make increasingly valuable contribution to the industrial and commercial world. The present generation has seen the start of a development which I hope and believe will continue.

Mr. J. E. Harris thinks

It is vital to maintain as a separate and distinct function the work of the public accountant in his capacity as auditor from work which is either voluntary on his part or requested of him in extension of that necessitated by the audit and that:

The public accountant in his capacity as auditor is called upon to report on what has happened and not to give advice or to say what might have happened if an alternative set of circumstances had been in existence.

The separation of the function as auditor from the mission as consultant being clearly defined and strongly emphasized, and the possible extension of the function of the accounting profession examined, Mr. J. E. Harris states:

There has been, however, in my country a further development whereby some of the larger firms of public accountants have set up within their organizations departments which specialize in what has become known as Management Consulting.

Mr. G. L. Phillippe from the United States brings his experience with one of the biggest American Corporations.

This company has a galaxy of top accounting talent, a well developed internal audit programme and a staff capable of solving our accounting problems. What use then have we for public accountants? What service can the public accountant perform for us that cannot be performed equally well by our own organization? The first thing that the public accountant can and does contribute is 'independence'.

Mr. G. L. Phillippe recognizes that

Their background of experience gives us a valued test of the procedures and recommendations our own staff has developed. Other times we are merely seeking someone who understands our business and background with whom we can talk over our problems. I know that our public accountant's viewpoint and mature judgement has been of great personal benefit and reassurance to me.

Mr. Bakkenist's paper, from Holland, gives a very comprehensive and complete survey of the development of the function of public accountant in this country

The knowledge and experience which the accountant acquires for and through the exercise of his profession make him an expert in the field of business economics, administrative organization and audit. Thus it was possible for the accountant to become a *business-consultant of the management*. This consulting function is, however, always exercised as an additional function to the audit task. It is an almost logical outcome of this work.

Especially as a result of the growth of the enterprises the need for tools in the hands of the management for the purpose of managing has become imperative. An effective system of accounting and record keeping has proved to be one of the most valuable tools for this, which, however, does not imply that in the greater part of the Netherlands enterprises where an organization of this kind might be expected this up-to-date organization actually does exist already.

A good system of accounting and record keeping keeps comparing costs and output and regularly submits deviations from the standards to the responsible executives. Moreover the top-management can base on such surveys their judgement on the efficiency of the various departments. This way of improving the productivity, which I would like to call the indirect method, must surely be mentioned beside the direct approach by means of business consultants and efficiency engineers.

The accountant is justified in entering the field of the business consultant if two conditions have been satisfied:

1. He must possess the necessary expert knowledge.
2. He must not prejudice the effective, carrying out of his basic function, the audit function.

Mr. Bakkenist concludes his paper by

With the hope I have succeeded in giving an outline of the wide and fascinating field which the organization of accounting and record keeping opens up for the public accountant.
and that:

There is in the Netherlands a great shortage of good consultants in the field of organizational and management problems in proportion to the potential need. Up to this moment there is no official training course for this free profession either in the Universities or in the Commercial Colleges. The consultants that are practising at the present moment are all self-made men.

Preparations by the Netherlands Universities for the establishment of a course for business consultants are in an advanced stage. In 1953 a Royal Commission especially established for this purpose has published a report on this course. Not only the government, business and the universities are interested in this question, but also the accountants.

One wonders whether the accountants, if they do not extend their field of action in this direction are not in danger of the reproach in later years that they have failed in this respect.

In France, the same problems of evolution in business have brought the public accountant to take a keen interest in Management Accounting.

It seems possible in the near future that French public accountants in a greater number will be attracted by Controllership. As such, the public accountant will be consulted to organize Control departments and their methods and supervise their efficiency.

Large firms will seek the skill, experience and independence of the public accountant to organize their Control and Budget Departments, or to evaluate their existing departments in comparison with others.

Medium size firms will ask from the public accountant the creation and setting up of: forecasting, planning, budgeting, control, the appraisal of their overall organization.

The public accountant will either specialize in Controllership or will enter into partnership with specialized practicians in order to meet the needs of industry, but their basic education will remain public accountancy.

Several projects for education and training in Controllership are on the way, in particular the 'Institute for the Development in Methods of Controllership' has been founded.

As to ethics, the rules of professional conduct of the existing bodies of public accountants will be applicable to the new tasks assigned to and accepted by the public accountants in the field of controllership. It implies therefore that public accountants will accept such missions only if they feel fully qualified, either personally or in co-operation with qualified colleagues.

MR. H. REINOUD (Netherlands)

Thank you, Mr. Richard, for your useful summary. Now, when dealing with the term business organization and its meaning, we can make several distinctions, but we should, I think, distinguish, at any rate according to the papers, between the accounting organization and the rest of the organization; and the accounting organization, again according to the papers, we can subdivide into the financial accounting system and the system of management. The evaluation of the accounting organization as a thing apart, as an independent question of efficiency, can be treated either in connection with the accounting organization or with the business organization. I will leave that to the course the discussion takes. For our purpose we will start with the accounting organization and consider the rest of the organization later. I should not be surprised, however, if the relationship between these two departments of the business organization will be revealed. As regards the public accountant, we will first think of his main function, namely that of auditor; the auditor on behalf of the shareholders and others concerned with the business, and after that we will discuss his optional function as auditor for and adviser to management. Now, with regard to the accounting organization, all panel members agree, in the papers, that with regard to this, the public accountant in his capacity as auditor has a task, an obligatory task, to fulfil. He has to see, in his function as auditor, that the financial accounting organization meets minimum requirements and all of the panel members agree that if the examination of the financial accounting system shows defects the public accountant is competent to make recommendations for its improvement. So there is no difference of opinion on this point and I will leave this part of the relationship between business organization and the public accountant aside.

But if we consider that other department of accounting organization, named in the English terminology 'management accounting', then there is, I believe, a slight difference in the opinion of the panel members. Before asking Mr. Harris to give his opinion about that point, I will first bring to the notice of the audience that three colleagues have delivered some comments with regard to the papers or to the subjects of our discussion. They are Mr. Carrol from Dublin, Mr. Douglas Clarke from London and Mr. Armstrong from London. We will try to take up their questions in our discussion. May I now ask Mr. Harris: is it your opinion that the public accountant is qualified to organize that part of the organization concerning the accounting and record systems referred to as 'management accounting', that is, budgetary control and interim calculation?

MR. J. E. HARRIS (United Kingdom)

Mr. Chairman, If I may first generalize, I do not think that the average public accountant is necessarily qualified to organize a management accounting system—if we mean by being qualified, to be a specialist in the matter. Firstly, his training, both academically and practically, has a considerable bias in favour of what may be termed financial, historical accounting, in spite of the changes that have been and are being made in the examination curricula of the accounting bodies in the United Kingdom. Secondly, the increasing amount of detailed knowledge now required by the public practising accountant compared with, let's say, a generation ago, particularly, for instance, as a result of the increased incidence of taxation, makes it almost impossible to be a specialist in the various branches of the accounting field. But perhaps equally important is the difference in outlook which is required, what may be called the difference in psychological approach. In management accounting, for instance, a relatively accurate trend, obtained with speed, is infinitely more valuable than a precise assessment obtained after a longer interval of time. And thus the public accountant as an auditor, who must necessarily place great importance on precision, has to make a mental readjustment when turning to management accounting. However, to be more specific, in this sphere, as I think in most spheres in this life, it is the possible, not the desirable, which really sets the pattern. A small growing company, unable to afford the services of a specialist, may well obtain useful assistance from the public accountant; although he may not necessarily be an expert in management accounting, he is, however, still able to offer valuable advice which somebody without an accountant's training could not possibly give. In fact, in my experience, unless such a public accountant takes the initiative in these cases, very often the management of small companies do not even know of the term 'management accounting'. Furthermore—and this I think is the development which will be of most value in the future—in the larger firms of public accountants, one or more of the partners may specialize in this particular branch of accounting. There, I think, is the most fruitful line of inquiry; the extent to which we can develop the specialist within the larger public accountant firms. To summarize, therefore, Mr. Chairman, it is quite clear, and I'm certainly very pleased to see it, that management accounting as an art, will increase with increasing rapidity. I think it would be a tragedy if the accounting profession were to lose its opportunity in this sphere, but I think that it is equally important for us all to realize that the public accountant himself, as a result of his first training, is not necessarily qualified to act in the sphere of management accounting. I think that it is essential in order that the accounting profession may do justice to itself, that public accountants, either in the academic field, or through further experience in the practical field, equip themselves quite consciously towards the end of becoming assistants in the management accounting sphere.

MR. H. REINOUD (Netherlands)

Thank you, Mr. Harris. May I ask Mr. Bakkenist, what his opinion is?

MR. S. C. BAKKENIST (Netherlands)

Ja, mijnheer de voorzitter, in mijn prae-advies (pagina 401) heb ik duidelijk laten uitkomen, dat naar mijn oordeel het terrein, dat dan bij ons wordt omschreven als de administratie ten behoeve van het bedrijfsbestuur en waarvoor we in deze bijeenkomst misschien maar het beste de Angelsaksische term 'management accounting' kunnen gebruiken, dat dat terrein binnen de deskundigheid van de accountant valt. Op dat punt verschil ik dus wel enigermate met de heer Harris, zij het ook, dat ik wel weer met hem instem, dat misschien die conclusie niet voor iedereen en in dezelfde mate voor iedereen geldt. Maar m.i. ligt dit werkterrein binnen de deskundigheidssfeer van de accountant en ik geloof ook, dat deze opvatting in Nederland vrij algemeen in accountantskringen wordt gehuldigd, en dat men het dus ook als de taak van de accountant ziet om de bedrijfsleiding te helpen en terzijde te staan bij de ontwikkeling van dit deel van de administratie.

Yes, Mr. Chairman, In my paper (page 401) I clearly pointed out that what we refer to as 'accounting on behalf of the management' or 'management accounting', lies within the competence of the public accountant. So here I differ from Mr. Harris, although I do agree with him in that this conclusion is not, perhaps, applicable to everyone and not to everyone to the same extent. But I am of opinion that this work is within the competence of the accountant. I think that Dutch accountants, in general, share this opinion and agree that the accountant should certainly assist the management in developing this part of the accounting system.

MR. H. REINOUD (Netherlands)

Thank you, Mr. Bakkenist. Mr. Yorston, will you give your views on this point?

MR. R. KEITH YORSTON (Australia)

Mr. Chairman, My view is that the training and the education of the accountant should be such that he should at least be capable of, although he need not be an expert in, handling so called 'management accounting'. I feel that unless the training is such, unless his experience is such, so that he can deal with these new things, we call them new, management accounting, company practice and those sort of things, the practising accountant will be left purely with the green ink and the auditing. I feel that we have to arrange our training and our education, so that the practising accountant can handle management accounting. I don't know, Mr. Chairman, whether in the last ten years or so, some harm has not been done by the use of the term 'management accounting'. We tend to put into watertight compartments financial accounting, and management accounting, there are many other types of accounting we do not sort of put them aside. We have in my country accountants who deal with what you would call fiduciary accounting; deceased estates, people going bankrupt, companies winding up and so on, we don't segregate these accountants and say they perform a special type of accounting. My view is that we would have done better to have kept to the term, purely 'accounting', and not to specially try and say this is in the 'financial accounting' basket, and that this is in the 'management accounting' basket. It is all accounting.

MR. H. REINOUD (Netherlands)

Thank you, Mr. Yorston. I think that we all see this point, thus, that it is more a difference of degree than of principle between Mr. Harris and the other panel members. But, now assume that the accountant is capable of organizing the management accounting system, the question arises: is it necessary for him to evaluate such a management accounting organization in his capacity as auditor? In other words, is it inescapable for him? Mr. Yorston, what is your opinion about that?

MR. R. KEITH YORSTON (Australia)

This came up, I think, Mr. Chairman, in yesterday's session. I don't think it's the job of the practising accountant as such to evaluate the so-called management accounting but obviously in his audit if there is management accounting in operation, budgetary control and so on, he will evaluate them as part of the internal check. I think it is his job and he would be most unwise not to use these aids in his audit.

MR. H. REINOUD (Netherlands)

So I think he has an interest in management accounting because that contributes to the efficiency of his audit. Now a second question: is the accountant, the public accountant, also competent to evaluate the *efficiency* of the accounting organization, as an independent subject; that is, quite apart from the other questions we have dealt with, but as an independent subject of investigation. Mr. Richard, what is your opinion about that?

MR. F. M. RICHARD (France)

Je pense que l'expert-comptable doit incontestablement être en mesure, non pas en tant qu'extension de ses services de révision des comptes, mais comme étant une fonction supplémentaire, d'apprécier le fonctionnement, éventuellement de faire des recommandations en vue de redressement des services comptables qui tendent à mettre sur pied des services de contrôle budgétaire, de prix de revient standards, de 'management accounting', de contrôle de gestion, c'est incontestablement le rôle de l'expert-comptable. Je ne dis pas que actuellement il est toujours compétent, parce qu'il a peut-être d'autres spécialisations fussent-elles fiscales ou juridiques, mais le point est que ce devrait l'être à l'avenir.

I believe that the accountant must obviously be in a position to do this, not as an extension of his auditing capacity, but as an additional function. The accountant, I say, must be in a position to assist the operation of the concern, and if necessary make recommendations for changes to be made in the accounting system setting internal control on foot, systems for standard cost prices. The check of the management accounting, I think, is definitely a role the accountant must play. I don't say that he is always qualified to do so at the moment, because he may be more qualified in other fields, fiscal or juridical, but nevertheless I think he should be qualified in the future in this respect too.

MR. H. REINOUD (Netherlands)

And what is your opinion, Mr. Harris, about that?

MR. J. E. HARRIS (United Kingdom)

Well, I would agree with the opinion expressed just now by Mr. Richard; I certainly think that the public accountant has the ability to judge the efficiency of the accounting and record machinery. Usually, of course, it is easier to appraise something than to construct it.

Moreover, the public accountant's experience with the function of other systems is, of course, most valuable in this connection. Equally important in my view, however, is that in his position, external to the organization, it allows him to get, as we say, a bird's eye view of the whole system. In any case, he can judge it on the results it actually produces; whether it produces them with accuracy, precision, speed and without undue cost. I think they are the factors which one would take into account.

MR. H. REINOUD (Netherlands)

And you, Mr. Phillippe, have you any ideas about this point?

MR. G. L. PHILLIPPE (United States of America)

Well, Mr. Chairman, I would like to divide my remarks concerning this question into two parts, by that I mean I would segregate medium-sized or small companies from the larger organizations. Certainly in any event the public accountant *should* be in the best position of anyone to evaluate the accounting system of the organizations which he audits. In the small and medium size companies this might very well be a part of his regular annual audit. In the case of the larger concerns this I doubt, because I think the magnitude of the task would be such as to necessitate his taking it on, if taken on at all, as a special assignment rather than as a part of his regular annual audit. I would not like to detract from the value of his annual audit for such a formal appraisal, but, of course, informal comments can be received by the client at any time and they are always happy to receive them.

MR. H. REINOUD (Netherlands)

Thank you. Mr. Proshan, what is your opinion on this subject?

MR. SHALOM PROSHAN (Israel)

Well, being qualified to organize management accounting as well as financial accounting it seems that the public accountant should also be qualified to judge the efficiency of the whole of the accounting and record machinery. This should, however, be a service complementary to his audit service and not part of the audit, and should not bring him into conflict with his basic function of auditor. Such evaluation should be restricted to the application of generally accepted minimum standards of organisation. In my opinion the educational programme of the profession laid inadequate stress on this subject, and it can therefore be claimed that until this deficiency is repaired, it cannot automatically be assumed that every public accountant is qualified for this function, and, in particular, where expert knowledge is required. It is for the accountant to decide when, according to circumstances, external expert advice should be required. It would be well to consider the desirability of laying greater stress on the subject in the educational syllabus and professional training. The enlargement of the basic knowledge by modern methods, systems and techniques will ensure service in this field to the business community.

MR. H. REINOUD (Netherlands)

Thank you, Mr. Proshan. And Mr. Bakkenist, have you any comments?

MR. S. C. BAKKENIST (Netherlands)

Ja, mijnheer de voorzitter, ik zou willen aansluiten bij wat de heer Proshan zo juist heeft gezegd, omdat daarmee duidelijk het verschil tot uitdrukking komt met wat, naar ik meen, het standpunt van de Nederlandse collega's in deze is. Als we aanvaarden de opvatting, dat de accountant de deskundigheid heeft – in ieder geval behoort te hebben – voor het ontwikkelen van een doeltreffend systeem van „management accounting", dan vloeit daar toch ook uit voort, dat hij er zich periodiek rekenschap van geeft of een bepaalde administratieve organisatie doeltreffend functioneert, en of zij nog voldoet aan de standaard, die – gezien de snelle ontwikkeling die plaatsvindt – zal moeten worden gesteld. Ik geloof dus, dat de Nederlandse accountants meer de neiging zullen hebben om te vinden dat het hun taak is om erop toe te zien, dat die organisatie in ieder geval overeenstemt met redelijke en ik zou bijna willen zeggen met optimale eisen die hieraan worden gesteld. Er is nog een heel belangrijk punt dat daarbij meetelt: hoe staat de opdrachtgever ertegenover? Ik heb het gevoel, dat vele opdrachtgevers toch van de accountant – in ieder geval in Nederland – verwachten, dat hij erop toeziet, dat hun administratieve organisatie up to date is en up to date blijft. En als zij op een bepaald moment zouden bemerken, dat er ernstige tekortkomingen zijn, of dat hun organisatie niet met haar tijd is meegegroeid, dan geloof ik toch dat vele opdrachtgevers er hun Nederlandse accountants op zouden aanzien. Ik geloof dus dat het naar Nederlandse opvattingen noodzakelijk is dat de accountant daar aandacht aan besteedt en er dus voor oppast, dat hij niet ten gevolge van de dagelijkse routine uit het oog verliest, dat hij zich periodiek rekenschap moet geven van de stand van zaken op dit punt in de bedrijven waar hij werkzaam is.

In addition to what Mr. Proshan has said, I should like to make some remarks that clearly show the different view, as I take it, of the Dutch colleagues. If we accept the opinion that the accountant has the competency—that he ought to have it, in any case—to develop an efficient system of management accounting, it follows that he should periodically examine whether a specific accounting organization operates efficiently, and whether it is still 'up to standard', for these standards have been developing rapidly in the last few years. So I believe that Dutch accountants are more inclined to think it is their duty to supervise this management accounting system; to see that at any rate it meets reasonable—and I would almost say optimal—requirements. There is another important aspect of the question: what does the client expect in this respect? I feel that a large number of concerns—in the Netherlands anyway—require that the accountant shall see that their accounting organization is up to date and remains up to date. And if some day they would find that the accounting system no longer corresponds to modern practices in this field, I think that many clients might be inclined to blame their accountant for not having drawn their attention to it.

I think that, according to the Dutch opinion in this matter, the accountant must necessarily be concerned with that aspect of his work, and the daily routine work should not prevent him from periodically investigating the accounting system of his clients in this respect.

MR. H. REINOUD (Netherlands)

But let us take an extreme example: let us say that in a large accounting system it is necessary or desirable to have a time and motion study to a certain degree of refinement. Do you think it lies within the competence of the public accountant to make this study or do you think in that case he ought rather to co-operate with other persons more specialized in the field?

MR. S. C. BAKKENIST (Netherlands)

Ja, mijnheer de voorzitter, wanneer het gaat om grote bedrijven, waarover Mr. Phillippe van de United States ook heeft gesproken, is er in die grote bedrijven natuurlijk veelal ook al een interne accountants-afdeling en ook vaak een interne organisatie-afdeling. Dan wordt het dus zaak dat de accountant met die interne afdelingen tot een duidelijke taakverdeling komt. Als er dan wordt besloten, dat bepaalde zaken liggen en beter kunnen liggen op het terrein van de interne afdelingen, is daarmede ook de verantwoordelijkheid bepaald. Ik geloof dus, dat de accountant er wel goed aan doet, op dat punt geen twijfel te laten. Gaat het om eenvoudige tijd- en bewegingsstudies voor wat betreft administratieve handelingen, dan denk ik toch, dat als de accountant met zijn tijd wil blijven mee gaan, hij ook op dat punt moet zorgen dat hij deze werkzaamheden kan uitvoeren. Ik geloof dat het ook niet zo moeilijk is om assistenten in zijn organisatie daarvoor een eenvoudige opleiding te laten doorlopen; u weet ook dat de opleiding voor tijd- en bewegingsstudie nu niet zo omvangrijk is.

Mr. Chairman, If we are talking about large concerns, the type which Mr. Phillippe referred to, we would find that in such enterprises there is probably an internal audit department, and often also an internal organization department. Then it is necessary to come to a clear division of functions between the accountant and those internal departments. If it is decided then, that certain activities will be, and can better be performed by the internal departments, the question of responsibility is automatically settled.

I think the accountant does well to leave no doubt on this point. If simple time and motion studies for accounting activities are in question, I believe that the accountant who wants to keep in step with the modern evolution of his profession, must see that he is able to apply these techniques. I do not think that it would be very difficult to provide some basic training for his assistants in this respect. This training, as you probably know, does not take a very long time.

MR. H. REINOUD (Netherlands)

Thank you, Mr. Bakkenist.

Now, we have seen that we all come to the conclusion that a public accountant is to a certain extent competent to judge the efficiency of the accounting organization, though there are perhaps limits, and moreover we have seen that it is not an inescapable duty of his function as auditor. Now, keeping to this function of his as auditor, we come to the question: is the accountant, as auditor on behalf of the shareholders and others financially interested in the company, obliged also to judge, to assess, the rest of the organization, not the accounting organization but *the rest of the organization*. In other words, is such an assessment inescapable in that function? I leave aside for the moment (we will discuss that later) whether he is competent to perform such an assessment, but assume that he is, is it then necessary for him, in his function as auditor, to evaluate the rest of the organization? Mr. Harris, do you have an opinion on this matter?

MR. J. E. HARRIS (United Kingdom)

Yes, most definitely, Mr. Chairman, I have a very strong opinion about this particular aspect, a stronger opinion than I hold in respect to some other parts of our subject for discussion this afternoon. Certainly the short answer is that in the U.K. the auditor, acting as such, is neither obliged nor does he attempt to appraise or evaluate the rest of the organization, and adding my own comment, nor would I wish to see him legally enforced to do so. There are, of course, one has to admit, circumstances, shall we say the limiting cases, where a part of the organization—for example physical control of stores—may be so inefficient, that an auditor does not feel himself enabled to give an unqualified certificate; but in my view this is essentially because of the reaction of that inefficient part of the organization on the record and accounting system, which is the purview of the auditor. I think one can easily distinguish those circumstances from the others where, for instance, the company concentrates, shall we say, on a lot of general advertising, and does not employ many technical representatives. Such a case, I think, is entirely outside the scope of the auditor for comment. Similarly one can argue that the auditor may form the opinion that the layout of an assembly shop in a factory results in excessive handling of component parts. But in my view, these are matters for management, and for management alone. The directors are entrusted, as I see it, by the shareholders with the responsibility of running the business; I think equally that they must have the power to run it. The general premise or axiom that responsibility and control ought not to be divorced, is essentially applicable, I think, in these particular cases. I do not think that the directors ought to be subjected to an outside assessment of their efficiency, except that automatically provided by the financial results which are achieved either in the short or the long run. I will add and qualify, Mr. Chairman, perhaps to this extent, that an auditor, quite obviously, forms an assessment in his own mind of a firm's efficiency, and certainly from time to time it may be very helpful if he gives those views to the management. But as I see it, the essential difference is this: it is a fundamentally different position from giving advice in those circumstances, advice and not directives, than it would be in the case where he was forced to give directives, as a result of his legal position.

And that is one which at the moment doesn't exist in the U.K., and I certainly hope it never will.

MR. H. REINOUD (Netherlands)

Thank you, Mr. Harris, that is a very clear statement. Mr. Richard, what is your opinion?

MR. F. M. RICHARD (France)

Pour répondre à la question précise qui est posée, dans l'état actuel de la législation en France, c.à.d. la loi sur les sociétés et les statuts des sociétés, le réviseur des comptes, c.à.d. le commissaire aux comptes, n'a pas l'obligation de juger le reste de l'organisation. Il ne paraît d'ailleurs pas souhaitable qu'en tant que commissaire aux comptes mandaté à ce titre par les actionnaires il prenne de lui-même un rôle qui ne lui a pas été dévolu.

In reply to the precise question which has been put to us, according to present French Company Law and Company Statutes, the auditor is not abliged to assess the rest of the organization. It does not seem desirable either that, as an auditor, entrusted to carry out his task by the shareholders, he should embark on an activity for which he has no mandate.

MR. H. REINOUD (Netherlands)

Merci, M. Richard. Mr. Phillippe?

MR. G. L. PHILLIPPE (United States of America):

Well, with respect to my country we would expect that the public accountants, the auditors, would not be in a particularly good position to evaluate the activities of other functions of the business, except as they might come into contact with things which they might criticize in the ordinary course of their audit. In the United States we would expect evaluations of other areas of the business to be done by those particularly qualified in those areas. This is not in any sense to criticize the public accountant at all, this is merely to say that the public accountant is fully qualified in the accounting area, and would be expected to make whatever comments he cared to make concerning the financial activity, but in the other areas, perhaps a little knowledge is a dangerous thing, and it might be better for the accountant to step aside in those other fields and allow the experts in those particular areas to express their opinions and give management their judgements on activities in those areas.

MR. H. REINOUD (Netherlands)

Mr. Yorston, do you agree with this?

MR. R. KEITH YORSTON (Australia)

I agree with Mr. Harris, there is no statutory obligation in Australia for the auditor to evaluate the organization as a whole. I agree with what Mr. Harris says.

MR. H. REINOUD (Netherlands)

I feel that most of the panel members are of the opinion that in his function as auditor, the public accountant is not obliged to make an expert evaluation of the rest of the organization. But we have been confronted on our panel, as you will have read in the paper by Mr. Kihlman, with a rather different point of view, namely, the Swedish-Finnish point of view. There you will see that the public accountant has the statutory obligation with regard to the business organization, that is to say, the business organization as a part of management. He has statutory obligations to make an evaluation of the management. And I think that this point brings us to the heart of some interesting questions, and therefore, I would ask Mr. Kihlman to tell us at greater length what the situation is in his country.

MR. SVANTE KIHLMAN (Finland)

Mr. Chairman, In order to give a full and clear reply regarding the special circumstances in my country, Finland, as well as in Sweden, I have to begin by reading some sentences from my paper.

'According to old custom in Finland, which in the year 1895 was incorporated in the law, regarding a share company, which is the most usual form of company, it is the auditors' liability to examine and to present to the annual general meeting a report, not only upon the company's 'räkenskaper', meaning accounting, record keeping, balance sheet and profit and loss account, but also upon the company's 'förvaltning', which may be translated as 'management'. 'Förvaltningen' is defined by Prof. Oskar Sillén, Sweden, as comprising, in translation 'all measures and actions which the management of a business makes, or ought to make, in order to achieve the aims of the enterprise's activity (usually understood) within the framework of the prevailing law and good business practice'. It is incumbent upon the general meeting, annually, after having read the auditors' report, to confirm the balance sheet and profit and loss account, and to determine either to discharge the management from responsibility for the activities up to the end of the year of work, or otherwise to withhold this release from responsibility, with its resultant consequences. Sweden has corresponding legal regulations.

'Förvaltningen' is, as may be understood from the definition, given a very wide conception which embraces the enterprise's activity in its entirety, and business organization, now under discussion, is only a part of this management.

Accountants in Finland, as well as in Sweden, have thus a legal liability to examine, and also to form an opinion of the business organization in its entirety. In this respect there may exist a difference, at least in principle, as compared with other countries. Consequent upon this, the basis for the accountant's attitude in the present questions is different. It should be specially observed, that, in the question of the accountant's liability of examination, it is not justifiable in Finland to make any difference between that part of the business organization which comprises accountancy, or has direct connections with it, and the other part of business organization.'

To avoid misunderstandings it should be pointed out that neither the Finnish law, nor the Swedish law, prescribes any special statement in the auditors' report about the business organization only. The statement, which the auditors in Finland and Sweden according to the law have to give, is, in addition to one on the accounts, a statement upon 'förvaltningen', in translation 'management', comprising the enterprise's activity in its entirety. The organization is, as already stated, only a part thereof, which is not dealt with separately in the statement unless very considerable faults or shortcomings make it necessary to do so.

MR. H. REINOUD (Netherlands)

Well, we see that is quite an interesting situation in these countries, and I am interested to hear Mr. Harris's point of view with regard to this situation.

MR. J. E. HARRIS (United Kingdom)

My first reaction, Mr. Chairman, having just heard that statement, is that if I were an auditor in Finland, I would expect a fee not only equal to that of the Chairman but to the whole emoluments of the board of directors as well. And they certainly have a liability which we in other parts of the world don't have.

MR. H. REINOUD (Netherlands)

Would you like to have a part of the profits?

MR. J. E. HARRIS (United Kingdom)

I won't pursue that at this particular stage, but I would like to ask Mr. Kihlman some questions, arising from that, specifically with reference to the accountant's responsibility in Finland and in Sweden, which I think is substantially the same in both countries. Is the responsibility restricted to, say, drawing the attention of stockholders to weaknesses in the system of internal control, or in the custody of assets, for example, or on the other hand, does it, Sir, include a necessity to report on obvious shortcomings in organizational management which can be recognized by any normal business man of, let us say, average education and experience? Or does his responsibility as regards organization and management extend beyond this minimum and is he expected to give his opinion more or less as an expert on the subject? If the latter is the case, are not accountants in Finland and Sweden embarrassed by lack of objective standards by which to judge the organization and management?

MR. SVANTE KIHLMAN (Finland)

The questions which I have been asked to answer no longer concern only business organization but the larger conception 'management'. The discussion will thus go beyond the limits of the subject.

The task, as well as responsibility, of the auditor in Finland and Sweden is neither restricted to the points mentioned nor to any other points, but goes far further comprising, as described in my previous answer, the enterprise's activity in its entirety.

When replying to this question it should be mentioned that faults, shortcomings and weaknesses in the organization and internal control are usually discussed with the management and corrected earlier during the year and therefore very seldom are taken up in the auditors' final report to the shareholders. This occurs only when the shortcomings are very severe and the management, despite remarks, has not made the necessary corrections.

It is asked, whether the auditor restricts his report only to faults which can be recognized by each normal business man of average education and experience. This is not the case, and moreover it must be considered very difficult to determine what such a theoretical 'normal' business man is expected to recognize, and it would certainly involve considerable trouble and uncertainty. On the other hand, the auditor is not expected to give his opinion as an expert on every sphere of management. The auditor has to pay attention to and give his opinion on the objects of his examination as far as his personal capacity admits it. His knowledge and experience are to be considered greater than those of the supposed average business man and it is expected that he uses them to the full extent, when he gives his opinion.

The accountants are not embarassed by lack of objective standards for giving an opinion on management. The numerous objects to be examined, the differences depending on the size and nature of enterprises, branches, ownership, etc., involve such great variations, that it is to be considered almost impossible to establish any objective standards. On the contrary, such standards could more likely prove to be obstacles for forming a concise report in each special case.

MR. H. REINOUD (Netherlands)

Thank you, Mr. Kihlman. You were in a difficult situation. You have already felt that most of the panel members have different feelings about this subject and, therefore, I thought it fair that you should have time to defend yourself. Perhaps you have the idea that you are not on the defence but on the attack! But let us now see what Mr. Yorston thinks about the situation.

MR. R. KEITH YORSTON (Australia)

Mr. Chairman, I was surprised at yesterday afternoon's session to hear one of the speakers say that in Sweden, I think it was, or Finland or both, you usually have two or three different auditors. I can now see why. I was quite amazed to find that in Finland and Sweden there is such a thing as a management audit, I do not think there is such a thing elsewhere in the world, such as a statutory management audit, and I'd like to ask Mr. Kihlman, does that mean that if the auditor forms the opinion, let's say, that the company is making an incorrect product; should make one product instead of another; or that the company has started a store or shop in a place where it shouldn't have, the auditor should report that to the shareholders? And does not a management audit, Mr. Kihlman, place the directors in an invidious position?

MR. SVANTE KIHLMAN (Finland)

It should be emphasized that the auditor must not usurp influence on the management of the enterprise. He should not criticize the economical suitability of steps taken by the management unless these are illegal or indefensible, involving, for instance, that the managers act in their own benefit at the expense of the enterprise and the shareholders, that they neglect their duties or obviously do not exercise reasonable care and skill. Such cases may give cause for the General Meeting to withhold discharge of responsibility from the managers and to claim compensation for the damages caused, and it is therefore the auditor's duty to report his observations of this nature to the shareholders.

Thus it is not a sufficient reason for the auditor to report to the shareholders when he only *thinks* the management was unwise in starting a new branch. But if he can show, for instance, that other interests than the company's seem to have been the main reason for the step or that the calculations made were incomplete or wrongly performed, so that the step taken will evidently result in considerable losses, the auditor has to interfere, in the first place by contacting only the management, if he considers this sufficient, but in severer cases by reporting to the shareholders.

It is further asked whether the auditor would advise the company to change from one product to another. If the audit discloses that a product causes losses or leaves an unsatisfactory profit, the auditor has to contact the managers about this. As to consideration of new products, this belongs to the planning of the enterprise's activity in which the auditor has not to interfere, especially as his objectivity would otherwise be endangered.

MR. R. KEITH YORSTON (Australia)

Mr. Chairman, I can only say that I hope that the Swedish or Finnish Company Acts are never translated into English so that our legislators read them.

MR. G. L. PHILLIPPE (United States of America)

Mr. Chairman, May I ask a question also . . . This is a very intriguing subject, and may I first say that in the United States, so far as I know, there is nothing like it. I noticed you used the words illegal or indefensible. Illegal I can understand, but it seems to me that in the term indefensible there enters an element of time. In the United States we have a term called 'Monday morning Quarter-backing', which means that with respect to a football game played on Saturday, there are many coaches who would have played the game differently on Monday morning. In this particular case, if a decision were made to start a new product, or open a new branch, at the end of the year, at the time the auditor is making his review, it seems to me that at that particular time, it might have been the best judgement of the auditor also that this was a good move, but that perhaps two or three years later, this move could have been proved to be indefensible, on the basis of the losses sustained by opening the branch or starting the new product, and it seems to me that this places the management or the directors in an impossible position—that the auditors have not the responsibility for having opened the branch, and yet having acquiesced in it, at the end of the year, they may later criticize the management for having done so. This would be almost impossible in our situation, I think.

MR. H. REINOUD (Netherlands)
Mr. Proshan, would you like to make some remarks?

MR. SVANTE KIHLMAN (Finland)
May I answer this?

MR. H. REINOUD (Netherlands)
Mr. Proshan, too, has something to ask you. Perhaps you can answer both speakers at the same time.

MR. SHALOM PROSHAN (Israel)
I would also like to ask a question, Mr. Kihlman—whether public accountants in Sweden or in Finland have ever been sued in court, either for neglecting to report on poor management, or for alleged undue criticism made in their reports. If so, what tendencies do the verdicts show?

MR. H. REINOUD (Netherlands)
Thank you. That is a useful question, because the law has already existed a fairly long time, if I understood Mr. Kihlman properly, since '95, so you must have had some court cases or something like that, unless your managers managed their businesses very well during all that time. May I ask you to reply now, Mr. Kihlman?

MR. SVANTE KIHLMAN (Finland)
Well, to Mr. Phillippe I can only answer that of course the auditor has to consider the circumstances prevailing at the moment when the step was taken by the management, and not to consider what has happened later on. It would otherwise be unfair.

And of course I cannot agree with the questioner who felt that the audit of management would tend to place the directors in an invidious position. In addition to what has already been explained, it may furthermore be stressed that the auditor is neither expected to examine every year all parts of the management, nor to investigate any detail of the parts examined. But he is expected to convince himself yearly that the enterprise is, in its most important respects, properly managed, with due care and skill. To have it stated by a public accountant that the management is considered satisfactory cannot but be pleasant for a good director. This matter has not caused any problem in Finland.

As to Mr. Proshan's question, as far as I know, no public accountant neither in Finland nor in Sweden has been sued in court either for neglect in reporting on poor management, or for alleged undue criticism in his reports. This may be due to the lack of objective standards for the auditing and reporting on management. It is a question of a personal evaluation and it seems difficult to have anybody sentenced for having arrived at his own opinion, provided the audit has been made with reasonable care. It may, however, perhaps also be assumed that the public accountants have succeeded fairly well in carrying out this difficult task.

I hope my answers have together given an idea of our audit of management. As it appears from the answers that remarks rather seldom are presented in the auditors' reports to the shareholders, it might possibly be asked whether the auditor's work in this respect perhaps can be considered to be fairly meaningless. To this can be replied, that the audit of management is to a great extent carried out during the year before the final audit and thereby detected faults are discussed with the management and corrected in good time so that criticisms in the final report can mostly be avoided. As the managers of course are anxious to avoid remarks in the auditors' report to the shareholders, they are inclined to be careful so as to avoid faults and to make corrections as soon as possible in co-operation with the auditor. The audit of management is thus of great importance even as an effective way to prevent faults and mistakes at an early stage.

MR. H. REINOUD (Netherlands)

Thank you, Mr. Kihlman. Mr. Boter, is there any Spanish comment about this intriguing situation?

DR. FERNANDO BOTER (Spain)

Mr. Chairman, Ladies and Gentlemen, D'accord avec la législation de mon pays, je crois que l'expert-comptable doit être obligé de faire son rapport sur la question comptable, c.à.d. c'est là la limitation de sa responsabilité et de son métier. Il ne doit pas être obligé d'amplifier sa mission dans d'autres branches des activités de l'entreprise. Il y a une question de compétence; la question comptable et la gestion des affaires sont si complexes à présent qu'il est difficile de pouvoir posséder toutes les connaissances nécessaires pour avoir une vision complète du problème. Au moyen-âge, les savants savaient tout ce qu'on pouvait savoir à ce moment-là, mais après, à présent il y a des spécialistes; les savants ont amplifié leurs connaissances en profondeur mais pas en extension. Pour le comptable c'est la même chose. Il y a beaucoup de problèmes extrêmement difficiles qui ne sont pas précisément ceux de la comptabilité, qui sont déjà une matière d'études tout à fait spéciales.

Alors on ne peut pas prétendre que l'expert-comptable possède aussi les connaissances spéciales pour les autres branches de l'entreprise. C'est une question de compétence. Je ne suis pas d'accord que la question de compétence doit être résolue par l'expert-comptable lui-même, mais je suis d'accord que cette question de compétence peut être résolue s'il y a deux circonstances. D'abord s'il arrive que l'entreprise demande à l'expert-comptable de donner son opinion, outre la question comptable, sur d'autres secteurs, d'autres branches de l'entreprise. C'est la première condition. Ensuite, il doit y avoir une autre condition: que l'expert-comptable reconnaît lui-même être capable de cette compétence. Si l'expert-comptable est un homme honnête, comme on doit le supposer toujours, il résoudra en conscience s'il est compétent ou non. Alors s'il y a cette coincidence à savoir: que l'entreprise lui demande son opinion sur l'organisation, sur l'organisation juridique par exemple, ou sur l'organisation technique et que le comptable croit à son tour qu'il est compétent de résoudre cette question, alors il se peut que le rapport de l'expert-comptable s'occupe de la partie de la comptabilité et en plus de cette partie de l'organisation. C'est à dire, en résumant, que l'expert-comptable est obligé de donner son opinion sur la comptabilité. Il n'est pas obligé de donner son opinion sur les questions non-comptables, mais ses opinions sur les questions techniques sont des opinions qui ne lui sont pas défendues. C'est tout ce que j'ai à dire.

Mr. Chairman, Ladies and Gentlemen, In accordance with the legislation in our country, I believe that the accountant should be obliged to base his report on the accounting side; that is the limitation of his responsibility and of his profession. He is not required to amplify his task to cover other of the company's activities. There is a question of competence. Accounting questions and management questions are so complex nowadays that it is difficult to obtain sufficient understanding of all their aspects to acquire a general, overall picture of the problem. In the Middle Ages men of learning knew everything there was to be known about everything, but since then we have acquired specialists. Men of science have gone more deeply into their particular branch of knowledge but have not widened their knowledge generally.

The accountant is in the same position. There are a number of extremely difficult problems, not precisely accounting problems, which have already become a matter of special study. One must not expect the accountant to possess special knowledge covering other branches of the business, besides the accounting. It is really a matter of competence. Personally, I don't think that the question of competence can be settled by the accountant himself. It may be solved, however, in two circumstances. First of all, that is, if the concern itself requests the accountant to give his views on matters outside purely accounting questions. That is the first condition. Then there must be a second condition: the accountant must feel himself competent to do this. If he is an honest man, as we must expect him to be, he will have to ask himself: 'Am I or am I not competent to do this?'

But if these two conditions are fulfilled, that is, if the enterprise asks the accountant to give his views on the organization, the juridical or technical organization, for instance, and he feels he is competent to do this, the accountant's report will also deal, in addition to the accounting, with the organizational side of the firm. The accountant, therefore, must give his views on the accounts; on the other hand, there is nothing to force him to give his views on the non-accounting side of the business, though he may give them on technical questions. That is all I have to say.

MR. H. REINOUD (Netherlands)

Merci. I believe that we can come to the conclusion that the majority of the panel members are not in favour of the Swedish-Finnish situation, nevertheless the situation there, in regard to our subject, is very interesting and it may be very useful, Mr. Kihlman, to study it more elaborately, when the congress is over; at home, I mean. Now, we are still discussing the situation of the relationship between the public accountant in his capacity as auditor and business organization. As a kind of recapitulation we may formulate the relationship in this way: the efficiency of the audit is dependent on the efficiency of the accounting organization and the efficiency of the accounting organization is, in turn, dependent on the efficiency of the whole organization. I think that formulated in this way, the majority of us will have objections. Mr. Harris, would you comment on that?

MR. J. E. HARRIS (United Kingdom)

Yes, Mr. Chairman, there is a relationship, just to clarify my thoughts, for a moment, while I am thinking aloud as it were, there is a relationship and indeed, obviously, a very positive relationship, in my view, between the work carried by an auditor during the course of his statutory audit, and the internal organization of a firm. Firstly, since in all but the very smallest cases, an auditor is not expected to carry out an exhaustive check, then it follows that both the structure and the efficiency of the organization influence the auditor in his approach to the audit. For instance, the existence of internal check, and/or internal audit, the existence of clearly defined spheres and responsibilities of the executives and their staffs within the accounting division, the system of routing documents and information and the type of costing system are but some of the factors which come to mind, which obviously determine the type and extent of the audit necessary by the statutory auditor. Secondly, to the extent that the auditor finds shortcomings in the system which the management has instituted, or where there is no particular part of such a system yet in force, where it ought to exist, then clearly it is also in the interest of all, both management and the auditor, that the auditor expresses his view as quickly as possible, if he is doing a continuous audit, and also for the auditor to express or give advice. Most managements, I think it is safe to say, ask for and welcome such advice and in practice the exchange of views is regular and in fact an interflow of information. I think in this way, one could argue that the auditor may well, inescapably, shall we say, meddle with some parts of the organization, which is not directly within the accounting division, but it is an auxiliary meddling and not a direct meddling, and it comes about, in my view, only because of his correct course in commenting, as and when the auditor thinks fit, on the accounting division, and any part thereof. I cannot see any harm in this kind of approach, I think in fact it is vitally necessary if the auditor is to do his job properly. The essential point, to go back on a previous question we are discussing, is that in these circumstances, the relationship results in the auditor giving advice, as I said before, and not directives. And what I think is also equally essential is that the auditor gives advice to the management, and not directly to the shareholders as to the management's efficiency. And the management, in turn, in those circumstances, is obviously free to accept or to reject it as it thinks fit.

MR. H. REINOUD (Netherlands)

Thank you, Mr. Harris. I think we can now switch over to the relationship between the public accountant, as an independent adviser in the field of business organization on behalf of management. Now the first point is: is the accountant's firm qualified to carry out such investigations in the field of the rest of the organization; here we are not speaking about the accounting organization, but about the rest of the organization. Is the accountant's firm qualified to carry out such investigation or can it become qualified to do so? Mr. Richard, will you perhaps reply briefly?

MR. F. M. RICHARD (France)

Je crois que cette question est plus ou moins liée à celle de savoir si l'expert-comptable peut ou non s'entourer de collaborateurs spécialisés, c.à.d. de certains experts. Deux de nos collègues ont déjà presque répondu pour moi tout à l'heure. M. Phillippe a dit un petit peu de connaissance est pire que pas de connaissance du tout et notre collègue espagnol nous a dit qu'il n'est pas possible que le comptable puisse acquérir, quel que soit son talent et même s'il veut devenir un savant comme au temps du moyen-âge, il ne pourra jamais acquérir toutes les connaissances qui lui permettraient d'apprécier, de juger, de redresser les différents secteurs de l'entreprise. Il lui est donc nécessaire de s'entourer d'experts qui traiteront les questions d'organisation du travail, les questions d'organisation de la production ou les études de temps et de mouvements, qui sont tout de même assez complexes, les questions d'implantation d'usines au point de vue commercial, les études de marchés, sur d'autres domaines la recherche opérationnelle ou les statistiques et un domaine qui s'ouvre à nous et qui est la manipulation intégrée des informations au moyen des machines électroniques. Eh bien, je pense que si l'expert-comptable prend le soin de grouper autour de lui un certain nombre d'experts, de collaborateurs, qui peuvent être des ingénieurs à qui il donnera une formation comptable suffisante, il doit être à même de pouvoir apporter son concours dans les entreprises en tant que appréciation et conseil d'organisation en général.

I think, Mr. Chairman, that this question is more or less connected with the question as to whether or not the accountant can call upon the assistance of specialized collaborators, that is, experts. Two of our colleagues have already as good as answered this point. Mr. Phillippe has said that a little knowledge is worse than no knowledge at all, and our colleague from Spain said that it is impossible for the accountant to acquire whatever his qualifications and even if he wanted to become a learned man, as in the Middle Ages, it is impossible for him to acquire the full knowledge that will enable him to appraise, judge, and correct any mistakes in all the various sectors of the enterprise. Thus he has to call upon the assistance of experts in matters of work organization and production organization, or in time and motion studies, which are all the same fairly complex. Also questions of factory siting, market research, and even the use of electronic machines in statistical data. Now if the accountant surrounds himself with a number of collaborators, 'engineers', whom he has given sufficient accounting training, he can advise on the matter of general organization as well.

MR. H. REINOUD (Netherlands)

Merci, M. Richard. Will you please give your opinion, Mr. Harris, very briefly?

MR. J. E. HARRIS (United Kingdom)

Yes, Mr. Chairman.

It seems to me essential that if a firm of public accountants are going to cover such a wide field then they must necessarily have these additional experts, and that it would be hopeless for anyone or two or three people, three partners shall we say, to try to acquire the knowledge whereby they could do themselves justice in dealing with such diverse problems and techniques. Furthermore is it desirable that a firm of public accountants should develop in that way, and whether, we are now thinking along a slightly different line, a much wider field, I do not know off hand. Previously we have been talking about financial accounting and management accounting, but now we are going into another sphere, which I think we want to develop at a later stage.

MR. H. REINOUD (Netherlands)

Mr. Phillippe, what is your opinion? We are still speaking about the rest of the organization.

MR. G. L. PHILLIPPE (United States of America)

I believe I have already expressed what I feel to be the case, but I should like to add one thing to it. In my company we have come to find that the management of a large diverse organization is a very difficult thing, for any one man or a group of men, a small group of men, to comprehend and administer. As a result, as perhaps many of you know, we have come upon a policy of decentralisation where we actually practice the delegation of authority to each of our decentralised departments and operations. I think that we might draw a corollary here, that there are many wide, diverse functions of a business and to expect one type of activity, to become expert in all of them is to my mind expecting a little too much of any one firm or any one group of individuals. To my mind the accountant can make very valuable contributions in other fields on a general basis but to make suggestions and recommendations in many fields without having the necessary spadework, background, experience may do more damage than good. I would hope that we accountants continue to specialize in all things for which we have a special training, background and experience and leave other areas for the development of the same type of experience, expertness and background by other people, rather than try to acquire all of those skills on the part of a relatively small organization. I do not criticize in any way the valued advice and counsel which public accountants, as good businessmen, can give in other fields to small organizations. They can bring to those organizations a wealth of experience and this advice and counsel will be sought and, when received, will be valued highly. But to take further interest and to go further down that road is to my mind going a little off the beaten path so far as the accounting profession is concerned.

MR. H. REINOUD (Netherlands)

Thank you, Mr. Phillippe. And your opinion, Mr. Bakkenist?

MR. S. C. BAKKENIST (Netherlands)

Ja, mijnheer de voorzitter, ik sluit wel aan bij wat mr. Phillippe heeft gezegd. Naar mijn oordeel eist het hebben van bemoeienis met de rest van de organisatie vaak toch wel een deskundigheid, die niet door de individuele accountant, die ook deskundig moet zijn op het terrein van de contrôle, kan worden bestreken. Daarom heb ik dus betoogd, dat wellicht *het kantoor* die deskundigheid zich eigen kan maken, maar dan is er in dat kantoor weer een bepaalde specialisatie op dat organisatieterrein nodig en, zo heb ik ook gezegd, dat organisatieterrein is op zich zelf weer zo ruim, dat er binnen die specialisatie weer een behoefte komt aan specialisatie op onderdelen. Dat sluit dus wel aan bij wat mr. Phillippe heeft gezegd. Ik wil nog deze kanttekening maken, dat naar mijn oordeel het organisatiewerk, met name wanneer het ligt buiten de sfeer van de administratieve organisatie, ook een ander soort man vraagt dan verlangd wordt voor de contrôlearbeid. Ik geloof dat er een verschil in habitus is en een verschil in karaktereigenschappen en ik geloof dus, dat we daarom dit punt ook met een bepaalde bedachtzaamheid moeten benaderen.

I must say that I share the views which have just been expressed by Mr. Phillippe. In my opinion, too, the intervention by the accountant in the other parts of the organization of the enterprise, requires competence which is not always available to the accountant, who after all must already be fully competent and qualified in the field of auditing. But it may become available, as I argued, to a *firm* of accountants when one or more of its members specialize(s) in this particular field. And this field, I also have said, is so large of itself that within this specialization it is necessary to specialize again in various sectors. So this corresponds with what Mr. Phillippe has said. I should like to add this marginal note: in my opinion the organizational activities, especially those outside the sphere of the accounting organization, also require another type of personality than auditing activities do. I think there is a difference in habits of thought and in qualities of character. Therefore, if we're going to take this up we've got to be very careful.

MR. H. REINOUD (Netherlands)

Thank you, Mr. Bakkenist. May I ask, is that the opinion of all the members that you need another type of personality, another character structure for doing advisory work in the field of business organization than that required in the field of auditing? Mr. Yorston? What is your opinion?

MR. R. KEITH YORSTON (Australia)

I would just say my view is that the professions of accounting and management consultancy are not competitive but complementary. It is just a matter how far you develop along the lines of management work in an accountant's firm, how far you can go.

MR. H. REINOUD (Netherlands)

But the question, Mr. Yorston, is: do you need, for the different types of work, different types of personality; thus, one person may be the right person for auditing but not the right person for doing business organization work.

MR. R. KEITH YORSTON (Australia)

Mr. Bakkenist deals in his paper with this aspect. I agree with what he states there. A slightly different type of personality is needed for the man who is dealing with historical work only. The man who does management consultancy work looks ahead, the man doing public accounting, as auditor, is inclined to concentrate on historical work mainly. In any case I do think that the man who is trained in accounting will make a better adviser for management consulting work.

MR. H. REINOUD (Netherlands)

Mr. Proshan, what do you think about the character question? About the psychological difference?

MR. SHALOM PROSHAN (Israel)

I would say that the foremost asset of the auditor is his independence. This by itself requires a strong character and I would not say that the accountant is required to possess special or different psychological attitudes in order to take an organizing task on himself. There is no reason to suppose that a situation may arise where in his advisory capacity on the rest of the organization he may come in conflict with his basic duties. It is for the accountant to decide from case to case whether he is sufficiently informed and possesses sufficient expert knowledge to act as adviser in given circumstances, and whether he possesses sufficient strength of character to withstand management's opposition to advice given by him. In any case, I would not recommend that a public accountant should give advice based on a synthesis of experts, without his mastering the problem personally.

MR. H. REINOUD (Netherlands)

Thank you. Now Mr. Bakkenist has raised another important point in his paper. He says organization experts in the employ of the accountants' firms will meet with the difficulty of having no opportunity to be a partner in the accountants' office unless they pass the accountant's examination. May I ask the other members to say very briefly, just with 'yes' or 'no', whether that is the situation in their country, too. So, if in one of your countries there is a situation whereby you have an expert in the field of business organization who has not passed the accountant's examination, would it then be impossible to make him a partner in the firm? Mr. Phillippe?

MR. G. L. PHILLIPPE (United States of America)

I had better not answer that question, Mr. Reinoud, not being in the public accounting profession myself.

MR. H. REINOUD (Netherlands)

Mr. Boter?—
Mr. Yorston?

MR. R. KEITH YORSTON (Australia)

In Australia you could not become a firm of chartered accountants, and the same would apply in the United Kingdom, if a person non-qualified as a chartered accountant was a member of the firm. Thus you would meet with the same difficulties in Australia as Mr. Bakkenist has pointed out in his paper.

MR. H. REINOUD (Netherlands)
Et en France?

MR. F. M. RICHARD (France)
En France même difficulté. Un organisateur ne pourrait pas devenir associé d'une société d'experts-comptables s'il ne passait pas au préalable le diplôme d'expert-comptable.

The same difficulty arises in France, Mr. Chairman. An organizer could not become a partner in a firm of accountants, if he had not first passed the accountancy examination.

MR. J. E. HARRIS (United Kingdom)
Mr. Yorston has already answered for the U.K., I'll just qualify it in this way that it would be legally possible for such a partnership to be formed, but that partnership could not describe itself as e.g. Certified Accountants, where you have a mixture of people with different qualifications or one without any qualifications at all. It would therefore detract from their public standing.

MR. H. REINOUD (Netherlands)
Mr. Kihlman, in your country?

MR. SVANTE KIHLMAN (Finland)
I am of the same opinion.

MR. H. REINOUD (Netherlands)
Mr. Proshan?

MR. SHALOM PROSHAN (Israel)
In Israel it is prohibited to practice as public accountants, in partnership with un-qualified accountants.

MR. H. REINOUD (Netherlands)
Thank you. Thus we have heard that there is almost everywhere the same difficulty as Mr. Bakkenist has raised in his paper, with regard to the possibility of an expert in the accounting field and an expert in the organization field becoming partners; that may be a handicap, I think, for the development of a management consultant department within an accountant's office. Now the small firm or medium size business has perhaps more need of the public accountant's organizing talent and knowledge than has a large concern. But let me ask first Mr. Phillippe who, as you know, is controller of the General Electric whether in a large organization like his, he, in the field of the rest of the organization, can make use of the management consultant department of a public accounting firm.

MR. G. L. PHILLIPPE (United States of America)
Mr. Chairman, As I have mentioned, the General Electric Company found it had some very serious organization problems, as it grew in size. We found also that we did not have internally the men competent to deal with this type of

organization problem and we therefore recruted from the ranks, principally of management consultation firms in the United States, men who were qualified along purely organizational lines, to help us in this regard. We then established these men as a separate organization consulting service in the General Electric Company and our organization problems were delegated for solution to this group. This group came up with their recommendations of five functional organizations in each of our business and made recommendations to each functional manager as to the organization which it should develop within that function. The responsibility, however, for the organization of that function, namely let us say financial, was the responsibility of the officer in charge of that particular function. For clarification I might mention that these five principal functions are the usual ones I believe of engineering, manufacturing, marketing, employee and public relations, and financial.

After having established those five functions for any business the responsibility for organizing within that function was assigned to the manager of that function in that business and the organization consulting service became what its name implies—an adviser and consultant. We, of course, obtained advice from the public accountants with respect to the organization of the financial department, but then proceeded, because of the responsibility delegated to us, to organize that particular function as we saw fit. Our organizing and consulting service is a department of the Company and is, as its name implies, an adviser and consultant on organization to all managers and officers.

MR. H. REINOUD (Netherlands)

Thank you so much, Mr. Phillippe. And what is your opinion, Mr. Richard?

MR. F. M. RICHARD (France)

Je pense que c'est précisément dans les entreprises de moyenne importance que les experts-comptables devraient le plus facilement trouver leurs techniques employées. Les grandes entreprises ont leur propre organisation.

I consider that it is precisely in the medium size business, that the accountants should find it easiest to use their technique. The larger enterprises have their own organization.

MR. H. REINOUD (Netherlands)

Finally, a few questions on the topical subject which in the foregoing was provisionally left out of consideration, namely the Public Accountant and Data Processing Equipment. We thought that it would perhaps be interesting to raise this point, just for some minutes, with regard to our subject. The first question that arises is this: Can an accountant's firm develop into an expert adviser in the field of electronic data processing? May I first ask Mr. Harris for a brief answer, please.

MR. J. E. HARRIS (United Kingdom)

Well, I should say the response to that is yes, it certainly can, if one or more of the partners are prepared to give the time and study to acquire the necessary knowledge, but this is a clear case where quite obviously academic training itself would never, as far as we can see, be sufficient to cope with the problem.

And therefore it is essentially a new development which firms of public accountants have got to turn their minds to more and more in the coming years.

MR. H. REINOUD (Netherlands)

Thank you. Mr. Bakkenist?

MR. S. C. BAKKENIST (Netherlands)

Ja, mijnheer de voorzitter, ik zie dit in de eerste plaats als een probleem van administratieve organisatie. Ik geloof, dat we bij die 'data processing' twee zaken moeten onderscheiden. De accountant zal zich naar mijn oordeel op de hoogte moeten stellen van de capaciteiten, van de mogelijkheden van de nieuwe apparatuur. Dat is misschien niet eens zo moeilijk als het aanvankelijk lijkt. Maar ik geloof, dat met name de problemen komen, als het gaat om het benutten van die apparatuur in de administratieve organisatie. En de programmering, daarbij kan de accountant een belangrijke rol vervullen. Ik geloof, dat op dit moment bij de bedrijven die er over denken en die ermee bezig zijn – ook in het buitenland – de moeilijkheden vooral liggen op het punt van de programmering. Hoe kunnen we die apparatuur met zijn enorme capaciteiten benutten in het geheel? Daarvoor is eigenlijk nodig een 're-thinking' van de hele administratieve procedure. En dat is een moeilijke opgaaf, waar ik een taak voor de accountant zie, mijnheer de voorzitter.

Yes, Mr. Chairman, I consider this problem in the first place as a problem of accounting organization. I think that when we talk about data processing, there are two points of view to be borne in mind. The accountant must first of all make himself acquainted with the possibilities offered by these new electronic machines. Maybe that is not such a difficult job as it looks at the outset. But the problems arise when we come to the use of such machines in the accounting system.

In the programming of such machines the accountant can play an important part. I think the main difficulties are those of the programming and how to ensure the optimum and best use of such appliances. For that purpose it is necessary to 're-think' the whole accounting procedure. And that is a difficult job, where I see, however, a task for the accountant, Mr. Chairman.

MR. H. REINOUD (Netherlands)

Mr. Proshan, have you any ideas about this?

What is your opinion, can the accountants' firm develop itself in the field of electronic data processing?

MR. SHALOM PROSHAN (Israel)

I share the view of Mr. Harris that of course it needs specialization and training, and if the accountant's firm will specialize in this field, it will certainly succeed in it.

MR. H. REINOUD (Netherlands)

I feel that the majority or perhaps all of us are of opinion that the public accountant, if he studies the problem and follows the techniques, will be able to become an adviser in the field of data processing. Now my experience is that the United States are rather far ahead in the field of electronic data processing, not only in the techniques, but also in the application of data processing. And, therefore, I would ask Mr. Phillippe whether he can tell us something about the application in the United States, and perhaps he will also pay attention to the question which may interest the accountants, in how far the accountants' firms in the United States have taken steps in order to ensure that expert advice can be given in this field.

MR. G. L. PHILLIPPE (United States of America)

Mr. Chairman, First I would like to say that I believe it to be a fact in the United States that the public accounting profession has taken a very substantial interest in developing electronic data processing. I hardly know where to start on this kind of a question, but we made use, in our electronic data processing problems, of several accounting firms to help us understand, design, and make effective the data processing systems which we have put into effect. I do not want to leave the impression that my company is by any means any leader in this area. I expect that perhaps there are many to whom I am speaking who are far ahead of us. Nevertheless, I should like to mention to you some of the problems so that they will not be under-estimated. First I believe the accountant, the industrial accountant and the public accountant, in approaching data processing must almost forget the methods by which he has previously accomplished his work. Electronic machines do not work in the same way as do individuals and I believe someone has characterized an electronic data processing machine as the fastest, the largest, the most expensive and the dumbest clerk you have in your organization. And this is certainly true—I do not want to bore you with a lot of details—but for example, when we did one job of programming in the payroll area as most companies have, we designed an electronic data processing system for a payroll of 30,000 employees. The 30,000 are now paid by an IBM 702 Computer, the payroll is up-dated, the deductions up-dated, and the payroll register prepared by the use of 20 hours of machine time. This means about 1 ½ seconds per employee. And this is wonderful as I sit here and tell you about it. But before we got to that point, we spent 20 man-years in programming the IBM 702 so that it would process our payrolls, and we consider our payrolls to be the simplest form of data processing that we have. We are also using our 702 for the purpose of consolidating our financial information, the balance sheet and operating statements of some 100 departments are transmitted by wire to the computer—they are consolidated without being touched by individuals and we can issue a consolidated company statement within 24 hours of the date of receiving the financial statements of the individual departments of which there are 125. The 125 also use some forms of data processing equipment and are able to issue their financial statements within 5 working days of the close of any fiscal period. Thus we have a consolidated financial statement for the company, balance sheet and operating statement, in 6 working days from the date of the close of the fiscal month, or fiscal quarter, or fiscal year. We still have a lot of work to do. Ahead of us is a sort of vision, if I may be permitted the expression, that this is much too slow for management's decision making, promptly as this action occurs. We visualize out in front of us the elimination of all financial statements, balance sheets, operating statements, except as may be required for record purposes, that is to file away so that you can look at them and refer to them as you need to. We visualize in place of that a television screen on each manager's desk, with several buttons in front of him so that he may push the appropriate one and have the information which he desires flash immediately ahead of him so that he may take whatever action the information seems to indicate. For example, if a general manager is interested in his profit and losses results, by pushing his profit and loss button, he would have the information for the current period up until let us say one minute ago, upon the screen in front of him. We anticipate that each department will have such an electronic data processing system and that he will be able to see the results of his particular department immediately, for the immediately preceding period, together with whatever comparisons he wished to make. I'm sorry I've taken up so much time, Mr. Chairman, but you indicated that this audience might have some interest in the activities that we have carried on in this area.

MR. H. REINOUD (Netherlands)

In trying to sum up our discussion, I would start with stating that the papers and discussions in the first place show that all of the participants in the discussion agree that the public accountant is being confronted with the problems of management and organization in an ever-increasing measure and that therefore the relation between business organization and the public accountant is an important subject both for the present and the future.

When speaking about 'business organization' there is a slight difference of opinion about the contents of this expression. Mr. Harris, for instance, thinks in this respect primarily of the accounting organization and particularly of that part which has to do with management accounting. Although in his paper he also speaks of administrative organization, methods and clerical routine. The other participants in the discussion have a somewhat wider definition in mind although they do not want to extend the activities in the field of business organization without limits. Leaving the situation in Finland and Sweden for a moment out of consideration—I will come to that presently—all members are of the opinion that there is not the slightest doubt that the public accountant in his capacity as auditor—and I emphasize that for the time being I only want to speak about the relation between business organization and the auditor—has close bonds with the accounting organization because he is, in a wide sense, dependent on it.

However, most of the members restrict the *obligatory* duties of the auditor to that part of the accounting organization that has to do with the financial statements and accounting data of the past, or in the English terminology, to the financial accounting organization. And here, all agree, he is completely competent to evaluate the organization and, if necessary, make recommendations to improve it.

With regard to the so-called management accounting, to the efficiency of the accounting organization as such, and to office equipment, the same members do not see an obligatory task resulting from the function of the accountant as auditor. This is a distinction in principle, for in practice all recognize, for instance, the benefits of management accounting for the auditor, because it leads to better insight into the accounts and to greater efficiency in the audit. And almost all agree that the accountant is qualified to evaluate and construct the management accounting system. With regard to the efficiency of the accounting organization and of the office equipment, the majority of us think he is capable to make recommendations but perhaps he may sometimes need the help of specialists.

The relation, as I have put it in one of the questions, viz. 'the efficiency of the audit is dependent on the efficiency of the accounting organization and the efficiency of the accounting organization is, in turn, dependent on the efficiency of the whole organization' is to a large extent recognized by all the participants in the discussion. All emphasize the importance of cost, performance and yield standards for the efficiency of the audit. But nobody will think it desirable that, due to this relationship, the total organization of a firm has to be the object of a systematic and overall evaluation by the public accountant in his capacity as auditor, if he has not to report thereon to shareholders.

I am still speaking of the relation between business organization and the auditor. If I now say something about the Finnish-Swedish situation, I think all of us have been struck by the interesting relationship between organization and the public accountant as described so clearly by Mr. Kihlman.

'Accountants in Finland, as well as in Sweden, have', says Mr. Kihlman, 'a legal liability to examine, and also to form an opinion of the business organization in its entirety', and they have to report about their findings to the shareholders.

Although Mr. Kihlman has made it clear that the shareholders do not expect expert knowledge and advice in this respect from him, and that too serious and perfectionist a view of his duties in this additional function must not be taken, the other participants in the discussion, I believe, reject obligatory duties of this kind for an auditor, on these grounds:

1. that an opinion on management and organization may be too subjective,
2. that it is difficult to reconstruct the situation and all the circumstances under which a management decision has been taken,
3. that there is the danger of confusion as to the respective functions of management and auditor,
4. that it is to be doubted whether an effective evaluation of the management or organization of a large company would be possible on an annual basis, even for the largest public accounting firms,
5. all kinds of less serious objections regarding management or organization, possibly resulting in the shareholders to a certain extent losing faith in the capacities of the management and directors.

Mr. Kihlman has denied at length the importance of these objections in practice, and it will be of interest to study more thoroughly the situation in Sweden and Finland and the experience gained with this remarkable relationship between management and auditor.

Thus far we have been concerned with the adequacy of the organization, as a subject of evaluation in the scope of a general audit.

As soon as we no longer connect business organization in the wider sense and the public accountant's auditing function, but see our point of discussion as Mr. Harris has formulated it on page 423:

'is it useful and/or desirable to utilize the public accountant in reviewing and commenting upon the organization and procedures of a business, not as part of any obligatory audit but as a function suggested either by the public accountant himself or requested by the company concerned',

then all fundamental objections, I mean objections in principle, against rather extensive interference by the public accountant in matters of business organization seem to disappear, although here, too, there are differences as regards the interpretation of the meaning and contents of the term 'business organization.'

Almost all of the speakers draw attention to the fact that there is a great and still-growing need in the field of management consultancy on one hand, but that there are only very few real capable management consultants on the other hand. Therefore, apart from their own interest, public accountants have to consider whether they have not a task in this field.

When dealing in this connection with the term 'public accountant', it is generally held that we have to think primarily of an accountant's firm inside which a certain specialization in the field of business organization has come about. In this respect the term 'Management consultant department' is used.

The majority of the members emphasize in this respect that a public accountant's firm should not widen its field of activity in this respect too much. They are not in favour of engaging all kinds of specialists, for instance, advertising experts. The accountant's work with regard to business organization must remain within the sphere and climate of the accountant's profession.

Intensive contact between the public accountant and organizational activities has its pros and cons. The pros are clearly stated in the papers. Messrs. Harris, Bakkenist and Kihlman mention, I believe, five or six advantages which lie in the public accountant's assessing the business organization of the firm, for which he already acts as an auditor. Let me mention three of them:

1. many firms may prefer to involve their auditors in organizational matters instead of introducing an outside consultant;
2. the accountant's firm is already *au fait* with the firm's organization and knows the staff;
3. the public accountant can take care of the follow up of a proposed re-organization, which so far has always proved a weak point when outside management consultants are called in.

As to the cons, the problems, there is first the question to what extent concern with the business organization may endanger the objectivity of the public accountant's work in the event of his combining the functions of auditor and adviser on organizational matters. Though admitting that a certain conflict is possible in principle, none of the participants are very much afraid about conflict between these functions in practice.

An important problem seems to be the fact that organization experts in the service of an accountant's firm cannot become partners, unless they have passed the accountant's examination. This, added to the situation that, in the Netherlands, the rules and regulations of the profession lay down the partners' joint responsibility to the accountancy body for each other's work, makes Mr. Bakkenist think that the development of a management consultant department for giving advice with respect to the rest of the organization of an enterprise, may prove to be a transitory phenomenon.

However, most of the participants in the discussion do not completely agree with Mr. Bakkenist about this.

As a difficulty in the way of extending the public accountant's activities to the business organization, the extent to which there are differences of psychological attitudes as between auditing financial statements and accounts on the one hand, and assessing the organization of a firm on the other. Almost all the members think that as long as the accountant's activities remain within the *advisory* field, differences in psychological attitude do not count for much. When there is a management consultant department in a public accountant's office, this may lead to a natural selection on the basis of differences in character and personality.

Next, the very topical case of electronic accounting. All of us are of the opinion that there exists a very important task for the public accountant as an adviser on electronic data processing equipment. In the near future the development of electronic data processing will have a far-reaching effect on the accounting and administrative organization of the enterprises and it is in the accountants' own interest to maintain their traditional function and role as advisers on office equipment. And almost all of us think that if they study and follow the new techniques intensively, they can certainly be reliable advisers in this field on behalf of top-management.

The task which eventually has to be performed by the accountants' organizations in the different countries with regard to the growing significance of the business organization for the business community, for instance with respect to the education for the profession, has not been intensively discussed. This does not lie along our path, I believe.

The purpose of our discussions was primarily to make us all conscious of the different aspects of an extension of the public accountant's activities in the field of business organization. However, I will end my summary by reading to you an observation by Mr. Proshan, which he sent to the panel members some time ago and which, I believe, has found some resonance in our discussion. He says:

'In conclusion, it may be stated that economic developments in commerce and industry are forcing the public accountant into the field of business organization, and it is for the profession to decide whether it will drift, without leadership, into this new activity, or whether it will chart such a course as will ensure the maximum benefit to the economic society in which our profession plays its not unimportant part.'

Mr. Chairman, with this my summary has come to an end.

CHAIRMAN:

Ladies and Gentlemen, This afternoon, I think, we have heard a most interesting discussion and I am sure that you want me to ask Mr. Orreby to thank the members of the panel most sincerely for the contribution they have made to the success of this congress.

Vice-chairman, MR. ERIC ORREBY (Sweden)

Mr. Chairman, Ladies and Gentlemen, In accordance with the procedure at these sessions, I have now been given the opportunity and the privilege of addressing a few words to the members of the panel. And what could those words be but expressions of gratitude? Most of us have had the opportunity of reading well in advance the interesting papers prepared for the sessions by eminent colleagues from different parts of the world. We had therefore every reason to expect a stimulating discussion to-day, and I am glad to be able to say that our expectations most certainly were not unfounded. The papers and the summary ably presented to us by the rapporteur of this session, Mr. Richard, have definitely been the means of raising interesting and important questions, and under the skilful guidance of the discussion leader, Mr. Reinoud, those questions have been efficiently dealt with by all members of the panel. I feel convinced that all these contributions will prove to be of great importance in our endeavour for the furtherance of our profession. And I do know that I am speaking on behalf of all colleagues present when I now express the sincere gratitude of this house to the members of this panel.

Thank you.

CHAIRMAN:

Ladies and Gentlemen, I shall now ask Mr. O'Connell to close the proceedings.

Vice-chairman, MR. B. W. S. O'CONNELL (South Rhodesia)

Ladies and Gentlemen, Our time unfortunately has passed. How dearly I would have loved to have added the last words to some of these arguments. There is so much that could be said on this subject, but our time has come to an end. It remains for me, before bringing the session to a close, to thank Prof. Wimble on behalf of you all for acting as chairman of this session.

Ladies and Gentlemen, the session is now closed.

THE INTERNAL AUDITOR

Afternoon session: Wednesday, 11th September 1957

Papers by: page

Chairman:	WP. F. C. J. Busch, Germany
Vice-chairmen:	G. H. L. Davies, B. Com., F. P. A. N.Z., F. S. A. A. New Zealand Federico Rioseco, Mexico C. J. Idman, Finland
Panel members:	
Discussion leader:	B. Smallpeice, B. Com., A.C.A. *Institute of Chartered Accountants in England and Wales*
Rapporteur and author of a paper:	W. A. Walker, C.P.A. *Controllers Institute of America*
Authors of papers:	R. A. Irish, F.C.A. (Aust.) *The Institute of Chartered Accountants in Australia*
	L. G. Macpherson, F.C.A. (Canada) *Canadian Institute of Chartered Accountants*
	Ernest Sinnott, F.I.M.T.A., F.S.A.A. *Institute of Municipal Treasurers and Accountants, U.K.*
	W. N. A. F. H. Stokvis *Nederlands Instituut van Accountants*
Other members of the panel:	W. R. Davies *The Institute of Internal Auditors, U.S.A.*
	Børge Hansen *Foreningen af Statsautoriserede Revisorer, Denmark*

PAPER

by

W. A. WALKER, C.P.A.

Controllers Institute of America

A complete coverage of all of the important phases of such a broad subject as the 'Internal Auditor' would take considerably more space than can be devoted to a paper of this type. There are, however, certain of the more important facets of the internal auditor's work and objectives which I should like to cover in some detail.

Objectives—in Brief

A practical guiding policy for the operation of an internal audit staff can be condensed into a very short set of objectives which may well be adopted by any company:

1. determination that all procedures involved in the recording and physical handling of all or any of a company's business are such that a minimum possibility of loss exists, considering also the cost of providing protection, and

2. determination by test that such procedures are properly applied so that a company's assets, liabilities, income, and expense are properly accounted for; that value is received for expenditures; and that collectible income to which the company is entitled is received;

3. determination of the extent of compliance with established rules and policies of the company.

Relation of Internal Auditing to Management

Since internal auditing is basically the auditing of internal affairs or the policies and procedures adopted by management, the auditing approach must be harmonious with the viewpoint of management.

It is only when management sits for the most part in the 'ivory tower' and lays down policies and observes results from pieces of paper that 'management by exception' becomes a necessity, since the details are so voluminous that they cannot all be viewed by management. It is then that management needs a group which can sift the chaff from the wheat and let them know where the points of special interest are in their companies. When speaking of 'management by exception' it is meant those departures which are exceptionally good and deserve the commendation of top management, as well as those which are departures from management's policies and procedures or good sound business practices. These latter need to be called to management's attention for correction.

Probably the most widely accepted reason in the minds of top management in the majority of companies for the existence of an Internal Audit Division is for verification, the assurance that the figures presented to them on financial and operating statements are reasonably correct and that there are no material irregularities in the accounts. However, while verification is necessary and is a primary reason for the existence of an Audit Division, organizations which limit their audit staffs to this function alone are certainly not deriving the full benefits which may be had from their staffs. It is the suggestions for improvement developed by the auditors while engaged in their verification work which permit us to sell management the principle that an Audit Division can be a definite and positive factor in the search for improvement, rather than merely of negative benefit by attesting to the correctness of figures.

Management should have the definite knowledge and feeling that the work of the internal auditors is being done for their benefit and that it is their right arm sorting out for them those points which need their administrative action. By management, in this connection, it is meant management at all levels, including the Board of Directors, the President, Vice Presidents, Plant Superintendents, Plant Accountants, Foremen, Department Heads, etc. All these people should feel that the job is being done for them, not that they are being audited. This is a 'must' in order to create a successful internal auditing organization. For it is only by utilization of the auditor's findings in order to correct or improve conditions that the work of the internal auditor is justified. Without the utilization of these findings, he has wasted his time. Because a great majority of these findings for improvement will be of a character which will not warrant action by the President or Board of Directors, but should be handled at lower levels, this utilization will come about through the acceptance by management at these lower levels of the recommendations of the auditors. Accordingly, it behooves the auditor to gain this acceptance in order that this work may be utilized and may be profitable.

Acceptance must not be gained by merely overlooking those matters which may engender controversy or by creating a cordial feeling toward the auditor by reason of the fact that the auditor never causes any trouble since all the audit reports are written with a whitewash brush. To reiterate, acceptance must not be gained in that way; a mutual feeling must be created by which both the auditor and the person being audited feel that they are working together to enhance the company's profits to the greatest possible extent. The person being audited must have a heartfelt feeling that the auditor is trying to help him disclose those conditions within his jurisdiction which he wants to know, so that he can get his work in the shape he would like to see it. He must not feel that the auditor is out to 'get him'. It is up to the auditor to see that every person gets that understanding of his attitude. Accordingly, his attitude must be just that. The auditor cannot expect the other fellow to get that sort of feeling toward him if, in his mind, he gloats over 'getting' someone, rather than feeling merely a justifiable satisfaction in having helped the supervisor. The auditor's innermost feelings will be reflected in his attitude. His attitude will be reflected in the acceptance. The acceptance will be reflected in the utilization of the findings and, accordingly, govern the success or failure of the audit program.

The auditor's viewpoint, then, must be helpful, not critical. There are several definite things which the auditor must do to maintain this viewpoint. In the first place, it is very essential that the auditor keep the faith with local and lower levels of management. In other words, each item of an audit must be frankly discussed with the immediate supervisor of that function before it is discussed in any way with his superiors. He should be given the opportunity to make such comments as he may wish, either in support of the present practice, or to straighten out the auditor on certain phases which may be pertinent, or to agree with the auditor and outline the general principles which he will employ to improve the situation. This is very important in order that no level of management will feel that the auditor is going over his head.

It is a sales job, and it is therefore necessary that the auditor's constructive remarks be presented in such a fashion that they will be accepted as helpful suggestions. It is necessary that all supervisory personnel know in so many words that the audit staff is not a 'gestapo' and, subsequently, that they can see for themselves, day in and day out, that the members of the audit staff do not consider themselves as a 'gestapo'.

Implementing the Internal Audit Program

In order to accomplish the objectives set forth above, it is essential that top management establish a clear understanding throughout the company that the audit staff has full and free access to all departments and records of the company and that there are no restrictions on its audit activities. It is essential to providing proper service to management that auditing be operated as a staff function as distinguished from a line function. By this is meant:

1. Auditing is not a substitute for management. The auditors have no authority to set up procedures, make policies, or direct or instruct anyone as to how he should conduct his activities. Auditing is a purely staff function of co-ordinating, investigating, and advising. It is the auditor's function to determine whether the company procedures and good accounting practices are in effect and whether the practices in effect are adequate to provide proper internal control for the company.

2. The audit staff should not be used for special line assignments not connected with the auditing function. To do this sets a precedent which sometimes leads to the use of auditors as fill-ins for line absentees and results in inadequate audit coverage.

3. The auditor should not be used as a glorified line clerk. In other words, routine checking which is performed on a day by day, week by week, or any other periodic basis in connection with the checking of accounts payable vouchers, etc., is a part of the line function, and it is the responsibility of the line supervisor to provide adequate assurance that the work turned out is accurate. This type of work does not deserve the name of auditing. It is merely checking

and should not be a part of an internal staff function. This much abused concept of auditing is one which tends to weaken the function of internal auditing staff in many companies.

Relative to the technique of internal auditing, there are various methods of approach and types of coverage which should be made in order that the Internal Audit Division can be of the greatest possible service to management, consistent with maintaining the staff at a reasonable cost.

In the first place, it is imperative that top management understand that the Audit Division cannot possibly cover any great percentage of the matters subject to audit scrutiny in any given year, assuming, of course, that the Internal Audit Division works, as it must, with an intensive, comprehensive, searching coverage. The viewpoint, that the analysis of a particular subject, to be beneficial to management, must be complete, should be emphasized. That is one of the main differences between an audit of a function performed by the Internal Audit Division and the coverage given by the public accounting firm to any particular function in the course of a balance sheet audit.

In the second place, an internal audit done for the benefit of management cannot be a check list type of audit, but must be one in which the auditor goes in with a general program for a known purpose and uses all the ingenuity, imagination, and ability that he can command to develop improvements which he would want to see in effect if it were the money out of his own pocket with which he was dealing. Because of the need for exhaustive investigation, it has been found that, in general, a more productive survey is gained by narrowing the scope of the review and performing what is called a functional audit, as compared with a responsibility audit. A responsibility audit is one which covers, in a general way, all the matters within the jurisdiction of a particular department. Because of the breadth of functions usually embraced in such an audit, it is virtually impossible to do more than to touch upon various points; whereas, in a functional audit, the auditors concentrate on particular points within a responsibility and dig into them, leaving no stone unturned. However, in the performance of a functional audit, intensive investigation does not comprehend coverage of all the details of clerical accuracy. Clerical accuracy is, as previously stated, the responsibility of line management. However, the audit must ascertain in detail whether or not the policies of the company and sound business practices are being adhered to, that the procedures adequately furnish complete internal control and protection, that revenue is fully protected, and that costs are consistent with proper control and are at a minimum. In the audit of any function, a certain amount of test checking of details must be done. If, in doing that, an exorbitant number of clerical errors are encountered, these errors are not important in themselves but merely point to another principle which is that adequate control over accuracy is not present. In order that the Audit Supervisor may perform the most helpful service to management, it is necessary that he have a rather broad and thorough acquaintanceship with all phases of the company's business, so that in the selection of the functions which the Audit Division will have the manpower to audit, the most productive and most vital matters will be done first. Therefore, he should attempt to cover those matters where lack of control can, and will, result in an actual loss of money as compared with those audits which pertain merely to distribution accounting.

Thirdly, the Audit Division does not confine itself solely to the Accounting Department, or Treasury Department, but makes itself available to any department for examination of any function in which the protection of assets, revenue, or costs is involved. This includes, therefore, virtually everything which the company does, including the work of the Sales Department, Operating Department, Purchasing Department, Treasury Department, Production Planning Department, etc. We believe that the greatest benefit from the audit is achieved if the auditor follows all the processes connected with a function of a business straight through from beginning to end without limitation as to the crossing of departmental lines. It is only in this way that a complete conception of the internal control over the subject as a whole can be observed and weaknesses or duplication detected. This being the case, the auditor must not forget, however, that he is not an industrial engineer, a management engineer, a metallurgist, an industrial relations expert, or the president of the company. Few practices have gotten the auditor into more hot water, and justifiably so, than that of pretending to know more about the technical phase of a subject than the technician himself. The auditor must try to arrive at a delicate balance which permits him to examine and render help in any department having a bearing on the financial status of the corporation while, at the same time, confining himself to those matters on which he can render sound opinions. An auditor is essentially a fact-finding examiner, and the judgment is up to the appropriate management group.

Position of the Audit Staff in the Company Organization

A great deal of discussion has transpired, and more will ensue on this subject and we predict that no firm answer acceptable to all will be determined. In our opinion, as long as the program has the support of the chief administrative officer or body along the lines set forth in the preceding paragraphs, the internal audit function can report to any member of management under whom the audit program can work smoothly and efficiently with support from all segments of management. In certain companies, depending upon the personalities involved or the over-all organizational structure, this may be the President, a Vice President, the Controller, the Treasurer, or (as stated in our Institute of Internal Auditors' Statement of Responsibilities of the Internal Auditor) 'to any officer of sufficient rank as will assure adequate consideration and action on the findings and recommendations'.

Some writers have advocated that the internal auditors should report directly to the board of directors. Although this may be feasible in some organizations, in our opinion it is not practical in most cases because we believe internal auditing can be most effective as a tool in the hands of active management.

The Auditor himself

With all his effort to perform a constructive service and to sell it, the auditor must maintain his own independence of thinking and exploration. He cannot permit his boss to dictate to him what his thoughts should be. This is another selling job. He should try to arrive at the facts and, after careful consideration, present these facts in such a manner that, even though they may be in conflict with present company polices or thinking, they will be accepted and given the proper consideration due them; since, by the method of presentation, they are obviously the sincere and considered viewpoint of the auditor, presented for what he believes is for the best interest of the company. There is no set rule as to how this independence should be accomplished organizationally, but regardless of the auditor's position on the organization chart, there is only one way of achieving independence, and that is by being independent.

The most important requirement of an auditor is that he use good common sense. Possessing this characteristic, an auditor can examine and analyze conditions and offer constructive suggestions to line supervision, even though they have been daily concerned for years with their functions and admittedly know more about them.

Effectiveness of the Audit Division

The value of an internal audit staff cannot be measured in dollars and cents alone; for it is not possible to set down a column of figures which represents the savings made by the Audit Division and balance them against another group of figures which represents the cost of the Audit Division.

Management will judge the effectiveness of the Audit Division on the quality of the report rendered and the effect of the action taken.

The report must indicate the action that has been taken or planned, and it should be a part of the Audit Division's function to follow up, within a reasonable time, to see that line management has made the corrections indicated.

Another service that the Audit Division should perform is the training and supplying of men qualified to accept responsibilities and, with the background of management's viewpoint, to assume executive positions in the various functions throughout the corporation. Men in the Audit Division will get a complete education as to the company's policies and how these policies tie together for a smoothly operating business. It should be the ambition of the Audit Supervisor to be constantly losing his best men to other departments of the business, where training of this type is needed to fill executive positions. Not only will this tend to create an organization of men with broad vision, but it will enable the Audit Division to maintain a staff of men of the caliber needed to do the job at hand because they know what opportunity exists for a job well done.

Relation to Public Accountants

Normally, the audits performed by the public accountant take the form of a balance sheet audit requiring, principally, the verification of the assets and liabilities as of a certain date and such analysis of the income statement as will enable the auditor to certify that they have been stated properly. In brief, the audit approach of the independent public accountant is to establish accuracy of accounts, account by account, while the internal auditor's approach is department by department, or function by function, and to establish that good business practices are in effect in each. Thus, it is apparent that the work of the two need not conflict, because basic approach and emphasis are different.

The greater portion of written matter devoted to auditing has been directed to the procedures for Balance Sheet audits.

In other words, contemporary literature on auditing has been concentrated largely from the viewpoint of the independent public accountant. Indeed, many of the articles, etc., purporting to address themselves to the subject of internal auditing have been actually more applicable to the work of the public accountants. This has been true because many persons, whose experience has been in public accounting, found themselves commissioned by their companies to establish and maintain internal audit programs, and in the absence of data on the most recent concepts of internal auditing as compared with public accounting, have not, in all cases, eliminated the duties of the public accountants from their programs.

In fact, we have heard internal auditors in some companies cite as an accomplishment the fact that the work performed by their staff during the past year reduced the fee of the company's public accountants by a significant sum. In our opinion, this admission, or assertion, is a definite indication of a lack of appreciation of the scope and responsibilities of the internal auditor. The activities of the internal auditor are, in the main, so divorced from the usual procedures of the public accountant that, if the internal auditor takes the time for such work, either (1) he is omitting the performance of audits which fall within his peculiar province and which would be of considerable benefit to the company, or (2) he is overstaffed.

Much has been written and said about coordination and cooperation between the external and internal auditor, but it boils down principally to this:

1. Each must stay out of the other's road, for although the emphasis varies, use of the same records is sometimes necessary. Accordingly, their audit time schedules should be so correlated as not to interfere with each other's programs and not to burden the line personnel who prepare and use the records.

2. The coverage of the internal auditor may reduce the detail work necessary to satisfy the external auditor of the existence of adequate internal control.

Standards for Internal Auditing

For years the preponderance of accounting literature has set forth auditing 'procedures' for various activities. Recently, however, our public accounting profession has attempted to distinguish between 'auditing procedures' and 'auditing standards' and has outlined certain standards particularly applicable to their work.

In any endeavor, such as auditing, in which no objective measurements are possible, such standards are necessarily of a very abstract character. Nevertheless, there are some standards of performance against which the activities of an internal auditing staff can be compared in a general way, as follows:

1. The staff must have a 'professional approach' to the task—with a spirit of complete helpfulness—without a thought of destructive criticism—and, above all, with the attitude that they are professional auditors and not detectives.

2. All thinking members of management, at every level, must wholeheartedly accept the audit staff as their right arm. Only adherence to all internal auditing standards by all members of the staff will win and hold such acceptance.

3. The auditor's factual data must be meticulously correct. Almost superhuman accuracy is expected and demanded of the auditor. He cannot be too careful. He must check his facts and have them carefully rechecked. The natural tendency of the groups under audit is to concentrate to such an extent on discussion of any error committed by the auditor that often the constructive effect of the balance of the audit findings is nullified.

4. The auditor must be qualified by education, training, experience, and tact to deal with the company executives in a manner which will engender their respect and assure proper consideration of his recommendations.

5. The auditor must not be a theorist. He must know good theory, but, primarily, he must view matters as a practical businessman. His recommendations must be workable and always reflect good business judgment.

6. The staff must have the degree of independence of thought and action previously commented upon, while still being in harmony with the viewpoint of management.

7. His reports must be interesting, constructive, easily understandable, generally well prepared, and, most important of all, must be unobtrusively forceful and convincing, with the effect that they get action.

8. The programming and planning of audits must be timely; show evidence of careful selection of most important and productive subject matter; result in no duplication with other staffs, other audits, or the public accountants; and must not waste staff and company time on nonessential matters.

9. The auditors should review all the significant control points and be thoroughly familiar with the internal control procedures covering all important functions. They must persistently work for the ultimate in controls that can be achieved at a cost consistent with the risks involved.

10. The auditor must be thoroughly discreet. No loose talk, gossip, or tale-telling can be a part of any auditor's make-up. Further, his reporting must be complete and unbiased, with no attempts to glorify the auditor whether at another's expense or not.

PAPER

by

R. A. IRISH, F.C.A. (AUST.)

The Institute of Chartered Accountants in Australia

Internal auditing is in reality an atavistic movement, for the embryo of the modern auditing profession emerged in bygone centuries when the auditor was a trusted employee of the master. The awakening of industry in the nineteenth century and the concomitant development of the limited liability company led the independent external audit to the fore, but the subsequent growth and increasing complexity of business have gradually turned the clock back. For reasons of cost and physical capacity alone there has been an advantageous and increasing reversion to the original type of auditor.

It is important to register that internal auditing first reappeared as an adjunct to the outside audit. Wherever it is introduced to an enterprise, there tends to be an initial emphasis in this direction. It has come to be appreciated, however, that internal audit can provide a constructive as well as a protective service, an advance in thought which lifts the functions far above mere clerical routine.

The Functions of the Internal Auditor

The external auditor's duties and responsibilities are defined by statute, regulation or contract, and are often interpreted in judgments of the Courts. He is legally responsible to his client but professionally has at least a moral obligation to others who may rely upon his report. The extent of his functions depends primarily upon his legal commitment, but the central objective is the verification of the financial statements. In this objective, legality and honesty are his prime concerns.

For internal audit there are no publicly defined boundaries and each business unit may accommodate it within its framework as it wills. There is rather less emphasis on the verification of financial statements and much more on the efficiency of internal procedures, the effectiveness of designed controls, and the economy of both. It will also have regard to protection against misappropriation whereas external audit is rather more strongly directed against falsity in the published financial statements.

Ideally, the internal auditor should be the apex of a triangle in which external audit and management are the base, with neither dominating the other. This concept of the three-way relationship upholds the place of financial audit objectives, yet expands the horizon to encompass what is generally called 'management audit'. In that form the internal audit may reach the peak of fulfilment.

Historically, the internal auditor's functions are ancillary to external audit. They are pointed in that capacity towards detailed examination of accounting and financial data and related internal control, with due stress on the end purpose of balance sheet verification by the public auditor. There is distinct benefit to the entreprise in this relationship. It minimises the cost of proving detailed clerical accuracy and enables quicker corrective action on errors or misappropriation. In controlling these situations, it allows the outside auditor to review procedures and questions of principle with more detachment and in broader perspective. Appropriate division of work between the two auditors should produce greater reliability and efficiency at a relatively lower cost.

It would be a mistake to play down the great importance of internal audit in the prevention or discovery of fraud, especially in the more petty fields of defalcation. The development of the science of internal control may be liable to create a false feeling that fraud is either impossible or must automatically be discovered. The truth is that the fear of audit is often the best preventative, but effective only if there is enough probing into detail. It is self-evident that that is most effectively done in a large-scale organisation through internal audit rather than external.

This phase of internal audit may be said to be probative and corrective. It remains to consider the directly constructive functions which can support management and promote good organisation.

Personal supervision is the most fundamental and effective form of control, yet expansion of any undertaking of necessity draws top management more and more away from detail. It leads to delegation of authority to subsidiary levels of management and, because personal supervision of all detail from the top is impossible, there follows a more precise definition of organisation, procedures and allied controls. Top management must then have a ticker-tape intelligence service which reports how its requirements are being met, whether there have been unauthorised deviations, and where standards of performance may be improved.

This is the area where the internal auditor's special training and qualifications and his ready access to detail have been harnessed with great benefit to management. It has extended his routine auditing functions to include evaluation of business policies, plans, records, procedures, controls and performance, sometimes moving outside the ambit of accounting and finance to physical operation. The internal auditor thus acts on management's behalf to sift the detail of daily operational efficiency and so to identify those features needing executive review, judgment, and decision.

Viewed in their highest concept, the dual functions give the internal auditor a secondary responsibility to the proprietors. In one, he is accountable through the external auditor, in the other through management. This ability to fulfil this concept of duty rests on two important principles:

a. That the internal audit is separate and distinct from internal check.

b. That the internal auditor has no positive management functions.

Internal control has a wider connotation than internal check and is generally held to embrace internal audit. However, internal audit has a relationship to internal control which is quite different from other controls or checks.

Internal control signifies primarily a process of check and cross-check among those who execute positive accounting operations, however remote their actions may be from the physical entry of the financial books. Employees so involved have a direct responsibility for appropriate skill and for complete honesty and accuracy which should never be lessened because internal or external audit is imposed.

Audit of any kind has a judicial flavour which calls for complete detachment of mind. It is something to be done after the event, not while it is taking shape. Control must be regarded as preventive, whereas audit is corrective, and the functions and responsibilities of each should be distinguished clearly. Therefore, it is probably best if internal audit is complementary to, but not directly part of internal control.

For a similar reason, the internal auditor should not have active management functions. His task of unprejudiced investigation and appraisal must suffer if he is charged with executive duties. He must be advisory rather than operational.

Relationship to the External Auditor

The public auditor's legal and moral responsibility to his client cannot be delegated to an internal auditor. In accepting the engagement he pledges his skill, care and integrity to produce an honest, well-founded opinion. If he falls short, his reputation suffers and at least some of his potential income growth is affected. This may be more serious in the long run than any legal penalty he might incur.

Contemporary auditing practice, evolved to meet the needs of modern business, places great reliance on the effectiveness of internal control. Excursions into detail are made by the public auditor to decide whether internal control is dependable in preventing or discovering errors or fraud. If reliable internal control is subject to internal audit, in the true sense of financial audit, the external auditor's work may be modified or sometimes supplanted —but it follows that both forms of audit should work in harmony.

Although a method of coordination is essential, it cannot be overlooked that the internal auditor is an employee, and management is entitled to say what his duties shall comprise. It is perfectly entitled to restrict his work or to extend it to other fields immaterial to the financial audit. In a sense, such decisions do not matter so long as the public auditor knows what the internal auditor is to do and how he is doing it. The external audit must always be adapted to the facts of a given case; if internal audit is any way ineffective for his purpose, the external auditor must take up the slack.

Effective coordination is practicable only if the external auditor is satisfied as to the competence of the internal audit staff and that its status and accountability within the organisation ensure integrity of results.

As the internal auditor is an employee, the public auditor cannot have any direct or absolute jurisdiction over him, but a de facto jurisdiction may be built if a proper form of coordinated relationship is organised with formal management approval.

Thus, the external auditor should participate in planning the internal audit programme, and management should preferably require his unreserved approval of its final form. Naturally, no changes should be made without his prior approval. It will be best if the two auditors settle the scope of the work and its subsequent execution as between themselves. This liaison bears upon the financial audit and does not prevent management imposing further duties for its own purposes.

To avoid purposeless duplication of audit work, the internal auditor must keep full and proper working papers carefully filed, and the external auditor must have a right of free access to all of them. He should also receive direct and, as of right, an unexpurgated copy of every internal audit report. Given this information and knowing the prescribed programme, he can judge how far his own procedures may be varied justifiably.

Through this method of alliance, the public auditor is placed in a position of psychological seniority; the internal auditor is impressed more indelibly with the duty he must feel towards him and the significance of the work he is doing. If the internal auditor knows he has the backing and co-operation of the public auditor and is given direct access to him, he will have an added desire to carry out his functions and report his findings fearlessly. The strength of the public auditor will reflect itself in the internal auditor.

The importance of conveying reports directly to the public auditor cannot be minimised, because a major defect in the relationship between the two parties is the absense of financial or legal responsibility imposed personally on the internal auditor. The public auditor is therefore dependent solely upon the moral integrity, and sometimes the courage, of the staff auditor, though he himself carries such responsibilities to the proprietors.

The public status of internal auditors would be greatly strengthened if some way of penalising a breach of duty could be found. It is questionable whether any Institute could do this successfully, except to the extent of disciplinary action for blatant dishonesty or fraud, but that is poor solace to the external auditor and leaves untouched the deeper problem of failing to exercise a proper standard of care and skill.

A system of licensing under appropriate legislation might have some value in so far as the licensee might lose his occupation for serious breach of duty in the form of unskilful or negligent work. As against that, practical experience shows the difficulty of proving culpability conclusively.

Doubtless the best answer lies (as it generally does in a profession) in the voluntary advancement of standards through specialist Institutes. From them we should expect high codes of performance to be inculcated and perhaps they might find a way of protecting members who face the alternative of smothering conscience or losing employment.

Relationship to Management

The internal auditor's functions are such that he must be able to act without fear or favour. His position must be so defined that he will not be pilloried if he speaks unpalatable truths.

Superficially at least, this would seem to demand he be given some element of independence.

It seems idle to use the term 'independence' as between employer and employee, nor am I convinced that alleged independence, whether in internal or external audit, is a conclusive force which guarantees impartiality and right moral behaviour. At best it is a psychological supporter for the more basic qualities of unswerving integrity and the will to do what is right regardless of the personal consequences.

These basic qualities will be fortified if management has the wisdom to give complete trust and support to internal audit activities and to couple that with a status which makes it independent of those whose work is audited. Without these the whole exercise is futile.

Internal audit is top management's medium for objective review of business controls and performance. It is a process of voluntary self-analysis; it is effective only if it is impersonal and realistic. In this specific field it is the meeting point between upper and lower management, the nerve centre for the top executive judgments. Confidence and support will flow strongly to the internal auditor if he proves impartial, factual, reliable, and appreciative of practical business operation.

Success in this fundamental objective will depend on clear definition at the outset of his place in the organisation. The scope of his responsibilities must be specified with precision and he must be kept advised of all management policies and decisions. He must have a status which entitles him to demand information from any source and which places him outside departmental influence, though this is not to say his activities may not be criticised from down the line. He must therefore be accountable only to the highest strata of management. Obviously, he must have no active managerial responsibility and no direct authority over any section of the undertaking other than his own department. Care must be taken that his duties are not incompatible with the objectivity underlying his functions.

Such a status may place him in a seemingly impregnable position, but abuse of the status can nullify the envisaged benefits. The department must not be allowed to operate as a secret service or detective force which could undermine the loyalty and morale of staff in general or the authority of under-management. The personal qualities of the internal auditor are the best guardian against abuse.

There seems to be a tendency to limit the so-called 'management audit' to an appraisal of procedures and controls and of performance in each sphere, but the internal auditor may have considerable constructive value in what might be termed the 'economics' of the particular business. To illustrate, his review of sales may lead him to study the effect on finances of variations in the terms of certain types of sale and so produce better financial returns from available funds. He may note areas where savings may be possible through changed methods or techniques. His review of bad debts may induce an analysis of credit policy to eliminate unprofitable risks. Again, he may suggest changes in reports or statistics which will more quickly highlight harmful tendencies. In many such ways he may be the vehicle to initiate ideas for improvements, but while this may be fostered it should not obscure the basic functions.

Likewise, internal audit should never become a super-imposed top management to criticise the operational top management's decisions. Successful business activity is still a product of judgment, and its achievement is gauged by the degree of profit and financial strength which results. The necessity for judgment implies that the element of risk is present, and maximum business development comes basically from a readiness to take calculated risks. If there is to be a studied post-mortem on such judgments initiative will be killed and there will be uncertainty of decision or disinclination to make one, which so often is the root of failure. There can be no advantage in such an inquisition. The position is different if top management requests an analysis of the reasons why judgment proved mistaken. The process then meets the principle of audit for management, not of management.

The manner of reporting to management is a crucial phase of the relationship. A busy executive has no time to study pointless detail and must expect reports to give him the essence of a matter with a minimum of words. This will often mean that the internal auditor has to be selective, an exercise to be practised with scrupulous fairness and acute appreciation of the relative materiality in the data. It will be helpful if he can crystallise his findings into recommendations and state how they may best be implemented. In conference, he can supplement the essence with detail, if detail is called for.

Obsession with the virtues of management audit must not submerge the protective financial auditing function. In that field there is a different relationship to management and especially where the work interlocks with external audit. The function may involve disagreement with the top executive on accounting treatment of certain items. The task is no easier if a close accord of minds has developed in the constructive efforts of the broader phases of management. The problem may be eased if his preliminary charter specifies firmly the course of duty in such cases, for worthwhile management will never resent an honest performance of duty.

The Internal Auditor's Qualifications

The ideal concept of internal auditing can be met only by a person with exceptional qualities and qualifications. The traditions behind his functions demand complete trustworthiness and integrity, but these must go hand in hand with the skill which is born of study, training and experience.

At the foundation he must place a sound knowledge of the principles and methods of general accounting and auditing, and demonstrate it by passing examinations of a reputable accountancy body. However, internal auditing is subtly but distinctly different from external auditing, and particularly so when it veers into management audits. The basic knowledge of accounting and auditing must be built on by specialised study of such things as control systems, office procedures, production and distribution problems, and internal auditing techniques. The examinations of a recognised body of internal auditors are probably the best test of this knowledge.

Theory is not self-sufficient qualification and practical training is essential. The question which follows is whether this is best secured in a public auditor's office or in the undertaking itself. The best answer would appear to be a combination of both.

Training in a professional office may be expected to yield a wider experience of accounting and auditing. It should stimulate an appreciation and acceptance of personal responsibility. It should bring out a critical and judicial attitude to accounting facts and should engender basic honesty and courage in holding to a well-formed opinion.

The internal auditor trained only in the particular undertaking should have at the outset a more profound understanding of its ramifications and problems but there is danger in the narrower outlook, in the lack of experience of other methods, and in the closer association with other employees. The net result may be comparatively ineffective work.

The problem of practical training for this specialised activity needs definite attention. The main recruiting ground to date has probably been the professional offices, but this is a somewhat negative approach to the present and future problem. Industry will cry out for more and more people of high executive calibre for this work, but they will not be there when wanted unless they are recruited and trained beforehand. The initial selection of recruits should look past mere clerical ability to the capacity for higher functions. The training in the business may be followed at an early stage by a specific period of engagement in the external auditor's office. The important thing is that whatever is done shall be a planned course to provide the essential equipment.

Because the functions must involve a fair degree of repetitious detailed work, it is all the more essential that he should be an active member of a body of internal auditors. Through this medium he will have a greater opening for exchange of ideas, he will be more self-critical, and he will keep on top of developments in his profession. A spirit of research and a willingness to look at new ideas round off the technical equipment he must have.

The Future

Auditing, in its widest sense, continues to undergo a process of evolution, a process which is inescapable if the advancing needs of large-scale business are to be serviced adequately. The evolution must be soundly conceived because auditing is the key to confidence in commercial accounting, and our economic system could not function without that basis of confidence and trust.

The size and spread of activity in so many businesses have led the external auditor more and more away from the old form of detailed audit. His attentions go more to matters of policy and principle and I foresee this becoming firmly implanted as his true role. Such a development is only possible if there is a marriage of internal audit functions which will take care of detailed accuracy and protection against staff dishonesty, but the internal auditor will have a continually expanding future as management appreciates that he, out of all executives, is best equipped to audit for management. It is a brilliant future, attainable if deserved.

PAPER

by

L. G. MACPHERSON, F.C.A. (CANADA)

Canadian Institute of Chartered Accountants

I. The Nature of Internal Auditing

As a recognizable business function, internal auditing is a very modern development. While its roots reach back at least to the efforts of feudal lords to confirm the accounts of their agents, the form and status of internal auditing received their first public recognition upon incorporation of the Institute of Internal Auditors in New York in 1941.

Subsequent developments in internal auditing have been so rapid that it is difficult today to mark its boundaries. Some writers seem to suggest that internal auditing embraces the whole field of business operation, while some cautiously believe that it should be confined to the traditional auditing function.

A reasonable approach to the nature of internal auditing emphasizes the two aspects of protection and verification, to which a third, the advisory function, is often added.

The importance of verification as the earliest function of the company-employed auditor is suggested by the work of the nineteenth century railway auditor who checked ticket agents' sales reports and stocks of tickets, and by the system of bank inspection which has long been a significant factor in branch banking. The internal auditing of branch banks has developed to such a highly efficient operation that shareholders' auditors of Canadian banks are able to devote most of their attention to head office records. An examination of the very large branches and possibly a few smaller branches, together with the work of the bank inspection staff, provides an adequate review of branch affairs.

The function of protection is inseparable from the function of verification unless the latter is looked upon merely as a matter of clerical proof of accuracy. Checking, however, is not carried on for its own sake, but for the results that it will help to obtain, and the chief of these is that of safeguarding the company's assets and, in a broader sense, their proper use and disposition.

Here we have a natural environment for great expansion of the internal auditor's responsibilities, since the broad protective function, embracing much more than accounting accuracy, may reach out to every part of the business operation.

The protective activities in any enterprise are related to the problems of planning, organization and methods. Governmental bodies have established organization and methods sections to perform important functions of investigation, consultation, planning and advice. Similar sections have been set up as methods divisions in some firms of public accountants. Industry relies for this service not only upon its executive officers but also upon external management consultants.

The developments which have been traced present a number of questions concerning the function and status of the internal auditor, including his status within the company, the desirable degree of independence, the scope of his duties and responsibilities, and the relations of the internal auditor to the external auditor. These questions have all received such able attention at conferences and in the literature of internal auditing, that one might think that any further comments would reflect either temerity or brilliance. The task, however, has been undertaken in the humble belief that discussion of auditing and accounting subjects at an international congress is bound to advance mutual understanding of an increasingly complex field, and to that end neither an excess of courage nor the talents of a genius need be sought.

II. Status and Independence

So much has been said and written on the subject of the auditor's independence that I shall direct only a few remarks to this topic. Independence is relative, not absolute. It is a function of the mental attitude of the individual concerned, influenced probably by his personal economic situation and the social relationships involved.

Professional independence is such an important attribute of public accounting that the idea of independence carries over inevitably into the theory of internal auditing. The internal auditor cannot, however, attain the degree of independence in his operations that is characteristic of the shareholders' auditor. Top management would surely be in an unenviable position if a company employee, located somewhat lower on the organization chart, reported independently to the shareholders. The unlucky employee designated as internal auditor in such an arrangement would find his position wholly untenable unless he confined his attention strictly to routine matters. Soon the conclusion would be reached that the more independent the internal auditor might be in his relationship to top management, the less valuable would he be to that management.

Nevertheless, a psychic independence is vital to the auditing process, and should be supported by suitable status within the organization. It is appropriate to expect, in the internal auditing, an independence with respect to audits of operations at all levels below but not at levels above the organizational status of the audit department. The degree to which the internal audit will facilitate the shareholder's audit will bear a close relationship to the internal auditor's independence of the departments subject to the internal review. In terms of general organization, this means that the audit section should not be part of the accounting department. It may well be part of the staff of the chief financial officer, if the latter is a senior executive and a member of the management committee. In terms of operations, it means that management should not allow audit staff to be substituted for accounting staff in temporary situations without recognizing the corresponding loss of independence and, in consequence, the reduction in reliance to be placed on the internal audit by the external auditor and by management itself.

In each case the external auditor tries to evaluate the independence of the internal auditor with respect to each department separately, knowing that it will vary according to the plan of organization and according to the degree to which the audit staff has actually participated in the work of the various departments by supplying temporary help, by originating entries, and so on. The significance of the internal audit as a part of the internal control will be measured to a considerable degree by this evaluation.

III. An External View of the Functions of the Internal Auditor

Some observers have made a distinction between the protective functions and the constructive functions of the internal auditor. The protective responsibilities are those related to the control of assets, authority for expenditures, adherence to established policy, and acceptability of accounts and reports while the constructive functions include the critical evaluation of policies, techniques and performance with recommendations for improvement and correction. A well developed internal audit will integrate the two types of functions, but if a choice must be made between them, the emphasis should be placed on the protective aspects, since occasional employment of the specialized services of management consultants can provide good doses of critical evaluation.

The protective functions direct the internal auditor's attention to the quality of the whole system of internal control. He should be expert in the methods of internal control, and knowledgeable as to his company's control procedures. His examinations and reports should stress the importance of the separation of operating responsibilities, custody of assets, and initiation of transactions from the recording and accounting aspects. He should be wholly familiar with the actual operation of the company's system of built-in accounting controls known generally as the system of internal check.

Where the accounting is decentralized, as in many multiple unit enterprises, an obvious need exists for constant review and direction as to consistency in the application of accounting principles. Where the company employs integrated or electronic data processing methods, accompanied perhaps by centralized accounting, a continuous familiarity with the techniques and especially with the programming in use, is essential. In every case, proficiency in procedures and methods will contribute to accounting control, and in these matters the internal auditor should be an effective influence.

The evaluation of procedures and methods often leads the internal auditor into a function similar to the systematic 'organization and methods' work already established in governmental services and in some business concerns. To a degree this is a corollary of the protective function of the auditor, since conservation of assets includes their efficient use and the prevention of fraud, but beyond a point it will absorb the time of the internal auditor at the expense of the functions which warrant his title. In many instances, organization and methods services can be provided better by external practitioners with broad experience, and many public accounting firms now have methods divisions devoted to this work.

From the viewpoint of the external auditor, any pronounced tendency on the part of the internal auditor to move from the protective function toward the advisory function and the appraisal of policy is regrettable. There is still a great need for the proof of accuracy and the application of accepted principles and policies, and the avoidance and detection of fraud and error. There is always a danger that the activities of the internal auditor will penetrate so far into the advisory or so-called constructive duties that he may be tempted to provide expert advice on the whole range of operations. He must then become an expert not only in accounting but in finance, procurement, production, warehousing, marketing, personnel administration and public relations. In other words, he would need to function as might a completely diversified management consulting group. The existence of such a superman, giving advice on every business activity would surely distress top management and alarm the consulting specialists.

The prime responsibility of internal auditing should be the maintenance of internal control. This of course includes what is called the prevention of fraud, although no absolutely fraud-proof system is likely to be devised. The position of the chief financial officer of any large company emphasizes the importance of detection and prevention of fraud. He is dependent upon the internal auditor for whatever information and sense of security he has with respect to the operation of the internal controls. The auditor who recognizes this relationship will accept not only the function of review and measurement of the application of company policy, but also the responsibility to advise and recommend with respect to defective control and the means of improvement.

IV. Significance of the Internal Audit to the Shareholders' Auditor

The shareholders' auditor must form and express his independent opinion on the annual financial statements of the company. To do so he must, amongst other things, satisfy himself as to the reliability of the accounting records. An important part of this process is the investigation of the system of internal control, including any internal audit in operation.

It is a well established principle that an external auditor may rely extensively on the work of an internal audit department if, by review and appraisal of the operations of that department, he has satisfied himself as to its effectiveness. He may, in his examination of the system of internal control, benefit from the internal auditor's knowledge of the system; he may focus his attention on parts determined by the reports and program of the internal auditor; but he must satisfy himself by tests and inquiries that things are as they seem, and that the internal controls are operating as they are supposed to do.

Audits by public accountants will never be compressed entirely into audits of internal audit departments even in the case of very large companies, although to some this might seem to be a logical result of certain current trends. There are, however, many ways in which an effective internal audit will assist the external auditor, especially in minimizing his examination and review of ordinary operations and transaction details, and to some extent in the balance sheet verifications, but these cannot eliminate the tests and examinations which are essential if he is to form an independent professional opinion on the credibility of the representations of the company's officers.

The staff of a client cannot be allocated suitably to the duties of the external auditor. The clients' staff will almost certainly lack appropriate indoctrination and training, especially where the person is not part of the internal audit staff; there is likely to be a failure to switch viewpoints; and there is a danger of conflicting loyalties. But this does not bar the use of client staff to minimize the detail work.

The internal audit staff can assist, for example, in the confirmation of receivables either by rotating the sections confirmed or by preparing the documents for mailing; they can participate in cash counts and in the observation of stock-taking procedures; and they can prepare required schedules and analyses with a skill and understanding, based on their experience as auditors, which is not likely to be found in the accounting department.

The great value of co-operation between the internal auditor and the external auditor is evident. It is almost painfully clear in some instances, where the external auditor does not share the internal auditor's technical facility in the industry. Where, for example, the external auditor is verifying stock in trade, he may find that personal contact with some products is useless, if not even dangerous, in the absence of highly specialized skill, knowledge and judgment. This may be so in the case of isotope products, wholesale drugs, gas in storage wells, pulp wood in block piles, logs in booms, and specialized electronic instruments. In some such cases there will be an understandable willingness to rely greatly on the internal auditor.

An able internal auditor will be fully informed as to his company's system of internal control and its effectiveness in operation, and this may serve to shorten the usual process of review of internal check, if he is given the opportunity of conveying his knowledge of the system to the shareholders' auditor. Shareholders' auditors who have found that the internal control questionnaire can be a tedious and sometimes exasperating device may restore their faith in its usefulness by inviting the co-operation of the internal auditor in its completion. This is to be preferred over an alternative method sometimes used, in which the internal auditor is blandly requested to supply a detailed description of the system of internal control in use. The auditor who recognizes that the control points in an extensive system may be virtually innumerable will suffer a moment of consternation before he decides that what is wanted is a complete copy of the company's procedures manual.

All of these possibilities of co-operation—in verifying cash, confirming receivables, examining stock in trade, surveying the system of internal control, and preparing working papers—present valuable opportunities, but they are secondary to the most important consequence of an internal audit insofar as its effect on the external audit is concerned. That is the possibility of greatly reducing the shareholders' auditor's attention to transaction details, freeing him to devote reasonable time to the assets and liabilities, the analysis of operations, and the appraisal of the fairness of the financial statements.

The external auditor cannot accept the work of the internal auditor as part of his own; he cannot merge the internal audit staff temporarily with and as his own; he cannot avoid responsibility for satisfying himself as to the fairness of statements simply because the internal auditor has reported his firm and clear opinion. Nevertheless, he can, by review and examination, assure himself of the attitude of independence of the internal auditor at each level of operation. He can and should review the internal auditors' completed program of work and his reports; and, if conditions are favourable, he can come to his own substantiated opinion by a much shorter route and by a more specialized examination than would otherwise be the case.

A few thoughts on the differences between the internal auditor and the external auditor, as to viewpoints and responsibilities, may be relevant to the possibilities of co-operation.

The respective attitudes towards company policy and accounting principles on the part of internal and external auditors serve as a good example of such differences. The internal auditor must be concerned to see that company policy is followed even if that policy conflicts with accounting principles; he may of course make recommendations to change the policy, but failing success in such recommendations, he has a responsibility to see that the policy is followed regardless of the conflict. The external auditor, on the other hand, is concerned with the application of accounting principles, even though company policy may be opposed. The internal auditor will report serious deviation from company policy, whereas the external auditor will report serious deviation from generally accepted accounting principles.

Consider, also, the relative positions of the internal and external auditor in circumstances where the accounting treatment of certain material transactions is grossly objectionable. The internal auditor has no way of carrying his views beyond the level of management to which he reports; but the external auditor must, as a matter of conscience and ethics, see that the matter is either adjusted or reported on, and his report, if he is serving as shareholders' auditor, will become public to a degree.

Another contrast is evident in the grounds for mutual interest in the effectiveness of internal control. The internal auditor is charged with the protection and conservation of the company's assets, and an adequate system of internal control is the means of discharging that responsibility. The external auditor's concern with internal control is in its bearing on the scope of his audit. In his view the extent and quality of internal control is a matter of decision by management. He may be prepared to advise, but when he does so he serves as a business consultant and not as auditor.

Further differences in viewpoint may be found in the fact that, to the external auditor, the work of the internal auditor is a part of the whole system of internal control while the internal auditor will view his own work largely as the employment of audit procedures common to both internal and external audits, including the review of internal check.

Finally, I must add that I have found only one unique term used to describe an internal audit technique. This is the word perambulation. Research has convinced me, however, that perambulation is not limited to internal auditing, for external auditors also indulge in the practice of walking about and observing things. This is just one more bit of evidence to support my belief that internal auditors and external auditors, with mutual respect and confidence, and with similar attitudes of mind and spirit, but from somewhat different viewpoints, are working toward the same ideals. That is a word the cynics avoid but its recognition and acceptance appear in business leadership to-day. It is a word for the objectives of those who look beyond selfish interests to the common good, and it should mark the character of the professional in any field.

PAPER

by

ERNEST SINNOTT, F.I.M.T.A., F.S.A.A.

The Institute of Municipal Treasurers and Accountants, U. K.

THE GROWTH OF INTERNAL AUDIT

1. The development of internal audit as an accepted commonplace in medium-sized and large scale business enterprises and in local government and public authorities is a thing of the present century. The more widespread adoption of internal audit has corresponded with the tendency for growth in size and complexity of these organisations and with advances in techniques of management.

2. Although the constitutions and the purposes and objects of these organisations vary widely, and they pursue independently their search for efficiency, they are alike in according to internal audit a status sufficient to make a practical contribution to efficiency and economies.

3. The proprietor of a small business, exercising personal control and supervision, can himself perform the simple internal audit work necessary. As the business expands and he must delegate some or all of his responsibilities to employees, he will resort to internal check in the arrangement of their activities. He will also ensure the installation of an accounting system which will provide him with the information he needs to exercise top control and direct the policy of the business.

4. Relative smallness in the numbers of staff employed limits the extent to which internal check can be a substitute for internal audit. In the earlier stages of the expansion of the business the proprietor will not wish to add to his overhead expenses by the employment of an internal auditor and he will turn to the external (public) auditor to advise him on the best methods of accounting and internal check to give him the information and security he seeks.

5. Interchange of staff duties, close cash and stock control and an external audit going beyond the books of final accounts and into details of transactions may postpone the time when it becomes necessary or desirable to employ internal auditors.

6. The growth of joint-stock finance and in the scale of business operations, giving rise to the emergence of management distinct and separate from ownership, have fostered the development of internal audit.

7. As a general proposition it may be said that the employment of internal

auditors becomes necessary or desirable when the size of the business, or the local or public authority is such that:

a. Managers immediately responsible to the proprietors or policy-making body are themselves not in constant touch with operations.

b. Authority to make significant decisions must be delegated to employees holding positions of trust remote from the controlling body.

c. Systems and procedures have become sufficiently complex to involve the risk of unauthorised variations or delays.

d. Transactions are too voluminous or technical in nature for an external auditor to have sufficient regard to matters of detail.

Functions of the Internal Auditor

8. In practice, the functions of the internal auditor will be governed by the attitude of the top management towards the purposes and objects of internal audit. His powers and duties vary as between different organisations but frequently he is regarded as a protective device for management and as forming a link between the controlling body and the operatives in the field. His activities will also be governed by the extent of the internal check practised in the organisation. Modern thought, it seems, extends his functions beyond those traditionally associated with his origins.

9. It is not considered that the investing public in the case of private enterprises, or the ratepayers or consumers in the case of local authorities and public boards, are concerned whether or not there is an internal audit in these organisations, except to the extent that they expect them to be administered efficiently and properly, and profitably in the case of trading concerns. The public would look rather to the published results and external auditors' certificates and reports or to the level of local taxation and the standard of public services.

10. It follows, therefore, that the duties of the internal auditor lie towards the management and controlling body of the organisation he serves, and these might be laid down at the time of his appointment.

11. Management is entitled to look to the internal auditor for the performance of the following functions:

a. Prevention and detection of theft, fraud or any other losses of a like nature. The emphasis should be on prevention through the continual appraisal of the system of internal check.

This aspect of the internal auditor's work is historically pre-eminent and should be a foremost consideration in the planning of audit work, because there will generally be a deliberate attempt to conceal this type of loss.

b. Prevention and detection of error, again with continual appraisal of the internal check.

Error and waste are less likely to be the subjects of deliberate concealment, though sometimes they might be in order to cover up an inefficiency. Management should rely on the internal audit to bring these matters to light, not only to prevent any repetition but also because management policy might be wrongly framed if based on data which is erroneous.

c. Detection and reporting of non-compliance with financial regulations and accounting instructions.

The words 'financial regulations' may be interpreted broadly, including powers of incurring expenditure, the disposal of assets, tendering and purchasing procedures, placing of contracts, etc. and all standing instructions with a financial significance.

In covering this wide field the internal auditor must use judgment and discretion. Rigid inflexibility may gain for the internal auditor a reputation for the stifling of initiative. Thus, where he finds that, though the spirit and intention of standing instructions have been observed, there has been some variation in detailed operation because of local circumstances, his report should indicate the reasons for, as well as the fact of the variation.

Accounting instructions, on the other hand, should be rigidly observed because departure from them can, where necessary, be agreed in advance with the chief accountant. The internal auditor should also give some attention to verifying that accounting records are kept up to date.

d. Suggestions for improvements in systems and methods, the presentation of financial and statistical data, the securing of further possible economies and ways of increasing income.

The internal auditor has, or should have, full authority to cross departmental lines. With this authority and his experience in conducting audits, allied to professional skill and training, he must constantly use a critical sense to assess the possibilities of improvements of the kind set out above.

This does not mean that the internal audit staff should also be the Organisation and Methods staff, though this dual function is performed in some organisations. It is true that the review and improvement of systems and methods is one of the primary objects of Organisation and Methods and that care must be taken to avoid duplication of work between the two staffs in this field. But in the course of their work, the internal audit staff have unique opportunities of appraising systems and methods, and it may well be that there should be some co-operation between the internal audit and the Organisation and Methods staff. Useful information may be supplied by the internal auditor which may become the basis for an Organisation and Methods investigation, but it is considered that the primary functions of internal audit may be impaired unless the two staffs are kept separate.

Fundamentally, the internal audit staff should have a right of access, whilst Organisation and Methods staff should investigate only by invitation.

12. It may be useful at this juncture to mention a number of functions which it is considered, ought not to be the concern of the internal auditor. They include:

a. The design of systems.

In order to be free to pursue his activities of continual appraisal of the efficiency and effectiveness of systems in use, it is preferable that the internal auditor should stand aside from their design and prescription. But he should always be ready to advise on them.

b. He should not be part of the internal check system. An internal auditor should not have executive functions and he should be independent of and helpfully critical towards the internal check system.

c. Special investigations.

There is a temptation to employ internal audit staff on special investigations which arise from time to time. Though quite proper to use them on investigations relating to suspected fraud or falsification of accounting records, it is thought that they should only be sparingly used in other kinds of investigation. These may include, for example, a proposed new system or procedure, an enquiry into the reasons for falling profits in a particular department, compilation of data for recruiting policy, etc. Too many assignments of this nature, however, detract from the comprehensive and continuous review which is the first responsibility of internal audit.

Qualifications and Attributes of the Internal Auditor

13. The main emphasis (though not the only one) of the internal auditor's activities is in connexion with the accounting and financial operations of the organisation he serves.

14. The most appropriate qualification for him is an accountancy one and it is most desirable that he should be a member of a recognised professional accountancy body. In the course of his duties he will be required to audit the records of staff, some of whom are likely to be qualified accountants, to conduct discussions with them and possibly to criticise their performances in his reports. Unless, therefore, he has a professional qualification at least equal to those possessed by staff whose work he examines, his views may not be accorded the respect and attention which they should receive.

15. A good internal auditor will go beyond the learning and experience which he has gained in the course of acquiring his professional accountancy qualification. He should seek to acquire as much information as possible about the technical production or service processes, economic and legal considerations and administrative techniques pertaining to the organisation he serves. Only with this knowledge added to his professional accountancy skill can he adequately and ideally perform his duties.

16. In addition, there are other attributes of character necessary to a successful internal auditor. He should have an enquiring mind, a well developed critical faculty and the qualities of patience, tact, integrity and determination. He should have a pleasant personality and although he should be a good mixer and gain the confidence of the staff of the organisation, his friendliness and helpfulness must not extend to familiarity.

Status in the Organisation

17. The question of his status in the organisation and of to whom he is responsible may be one for some differences of opinion. A degree of independence is vital to the proper effectiveness of internal audit, but in the view of the writer this does not signify that he should be directly responsible to top management.

18. The number of higher executives responsible to top management should be limited if top management is not to be overburdened. The head of the finance branch, whether he be titled Treasurer, Comptroller, Chief Accountant or Chief Financial Officer should be responsible for the whole of the financial operations and it is to him that the internal auditor should be responsible.

19. If the internal audit is developed independently of the finance branch or department, there is a danger of parallel internal audit sections, by whatever name they may be called, being set up within the same organisation.

20. To obtain the best results, a wise chief financial officer will accord to the internal auditor a status within his department as senior as is reasonably possible, and will allow him wide freedom of action in the matters to be audited and the methods of doing so.

21. The arguments of those favouring the complete independence of the internal auditor from the chief financial officer are usually centred upon the difficulties arising if the latter were himself involved in financial irregularities or if he ignored or suppressed legitimate accounting criticisms. Undue emphasis must not be attached to these points. One must pay regard also to the likely standing in the organisation of the chief financial officer, and the system of internal check which can be installed to limit the possibilities of irregularities. A chief financial officer, too, is more likely to react favourably to constructive criticism of the accounting system and procedures if it comes from inside, rather than outside, his own department. Moreover, the support of the chief financial officer lends more power to the internal auditor in carrying out his duties.

22. It should be laid down, however, that the internal auditor has the right of access and direct report to top management in extreme circumstances.

Restrictions on the Scope of Activities

23. There is a difference between the responsibilities of an internal auditor and those of an external auditor. Those of the latter are placed upon him by statute, his certificate on the organisation's final accounts is relied upon (as relevant to the particular organisation) by shareholders, the general public, taxpayers and the national taxing authorities. An external auditor must have these responsibilities constantly in mind and cannot accept any restriction whatever upon professional standards.

24. An internal auditor, on the other hand, is employed by the organisation to perform the functions discussed earlier. He owes his responsibility to those who employ him and it cannot be regarded as unethical for him to accept and carry out the legitimate instructions of his employers. Towards such functions as he performs he must bring to bear the highest professional standards, but the scope of those functions will quite properly be prescribed by top management. If he considers that the scope is so restricted as to render his employment virtually abortive it would be his duty to point it out at the time of his appointment and, if he thinks fit, to decline the position.

25. This, however, would be so rare and extreme a case as to be most unlikely in practice. The internal auditor should have his scope of activities clearly

defined and his reports should indicate any shortcomings due to restrictions imposed on his activities. The external auditor, in his collaboration with the internal auditor, should become acquainted with any limitations in the scope of the latter's duties and arrange his audit programme accordingly.

Audit of the Activities of Top Management

26. This matter is closely related to that discussed in the paragraphs immediately preceding. Since his appointment will derive from top management, the question of the audit of their activities will be decided by them. A position of some delicacy may well arise, for the ultimate authority to which the internal auditor can report is top management itself. It is considered that the internal auditor might best discharge this onerous task by offering advice on a sound system of internal check upon top management activities. Should top management welcome internal audit of their own activities the internal auditor's position will be eased. If, on the other hand, the scope of his activities is restricted to exclude top management, he can quite properly leave this field to the external auditor, having made his own restricted position clear to that auditor and having proffered advice on the appropriate internal check. In local and public authorities, considerations of public accountability would tend to make it more desirable that access to the activities of top management be accorded to the internal auditor.

Relationships between the External and Internal Auditors

27. The fact that the internal auditor is an employee of the organisation should in no way prejudice his relationships with the external auditor.

28. The Institute of Chartered Accountants in England and Wales has considered this matter and has recorded its views in a publication of 1953 entitled 'Notes of the relation of the internal audit to the statutory audit'.

29. In this publication the Institute records that the statutory auditor may (inter alia):

a. 'derive much assistance from the internal auditor's intimate knowledge of the accounting system and technical knowledge of the business';

b. 'where satisfied that the internal auditor has adequately covered part of the work... be able to reduce the extent of his examination in detail';

c. 'be able to rely to a large extent on the internal auditors in determining whether the system of internal check is operating satisfactorily and in assessing the general reliability of the accounting records'.

30. Coming from such an authoritative body these pronouncements are significant and exemplify the beneficial results flowing from co-operation between the external and internal auditors. Each of the two classes of auditors, however, has different functions outside this band of common interest. Both have been referred to already; the external auditor's responsibility to the public, his emphasis upon the accuracy and reliability of the final accounts and his attention to that part of the work which may not be adequately covered by internal audit (e.g. top management activities). The internal auditor will have

paid close attention to detailed records and documents, the operation of the internal check, more efficient or cheaper methods of performing accounting and clerical duties, and the other duties for management referred to in paragraph (11).

31. It is usual for Government auditors of local authorities (the District Audit) to make extensive use of the knowledge and activities of the internal auditors.

32. The internal audit programmes and reports should be made available for the scrutiny of the external auditor and the two forms of audit may be regarded as complementary.

The Organisation of the Internal Audit

33. Where the area of operations of an organisation is reasonably compact little difficulty presents itself in considering the best form of organisation for the internal audit staff. It is located at the headquarters seat of the organisation's operations.

34. Where, however, the operations are over a wider area such as that, for example, of a public electricity board, considerations of geography enter into the problem. In the writer's view, internal audit must be regarded as a headquarters service but beyond this it is not possible to generalise, and three main variations are possible:

a. Base the entire staff at headquarters and travel to the outlying branches or districts to carry out audit work.

The advantages are: the facility for changing auditors' duties, prevention of undue familiarity with locally based staffs, a better team spirit among audit staffs and a greater moral effect of the audit.

The disadvantages are: the increased expenses involved, the loss of travelling time and fewer opportunities for gaining local knowledge.

b. The attachment of internal audit staffs to sub-organisations of the main organisation, when they are no longer regarded as part of the headquarters service but a tool in the hands of local management. Some form of reporting and remote supervisory link with main headquarters would need to be established.

Under this method, the advantages and disadvantages of method *a* are, roughly, reversed.

c. The establishment of audit teams or groups at convenient centres throughout the area of the organisation's activities, under close supervision of, and receiving frequent visits from, the chief internal auditor. The staffs are regarded as headquarters services sited 'in the field' for ease of operations.

This arrangement, which is an attempt to gain the best of both methods *a* and *b* is, on the whole, thought to be the best.

Internal Audit Reports

35. The reporting system of the internal auditor is of great importance in securing the effectiveness of internal audit. Leading considerations are —to whom should he report, at what intervals and what sort of matter should he include in his reports? The answers to these questions will depend largely upon the type of

organisation he serves and his status in it. In the context of this paper, internal audit is regarded as a management service and the internal auditor as a senior officer in the department of the chief financial officer. The reporting system would be designed accordingly, and the internal auditor would report through the chief financial officer to the manager (or departmental head) of the district, branch, or department which is the subject of the report. Top management would be apprised by the chief financial officer of anything in the report of sufficient importance to bring to their notice.

36. The general rule should be for reports to be made as soon as audits are completed, rather than at fixed intervals of time. The latter system has the disadvantage of requiring management to piece together two or more reports in order to get a complete picture of the department or branch in which they are interested. Regular reporting at fixed intervals of time may carry with it the corollary of audit visits at regular intervals, so destroying the value of the surprise element.

37. The content-matter of audit reports, whilst being reasonably full, should not be overburdened with detail or references to minor clerical errors corrected during the course of audit. They should, as a rule, be strictly factual and where comments or recommendations are made, reasons must be given. Management is not usually concerned with the audit programme or procedure followed, but with the end results of the work.

38. Special considerations may apply to reports of surprise audits which have been specifically commissioned.

The Effect of Developments in Electronic Accounting

39. The object of internal audit will not be altered by changeover to electronic accounting. There have been continuous changes in accounting processes throughout the twentieth century, and the transition from the commonly used punched card and other types of accounting machines to the newer forms of electronic machines is no more fundamental than has been experienced in the past.

40. Increased centralisation of accounting, which may follow the newer devices, may tend to increase the reliance upon the internal auditor by removing executive accountants further away from operational districts and branches.

41. Appraisal of computor programmes may become one of the internal auditor's functions, and it will continue to be at the early stage of original records and base documents, upon which the worth of future accounting processes rests, that the value of the internal auditor's activities will continue to be felt.

Tests of Efficiency of the Internal Auditor

42. Just as the necessity for a fire brigade ought not to be judged by the number of incendiary outbreaks being few, or of a police force by the number of crimes committed being few, so the internal auditor ought not to be judged by the number of frauds or mistakes uncovered. Indeed, with an important part of the internal auditor's role being that of the prevention of such occurrences, it may

be a good thing if none at all come to light, for his activities may be responsible for there being none.

43. A list of economies or increased income resulting from audit suggestions is one interesting test. More important, however, is the degree to which internal audit has been accepted by management, and to which its recommendations have been acted upon, for this denotes confidence in audit activities.

44. A scrutiny of audit reports may also be revealing in assessing the efficiency of the internal auditor. The extent of his activities, his command of the subject and approach to his work will be recognisable from the reports.

INLEIDING

van

W. N. A. F. H. STOKVIS

Nederlands Instituut van Accountants

Het arbeidsveld van de interne accountant kan liggen in de private ondernemingen en in de overheidshuishoudingen. In deze inleiding zal uitsluitend worden onderzocht welke de functie en de taak zijn van de interne accountant in de private onderneming.

Ongetwijfeld liggen vele problemen welke in deze inleiding aan de orde komen voor de interne accountant in de private onderneming en in de overheidsbedrijven in principe gelijk, maar de beperking in het behandelde heeft het voordeel, dat niet in de bijzondere aspecten van de leiding van de overheidshuishoudingen behoeft te worden getreden.

Aangezien de functie van intern accountant is ontstaan uit de behoefte van de leiding van de onderneming is het wenselijk aan het onderzoek betreffende functie en taak van de interne accountant een beschouwing omtrent de functies van de leiding vooraf te laten gaan.

I. De functies van de leiding

De eerste functie van de leiding – de constituerende – omvat de opbouw van de structuur van de onderneming. De leiding zal o.m. plannen moeten maken zowel ten aanzien van arbeidsverdeling als van productie, nieuwe wegen moeten zoeken en bij voortduring de bedrijfspolitiek moeten bepalen.

De tweede functie van de leiding is de dirigerende. Deze bestaat uit het besturen van het apparaat, waarin haar initiatieven uitgevoerd kunnen worden. De uitvoering geschiedt door het delegeren van taken en het geven van instructies betreffende de vervulling dezer taken aan de onder de leiding gestelden.

In de derde functie van de leiding ligt besloten het toezicht houden op en controleren van de uitvoering door het in de dirigerende functie door de leiding opgebouwde apparaat. Deze derde functie is de controlerende.

II. De gevolgen van de groei van een onderneming

Voor de vervulling van de functie van de leiding

In elke onderneming – zelfs in de allerkleinste – zullen de genoemde drie

The platform during the Closing Session on Friday afternoon

The opening of the Ball

elementen in de leiding aanwezig moeten zijn om het voortbestaan van de onderneming mogelijk te maken.

In de zeer kleine onderneming zal de leider de drie functies nauwelijks onderkennen. De leider ontwerpt zijn plannen, hij voert ze zelf uit en controleert de uitvoering (zelf-contrôle en bezinning op de doelmatigheid van eigen handelen). Zeer duidelijk spreekt hieruit, dat de drie functies niet los van elkaar gezien kunnen worden, maar elkaar wederkerig beïnvloeden.

Bij de groei van de onderneming zal de leider al zeer spoedig taken, welke uit de functies voortvloeien, ten dele moeten overdragen aan ondergeschikten. Eerst zal het nog mogelijk zijn de opdrachten en instructies aan de aan de leider gesubordineerde krachten mondeling te verstrekken. Bij een verdere groei van de onderneming zullen behalve mondelinge ook schriftelijke instructies worden gegeven, terwijl tevens bevoegdheid tot het nemen van initiatieven zal worden overgedragen.

De contrôle op de uitvoering wordt steeds moeilijker en meer omvattend; de daaraan verbonden werkzaamheden zullen in toenemende mate aan anderen moeten worden opgedragen.

Voor de administratie

Met de groei van de onderneming groeien de problemen, welke verband houden met de inrichting van de administratie. Zij is immers het middel, dat de leiding ten dienste staat om bij een toenemende omvang van de onderneming, waarbij onvermijdelijk de functionele en geografische afstand tussen leiding en de verschillende niveaux van uitvoering wordt vergroot, contrôle te houden op de wijze, waarop de opdrachten en instructies zijn uitgevoerd, inclusief het beheer van de waarden toevertrouwd aan ondergeschikten.

Wel moet in het oog worden gehouden, dat in de structuur van de organisatie al naar de grootte en aard van de onderneming vereist, technische contrôle moet zijn opgenomen. Deze omvat echter uitsluitend het technische aspect van het bedrijfsgebeuren, terwijl de administratie het gehele bedrijfsgebeuren omvat.

Niet alleen ter verschaffing van een grondslag voor beslissingen in de beleidssfeer, maar ook voor de verslaggeving betreffende hetgeen is geschied, is de leiding van de onderneming verplicht het bedrijfsgebeuren te registreren. In deze gecompliceerde wereld zijn het velen, die geïnteresseerd zijn bij juiste verslaggeving of aan wie verantwoording moet worden afgelegd: aandeelhouders, bankiers, de Staat, winstdelenden, prestatieloon-arbeiders, crediteuren, enz.

Wil de administratie aan deze behoeften van de leiding voldoen, dan moet zij zodanig zijn ingericht dat zij op de juiste tijdstippen een betrouwbaar beeld kan geven van het bedrijfsgebeuren.

III. De taak van het hoofd van de administratie

Met de toenemende betekenis van de administratie zal steeds meer kennis worden verlangd van degene, die met de leiding ervan is belast. Lagen de zorgen van de administratie eerst nog vrijwel uitsluitend op het terrein van de zorgvuldige geschiedschrijving, steeds meer zal de leiding ook behoefte voelen aan gedocumenteerde begrotingen. Ongetwijfeld zal de kennis, welke hiervoor noodzakelijk is op het gebied van de administratie, de statistiek en bedrijfseconomie geen onoverkomenlijke bezwaren opleveren voor de theoretisch en praktisch bekwame leider van de administratie. Hij zal op het tijdstip, dat de omvang of de aard van het bedrijf dit doelmatig maakt de administratie zodanig kunnen organiseren, dat de onder zijn verantwoordelijkheid te verrichten arbeid twee terreinen bestrijkt.

Het ene terrein omvat de nauwkeurige geschiedschrijving betreffende het gehele bedrijfsgebeuren, het andere het analyseren van de geschiedschrijving, de bewaking van de efficiency in het bedrijf, de bezettingsmeting van de productiemiddelen en het bestuderen van alle vraagstukken waaromtrent de administratie licht kan verschaffen ten behoeve van de leiding in de onderneming.

In sommige landen geschiedt de laatst besproken arbeid onder leiding van een 'controller'. Omtrent de functionele plaats van deze functionaris bestaat nog geen eenstemmigheid.

IV. Betrouwbaarheid van de uitkomsten van de administratie

Wil de administratie tot een betrouwbaar beeld van het bedrijfsgebeuren voeren en de leider van de administratie de verantwoordelijkheid kunnen dragen, dan zal hij de contrôlemethoden toepassen, welke hij noodzakelijk acht en met eigen apparaat kan bereiken.

Deze op zichzelf toegepaste contrôle kan echter niet voorzien in de functionele behoefte van de leider van de onderneming aan contrôle op de administratie, welke immers voor hem het enige waarnemingsmiddel is, dat het gehele bedrijfsgebeuren in de onderneming omvat.

De oordeelvorming door de leiding geschiedt in belangrijke mate op grond van gegevens, welke uit de administratie kunnen worden geput. Er moeten beslissingen worden genomen, waarvan het wel en wee van de onderneming en van hen, die hun vermogen of arbeid aan de onderneming hebben toevertrouwd, kan afhangen. Het is daarom voor de leiding noodzakelijk, dat de haar verstrekte administratieve gegevens aan de hoogste eisen van betrouwbaarheid voldoen.

V. Behoefte van de leiding aan contrôle op de administratie

De zekerheid, welke de leider van de onderneming nodig heeft om verantwoordelijkheid te kunnen dragen, kan hij verkrijgen door zijn controlerende functie, voor wat betreft de bedrijfseconomische contrôle te delegeren aan een contrôlefunctionaris, die geen deel heeft aan het registrerende noch aan het informatieve element van de administratie.

Welnu, deze functionaris is de accountant.

De leider van de onderneming zal de te delegeren administratieve contrôlefunctie aan een openbare accountant dan wel aan een accountant in dienst van de onderneming kunnen opdragen. Slechts bij een bepaalde omvang van de onderneming zal doelmatig een interne accountant kunnen worden aangesteld.

Is de onderneming niet groot genoeg, dan kan de functie doelmatig vervuld worden door een openbare accountant met zijn staf.

Wordt de onderneming ten behoeve van het maatschappelijk verkeer gecontroleerd door een openbare accountant, dan zal deze de arbeid, welke in die functie nodig is, aanvullen ten aanzien van die aspecten van het bedrijfsgebeuren, die voor de leiding van belang zijn, doch niet of in mindere mate voor de contrôle ten behoeve van het maatschappelijk verkeer. In het bijzonder zal de aanvulling zich richten op het constateren, dat de administratie zodanig is ingericht en functionneert, dat de leider van de onderneming op betrouwbare en zinvolle wijze wordt geinformeerd omtrent het resultaat van de uitvoering zijner instructies.

Zoals uit de verdere inhoud van deze inleiding zal blijken, zijn in het bijzonder in de grote ondernemingen belangrijke nadelen verbonden aan het koppelen der functies van openbare en interne accountant aan één persoon, zowel bezien uit het oogpunt van de leiding van de onderneming, als voor de openbare accountant en voor het maatschappelijk verkeer.

VI. Functie en taak van de interne accountant

Ter verkrijging van het grootste nut van het fungeren van een interne accountant moet zijn opdracht inhouden dat hij zijn deskundig oordeel uitspreekt op grond van zijn contrôle van de interne jaarrekening. Hieronder zijn begrepen de volledigheid en betrouwbaarheid van de voor het bedrijfsbeleid nodige administratieve gegevens.

Ter vervulling van deze opdracht moet hij binnen het kader van zijn deskundigheid grote aandacht hebben voor de interne organisatie in de onderneming en wel in het bijzonder ten aanzien van:

de doelmatigheid van de administratie;
de doelmatige scheiding van functies ter bevordering van interne contrôle;
de afbakening van de verantwoordelijkheid voor en de doeltreffendheid van de instructies voor de sub-alterne leiders, uitvoerende personen of afdelingen;
de contrôle op de naleving van de instructies.

Wil de interne accountant deze opdracht naar behoren kunnen uitvoeren, dan zal hij een grondige kennis moeten verkrijgen omtrent de bestaande organisatie, omtrent de factoren, welke tot die organisatie hebben geleid en omtrent de doeleinden, welke de leiding van de onderneming nastreeft.

Is aan de functie van interne accountant de inhoud gegeven als hiervoor vermeld, dan zal het hem mogelijk zijn:

a. een oordeel uit te spreken over de betrouwbaarheid der administratie, met inbegrip van de verslaggeving;

b. vast te stellen, dat de organisatie van de administratie zodanig is, dat fraude zover mogelijk wordt voorkomen of spoedig wordt ontdekt;

c. de leiding zonodig te adviseren in alle zaken, welke een grondige kennis van het bedrijf en de organisatie vereisen.

VII. Het principiële verschil tussen interne contrôle en interne accountantscontrôle

In het kader van deze inleiding zou het te ver voeren alle facetten van dit probleem te behandelen. Beperking tot de hoofdzaak is geboden.

Interne contrôle is het geheel van contrôlehandelingen en -middelen, voorzover niet opgedragen aan een verbijzonderd contrôleorgaan. De interne contrôle heeft derhalve betrekking op het commercieel, het technisch en het financieel gebeuren in de onderneming.

Er is een gehele reeks van middelen, welke tot interne contrôle kunnen leiden. Als voornaamste uit deze reeks worden genoemd scheiding van functies, meervoudige administratieve verwerking, waardoor langs minstens twee onafhankelijk van elkaar lopende wegen eenzelfde resultaat moet worden verkregen, de budgettering en de visuele contrôle.

Daarnaast staat dan de contrôle ten behoeve van de leiding, die niet in de organisatie is geincorporeerd, maar door verbijzonderde contrôle-organen moet worden uitgevoerd. Heeft deze contrôle betrekking op technische vervaardiging, dan moet de controleur een technisch contrôle-deskundige zijn; betreft zij de contrôle van de administratie dan is het een administratief contrôle-deskundige, een accountant, die deze arbeid verricht.

De vervulling van de hem gedelegeerde contrôlefunctie vereist, dat de interne accountant al die contrôle-arbeid verricht, nodig voor het verkrijgen van een eigen oordeel omtrent de betrouwbaarheid van de verslaggeving aan de leiding. Dit houdt in, dat hij de toegepaste interne contrôle-methoden bestudeert op hun volledigheid en doeltreffendheid, de detailarbeid verricht, welke in dat verband noodzakelijk is en voorts al datgene doet wat nodig is voor het bereiken van een volkomen contrôle.

VIII. De interne accountant moet lid zijn van een erkende organisatie

Alleen indien de interne accountant lid is van een erkende accountantsorganisatie is er een objectieve waarborg, dat de kennis van de accountant verkregen is door een opleiding, welke hem in staat stelt als deskundige op te treden op het gebied van de bedrijfseconomie, de administratie en de contrôle.

Indien de interne accountant fungeert in een onderneming, die door een openbare accountant wordt gecontroleerd, is het voor een rationele samenwerking noodzakelijk, dat de interne accountant lid is van een organisatie gelijkwaardig aan die waarvan de openbare accountant lid is. Hierdoor zijn beide accountants onderworpen aan overeenkomstige arbeids- en tuchtregelen.

IX. Functionele plaats van de interne accountant in de onderneming

Eerder is in deze inleiding betoogd, onder welke omstandigheden de leiding van de onderneming er toe zal komen een deel van de taak, welke voortvloeit uit haar controlerende functie te delegeren aan de interne accountant. Deze ontleent zijn functie rechtstreeks aan de leiding en hij zal zijn bevindingen aan de leiding moeten rapporteren zonder tussenschakeling van welke functionaris dan ook.

Het is duidelijk, dat er voor de interne accountant onaanvaardbare conflicten zouden ontstaan, indien hij niet – zo hij dit nodig acht – ongehinderd zijn oordeel rechtstreeks ter kennis kan brengen van de leiding. Is er een meerhoofdige directie, dan zal de interne accountant zijn bevindingen moeten kunnen rapporteren aan de gezamenlijke directie.

De grondslagen voor het oordeel en de adviezen van de interne accountant zullen voor een deel verkregen worden uit de resultaten van de arbeid door zijn assistenten verricht. De interne accountant moet daartoe binnen de onderneming een zodanige positie hebben, dat de objectiviteit van zijn staf niet in het gedrang komt.

De interne accountant zal o.a. daartoe zelf het personeel voor zijn afdeling moeten selecteren en zelf hun salarissen binnen de daarvoor in de onderneming geldende regelen moeten vaststellen; hij moet de opleiding van zijn assistenten er op richten zich als zelfstandige, objectieve beschouwers van het bedrijfsgebeuren te gedragen. Zij moeten alleen van hem instructies aanvaarden. De interne accountantsafdeling mag niet als opleidingsinstituut voor administratief personeel voor de onderneming worden gebruikt, noch is het wenselijk, dat omgekeerd administratief personeel uit de onderneming wordt overgeplaatst naar de interne accountantsafdeling.

X. Bepaling van de omvang van de arbeid van de interne accountant

Als deskundige op het gebied van de contrôle kan het alleen de accountant zijn, die de uit zijn functie voortvloeiende taak bepaalt. Dit geldt ook indien hij bijzondere onderzoekingen verricht, welke hij noodzakelijk acht of die hem zijn opgedragen door de leiding.

Zijn arbeid moet de gehele activiteit van de onderneming omvatten en voldoen aan de vaktechnische eisen, welke voor accountantscontrôle gelden.

XI. De accountant moet ook de gestes van de hoogste leiding in zijn contrôle betrekken

In een goede organisatie zullen de gestes van de leiding welke o.a. tot uiting komen in instructies, doorwerken tot op het laagste niveau.

Het is de taak van de interne accountant te onderzoeken of de instructies zijn uitgevoerd in overeenstemming met de wensen van de leiding; uiteraard wordt hij daardoor ook geconfronteerd met de doelmatigheid van de instructies.

Van al zijn bevindingen voorzover voor de leiding interessant moet de accountant krachtens zijn aan de leiding ontleende functie verslag uitbrengen.

Uit het voorgaande vloeit logisch voort, dat de interne accountant ter volledige vervulling van zijn functie niet anders kan dan de gestes van de leiding in zijn contrôle betrekken.

Het kan nuttig zijn ter voorkoming van misverstand hierbij op te merken, dat de contrôle van de interne accountant niet resulteert in critiek op de leiding, maar in een oordeelvorming nodig om de leiding een doeltreffend verslag te geven betreffende dit beleid.

Zijn contrôlefunctie kan niet samengaan met het deelhebben in de directie en daardoor in de leiding, omdat de interne accountant dan omtrent eigen beleidsactiviteiten zou hebben te rapporteren. Wel moeten alle documenten waaruit beslissingen van de leiding blijken, zoals notulen, begrotingen enz. ter beschikking staan van de interne accountant.

XII. Het voorzien door de interne accountant in de behoefte van de leiding aan adviezen

De interne accountant moet voorzover zijn deskundigheid reikt, de vrijheid hebben de leiding naar aanleiding van zijn contrôle voorstellen in overweging te geven, welke hij nuttig acht voor de onderneming. Deze deskundigheid zal in algemene zin op het terrein van de bedrijfseconomie en administratieve organisatie liggen, zoals methode en vorm van administratieve verslaglegging, kostprijs- en financieringsvraagstukken.

XIII. De interne accountant en zijn contrôle van dochterondernemingen

Al of niet gepaard gaande met een geografische spreiding kan een onderneming haar organisatie gericht hebben op een functionele decentralisatie. Hoe consequenter deze is doorgevoerd, des te meer rijst de behoefte voor de centrale leiding aan toezicht en contrôle op de verslaglegging van de gedecentraliseerde eenheden en op de uitvoering van de centraal gegeven instructies ter verzekering van de economische eenheid van de gezamenlijke ondernemingen.

In het algemeen zal de contrôle van de dochterondernemingen door een openbare accountant, gericht op de verklaring omtrent de jaarrekening, niet alle specifieke behoeften van de contrôleleiding dekken.

Met behoud van de voordelen van decentralisatie ook ten aanzien van de administratie, zal de interne accountant als een van het betrokken onderdeel onafhankelijk functionaris de aangewezene zijn om de ten behoeve van de centrale leiding bedoelde contrôle uit te oefenen.

XIV. De interne accountant kan niet tevens de functie van openbare accountant vervullen ten behoeve van eenzelfde onderneming; in grote ondernemingen is het omgekeerde evenmin rationeel

De interne accountant behoort tot de structuur van de onderneming; hij is in dienst van de onderneming en vervult zijn taak ten behoeve van de leiding van die onderneming.

In de voorgaande bladzijden is reeds uiteengezet, dat de leiding van de onderneming voor de vervulling van haar functies goed georganiseerde interne accountantscontrôle behoeft. Is de onderneming hiervoor te klein, dan zal veelal door de openbare accountant in deze behoefte worden voorzien.

Toch zal, indien een intern accountant fungeert, deze niet alle behoeften van de leiding ten aanzien van diensten van accountants kunnen dekken, omdat er bepaalde bedrijfseconomische vraagstukken zullen opkomen waarvoor het advies van een openbare accountant zal worden ingewonnen om, gebruikmakende van diens ervaring welke veelal meer gespreid zal zijn dan in het algemeen die van de interne accountant, goed gefundeerde beslissingen te nemen. Voorts staat tegenover de grotere detailkennis van de interne accountant de omstandigheid, dat de openbare accountant verder afstaat van de dagelijkse bedrijfshandelingen in de onderneming.

Ook kan de interne accountant functioneel niet worden geacht een ten behoeve van het maatschappelijk verkeer onafhankelijke verklaring te kunnen afleggen. Dit is niet omdat het maatschappelijk verkeer een negatief standpunt inneemt ten aanzien van de integriteit en onafhankelijkheid van karakter van de interne accountant, maar omdat de onafhankelijkheid van de openbare accountant functioneel is verzekerd. Met de wens van het maatschappelijk verkeer de juistheid van een verslaglegging te laten certificeren door een openbare accountant, zal de leiding der onderneming rekening moeten houden.

Thans kan nader worden ingegaan op de vraag waarom de openbare accountant niet in alle behoeften van de leiding aan administratieve contrôle kan voorzien.

Het is onmogelijk, dat de openbare accountant, die een grote onderneming controleert, te allen tijde beschikbaar is voor de leiding. Ook zou hij tekort schieten in gespecialiseerde ervaring en detailkennis de onderneming betreffende om voor de leiding van de onderneming de meest aangewezen deskundige te zijn ter behandeling van de dagelijks opkomende vraagstukken. De voordelen van de gespreide ervaring en van de grotere afstand van de dagelijkse gang van zaken in de onderneming zouden verloren gaan en hem minder waardevol maken voor de onderneming en als vertrouwensman van het maatschappelijk verkeer.

Als conclusie van het voorgaande wordt dus gesteld, dat de behoefte van de grote onderneming aan accountantscontrôle moet worden verdeeld over twee functionarissen, de interne en de openbare accountant, die elkaar aanvullend de taak verrichten.

XV. Samenwerking tussen de openbare en interne accountant

Het beste resultaat van de samenwerking tussen beide functionarissen wordt verkregen, indien de interne accountant:

1. lid is van dezelfde of een gelijkwaardige beroepsorganisatie als de openbare accountant;

2. is opgedragen zijn deskundig oordeel te geven over de interne verslaggeving tot en met de jaarrekening;

3. van de leiding de onvoorwaardelijke opdracht heeft gekregen alle gegevens en inlichtingen, welke hij van belang acht voor de openbare accountant aan deze door te geven;

4. aanvaardt zijn contrôleprogramma op te stellen in overleg met de openbare accountant en zijn contrôle uit te voeren overeenkomstig dat programma;

5. op zich neemt aan de openbare accountant een afschrift te geven van alle door hem verstrekte rapporten.

Is aan al deze eisen voldaan, dan kan de openbare accountant bij het bepalen van zijn contrôlewerkzaamheden ter ondertekening van de jaarrekening rationeel rekening houden met het resultaat van de werkzaamheden van de interne accountant. De openbare accountant zal zich ervan moeten vergewissen, dat de interne accountant de werkzaamheden van het contrôleprogramma, dat in gemeenzaam overleg tot stand is gekomen, heeft uitgevoerd. De openbare accountant kan het in de vorige zin gestelde bereiken o.a. door het bestuderen en bespreken van contrôleprogramma's en contrôledossiers en door het steekproefsgewijze herhalen van delen van de contrôle-arbeid van de interne accountant.

Het verdient de aandacht, dat deze herhaling van arbeid geen doublure inhoudt. De doeleinden van beide werkzaamheden zijn verschillend, omdat het ene namens en voor de leiding een onderzoek is naar de betrouwbaarheid van de interne verslaggeving, terwijl het andere de verificatie is van de juiste uitvoering van die werkzaamheden door de interne accountant.

Inefficiënte herhaling van contrôlewerkzaamheden wordt vermeden, doordat de openbare accountant de interne zal inlichten omtrent de werkzaamheden, welke de openbare accountant in elk geval zelf wenst te verrichten. De interne accountant zal daarmede rekening kunnen houden bij het ontwerpen van eigen contrôleprogramma.

De openbare accountant zal bijzondere aandacht geven aan al die werkzaamheden en oordeelvellingen, waarbij de mogelijkheid aanwezig is, dat de zienswijze van de interne accountant – omdat hij onbewust beïnvloed wordt door de meningen van de leiding – afwijkt van die van de openbare.

Tenslotte zal de externe accountant alle rapporten zorgvuldig bestuderen en zonodig bespreken met de interne accountant. Het is noodzakelijk voor de openbare accountant, dat hij de interne accountant steunt in zijn wensen, welke er toe bijdragen onvolkomenheden in bijv. de administratieve organisatie van de onderneming of in de verslaggeving op te heffen.

XVI. Besluit

Vertrouwd wordt, dat deze inleiding van nut zal zijn voor de beantwoording van enige van de vele vragen, welke er ten aanzien van dit onderwerp voor de leiding van de grote onderneming en de openbare accountant zijn.

De hiervoor ontwikkelde grondslagen maken het mogelijk, dat de openbare accountant een volkomen contrôle van de jaarrekening kan uitvoeren in overeenstemming met zijn functie van vertrouwensman van het maatschappelijk verkeer. De interne accountant zal in de onderneming een zodanige functionele plaats innemen, dat hij van het grootste nut is voor de onderneming en de openbare accountant.

Gehoopt wordt, dat bij de behandeling van dit onderwerp zowel ten aanzien van de algemene lijn als van de details zal blijken, dat de geschetste samenwerking van accountants de meest doelmatige is voor de onderneming en het maatschappelijk verkeer.

De onderneming en daardoor het maatschappelijk verkeer zullen het grootst mogelijke profijt van de diensten van accountants krijgen, omdat de interne accountant in staat wordt gesteld zijn capaciteiten ten volle te ontplooien ten dienste van de onderneming en de onafhankelijkheid van de openbare accountant gewaarborgd blijft.

Translation

PAPER

by

W. N. A. F. H. STOKVIS

Nederlands Instituut van Accountants

The internal auditor's function is to assist management in the performance of certain of its duties; it is, therefore, appropriate to consider the function and duties of management before examining those of the internal auditor.

I. Functions of Management

Management functions can be sub-divided into three different categories, the fulfilment of each of which requires specific abilities, viz:

1. determining the general policy of the company;
2. directing the company's activities by delegation of executive powers and by instructing the lower managerial and operational levels;
3. supervising and controlling delegated activities in order to ascertain whether they are performed in accordance with management's intentions as reflected in instructions.

II. Effect of Size of Enterprise on Management's Duties

When the enterprise is still a small unit all the activities enumerated above can be readily performed by the boss himself; his instructions are given orally, he himself watches what is being done and the accounting records serve primarily to support his memory.

It is important to note that even in the smallest businesses it is necessary to keep accounts which disclose the financial position and results and which provide the data required by statutory regulations governing taxes, social insurances, etc. When management is delegated to persons other than those who supply the necessary capital, the accounts also provide the data enabling the management to render an account of its stewardship. In addition the accounts should be capable of producing such information as may reasonably be required by third parties interested in the financial position and results of the company.

At a certain stage the increase in size or complexity of the enterprise makes it necessary for the management to delegate more of its activities. The distance between the management and operatives and the introduction of executives on different operational levels will force the management to devote more of its time to controlling the execution of its instructions. Direct supervision and memory fail.

Eventually it is only the records of activities which enable the top-management to form an opinion about the correctness and the proper performance of its orders. An organized accounting system alone can provide a comprehensive picture of the business' activities. In addition an adequate system of qualitative control over materials and products must, of course, be incorporated in the organizational set-up of the enterprise.

III. Function of Chief Accountant and Controller

The chief accountant, being the head of the accounting department, is reponsible not only for the correct recording of all activities, but is also expected by the management to interpret the figures produced by the accounting department, make constructive suggestions and provide the management with the data necessary to make decisions as regards strengthening the company's earning power, valuation of assets, setting aside necessary provisions and reserves, etc.

The chief accountant, therefore, sifts and selects important data for the management and passes them on in a form adapted to serve the management's purpose best.

In some countries the last mentioned elements of the chief accountant's task are in the larger enterprises often commissioned to a controller, leaving the chief accountant primarily responsible for the proper recording of activities.

The controller should study the picture of the activities of managerial and operational executives, the chief accountant included, as given in the detailed accounts and should report to the management thereon.

IV. Reliability of Accounting Data

As soon as the enterprise reaches such a size or complexity that the top-management can only exercise a proper control of the business' activities through the medium of data supplied by the accounting records, the accuracy of such records becomes a prerequisite for this control.

The ability to form an opinion on the reliability of accounting data requires a specialized knowledge and experience in the fields of accounting, including management accounting and managerial organization, and of auditing. In general, therefore, the performance of this task is delegated by management to specialists. Thus, in medium-sized companies, even if they are privately owned, it is common practice for the management to enlist the aid of a public accountant in order to maintain adequate accounting control.

When persons who do not take part in the management of an enterprise supply the necessary capital, they require an account of the management's stewardship. Confidence in the financial statements produced by management is strengthened if they are audited and certified by a public accountant. This public accountant will normally be the most suitable person to assist the management in exercising control over the activities of the business (as described in the first paragraph). He can readily expand the scope of his audit with a view to ascertaining that the accounting data form a reliable basis to judge the execution of managerial instructions at all levels. His examination on behalf of management will reduce the extent to which the figures can be affected, perhaps unintentionally, by the personal views of either the executives at the various managerial levels or the persons who combine these figures into a form suitable for use by management.

V. Needs of Management Affect Scope of Audit

In order to give management an expert opinion on the internal accounting data, the statutory auditor will have to cover many aspects of the business activities in much greater detail than would be necessary for his statutory audit.

In medium-sized enterprises this expansion of the scope of his audit will, however, not make it necessary for either the public accountant or part of his staff to be engaged full-time on the job, nor will the needs of management in respect of accounting control normally justify the fulltime employment of a qualified internal auditor.

During the past decades, however, an appreciable number of companies have greatly expanded, thereby becoming of such a complexity that their administrative requirements have increased enormously. Consequently the gap between the needs of management as described above on the one hand, and the requirements of all other persons interested in the overall financial position and results on the other hand, has widened accordingly.

These circumstances lead to the management feeling the necessity of engaging a specialist who can properly direct the audit of the internal accounting data and who will continuously be available to give support in the various fields of managerial control. Under XIV below it will be explained why in large concerns conditions give rise to the statutory auditor feeling that he cannot properly meet the various needs of management without being impeded in the fulfilment of his primary task—giving an independent opinion on the published accounts. At this stage, therefore, an efficient organization demands the employment of a qualified internal auditor, head of an internal audit department.

VI. Function of Internal Auditor

In order to reap the best fruits of such an employment the internal auditor should be commissioned:

1. to give his expert opinion on the internal financial statements;
2. to judge the efficiency of the accounting system;
3. to provide the management, within the orbit of his specialized knowledge, with all information which in his opinion can be of assistance in running the business, especially as regards:

planning and delegation of the duties of subordinate executives;
control of the performance of delegated tasks.

For a proper fulfilment of these functions the internal auditor should obtain all information necessary for a critical judgment of the activities of all departments.

The continuous activity of the internal audit department increases the probability of an earlier detection of organizational defects and the internal auditor's position on the staff of the organization enables management to consult him on those problems where an intimate knowledge of facts and internal conditions is needed.

VII. Fundamental Difference between Internal Audit and Internal Check

From the foregoing description of the internal auditor's function it will be seen that there is an essential difference between internal audit and internal check.

A system of internal check is a series of procedures designed to exercise accounting control through a division of duties and through routine checking by officers of the company who need not be trained in the field of auditing. The system is established in order to ensure proper recording of all activities, prevention of fraud and detection of fraud, if any, at the earliest possible moment.

Where a division of duties is not feasible, e.g. in the chief accountant's or controller's presentation of the results of their activities, internal check fails. Particularly here the functioning of an internal auditor, who ascertains on behalf of management that the duties of senior executives are carried out properly, provides the necessary control.

Moreover, the internal auditor's continuous testing of the system of internal check will act as a safeguard on the adequacy of its functioning. A well devised system of internal check is a prerequisite for a satisfactory audit.

VIII. Internal Auditor should be member of Recognized Professional Organization

The internal auditor should be a qualified member of the profession since only a diploma issued by a recognized body of accountants or a government organization gives an objective guarantee that his knowledge is based on an education which enables him to give an expert opinion on financial statements and on all other accounting matters.

His collaboration with the public auditor (see below) makes it necessary for both auditors to be members of the same organization or of organizations of the same professional standing. Then both have to comply with similar professional regulations and both are subject to professional jurisdiction.

IX. Status of Internal Auditor and his Department

In order to meet the requirements of management, the internal auditor must include activities on all executive levels in the scope of his audit. It is, therefore, essential that he should receive his instructions from top-management alone. Although the internal auditor will, naturally, give the controller and chief accountant such help as is compatible with his primary duties, neither of these officials should functionally be in a position which entitles them to give him instructions. Thus, the internal auditor's position within the organization will be as strong and independent as possible. He will be solely responsible to the highest managing authority in the company to whom he will address his report on the annual internal accounts, which summarize the accounts rendered by the various individual departments.

The internal auditor should select the members of his staff and, within the general standards of the organization, he should fix their salaries. He alone should determine the audit procedures and, consequently, the duties of his employees. His staff should be forbidden to accept audit instructions from the executives of the departments they audit. The internal audit department should not be considered as a training ground for accounting personnel, offering promising possibilities for speedy promotion to other departments, nor should the company's accounting personnel be engaged as employees of the internal audit department. Both conceptions would result in the internal audit staff losing much of their independence; for example, they might be afraid of 'stepping on the toes' of executives who might some day be their superiors.

In order to obtain the required standard of internal audit work, it is essential that the audit personnel should be properly trained, that they should use detailed audit programmes and that their work should be planned and periodically reviewed by professionally qualified auditors.

X. Determination of Scope of Internal Auditor's Activities

The internal auditor, being an expert in auditing, should be entitled to lay down the minimum scope of his audit, which should cover all parts of the organization. Similarly, he should determine the procedures to be used for specific investigations, which either arise from his main job or have been specially commissioned by management. As a qualified accountant the internal auditor is bound to comply with the standards of the professional body to which he belongs.

XI. Internal Audit should Include Top-Management's Activities

In a well-organized enterprise the management's initiatives and instructions will be reflected in the performances of the staff at all executive levels. To assist the management in carrying out its function of supervising and controlling delegated tasks, the internal auditor must report as to whether and to what extent these delegated tasks have been performed in accordance with the management's intentions. His audit function precludes him from taking part in managerial activities lest he should have to report on his own actions. Thus the internal auditor, though being a highly ranked member of the organization, should not be a member of the board.

It is essential to note that the internal auditor can only give his expert opinion on the internal accounts if he is entitled to include all the activities of the management in the scope of his audit. He should, therefore, be allowed to take cognizance of all documents which reflect the decisions of management, e.g. minutes, budgets, etc.

If his findings give rise to any comment on top-management's activities he should be able to report direct to the president and to any or all of the managing directors, thus ensuring that his position has the greatest possible independence within the organization.

XII. Extent of Internal Auditor's Advisory Function

Within the field of his specialized knowledge the internal auditor is in the position to give management as a by-product of his audit such suggestions as he deems to be in the interest of the business. His recommendations may be on accounting matters in general, e.g. collation and presentation of accounting and costing information, on organizational matters, e.g. the efficiency of the system of internal check, or on matters of general policy, e.g. financing, market research, etc.

XIII. Internal Auditor's Assistance to Management in Control of Subsidiary Companies

The degree of functional decentralisation within the organization has a bearing on the character of the internal auditor's task. A geographical spreading of the units which together form one group implies a certain minimum of functional decentralisation. The more independent the set-up of the individual unit, the more the group's central management requires supervision of the financial reporting by local units and an examination of the records underlying such reports to ensure that uniform principles have been properly applied and the unit's activities duly accounted for.

Normally, the scope of the statutory audit performed by local public auditors would not cover these aspects of supervision to the extent needed by central management. Moreover, the control exercised by central management must to some extent be limited, if the advantages resulting from functional or geographical decentralisation are not to be jeopardized. The employment of an internal auditor, acting functionally and independent of local management, enables central management to exercise the required elements of control.

XIV. Internal Auditor's Unsuitability to Function as Statutory Auditor and vice versa

In the foregoing analysis it has been explained that the management of a large enterprise cannot properly fulfil its functions without establishing a well-organized internal audit department. Such a department cannot, however, meet all management's requirements as regards the services rendered by auditors since:

1. the internal auditor's opinion on certain problems presented to him may not be the best possible as his experience with regard to certain aspects of

managerial accounting and policy, e.g. financing and compliance with stock exchange regulations, is limited;

2. the internal auditor, however great his personal integrity and independence of character, cannot be deemed to give an independent opinion on accounts presented by the management to shareholders and third parties, because his opinion is given in his capacity as a staff-member of the company.

The above mentioned requirements of management can only be met through the services of a public accountant. Why then should not a public accountant cover all of the management's requirements?

When auditing a large enterprise he cannot do so since:

1. it is impossible for him to be continuously at the disposal of the management;

2. he would have to acquire specialized experience and intimate knowledge of the details of the organization to an extent which would be incompatible with his primary function, i.e. to perform a statutory audit. In other words impediments similar to those explained above as regards the functioning of an internal auditor would arise.

It is, therefore, considered that the audit requirements of a large undertaking should be divided between two distinct functionaries, i.e. an internal auditor and a public accountant, complementary to and collaborating with each other.

XV. Arrangements to Ensure Proper Co-operation between Public Accountant and Internal Auditor

When an enterprise employs a qualified accountant as internal auditor collaboration between the statutory auditor and the internal auditor can best be effected if:

1. the internal auditor is a member of an equivalent professional organization as the public accountant (see above under VIII);

2. the internal auditor is required to give his expert opinion on the internal financial statements;

3. the internal auditor is unconditionally allowed by management to forward any information which he deems to be of importance to the public accountant;

4. the internal auditor undertakes to perform an audit programme covering, as a minimum, all the procedures deemed essential by the public accountant;

5. the internal auditor undertakes to forward to the public accountant a copy of all reports issued by him.

If the foregoing arrangements have been made, the statutory auditor is justified in taking account of the results of his internal colleague's activities when determining the procedures to be followed in performing his statutory audit. He will have to satisfy himself that the internal auditor continuously performs his audit in compliance with the above-mentioned arrangements. This implies, inter alia, that the public accountant will keep himself informed as to the contents and execution of the internal audit programmes. He will do this by studying and discussing newly-issued programmes, by reviewing the working-papers on the files of the internal audit department and by repeating part of the audit work carried out by the internal auditor and his staff. It should be noted that this repetition of work is not in fact a duplication of the internal auditor's, since the purposes of the two activities differ; one is an ascertainment on behalf of management as to whether the company's internal accounts are reliable, whereas the other is an investigation as to whether the internal audit department's activities have been duly performed. Thus the public accountant's review includes an examination of the work of the internal audit department on a test basis.

Furthermore, the public accountant will direct his attention to those activities on which the internal auditor's opinion might have been influenced by his subjectivity, having in mind that he is an integral part of the organization of the company and that he, to some extent, may think along the same lines as management.

Last but not least the public accountant will carefully study all reports issued by the internal audit department. If his study gives rise to any comments he will discuss the reports with the internal auditor. In some cases the internal auditor will arrange to have discussions with the public accountant when drafting his report in order to establish whether the latter shares his views. The public accountant will also ascertain whether the internal auditor is satisfied that his reported findings are properly followed up.

XVI. Effect of Public Accountant's Audit on Internal Auditor's Activities

In performing his audit as described above, the public accountant must determine, in the light of his professional standards, the extent of his verification of the figures in the published annual accounts. In order to give his opinion on the internal accounts the internal auditor, on the other hand, will have to cover all fields of activities in his audit.

The procedures carried out by each auditor will result from a rational division of duties between them so as to avoid unnecessary duplication of work. To this end the public accountant will also give his internal colleague the appropriate information as regards the scope and results of his work.

When advising the management on important questions the internal auditor may previously discuss them with the public accountant, especially in those instances where the internal auditor expects the public accountant's views to be at variance with his own. This policy enables the public accountant to become acquainted with the problems arising within the enterprise and at the same time to form an opinion on the degree to which his internal colleague's independence of judgment is influenced by his being a staff-member of the company.

XVII. Conclusion

It is felt that the set-up of the internal and statutory audits as described above will be helpful in solving some of the many problems encountered by the management and the public accountant when performing their respective tasks in a large enterprise.

This set-up leaves the public accountant with all that is essential to justify his professional opinion on the annual accounts and enables him to direct a major part of his activities to the essential elements of his job. It is hoped that the audit approach for both the internal and the public auditor, as outlined above, when discussed in principle and in detail during the forthcoming congress, will be confirmed as being professionally sound. It is felt that this approach removes the conditions endangering the independence of the public accountant, leaving his impartiality unimpaired. On the other hand it results in the internal auditor functioning at a level where, as a qualified accountant, he can be of the greatest value both to management and the public accountant.

DISCUSSION

CHAIRMAN: WP. F. C. J. BUSCH

Institut der Wirtschaftsprüfer in Deutschland e.V.

CHAIRMAN:

Meine sehr geehrten Damen und Herren! Am gestrigen Tage der verschiedenen Arbeitssitzungen hier in diesem schönen Hause haben wir die sorgfältig ausgewählten und vorbereiteten Referate und Diskussionen angehört. Diese waren außerordentlich berufswichtig und wir alle haben sie mit großem Interesse vernommen. Es hat sich bei den Diskussionen herausgestellt, wie unterschiedlich die Auffassungen über die Durchdringung und Anwendung der gestellten Themen sind und wie dringend notwendig es erscheint, auf internationaler Basis die Zusammenarbeit der Berufsangehörigen zu fördern. Heute, meine sehr geehrten Damen und Herren, soll uns ein anderes Thema in Anspruch nehmen und zwar: Der Interne Accountant, auch ein Juwel in dem großen Rahmen dieses Kongresses, zweifelsohne ein Gebiet, welches den übrigen Gebieten, von denen wir bisher gehört haben, an Bedeutung sicherlich nicht nachsteht und für alle Berufsangehörigen von großer Wichtigkeit ist. Ich glaube, daß auch hier von verschiedenen Gesichtspunkten an das Thema herangegangen wird. Meine Damen und Herren, ich hoffe, daß Sie Gelegenheit gehabt haben, in den Monaten vor Beginn dieses Kongresses einen Blick in die verschiedenen Papiere der Herren Referenten zu werfen, so daß Sie schon etwas auf die Diskussion vorbereitet sind.

Möglicherweise ergeben sich bei der Behandlung dieses Themas Meinungen, die nicht auf einen einheitlichen Nenner gebracht werden können. Ich hoffe aber, daß die Diskussion zeigen wird, daß wir uns in dieser Beziehung keinen großen Meinungsverschiedenheiten hinzugeben haben.

In der Diskussion, die gestern über das Thema 'Grundlagen des Wirtschaftsprüferberufs's tattfand, hat ein Mitglied des Panels darauf hingewiesen, daß es in den Vereinigten Staaten – soweit ich ihn richtig verstanden habe – im allgemeinen nicht üblich ist, einen längeren Bericht an größere Gesellschaften zu erstatten, weil hierfür primär andere Organe, z.B. die internen Prüfer oder die Revisionsabteilungen zuständig sind. Und ich glaube, damit haben wir die beste Brücke zu unserem Thema. Ich habe die Ehre, meine Damen und Herren, Ihnen nunmehr die mitwirkenden Herren vorzustellen, und zwar zunächst im Präsidium:

Mr. Davies aus Neu-Seeland; Mr. Idman aus Finland; Mr. Rioseco aus Mexiko,

dann den Herrn Diskussionsleiter Mr. Smallpeice aus England, den Herrn

Rapporteur, Mr. Walker aus USA und die Herren Autoren Mr. Irish, Australien, Mr. Macpherson, Kanada, Mr. Sinnott, England und Mr. Stokvis, Holland, ferner die übrigen Mitglieder des Panels: Mr. Davies aus USA und Mr. Hansen aus Dänemark.

Indem ich nunmehr offiziell die Sitzung eröffne, darf ich den Herrn Diskussionsleiter bitten, die Diskussion aufzunehmen.

Ladies and Gentlemen. Yesterday, at one of the several business sessions we are holding in this beautiful house, we listened with interest to carefully selected and well-prepared papers and discussions of extreme importance to our profession. In the course of the discussions, it became clear what a great difference of view exists on the subjects with which we are concerned, on the degree of penetration of the ideas involved and of their application. It also became clear how important it is to foster international co-operation among all belonging to our profession.

Ladies and Gentlemen. This afternoon we shall be devoting our attention to another subject, entitled 'The Internal Auditor', another highly important item on our programme, without doubt a field equal in importance to the other subjects we have discussed so far and of interest to all of us. I believe that this subject, too, will be approached from differing points of view.

Ladies and Gentlemen. I hope that during the months preceding this congress, you have found an opportunity to glance at the various papers drawn up by the authors, and that you are, to some extent, already prepared for the discussion. In treating this subject, we shall probably encounter opinions which cannot be reconciled, though it is my hope that here, too, no very great differences of opinion will be thrown up.

In yesterday's discussion on the problem of Principles for the Accountant's Profession, a member of the panel pointed out that in the United States, it is not—as far as I gathered—customary to make long-form reports to the management of larger concerns, since this is primarily a job for other organs, e.g. the internal auditor or the internal audit department. I think this provides us with a bridge whereby we can cross over to our present subject.

Now, Ladies and Gentlemen, I have the honour to introduce to you the gentlemen on the platform, who will be taking part:

The vice-chairmen: Mr. Davies from New Zealand; Mr. Idman from Finland; Mr. Rioseco from Mexico;

further, Mr. Smallpeice from England, who will lead our discussion; our rapporteur, Mr. Walker from the U.S.A., and the authors of papers: Mr. Irish, Australia; Mr. Macpherson, Canada; Mr. Sinnott, U.K. and Mr. Stokvis from the Netherlands. The other members of the panel are: Mr. Davies, U.S.A. and Mr. Hansen, Denmark.

I herewith open this afternoon's meeting and I now call on the leader of our discussion to start the proceedings.

MR. B. SMALLPEICE (United Kingdom)

Mr. Chairman, Ladies and Gentlemen: We have first the report of the rapporteur Mr. Walker and I would like to call upon him to make his report.

MR. W. A. WALKER (United States of America)

Mr. Chairman, Gentlemen, Now we have all the mechanical troubles fixed up, I will try to summarize as I see it, what these very fine gentlemen have said about the work of the internal auditor.

In preparing this summary I was privileged to compare my own thoughts and experiences with those of four gentlemen who obviously had given considerable study to the subject at hand. They are:

Mr. W. N. A. F. H. Stokvis of the Netherlands
Mr. R. A. Irish of Australia
Mr. Ernest Sinnott of England
Mr. L. G. Macpherson of Canada

Such a comparison brought home to me the realization that Internal Auditing, the youngest branch of the accounting profession, is growing up, although it has yet to reach the state of stabilization of scope, standards, and procedures attained by the public accounting profession.

It was encouraging to find that the papers presented seemed in general agreement on a number of points.

For example:

a. Regarding the effect of size on management duties, Mr. Sinnott expressed the common viewpoint—'Widespread adoption of internal audit has corresponded with the tendency for growth in size and complexity... and with advances in techniques of management'.

b. On the subject of accessibility to records, Mr. Stokvis stated—'The internal auditor should obtain all information necessary for a critical judgment of the activities of all departments'.

c. In commenting on differences between internal auditing and internal check, Mr. Irish most ably indicated the various authors' thinking—'Internal control signifies primarily a process of check and cross check... It is probably best if internal audit is complementary to, but not directly part of, internal control'.

d. On the relationship between the internal auditor and public accountant, Mr. Macpherson stated—'An effective internal audit will assist the external auditor, especially in minimizing his examination... he may in his examination of the system of internal control benefit from the internal auditor's knowledge of the system'.

e. All indicated that the function of the internal auditor is a 'staff' function without direct authority over any functions other than his own.

f. Those who mentioned the organization of the internal audit staff itself seemed in agreement with the statement of Mr. Sinnott recommending audit groups at convenient centres under close supervision of the chief internal auditor.

g. As might be expected, prevention or discovery of fraud was mentioned as related to the duties, but relatively little emphasis was placed on this function.

h. As stated by Mr. Macpherson—'Management should not allow the audit staff to be substituted for the accounting staff in temporary situations'.

i. Those who commented on the problem of judging the effectiveness of the internal audit staff seemed to agree with Mr. Sinnott who said—'A list of economies or increased income resulting from audit suggestions is one interesting test. More important, however, is the degree to which internal audit has been accepted by management, and to which its recommendations have been acted upon'.

However, I admit to some disappointment that there seems still to exist a considerable difference in viewpoint on the more fundamental concepts of the functioning of the internal auditor.

For example: Normally, audits by public accountants involve principally the verification of assets and liabilities as of a certain date and such analysis of the income statement as will enable certification that they are properly stated. In other words, the public accountant establishes the accuracy of accounts, while I have always held that the internal auditor's approach is by department or function to establish that good business practices and controls are in effect. Thus, the work of the two need not conflict because basic approach and emphasis are different.

Unfortunately, contemporary literature on auditing has been concentrated largely on the viewpoint of the public accountant. Indeed many articles, purporting to address themselves to the subject of internal auditing, actually have been more applicable to the work of the public accountants. This has been true because many auditors, whose experience has been in public accounting, found themselves commissioned by their companies to establish internal audit programs, and in the absence of adequate data on the concepts of internal auditing have not eliminated the duties of the public accountant from their programs.

In fact, some internal auditors have cited as an accomplishment the fact that the work performed by their staff reduced the fee of the public accountant. It is my belief that such an assertion is a definite indication of a lack of appreciation of the scope and responsibilities of the internal auditor.

Of course, in the coverage of his proper function, the internal auditor will perform a certain amount of verification work —not as an end, but as a means to an end—and such coverage may reduce the detail work of the public accountant necessary to satisfy the existence of adequate internal control. Mr. Sinnott seemed to be in accord with this latter concept.

But this basic concept seems not to be completely shared by several of the other gentlemen. One stated—'An effective internal audit will assist the external auditor, especially in minimizing his examination and review of ordinary operations and transaction detail, and to some extent in the balance sheet verifications'. Another indicated the internal auditor should be required to give his expert opinion on the financial statements and should undertake a program covering, as a minimum, all the procedures deemed essential by the public accountant. He further stated that in order to give his opinion on the internal accounts, the internal auditor will have to cover all fields of activities in his audit, and that there must be a rational division of duties between the external and internal auditor to avoid duplication.

In connection with that same thought, I find myself agreeing wholeheartedly with Mr. Irish, and hoping that he is right, when he says that internal auditing was first an adjunct to the outside audit but it 'has come to be appreciated, however, that internal audit can provide a constructive as well as a protective service, an advance in thought which lifts the functions far above mere clerical routine. The internal auditor thus acts on management's behalf to sift the detail of daily operational efficiency and so identify those features needing executive review, judgment and decision'.

One of the gentlemen, however, has the view that, 'within the field of his specialized knowledge, the internal auditor is in the position to give management as a by-product of his audit such suggestions as he deems to be in the interest of the business'.

Again, another gentleman indicated that a well-developed internal audit will integrate the constructive and protective functions, but if a choice must be made, emphasis should be placed on the protective aspects.

Another facet of the problem about which there seems to be a rather wide diversity of opinion is in connection with the broad subject of the internal auditor's status in the company. Generally it seemed to be felt that the auditing approach must be harmonious with the viewpoint of management, and a majority seemed to agree that as long as the program has the support of the chief administrative officer or body, the function can report to any member of management under whom the total program can work efficiently. However, one view was expressed that if the auditor's findings give rise to any comment on top-management's activities, he should be able to report direct to the president and to any or all of the managing directors, thus ensuring that his position has the greatest possible independence. Another view was that he must be accountable only to the highest strata of management.

However, this difference in views may be apparent rather than real, for through it all I gather the impression that there would be universal agreement with the following principle: The internal auditor should try to arrive at the facts and, after careful consideration, present these facts in such a manner that, even though they may be in conflict with present company policies or thinking, they will be accepted and given the consideration due them. A proper method of presentation will reflect the obvious sincerity of the auditor in presenting findings which he believes to be in the best interest of the company.

Among those who touched on the problem there was quite a wide difference in view as to whether the audit department should be considered as a training ground for accounting personnel. One view is that it should not, as they might be afraid of stepping on the toes of executives who might someday be their superiors. The other view expressed was that men in the audit department get a complete education as to the company's policies and how these policies tie together for a smoothly operating business. Accordingly, it should be the ambition of the Audit Supervisor to be constantly losing his best men to other departments of the business where training of this type is needed to fill executive positions. It was contended that not only would this tend to create an organization of men with broad vision, but it would enable the audit staff to maintain a staff of men of the caliber needed to do the job at hand because they know that opportunity exists for those whose work is well done.

In connection with the so-called 'management' types of audit, some concern was expressed that adequately qualified men would not be available, as it would take a 'superman' to give advice on every business activity. My own experience indicates that this is a problem which must be recognized; but that if it is so recognized and handled with common sense, the 'management' type of audit can be most beneficial. Each auditor must remember that he is not an industrial engineer, a metallurgist, an industrial relations expert, or the president of the company. Few practices have got the auditor into more hot water, and justifiably so, than that of pretending to know more about the technical phase of a subject than the technician himself. The auditor must try to arrive at a delicate balance which permits him to examine the facts and to render help in any department having a bearing on the financial status of the corporation while, at the same time, confining himself to those matters on which he can base his opinions. An auditor is essentially a fact-finding examiner, and the judgment should be left to the appropriate management group.

In ending this summary, I felt I could do no better than state the conclusion with which Mr. Irish ended his paper quoting: 'The size and spread of activity in so many businesses have led the external auditor more and more away from the old form of detailed audit. His attentions go more to matters of policy and principle and I foresee this becoming firmly implanted as his true role. Such a development is only possible if there is a marriage of internal audit functions which will take care of detailed accuracy and protection against staff dishonesty, but the internal auditor will have a continually expanding future as management appreciates that he, out of all executives, is best equipped to audit for management. It is a brilliant future, attainable if deserved.

MR. B. SMALLPEICE (United Kingdom)

Thank you, Mr. Walker, for the very lucid and brilliant summing up of these papers and I am sure that it will help all of us to bring this subject into focus.

Now for the purposes of this discussion I think it might be a good idea, so as to make it as interesting as possible and to give it practical content, if we suppose that I as discussion leader have assumed the position of managing director or president of a medium size business employing some 10,000 people, and that I want to get the best advice that I can get about the working of internal audit in that business. Let us also suppose that a certain amount of internal auditing is already taking place, and limited, I think, to its protective function, that is to say the protection, prevention and detection of fraud, and mis-appropriation, inaccuracies and deviation from prescribed procedures and that I have this very unique opportunity of being able to consult these gentlemen on the platform, occupying the very eminent positions which they hold all over the world. As you know, four of them are in public practice, three of them on the financial side of industry in the United States and the United Kingdom, and in addition, one of those in public practice is also an internal auditor in an industrial organization, and another one, engaged in industry, was at one time in the accounting firm of Ernst and Ernst in America. So it is difficult to imagine a more distinguished or more representative cross-section of experience to advise me, and all of you, on this subject. Now I propose to divide the discussion up a bit and the first general subject that I would like to discuss is—'What is the Scope of the Internal Audit Function within a Business?' Should it be the main function of the internal auditor just to be protective, as we will assume that I have it already in the business that I am responsible for, or should he have a constructive function, and if a constructive function, then in what sort of ways?

Now first of all I would like to ask Mr. Davies, who is not the author of a paper but whom we are very glad to have with us to-day, if he would like to answer on that point.

MR. W. R. DAVIES (United States of America)

Mr. Managing Director,

In 1947, the Institute of Internal Auditors prepared and issued its first 'Statement of the Responsibilities of the Internal Auditor', in which, and among other things, it discussed the 'Scope of Authority and Responsibility' of internal auditing. It said, and I quote, 'Internal auditing is a staff or advisory function rather than a line or operating function. Therefore the internal auditor does not exercise direct authority over other persons in the organization. The internal auditor should be free to review and appraise policies, plans and procedures but his review and appraisal does not in any way relieve other persons in the organization of the primary responsibilities assigned to them'. In discussing the nature of internal auditing, at that time, it further stated that 'internal auditing is the independent appraisal activity within an organization for the review of the accounting, financial, and other operations as a basis for protective and constructive service to management. It is a type of control which functions by measuring and evaluating the effectiveness of other types of control. It deals primarily with accounting and financial matters but it may also properly deal with matters of an operating nature'.

Ten years later, in May, 1957, on account of the continuing development of the profession, the Institute issued a revised statement in order to express the still broader concept of internal auditing which it holds to-day. Under the heading of 'Objective and Scope of Internal Auditing', this revised statement states, and I quote, 'The over-all objective of internal auditing is to assist all members of management in the effective discharge of their responsibilities, by furnishing them with objective analyses, appraisals, recommendations and pertinent comments concerning the activities reviewed. The internal auditor therefore should be concerned with *any* phase of business activity wherein he can be of service to management. The attainment of this over-all objective of service to management should involve such activities as:

Reviewing and appraising the soundness, adequacy and application of accounting, financial and operating controls.

Ascertaining the extent of compliance with established policies, plans and procedures.

Ascertaining the extent to which company assets are accounted for, and safeguarded from losses of all kinds.

Ascertaining the reliability of accounting and other data developed within the organization, and finally

Appraising the quality of performance in carrying out assigned responsibilities'.

This, then, is the approved framework within which the best internal audit practice to-day operates. After the original statement was issued, the concepts and practice of internal auditing continued to advance, particularly in the extension of internal auditing in the operating departments of business. Like the earlier statement, at the time of its issue, the present statement presents an advanced conception of the nature, scope, and responsibility of the internal auditor's work.

Needless to say, as President of the Institute of Internal Auditors, I agree with this advanced concept which entails greatest emphasis upon constructive service to management. This requires, as Mr. Walker has stated in his paper, that internal audit does not confine itself solely to the protective phases of internal auditing in the accounting and financial departments. Rather, it requires that it extends its investigations of the financial effects in any department of the business, including sales, production, engineering, purchasing, etc. This is usually the area in which the so-called 'Management' type of audit is generated. The Management type of audit programme very practically evolves over a period of time from the gradual establishment of a sound functional audit programme the original emphasis of which was accounting and financial. This evolution involves such basic considerations as:

1. Training the auditors to gradually assume more and more responsibility as their knowledge of the business increases, which

2. Makes it easier to convince the various department heads that a capable auditor can be of helpful service to them, which in turn

3. Convinces top management, whose backing was necessary from the start and all along the way, that they have made no mistake in supporting the Internal Audit Programme.

My conclusion, therefore is that the constructive phase of Internal Auditing, concerned as it is with the operations of the business, is even of more importance than the time-honoured protective phase. I thank you.

MR. B. SMALLPEICE (United Kingdom)
Thank you very much, Mr. Davies. Now I would like to pursue this question of the constructive phase a little further. In the course of your paper, Mr. Stokvis, you referred to one of the duties, one of the constructive duties which the internal auditor might undertake, as being to control the performance of delegated tasks, and there are other thoughts associated with that. I would just like to be clear what it is specifically you have in mind.

MR. W. N. A. F. H. STOKVIS (Netherlands)
Mijnheer de directeur, Ik vind het bijzonder prettig, dat u mij gelegenheid geeft na de schriftelijke uiteenzetting, die ik u enige tijd geleden deed toekomen, mij verdere inlichtingen te vragen omtrent het door mij geschrevene. In het bijzonder wijst u op dat fragment uit hoofdstuk VI van het door mij geschrevene, waarin wordt opgesomd wat tot de taak van de interne accountant behoort en wel op de laatste zinsnede, waarin tot uitdrukking wordt gebracht, dat 'one of the constructive duties which the internal auditor might undertake is the control of the performance of delegated tasks'.

Ik kan mij voorstellen, mijnheer de directeur, dat u onzekerheid heeft omtrent de plaats welke de constructieve taak in het geheel van plichten van de interne accountant inneemt en de begrenzing van die constructieve taak. Uw onzekerheid wordt wellicht vergroot door hetgeen uw andere adviseurs hieromtrent hebben geschreven.

Mr. Davies stelt aan het slot van zijn betoog, dat 'the constructive phase of Internal Auditing concerned as it is with the operations of the business, is even of more importance than the time-honoured protective phase'.

In deze uitspraak zie ik een ernstig gevaar, omdat zij uit het oog verliest hoe en waarom de functie van de internal auditor is ontstaan. Deze uitspraak gevoegd bij het feit, dat uw vraag aan mij betrekking heeft op het laatste deel van mijn opsomming van de taak van de interne accountant, geeft mij de vrijheid u erop te wijzen, dat ik als nummer 1 en 2 van de plichten stel de beschermende taak van de interne accountant en daarna op de derde plaats de constructieve taak. Voor een goede beantwoording van uw vraag moet u mij toestaan daaraan te laten voorafgaan een kort overzicht omtrent de historische ontwikkeling van de interne accountant, zoals die zich volgens mij heeft voltrokken.

Ik heb u geschreven, mijnheer de directeur, dat, wilt u uw organisatie zo goed mogelijk opbouwen en de leiding van uw onderneming in handen houden, u hebt te zorgen voor een controlerende functie. Weliswaar heeft uw onderneming nog niet de grootte bereikt van een 'giant enterprise', maar toch zijn er in uw organisatie reeds zovele functionele geledingen, dat u onder u vele personen hebt, die instructies ontvangen en doorgeven.

Mijnheer de directeur, u kent wellicht het gezelschapspel waarbij een kring van personen een gefluisterde opdracht moet doorgeven aan de volgende in de kring. Uiteindelijk komt deze opdracht weer terug bij de oorspronkelijke gever van de opdracht maar met geheel verwrongen en afwijkende inhoud. Precies hetzelfde gevaar is ook aanwezig in uw onderneming, als u niet – nadat uw instructies van boven naar beneden zijn gestroomd – weer terugkrijgt het verhaal zoals het uiteindelijk in uw onderneming is terechtgekomen. Door de verschillende adviseurs is gewezen op het gevaar, dat er van de kant van de public accountant wel eens een te eenzijdige nadruk kan gelegd worden op de controlerende functie van de accountant en vooral, zoals ik het gesteld heb, op de controlerende functie van de accountant, die uitmondt op de interne certificering van de jaarstukken. Mag ik daarom proberen u nog op een andere wijze te laten zien hoe ik mijn overtuiging heb opgebouwd?

Ik zou u graag in gedachten mee terug willen nemen naar een boekhouder en naar een boekhouding van laten we zeggen 50 jaar geleden. We waren er waarschijnlijk allebei nog niet; maar we kunnen ons dit wel voorstellen.

Vijftig jaar geleden vonden wij in de onderneming een boekhouder, die het als zijn taak beschouwde een grootboek bij te houden. Dat grootboek was voor hem eigenlijk meer een doel dan een middel. Hij vond het betrekkelijk maar een onaangename taak uit die boekhouding een jaarrekening te moeten opstellen. Waarom vond hij het zo onaangenaam? Omdat hij op het moment, dat hij zich met de jaarrekening bezig zou houden, bemerkte, dat zijn algemene grootboek niet klopte met de specificaties die daarbij hoorden. Z'n debiteuren klopten niet, z'n crediteuren klopten niet, z'n onkosten klopten niet; er waren allerlei zaken die hij had uit te zoeken en, Mijnheer de directeur, kunt u zich nu voorstellen, dat deze boekhouder, die een denkend wezen was, niet ontbloot van gezond verstand, zo langzamerhand ging denken aan methodes, die het hem mogelijk zouden kunnen maken om niet één keer per jaar deze Augiasstal te moeten uitmesten? Hij ging daarom zinnen op allerlei maatregelen, die het hem mogelijk maakten om periodiek tot verschillende contrôlemaatregelen te komen, zodat hij niet één keer per jaar overvallen zou worden door allerlei verschillen, maar dat hij dus zo in de loop van het jaar kon concluderen, dat het grootboek aansloot met de specificaties. En dan, Mijnheer de directeur

– gelukkig hebben wij het in onze onderneming nog niet meegemaakt – deze boekhouder werd op een goede dag ook geconfronteerd met een fraude-geval en zo kwam hij ook tot de idee, dat hij maatregelen moest nemen om fraude te voorkomen en allengs zien wij in het hoofd van deze boekhouder ontstaan de idee van wat we thans noemen 'interne contrôle'. Interne contrôle die we kunnen toepassen door toezicht, door langs twee verschillende wegen tot één doel te komen en door alle andere zaken die we onder interne contrôle willen bevatten.

Mijnheer de directeur, zo langzamerhand kwam die boekhouder verder af te staan van het dagelijks boekhouden; hij liet het grootboek over aan een ander, hij ging zich alleen bemoeien met contrôle- en organisatiemaatregelen, maar hij was toch steeds een lijn-employé en weinig onafhankelijk van zijn directeur. En nu krijgen wij een zeer interessant punt in zijn evolutie. Het is namelijk zo, dat op een goede dag deze boekhouder op een morgen wakker werd, niet meer in zijn gedachte als een lijn-employé; hij was gegroeid tot een staf-employé. En zo ziet u dan ook in de loop van de jaren in verschillende landen, dat een boekhouder zich ging noemen accountant. In feite was deze man een amphibie. Aan de ene kant was hij nog een boekhouder, aan de andere kant trachtte hij te zijn accountant en na een evolutie door de verderschrijdende wetenschap, door de opleiding die verder is gegaan, zien wij dat deze boekhouder-accountant zich heeft ontwikkeld tot een interne accountant. En nu ziet u, waarom ik zo sta op het punt, dat de interne accountant moet instaan voor de jaarrekening. Heeft u niet meegemaakt, dat die oude boekhouder op een goede dag bij zijn directeur binnenkwam en zei: 'Mijnheer de directeur, hier heeft u mijn balans en winst- en verliesrekening'. Hij bedoelde daarmede: 'Ik getuig, dat gezien mijn functionele plaats, mijn kennis en ervaring, deze balans en winst- en verliesrekening goed zijn'.

Welnu deze boekhouder gaf eigen getuigenis omtrent zijn arbeid. Met de ontwikkeling van de administratieve wetenschap en de wijziging van de organisatorische plaats van de boekhouder van lijn-employé tot de interne accountant als staf-employé, kon en mocht u als leider van de onderneming meer toevertrouwen aan uw functionaris. Het werd de taak van de interne accountant om de getuigenis af te geven omtrent de juistheid van de jaarrekening. Indien de interne accountant deze verantwoordelijkheid niet zou wensen te aanvaarden, zou hij deze geheel of ten dele weer terugschuiven naar 'de boekhouder', de 'lijn-employé'. Dit zou een stap terug zijn in de historische ontwikkeling en een verzwakking van de verantwoordelijkheid van de leider der onderneming.

Zie hier, mijnheer de directeur, waarom ik deze omweg gekozen heb ter beantwoording van uw vraag ten aanzien van de constructieve plicht van de accountant. Uit de historische ontwikkeling, zoals door mij geschetst, blijkt, dat primair de accountant een beschermende taak heeft, welke hij vervult door de contrôle van de administratie, inclusief de balans en winst- en verliesrekening, op welker gebied bij uitstek zijn deskundigheid ligt.

Deze taak heb ik in hoofdstuk VI omschreven als:

1. to give his expert opinion on the internal statements;
2. to judge the efficiency of the accounting system.

Met deze doelstellingen voor ogen zal de constructieve taak logisch daaruit

voortvloeien en zal de interne accountant zich tevens bewust zijn van de grenzen, waarbinnen hij daarbij zal moeten blijven.
En zo heb ik, na de beschermende, controlerende, taak van de interne accountant voorop te hebben gesteld, op de eerder genoemde plaats ten slotte laten volgen:

3. to provide the management, within the orbit of his specialized knowledge with all information which in his opinion can be of assistance in running the business, especially as regards:
planning and delegation of the duties of subordinate executives;
control of the performance of delegated tasks.

Mr. Managing Director, I am highly gratified that, after receiving the written statement I sent you some time ago, you should ask me for further information regarding what I have written. You have referred to that passage in Chapter VI of what I have written in which I sum up the functions which go to make up the Internal Auditor's task and mentioned in particular the last sentence, which says that 'one of the constructive duties which the Internal Auditor might undertake is the control of the performance of delegated tasks'.

I can well appreciate, Mr. Managing Director, that you may be in some doubt as to the place, occupied by the Internal Auditor's constructive task in the whole complex of his duties and to the limits of that constructive task. Your uncertainty on this point has, perhaps, been increased by what your other advisors have written you on the matter.

At the end of his exposition, Mr. Davies states that 'the constructive phase of Internal Auditing, concerned as it is with the operations of the business, is even of more importance than the time-honoured protective phase'.

I detect a grave danger in this view, since it loses sight of how and why the Internal Auditor's function has come into being. This view, and the fact that your question to me refers to the last part of my summing up of the Internal Auditor's task afford me the liberty of pointing out to you that I put the protective function of the Internal Auditor as number 1 and 2 of his duties, preceding number 3, his constructive function. Before answering your question proper, I feel I should preface it with a brief historical review of the Internal Auditor and his task. I wrote to you, Mr. Managing Director, that if you wish to build up an effective organization in your business in order to ensure that you keep the management on your own hands, you need a proper auditing function in your enterprise. It is true that your firm has not yet taken on the proportions of a giant enterprise, yet there are already so many functional departments in the business that you have many persons under you who receive and pass on instructions. Mr. Managing Director, I don't know whether you know that game in which a message is passed round, in whispers, from one person to the next, until, at the end, the final version is compared with the original message. There is usually no resemblance between the two. Mr. Managing Director, precisely the same danger is also present in your business, if, after your instructions have filtered down from top to bottom, you do not get the outcome as it was planned when the instructions were given. Other advisors have pointed to the danger that the Public Accountant may sometimes lay too one-sided an emphasis on his primary function, i.e. the function which leads up to his internal report on the annual accounts. May, therefore, I try to explain in another way, how I have arrived at my point of view?

I should like to take your mind back to a bookkeeper and a bookkeepingsystem of, let us say, 50 years ago. We were probably not there at the time, Mr. Managing Director, but we are able to form an idea of how things were. Fifty years ago we found in the firm a bookkeeper who, standing in front of his desk, confined himself to keeping his ledger posted. This task was to him more of an aim in itself than a means. He regarded it as a comparatively unpleasant task to have to draw up the annual accounts on the basis of his bookkeeping. And why did he find it so unpleasant? Because when he went to make up the annual accounts, he discovered that his general ledger did not agree with the underlying details. His individual debtor accounts didn't agree with the general account. His creditor accounts didn't agree, his expense accounts didn't agree. There were all sorts of details he had to go into. And, Mr. Managing Director, you can imagine that this bookkeeper, who was a thinking creature, not devoid of common sense, gradually began to develop methods which would save him the task of having to clean out this Augean stable once every year.

He therefore began to ponder all manner of measures that would enable him to apply various periodical checks, so that he would no longer be caught once a year with a great variety of discrepancies, but could easily keep checking up during the course of the year to see that his ledger agreed with the underlying specifications. And then, Mr. Managing Director—I presume that you haven't yet experienced it in your business—one day this bookkeeper may well have been confronted with a case of defalcation. This gave rise to his taking measures to prevent fraud; gradually, therefore, his mind was forming the idea we now know by the name of 'Internal Audit'. Internal audit that can be applied by supervision, by arriving at one goal along two paths and by achieving all the other things now covered by internal audit.

Mr. Managing Director, in this way that bookkeeper gradually became further and further removed from day-to-day bookkeeping; he left the posting up of the ledger to someone else, he began to concern himself exclusively with organizational measures; but he was still a low-grade employee and he enjoyed little independence of his manager. And now we come to a very interesting point in his evolution. It so happened that one fine day this bookkeeper woke up no longer feeling himself to be an ordinary employee; he had developed into a member of the staff. And thus in various countries in the course of time, we see the bookkeeper beginning to call himself an auditor. In actual fact, this man was two things in one. On the one hand, he was still an accountant, and on the other, he tried to be an auditor; by means of an evolutionary process, by advancing knowledge, by improved training, this bookkeeper-accountant has developed into an Internal Auditor. And now, Mr. Managing Director, I should like to say why I take the view that the Internal Auditor must bear the responsibility for the fairness of the annual accounts. You can imagine that old bookkeeper enter his manager's office one day and say: 'Here you have my balance sheet and profit and loss account, Sir'. By this he meant: 'I declare, by virtue of my function, knowledge and experience, that this balance sheet and this profit and loss account are correct and in order'.

Thus, however, this bookkeeper testified to the accuracy of his own work. With the development of administrative science and the shift in the position the bookkeeper occupies in the organization of the business—from being an ordinary employee to being the Internal Auditor and a member of the staff—the management was able (and justified) to entrust him with greater responsibilities. It became the Internal Auditor's task to give an opinion on the accuracy of the annual accounts. If the Internal Auditor were not willing to accept this responsibility, he would pass the whole or part of it back to the bookkeeper, the ordinary employee. This would be a step backwards in the historical trend of development and would weaken the responsibility of the head of the firm.

See here, Mr. Managing Director, why I have chosen this roundabout way of answering your question concerning the auditor's constructive task. It is clear from the historical development of the auditor's function, as I have outlined it, that his primary task is a protective one, which he performs by auditing the books and accounts, including the balance sheet and the profit and loss account, a field in which he is qualified by virtue of his education and experience.
In Chapter VI, I have described this task as follows:

1. to give his expert opinion on the internal statements;
2. to judge the efficiency of the accounting system.

If these aims are kept in view, the constructive task will logically follow, and the Internal Auditor will at the same time be aware of the limits set to the performance of that task.
And so, after having put the protective and auditing task of the Internal Auditor first, as already mentioned, I have put in the third—but not least—place the following:

3. to provide the management, within the orbit of his specialized knowledge, with all the information which in his opinion can be of assistance in running the business, especially as regards:
   planning and delegation of the duties of subordinate executives;
   control of the performance of delegated tasks.

MR. B. SMALLPEICE (United Kingdom)

Thank you, Mr. Stokvis. I think I understand the general point which you made in the earlier part of your remarks, that there is a function to be performed in every business, that of ensuring that instructions are carried out. But what I am not quite clear about, and perhaps we could hear some other people on this point, is whether that task of seeing that instructions are carried out properly falls to the internal auditor as such, who is, I take it, primarily concerned with the financial aspects of the business. I am just wondering whether in point of fact, if he embarks on that field, he won't very soon cut across the responsibilities of other executives within the business. Mr. Macpherson, would you like to come in at this point and, if I might just ask you to be very brief, I think we ought to pass on very shortly to our other subjects.

MR. L. G. MACPHERSON (Canada)

It seems to me that if we think in terms of the medium sized company (without trying to define that, because in Canada we think of a medium size company as employing much fewer than 10,000, which is to us a large company), it is right to expect that the internal auditor will perform much more than the protective function. Indeed, it is difficult to imagine how the internal audit could be properly conducted at all, even in the smaller enterprise, without embracing the advisory or so-called constructive function. The internal auditor should emphasize examination in depth, rather than the detailed checking of transactions, because the audit in depth will reveal the effectiveness of the internal control, providing the best review of the organization and the operations. Here though I think a danger develops because the auditor with a constructive viewpoint may be tempted to go too far into the technical operations as distinct from the more clerical activities. If he should go beyond the field of his own competence, his recommendations to management may be impractical, or unsound, and this will certainly cast doubt on the reliability of his whole report. I think management has the right to expect from the internal auditor assurances as to what is right, and recommendations with respect to what is not good, but only in the areas of the auditor's technical competence. The wise auditor will avoid the temptation to go beyond that field in tendering his advice. Mr. Chairman, I might clarify with an example but to cut it short I shall stop there.

MR. B. SMALLPEICE (United Kingdom)

Thank you very much, Mr. Macpherson, I think that in view of the importance of adhering to the time schedule, perhaps we ought to go on now to consider another aspect of this subject, and that is: What is the status which the internal auditor should hold in the business? Mr. Irish, I think on page 17 of the printed documents you suggested that he should be accountable to the highest strata of management. I wonder if you would just develop that for a moment. Would you bear in mind particularly the problem of the effect of the status of the internal auditor on the responsibility of the various department heads, whether they are works managers, engineers, sales managers and so on?

MR. R. A. IRISH (Australia)

Yes, Mr. Managing Director, with the size of organization that you have in mind it is very obvious that your internal auditor must be a man who has a psychological sense of independence, and while I have no fixed views as to the particular person who should be his ultimate controller, I do feel that basically that person, the person to whom he ultimately reports, must be very high up the line of top-management, and I think, equally, that top-management must have a very sensible attitude toward the internal auditor, because if he is not backed from that quarter, he will not succeed in his particular function. I think you are raising also the question of his ability to extend further into the departments down the line and I would suggest to you, Sir, that in the size of organization you have, the internal auditor must obviously be a man of more than ordinary ability. You have a business which is beyond any one man's capacity to absorb in detail, and I would suggest to you, therefore, that this internal auditor would quite valuably strengthen your organization, if part of his duties included the review of operations of department heads in accordance with your instructions. I don't know if that covers precisely the point you had in mind, Mr. Managing Director.

MR. B. SMALLPEICE (United Kingdom)
Thank you very much. Yes, I think it does very clearly. Mr. Sinnott, I wonder if I could call on you for your view on this important subject.

MR. E. SINNOTT (United Kingdom)
I think that the question of status of the internal auditor would depend largely upon what functions are allotted to him. If, for example, we can see that his functions are the fundamental protective ones, then in my view the ultimate responsibility is in the financial field. I take that to be the responsibility of your chief finance officer, whatever you might call him. If you accord a higher status to the internal auditor I feel that your chief finance officer would be placed in an invidious position. If, however, we have the superman sort of internal auditor, who is going to be a Metallurgist, Industrial Engineer, Economist, Accountant and everything else all rolled into one, then I think he is ultimately going to be the general manager, or the personal assistant to the general manager, in which case you would have to appoint another internal auditor, to do the basic internal audit protective duties. I feel that I must get the scope in perspective. That is the perspective, Mr. Managing Director, in which I see it. I don't see where you are going to find a man who is going to do all these extended functions, I don't think he'll be an accountant; this may well be debated at the Society of Industrial Engineers at some time. In my view, therefore, the status should be this—that he should be under the wing of the chief finance officer and should report to you, through him, and direct to you in special circumstances only.

MR. B. SMALLPEICE (United Kingdom)
Well, now I think, Ladies and Gentlemen, that we might pass on to considering the relationship between the Internal Auditor and the Public Accountant. I think it has been useful to traverse what is evidently a very controversial ground, before getting to this point, because in a sense, the relationship between the Internal Auditor and the Public Accountant will depend on the function which the Internal Auditor is performing within the organization. In approaching this question, I would suggest that we start by considering what is the

The Rotterdam Harbour

Amsterdam in September

fundamental difference between their functions, and I would like to ask Mr. Hansen from Copenhagen, to deal with that and to consider, in the light of those fundamental differences, whether they each have a separate task and to what extent there should be co-ordination of work and whether, for example, the Internal Auditor can suggest modifications in the scope of the Public Accountant's audit, or vice versa.

MR. BØRGE HANSEN (Denmark)

I feel favoured, by your questions, Mr. Managing Director, and with regard to your first question—what is the fundamental difference between their functions—I should like to point out the following to you. The Internal Auditor in the organization is an employee of the company, engaged by you, to assist and to serve the management, and he is responsible solely towards the management. The Public Accountant is appointed by the general meeting of the shareholders and is responsible not only towards the shareholders, but towards third parties who must rely on his certification. This means, in my opinion, that the Public Accountant's function must cover the whole enterprise, including decisions taken by the board and by the management. The Internal Auditor's function covers that part of the enterprise below management level, and his main function is probably to check that the policy of the management is carried out, and that the results of same are correctly expressed in the records of the accounting department. You can understand the difference in their functions from the titles. The Internal Auditor serves internally, the Public Accountant serves the public, and in doing so, he also renders a service to your company. Then you ask me whether each of them has a separate task, or if there should be some co-ordination of their work—I should say that the two auditors have, to a certain extent, a common task as far as serving the enterprise is concerned. And they have a deviating task, because of the fundamental difference in the nature of their responsibility. Of course, you could think of co-ordination of the work as far as the common task is concerned, but in my opinion, only to avoid too much duplication of work. I take it for granted that both of the auditors are on the same professional level, and I should recommend not to organize any co-ordination beforehand but to do it thus: the Internal Auditor should devise his working programme according to the scope of his duties, as they have been determined by the management. Once the Public Accountant has received this programme, he will be able to build up his own programme. A section of the Public Accountant's programme is certainly to check to which extent he can rely on the work carried out by the Internal Auditor, because he must always keep in mind his own responsibility, which cannot be borne for him by the Internal Auditor. I should think that the Internal Auditor could modify a good deal of the volume of test and checking work for the Public Accountant, and vice versa, but he certainly cannot exert any influence upon the scope of the Public Accountant's audit. This is only natural because it would imply that the management, whose decision is under the audit of the Public Accountant, would be able to modify the scope of the Public Accountant's audit through the Internal Auditor, and you 'll understand that this would be an impossible situation. I think Mr. Walker is not very far from a good definition when he determines the scope of the Internal Auditor's work to be a control of the efficiency of the departments in every respect, and a test of the results of the policy prescribed by the management, whereas the scope of the Public Accountant's audit is the certification of the annual account. As far as the scope of the Internal Auditor's work is determined by the management, I cannot see how the Public Accountant could modify this scope, at least, not without agreement from your side.

MR. B. SMALLPEICE (United Kingdom)

Thank you, Mr. Hansen. I think you have made it very clear that without agreement, the internal audit programme could not necessarily be altered by the External or Public Accountant. But, Mr. Stokvis, you've had experience of being both inside an industrial organization and in practice, do you think that the internal audit programme should require the approval of the Public Accountant?

MR. W. N. A. F. H. STOKVIS (Netherlands)

Mijnheer de directeur, Approval, goedkeuring, is een beetje eenzijdig woord. We hebben tegenover elkaar twee mensen, die het vak verstaan. Er moet zijn overleg en door dit overleg moet de goedkeuring van het programma naar voren komen. In deze geest, Mijnheer de directeur, kan ik zeggen: ja, de public accountant moet het programma van de interne accountant goedkeuren. Maar nogmaals, omdat het zijn twee mensen die beiden een zelfde vak beheersen, is het meer een kwestie van overleg dan van het opleggen van de mening van de een op de ander. Bovendien kunnen wij in het algemeen nergens waar wij de mening moeten opleggen aan een ander, een goede samenwerking bereiken.

Mag ik hieraan nog iets toevoegen naar aanleiding van wat ook Mr. Hansen heeft gezegd over het bepalen van de omvang van het werk van de interne accountant. Dat begrijp ik nu niet goed. Als een directeur van een onderneming o.a. geschoold is op het gebied van de administratie, dan kan ik mij voorstellen, dat hij zekere ideeën heeft over het werk van de interne accountant. Als echter de directeur niet administratief geschoold is, hoe zou hij dan kunnen voorschrijven aan de interne accountant wat zijn taak is? Als hij een commercieel directeur is zonder bepaalde technische kennis, hoe zou hij dan willen voorschrijven aan zijn technische beambten, hoe zij hun techniek moeten uitoefenen? Ik geloof toch, dat het een kwestie is van leiding, van organisatie, om als men eenmaal de mensen heeft uitgezocht en hun functie heeft bepaald, hen deze functie te laten vervullen zoals zij het geleerd hebben en niet zoals de directeur meent het hun te moeten voorschrijven, want dan ontstaan aan alle kanten gebreken in deze organisatie.

Mr. Managing Director, Approval is a rather one-sided word. Here we have two people, face to face, who both know their profession. There must be consultation, and out of this consultation must come the joint approval of the working programme. In this sense, Mr. Managing Director, I can say: 'Yes, the Public Accountant must approve the Internal Auditor's working programme'. But, since we have here two people who are both masters of the same profession, in my view it is more a question of consultation than of imposing the opinion of the one upon the other.

Moreover, good collaboration can, generally speaking, never be achieved if an opinion is to be forced on someone else.

May I just add a word regarding what Mr. Hansen has said, too, about determining the scope of the Internal Auditor's work? I don't understand that very well. If a company's director has been properly trained in bookkeeping and accounting, I can understand that he has certain views regarding the Internal Auditor's work.

But if a Managing Director has had no special training in bookkeeping and accounting, how could he tell the Internal Auditor what his task ought to be? If he were a Commercial Manager, without any special technical knowledge, how could he tell his technical staff how to carry out their side of the business? I think that it is a question of good management, of organization, once one has selected the right people and put them in charge of some task or other, to allow them to perform that task the way they have learnt to do it, and not the way the Managing Director thinks they ought to do it—for in that case weaknesses will result in the organization all along the line.

MR. B. SMALLPEICE (United Kingdom)

Mr. Walker, you have been on both sides of the fence, if I might call it that. What would you advise me on the question of how the Internal Auditor should work with or not work with the Public Accountant?

MR. W. A. WALKER (United States of America)

Well, as You say, I have been on about three sides of this fence, having been in public accounting and internal auditing and then part of the management of the company using both internal auditing and external auditing. So if there can be three sides to a fence, well that's it. I would certainly recommend that the Public and the Internal Auditor must have a very good speaking acquaintance with each other. They must work with each other quite closely to be sure that they do not overlap and interfere with each other on a particular audit. For example, the Public Accountant does certain work in the audit of things which apply to his own audit, the balance sheet audit so-called. The Internal Auditor may be doing certain work in the same area, aimed, generally, at a different objective, aimed at finding out whether that department is functioning well and with good common sense, with good business practices or whether the whole function, as it crosses one department and another, is integrated in its functioning in a good businesslike manner.

They may be working in the same area but with different objectives, and they certainly do not interfere with each other as far as their objective and their function is concerned, in my opinion, although they could interfere with each other as far as both are going into a certain department the same day, trying to use the same people and the same records and so forth. So they must integrate their activities in that respect. But the fee that we pay a Public Accountant certainly is paid for a different thing than the cost that the Internal Auditor is incurring in his department. So I think you need have no fear if you properly plan the function and the objective of these two, that they will cross lines, if the two of them co-ordinate to be sure to keep out of each other's way in the functioning of their job.

MR. B. SMALLPEICE (United Kingdom)

Mr. Macpherson, In your paper, you have expressed the view that the Internal Auditor does give the possibility to a Public Accountant of reducing the attention he pays to detail and therefore freeing his time for the appraisal of more important matters, in particular the fairness of the public statements. How far do you think that that could be taken?

MR. L. G. MACPHERSON (Canada)

There is nothing but gain to be derived from co-operation between the two auditors, especially from the viewpoint of the External Auditor, with respect to the planning of the Internal Auditor's programme. I do not mean to imply that the External Auditor should have any control over this at all, but joint planning can be nothing but good for the company. Beyond that, if this internal audit programme embraces procedures that are really auditing, I think this is bound to have its effect upon the scope of the duties of the External Auditor. For example the Internal Auditor, it seems me, should always be the best informed person as to the efficiency of the operation of the internal control system as a whole, and his knowledge being passed on to the External Auditor will save the latter a great deal of effort in tracing the operation, even though it will not eliminate the essential work that the External Auditor must do in his independent capacity.

MR. B. SMALLPEICE (United Kingdom)

Thank you. Mr. Sinnott, I wonder if you could give me the benefit of your advice from the point of view of somebody employed in a public utility undertaking.

MR. E. SINNOTT (United Kingdom)

Well, I can see it in the same way as Mr. Macpherson, that there can be nothing but benefit derived by close co-operation between the External Auditor and the Internal Auditor. Now I conceive the functions of the Internal Auditor to be protective very largely, on the prevention and detection of fraud and error and ensuring that financial regulations of the organization are complied with by the personnel. If the Internal Auditor is carrying out those duties according to his auditing programme, then I see that a good deal of detail work must be taken off the shoulders of the Public Auditor. He may wish to testcheck a few things that the Internal Auditor purports to have done in his programmes, and having satisfied himself then, I think he would be able to rely very largely on the efficacy of the internal audit. I do not conceive, however, that the Internal Auditor's programmes ought to be subjected in any way to the approval of the Public Auditor, although I am quite sure that a good Internal Auditor would discuss the construction and extent of his programme with the External Auditor. There is what I call a band of common interest between the two. But then the Internal Auditor has functions, in addition, which are hardly the concern of the Public Auditor and the Public Auditor has responsibilities to the public shareholders and third parties, as Mr. Hansen said, which are not the concern of the Internal Auditor.

So it is within this band of common interest that relationships arise between the Internal Auditor and the External Auditor. I do not conceive of it in any way as a senior-junior partnership, I think it is one for mutual regard and esteem, goodwill and co-operation, and I do not think that the Internal Auditor should take any instructions from the Public Auditor. If he is wise, however, he will, as Mr. Walker said, arrange his affairs so that the utmost co-operation beneficial to the organization results from the integration of their problems.

MR. B. SMALLPEICE (United Kingdom)

I think it is quite fundamental, in fact it goes without saying, that anything the Internal Auditor may do in his business does not in any way take away the responsibilities of the Public Accountant. But what I would like to hear from you, Mr. Irish, if I might, is whether, as regards the shortcomings of the Internal Auditor, if there are any—I mean if he slips up in part of his work and the Public Accountant has been relying on that work—whether is the Public Accountant in any way responsible for those shortcomings?

MR. R. A. IRISH (Australia)

Mr. Managing Director, It has been said that the Public Accountant and the Internal Auditor have two distinct functions. I believe that the Public Accountant in his review of internal control will take into account the existence of an internal audit, which I have always regarded as being not part of the internal control but complementary to it. In consequence, I think the Public Accountant needs to be satisfied that in so far as internal audit may be affecting his programme, the internal audit is being carried out properly according to the programme as he understands it to be. For that reason alone I would like to see an Internal Auditor refrain from making any change in his programme without first informing the External Auditor, that is, at least so far as it affects financial matters. I think under such an arrangement, too, you prevent management perhaps forcing the Internal Auditor into an unsatisfactory position, and in view of the fact that the Internal Auditor really lacks the protection which would ensure his independence, I think anything which can hedge him round in that way is all to the good. Thus I think that any shortcoming of the Internal Auditor is not necessarily the Public Accountant's responsibility, nor is he relieved by the existence of the internal audit. He must examine what the Internal Auditor is doing, satisfying himself that it is reliable, as far as it affects his programme, and if he sees shortcomings, then he must make up the gap.

MR. B. SMALLPEICE (United Kingdom)

One further point I would like to take up before we bring this panel discussion to an end, and open it to everybody else here, is this. I would just like to consider whether it ought to be regular practice for the Internal Auditor's report to go automatically to the Public Accountant or not?

Mr. Hansen, you started off the discussion on this question. Please let us have your views on that.

MR. BØRGE HANSEN (Denmark)

In my opinion the report should not automatically go from the Internal Auditor to the External Auditor. It has been said several times by the gentlemen present here that we see that the External Auditor obtains the programme from the Internal Auditor, and I want to add that he should have access to the working papers and to the copies of the reports issued by the Internal Auditor during his audit. When checking the reliability of the Internal Auditor's work, he will also take cognizance of the internal auditor's reports. How much he will do depends upon his findings, but I do not see any reason why he should get the reports automatically.

MR. B. SMALLPEICE (United Kingdom)

I think that it might be of assistance to the Public Accountant to have them.

MR. BØRGE HANSEN (Denmark)

He should have access to them.

MR. B. SMALLPEICE (United Kingdom)

Yes. The discussion is now opened to everybody present here, and I have already received three questions. If I start by taking those, I think that will be the best thing to do. I have received a question from Mr. J. S. Seidman of New York and if I might, having the microphone in front of me, just put it on behalf of Mr. Seidman, the question is this: The authors of the papers say that the Internal Auditor should have a certain amount of independence. How much independence can be allowed, Mr. Seidman asks, to a mere employee who is in the position of being fired or discharged for disagreeing with his superior? Mr. Macpherson, would you like to deal with that?

MR. L. G. MACPHERSON (Canada)

I should say that I do not think the modern attitude towards employment at the administrative or executive level denies the quality of independence. It is too easy for the able executive to move around from post to post, for him to be tied down by any fear of loss of his economic independence, and at the sacrifice of his spirit, shall we say. I think that in this situation independence is much more an attitude of mind than a problem of economics and with that attitude of mind, of independence, he is in a proper position to behave as an auditor. Without it he should not be in the position of an auditor. The auditor should be prepared to present his independent opinion, and I am speaking of the Internal Auditor, and he should be prepared to defend that opinion and subject it to discussion, and then, I think, he should be prepared to abide by the decision that has to be made by management, since it is management that is responsible for the operation. At least, he must abide by that decision until another opportunity arises for him to press the point.

MR. B. SMALLPEICE (United Kingdom)

Mr. Walker, can you add anything to that?

MR. W. A. WALKER (United States of America)

I might just say that the Internal Auditor has to have independent thinking all up and down the line, not only with his own supervisors but with everybody up and down the line with whom he comes in contact. Those he makes audits of, so to speak. That means that he has to have a wider presentation, he has to sell his services in such a manner that people will like to see him come and not put up the iron curtain, so to speak, every time he comes down the hall. He must, therefore, sell his services to those whom he is auditing. Likewise, he has to sell his ideas to his boss, and I think that, as long as he does not become obnoxious about it but tries to sell it, and make it understood that this is his considered judgment that he is putting forward to the best interest of the company, he is going to get a good reception. I think that, because I am now on the other side of the fence, where I certainly would hate to think that our Internal Auditors are trying to be Yesmen to their superiors. The superiors certainly want to know what, independently, the Internal Auditor thinks; if they thought he was just echoing what they thought, he would not be of any use to them. So I think independence is something which the Internal Auditor certainly can maintain, possibly to the ultimate degree that the Public Accountant can maintain it. On the other hand, the Public Accountant can't afford to be hard to get along with either, as far as that's concerned; he too has a selling job to do. Thus independence can be, and is being, achieved by the Internal Auditor.

MR. B. SMALLPEICE (United Kingdom)

Thank you. I have also had a question from Mr. A. Rayner of Leeds, England, and in introducing this question I would just like to refer to a question which may have been in the minds of many of you, that is, why in the original outline I gave for setting the discussion, I chose to talk about a business employing several thousands of people. It was for this reason, that it can be, I think, taken as obvious that there is a function of Internal Audit to be performed within a business of that size. But Mr. Rayner has raised a question in regard to the small firms, and I am very grateful to him for doing so, because this discussion would not have been in any way complete without reference to them. I think the easiest way of summing up his question is to take some words out of this paper which he has handed to me and ask 'at what stage in the growth of a business is an internal audit warranted'. Now that is a very important question and I do not know that there is any absolute answer, but I wonder if you, Mr. Irish, would like to have a shot at it.

MR. R. A. IRISH (Australia)

Mr. Managing Director, I think you almost ask me to do the impossible; there is obviously no absolute answer to such a question, but I feel sure that each member of this panel has been concerned as to the scope of the Internal Auditor's function. The maximum scope which was enunciated by Mr. Davies at the outset is something which I would frankly not like to see universally applicable to all Internal Auditors, because it obviously embraces certain functions which almost go beyond internal auditing and which I might best illustrate by saying that your Public Accountant may be a good financial adviser, but if he is appointed as auditor, it does not follow that he must automatically be your financial adviser, nor even that he is the best man to do that particular job. And also we must be conscious of the fact that management can vary the duties of the Internal Auditor, as it wishes. But certainly within the purely protective field as well as the constructive field I think there is a point in the development of a business which would warrant at least the consideration of whether an Internal Auditor would not greatly strengthen the organization. I think that the yardstick might perhaps come in two ways, possibly there are others. The first one, obviously, is the volume of transactions and we may well find that in a relatively small business with a limited number of employees, which, however, has multitudes of transactions of small value, on the strictly protective side an Internal Auditor might be a very valuable person. On the other hand, where you run into large numbers of personnel, and you have to delegate responsibilities to individuals, so that personal supervision is not so practicable, unquestionably the use of internal audit should be considered, and for what it is worth I would suggest that any business having a staff of say 500 people should consider whether the appointment of an Internal Auditor would be advantageous at that stage. And, more emphatically, I think with a thousand people I would find almost inevitably it was very advantageous.

MR. B. SMALLPEICE (United Kingdom)

Thank you. What do you think, Mr. Sinnott?

MR. E. SINNOTT (United Kingdom)

Although I agree very largely with what Mr. Irish has said, I would be very hesitant to fix any actual size of the business by relation to the number of employees. It is very difficult indeed to give a number like that. I did try in my paper to paint a picture, as it were, of an abstract proposition of the stage at which it might well be beneficial to install an internal audit. I conceived it to be the stage when the business had reached such a point that the managers, who are responsible to the policy-making body, could not give personal supervision themselves, nor could they rely upon the Public Accountant to check in detail the financial records, because they had got too extensive. I think it would be at that point that some system of internal check on financial procedures or regulations would have to be drawn up for the information of all personnel of the company, and I think it would be then that you would require an internal audit to ensure compliance with your laid-down procedures and to provide some sort of detail check, which the Public Accountant could no longer do. I would hesitate to give a number to it, but that is about the stage I would visualize an internal audit as being worth while.

MR. B. SMALLPEICE (United Kingdom)

That I feel, Mr. Rayner, will answer the main question which you put to us. Now I have another question here from Mr. D. de la Garza of Mexico. He asks if the panel consider that an Internal Auditor, with the personal qualifications referred to in the various papers and the desired independence of mind, could be in a safe position to do a balance sheet audit for external purposes or submit to the shareholders a report on the balance sheet of the company in which he acts as an internal auditor. Mr. Macpherson, could you help us on this?

MR. L. G. MACPHERSON (Canada)

Well, it looks to me that this question calls for a very simple answer which is not in any conflict with what has been said about independence being largely an attitude of mind. There is something more to it than that. It is necessary that those who are to rely on the auditor have absolute assurance of his independence. It is not just enough for him to be in an independent state of mind, and this absolute assurance cannot possibly, I think, be conveyed to shareholders or the general public by one who is in the position of an employee at any level. I think it needs the professional relationship to support the public view.

MR. W. N. A. F. H. STOKVIS (Netherlands)

Mijnheer de directeur, Zou ik nog één punt van de vraag van mijnheer Rayner naar voren mogen brengen, omdat ik geloof, dat hij met de vraag, die hij o.a. stelt in zijn brief een tere plek aanraakt in de gehele behandeling van dit onderwerp. Hij vraagt namelijk of 'Internal Auditor' is still an appropriate term; it seems that in at least one other language he is referred to as the 'Internal Accountant'. Namelijk de 'Internal Auditor' krijgt zoveel dingen te doen, die – ik zou haast tussen de regels door kunnen lezen – niet meer tot zijn taak behoren, dat het beter zou zijn, volgens de heer Rayner, om die mijnheer 'Internal Accountant' te noemen. Ik geloof nu, dat hij hier op een bijzonder kwetsbaar punt komt, namelijk dat wij in onze terminologie, die wij gebruiken in de verschillende talen, maar ook in de terminologie die wij gebruiken in de Nederlandse taal, ons eigenlijk zouden moeten voorstellen, wat bedoelen we nu precies met 'internal auditor'. Als ik de verschillende 'papers' lees, Mijnheer de directeur, die voorgelegd zijn, dan kom ik tot de conclusie, dat men, sprekende over de 'Internal Auditor' in vele gevallen bedoelt de interne adviseur op administratief-organisatorisch gebied. Vandaar dus ook, dat men de vraag krijgt, komt hij niet op een gegeven moment in strijd met allerlei andere adviserende instanties, die in deze onderneming aanwezig zijn?

Zou het niet goed zijn, dat wij het eens zouden zijn over wat nu precies 'internal auditor' betekent.

Om mijn bijdrage hiertoe te leveren stel ik, dat bij een perfecte organisatie in de onderneming van voldoende omvang de 'internal auditor' de enige 'auditor' is, waaraan de onderneming behoefte heeft voor de uitoefening van de controlerende, beschermende taak ten behoeve van de leider der onderneming en de daaruit volgende constructieve taak. Ieder ander administratief deskundige in de onderneming geve men een andere titel.

Aan dit beginsel doet niet af, dat de openbare accountant ook in deze onderneming zijn intrede zal doen ten behoeve van deze onderneming in zijn adviserende taak en ten behoeve van de financieel geïnteresseerden buiten de onderneming in zijn controlerende taak.

Mr. Managing Director, There is just one more point with regard to Mr. Rayner's question that I should like to bring forward, because I believe that the question he poses, among other things, in his letter touches a tender spot in the whole treatment of this subject. He asks if 'Internal Auditor' is still an appropriate term; it seems that in at least one other language he is referred to as the 'Internal Accountant'. That is to say, the Internal Auditor gets so many things to do, which —I could practically read through the lines here—do not really belong to his task, that, according to Mr. Rayner, it would be better to call him the 'Internal Accountant'. Now I think that he touches on a very vulnerable point here; that is to say, in the terminology used in Holland, we ought really to ask ourselves what we mean precisely by the term 'Internal Auditor'. When, Mr. Managing Director, I read all the papers that have been submitted I come to the conclusion that in many cases, in speaking of the 'Internal Auditor' what is meant is the Internal Advisor on accounting and organizational matters. And this is why the question arises as to whether he comes into conflict, sooner or later, with all the other advisory officials working in the business. Would it not be a good thing if we were to agree as to what the term 'Internal Auditor' really means. To make my contribution to this, I would say that in the case of a perfect organization in a firm of adequate size, the 'Internal Auditor' is the only 'auditor' the firm requires for the performance of the auditing and protective task on behalf of the Management, and for the performance of the constructive function ensueing from this. Every other accounting expert in the business should be given a different title.

The fact that the Public Accountant also performs a function in the firm, both on behalf of the firm itself in his advisory capacity, and on behalf of financially interested parties outside the firm in his auditing capacity, does not alter this principle.

MR. B. SMALLPEICE (United Kingdom)

Thank you. Those are all the questions I have received so far. Are there any other questions which any member present would like to put? If there are none, there is one point which I think we might take up for a moment, and it is related to this question of the independence of an Internal Auditor: what qualifications should he have and ought he to be a member of a recognized body of accountants? Mr. Irish, have you any view as to whether it is desirable for the Internal Auditor to be a member of a professional body?

MR. R. A. IRISH (Australia)

Yes, I think it is most desirable, Mr. Smallpeice. First of all it is an indication that he has covered a basic field of academic knowledge, and secondly I think, too, that membership or qualification through such a channel, is more inclined to instill into him the professional principles which, after all, should characterise his work, although he might not be in public practice.

MR. B. SMALLPEICE (United Kingdom)

Mr. Walker, do you have views on this subject?

MR. W. A. WALKER (United States of America)

I do not have any strong views on this subject at all, Mr. Smallpeice, because I do not think it necessary for an Internal Auditor to be C.P.A. or anything like that, Chartered Accountant and what, not as long as he knows the business and his objectives. I do think that, as long as an organization is available in his particular field, such as the Institute of Internal Auditors in the United States, it is beneficial to him to have that association with other people, where he can exchange views and give his views to them, so I think that he should belong to such an organization.

MR. B. SMALLPEICE (United Kingdom)

Is there anybody who wants to put a question? (question from floor) Can I just try to repeat in a few words what you have said because of the impossibility of translation unless it comes through the microphone.

As I understand it, what you are asking is whether there is any measure by which the cost of the internal audit department or system can be gauged as being of value to the undertaking. Mr. Sinnott, you must have asked this question of yourself a good many times, what would you say?

MR. E. SINNOTT (United Kingdom)

I have tried to deal with it in my paper. It is very difficult. As you would not judge the cost of the fire brigade by the number of fires that broke out, so you should not judge the cost of an Internal Audit by the number of frauds or falsifications it turns up. Because the existence of the internal audit may prevent them. Nevertheless there are several tests: I have applied tests of suggestions for improvements in procedures which the Internal Audit has made and we have attempted calculations of resultant savings. You can get a quantitative figure that way to measure against the cost of the audit, but you know that it is the moral presence of the audit which is worth a good deal. And I think it is quite impossible to put an absolute figure on the points at which your audit becomes remunerative to you in terms of cold cash. It is almost like a police force: it sometimes stops the murder. And we hope that we get less murders, i.e. less fraud, by the existence of the internal audit. Also in the sense of the internal audit giving a continuous appraisal of systems, procedures and internal check, they do improve the organization with benefits to its payroll. Those are a few tests you can apply, but there is no one single short test, which I know of.

MR. W. R. DAVIES (United States of America)

I would like to echo what Mr. Sinnott has said, because I do not think it is possible to evaluate the total value of an audit and internal audit division to a company in terms of dollars and cents, as we would say in the U.S. I think that the preventive phases of internal auditing cannot be evaluated in all circumstances. It is entirely possible, however, to evaluate, say at the year end, how much you have saved the company. I know we have done it in our company, and it sometimes amounts up to quite a figure. If you're auditing the contracts, contractor's charges, expansion costs, plant construction and so forth, and if it is in any great volume, you can certainly pay your way. But largely I think that you should not attempt to dollarize or evaluate, add up a lot of figures in order to say: this is what the Internal Auditor's vision has saved you and this what it has cost and therefore this is the profit.

MR. B. SMALLPEICE (United Kingdom)

I think that an interesting point arising out of this subject, which might be worth spending a few moments on, is the question of the relation between internal audit and internal control. Is internal audit part of the general system of internal control, and how is it different from internal check and so on, because it depends very much, I think, on how we answer this question what value we would place on internal audit. Mr. Irish, may I ask you for your views on this point?

MR. R. A. IRISH (Australia)

Yes, Mr. Smallpeice. I suggested earlier that while internal audit may be regarded as part of internal control, I am rather more partial to the view that it should be regarded as complementary to it, because internal control signifies primarily a process of check and cross check from within the organization by those who have positive accounting functions—the people in your accounting department, for example. And I don't think that they should be relieved of any of their basic duties in the internal control system by the mere knowledge that there is an internal audit following on behind. And for internal audit to be truly an audit, I think it should preferably not be regarded as part of your internal check system, if not your internal control.

MR. B. SMALLPEICE (United Kingdom)

May we have your views, Mr. Stokvis?

MR. W. N. A. F. H. STOKVIS (Netherlands)

Mijnheer de directeur, Interne contrôle (Internal control) is het *geheel* van contrôlehandelingen en -middelen. De interne contrôle kan derhalve betrekking hebben op het commercieel, het technisch en het financieel gebeuren in de onderneming.

'Internal check' is interne contrôle, toegepast in de administratie, en uitgeoefend door niet bij uitstek contrôle-deskundigen. 'Internal check' ontstaat o.a. door functiescheiding en meervoudige administratieve verwerking, waardoor langs minstens twee onafhankelijke wegen een zelfde resultaat moet worden verkregen.

'Internal audit' wordt uitgevoerd door personen, 'Internal Auditors', die deskundig zijn op het gebied van contrôle en functioneel zijn samengevoegd in een 'internal audit department'.

'Internal Audit' verschaft o.m. de bewaking van de 'Internal control' en de 'Internal check'.

Mr. Managing Director, 'Internal control' is the whole complex of verification operations and means of accounting control. Consequently, internal control can relate to the commercial, technical and financial sides of the business. 'Internal check' is the complex of internal control procedures, applied in the field of accounting and exercised by other than specialized 'control' functionaries. 'Internal check' is arrived at by a division of functions and by multiple accounting processes, which should produce the same result, working along at least two independent paths. 'Internal audit' is performed by persons, known as 'Internal Auditors', who are experts in the field of auditing and who form a functional unit, known as the 'internal audit department'. Thus, 'Internal audit' provides, among other things, a control on 'internal control' and 'internal check'.

MR. B. SMALLPEICE (United Kingdom)

Now, Ladies and Gentlemen, it seems that it is up to me to try to sum up this discussion. It is not a task that I much envy myself, because it is very evident, I think, that there are considerable differences in viewpoint on fundamental points. That, I think, is a good thing; it is very healthy that it should be so, and it would be dull if we were all of one mind.

On this first question of the scope of the Internal Audit function within a business we all entirely agree that the basic function is that of protection, but beyond that it is suggested that there should be a constructive approach.

I think that it is generally felt that the Internal Auditor, if he is going to be of value to a business, must be not only protective but also constructive and in fact if he is not so, then he will tend not to be so highly regarded by the other members of the management. It is when he extends beyond the strictly financial field that we find differences between us; and I am wondering now—Mr. Stokvis referred to it in one of his earlier remarks—whether we are not in danger of being led into confusion by uncertainty as to what this function is which we call internal audit. I mean, if it's pressed very far, it can be stretched to cover almost everything in the business. Looking at it from my assumed position as Managing Director of a business, then I can only assume that, as Mr. Sinnott suggested, if the Internal Auditor tries to cover everything he is almost the Managing Director himself, or at any rate nothing less than his personal assistant. And when it comes to questions of evaluating business policies or selecting matters which require corrective action in a business, I am wondering whether the Internal Auditor is not in point of fact setting out to do work which in many businesses would be undertaken by the comptroller or by some other executive. I don't think we want to establish agreement upon this. I think it is a good thing to know that there are these conflicting views. But it seems to me that an Internal Auditor can be used for very many different things, depending on his personal qualities, and if in some cases it is desirable to use him outside the strictly financial function, then it is necessary to remember that he is being used to do other things, which may not really be within the definition of an Internal Auditor at all. At the same time I am sure we will all have gained the general impression from this panel that the Internal Auditor has to be constructive, because if he is not, he will not gain the support of his colleagues in the management. In fact, it was very well put by one speaker when his duties were described as being to assist all members of management in the discharge of their responsibilities. And if he can help them to do that through his checking of all that goes on, on the financial side of their responsibility, then that must be an advantage to them.

I think that is evident not only from the papers but also from the remarks that have been passed to-day, that the question of what status he should have in the business is one which does not allow of a very firm answer but it would seem that he must have sufficient authority within a business to ensure that what he says receives due consideration. Businesses differ so much from one another that we might get different answers in different sorts of circumstances. On the question of the relationship between the Internal Auditor and the Public Accountant, there is, of course, the fundamental distinction between their different duties. This is one thing that is easy in a body of professional accountants to dogmatize about, and I think that there can be no question of the Internal Auditor taking away any part of the responsibility of the Public Accountant. But it seems to me—this is an impression I have gained, anyway, from what has been said—that the work of the Internal Auditor is done primarily for the better working of the business, and if his work can contribute to the work which the Public Accountant would have to do, or if his work would indeed relieve the Public Accountant of detail work, then so much the better; and indeed any collaboration that can be achieved between the two is to the general advantage.

Mr. Chairman, I think that brings me to the end of my remarks, and if I might, I shall hand the session over to you.

CHAIRMAN:

Meine sehr geehrten Damen und Herren, Die Zeit ist bereits ziemlich vorgeschritten, so daß ich mich bemühen werde, eine Abkürzung der Schlußausführungen vorzunehmen. Die Diskussion und die Referate und auch die Zusammenfassung der Diskussion haben gezeigt, daß dem verhältnismäßig jungen Sproß in unserer prüfenden Tätigkeit – Interne Kontrolle – doch eine sehr große Bedeutung beizumessen ist. Wir haben weiter, glaube ich, aus den Referaten zu unserer großen Freude eine positive Feststellung entnehmen können, daß doch in sehr vielen Punkten bei den Herren Autoren Uebereinstimmung besteht hinsichtlich der Art der Tätigkeit, der Eingliederung und der besonderen Aufgaben des internen Accountants. Weiterhin glaube ich festgestellt zu haben, daß in diesem Punkte eine volle Uebereinstimmung bei den Autoren vorhanden ist, nämlich in der Frage, daß der interne Accountant mit seiner ganzen Einrichtung eine außerordentlich wertvolle Arbeit und Vorarbeit und Mitarbeit für den externen Accountant für den Abschluß leisten kann. Wenn er ihm auch nicht die Verantwortung für den vollen Umfang seiner Tätigkeit abnimmt, so hat er doch, glaube ich, ihm ein wesentliches Stück Arbeit durch seine Tätigkeit im Laufe des Jahres abnehmen können. Die Ausführungen der Referenten begegneten, wie ich feststellen konnte, großem Interesse und geben Veranlassung, in der täglichen Berufsarbeit die Nutzanwendung zu praktizieren. Darin erblicke ich den großen Wert des Kongresses. Ich hoffe mit Mr. Irish, der in seiner Broschüre, soweit ich gelesen habe, ausgeführt hat, daß dem internen Accountant eine verheißungsvolle und glückliche Zukunft bevorsteht, auf eine Erfüllung dieser Prophezeiung. Ich darf jetzt Mr. Davies bitten, zu den Mitgliedern des Panels zu sprechen.

Ladies and Gentlemen, We are almost behind time and therefore I shall try to be as brief as possible. The discussion, the papers which have been presented, and the summary of the discussion have shown us that this comparatively young offspring of our audit activity, the Internal Audit, is nevertheless of very considerable importance. And I think I might say that the papers which have been presented here have shown us, to our gratification, that there is a great deal of agreement among our authors concerning the nature of the work, the position and the special duties of the Internal Auditors. I think I may also say that there is complete agreement on one point, that is that the Internal Auditor, with his entire apparatus, can perform very valuable work for the External Auditor—preparatory work and work in collaboration with him—to help him arrive at his final balance. Although he cannot relieve the External Auditor of the responsibility for the full extent of his work, he can nevertheless relieve him of a great deal of work by the operations he himself performs during the course of the year.

As far as I could make out, the detailed accounts given us by the authors have been followed with great interest and I hope that they may give us occasion to make use of what we have heard, in our daily work. Here, in my opinion, lies the great value of this congress. I think it was Mr. Irish who said in his report, as far as I have understood, that a promising and happy future lies ahead of the Internal Auditor, and I hope that this prophecy may be fulfilled. Now, I should like to call on Mr. Davies to address the members of the panel.

Vice-chairman, MR. G. H. L. DAVIES (New Zealand)

Mr. Chairman, Ladies and Gentlemen, I consider it a privilege indeed to be asked on your behalf to propose a vote of thanks to Mr. Smallpeice, Mr. Walker and the other distinguished gentlemen on the platform who have given us to-day such an interesting discussion. From the matters discussed, and as mentioned by other speakers, we can see that there are a number of points on the subject of the internal audit where we have had differences of opinion. Perhaps I might say that that could be the reason why I have been asked to thank them, because coming from the very small country of New Zealand, where the process of development of the accounting functions has not come to the stage of internal audit, we have very few Internal Auditors. So it could be fairly commented that I have no views one way or the other, and therefore am not subject to prejudice! There may be in the audience other accountants from the smaller countries and I think they will appreciate the interest raised by the discussion to-day. It would serve as a very good introduction to what we may expect when business activities grow to the size where the employment of an Internal Auditor is warranted. The papers presented, of which, of course, we all have copies, I suggest will remain of much value for some years to come, and will be re-read quite often. I feel I shall be looking at mine quite a number of times in view of the comments passed to-day. So, Ladies and Gentlemen, we are over our time, and I ask you to join with me in thanking all these gentlemen for the long preparation and hard work which has been necessary to ensure this most successful session to-day.

Vice-chairman, MR. FEDERICO RIOSECO (Mexico)

Mr. Chairman, Ladies and Gentlemen, It is a very great privilege to have this opportunity to thank and congratulate you and the other members of the panel for the successful manner in which this discussion has been conducted. This business session, entitled 'The Internal Auditor' rather than 'Internal Auditing' has a surprisingly significant connection with the brilliant allusion made by His Royal Highness, The Prince of The Netherlands, in the opening session, to the higher aspects of the profession —when reference was made to the importance of the spiritual integrity of the accountant as his fundamental qualification. This trend which leads to successively higher goals, in all phases of our activity, has also been constantly promoted in my country by practitioners and teachers of accountancy. For this reason, I proudly present to you all the sincere and warm compliments of the accountants of Mexico. I thank you.

CHAIRMAN:

Meine sehr geehrten Damen und Herren, Mit einem besonderen Dank an Sie darf ich jetzt diese Arbeitssitzung schließen.

Ladies and Gentlemen, I should like to express my thanks to you once again and I herewith close this afternoon's meeting.

ASCERTAINMENT OF PROFIT IN BUSINESS

Morning session: Friday, 13th September 1957

Papers by: Page

Chairman:	A. VEYRENC, France
Vice-Chairmen:	R. GERBÈS, Luxembourg G. E. FITZGERALD, B.A., B. COM., F.A.S.A., F.C.I.S., Australia RAHIM JAN, Pakistan
Panel members:	
Discussion leader:	WELDON POWELL, C.P.A. *American Institute of Certified Public Accountants*
Rapporteur and author of a paper:	G. L. GROENEVELD, Ec. Drs. *Nederlands Instituut van Accountants*
Authors of papers:	IRA N. FRISBEE, C.P.A. *American Institute of Certified Public Accountants*
	PROF. PALLE HANSEN [1] *Foreningen af Statsautoriserede Revisorer, Denmark*
	C. I. R. HUTTON, B.A. (Oxon), C.A. *Institute of Chartered Accountants of Scotland*
	PROF. DR. LEOPOLD L. ILLETSCHKO [1] *Kammer der Wirtschaftstreuhänder, Austria*
	EMILE MANGAL [1] *Collège National des Experts Comptables de Belgique*
Other members of the panel:	HELGE BRÆNDE *Norges Statsautoriserte Revisorers Forening*
	BÖRJE FORSSTRÖM *Föreningen C. G. R., Finland*
	PROF. DR. KARL KÄFER *Verband Schweizerischer Bücherexperten*

[1] Prof. Hansen, Prof. Illetschko and Mr. Mangal were not able to attend the congress; the following gentlemen were their deputies on the panel:

L. J. M. Roozen, ec. drs. *(Nederlands Instituut van Accountants)*
Dr. Ernst Allet *(Kammer der Wirtschaftstreuhänder, Austria)*
E. K. P. Darden *(Collège National des Experts Comptables de Belgique)*

INLEIDING

van

G. L. GROENEVELD, EC. DRS.

Nederlands Instituut van Accountants

I. Doelstelling en betekenis van de winstbepaling

De winstbepaling in de onderneming beoogt antwoord te geven op de vraag of de onderneming aan haar doelstelling heeft voldaan. De ondernemingsgewijze produktie wordt immers door het winststreven gekenmerkt. Mag dit sommigen te beperkt voorkomen, gezien de moderne tendenties waarin ook sociale doeleinden der onderneming naar voren treden, zo moet worden vastgesteld dat met deze ontwikkeling geen afbreuk wordt gedaan aan het feit, dat de maatschappelijke produktie door het economisch principe wordt beheerst, noch aan de conventie, dat wij in de bedrijfseconomie in het bijzonder de werking van het economisch motief bestuderen en dus de vraagstukken vanuit dit gezichtspunt bezien.

Met de produktie moet een overschot worden verkregen van opbrengst aan nuttigheid boven offers aan nuttigheid. Regelmatig moet de producent er zich rekenschap van geven of en in hoeverre hij daarin slaagt. Hierbij wordt het retrospectieve standpunt steeds meer verlaten. Sinds Emerson en Harrison de standaardkostprijsmethode in het leven riepen, sinds bedrijfsbegroting en budgettering nadrukkelijk dringen naar vooruitzien en begroten, is in de moderne onderneming de prospectieve beschouwingswijze doorgedrongen. Er zijn maatstaven ter beoordeling, er zijn normen, en daarmede is toetsing van de werkelijkheid aan hetgeen bereikt behoorde te worden mogelijk. Op korte termijn, per maand, per vier weken, per tien dagen, per week kunnen de bereikte resultaten worden beoordeeld aan de hand van de begrotingen. Het tot standkomen van de jaarstukken behoeft niet te worden afgewacht om de resultaten te kennen, zoals in het verleden regel was en bij de middengrote ondernemingen nog te veel voorkomt. De resultaten zijn in de goed geoutilleerde ondernemingen na de tiende, elfde maand reeds voldoende bekend. Voor bedrijfsbeoordeling is de jaarbalans dan van geen andere betekenis dan dat zij er een is uit de reeks van periodieke balansen op korte termijn. Wel heeft de publikatie van de over de jaarperiode bepaalde winst een typisch maatschappelijke functie. Het jaarverslag is de presentatie naar buiten. Het moge duidelijk het karakter dragen van een publikatie voor niet-insiders, het geeft toch de verslaglegging van het afgelopen jaar en de verantwoording over het gevoerd beheer. Met de voorstellen tot winstverdeling is het beslissend voor wat uit de winst der onderneming door de winstgerechtigde tot vertering zal kunnen worden gebracht. Het behoudt deze functies ook wanneer tussentijdse publikaties worden gedaan en interim-dividenden worden uitgekeerd.

Wanneer in de sociale economie over winst- of ondernemersinkomen wordt gesproken, worden de criteria ter afgrenzing van het inkomen in velerlei richting gezocht. Sommigen denken aan surplussen van geld of in het algemeen eenheden van koopkracht, anderen aan surplussen van reële goederen, weer anderen onderscheiden tussen surplussen uit permanent vloeiende bronnen en incidentele surplussen, en dit alles veelal herleid tot het inkomen van natuurlijke personen. Onze beschouwingen daarentegen zullen in het bijzonder de winst van de onderneming betreffen, deze laatste gezien als de produktieve eenheid in ons maatschappelijk bestel, die in economisch financieel en organisatorisch opzicht de zelfstandigheid heeft verworven die past in het kader van de maatschappelijke organisatie.

Die zelfstandigheid heeft in de loop der tijden een wisselende inhoud. Denken we ons de economische samenleving in de negentiende eeuw voornamelijk als die van een vrije economie, waarin het laisser-faire-stelsel domineert, thans kan men beter spreken van een 'économie orientée'. Naar de uiterlijke vorm is er vrijheid. De ondernemingen zijn autonoom. De ondernemingsleiding moet haar eigen zaken zelf regelen, alsof nog het laisser-faire-stelsel heerste. Er is vrije beschikkingsmacht over inkomens- en vermogensbestanddelen en over arbeidskracht. Het ruil- en prijsvormingsmechanisme van de vrije verkeershuishouding blijft gehandhaafd, maar de overheid en de centrale bank trachten door het prijsvormingsmechanisme zelf bepaalde resultaten te bereiken: volledige werkgelegenheid, spreiding van inkomen, monetair evenwicht. De fiscale politiek van de overheid en de monetaire politiek van de centrale bank verschaffen de machtsmiddelen om de gestelde doeleinden te bereiken of na te streven. Men kan spreken van globale, niet-specifieke beïnvloeding van de geldstroom, die het economisch proces als het ware draagt. Er is een indirecte ordening, waarbij voornamelijk gebruik wordt gemaakt van fiscale en monetaire beleidsvormen, waardoor de afloop van het economisch proces indirect wordt beïnvloed.

Gezocht wordt een synthese tussen vrijheid van het individu en gebondenheid van de volkshuishouding aan bepaalde normen. In dit milieu heeft de hedendaagse onderneming haar plaats. Gespeeld wordt als het ware het spel van de vrije economie, waarbij uiteraard de onderneming naar 'winst' streeft. Op de achtergrond staat dan het globale beleid, dat de overheid tracht te voeren.

De instelling bij de onderneming en haar leiding is dus typisch microeconomisch, doelgericht, met concrete oogmerken en motieven – maar er is maar een beperkte horizon. De ondernemingsleiding heeft slechts kennis van haar naaste omgeving; het gezichtsveld is beperkt en zij reageert onmiddellijk op de direct waarneembare verschijnselen: vraag, aanbod, produktie, afzet, en... winstmogelijkheden. Ook wij zullen het vraagstuk van de winst bezien vanuit het gezichtspunt van de onderneming. De conclusies zullen gewoonlijk niet zonder meer in overeenstemming zijn met die welke vanuit het gezichtspunt van de gemeenschap zouden worden bereikt. Maar evenmin als de ondernemingsleiding zullen wij ons erin verdiepen, in hoeverre de macro-economische samenhang kan worden herleid tot de micro-economische relaties die eraan ten grondslag liggen.

Welk winstbegrip is onder deze omstandigheden voor de onderneming doelmatig? 'Economisch', aldus Limperg, 'heeft het begrip 'winst' slechts zin als grondslag voor de rationele behoeftebevrediging van hen wier inkomen in grootte afhankelijk is van de uitkomst van het produktieproces'. De vermogensvermeerdering der onderneming, die in beginsel verteerbaar is, is derhalve voor haar als winst te beschouwen. Verteerbaar voor háár, voor de onderneming, dus niet altijd voor de maatschappij in haar geheel. Sommigen menen dit onderscheid te moeten onderstrepen door van misbaarheid voor de onderneming te spreken. Voor ons echter heeft de gehanteerde eis van verteerbaarheid van het inkomen een logisch kader, wanneer wij het winststreven plaatsen tegen de achtergrond van de maatschappelijke produktieverdeling. Deze is immers zo dat de produktie onzer ruilverkeersmaatschappij overwegend is gericht op een indirecte behoeftebevrediging, d.w.z. op een behoeftebevrediging via de verwerving van een inkomen in geld. Hoe groot dit inkomen is, welke de vertering kan zijn, is dan de wezenlijke inhoud van de vraag, die met betrekking tot de uitkomsten van de produktie over de jaarperiode wordt gesteld. Met name zij, die hun inkomen in grootte afhankelijk stellen van de uitkomsten van het bedrijf, dienen de grootte van dat inkomen te kennen, opdat zij weten wat zij mogen verteren zonder het vermogen van het bedrijf waarin het inkomen wordt gevormd, in te teren.

De vraag welk deel van de vermogensvermeerdering in beginsel voor vertering beschikbaar zal zijn, en dus als inkomen kan worden beschouwd, blijkt verre van gemakkelijk te beantwoorden. Raadpleegt men de literatuur, dan zal men ervaren dat het criterium voor de verteerbaarheid veelal wordt verbonden aan een bepaalde doelstelling, waarvan men de verwezenlijking van belang of noodzakelijk acht. Wel wordt in het algemeen gezegd, dat de vermogensvermeerdering verteerbaar wordt geacht, indien de vertering kan geschieden zonder dat schade aan het bedrijf wordt toegebracht, maar het schade-element wordt in verschillende richting gezocht. Zo stelt men als eis de handhaving van vermogen of kapitaal, de handhaving van de continuïteit van de produktie en van de inkomensstroom, de instandhouding van de inkomensbron of ook de handhaving van de organische plaats van de onderneming in het bestel van de maatschappelijke produktie.

In Nederland heeft de vervangingswaardetheorie van Th. Limperg Jr. veel gezag verworven en vernieuwde belangstelling in het leven geroepen voor vraagstukken van waarde en winst, kostprijsberekening en resultaat, ruilwinst en speculatieve winst, transactie-winst en perioden-winst enz. In deze theorie ziet Limperg het vraagstuk van winstbepaling als een vraagstuk van waardebepaling. De waardering op de balans is tezelfdertijd en houdt in de waardering van de verbruikte werkeenheden in de winst- en verliesrekening. Het is de vervangingswaarde die bij de waardebepaling van de aanwezige werkeenheden op de winst- en verliesrekening moet worden gehanteerd. De betekenis van de goederen voor onze welvaart en in het bijzonder de betekenis van de produktiemiddelen voor het inkomenstreven van de producent, wordt volgens deze theorie ten enenmale uitgedrukt door de vervangingswaarde dezer goederen respectievelijk produktiemiddelen. Van die waarde is de producent afhankelijk wanneer hij het oog richt op de voortzetting van zijn produktieproces. Die waarde ook doet hem onderscheiden welke resultaten te danken zijn aan produktie en ruil en welke resultaten het gevolg zijn van prijsfluctuaties. Calculatie tegen vervangingswaarde verzekert de producent in belangrijke mate van het vermogen dat nodig zal zijn om het produktieproces in de continuïteit die onze produktie kenmerkt, te kunnen blijven financieren.

Van de grondslagen der vervangingswaardetheorie is een duidelijke uiteenzetting gegeven door A. Goudeket, welke is opgenomen in het gedenkboek van het zesde congres in 1952: Fluctuating price levels in relation to accounts. Wij mogen er ons daarom van ontslagen achten deze theorie thans als zodanig weer te geven. Wel dienen wij de conclusie te geven, waartoe deze theorie voor ons probleem leidt. Aanvaardt men daarvan de grondgedachte, dan is de vermogensvermeerdering verteerbaar en dus 'inkomen', wanneer de verbruikte werkeenheden voor hun vervangingswaarde van de opbrengsten in mindering zijn gebracht.

De stelling, dat als inkomen wordt beschouwd de vermogensvermeerdering die boven de vervangingswaarde der verbruikte eenheden uitgaat, heeft ten gevolge dat moet worden onderscheiden tussen de verteerbaarheid van het inkomen en de besteding daarvan. Nog veel verbreid is de opvatting dat alleen als inkomen kan worden beschouwd die vermogensvermeerdering, die in feite kan worden uitgekeerd. Het accent dient echter niet op de feitelijke mogelijkheid tot uitkering, maar op de principiële mogelijkheid tot vertering te liggen. Men moet zich losmaken van de vraag of de liquiditeiten voor de uitkering beschikbaar zijn, hetgeen bijv. in het geval van reeds voltrokken en intern gefinancierde expansie niet het geval is. Er zijn nog andere facetten: de gehele financiële structuur van de onderneming spreekt mede bij de bestemming die aan het inkomen wordt gegeven. Wij noemen de invloed van de liquiditeitspositie, de talrijke facetten van de dividendpolitiek en de reserveringspolitiek. De belangen van diverse categorieën van winstgerechtigden moeten worden afgewogen en in het algemeen de verhouding tot de vermogensmarkt worden omlijnd. Verhoudingen van macht en invloed spelen hierbij een rol naast die van calculatorische aard. Het zijn echter alle factoren van bestemming van het inkomen, zoals deze door beleidsoverwegingen worden ingegeven, maar geen factoren van de bepaling van het inkomen.

Niet kan worden ontkend, dat de praktijk soms in tegenstelling schijnt met onze stelling. In de gepubliceerde jaarrekeningen der naamloze vennootschappen is veelal de tendentie merkbaar om winst en uitgekeerde winst te doen samenvallen. Hiermede staat in nauw verband het rijkgeschakeerde vraagstuk van de geheime en stille reservering. Interessant voor het bedrijfsleven, interessant in het bijzonder voor de accountant, wiens verantwoordelijkheid voor de aanvaardbaarheid van de verslaglegging der vennootschappen hem rechtstreeks confronteert met de betekenis van dit vraagstuk voor zijn verklaring. Hoe nauw de relatie met ons onderwerp ook moge zijn, toch moeten wij ons ervan onthouden op dit vraagstuk in te gaan. De usantie der praktijk heeft in de theorie de neiging tot gelijkschakeling van winst en uitkeerbare winst versterkt. Ze is onjuist. De reservering is een winstbestemmingsvraagstuk en geen vraagstuk van winstbepaling. De reservering als winstbepalend element te zien zou het winstbegrip op losse schroeven zetten en de inhoud doen vervagen zowel van het begrip kosten als van onze opvatting over het begrip reserveren. Reserveren betekent het afscheiden van en het geven van een bestemming aan een deel van het inkomen, maar is geen oorzakelijk bepaalde voorziening en daarmede geen bestanddeel van de op vervangingswaarde gebaseerde kosten en geen factor ter bepaling van de inkomensgrootte.

Wij willen deze korte inleiding over doelstelling en betekenis van de winstbepaling niet besluiten zonder enkele woorden te wijden aan de betekenis van de winstbepaling voor de functie van de jaarrekening als administratief instrument.

In de aanvang van ons betoog hebben wij gerefereerd aan de ontwikkeling van de prospectieve oriëntering in de administratie, gepaard gaande met resultatenbepaling op korte termijn en vergelijking tussen hetgeen prospectief werd verwacht en retrospectief werd verkregen. De jaarrekening, samengesteld uit balans en winst- en verliesrekening, zien wij bij voorkeur als een uit de reeks der overzichten op korte termijn. Ze is dan het verlengstuk van de administratie, vloeit voort uit en is tevens het sluitstuk van de administratieve verslaglegging. De uitkomsten daarvan geven de uiteindelijke toets op de rentabiliteit en op de vervulling van het algemene doeleinde der onderneming. Voor de beoordeling van tal van vraagstukken moet in eerste aanleg worden teruggegrepen op de resultaten der winstbepaling. Ziedaar het grote belang van een verantwoorde grondslag voor de winstbepaling. In de theorie der vervangingswaarde, zoals deze in Nederland door Limperg is ontwikkeld, menen wij deze te hebben gevonden. Niet alleen bij de beoordeling van de gevolgen van prijsstijging respectievelijk prijsdaling, maar evenzeer bij de beoordeling van de efficiëntie van de produktie vindt deze theorie toepassing. Zij legt een dwingend verband tussen de vraagstukken van efficiëntie, kostprijsberekening en winstbepaling. De vervangingswaardetheorie fixeert de kostprijs op de causaal bepaalde offers die voor de produktie zijn vereist. Alleen doelmatig gebrachte offers kunnen causaal bepaald zijn. Standaardisatie der offers is daardoor een logisch gevolg van het toepassen van de vervangingswaarde.

De kostenstandaard krijgt een theoretisch verantwoorde inhoud als ze op de vervangingswaarde wordt gebaseerd. Afwijkingen van de werkelijkheid naar boven zijn geen bestanddeel van de kosten, maar vormen verliezen door verspilling. Bij toepassing van de budgettering kunnen standaard en werkelijkheid meelopen in de administratieve verslaglegging en wordt de winst- en verliesrekening opgebouwd naar de oorzaken, die leiden tot winst of verlies en wordt inzicht verkregen in de problemen die voorwerp van bedrijfsbeleid moeten zijn.

II. Waardering van grondstoffen en werkeenheden van duurzame produktiemiddelen in de verbruiksrekening

Ongetwijfeld is er behoefte aan een kritische beschouwing van de argumenten, die nog worden aangevoerd voor het handhaven van de uitgaafprijs als basis bij de bepaling van kosten en winst. Velen die nog niet ten volle bevredigd zijn door de vervangingswaarde-leer of daarmede nog niet volledig bekend zijn, beroepen zich op de onbepaaldheid of moeilijke bepaalbaarheid van de vervangingswaarden, op de mogelijkheid van persoonlijke beïnvloeding der resultatenrekening of op de onduidelijkheid van de uitkomsten bij hantering van de vervangingswaarden. Argumenten, die bij belangrijke toepassingen in de praktijk reeds zijn overwonnen en eigenlijk niet anders meer kunnen worden verklaard dan uit de kracht der traditie. Veelal ook ziet men de betekenis van de vervangingswaardetheorie te beperkt en erkent of wenst men als enig effect een zekere uitschakeling van de gevolgen van prijsfluctuaties. Het gevolg is, dat de toepassing van de vervangingswaarde wordt verbonden aan deze doelstelling. Ze wordt dan alleen in perioden van uitgesproken prijsbeweging noodzakelijk geacht, bovendien wordt dan naar andere technieken omgezien, waarlangs men een soortgelijk effect kan bereiken. Deze houding berust op een gebrek aan inzicht in de universaliteit der theorie en in haar wezen als theorie van waarde en daardoor van algemene geldigheid. Wel zullen de grootste kwantitatieve effecten zich daar voordoen, waar voorraden worden gehouden en aldus bij de ruil verschillen worden geconstateerd tussen hetgeen bij de verwerving der produktiemiddelen werd uitgegeven en datgene wat als vervangingswaarde bij de ruil wordt geofferd.

Bij de duurzame produktiemiddelen zijn de voorraden zelfs voor zeer lange tijd gebonden, in de vorm van werkeenheden van het duurzame activum, die daaruit eerst in de loop der jaren kunnen worden losgemaakt. Hier loopt de producent een veeljarig risico ten aanzien van de prijsontwikkeling, dat zich op verschillende wijze manifesteert. In de loop van zijn gebruiksduur ondergaat het duurzaam produktiemiddel prijsbewegingen, die zowel van structurele als van conjuncturele aard zijn. Bepaling van de levensduur van het produktiemiddel en keuze van afschrijvingssysteem dienen daarom te worden gezien tegen de achtergrond van de economische betekenis van het vervangende werktuig. De gevolgen van techniekverbetering moeten onder het oog worden gezien, evenals die van schommeling in de conjunctuur respectievelijk van inflatoire tendenties in de prijsbeweging. De vervangingswaardetheorie eist toepassing dezer factoren op de waarde der werkeenheden bij hun aanwending in de produktie: de (calculatorische) afschrijvingen moeten een realisatie inhouden van de opgetreden wijzigingen en moeten zijn aangepast aan het gewijzigd niveau van waarde. Door deze zelfde waarderingsgrondslag toe te passen op elk moment waarop de producent zich van de waarde zijner produktiemiddelen rekenschap geeft, ontstaat eenheid tussen balans en resultatenrekening en tussen resultatenrekening en kostprijscalculatie.

Er zijn verderstrekkende gevolgen: wat in de theorie van de uitgaafprijs als risico's moet worden gezien, wordt bij aanpassing aan gewijzigde omstandigheden ten dele omgezet in calculeerbare offers. De gevolgen van de onzekerheid over de waarde der werkeenheden gedurende de levensduur van het werktuig worden, voor zover het menselijk inzicht reikt, opgevangen in calculatie en winstberekening. Naarmate de diversiteit in levensduur van de duurzame activa groter is verdwijnt het prijsrisico ten aanzien van de werkeenheden die in voorafgaande perioden zijn verbruikt en wordt de financiering van de aanschaffing der vervangende werkeenheden verzekerd.

Reeds is men in het algemeen meer vertrouwd met de toepassing der vervangingswaarde-idee op de waarde der verbruikte grond- en hulpstoffen. Komt dit enerzijds doordat voor de producent grondstoffenprijzen en produktprijzen nauwer aan elkaar verbonden zijn dan de produktprijzen en de prijs der in het verleden door hem aangeschafte duurzame activa, zodat de gevolgen der prijsfluctuatie voor grond- en hulpstoffen duidelijker voor ogen staan, anderzijds is hieraan zeker niet vreemd, dat voor fiscale toepassing een uit de theorie ontstane gedachte hanteerbaar werd geacht; het ijzeren-voorraadstelsel deed zien dat men door bestendige waardering van een constante voorraad aan het begin en het einde ener boekingsperiode het effect van de prijsstijging in het verbruik doet uitkomen. In de vorm van het last-in-first-out-principe vond deze gedachte ook ingang in de V.S., wat niet zonder invloed bleef op de fiscale wetgeving in Nederland. De Wet Belastingherziening 1950 stond onder bepaalde voorwaarden een lifo-stelsel toe, dat enigermate dat van de V.S. benaderde. Met het arrest van de Hoge Raad van 7 maart 1956 nr. 12623 werd een verdere stap gezet op de evolutie van het fiscale winstbegrip, doordat ook de toepassing van de manco-regel tot goed koopmansgebruik werd verklaard.

In Amerika is de toepassing van het lifo-stelsel nog verbreed door de aanvaarding van de zogenaamde dollar-value-method, waarbij de confrontatie van begin- en eindvoorraad niet in hoeveelheden goederen maar in geldbedragen plaats vindt, hetgeen van bijzonder belang is voor zover begin- en eindvoorraden niet uit identieke goederen bestaan, doch uit goederen die in het produktieproces dezelfde functie vervullen. Het genoemde arrest geeft goede hoop, dat de ontwikkeling van de jurisprudentie van de Hoge Raad tot overeenkomstige resultaten voor Nederland zal leiden.

Wordt het stelsel toegepast op de economische voorraad, dan zal het ten aanzien van de winstberekening veelal een uitkomst geven die nagenoeg gelijk is aan die welke op basis van de vervangingswaardetheorie zou worden verkregen. Echter kent het ijzeren-voorraadstelsel in beginsel niet het alternatief van waardering tegen lagere opbrengst (markt)waarde. Voor de vermogensbepaling der balans voldoet het stelsel niet aan de eisen, omdat de voorraden in plaats van tegen de werkelijke waarde worden opgenomen tegen een neutrale of indifferente waarde. Voor de inkomensbepaling van de winst- en verliesrekening voldoet het daaraan evenmin, omdat in beginsel een nadelig verschil tussen opbrengst- of marktwaarde en de vaste (neutrale) waarde niet als verlies wordt genomen. Zo bleek de ijzeren-voorraadwaardering minder eenvoudig hanteerbaar dan zij zich voordeed. De ontwikkeling tot lifo-stelsel, normale voorraadstelsel, manco-stelsel, dollar-value-method, deed wel het aantal methoden toenemen, maar reeds blijkt in de Nederlandse opinievorming een zekere onvoldaanheid indien men de uitwerking van al deze regels toetst aan datgene wat men op grond van de vervangingswaardetheorie zou willen bereiken. Het ijzeren-voorraadstelsel is dan ook zwakker gefundeerd: het berust weliswaar op een inzicht in de gevolgen van prijsschommelingen op het resultaat, en gaat terecht uit van de complementariteit der produktiemiddelen en de continuïteit van de produktie, doch behelst niet meer dan een methodiek om deze fluctuaties te elimineren. De vervangingswaardetheorie daarentegen berust op een eigen opvatting omtrent het wezen van de waarde als zodanig en is daardoor bij de praktische toepassing beter opgewassen tegen de grote verscheidenheid van gevallen die zich in het bedrijfsleven voordoen. De vervangingswaardetheorie legt een causaal en dwingend verband tussen verbruik en vervanging en legt ook het eigenlijk moment van noodzakelijke vervanging, als bepaald door het moment van de ruil, vast. Daardoor doet zij ons in de bedrijfsresultaten een onderscheid maken tussen transactie-resultaten en voorraad-resultaten, terwijl van deze laatste nog weer de speculatie-resultaten moeten worden onderscheiden.

Deze belangrijke verrijking van de resultaten-analyse in de vervangingswaardetheorie wordt bij het ijzeren-voorraadstelsel gemist. Men onderschatte de betekenis van deze onderscheiding niet: doel van de onderneming is het verwerven van een inkomen uit produktie en ruil en niet het behalen van voordelen uit speculatieve voorraadmutaties. Produktie en ruil geven aan de onderneming haar specifieke en functionele plaats in het maatschappelijk bestel en niet de speculatie. Alleen door deze analyse is het derhalve mogelijk om na te gaan of de onderneming aan haar doelstelling heeft voldaan.

III. Winstbepaling op fiscale en bedrijfseconomische grondslag

Uit het voorgaande volgt reeds, dat de fiscale winstbepaling zal afwijken van die op bedrijfseconomische grondslag. Bedrijfseconomische overwegingen mogen dan al mede een rol spelen bij de conceptie van de fiscale wetgeving, er mag zelfs naar zijn gestreefd zo nauw mogelijk bij bedrijfseconomische grondslagen aan te sluiten, dit neemt niet weg dat er sterke divergenties zijn tussen fiscale en bedrijfseconomische winstbepaling. De fiscale winstbepaling volgt ten dele haar eigen principes. De fiscale politiek heeft ten enenmale haar eigen algemene, economische, financiële en sociale doeleinden, die niet altijd met strikt bedrijfseconomische desiderata in overeenstemming zijn (werkgelegenheid, redelijke verdeling van het nationale inkomen, bevoordeling van achtergebleven groepen van de bevolking, internationale betalingsverhoudingen, conjunctuurstabilisering e.d.). Bovendien moet de fiscus zich veilig stellen voor het incasso en er dus voor zorg dragen dat inderdaad alle winsten van het belastingplichtig subject worden belast. Daardoor moet zij zware eisen stellen aan de continuïteit der principes van winstbepaling en mist zij de dynamiek ter aanpassing aan gewijzigde omstandigheden, zoals deze aan het bedrijfsleven eigen is. Afweging van de zo zeer uiteenlopende belangen zal voortdurend plaats moeten vinden. Van het standpunt van de onderneming gezien kunnen bepaalde heffingen volkomen onjuist zijn, bijv. bij het niet-toelaten van afschrijvingen die hoger zijn dan die over de historische aanschaffingsprijs, de fiscale overheid zal zich echter meer afvragen welke lasten diverse onderdelen van het economisch apparaat kunnen dragen, zo dat het geheel zo goed mogelijk functioneert; dat deze goede functionering beperkt is wanneer tegen bedrijfseconomische grondslagen in wordt gehandeld, moge hier als waarschuwing worden uitgesproken. Wanneer nog in aanmerking wordt genomen, dat voor de formulering in de fiscale wetgeving juridische zienswijzen en overwegingen niet zonder betekenis zijn, volgt de conclusie, dat het niet redelijk is de eis te stellen dat de fiscale winst volledig zal corresponderen met de bedrijfseconomische winst, die toch ook nimmer op algehele exactheid zal kunnen bogen. Wel is noodzakelijk, dat men, gegeven de eigen aard van de fiscale winstbepaling, naar een zo ver mogelijk gaande toepassing der bedrijfseconomische beginselen streeft.

Vindt in de onderneming afzonderlijke vaststelling van bedrijfseconomische en fiscale winst plaats, dan ontstaat de mogelijkheid van discrepantie tussen de fiscale lasten die in feite ontstaan en de fiscale lasten welke zouden worden geheven van de winst die op bedrijfseconomische grondslag is bepaald, respectievelijk van de winst die als zodanig door de onderneming wordt gepubliceerd. Verschillen kunnen ontstaan naar beide zijden: de bedrijfseconomische winst kan zowel groter als kleiner zijn dan de fiscale.

In Nederland leiden sommige fiscale bepalingen op zichzelf ertoe, dat de fiscale winst tijdelijk lager wordt berekend dan de bedrijfseconomische winst. Te denken is aan de bepalingen volgens welke bepaalde winstbestanddelen in een zogenaamde overgangsreserve mogen (mochten) worden opgenomen, alsook aan de zogenaamde vervroegde afschrijvingen, die op de belangrijkste investeringen worden toegestaan. In beginsel is echter alle economische winst op de lange duur fiscaal belast. De fiscus vraagt haar deel soms vroeger, soms later dan de economische principes aangeven, maar zal onherroepelijk haar tol eisen, ook al verschijnt zij pas op het moment van liquidatie.

Hieruit volgt de eis tot normatieve calculatie van de winstbelasting bij het bepalen van het verteerbare inkomen, d.w.z. dat als jaarlast wordt genomen het normale percentage winstbelasting over het inkomen zoals dat wordt gepubliceerd. Dit houdt in de eis tot het opnemen van latente en uitgestelde belastingverplichtingen in de balans. Tussen deze beide, de latente en de uitgestelde belastingschulden, kan nog worden onderscheiden omdat de latente belastingschulden moeilijker bepaalbaar zijn, met name wanneer de vraag naar de contante waarde dezer claims wordt opgeworpen. Deze vraagstukken zijn thans niet aan de orde. De algemene grondslag is voorshands alleen van belang en deze eist, dat het vermogen en de winst, die in de jaarrekening worden getoond, de aftrek voor belastingheffing hebben ondergaan. Is dit niet het geval dan moeten de daarop rustende fiscale claims tot uitdrukking worden gebracht.

IV. De voorziening voor latente risico's bij de winstbepaling

De jaargrens moge voor de bepaling van de inkomensperiode doelmatig gekozen zijn, dit neemt niet weg dat zij een willekeurige scheidingslijn aanbrengt. De totale winst van de onderneming gedurende haar bestaan zou een afgebakend begrip zijn, maar de winst ener periode, die wij voor ons inzicht nodig hebben, is dat nu juist niet. De onderneming is in haar conceptie en activiteit ingesteld op duurzaamheid en continuïteit. Een continuele reeks van produktieprocessen verbindt de jaarperioden tot een organische reeks. Bij voortduring worden in de ene periode offers gebracht, die eerst in volgende perioden hun nut zullen afwerpen of zullen worden aangewend; de reeds besproken voorraden vormen hiervan de manifestatie. Daarnaast zien wij kosten, die zich met groter periodiciteit dan het jaar voordoen en ten laste behoren te komen ook van het jaar waarin zij niet optreden. Verliezen op debiteuren, op incourante voorraden, op garantieverplichtingen, doen zich niet met jaarlijkse regelmaat voor. Identieke verschijnselen kan men waarnemen bij reparatie en onderhoud, survey-verplichtingen en bij uitstek bij de risico-dragende activiteit der verzekeringsbedrijven.

Er is de noodzaak tot calculatie van deze vaak schijnbaar incidentele offers, ook in het jaar waarin zij niet in feite optreden. Er moeten volgens normatieve grondslagen voorzieningen worden getroffen. De grondslagen voor de calculatie van deze normen zijn vaak moeilijk aanwijsbaar. De meest exacte gegevens moeten voortvloeien uit de ervaringen in het verleden opgedaan, die moeten worden geëxtrapoleerd naar wat voor de toekomst het meest waarschijnlijk lijkt. De toekomst is echter onbepaald en zo blijft een schattings-element in de calculatie. Deze schattings-elementen kunnen worden aanvaard voor wie, zoals voor de aanhangers van de vervangingswaardetheorie, de winstbepaling een ex-post begrip is.

Voor velen draagt de winstbepaling echter een ex-ante karakter. Bij hen grijpt de onzekerheid der toekomstige ontwikkeling naar een veel groter terrein der winstbepaling over. Men wil de toekomstige ontwikkeling over de gehele lijn weerspiegeld zien in het oordeel over het heden. Waar die toekomst mede wordt beïnvloed door het beleid van de producent, worden beleidsoverwegingen betrokken in de winstbepaling der voorbije jaren. Subjectieve schattingen en beslissingen van de producent gaan daardoor mede een rol spelen in de winstbepaling.

Ook de onzekerheden die niet door het beleid van de producent kunnen worden bestreken, acht men van betekenis voor de winstbepaling. Soms samenhangend met de aloude risicotheorieën van de ondernemerswinst ziet men een hoge winst als uitvloeisel van een groot risico, waarop de terugslag zal volgen. Boven de kosten van het heden uit wil men de onzekerheden der toekomst herleiden tot offers van heden en verleden, waarvan men de grootte echter nog niet kent. Deze gedachtengang leidt tot de conclusie, dat er eigenlijk geen winst meer is, omdat de winst immers tot functie krijgt om de onzekere offers der toekomst op te vangen. De winstbepaling is afhankelijk van de toekomst en de bestemming tot uitkering zou eigenlijk niet meer mogen worden gegeven. Voor zover dit toch geschiedt berust deze beslissing, die voor winstbepaling en winstbestemming gezamenlijk geschiedt, op de subjectieve overwegingen van de producent.

Deze opvatting is niet zonder gevolgen voor de houding van producent en accountant. Reeds is in de Nederlandse literatuur door B. Pruyt de mening uitgesproken, dat de verklaring van de accountant omtrent de juistheid van de berekende winst in feite vrijwel steeds een geclausuleerde verklaring zou moeten zijn. De bedrijfseconoom zou geen juist winstbegrip kunnen vaststellen en op de vraag 'wat is winst' geen voor alle gevallen geldend antwoord kunnen geven. Soortgelijke uitlatingen uit de buitenlandse literatuur zijn niet onbekend. Het inkomensbegrip behoort dan bijv. tot de 'rough approximations, used by the business man to steer himself through the bewildering changes of situation which confront him. For this purpose, strict logical categories are not what is needed; something rougher is actually better' (Hicks).

Het behoeft geen betoog dat dergelijke opvattingen tegengesteld zijn aan de onze. Naar onze mening moeten vraagstukken van bedrijfsbeleid en winstbepaling scherp van elkaar worden onderscheiden. De beleidsvraagstukken doen zich op het circuit van winstbepaling naar winstbestemming voor. Hierbij kan, of zelfs moet, het beleid op de toekomst zijn gericht. Maar wil over winstbestemming worden gesproken, dan moet eerst de winst vaststaan en daartoe moet klaarheid bestaan over het winstbegrip. De toepassing van de uitgaafprijs als waardebeginsel vormt een hinderpaal in deze oordeelvorming. Ze leidt tot wisselvallige uitkomsten der winstberekening en creëert daardoor een sfeer van onzekerheid, waarin men voorzieningen voor latente risico's in de ruimste zin als onmisbaar element van winstbepaling gaat zien. De uitgaafprijs is een grootheid die uitdrukking geeft aan een dood verleden. Ze geeft een cijfer dat interessant was op het moment van besteding, maar faalt bij de vaststelling van kosten en van inkomen dat verworven wordt bij de ruil in latere perioden. De vervangingswaarde daarentegen is de waarde van het ogenblik, waarin de waardering naar het momentele inzicht van de verkeersmaatschappij is voltrokken. Wanneer de winstbepaling zich bij dit proces aansluit, voldoet zij aan de behoeften van producent en maatschappij.

Zij die niet naar het verleden maar naar de toekomst zien en de bepaling van de vervangingswaarde naar het toekomstige moment van vervanging willen verschuiven, verwarren waardebepaling met schatting van de financieringsbehoefte ten tijde van de vervanging. De prijsfluctuatie der toekomst is een element van die toekomst, maar heeft geen gevolgen voor de winstberekening over het afgelopen tijdvak. Handelt men anders, dan incorporeert men elementen van onzekerheid en beleid in een winstbepaling, die strijdig zou zijn met de ex-post-opvatting van de aanhangers der vervangingswaardetheorie.

Nog een andere visie op de toekomst blijkt mogelijk, wanneer wij zien hoe sommigen de waardebepaling willen voltrekken op basis van de gekapitaliseerde waarde der toekomstige opbrengsten, waarvan de schatting uiteraard grote moeilijkheden inhoudt. Op deze wijze wordt echter niets anders berekend dan de (indirecte) opbrengstwaarde der produktiemiddelen, welke waarde alleen onder bijzondere omstandigheden relevant is.

Wij menen uit het voorafgaande te mogen concluderen, dat de vervangingswaardetheorie door de winstbepaling te koppelen aan de momentele waarde een belangrijke bijdrage heeft gegeven tot een kwantitatieve bepaling en exacte omlijning van het winstbegrip. Het wil ons voorkomen dat in de opbouw van zekerheid over het winstbegrip een van de belangrijkste taken ligt die bedrijfseconomen en accountants hebben te vervullen. Moge de gedachtenwisseling van het Congres ertoe bijdragen ons inzicht en onze oordeelvorming in deze materie te verrijken.

Translation

PAPER

by

G. L. GROENEVELD, EC. DRS.

Nederlands Instituut van Accountants

1. *Purpose and significance of the ascertainment of profit*

The ascertainment of business profits is aimed at answering the question whether the business has reached its target. The characteristic of our system of production is the object of making profits. Possibly some may feel this definition to be too narrow, bearing in mind the modern tendency to stress the social purposes of the business. This development, however, does not alter the fact that production in a community is governed by economic principle, nor does it affect the convention that in business economics the working of economic motives is the particular object of study and that the problems must be dealt with from this point of view.

Production should yield a surplus of proceeds over the value of the utilities sacrificed in production. The entrepreneur must regularly ascertain whether and to what extent he has succeeded in doing this: the retrospective viewpoint is being abandoned more and more. Since Emerson and Harrison developed the method of standard costing, since business forecasts and budgeting emphasize the necessity of looking ahead, the prospective view has entered into modern business philosophy. Standards are set to compare reality with what ought to be achieved. Actual results can be critically examined at short intervals —monthly, four-weekly, per ten days, weekly—with the aid of budgets. It is not necessary to wait for the preparation of the annual accounts in order to be informed about the results, as was customary in the past and still is sometimes found in medium-sized companies. In well-equipped enterprises the results are known with an acceptable degree of reliability after only a small lapse of time. For business control purposes the yearly balance sheet then has no other significance than any one of the periodical short-term balance sheets.

The publication of the profit for the year does have a typical social function. The annual report is the presentation of financial position and results to shareholders and third parties interested. Although it has clearly the character of a publication for outsiders, it nevertheless accounts for the stewardship of the management during the past year. With its proposals for the distribution of profits, it is decisive, as to what those who are entitled to the profits will be able to spend. The financial statements also maintain these functions when published at shorter intervals and when interim dividends are paid.

When writing of profit or rent, economists have sought in several directions for the criteria to define income. Some writers think of surpluses of money or of units of purchasing power in general, others of surpluses of real goods, still others distinguish between surpluses derived from permanently flowing sources and incidental surpluses, all these generally being converted into income of individuals. This paper, however, will deal particularly with the profits of enterprises, seen as the productive units in our society, which are economically, financially and organizationally independent and yet form part of the whole structure of society.

In the course of time the significance of this independence has undergone many changes. If the economic life of the nineteenth century in which the laisser-faire system dominated may be considered as one of free economy, so the present situation may be defined as an economy under limited control. To all outward appearance there is freedom. The enterprises are autonomous: the managements of enterprises have to settle their own affairs, as if the laisser-faire system were still in force. There is free disposal of income and property and of labour. The mechanism of value and exchange as developed under the free society is being maintained, but the government and the central bank try to achieve certain objects by means of that very price-mechanism: full employment, an even distribution of income, monetary equilibrium. The government's taxation policy and the monetary policy of the central bank provide powerful means to achieve or to pursue these objects. One can speak of a general, not direct, influencing of the flow of money, which keeps the economic process going. There is indirect control in which mainly tax and monetary measures are used, influencing indirectly the outcome of the economic process.

A synthesis of the freedom of the individual and his integration in society is being sought. This is the atmosphere in which the present-day enterprise has its place. The game of free enterprise is still being played, with the enterprise striving for profits. In the background there is, however, the general control that the government tries to excercise. Thus the attitude of the enterprise and its management is typically micro-economic, with well-defined intentions and motives, but with a limited horizon. The management of the enterprise is well acquainted with its immediate surroundings, but its field of vision is limited: it reacts immediately to what is directly perceptible: demand, supply, production, sales and opportunities for profit.

In this paper the problem of profit will be considered from the point of view of the enterprise. The conclusions will not always agree with those which would be reached from the point of view of society. Accountants, like management, are not concerned with the problem how to convert the macro-economic interdependence into the micro-economic relations which are underlying them.

What conception of profit is appropriate to the enterprise? 'Economically', Limperg says, 'the conception of 'profit' is understandable only as the underlying basis for a rational satisfaction of the wants of those whose income depends on the result of the production process'. Consequently only that part of the increase in the net assets of the enterprise which can be consumed without impairing the productive capacity of the enterprise is to be considered as profit.

The conception of the consumability of income can be explained if we place the object of making profit against the background of the social division of labour, for production in our society is such as to satisfy the wants indirectly, in other words: the wants are satisfied through obtaining an income in money. Thus, the real significance of the ascertainment of the size of the income resulting from the year's production is to determine the possible scope of consumption. Those whose income depends on the results of the enterprise must know the size of such income, in order to know what they may consume without reducing the productive capacity of the business from which the income is derived.

The question which part of the increase in surplus during the year is in principle available for consumptive spending and, consequently, may be regarded as income, is not at all easy to solve. When consulting the literature on this problem, it will appear that the criterion determining consumability is generally connected with a given purpose, the realisation of which is thought to be important or necessary. It is generally upheld that the increase in money value is consumable if consumption can take place without the enterprise suffering damage, but the damage criterion is defined in different ways. Some authors advocate the maintenance of asset or capital values, others the maintenance of the continuity of production or of the flow of income, or the maintenance of the source of income; elsewhere the maintenance of the relative position of the enterprise in the total social production is the purpose emphasized.

In the Netherlands the theory of replacement value of Th. Limperg Jr. has gained much authority and has given rise to a renewed interest in problems of determining value and profit, of calculating costs and results and of distinguishing between trading profits, speculative profits, transaction profits, and period profits etc. In his theory Limperg regards the problem of determining profit as a problem of determining value. The valuation in the balance sheet is to be seen as a corollary of the valuation of the work units consumed in the profit and loss account. In a going concern it is the replacement value that must be applied for the valuation of both the available work units in the balance sheet and the consumed work units in the profit and loss account. According to this theory, the significance of the production of goods for our wealth and in particular the significance of the means of production to the producer striving after an income, must be expressed in terms of replacement value of such goods and means of production. The producer must base his decision on this valuation when considering whether a continuation of production is justified. This valuation enables him to distinguish between the income resulting from production and trading and the results arising from price fluctuations. Calculation at replacement values assures the producer to a large extent of the financial means necessary to finance the production process in a continuity which is the characteristic feature of our social system of production.

The principles of the theory of replacement value were clearly explained by A. Goudeket, in his paper 'Fluctuating price levels in relation to accounts' delivered at the Sixth International Congress in London, 1952 and reported in the proceedings of the Congress. It is, therefore, considered to be unnecessary to give an elaborate explanation of the theory itself: only the conclusions resulting from this theory in relation to our problem need be explained. If the principles are accepted, the increase of business capital in terms of money is spendable, and may thus be considered as 'income', so long as the work units consumed have been deducted from the proceeds of production at their replacement value.

The above thesis leads to a clear distinction between the spendability of income and its distribution.

The conception that only an increase of capital which in fact is distributable may be considered as income, is still widely spread. The actual possibility of distribution should, however, not be stressed, but rather the fundamental possibility of consumption. One should dissociate oneself from the question whether sufficient liquid resources for the distribution are available. This is, for instance, not the case when an expansion has been financed out of own funds. In general the entire financial structure of the enterprise should be taken into account when a distribution of income is considered. Reference is made to the bearing of the liquid position on the financial position and to numerous other aspects of the dividends and reserve policies. The interests of the various categories of persons entitled to the profit should be weighed and the position viz a viz the capital market should be determined. Over and above the problems of calculation, conditions of power and influence have a bearing on the actual distribution of income. The latter factors, however, determine the appropriation of income and are resulting from the various policies of the management; they do not determine income itself.

It cannot be denied that actual practice sometimes seems to be in conflict with our thesis. In drafting the annual accounts there is a noticeable tendency to strive for an equalization of profits and distributed profits. Closely connected with this is the many-sided problem of secret reserves, which is of interest to the business world and in particular to the auditor, whose responsibility as to the acceptability of the reports of companies confronts him directly with the bearing of this problem on his certificate. However close the relation with our subject may be, we must refrain from going into this problem. Actual practice has given a stimulus to the theory which identifies profit and distributable income, but this is incorrect. The building up of reserves is a problem of the appropriation of profit and not a problem of the ascertainment of profit. When the building up of reserves is regarded as an element of profit determination, the conception of profit is upset. Both the conception of costs and of reserves would then become blurred.

The building up of reserves being an appropriation of a part of the income is not connected with the setting aside of necessary provisions. The profit appropriations are no part of the cost based on replacement value and are no factors which determine income.

This introduction is not concluded without devoting a few words to the significance of a proper ascertainment of profit with a view to the function of the annual accounts as a tool of management.

At the beginning of this paper the development of a prospective view with a forward looking orientation in accounting was mentioned in connection with the calculation of results on a short term and with the critical comparison of forecasts and actual achievements. It is felt that the annual accounts, comprising the balance sheet and the profit and loss account, should be considered to be one in a series of periodic short term publications. Thus, the resulting extension in the accounting technique provides the key-stone of the information of management. The results disclosed in the periodic accounts give the ultimate test of profit-earning capacity and of whether the general aims of the enterprise have been achieved. To arrive at an opinion on a number of problems one must in the first instance look back at the results shown in the statement of income. This shows the great importance of having a reliable foundation for determining the profit. It is felt that such foundation can be derived from the theory of replacement value as developed by Professor Limperg. This theory not only offers a solution for dealing with the consequences of increases or decreases in prices, but it also provides an aid in testing the efficiency of production. It combines the problems of efficiency, cost calculation and profit determination into one integrated system. The theory of replacement value defines cost as being the sacrifices which are causally required for the production. Only those sacrifices which are appropriate to efficient working can have a causal relationship with production. Standard costs are a logical consequence of the application of the theory of replacement value.

The justification of the cost standard is theoretically sound when it is based on the replacement value. To the extent that actual quantities used exceed the standard quantities the excesses do not constitute part of the cost, but are a loss due to waste. When applying the system of budgeting, standard and actual performance can both be reflected in the accounting records and the profit and loss account can be built up so as to show the causes which have led to profits and losses and to provide an insight into the problems that ought to be the concern of management.

2. *Valuation of raw materials and work units of fixed assets in the profit and loss account*

The arguments which are still advanced for maintaining historical cost as a basis for the ascertainment of cost price and profit will now be reviewed. Opponents of the theory of replacement value mostly point to the difficulties of determining the replacement values, and the resulting opportunities of influencing the profit and loss account: they hold that the results are not sharply defined when replacements values are applied. These are arguments which have already been refuted by important applications in practice, proving that their origin is to be found in tradition. Often the views held as to the significance of the theory of replacement value are too restricted and alone the effect that it eliminates the consequences of price fluctuations is recognized or stressed. Accordingly these advocates stress the application of replacement value with a view of attaining this purpose: and they only consider an application to be necessary in periods of pronounced price fluctuations, at a time when other techniques can be applied aiming at reaching a similar effect. This attitude follows from a lack of insight into the universality of the theory and into its nature as a general theory of value.

With regard to stocks the effects of an application of the theory are seen when differences arise between what was spent on buying the means of production and their replacement value which is borne at the moment when the product is marketed.

With fixed assets work units are for a very long time stored in the equipment and are only released over the course of years. Here the producer runs a price risk for many years to come, which manifests itself in different ways. During the period of its use the equipment is subject to price changes which fluctuate by reason of the nature and life of the particular equipment and also through changes in the value of money during the trade cycle. The fixing of the life of these assets and the choice of the system of depreciation must therefore be seen against the background of the economic significance of the equipment being replaced. The consequences of technical improvement must be considered as well as those of fluctuations in the business cycle and of inflationary tendencies. The theory of replacement value requires these factors to be taken into account when evaluating the work units used in production: the (calculated) depreciation should take into account changes in value which have occurred and be adapted to changes in the level of values. The application of the same principle of valuation every time the producer is ascertaining the value of the assets means that uniformity is reached between balance sheet and profit statement and between profit statement and cost calculation.

There are even more far-reaching consequences: what in the theory of historical cost is regarded as being risks, is to a great extent converted into calculable sacrifices when the accounting system is being adapted to changed circumstances. The results of uncertainty as to changes in the value of work units during the life of the assets is, to the extent within the reach of human insight, absorbed in the calculation of costs and in the determination of profits. The greater the diversity in the life times of the various fixed assets, the more the price risk on the work units used in previous periods has been absorbed and, as a corollary, the more the financing of the replacement of the work units is secured.

The application of the replacement value theory to the value of raw materials used is becoming more generally accepted. Possibly this is due to the fact that in the producer's mind the prices of raw materials are more closely related to the cost of finished products than are the prices of equipment bought in the past. Thus the producer has a clearer idea of the consequences of fluctuations in the prices of raw materials than of fluctuations in the prices of fixed assets.

This opinion will also have been influenced by the fact that some views derived from the theory have proved to be useful when applied to the ascertainment of income for tax purposes: the 'base-stock' procedure showed that the fixed valuation of a constant base-stock volume at the beginning and the end of the accounting period brings out the effect of price increases in the quantity of goods used. In the form of the last-in-first-out principle this idea found acceptance in U.S.A. and was also embodied in the Dutch tax law. In certain circumstances the 'Wet Belastingherziening 1950' (Tax-Revision Act 1950) allowed the application of a lifo-system similar to the one adopted in the U.S.A. With the decision of the 'Hoge Raad' (Supreme Court) dated 7th. March 1956 No. 12623 a further step forward was taken in the evolution of the conception of taxable profits, by stating that it is accepted accounting practice to evaluate the liability to cover shortages in inventories on the basis of replacement cost.

In the U.S.A. the application of the lifo-system has further been extended by the acceptance of the so-called dollar-value method, whereby the comparison of opening and closing stock is not effected in quantities but in money, which is particularly important to the extent to which the opening and closing stocks do not consist of identical goods but of goods having the same function in the production process. The decision mentioned in the previous paragraph raises the hope that the development of the case law of the Supreme Court will lead to similar results in the Netherlands.

In certain circumstances such a system may result in a profit calculation which nearly equals the result which would be reached on the basis of the replacement value theory. However, the 'base-stock system' does not, in principle, recognise the alternative of valuing at the lower market value. In measuring the money value of business capital on the balance sheet, this system does not meet requirements, since the stocks are shown at a notional value instead of at their real value. Nor does it suffice when determining income, since in principle an adverse difference between market value and the fixed (notional) value is not recognized as a loss.

Consequently the 'base-stock-system' proved to be less simple to handle than it first appeared. The development into lifo-system, normal stock-system, shortage-replacement system, and dollar-value-method certainly increased the number of methods, but in the Netherlands' opinion the outcome of alle these rules when compared with what should be reached by virtue of the theory of replacement value gives cause for dissatisfaction. The 'base-stock-system' has indeed a weaker foundation: admittedly it is based on an insight into the bearing of price fluctuations on the result; correctly it accepts that the means of production are complementary to each other and that the process of production should be viewed as a going concern; but it offers no thing more than a method of eliminating the price fluctuations.

The replacement value theory, on the other hand, rests on a definite conception of the nature of value as such, and so, in its practical application, is more fitted to meet the great diversity of circumstances which arise in business life. This theory bases itself on a causal and necessary relation between consumption and replacement and also fixes the proper moment for replacements, namely the moment of exchange of quantities used. By this it distinguishes in business accounts between transaction profits and stock profits or losses, the latter furthermore to be distinguished from speculation results.

This important enlargement of the faculty of analysing results offered by the theory of replacement value is lacking in the base-stock-system. The significance of this distinction should not be underestimated: generally the primary object of the enterprise is to obtain an income from production and exchange and not to benefit from speculative stock transactions. Production and exchange, not speculation, give the enterprise its specific and functional place in society. This analysis alone makes it possible to examine whether the enterprise has reached its target.

3. *Principles of taxation versus economic principles in the determination of profits*

From the foregoing it appears that the taxable profit differs from what is felt to be the real profit. Though proper accounting principles do have a bearing on tax law—there even is a tendency to a close relation with economic principles—there is no denying that a considerable divergency exists between the ascertainment of profit for tax purposes and for management purposes. The computation of taxable profits partly follows its own rules. The policy laid down in tax regulations has its own general, economic, financial and social purposes (employment, reasonable distribution of national income, favouring of underprivileged groups of the population, balance of payment problems, business cycle stabilization, etc.), which are not always in accordance with strictly micro-economic desiderata. Moreover the tax authorities must safeguard the revenue and, therefore, take care that indeed all profits of the taxpayers are taxed. Thus, they must place particular emphasis on the continuity of the principles of ascertaining profits for taxation purposes and accordingly they lack the dynamic faculties which enable a business to adjust itself to changing circumstances.

Such widely diverging purposes will have to be weighed continuously. From the standpoint of the enterprise certain taxes may seem thoroughly unfair, for instance when depreciation charges exceeding those calculated on the basis of historical cost are disallowed. The tax authorities will be more inclined to investigate which taxes the various branches of society can bear, so that society as a whole can function as smoothly as possible. It may be said as a warning that this smooth functioning is impaired when the incidence of taxation is in conflict with economic business principles.

When furthermore it is realised that juridical views and considerations have a bearing on the drafting of tax regulations, it is clear that it would not be reasonable to demand that the conception of taxable profit should agree in all respects with the profit calculation based on accounting principles, the more since the latter will never be able to attain complete exactness. While recognizing the special character of the principles of taxation, an application of good accounting principles should, as far as possible, be striven for.

When the enterprise makes separate profit calculations for accounting and for tax purposes, a difference is likely to arise between the actual tax payable under the tax assessments and the amounts of tax which would be payable on the basis of the profit calculated for management purposes and published by the company. Differences can arise because the actual profits are higher or lower than the taxable profits.

In the Netherlands like in other countries special tax allowances may lead to taxable profits which are temporarily lower than the actual profits, e.g. in the case of stipulations which allow certain parts of the profit to be assigned to a temporary fund or to be used for an 'accelerated depreciation' on new investments of special importance. In principle, however, in the long run all business profits will be taxed. Sometimes the Treasury demands its share earlier, sometimes later than would be indicated by proper accounting principles, but irrevocably the toll must once be paid, although in some cases this may not be earlier than at the moment of liquidation.

From this it follows that the burden of taxation based on the actual business income must be computed when calculating the spendable income, i.e. the normal rate of tax should be applied to the income ascertained and published in the annual report. This leads to the necessity of carrying in the balance sheet provisions for contingent and deferred tax liabilities. A distinction should however be made between these two kinds of provisions since it is more difficult to estimate contingent or latent tax liabilities, especially when the question is raised how to establish the discounted value of such liabilities. These detailed questions are not here under discussion: but the general principle is of importance and requires the business capital and the profits to be shown in the annual accounts after a commensurate deduction for taxes.

4. *Provision for contingent risks in the ascertainment of profits*

Although the year is appropriately chosen for the determination of income, it nevertheless constitutes an arbitrary period. It is possible to define the total profit of the enterprise arising during its life-time, but the profit for a period, needed for an insight into the state of affairs is, however, far from exactly definable.

Under normal conditions the establishment and running of a business is based upon the conception of a going concern. A continual flow of productive processes joins the yearly periods into an organic flow. Many of the outlays made in one period will not render their utility or be productive until a future period, stocks and purchases of fixed assets being a case in point. These latter are outlays made at longer intervals than a year which must be charged to years in which they are not incurred.

Losses on debtors, obsolete stocks and guarantee obligations, do not arise with yearly regularity. Similar items of irregular appearance can be observed in respect of repairs and maintenance, survey obligations and particularly in connection with the risk-bearing activities of insurance companies. It is necessary to charge such seemingly incidental burdens to years in which they are not in fact incurred. Provisions must be built up according to standard expectations. The bases for the setting of such standards are often difficult to indicate. The most appropriate data are likely to result from past experience and should be extrapolated to what seems most probable for the future. The future, however, is uncertain and so there remains an element of estimation in the valuation of the moment. For those adhering to the theory of the replacement value the determination of profit is an ex-post conception and they consider arbitrary estimates to be acceptable if properly devised.

To others the determination of profit has an ex-ante character. They regard the uncertainties of developments in the future as having a greater bearing on the ascertainment of profit in the present: they want the uncertainties as to future development to be reflected when forming their opinion of the present. Since the future is influenced by the decisions of the producer and management considerations have a bearing on the determination of profits of the years as they go by, subjective estimates and decisions made by the producer thus play some part in the determination of profit.

Even uncertainties which cannot be forecast by the management, may still have to be taken into account when determining the profit. Guided by ancient risk theories of the producer's rent a high profit is seen by some writers as resulting from the acceptance of heavy risks which will eventually be followed by a reaction. In addition to present-day costs, they would like to convert the risks of loss in the future into charges on the profits of the past and the present, without, however, knowing what yardstick to use. This train of thought would lead to the conclusion that there is no profit, for what is indeed a profit is thus given the function of covering uncertain future cost elements. In this way the determination of profit would depend on the future, making it impossible to fix proposals as to its appropriation for dividends and other purposes. Whenever this policy is followed the decision made in determining the profit and its appropriation would rest on subjective decisions and recommendations of the management.

Apparently, this conception of profit is not without consequence for both the producer and the auditor. In the Netherlands literature B. Pruyt has already expressed his opinion that the auditor's certificate as to the correctness of the calculated profit should in fact always be a qualified certificate. According to this author an accountant, however expert, would not be in a position to establish a correct conception of profit nor could he give an answer to the question: 'What is profit?' thus, that it would be valid under all circumstances. Similar opinions are not unknown in the literature of other countries. The conception of profit has been expressed to be based on 'rough approximations, used by the business man to steer himself through the bewildering changes of situation which confront him. For this purpose, strict logical categories are not what is needed; something rougher is actually better' (Hicks).

It is self-evident that such conceptions are contrary to the one described above. It is felt that accounting philosophy and management policy in making the profit appropriations must be clearly distinguished. When appropriating the profit, management can or even must take into account its expectations as regards future events. But an appropriation of profit comes only after the profit has been determined and for that purpose the profit conception should be clearly defined. The customary use of the historical cost price as a basis of valuation forms an obstacle in achieving this. It leads to capricious results in the profit calculation and thus creates a sphere of uncertainty in which provisions for contingent risks in the widest sense are considered to be essential elements of profit determination. The historical cost price is an amount which expresses a fact from the past: it gives a figure that had a meaning at the moment of buying, but it is of no use for the ascertainment of cost and income in later periods. The replacement value on the other hand is the value at the moment at which the valuation is made, reflecting the value attached by the economic society to the goods at the moment of exchange. When the profit is determined in conjunction with this method it meets the requirements of both producer and society.

Those who look towards the future and wish to postpone the fixation of the replacement value to the future moment of replacement, mistake valuation for an estimation of the financing requirements at the time of replacement. The future price fluctuation is an element of the future but has no bearing on the profit calculation of the expired period: otherwise, elements of uncertainty and management policy are incorporated in a profit determination which would be contrary to the ex-post conception of the theory of replacement value.

Still another outlook on the future is provided by some theorists who want to base valuations on the capitalized value of future proceeds, the assessment of which naturally involves great difficulties. The calculation reflects only the (indirect) selling value of the means of production and this method of valuation is only relevant in special circumstances.

From what has gone before, we reach the conclusion that the replacement value theory has—by linking the profit determination to the value at the moment of exchange—made an important contribution to a quantitative determination of the profit conception. One of the most important duties of business economists and accountants lies in the building up of certainty as to the conception of profit. May the exchange of views at this Congress contribute to our understanding and judgement of this matter.

PAPER

by

IRA N. FRISBEE, C.P.A.

American Institute of Certified Public Accountants

In the United States the number of investors in large businesses has been increasing rapidly. The number of stockholders in General Motors Corporation, for example, increased 27 % between January 1, 1955 and June 1956 to a total of 621,000. General Electric Company had a 22 % increase in the average number of stockholders in 1955 as compared with 1954.

These numerical increases in stockholders do not give the complete picture. The number who *indirectly* are the owners of the capital stock has been increasing also. Pension funds and profit-sharing funds have been established by many corporate employers. Health and welfare funds are now common in the labor unions and pension funds have been introduced in these organizations. Some of these savings are invested in the capital stocks of American corporations. Thus, we find that the number of people who have reason to be interested in the results of such investments is much larger than the number of stockholders. A large part of these investments is made for the primary purpose of accumulating wealth to provide future income, rather than current income for the participants.

Accompanying the increases in stockholders there has been more extensive and more frequent financial reporting by the corporate officers, particularly as to profits. A considerable number issue quarterly statements of income, in addition to the annual audited financial statements dealing more extensively with the operations of the year. These frequent reports recognize that the chief interest of the stockholder is in the earnings of the business. How much is the profit per share this year or this quarter or this month? How much was it last year? How much can be expected next year? And how much will be paid in dividends?

Nevertheless, business profit is a term which is quite indefinite and nebulous. Certainly for the intermediate periods in the life of a business it cannot be determined with exactness. A carefully worded annual statement of income might be called a 'tentative statement of profit'. Only a statement covering the entire life of a business can be deemed to be accurate in the determination of profit.

Such a statement, although accurate in the monetary units in which it is presented, is not likely to be accurate from the standpoint of economic income because of changes in economic value of those monetary units. For example, if a person invests $ 100,000 in a business and ten years later, upon the winding up of the business and without any previous withdrawals, he receives exactly $ 100,000 as his entire recovery, we may say accurately that he has had no monetary profit or loss. But if the value of those dollars has changed in the ten years so that they will buy only one-half of what they would purchase at the beginning of the period, it is obvious that there has been an economic loss of 50,000 of his original dollars, or one-half of his investment. We cannot deny the occurrence of such a loss even though the only factor affecting the value of his original $ 100,000 was the changing price level. In fact, in terms of current dollars his loss is not $ 50,000 but is $ 100,000. Instead of having 200,000 current dollars from his $ 100,000 investment of ten years ago, he has only 100,000 current dollars.

Even if the investor were to receive $ 200,000 in return for his $ 100,000 investment under the circumstances just described, would he have any satisfaction in recovering the same purchasing power that he originally invested if he has had no spendable income during the period of his investment? Certainly the receipt of $ 200,000 in this case would not result in any spendable income. All the investor could say is that his capital was not dissipated. Is this not something he should know during the ten-year period when operating results are being reported to him in each interim period? If dividends had been paid to him during the ten-year period as a result of accounting methods which failed to recognize the decreasing value of the dollars, the stockholder would think that he was receiving spendable income whereas he might only be receiving part of his original investment.

Economic profit also should be recognized as important to the corporate officials who are responsible for the management of business enterprises. It is the duty of management executives to protect the investment of the stockholders. This requires a measurement of the effect of price increases upon the capital requirements of the enterprise. A comprehensive picture of the financial status of a business and of its future capital requirements is not necessarily obtained by stating assets on the basis of historical cost. If a portion of the assets are stated at 1939 dollars whereas other assets are at 1946 dollars and still others are quoted in a mixture of 1956 and 1957 dollars, the resulting measurement of the capital requirements may be quite misleading. If, in ascertaining profit, the expenses are determined by recording either the sale or use of assets which are stated in out-of-date dollars, the resulting 'net profit' may not be available to the investors. It may be partly or entirely needed to replace the assets sold or consumed. In other words, it may be capital required to continue the business—that is, to continue the same volume of operations without expansion of plant or of inventories. To the extent that such a monetary profit is required to continue operations which are identical with the past operations, it is difficult to find any basis for labelling it as 'profit'. However, to measure the extent of the misnomer, or to avoid its creation in the accounts, requires continuing adjustments within or without the books of account.

At the Sixth International Congress on Accounting in 1952 eight papers were presented on the subject 'Fluctuating Price Levels in Relation to Accounts'. Within the limits of the present discussion it is not possible to review all of the excellent presentations or to summarize all of the points of view expressed.

Nearly all of the speakers were in favor of eliminating at least part of the effects of fluctuating price levels in the ascertainment of profits. The methods of accomplishment differed. Some favored an adjustment only in the historical cost of fixed assets, and of depreciation, to be made at periodic intervals when an appreciable change in value has occurred. Apparently the revaluation dates would be infrequent. At those dates the plant assets would be valued at current prices and for a time thereafter, until inflation became marked, the resulting expression of depreciation would not differ materially from the current level of prices. This point of view has been followed in England. For example, the financial statements of the Imperial Chemical Industries, Limited, show that a revaluation of physical assets took place as of January 1, 1950, with the allowance for depreciation determined on the revaluation basis.

Other participants at the Sixth International Congress supported the thesis that replacement values should be recorded annually upon the books and in the financial statements in order to state correctly the profits of the enterprise and the amount of capital employed. It is interesting to note that the replacement-value theory is being used by important companies in the Netherlands. The annual reports of N.V. Philips' Gloeilampenfabrieken present the property, plant, and equipment on the basis of replacement value less depreciation, and the inventories also are shown at replacement value. These replacement values are determined by means of indexes measuring the price trends of the various assets. An account called 'revaluation surplus' is credited or charged with the changes in the replacement values. Profits are ascertained by calculating depreciation expense on the replacement values of the property, plant, and equipment, and by using replacement values for raw materials and other elements of the cost of sales.

Replacement values instead of historical costs are similarly used by the Algemene Kunstzijde Unie N.V., a Netherlands corporation, as stated in a prospectus issued in the United States in 1953 in connection with its offering of American shares. This prospectus stated that the net income 'has been determined on the basis of generally acceptable accounting principles in the Netherlands, which principles include, in the determination of net income, provision for depreciation on the basis of estimated replacement value rather than historical cost... and costing of sales at replacement value rather than cost...'

One speaker at the Sixth Congress, Professor Willard J. Graham of the American Accounting Association, presented 'adjusted historical cost' as the preferred basis for the periodic reporting of income and compared this method with replacement cost. His paper embodies the recommendations of the American Accounting Association Committee on Concepts and Standards Underlying Corporate Financial Statements presented in their 'Supplementary Statement No. 2' which was issued August 1, 1951, and is published in the Accounting Review for October, 1951.

Adjusted historical cost is stated to be 'historical dollar cost adjusted to a current dollar basis by the application of a broadly accepted index of general prices'. Professor Graham further states that 'net income based on 'adjusted historical cost' is also a clear-cut, definite concept... the excess of revenue, expressed in current dollars, over the incurred cost of the capital (assets and services) consumed in producing that revenue, expressed in the same sized current dollars'.

There are several advantages of the adjusted historical cost method. One is that the primary financial statements, as prepared by management and verified by independent accountants, can continue to reflect historical dollar costs if this is desired. The committee of the American Accounting Association has so recommended. The conversion of the conventional financial statements to reflect the changes in the price level is accomplished without changes in the books of account. The American Accounting Association has issued two publications which explain and illustrate the technique to be used in making the price-level adjustments. The first of these publications is entitled 'Case Studies of Four Companies', which was prepared under the direction of Professor Ralph C. Jones and was published in 1955. The other publication is a pamphlet on 'Basic Concepts and Methods' prepared by Professor Perry Mason and issued in 1956. This latter pamphlet provides a brief explanation of the problem and illustrates the technique which was used in the case studies.

The committee of the American Accounting Association believes that it is essential to full disclosure to adjust all of the items on the financial statements to the current dollar amounts. By use of a general price index, such as the Consumers' Price Index of the U.S. Bureau of Labor Statistics, the various items on the income statement and on the balance sheet are converted to current dollars. As illustrated by Professor Mason in 'Basic Concepts and Methods', this procedure of conversion starts with the published price index numbers which are converted into a purchasing power index and the latter is expressed decimally with the current date as the basis of reference. The resulting decimals, known as conversion factors, can be applied easily to the historical cost amounts requiring adjustment. For example, if the price index has doubled since the date of acquisition of the plant assets, the conversion factor will be two and the valuation of the plant assets on the adjusted historical cost basis will be twice the book amount of historical cost. Similarly, if the same change in price level has taken place since the capital stock was issued, the adjusted balance sheet will show the capital stock account at twice as many dollars as were paid in at the time of issue. Bonds or other long-term obligations, however, will not be adjusted at the balance sheet date because these, and the other liabilities to outsiders, now might be paid with current dollars. Extensive adjustments also are made on the income statement.

Several advantages may be suggested for the adjusted historical cost method. First, it offers considerable convenience and flexibility in ascertaining and refining the adjustments. Because these adjustments ordinarily are not to be placed upon the books, decisions as to refinements do not have to be made in advance of preparing the conventional financial statements. Second, on the whole it is probable that the best purpose is accomplished by basing adjustments upon an index which measures the general level of prices rather than on indexes which measure price changes in specific commodities or types of commodities. Were the latter type of index to be used, the corrections would result in the use of replacement costs at the current market, which, in the case of plant assets particularly, may not be the costs when the so-called 'replacements' occur.

Actually, literal replacement seldom, if ever, happens. Third, by applying a general purchasing power index to the original historical costs, the resulting financial statements are still on the basis of original cost, although adjusted to current monetary units. The *principle* of original cost still endures. The only change is in the *measurement* of original cost, which is done at approximately current dollars rather than partially at out-of-date dollars. The resulting profit has been determined on the cost principle: current revenues have been reduced by the cost of current expenses, which are all expressed in monetary units having the same general purchasing power as those in which the current revenues are stated.

As yet there has been little, if any, use of the adjusted historical cost, or of any other method of adjusting for price-level changes, among accountants and business enterprises in the United States. One of the four companies, studied by Professor Ralph C. Jones[1] has continued the study and has published the adjusted figures as a supplement to its annual statement. One of the other companies that was included in the studies has made subsequent references to the variation between the rate of return on present day values and on book values.

Interest in the effects of the changing price levels upon business profit appears likely to vary according to the amount of inflation currently experienced. The problem receives little attention if prices are relatively stable or slowly creeping upward. Interest is stimulated when prices are advancing rapidly, as was the case in the United States during the six years from 1946 to 1951, inclusive. The average annual increase in consumer prices was 6.4% during this period. In contrast, this was followed by a period of price stability during the four years of 1952–1955, inclusive.

In 1948 a Study Group on Business Income was organized by the American Institute of Accountants for an intensive study of the uses of the word 'income' and 'terms associated therewith in accounting and in business, economic, and political fields'. Outstanding accountants and economists comprised the study group, whose report was published in 1952 under the title 'Changing Concepts of Business Income'. A majority of the group recognized the need for accounting statements that would be more broadly meaningful by measuring profits in units of equal purchasing power during periods when the value of the monetary unit was not stable. The conclusion was expressed that methods should be developed to expand the framework of accounting to recognize the changes in value, but that for the present, the primary statements of income should continue to be on bases now commonly accepted. It was suggested, however, that corporations should be encouraged to furnish information to stockholders which will facilitate the determination of income measured in units of approximately equal purchasing power. The report did not indicate the methods to be followed in obtaining this information for the stockholders.

Apparently, as yet the report of the Study Group has had little, if any, effect upon accounting methods in the United States. Nevertheless, we cannot conclude that the work of the Study Group and of the committee of the American Accounting Association has not been important or beneficial. The research, the

[1] 'Case Studies of Four Companies', Ralph Coughenour Jones, American Accounting Association, 1955.

thinking, the exchange of ideas all have resulted in publication of useful materials. It may be that the use of the work of these pioneering groups will be delayed until another inflationary period is upon us. Even at such a time many businessmen will be slow to change their accounting methods or to interest themselves in supplementary information unless it is useful in reducing their income taxes. Among American business executives and accountants, the concept of profit that receives the chief attention is 'taxable profit'.

The importance that income taxes have upon our accounting thinking in the United States is evidenced by the growing use of the 'Lifo' method of accounting for inventories and cost of sales. In 1949 less than twenty percent of the companies surveyed by the research department of the American Institute of Accountants and reported upon in 'Accounting Trends and Techniques' were using the Lifo method. In the ninth edition of this survey, it is shown that almost one-third of the 600 companies surveyed were using Lifo in 1954.

The Lifo method is generally referred to as a cost method. As to the balance sheet, it results in an out-of-date cost if prices are changing. If prices are rising, the cost of unsold merchandise will be too low in relation to current dollar valuations. In periods of declining prices, however, inventories will be priced too high if these out-of-date cost valuations are used.

The principal justification for Lifo is in its effect upon profits, and upon the income taxes on these profits, when prices are rising. The amounts charged to cost of goods sold are for the latest purchases and tend to be, or to approximate, current replacement costs. Thus, the level of prices at which the cost of sales is stated is near to the same level as that at which the sales are stated, particularly if the physical goods sold are 'replaced' near to the time of the sale.

The inconsistencies of Lifo are fairly obvious. In order to use current values for the cost of goods sold, the balance sheet must use 'ancient' values, which may either be lower or higher than current prices depending upon the forces of inflation or deflation. Also, the use of a replacement value in the cost of sales depends upon the occurrence of replacement within the accounting period. If specific items are not replaced until later, the last-in cost may be a prior, out-of-date cost. Furthermore, the Lifo method is not likely to be popular during a period of deflation. In fact, under the cost or market, whichever lower, method it then will usually be replaced by market.

Turning from the problem of the effect of general price changes upon profits, we shall now consider questions that arise because of dormant risks involved in reporting profit according to annual or other periods of time. It should be noted that the adoption of a 'natural business year', rather than the calendar year, may diminish the problems of assigning income and expenses to the proper accounting period. Also, these problems would not require attention if the cash basis were acceptable in recognizing profits. Actually, the cash basis is used by a considerable number of business enterprises, except that depreciation usually is recognized. For example, in farming operations, the accounting is likely to be essentially on the cash basis. Among professional people, such as doctors, attorneys and even accountants, the recording of income sometimes awaits its receipt in cash, and the recognition of expenses, except depreciation, may occur only when cash is paid out. Other businesses that render personal services, such as real estate agents and insurance brokers, sometimes use accounting methods that are essentially on the cash basis.

The cash basis is an acceptable basis for income tax purposes in the United States. This, of course, has encouraged its use, particularly where there are uncertainties as to the realization of the income. For example, farmers seldom inventory the growing crops and therefore have no accumulated cost values for the unsold harvested crops. This may be due partly to the hazards of farm prices, and partly to accounting inertia. Nevertheless, for financial reporting purposes the cash basis is not acceptable, because it does not match revenues with expenses in the period to which they both belong.

The accrual basis is essential but it raises many questions as to the time when income is to be included, and when the expenses and provisions for losses are to be deducted to ascertain business profit. Some risks can readily be ascertained and provided for, but in other cases accounting options appear to exist, although sometimes a logical justification may not be evident. For example, a complete accrual basis would require that profit on installment sales be recognized fully at the time of the sales with appropriate provision for collection risks. Yet there are occasions when the risks of collection are such that all profit is deferred until cost has been recovered, while in other instances each collection may be treated as partly a recovery of cost and partly a receipt of profit. From a theoretical point of view there appears to be no difference between sales 'on account', without initial or 'down' payments and without specified dates for installment payments, and sales that provide for such installment payments. If the sale is complete and no service remains unperformed, the time for recognizing income and for recognizing and providing for the risks of collection has arrived.

Provision for the risk of loss on accounts receivable is a required procedure but is this true for the risk of obsolescence and supersession of merchandise? Admittedly, the provision for obsolescence is required if it actually has occurred, but this is for an accomplished event. It is not for the risk that future obsolescence may occur or be discovered. There may be items of merchandise in stock which gradually are being superseded. Ordinarily, obsolescence or supersession is not a sudden occurrence; new products gradually are accepted and replace the old. But the occurrence of complete obsolescence may happen suddenly even though the unrecognized event or events responsible for it occurred in a prior accounting period. It is the risk that such events are occurring which is not provided for in the usual provisions for obsolescence of merchandise.

Many manufacturing concerns engage continually in research and experimental work with the expectation that future benefits will result. Because of the uncertainty as to the benefits which will be obtained and as to the duration of these benefits, common practice is to choose between two options. Usually it is considered practical to charge such expenditures to current expense, particularly if the company engages continuously in experimental and development work. It is generally considered to be permissible, however, to capitalize these expenses during the course of a specific project and to write them off if the project is unsuccessful when that fact is ascertained. If the project is beneficial, the capitalized costs may be charged to operations by amortizing them on a time basis or according to the expected production. It is likely that the total time, or sometimes the quantity of production, chosen as the basis for the annual write-off will be determined arbitrarily. In fact, in most cases the uncertainties will encourage the method of an immediate charge-off to expense. But, under either method, the result is likely to be an arbitrary, instead of a scientific, determination of profit.

In appraising the losses for which provisions are needed in ascertaining the profit of one year, changes in the business cycle may need to be anticipated if possible. In prosperous 'boom' periods of production, recognition should be given to the possibility of a depression or recession in activity. The allowance for loss in the collection of receivables, for example, will need to be larger if collections will extend into a period of hard times. The least desirable merchandise may sell in a period of great activity when quantities are inadequate, whereas types of items that seemed very popular during prosperity may be found to have been superseded when merchandise stocks are found to be adequate or excessive.

It is well known that the profits under fixed-price contracts for long-term construction projects are hazardous to estimate in periods of inflation. Logically, the total profit should be apportioned over the period of the contract on a percentage-of-completion basis, instead of being recognized only upon fulfilling the contract. But this requires provisions for increasing costs and for other non-calculable risks. Even if no inflation is occurring during a period of full employment and production, work stoppages may be caused by a lack of materials or by a shortage of skilled workmen. The danger of strikes is greater at this time. Theoretically, the risks should be recognized and provided for but this seldom is possible until the arrival of the events causing the losses.

In the United States, the difficulties encountered in reaching only one logical result in deciding each problem of business profits have resulted in a general recognition of the concept of 'generally accepted accounting principles' in preference to an insistence upon adherence to economic concepts of profits. The principles to be used in ascertaining profit, according to this doctrine, must be generally accepted. It does not need to be shown that they are 'sound' or even logical in all particulars. Merely, they must have found general acceptance among accountants and businessmen. Sometimes choices or options exist as to the generally accepted principles. Often the particular circumstances affect the options, limiting the application of the principles.

These accepted principles are not immutable. They are not unchangeable laws. Rather they are rules that have evolved from the thinking of men which have come to be accepted, at least temporarily. In fact, very important changes have occurred; one example is in the accepted principles for valuing inventories, which were first expanded to include 'cost or market, whichever is lower' and now include 'Lifo' as a method of costing.

The principles that receive recognition undoubtedly have been influenced by economic concepts of profit. The need for price level adjustments, for instance, is gaining some recognition. But another influence, which often supersedes the concepts of economic profit, is that of 'taxable profits'.

As a practical matter, businessmen and corporate investors are justified in their interest in taxable profits because only about one-half of these profits remain after federal and state income taxes. In some respects the divergence between economic and taxable profit is so great that one can scarcely justify the use of the word 'profit' in both instances. Taxable profits have been determined mostly by legislators although partly by court interpretations. In too many cases the rules prescribed by the legislators have resulted from propaganda for reductions, exemptions and special privileges. In our latest Revenue Code, in 1954, a little progress was made in changing a few sections to conform with generally accepted accounting principles. Unless taxable profit is determined according to these accepted accounting principles, it cannot be used for reporting the financial results, except in income tax returns. Too often this limitation is overlooked in financial accounting.

But the taxation of business profit which has been ascertained according to current concepts of generally accepted accounting principles would not prevent the partial confiscation of economic wealth. Accepted principles today fail to require adjustment for changing price levels in periods of inflation. For instance, an investor who invests $ 100,000 in capital stock and receives $ 200,000 either upon liquidation of the corporation or upon sale of the stock is taxed on $ 100,000 as a capital gain. It does not matter if the liquidation dollars are worth only one-half what the invested dollars were worth in purchasing power, so that there is no economic profit. The monetary result is the measure of the taxable profit. And if dividends are received out of monetary profits where in fact no economic profit has occurred, these also will be partly 'confiscated' by income taxes which may be as high as 91 % at present federal rates of tax.

Summarizing, this paper has argued that both the corporate investors and the management executives who have the stewardship of business should be interested in ascertaining periodically the economic profit rather than the monetary profit. For this, the preparation of accounting statements on the basis of adjusted historical cost is urged. It is believed that this method is more useful in approximating the economic profit than the method of replacement cost. Another problem in ascertaining profits arises from arbitrary divisions of the life of a business into years or other periods of time. In determining the profit of each period it is probable that too little attention has been given to the most uncertain of income and expense items. Risks that can be calculated must be provided for and expense and income accruals must be made whenever dependable estimates are possible. Other risks that cannot be calculated far in advance of governing events may logically await recognition. Although concepts of economic profit have received some attention from accountants and businessmen, currently the ascertainment of profit in the United States is based upon generally accepted accounting principles. Unfortunately, concepts of taxable profits do not as yet always coincide with either the economic concepts or the generally accepted accounting principles.

PAPER

by

PROF. PALLE HANSEN

Foreningen af Statsautoriserede Revisorer, Denmark

'A properly determined profit will enable Management to judge by means of analysis the efficiency of production, the yield on invested capital, the appropriateness of expansion etc.' (From Seventh International Congress of Accountants 1957 Information for Authors of Papers).

Before we enter a discussion of the Accountant's concept of profit and try to make suggestions towards improved methods of ascertaining these concepts, it will be necessary first to attempt to determine the actual content of *profit* in accounting practice. In doing so I will have to bring out some theoretical reflections which might seem academic and unrealistic to the practical auditor. Nevertheless it is my conviction that in the time to come we auditors and accountants will have to dig further into the theory in order to find a firmer more sound basis for our opinions. With very few, prominent exceptions Canning's[1] remarks of 1929 still depict the general situation:

'A diligent search of the literature of accounting discloses an astonishing lack of discussion of the *nature of income*. One should hardly expect that the profession which, above all others, is most constantly engaged in the statistical treatment of income should have found almost nothing at all to say about the nature of the thing they measure so carefully.'

Generally speaking we can hardly claim reasonable to agree on anything but the quite formal definition of profit which says that:

'*The profit earned during a period of time equals the consumption plus the change (positive or negative) in capital value taken place during that period*, i.e. expressed in the equation:

$$P = W + E_u - E_p$$ [2]

Unfortunately the three factors of this equation are not precise, clear-cut concepts. The factor W may be determined with the highest degree of objec-

[1] John B. Canning: „The Economics of Accountancy", New York 1929.

[2] P = profit; W = the withdrawals of the period; E_u = the equity at the end (ultimo) of the period; E_p = the equity at the beginning (primo) of the period.

tivity, as predominantly it takes the form of withdrawals of cash or of private consumption of goods[1]. The real problems present themselves when we go into the debate of how to determine the factors E_u and E_p which represent the capital values in the balance sheets.

I. Does a concept of Profit exist which may be termed 'true'?

In case we base our discussion on the economic theory the factors just mentioned *may* be given a very definite content and consequently we shall also be able under these circumstances precisely to define the concept of profit. It will be possible to state what we understand by the term 'economically *true* profit'. Therefore, in order to give the following discussion a better background, I shall dwell for a moment on these theoretical viewpoints.

To possess *capital* in economic terms means to have title to all *future* yields from one or more assets. The *capital value* of an asset thus is entirely determined by the amounts it will *produce* to the owner *in the future*. In the case of a business the capital value (E) therefore is determined by the amount of withdrawals or yields which the owner may expect to receive from the business as long as it is in his possession (thus including any future amount he might receive when handing over his ownership to someone else).

The economic theory points out the equation of discounting as the means for determination of capital value[2]):

$$Ct_0 = W_1\ (1 + r)^{-1} + W_2\ (1 + r)^{-2}$$
$$W_n\ (1 + r)^{-n}$$

in which Ct_0 = the capital value at the time of the evaluation
W = the withdrawals (Yields) at the different times
r = the rate of interest

In order at any time to compute the *true* capital value of a business (or of an individual asset) we need to have a complete knowledge of what the future will bring, regarding the yields the business will give the owner as well as the rate of interest to be used.

This abstraction from the real world enables us precisely to define the content of E_p and E_u and consequently we are in a position to set up an exact clear-cut theoretic concept of profit, which we may term '*the ideal profit*'. This concept is simply defined as *interest of the capital value of the asset*[3].

It goes without saying that the assumptions of *complete knowledge* of the future

[1]) Obviously a very important problem of the purchasing power presents itself, but this problem will not be dealt with here.

[2]) The reality behind this equation may be illustrated by the following example: An amount of kr. 1,000, which cannot be withdrawn until one year from now, is not worth its par value to-day but only its par minus rate of interest. If the rate of interest is 8%, kr. 1,000 to be withdrawn one year from now is only worth kr. 926 to-day. 8% of kr. 926 in one year equals kr. 74. Kr. 926 + kr. 74 = kr. 1,000.

[3]) According to the example in footnote [2]) the capital value on 1/1 is kr. 926 and the profit is kr. 74, i.e. 8% of the capital value.

cannot come true in actual life. We will have to revise our assumptions about the future at the end of each accounting period. Consequently we must adjust the capital value, although at this point of the discussion this fact is not of main importance. The most essential for the following discussion is the fact that:

The economic way of thinking rests on the theorem that the evaluation of capital value must be made on the basis of the expected future and not on the basis of socalled facts about the past.

II. The accounting Concept of Profit deviates from the Ideal Concept

Before I go into a more detailed analysis of the accountant's technique in computing his profit I should like on the background of the previous remarks to present the results of the investigations I made of a case in actual businesslife. My aim in this case was to show how big deviations *may* occur between profits computed as the *ideal profit* and profit computed in accordance with generally accepted socalled *conservative principles of accounting.*

The business in case was run as a joint-stock company, and after 10–11 years of operation it ran into financial difficulties. The stockholders were forced to sell their shares so that the company could be carried on by new owners. The sale of the old shares was made at kr. 72,000, which amount in computing the ideal profit is considered an indication of the end-value of the shares (liquidation value). This end-value together with the periodic *withdrawals* (dividends) shown in the accounts formed the basis for a computation partly of the actual (true) capital value (of the entire business) at the end of the different accounting periods and partly of the ideal profits (realized capital interest) of the different accounting periods. The capitalization has been carried out on an interest rate of 8 % pro anno.

This case enables us to measure the extent to which computations of profit according to generally accepted accounting principles and according to the most perfect, economic concepts may differ in actual life.

The computation of profit, withdrawals (inclusive of the liquidation price) and capital value *according to the accountant's principles* disclosed the following development (see figure 1).

The ideal profit and true capital value at the end of the different accounting periods were computed by means of the equation of discounting on the basis of the withdrawn dividends and the realized liquidation value of the shares kr. 72,000 which together form the total withdrawals received by the stockholders in the period 1/1-1941 to 1/1-1952 (see figure 2).

The two computations of capital are shown in the diagram of figure 3. It appears that the capital according to the two different methods of computation has developed along trends which are practically diametrically opposed. The graph of the accounting computations (1) shows for all years except the last that the earned yearly profits exceed the withdrawals resulting in an ever increasing capital accumulation from kr. 44,000 to kr. 126,000. On the other hand the graph representing the true capital (2) shows that in all years except the first two and the last the withdrawals have exceeded the profits (i.e. the interest on the capital). Therefore, the true value of the net assets has not increased but fallen from kr. 143,000 to kr. 72,000.

For the first 5 years the accounting figures show under-estimated capital values (in other words an *invisible capital value* has prevailed) but from 1/1-1947 and up to the liquidation the situation was the opposite. In these years the accounting figures show an ever increasing *over-estimation* of the net assets (the invisible capital value has been negative). A closer examination of the two different computations of profit shows clearly that the accounting figures, *besides coming up with far bigger profits than the true capital interest* (except the last year), *do not show any correlation neither with the ever increasing accounting asset value nor with the ever decreasing true capital value.*

A difference in principle exists between the results of the two computations and therefore also between the content of the two concepts of profit.

Even though this represents just one case from accounting practice it will nevertheless be secure on this basis to draw certain conclusions, as these accounting figures were arrived at according to generally accepted, so-called 'conservative' accounting principles.

These conclusions say that by adhering to conservative accounting principles we have *no guarantee whatsoever that our capital computations will be conservative* (see the years 1946–51) and furthermore that apparently *we definitely cannot expect the accounting computations to give us conservative profit figures* (confirmed by all the years except 1951).

The main impression remains that by using the traditional accounting methods of evaluating assets and liabilities we are not able to inform owners or management of where the dividing line goes between *true* profit and consumption (or accumulation) of capital. The accounting concept of profit *may include consumption of capital* and *may be exclusive of accumulation of capital* (completely or in part) which is in keeping neither with the economic definition of profit nor with the formal accounting definition of profit stated above.

In the case cited it is obvious that the accounting profits were far too high which in turn has led to the big, actual withdrawals of capital. During the first 5–6 years this was done under shelter of an *under-estimation of the total-value of the business.* This under-estimation (i.e. invisible positive capital value) amounted to kr. 99,000 (143,000–44,000) at the start of the business. On the other hand, during the last 6 years the employed accounting methods led to a successive accounting *over-estimation of the total-value.* At the liquidation 1/1-1952 the over-estimation amounted to kr. 54,000 (126,000–72,000).

From figure 1 will be seen that the total accounting profit for the entire life time of the business amounted to kr. 205,000, but this amount consists of *true profit* (realized capital interest) kr. 106,000 (see figure 2) and consumption of capital corresponding to the invisible capital value as of 1/1-1941 of kr. 99,000.

III. The reason why 'Conservative' accounting Profits can be 'Un-conservative'

On the background of this practical case the question presents itself: What reason or possibly reasons may be printed out as responsible for the fact that accounting profits as we have seen can be termed neither *realistic* nor *conservative* but quite contrarily are most *unrealistic* and in addition apparently at times even *over-optimistic?* Or phrased in a different way: *Why does invisible capital value (positive-or negative) exist?*

It will be natural to ask if all the trouble cannot be traced back to the fact that we cannot predict the future with a sufficient degree of certainty.

To this may be said that this fact naturally contributes to the deviations but it is very important to stress, *that it is not solely to blame.* As earlier granted it is naturally evident that in actual life we cannot determine capital values and yearly profits as exactly as in the business case cited, in which we assumed complete knowledge of the actual development through all the accounting periods. Consequently we will always have to make capital adjustments in accounting practice. But still *a distinct difference remains between profit based on economic viewpoints and profit determined through accounting methods.* This difference is attributable to the fact that: *The annual accounting figures rest on a set of rules (in the following termed 'conventions'), which by necessity must make accounting something different from true economic computations.*

Even though it may sound very daring in such a circle as this, one is tempted to ask: Are we accountants really aware of the impacts the conventions may have on the determination of profit and capital value?

In other words, do we fully realize *the limitations of the contents of the concepts we call profit and capital? And specially, are we aware of the fact that we have absolutely no guarantee that our methods are conservative?*

It would take us too far to try this place to go into all phases of these problems. I will have to confine the discussions to a few characteristic examples from accounting practice in order to try to determine what conventions are actually guiding our work and thus get an impression of the consequences they may have with respect to the determination of profit.

IV. Some typical accounting Conventions which influence the Computation of Profit and Capital Value

If we start looking into ordinary commodity accounts of a commercial business we immediately meet one of the most characteristic accounting conventions which can be traced all through the balance sheet and profit and loss account. *It is the principle of using realization as the criteria of determining sales.*

The income from a sale is not entered into the profit and loss account till it has reached that phase in the whole transaction cycle, in which an actual realization has taken place from the business to the outside world; usually this phase coincides with the passing of the title to the commodities sold. This is termed *accounting on sales basis.*

As a consequence 1. saleable goods in stock at the end of the accounting period can only be entered in the inventory account at cost, 2. the balance sheet cannot contain items representing the value of other activity regarding commodity transactions, which will result in income or expenses in the future.

This accounting convention therefore does not only regulate the flow of income to the profit and loss account but also the flow of expenses. We encounter the situation which is so characteristic for accounting but at the same time so irrelevant from an economical viewpoint:

It is the view on what should be included in the profit and loss statement as income which determines which items may be included in the balance sheet and how they should be *evaluated.*

From an economic viewpoint the procedure would be the opposite:

First the value of the assets and liabilities should be determined on the basis of an estimate of their future yields, where upon the incomes and expenses are derived as a consequence thereof.

In '*cost or market whichever is lower*' we find a modification of the basic rule that the goods should be evaluated at cost. We accountants generally are very content with this principle because we feel that it leads to conservative computations of profit and capital value. However, use of the principle of 'cost or market whichever is lower' does not influence the convention of *realizing income on sales basis;* it is universal irrespective of which evaluation basis we use. At the most it may be claimed that the principle represents a certain advance towards an economic evaluation, confined to the stock account, and only when a future decline in the commodity prices is expected. Consequently the accounting results are seemingly given a slight similarity with economic computations. And which is even more dangerous: One is led to believe that their use brings about conservative accounting reports of an economic content.

Whether we use 'cost or market whichever is lower' or cost as a basis for the evaluation of the inventory a host of future effects originating in buying and sales transactions started before the end of the accounting period will not be anticipated and consequently will not be included in the capital value. Their effect will in other words not be registered till the transaction has been completed. Therefore invisible capital value (positive as well as negative) is bound to exist and, first of all, the profit will include either consumption of invisible capital value (i.e. the profit is over-estimated) or will be exclusive of capital accumulation from these invisible values (i.e. the profit is under-estimated). The convention of *realizing income on a sales basis* therefore is highly responsible for the fact that the profit and loss statements show 'good' and 'bad' years to an extent which no doubt is often quite unrealistic.

Turning to other areas of the accounting reports we will be able to point out similar deviations between the accounting and the economic procedures.

Concerning the accounting for *fixed assets* it may be said that the value of these assets to be included in the balance sheet is *not* determined by viewpoints of any similarity with those of the economic theory of evaluation. When the straight line method of depreciation is used, and a socalled 'depreciation schedule' has been made, the values to go into the future balance sheets have in fact been determined in advance without considering that the economic value (i.e. the ability of the asset to bring in yields) probably will vary in a completely different way from one accounting period to another.

Again, the accountant works backwards. First he determines what shall be included in the profit and loss statement and then the asset value is derived as a residual.

An interesting situation is found when we look into the accounting of the *work performed of employees and owners.* Here we have entered an area where accounting practice deviates considerably from a true, economic computation. It goes for all work performed that in principle it is creative of income. Consequently these contributions of work have a capital value for the business and this value like all other capital value can fluctuate from time to time. Nevertheless it is an unwritten law in the accounting world that such a capital value of human working power is not entered into the balance sheet[1]).

As a consequence the computation of profit is not influenced by any decline in this capital value, whereas on the other hand no increase in this capital value is included in the profit.

A number of other examples could be cited which all point to accounting practices which clearly differ from economic viewpoints.

It will, however, take us too far afield to bring out more examples. Only one important thing has still to be pointed out. Even if we supposed that the balance sheet and profit and loss statement were brought better to reflect the many rather palpable items which today are not included in the accounting reports; we still would not have a capital evaluation which would be economically realistic. We would also have to evaluate and include in the balance sheet a number of more immaterial items which influence the future income and expenses, influences which normally are hardly distinguishable neither from each other nor from those of the items already in the balance sheet. In trying to determine these capital values we would encounter impacts which originate outside of the business, for example in the favourable or unfavourable conditions created by society, and also we would meet circumstances created within the business itself which will also influence the earning power in positive or negative direction.

All these factors *may* be included in the *goodwill*, but this item may only be entered in the balance sheet, when an amount was paid for it at the purchase of the business, and furthermore goodwill may not be entered in the balance sheet above cost. Besides that goodwill is normally depreciated very fast, usually according to strict rules in the accounting law.

In business which has only been in the possession of the new owner for a few years, goodwill therefore will not be found in the balance sheet, even though a *positive* or *negative* goodwill may very well exist.

On the basis of the previous discussion we can now sum up that the fact that the annual accounting reports can not be characterized as real economic reports is *not only due to our lack of ability clearly to look into the future; also to blame is the accountant's adherence to certain conventions which prevent him from giving his reports an economic content.*

Among the most characteristic of these conventions, which we have met, are:

1. The convention of realizing income on a *sales basis*, which, as we have seen,

[1] By these remarks I do not voice any opinion that this should be done, but the remarks about the human working power are made, because this is a clear case of a missing capital value, which in many businesses amounts to a considerable size. The invisible capital value in the case above of kr. 99,000 was mainly caused by the ability of the management during the war to keep the business going in spite of many difficulties. And note that the invisible capital value amounted to kr. 99,000 as compared to an equity of kr. 44,000, i.e. more than 200% of the norminal equity was not shown in the balance sheet!

brings us in conflict with economic viewpoints of evaluation, as at the inventory evaluation we work backwards, so to speak.

2. Secondly, we have met the convention within which the accountant *can only include those items in the balance sheet for which payment has been (or will be) made.* This convention prevents the accountant from including in the balance sheet a host of factors that influence the economy of the business in the future, and which, consequently, ought to affect the computation of the profit.

3. We have met the convention of *cost or market whichever is lower*, which at first glance may seem to serve the accountant's wishes and the requirements of law concerning conservative computations of profit. We have, however, proved that this is only a measure of very limited importance, which furthermore is economically relevant only when a loss is imminent.

4. We have also met the convention of *fixed rules of depreciation for long term assets* as a result of which the value of such very essential assets is determined for many years into the future, which must also be termed irrelevant from an economic viewpoint.

5. Finally, we have been confronted with the convention that the *value of human working power must be excluded from the balance sheet*, which will also influence the content of the concept of profit.

Especially for these reasons we have been able to prove that the accounting concept of profit, as compared to theoretical, economic concepts, is most *unclear, that it lacks consistency; and that it does not deserve the term: economic computation of profit.* This we see in the balance sheet items, the values of which could be traced to many different origins. Some items are entered at *present value* (for example, cash-on-hand); others at their *future value* (for example, receivables, bills of exchange, etc.); still others at their '*historical cost*' *value* (this often holds true for the inventory and for various procurements for which the expense is spread out over a period of time). Furthermore items are found that are evaluated according to a fixed plan which pertains to several future accounting periods and which is based on an *arbitrary distribution of the* '*historical cost*' over a certain number of accounting periods (fixed assets); and regarding the liabilities and pre-payments received, the main rule calls for evaluation at *future value*. With respect to long term debts this means an over-estimation of the liabilities.

Finally we have found that elements of positive capital value, which at times are probably quite substantial, are never included in the balance sheet but to the contrary are included successively in the profit and loss statements as profit (see the invisible capital value kr. 99,000 in the above case).

The total effect is the same as if we put Dutch guilders in front of one balance sheet item, English pounds in front of another, French francs in front of a third, German marks in front of a fourth, and nothing in front of a fifth, whereupon these heterogeneous amounts are added and used to indicate the size of the capital value or, at least, to indicate the *conservative* size of this value.

V. Should the Accounting Concept of Profit have another Content?

Even though time has not allowed me to make my analysis of the accounting concept of profit as extensive and systematic as probably is desirable, I do hope that my readers from the above discussion have been able to follow me in concluding that the accounting concept of profit consists of such incompatible elements that it must be doubted very much that the *accountant can have any clearly defined concept of profit in view when working out his annual accounting reports.*

It seems to me that, in fact, we are sitting between two chairs, that is, on the one side: *computations which do not pretend at all to be economic;* and on the other side: *accounting reports aimed at conforming with the requirements of the economic theory as far as possible, but at the same time being ruled by the realistic conditions.*

Generally it appears to me that, if we want to strive toward greater consistency regarding the goal of our computation of profit, we have two main alternatives from which to choose: 1. We can decide that the annual accounting reports shall not be economic reports, but instead what has been termed a 'narration of history', i.e. attempt to record what has been gained, *not considering whether it is income gain or capital gain;* 2. We can attempt to anchor the annual accounting reports in economic evaluations, and *thereby try to distinguish profit from capital gain.*

Some authorities maintain that the accounting reports shall not be economic reports, but '*narration of history*'. These people feel that, by means of the procedures we now employ, it should be possible to record with historical accuracy what has been *earned.* This is claimed to be the case as the computation of profit is based on the convention of realization of income on a sales basis. Thus the profit shows what has been gained through realization.

It cannot be debated that a concept of profit can be based on this ground.

It must, however, be made completely clear to the accountant and not least to the reader of the accountant's report, that the concept of profit thus created *has consistency only regarding the criteria for realization of income.* It does not record anything historically correct about the economic profit earned to date, *but is bound to represent a mixture of capital gains (or losses) and true profit in the economic sense.*

Furthermore, this procedure will not provide any guarantee that too favourable profits or capital values are not recorded.

Considering the fact that other areas of accounting are influenced increasingly by the viewpoints of the economic theory, it does not seem too early now to raise the question of switching the accounting concept of profit from the principle of 'narration of history' to the viewpoints of the economic theory of income and capital.

It is an established fact that management, in carrying out its most important function of deciding the business policies must base its decisions (if made on a realistic basis at all) on computations in deeping with the economic theory, that is, on computations concerning the future. As the annual accounting report is one of the tools management and owners must use in controlling the business policy, it is natural to claim that this report should have an economic content as far as possible.

PALLE HANSEN

VI. Future Problems in writing Annual Accounting Reports

In conclusion I shall try to sketch the problems and the nature of the procedures with which the accountant is confronted if he wants to adapt his reports to the theory of the *economic concept of profit*. First of all, *he will have to discard the convention of realization on sales basis, and instead adopt a principle of anticipation*, which does not aim exclusively at evaluating unfavourable future events, but also tries to register the impact of the favourable events. He must advocate the basic viewpoint *that a most likely estimate in connection with indication of the probable margin of error, everything considered, is bound to be more appropriate as it should be obvious that the sooner management and owners can predict or estimate with a certain degree of reliability the final effect of the actions taken the better they can exercise control and plan future activities.*

In all his work the accountant must turn from the past to the future.

It goes without saying that this does not give him fewer or less complex problems of evaluation. In many cases it will probably be limited how far one dares go in giving the anticipations the shape of numerical evaluation included in the accounting reports.

A changed attitude towards a true economic evaluation of balance sheet items will *allow*, but also *demand*, inclusion in the balance sheet of other *visible* items than those acquired by purchase. This, however, cannot be expected to be sufficient to secure the best possible adherence to the perfect, economic concept of profit. In most cases it probably will be necessary to try to adjust the net asset value regarding any invisible capital value in order to give the best possible picture of the *entire value* of the business. This means that, in addition to the evaluation of the visible assets, carried out with a future viewpoint, we must try to indicate the size of the existing positive or negative goodwill.

Since this question is so vitally important, however, another form of reporting can be sought which might enable the reader himself to form an opinion of the invisible capital value. Attention must be called, therefore, to the fact that it is possible to *make the report, which accompanies the balance sheet and the profit and loss statement, more inclusive* than it usually is today. This report may contain information of the factors (positive or negative) which presumably will influence the earning power of the business, and which the accountant has not dared to include on the balance sheet. This can be done if the profit and equity items are provided with references to the accompanying report.

An important consequence of the proposal set forth here will be that the reader of the accounting report is clearly informed that the profit and loss statement and the balance sheet can be considered neither *correct* nor *conservative*. Rather, it ought to be underlined wherever an opportunity is given that the balance sheet, at best, is pieced together from different factors of value. Therefore, the reader of an annual accounting report in fact will have to make the final adjustments himself in order to arrive at the capital value of the business which he deems realistic. An optimistic view of the future will make the reader add a factor representing 'invisible capital value'. A pessimistic view of the future, on the other hand, may result in a deduction in the accountant's capital computation; that is to say that cases may be found like the one cited above, in which the balance arrives at an over-estimated capital value.

I have dwelt extensively upon the 'economically inspired' accounting report. This, however, does not indicate that personally I have taken sides in this important matter. On the shoulders of the Certified Public Accountants rests a heavy responsibility, and in the future ever increasing demands will be made up on their reports. In order to serve business owners, and especially management, the auditor must be able clearly to point out what his reports do say as well as what they do not say. In this the theoretical tools can guide us.

In the brief time allotted to me I have attempted to point out some important problems which present themselves to us more and more urgently.

	Accounting profit	*Withdrawals (dividends)*	*Accounting equity*
1/1 1941			44.000
1/1 1942	16.000	11.000	49.000
1/1 1943	28.000	5.000	72.000
1/1 1944	36.000	17.000	91.000
1/1 1945	37.000	18.000	110.000
1/1 1946	23.000	13.000	120.000
1/1 1947	34.000	27.000	127.000
1/1 1948	29.000	27.000	129.000
1/1 1949	19.000	19.000	129.000
1/1 1950	27.000	21.000	135.000
1/1 1951	20.000	19.000	136.000
1/1 1952 (before liquidation)	— 10.000	0	126.000
1/1 1952 (after liquidation)	— 54.000		72.000
	205.000		

Fig. 1. Accounting computation of profit and capital value

	Ideal profit (capital interest)	*Withdrawals (dividends)*	*True capital value*
1/1 1941			143.000
1/1 1942	12.000	11.000	144.000
1/1 1943	11.000	5.000	150.000
1/1 1944	12.000	17.000	145.000
1/1 1945	12.000	18.000	139.000
1/1 1946	11.000	13.000	137.000
1/1 1947	11.000	27.000	121.000
1/1 1948	10.000	27.000	104.000
1/1 1949	8.000	19.000	93.000
1/1 1950	7.000	21.000	79.000
1/1 1951	7.000	19.000	67.000
1/1 1952	5.000		72.000
	106.000		

Fig. 2. True (ideal) profit and capital value based on a discounting at 8 % interest.

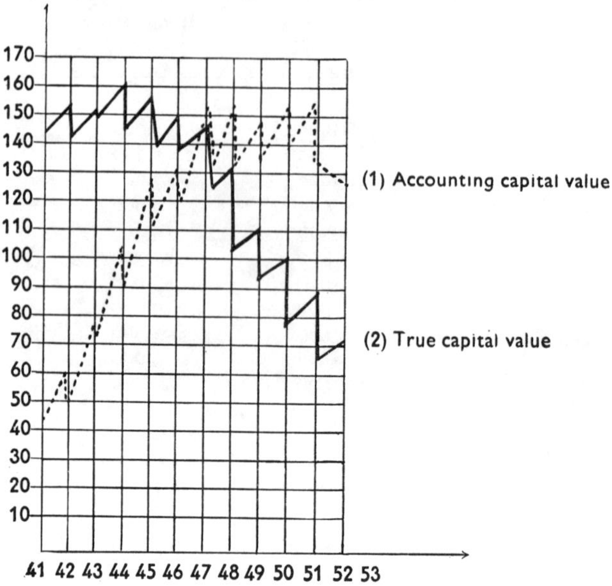

Fig. 3. True and accounting computation of capital value.

PAPER

by

C.I.R. HUTTON, B.A. (OXON), C.A.

The Institute of Chartered Accountants of Scotland

> *'I can easier teach twenty what were good to be done than be one of twenty to follow my own teaching.'*[1]

I. Mathematics and Politics

Aristotle said that it is the mark of an educated person to seek that degree of accuracy on any subject which the nature of the subject admits: and that to accept a plausible estimate from a mathematician is on a par with asking a politician for demonstrative proof.[2]

Can there be any question whether the ascertainment of profit in business ranks as mathematics or politics? Apparently the Council of The Institute of Chartered Accountants in England and Wales (generally known outside England as the 'English Institute') had no such doubts when they recorded their approval of a basis of preparing annual accounts which 'reduces to a minimum the extent to which the accounts can be affected by the personal opinions of those responsible for them'.[3]

Possibly, however, the question merits some brief examination. The English Institute itself points out that accounts affected by the minimum of personal opinion 'are not necessarily suitable for purposes such as price fixing, wage negotiations and taxation unless in using them for these purposes due regard is paid to the amount of profit which has been retained in the business for its maintenance'.[4]

Whether the amount which has been retained in the business for its maintenance is profit or not seems to depend on the meaning not only of the word 'profit' but also of the word 'maintenance'.[5] Clearly, in its context here, mainte-

[1] Shakespeare, The Merchant of Venice, Act I, Scene 2.

[2] Aristotle, Nicomachean Ethics, I, 3.

[3] The Institute of Chartered Accountants in England and Wales – Recommendations on Accounting Principles, No. XV, para. 287.

[4] Op. cit., para. 312.

[5] cf. Lewis Carroll – Through the Looking Glass.

'When I use a word', Humpty Dumpty said in rather a scornful tone, 'it means just what I choose it to mean – neither more nor less'.

nance means preservation of the continuity of the business. And no doubt the Chancellor of the Exchequer may have had this meaning in mind when he said, as quoted recently in 'The Accountant', that 'about 15 per cent of profits earned is needed to keep factories and plant in good repair and up to date'.[1]

If it were as easy as might appear from the Chancellor's observation to calculate the amounts required for the maintenance of a business there would be no difficulty in deducting the amount before arriving at the annual profit figure. But a strong body of professional opinion in the U.K. holds that calculations which must be based in the main on personal experience, knowledge and judgment are insufficiently 'mathematical' by nature to justify their admission to the list of expenditure incurred in earning the profits. The result achieved by the exclusion of such amounts is a mathematical answer, but the value of the answer to the reader will depend on the extent to which he is trained to pay 'due regard' to the more subjective factors omitted from the calculation.

The attachment to mathematical accounts in the U.K. is perhaps, in part, a reaction from the excessive exercise of 'personal opinion' permitted by earlier Acts of Parliament. Prior to the passing of the Companies Act, 1948 the Balance Sheet of a U.K. Company showed a legally 'true and correct view' of the state of affairs even if the fixed assets had been over-depreciated, the stock-in-trade undervalued and the liabilities swollen by provisions for unimaginable contingencies. There was no statutory obligation that the Profit and Loss Account should be 'true and correct' and it was not illegal to make undisclosed transfers to hidden reserves before striking the disclosed profit of the year. Undisclosed transfers from hidden reserves to swell the disposable profits had gone out of fashion after the Royal Mail case, but Consolidated Accounts were not called for and Holding Companies could, and many did, disclose only such part of the subsidiaries' profits as they chose to receive by way of dividend.

Informed professional opinion had for some years been pressing for reform and a favourable climate awaited the accounting requirements contained in the 1948 Act in which attention was for the first time given to the contents of the Profit and Loss Account and somewhat rigid regulations were included, designed to disclose the 'true and fair' profit of each year and to reveal the fluctuations between one year and another.

What had not perhaps been fully foreseen was the effect of the change, in an inflationary era, upon unprofessional opinion among politicians and trade-unionists. The freedom of manoeuvre available under previous legislation had made it possible to disclose a profit not substantially in excess of what could in effect be disposed of without adversely affecting the continuity of the business. Now that the application of the sums so set aside is shown in the accounts – and shown as appropriation of profit – the amounts tend to be ignored by politicians and Trades Union leaders in assessing the social justification for the profits earned and the ability of the business to meet claims for higher wages. Indeed a wide range of opinion, from the Prime Minister downwards, has come to regard a growth in profits as at least reprehensible and an increase in dividends as positively anti-social – a surprising state of affairs in a nation which reached its peak of power on the basis of profitable trade!

[1] 'The Accountant', Leading Article – 8/9/56.

These problems have not been solved and will not solve themselves while we do no more than continue to produce accounts which, though mathematically correct and conforming to the requirements of the Statutes, are unsuitable, without re-interpretation, for the other purposes in which they find themselves employed. Some 'further education' seems to be needed if a better understanding is to be reached, and if we are satisfied with our own attainments we must presumably concentrate our efforts on those of our readers who credit our accounts with a higher degree of accuracy than the nature of the subject admits.

There are, of course, as always in the U.K., exceptions to any general rule. Our Banks and Insurance Companies are exempt from the obligation to disclose a true and fair profit for the year on the grounds that to do so might endanger the confidence which these important institutions enjoy both at home and abroad. Shipping Companies can claim similar exemptions, presumably for the reasons expressed so succinctly in Note 1 of this page[1]. Other giant institutions of national importance such as Imperial Chemical Industries Ltd. are obliged to disclose the true and fair profit of each year and it can only be supposed that in such cases disclosure is considered unlikely to endanger confidence, or to attract the 'curiosity of foreign countries', to an extent likely to damage our national interests.

Again there is nothing except the disapproval of the English Institute to prevent a company from revaluing its fixed assets, thus attracting a charge for depreciation on the basis of replacement cost; and even the Institute's disapproval does not apply 'in cases where a subsidiary is acquired and the assets are written up to reflect the cost to the acquiring company, or where subscriptions for new capital are invited on the basis of a current valuation of the assets'.[2]

II. Astronomical figures

The reference to 'annual accounts' in the English Institute's observation (Note 3, page 609) indicates general acceptance of the principle that accounts should be produced at regular intervals measured by the time that it takes the earth to go round the sun. Nevertheless some of the difficulties met in ascertaining profits in business arise from the artificial concept that a true and fair view of the profit of a continuing business can be ascertained at annual and only at annual intervals.

Businesses engaged in long-term contracting are particularly affected by these difficulties. An exceptionally interesting professional paper written some years ago includes an entertaining reference to their problems: –

> 'If the orthodox principle of bringing into account only realised profits is accepted, the accounts for any year might, by themselves, be almost meaningless. While the practice is not uniform, it is quite common for sums on account of profit on uncompleted contracts to be brought in. Whether the effect of this is to produce results which really reflect the varying fortunes of the business will depend on the objectivity with which the

[1] *Excerpt from a letter to 'Accountancy' – July, 1956 – written by Mr. Charles W. Aston, A.C.A., for the Managing Directors, Peninsular and Oriental Steam Navigation Company.*

'The curiosity of foreign countries in the profits of British shipping companies is a very real threat to the interests of this country.'

[2] Op. cit., para 297

uncompleted contracts are assessed – in other words, the success with which the temptation to aim at equalising profits has been resisted.'[1]

The excerpts from two recent advertisements quoted below indicate that both companies concerned prefer the use of the 'orthodox principle' but it will be noted that whereas in one case provision for any loss is anticipated, in the other case a loss is not taken up until the year in which it is realised.[2 and 3]

The question of interim accounts lies somewhat outside the scope of this paper. In response to demands in the financial Press a small number of U.K. companies now furnish quarterly or half-yearly figures, almost invariably 'subject to audit'. Obviously, the value of interim accounts varies largely as between one business and another according to its nature.

Notwithstanding the inevitable problems (and the inevitable exception)[4] the U.K. pays homage to astronomy and accepts the solar year as the appropriate interval at which to ascertain business profits. But, except in the case of businesses with a very rapid turnover the profits of a single year may not be very informative until viewed as one of a series.

III. Ascertainment of Profits for Valuation Purposes

Indeed, the profits of a single year are seldom examined in isolation. The Companies Act, 1948 requires disclosure of the 'corresponding amounts' for the immediately preceding financial year of all items shown in the Balance Sheet and Profit and Loss Account. For prospectus purposes the Act requires disclosure of the profits or losses in respect of each of the five financial years immediately preceding the issue of the prospectus and, in practice, the five years are usually increased to ten in order to meet Stock Exchange requirements.

For prospectus purposes profits are often compared in relation to fixed assets

[1] Accounting Statements – A General Formula, by Thomas Lister, C.A. (Edinburgh & Glasgow C.A. Students' Societies Transactions – 1950/51).

[2] *Excerpt from an advertisement issued by Holst & Co. Ltd. and published in The Financial Times dated 2nd May, 1956*

'The bulk of the Company's business comprises important contracts, some of which may take several years to complete. The practice is to take no profit into account until the contract is complete apart from maintenance obligations for the cost of which provision is made. Exceptionally, where a contract takes the form of a number of separate orders and runs over several years, profit is taken on work carried out in each financial year. Provision is made against contracts in progress the position of which is such that a loss may be expected.'

[3] *Excerpt from an advertisement issued by Crowley, Russell & Co. Ltd. and published in The Financial Times dated 9th May, 1956*

'*Valuation of Work in Progress.* The value of the work in progress at the end of each financial year is arrived at by aggregating for the various contracts the costs of labour and materials, direct contract expenses, and either (a) the cost of plant purchased for the various contracts or (b) in the case of plant not so purchased, the Directors' valuation of plant transferred to these contracts, such valuation not being in excess of cost, and deducting therefrom in both cases the Directors' valuation of plant withdrawn from these contracts.

...The profit or loss on each contract is brought into account in the year in which the final price is substantially agreed.'

[4] *Companies Act, 1948, Section 455, (1)*

'..."financial year" means... the period in respect of which any profit and loss account of the body corporate laid before it in general meeting is made up, whether that period is a year or not.'

revalued on a replacement basis and on these occasions the English Institute finds itself obliged to depart from the theory of 'historic costs' and to recommend[1] that the prospective investor should be acquainted with the excess of the future depreciation to be provided out of future profits and be reminded that the tax collector will continue to base his allowance for depreciation on the historic cost.

Since the prospective investor examines a series of past years' profits as a guide to future maintainable revenue it is important that the series of figures should reflect the trend as accurately as possible. It follows that any exceptional or non-recurring debits or credits should be picked out and it is also necessary to ensure, so far as practicable that the results of each year are arrived at on a consistent basis. Natural over-caution in the preparation of the original accounts will have largely eliminated itself over a ten year period but some readjustments may be needed, as between one year and the next, in order to clarify the trend of results.

IV. Ascertainment of Business Profits for Tax Purposes

It is self-evident that so long as accountants are satisfied to ascertain profits on a basis which admittedly contains an element of inflation it is illogical to expect the taxing authorities to accept some other basis designed to exclude the inflationary element.

The English, however, are respected for virtues other than logic and for some time past and for various reasons the Inland Revenue have given rather more generous allowances for depreciation on Machinery and Plant than the historic cost basis would warrant.

These allowances are determined by the Commissioners of Inland Revenue by reference to the original cost to the owner and having regard to the anticipated normal working life of machinery or plant of that class. For many years, and as now codified in Section 281 of the Income Tax Act, 1952, the annual allowance has been five-fourths of the percentage thus computed by the Commissioners. This pleasant but illogical arrangement operates in a minor way to accelerate depletion allowances.

A faster, but more erratic method of acceleration is the 'Initial Allowance' introduced in 1945 as an encouragement to Industry to renew its capital assets after the ravages of war. The allowance, originally 20% on cost, was increased to 40 % in 1949, was withdrawn altogether, owing to a financial crisis, in 1952, was restored at 20 % in 1953, was withdrawn again in 1954 when an Investment Allowance of 20 % took its place, and was restored, also at 20 % in 1956 when (subject to certain special cases) the short-lived Investment Allowance disappeared in the course of another financial crisis. Writing in the Autumn of 1956 one hesitates to conjecture what the situation will be by the time we meet in Amsterdam in September, 1957.

These arrangements raised some problems in business accounts from the point of view of relating the charge for tax to the disclosed profits of the year. An

[1] The Institute of Chartered Accountants in England and Wales – Recommendations on Accounting Principles – No. XIII, para. 206 and 207.

early tendency to equate the charge for depreciation to the aggregate of the Inland Revenue allowances foundered owing to the erratic course of the allowances and the most popular plan now is to suspend the benefit of the Initial Allowances as if they were (and in fact they are) a kind of temporary loan from the Revenue, free of interest and repayable by annual instalments. The Reserve representing the temporary loan will be found in many accounts described in some such words as 'Tax Equalisation Reserve'.

The Inland Revenue have not, so far, responded to any suggestions for the adoption of LIFO in computing profits for tax purposes and indeed they have succeeded in getting the 'base stock' method of valuation rejected in the Court of Appeal to the detriment of those few stalwarts in the U.K. who still adopted this old-fashioned, but LIFO-like method and in the face of evidence given by a future President of the English Institute that he had himself given his unqualified audit certificate to accounts of cotton spinners using the base stock method.[1]

A Royal Commission appointed by the Government to consider and report on the taxation of profits and income gave some thought to the method of valuing stock-in-trade and in its report, issued in 1955, suggested that the trader should have an option to value his stock on any one of a number of bases including one transported from North America by the Commission which seems to owe something to both the base stock and LIFO methods.[2] These suggestions aroused some interest in professional circles, but it has not been the practice of the Government to pay much attention to reports by Royal Commissions on tax matters and there seems little prospect that these particular suggestions will be translated into legislation at an early date.

On the need for provision against contingencies the Inland Revenue tends to take a narrower view than business men and their accountants, preferring to await the actual expenditure before allowing the charge against taxable profits. Thus, provisions by a Catering Company against equipment shortages which could not meantime be replaced owing to war-time scarcity were rejected in the face of evidence by an eminent accountant that he would not have been prepared to certify the accounts as correct if the provisions had not been made[3]. And a Company operating a railway in Peru has recently lost its case relating to provisions made for anticipated compensation payable under Peruvian law to its employees upon the termination of their services.[4]

But the Inland Revenue is not always blind to changing fashions[5] and it is fair to say that in the United Kingdom, subject to exceptions such as I have indicated above which are not all unfavourable to the taxpayer, profits for tax purposes are not normally very different from the profits as ascertained in business accounts. If there is anything basically wrong with the methods by which we ascertain our business profits we cannot reasonably expect the Inland Revenue to pioneer the field of reform.

[1] Patrick v. Broadstone Mills Ltd. – 1953

[2] Report of Royal Commission on the Taxation of Profits and Income – Appendix II, p. 477.

[3] Peter Merchant Ltd. v. Stedeford – 1948.

[4] Southern Railway of Peru Ltd. v. Owen – 1956.

[5] The word 'horse', which appears in the Ninth Schedule of the Income Tax Act, 1952, is already deemed to include 'motor car' and, according to an obiter dictum of the Judge in the recent case of Maclean v. Trembath, should also include 'aeroplane'.

No doubt the real trouble with tax in the U.K., which lies outside the scope of this paper, is that the percentage of profits taken is too high a burden to be indefinitely supported.

SUMMARY

The main features of the ascertainment of profit in business may be summed up as follows: –

1. The annual statement rendered to the proprietor by the steward whose duty it is to account for the possessions entrusted to him and for the fruits thereof.

This statement is normally prepared in the U.K. on the historic cost basis, a basis admittedly unsuitable for eyes other than those of the proprietor. Good stewards are cautious by nature but modern legislation has gone some way to obstruct the natural bias towards under-statement with results which are politically unfortunate. No attempt is made, in this short paper, either to apportion the blame or to suggest a solution.[1]

2. The series of annual statements collated, adjusted and re-interpreted as may be thought necessary in order to provide a guide to the valuation of the business.

Natural caution in the preparation of annual statements tends to eliminate itself over a period of years, but if the series of figures is to serve as an accurate guide some readjustment may be needed in order to clarify the trend.

3. The annual statement prepared for tax purposes.

In the U.K. the result does not normally differ very much from the result arrived at on the historic cost basis, and, when it does, any over- or under-assessment to tax in any one year tends to correct itself over a longer period.

By way of apology for this paper and, in particular, for the large number of notes, a final quotation is offered, again from The Merchant of Venice.

> 'What damned error but some sober brow
> Will bless it and approve it with a text'[2]

[1] 'How long halt ye between two opinions?' I Kings, XVIII, 21.
[2] Op. cit., Act III, Scene 2.

REFERAT

von

PROF. DR. LEOPOLD L. ILLETSCHKO

Kammer der Wirtschaftstreuhänder, Österreich

1. Der Gewinn der Unternehmungen ist durch verschiedene Ursachen bewirkt. Auf die Umsatztätigkeit wirken ein: die konkrete Konkurrenz- und Konjunkturlage, die Kaufkraftentwicklung des Geldes, das Führungsgeschick der Unternehmungsleiter, die Arbeitsgeschicklichkeit und Arbeitsintensität der Belegschaft, der Standort im Wirtschaftsraum, die Förderungen und Bedrohungen aus der Umwelt, welche unter den Bezeichnungen Chance und Risiko sich zusammenfassen lassen und manches andere mehr. Eine Gewinnberechnung kann nur von den *quantitativ erfaßbaren* Daten aus diesem Verursachungsbündel ausgehen, wobei als Gewinn ein in Zahlen ausdrückbares Plus (Verlust ein Minus) gegenüber einem zu einem früheren Zeitpunkt ermittelten Zahlenansatz sich definieren läßt. Diese Definition impliziert einmal, daß nur *ein Teil* der Verursachungen durch jenes Plus sich rechnerisch darstellen läßt, weil nur die quantitativ erfaßbaren Daten eine Differenzbildung erlauben, und zum anderen, daß der Zahlenansatz für die beiden Größen, aus denen die Differenz gefunden wird, in *formal gleicher Weise* gebildet sein muß, wenn nicht Ungleiches verglichen werden soll. In der Wirtschaftsrechnung ist daher eine Mehrzahl von Gewinnberechnungen möglich, je nach dem erfaßten (größeren oder kleineren) Teil der Gewinnverursachungen und je nach Art der Findung der Zahlenansätze.

Werden die Zahlenansätze für den früheren und für den späteren Zeitpunkt durch Anschlag in Geld für die ganze Unternehmung (oder von Bestandteilen, die für die Unternehmung repräsentativ sind) gefunden, dann spricht man von *Bewertung*. Die materielle Bedeutung des Gewinnes nach dem erfaßten Teil und seine formale Bedeutung nach der Art der Findung der Zahlenansätze geht somit in den *Bewertungsformen* und *Bewertungsmethoden* unter.

2. Die umfassendste Form solcher Bewertungen zu verschiedenen Zeitpunkten ist der Kauf und Verkauf von ganzen Unternehmungen überhaupt, weil bei diesen von Käufer und Verkäufer möglichst alle erkennbaren Gewinnverursachungen mitveranschlagt werden können. Ein Kauf zu einem Zeitpunkt und Verkauf zu einem anderen ergibt zwei konkret ermittelte Anschläge in *Geld*, die eine Differenzbildung zulassen. (Es müssen dabei wohl die privaten Geldzu- und -abflüsse in dem Zeitraum, den die Differenzbildung überbrückt, berücksichtigt werden.) Ein solcherart ermittelter Gewinn ist ein Geldbetrag. der als Plus

gegenüber dem seinerzeitigen Erwerbspreis nunmehr in Händen des Verkäufers liegt. Auf seinen *realen Gehalt* ließe er sich durch entsprechenden Kaufkraftvergleich (der Zeitpunkte von Erwerb und von Verkauf unter stufenweiser Berücksichtigung der privaten Geldzu- und -abflüsse) bringen. Welche Indices hiefür in Anwendung kommen können, hat bisher noch keine allgemein anerkannte Klärung gefunden, weil eine solche Art der Gewinnberechnung eine private Unternehmerrechnung ist. Der so ermittelte Differenzbetrag sei *Veräußerungsgewinn* genannt.

Immer noch das ganze Unternehmen mit allen Gewinnverursachungen im Auge behaltend, kann an die Stelle des Verkaufes im Ganzen eine Abwicklung (die Liquidation) treten. Bei einer solchen werden *nur die markt- und verkehrsfähigen Bestandteile* der Unternehmung zu einem Geldbetrag führen. Wird daher einem Erwerbspreis für ein ganzes Unternehmen das geldmäßige Liquidationsergebnis (wieder unter Berücksichtigung der privaten Geldzu- und -abflüsse in dem Zeitraum, der der Differenzbildung zugrundeliegt) gegenübergestellt, ergibt sich ein Geldbetrag, der ebenso als ein Plus in den Händen des Liquidators liegt und für dessen realen Gehalt dasselbe gilt, wie vom Veräußerungsgewinn. Die dieserart ermittelte Differenz sei *Liquidationsgewinn* genannt. Er muß sich in seiner materiellen Bedeutung vom Veräußerungsgewinn unterscheiden, weil er nur die markt- und verkehrsfähigen Bestandteil im Liquidationserlös enthält, im Erwerbspreis aber darüber hinaus als Teile auch anderer Gewinnverursachungen mit veranschlagt sein können.

Wird weiter an Stelle eines Erwerbspreises eines ganzen Unternehmens der Aufbau des Unternehmens in Verfolgung des Erwerbs der markt- und verkehrsfähigen Bestandteile gesetzt und der Summe aller dieser Erwerbungen ein Liquidationserlös gegenübergestellt, dann ergibt sich in formaler Hinsicht als Ergebnis ein homogeneres Zahlenbild, weil dann nur die Bewertungsdifferenzen der markt- und verkehrsfähigen Bestandteile sich auswirken können. Diese Differenz sei *Totalgewinn* genannt. Für seinen realen Gehalt hinsichtlich der Kaufkraftschwankungen des Geldes gilt das bereits Gesagte. Da bei seiner Ermittlung einzig und allein von den markt- und verkehrsfähigen Bestandteilen des Unternehmens ausgegangen wird, läßt sich die Liquidation auch fingieren und somit eine Differenzbildung zu jedem beliebigen Zeitpunkt vornehmen. Nach einer beliebigen Periode des Aufbaues und Bestehens der Unternehmung kann durch einen Anschlag in Geld *ohne* Verkaufsakt (durch bloße Fingierung eines solchen) der für die Differenzbildung erforderliche zweite Zahlenansatz gefunden werden. Auf diese Art und Weise ermittelt sich ein *Periodengewinn.* Sowohl Totalgewinn wie Periodengewinn sind zum Unterschied von Veräußerungs- und Liquidationsgewinn kein Plus an Geld, sondern lediglich in Geld angeschlagene *Rechendifferenzen.*

3. Die angeführten Gewinnbegriffe decken sich nicht. Im Veräußerungsgewinn sind *alle* Gewinnverursachungen in einer dem Käufer und Verkäufer überlassenen *subjektiven* Veranschlagung enthalten. Im Liquidationsgewinn liegt eine Reduzierung vor, weil *nur die markt- und verkehrsfähigen Bestandteile* veräußerbar sind, wobei ein Zeitdruck in der Liquidation zudem den Wertanschlag gegenüber dem beim Erwerb herabsetzen kann. In beiden Fällen erfolgt die Gewinnermittlung aus der Differenzbildung zwischen *effektiv bezahlten Preisen.* Beim Total-

gewinn und beim Periodengewinn erfolgt die Differenzbildung nur hinsichtlich des Erwerbs an Hand von effektiv bezahlten Preisen, dagegen hinsichtlich der fingierten Liquidation oder Veräußerung an Hand von Vergleichspreisen. Dazu kommt, daß diese beiden Formen *ausschließlich* sich auf die markt- und verkehrsfähigen Bestandteile des Unternehmens beschränken, so daß statt aller Gewinnverursachungen nur *ein Niederschlag* aus diesen in die Rechnung eintritt. Ein allerdings sehr repräsentativer Teil vertritt das Gesamte. Als Vergleichspreise für eine fingierte Veräußerung lassen sich über den Markt der markt- und verkehrsfähigen Bestandteile durch Schätzung die entsprechenden Daten finden.

4. Es stehen sich somit Veräußerungs- und Liquidationsgewinn als fallweise Ermittlungen auf Grund *effektiver* Kauf- und Verkaufsabschlüsse und Total- und Periodengewinn als zu wählbaren Zeitpunkten durchführbare Ermittlungen auf Grund *rechnerischer* Betrachtung gegenüber. Inhaltlich umfassen Veräußerungs- und Liquidationsgewinn mehr als Total- und Periodengewinn, die Form der Findung der Zahlenansätze ist zudem nicht homogen. Total- und Periodengewinn sind inhaltlich enger, aber durch eine homogenere Art der Findung der Zahlenansätze ausgezeichnet.

5. Die Gewinnberechnung der Unternehmung wird daher, wenn sie zu einer *Periodisierung* des Vorganges führen soll, auf die Differenzbildung von markt- und verkehrsfähigen Bestandteilen des Unternehmens sich beschränken müssen; das bedeutet, daß der Gewinn nicht nach seinen Verursachungen ermittelt wird, sondern lediglich einer als repräsentativ genommenen Reihe von Veränderungen abgenommen ist. Der Periodengewinn ist also ein *formaler Rechenbegriff*, der nur einen quantifizierbaren Niederschlag der Gewinnverursachungen umfaßt und der die Zahlenansätze aus der Verfolgung von echten und fingierten Erwerbsvorgängen findet. Damit läßt er sich aus einer Zu- und Abgangsrechnung an Hand bezahlter Preise, also von Zahlungsvorgängen aufbauen. Er wird aus einer kontinuierlichen 'Bewegungsrechnung' ermittelbar, wenn diese eine 'Periodisierung' durch Auseinanderhaltung von Anfall und Verrechnung der Zahlung erlaubt.

Wie alle Gewinnberechnung ist aber auch diese, infolge der Heranziehung *bezahlter* Preise beim Erwerb der markt- und verkehrsfähigen Teile, an die Entwicklung der Kaufkraft gebunden, sie enthält daher einen *Störungs-* bzw. *Verzerrungsfaktor*, der schwierig zu eliminieren ist, weil die Kaufkraftänderung die verschiedenen Schichten der markt- und verkehrsfähigen Bestandteile der Unternehmung in verschiedener Weise und in verschiedener zeitlicher Auswirkung erfaßt. Der formale Rechenbegriff erfährt zwar durch die Wahl der in Geld ausgedrückten Preise als Maßeinheiten eine starke substanzielle Einfärbung, das darf über seine durchaus formale Herkunft nicht hinwegtäuschen.

6. Die fingierte Veräußerung von markt- und verkehrsfähigen Bestandteilen bringt in der Gewinnberechnung die Datenfluktuationen im Auf und Ab des konjunkturellen und strukturellen Ablaufs der Gesamtwirtschaft zur Geltung. Jeder markt- und verkehrsfähige Bestandteil (Immobilien, Einrichtung, Vorräte, Nominalwerte) nimmt in anderer Weise an dieser Entwicklung teil. Eine Eliminierung dieser Einflüsse ergibt sich nur dann, wenn für die fingierte Veräußerung (Schätzung) von vorhandenen Bestandteilen die *Erwerbspreise* (Anschaffungspreise) beibehalten werden. Dann wird bei der Differenzbildung nur

jene Preisänderung in Erscheinung treten können, welche aus der *Realisierung* erworbener Bestandteile sich ergab. Der materiell auf die Verfolgung von Zu- und Abgang der markt- und verkehrsfähigen Bestandteile eingeschränkte formale Rechenbegriff des Periodengewinnes bedient sich dann formal eines sehr einheitlichen Maßes, welches Geldwert-, Kaufkraft- und Konjunkturschwankungen unberücksichtigt läßt. Aber durch bedeutendere Schwankungen dieser Art wird der auf Anschaffungspreise abgestützte formale Rechenbegriff sehr irreal. Sind die Schwankungen langwellig und ist die Periodenbildung kurzfristig, also im kurzen *Intervall* (in Bezug auf Kaufkraft- und Konjunkturschwankung), dann ist eine vertretbare Näherung des formalen Ergebnisses an reale Sachverhalte möglich, im langen Intervall treten Verzerrungen nach oben oder unten auf.

7. Um diese Verzerrungen zu analysieren, sind konjunkturelle Schwankungen und Kaufkraftschwankungen getrennt zu betrachten. Die *konjunkturellen Schwankungen* finden ihren realen Niederschlag bei Realisationen. Insolange markt- und verkehrsfähige Bestandteile im Verband der Unternehmung verbleiben, also insolange sie nicht realisiert werden, sind sie dem Auf und Ab der Konjunktur entzogen. Steigen die Vergleichspreise über die Anschaffungspreise für diese Bestandteile, ergibt sich bei Fortführung der Unternehmung, bei ihrem kontinuierlichen Betrieb bis zu deren Realisierung, nichts, während bei der Ermittlung des Veräußerungs- bzw. des Liquidationsgewinnes er im Gewinnermittlungszeitpunkt zu einer Berücksichtigung dieser Preisdifferenzen käme. Fallen die Vergleichspreise unter die Höhe der Anschaffungspreise für solche Bestandteile, dann allerdings wird auch bei kontinuierlichem Betrieb eine Rücksichtnahme erforderlich, weil Gefahren für die künftige Realisation entstehen. Die Verluste, die realisationsmäßig erst in künftigen Perioden entstehen würden, sind im Zeitpunkt des Fallens der Vergleichspreise bereits begründet. Man könnte einwenden, daß dies auch für ein Steigen der Vergleichspreise hinsichtlich künftiger Gewinne gelte und dies trifft auch zu. Es ist aber zu bedenken, daß der *formal ermittelte* Gewinn zugleich ein *Rechtstatbestand* hinsichtlich von Gewinnbezugsrechten ist, daß ihm also eine Notwendigkeit der Ausschüttung folgt. Eine Ausschüttung bedeutet Entrichtung in Geld und erfordert die Transferierung des Gewinnes (der Preisdifferenzen markt- und verkehrsfähiger Bestandteile) in Geld, welche, wenn von der Kreditaufnahme abgesehen wird, nur durch vorgängige *Realisation* möglich ist.

Weil also der formale Rechenbegriff *zugleich* eine Rechtsfigur darstellt, muß die *sofortige* Realisationsmöglichkeit in Betracht gezogen werden. Das bedeutet aber, daß ein Fallen der Vergleichspreise die sofortige Realisation der Gewinnauszahlung gefährdet, während ein Steigen der Vergleichspreise die Gewinnauszahlung sichert. Zur formalen Rechnung tritt auf diese Art und Weise *ein Verhalten* des Rechnenden, er wird ein Fallen der Vergleichspreise zur Kenntnis nehmen, ein Steigen aber zunächst unbeachtet lassen können. Die formale Rechnung wird, wenn alle gleichartig dieses Verhalten an den Tag legen oder wenn alle durch Vorschriften dazu gezwungen werden, *konventionell* beeinflußt werden, weil der 'Gewinn' nicht allein Rechenbegriff, sondern auch Rechtsfigur ist. Gäbe es keine Ansprüche auf errechnete Gewinne, könnte die (konjunkturelle Preisänderungen unberücksichtigt lassende) Rechnung mit Beibehaltung der Anschaffungspreise für alle noch vorhandenen markt- und verkehrsfähigen Bestandtteile der Unternehmung genügen. Es gibt aber durch die rechtliche Lage solche Ansprüche und daher sind Preisabweichungen nach unten zur Kenntnis zu nehmen, d.h. diese kürzen den formalen Rechenbegriff auf den Rechtstatbestand 'Gewinn'. Da ein solches konventionelles Verhalten nur einseitig, imparitätisch sich bei Anwendung der Vergleichspreise auswirkt, wird es auch als Imparitäts-, Niederstwertregel usw. bezeichnet. Sein Einfluß schafft aus dem Periodengewinn den *Rechtstatbestand 'Unternehmungsgewinn'* und berücksichtigt Einflüsse der konjunkturellen Schwankungen in der Gewinnberechnung.

8. Die *Kaufkraftschwankungen* sind bei dieser Form der Rechnung nicht ausgeschaltet, sie wirken einem solchen Verhalten geradezu entgegen. Verminderungen und Vermehrungen der Kaufkraft finden ihren Ausdruck in den Preisen, daher auch in den für den formalen Rechenbegriff konstitutiven Vergleichspreisen. Fallende Kaufkraft bedeutet steigende Vergleichspreise; steigende Vergleichspreise beeinflussen die Ermittlung des Rechtstatbestandes 'Unternehmungsgewinn' nicht. Steigende Kaufkraft läßt die Vergleichspreise sinken; dieser Sachverhalt wird jedoch durch die Imparitätsregel zur Kenntnis genommen. So sicher und eindeutig im Hinblick auf die Realisation der Unternehmungsgewinn konjunkturelle Schwankungen berücksichtigen kann, so wenig kann er es hinsichtlich der Kaufkraftschwankungen. Es hat sich auch keinerlei feste Konvention zur Berücksichtigung dieser ausgebildet, sondern bisher nur ein ganzes Instrumentarium von Hilfskonstruktionen entwickelt. Die einfachste Form der Berücksichtigung von Kaufkraftschwankungen liegt in der Aufspaltung des Unternehmungsgewinnes in einen ausschüttbaren und einen im Unternehmen zurückbleibenden Teil. Die Aufspaltung ist dem subjektiven Ermessen derjenigen überlassen, welche Ansprüche auf den Rechtstatbestand 'Gewinn' haben. Eine objektivere Form liegt dann vor, wenn auf Grund von (zumeist nur steuerrechtlich fixierten) Normen der Rechtstatbestand 'Gewinn' durch Kürzung von vervielfachten Abschreibungen oder durch Vorratsaufwertungen korrigiert wird. Die Tatsache, daß die Kaufkraftänderungen einen Störungsfaktor in die Rechnung bringen, wird auch so formuliert, daß der errechnete Gewinn einen 'Scheingewinn' enthalte, also einen Teil, der nur durch den Ermittlungsmodus an Hand der Entwicklung der Preise der markt- und verkehrsfähigen Bestandteile bedingt ist. Der Sachverhalt verkompliziert sich dadurch, daß markt- und verkehrsfähige Bestandteile auch in nominaler Form (Geldwerte und auf Geld lautende Werte) im Unternehmen vorhanden sind und bei den letzteren Entwertungen durch die Kaufkraftänderung *die Rechnung* überhaupt nicht beeinflussen können.

9. Wird der Rechtstatbestand 'Gewinn', der sich in formaler Rechnung aus einem Periodengewinn auf Grund der Anschaffungspreise unter Anwendung der imparitätischen Niederstwertregel ergibt, kurz als *Unternehmungsgewinn* bezeichnet, so zeigt die vorgebrachte Analyse, daß der Unternehmungsgewinn von *Realisationsgesichtspunkten* überschattet ist und Verzerrungen durch Kaufkraftänderungen *nicht* abwehren kann. Die Kaufkraftänderungen zwingen zu einer Modifikation des Unternehmungsgewinnes, die in Zeiten ruhiger Kaufkraftentwicklung unbeachtet bleiben kann, in Zeiten bewegter Kaufkraftver-

änderung aber an Bedeutung gewinnen muß. Ob eine Kaufkraftentwicklung als ruhig oder bewegt zu bezeichnen ist, bestimmt sich nach der Länge der Periode der Ermittlung des Unternehmungsgewinnes, denn wäre der Intervall kurz, würde auch eine dynamische Kaufkraftänderung immerhin noch eine 'scheingewinnfreie' Ermittlung des Unternehmungsgewinnes erlauben, wenn der Anteil jener markt- und verkehrsfähigen Bestandteile der Unternehmung, der aus zurückliegenden Perioden stammt, klein ist. Unternehmungen ohne nennenswerte Anlagen und ohne Vorratshortungen können bei kurzer Intervallbildung in starker Annäherung den Scheingewinnanteil im Unternehmungsgewinn fast auf Null reduzieren. Markt- und verkehrsfähige Bestandteile, die nicht der alsbaldigen Realisierung, sondern dem Gebrauch, der Nutzung bestimmt sind, oder die über viele Intervalle gehalten werden, vergrößern die verzerrende Wirkung des Störungsfaktors einer 'schwankenden Maßgröße'. In richtiger Erkenntnis dieser Tatsache hat die Wirtschaftspraxis neben die Ermittlung des Unternehmungsgewinnes die *kurzfristige Erfolgsrechnung*, die stückbezogene Kalkulation, welche mit *aktuellen* Preisansätzen arbeiten kann, gesetzt. Das betriebliche Rechnungswesen entwickelt sich daher zu zwei durch ihren Charakter verschiedenen Werkzeugen, einmal zur dokumentierenden, den Unternehmungsgewinn in der Periode des Geschäftsjahres ermittelnden Buchhaltung, bei der die formale Rechnung auf Grund der Anschaffungspreise unter Berücksichtigung der imparitätischen Niederstwertregel durch Rechtsvorschriften konventionell gesichert ist und zum anderen zur für die Geschäftsdisposition kalkulatorisch Stückgewinne ermittelnden Kostenrechnung, welche auf Grund aktueller Preisansätze konjunkturelle und monetäre Einflüsse bei Bildung von Kurzintervallen möglichst berücksichtigt. Werden im betrieblichen Rechnungswesen beide Werkzeuge zusammengefaßt betrachtet, so hat dieses einmal einen *rechtlich* begründeten *Dokumentarcharakter* und zum anderen einen für die Geschäftsdisposition unerläßlichen *Instrumentalcharakter*. Die Rechtsfigur Unternehmungsgewinn hat nur in dem Teil des betrieblichen Rechnungswesens, der Dokumentarcharakter hat, Raum.

10. Eine Untersuchung der tatsachlichen Bilanzierungspraxis im internationalen Vergleich beweist das Vorgebrachte. Die Commission de Droit Comptable der UEC (Union européenne des experts comptables et financiers) hat für die Kongresse in Florenz 1952 und Brüssel 1955 die Bilanzbewertungsvorschriften aus zehn europäischen Ländern synoptisch einander gegenübergestellt und eindeutig eine Ermittlung des Unternehmungsgewinnes aus einer Differenzbildung zwischen Anschaffungspreis und Realisationsergebnis bzw. bei noch fehlender Realisation durch Beibehaltung des Anschaffungspreises unter Berücksichtigung der imparitätischen Niederstwertregel gefunden. Es fanden sich lediglich Ausnahmen von diesem ganz allgemein angewendeten Verfahren der Ergebnisbildung bei der Bewertung von Finanzanlagen, börsefähigen Wertpapieren usw., die ohne nähere Besprechung hier übergangen werden können. Ebenso ist im anglo-amerikanischen Bereich die Ermittlung des Unternehmungsgewinnes auf Anschaffungswert und imparitätischen Niederstwertregel gestützt. Daraus kann gefolgert werden, daß die Ermittlung des Unternehmungsgewinnes zwei Quellen der Herkunft hat, einmal die formale Rechnung, welche nur Zu- und Abgang markt- und verkehrsfähiger Bestandteile der Unter-

nehmung verfolgt und zum anderen die sehr gesicherte Konvention, bei der Ergebnisbildung dieser Rechnung *künftige* Realisierungsmöglichkeiten an Hand der Vergleichspreise zu berücksichtigen. *Rechnung* und *Erwartung* sind daher letzten Endes die Quellen, aus denen Bewertungsvorschriften und Bewertungsmethoden sich bilden.

11. Zur Rechnung ist zu sagen, daß sie durch ihre Beschränkung auf Anschaffungspreis, Vergleichspreis und Realisationserlös lediglich markt- und verkehrsfähiger Bestandteile die Sachverhalte der Gewinnverursachung nicht bloßzulegen vermag. Eine gesteigerte Umsatztätigkeit infolge der besseren Erfassung der Marktlage durch die Unternehmungsleiter oder durch unabhängig von diesen Entschlüssen eintretende Standortvorteiländerungen; eine verminderte Umsatztätigkeit aus von den Unternehmungsleitern nicht rechtzeitig erkannten Schädigungen des Produktionsapparates oder aus einer eingetretenen Einkommensumschichtung der bisherigen Bezieher; eine gleichbleibende Umsatztätigkeit, in der gewinnverursachende und gewinnverhindernde Faktoren sich kompensiert haben usw., alles dies in vielerlei Kombination und Variation wird bei der rechnerischen Ermittlung des Unternehmungsgewinnes nicht aufgehellt. Er ist eine Zahlengröße, die durch die formale Art ihres Entstehens die reale Sachlage nicht abbildet, die Zahlengröße zeigt nur ein Resultat des Zusammenwirkens vieler Sachlagen. Die Realität liegt hinter dieser Zahlengröße und ist nur durch eine gesonderte Untersuchung nachkonstruierbar, entzieht sich in manchen Fällen gänzlich der Aufhellung.

12. Die Beschränkung der Herkunft dieser Zahlengröße *nur* auf die Veränderung der markt- und verkehrsfähigen Bestandteile aus Erwerb, Vergleichspreis und Realisation muß zudem wesentliche Gewinnbeeinflussungsgrößen außerhalb der Rechnung lassen. Die Wahl eines besseren Erzeugungs- oder Vertriebsverfahrens, das nicht von außen her erworben, sondern in der Unternehmung durch Geschick der Leitung und Arbeitsgeschicklichkeit der Belegschaft durchführbar wird, findet einen direkten Anschlag in Zahlen nur insoweit als hiefür markt- und verkehrsfähige Wirtschaftsgüter als Mittel erworben werden mußten. Standortvorzüge und -nachteile, die während des Bestehens der Unternehmung durch Veränderungen im Transportsystem der Gesamtwirtschaft sich bilden, kommen nur im Wege der veränderten Transportkostenbelastung ins Zahlenbild, der Aufbau von public relations, eines goodwill, ist lediglich im günstigeren Resultat des Unternehmungsgewinnes sichtbar. Überdies hat die Rechtsform der Unternehmung einen nachhaltigen Einfluß, weil bei Kapitalgesellschaften das Leitungsgeschick durch Gehälter und Tantièmen belohnt, also erworben wird, während bei Personengesellschaften nicht einmal die fertigende Arbeit des Leitenden in die formale Rechnung eingeht. Im Veräußerungsgewinn werden solche Elemente des Aufbaues *originärer* Gewinnverursachungen in Anschlag gebracht (in Form von Bewertungen des Kundenstocks, der Rezepte, der Verfahren, der Erfindungen, der Organisationsvorteile, der Standortvorteile, der Markterwartungen und dergl. mehr) und im Liquidationsgewinn sind sie, sofern sie zu einem markt- und verkehrsfähigen Substrat (Rechte, vertragliche Sicherung, Konzessionserteilung, Kartellquoten usw.) führen, in *derivativer* Form berücksichtigt. Vom Unternehmungsgewinn auf Veräußerungs- oder Liquidationsgewinn zu schließen, ist schwierig, weil originäre

Gewinnverursachungsquellen, die im Unternehmungsgewinn nur einen unvollständigen resultatsmäßigen Niederschlag gefunden haben, erfordern, daß dieser Niederschlag vor einen Vergleich von Unternehmungsgewinn und Veräußerungsgewinn (Liquidationsgewinn) bereinigt werden muß. Erst nach dieser Eliminierung darf eine rechnerische Brücke gesucht werden, und dem Ergebnis sind sodann die originären Gewinnverursachungen durch Anschlag in Geld (also derivativ) wieder hinzusetzen. Jede solche Umwandlung originärer Formen in derivative Ansätze ist weitgehend von Erwartungen überschattet, so daß aus diesem komplizierten Sachverhalt geschlossen werden darf, alle Gewinnermittlung (Veräußerungs-, Liquidations-, Perioden-, Unternehmungsgewinn) überhaupt spielt in einem *Spannungsfeld* von formaler Rechnung und Zukunftserwartung und je nach dem Hinneigen zu dem einen oder dem anderen Pol dieses Spannungsfeldes realisiert sich eine der angeführten Gewinnermittlungsformen. Unter diesen ist der Unternehmungsgewinn gekennzeichnet durch seine stärkere Abstützung auf die formale Rechnung (weil er nicht fallweise, sondern in regulären Perioden ermittelt wird) und durch das konventionell gesicherte Ausmaß der zu berücksichtigenden Erwartungen. Diese Stabilisierung im Spannungsfeld von Rechnung und Erwartung macht ihn für die allgemeine Anwendung tauglich, aber er bleibt nur *eine Form unter vielen Formen.*

Translation

PAPER

by

PROF. DR. LEOPOLD L. ILLETSCHKO

Kammer der Wirtschaftstreuhänder, Austria

1. Business profit is brought about through various causes. The turnover is influenced by: the existing competition and the turn of the economic cycle; the development of the purchasing power of money; managerial ability; the skill and efficiency of the staff; the location in the economic area; the dangers and encouragements of the surroundings, which may be summarized by the terms 'opportunity' and 'risk'; several other factors. A computation of profit—profit being defined as an increase (loss equals decrease) in terms of figures, over a figure established at an earlier date—can be based only on those data from amongst these many causes, as can be *expressed in quantity*. The above definition implies, first, that *only some* of the causes can be expressed in a figure of increase, because only data expressed in terms of quantity permit establishing a difference; and secondly, the figures for the two amounts, on the basis of which the difference is computed, must be arrived at by the *same formal method*, so as to avoid comparing what is not comparable. There are, therefore, several ways of computing profit, of a business dependent on the number of profit causes taken into account, and on the manner in which the figures are determined.

If the figures for the earlier and the later dates are in terms of money for the enterprise as a whole (or for representative parts of it) we speak of *valuation*. The significance of profit in terms of real causes, and its formal significance in terms of figures used, are due, therefore, solely to the *forms and methods of valuation*.

2. The most comprehensive form of such valuations at different dates is the purchase and sale of business enterprises as a whole, because, on these occasions, all perceivable causes of profit can be taken into account by the purchaser and the seller. Purchasing at one date and selling at another furnish two concrete figures in terms of *money*, which permit computing the difference. (Allowance must, of course, be made for any investments and withdrawals of money by the entrepreneur during the period concerned.) The profit thus arrived at, is a sum of money, representing the increase over the former purchase price, now in the hands of the seller. Its *real value* can be ascertained by an appropriate comparison of purchasing power (as per the dates of the purchase and sale, also taking account, step by step, of the investments and withdrawals of money by the entrepreneur). A generally accepted solution as to the kind of indices to be used for this purpose has not yet been found, because this kind of profit computation

is a matter of private accountancy of the entrepreneur. The difference thus arrived at, may be termed *'disposal profit'* (Veräusserungsgewinn).

Still considering an enterprise as a whole, and all its profit causes, there may be a winding-up (liquidation) instead of a sale. Under the former, *only the marketable and realizable assets* of an enterprise will produce a sum of money. If, therefore, the purchase price of an enterprise as a whole is set against the proceeds of liquidation (again taking into account the entrepreneur's additions and withdrawals of money during the period concerned), a sum of money results which also represents an increase in the hands of the liquidator. As to its real value, the same applies as was said about 'disposal profit'. The difference thus arrived at, may be termed *'winding-up profit'* (Liquidationsgewinn). Its significance in real terms is bound to differ from that of 'disposal profit', since the former will comprise only the winding-up proceeds of the marketable and realizable assets, whereas a purchase price may reflect, over and above that, a valuation of other causes of profit.

If one considers, not the purchase price of a business enterprise as a whole, but the gradual building-up of an enterprise by the acquisition of marketable and realizable assets, and then sets the winding-up proceeds against the cost of all these acquisitions, the result is, from a formal point of view, a more homogeneous set of figures, because only the difference in the valuation of the marketable and realizable assets can have any effect. This difference may be termed *'total profit'* (Totalgewinn). As to its real value, the above suggestions about elimination of fluctuations in the purchasing power of money apply. Since the computation of 'total profit' is based solely on the marketable and realizable assets of the enterprise, a hypothetical winding-up may be assumed, and the amount of difference ascertained at any date desired. At some unspecified period after the establishment of an enterprise, the second set of figures, which is required for ascertaining the difference, can be arrived at by a valuation in terms of money, *without* an actual sale taking place (only a hypothetical one). In this way a *'period profit'* (Periodengewinn) results. Neither 'total profit' nor 'period profit', in contrast with 'disposal profit' and 'winding-up profit', represent an increase in money, but are both just *accounting differences* expressed in money.

3. The concepts of profit mentioned above are not alike. 'Disposal profit' reflects *all* the causes of profit as valued *subjectively* by the purchaser and the seller. 'Winding-up profit' falls short of the former, because *only the marketable and realizable assets* can be sold, and time pressure in the case of when liquidation may lower the price still further as compared with that paid on acquisition. In both cases the computation of profit is based on the difference between *actually paid prices*. In the case of 'total profit' and 'period profit' the difference is based on actually paid prices only in so far as the acquisitions are concerned, but on comparative prices as regards the hypothetical winding-up or sale. What is more, both these forms are *strictly confined* to the marketable and realizable assets of an enterprise so that, instead of all causes of profit, only these assets enter into the computation. The part thus standing for the whole is, however, very representative. Comparative prices for a hypothetical sale can be estimated on the basis of market conditions for the marketable and realizable assets of the enterprise.

4. On the one hand, therefore, there are 'disposal profit' and 'winding-up profit' as computed on the basis of actual purchase and selling agreements, and, on the other hand, 'total profit' and 'period profit' as computed up to any selected dates on the basis of *accounting*. 'Disposal profit' and 'winding-up profit' cover a wider range than do 'total profit' and 'period profit', and the method of ascertaining their account is not homogeneous. 'Total profit' and 'period profit' cover a smaller range, but are distinguished by a more homogeneous way of ascertaining their account.

5. The computation of business profit, if it is to become a regular periodical procedure, must for this reason be confined to ascertaining the differences in the marketable and realizable assets of the enterprise, i.e. profit is computed not on the basis of its causes, but on a series of changes which are considered representative. 'Period profit' is thus a *formal accounting concept*, reflecting only those causes of profit which can be expressed quantitatively, and arriving at the appropriate figures on the basis of actual and hypothetical acts of acquisition. It may, therefore, be ascertained by taking account of additions to and subtractions from assets, in terms of paid prices, i.e. on the basis of actual payments. It is taken from a continuous 'accounting of changes' ('Bewegungsrechnung'), if the latter allows for clear-cut accounting periods by keeping apart the incidence of payments and their inclusion in the accounts.

By using prices *paid* at the acquisition of the marketable and realizable assets, this way of computing profit, like all the others, is also subject to the changes in purchasing power. It thus contains a *factor of inaccuracy and distortion* which is difficult to eliminate, because changes in purchasing power affect differently, and with a different time effect, the various strata of the marketable and realizable assets of an enterprise. The formal accounting concept indeed becomes more real by the choice of prices expressed in money units as a measure-stick, but this should not reader us blind to its absolutely formal origin.

6. The hypothetical sale of the marketable and realizable assets reflects, in the computation of profit, the fluctuations of data due to the ups and downs of cyclical and structural changes in the whole economy. Of the marketable and realizable assets (real estate, equipment, stocks, nominal values) each is affected in a different way by these developments. Elimination of these influences is possible only if the *cost prices* of the existing assets are retained for the hypothetical sale (valuation estimate). In this way, the computation of the difference is based only on that change of prices as arises from the *realization* of previously acquired assets. The formal accounting concept of 'period profit', confined to the marketable and realizable assets entering and leaving the enterprise, thus makes use of a very homogeneous yardstick from a formal point of view, a yardstick which ignores any fluctuations in the value of money, in purchasing power and the trade cycle. When these fluctuations are relatively important, the formal accounting concept based on cost prices however, becomes very unrealistic. When fluctuations occur in long-term waves, and accounting periods are in respect of short *intervals* (in relation to cyclical and purchasing power fluctuations), an acceptable approximation of the formal results to the real state of affairs can still be achieved, but, over long intervals, distortions, upwards or downwards, are bound to arise.

7. In order to analyse these distortions, cyclical fluctuations and the fluctuations of purchasing power have to be considered separately. *Cyclical fluctuations* are reflected in concrete terms when assets are realized. As long as marketable and realizable assets remain within the framework of the enterprise, i.e. as long as they are not realized, they are not affected by the ups and downs of the trade cycle. It is of no consequence when comparative prices rise over the cost prices of these assets, as long as the enterprise is carried on right up to their realization; whereas, with 'disposal profit' and 'winding-up profit', that difference in prices at the date of computation would be taken into account. However, when comparative prices drop below the level of the cost prices of such assets, this must be taken notice of, even if the business is continued, because there is the danger of possible losses on future realizations. Although these losses would not actually occur until future periods, their cause dates back to the decline in comparative prices. It might be objected, and quite rightly, so that, with regard to future profits, this also applies to a rise in comparative prices. However, it must be borne in mind that the *formally computed* amount of profit constitutes at the same time a *legal fact* on which claims to profit distributions are based, i.e. it entails distributions. Distributions mean disbursements in cash, i.e. they necessitate the transfer in cash of the computed profit (due to the price differences of the marketable and realizable assets). Excluding a loan, however, this is not possible without preceding *realizations*.

Since the formal accounting concept is thus *at the same time* a legal fact, the possibility of a *sudden* realization must be taken into consideration. This implies that a decline in the comparative prices endangers the prompt realization of the profit distribution, while a rise in comparative prices ensures this distribution. Formal accounting is in this way supplemented by an *attitude* of the computer: he will take account of a decline in comparative prices, but, for the time being, ignore any rise. With everybody voluntarily assuming the same attitude, or compelled to do so by regulations, formal accounting will thus become more *conventional* by the fact that 'profit' is not just an accounting concept but also a legal fact. If there were no claims to computed profits, a computation retaining the cost prices of all assets still in the enterprise (while ignoring cyclical price changes) would be sufficient. But since there are such claims according to the law, downward changes of prices must be taken account of, i.e. the formal accounting concept of 'profit' is reduced to the legal concept of 'profit'. As this conventional attitude to the use of comparative prices works only one way, the 'rule of the lower value of cost or market' (Niederstwertregel) is also termed the 'rule of imparity' (Imparitätsregel). Its influence converts 'period profit' into the *legal* (*fact of*) '*business profit*', and takes into account the effects of cyclical fluctuations on the computation of profit.

8. *Fluctuations in purchasing power* are not eliminated by this kind of computation, and work right against the above-mentioned attitude. Any decrease or increase in purchasing power is reflected in prices, and thus also in the comparative prices on which the formal accounting concept is based. A decrease in purchasing power means an increase in comparative prices, but higher comparative prices have no bearing on the computation of the legal (fact of) 'business profit'. An increase in purchasing power means a fall in comparative

prices, which fact is taken into account in complying with the 'lower of cost or market value rule' (rule of imparity). While a computation of business profit can make definite allowances for cyclical fluctuations, keeping realization in mind, it cannot do so as regards fluctuations in purchasing power. Nor has any firm convention been established for dealing with them. So far, only a host of makeshift devices has been developed. The simplest form of taking account of fluctuations in purchasing power consists in dividing business profit into two parts, one to be distributed, and the other to be retained in the enterprise. The making of this division is left to the subjective judgement of those who have a claim to 'profit' as a legal fact. A more objective way is to reduce the legal 'profit' by accelerated or increased depreciation, or by a write-up of stocks, on the basis of standard rules (which in most cases are laid down by fiscal law). The fact that changes in purchasing power introduce a distorting factor into the computation is also recognized by saying that the computed profit contains a 'fictitious (illusory) profit', i.e. a part which is due to the computation being based on changes in the prices of the marketable and realizable assets. The matter is rendered more complicated by the fact that there are in the enterprise marketable and realizable assets in the form of money, or values expressed in money, the reduction in value of which, through changes in the purchasing power, can in no way affect the *computation*.

9. The above analysis shows that business profit is overshadowed by *considerations of realization*, and that it is not possible to eliminate distortions due to changes in purchasing power. The term '*business profit*', as used here, stands for the legal concept of 'profit', as it arises from 'period profit' by formal computation on the basis of cost prices and the 'lower of cost or market value rule'. Changes in purchasing power necessitate an adjustment of 'business profit', which may be neglected in times of a steady development of purchasing power, but is bound to increase in importance in times of considerable changes. Whether a development of purchasing power is to be considered steady or lively, depends on the length of period for which business profit is to be computed. If the period is short, a dynamic change in purchasing power will still permit a computation of business profit which is free of fictitious profit, provided the share of the marketable and realizable assets in the enterprise which date from preceding periods is small. Enterprises without considerable equipment and without stockpiles can, in the case of short periods, reduce the portion of fictitious profit included in their business profits to nearly zero. The distorting effect of an 'unstable yardstick' is enhanced by those marketable and realizable assets which are designed not for early realization but for use, and which are retained over longer periods. In recognition of this fact, business practice has introduced, side by side with the computation of business profit, *short-term operating accounting* and unit cost accounting which are based on *current* prices. Business accounting thus produces two tools which are distinct in character. On the one hand, there is bookkeeping which serves as documentary evidence and shows the business profit for the period of the fiscal year, the formal computation being conventionally determined by legal regulations (cost price and 'lower of cost or market value rule'). On the other hand, there is cost accounting, by which unit profits are ascertained for the purpose of operating policy, and which, by considering

only short periods and using current prices, takes cyclical and monetary influences as much as possible into account. Business accounting, providing these two tools, is in the nature, first, of a *legally recognized document*, and secondly, of an *instrument* which is indispensable to operating policy. The legal (fact of) 'business profit' can be found only in that part of business accounting which is in the nature of a document.

10. An investigation, based on international comparisons, of actual accounting practices corroborates what has been said above. The 'Commission de Droit Comptable' of UEC (Union européenne des experts comptables et financiers) compiled, for their conferences at Florence in 1952 and at Brussels in 1955, the accounting regulations concerning balance sheet valuations, of ten European countries, and it was clearly established that the computation of business profit is based on the difference between cost price and realization proceeds, or, in the absence of realization, on retaining the cost price and applying the 'lower of cost or market value rule'. The only exceptions to this generally employed practice of computing profit concerned the valuation of investments, listed securities, etc. For our purposes, these exceptions may be passed over without detailed discussion. In the British and American spheres, the computation of business profit is also based on cost prices and the 'unilateral lower of cost or market value rule' (imparitätische Niederstwertregel). From this it may be inferred, that the computation of business profit results from two sources, the one being the formal accounting which deals with nothing but the arrival at and the departure from the enterprise of the marketable and realizable assets, the other, the well established convention of taking into account the *future* possibilities of realization, in the light of comparative prices. In the last ressort, therefore, it is *formal accounting* and *expectations* which constitute the sources of the rules and methods of valuation.

11. Formal accounting, being based solely on cost, comparative prices, and realization proceeds of the marketable and realizable assets, fails to disclose the real facts which give rise to profit. The formal computation of business profit fails to throw light on many facts, such as an increase in turnover due to a better interpretation of market conditions by the management, or to favourable changes in the advantages of location, occurring independently of managerial decisions; a decrease in turnover due to failure by the management to realize in time an impairment of the production plant, or to a shift in the income stratification of customers; an unchanged turnover due to factors conducive to profit being offset by factors impairing profit,—and many combinations and varieties of all these conditions. Business profit is a figure which, owing to the formal manner of its computation, does not reflect the real state of affairs, but just shows the result of the interaction of several states of affairs. Reality is hidden behind this figure, and may be reconstructed only by separate investigations, but in some cases it completely defies clarification.

12. Confining the origin of this figure to changes of the marketable and realizable assets, due to acquisition, comparative prices, and realization, leaves important factors affecting profit out of account. The adoption of improved methods of production and distribution, which are not bought from outside but become practicable in the enterprise by managerial ability and the working

skill of the staff, is reflected in terms of figures only in so far as marketable and realizable goods have to be acquired as the means of the new procedures. Advantages and disadvantages of location, which arise in the course of the enterprise existence because of changes in the transport system of the whole economy, enter into the sets of figures only by way of a change in transport charges; and the building up of public relations and goodwill can be seen only in terms of a more favourable business profit. The legal status of an enterprise also exercises a profound influence, because, in the case of corporations, managerial ability is rewarded with salaries and bonuses, i.e. it is acquired; whilst, in partnerships, not even the work of the manager-owner enters into formal accounting. 'Disposal profit' (Veräusserungsgewinn) does contain such elements of *primary* causes of profit (by placing a value on clientèle, recipes, processes inventions, advantages of organization and location, market expectations, etc.), and 'winding-up profit' takes account of them in a *derived* form, in so far as they are expressed in marketable and realizable assets (rights, contractual guarantees, licences, cartel quotas, etc.). It is difficult to try to arrive at 'disposal profit' or 'winding-up profit' on the basis of 'business profit', because it is necessary to eliminate first the primary causes of profit which are only imperfectly reflected in business profit, before a comparison can be made between business and disposal profit (liquidation profit). Not until such elimination may a connection be attempted between the two, and then the primary causes of profit are to be added again in terms of money (i.e. in a derived form). Any such conversion of primary causes into derived figures is largely influenced by expectations, so that the conclusion to be drawn from this complicated state of affairs is that all computations of profit (disposal profit, winding-up profit, period profit, business profit) take place in a *field of tension* of formal accounting and expectations for the future. The nature of the profit computation is determined by the way in which it tends towards one of these poles in the field of tension: Business profit is characterized by being based largely on formal accounting (because it is computed, not just occasionally, but at regular intervals) and on conventions, which fix the extent of expectations to be taken into account. Its stabilization in the said field of tension renders it satisfactory for general use, but it remains just *one way of several.*

RAPPORT

de

EMILE MANGAL

Collège National des Experts Comptables de Belgique

Ce rapport examine trois questions proposées pour la discussion du sujet ci-dessus.

PREMIÈRE QUESTION

'Existe-t-il une relation calculable entre les excédents et les déficits résultant d'un pourcentage d'emploi de la capacité de production respectivement supérieur ou inférieur au pourcentage normal, le tout se produisant au cours du cycle conjuncturel'.

1. Les services de Comptabilité sont toujours en mesure de justifier 'à posteriori' les écarts de résultats que l'on enregistre en période de sous-activité ou de suractivité par rapport à une période d'activité normale.

Ces justifications peuvent être poussées aussi loin qu'on le veut. Mais il est alors parfois difficile de dégager le facteur prédominant.

Or, entre une période de sous-activité et une période de suractivité, la différence de résultats réside essentiellement dans le bénéfice des ventes supplémentaires. Il semble donc, à première vue, qu'il doit être aisé de calculer 'à priori', toutes choses étant égales, les excédents ou déficits par rapport à un bénéfice normal lorsque l'activité varie.

2. Notre propos est d'attirer l'attention sur le fait que ces excédents ou déficits sont fonction:

a. de la méthode d'enregistrement des prix de revient;

b. de la politique de gestion en matière d'adaptation de la production au volume des ventes.

3. Pour le montrer, nous allons schématiser, par un exemple, un cycle complet en prenant comme référence un volume de production représenté par 100.

Sous-activité de production	90	Ventes	80	Mise en stock	10
Suractivité de production	110	Ventes	120	Déstockage	10
Total	200		200	Variation du stock	0

4. Comme on le voit, ce schéma définit déjà une politique de gestion de l'exploitation consistant à stocker légèrement pendant la période de récession des ventes, pour déstocker lors de la reprise.

Les conséquences de cette politique apparaîtront clairement par la suite (Voir 8).

5. Considérons à présent les différentes méthodes possibles d'enregistrement des prix de revient.

5a. Si on calcule les prix de revient correspondant à chaque niveau d'activité en y incorporant tous les frais fixes, il est clair que le prix de revient en période de suractivité sera plus avantageux qu'en période de sous-activité, les frais fixes étant répartis sur un tonnage plus important.

Aucune difficulté ne se présente pour prédéterminer les prix de revient à des niveaux d'activité de 90 ou de 110. Les bénéfices sur des volumes de vente de 80 et de 120 peuvent donc être prédéterminés et, par conséquent, les écarts par rapport à un bénéfice moyen correspondant à l'activité normale.

Il y a toutefois lieu d'apporter une correction aux inventaires de produits en stock dont les prix de revient se trouvent modifiés.

L'importance de cette correction, à faire chaque année, dépendra du niveau absolu des stocks en magasin. Elle tend à diminuer le bénéfice en période de sous-activité par l'effet de la plus-value sur stocks comptabilisés à un prix de revient supérieur à la normale. Or, cette correction est sans signification particulière puisqu'en période de suractivité elle devra se faire en sens contraire.

5b. Un des avantages des comptabilités utilisant un prix de revient standard, qui serait calculé, dans l'exemple cité, sur une production moyenne de 100, consiste dans le fait qu'aucune correction n'est nécessaire dans l'évaluation du prix des produits finis en stock, ceux-ci étant toujours comptabilisés au prix de revient standard qui reste théoriquement immuable pendant la durée d'un cycle, sauf variations dans les postes du prix de revient standard qui sont nettement mises en lumière par la méthode des écarts.

6. Examinons dès lors le cas d'utilisation d'une comptabilité avec prix de revient standard.

Nous pouvons prendre deux cas extrêmes en considération suivant qu'on utilise les prix de revient marginaux, sans aucune incorporation de frais fixes, ou les prix de revient complets incorporant la totalité des frais fixes. Les cas intermédiaires peuvent être examinés à la lumière des constatations qui seront faites sur les cas extrêmes.

6a. *Cas des prix de revient standards marginaux*

Le résultat normal d'exploitation pour un niveau de production et de vente de 100 s'obtiendrait en déduisant du montant global du bénéfice marginal, le montant global des frais fixes.

En représentant par b_m le bénéfice marginal par unité de production et par F le montant des frais fixes pour l'activité 100, on aura:

$$\text{Résultat en activité normale: } 100\, b_m - F.$$

Nous admettrons, pour simplifier l'exposé, qu'en sous ou suractivité les frais catalogués comme fixes restent rigoureusement à leur niveau standard de l'activité normale. Pratiquement, il n'en est jamais ainsi, certaines réductions pouvant être opérées sur les frais classés comme fixes en cas de diminution d'activité.

Mais dans ce cas, on en déduit immédiatement un écart sur frais fixes standards qui peut être prédéterminé, surtout quand les budgets d'exploitation sont établis, à posteriori ou en prévisionnel pour différents paliers de production.

Le résultat en suractivité sera dès lors $120\ b_m—F$

et en sous-activité $80\ b_m—F$.

L'excédent en suractivité par rapport à l'activité normale est donc de

$$120\ b_m—F—(100\ b_m—F) = 20\ b_m$$

Le déficit en sous-activité sera de $100\ b_m—F—(80\ b_m—F) = 20\ b_m$.

En comptabilité avec prix de revient standards marginaux, les excédents et déficits par rapport au résultat normal ont la même valeur dans l'exemple considéré, sous réserve d'écarts à enregistrer sur les standards de consommation et de prix unitaire.

On remarquera que ces excédents et déficits sont proportionnels aux écarts sur les volumes de vente et non aux écarts sur les volumes de production. Nous reviendrons plus loin sur cette constatation (Voir 7).

6b. *Cas des prix de revient standards incorporant tous les frais fixes*

Désignons par i l'incidence des frais fixes dans le prix de revient à activité normale. On aura

$$i = \frac{F}{\text{Production normale}} = \frac{F}{100} \text{ dans l'exemple étudié.}$$

Le bénéfice unitaire étant représenté par b, le résultat à l'activité normale sera 100 b.

En utilisant un prix de revient standard immuable, quelle que soit l'activité de production, la comptabilité enregistrera toujours le même bénéfice commercial par unité de production, pour autant que le prix de vente reste invariable pendant la durée du cycle.

Le résultat commercial sera dès lors 80 b en sous-activité

et 120 b en suractivité.

Mais ce résultat commercial doit être corrigé car le prix de revient varie effectivement avec l'activité de la production.

Comment procéder à cette correction?

Remarquons que lorsqu'on se trouve à l'activité 110 et qu'on valorise les entrées en magasin à un prix de revient comprenant i de frais fixes par unité de production, le montant global des frais fixes pris en charge par les entrées de magasin est de $110 \times i$, alors que les frais fixes ne s'élèvent qu'à 100 i dans l'hypothèse adoptée.

Les frais fixes sont donc, en suractivité de 110, surestimés de 10 i, c'est-à-dire que la rentabilité commerciale de 120 b est trop faible de 10 i. La rectification s'opérera pratiquement en imputant au compte P.P. le supplément de couverture de frais fixes résultant de l'utilisation d'un prix de revient standard immuable.

Le résultat d'exploitation en *suractivité* se présentera donc comme suit:

Résultat commercial	120 b
Supplément de couverture de frais fixes	+ 10 i
Résultat net	120 b + 10 i
Excédent sur résultat normal de 100 b	20 b + 10 i

En *sous-activité*, on aura:

Résultat commercial	80 b
Manque de couverture de frais fixes	— 10 i
Résultat net	80 b — 10 i
Déficit sur résultat normal de 100 b	100 b — (80 b — 10 i) = 20 b + 10 i

7. Comme dans le cas de l'utilisation des prix de revient marginaux (Voir 6a), et pour l'exemple cité, les excédents et déficits sont de même importance.

Par contre, leur expression dépend à la fois des écarts de volume de vente (20 b) et des écarts de volume de production (10 i).

8. C'est ici qu'apparaît l'influence de la politique d'adaptation de la production au volume des ventes, lorsqu'on utilise les prix de revient complets.

Par exemple, si la production ne devait entraîner aucun stockage et équilibrait toujours les ventes, les excédents et déficits auraient comme valeur 20 b + 20 i puisqu'avec une production réduite à 80 en période de récession, le manque de couverture de frais fixes atteindrait 20 i, le déficit de production étant de 100 — 80 = 20.

8a. En cas d'utilisation des prix de revient complets, les résultats apparaissent donc plus favorables en période de sous-activité quand on procède à un certain stockage. On en comprend immédiatement la raison en constatant qu'une mise en stock de 10 évaluée au prix de revient standard, absorbe un montant de 10 i de frais généraux qui se trouvent imputés aux inventaires.

8b. Une autre constatation est que les excédents et déficits, pour une politique déterminée d'adaptation de la production aux ventes, ont une valeur différente suivant qu'on utilise les prix de revient marginaux ou les prix de revient complets.

9. Dans l'exemple étudié, comportant un déséquilibre entre les productions et les ventes, on a en effet:

excédent ou déficit $20\ b_m$ (1) avec les prix de revient marginaux
$20\ b + 10\ i$ (2) avec les prix de revient complets.

Pour mettre en évidence la différence de valeur entre ces deux expressions, ajoutons et retranchons 10 i à l'expression (2). On aura:

$$20\ b + 10\ i = 20\ b + 20\ i - 10\ i = 20\ (b + i) - 10\ i = 20\ b_m - 10\ i$$

en se souvenant que $b_m = b + i$.

La différence entre ces deux expressions de l'excédent ou du déficit est représentée dans cet exemple par 10 i, c'est-à-dire par le montant des frais fixes imputés au magasin en cas de stockage et d'utilisation des prix de revient complets. Par contre, d'après ce que nous avons vu plus haut, les deux expressions sont identiques s'il n'y a pas de stockage en période de sous-activité.

10. En conclusion de l'examen de ce schéma, on peut dire que l'utilisation de la comptabilité avec prix de revient standards met bien en évidence la relation qui existe entre les excédents ou déficits par rapport au résultat normal, en cas de variation d'activité, toutes autres choses restant égales.

Par ailleurs, les écarts observés sur les standards de prix ou de consommation indiquent comment le bénéfice d'une amélioration d'activité peut être influencé par l'évolution de facteurs défavorables, tels que hausse de salaires, baisse des prix de vente etc....

Mais pour que la relation soit calculable lorsqu'on utilise des prix de revient standards non marginaux, il est nécessaire de définir au préalable la politique de production et de vente, ce qui fait du reste partie intégrante de l'utilisation des méthodes budgétaires.

DEUXIÈME QUESTION

Valorisation des stocks

Devant la grande diversité des cas qui peuvent se présenter, il est difficile de porter un choix sur une seule méthode. Devant l'impossibilité de tracer des règles pour chaque cas, il y a lieu de permettre à chaque entreprise de choisir la méthode d'évaluation qui s'adapte le mieux au problème qui se pose.

Mais il y a des principes, applicables à toutes les entreprises, qui devraient être respectés, notamment:

1. Les évaluations doivent être inspirées par la *prudence;* il faut éviter toute surestimation possible, pouvant donner lieu à la distribution de dividendes fictifs;

2. Un autre principe de base de l'évaluation des stocks réside dans l'application *constante* de la méthode choisie. En cas de changement de la méthode d'évaluation, l'entreprise doit le signaler et faire apparaître son incidence sur le revenu;

3. A l'intention des tiers, les bases de détermination de l'évaluation des stocks doivent être renseignées;

4. En cas de baisse des matières, l'évaluation ne peut être faite qu'au coût de remplacement et la perte provenant de la baisse doit être portée à un compte approprié dans le compte de profits et pertes;

5. En cas de hausse, l'évaluation doit être faite au coût historique pour respecter le principe que le bilan doit renseigner le bénéfice consommable;

6. On admet que le prix de revient des produits fabriqués doit comprendre aussi bien les coûts indirects que les coûts directs, pour autant que les premiers correspondent à une activité normale et pour autant que le stock lui-même soit normal. En effet, si le dégagement du stock devait se faire ultérieurement par une réduction de l'activité, on aurait simplement reculé la constatation d'un manque de couverture des frais fixes;

7. Il est nécessaire de traduire séparément dans les comptes, d'une part, les opérations normales et, d'autre part, toutes les contingences qui ajoutent leur effet à ces opérations et en altèrent l'expression, tels les ajustements de stocks consécutifs aux fluctuations de prix, les charges d'entreprises résultant d'un fléchissement dans le degré d'activité etc....

8. Il faut condamner toute surestimation d'actif et toute sous-estimation de passif favorisant les comptes de résultats:

a. si ces redressements sont normalement à considérer comme indisponibles, c'est-à-dire comme des prolongements du patrimoine social dont on veut exprimer la valeur en signes monétaires actuellement dévalués;

b. s'ilssont inspirés par une politique spéculative de distribution de dividendes;

c. si des évaluations défavorables inverses (sous-estimation d'actif et surestimation de passif) sont simultanément négligées.

Il est, par contre, impératif de constater les moins-values d'actif et les plus values de passif, même si des réévaluations inverses, donc favorables, existent en potentiel et ne sont pas enregistrées.

9. Pour les matières se raréfiant rapidement, en cas de haute conjoncture ou d'évènements internationaux bousculant les marchés, il faudra être prudent si l'exercice se clôture en plein 'boom' avec des stocks importants et récemment acquis. En effet, dans ce cas, ni la valeur vénale, ni la valeur de revient ne seraient opportunes à adopter. Il faudrait se référer à une période normale pour la valeur à donner.

Troisième question

'Un bénéfice établi sur des bases exactes, ouvrira-t-il, moyennant l'analyse, la voie vers un jugement sain sur l'efficience de la production, la rentabilité, le bien fondé d'une expansion?'.

L'expert-comptable sera toujours impuissant à satisfaire à la vérité objective. C'est un idéal tellement insaisissable.

Comme l'a déclaré le Professeur Masoin à la séance de clôture du Congrès de l'Union Européenne des Experts-Comptables Economiques et Financiers, tenue à Bruxelles en septembre 1955:

'La vérité objective n'existe pas dans l'appréciation de la valeur. La valeur des biens n'existe pas en soi. C'est une réalité mouvante dans le temps, variable selon les lieux et les personnes. La valeur d'un objet d'apprécie par rapport à un besoin et ce besoin luimême est relatif. En toutes ces matières d'évaluation, il faut tendre non à la vérité, mais à la correction, c'est-à-dire à l'appréciation juste des choses et à la loyauté envers les tiers.'

Si l'expert-comptable doit donc s'efforcer de s'en rapprocher le plus consciencieusement qu'il le peut, il doit surtout attacher beaucoup d'importance à préciser ses bases de détermination et à décomposer ses évaluations par tranche homogène dans le temps et dans l'espace.

Cette précision est nécessaire à quiconque, actionnaire, créancier, assureur, fiscaliste, économiste, acquéreur, dirigeant, devant traiter des problèmes intéressant l'entreprise en fonction de ce bénéfice.

Non seulement les critères de détermination du bénéfice doivent être précisés, mais il faut encore indiquer quelles sont les modifications apportées à ces critères d'un exercice à l'autre.

Au surplus, ces modifications ne devraient se concevoir que dans le sens d'un effort de rapprochement constant vers la qualité, la précision et la clarté des informations. Il faut donc condamner toute instabilité des critères qui ne serait que la conséquence de manoeuvres déloyales ou incorrectes ou la manifestation d'un opportunisme de mauvais aloi.

Il n'y a pas que l'instabilité des critères qui rend difficiles les comparaisons de bilans successifs, il y a aussi l'instabilité des valeurs. Il convient donc d'utiliser tous les moyens de mettre en évidence les incidences de volume, de prix, de composition en ce qui concerne les stocks, le chiffre d'affaires et le prix de revient des ventes. Il s'agit également d'apprécier la composition des stocks en ce qui concerne leur activité (stocks morts, stocks dormants). Il faut apprécier encore l'évolution de la durée du crédit en ce qui concerne les clients et les fournisseurs. Il faut décomposer les immobilisations, les capitaux propres et les réserves, selon leur année d'origine. Au point de vue des immobilisations, il est utile de connaître quelles sont les immobilisations actives mais qui sont complètement amorties de même que celles qui sont devenues inactives mais qui ne sont pas complétement amorties.

Certes, certains critères d'évaluation, de présentation et d'imputation peuvent être universalisés, mais il sera toujours impossible, en raison de contingences propres à chaque entreprise, de codifer à l'extrême. Il faut alors connaître les effets de ces contingences particulières sur la détermination des bénéfices.

Les points les plus délicats sont précisément les stocks et les immobilisations.

Si le jugement sur l'efficience de la production, la rentabilité et le bien fondé d'une expansion doivent trouver une base dans une *saine* détermination du bénéfice, la voie de ce jugement se trouve dans les procédés de cette détermination.

Il faut utiliser des comptes ramenant à une seule variable les opérations conduisant vers les comptes de résultats. Il s'agit d'une adaptation de la comptabilité pour l'orienter vers son utilisation en vue de la gestion. C'est dans la conception et la présentation de ces comptes particuliers que l'on trouvera les éléments d'une politique ou d'une action directoriale. Si ces comptes sont invisibles dans le bilan, ils ne font cependant pas double emploi. Ils devraient d'ailleurs apparaître dans l'analyse des comptes de résultats. C'est uniquement une question de classification selon la nature des opérations, et les responsabilités mises en jeu. Il faut que ces comptes expriment des résultats en termes de gestion, qui soient faciles à étudier et à interpréter en mettant en évidence des écarts par rapport à des standards. La comptabilité et le contrôle budgétaire sont tout indiqués à cet effet.

Propositions

Nous proposons au Congrès:

1. De définir d'une façon très précise les différentes méthodes d'évaluation des stocks de matières et de produits finis, des encours de fabrication et travaux en cours, des valeurs immobilisées et des amortissements.

2. De réunir ces différentes définitions dans un code.

3. De recommander aux experts-comptables de se référer à ce code pour les évaluations faites dans leurs rapports.

4. De recommander aux experts-comptables des différents pays, lorsqu'ils appliquent des méthodes d'évaluation différentes pour deux bilans successifs, de le signaler expressément dans leurs rapports, tout en indiquant l'incidence chiffrée qui en résulte.

Translation

PAPER

by

EMILE MANGAL

Collège National des Experts Comptables de Belgique

This report covers three questions proposed for discussion in connection with the above mentioned subject.

FIRST QUESTION

'Is there any computable relation between surplus and deficiency resulting from a percentage of utilisation of production capacity either above or below normal rate, all occurring during the conjunctural cycle?'

1. The Accounts Departments are always able, a posteriori, to explain variations in the results recorded during periods of below-normal or above-normal activity as compared with a period of normal activity.

Such explanations can be made as detailed as is required but it is then sometimes difficult to bring out the predominant factor.

Now, between a period of below-normal activity and a period of above-normal activity the difference in results lies essentially in the profit on supplementary sales. It seems therefore at first sight that, all other things being equal, it should be easy to compute 'a priori' excesses and deficiencies as compared with a normal profit when activity varies.

2. Our purpose is to draw attention to the fact that excesses or deficiencies are related to:

a. the method of recording cost price, and

b. management policy in adapting production to sales volume.

3. To illustrate the fact, we shall schematize, by an example, a complete cycle, taking as reference a volume of production represented by 100.

Below-normal production	90	Sales	80	Taken into stock	10
Above-normal production	110	Sales	120	Issued from stock	10
Total	200		200	Stock variation	0

4. It will be noted that this example already outlines management's policy, consisting in slightly increasing stocks during a period of sales recession and releasing stocks in the period of business revival.

The consequences of such a policy will be clearly shown further on (See § 8).

5. We shall now consider the various methods of recording cost prices.

5a. If cost prices for each level of activity are established inclusive of fixed charges, it is obvious that the cost price in a period of above-normal activity will be more profitable than that in a period of sub-normal activity, since fixed charges will be spread over a larger load.

No difficulty arises in predetermining cost prices at activity levels of 90 or 110. Profits on sales volumes of 80 or 120 may therefore be predetermined, with the result that variations from an average profit at a normal operation level can as easily be determined.

It will, however, be necessary to adjust the inventories of products in stock as their costs are modified.

The importance of this adjustment, to be made every year, depends upon the actual level of the stocks on hand. It will tend to decrease profits in periods of sub-normal activity because of the surplus value on stocks entered at a cost price above normal. Such adjustment is, however, not significant since in periods of above-normal activity it will have to be effected in the opposite way.

5b. One of the advantages of accounts using standard costs, which in our example would be computed on an average production of 100, lies in the fact that no adjustment is required in the valuation of the finished goods in stock, the latter always being entered at standard cost, which remains theoretically fixed during the whole cycle, except for variations in items included in standard costs, which are clearly brought to light by the method of variations.

6. Let us then examine the case of an accounting system using a standard cost price.

Two extreme instances can be considered: either the use of marginal cost prices without any inclusion of fixed charges, or the full cost prices inclusive of all fixed charges. Intermediate cases may be examined in the light of the facts established by survey of both these extreme cases.

6a. *Marginal cost prices system*

The normal result of operations for a production and sales level of 100 would be obtained by deducting total fixed charges from the gross marginal profit.

Taking b_m to represent the marginal profit per production unit, and F the fixed costs at activity 100, we obtain:

Result by normal activity: $100\ b_m—F$.

To simplify matters, let us assume that in periods of either sub-normal or above-normal activity all charges classified as fixed charges remain strictly at standard level of normal operation. This never occurs in practice, since some reduction can be effected on certain of the charges classified as fixed when activity is reduced.

In this case, however, there is immediately deducted a variation in standard fixed charges which may be predetermined, especially if operation budgets are established, either 'a posteriori' or in advance, for different levels of production.

Hence, in above-normal activity the result would be: $120\ b_m—F$

and in sub-normal activity: $80\ b_m—F$.

The excess in above-normal activity as compared with normal activity is thus:

$$120\ b_m—F—(100\ b_m—F) = 20\ b_m$$

The deficiency in sub-normal activity would be:

$$100\ b_m—F—(80\ b_m—F) = 20\ b_m.$$

Under an accounting system with standard marginal cost prices, excesses and deficiencies with respect to normal results have the same value in the example considered, subject to recording variations on standards of consumption and unit prices.

It will be noted that these excesses and deficiencies are proportionate to variations in sales volume and not to variations in production volume. We shall revert to this observation further on (See § 7).

6b. *Case of standard cost prices including all fixed charges*

If 'i' stands for the incidence of fixed charges in the cost price at normal operation level we find:

$$i = \frac{F}{\text{normal operation}} = \frac{F}{100}$$

in our example.

The profit per unit being represented by 'b', the result at normal activity will be 100 b.

By using an unchanging standard cost price, whatever be the production activity, the accounts will always reflect the same trading profit per production unit provided sales prices remain unchanged during the whole cycle.

The trading profit will therefore be: 80 b in sub-normal activity and
120 b in above-normal activity.

However, this trading profit must be adjusted, since cost price actually varies with production activity.

How is this adjustment to be effected?

It should be observed that when at operation level 110 the stock entries are valued at a cost price including i fixed charges per production unit, the total of fixed charges included in stock entries is $110 \times i$, whereas the fixed charges are only 100 i in the hypothesis adopted.

The fixed charges are therefore, in above-normal activity of 110, over-estimated by 10 i, that is to say, the earning power of 120 b is too low by 10 i. In practice, the adjustment will be effected by transferring the extra coverage of fixed charges resulting from using unchanging standard costs to the profit and loss account.

Operation results in case of above-normal activity will thus appear as follows:

Commercial result	120 b	
Extra coverage of fixed charges		+ 10 i
Net result	120 b	+ 10 i
Excess over 100 b normal result	20 b	+ 10 i

In sub-normal activity it will show:

Commercial result	80 b
Lack of coverage of fixed charges	10 i
Net result	**80 b — 10 i**

Deficiency as compared with 100 b normal result

$$100\text{ b} - (80\text{ b} - 10\text{ i}) = 20\text{ b} + 10\text{ i}$$

7. As in the case of the use of marginal cost prices (See § 6a) and for the present example, excesses and deficiencies are equal.

Their expression however depends both on variations in sales volume (20 b) and on variations in production volume (10 i).

8. The influence of a policy of adjusting production to sales volume when full cost prices are used here becomes apparent.

For instance, if production did not involve any stocking and would always be equal to sales, the value of excesses and deficiencies would be 20 b + 20 i since with production reduced to 80 in slack periods the lack of coverage of fixed charges would amount to 20 i, production deficiency being 100 — 80 = 20.

8a. When using full cost prices, the results in periods of sub-normal activity therefore appear more favourable when a certain amount of stocking is effected. The reason is readily understandable when it is considered that a stock entry of 10 valued at standard cost price absorbs on amount of overheads of 10 i which are thus charged to the inventories.

8b. Another fact to be noted is that excesses and deficiencies for a given policy of adapting production to sales have different values depending on whether marginal cost prices or full cost prices are used.

9. In the example under consideration, where production is not in harmony with sales, we have:

excess or deficiency $20\ b_m$ (1) with marginal cost prices
$20\ b + 10\ i$ (2) with full cost prices.

To evidence the difference in value between these two expressions, let us add and substract 10 i from expression (2). The result is:

$$20\ b + 10\ i = 20\ b + 20\ i - 10\ i = 20\ (b + i) - 10\ i = 20\ b_m - 10\ i,$$

bearing in mind that $b_m = b + i$.

The difference between the two expressions of excess or deficiency (in our example) is thus 10 i, which is the amount of fixed charges debited to inventories in the event of stocking, when using the full cost prices method.

On the other hand, from what has been seen above, both expressions are identical when no stocking is effected in a period of sub-normal activity.

10. The conclusion to be drawn from the study of this case is that the use of standard costs in accounting places clearly in evidence the relation existing between excesses and deficiencies as compared with normal results, in the event of variation in activity, all other factors remaining equal.

Besides, variations observed in the standards of prices or consumption show to what extent the gain to be derived from improved activity can be influenced by the development of unfavourable factors, such as a rise in labour costs, a drop in sales prices etc.

But if this relation is to be computable when non-marginal standard cost prices are used, it is necessary to define in advance the production and sales policy, this being in any case an integral part of the use of budgeting methods.

Second Question

Stock Valuation

Because of the great variety of cases that may arise, it is difficult to fix one's choice on one single method. In view of the impossibility of laying down rules for each case, it is advisable to let each business choose the method of valuation best suited to its own problems.

There are, however, principles applicable to every business which should be taken into account, in particular:

1. *Caution* should be the leading thought in stock valuation; any possible over-estimation should be avoided, as this might lead to payment of fictitious dividends.

2. Another basic principle of stock valuation is *consistency* in applying the system selected. Any change therein must be disclosed and the incidence of the change on profit should be shown.

3. For the benefit of third parties, principles of stock valuation should be described.

4. In the event of a drop in price of raw materials, valuation may only be made at replacement cost and the loss resulting from such drop must be written off to an appropriate account in the Profit and Loss Account.

5. In the event of increase in prices, valuation must be made at historical cost to respect the principle that the balance sheet must show the realised profit.

6. It is accepted that the cost price of manufactured products should include both indirect and direct costs, in so far as the former correspond to normal activity and the stock itself is normal. In fact, if stocks were reduced at a later date because of reduced activity, the recording of a lack of coverage of fixed charges would merely have been postponed.

7. The accounts should show separately, on the one hand, normal operations and, on the other, all contingencies which affect such operations and alter their expression, such as stock adjustments following on price fluctuations, increased pressure on the company because of a drop in activity level, and so on.

8. All revaluation of assets and revaluation of liabilities which tend to overstate profits should be condemned:

1. if these adjustments are normally to be considered as unavailable for distribution, that is to say, as extensions of the networth of the company which is desired to be expressed in terms of devalued currencies;

2. if they are motivated by a speculative policy in connection with payment of dividends;

3. if unfavourable valuations (under-estimation of assets and over-estimation of liabilities) are at the same time omitted.

On the other hand, it is essential that depreciation of assets and appreciation of liabilities be recorded, even if opposite and therefore favourable revaluations potentially exist and are not recorded.

9. When raw materials become scarce suddenly, as a result of a 'boom' or international events upsetting markets, much caution will be needed if the financial year closes in full 'boom', with large and recently acquired stocks on hand. In this case, neither the market value nor the cost price could appropriately be used. A normal period should be referred to for determining appropriate valuation.

Third Question

'Is profit computed on accurate bases and subjected to careful analysis the key to a sound judgment on production efficiency, profitability, and advisability of development?'

The accountant will always be incapable of laying bare objective truth. It is such an elusive ideal.

As Prof. Masoin declared at the closing session of the Congress of the Union Européene des Experts-Comptables Economiques et Financiers, held in Brussels in September 1955:

'There is no objective truth in the estimation of value. The value of goods does not exist as such. It is a reality that moves in time, and varies with place and person. The value of an object exists only in relation to a need, and the need itself is relative. In all matters of valuation, it is not truth that should be aimed at, but correctness which means the just appreciation of things and loyalty towards third parties.'

The accountant should thus endeavour to approach this truth as conscientiously as he can, but he should put particular stress on a clear statement of his valuation bases, and break them up into homogeneous sections in time and space.

Such precision is essential to anyone, shareholder, creditor, insurer, fiscalist economist, buyer, manager, to all in fact who are to deal with the company's problems involving profit.

Not only should the criteria for establishing the profit be clearly specified, but any alteration occurring therein from one financial year to another should be revealed.

Moreover, such alterations should only be conceived as an endeavour ever to improve quality, precision and clarity of information. Any inconsistency in these criteria, which could only result from unfair or improper practices or from an unsound opportunism, should be condemned.

Besides inconsistency of the criteria, instability of values may also hamper comparison between successive balance sheets. All means which may bring to light the incidence of volume, price and composition of stocks, turn-over and cost of sales should therefore be used. Also, valuation of stock composition should take into account the 'vitality' of the stock (dead stock, dormant stock and so on). Changes in credit terms concerning customers and suppliers should also be considered. Fixed assets, capital and reserves should be divided according to their year of origin. Regarding fixed assets, it is advisable that those fixed assets that are active but fully depreciated be recognized as well as those that are inactive but not yet fully depreciated.

It is true that certain criteria of valuation, presentation and charging to accounts can be made universal, but because of the individual contingencies of each business, it will always be impossible to codify them to extremes. The effect of such special contingencies on determining profits should therefore be known.

The more delicate points are precisely those related to stocks and fixed assets.

If judgment of production efficiency, profitability and advisability of development is to be based on a *sound* determination of profit, then the methods of such determination will prove the key to this judgment.

Accounts reducing to a simple variable all operations leading to the profit and loss accounts should be in general use. The problem is to adapt accounting towards its utilisation as a management tool. The elements of management policy and action will be found in the conception and presentation of these special accounts. Although these accounts will not appear on the balance sheet, they are not duplications of existing accounts. They should, moreover, appear in the analysis of profit and loss. They are a method of classification according to the nature of the operations and the responsibilities involved. The results in these accounts should be expressed in terms of management, easily studied and easily interpreted, clearly evidencing any variations from standards. The accounts and budgetary control are obviously to be used for this purpose.

PROPOSALS

We suggest to the Congress:

1. To define very clearly the several methods of valuing stocks of raw material and of finished products, work in progress, fixed assets and amortisations.

2. To gather these several definitions into a code.

3. To recommend to accountants that they refer to this code for valuations given in their reports.

4. To recommend to accountants of all countries that, when there are applied different valuation methods to two successive balance sheets, they should call particular attention to the fact in their reports and disclose the resulting incidence in figures.

DISCUSSION

CHAIRMAN: MR. A. VEYRENC (France)

CHAIRMAN:

Mesdames, Messieurs,

En ouvrant cette dernière séance de travail, permettez-moi d'abord de remercier très vivement Monsieur le Président et les organisateurs de ce congrès pour l'honneur qu'ils m'ont réservé en m'en confiant la présidence. L'objet de notre étude et de nos discussions va porter, comme vous le savez, sur la 'détermination du bénéfice de l'entreprise'.

C'est une question à la fois très importante, et fort délicate. Elle intéresse au plus haut point les experts-comptables de tous les pays du monde dans le rôle de conseiller et de contrôleur de gestion qu'ils assument auprès des entreprises.

Le bénéfice d'une entreprise ne peut-il, en effet, être dégagé en fonction de conceptions diverses et parfois même divergentes, par exemple: légales, fiscales, économiques? Suivant les critères retenus, les résultats pourront apparaître fort différents les uns des autres et parfois même contradictoires.

La conception économique du bénéfice n'est-elle pas nécessaire si l'on veut assurer le développement normal et la pérennité d'une entreprise? Ne convient-il pas, alors, d'évaluer tous les biens fongibles à leur valeur de remplacement, de prévoir les amortissements nécessaires en fonction de l'accélération de renouvellement des matériels et des équipements imposée par les progrès rapides des techniques modernes, de dissocier des bénéfices purement commerciaux, les résultats provenant de variations monétaires, de tenir compte des flux économiques et de l'incertitude de l'avenir?

Quel est donc le bénéfice réel qui doit être déclaré aux associés, aux actionnaires, au personnel, au public en général, à l'Etat? Où est la vérité? Et si la vérité absolue n'existe pas en cette matière, quelles sont donc les directives et suggestions raisonnables qui peuvent être retenues dans la détermination périodique des bénéfices de l'entreprise?

Outre les remarquables rapports qui vous ont été remis, les membres du panel que vous allez entendre vont s'efforcer de répondre à ces préoccupations d'ordre général.

Je suis heureux de vous présenter ces personnalités éminentes:

Vice-présidents: Monsieur Fitzgerald d'Australie, Monsieur Gerbès, Luxembourg, Monsieur Rahim Jan du Pakistan.

Directeur des discussions: Monsieur Weldon Powell des U.S.A.

Rapporteur général: Monsieur Groeneveld de Hollande.

Auteurs des rapports: Monsieur le Docteur Allet d'Autriche, Monsieur Frisbee des U.S.A., Monsieur Roozen de Hollande, Monsieur Hutton d'Ecosse, Monsieur Darden de Belgique.

Autres membres du panel: Monsieur Braende de Norvège, Monsieur Forsström de Finlande et Monsieur le Professeur Käfer de Suisse.

Et maintenant, Mesdames et Messieurs, j'ai le plaisir de remettre la direction de la discussion à Monsieur Powell.

Ladies and Gentlemen, In opening this last business session of the congress please allow me, first of all, to thank the President and organizers of this congress very cordially for the honour done me in appointing me to the Chair. Our discussion to-day will, as you already know, deal with the ascertainment of profit in business. This is a question which is both very important and extremely delicate. Indeed, it is of the highest interest to accountants throughout the world as consultants and auditors of enterprises. The profit of an enterprise can be determined by reference to various concepts, and I would say, sometimes even to differing concepts, legal, fiscal, economic and others. According to the criteria which you choose, the results at which you will arrive, may appear to be utterly different one from another, and sometimes even contradictory. The economic concept of profit is, I believe, the most important for ensuring the normal development and continuity of a business. It is therefore necessary to calculate all tangible assets at their replacement value, in order to allow for necessary reserves for depreciation of equipment in view of accelerated replacements due to the rapid progress of modern techniques. It is also necessary to separate profits derived purely from commercial sources from profits originating from monetary fluctuations, and to take into consideration economic fluctuations and the lack of certainty as to the future. What is the profit which has to be presented to the partners, to shareholders, to the staff, to the public and to the State? Where do we find the truth? And if there is no absolute truth in this matter, then we must ascertain what are the reasonable recommendations and suggestions which may be made in determining periodically the profit of a business. In addition to the very interesting papers which you have all read, the members of the panel whom you are going to hear this morning will now attempt to provide answers to questions of a more general nature. Ladies and Gentlemen, I am very happy to have the opportunity to introduce this panel to you: Mr. Fitzgerald of Australia, our Vice-Chairman; Mr. Gerbès of Luxembourg, Vice-Chairman; Mr. Rahim Jan of Pakistan, Vice-Chairman. Mr. Weldon Powell, the Discussion Leader of the U.S.; Mr. Groeneveld, our rapporteur of Holland; Dr. Allet of Austria, Mr. Frisbee of the U.S., Mr. Roozen of Holland, Mr. Hutton of Scotland, Mr. Darden of Belgium, Mr. Braende of Norway, Mr. Forsström of Finland and Prof. Käfer of Switzerland. And now, Ladies and Gentlemen, I will hand over the discussion to Mr. Powell.

MR. WELDON POWELL (United States of America)

Thank you, M. Veyrenc. Ladies and Gentlemen, you have had the panel introduced to you. Some of them, as you know, are authors of papers, others are not. Unfortunately, three of the authors of papers are absent this morning, having been prevented by illness from attending this session. They are Prof. Illetschko of Austria, M. Mangal of Belgium, and Professor Hansen of Denmark. Fortunately, we have been able to make three substitutions, three very able substitutions I might say, for them, Dr. Allet of Austria, M. Darden of Belgium, and Mr. Roozen of the Netherlands. You will understand, of course, that these three gentlemen who are substituting for the three absent authors cannot be expected to be responsible fully for the views expressed by the three authors of papers.

As to procedure, our programme is not entirely unrehearsed. On the other hand, it is to a large extent unrehearsed. We are going to try to have a free exchange of views on aspects of the subject 'Ascertainment of Profit in Business', of questions back and forth, and to a large extent I hope that you will be able to observe us thinking out loud.

I might say also that our announced subject is perhaps not precisely expressed. Ascertainment of profit in business is a very broad subject. It covers a lot of territory, and there is not sufficient time this morning for us to get into all aspects and cover all facets or areas of the subject. Accordingly, we shall confine our discussion to a few of these aspects and try to explore them somewhat intensively.

A number of years ago there was an income study group in the United States, constituted by the American Institute of Certified Public Accountants, which spent months on the study of business income without coming to any very firm conclusions. As a matter of fact, in its report I think there probably were as many dissents as there were concurrences. Accordingly, you will not expect us this morning to tell you exactly and precisely how to compute income and to give you definite rules for it.

In accordance with the practice of the sessions, one of our panel members, Mr. Greoneveld of the Netherlands, who is also the author of a paper, will open our programme by summarizing for you the six papers that have been presented on this subject. And I would now like to ask Mr. Groeneveld to do this.

MR. G. L. GROENEVELD (Netherlands)

When the Netherlands economist N. G. Pierson in his 'Principles of Political Economy' of 1896 speaks about business profit, he begins his explanations with the observation that the word 'profit' has no definite meaning in the language of daily life, but that the scope of its meaning varies considerably.

Even to-day, 60 years later, this remark still holds. If we try to draw a general conclusion from the papers, we feel that there is still little uniformity in views on the concept of profit. This is the more regrettable since there is no difference of opinion as to the importance of the problem of profit determination.

Neither the studies of more than half a century, nor the progress of economic science, nor the specialization in industrial economics, have led to generally accepted views on the concept of profit, nor even to an acceptable diversity of opinions. The impression we obtain from the present international review of opinions may be said to be almost confusing on account of the diversity it reveals.

I shall now proceed to deal with the main aspect of the views taken, and in doing so, I would first mention those authors, who have put before us some of the least conventional ideas on profit determination.

PROF. PALLE HANSEN (Denmark) has based his concept of profit in particular on the general economic theory on utility, which states that productive goods derive their value from goods of a lower order. Proceeding along these lines, he states that the value of capital goods is determined by the discounted value of their future yields. He holds that on this basis only the true capital value of an enterprise or of individual assets can be determined and a definition of economically true profit can be given. He defines the ideal profit as being the normal interest on the capital value of the assets, the latter being determined by their future yields.

Then it is not difficult for Prof. Hansen to demonstrate that the conventional principles of management and accountancy are not in harmony with his thesis. For instance, he indicates that only those items which have been paid for are taken up in the balance sheet, that the rules for depreciating fixed assets are inflexible and thus not influenced by economic development and that the value of human energy is generally not included in the balance sheet. In other words, traditional valuation hardly ever takes into account the future yields of the assets. Prof. Hansen feels that it is necessary to make a choice between the conventional and the economic determination of profit.

Furthermore, Prof. Hansen elaborates on the problems connected with the drafting of annual accounts. Here, too, the accountant must anticipate the future. His statement 'In all his work the accountant must turn from the past to the future' summarizes his view.

Although Prof. Hansen does not specifically take sides as to the 'economically inspired accounting report', his sympathies definitely go in this direction.

Contrary to the views of Prof. Hansen, the concept of Prof. ILLETSCHKO (Austria) reaches back to the past. In order to obtain a solid basis for the periodical determination of profit, the author starts from the concepts liquidation-profit and total-profit. He converts periodical profits into a total profit by introducing a hypothetical liquidation. The periodical profit is then a formal accounting concept, built up of those components only which can be expressed in terms of money.

The prices actually paid entail the disadvantage that they do not recognize possible changes in purchasing power. Thus, the profits contain a factor of distortion, which can only be eliminated if the estimate of the proceeds in case of a hypothetical liquidation is based on the historical cost of the assets.

If and when fluctuations in purchasing power become significant and if they show a long term trend, the formal accounting concept of profit will become very unrealistic. According to Prof. Illetschko fluctuations in purchasing power are in this respect more important than cyclical fluctuations since the distortion caused by the latter can be eliminated by evaluating in accordance with the so-called lower-value-rule.

The elimination of changes in purchasing power, however, requires a subjective break-down of the profits into distributable and non-distributable profits.

Another factor of importance is the length of the period for which the business profit is to be computed. The shorter the period, the smaller the influence of distorting factors. Therefore, current prices can be used in short-term operating accounts.

Prof. Illetschko regards short-term operating accounts and annual profit and loss accounts as two different instruments. The short-term operating account which is based on cost accounting and on current prices has an instrumental function for management. The annual business profit on the other hand is derived from the documentary bookkeeping, whose formal accounts contain a registration of historical prices, taking duly in consideration the precepts of the lower-value-rule. Besides, this formal computation is conventionally determined by statutory regulations and thus acquires a documental character.

Whereas Prof. Hansen comes to a conclusion which completely deviates from generally accepted accounting principles, Prof. Illetschko states in his summary that he is in accordance with international conventions.

Apart from these concepts, which in principle are based either on the future or on the past, we see that other authors take into account the changes in value of the means of production and that, consequently, they draw our attention to the present value of the assets.

Mr. Hutton (U.K.) gives in this respect no definite opinion. In his paper he has repeatedly stated his objection against maintaining historical cost in a period of inflation, especially to prevent the proprietor from drawing false conclusions. Above all, Mr. Hutton notices the danger of politicians and trade-unionists ignoring the amounts that must be eliminated from profit in order to maintain the continuity of the business, since generally such amounts are shown as an appropriation of profit. Mr. Hutton does not attempt as he says either to apportion blame or to suggest a solution, but concludes with the quotation: 'How long halt ye between two opinions'?

In the paper of Ira N. Frisbee (U.S.A.) a more pronounced view is taken. The author clearly states that the investor will have to know, not only at the moment of liquidation but also during the lifetime of the business, that his dividend is really 'spendable income' and not a part of his original investment. Besides, economic profit should be recognized as such by the corporate officials and a measurement of the effect of price increase upon the capital requirements of the enterprise is therefore necessary.

The author explains how earned surplus may be necessary for the replacement of assets sold or consumed, in order to continue the same volume of operations. Investors and managers should be more interested in economic profit than in monetary profit. When eliminating the effects of fluctuating price levels in the ascertainment of profit, Mr. Frisbee sees more advantages in an adjustment of historical cost than in the application of replacement cost. This adjustment of historical cost will probably better be accomplished by using an index which measures the general price level than by using indexes which measure changes in the prices of specific commodities. In this way he succeeds in maintaining the principle of original cost but the original cost is measured in current dollars rather than in out-of-date dollars.

Mr. Frisbee notes, however, that this method would not be in accordance with generally accepted accounting principles. He states that the difficulties encountered in reaching only one logical result in deciding each problem of business profits have resulted in the U.S.A. in a general recognition of the concept of generally accepted accounting principles, in preference to an insistence upon adherence to economic concepts of profits or to principles which are sound or even logical in all particulars.

Fortunately the accepted principles are not immutable. They have evolved from the economic thinking of man and so they will continue. In the U.S. very important changes have occurred in the past and the possibility for recognition of new principles of ascertaining business profits will always be open.

A pronounced plea for the ascertainment of profits on the basis of valuation of the means of production at their present-day value is particularly found in *my paper*. Like Prof. Hansen, I stand for a co-ordination with the valuation based on the principles of social economics. Consequently, I base my views on the fundamental principle that the value of the goods is determined by their utility. In social economics this principle is also applicable to means of production; it states that their value depends on the value of the goods which have been used to satisfy the needs in question and which can thus no longer be used for other purposes.

This principle of substitution, when applied to the value of the means of production in the individual enterprise, leads to a valuation at the lower of either the utility value or the replacement value.

For simplicity's sake this principle of alternative valuation has been mentioned in my paper as a valuation at replacement value, because in the continuity of production this value is normally the lower of the two. Neither the elimination of price fluctuations, nor the safeguarding of financing possibilities is my starting point, and I do not expressly aim at achieving a continuity of the production process. Not choosing between the various methods of profit ascertainment, I base myself in full on the theory of replacement value.

However, when working out the principle of replacement value it appears that such purposes as have just been mentioned can all be achieved and we find that for the management of the enterprise the application of the theory of replacement value leads to a sound business policy. The actual applications lie in the fields of cost calculation, price policy, finance, profit determination and profit appropriation. Finally I explained in my paper—though briefly—that this application results in a uniform concept in the fields of cost accounting, accounting for stock movements, profit calculations, profit analyses and efficiency judgments. In passing I pointed out what effects this may have on accounting in general.

So far this summary was confined to what was said in the papers on the fundamentals of profit and its ascertainment; this was really the most important subject of most papers. Although the Congress Committee has also asked for a discussion of other interesting features, such as the valuation of work units of plant and equipment and raw materials used, the problem of latent contingencies including the provisions for profit taxes, it appeared that the limited space granted to each paper did only permit a scanty discussion of these subjects.

In this connection I would draw the attention to some observations made with regard to the *fiscal ascertainment of profits*.

There is a rather easy going view which states that economic and fiscal profits ought to harmonize in order to fulfil the condition that business must be taxed for real profits only. I have, however, also pointed to the reasonable view that the levying of taxes on income and profit is a problem that differs from that of profit calculation in business. Of course I did not do so without warning against the detrimental consequences of deviations for the enterprise.

Mr. Frisbee states in his paper that in the U.S.A. there is a considerable divergence between economic and taxable profit. In some respects he deems the divergence to be so great that one can scarcely justify the use of the term 'profit' in both instances. The high tariffs make it understandable that business men are especially interested in taxable profits, but too often the fact is overlooked that taxable profits cannot be used for reporting on the financial results. He stresses that even the tax levied on business profit ascertained in accordance with generally accepted accounting principles would not prevent a partial confiscation of economic wealth. Currently accepted principles fail to make adjustments for rising price levels in periods of inflation.

A similar reproach is made by Mr. Hutton to English accountancy. He is, however, not dissatisfied with the rather generous allowances of the Inland Revenue for depreciation of machinery and plant. Mr. Hutton's conclusion that accountants cannot with reason expect the Revenue to pioneer in the field of profit calculation so long as there is something basically wrong with the methods employed to ascertain our business profits, is I feel, not only applicable to English accountants.

Although time does not permit me to continue my summary, I must make an exception for the paper of Mr. E. Mangal (Belgium).

Mr. Mangal did not so much speak of the general problems relating to profit as of three special questions. In his first explanation, Mr. Mangal deals with the relation between surpluses and deficits resulting from over- and under-utilization of capacity. In his second explanation and to some extent also in his third, Mr. Mangal gives a summary of the fundamental rules for the valuation of stocks. His careful considerations lead to a conservatism that is disputed by Prof. Hansen, and they induce the author to make a proposal to the Congress, namely to stimulate that the methods of valuation will be sharply defined and will be made the object of a codification. Mr. Mangal would recommend to refer to such code when defining the principles of valuation in annual reports and he pleads to indicate in such reports the effects of a change in the method of valuation.

This suggestion of Mr. Mangal calls for an investigation of the possibilities of a wider codification of conventions of profit determination in order to promote the objectivity which so urgently is needed.

In the Netherlands the report 1955 of the Committee on Financial Reporting of the four Unions of Employers which of course does not hold a regulation but confines itself to general principles and recommendations—proves that a certain codification can be effected and that this may work out as an incentive to establish uniformity in the field of financial reporting.

MR. WELDON POWELL (United States of America)

Thank you, Mr. Groeneveld, for your very clear summary of the six papers that have been presented on this complex subject.

I might say one further word to the audience, and that is that unfortunately audience participation in this programme will have to be severely limited for obvious reasons. Several of you have presented questions or indicated your desire to make comments, and at appropriate points during the discussion I expect to ask a few of you to come to the microphone to present your comments, but there will not be, unfortunately, time for much free discussion after the panel concludes its work.

Now, Gentlemen of the panel, you have heard Mr. Groeneveld's summary, you have read the papers, and you are ready to go to work. I hope we can have in this discussion insofar as possible a free exchange of views. Will each of you please say what he has to say in as few words as possible, in order to give all of you an opportunity to be heard, and will you please feel free to ask questions of anyone who makes a remark that you do not agree with. If we do not have a free discussion, then I am sure from preliminary canvassing of your views, that it will not be because you are in agreement, because I am satisfied that there are considerable divergencies of opinion among you.

To begin with, it occurred to me when I read the papers, to wonder whether any of the authors were thinking of the possibility of equalizing income from year to year. Mr. Forsström, I think you had some comments on that point. Would you like to present them at this time?

MR. BÖRJE FORSSTRÖM (Finland)

Mr. Chairman, There is an old convention which has not in my opinion got a fair representation in the papers delivered to the Congress. It is what we in Finland use to call The European or Continental Convention of the cautious businessman.

The profit in the final statement of results for one year in an industry or an enterprise is primarily an indication of the stewardship of the management. It tells the shareholders how much the company has earned during the year. An enterprise is a complicated organism. It is impossible to arrive at a correct value of the whole, simply by adding up the values of the individual assets and deducting the liabilities from the sum, although there are different methods for valuing different groups of assets. Through research, maintenance, marketing, training of staff and so on the enterprise continues looking forward. The values of these invisible assets fluctuate considerably, they are never shown as assets. There are also many risks to provide for. Some are more specific than others and in anticipation of them mathematically correct reserves can be created before arriving at the profit for the year. But there are many other risks, which the natural instinct of every prudent businessman will inevitably recognize and take into account. This should also be done before arriving at the profit for the year. The assets should be valued with prudent care and foresight, creating in reality no reserves and making no undue undervaluation.

The method of the cautious businessman tends to result in equalizing profits, but this is not the aim of the method and besides, it is also possible to equalize profits through budgeting, which is a more dangerous way, as it might lead to unwise planning and excessive expenditure, benefiting no one.

In countries where yearly inflation of the currency is a disturbing factor and in which it is therefore difficult to distinguish between earnings and capital movement, and in countries where the tax system does not permit the deduction of losses from past or future profits, this method has proved to be a necessary complement to the other conventions.

I thus recommend as a complement to the replacement value method or the index-corrected historical cost method in connection with the cost or market (whichever lower) method, that when the result arrived at does not show correctly the trend in the results of the enterprise, taking the future into consideration, that the method of the *cautious* businessman should be applied. I am quite aware of the dangers. However, the upper limits for valuing assets must be clearly defined for the benefit of the creditors. There should be no further limits downward than required to make the profit and loss accounts still give a true and fair view of the results of the enterprise. As it is in the interest of the Board of Directors to show as good results as possible for the period of their mandate, this will act as a regulatory factor. Unduly low results will thus not appear. It is the capital market and especially the minority-shareholders which might suffer, at least for a shorter period, and this especially when the Board of Directors have an interest in keeping the value of the shares down for some time. It sets a difficult task for the auditors of companies, to analyze the valuing of assets and to appreciate the risks, to be able to report on the closing of the books.

Mr. Chairman, I only ask: can any specified rules be applied in order to avoid the influence of unethical thinking?

MR. WELDON POWELL (United States of America)

This is quite a question. It puts great responsibility upon the accountant. Mr. Hutton, what would you think about it?

MR. C. I. R. HUTTON (United Kingdom)

Mr. Powell, I will take that question, but I do not know that I can answer it. I do not know whether you are right in thinking that the audience may have read some of the papers, but if they read mine, they will know that I am not very good at answering questions. But I think what you have here is an age-old conflict between the human factor and the academic. All the old religions and philosophies teach man, and I think he is quite willing to be taught on the whole, to be moderate in his claims and not to go to extremes. The English language is full of proverbs: we like 'not to count our chickens before they are hatched' and we like 'to put something by for a rainy day'. In our private life I think we do like to equalize our good fortune and bad fortune as best we can. It is perhaps a quality of the heart, whereas the full disclosure represented by the 'true and fair view' is a quality of the head. The man who allows his heart to rule his head is not a prudent man, but I suppose we must agree in business that the head must rule and we must attempt to resist equalization of profits, though as in any good government the rules should not be enforced to the limit. I make that last reservation purely so that I can offer some sort of answer and it is very much the answer which has been offered to you by other speakers on other problems, that in the end everything depends upon the facts of the particular case.

MR. WELDON POWELL (United States of America)

This is an answer from Britain. May we now move across the ocean. Mr. Frisbee, what would the opinion in the United States be on the points that Mr. Forsström has raised?

MR. IRA N. FRISBEE (United States of America)

Well, Mr. Powell, I think that we have sympathy with management for wanting to equalize profits, but we have found that this is subject to abuse if it is allowed. And so we strongly oppose means of attempting to equalize profits over the years. We particularly do not like to see reserves for general contingencies, or even for special contingencies unless they are definitely measurable and likely to occur as set up in the accounts. In one of the papers reference was made to a suggestion of some thirty years ago by Prof. John B. Canning of Stanford University, who had a very interesting idea, which, in effect, might mean that during periods of high production we should include some costs to take care of the periods of low production and depression, and thus help to level off the peaks of prosperity. But I must say that this did not gain any appreciable support in the United States, and we just do not accept that sort of thing in practice.

In fact, we had rather an interesting experience, I think, during the Second World War. At that time—at the beginning of the war—we determined that it was proper to set up some reserves to take care of events that would happen after the close of the war. Special and general contingency reserves were set up by companies particularly affected by war work for such things as to convert their plants over to peacetime production and to get business back on a peacetime basis at the close of the war, and even for strikes which probably would occur then. Also, reserves were provided for the deflation or downward trend in prices which was going to happen after the war,—and we are still waiting for those falling prices. Actually, the adjustments needed on account of the war were not nearly as great as had been expected; in fact they were not very considerable. As a result, the setting up of reserves was overdone and at the end of the war many companies had reserves for which they had no use. Finally, the Committee on Accounting Procedure of the American Institute of Certified Public Accountants determined and recommended that those war reserves should be disposed of, preferably by returning them to surplus.

This brings up an interesting question as to whether the unused reserves should be put back into surplus directly or should be put back into the income of the year. I have noticed that, here on the continent, reserves are provided for general and for special contingencies. I am wondering whether, if they are not used after they have been set up, they are put back into surplus directly or whether they go back into the income account. It seems to me that two wrongs cannot make a right. If the reserve is not needed in the first place, then when the reserve is determined not to be needed we should not make a second mistake and put it into the income, where it does not belong, just because it previously was taken from the profit of another year.

MR. WELDON POWELL (United States of America)

Thank you, Mr. Frisbee. I rather gather from your remarks that you are just a little bit afraid of the principle of the cautious businessman because you think he might be a little too cautious. Mr. Groeneveld, would you care to comment on this point?

DISCUSSION

MR. G. L. GROENEVELD (Netherlands)

Ja, mijnheer de voorzitter, de heer Forsström heeft vooral gepleit voor het toepassen van het voorzichtigheidsbeginsel, maar uit de woorden van de heer Frisbee valt op te maken dat deze bevreesd is voor een te vergaande toepassing daarvan. Het beginsel van voorzichtigheid zal verschillend uitwerken in verschillende sferen. Ik stel mij voor, dat wanneer men de resultaten opmaakt voor derden, voor aandeelhouders bijvoorbeeld, dat men dan misschien voorzichtiger is dan wanneer men de resultaten opmaakt voor de leiding of in 't algemeen voor interne doeleinden. Onder omstandigheden kan het heel verstandig zijn om voorzichtig te zijn en niemand zal dat willen bestrijden, maar wel heb ik een principieel bezwaar tegen het voorzichtigheidsbeginsel als methode van winstbepaling, namelijk dat het een kwantitatief onbepaald beginsel is, dat ik daarom niet geschikt acht voor de benadering van een kwantitatief vraagstuk. Ik ben er dan ook voorstander van om te zoeken naar andere methoden die meer calculeerbaar zijn en daarbij gebruik te maken van de vooruitgang in onze bedrijfseconomische denkwijze, die er wel degelijk is. Als voorbeeld moge ik noemen een beginsel als dat van normale bedrijfsdrukte en overeenkomstige concepties, die ons de mogelijkheid geven om de resultaten van over- en onderbezetting te calculeren, ook als ze over de jaargrenzen heen grijpen. Ik denk verder aan wat prof. Hansen heeft gezegd over de behoefte om ons nauwkeuriger rekenschap te geven van de calculatie van de kosten van research en ontwikkeling, die vooral in de grote bedrijven kwantitatief van steeds groter betekenis worden, zodat wij daaraan ook in het kader van de winstbepaling onze aandacht zullen moeten geven. Ten slotte moge ik herinneren aan de sterk nivellerende betekenis, die in tijden van fluctuerende prijsbeweging uitgaat van toepassing van het beginsel van de vervangingswaarde. Zo zijn er meer, maar ik zal het hierbij laten.

Ik zou willen bepleiten in die richting te gaan, om aldus de gelegenheid aan te grijpen om in het vraagstuk van de nivellering van de winsten het willekeurig element, dat nu vaak door voorzichtigheidsoverwegingen moet worden opgevangen, terug te dringen ten gunste van elementen van calculatie.

Thank you, Mr. Chairman.
Mr. Forsström has mainly advocated the application of the principle of caution, but from Mr. Frisbee's comments it would appear that he fears an excessive application of this principle. This principle may have different results in different fields. I feel that when the results are determined for third parties, shareholders, for instance, more caution is taken than when this is done for internal purposes, e.g. for the management of the business. Although in some cases caution as such may be excellent, I feel that there is a fundamental objection to the principle of caution as a basis for the determination of profit. A quantitative problem cannot be solved on the basis of a principle that cannot be expressed in quantitative form. I would here make a plea that we should search for other principles, which give better computable rules and yardsticks and in this respect I suggest the recent progress in the science of management accounting should be taken into account. As an example, I would like to mention the application of the yardstick of normal capacity, which affords the possibility of calculating the results of over and underemployment of the capacity of the enterprise, even if such variations in volume extend beyond the actual period of a financial year. Furthermore, I would refer to what Prof. Hansen has said in his paper about the necessity of taking into consideration the increasing importance of the cost of research and development, particularly in large undertakings. This feature induces us to give this problem our attention as well, when ascertaining the profit. Finally I may mention the considerable equalizing influence resulting from the application of the principle of replace-

ment value in times of fluctuating price levels. I will confine myself to these examples and I would suggest that we proceed in the direction indicated by the advocates of the replacement value. Then the problem of equalization of profits can be approached in such a manner that elements that are computable are indeed calculated, rather than being determined by arbitrary factors, inspired by the principle of caution.

MR. WELDON POWELL (United States of America)

Prof. Käfer, Would you care to comment on this subject?

PROF. DR. KARL KÄFER (Switzerland)

Herr Vorsitzender, Ich möchte zu diesem Punkt nur kurz bemerken, daß wir auch in der Schweiz mit diesen Problemen schwer gerungen haben, aber schließlich bei der letzten Revision des Handelsrechts zu einer Lösung gelangt sind, welche der bei uns fast allgemein vertretenen Meinung entsprechend der Unternehmungsleitung auch von Gesetzes wegen weitgehende Freiheit gibt.

Ich weiß nicht, ob noch in vielen anderen Ländern die Verwaltung der Aktiengesellschaft durch gesetzliche Bestimmungen ermächtigt wird, zur Ausgleichung der Dividende, und demnach auch schon vorher zur Ausgleichung der Gewinne, stille Reserven zu schaffen. Diese stillen Reserven haben die Aufgabe, die Unternehmung gegen Rückschläge zu stärken und sollen auch verhindern, daß unvorsichtige Aktionäre durch Anträge in der Generalversammlung die Auszahlung zu hoher Dividenden durchsetzen können. Durch stille Reserven dürfen also Gewinne versteckt werden, die später wahrscheinlich zur Stabilisierung der Dividende benützt werden müssen. Bekanntlich sind in anderen Ländern in dieser Beziehung andere Maßnahmen getroffen worden; zum Beispiel wird festgesetzt, daß nicht die Aktionäre die Gewinnverteilung bestimmen, sondern das 'Board of Directors'. In einem Land, in dem die Generalversammlung maßgebend ist für die Gewinnverteilung, muß natürlich die Berichterstattung wesentlich vorsichtiger sein als in einem Lande, in dem die Verwaltung die Dividenden festsetzt.

Mr. Chairman, on this point I would like to say briefly that, in Switzerland too, we have had various controversies On the legal aspect of this problem, but that in the last revision of Company Law we have found a solution which gives the enterprise a wide measure of freedom. I don't know if there are many other countries which have a system whereby legal regulations leave it to the management of the companies themselves to form secret reserves in order to balance out dividends, and therefore also profits. These secret reserves serve to strengthen the undertaking in case it should suffer reversals later on, and are also intended to render it impossible for imprudent shareholders to secure the payment of too high a dividend by putting forward a motion to this effect at the general meeting of shareholders. By means of secret reserves such profits which might probably be needed later on for equalization, can be kept in reserve.
I know that similar measures do exist in other countries, for instance, the regulation that the Board of Directors and not the shareholders should determine the use made of the profits. But, of course, in those countries where the general meeting has the final say as regards the distribution of profits, the reports have to be formulated a great deal more cautiously than in a country where the dividends are determined by the directors.

MR. WELDON POWELL (United States of America)

Prof. Käfer, Gentlemen, has mentioned the subject of secret reserves. The use of secret reserves, of course, is one way of equalizing profits. Would any of the rest of you care to comment on this matter? I think it possibly would be interesting to know how secret reserves are being disposed of, once having been created. Are there disclosure problems? Does it have to be brought out in the report when the secret reserves are disposed of? Is it possible to use secret reserves to conceal losses? Would any of you have any comment on this point?

MR. HELGE BRAENDE (Norway)

Mr. Chairman, Ladies and Gentlemen, Equalization of profits leads to the increasing and reducing of secret reserves. It goes without saying that the increasing as well as reducing of secret reserves ought to be mentioned in the accountant's report. As far as I know, Norway is among those countries where the amount of secret reserves is on a rather high level, and the principle is acknowledged in the law. In the new Norwegian Limited Company's Act, which was passed on the sixth of July this year, the management is obliged, in its annual report to the shareholders, to mention and explain the effects on the Profit and Loss Account, if secret reserves have been reduced.

I am on the line with Mr. Forsström; however, I should like to stress the significance of and the reason for the tendency to equalize profits in the annual accounts. We hold it from the paper of Prof. Palle Hansen that the economically true profit can only be produced, if we know the future yields of the capital. However, the future is hidden behind this next split second, and so we are not able to produce this economically true profit. True profit in the accounts must be an economic concept of its own, which I prefer to call accountable true profit. This accountable true profit is a synthesis of many different components. Some of these components are known and must, of course, figure in the true expression in the accounts. Other components might be estimated, there are, however, also components, which we do not know at all, because they are hidden in the future. It is these last mentioned components which are the logical argument for equalization of profits in a going concern. In an apparently good year there might be hidden sources of misfortunes and losses which will be apparent in following years, and, seen the other way round, the sources for a bad year are very often to be found in previous years, therefore in my opinion the equalization of profits in the annual accounts will in the long run prove to be the best qualified method of producing 'accountable true profit'.

MR. WELDON POWELL (United States of America)

M. Darden, You had a specific question, I believe, that ties in with this general subject. Would you like to present it?

MR. E. K. P. DARDEN (Belgium)

Monsieur le Président, Pour répondre d'abord directement au sujet qui a été traité par Monsieur Forsström, je dois dire qu'en Belgique nous avons également constaté après la seconde guerre que des réserves occultes ont été constituées par certaines firmes pour faire face aux fluctuations de la monnaie. Si économiquement cette mesure était défendable, je ne crois pas qu'en général dans un période normale, nous puissions nous déclarer d'accord avec un nivellement de bénéfice.

J'avais en outre à poser une question indirecte. Pour bien préciser ma question, je vais d'abord donner lecture d'un passage du rapport de Monsieur Hutton, ici présent. Je lis le texte anglais:

'Some of the difficulties met in ascertaining profits in business arise from the artificial concept that a true and fair view of the profits of a continuing business can be ascertained at annual and only at annual intervals.

Businesses engaged in long term contracting are particularly affected by these difficulties. An exceptionally interesting professional paper written some years ago includes an entertaining reference to their problems:

If the orthodox principle of bringing into account only realised profits is accepted, the accounts for any year might, by themselves, be almost meaningless. While the practice is not uniform, it is quite common for sums on account of profit on uncompleted contracts to be brought in. Whether the effect of this is to produce results which really reflect the varying fortunes of the business will depend on the objectivity with which the uncompleted contracts are assessed —in other words, the success with which the temptation to aim at equalizing profits, has been resisted.'

Je continue mon exposé en français. Il résulte de ce texte que pour les entreprises traitant des contrats à long terme, comme par exemple les chantiers de constructions navales, les entreprises de travaux publics, deux méthodes différentes sont suivies pour enregistrer le résultat; la première consistant à dégager le résultat seulement au moment où les contrats sont terminés, tandis que la seconde consiste à faire ressortir le résultat également sur la partie exécutée des contrats inachevés. A mon avis ce n'est que la seconde méthode qui conduit au résultat réel de l'exercice. Pour illustrer mon opinion, je vais citer très brièvement un cas typique personnellement vécu. En 1952 je fus délégué en Afrique pour aider le personnel local d'une firme importante de travaux publics à dresser le bilan. A mon arrivée le chef-comptable me soumettait un projet de bilan clôturant par un léger bénéfice. Ayant eu l'occasion de contrôler pendant quelques mois l'évolution de la situation financière de cette même société et d'en déduire que la situation générale ne pouvait être que déficitaire, je ne pouvais pas admettre la vérité des chiffres qui furent présentés. L'analyse me permettait de constater que le chef-comptable n'avait passé en compte de pertes et profits que le résultat des entreprises terminées, alors qu'il existait des pertes très importantes sur les entreprises non achevées. En pratiquant la méthode d'évaluation que je préconise, je constatais qu'il y avait 9.000.000.— de pertes au lieu d'un léger bénéfice; je parle de francs congolais qui sont équivalents à des francs belges. Je m'excuse de cet exposé assez long, mais qui était nécessaire à mon avis pour montrer à quels risques on s'expose, si l'on attend la fin du contrat pour dégager le résultat. On me fera, peut-être, remarquer que dans un cas extrême comme celui-ci, il faut évidemment suivre l'autre méthode, mais il est tout de même inconcevable, qu'il existe une méthode pour en cas de pertes et une autre méthode pour en cas de bénéfices. Je me demande donc, si, pour faire ressortir le résultat exact d'une entreprise du genre qui nous occupe, il ne faut pas toujours adopter la méthode consistant à dégager le résultat également sur les contrats inachevés. On me fera peut-être remarquer que bien entendu dans un cas exceptionnel comme celui que je viens de citer, il faut créer une provision pour pertes sur travaux en cours, si l'on applique la première méthode, mais je ferai observer qu'en suivant la première méthode, on ne sait pas toujours déterminer cette perte d'une façon précise et encore faut-il que l'expert sache qu'il y ait perte, tandis que la seconde méthode conduit inévitablement à la détermination exacte du résultat.

Mr. Chairman, First of all, to give a direct answer to Mr. Forsström's question, I would say that in Belgium we have also found after the Second World War that secret reserves have been built up by certain concerns in order to be able to meet fluctuations in the value of money. Although from the economic point of view a measure of this sort could be justified, I do not believe that in normal times we should as a general rule approve an equalization of profits. In addition, I had an indirect question to ask. In order to make my point quite clear, may I first refer to a point which was made by Mr. Hutton, I will read it in English:

'Some of the difficulties met in ascertaining profits in business arise from the artificial concept that a true and fair view of the profits of a continuing business can be ascertained at annual and only at annual intervals.

Business engaged in long term contracting are particularly affected by these difficulties. An exceptionally interesting professional paper written some years ago includes an entertaining reference to their problems:

If the orthodox principle of bringing into account only realised profits is accepted, the accounts for any year might, by themselves, be almost meaningless. While the practice is not uniform, it is quite common for sums on account of profit on uncompleted contracts to be brought in. Whether the effect of this is to produce results which really reflect the varying fortunes of the business will depend on the objectivity with which the uncompleted contracts are assessed—in other words, the success with which the temptation to aim at equalizing profits, has been resisted'.

To continue now, Mr. Chairman, I think it will be clear from this text that for enterprises which engage in the conclusion of long term contracts, such as shipbuilding yards and contract builders, two different methods are used to record the results of their activities, the first one being that of establishing and computing the results at the moment the contract is completed, the second method being one of computing the results with reference to uncompleted contracts.

In my opinion, Mr. Chairman, it is only the second method which can give a true picture of the year you are assessing. To show what I have in mind, may I quote a practical example which I have come across. In 1952 I was sent to Africa to assist the local staff of a large firm engaged on a public works contract in preparing their balance sheet at the end of the year. When I arrived, the accountant submitted to me a balance sheet which showed a very slight profit. Having checked the evolution of the financial situation of this concern over a period of a few months, and having concluded that the general position must show a loss, I simply could not accept the figures submitted to me as correct. An analysis of the figures showed that the accountant had, in fact, taken into his profit and loss account only the results of completed contracts, whereas there were important losses in respect to uncompleted contracts. The evaluation method which I use showed that there was a loss of nine million francs, instead of a small profit. I'm speaking of the Congo franc, having the same value as a Belgian franc. I apologize, Mr. Chairman, for having gone into these details, but I think it was necessary to make the point I have in mind and to show the risk which is involved in waiting for the completion of the contract, before establishing and computing the results. It may be said that in an extreme case, such as the one I have illustrated here, one must apply the other method. Nevertheless, it is simply inconceivable that such a method should be used in case of losses and another method in case of profits.

For these reasons it seems to me that in order to show the correct position of enterprises of the type we are concerned with, only the method by which losses or profits on uncompleted contracts are brought in can be accepted.

One may say that when applying the orthodox principle, a provision can be made for possible losses on work in progress, but I would reply that such provision cannot be calculated with the required precision, while the recommended method automatically leads to the ascertainment of the true result.

MR. WELDON POWELL (United States of America)

If I may comment on M. Darden's question myself, I would like to do so briefly, because I have had a little to do with that in the United States recently. One of the technical committees of the American Institute of Certified Public Accountants has recently adopted a statement on accounting for long-term construction-type contracts, which in effect provides that you take up all known losses as soon as you know that there are going to be losses. As far as profits are concerned, you may account for them either as the contracts are completed or as the work is completed on the contracts during the construction period, provided you disclose clearly what you are doing.

We have had a number of comments concerning the use of equalization as a means to depress profit. Possibly at times equalization may have worked in the other direction. One of the audience, Mr. Armstrong, had a point in this connection. Would he like to come to the microphone to present his comment?

MR. P. LIVINGSTONE ARMSTRONG (United Kingdom)

Mr. Chairman, Ladies and Gentlemen.

One aspect of this question of profit has not, I think, been brought out sufficiently, and is one which may be of importance in other countries, as in my own. This is whether, under to-day's conditions, profits are high enough in many industries, and what should be done about this.

We have seen in recent years a great increase in Government interference in business, and a greatly increased burden of taxation, which has reacted to the detriment of savings, of initiative, and of enterprise. Profits have been much criticized as too high—yet the effect of inflation, as to-day's papers and discussions show, is exercising all our minds.

Mr. George O. May, who is such an inspiration to so many of us, has recently pointed out that many corporations in the U.S., in real money terms, have made losses and not profits, over the last decade. The same applies in the United Kingdom and no doubt elsewhere.

Mr. May has said that as accountants we have a public duty to perform in bringing out the facts of this vital matter.

Not only does the continued existence of private enterprise depend upon this, but in my belief also our freedom as individuals. It seems to me that if we, as accountants, do not take the lead in this, nothing effective will be done until too late. May I therefore humbly suggest that this is a matter for most urgent attention, and on which we should greatly welcome the guidance of our leaders?

MR. WELDON POWELL (United States of America)

Mr. Armstrong, I do not see any hands. Is anyone going to answer that question and present a solution in about 30 seconds? If not, I am going to pass on to another facet of this matter of determination of income. During the preceding discussion mention has been made of determination of income for taxation purposes, economic income, the use of reports by different groups of persons—shareholders investors and creditors, in addition to the government. I wonder if we could discuss a few of these matters, just a little bit.

Prof. Käfer, would you like to lead off the discussion of this matter of economic and fiscal determination of income?

PROF. DR. KARL KÄFER (Switzerland)

Mr. Powell, Ich muß hier im wesentlichen eine Frage stellen. Wer die Aufsätze gelesen hat, die uns vorgelegt wurden und die so viele wertvolle Gedanken enthalten, ist sicher erstaunt gewesen über die große Verschiedenheit, mit der das Problem der Feststellung des Gewinnes einer Unternehmung angepackt worden ist. Immer wieder aber mußte er dabei auf die Frage stoßen, wie weit der Buchhalter oder der 'Accountant' – wir haben für ihn im Deutschen keine ganz zutreffende Bezeichnung – wie weit der Accountant den handelsrechtlichen oder steuerrechtlichen Vorschriften nachgeben muß, wenn er seinen Bericht der Verwaltung oder der Generalversammlung vorlegt. In früheren Zeiten waren es namentlich die handelsrechtlichen Vorschriften, die für die Revisoren einen gewissen Stein des Anstoßes bedeuteten; aber diese Vorschriften waren doch immerhin noch in der Regel aufgebaut auf den aus früherer Erfahrung stammenden kaufmännischen Grundsätzen. Bei den steuerrechtlichen Bestimmungen besteht ein viel größerer Gegensatz, und deshalb scheint mir die Hauptfrage folgende zu sein: wie hat sich der Accountant einzustellen zu jenen Vorschriften des Steuerrechts und der Steuerverwaltungen, die ihm wirtschaftlich als unannehmbar erscheinen?

Ich glaube, um ganz kurz zu sagen was ich dazu meine, der Buchhalter oder Bücherexperte wird dem Kaiser geben was des Kaisers ist, er wird sich aber nicht damit abfinden, den Aktionären eine Bilanz oder Erfolgsrechnung vorzulegen, die er eigentlich als falsch empfindet, die er jedoch in dieser Art vorlegen muß, z.B. weil die steuerlichen Bewertungsvorschriften ihn zu bestimmten Ansätzen zwingen. Eine Antwort auf die Frage, wie sich der Accountant in solchen Fällen einzustellen hat, scheint mir sehr dringend zu sein. Sollte es ihm nicht möglich gemacht werden, mit der Steuerverwaltung über eine Steuerbilanz zu verhandeln, die allein als Grundlage für die Besteuerung gilt, dagegen dem Verwaltungsrat und den Aktionären eine Bilanz vorzulegen, die nach seinen Grundsätzen die wirtschaftliche Lage der Unternehmung richtig wiedergibt? So daß er also z.B. nicht gezwungen wäre Forschungskosten in die Bilanz zu übernehmen, obwohl er die Ergebnisse als wertlos erachtet, bloß weil die Abschreibung durch die Steuerverwaltung nicht gestattet wird. Es ist sicher Aufgabe der Verbände der Bücherexperten, jedesmal sehr energisch ihre Stimme zu erheben, wenn Steuergesetze in Beratung stehen. Leider ist das auch bei uns nicht immer in genügender Stärke geschehen, vielleicht wären dann manche Vorschriften etwas anders gefaßt worden.

Mr. Powell, In actual fact I have to ask a question myself here. Anybody who has read the papers submitted to us, and which contain so many valuable ideas, will have been surprised at the great variety of aspects there is to the question of the determination of profits. But he will constantly encounter the question of the extent to which the accountant must comply with the statutory provisions, whether it is a matter of fiscal or other regulations, when submitting his report to the Board or to the General Meeting. In the past it was mainly the provisions of Company Law which were the stumbling block to the auditors. But these provisions were largely based on standards derived from the past experience of businessmen. In the case of fiscal regulations, we see a much greater contrast and the main question appears to me to be the following: what should the attitude of the accountant be to the provisions of fiscal law and tax authorities which do not appear acceptable to him?

I think the accountant should give to Caesar what is Caesar's. But he will certainly offer resistance, if such regulations mean that he has to submit a report to the shareholders which he feels to be wrong, but which he has to submit nevertheless, because the fiscal regulations force him to assess matters in a certain way. It appears to me that the question is what the attitude of the accountant should be in these cases. Should it not be possible for him to get together with the tax authorities to negotiate the fiscal balance sheet and to take that as the basis for taxation, while at the same time giving the Board of Directors and the shareholders a balance sheet which he has drawn up according to his own principles and which provides a proper picture of the economic position of the enterprise? So that he should not, for instance, be forced to include research costs in the balance sheet, even though he considers the results to be valueless, simply because the tax authorities do not permit them to be written off.

I wonder if this is not a point on which societies of accountants and auditors should always intervene very energetically and get a hearing when such laws are being framed. Unfortunately, sufficient is not always done in our country in this respect; and, perhaps if sufficient had been done, some laws might have turned out a little differently.

MR. WELDON POWELL (United States of America)

Thank you, Prof. Käfer. As I understood what you were saying, it is to the effect that tax considerations have an effect on the accounting, and we ought to try to get the tax laws adjusted, so as to present results in a proper manner.

Mr. Frisbee, would you like to comment on the United States approach to this matter?

MR. IRA N. FRISBEE (United States of America)

Mr. Powell, I certainly can agree with that last statement, that we would like to get the tax people to do as we think they ought to do. However, I feel strongly that we should not let the tax people or any other governmental body determine for us what the profits of the business are. We should report as Prof. Käfer said 'to Caesar what is due to Caesar'.

But when it comes to reporting to the stockholders, the creditors and the employees we are then reporting to the people to whom the business is responsible. In doing this, we must report correctly, irrespective of what the governmental authorities have said as to the proper methods of determining profits. This is quite important because for tax purposes there are special write-offs, such as for amortization of plant, depletion, and intangible assets, which may not be properly written off for other reporting purposes.

Also, there are items which are included in income for tax purposes, which we do not accept as income, and which are not properly income items as yet, but which must be reported currently for tax purposes. So I would say that, in our country, it very definitely is our practice to report different profits in some instances than the profits reported for income tax purposes.

We have other governmental authorities or regulatory bodies. For example, we have public utility commissions and railroad commissions that prescribe certain methods which must be followed, and in preparing reports to these commissions they are followed. But it is certainly coming to be strongly felt that, for other purposes, we must take exception to their methods when they are contrary to our generally accepted accounting principles. There is one governmental authority which has had quite a bit of influence upon our principles of accounting in the United States. It was referred to the other day, I think, in the first session of this Congress, particularly by Mr. Blough. This is our Securities and Exchange Commission, which has been interested in seeing that stockholders, prospective investors and creditors receive a correct or fair statement of profits, not only for the current year, but for past years, and that each year the financial statements of companies whose securities are sold on the Exchange or over the counter are fair presentations. In the case of this Commission I think it is accurate to say that the accounting profession and the governmental authorities have worked together pretty much hand-in-hand. There have been some arguments but they have been ironed out so that the accounting profession and the accountants for the Securities and Exchange Commission usually are in agreement upon the principles governing the preparation of accounting statements.

MR. WELDON POWELL (United States of America)

Dr. Allet, You have been quiet during this meeting. What would you like to say about this point?

DR. ERNST ALLET (Austria)

Die Frage der verschiedenen Bilanzierungsbestimmungen handelsrechtlicher und steuerrechtlicher Natur ist auch bei uns in Österreich sehr aktuell. Infolge der hohen Steuersätze, die wir seit 1945 haben, wird über sehr viele Einzelfragen der Bewertung gerade in steuerrechtlicher Hinsicht sehr viel diskutiert und es werden sehr viele Rechtsmittel, Berufungen u.s.w. darüber geführt. In Einzelfällen hat es oft Jahre gedauert bis sich in steuerrechtlicher Hinsicht eine richtige Bewertungsbestimmung durch die Spruchpraxis der obersten Verwaltungsgerichtshöfe herausgebildet hat. Es ist dazu noch zu erwähnen, daß wir in steuerlicher Hinsicht Begünstigungen für Abschreibungen seit vielen Jahren genießen, um die Investitionstätigkeit zu fördern.

Handelsrechtlich, also nach den Grundsätzen des Handelsgesetzbuches, ist die Bewertung nicht sehr schwierig, weil das Handelsgesetzbuch ja nur den Schutz der Gläubiger im Sinn hat und daher eine Bewertung nach niedrigsten Grundsätzen vorzieht als nach höheren Grundsätzen. Die Finanzbehörde dagegen hat ihre fiskalischen Interessen und möchte natürlich möglichst große Bewertungsansätze herausholen.

The question of the various regulations governing the determination of the balance contained in commercial and fiscal laws is a very topical one with us in Austria too. Owing to the high rate of taxation we have known since 1945, a host of individual questions relating to valuation has given rise to much discussion, especially in regard to fiscal laws, and a great deal of legal action, appeals, etc., has been taken. In some cases, it has frequently taken years before decisions by the supreme administrative courts have resulted in proper valuation according to fiscal law. It must be mentioned in addition that fiscal regulations have for many years allowed certain privileges as regards depreciation in order to stimulate investment. According to commercial law, i.e. according to the principles of the commercial law code, valuation is not very difficult because this code has only the protection of creditors in mind, and therefore prefers a valuation in accordance with the lowest basic rates to one according to the higher ones.
On the other hand, the fiscal authorities have their fiscal interests and would naturally like to squeeze out the highest basic rates of valuation possible.

MR. WELDON POWELL (United States of America)
Mr. Braende wants to comment.

MR. HELGE BRAENDE (Norway)
Economic and fiscal determination of profit might be looked upon as two different things, but only to a certain extent. The treasury might well impose income taxes without taking into account the economic way of determining profit, but it would be unrealistic in economic determination of profit to elude the problem of taxation. This becomes the more evident the higher the degree of progression in income taxation. The taxable profit and the taxes derived therefrom are of such influence to the various concerns, that they have a bearing upon the economic determination of profit in addition to other expenses. Nevertheless, we might theoretically examine and discuss the economic determination of profit apart from the problems of taxation, with the faint hope that the economic principles we eventually might agree upon through the years will enter into the fiscal determination of profit. The main principle in the income taxation in Norway is that the fiscal determination of profit shall be based upon the annual profit and loss account, as long as this profit is produced in accordance with sound business principles. However, the tax law establishes certain rules which must be followed. And it is in the field between these rules and the sound business principles that the real problems are to be found.

MR. WELDON POWELL (United States of America)
I think we should all go to Norway.

MR. HELGE BRAENDE (Norway)
I am glad to say that owing to the growing respect for the accountants' profession, nationally as well as internationally, in my country the opinion of the accountant is asked as often as alterations in the business taxation are at stake. So we may hope for the future.

MR. WELDON POWELL (United States of America)
What is the Finnish view on this point?

MR. BÖRJE FORSSTRÖM (Finland)
I quite agree with the foregoing. I should only just mention an example which shows how dangerous the mixing up of the tax principles and economic principles will prove to be. When, for instance, tax relief is given for expansion of enterprises which the government sometimes promotes, there should be no claim from the tax authority side that the depreciation in question must be booked, otherwise the tax relief would not be given, which I think is a dangerous thing.

MR. WELDON POWELL (United States of America)
Mr. Roozen, You have kept quiet during this meeting. Possibly you would like to comment on this point.

DISCUSSION

MR. L. J. M. ROOZEN (Netherlands)

Mijnheer de president, Het zou verwonderlijk zijn, wanneer de verschillen van mening over de ter sprake gebrachte thema's juist zouden overeenstemmen met de landsgrenzen. Ik zou zelfs willen zeggen, dat zou enigszins te betreuren zijn. En om nu een demonstratie te geven van het tegenovergestelde, zou ik gaarne in willen gaan op een van de punten, die collega Groeneveld in zijn uiteenzetting ter sprake heeft gebracht, juist aangaande dit onderwerp. En ik kan dit doen, zonder mijn grote bewondering voor het geheel van de uiteenzetting van de heer Groeneveld ook maar enigszins onder stoelen of banken te steken. De heer Groeneveld is van mening, dat wij moeten berusten in het feit, dat de fiscus zijn eigen regels en zijn eigen overwegingen heeft. Hij zegt nl.: 'the policy laid down in tax regulations has its own general, economic, financial and social merits, which are not always in accordance with strictly micro-economic desiderata, e.g. employment, reasonable distribution of national income, favouring of under-privileged groups of the population, balance of payment problems, business cycle stabilization, etc.'

Daarnaast noemt de heer Groeneveld als tweede reden van een afwijking tussen fiscale en economische waarderingsregelen, dat, 'Moreover the tax authorities must safeguard the revenue and therefore take care that indeed all profit elements of the taxable subject are taxed'. Van dit tweede punt noemt hij dan nog een voorbeeld als het ware, dat zou men met een derde punt kunnen samenvoegen, waar hij zegt: 'it is further realised that juridical views and considerations have a bearing on the drafting of tax regulations'.

Sta mij nu toe, mijnheer de president, om speciaal het eerste punt ter sprake te brengen, de vraag dus, of inderdaad op grond van macro-economische overwegingen de overheid kan stellen, dat zij eigen regelen moet hebben voor de winstbepaling.

Ik zou dat willen ontkennen, mijnheer de voorzitter, ik geloof namelijk dat de overheid alleen op haar macro-economische overwegingen kan besluiten om een winstbelasting in te voeren en in tweede instantie, onder de gegeven omstandigheden, besluiten kan de tarieven van die winstbelasting op een bepaalde hoogte te stellen. Dit neemt dan echter niet weg, dat, wanneer zij zich aldus op grond van haar macro-economische overwegingen deelgerechtigd heeft gemaakt aan de winst, daarna haar positie als deelgerechtigde volmaakt dezelfde is als die van de andere deelgerechtigden in de winst, met name de aandeelhouders.

En ik geloof dus, dat de Staat hetzelfde belang heeft bij een zo juist mogelijke benadering van de voor vertering beschikbare vermogensaanwas binnen die onderneming. Ook de Staat heeft, naar mijn overtuiging, naast zijn specifieke medeverantwoordelijkheid voor de instandhouding van het produktieapparaat, er nu ook financieel belang bij dat de winstbron blijft vloeien.

Ik concludeer dus hier, dat de eigen macro-economische overwegingen van de Staat geen andere inhoud kunnen geven aan de winst, die immers blijft de winst van de onderneming, m.a.w. een micro-economisch bepaald gegeven.

Mr. Chairman, It would be surprising if the differences of opinions concerning our questions were to correspond exactly with the national frontiers of our countries. I would say it would even be regrettable if it were so. To illustrate my point, which is, in fact, the opposite view to that which has been advanced here, may I quote the details of one of the points made by Mr. Groeneveld in this respect. I can do so, without detracting from my sincere admiration for Mr. Groeneveld's paper.

Mr. Groeneveld considers that we shall have to reconcile ourselves to the fiscal authorities having their own rules and considerations and here I will quote his paper:

'the policy laid down in tax regulations has its own general economic, financial and social merits, which are not always in accordance with strictly micro-economic desiderata, e.g. employment, reasonable distribution of national income, favoring under-privileged groups of the population, balance of payment problems, business cycle stabilization, etc.'.

In addition, as a second argument for a deviation between economic and fiscal rules Mr. Groeneveld says:

'Moreover, the tax authorities must safeguard the revenue, therefore they have to take care that all profit elements of the taxable subjects are taxed'. He then gives an example of this second point and this could be read in conjunction with a third one, where he states: 'it is further realised that juridical views and considerations have a bearing on tax regulations'. If I may now, Mr. Chairman, mention in particular the first point, which is whether the government may indeed maintain, on macro-economic grounds, that it should establish its own rules for the ascertainment of profit. I would deny this, for I feel that the government can only decide, on macro-economic considerations, to levy taxes on profits and secondly to set rates for the taxation of profits, under the given circumstances. Nevertheless, when on the basis of these macro-economic considerations the government has entitled itself in this way to a share in the business profits, its position is then identical with that of other parties entitled to a share in the profits, in particular the shareholders. And consequently I feel that the Government has the same interest in a correct assessment of the expendable increase of the capital within the enterprise. In my opinion, besides its specific joint responsibility for the maintenance of production, the Government has also a financial interest in seeing that the source of the profits does not dry up. Therefore my conclusion is that macro-economic considerations cannot lead to a different concept of profit, for it is obvious that the latter remains the profit of the enterprise, which is a datum determined by micro-economic considerations.

MR. WELDON POWELL (United States of America)

Well, We have developed up to this point, that there are taxation considerations in the determination of income and also economic considerations. The latter subject leads us into consideration of accounting for inflation, price-level adjustments and what not. We are not going to discuss that at this meeting in detail, because it was covered in the 1952 congress. However, I think it should be noted that everyone of the authors of the papers has referred to it, and that of the questions we have had from the audience, at least three or four have referred to it. In order to just round out the record I would like to ask one or two of the audience just to come to the microphone and very briefly put their question. The first is Mr. Saunders of England. Is Mr. Saunders here?

MR. G. F. SAUNDERS (United Kingdom)

Mr. Chairman, Ladies and Gentlemen,

In 1952, a few weeks before the 6th International Congress was held in London, the English Institute issued No. XV in its Series of Recommendations dealing with 'Accounting in Relation to the Changes in Purchasing Power of Money'.

After setting out the limitations of accounts drawn up on the customary basis of historical cost it invited its members to experiment with the methods of measuring the effect of changes in the purchasing power of money on profits.

During the intervening period little progress has been made in developing new methods, possibly because the rate of inflation has slowed down and also as a greater proportion of fixed assets now included in a company's Balance

Sheet has been acquired at the enhanced postwar cost so that the normal charge for depreciation is based upon figures which have a closer relation to replacement cost.

In some published accounts the method employed has been that of setting sums aside to reserve to cover the enhanced cost of asset replacement without in most cases indicating the basis of computation. In other instances, the calculation has been made on the basis of price indices and is shown as an additional provision in the Profit and Loss Account and not as an appropriation to Reserve. In most cases, however, as a policy of financial prudence an amount has been set aside to Reserve to cover both the needs of asset replacement and business expansion without attempting to differentiate between the two separate elements. Whatever method is adopted there are three important questions which arise.

In times of continuous inflation an amount set aside on the basis of current price indices will not provide the full amount required for replacement unless additional provision is made from time to time to cover the shortage in the amounts set aside in previous years when prices were at a lower level. How is this additional sum to be shown?

If prices are increased by charging depreciation on the basis of the replacement cost of existing assets, has an unnecessary twist been given to the spiral of inflation if the assets are ultimately replaced by others of modern design which enable the subsequent cost of production to be reduced? If this is so, as undoubtedly is the case in some instances, then the charging of depreciation on replacement cost is of itself a contributory cause of inflation. If the effect of inflation on the business as a whole is considered then regard must be given to the liabilities as well as to the assets. With the result that the amount required to be set aside will be less in those concerns which have a proportion of their capital raised by loan stock and preference shares than in those which are capitalised solely on a basis of equity capital.

All these difficulties lead one to the conclusion that there is no method which can be of universal application and attention should be concentrated on setting out the Profit and Loss Account in such a way that it is clearly shown to what extent provision has been made for the maintenance of the company's trading capacity before arriving at the balance of profit which is available for appropriations.

MR. WELDON POWELL (United States of America)

A similar point has been made by Mr. Francisco Lopez Dominguez of Zaragoza, Spain. Mr. J. S. Seidman of the United States has, I think, a somewhat contrary view. Mr. Seidman, would you like to express yourself very briefly?

MR. J. S. SEIDMAN (United States of America)

Mr. Chairman, I wonder whether the economic concept of profit is practicable and whether from the accountant's standpoint, in any event, it has any place at all in the accountant's report. As to the practicability of it, I call attention to the fact that implicit in that concept is the task of valuing the business assets of the entire world, either annually or at other intervals. Now to be sure, indices can be used, but as applied to any one particular business, an index is merely an arbitrary average and I question whether it brings us any nearer to the concept of real profits. As to the use of this concept in the accountant's report, I think that there are various types of reports from different professional sources, all of which have significance to an enterprise. Just as a doctor or a physicist or an artist can look at the same body and come away with different meaningful conclusions, so also in business there is room for the report from an economist, from an engineer, from a market consultant and from the accountant. The accountant provides the record of history, and I submit, Mr. Chairman, that a page of accounting history may very well be worth far more than a volume of economic theoretical logic.

It does seem to me that with cost as the basis for the accounting, the accountant has a known, reasonably reliable anchor. When he wanders away from that, he loses his mooring. I submit that the accountant will be far better off, and so will management and the public, if the accountant keeps his feet on dry ground and lets the other professionals drift to sea. Thank you.

MR. WELDON POWELL (United States of America)

I told you we were going to have differences of opinion. This discussion leads us into a point which has become evident, that accounting is determined by rules and conventions, but that also the human element plays a substantial part in it. Could we spend just a few minutes, we are running a little behind schedule, to discuss the part the judgment and similar matters play in accounting determinations. The accountant, of course, aims to be objective, but he is affected by subjective considerations also. M. Darden, could you comment very briefly on that for us?

MR. E. K. P. DARDEN (Belgium)

Monsieur le Président, Pour déterminer le résultat d'une entreprise certains éléments du patrimoine doivent nécessairement faire l'objet d'une évaluation. Citons à titre d'exemple les stocks des matières et des produits fabriqués, les travaux en cours. La discipline professionnelle veut que cette évaluation soit faite d'une façon consciencieuse, honnête et abstraction faite de tout intérêt personnel, en un mot, d'une façon objective. Il est généralement admis, également par les auteurs des différents rapports qui ont été introduits qu'il est difficile de trouver une base objective d'évaluation; par ailleurs on constate que l'étude de ce problème mène à des points de vue divergents. Ceux qui sont très optimistes sont d'avis que cette incertitude peut être écartée si on voulait procéder à un raffinement toujours croissant des principes théoriques et des méthodes pratiques comptables.

Cette conception renferme une surestimation de la possibilité de la science appliquée dans le secteur économique et tend à faire croire que la valeur essentielle des services à rendre par l'expert-comptable réside dans l'art de manipuler les chiffres d'une main de maître. Quant aux pessimistes, qui, en réalité, sont aussi désireux d'atteindre ce degré élevé d'objectivité, ils considèrent que la détermination du résultat réel d'une entreprise est une impossibilité. Leur conception aboutit à une espèce de nihilisme, ils condamnent la science à la stérilité tout en discréditant la fonction de l'expert-comptable. Entre ces deux extrêmes se situent d'autres conceptions d'ordre pratique. Il y a par exemple la conception anglaise en vertu de laquelle la théorie de la valeur de remplacement ne constitue pas un principe scientifique pour calculer le résultat. Suivant la même conception le coût historique, auquel se rattache une date réelle représente une bien meilleure base d'évaluation. Il y a aussi la conception américaine qui veut faire dépendre le calcul du profit de règles fixes, qu'elles soient bonnes ou mauvaises.

La question est de savoir si une réconciliation de ces différentes conceptions est possible, en supposant qu'il soit généralement admis:

1. que le profit objectif existe d'une façon concrète, mais qu'il est difficile de le déterminer à cause d'une défaillance des capacités humaines.

2. que l'inévitable subjectivité naturelle inhérente à tout jugement humain n'est dangereuse que si un jugement est rendu par une personne, qui par sa position sociale a un certain intérêt dans le profit à déterminer.

3. qu'en conséquence la signification essentielle du certificat posé à la suite du bilan annuel par l'expert-comptable ne réside pas dans son jugement rendu en qualité d'expert, mais plutôt dans le caractère indépendant de ce jugement.

Pour terminer je me permets de suggérer si la solution n'est pas à rechercher dans l'établissement de normes sous forme de définitions des différentes méthodes d'évaluation pratiquées dans les divers pays.

Mr. Chairman, In order to determine the results of an enterprise, certain elements of the assets must of course be evaluated, e.g. stocks of raw materials, finished products, work in progress. Professional discipline requires that such valuations should be carried out conscientiously, honestly and setting aside any personal considerations. In other words, it must be done objectively.

It is usually accepted, and this also holds good for the authors of the various papers which have been submitted to us, that it is difficult to find an objective basis for the purpose of valuation. On the other hand, it is also clear that the study of this problem leads us to divergent views. Those who are very optimistic consider that this lack of certainty might be overcome by an ever-increasing refinement of our economic principles and accounting procedures. This notion involves an over-estimation of our science, in the economic field at least, and indicates that the essential value of the services to be rendered by the accountant are to be found in the art of handling figures in a masterly way. On the other hand, those of us who are pessimistic about it and who also want to reach the best possible results, nevertheless consider that the true results of an enterprise just cannot be established. Their concept leads to a sort of nihilism; they condemn totally any scientific approach and discredit the function of the accountant.

Between these two extremes, however, there are various other concepts, practical ones. There is the British concept, for instance, according to which the theory of the replacement value does not constitute a scientific principle for the calculation of the results. According to this same concept the historical cost, related to an actual date, would be a better basis for valuation. There is also the American concept, according to which the calculation of profit must depend on fixed rules, whether good or bad. The question then is whether it is possible to find a middle way which would combine all these concepts, assuming that it was agreed, first of all, that the objective profit actually exists, but that it is difficult to determine it, because of some lack of perfection in human capacities; secondly, that the subjectivity natural to any human judgement is dangerous, only if such a judgement is delivered by a person who, due to his social position, has some interest in the profits to be assessed; thirdly, that accordingly the main significance of the auditor's certificate which is issued after preparation of the yearly balance sheet, does not lie in his expert judgement but in the independent character of that judgement. In conclusion, therefore, I take the liberty of suggesting that the solution may be found in the establishment of standards which might be expressed as definitions of the various methods of valuation applied in the different countries.

MR. WELDON POWELL (United States of America)

We are running on. I am not going to try to summarize the discussion up to this point. We have discussed a wide range of views under the subject of equalization of income. We have discussed also the effects of taxation and of economic considerations on the determination of income. We have discussed further, although not as fully as I had hoped, because of lack of time, the subjective versus the objective nature of the accountant's work.

We probably have settled nothing, but maybe we have stimulated your thinking a little. I hope that one result may be to have brought home to all of us a greater appreciation that the accounting in the respective countries is affected by differences in outlook and conditions and business practices, without attempting to impose anyone's ideas on anyone else. Possibly the exchange of views in a meeting like this is very helpful towards international understanding.

I would stress the importance of judgment and independence on the part of the accountant. I would call attention to the fact that convention does play quite a large role in accounting. The matter of consistency from period to period has not been mentioned before, but it seems to me that this also is important. As is also one point that has been mentioned, disclosure of the basis on which accounts are prepared and offered. In coming to this point I wonder whether it is possible for anyone to codify accounting principles, rules, and conventions.

Mr. Henry Benson of England has offered some very pertinent comments. I had intended to ask him to come up here to present them, but time will not permit me to do so. I would like to give you the gist, however, of what he says. He says, 'I do not believe that profit can be determined by any universal or absolute formula. Profit is determined partly on the facts but also, to a large extent, by the nature of the business, the exercise of judgment and of opinion and management's individual interpretation of general principles'. He goes on to illustrate that, and winds up with a statement that in his view 'each business in preparing and presenting its annual accounts should observe three things:

a. it should interpret these principles consistently year by year;
b. it should disclose any departure from the principles;
c. it should declare the effect of any change of basis in preparing its accounts as between one year and another.'

Mr. Groeneveld, you started out this session with a summary of the papers. Possibly you would like to wind it up by giving your own comments and any thoughts that you might have on codification and any recommendations that this congress might make in that regard.

MR. G. L. GROENEVELD (Netherlands)

Mijnheer de voorzitter, De heer Mangal heeft zijn inleiding besloten met het Congres te verzoeken aanbevelingen te maken voor een zekere codificatie van waarderingsgrondslagen. Die gedachte van de heer Mangal heeft bij verschillende leden van ons panel en bij verschillende auteurs van prae-adviezen ondersteuning gevonden en onder meer is dat ook de reden geweest, dat ik er in mijn resumé aandacht aan heb gegeven. De gedachte aan een dergelijke codificatie is buitengewoon aantrekkelijk, gezien de grote verscheidenheid van begrippen, terminologie en meningsvorming waarmee wij worden geconfronteerd. Het zou van zeer groot belang zijn om daaraan in internationaal verband te kunnen werken. Maar nauwelijks heeft men die gedachte uitgesproken of men ziet de berg van moeilijkheden en vraagstukken, die een dergelijke arbeid met zich zou meebrengen, vooral waar het ons vooralsnog aan een permanente internationale organisatie, die daarvoor toch wel nodig zou zijn, ontbreekt. Internationale codificatie zal dus zeker nog toekomstmuziek blijven. Niettemin kunnen wij de wenselijkheid daarvan in gedachten houden en er bij verschillende gelegenheden naar streven iets tot stand te brengen. Persoonlijk, mijnheer de voorzitter, geloof ik dat al veel gewonnen is als wij tot de opinie zouden komen, dat wij niet bij voorbaat moeten uitsluiten dat wij op dit gebied iets kunnen bereiken.

Mr. Chairman, Mr. Mangal concludes his paper by asking the Congress to prepare recommendations as to some possible codification of principles of valuation. This was supported by various authors of other papers and by other members of the panel, and this is why I drew attention to this request in my summary of the papers. The idea that some codification should be introduced is, indeed, an attractive one, the more so, since approach, terminology, and concepts differ widely from one country to another. It would certainly be of great significance, if greater uniformity on an international level could be achieved.

However, the idea has hardly been expressed when one is immediately confronted with the difficulties that would be encountered in attempting to perform such a task. The more so, since there is as yet no permanent international organization, which would certainly be needed for such work.

Nevertheless, I hope that it may be possible in the future to do something along these lines, and this idea of a future international codification could undoubtedly be fostered.

Mr. Chairman, I believe that if we were able to reach the conclusion that such codification is not an impossibility, this in itself would be a step forward.

MR. WELDON POWELL (United States of America)

Thank you, Mr. Groeneveld. M. Veyrenc, I now return the meeting to you.

CHAIRMAN:

Mesdames, Messieurs. Au terme de cette dernière séance de travail où nous avons entendu une discussion et des exposés très objectifs, qui seront certainement profitables à chacun d'entre nous, qu'il me soit permis d'adresser toutes mes félicitations aux membres du panel et aux personnes qui ont bien voulu entrevenir. A la lumière des discussions il nous apparaît bien que parmi les missions diverses confiées à l'expert-comptable la détermination du bénéfice et son appréciation est une de celles qui requiert de sa part beaucoup d'expérience de jugement et d'autorité. Mais en dépit de toutes les difficultés d'ordre fiscal, économique ou autre, nous savons tous aussi que la noblesse de notre profession réside justement dans la recherche constante et passionnée de la vérité au service du bien public. Dans cette ambiance que la devise de l'ordre national français traduit en ces termes: science, conscience, indépendance, et c'est alors en me permettant de reprendre les termes élevés de Son Altesse Royal, le Prince Bernhard que par la promotion de l'honnêteté dans les documents financiers de tout genre, les experts-comptables contribueront en une large mesure à l'établissement de relations humaines basées sur les principes de la vérité et de la justice. Je vais maintenant, Mesdames et Messieurs, avoir le plaisir de donner la parole successivement à Monsieur Jan, vice-président, puis à Monsieur Fitzgerald, vice-président, qui voudra bien clôturer cette session.

Ladies and Gentlemen. As we reach the end of this last business session, after having heard a very enlightening and objective discussion, and a number of explanations which undoubtedly will be of great use to each one of us, may I be allowed to congratulate, very sincerely, the members of the panel and all those who were good enough to participate in the discussion. Having heard all these discussions, I think it must be clear that among all the tasks which are entrusted to the accountant, profit determination and its appreciation is indeed one which requires the highest experience, judgement and authority from the accountant. But despite all the difficulties, fiscal in particular, economic, or others, we all know, too, that the high standing of our profession is based on this very constant pursuit of truth on behalf of public welfare. It is from this point of view that I would remind you of the motto of the French Institute: 'Science, Conscience, Indépendance'. Thus, now reverting to Prince Bernhard's statement to us on the first day, that 'by promoting honesty in financial documents of all kinds, accountants will be able to contribute to a large extent to the foundation of human relations based on principles of truth and justice'.

Now, Ladies and Gentlemen, I will call successively on Mr. Jan, Vice-Chairman, and then on Mr. Fitzgerald, Vice-Chairman, to close the session.

Vice-chairman, MR. RAHIM JAN (Pakistan)

Mr. Chairman, Ladies and Gentlemen. It is an honour and my pleasant duty to thank the members of the panel for the very informative discussion of this morning. As we have just heard, the subject of the ascertainment of profit is not one which lends itself to easy agreement. Particularly when the definition of profits has not been or cannot be agreed upon. Nevertheless, the discussion has been successful in giving us the view of accountants in various parts of the world. Although the interesting points that we had expressed this morning do not entirely exhaust the subject they will certainly prove to be a useful contribution and a subject for further reflection for all of us in the future. Thank you.

Vice-chairman, MR. G. E. FITZGERALD (Australia)

Ladies and Gentlemen. My task is a simple and pleasing one. I am sure you are all grateful to the President for the courteous and efficient manner in which he has carried out his duty, and on your behalf I would like to express to him sincere thanks. And now I might exercise a woman's privilege and say the last word: thank you, Ladies and Gentlemen, for your attendance and the way in which you have attended to the proceedings, and I now declare this session closed.

PART THREE

APPENDICES

LIST OF BODIES
REPRESENTED AND ALPHABETICAL LISTS OF PARTICIPANTS FROM ABROAD

A = *delegate* Aa = *leader of delegation* B = *visitor* C = *guest*

The numbers shown with the characters behind the names of the participants refer to the numbers given to the bodies invited, mentioned under the heading of their country.

AUSTRALIA

1 *The Institute of Chartered Accountants in Australia*
2 *Australian Society of Accountants*

Digby, Mr. and Mrs. W. H. M.	Sydney	A	1
Fitzgerald, Mr. and Mrs. G. E.	Melbourne	Aa	2
Wedd, Mr. and Mrs. J.		C	
Irish, R. A.	Sydney	Aa	1
McAlister, Ian M. and Mr. Dunster	Mont Albert	A	1
Yorston, Mr. and Mrs. R. Keith	Roseville	A	1

AUSTRIA

Kammer der Wirtschaftstreuhänder

Albeseder, Herr und Frau Walter	Wien	B
Allet, Dr. und Frau Ernst	Innsbruck	Aa
Alvarado-Dupuy, Herr und Frau Alfons	Wien	A
Fischer, Frau Dr. Blanche	Wien	B
Hafner, Herr und Frau F.	Klagenfurt	B
Petras, Herr und Frau Paul	Innsbruck	B
Radey, Dr. Christian	Wien	B
Reichart, Frau Maria	Wien	B
Schick, Dr. und Frau Hans	Wien	A
Wunder, Friedrich	Wien	B

BELGIUM

1 *Collège National des Experts Comptables de Belgique*
(Nationaal College der Accountants van België)
2 *Chambre Belge des Comptables*

Aldeweireldt, Hr. en Mevr. E. E.	Antwerpen	B	1
Bastin, M. et Mme. Jean G.	Bruxelles	B	1
Brisé, M. et Mme. Robert	Gand	B	1

Brisé, Jean-Pierre		C
Charels, Dr. Leo F. H.	Brussel	B 1
Darden, E. C. P.	Antwerpen	A 1
Deheuvel, M. et Mme. Charles	Bruxelles	A 1
Eeckhoven, M. et Mme. J. J. M. van	Anvers	B 1
François, A.	Watermael	B 2
Genard, M. et Mme. S.	Gosselies	B 1
Goffin, M. et Mme. J.	Wemmel	B 2
Henry, Maurice G.	Bruges	B 1
Inslegers, Hr. en Mevr. R. A. J.	Brugge	B 1
Iper, R. J. van	Antwerpen	Aa 1
Lambert, M. et Mme. Maurice	Bruxelles	B 1
Maartense, Hr. en Mevr. Jacques J.	Deurne Zuid-Antwerpen	B 1
Marchal, M. et Mme. F.	Bruxelles	B 1
Mercier, M. et Mme. L.	Rixensart	B 1
Peumans, Hr. en Mevr. H. M. J.	St. Lambrechts-Woluwe	B 1
Pirenne, Theo	Anvers	A 1
Schellekens, J. J.	Antwerpen	A 1
Trefois, Madame N.	Bruxelles	A 2
Verbert, M. et Mme. A. H.	Anvers	B 1
Verhaegen, Hr. en Mevr. Louis	Antwerpen	B 1
Verheyen, A.	Antwerpen	B 1
Vestel, Maurice de	Sterrebeek	B 1

BRAZIL

Sindicato dos Contabilistas do Rio de Janeiro

Machado Sobrinho, Prof. P. J. A.	Rio de Janeiro	Aa
Mandina, Mr. and Mrs. S.	Rio de Janeiro	B

BURMA

Burma Accountancy Board

Maung Maung, U.	Rangoon	Aa
Shein, U.	Rangoon	A

CANADA

1 *The Canadian Institute of Chartered Accountants and the Provincial Institutes*
2 *The Canadian Institute of Certified Public Accountants*

Brown, Mr. and Mrs. J. G.	Kitchener	A-Ontario
Carter, Mr. and Mrs. Kenneth LeM.	Toronto	A-Ontario
Church, Mr. and Mrs. John R.	Montreal	A-Quebec
DeLalanne, James A.	Montreal	Aa-Inst.
Farish, Mr. and Mrs. David M.	Montreal	B 1
Hart, G.	North Vancouver	B 1
Hesford, Mr. and Mrs. A.	North Vancouver	B 1
Jephcott, Mr. and Mrs. Gerald	Toronto	A-Ontario
Keeping, George P.	Montreal	A-Quebec
Kidd, Mr. and Mrs. Robert N. A.	Montreal	B 1

King, Clem L.	Toronto	A-Ontario
Kreeft, Mr. and Mrs. H.	Sarnia	B 2
Macpherson, Mr. and Mrs. Lawrence G.	Kingston	A-Inst.
McDonald, Mr. and Mrs. W. Leslie	Toronto	A-Inst.
McKean, Mr. and Mrs. Robert T.	Victoria	B 1
McLean, Mr. and Mrs. Lorn	Vancouver	A-Br.Col.
Miller, Mr. and Mrs. A. K.	Edmonton	B 1
Rabnett, Mr. and Mrs. F. H.	Owen Sound	A 2
Sorley, Mr. and Mrs. Stewart H.	Toronto	A-Ontario
Sprague, Mr. and Mrs. D.	Winnipeg	A-Manitoba
Stanley, A. D. Peter	Vancouver	A-Br. Col.

CEYLON

Board of Accountancy

Eliatamby, James S.	Colombo	personal
Henderson, Mr. and Mrs. J.	Colombo	Aa
Hulugalle, Upatissa	Colombo	A
Velupillai, S.	Colombo	A

DENMARK

Foreningen af Statsautoriserede Revisorer

Allum, Mr. and Mrs. Erik	Copenhagen	B
Askgaard Olesen, Mr. and Mrs. C. E.	Copenhagen	B
Berthelsen, Mr. and Mrs. J. E.	Hellerup	B
Boesberg, Mr. and Mrs. I.	Copenhagen	B
Christensen, Mr. and Mrs. Holger	Sønderborg	B
Christensen, T.		C
Engblom, Mr. and Mrs. Aksel	Copenhagen	B
Hansen, Mr. and Mrs. Børge	Copenhagen	A
Hjernø Jeppesen, Mr. and Mrs. H.	Copenhagen	Aa
Hjernø Jeppesen, Master M.		C
Holm, Mr. and Mrs. Gunnar V.	Copenhagen	B
Iverson, Mr. and Mrs. Iver H.	Copenhagen	B
Jensen, Mr. and Mrs. K. G.	Copenhagen	B
Jensen, Mr. and Mrs. O. B.	Viby J.	B
Jensen, Vilh.	Copenhagen	B
Jørgensen, Mr. and Mrs. Erling	Gentofte	B
Klevel, Mr. and Mrs. J. V.	Odense	B
Kliim, Mr. and Mrs. Knud	Copenhagen	B
Olsen, Mr. and Mrs. C. O.	Copenhagen	B
Olsen, Poul		C
Ørkild Hansen, Mr. and Mrs. I.	Copenhagen	B
Pedersen, Mr. and Mrs. K. A.	Aarhus	B
Sörensen, Mr. and Mrs. S. A.	Copenhagen	B
Spang-Thomsen, Mr. and Mrs. V.	Copenhagen	B

EAST AFRICA

The Association of Accountants in East Africa

Highwood, Mr. and Mrs. J. G.	Nairobi	Aa

FINLAND

K.H.T. – Yhdistys – Føreningen C.G.R.

Anttonen, Herr und Frau Jonne	Helsinki	B
Blomquist, Mr. and Mrs. Tyrgils	Vasa	B
Colliander, Mr. and Mrs. S.	Helsingfors	B
Forsström, Mr. and Mrs. B.	Helsinki	Aa
Grandell, Prof. und Frau Axel	Åbo	B
Hamberg, Mr. and Mrs. Gunnar	Helsingfors	B
Havu, Mr. and Mrs. Viljo	Helsinki	B
Idman, Mr. and Mrs. C. J.	Tampere	A
Kihlman, Svante	Helsingfors	A
Kumlander, T.	Helsingfors	B
Laxström, Mr. and Mrs. G.	Helsingfors/Drumsö	B
Lönnqvist, Mr. and Mrs. Uno	Helsingfors	A
Mellberg, Herr und Frau G.	Grankulla	B
Österman, Herr und Frau Bruno	Helsingfors	B
Steiner, Mr. and Mrs. G. L.	Fiskars	B
Usva, Mr. and Mrs. Erkki	Helsinki	A
Uunila, Mr. and Mrs. Bengt	Helsingfors	B

FRANCE

1 *Ordre National des Experts Comptables et Comptables Agréés*
2 *Chambre Nationale des Experts Comptables diplomés par l'Etat*
3 *Compagnie Nationale des Experts Comptables*
4 *Conseil National de la Comptabilité*
5 *Société de Comptabilité de France*
6 *Société des Experts Comptables Français*
7 *Union Professionnelle des Sociétés Fiduciaires d'Expertise Comptable*
8 *Compagnie des Chefs de Comptabilité*
9 *Fédération des Associations de Commissaires de Sociétés inscrits par les Cours d'Appel*

Archavlis, E.	Marseille	A	1
Auguste, M. et Mme. P. H. A. et fils	Bordeaux	A	2
Bérard, M. et Mme. Francis	Marseille	A	2
Beras, M. et Mme. R.	Nîmes-Gard	B	1
Bergeon, P.	Paris	A	3
Blois, M. et Mme. J. D.	Evreux	A	1
Boulogne, M. et Mme. M. et fils	Lixing-les-St. Avold	B	2
Brissaud, Jean	Paris	B	2
Butin, Mme. J. et Monsieur	Paris	B	1
Caudron, M. et Mme. J.	Saint-Quentin	A	2
Casiez, Mlle. M. L.	Paris	B	2
Corbin, M. et Mme. Charles	Alger	B	1
Cordoliani, Alfred	Paris	B	1

Coste, R.	Clermont-Ferrand	B 1
Danet, M. et Mme. René	Rouen	B 2
Dhyvert, M. et Mme. A.	St. Gratien	B 1
Duchesne, M. et Mme. Lucien R.	La Celle Saint-Cloud	Aa 5
Duchesne, Mlles. C. et M.		C
Durando, M. et Mme. M. E.	Paris	B 1
Fleury, M. et Mme. Jean	Paris	B 2
Gineste, M. et Mme. A.	Avignon	B 2
Goubaux, Jacques	Paris	B 1
Grévoul, M. et Mme. A.	Paris	A 5
Guillard, M. et Mme. R.	Toulouse	B 1
Guillard, Mlle. J.		C
Guillet, M. et Mme. H. F.	Grenoble	B 1
Debon, Mme. M.		C
Ripert, Mlle. D.		C
Herning, Alf. R.	Strasbourg	B 1
Houlez, M. et Mme. R.	Paris	Aa 8
Jaume, M. et Mme. L. B.	Paris	B 1
Juillard, M. et Mme. A.	St. Mandé	B 2
Laboissière, Pierre et Mlle. J. Dawkins	Nogent sur Marne	A 3
Lebreton, Marcel	Angers	A 1
Lievens, M. et Mme. J.	Paris	Aa 7
Loeb, M. et Mme. Paul	Paris	Aa 6
Marchand, M. et Mme. Bernard	Nogent sur Marne	B 1
Marinier, M. et Mme. A.	Paris	B 1
Maugras, M. et Mme. P.	Nîmes-Gard	B 1
Mazars, Robert	Rouen	A 6
Mégard, M. et Mme. M.	Lons le Saunier	A 3
Miller, Mme. A.	Paris	B 1
Mollier, M. et Mme. Paul	Besançon	B 1
Mollier, Mlle. J.		C
Montagner, M. et Mme. A. L. M.	Rouen	A 2
Mouret, M. et Mme. E.	Paris	B 1
Naudy, J. P.	Paris	B 2
Niquet, M. A. et Mlle. L.	Boulogne sur Seine	B 2
Mérienne, Mlle. R. G.		C
Noclain, M. et Mme. M.	Roubaix	B 1
Paquet, M. et Mme. Claude	Neuilly sur Seine	B 2
Poirier, M. et Mme. P.	Saint Avold	B 5
Porcher, M. et Mme. M.	Rueil	B 2
Poujol, M. et Mme. G. J. E.	Paris	Aa 4
Rateau, Mlle. J.	Cognac	B 2
Richard, F. M.	Paris	Aa 3
Rousseau, Julien	Lyon	B 1
Sacksteder, M. et Mme. Paul	Metz	B 2
Samson, M. et Mme. F.	Paris	Aa 2
Spanneut, M. et Mme. J.	Lille	B 2

Steiger, M. et Mme. A.	Strasbourg-Neuhof	B 5
Suire, Pierre	Casablanca (Maroc)	B 3
Vandriesse, Georges et Mme. R.		
Reuche-Vandriesse	Dyon – Côte d'Or	B 1
Veyrenc, M. et Mme. Albert	Montreuil	Aa 1, Aa 9
Veyrenc, Mlle. M.		C
Villeguerin, M. et Mme. J. de la	Paris	B 7

GHANA

Association of Accountants in Ghana

Hewson, Mr. and Mrs. D.A.W.	Accra	Aa

GERMANY

1 *Institut der Wirtschaftsprüfer in Deutschland e.V.*

2 *Bundesverband der vereidigten Buchprüfer*

Baier, Dr. und Frau Karl	Gelsenkirchen-Buer	B 1
Bauer, Herr und Frau Erwin	Pforzheim	B 2
Bengs, Dr. und Frau P.	Bad Homburg	A 1
Berg, Herr und Frau Karl	Düsseldorf	B 1
Berg, Frl. Ruth		C
Bredt, Dr. und Frau Otto	Hannover-Kleefeld	Aa 1
Busch, Friedrich C. J.	Hamburg	A 1
Dieterich, Dr. und Frau Wilhelm	Düsseldorf	A 1
Dietze, Herr und Frau Karl W. M.	Berlin-Wilmersdorf	A 2
Eickhoff, Herr und Frau J.	Hamm	B 2
Elmendorff, Herr und Frau W.	Düsseldorf	A 1
Engel, Herr und Frau W.	Frankfurt/Main	B 1
Ewald-Schroff, Frau M.	Berlin-Lichterfelde	B 2
Eyerich, Dr. und Frau H.	Mannheim	B 1
Fervers, Dr. und Frau Paul	Solingen-Ohligs	B 1
Gerhard, Herr und Frau Karl-Heinz	Stuttgart	B 2
Germann, Dr. und Frau H.	Hannover	B 1
Götze, Herr und Frau Hermann	Berlin-Charlottenburg	A 1
Graf, Herbert P. R.	Luebeck	B 1
Grah, Herr und Frau Walter	Düsseldorf	B 1
Günther, Dr. und Frau Hans	Bentheim	B 1
Heer, Herr und Frau Willem H. A. de	Köln-Lindenthal	B 1
Heiken, Herr und Frau H.	Essen	Aa 2
Herberger, Dr. und Frau H.	Konstanz	B 1
Hesse, Dr. und Frau Werner	Bünde	B 1
Hinst, Ernst und		
Pegels-Hinst, Frau K. M.	Duisburg	B 1
Hunscheidt, Dr. C. und Frl. B.	Aachen	B 2
Huppertz, Dr. und Frau Hubert	Köln-Braunsfeld	B 1
Ihne, Herr und Frau Willi	Grevenbrück	B 1
Ihne, Frl. R. und Herr W.		C
Jäger, Dr. A.	Hamburg	B 1

Jünger, Dr. und Frau Hans	Darmstadt	B	I
Heil-Jünger, Frau E.		C	
Kenntemich, Dr. und Frau Robert	Düsseldorf	B	I
Kilb, Herr und Frau Heinrich	Düsseldorf	B	I
Kneipel, Herr und Frau Paul L.	Wuppertal-Elberfeld	B	2
Knorr, Prof. Dr. und Frau E. R.	Köln	A	I
Kolsch, Herr und Frau Gerhard	Hannover	B	I
Kraus, W.	Coburg	B	I
Krieger, Dr. Otto	Stuttgart	B	2
Krönke, Herr und Frau Ludwig	Hamburg	A	2
Laan, Herr und Frau Walther van der	Hamburg	B	I
Lemme-Stohl, Frau Dr. Hertha	Berlin-Charlottenburg	B	2
Lieffering, Herr und Frau W. A.	Berlin-Wilmersdorf	B	2
Lipfert, Dr. und Frau F.	Stuttgart	A	I
Luettges, Dr. Karl-Heinz	Hamburg-Wandsbek	B	I
Lutwitzi, Dr. Karl	Pforzheim	B	I
Magnussen, Dr. und Frau J. P.	Mülheim/Ruhr	B	I
Matthiessen, Dr. und Frau H. P. W.	Hamburg	B	I
Mauve, Herr und Frau Hans	Gräfelfing vor München	A	I
Mauve, Frl. C.		C	
Meier, Dr. und Frau Albert	Frankfurt/Main	A	I
Merckens, Dr. und Frau Reinhold	Berlin-Dahlem	A	I
Merckle, Dr. und Frau Franz	Stuttgart-N.	A	I
Minz, Dr. und Frau Willy	Köln-Mariënburg	A	I
Moebis, Dr. und Frau R.	Düsseldorf	B	I
Mohren, Dr. und Frau Leo	München	B	I
Müller, Dr. und Frau Karl-Heinz	Gummersbach	B	I
Müller, Dr. und Frau Ludwig	Aschaffenburg	B	I
Fäth, Hans		C	
Nienheysen, Herr und Frau Leo	Essen/Ruhr	B	I
Ostrowski, Dr. Ulrich	Wiesbaden	B	I
Prümers, Herr und Frau R.	Burgsteinfurt	B	2
Prüsener, Herr und Frau H.	Stuttgart	B	I
Rätsch, Herr und Frau Herbert	Düsseldorf	A	I
Rätsch, Claus P.		C	
Reiszmann, Herr und Frau Karl	Stuttgart	B	2
Remmlinger, F.	Stuttgart-Hofen	B	I
Rentrop, Dr. und Frau Siegfried	Köln	B	I
Robens, Dr. Hans	Köln	B	I
Ronneberger, Herr und Frau R.	Düsseldorf-Oberkassel	B	I
Röver, Frau Dr. Maria und Herr H. L.	Berlin-Schlachtensee	B	I
Runte, Dr. und Frau Theo	Essen/Ruhr	B	I
Schiffmann, Dr. und Frau W.	München	B	I
Schmid, Herr und Frau Richard	Stuttgart	A	2
Schmidtberg, Frau Dr. Mia	Solingen-Ohligs	B	I
Schneider, Herr und Frau Karl	Hannover	B	I
Schneider, Dr. und Frau Karl	Düsseldorf	B	I

Scholich, Herr und Frau L.	Düsseldorf	B 1
Scholich, Roland		C
Schubert, Dr. und Frau Hans Theodor	Hannover	A 1
Schultheis, Dr. und Frau Helmuth	Bad Wildungen	B 1
Schulz, Dr. und Frau C. E.	Düsseldorf	B 1
Schumacher, Dr. und Frau W.	Münster	A 1
Schumacher, Dr. Hans Jürgen		C
Schürer, Herr und Frau K. K.	Coburg	B 1
Schwarz, Dr. und Frau Max	München	A 1
Steffen, Herr und Frau R.	Braunschweig	B 2
Steinrücke, Herr und Frau A.	Hamburg	B 1
Strack, Herr und Frau Wilhelm	Krefeld	B 1
Strathus, Herr und Frau Max	Hamburg	A 1
Ullmann, Herr und Frau H.	Berlin-Grünewald	B 1
Volkmer, Herr und Frau Bruno	Karlsruhe	B 1
Voors, Herr und Frau Willem	Hamburg-Nienstedten	B 1
Warth, Karl	Düsseldorf	B 1
Weickert, Herr und Frau Hans	Faurndau-Göppingen	B 1
Winker, Herr und Frau Paul	Frankfurt/Main	A 2
Wöhl, Dr. Kurt	Hannover	B 1
Wollert, Dr. und Frau Heinrich A.	Düsseldorf	A 1
Zachow, Herr und Frau Erich	Berlin-Spandau	B 2

GREAT BRITAIN AND IRELAND

1 *The Institute of Chartered Accountants of Scotland*
2 *The Institute of Chartered Accountants in England and Wales*
3 *The Society of Incorporated Accountants*
4 *The Institute of Chartered Accountants in Ireland*
5 *The Association of Certified and Corporate Accountants*
6 *The Institute of Municipal Treasurers and Accountants*
7 *The Institute of Cost and Works Accountants*

Adams, H. A.	London	B 2
Adams, Mr. and Mrs. R.	London	A 1
Adams, Mr. and Mrs. W. G.	South Croydon	B 3
Allsop, Mr. and Mrs. F. J.	Wolverhampton	B 2
Allsop, Mr. and Mrs. H. P.	Birmingham	B 2
Amor, Mrs. W.	London	A 2
Archbold, Mr. and Mrs. Roger	Edinburgh	B 1
Armstrong, Mr. and Mrs. P. Livingstone	London	B 2
Armstrong, Miss Rosemary		C
Atkinson, Mr. and Mrs. W. O.	London	Aa 6
Bailey, Wilfrid	London	B 6
Baird, James	Belfast	B 3
Baldry, Edward	London	A 3
Bannon, Mr. and Mrs. John William	Dublin	B 5
Barrowcliff, Mr. and Mrs. Ch. P.	Biddlesbrough	A 3
Barrows, P. W.	Birmingham	B 2

Barrows, Mr. and Mrs. W. L.	Birmingham	A 2
Barsham, Mr. and Mrs. A. J.	London	B 2
Baskin, R. S.	Dublin	B 3
Bateman, Mr. and Mrs. R. D. R.	Burton upon Trent	B 2
Baynes, Mr. and Mrs. T. A. Hamilton	Birmingham	A 2
Bedford, R.	York	B 2
Bennett, Mr. and Mrs. C. J. M.	London	B 2
Benson, Mr. and Mrs. H. A.	London	A 2
Berger, Mr. and Mrs. Stanley J. D.	London	A 7
Biddle, Mr. and Mrs. Kenneth B.	Bournemouth	B 2
Bird, Mr. and Mrs. H. G.	Sheffield	B 5
Blumer, Mr. and Mrs. J. C.	Purley	B 2
Body, J. F.	Nr. Sheffield	B 2
Bond, Mr. and Mrs. Thomas James	London	B 2
Borsay, Mr. and Mrs. James	Sale	Aa 7
Bostock, Mr. and Mrs. Christopher	London	B 2
Bottomly, Mr. and Mrs. A.	London	B 2
Bracher, Mr. and Mrs. J. Charles	Highnam	B 2
Bray, A. J.	London	B 2
Brown, Mr. and Mrs. H.	Rochester	B 6
Brown, Mr. and Mrs. J. G.	Kilmarnock	B 1
Brown, Mr. and Mrs. N. S.	Glasgow	B 1
Browning, R.	Glasgow	A 1
Bundy, Mr. and Mrs. A.	Glamorgan	A 5
Burgess, Miss M. R.	Radlett	B 2
Burn, Mr. and Mrs. William A.	London	B 2
Burton, Miss V. M. and Larking, Mrs. A. H.	Bedford	B 2
Callaby, F. A.	London	A 5
Callan, Mr. and Mrs. Paul	Dublin	B 5
Cameron, Mr. and Mrs. D. I.	Edinburgh	B 1
Campbell, Mr. and Mrs. H. K.	Nr. Bristol	B 2
Campbell, Miss S. A. and Master J. O.		C
Carnelley, Mr. and Mrs. William Edmund	London	B 2
Carpenter, Mr. and Mrs. Percy F.	London	A 2
Carrington, Mr. and Mrs. W. S.	London	A 2
Carroll, Mr. and Mrs. E. J.	Dublin	B 2
Cemach, Mr. and Mrs. H. Paul	London	B 2
Channon, Mr. and Mrs. Eric H.	Woodford Green	B 2
Cherry, Mr. and Mrs. G. A.	London	B 2
Cheyney, Mr. and Mrs. L. F.	London	A 6
Church, Mr. and Mrs. A. G.	London	B 2
Clark, Mr. and Mrs. J. B. L.	Northwood	B 2
Clark, Miss S. J.	London	B 2
Clarke, Mr. and Mrs. Douglas A.	London	A 2
Cole, Mr. and Mrs. D. Davey	Birmingham	B 2

Cooksey, Mr. and Mrs. I. D. C.	Innerleithen	B 7
Cooper, Mr. and Mrs. G. M.	Glenfield	B 2
Covington, Mr. and Mrs. R. W.	London	B 2
Crafter, Mr. and Mrs. W. J.	Loughton	A 3
Craig, Mr. and Mrs. I. A. F.	London	A 3
Crane, Mr. and Mrs. G. F.	London	B 1
Crawford, Mr. and Mrs. R. Norman	Belfast	B 4
Crawshaw, Mr. and Mrs. J. S.	Enugu (Nigeria)	B 2
Crowe, Mr. and Mrs. F. X.	Rome (Italy)	B 5
Cusworth, Mr. and Mrs. G. E.	Frankfurt /Main (Germany)	B 2
David, Mr. and Mrs. L. C.	Paris (France)	B 2
Deeker, Mr. and Mrs. H. A.	London	B 2
Densem, Mr. and Mrs. W. G.	London	A 2
Dessauer, Mr. and Mrs. K. J.	London	B 2
Dixon, Mr. and Mrs. R. B.	Birmingham	B 2
Dobson, Mr. and Mrs. Peter H.	Leeds	B 2
Dowling, Mr. and Mrs. James T.	Glasgow	Aa 1
Downing, Mr. and Mrs. F.	Sheffield	B 2
Drysdale, Mr. and Mrs. A. M.	Buenos Aires (Argentine)	B 2
Dunlop, R. L.	London	B 2
Dunn, Mr. and Mrs. J. B.	Altrincham	B 2
Dunn, Mr. and Mrs. P. H.	London	B 3
DuPré, Mr. and Mrs. Derek	London	A 7
Durnin, Mr. and Mrs. John C.	Kew Gardens	B 2
Earley, Mr. and Mrs. W. P.	The Hague (Holland)	B 2
Eaton, Desmond T.	Waltham Cross	B 2
Eden, Mr. and Mrs. H. A.	Langley	B 7
Edgcumbe, Mr. and Mrs. Stanley J. P.	Plymouth	B 2
Edgcumbe, Miss C.		C
Edney, Mr. and Mrs. George	Sutton	B 6
Edwards, Harold	London	B 2
Edwards, Mr. and Mrs. W. F.	London	A 3
Elliott, Mr. and Mrs. M. C.	London	B 6
Elliott, Mrs. L., Miss G., Master R.		C
Elmitt, Mr. and Mrs. Sidney	Reading	B 6
English, Mr. and Mrs. A. R.	Woodford Green	B 2
Esslemont, Mr. and Mrs. G. B.	Glasgow	B 6
Eva, Mr. and Mrs. W. F.	Pinner	B 1
Fielder, Mr. and Mrs. L.	London	B 1
Flint, D.	Glasgow	B 1
Foster, Mr. and Mrs. D. U.	Sheffield	B 2
Fox, Miss Margaret	London	B 2
Freeborn, Mr. and Mrs. Norman	Nr. Leeds	B 2
Freeman, Mr. and Mrs. J. McD.	Newbury	B 2
Freeman, Mr. and Mrs. S.	London	B 2

French, William I.	Glasgow	A	1
Gilbert, Mr. and Mrs. Michael John	Beckenham	B	2
Glendinning, Mr. and Mrs. R. and daughters	Beaconsfield	A	7
Gold, Mr. and Mrs. Robert	London	B	2
Goult, Mr. and Mrs. Garfield G.	Ipswich	B	2
Granger, Mr. and Mrs. P. F.	Nottingham	A	2
Grant, Robert	Bagdad (Iraq)	B	2
Gray, Mr. and Mrs. W. Macfarlane	Stirling	A	5
Greaves, J. F.	Brussels (Belgium)	B	2
Green, Mr. and Mrs. J. Donald	London	B	2
Griffiths, Mr. and Mrs. C. W.	Keston Park	B	2
Griffiths, Mr. and Mrs. F. C.	Nr. Chaltenham	B	2
Guilbride, Mr. and Mrs. F. P.	Dublin	B	4
Halliday, Mr. and Mrs. H. E.	Newport	B	2
Harris, J. E. and Miss E.	London	A	5
Harrison, Mr. and Mrs. Herbert	Chingford	B	6
Hawkins, Mr. and Mrs. P. F.	London	B	2
Hayden, Mr. and Mrs. Leslie	London	B	2
Hayes, Mr. and Mrs. H. R.	Thelwall via Warrington	B	2
Hayhow, Mr. and Mrs. Henry	London	B	6
Hayhurst, Mr. and Mrs. W.	London	B	6
Hayward, Mr. and Mrs. E. J.	Northampton	B	6
Heywood, Mr. and Mrs. G. W.	Exeter	B	2
Hill, Mr. and Mrs. J. M.	London	B	2
Hiscocks, Mr. and Mrs. Frank	Liverpool	B	2
Hodgins, Mr. and Mrs. L. T.	London	B	1
Hodgson, Mr. and Mrs. H.	London	B	2
Horne, Mr. and Mrs. O. W.	Portsmouth	B	2
Horsfall, Mr. and Mrs. W. T.	Liverpool	B	2
Hough, Mr. and Mrs. J. W.	London	B	6
Houghton, D. S.	Dar es Salaam (Tanganyika)	B	1
House, Mr. and Mrs. D. V.	London	A	2
Howitt, Sir Harold and Lady	London	A	2
Hussey, Mr. and Mrs. A. V.	London	A	3
Hutton, C. I. R.	London	A	1
Jackson, Mr. and Mrs. P. M.	Perth	A	1
Jackson, Mr. and Mrs. W.	Bearsden	B	5
Jeffreys, Mr. and Mrs. T. W.	Cardiff	B	3
Johnston, Mr. and Mrs. R. C.	Birkenhead	B	2
Jones, Mr. and Mrs. J. D. R.	Newport	A	3
Keeble, Mr. and Mrs. R. ML.	Ipswich	B	5
Keeling, Mr. and Mrs. G.	Styal	B	5
King, H. R. and Newmarch, Miss N.	Beckenham	B	5
Kirkham, Mr. and Mrs. H. and son	Manchester	B	7

Kitchen, Mr. and Mrs. Stanley	Birmingham	B 2
Klingner, Mr. and Mrs. G. Francis	Dublin	Aa 4
Latham, Mr. and Mrs. J. C.	London	A 5
Latham, Lord and Lady	Maide Vale	A 5
Lawson, Mr. and Mrs. W. H.	London	Aa 2
Leech, Mr. and Mrs. R. B.	Coventry	A 2
Leitch, Mr. and Mrs. J. R.	London	B 1
LeMaistre, Mr. and Mrs. J. V.	London	B 2
Leppard, Mr. and Mrs. A. H.	London	B 2
Little, Leo T.	London	A 3
Loryman, Mr. and Mrs. L. W.	Dorking	B 5
Loryman, Miss D.		C
MacCormac, Mr. and Mrs. M. F.	Dublin	B 5
MacDonald, Mr. and Mrs. E. N.	Liverpool	B 2
MacIver, Mr. and Mrs. Alan S.	London	A 2
Mac Mahon, J. G. J.	Wembley Park	B 5
MacTaggart, Mr. and Mrs. Hugh	Edinburgh	B 1
Mair, G.	London	B 5
Makin, Mr. and Mrs. S.	Nr. Amersham	B 2
Makin, Miss		C
Maples, Mr. and Mrs. C. J.	Groombridge	B 2
Marshall, Mr. and Mrs. R. Ian	Edinburgh	A 1
Mathias, Mr. and Mrs. Noel J.	Jamshedpur (India)	B 2
Matthews, Mr. and Mrs. R. P.	London	B 2
McDonald, Mr. and Mrs. H.	Birmingham	B 2
McDougall, Mr. and Mrs. E. H. V.	Edinburgh	A 1
McHaffie, Mr. and Mrs. A. N. E.	London	A 1
McKelvey, Mr. and Mrs. D. A.	Bolton	B 2
McMillan, Mr. and Mrs. E. D.	London	B 2
McNeil, Mr. and Mrs. R.	Hove	A 2
Mead, Mr. and Mrs. B. K.	Kenilworth	B 3
Meynell, Mr. and Mrs. A. C. S.	London	Aa 5
Middleton, Mr. and Mrs. W. R.	London	B 2
Millar, T. Ford	London	B 1
Miller, Miss D. H.	London	B 2
Mills, Mr. and Mrs. L. V.	London	B 2
Milstone, D. M.	Wembley Park	B 2
Montgomery, Mr. and Mrs. J. K.	Belfast	B 4
Morgan-Jones, Mr. and Mrs. G. P.	Eastbourne	A 2
Morris, Mr. and Mrs. G. F.	Chester	B 3
Morse, Mr. and Mrs. Dudley	London	B 2
Muir, Mr. and Mrs. G. David	Compton	B 2
Murison, Mr. and Mrs. A. B. L.	London	B 2
Nathan, Mr. and Mrs. C. H.	London	B 2
Nelson, Mr. and Mrs. Bertram	Liverpool	A 3
Newell, Mr. and Mrs. A. E.	Bridgend	B 6
Newhouse, Kenneth Theodore	London	B 2

Nicholson, Mr. and Mrs. Ernest	Nr. Warrington	B	2
Nicholson, Mr. and Mrs. George	Stoke on Trent	A	7
Nicholson, Mr. and Mrs. Robert G.	London	B	1
Nicol, Mr. and Mrs. James A.	Hatch End	B	2
Calder, Miss M. D.		C	
Norman, Mr. and Mrs. L. H.	London	B	2
O'Brien, Mr. and Mrs. G. W.	Dublin	B	4
Oldfield, Mr. and Mrs. G.	Norwich	B	2
Orr, Mr. and Mrs. W. S.	Dublin	B	4
Osbourn, F. Cameron	London	A	5
Padgham, Mr. and Mrs. F. N.	Jersey (Channel Islands)	A	3
Parker, Mr. and Mrs. A. R.	Manchester	B	2
Payne, Mr. and Mrs. A. T.	Smethwick	B	2
Payne, Master J. T.		C	
Neale, Mrs. H. and Master G.		C	
Peacock, Mr. and Mrs. F. G.	London	B	2
Pears, Mr. and Mrs. S. John	London	A	2
Penfold, Mr. and Mrs. W.	Beckenham	B	2
Perry, Mr. and Mrs. V. F.	Bedford	B	2
Peyton, Mr. and Mrs. C. J.	Nantwich	B	2
Peyton, Miss V. K.		C	
Pollard, Mr. and Mrs. C. H.	Kingston upon Hull	B	6
Powell, Mr. and Mrs. T. R.	Belfast	A	5
Pratley, Mr. and Mrs. L. J.	London	B	2
Pratt, Mr. and Mrs. D. W.	Dublin	B	4
Procter, Mr. and Mrs. Leslie	Rossendale	B	5
Rainey, Miss B. I.	London	B	2
Ramus, E.	London	B	2
Ravenhill, Mr. and Mrs. A. P.	London	B	2
Rawlins, Mr. and Mrs. Richard C. C.	London	B	2
Rayner, Mr. and Mrs. Albert	Leeds	B	2
Reisler, Mr. and Mrs. Leo H.	Isleworth	B	2
Richardson, Mr. and Mrs. J. P. C.	London	B	2
Ridgway, Miss Phyllis E. M. and Newsome, Mrs.	Hull	A	3
Ritchie, Mr. and Mrs. W. R. S.	London	B	1
Roberts, Miss Joan R.	Welling	B	2
Roberts, P. V.	Bristol	A	2
Robinson, H. W.	Dublin	B	4
Robinson, Mr. and Mrs. P. H.	Manchester	B	2
Robson, Mr. and Mrs. Lawrence W.	North Woodstock	A	2
Robson, Sir Thomas B. and Lady	London	A	2
Ronson, Mr. and Mrs. George	Rangoon (Burma)	B	2
Russell, E. S.	Birmingham	B	2
Russell, Mr. and Mrs. John D.	London	B	2
Russell, Mr. and Mrs. W. G. A.	Birmingham	A	3
Sadd, Mr. and Mrs. M. J. G.	London	B	2

Sainer, Mr. and Mrs. H.	London	B	2
Sarson, Mr. and Mrs. A. Wilfred	London	B	2
Saunders, Mr. and Mrs. G. F.	Liverpool	A	2
Scott, Mr. and Mrs. Alec G.	London	B	2
Scott, Miss Elisabeth		C	
Scott, Mr. and Mrs. A. G. W.	Surbiton	B	2
Shepherd, Mr. and Mrs. Edgar T.	Cardiff	B	2
Shepherd, Gilbert D.	Cardiff	A	2
Sillem, Mr. and Mrs. S. G.	London	B	2
Sim, Mr. and Mrs. K. G.	Caerleon	B	3
Simpson, Mr. and Mrs. Ronald	Leeds	B	3
Singer, Mr. and Mrs, A. E.	London	B	5
Sinnott, Mr. and Mrs. Ernest	Hove	A	6
Small, Mr. and Mrs. M. W.	Lagos (Nigeria)	B	2
Smallpeice, Basil	Hounslow	A	2
Smith, Miss E. M. and Charles, Miss J.	London	B	2
Smith, Mr. and Mrs. R. T.	Rhyl	B	2
Smith, Miss A. Louise and Andrew		C	
Smith, Mr. and Mrs. R. W.	Maidstone	B	2
Solomons, Prof. and Mrs. D.	Bristol	B	2
Spence, Joseph	London	B	2
Spencer, Mr. and Mrs. Edgar	Notts	A	5
Spencer, G. A.	Bramhall	B	2
Sproull Senr., Mr. and Mrs. Robert	London	B	1
Statham, Mr. and Mrs. Reginald	New Castle	B	5
Statham, Miss H. Z.		C	
Steele, Robert A. and Miss Barbara	Grimsby	B	2
Stepto, W. E.	Bristol	A	5
Stevenson, Mr. and Mrs. J. L.	Sutton	B	2
Stewart, Mr. and Mrs. Jas. C.	Glasgow	A	1
Stott, Alistair J.	Bethlehem P. A. (U.S.A.)	B	1
Strachan, Chas. M. and Maxwell-Melville, Mrs. E.	Hull	A	2
Summerscale, Mr. and Mrs. N. T.	Paris (France)	B	2
Sumner, Mr. and Mrs. R. F.	London	B	2
Tabaxman, S. B.	London	B	2
Taffs, Mr. and Mrs. A. F.	Thames Ditton	B	3
Tanfield, Mr. and Mrs. D. E. T.	Brierley Hill	B	2
Taylor, Mr. and Mrs. Ronald R.	Kamarhati (India)	B	7
Taylor, Mr. and Mrs. William C.	Edinburgh	B	1
Tems, Mr. and Mrs. J. S.	Abingdon	B	2
Tester, Mr. and Mrs. R.	Otford	B	1
Tetley, Mr. and Mrs. F.	Leeds	B	2
Thomason, Mr. and Mrs. R. E.	Coventry	B	7
Thomason, Miss A.		C	
Thomson, Mr. and Mrs. T. Hunter	Edinburgh	B	1

Tollit, O. T.	Chester	B 2
Troy, James and Miss E.	Dublin	B 4
Trump, Mr. and Mrs. T. H.	Cardiff	B 3
Unthank, Mr. and Mrs. A. C.	London	B 2
Valentine, Mr. and Mrs. J. R. M.	Chalfont St. Giles	B 1
Veysey, Mr. and Mrs. F. H.	Birkenhead	B 2
Vieyra, S. J.	Johannesburg (S. Africa)	A 7
Waldron, Mr. and Mrs. E. J.	Southampton	B 3
Walker, Mr. and Mrs. Alex D.	Liverpool	A 2
Walker, J. C.	Nr. Newdigate	B 2
Waller, R.	Paris (France)	B 2
Warmington, Cyril Bernard	Nr. Maidstone	B 2
Watson, Mr. and Mrs. D. McC.	Dublin	B 4
Webb, Mr. and Mrs. Arthur E.	London	personal
Welsford, Mr. and Mrs. P. A.	London	B 2
White, Miss Patricia B.	Coulsdon	B 2
Whitton, Mr. and Mrs. James	Glasgow	A 1
Wilkins, Mr. and Mrs. S. P.	London	B 2
Wilkinson, F. M.	London	A 2
Wilson, Mr. and Mrs. J. P.	Kenilworth	A 7
Windle, Peter	Birmingham	B 2
Winter, Mr. and Mrs. D.	London	B 2
Winterbottom, Mr. and Mrs. E.	Altrincham	B 2
Withnall, G.	Birmingham	B 2
Worrall, Mr. and Mrs. J. O.	Liverpool	B 3
Wright, Mrs. Elizabeth M.	Codicote	B 2
Wright, F. Th.	Codicote	B 2
Yeabsley, Sir Richard and Lady	London	Aa 3

INDIA

1 *The Institute of Chartered Accountants of India*
2 *The Institute of Cost and Works Accountants*

Chopra, Suraj Prakash	New Delhi	Aa 1
Desai, Shantanu Nanubhai	Bombay	B 1
Mody, Mr. and Mrs. Naval R.	Bombay	Aa 2, A 1
Puri, Mohinder Pal	New Delhi	B 1
Sahgal, A. L.	New Delhi	A 1
Sambiah, P.	Bangalore	B 1
Srinivasan, E. V.	New Delhi	B 1
Venkatesan, Mr. and Mrs. R.	Madras	B 1

ISRAEL

Association of Certified Public Accountants in Israel

Goldsmith, L. E.	Tel-Aviv	B
Proshan, S.	Tel-Aviv	A
Rojansky, Dr. A. R.	Tel-Aviv	Aa

ITALY

1 *Consiglio Nazionale dei Ragionieri e Periti Commerciali*
2 *Consiglio Nazionale dei Dottori Commercialisti*

Arrighi, M. et Mme. Alfredo	Florence	B 1
Arrighi, Mlle. Albertina		C
Borelli, M. et Mme. Mario	Turin	B 1
Denari, P.	Voghera	B 1
Marcantonio, Arnaldo	Roma	B 2
Palamara, M. et Mme. A.	Milano	B 1
Sensini, Prof. et Mme. Giovanni	Firenze	Aa 1
Zantonelli, A.	Monza	B 1

JAPAN

1 *Shadan Hojin Nippon Konin Kaikeishi Kyokai*
2 *Shadan Hojin Nihon Keirishi Kyokai*
3 *Nippon Kaikeijin Renmei*

Aizaki, Kenji	Tokyo	personal
Harada, T.	Tokyo	B 2
Katoh, S.	Tokyo	Aa 2
Kawakita, R.	Tokyo	B 2
Kurosawa, Prof. K.	Yokohama	Aa 1
Natake, M.	Tokyo	B 1
Ohyama, J.	Tokyo	A 2
Yamamoto, Y.	Tokyo	B 1

LUXEMBURG

Ordre des Experts Comptables Luxembourgeois

Faber, F.	Luxembourg	A
Gerbès, R.	Luxembourg	Aa

MALTA

The Malta Institute of Accountants

Busuttil, Mr. and Mrs. Paul	Sliema	Aa
Vincenti, Mrs. M.		C

MEXICO

Instituto Mexicano de Contadores Publicos

Alatriste Jr., Mr. and Mrs. Sealtiel	Mexico D.F.	A
Cárdenas C, Ramón	Monterrey	B
Carrasco, Alfonso G.	Mexico D.F.	B
Casas-Alatriste, Mr. and Mrs. Roberto	Mexico D.F.	Aa
Casas-Alatriste H., Mr. and Mrs. Rogerio	Mexico D.F.	B
Castillo-Miranda, Mr. and Mrs. Wilfrido	Mexico D.F.	B

Garza, Mr. and Mrs. Daniel de la	Monterrey	B
Marrón González, Mr. and Mrs. Manuel	Mexico D.F.	B
Mora Montes, Ricardo	Mexico D.F.	B
Pineda Léon, Rafael	Lomas de Sotelo D.F.	B
Rioseco, Mr. and Mrs. Federico	Mexico D.F.	B
Roldán Román, Mrs. Dolora and		
Roldán, J. Hoyos,	Mexico D.F.	B
Cortes, E. and son		C
Román Almonte, Refugio	Mexico D.F.	B
Tovar Y Córdova, Mr. and Mrs. Manuel	Mexico D.F.	B

MONACO

Ordre des Experts Comptables de la Principauté de Monaco

Mascarel, M. et Mme. F.	Monte-Carlo	Aa

NEW ZEALAND

1 *New Zealand Society of Accountants*
2 *Incorporated Institute of Accountants of New Zealand*

Campion, Miss Diana	Levin	B 1
Coburn, R. H.	Christchurch	B 1
Davies, Mr. and Mrs. G. H. Lloyd	Wellington	Aa 1, Aa 2
Frethey, A. R.	London (England)	B 1
Gibbs, Mr. and Mrs. H. M.	Glasgow (Scotland)	B 1
Macaulay, P. U.	Invercarhill	B 1
Starke, Mr. and Mrs. Lawrence J. R.	Wellington	B 1
Stewart, Mr. and Mrs. Gordon D.	Wellington	A 1, A 2
Wilson, Mr. and Mrs. B. D.	London (England)	A 2

NORWAY

Norges Statsautoriserte Revisorers Forening

Bache-Wiig, Mr. and Mrs. K. F.	Sandvika	B
Braende, Mr. and Mrs. Helge	Oslo	A
Carlsen, Mr. and Mrs. Alf R.	Oslo	A
Carlson, Erik	Oslo	B
Corneliussen, Mr. and Mrs. Otto	Oslo	B
Ekevik, Mr. and Mrs. Odd	Oslo	B
Endresen, Mr. and Mrs. Karl-Johan	Stavanger	B
Eng, Mr. and Mrs. Asbjörn	Oslo	B
Fostvedt, Mr. and Mrs. A.	Bergen	B
Klingenberg Knudsen, Miss M.		C
Glomstein, Mr. and Mrs. A.	Oslo	Aa
Gran, Torstein and Miss M.	Oslo	B
Haegstad, Mr. and Mrs. Gunnar	Oslo	B
Ildal, Mr. and Mrs. Olav	Oslo	B
Ingebrethsen, Mr. and Mrs. Odd	Oslo	B
Kittelsen, Mr. and Mrs. J. A.	Oslo	A

Kjeldsberg, Mr. and Mrs. Th.	Oslo	A
Klette, Mr. and Mrs. R. M.	Stavanger	B
Klyve, Mr. and Mrs. Carl	Oslo	B
Kvalstadt, Mr. and Mrs. A.	Bergen	B
Lodding, Mr. and Mrs. Kåre B.	Oslo	B
Lorentzen-Styr, Mr. and Mrs. F.	Oslo	B
Minken, Mr. and Mrs. B.	Oslo	B
Nordli, Mr. and Mrs. Einar	Oslo	B
Rieker, Mr. and Mrs. Louis	Oslo	B
Rosef, Mr. and Mrs. Jens	Oslo	B
Rosenlind, Mr. and Mrs. Fridtjov E.	Oslo	B
Skreen, Herr und Frau O.	Trondheim	B
Steffensrud, Mr. and Mrs. Karl	Oslo	B
Thorbjörnsen, Mr. and Mrs. Johan	Oslo	B
Treider, Herr und Frau Jacob	Oslo	B
Wulff-Pedersen, Mr. and Mrs. Emil	Oslo	B

PAKISTAN

Pakistan Council of Accountancy

Hussein Chaudhury, Mr. and Mrs. M.	Lahore	A
Jan, Mr. and Mrs. Rahim	Lahore	Aa
Masood, S. M.	Lahore	A

PHILIPPINES

Philippine Institute of Accountants

Velayo, Alfredo M.	Manila	Aa

RHODESIA

1 *The Rhodesia Society of Accountants*
2 *The Northern Rhodesia Association of Accountants*

Farmer, Mr. and Mrs. R. E.	Ndola	Aa 2
O'Connell, Mr. and Mrs. B. W. S.	Salisbury	Aa 1

SOUTH AFRICA

1 *The Transvaal Society of Accountants*
2 *Cape Society of Accountants and Auditors*
3 *The Institute of Municipal Treasurers and Accountants*

Chambers, Mr. and Mrs. R. D.	London	B 3
Charles, Mr. and Mrs. J. B.	Johannesburg	B 1
Danks, Mr. and Mrs. W. B.	Johannesburg	B 1
Greenwood, Prof. and Mrs. H.	Cape Town	Aa 2
Holmes, Dr. I. Q.	Johannesburg	Aa 3
Read, Mr. and Mrs. E. J.	Johannesburg	B 1
Rissik, A. G.	London (England)	B 1
Stuart, Mr. and Mrs. C. M.	Johannesburg	A 1
Wimble, Prof. and Mrs. B. J. S.	Johannesburg	Aa 1

SPAIN

1 *Colegio Oficial de Titulares Mercantiles de Madrid*
2 *Ilustre Colegio Oficial de Titulares Mercantiles de Barcelona*

Boter y Mauri, Dr. Fernando	Barcelona	Aa 2
Buira Rovira, Juan	Barcelona	B 2
Diaz Martin, M. et Mme. L.	Madrid	Aa 1
Garcia Cairo, M. et Mme. Robert	Barcelona	B 2
Lopez Dominguez, M. et Mme. F.	Zaragoza	personal
Martinez-Comin, M. et Mme. Antoin	Barcelona	B 2

SWEDEN

1 *Foreningen Auktoriserade Revisorer*
2 *Svenska Revisorsamfundet*

Ahrén, Mr. and Mrs. Claes E.	Göteborg	A 1
Andersson, Mr. and Mrs. C. S.	Helsingborg	B 1
Barkland, Mr. and Mrs. Olof	Stockholm	B 2
Björfors, Mr. and Mrs. G.	Bromma	Aa 2
Björner, Mr. and Mrs. T.	Stockholm	B 1
Brantberg, Mr. and Mrs. Inge	Malmö	B 1
Cassel, Mr. and Mrs. Ö.	Stockholm	A 1
Danielson, Mr. and Mrs. Stig	Göteborg	B 1
Elinder, Mr. and Mrs. Rickard	Stockholm	B 1
Fritzdorf, Mr. and Mrs. Tore	Stockholm	B 1
Hafström, Mr. and Mrs. S.	Bromma	A 2
Henckel, Mr. and Mrs. T. G.	Stockholm	B 1
Höjeberg, Mr. and Mrs. O.	Stockholm	B 1
Hultgren, Mr. and Mrs. B.	Göteborg	B 1
Jonsson, Mr. and Mrs. Bertil	Stockholm	B 1
Karlgren, Mr. and Mrs. Nils	Göteborg	B 1
Kollén, Mr. and Mrs. Ingvar	Bromma	B 1
Löfgren, Mr. and Mrs. Sigurd	Bromma	B 1
Nelson, Sten	Stockholm	Aa 1
Nordenham, Mr. and Mrs. F.	Göteborg	B 1
Orreby, Mr. and Mrs. Eric V.	Stockholm	A 1
Rilby, Mr. and Mrs. Nils	Göteborg	B 1
Rohlin, Mr. and Mrs. Sven-Rune	Göteborg	B 1
Samuelsson, Mr. and Mrs. S.	Malmö	B 1
Samuelsson, Miss M. and Master B.		C
Stenberg, Mr. and Mrs. Sten	Stockholm	B 1
Svensson, Mr. and Mrs. B.	Stocksund	B 1
Thorée, Herr und Frau Elis	Arvika	B 2
Westberg, Mr. and Mrs. Bertil	Halmstad	B 1
Wisén, Mr. and Mrs. S. O.	Stockholm	B 1
Witt, Mr. and Mrs. C. H.	Stockholm	A 1

SWITZERLAND

1 *Schweizerische Kammer für Revisionswesen*
2 *Verband Schweizerischer Bücherexperten*
3 *Vereinigung Schweizerischer Treuhand- und Revisionsgesellschaften*

Bossard, Dr. E.	Zürich	A 2
Dober, Dr. W.	Aarau	B 2
Dreyfus, M. et Mme. M. Georges	Lausanne	B 2
Fahrni-Lenz, M. et Mme. A. R.	Biel-Bienne	B 2
Hoessli, M.	Küssnacht	A 2
Hofmann, Dr. und Frau H.	Zollikon-Zürich	Aa 3
Honold, Herr und Frau A.	Zürich	A 2
Käfer, Prof. Dr. und Frau Karl	Zürich	A 2
Muggli, Herr und Frau Emil	Solothurn	Aa 1
Rognon, M. et Mme. P.	Neuchâtel	B 2
Ruetschi, W.	Zürich	B 2
Santschi, R.	Bern	B 2
Viel, Dr. und Frau Jakob	Zürich	Aa 2, A 1
Weisser, Herr und Frau O. M.	Zürich	B 2
Wohlers, M. et Mme. Ed. G.	Genève	B 2
Zweifel, Herr und Frau J. J.	Zürich	B 2

THAILAND

The Association of Certified Accountants of Thailand

Buranasombati, Mr. and Mrs. Leck	Bangkok	Aa

TRINIDAD AND TOBAGO

The Association of Chartered Accountants in Trinidad and Tobago

Hort, Mr. and Mrs. T. Jeffrey	Port of Spain	Aa

TURKEY

Ferman, Dr. Cumhur	Ankara	personal
Oluç, Mehmet	Istanbul	personal
Sihay, Mrs. Jale	Ankara	personal

UNITED STATES OF AMERICA

1 *American Institute of Certified Public Accountants and State Societies*
2 *National Association of Accountants*
3 *The Institute of Internal Auditors*
4 *American Accounting Association*
5 *Controllers Institute of America*

Addison, Mr. and Mrs. James	Des Moines	B 1
Ameryckx, A.	La Celle St. Cloud (France)	B 3
Anthony, Prof. and Mrs. Robert N.	Boston	B 2
Bachrach, Mr. and Mrs. Michael	Pittsburgh	A 1
Bailey, Geo. D.	Detroit	A 1

Bartle, Mr. and Mrs. W. O.	Houston	B 1
Barton, Mr. and Mrs. Meyer	New Orleans	B 1
Barton, Miss Gay		C
Batzer, R. Kirk	New York	A 1
Bennett, Mr. and Mrs. Clinton W.	Winchester	B 2
Bevis, Mr. and Mrs. Donald J.	Detroit	A 1
Troost, Mrs. Louise		C
Blough, Carman G.	New York	A 1
Bock, Mr. and Mrs. Russell S.	Los Angeles	A 1
Boland, Mr. and Mrs. R. G. A.	Paris (France)	B 1
Bold, Mr. and Mrs. Joseph	Kansas City	B 1
Buccalo, Mr. and Mrs. James N.	Columbus	A 1
Caffyn, Mr. and Mrs. Harold R.	New York	A 1
Carey, Mr. and Mrs. John L.	New York	A 1
Carey, Master C.		C
Carson, J. R.	Bay City	B 1
Char, Mr. and Mrs. Theodore	Honolulu	B 1
Chubbuck, Mr. and Mrs. Arthur C.	South Weymouth	B 2
Cobun, Mr. and Mrs. Charles C.	Los Angeles	B 1
Conick, Mr. and Mrs. M. C.	Pittsburgh	A 1
Coursen, Mr. and Mrs. W. M.	New York	B 1
Cowan, Mr. and Mrs. John R.	Chicago	A 1
Davies, Mr. and Mrs. J. O.	London (England)	A 3
Davies, Mr. and Mrs. W. R.	Pittsburgh	Aa 3
Deeming, Mr. and Mrs. William S.	Chicago	A 1
Deering, Mr. and Mrs. John J.	New York	A 1
Dohr, Prof. and Mrs. James L.	New York	A 4
Eaton, Mr. and Mrs. Marquis G.	San Antonio	Aa 1
Fariss, Mr. and Mrs. Aubrey	Houston	A 1
Fielding, Mr. and Mrs. Andrew B.	Winchester	B 1
Flynn, Mr. and Mrs. Thomas D.	New York	A 1
Fincham, Mr. and Mrs. James M.	Baltimore	B 1
Foye, Mr. and Mrs. Arthur B.	New York	A 1
Frederick, Mr. and Mrs. Wayne D.	Canton	B 1
Frisbee, Mr. and Mrs. I. N.	Long Beach	A 1
Garner, Paul	University	Aa 4
Gillette, David O.	Honolulu	B 1
Gilman, Mr. and Mrs. Stephen	Chicago	B 1
Goldberg, Mr. and Mrs. Louis S.	Sioux City	A 1
Greene, Mr. and Mrs. U. S.	Binghamton	B 1
Church, Mrs. E. D.		C
Gregory, Mr. and Mrs. Robert H.	Cambridge	B 1
Gunnarson, Mr. and Mrs. Arthur B.	Scarsdale	A 2
Hammond, Mr. and Mrs. James E.	San Francisco	A 1
Harrow, Mr. and Mrs. Benjamin	New York	A 1
Heilman, Prof. E. A.	Ankara (Turkey)	B 4
Heims, Mr. and Mrs. H. S.	Rapid City	B 1

Herrick, Mr. and Mrs. Anson	San Francisco	A	1
Hewitt, Mr. and Mrs. George A.	Philadelphia	A	1
Higgins, Mr. and Mrs. Thomas G.	New York	A	1
Hill, Gordon M.	New York	A	1
Himmelblau, Prof. and Mrs. David	Chicago	B	1
Hintze, Mr. and Mrs. H. J.	Stockholm (Sweden)	A	3
Inglis, Mr. and Mrs. John B.	New York	A	1
Jennings, Mr. and Mrs. Alvin Randolph	New York	A	1
Johnson, Mr. and Mrs. Gerald M.	Sacramento	B	1
Jones, James W.	Baltimore	B	1
Keller, Mr. and Mrs. I. Wayne	Lancaster	B	2
Kohler, E. L.	Chicago	B	4
Kornfeld, Mr. and Mrs. Raymond J.	Los Angeles	B	1
Krekstein, Mr. and Mrs. I. H.	Philadelphia	A	1
Landau, Mr. and Mrs. Bernard	Chicago	B	1
Lang, Mr. and Mrs. John J.	St. Louis	B	1
Lenhart, Mr. and Mrs. Norman J.	New York	B	1
Lindsay, Mr. and Mrs. Alexander J.	Denver	A	2
Loflin, Mr. and Mrs. Wm. F.	Columbus	A	1
Love, Mr. and Mrs. Percy	Pittsburgh	B	1
Love, Master Paul A.		C	
Marder, Mr. and Mrs. John I.	Los Angeles	B	1
Marsh, Mr. and Mrs. William F.	Pittsburgh	B	2
McCloskey, Mr. and Mrs. William B.	Baltimore	B	2
McLaren, Mr. and Mrs. N. Loyall	San Francisco	A	1
Miller, Edward O.	Butler	B	1
Minor, Mr. and Mrs. W. T.	Charlotte	B	1
Olive, Geo. S.	Indianapolis	A	1
Pearce, Mr. and Mrs. Harry L.	Stockton	B	1
Pelej, Mr. and Mrs. Joseph	New York	A	1
Peloubet, Mr. and Mrs. Maurice E.	New York	A	1
Penney, Mr. and Mrs. Louis H.	San Francisco	A	1
Perlysky, Mr. and Mrs. Louis	Hartford	B	1
Phillippe, Mr. and Mrs. Gerald L.	New York	A	5
Pilié, Mr. and Mrs. Louis H.	New Orleans	A	1
Powell, Mr. and Mrs. Weldon	New York	A	1
Prest, Mr. and Mrs. Alan P. L.	Darien	B	1
Prest, Miss J.		C	
Queenan, Mr. and Mrs. John W.	Greenwich	A	1
Reid, Mr. and Mrs. R. A.	Sanderstead (England)	B	3
Ring, Mr. and Mrs. R. Warner	Miami	A	1
Robinson, Mr. and Mrs. J. R.	London (England)	B	3
Rossdutcher, C.	Wichita	A	1
Schaffer, Mr. and Mrs. Walter L.	New York	A	1
Scott, Mr. and Mrs. Harold W.	Grosse Pointe	Aa	2
Seeber, Mr. and Mrs. Taylor H.	Grosse Pointe Farms	B	1
Seidman, Mr. and Mrs. J. S.	New York	A	1

Shapiro, Sherman G.	Lewiston	B 1
Smith, Mr. and Mrs. Alden C.	New York	A 1
Stephenson, Mr. and Mrs. J. Bryan	Albuquerque	A 1
Stewart, Mr. and Mrs. Andrew	New York	A 1
Stewart, Mr. and Mrs. J. Harold	New York	A 1
Tanner, Mr. and Mrs. Louis F.	Morgantown	B 1
Thomas, Mr. and Mrs. Marshall M.	Montclair	A 1
Timmons, Mr. and Mrs. B. A.	Knoxville	B 1
Tout, Robert E.	Stockton	B 1
Trautlein, Mr. and Mrs. D. H.	Bethlehem	B 1
Troub, Mr. and Mrs. Leonard M.	Hartford	B 1
Vincent, Mr. and Mrs. Norman H. S.	Boston	B 2
Wade, Mr. and Mrs. Alvin C.	Cheyenne	A 1
Wagner, Mr. and Mrs. George	New York	B 1
Walker, Mr. and Mrs. Wilbert A.	Short Hills	Aa 5
Weil, Carl	New York	B 1
Weisbard, Mr. and Mrs. George L.	Chicago	B 1
Weisbard, Miss P.		C
Weiss, Mr. and Mrs. Louis Carl	Cleveland	A 1
Williams, Mr. and Mrs. J. Harry	New York	A 1
Williams, Mr. and Mrs. Thomas A.	New Orleans	B 1
Wiseman, Mr. and Mrs. John	Wheeling	A 1
Witschey, Mr. and Mrs. Robert E.	Charleston	A 1
Witte, Mr. and Mrs. Arthur E.	Chicago	B 1
Wynhoff, Mr. and Mrs. Louis A.	Houston	A 1
Yaverbaum, Mr. and Mrs. Irving	Harrisburg	A 1

VENEZUELA

Colegio Nacional de Tecnicos en Contabilidad

Tinoco, P. J.	Caracas	Aa

LIST OF THE PARTICIPATING MEMBERS OF THE SPONSORING BODIES

Aa, heer en mevr. H. van der, Amsterdam
Aaftink, heer en mevr. H., Laren (N.H.)
Aarts, heer en mevr. P.M., Maastricht
Abbema, heer en mevr. W.T.J., Gouda
Achilles, heer en mevr. S.L., 's-Gravenhage
Ackermans, E.J.M., Voorburg
Afman, R.N., Almelo
Alsem, heer en mevr. D.M., Leeuwarden
Amerongen, heer en mevr. F. van, Heemstede
Amesz, B.J., Rotterdam
Apers, J.P., 's-Hertogenbosch
Appelboom, heer en mevr. T.J., Eindhoven
Ark, heer en mevr. H.H. van, Haarlem
Arkel, heer en mevr. S. van, 's-Gravenhage
As, E. van, 's-Gravenhage

Baak, heer en mevr. J.G., Aerdenhout
Baarsen, heer en mevr. K., Amsterdam
Bak, heer en mevr. J.P., 's-Gravenhage
Bakergem, heer en mevr. Th. van, Amsterdam
Bakkenist, heer en mevr. S.C., Laren (N.H.)
Bakker, heer en mevr. A.C., Amsterdam
Bakker, heer en mevr. C., Amsterdam
Bakker, H.A., Rijswijk (Z.H.)
Bakker, L.A., Bentveld
Bakker, heer en mevr. P.Th.A., Amsterdam
Bakker, heer en mevr. B. de, Rotterdam
Bakker, heer en mevr. J. de, Zeist
Bakkes, heer en mevr. J., 's-Gravenhage
Bakx, heer en mevr. F.P.J., Eindhoven
Balk, heer en mevr. J., Amstelveen
Batenburg, heer en mevr. I.E., Leiden
Bausch, heer en mevr. J.E., Rotterdam
Baijens, heer en mevr. W.J.B., Breda
Beck, heer en mevr. J.A.C., Cormeilles en Parisis (Frankrijk)
Beck, heer en mevr. J.C., Amsterdam
Bedeaux, F.Th., Voorburg
Beek, heer en mevr. A. van der, Badhoevedorp
Beekman, E., Amsterdam
Beens, heer en mevr. H., Amsterdam
Belt, heer en mevr. J.N., 's-Gravenhage
Bennink, D., Zwolle
Bergh, heer en mevr. A. van den, Arnhem
Berkel, heer en mevr. S. van, Amsterdam
Bertelsmann, heer en mevr. W.H., Amsterdam
Besançon, heer en mevr. R., Wassenaar
Besseling, heer en mevr. J.Ph.F.J., Groningen
Bins, heer en mevr. W., Zeist
Blaey, heer en mevr. W.J. de, Rotterdam
Blacy, W.N. de, 's-Gravenhage
Bliek, W., Voorburg
Bloemendaal, heer en mevr. H.G., Zwolle
Blok, heer en mevr. D., Haifa (Israël)
Turksma, mevr. E.E.,
Blomhoff, heer en mevr. J.A.N., Amsterdam
Bockel, Chr. D. van, Eindhoven
Bockel, H.H.H. van, Rotterdam-Schiebroek
Boer, D. de, Naarden
Boer, heer en mevr. H.P. de, Rotterdam
Boer, heer en mevr. J.W. de, Velp
Boer, heer en mevr. Th. de, Haarlem
Boer, heer en mevr. W. de, Amsterdam
Boer, W.R., 's-Gravenhage
Bolhuis, heer en mevr. P., Groningen
Bonenberg, heer en mevr. J., Amsterdam
Boom, L.C. van den, Haren (Gr.)
Boomkens, H., Heerlen
Boon, heer en mevr. J. van der, Bodegraven
Borrie, heer en mevr. W.B., Rotterdam
Borstlap, heer en mevr. J.M.A., 's-Gravenhage

Bos, B. J. M., Amsterdam
Bos, G. J. J. J., Amsterdam
Bos, J. Chr. G., 's-Gravenhage
Bosboom, heer en mevr. C. H., Amsterdam
Bosch, heer en mevr. H. H., Utrecht
Bosch, heer en mevr. H. L. van den, De Bilt
Boschma, heer en mevr. P. H., Amsterdam
Bose, Jhr. W. M. E. C. von, Arnhem
Bosman, heer en mevr. A. J., Amsterdam
Bosman, heer en mevr. J. M., 's-Gravenhage
Boter, H. L., Haarlem
Botman, heer en mevr. F., Nijmegen
Bots, heer en mevr. F. J. P. M., Amsterdam
Bouma, T. B., Overschie
Bouricius, R., Utrecht
Bouwman, M. C. H., Driebergen
Bovenberg, heer en mevr. C., Oosterbeek
Brackel, Dr. en mevr. G. J. L., Amsterdam
Brandenburg, D. J., Breda
Brandenburg, heer en mevr. H., Huizen
Brandhof, heer en mevr. J., Bussum
Brandhof, heer en mevr. J. A. N., 's-Gravenhage
Brands, Professor en mevr. J., 's-Gravenhage
Brandsma, F. A., Nijmegen
Braun, heer en mevr. C. F. H., Amsterdam
Breejen, K. A. den, Bussum
Breek, heer en mevr. P. C., Aalst-Waalre
Brenkman, heer en mevr. W. J., Rijswijk (Z.H.)
Brenkman, heer en mevr. W., Rotterdam
Breukelaar, J., Amsterdam
Breijinck, heer en mevr. H., Oosterbeek
Broek, C., Amsterdam
Broekhuizen, heer en mevr. P., 's-Gravenhage
Broekhuijsen, P. J., Dordrecht
Broeksma, heer en mevr. C., Amsterdam
Broere, G., Rotterdam
Broers, heer en mevr. J. H., Amsterdam
Brok, A. L., Rotterdam
Brouwer, heer en mevr. S., Voorburg
Brugge, heer en mevr. W. G., Amsterdam
Bruin, heer en mevr. W. de, Amsterdam
Bruinessen, heer en mevr. W. van, Egmond aan Zee
Brunner, heer en mevr. G. J. R., Amsterdam
Bruijn, C. D. de, Dordrecht
Bruijn, J. de, Amsterdam
Bruijn, heer en mevr. W. K. de, Amsterdam
Bruijne, heer en mevr. M. de, Middelburg
Bueren, heer en mevr. D. van, 's-Gravenhage
Buning, J. J., 's-Gravenhage
Burg, heer en mevr. C. van der, Amsterdam
Burg, heer en mevr. W. A. M. van der, Amstelveen
Burgert, heer en mevr. R., Rotterdam
Busnac, heer en mevr. A. B., Arnhem
Buuren, heer en mevr. H. van, Amsterdam

Caaij, heer en mevr. G. van der, Delft
Carlée Jr., W., Amsterdam
Cassing, heer en mevr. F., Louveciennes (Frankrijk)
Cohen, heer en mevr. J., Amsterdam
Coini, heer en mevr. J. A., Amsterdam
Cok, J., Amsterdam
Conradi, T. A., Rijswijk
Rollema, mej.
Convent, heer en mevr. J. M. F., Amstelveen
Coppens, heer en mevr. A. L. A., 's-Gravenhage
Corbet, J., Rotterdam
Cornelisse, J. A. P., Eindhoven
Corput, E. C. van den, Voorburg
Cremer, P. Ch., Beverwijk
Crop, H., Arnhem
Crouse, J., 's-Gravenhage

Daamen, heer en mevr. P. F., Zaandam
Dalhuizen, heer en mevr. G. L., 's-Gravenhage
Damme, heer en mevr. J. P., Amsterdam
Dechesne, J. H., Tilburg
Dekker, A., Rotterdam
Dekker, heer en mevr. C., Amsterdam
Dekkers, heer en mevr. B. A. W. C. M., Eindhoven
Dekkers, H. G., Eindhoven
Demenint, heer en mevr. A. L., Oegstgeest
Derks, heer en mevr. A. F., Utrecht
Dessing, Chr. J. P., Amsterdam
Deurloo, heer en mevr. A. J., 's-Gravenhage
Deijs, S., Amstelveen
Diekema, T., Bussum

Dielen, heer en mevr. A., Breda
Dien, heer en mevr. D. van, Amsterdam
Diephuis, heer en mevr. G., Hengelo (O)
Dingemans, heer en mevr. W. J. C., Oudenbosch
Dirksen, heer en mevr. M., Voorschoten
Djie, Dr. T. L., Amsterdam
Dolmans, A. Th., Arnhem
Dongen, heer en mevr. A. van, 's-Gravenhage
Donk, J. G. T., Amstelveen
Donker, P. L. J., Naarden
Donkers, heer en mevr. M. J. F., Oegstgeest
Doorn, heer en mevr. P. van, Bussum
Doorne, heer en mevr. B. A. E. van, Rotterdam
Doorne, heer en mevr. F. F. van, 's-Gravenhage
Doppegieter, A., Rotterdam
Dorssen, heer en mevr. H. G. van, Aerdenhout
Draaijer, H. J., Bussum
Driessen, heer en mevr. E., Amsterdam
Duchâteau-Fennema, mevr. E., Monte Carlo
Duchâteau, Dr. W.,
Duin, W. J. van, Heemstede
Duivenbooden, F. G. van, 's-Gravenhage
Dunselman, heer en mevr. H. J. J. M., Amsterdam
Duyn, H. van, Leersum
Duyverman, heer en mevr. J., Wassenaar
Dijk, heer en mevr. D. C. G. van, 's-Gravenhage
Dijk, heer en mevr. H. J. H. van, 's-Gravenhage
Dijk, J. F. van, Zwolle
Dijkman, heer en mevr. H. G., Amsterdam
Dijkshoorn, heer en mevr. A., Amsterdam

Eckhardt, heer en mevr. M. J. W. J., Amsterdam
l'Ecluse, heer en mevr. J. H. P. de, 's-Gravenhage
Eikenaar, heer en mevr. H., Rotterdam
Ek, heer en mevr. P. L., Voorschoten
Elgershuizen, W. N. D., 's-Gravenhage
Elgersma, N., Rijswijk
Elzinga, R., Eefde (Gld.)
Ende, M. D. L. van den, Rotterdam
Engelgeer, A. G. C., Haarlem
Engels, heer en mevr. J. H., Amsterdam
Entrop, heer en mevr. E. A., Amsterdam
Erdman, heer en mevr. J. E., Amsterdam
Erp, G. van, Arnhem
Essen, L. van, Amersfoort
Essen Lzn., heer en mevr. L. van, Bloemendaal
Essink, D., Amsterdam
Eyden, heer en mevr. J. W. van, Amstelveen
Eys, heer en mevr. J. van, Hilversum

Feenstra, heer en mevr. D., Wassenaar
Felten, G. A. L., 's-Gravenhage
Ferdinandusse, J., 's-Gravenhage
Flipse, heer en mevr. E. J., Heemstede
Flothuis, heer en mevr. J. W. P., Amsterdam
Fock, heer en mevr. J. A., Voorburg
Foppe, heer en mevr. H. H. M., Amsterdam
Frank, heer en mevr. P., Amsterdam
Frese, heer en mevr. B. H., Bussum
Frielink, heer en mevr. A. B., Amsterdam
Frijns, J. W., Heerlen

Gent, heer en mevr. M. van, Utrecht
Gerlagh, L. P., Amstelveen
Gerretsen, heer en mevr. A. L., 's-Gravenhage
Gerritsen, heer en mevr. H., Wassenaar
Gerritsen, heer en mevr. H. P. W., Naarden
Gestel, H. P. L. van, Wassenaar
Geuns, heer en mevr. J. H. J. van, Huizen
Ginkel, J. Th. van, Amsterdam
Glavimans, F. N., Rotterdam
Godhart, heer en mevr. J. J., Amsterdam
Goossens, H., Bussum
Goudeket, Professor en mevr. A., Eindhoven
Graaff, heer en mevr. C. de, Naarden
Grand, heer en mevr. H. le, 's-Gravenhage
Greebe, E., Amsterdam
Groenenboom, heer en mevr. M., Huizen
Groenendijk, W., Rotterdam
Groeneveld, heer en mevr. F., 's-Gravenhage
Groeneveld, heer en mevr. G. L., Eindhoven
Groenewegen, Q., Rotterdam
Grondel, A. H., Bussum
Groothoff, heer en mevr. J., Amsterdam

Guittart, F., Rotterdam

Haan, A. de, Rotterdam
Haan, heer en mevr. J. H. de, Amsterdam
Haantjes, J. J., Breda
Haar, K. van de, 's-Gravenhage
Haarbosch, heer en mevr. F., Amsterdam
Haas, heer en mevr. G. G. de, Tiel
Hacquebard, P. C., Bloemendaal
Hage, heer en mevr. I. M., Rotterdam
Hageman, heer en mevr. Ch., 's-Gravenhage
Hageman, heer en mevr. H. W., Rotterdam
Hagenbeek, heer en mevr. J. G., 's-Gravenhage
Hagers, heer en mevr. L. A., 's-Gravenhage
Haks, heer en mevr. H. D. A., Wassenaar
Haks, heer en mevr. J. W. F., Rotterdam
Halders, B. L. L., Maastricht
Hamelijnck, heer en mevr. M., 's-Hertogenbosch
Haring, heer en mevr. F. L. M., 's-Gravenhage
Haring, J. C. M., Rijswijk (Z.H.)
Harms, heer en mevr. A., Bussum
Harmsen, E. E., Amsterdam
Hartog, G., Amsterdam
Hartog, heer en mevr. W. D. A. den, Rotterdam
Hauw, F. van der, Huis ter Heide (Utr.)
Heaviside, heer en mevr. J. F., Eindhoven
Hebly, heer en mevr. H. J. ,Amsterdam
Heerden, heer en mevr. A. van, Chipstead (Engeland)
Heiser, heer en mevr. J. G., Rotterdam
Hellendall, heer en mevr. A., Amsterdam
Hendriks, A. J., Haarlem
Hendriks, W. A. H., Rotterdam
Hengel, heer en mevr. C. van, Amsterdam
Hennephof, heer en mevr. G. J., 's-Gravenhage
Heuvel, heer en mevr. C. A. van den, Naarden
Heykoop, Ch. A., 's-Gravenhage
Heyligers, R., Badhoevedorp
Hinnen, heer en mevr. G. K. H., Amsterdam
Hoefsmit, R., 's-Gravenhage
Hoek, heer en mevr. L. G. van der, Rotterdam
Hoeting, heer en mevr. J. F. J., IJmuiden
Hoeve, P. Ph., Aalst (N.Br.)
Hofman, Mr. en mevr. E. A., Londen (Engeland)
Hogeweg, G. P. J., Amsterdam
Holthuyzen, heer en mevr. A. J. J., Eefde (Gld.)
Homan, heer en mevr. A. J., Amsterdam
Hommel, heer en mevr. J., 's-Gravenhage
Hoogendijk, C. A., Voorburg
Hoogerdijk, heer en mevr. P., 's-Gravenhage
Hoogeveen, heer en mevr. J.W., Amsterdam
Hoogewerff, heer en mevr. J. J., 's-Gravenhage
Hoogheid, J. C., Rotterdam
Hoorn, heer en mevr. Th. van, Amsterdam
Hootsen, H. G., Almelo
Hordijk, Ph., Mortsel-Antwerpen (België)
Hout, J. J. N. van, Eindhoven
Hoving, heer en mevr. E. H., Deventer
Hueck, H. F., Rotterdam
Hueting, heer en mevr. B., 's-Gravenhage
Huiskamp, W. J., Voorburg
Huisma, R., Scheveningen
Huizer, heer en mevr. H., Rijswijk (Z.H.)
Hulst, heer en mevr. H. J. van, Utrecht

Ingwersen, heer en mevr. J., Bloemendaal
Iprenburg, C., Amsterdam

Jacobs, heer en mevr. G. J., Amsterdam
Jansen, heer en mevr. J., Voorburg
Jansen, M., Deventer
Janssens, C. H. A. J., Tilburg
Joanknecht, W. F., Eindhoven
Joëls, heer en mevr. E. J., Amsterdam
Jong, Professor en mevr. A. A. de, Rotterdam
Jong, heer en mevr. A. C. J. de, Leiden
Jong, C. de, Wassenaar
Jong, heer en mevr. G. de, 's-Gravenhage
Jong, heer en mevr. J. de, Amsterdam
Jongh, W. A. de, 's-Gravenhage
Jongstra, heer en mevr. P. J. B., 's-Gravenhage
Jonker, J., Voorburg
Jonker, heer en mevr. R., Zwolle
Jonkers, heer en mevr. A. C. J., Rotterdam

Kaay, heer en mevr. J. E. van der, 's-Gravenhage
Kamer, heer en mevr. C. F., Amsterdam
Kammer, Mr. Dr. en mevr. A., Overschie
Kampen Jr., Professor en mevr. L. van, 's-Gravenhage

Kampen, L. van, 's-Gravenhage
Kamphorst, A. J., Rotterdam
Karelse, heer en mevr. F. M. A., Rotterdam
Kastein, Mr. en mevr. A. Th. E., Amsterdam
Katan, heer en mevr. E., Scheveningen
Kauer, A., 's-Gravenhage
Keizer, heer en mevr. C. de, Rotterdam
Keuzenkamp, J., 's-Gravenhage
Kips, heer en mevr. H. B., Leiden
Kirchner, heer en mevr. W., Naarden
Klashorst, heer en mevr. G. van de, Nieuw-Loosdrecht
Kleerekoper, heer en mevr. I., Amsterdam
Klerk, K., Zaandijk
Klimbie, heer en mevr. J. G., Heemstede
Klinkenbijl, heer en mevr. C., Rotterdam
Kloet, J. C., Haarlem
Klok, heer en mevr. H. J., Groningen
Klomp, heer en mevr. F., Amsterdam
Klomp, heer en mevr. J. A., Rotterdam
Klooster, heer en mevr. A. J. van 't, Amsterdam
Kluin, heer en mevr. H., Amstelveen
Knegtmans, heer en mevr. G. C., 's-Gravenhage
Knopper, G. J., Rotterdam
Knulst, heer en mevr. L., 's-Gravenhage
Knijff, heer en mevr. J. van der, Utrecht
Koene, heer en mevr. J. J., Apeldoorn
Koetsier, heer en mevr. J., Meppel
Koetsveld, heer en mevr. J. E. van, Rhoon
Koning, J., Eindhoven
Koning, heer en mevr. J. A. A., Heemstede
Koning, heer en mevr. L. W. de, Santpoort
Koning, heer en mevr. R. de, Amsterdam
Kooiman, J., Amsterdam
Kool, A., Rotterdam
Koops, C., Rijswijk (Z.H.)
Kooy, T. van der, 's-Gravenhage
Koppenberg, W. C., Hengelo (O)
Korff, heer en mevr. A., Amsterdam
Korff, heer en mevr. Tj., 's-Gravenhage
Korte, Mr. en Mevr. J. P. de, Wassenaar
Koster, heer en mevr. J., Breukelen
Koster, heer en mevr. Ph., 's-Gravenhage
Kousbroek, heer en mevr. H. R., Den Helder
Kraa, heer en mevr. J., Amsterdam
Kraayenhof, heer en mevr. J., Amsterdam
Kramer, G. J., Eindhoven
Kramer, J. H., Heemstede
Kreiken, F. H. C., 's-Gravenhage
Krimpen, heer en mevr. L. H. van, Amersfoort
Krol, G. M., Leiden
Kruisbrink, heer en mevr. K., Amsterdam
Kruizenga, H., Eindhoven
Krul, A. P., Wassenaar
Krijger, L. P., Arnhem
Kuggeleijn, heer en mevr. F., Amsterdam
Kuipers, J., Rotterdam
Kuttschrütter, W. G. J., Bussum
Kuijl, heer en mevr. F., Almelo
Kuijper, Czn., D., Hilversum
Kuijper, heer en mevr. G. R., Heemstede
Kuijper, P. C., Hilversum
Kuijper, heer en mevr. H., Haarlem
Kuyper, R. M., Bussum
Kwantes, heer en mevr. C. R., Amsterdam

Laat, heer en mevr. J. Th. de, Amsterdam
Lafeber, A. F., Rotterdam
Laforêt, V. P. L., 's-Gravenhage
Lagendijk, W. H., 's-Gravenhage
Laman, J. H. C., Leiden
Lampe, heer en mevr. Jac., Amsterdam
Landeweer, heer en mevr. F. H., 's-Gravenhage
Lange, Dr. en mevr. A. Th. de, Amsterdam
Lange, G. de, Rotterdam
Lange, K. de, Wassenaar
Langedijk, K. J., Amsterdam
Lasance, J. H. A. A., 's-Gravenhage
Laterveer, heer en mevr. E. L. Th., Naarden
Lauterbach, heer en mevr. P. G., Amsterdam
Leede, H. de, Wassenaar
Leenheer, heer en mevr. E. B., Rijswijk (Z.H.)
Leeuw, heer en mevr. H. D. de, Arnhem
Leguyt, heer en mevr. J., Amsterdam
Lekanne Deprez, J. G. E. A., Eindhoven
Liem, T. S., Amsterdam
Lieve, R. H., Hilversum
Lim, H. T. G., 's-Gravenhage
Limperg, Professor Dr. en mevr. Th., Amsterdam
Lindner, heer en mevr. J. A. M. F., Tilburg
Linge, heer en mevr. R. van, Voorburg

Linge, heer en mevr. Th. N. van, 's-Gravenhage
Lokkerbol, heer en mevr. J. P., Rijswijk (Z.H.)
Loo, C. van der, Haarlem
Loon, P. C. van, Hengelo (O)
Loos, heer en mevr. J., Hollandse Rading
Los, heer en mevr. J., Amsterdam
Lotgering, G. W. F., Rotterdam
Lous, N.H., Helmond
Louwers, heer en mevr. P. C., Vught
Lubeck, A. H. van, Bergen op Zoom
Lulof, heer en mevr. J. H., Hilversum
Luyendijk, G. H., Middelburg
Lyre, heer en mevr. J. H., Amsterdam

Maan, Mr. en mevr. P. C., Amsterdam
Maas, heer en mevr. A. H., Hengelo (O)
Maas, heer en mevr. J., 's-Gravenhage
Mackloet, heer en mevr. S. P., Rotterdam
Made, heer en mevr. W. H. J. van der, Breda
Mallee, heer en mevr. A., Huizen (N.H.)
Mank, N., Rotterdam
Mast, heer en mevr. H. van der, Voorburg
Matthews, heer en mevr. J. H. D., Heemstede
Meeles, D. A. M., Rotterdam
Meer, Th. J. van der, Rotterdam
Meeuwen, heer en mevr. J. van, Amsterdam
Meinardi, H. A., Tilburg
Mélis, heer en mevr. F. B., Rotterdam
Melker, W. C. de, Rotterdam
Merckel, heer en mevr. W. H., Utrecht
Mesritz, heer en mevr. Jac. H., Amsterdam
Meulen, heer en mevr. H. B. J. ter, Tilburg
Meulen, heer en mevr. J. van der, Beverwijk
Meurs, J. G. van, Diemen
Mey, Professor Dr. A., Amsterdam
Mey, Professor Dr. J. L., Groningen
Mey-Koning, Mevr. M. G., Amsterdam
Meijer, C. J., Amsterdam
Meyer, heer en mevr. N., Amsterdam
Meijeraan, heer en mevr. J. F., 's-Gravenhage
Meyers, heer en mevr. J., Hilversum
Michael, heer en mevr. S., Voorburg
Modderaar, heer en mevr. J., Rotterdam
Modijefsky, heer en mevr. Ch., Utrecht
Moerbeek, heer en mevr. H. G., Rotterdam
Möhring, A. C., Alkmaar
Molhoek, heer en mevr. F. Th., 's-Gravenhage
Moor Jr., heer en mevr. A. H. K., 's-Gravenhage
Moormans, W., New York (V.S.)
Moret, Mr. en mevr. B., Rotterdam
Morren, F. W., 's-Gravenhage
Mouwes, heer en mevr. J. R., Alkmaar
Mulder, A., Overveen
Mulder, heer en mevr. J., Amsterdam
Mulder, heer en mevr. K., Amsterdam
Mulders, A. K., Amsterdam
Muller, heer en mevr. S., Voorburg
Munnik, heer en mevr. H., Hilversum
Munnik, heer en mevr. H. A., Amsterdam
Munnikes, H., Velp
Munting, heer en mevr. J., Oegstgeest

Namen, heer en mevr. H. van, Amstelveen
Naninck, A. A. C., Eindhoven
Nathans, J., Amsterdam
Neisingh, W., Amsterdam
Nelis, heer en mevr. W. A., Amstelveen
Nienhuis, K., Eindhoven
Nierhoff, A., Amsterdam
Niessen, heer en mevr. J. H., Haarlem
Nolson, R. D., 's-Gravenhage
Noorman, J., Alkmaar
Notebaart, J., Rotterdam
Nugteren, heer en mevr. A. M., Amsterdam
Nuij, W. H. A., 's-Gravenhage
Nije, heer en mevr. D., Amsterdam
Nijman, heer en mevr. J., Amsterdam
Nijst, J. A. M., Eindhoven

Okker, heer en mevr. T., Rotterdam
Okkerse, J., 's-Gravenhage
Oldenburger, Th., Velsen-Noord
Olie Jr., J., Amsterdam
Oost Jzn., heer en mevr. A.F., Amsterdam
Oosterholt, heer en mevr. H. F., Rotterdam
Oosterhuis, heer en mevr. A. D. L. W., Amsterdam
Oosterveld, heer en mevr. M. M., Amsterdam
Op 't Landt, J. G. A., Wassenaar
Oranje, heer en mevr. L., Hilversum
Ouboter, G. C., Rotterdam
Oudt, A., Wassenaar

Ouwehand, C., Rotterdam
Ouwerkerk, heer en mevr. J., Rotterdam
Overbeek, heer en mevr. A. R., Amsterdam
Ovezall, heer en mevr. R. J., Delfzijl

Paar, heer en mevr. G., Hilversum
Peelen, heer en mevr. J. A., Amsterdam
Pelgrim, C., Wassenaar
Pelt, heer en mevr. J. C. van, Oss
Philippus, G. M. M., Amsterdam
Pieters, Th. W., 's-Gravenhage
Pieterse, H. P., Rotterdam
Pieterse, J. H., Amsterdam
Pieterse van Wijck, heer en mevr. J. A., 's-Gravenhage
Pikaar, heer en mevr. A. W., Rotterdam
Pinxteren, heer en mevr. A. A. M. van, Amsterdam
Plas, heer en mevr. H. A. E., 's-Gravenhage
Poels, A. Th. J., Roermond
Poggemeier, heer en mevr. W. Th., Amsterdam
Polak, heer en mevr. M. J., Amsterdam
Pont, D., Naarden
Pool, A., Rotterdam
Poot, heer en mevr. E., 's-Gravenhage
Porrey, D. P., Rotterdam
Post, heer en mevr. J. F. A., Voorburg
Posthumus, heer en mevr. J. J., Bilthoven
Praal, heer en mevr. F. D. B., Rotterdam
Prause, F. J., Arnhem
Pruschen, heer en mevr. J. F. H., Haarlem
Putten, heer en mevr. L. A. A. M. van, Amsterdam
Pijl, heer en mevr. M. J., Rotterdam

Quispel, C., Barendrecht

Raadsen, J., Heemstede
Raakman, heer en mevr. K. P., Amsterdam
Rademaker, heer en mevr. L., Hilversum
Ramkema, G., Overveen
Ras, heer en mevr. L. F., Wassenaar
Rechtuyt, heer en mevr. C., Amsterdam
Reder, heer en mevr. H. R., Amsterdam
Ree, heer en mevr. G. van der, Tilburg
Ree, heer en mevr. J. van de, Voorburg
Regt, heer en mevr. A. de, 's-Gravenhage
Reinoud, H., 's-Gravenhage
Renes, heer en mevr. A. J., 's-Gravenhage
Reijn, A. J. F., Amsterdam
Reijn, heer en mevr. H. J., Amsterdam
Ribbink, heer en mevr. H. J., Hengelo (O)
Riemsdijk, heer en mevr. A. A. J. van, 's-Gravenhage
Rietschoten, Professor en mevr. A. M. van, Bussum
Rietveld, heer en mevr. C., Utrecht
Rinkel, heer en mevr. W. J., Willemstad (Cur.)
Rinkel, mej.,
Koeman, mevr. H. J.,
Rinsma, heer en mevr. F., 's-Gravenhage
Ritz, A., 's-Gravenhage
Rockland, C. J. F., 's-Gravenhage
Roelvink, P., Voorburg
Roest, C. W., 's-Gravenhage
Rombouts, L. M., Rotterdam
Rommelaar, H. C., Hengelo (O)
Roodenburg, heer en mevr. W., Noordwijk aan Zee
Roos, heer en mevr. Ph., Amsterdam
Rooy, heer en mevr. D. de, Rotterdam
Rooy, heer en mevr. J. de, Hoogeveen
Roozen, heer en mevr. L. J. M., Blaricum
Rosenboom-Kleerkoper, mevr. R., Antwerpen (België)
Rosenboom, J.
Rossum, heer en mevr. A. J. van, Bussum
Rozema, heer en mevr. H. J., Groningen
Ruygers, A. A. G. M., Ukkel/Brussel (België)
Rijnsburger, heer en mevr. W. J., Heemstede
Rijpkema, heer en mevr. J. A., Venlo

Sanders, H. B. J., Rotterdam
Santen, heer en mevr. J. B. H. A., Amsterdam
Sasburg, heer en mevr. J. W., Voorburg
Sauer, heer en mevr. C., Delft
Schatte Olivier, heer en mevr. Th. v. d., Ukkel/Brussel (België)
Schattinga, heer en mevr. W., Rotterdam
Schee, F. van der, Rotterdam
Schermers, H. L., Arnhem
Schilder, heer en mevr. A., Bennekom
Schipper, J. J., Eindhoven
Schluter, J. B., Rijswijk
Schoonderbeek, J. W., Amsterdam
Schoonhoven, F. W. H. B. van, Madrid (Spanje)
Schroeff, Professor Dr. en mevr. H. J. van der, Heemstede

Schuil, mevr. Professor G. C., Rotterdam
Schukking, heer en mevr. L. M., Almelo
Schutte, mej. M. J., Eindhoven
Schutte-Van Ingen, mevr. A. E., Amsterdam
Segall, mej. G., Amsterdam
Senn, W. J., Rotterdam
Seters, F. A. van, Beverwijk
Seyen, heer en mevr. H. van, Rotterdam
Siebesma, heer en mevr. R., Leeuwarden
Simons, Professor Mr. en mevr. D., 's-Gravenhage
Simons, R. K., Eindhoven
Sissingh, B. G., Amsterdam
Rees-Sissingh, mevr. J. G. van,
Slagt, heer en mevr. W. G., Rotterdam
Slooff, heer en mevr. F. P., Aerdenhout
Slot, G., Rotterdam
Slot, J. P., 's-Hertogenbosch
Sloten, heer en mevr. P. J. van, Amsterdam
Sluys, H. van der, Amsterdam
Sluys, mej. A. van der,
Sluijs, heer en mevr. J. van, 's-Gravenhage
Smeding, heer en mevr. J. P., Naarden
Smeele, L. J. M., 's-Gravenhage
Smit, G. H., Zwolle
Smit, heer en mevr. P., Amsterdam
Snoep, C., Rotterdam
Soeting, heer en mevr. P., Amsterdam
Spaan, J. C., Rotterdam
Spaanderman, heer en mevr. F. W., Bussum
Speydel, L. J., Amsterdam
Spil, J. C. A. van der, Wassenaar
Spil, heer en mevr. Th. A. van der, Wassenaar
Spits, heer en mevr. C. L., Amstelveen
Spits, F. G., Paterswolde
Splint, heer en mevr. P. G. E., Amsterdam
Spoormaker, J., 's-Gravenhage
Sprangers, heer en mevr. L. A. J., 's-Gravenhage
Stap, heer en mevr. J. F., Amstelveen
Starre, heer en mevr. G. H. van der, Driebergen
Starreveld, heer en mevr. R. W., Amsterdam
Staveren, J. van, Rotterdam
Stegeman, Mr. en mevr. H. J. W., Amsterdam
Steinhauer, heer en mevr. M., Amsterdam
Steneker, heer en mevr. C., Wezep
Stevenhagen, heer en mevr. W., 't Joppe
Stobbe, heer en mevr. J., Amsterdam
Stofkoper, J. A., 's-Gravenhage
Stokvis, heer en mevr. W. N. A. F. H., Laren (N.H.)
Stolte, H. M., Egmond aan Zee
Stouthandel, heer en mevr. A., Schiedam
Straatemeier, heer en mevr. A., Amsterdam
Straaten, A. van der, Utrecht
Strasters, E. J., 's-Gravenhage
Strieder, heer en mevr. J. Ch. E., Amersfoort
Stroomberg, J., 's-Gravenhage
Stuart, J., Brussel (België)
Stijl, C. Th., Rotterdam
Surber, heer en mevr. A. A., 's-Gravenhage

Tack, heer en mevr. J., Huizen
Talen, heer en mevr. H. A., Rotterdam
Tan, Eng Oen, Rotterdam
Tanis, heer en mevr. J. M., 's-Gravenhage
Teeseling, heer en mevr. G. van, Amsterdam
Teeseling, heer en mevr. M. F. Ch. van, Amsterdam
Tempelaar, heer en mevr. A. F., Hengelo (O)
Termohlen, heer en mevr. G. P., 's-Gravenhage
Thuijl, heer en mevr. J. van, 's-Gravenhage
Til, heer en mevr. D. G. van, Amsterdam
Til, heer en mevr. G. E. A. van, Heemstede
Timmer, heer en mevr. D. F., Amsterdam
Timmer, heer en mevr. G., 's-Gravenhage
Timmer, G. J., 's-Gravenhage
Timmers, heer en mevr. P., Eindhoven
Tjepkema, heer en mevr. J., Eindhoven
Tjitrosidojo, Raden Soemardjo, Kebajoran Baru (Indonesia)
Tombe, heer en mevr. W. J. de, Oegstgeest
Toutenhoofd, J., 's-Gravenhage
Treffers, heer en mevr. H. C., Amstelveen
Trouwborst, heer en mevr. J. Ch., Eindhoven
Turpijn, J., Bussum
Tuijn, heer en mevr. D. P., Hilversum

Uiterlinden, heer en mevr. J., Amsterdam
Utteren, heer en mevr. C. van, Amsterdam
Uijterwaal, heer en mevr. H. J. J., Utrecht

Valk, H. J., Rotterdam

Valk, W. R. G. van der, 's-Gravenhage
Veeling, B., 's-Gravenhage
Oltmans-Veeling, Mevr. G. E.,
Veen, G. van der, Zeist
Velden, heer en mevr. J. van der, Beccar (Arg.)
Verbruggen, heer en mevr. P. L. J., 's-Hertogenbosch
Verburg, N. M. Ch., 's-Gravenhage
Verdenius, Th. J., Arnhem
Verduyn, heer en mevr. G., Haarlem
Verhagen, heer en mevr. M. A. C., Nijmegen
Verhelst, heer en mevr. A. P. G., Tilburg
Verheij, C. A., Wageningen
Verheij, C. G., Voorschoten
Verhoeven, heer en mevr. Th. J. H., Heemstede
Verhoeven, W. A. A., Heerlen
Verhoog, P., Amsterdam
Verleur, heer en mevr. A., Amsterdam
Vermeulen, heer en mevr. P. G. A., Amsterdam
Verpoorte, D. F., Leiden
Verschoof, heer en mevr. J. J., Amsterdam
Verschoor, heer en mevr. N., Voorburg
Versteeg, J. H., 's-Gravenhage
Viegen, B. van, Vlaardingen
Vingerhoeds, L. J., Amby (L)
Vink, heer en mevr. P. J., Rotterdam
Visser, heer en mevr. A., Deventer
Viveen, J. C., Amsterdam
Vliet, heer en mevr. Th. J. van, 's-Gravenhage
Vogel, heer en mevr. H., Amsterdam
Vogel, heer en mevr. J., Wassenaar
Vonhoff, J. O., Eindhoven
Vooys, H., Rotterdam
Vos, heer en mevr. J., 's-Gravenhage
Vos, heer en mevr. Ph., Amsterdam
Vosse, heer en mevr. H. A. van de, Hengelo (O)
Vries, heer en mevr. N. J., Arnhem
Vries, heer en mevr. H. de, Scheveningen
Vries, N. de, Rotterdam
Vrind, heer en mevr. L., Rotterdam
Vroome, J. de, Velp

Waal, H. de, Danderyd (Zweden)
Waart, heer en mevr. L. J. J. van der, Amsterdam
Walgemoed, heer en mevr. H., Overveen
Wallis de Vries, heer en mevr. M., 's-Gravenhage
Waringa, heer en mevr. S. H., Amsterdam
Warmenhoven, P., Amsterdam
Wassink, heer en mevr. G. W., Badhoevedorp
Weger, heer en mevr. J. G. de, Bussum
Weisfelt, heer en mevr. J., Rotterdam
Welle, heer en mevr. F. A. van der, Voorburg
Werf, heer en mevr. J. van der, Bussum
Werf, heer en mevr. S. J. G. van der, Voorburg
Wesselius, heer en mevr. Ch. J., Haren
Westebring, heer en mevr. P. W., Almelo
Westendorp, heer en mevr. G. F., Aerdenhout
Westra, heer en mevr. J. T., 's-Gravenhage
Westra, W., Rotterdam
Wiegel, E., Amsterdam
Wiel, W. J. van de, Eindhoven
Wielenga, heer en mevr. G. Ph., Wassenaar
Wielenga, heer en mevr. J. J., Rhoon
Wientjes, B. E. J., Bentveld
Wieringen, G. van, Heiloo
Wiersum, K. A., 's-Gravenhage
Willig, heer en mevr. J., Amsterdam
Wilsem, heer en mevr. H. van, Amsterdam
Wingelaar, heer en mevr. H. A., Haarlem
Winter, J. D. de, Voorburg
Winter-Otto, mevr. F. J. de, Voorburg
Wintersteyn, M. C., Beverwijk
Wisse, J., Voorburg
Wisse, heer en mevr. P., 's-Gravenhage
Wit, heer en mevr. M. de, Wormerveer
Woelders, heer en mevr. M. J., Bussum
Wolferen, J. van, 's-Gravenhage
Wolff, J. W., Rotterdam
Wolfrat, J. H., Amsterdam
Wouters, M. J., Bussum
Wijs, heer en mevr. H. F. de, Utrecht

Zaat, heer en mevr. H. G. A., 's-Gravenhage
Zandstra, F. D., Amsterdam
Zant, heer en mevr. H. J. van der, Amsterdam
Zant, Z. M. van der, Amsterdam
Zanten, A. G. van, Amsterdam
Zee, heer en mevr. S. R. van der, Amsterdam
Zelders, G. K., Bloemendaal
Zwaan, heer en mevr. D. de, 's-Gravenhage

GUESTS OF HONOUR AT THE DELEGATES' DINNER

HIS ROYAL HIGHNESS

THE PRINCE OF THE NETHERLANDS

HIS EXCELLENCY THE STATE SECRETARY
OF ECONOMIC AFFAIRS

DR. G. M. J. VELDKAMP

THE GOVERNOR OF THE QUEEN
FOR THE PROVINCE OF NORTH HOLLAND

DR. M. J. PRINSEN

THE DEPUTY-BURGOMASTER OF AMSTERDAM

DR. A. DE ROOS

LIST OF GUESTS AT THE DELEGATES' DINNER

Adams, R., Great Britain
Ahrén, C. E., Sweden
Alatriste Jr., Sealtiel, Mexico
Allet, Dr. E., Austria
Alvarado-Dupuy, Alfons, Austria
Amor, Mrs. W. ,Great Britain
Archavlis, E., France
Atkinson, W. O., Great Britain
Auguste, P. H. A., France

Bachrach, M. D., America
Bailey, G. D., America
Bak, J. P.
Bakkenist, S. C.
Baldry, Edward, Great Britain
Barrowcliff, Ch. P., Great Britain
Barrows, W. L., Great Britain
Batzer, R. K., America
Baynes, T. A. Hamilton, Great Britain
Beck, J. C.
Bengs, Dr. P., Germany
Benson, H. A., Great Britain
Bérard, F., France
Bergeon, P., France
Berger, S. J. D., Great Britain
Besançon, R.
Bevis, D. J., America
Björfors, G., Sweden
Blois, J. D., France
Blough, C. G., America
Bock, R. S., America
Boer, H. P. de
Boertien, C., *Adj. Secretary of the Congress*
Borsay, J., Great Britain
Bosch, H. L. van den
Boschma, P. H.
Bossard, Dr. E., Switzerland
Boter, Dr. Fernando, Spain
Brackel, Dr. G.
Braende, Helge, Norway
Brands, Prof. J.
Bredt, Dr. Ing. O., Germany
Brok, A. L.
Brongers, J., *President of the Appeals Comm. of the Netherlands Inst. of Acc.*
Brown, J. G., Canada
Browning, Prof. R., Great Britain
Bruyne, A. L. de, *Secretary of the Congress*
Buccalo, J. N., America
Bundy, A., Great Britain
Buranasombati, Leck, Thailand
Burgert, R.
Busch, Friedrich C. J., Germany
Busuttil, P., Malta

Caffyn, H. R., America
Callaby, F. A., Great Britain
Carey, J. L., America
Carlsen, Alf R., Norway
Carpenter, Percy F., Great Britain
Carrington, W. S., Great Britain
Carter, Kenneth LeM., Canada
Casas-Alatriste, R., Mexico
Cassel, Ö., Sweden
Caudron, J., France
Cheyney, L. F., Great Britain
Chopra, S. P., India
Church, John R., Canada
Clarise, Jean, France
Clarke, Douglas A., Great Britain
Conick, M. C., America
Cowan, J. R., America
Crafter, W. J., Great Britain
Craig, I. A. F., Great Britain

Darden, E. K. P., Belgium
Davies, G. H. Lloyd, New Zealand
Davies, J. O., America
Davies, W. R., America
Dechesne, J. H.
Deeming, W. S., America
Deering, J. J., America
Deheuvel, Ch., Belgium
DeLalanne, James A., Canada
Demenint, A. L.
Densem, W. G., Great Britain
Desai, S. N., India
Diaz Martin, L., Spain
Diephuis, G.
Dieterich, Dr. Wilhelm, Germany
Dietze, K. W. M., Germany
Digby, W. H. M., Australia
Dohr, Prof. J. L., America
Dongen, A. van
Dowling, James T., Great Britain
Duchesne, Lucien R., France
DuPré, Derek, Great Britain

Eaton, M. G., America
Edwards, W. F., Great Britain
Elmendorff, Dr. W., Germany
Essen Lzn., L. van

Faber, F., Luxemburg
Fariss, A., America
Farmer, R. E., Rhodesia
Fitzgerald, G. E., Australia
Flynn, Th. D., America
Forsström, B., Finland
Foye, A. B., America
Frank, P.
French, William I., Great Britain
Frisbee, I. N., America

Garner, P., America
Gerbès, R., Luxemburg
Glendinning, R., Great Britain
Glomstein, A., Norway
Goldberg, L. S., America
Götze, Dr. Hermann, Germany
Goudeket, Prof. A.
Graaff, Dr. F. A. de, *Private Secretary to His Royal Highness the Prince of the Netherlands*
Granger, P. F., Great Britain
Gray, W. Macfarlane, Great Britain
Greenwood, Prof. H., South Africa
Grévoul, A., France
Groeneveld, G. L.
Gunnarson, Arthur B., America

Hafström, S., Sweden
Hammond, J. E., America
Hansen, Børge, Denmark
Harris, J. E., Great Britain
Harrow, B., America
Heiken, H., Germany
Henderson, J., Ceylon
Herrick, A., America
Hewitt, G. A., America
Hewson, D. A. W., Ghana
Higgins, T. G., America
Highwood, J. G., East-Africa
Hill, G. M., America
Hintze, H. J., America
Hjernø Jeppesen, H., Denmark
Hoessli, M., Switzerland
Hofmann, Dr. H., Switzerland
Hogeweg, G. P. J.
Holmes, Dr. I. Q., South Africa
Honold, A., Switzerland
Hort, T. Jeffrey, Trinidad
Houlez, R., France
House, D. V., Great Britain
Howitt, Sir Harold, Great Britain
Hulugalle, U., Ceylon
Hussain Chaudhury, M., Pakistan
Hussey, A. V., Great Britain
Hutton, C. I. R., Great Britain

Idman, C. J., Finland
Inglis, J. B., America
Ingwersen, J.,
Iper, R., van, Belgium
Irish, R. A., Australia

Jackson, P. M., Great Britain
Jackson, W., Great Britain

Jan, Rahim, Pakistan
Jennings, A. R., America
Jensen, K. G., Denmark
Jephcott, G., Canada
Jones, J. D. R., Great Britain
Jong, Prof. A. A. de,
Jong, J. de
Jonkers, A. C. J.

Käfer, Prof. Dr. Karl, Switzerland
Kampen, Prof. L. van
Kastein, A. Th. E.
Katoh, S., Japan
Keeping, George P., Canada
Kihlman, Svante, Finland
King, Clem L., Canada
Kittelsen, J. A., Norway
Kjeldsberg, Th., Norway
Kleerekoper, I.
Klingner, G. F., Ireland
Knorr, Prof. Dr. E. R., Germany
Koppenberg, W. C.
Kraayenhof, J., *President of the Congress*
Krekstein, I. H., America
Krönke, Ludwig, Germany
Kuyper Czn., D.

Laboissière, Pierre, France
Lange, Dr. A. Th. de
Latham, J. C., Great Britain
Latham, Lord, Great Britain
Lawson, W. H., Great Britain
Lebreton, Marcel, France
Leech, R. B., Great Britain
Leitch, J. R., Great Britain
Lievens, J., France
Limperg Jr., Prof. Dr. Th.
Lindner, J. A. M. F.
Lindsay, Alexander J., America
Lipfert, Dr. F., Germany
Little, L. T., Great Britain
Loeb, Paul, France
Loflin, Wm. F., America
Lönnqvist, Uno, Finland
Los, J.

MacIver, Alan S., Great Britain
Macpherson, Lawrence G., Canada
Marshall, R. Ian, Great Britain
Mascarel, F., Monaco
Masood, S. M., Pakistan
Mast, H. van der
Masthoff, Th. P. J., *President of the Disputes Comm. of the Netherlands Inst. of Acc.*
Maung Maung, U., Burma
Mauve, H., Germany
Mazars, Robert, France
McAlister, Ian M., Australia
McDonald, W. Leslie, Canada
McDougall, E. H. V., Great Britain
McHaffie, A. N. E., Great Britain
McLaren, N. L., America
McLean, Lorn, Canada
McNeil, R., Great Britain
Mégard, M., France
Meier, Dr. Albert, Germany
Merckens, Dr. Reinhold, Germany
Merkle, Dr. Franz, Germany
Mey, Prof. Dr. A.
Mey, Prof. Dr. J. L.
Meynell, A. C. S., Great Britain
Middleton, W. R., Australia
Minz, Dr. Willy, Germany
Modderaar, J.
Mody, Naval R., India
Montagner, A. L. M., France
Moret, B.
Morgan-Jones, G. P., Great Britain
Muggli, E., Switzerland
Munnik, H.

Nelson, B., Great Britain
Nelson, S., Sweden
Nicholson, G., Great Britain
Neppérus, F. L., *President of the Discipline Comm. of the Netherlands Inst. of Acc.*

O'Connell, B. W. S., Rhodesia
Ohyama, J., Japan
Olive, G. S., America
Orreby, E. V., Sweden
Osbourn, F. C., Great Britain

Paar, G.
Padgham, F. N., Great Britain
Paquet, C., France
Pears, S. John, Great Britain
Pelej, J., America
Peloubet, M. E., America
Penney, L. H., America
Phillippe, Gerald L., America
Pilié, L. H., America
Pirenne, Th., Belgium
Powell, T. R., Great Britain
Powell, W., America
Proshan, S., Israel

Queenan, J. W., America

Rabnett, F. H., Canada
Rätsch, Herbert, Germany
Reder, H.
Ridgway, Miss Phyllis E. M., Great Britain
Rietschoten, Prof. A. M. van, *President of the Netherlands Inst. of Acc.*
Ring, R. W., America
Roberts, P. V., Great Britain
Robson, Lawrence W., Great Britain
Robson, Sir Thomas B., Great Britain
Rojansky, Dr. A. R., Israel
Rossdutcher, C., America
Russell, W. G. A., Great Britain

Sahgal, A. L., India
Samson, F., France
Saunders, G. F., Great Britain
Schaffer, W. L., America
Schellekens, J. J., Belgium
Schick, Dr. Hans, Austria
Schmid, R., Germany
Schokking, Dr. W. F., *Member of the 'Raad van State'*
Schroeff, Prof. Dr. H. J. van der
Schubert, Dr. Hans-Theodor, Germany
Schumacher, Dr. W., Germany
Schwarz, Dr. Max, Germany
Scott, Harold W., America
Seidman, J. S., America
Sensini, Prof. G., Italy
Shein, U., Burma
Shepherd, Gilbert D., Great Britain
Simons, Prof. Dr. D.
Sinnott, E., Great Britain
Smith, A. C., America
Sörensen, S. A., Denmark
Sorley, Stewart H., Canada
Spencer, E., Great Britain
Spits, C. L.
Splint, P. G. E.
Spoormaker, J.
Sprague, D., Canada
Stanley, A. D. Peter, Canada
Starreveld, R. W.
Stephenson, J. B., America
Stepto, W. E., Great Britain
Stewart, A., America
Stewart, Gordon D., New Zealand
Stewart, Jas. C., Great Britain
Stewart, J. H., America
Stokvis, W. N. A. F. H.
Strachan, Chas. M., Great Britain
Strathus, Max, Germany
Stuart, C. M., South Africa

Tanis, J. M.
Tempelaar, A. F.
Thomas, M. M., America
Tinoco, P. J., Venezuela
Treffers, H. C.

Usva, Erkki, Finland

Velayo, Alfredo M., Philippines
Velupillai, S., Ceylon
Venkatesan, R., India
Veyrenc, Albert, France
Viel, Dr. Jakob, Switzerland
Vieyra, S. J., Great Britain
Vogel, J.
Vooys, H.

Wade, A. C., America
Walker, Alex. D., Great Britain
Walker, J., Ireland
Walker, Wilbert A., America

Webb, A. E., Great Britain
Weger, J. G. de, *President of the Ass. of Univ. Trained Acc.*
Weiss, L. C., America
Whitton, James, Great Britain
Wilkinson, F. M., Great Britain
Williams, J. H., America
Wilson, B. D., New Zealand
Wilson, J. P., Great Britain
Wimble, Prof. B. J. S., South Africa
Winker, P., Germany
Wiseman, J., America
Witschey, R. E., America
Witt, C. H., Sweden
Wollert, Dr. H. A., Germany
Wynhoff, L. A., America

Yaverbaum, I., America
Yeabsley, Sir Richard, Great Britain
Yorston, R. Keith, Australia

Zaat, G. H. A.

DELEGATES' DINNER

MENU

ESCALOPE DE HOMARD

OEUFS FARCIS AU CAVIAR

SAUMON FUMÉ

ANGUILLE FUMÉE — *Champagne Dumontel*

*

CONSOMMÉ QUEUE DE KANGOUROU — *Madère*

*

SELLE DE CHEVREUIL

À LA GRAND VENEUR

POMMES DAUPHINE — *Nuits St. Georges 1952*

*

PARFAIT SYMBOLIQUE

OUBLIES

*

FRUITS SUCRÉS

*

MOKA — *Cognacs et Liqueurs*

DELEGATES' DINNER

LIST OF TOASTS

HER MAJESTY THE QUEEN

PROPOSED BY THE PRESIDENT, MR. J. KRAAYENHOF

HEADS OF STATES OF ALL NATIONALITIES PRESENT HERE

PROPOSED BY HIS ROYAL HIGHNESS
THE PRINCE OF THE NETHERLANDS

THE GUESTS FROM ABROAD

in English:

PROPOSED BY PROF. A. M. VAN RIETSCHOTEN
RESPONDED TO BY MR. MARQUIS G. EATON

in French:

PROPOSED BY MR. R. BESANÇON
RESPONDED TO BY MR. A. VEYRENC

in German:

PROPOSED BY MR. J. G. DE WEGER
RESPONDED TO BY DR. ING. O. BREDT

THE ACCOUNTANCY PROFESSION

PROPOSED BY DR. W. F. SCHOKKING
RESPONDED TO BY MR. J. T. DOWLING

LIST OF PHOTOGRAPHS

Accounting Books Published by Garland

NEW BOOKS

- *Altman, Edward I., *The Prediction of Corporate Bankruptcy: A Discriminant Analysis.*
  New York, 1988.

- Ashton, Robert H., ed. *The Evolution of Accounting Behavior Research: An Overview.*
  New York, 1984.

- Ashton, Robert H., ed. *Some Early Contributions to the Study of Audit Judgement.*
  New York, 1984.

- *Bodenhorn, Diran. *Economic Accounting.*
  New York, 1988.

---

* Included in the Garland series Foundations of Accounting
† Included in the Academy of Accounting Historians, Classics Series, Gary John Previt, ed.

■ *Bougen, Philip D. *Accounting and Industrial Relations: Some Historical Evidence on Their Interaction.*
New York, 1988.

■ Brief, Richard P., ed. *Corporate Financial Reporting and Analysis in the Early 1900s.*
New York, 1986.

■ Brief, Richard P., ed. *Depreciation and Capital Maintenance.*
New York, 1984.

■ Brief, Richard P., ed. *Estimating the Economic Rate of Return from Accounting Data.*
New York, 1986.

■ Brief, Richard P., ed. *Four Classics on the Theory of Double-Entry Bookkeeping.*
New York, 1982.

■ Chambers, R. J., and G. W. Dean, eds. *Chambers on Accounting.*
New York, 1986.
Volume I: Accounting, Management and Finance.
Volume II: Accounting Practice and Education.
Volume III: Accounting Theory and Research.
Volume IV: Price Variation Accounting.
Volume V: Continuously Contemporary Accounting.

■ *Clark, John B. (with a new introduction by Donald Dewey). *Capital and Its Earnings.*
New York, 1988.

■ Clarke, F. L. *The Tangled Web of Price Variation Accounting: The Development of Ideas Underlying Professional Prescriptions in Six Countries.*
New York, 1982.

■ Coopers & Lybrand. *The Early History of Coopers & Lybrand.*
New York, 1984.

■ Craswell, Allen. *Audit Qualifications in Australia 1950 to 1979.*
New York, 1986.

■ Dean, G. W., and M. C. Wells, eds. *The Case for Continuously Contemporary Accounting.*
New York, 1984.

■ Dean, G. W. , and M. C. Wells, eds. *Forerunners of Realizable Values Accounting in Financial Reporting.*
New York, 1982.

■ Edey, Harold C. *Accounting Queries.*
New York, 1982.

■ Edwards, J. R., ed. *Legal Regulation of British Company Accounts 1836-1900.*
New York, 1986.

■ Edwards, J. R. ed. *Reporting Fixed Assets in Nineteenth-Century Company Accounts.*
New York, 1986.

■ Edwards, J. R., ed. *Studies of Company Records: 1830-1974.*
New York, 1984.

■ Fabricant, Solomon. *Studies in Social and Private Accounting.*
New York, 1982.

■ Gaffikin, Michael, and Michael Aitkin, eds. *The Development of Accounting Theory: Significant Contributors to Accounting Thought in the 20th Century.*
New York, 1982.

■ Hawawini, Gabriel A., ed. *Bond Duration and Immunization: Early Developments and Recent Contributions.*
New York, 1982.

■ Hawawini, Gabriel A., and Pierre A. Michel, eds. *European Equity Markets: Risk, Return, and Efficiency.*
New York, 1984.

■ Hawawini, Gabriel A., and Pierre Michel. *Mandatory Financial Information and Capital Market Equilibrium in Belgium.*
New York, 1986.

■ Hawkins, David F. *Corporate Financial Disclosure, 1900-1933: A Study of Management Inertia within a Rapidly Changing Environment.*
New York, 1986.

■ *Hopwood, Anthony G. *Accounting from the Outside: The Collected Papers of Anthony G. Hopwood.*
New York, 1988.

■ Johnson, H. Thomas. *A New Approach to Management Accounting History.*
New York, 1986.

■ Kinney, William R., ed. *Fifty Years of Statistical Auditing.*
New York, 1986.

■ Klemstine, Charles E., and Michael W. Maher. *Management Accounting Research: A Review and Annotated Bibliography.*
New York, 1984.

■ *Langenderfer, Harold Q., and Grover L. Porter, eds. *Rational Accounting Concepts: The Writings of Willard Graham.*
New York, 1988.

■ *Lee, T. A., ed. *The Evolution of Audit Thought and Practice.*
New York, 1988.

■ Lee, T. A., ed. *A Scottish Contribution to Accounting History.*
New York, 1986.

■ Lee, T. A. *Towards a Theory and Practice of Cash Flow Accounting.*
New York, 1986.

■ Lee, T. A., ed. *Transactions of the Chartered Accountants Students' Societies of Edinburgh and Glasgow: A Selection of Writings, 1886-1958.*
New York, 1984.

■ *Loft, Anne. *Understanding Accounting in Its Social and Historical Context: The Case of Cost Accounting in Britain, 1914-1925.*
New York, 1988.

■ McKinnon, Jill L.. *The Historical Development and Operational Form of Corporate Reporting Regulation in Japan.*
New York, 1986.

■ *McMickle, Peter L., and Paul H. Jensen, eds. *The Auditor's Guide of 1869: A Review and Computer Enhancement of Recently Discovered Old Microfilm of America's First Book on Auditing by H. J. Mettenheimer.*
New York, 1988.

■ *McMickle, Peter L., and Paul H. Jensen, eds. *The Birth of American Accountancy: A Bibliographic Analysis of Works on Accounting Published in America through 1820.*
New York, 1988.

■ *Mepham, M.-J. *Accounting in Eighteenth-Century Scotland.*
New York, 1988.

■ *Mills, Patti A., trans. *The Legal Literature of Accounting: On Accounts by Diego del Castillo.*
New York, 1988.

■ *Murphy, George J. *The Evolution of Canadian Corporate Reporting Practices: 1900-1970.*
New York, 1988.

■ *Mumford, Michael J., ed. *Edward Stamp—Later Papers.*
New York, 1988.

■ Nobes, Christopher, ed. *The Development of Double Entry: Selected Essays.*
New York, 1984.

■ Nobes, Christopher. *Issues in International Accounting.*
New York, 1986.

■ Parker, Lee D. *Developing Control Concepts in the 20th Century.*
New York, 1986.

■ *Parker, Lee D., ed. *Financial Reporting to Employees: From Past to Present.*
New York, 1988.

■ *Parker, Lee D., and O. Finley Graves, eds. *Methodology and Method in History: A Bibliography.*
New York, 1988.

■ Parker, R. H. *Papers on Accounting History.*
New York, 1984.

■ Previts, Gary John, and Alfred R. Roberts, eds. *Federal Securities Law and Accounting 1933-1970: Selected Addresses.*
New York, 1986.

■ *Reid, Jean Margo, ed. *Law and Accounting: Nineteenth-Century American Legal Cases.*
New York, 1988.

■ *Sheldahl, Terry K., ed. *Accounting Literature in the United States before Mitchell and Jones (1796): Contributions by Four English Writers, through American Editions, and Two Pioneer Local Authors.*
New York, 1988.

■ Sheldahl, Terry K. *Beta Alpha Psi, from Alpha to Omega: Pursuing a Vision of Professional Education for Accountants, 1919-1945.*
New York, 1982.

■ Sheldahl, Terry K. *Beta Alpha Psi, from Omega to Zeta Omega: The Making of a Comprehensive Accounting Fraternity, 1946-1984.*
New York, 1986.

■ *Sheldahl, Terry K., ed. *Education for the Mercantile Countinghouse: Critical and Constructive Essays by Nine British Writers, 1716-1794.*
New York, 1988.

■ Solomons, David. *Collected Papers on Accounting and Accounting Education (in two volumes).*
New York, 1984.

■ Sprague, Charles F. *The General Principles of the Science of Accounts and the Accountancy of Investment.*
New York, 1984.

■ Stamp, Edward. *Edward Stamp—Later Papers.* *See* Michael J. Mumford.

■ Stamp, Edward. *Selected Papers on Accounting, Auditing, and Professional Problems.*
New York, 1984.

■ *Staubus, George J. *Activity Costing for Decisions: Cost Accounting in the Decision Usefulness Framework.*
New York, 1988.

■ Storrar, Colin, ed. *The Accountant's Magazine—An Anthology.*
New York, 1986.

■ Tantral, Panadda. *Accounting Literature in Non-Accounting Journals: An Annotated Bibliography.*
New York, 1984.

■ *Vangermeersch, Richard G. *Alexander Hamilton Church: A Man of Ideas for All Seasons.*
New York, 1988.

■ Vangermeersch, Richard, ed. *The Contributions of Alexander Hamilton Church to Accounting and Management.*
New York, 1986.

■ Vangermeersch, Richard, ed. *Financial Accounting Milestones in the Annual Reports of the United States Steel Corporation—The First Seven Decades.*
New York, 1986.

■ *Walker, Stephen P. *The Society of Accountants in Edinburgh, 1854-1914: A Study of Recruitment to a New Profession.*
New York, 1988.

■ Whitmore, John. *Factory Accounts.*
New York, 1984.

■ *Whittred, Greg. *The Evolution of Consolidated Financial Reporting in Australia: An Evaluation of an Alternative Hypothesis.*
New York, 1988.

■ Yamey, Basil S. *Further Essays on the History of Accounting.*
New York, 1982.

■ Zeff, Stephen A., ed. *The Accounting Postulates and Principles Controversy of the 1960s.*
New York, 1982.

■ Zeff, Stephen A., ed. *Accounting Principles Through the Years: The Views of Professional and Academic Leaders 1938-1954.*
New York, 1982.

■ Zeff, Stephen A., and Maurice Moonitz, eds. *Sourcebook on Accounting Principles and Auditing Procedures: 1917-1953 (in two volumes).*
New York, 1984.

■ *Zeff, Stephen a., ed. *The U. S. Accounting Profession in the 1890s and Early 1900s.*
New York, 1988.

REPRINTED TITLES

- *American Institute of Accountants. *Accountants Index, 1920* (in two volumes).
  New York, 1921 (Garland reprint, 1988).

- American Institute of Accountants. *Fiftieth Anniversary Celebration.*
  Chicago, 1937 (Garland reprint, 1982).

- American Institute of Accountants. *Library Catalogue.*
  New York, 1919 (Garland reprint, 1982).

- Arthur Andersen Company. *The First Fifty Years 1913-1963.*
  Chicago, 1963 (Garland reprint, 1984).

- Bevis, Herman W. *Corporate Financial Reporting in a Competitive Economy.*
  New York, 1965 (Garland reprint, 1986).

- Bonini,. Charles P., Robert K. Jaedicke, and Harvey M. Wagner, eds. *Management Controls: New Directions in Basic Research.*
  New York, 1964 (Garland reprint, 1986).

- **The Book-Keeper and the American Counting Room.*
  New York, 1880-1884 (Garland reprint, 1988).

▪ Bray, F. Sewell. *Four Essays in Accounting Theory.* London, 1953. *Bound with* Institute of Chartered Accountants in England and Wales and the National Institute of Economic and Social Research. *Some Accounting Terms and Concepts.*
Cambridge, 1951 (Garland reprint, 1982).

▪ Brown, R. Gene, and Kenneth S. Johnston. *Paciolo on Accounting.*
New York, 1963 (Garland reprint, 1984).

▪ Carey, John L., and William O. Doherty, eds. *Ethical Standards of the Accounting Profession.*
New York, 1966 (Garland reprint, 1986).

▪ Chambers, R. J. *Accounting in Disarray.*
Melbourne, 1973 (Garland reprint, 1982).

▪ Cooper, Ernest. *Fifty-seven years in an Accountant's Office.* *See* Sir Russell Kettle.

▪ Couchman, Charles B. *The Balance-Sheet.*
New York, 1924 (Garland reprint, 1982).

▪ Couper, Charles Tennant. *Report of the Trial ... Against the Directors and Manager of the City of Glasgow Bank.*
Edinburgh, 1879 (Garland reprint, 1984).

▪ Cutforth, Arthur E. *Audits.*
London, 1906 (Garland reprint, 1982).

▪ Cutforth, Arthur E. *Methods of Amalgamation.*
London, 1926 (Garland reprint, 1982).

- Deinzer, Harvey T. *Development of Accounting Thought.*
  New York, 1965 (Garland reprint, 1984).

- De Paula, F.R.M. *The Principles of Auditing.*
  London, 1915 (Garland reprint, 1984).

- Dickerson, R. W. *Accountants and the Law of Negligence.*
  Toronto, 1966 (Garland reprint, 1982).

- Dodson, James. *The Accountant, or, the Method of Bookkeeping Deduced from Clear Principles, and Illustrated by a Variety of Examples.*
  London, 1750 (Garland reprint, 1984).

- Dyer, S. *A Common Sense Method of Double Entry Bookkeeping, on First Principles, as Suggested by De Morgan. Part I, Theoretical.*
  London, 1897 (Garland reprint, 1984).

- *† Edwards, James Don. *History of Public Accounting in the United States.*
  East Lansing, 1960 (Garland reprint, 1988).

- *† Edwards, James Don, and Robert F. Salmonson. *Contributions of Four Accounting Pioneers: Kohler, Littleton, May, Paton.*
  East Lancing, 1961 (Garland reprint, 1988).

- *The Fifth International Congress on Accounting, 1938 [Kongress-Archiv 1938 des V. Internationalen Prüfungs- und Treuhand-Kongresses].*
  Berlin, 1938 (Garland reprint, 1986).

■ Finney, A. H. *Consolidated Statements.*
New York, 1922 (Garland reprint, 1982).

■ Fisher, Irving. *The Rate of Interest.*
New York, 1907 (Garland reprint, 1982).

■ Florence, P. Sargant. *Economics of Fatigue and Unrest and the Efficiency of Labour in English and American Industry.*
London, 1923 (Garland reprint, 1984).

■ *Fourth International Congress on Accounting 1933.*
London, 1933 (Garland reprint, 1982).

■ Foye, Arthur B. *Haskins & Sells: Our First Seventy-Five Years.*
New York, 1970 (Garland reprint, 1984).

■ *† Garner, Paul S. *Evolution of Cost Accounting to 1925.*
University, Alabama, 1925 (Garland reprint, 1988).

■ Garnsey, Sir Gilbert. *Holding Companies and Their Published Accounts.* London, 1923. *Bound with* Sir Gilbert Garnsey. *Limitations of a Balance Sheet.*
London, 1928 (Garland reprint, 1982).

■ Garrett, A. A. *The History of the Society of Incorporated Accountants, 1885-1957.*
Oxford, 1961 (Garland reprint, 1984).

■ Gilman, Stephen. *Accounting Concepts of Profit.*
New York, 1939 (Garland reprint, 1982).

- Gordon, William. *The Universal Accountant, and Complete Merchant* ... [Volume II].
Edinburgh, 1765 (Garland reprint, 1986).

- Green, Wilmer. *History and Survey of Accountancy.*
Brooklyn, 1930 (Garland reprint, 1986).

- Hamilton, Robert. *An Introduction to Merchandise, Parts IV and V (Italian Bookkeeping and Practical Bookkeeping).*
Edinburgh, 1788 (Garland reprint, 1982).

- Hatton, Edward. *The Merchant's Magazine; or, Tradesman's Treasury.* London, 1695 (Garland reprint, 1982).
Hills, George S. *The Law of Accounting and Financial Statements.*
Boston, 1957 (Garland reprint, 1982).

- *A History of Cooper Brothers & Co. 1854 to 1954.*
London, 1954 (Garland reprint, 1986).

- Hofstede, Geert. *The Game of Budget Control.*
Assen, 1967 (Garland reprint, 1984).

- Howitt, Sir Harold. *The History of the Institute of Chartered Accountants in England and Wales 1880-1965, and of Its Founder Accountancy Bodies 1870-1880.*
London, 1966 (Garland reprint, 1984).

- Institute of Chartered Accountants in England and Wales and The National Institute of Social and Economic Research. *Some Accounting Terms and Concepts.* *See* F. Sewell Bray.

- Institute of Chartered Accountants of Scotland. *History of the Chartered Accountants of Scotland from the Earliest Times to 1954.*
  Edinburgh, 1954 (Garland reprint, 1984).

- *International Congress on Accounting 1929.*
  New York, 1930 (Garland reprint, 1982).

- Jaedicke, Robert K., Yuji Ijiri, and Oswald Nielsen, eds. *Research in Accounting Measurement.*
  American Accounting Association,
  1966 (Garland reprint, 1986).

- Keats, Charles. *Magnificent Masquerade.*
  New York, 1964 (Garland reprint, 1982).

- Kettle, Sir Russell. *Deloitte & Co. 1854-1956.* Oxford, 1958. *Bound with* Ernest Cooper. *Fifty-seven Years in an Accountant's Office.*
  London, 1921 (Garland reprint, 1982).

- Kitchen, J., and R. H. Parker. *Accounting Thought and Education: Six English Pioneers.*
  London, 1980 (Garland reprint, 1984).

- Lacey, Kenneth. *Profit Measurement and Price Changes.*
  London, 1952 (Garland reprint, 1982).

- Lee, Chauncey. *The American Accomptant.*
  Lansingburgh, 1797 (Garland reprint, 1982).

- Lee, T. A., and R. H. Parker. *The Evolution of Corporate Financial Reporting.*
  Middlesex, 1979 (Garland reprint, 1984).

■ *† Littleton, A. C.. *Accounting Evolution to 1900.*
New York, 1933 (Garland reprint, 1988).

■ Malcolm, Alexander. *The Treatise of Book-Keeping, or, Merchants Accounts; In the Italian Method of Debtor and Creditor; Wherein the Fundamental Principles of That Curious and Approved Method Are Clearly and Fully Explained and Demonstrated ... To Which Are Added, Instructions for Gentlemen of Land Estates, and Their Stewards or Factors: With Directions Also for Retailers, and Other More Private Persons.*
London, 1731 (Garland reprint, 1986).

■ Meij, J. L., ed. *Depreciation and Replacement Policy.*
Chicago, 1961 (Garland reprint, 1986).

■ Newlove, George Hills. *Consolidated Balance Sheets.*
New York, 1926 (Garland reprint, 1982).

■ North, Roger. *The Gentleman Accomptant; or, An Essay to Unfold the Mystery of Accompts; By Way of Debtor and Creditor, Commonly Called Merchants Accompts, and Applying the Same to the Concerns of the Nobility and Gentry of England.*
London 1714 (Garland reprint, 1986).

■ **Proceedings of the Seventh International Congress of Accountants.* Amsterdam, 1957 (Garland reprint, 1988).

■ Pryce-Jones, Janet E., and R. H. Parker. *Accounting in Scotland: A Historical Bibliography.*
Edinburgh, 1976 (Garland reprint, 1984).

- *Reynolds, W. B., and F. W. Thornton. *Duties of a Junior Accountant* [three editions].
  New York, 1917, 1933, 1953
  (Garland reprint, 1988).

- Robinson, H. W. *A History of Accountants in Ireland.*
  Dublin, 1964 (Garland edition, 1984).

- Robson, T. B. *Consolidated and Other Group Accounts.*
  London, 1950 (Garland reprint, 1982).

- Rorem, C. Rufus. *Accounting Method.*
  Chicago, 1928 (Garland reprint, 1982).

- Saliers, Earl A., ed. *Accountants' Handbook.*
  New York, 1923 (Garland reprint, 1986).

- Samuel, Horace B. *Shareholder's Money.*
  London, 1933 (Garland reprint, 1982).

- *The Securitites and Exchange Commission in the Matter of McKesson & Robbins, Inc. Report on Investigation.*
  Washington, D. C., 1940 (Garland reprint, 1982).

- *The Securities and Exchange Commission in the Matter of McKesson & Robbins, Inc. Testimony of Expert Witnesses.*
  Washington, D. C., 1939 (Garland reprint, 1982).

- Shaplen, Roger. *Kreuger: Genius and Swindler.*
  New York, 1960 (Garland reprint, 1986).

- Singer, H. W. *Standardized Accountancy in Germany. (With a new appendix.)*
  Cambridge, 1943 (Garland reprint, 1982).

- *The Sixth International Congress on Accounting.*
  London, 1952 (Garland reprint, 1984).

- Stewart, Jas. C. (with a new introductory note by T. A. Lee). *Pioneers of a Profession: Chartered Accountants to 1879.*
  Edinburgh, 1977 (Garland reprint, 1986).

- Thompson, Wardbaugh. *The Accomptant's Oracle: or, a Key to Science, Being a Compleat Practical System of Book-keeping.*
  York, 1777 (Garland reprint, 1984).

- *Thornton, F. W. *Duties of the Senior Accountant.* New York, 1932. *Bound with.* John C. Martin. *Duties of Junior and Senior Accountants, Supplement of the CPA Handbook.*
  New York, 1953 (Garland reprint, 1988).

- Vatter, William J. *Managerial Accounting.*
  New York, 1950 (Garland reprint, 1986).

- Woolf, Arthur H. *A Short History of Accountants and Accountancy.*
  London, 1912 (Garland reprint, 1986).

- Yamey, B. S., H. C. Edey, and Hugh W. Thomson. *Accounting in England and Scotland: 1543-1800.*
  London, 1963 (Garland reprint, 1982).